Lecture Notes in Computer Science 5643

Commenced Publication in 1973
Founding and Former Series Editors:
Gerhard Goos, Juris Hartmanis, and Jan van Leeuwen

Ahmed Bouajjani   Oded Maler (Eds.)

Computer Aided Verification

21st International Conference, CAV 2009
Grenoble, France, June 26 - July 2, 2009
Proceedings

 Springer

Volume Editors

Ahmed Bouajjani
LIAFA, University Paris Diderot (Paris 7)
Case 7014, 75205 Paris Cedex 13, France
E-mail: abou@liafa.jussieu.fr

Oded Maler
CNRS-VERIMAG, University of Grenoble
2 Avenue de Vignate, 38610 Gières, France
E-mail: oded.maler@imag.fr

Library of Congress Control Number: 2009929037

CR Subject Classification (1998): F.3, D.2.4, D.2.2, F.4.1, I.2.3, B.7.2, C.3

LNCS Sublibrary: SL 1 – Theoretical Computer Science and General Issues

ISSN 0302-9743

ISBN 978-3-642-02657-7 Springer Berlin Heidelberg New York

Typesetting: Camera-ready by author, data conversion by Scientific Publishing Services, Chennai, India
Printed on acid-free paper   SPIN: 12701841   06/3180   5 4 3 2 1 0

Preface

This volume contains the proceedings of the 21st International Conference on Computer-Aided Verification (CAV) held in Grenoble, France, between June 28 and July 2, 2009. CAV is dedicated to the advancement of the theory and practice of computer-aided formal analysis methods for hardware and software systems. Its scope ranges from theoretical results to concrete applications, with an emphasis on practical verification tools and the underlying algorithms and techniques.

Every instance of a conference is special in its own way. This CAV is special for at least two reasons: first, it took place in Grenoble, the place where the CAV series started 20 years ago. Secondly, there was a particularly large number of paper submissions: *135 regular papers* and *34 tool papers*, summing up to 169 submissions. They all went through an active review process, with each submission reviewed by four members of the Program Committee. We also sought external reviews from experts in certain areas. Authors had the opportunity to respond to the initial reviews during an author response period. All these inputs were used by the Program Committee in selecting a final program with *36 regular papers* and *16 tool papers*. In addition to the presentation of these papers, the program included the following:

- Four invited tutorials:
  - *Rachid Guerraoui* (EPFL Lausanne, Switzerland): *Transactional Memory: Glimmer of a Theory.*
  - *Jaeha Kim* (Stanford, USA): *Mixed-Signal System Verification: A High-Speed Link Example.*
  - *Jean Krivine* (Institut des Hautes Etudes Scientifiques, France): *Modelling Epigenetic Information Maintenance: A Kappa Tutorial.*
  - *Joseph Sifakis* (CNRS-VERIMAG, France): *Component-Based Construction of Real-Time Systems in BIP.*

- Four invited talks:
  - *Martin Abadi* (UC Santa Cruz and MSR Silicon Valley, USA): *Models and Proofs of Protocol Security: A Progress Report.*
  - *Luca Benini* (U Bologna, Italy): *Predictability vs. Efficiency in the Multicore Era: Fight of Titans or Happy Ever After?*
  - *Sumit Gulwani* (MSR Redmond, USA): *SPEED: Symbolic Complexity Bound Analysis.*
  - *Ofer Strichman* (Technion, Israel): *Regression Verification: Proving the Equivalence of Similar Programs.*

The conference was preceded by the following 14 affiliated workshops and events:

- SPIN - Model Checking of Software

- RV - Runtime Verification
- EC^2 - Exploiting Concurrency Efficiently and Correctly
- GASICS - Games for Design, Verification and Synthesis
- VETO - Computer Science Security and Electronic Vote
- MITACS - Foundations and Practice of Security
- BPR - Bit Precise Reasoning
- QA - Quantitative Analysis of Software
- PSY - Practical Synthesis for Concurrent Systems
- AFM - Automated Formal Methods
- FAC - Formal Verification of Analog Circuits
- CFV - Constraints in Formal Verification
- HWMCC - Hardware Model Checking Competition
- PADVES - Platforms for Analysis, Design and Verification of Embedded Systems

We gratefully acknowledge the support to CAV 2009 from public and industrial sponsors. The former included the Joseph Fourier University of Grenoble (UJF), the French National Center for Scientific Research (CNRS), the French National Institute for Research in Informatics and Control (INRIA), the MINA-LOGIC pole of excellence of the Rhône-Alpes region and the European network of excellence ARTIST2. On the industrial side, we received support from IBM, Intel, Jasper Design Automation, Microsoft Research and NEC Labs America.

Many individuals were very generous with their time and expertise that went into putting the conference together. We thank the Program Committee and the external reviewers for their efforts in the assessment and evaluation of the submissions. We thank Andrei Voronkov for creating and supporting the invaluable EasyChair conference management system. The organization of CAV 2009 could not have been achieved without the efforts of the Organization Chair Saddek Bensalem, aided by Ylies Falcone (web), Peter Habermehl (submissions and proceedings) and the conference team of Floralis (Laetitia Libralato, Audrey Dibilio and Cyrille Mathon). Numerous student volunteers at VERIMAG helped us as well. We thank Andreas Podelski for help in organizing the tutorials and workshops and the CAV 2008 Chairs and organizers Aarti Gupta and Sharad Malik, as well as the members of the Steering Committee for their help and advice.

July 2009   Ahmed Bouajjani
                                                                              Oded Maler

Organization

Program Chairs

Ahmed Bouajjani — LIAFA/University of Paris 7, France
Oded Maler — VERIMAG/CNRS, France

Program Committee

Parosh A. Abdulla — University of Uppsala, Sweden
Rajeev Alur — University of Penn, USA
Christel Baier — University of Dresden, Germany
Clark Barrett — NYU, USA
Armin Biere — Johannes Kepler University of Linz, Austria
Nikolaj Bjørner — MSR Redmond, USA
Roderick Bloem — TU Graz, Austria
Edmund Clarke — CMU, USA
Byron Cook — MSR Cambridge, UK
Martin Fränzle — University of Oldenburg, Germany
Aarti Gupta — NEC Labs, USA
John Harrison — Intel, USA
Klaus Havelund — NASA JPL, USA
Alan Hu — UBC Vancouver, Canada
Kevin Jones — Green Plug, USA
Daniel Kröning — University of Oxford, UK
Robert Kurshan — Cadence, USA
Yassine Lakhnech — VERIMAG/UJF, France
Kenneth McMillan — Cadence, USA
Markus Müller-Olm — University of Münster, Germany
Kedar Namjoshi — Bell Labs, Alcatel-Lucent, USA
Madhusudan Parthasarathy — UIUC, USA
Sriram Rajamani — MSR India
Andrey Rybalchenko — MPI-SWS, Germany
Philippe Schnoebelen — LSV/CNRS, France
Sanjit Seshia — UC Berkeley, USA
Natarajan Shankar — SRI International, USA
Fabio Somenzi — University of Colorado Boulder, USA
Ofer Strichman — Technion, Israel
Serdar Tasiran — Koç University Istanbul, Turkey
Tayssir Touili — LIAFA/CNRS, France
Stavros Tripakis — Cadence, USA
Helmuth Veith — TU Darmstadt, Germany

Organizing Committee

Saddek Bensalem (Chair)   VERIMAG/UJF, France
Ylies Falcone   VERIMAG/UJF, France
Peter Habermehl   LIAFA/University of Paris 7, France

Steering Committee

Edmund M. Clarke   CMU, USA
Mike Gordon   University of Cambridge, UK
Robert P. Kurshan   Cadence, USA
Amir Pnueli   NYU, USA

Sponsors

ArtistDesign, CNRS, INRIA, University Joseph Fourier (Grenoble, France), IBM, Intel, Jasper, Microsoft Research, Minalogic, NEC.

External Reviewers

Nina Amla
Flemming Andersen
Cyrille Artho
Cyrille Valentin Artho
Eugene Asarin
Faouzi Atig
Philippe Audebaud
Domagoj Babic
Sruthi Bandhakavi
Sharon Barner
Howard Barringer
Amir Ben-Amram
Beatrice Berard
Josh Berdine
Dietmar Berwanger
Ritwik Bhattacharya
Jesse Bingham
Nicolas Blanc
Jan Olaf Blech
Tobias Blechmann
Borzoo Bonakdarpour
Patricia Bouyer
Marius Bozga
Thomas Brihaye
Angelo Brillout

Robert Brummayer
Roberto Bruttomesso
Sebastian Burckhardt
Franck Cassez
Jonathan Cederberg
Pavol Cerny
Rohit Chadha
Krishnendu Chatterjee
Swarat Chaudhuri
Hana Chockler
Ching-Tsun Chou
Frank Ciesinski
Ariel Cohen
Christopher Conway
Scott Cotton
Pepijn Crouzen
Vijay D'Silva
Dennis Dams
Thao Dang
Aldric Degorre
Giorgio Delzanno
Stéphane Demri
Henning Dierks
Catalin Dima
Dino Distefano

Alexandre Donzé
Laurent Doyen
Bruno Dutertre
Andreas Eggers
Jochen Eisinger
Cindy Eisner
Tayfun Elmas
Cristian Ene
Constantin Enea
Georgios E. Fainekos
Ylies Falcone
Azadeh Farzan
Goerschwin Fey
Bernd Finkbeiner
Cormac Flanagan
Goran Frehse
Paul Gastin
Stephane Gaubert
Naghmeh Ghafari
Antoine Girard
Patrice Godefroid
Amit Goel
Dan Goldwasser
Alexey Gotsman
Susanne Graf

Karin Greimel
Andreas Griesmayer
Alex Groce
Marcus Groesser
Bhargav Gulavani
Sumit Gulwani
Arie Gurfinkel
Peter Habermehl
Moritz Hahn
Leopold Haller
Hyojung Han
Frédéric Haziza
Christian Herde
Philippe Herrmann
Georg Hofferek
Daniel Holcomb
Lukas Holik
Andreas Holzer
Gerard Holzmann
Benny Van Houdt
Hardi Hungar
Pierre-Cyrille Héam
Radu Iosif
Samin Ishtiaq
Franjo Ivancic
Ethan Jackson
Alok Jain
Visar Januzaj
Thierry Jeron
Susmit Jha
Sumit Kumar Jha
Ranjit Jhala
HoonSang Jin
Barbara Jobstmann
Rajeev Joshi
Dejan Jovanovic
Marcin Jurdzinski
Vineet Kahlon
Mark Kattenbelt
Mohammad Khaleghi
Hyondeuk Kim
Johannes Kinder
Joachim Klein
William Klieber
Sascha Klueppelholz

Eric Koskinen
Laura Kovacs
Jens Krinke
Sava Krstic
Andreas Kuehlmann
Orna Kupferman
Marta Kwiatkowska
Boris Köpf
Salvatore La Torre
Pascal Lafourcade
Akash Lal
Peter Lammich
Axel Legay
Jerome Leroux
Wenchao Li
Etienne Lozes
Roberto Lublinerman
Bernhard Möller
Stephen Magill
Patrick Maier
Rupak Majumdar
Alexander Malkis
Pete Manolios
Nicolas Markey
Richard Mayr
Michele Mazzucchi
Antoine Meyer
David Monniaux
Laurent Mounier
Leonardo de Moura
Peter Müller
Madanlal Musuvathi
Dejan Nickovic
Aditya Nori
Joel Ouaknine
Sam Owre
Catuscia Palamidessi
Gennaro Parlato
Corina Pasareanu
Flavio de Paula
Udo Payer
Michael Perin
Paul Pettersson
Claudio Pinello
Nir Piterman

Andre Platzer
Corneliu Popeea
Polyvios Pratikakis
Mitra Purandare
Shaz Qadeer
Pascal Raymond
Zvonimir Rakamaric
V.P. Ranganath
Kavita Ravi
Ahmed Rezine
Noam Rinetzky
Christophe Ringeissen
Adam Rogalewicz
Mirron Rozanov
Sitvanit Ruah
Philipp Ruemmer
Michael Ryabtsev
Vadim Ryvchin
Konstantinos Sagonas
Hassen Saidi
Ramzi Ben Salah
Roopsha Samanta
Marko Samer
S. Sankaranarayanan
Gerald Sauter
Christian Schallhart
Viktor Schuppan
Stefan Schwoon
Koushik Sen
Ali Sezgin
Mihaela Sighireanu
Jiri Simsa
Jan-Georg Smaus
Gregor Snelting
Saqib Sohail
Jeremy Sproston
Stefan Staber
Grégoire Sutre
D. Suwimonteerabuth
Mani Swaminathan
Paulo Tabuada
Muralidhar Talupur
Tino Teige
Nikolai Tillmann
Cesare Tinelli

Table of Contents

Invited Tutorials

Invited Talks

Regular Papers

Tool Papers

Transactional Memory: Glimmer of a Theory
(Invited Paper)

Rachid Guerraoui and Michał Kapałka

EPFL, Switzerland

Abstract. Transactional memory (TM) is a promising paradigm for concurrent programming. This paper is an overview of our recent theoretical work on defining a theory of TM. We first recall some TM correctness properties and then overview results on the inherent power and limitations of TMs.

1 Introduction

Multi-core processors are already common in servers, home computers, and laptops. To exploit the power of modern hardware, applications will need to become increasingly parallel. However, writing scalable concurrent programs is hard and error-prone with traditional locking techniques. On the one hand, coarse-grained locking throttles parallelism and causes lock contention. On the other hand, fine-grained locking is usually an engineering challenge, and as such is not suitable for use by the masses of programmers.

Transactional memory (TM) [1] is a promising technique to facilitate concurrent programming while delivering performance comparable to that of fine-grained locking implementations. In short, a TM allows concurrent threads of an application to communicate by executing lightweight, in-memory *transactions* [2]. A transaction accesses shared data and then either commits or aborts. If it commits, its operations are applied to the shared state *atomically*. If it aborts, however, its changes to the shared data are lost and never visible to other transactions.

The TM paradigm has raised a lot of hope for mastering the complexity of concurrent programming. The aim is to provide the programmer with an abstraction, i.e., the transaction, that makes concurrency as easy as with coarse-grained critical sections, while exploiting the underlying multi-core architectures as efficiently as hand-crafted fine-grained locking. It is thus not surprising to see a large body of work directed at experimenting with various kinds of TM implementation strategies, e.g. [1,3,4,5,6,7,8,9,10,11,12,13,14,15,16]. What might be surprising is the little work devoted so far to the formalization of the *precise* guarantees that TM implementations should provide. Without such formalization, it is impossible to verify the correctness of these implementations, establish any optimality result, or determine whether various TM design trade-offs are indeed fundamental or simply artifacts of certain environments.

A. Bouajjani and O. Maler (Eds.): CAV 2009, LNCS 5643, pp. 1–15, 2009.

From a user's perspective, a TM should provide the same semantics as critical sections: transactions should appear as if they were executed sequentially, i.e., as if each transaction acquired a global lock for its entire duration. (Remember that the TM goal is to provide a simple abstraction to average programmers.) However, a TM implementation would be inefficient if it never allowed different transactions to run concurrently. Hence, we want to reason formally about executions with interleaving steps of arbitrary concurrent transactions. First, we need a way to state precisely whether a given execution in which a number of transactions execute steps in parallel "looks like" an execution in which these transactions proceed one after the other. That is, we need a *correctness condition* for TMs. Second, we should define when a TM implementation is allowed to *abort* a transaction that contends for shared data with concurrent transactions. Indeed, while the ability to abort transactions is essential for all optimistic schemes used by TMs, a TM that abuses this ability by aborting every transaction is, clearly, useless. Hence, we need to define *progress properties* of TM implementations.

We overview here our work on establishing the theoretical foundations of TMs [17,18,19]. We first present *opacity*—a correctness condition for TMs, which is indeed ensured by most TM implementations, e.g., DSTM [4], ASTM [5], SXM [20], JVSTM [6], TL2 [21], LSA-STM [11], RSTM [7], BartokSTM [8], McRT-STM [12], TinySTM [14], AVSTM [22], the STM in [23], and SwissTM [24]. We then define progress properties of the two main classes of existing TM implementations: *obstruction-free* [4] and *lock-based* ones. The intuition behind the progress semantics of such TMs has been known, but precise definitions were missing.

It is important to notice that the paper is only an overview of previously published results. In particular, we do not give here precise definitions of many terms that we use (and describe intuitively) or any proofs of the theorems that we state. Those definitions and proofs, as well as further details and discussions of the results presented here, can be found in [17,18,19].

2 Preliminaries

2.1 Shared Objects and Their Implementations

Processes and objects. We consider a classical asynchronous shared-memory system [25,26] of n processes $p_1, \ldots, p_n$ that communicate by executing operations on *(shared) objects*. An example of a very simple object is a *register*, which exports only *read* and *write* operations. Operation *read* returns the current state (value) of the register, and operation *write(v)* sets the state of the register to value v.

An execution of every operation is delimited by two *events*: the invocation of the operation and the response from the operation. We assume that, in every run of the system, all events can be totally ordered according to their execution time. If several events are executed at the same time (e.g., on multiprocessor systems), then they can be ordered arbitrarily. We call a pair of invocation of an operation and the subsequent response from this operation an *operation execution*.

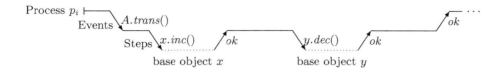

Fig. 1. An example execution of an operation *trans* on a shared object A by a process p_i. Operation *trans* is implemented using operations *inc* and *dec* on base objects x and y.

An object x may be provided either directly in hardware, or *implemented* from other, possibly more primitive, *base* objects (cf. Figure 1). We call the events of operations on base objects *steps*. We assume that each process executes operations on shared objects, and on base objects, sequentially.

Wait-freedom. We focus on object implementations that are *wait-free* [25]. Intuitively, an implementation of an object x is wait-free if a process that invokes an operation on x is never blocked indefinitely long inside the operation, e.g., waiting for other processes. Hence, processes can make progress independently of each other.

Computational equivalence. We say that object x *can implement* object y if there exists an algorithm that implements y using some number of instances of x (i.e., a number of base objects of the same type as x) and atomic (i.e., linearizable [27]) registers. We say that objects x and y are *equivalent* if x can implement y and y can implement x.

The power of a shared object. We use the *consensus number* [25] as a metric of the power of objects. The consensus number of an object x is the maximum number of processes among which one can solve (wait-free) *consensus* using any number of instances of x (i.e., base objects of the same type as x) and atomic registers.

The consensus problem consists for a number of processes to agree (*decide*) on a single value chosen from the set of values these processes have *proposed*. It is known that, in an asynchronous system, implementing wait-free consensus is impossible when only registers are available [28].

2.2   Transactional Memory (TM)

A TM enables processes to communicate by executing transactions. A transaction may perform operations on objects shared with other transactions, called *transactional* objects (or *t-objects*, for short), as well as local computations on objects inaccessible to other transactions. For simplicity, we will say that a transaction T performs some action, meaning that the process executing T performs this action within the transactional context of T. We will call *t-variables* those t-objects that are registers, i.e., that provide only *read* and *write* operations.

Every transaction has a unique *identifier* (e.g., T_1, T_2, etc.). (We use the terms "transaction" and "transaction identifier" interchangeably.) Every transaction, upon its first action, is initially *live* and may eventually become either *committed* or *aborted*, as explained in the following paragraphs. A transaction that is not live does no longer perform any actions. Retrying an aborted transaction (i.e., the computation the transaction intends to perform) is considered in our model as a new transaction, with a different transaction identifier.

TM as a shared object. A TM can be viewed as an object with operations that allow for the following: (1) Executing any operation on a t-object x within a transaction T_k (returns the response of the operation or a special value A_k); (2) Requesting transaction T_k to be committed (operation $tryC(T_k)$ that returns either A_k or C_k); (3) Requesting transaction T_k to be aborted (operation $tryA(T_k)$ that always returns A_k). The special return value A_k (*abort* event) is returned by a TM to indicate that transaction T_k has been aborted. The return value C_k (*commit* event) is a confirmation that T_k has been committed.

As for other objects, we assume that every implementation of a TM is wait-free, i.e., that the individual operations of transactions are wait-free. This is indeed the case for most TM implementations (including lock-based ones; see [19]).

If x is a t-object (provided by a given TM), then we denote by $x.op_k \rightarrow v$ an execution (invocation and the subsequent response) of operation op on x by transaction T_k, returning value v. We also denote by A_k (and C_k) an abort (commit) event of transaction T_k.

Histories. Consider any TM and any run. A *history* (of the TM) is a sequence of invocation and response events of operations executed by processes on the TM in this run. Let M be any implementation of the TM. An *implementation history* of M is the sequence of (1) invocation and response events of operations executed by processes on M, and (2) the corresponding steps of M executed in a given run.

We say that transaction T_k is *committed* (respectively, *aborted*) in H, if H contains commit event C_k (resp., abort event A_k). A transaction that is neither committed nor aborted is called *live*. We say that transaction T_k is *forcefully aborted* in H, if T_k is aborted in H but there is no invocation of operation $tryA(T_k)$ in H. We say that T_k is *commit-pending* in H, if H contains an invocation of operation $tryC(T_k)$ but T_k is still live in H (i.e., operation $tryC(T_k)$ has not returned yet).

We say that a transaction T_k *precedes* a transaction T_m in history H, and write $T_k \prec_H T_m$, if T_k is committed or aborted and the last event of T_k precedes (in H) the first event of T_m. We say that transactions T_k and T_m are *concurrent* in a history H, if neither T_k precedes T_m, nor T_m precedes T_k (in H).

We say that history H is *sequential* if no two transactions in H are concurrent. We say that H is *complete* if H does not contain any live transaction.

We assume that every transaction T_k in H is executed by a single process. Conversely, we assume that every process p_i executes only one transaction at a time, i.e., that no two transactions are concurrent at any given process.

Sequential specification of a t-object. We use the concept of a *sequential specification* to describe the semantics of t-objects, as in [29,27]. Intuitively, a sequential specification of a t-object x lists all sequences of operation executions on x that are considered correct when executed outside any transactional context, e.g., in a standard, single-threaded application.[1] For example, the sequential specification of a t-variable x, denoted by $Seq(x)$, is the set of all sequences of *read* and *write* operation executions on x, such that in each sequence that belongs to $Seq(x)$, every *read* (operation execution) returns the value given as an argument to the latest preceding *write* (regardless transaction identifiers). (In fact, $Seq(x)$ also contains sequences that end with a pending invocation of *read* or *write*, but this is a minor detail.) Such a set defines precisely the semantics of a t-variable in a single-threaded, non-transactional system.

3   Opacity

Opacity is a safety property that captures the intuitive requirements that (1) all operations performed by every *committed* transaction appear as if they happened at some single, indivisible point during the transaction lifetime, (2) no operation performed by any *aborted* transaction is ever visible to other transactions (including live ones), and (3) every transaction always observes a *consistent* state of the system.

To help understand the definition of opacity, we first consider very simple histories, and increase their complexity step by step. The precise definitions of the terms that correspond to the steps described here are given in [17].

Opacity is trivial to express and verify for sequential histories in which every transaction, except possibly the last one, is committed. Basically, if S is such a history, then S is considered correct, and called *legal*, if, for every t-object x, the subsequence S_x of all events in H executed on t-object x respects the semantics of x, i.e., S_x belongs to the sequential specification of x. For example, if a transaction T_i writes value v to a t-variable x at some point in history S, then all subsequent reads of x in S, performed by T_i or by a following transaction, until the next write of x, must return value v.

The situation becomes more difficult if S is sequential but contains some aborted transactions followed by committed ones. For example, if an aborted transaction T_i writes value v to a t-variable x (and no other transaction writes v to x), then only T_i can read v from x thereafter. A read operation on x executed by a transaction following T_i must return the last value written to x by a preceding *committed* transaction. Basically, when considering a transaction T_i (committed or aborted) in S, we have to remove all aborted transactions that precede T_i in S. We then say that T_i is *legal* in S, if T_i together with all committed transactions preceding T_i in S form a legal history. Clearly, for an arbitrary sequential history S to be correct, all transactions in S must be legal.

---

[1] An operation execution specifies a transaction identifier, but the identifier can be treated as part of the arguments of the executed operation. In fact, in most cases, the semantics of an operation does not depend on the transaction that issues this operation.

To determine the opacity of an arbitrary history H, we ask whether H "looks like" some sequential history S that is correct (i.e., in which every transaction is legal). In the end, a user of a TM should not observe, or deal with, concurrency between transactions. More precisely, history S should contain the same transactions, performing the same operations, and receiving the same return values from those operations, as history H. We say then that H is *equivalent* to S. Equivalent histories differ only in the relative position of events of *different* transactions.

Moreover, the real-time order of transactions in history H should be preserved in S. That is, if a transaction T_i precedes a transaction T_k in H, then T_i must also precede T_k in S.

There is, however, one problem with finding a sequential history that is equivalent to a given history H: if two or more transactions are live in H, then there is no sequential history that is equivalent to H. Basically, if S is a sequential history, then $\prec_S$ must be a total order; however, if a transaction T_i precedes a transaction T_k in S, i.e., if $T_i \prec_S T_k$, then T_i must be committed or aborted. To solve the problem, observe that the changes performed by a transaction T_i should not become visible to other transactions until T_i *commits*. Transaction T_i commits at some point (not visible to the user) between the invocation and the response of operation $tryC(T_i) \rightarrow C_i$. That is, the semantics of T_i is the same as of an aborted transaction until T_i invokes $tryC(T_i)$, but this semantics might change (to the one of a committed transaction) at any point in time after T_i becomes commit-pending. Hence, we can safely transform an arbitrary history H into a *complete* history H' (called a *completion* of H) by (1) aborting all live and non-commit-pending transactions in H, and (2) committing or aborting every commit-pending transaction in H.

To summarize the above steps:

Definition 1. *A history H is* opaque *if there exists a sequential history S equivalent to any completion of H, such that (1) the real-time order of transactions in H is preserved in S, and (2) every transaction in S is legal in S.*

Note that the definition of opacity does not require every prefix of an opaque history to be also opaque. Thus, the set of all opaque histories is not prefix-closed. For example, while the following history is opaque:

$$H = \langle x.write(1)_1, \ x.read_2 \rightarrow 1, \ tryC(T_1) \rightarrow C_1, \ tryC(T_2) \rightarrow C_2 \rangle,$$

the prefix $H' = \langle x.write(1)_1, \ x.read_2 \rightarrow 1 \rangle$ of H is not opaque (assuming the initial value of x is 0), because, in H', transaction T_2 reads value written by T_1 that is not committed or commit-pending. However, a history of a TM is generated progressively and at each time the history of all events issued so far must be opaque. Hence, there is no need to enforce prefix-closeness in the definition of opacity, which should be as simple as possible.

The way we define the real-time ordering between transactions introduces a subtlety to the definition of opacity. Basically, the following situation is possible (and considered correct): a transaction T_1 updates some t-object x, and then some other transaction T_2 concurrent to T_1 observes an old state of x (from before the update of T_1) even after T_1 commits. For example, consider the following history (x and y are t-variables with initial value 0):

$$H = \langle x.read_1 \to 0, \ x.write(5)_2, \ y.write(5)_2,$$
$$tryC(T_2) \to C_2, y.read_3 \to 5, \ y.read_1 \to 0 \rangle.$$

In H, transaction T_1 appears to happen before T_2, because T_1 reads the initial values of t-variables x and y that are modified by T_2. Transaction T_3, on the other hand, appears to happen after T_2, because it reads the value of y written by T_2. Consider the following sequential history:

$$S = \langle x.read_1 \to 0, \ y.read_1 \to 0, \ tryC(T_1) \to A_1,$$
$$x.write(5)_2, \ y.write(5)_2, \ tryC(T_2) \to C_2,$$
$$y.read_3(5), \ tryC(T_3) \to A_3 \rangle.$$

It is easy to see that S is equivalent to the completion $H \cdot \langle tryC(T_1) \to A_1, tryC(T_3) \to A_3 \rangle$ of H, and that the real-time order of transactions in H is preserved in S. As, clearly, every transaction is legal in S, history H is opaque.

However, at first, it may seem wrong that the *read* operation of transaction T_3 returns the value written to y by the committed transaction T_2, while the following *read* operation, by transaction T_1, returns the old value of y. But if T_1 read value 5 from y, then opacity would be violated. This is because T_1 would observe an inconsistent state of the system: $x = 0$ and $y = 5$. Thus, letting T_1 read 0 from y is the only way to prevent T_1 from being aborted without violating opacity. Multi-version TMs, like JVSTM and LSA-STM, indeed use such optimizations to allow long read-only transactions to commit despite concurrent updates performed by other transactions. In general, it seems that forcing the order between operation executions of different transactions to be preserved, in addition to the real-time order of transactions themselves, would be too strong a requirement.

4 Obstruction-Free TMs

In this section, we define the class of obstruction-free TMs (OFTMs). We also determine the consensus number of OFTMs and show an inherent limitation of those TMs.

Our definition of an OFTM is based on the formal description of obstruction-free objects from [30]. In [18], we consider alternative definitions but we show, however, that these are computationally equivalent to the one we give here.

4.1 Definition of an OFTM

The definition we consider here uses the notion of *step contention* [30]: it says, intuitively, that a transaction T_k executed by a process p_i can be forcefully aborted only if some process other than p_i executed a step of the TM implementation concurrently to T_k.

More precisely, let E be any implementation history of any TM implementation M. We say that a transaction T_k executed by a process p_i encounters *step contention* in E, if there is a step of M executed by a process other than p_i in E after the first event of T_k and before the commit or abort event of T_k (if any).

Definition 2. *We say that a TM implementation M is* obstruction-free *(i.e., is an OFTM) if in every implementation history E of M, and for every transaction T_k in E, if T_k is forcefully aborted in E then T_k encounters step contention in E.*

4.2   The Power of an OFTM

We show that the consensus number of an OFTM is 2. We do so by first exhibiting an object, called *fo-consensus*, that is equivalent to any OFTM, and then showing that the consensus number of fo-consensus is 2. (The proofs of the theorems stated here are in [18].)

Intuitively, *fo-consensus* (introduced in [30] as "fail-only" consensus) provides an implementation of consensus (via an operation *propose*). That is, processes can use an fo-consensus object to agree on a single value chosen from the values that those processes propose, i.e., pass as a parameter to operation *propose*. However, unlike classical consensus, an fo-consensus object allows *propose* to *abort* when it cannot return a decision value because of concurrent invocations of *propose*. When *propose* aborts, it means that the operation did not take place, and so the value proposed using this operation has not been "registered" by the fo-consensus object (recall that only a value that has been proposed, and "registered", can be decided). A process which *propose* operation has been aborted may retry the operation many times (possibly with different proposed value), until a decision value is returned. (For a precise definition of an fo-consensus object, see [18].)

Theorem 1. *An OFTM is equivalent to fo-consensus.*

Theorem 2. *Fo-consensus cannot implement (wait-free) consensus in a system of 3 or more processes.*

From Theorem 1, Theorem 2, and the claim of [30] that consensus can be implemented from fo-consensus and registers in a system of 2 processes, we have:

Theorem 3. *The consensus number of an OFTM is 2.*

Corollary 1. *There is no algorithm that implements an OFTM using only registers.*

4.3   An Inherent Limitation of OFTMs

We show that no OFTM can be strictly disjoint-access-parallel. To define the notion of strict disjoint-access-parallelism, we distinguish operations that modify the state of a base object, and those that are read-only. We say that two processes (or transactions executed by these processes) *conflict on a base object* x, if both processes execute each an operation on x and at least one of these operations modifies the state of x. Intuitively, a TM implementation M is *strictly disjoint-access-parallel* if it ensures that processes executing transactions which access disjoint sets of t-objects do not conflict on common base objects (used by M).

Theorem 4. *No OFTM is strictly disjoint-access-parallel.*

It is worth noting that the original notion of disjoint-access-parallelism, introduced in [31], allows for transactions that are *indirectly* connected via other transactions to conflict on common base objects. For example, if a transaction T_1 accesses a t-object x, T_2 accesses y, and T_3 accesses both x and y, then there is a dependency chain from T_1 to T_2 via T_3, even though the two transactions T_1 and T_2 use different t-objects. Disjoint-access-parallelism allows then the processes executing T_1 and T_2 to conflict on some base objects. Disjoint-access-parallelism in the sense of [31] can be ensured by an OFTM implementation, e.g., DSTM.

It is also straightforward to implement a TM that is strictly disjoint-access-parallel but not obstruction-free, e.g., using two-phase locking [32] or the TL algorithm [33].

5   Lock-Based TMs

Lock-based TMs are TM implementations that use (internally) mutual exclusion to handle some phases of a transaction. Most of them use some variant of the two-phase locking protocol, well-known in the database world [32].

From the user's perspective, however, the choice of the mechanism used internally by a TM implementation is not very important. What is important is the semantics the TM manifests on its public interface, and the time/space complexities of the implementation. If those properties are known, then the designer of a lock-based TM is free to choose the techniques that are best for a given hardware platform, without the fear of breaking existing applications that use a TM.

In this section, we define *strong progressiveness*—a progress property commonly ensured by lock-based TMs. We determine the consensus number of strongly progressive TMs, and show an inherent performance trade-off in those TMs. (The proofs of the theorems stated here can be found in [19].)

5.1   Strong Progressiveness

Intuitively, strong progressiveness says that (1) if a transaction has no *conflict* then it cannot be forcefully aborted, and (2) if a group of transactions conflict on a single t-variable, then not all of those transactions can be forcefully aborted. Roughly speaking, concurrent transactions conflict if they access the same t-variable in a conflicting way, i.e., if at least one of those accesses is a *write* operation. (We assume here, for simplicity of presentation, that (1) all t-objects are t-variables, i.e., they export only *read* and *write* operations, and (2) there are no *false* conflicts. We discuss those assumptions in [19].)

Strong progressiveness is not the strongest possible progress property. The strongest one, which requires that no transaction is ever forcefully aborted, cannot be implemented without throttling significantly the parallelism between transactions, and is thus impractical in multi-processor systems.

Strong progressiveness, however, still gives a programmer the following important advantages. First, it guarantees that if two independent subsystems of an application do not share any memory locations (or t-variables), then their transactions are completely isolated from each other (i.e., a transaction executed by a subsystem A does not cause a transaction in a subsystem B to be forcefully aborted). Second, it avoids "spurious" aborts: the cases when a transaction can abort are strictly defined. Third, it ensures global progress for single-operation transactions, which is important when non-transactional accesses to t-variables are encapsulated into transactions in order to ensure strong atomicity [34]. Finally, it ensures that processes are able to eventually communicate via transactions (albeit in a simplified manner—through a single t-variable at a time). Nevertheless, one can imagine many other reasonable progress properties, for which strong progressiveness can be a good reference point.

Let H be any history, and T_i be any transaction in H. Intuitively, we denote by $CVar_H(T_i)$ the set of t-variables on which transaction T_i conflicts with any other transaction in history H.[2] If Q is any set of transactions in H, then $CVar_H(Q)$ denotes the union of sets $CVar_H(T_i)$ for all $T_i \in Q$, i.e., the set of t-variables on which any transaction in set Q conflicts with any other transaction in history H.

Let $CTrans(H)$ be the set of subsets of transactions in a history H, such that a set Q is in $CTrans(H)$ if no transaction in Q conflicts with a transaction *not* in Q. In particular, if T_i is a transaction in a history H and T_i does not conflict with any other transaction in H, then $\{T_i\} \in CTrans(H)$.

Definition 3. *A TM implementation M is* strongly progressive, *if in every history H of M the following property is satisfied: for every set $Q \in CTrans(H)$, if $|CVar_H(Q)| \leq 1$, then some transaction in Q is not forcefully aborted in H.*

5.2   The Power of a Lock-Based TM

We show here that the consensus number of a strongly progressive TM is 2. First, we prove that a strongly progressive TM is computationally equivalent to a *strong try-lock* object that we describe in this section (and define precisely in [19]). That is, one can implement a strongly progressive TM from (a number of) strong try-locks and registers, and vice versa. Second, we determine that the consensus number of a strong try-lock is 2.

All lock-based TMs we know of use (often implicitly) a special kind of locks, usually called *try-locks* [35]. Intuitively, a try-lock is an object that provides mutual exclusion (like a lock), but does not block processes indefinitely. That is, if a process p_i requests a try-lock L, but L is already acquired by a different process, p_i is returned the information that its request failed instead of being blocked waiting until L is released.

---

[2] For a precise definition, consult [19].

Try-locks keep the TM implementation simple and avoid deadlocks. Moreover, if any form of fairness is needed, it is provided at a higher level than at the level of individual locks—then more information about a transaction can be used to resolve conflicts and provide progress. Ensuring safety and progress can be effectively separate tasks.

Every try-lock L guarantees the following property, called *mutual exclusion*: no two processes hold L at the same time. Intuitively, we say that a try-lock L is *strong* if whenever several processes compete for L, then one should be able to acquire L. This property corresponds to deadlock-freedom, livelock-freedom, or progress [36] properties of (blocking) locks.

While there exists a large number of lock implementations, only a few are try-locks or can be converted to try-locks in a straightforward way. The technical problems of transforming a queue (blocking) lock into a try-lock are highlighted in [35]. It is trivial to transform a typical TAS or TATAS lock [36] into a strong try-lock [19].

Theorem 5. *A strongly progressive TM is equivalent to a strong try-lock.*

Theorem 6. *A strong try-lock has consensus number 2.*

Hence, by Theorem 5 and Theorem 6, the following theorem holds:

Theorem 7. *A strongly progressive TM has consensus number 2.*

Corollary 2. *There is no algorithm that implements a strongly progressive TM using only registers.*

5.3   Performance Trade-Off in Lock-Based TMs

We show that the space complexity of every strongly progressive TM that uses *invisible reads* is at least exponential with the number of t-variables available to transactions.[3] The invisible reads strategy is used by a majority of lock-based TM implementations [7,8,12,14,21,24] as it allows efficient optimistic reading of t-variables. Intuitively, if invisible reads are used, a transaction that reads a t-variable does not write any information to base objects. Hence, many processors can concurrently execute transactions that read the same t-variables, without invalidating each other's caches and causing high traffic on the interprocessor (or inter-core) bus. However, transactions that update t-variables do not know whether there are any concurrent transactions that read those variables. (For a precise definition of invisible reads, consult [19].)

The *size* of a t-variable or a base object x can be defined as the number of distinct, reachable states of x. In particular, if x is a t-variable or a register object, then the size of x is the number of values that can be written to x. For example, the size of a 32-bit register is 2^{32}.

---

[3] In fact, the result holds also for TMs that ensure a property called *weak progressiveness*, which is strictly weaker than strong progressiveness [19].

Theorem 8. *Every strongly progressive TM implementation that uses invisible reads and provides to transactions N_s t-variables of size K_s uses $\Omega\left(K_s{}^{N_s}/K_b\right)$ base objects of size K_b.*

This result might seem surprising, since it is not obvious that modern lock-based TMs have non-linear space complexity. The exponential (or, in fact, unbounded) complexity comes from the use of timestamps that determine version numbers of t-variables. TM implementations usually reserve a constant-size word for each version number (which gives linear space complexity). However, an overflow can happen and has to be handled in order to guarantee opacity. This requires (a) limiting the progress (strong progressiveness) of transactions when overflow occurs, and (b) preventing read-only transactions from being completely invisible [19]. Concretely speaking, our result means that efficient TM implementations (the ones that use invisible reads) must either intermittently (albeit very rarely) violate progress guarantees, or use unbounded timestamps.

6   Concluding Remarks

We gave an overview of our recent work on establishing the theoretical foundations of transactional memory (TM). We omitted many related results. We give here a short summary of some of those.

An important question is how to verify that a given history of a TM, or a given TM implementation, ensures opacity, obstruction-freedom, or strong progressiveness. In [17], we present a graph interpretation of opacity (similar in concept to the one of serializability [37,38]). Basically, we show how to build a graph that represents the dependencies between transactions in a given history H. We then reduce the problem of checking whether H is opaque to the problem of checking the acyclicity of this graph. In [19], we provide a simple reduction scheme that facilitates proving strong progressiveness of a given TM implementation M. Roughly speaking, we prove that if it is possible to say which parts of the algorithm of M can be viewed as logical try-locks (in a precise sense we define in [19]), and if those logical try-locks are strong, then the TM is strongly progressive. In other words, if the locking mechanism used by M is based on (logical) strong try-locks, then M is strongly progressive.

The graph characterization of opacity and the reduction scheme for strong progressiveness do not address the problem of automatic model checking TM implementations. Basically, they do not deal with the issue of the unbounded number of states of a general TM implementation. In [39,40], the problem is addressed for an interesting class of TMs. Basically, it is proved there that if a given TM implementation has certain symmetry properties, then it either violates opacity in some execution with only 2 processes and 2 t-variables, or ensures opacity in every execution (with any number of processes and t-variables). The theoretical framework presented in [39,40] allows for automatic verifications of implementations such as DSTM or TL2 in a relatively short time. Work similar in scope is also presented in [41].

One of the problems that we did not cover is the semantics of memory transactions from a programming language perspective. A very simple (but also very convenient) interface to a TM is via an `atomic` keyword that marks those blocks of code that should be executed inside transactions. The possible interactions between transactions themselves are confined by opacity. However, opacity does not specify the semantics of the interactions between the various programming language constructs that are inside and outside atomic blocks. Some work on those issues is presented, e.g., in [42,43,44,45,46].

Acknowledgements

We thank Hagit Attiya, Aleksandar Dragojević, Pascal Felber, Christof Fetzer, Seth Gilbert, Vincent Gramoli, Tim Harris, Thomas Henzinger, Eshcar Hillel, Petr Kouznetsov, Leaf Petersen, Benjamin Pierce, Nir Shavit, Vasu Singh, and Jan Vitek for their helpful comments and discussions.

References

1. Herlihy, M., Moss, J.E.B.: Transactional memory: Architectural support for lock-free data structures. In: ISCA (1993)
2. Gray, J., Reuter, A.: Transaction Processing: Concepts and Techniques. Morgan Kaufmann, San Francisco (1992)
3. Shavit, N., Touitou, D.: Software transactional memory. In: PODC (1995)
4. Herlihy, M., Luchangco, V., Moir, M., Scherer III, W.N.: Software transactional memory for dynamic-sized data structures. In: PODC (2003)
5. Maranthe, V.J., Scherer III, W.N., Scott, M.L.: Adaptive software transactional memory. In: Fraigniaud, P. (ed.) DISC 2005. LNCS, vol. 3724, pp. 354–368. Springer, Heidelberg (2005)
6. Cachopo, J., Rito-Silva, A.: Versioned boxes as the basis for memory transactions. In: SCOOL (2005)
7. Marathe, V.J., Spear, M.F., Heriot, C., Acharya, A., Eisenstat, D., Scherer III, W.N., Scott, M.L.: Lowering the overhead of software transactional memory. In: TRANSACT (2006)
8. Harris, T., Plesko, M., Shinnar, A., Tarditi, D.: Optimizing memory transactions. In: PLDI (2006)
9. Spear, M.F., Marathe, V.J., Scherer III, W.N., Scott, M.L.: Conflict detection and validation strategies for software transactional memory. In: Dolev, S. (ed.) DISC 2006. LNCS, vol. 4167, pp. 179–193. Springer, Heidelberg (2006)
10. Herlihy, M., Moir, M., Luchangco, V.: A flexible framework for implementing software transactional memory. In: OOPSLA (2006)
11. Riegel, T., Felber, P., Fetzer, C.: A lazy snapshot algorithm with eager validation. In: Dolev, S. (ed.) DISC 2006. LNCS, vol. 4167, pp. 284–298. Springer, Heidelberg (2006)
12. Adl-Tabatabai, A.R., Lewis, B.T., Menon, V., Murphy, B.R., Saha, B., Shpeisman, T.: Compiler and runtime support for efficient software transactional memory. In: PLDI (2006)

13. Shpeisman, T., Menon, V., Adl-Tabatabai, A.R., Balensiefer, S., Grossman, D., Hudson, R.L., Moore, K.F., Saha, B.: Enforcing isolation and ordering in STM. In: PLDI (2007)
14. Felber, P., Riegel, T., Fetzer, C.: Dynamic performance tuning of word-based software transactional memory. In: PPoPP (2008)
15. Gramoli, V., Harmanci, D., Felber, P.: Toward a theory of input acceptance for transactional memories. In: OPODIS (2008)
16. Dragojević, A., Singh, A.V., Guerraoui, R., Singh, V.: Preventing versus curing: Avoiding conflicts in transactional memories. In: PODC (2009)
17. Guerraoui, R., Kapałka, M.: On the correctness of transactional memory. In: PPoPP (2008)
18. Guerraoui, R., Kapałka, M.: On obstruction-free transactions. In: SPAA (2008)
19. Guerraoui, R., Kapałka, M.: The semantics of progress in lock-based transactional memory. In: POPL (2009)
20. Herlihy, M.: SXM software transactional memory package for C#, http://www.cs.brown.edu/~mph
21. Dice, D., Shalev, O., Shavit, N.: Transactional locking II. In: Dolev, S. (ed.) DISC 2006. LNCS, vol. 4167, pp. 194–208. Springer, Heidelberg (2006)
22. Guerraoui, R., Henzinger, T.A., Singh, V.: Permissiveness in transactional memories. In: Taubenfeld, G. (ed.) DISC 2008. LNCS, vol. 5218. Springer, Heidelberg (2008)
23. Raynal, M., Imbs, D.: An STM lock-based protocol that satisfies opacity and progressiveness. In: OPODIS (2008)
24. Dragojević, A., Guerraoui, R., Kapałka, M.: Stretching transactional memory. In: PLDI (2009)
25. Herlihy, M.: Wait-free synchronization. ACM Transactions on Programming Languages and Systems 13(1), 124–149 (1991)
26. Jayanti, P.: Robust wait-free hierarchies. Journal of the ACM 44(4), 592–614 (1997)
27. Herlihy, M., Wing, J.M.: Linearizability: a correctness condition for concurrent objects. ACM Transactions on Programming Languages and Systems 12(3), 463–492 (1990)
28. Fischer, M.J., Lynch, N.A., Paterson, M.S.: Impossibility of distributed consensus with one faulty process. Journal of the ACM 32(3), 374–382 (1985)
29. Weihl, W.E.: Local atomicity properties: Modular concurrency control for abstract data types. ACM Transactions on Programming Languages and Systems 11(2), 249–282 (1989)
30. Attiya, H., Guerraoui, R., Kouznetsov, P.: Computing with reads and writes in the absence of step contention. In: Fraigniaud, P. (ed.) DISC 2005. LNCS, vol. 3724, pp. 122–136. Springer, Heidelberg (2005)
31. Israeli, A., Rappoport, L.: Disjoint-access-parallel implementations of strong shared memory primitives. In: PODC (1994)
32. Eswaran, K.P., Gray, J.N., Lorie, R.A., Traiger, I.L.: The notions of consistency and predicate locks in a database system. Commun. ACM 19(11), 624–633 (1976)
33. Dice, D., Shavit, N.: What really makes transactions fast? In: TRANSACT (2006)
34. Blundell, C., Lewis, E.C., Martin, M.M.K.: Subtleties of transactional memory atomicity semantics. IEEE Computer Architecture Letters 5(2) (2006)
35. Scott, M.L., Scherer III, W.N.: Scalable queue-based spin locks with timeout. In: PPoPP (2001)
36. Raynal, M.: Algorithms for Mutual Exclusion. MIT Press, Cambridge (1986)
37. Papadimitriou, C.H.: The serializability of concurrent database updates. Journal of the ACM 26(4), 631–653 (1979)

38. Bernstein, P.A., Goodman, N.: Multiversion concurrency control—theory and algorithms. ACM Transactions on Database Systems 8(4), 465–483 (1983)
39. Guerraoui, R., Henzinger, T., Jobstmann, B., Singh, V.: Model checking transactional memories. In: PLDI (2008)
40. Guerraoui, R., Henzinger, T.A., Singh, V.: Completeness and nondeterminism in model checking transactional memorie. In: van Breugel, F., Chechik, M. (eds.) CONCUR 2008. LNCS, vol. 5201, pp. 21–35. Springer, Heidelberg (2008)
41. O'Leary, J., Saha, B., Tuttle, M.R.: Model checking transactional memory with Spin. In: ICDCS (2009)
42. Vitek, J., Jagannathan, S., Welc, A., Hosking, A.: A semantic framework for designer transactions. In: Schmidt, D. (ed.) ESOP 2004. LNCS, vol. 2986, pp. 249–263. Springer, Heidelberg (2004)
43. Jagannathan, S., Vitek, J., Welc, A., Hosking, A.: A transactional object calculus. Science of Computer Programming 57(2), 164–186 (2005)
44. Abadi, M., Birrell, A., Harris, T., Isard, M.: Semantics of transactional memory and automatic mutual exclusion. In: POPL (2008)
45. Moore, K.F., Grossman, D.: High-level small-step operational semantics for transactions. In: POPL (2008)
46. Menon, V., Balensiefer, S., Shpeisman, T., Adl-Tabatabai, A.R., Hudson, R.L., Saha, B., Welc, A.: Practical weak-atomicity semantics for Java STM. In: SPAA (2008)

Mixed-Signal System Verification:
A High-Speed Link Example

Jaeha Kim

Center for Integrated Systems, Stanford University
Room 128, Paul G. Allen Building
420 Via Palou Mall, Stanford, CA 94305-4070, U.S.A.
jaeha@ieee.org

Abstract. This tutorial begins by visiting various mixed-signal circuit examples in high-speed interfaces, of which verification cannot be done via the established methods for digital systems and instead has relied on exhaustive time-domain circuit simulations. While recognizing the vast literature on trying to extending the prevailing digital verification methods to analog and mixed-signal systems, this tutorial suggests that a promising approach might be to extend the way that digital methods leverage the *design intent* and choose the proper abstraction for it. After examining the properties that the designers would most want to verify for the high-speed interface circuits, it is claimed that those are mostly the properties of a linear or weakly-nonlinear system, e.g. gain, bandwidth, local stability, etc. It is because most of the mixed-signal circuits in high-speed links are motivated by the need to replace analog circuits with digital for the ease of process migration. Although in digital forms, the resulting circuits are still supposed to have analog functionalities which are best described in linear or weakly-nonlinear system models. Therefore, a possible formal verification for those circuits might be to extend the traditional small-signal linear analysis. For example, this tutorial will demonstrate ways to extend the linear AC analysis in SPICE to measure the phase-domain transfer functions of PLLs or the noise transfer functions of delta-sigma ADCs. It also examines the limitations of linear analysis, for instance, the inability to detect start-up failures, which is the problem that can be more properly addressed by extending the digital verification methods and coverage concepts.

Keywords: analog and mixed-signal verification, analog design intent, linear system models.

A. Bouajjani and O. Maler (Eds.): CAV 2009, LNCS 5643, p. 16, 2009.
© Springer-Verlag Berlin Heidelberg 2009

Modelling Epigenetic Information Maintenance: A Kappa Tutorial

Jean Krivine[1], Vincent Danos[2], and Arndt Benecke[1]

[1] Institut des Hautes Études Scientifiques & Institut de Recherche Interdisciplinaire - CNRS USR3078 - USTL, 35 route de Chartres, 91440 Bures-sur-Yvette, France
[2] University of Edinburgh

The purpose of this tutorial is to explain and illustrate an approach to the quantitative modelling of molecular interaction networks which departs from the usual notion of (bio-) chemical reaction. This tutorial is self-contained and supposes no familiarity with molecular biology.[1]

We shall use a modelling language called Kappa [1], but much of what we will present equally applies to the larger family of rule-based modelling frameworks -and in particular to the BNG language [2] which is very close to Kappa. For a technical exposition of Kappa as a stochastic graph rewriting system, the reader can consult Ref. [3].

To demonstrate the interest of a rule-based approach we will investigate a concrete biological question, that of the maintenance of epigenetic information.

Our plan is to:
- articulate in purely biological terms an epigenetic repair mechanism (§1)
- capture this mechanism into a simple rule-based model (§2)
- equip this rule set with numerical information (rule rates, copy numbers of various intervening agents) to obtain a quantitative model (§3.1-3.2)
- exploit the said model by investigating various questions (§3.3-3.4)

Although the model we present here is congruent with the current evidence, and generates interesting results, it offers a -perhaps overly- simplified view of the relevant biological mechanisms. Its primary use is to introduce gradually the Kappa concepts and (some of its) methods in a concrete modelling situation, as we make progress in our plan.

1 Epigenetic Repair

Key epigenetic information is encoded in the human genome via a chemical modification of C bases into their methylated form mC. The resulting methylation patterns which are far from random, can be thought of as annotations of the DNA which determine the shutdown of their associated DNA segments. Such bookmarkings are inherited upon duplication -hence the qualifier epigenetic. This large-scale mechanism to manage the genome plays an important role in cell differentiation and unsurprisingly is very often found disrupted in cancers.

---

[1] The reference model can be obtained at `krivine@ihes.fr`, and the Kappa implementation used for this paper at `support@plectix.com`

A. Bouajjani and O. Maler (Eds.): CAV 2009, LNCS 5643, pp. 17–32, 2009.

The mCs form about 2% of the total number of Cs and are recognised by a suitable machinery -among which the MeCP2 protein- which drives the DNA compaction and subsequent gene silencing. Both the setting and maintenance of epigenetic information is under intense investigation [4]. In this note we will concentrate on the maintenance aspects.

Indeed, maintenance or repair is needed since there are problems inherent to the low-level biochemical substrate of epigenetic information. DNA base pairs can be either of the AT type or the CG one (Fig. 1), and as said, the latter can be further modified as mCG. The problem is that mCGs and CGs can endure spontaneous chemical transitions to TG and UG mismatches (roughly four times per second per genome). If not reset to their respective original values, such mismatches would inevitably lead to erratic and eventually damaging genetic expression profiles. It must be that there are various agents at work within the cell in charge of recognising and repairing these mismatches and thus stabilizing the epigenetic information.

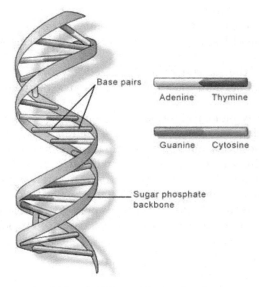

Fig. 1. The dual base pairs AT and CG provide a redundant representation of genetic information; not so for epigenetic information which is not redundantly represented in its sole biological mC substrate (Image from the U.S. National Library of Medicine)

1.1   The Repair Problem

Recent findings point at a surprising fact, namely that both kinds of mismatches seem to be recognised by the *same* agent TDG which is also in charge of excising the faulty bases T and U, before they can be replaced. Considering that after excision there is no way to tell from the local DNA state itself what the nature of the mismatch was (in sharp constrast with the redundancy of the representation of genetic information as in Fig. 1), one wonders how a proper resetting can ensue.

Let us examine the life cycle of C bases in more details to see what the problem is. As said, Cs and mCs are subject to spontaneous deaminations into U and T respectively. These are happening roughly at a rate of 1 per second and per billion bases (which give means of calibrating the time units used in the model, of which more in §3). As shown Fig. 2, the enzymatic repertoire of the host cell shows no way how to directly reverse those changes. Instead, the C life cycle has this enigmatic feature that both U and T converge to C after being processed by TDG and APE1. In other words the cycles used to reset faulty bases at their initial methylation state join ambiguously at a base pair CG. There the system in a state where it is unclear whether the last step -performed by Dnmt3A- should be taken, ie whether C should be methylated.

The system has no obvious local memory and is in the danger of making two kinds of mistakes, either by methylating a C that was not, or by forgetting to re-methylate a C that was.[2]

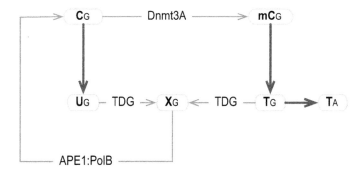

Fig. 2. C's deamination and repair cycle: Cs and methylated Cs are subject to deaminations into U and T; TDG can recognise and excise the induced mismatches (X stands for the lack of a base), while APE1:PolB can put back in place a C, and Dnmt3A can transfer the methyl group that is needed to make it an mC. The question is how does Dnmt3A know whether a C should be remethylated or left as is?

1.2   A Solution?

From the above it clearly follows that some memory of the mismatch type must be established before the excision of the faulty base by TDG. DNA-processing proteins are not monolithic objects and can be usefully decomposed into subunits providing different functionalities and usually called domains.

The structure of TDG reveals two DNA binding domains:

-*N140* (named after its position in TDG's amino-acid chain) responsible for the DNA-binding and excision activity,
- and *rd* (regulatory domain) which provides a second means to bind DNA.

---

[2] In fact there is a third possible mistake which is for the BER complex (base excision repair machinery) to correct the TG mismatch into a TA, but we are not taking this into account.

So it seems quite natural to hypothesize that:

- TDG binds both mismatches using its *N140* DNA-binding domain,
- TDG uses another domain *rd* to bind the DNA a second time in the *specific* case of a *TG* mismatch.

Such a mechanism leaves the system in an unambiguous state even after the excision of the faulty bases T or U -provided that the excision of a TG mismatch is only performed after the secondary TDG binding via *rd* has happened. This we will also suppose. We will refer to this mechanism as the transient memory assumption, and refer to the *rd*.

Note that the memory of the type of mismatch under repair is kept -not in the DNA substrate itself- but rather in the transient assembly of some of the repair agents. In other words the redundancy is buily dynamically during by the repair process itself. This is compatible with the now emerging picture of DNA-processing complexes as being assembled only ever partially, and with causal constraints implemented via enzymatic steps [5]. Another thing the reader might already have noticed, is that an immediate consequence of our hypothetic mechanism is that a knock-out of the *rd* domain on TDG should hinder the repair of mCs, and potentially lead to their complete loss. This is indeed observed experimentally. What is also known is that the TG mismatch is a much stronger perturbation of the DNA structure than the UG one, and hence it is plausible to suppose as we do here that TDG can tell the two apart.

In order to provide further support one could try out various other experiments as in the course of a normal biological investigation. However, at this stage it might be perhaps wiser and more economic to provide a quantitative model prior to any further experimental elaboration. Indeed, it is easy to get carried away and convince oneself of the general good-lookingness of an informal hypothesis. Not so with a numerical model which is a stronger stress test as it incorporates a proof of quantitative consistency of our starting assumption (of course not by any means a proof that the said assumption is indeed true). Constructing such a model is what we do in the next two sections (§2–3).

2   The Qualitative Model

One first difficulty in turning our informal assumption above into quantitative form is not even quantitative -as it is a matter of pure representation. The various agents involved in epigenetic repair will associate in so many different contexts that requiring a model to explicit all of these is unrealistic. A quick glance at Fig. 3 describing the domains and interactions of CBP, one of the biological agents we will be concerned with, reveals the potential combinatorics involved. Such cases are in no way exceptional. In fact, this combinatorial complexity is often amplified by the fact that proteins often have multiple modification states. One would like to specify molecular events which are conditioned only on partial contextual information, that is to say one would like to use *rules* and not simple reactions.

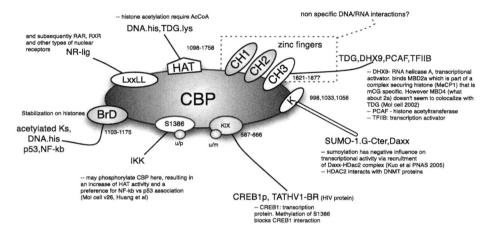

Fig. 3. Domains and interactions of CBP: the fine domain structure of CBP is far richer than what we will represent in our model (§2.3)

As our mechanism is formulated directly in terms of domain-domain binding, it would also be convenient if one were to use a quantitative formalism that offers binding as a primitive operation. The language Kappa -a stochastic calculus of binding and modification introduced in the context of cellular signalling networks- fits such representational needs well, and we shall use it here.

2.1 Agents

To begin with, we have to list the various agents that we want to describe in our model and decide at which level of resolution each will be made available.

Folowing Fig. 2, we will thus use the following inventory of agent types (of which there will be many copies in a given state of the system):

- an agent DNA representing a unit of closure and opening (one can think of it as a DNA double strand about a kilobase long)
- a pair of agents MeCP2, CBP controlling DNA segments closure and opening
- an agent TDG in charge of recognising/excising both types of mismatches
- a combined agent APE1:PolB to fill in the lacking C after excision
- and Dnmt3A to methylate Cs

Each of the agents above is equipped with an interface, that is to say a set of sites. Sites are a generic abstraction for meaningful subunits of an agent such a chemically modifiable site, a binding site, etc. As shown in Fig. 4 where all six agents are represented with their sites, some of these sites can bind together (note that the curvature of the various edges carries no signification and is purely there for aesthetic reasons). The resulting site graph is called the model *contact map*. As we wish to build a simple model, not all known sites are included in our map. For instance, CBP has several binding sites (Fig. 3) and yet in our map we consider only one for binding compact chromatin and one for binding TDG.

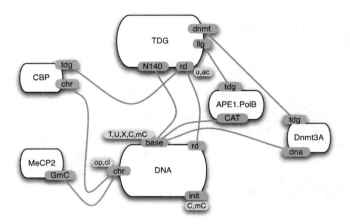

Fig. 4. The model's contact map: agents figure together with their sites and the potential values held by these sites (only TDG and DNA have sites holding values). Potential bindings are represented by edges.

A *state* of our model is any site graph, where each site is bound at most once and in a way that is compatible with the contact map, and each site has a definite internal state (if it has internal states at all). It is important to realise that the contact map does not specify under which conditions a binding/unbinding or a modification is possible, it merely registers which bindings are possible at all.[3] It is the role of rules to specify for each possible binding, unbinding or internal state modification, under which partial conditions it happens. We will describe rules in the next subsection.

The DNA *init* site in the contact map has no biological meaning and is used to keep a record of the base initial value and track repair mistakes (see §3 below). The DNA site *chr* abstracts the complex closure and opening mechanism of DNA segment; *chr* stands for chromatine which is the biological name for the DNA molecule and its associated cortege of structure-managing proteins, it can be either closed (compact) or open.

2.2   Rules

The language of rules on (site) graphs that we will be using to describe the dynamics of our system of interest can be neatly described in mathematical form, but we will not belabour this point in this tutorial and keep an intuitive approach.

We shall only consider here the essential rules, ie the ones that are directly in charge of setting and exploiting the transient memory. There are several other rules in the full model including the spontaneous deamination rules, as well the rules associated to the chromatin control, the APE1:PolB base synthesis rule,

---

[3] Genome-wide contact maps are beginning to appear improving spectacularly the level at which the mass action proteic systems can be described [6].

and those controlling the association of TDG with its various partners other than DNA, but these pose no particular problem and are not shown.

What we need first is a pair of *recognition rules* stipulating how TDG recognises the DNA mismatches, and how TDG tells apart the two kinds of mismatches. These two rules are represented Fig. 5 and embody half of our transient memory assumption. This is of course a very simplified view as in reality, it might well be that TDG can bind open DNA unspecifically and diffuse along the DNA strand [4]. Subtler and more realistic behaviours of this sort could be incorporated in the model, and one would have to concatenate explicitly our DNA segments, and specify rules for sliding. As said, for this tutorial we shall keep things simple.

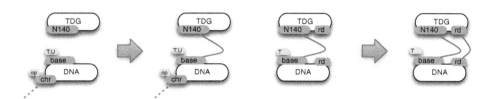

Fig. 5. TDG-DNA recognition rules: the dotted semi-edge means that the binding state of DNA(chr) is left unspecified, it can be free or not; the key second binding depends on the base being T (hence having been mC); the first binding presupposes that the chromatin is opened (the chr site holds the value 'op')

Then we need a pair of *excision rules* where TDG bites off the faulty base and brings along APE1:PolB to place a C at the place left vacant. These two rules are given Fig. 6. We could have decomposed these rules by separating the excision step from the binding exchange one. It is worth noticing that the excision rule in the T case does require the binding on the rd domain to be in place, as excising to soon would compromise the arming of our temporary memory, that is to say the rd-mediated binding to DNA. This is the other half our assumption.

To complete the repair triptych we need a *remethylation rule* where Dnmt3A comes into play. The rule is given Fig. 7, and as we can see it conditions this event on the presence of the memory binding at rd. It is interesting to see that at this stage we meet with the problem dual to the one dealt with in the T excision rule Fig. 6. Namely, we would like to make sure that the memory binding does not disappear too soon.

A way to do this is to let go of the rd binding only after remethylation of the base. This is easy to formulate as a rule but we choose not to because it seems too unrealistic. For one thing the rd binding is known to be weak experimentally, and it seems unlikely that the excision and subsequent loss of the $N140$ binding will help stabilize it. Even if that were the case, it seems that asking TDG to know if the base it is *no longer bound to* is methylated is too non-local an interaction. The good news is that this is actually not necessary and one can let this binding be quite weak without compromising the performance of repair.

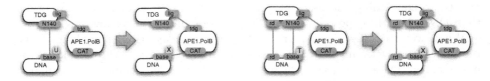

Fig. 6. TDG:DNA-APE1:PolB excision rules (abbreviated respectively as "repair U" and "repair T" below): TDG and APE1:PolB exchange connexions to the base under repair in order for APE1.PolB to replace the missing base, that was excised by TDG; importantly, and in accordance our basic assumption (§2), the excision of a T (second rule) presupposes the binding of rd

Fig. 7. DNA-Dnmt3A remethylation rule: Dnmt3A binds to the base left free by TDG and remethylates it; the memory is not local to any of the agents but resides in their assembly

We can only (and will in §3) elaborate on this point when we have a quantitative model. Indeed, rules in the absence of any kinetic information only specify a non-deterministic system. If we suppose as we do that the *rd* binding is even somewhat reversible, nothing prevents our memory binding to dissolve. The non-deterministic transition system associated to our rule set is wrong, it will make mistakes. Numerically however, such mistakes just never happens and the repair system is correct. This discussion begs the question of how one equips the model quantitatively, a matter to which we turn in the next section.

2.3   Stories

Before turning to the quantitative aspect, however, we can check the causal soundness of the rule set we have put together. We ask what minimal trajectories starting from a mC deamination event will lead to its proper repair. As in any rewriting system, one has a natural notion of commuting/concurrent events, which one can use to simplify trajectories leading to event of a given type - here a C remethylation- by eliminating spurious concurrent events. In practice this causal simplification leads to an overwhelming number of thumbnails. But one can simplify them further by asking that they contain no subconfiguration leading to the same observable. This notion of incompressible subtrace, where all steps matter, and which we call story, gives strong insights in the causal mechanisms of a rule set, and is a powerful tool to debug complex rule sets.

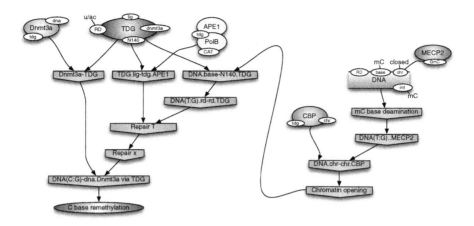

Fig. 8. A story leading to a C remethylation: nodes represent events, that is to say rule applications; causal precedence between events is indicated with arrows, eg the chromatin opening is a necessary step for TDG to bind at $N140$

An example is given Fig. 8. The right part depicts an mC deamination with the subsequent chromatin opening by CBP, while the left part shows a Dnmt3A:TDG:APE1.PolB trimer recognising and processing the ensuing mismatch according to the rules given previously. We will see later two other variant stories (§3.4). All observed stories are suffixes of these three archetypical ones in this case.

3   The Quantitative Model

Our rule set is a good start, however, as we just mentioned, there are pending questions that need numerical information to begin to be answered. We first need to understand how one can use a rule set to create a dynamical system, specifically an implicit continuous time Markov chain (CTMC). By implicit, we mean that there is no need to construct the explicit state space of the system, which is fortunate since combinatorial complexity forbids an explicit representation of all but the simplest systems [7].

3.1   The CTMC

The needed CTMC structure is as follows. Define the activity of a rule r in a given state x as $\mathbf{a}(r, x) := k_r[s_r, x]$ where $k_r \in \mathbb{R}^+$ is the rule intrisic rate (a parameter), s_r is the rule left hand side, and $[s_r, x]$ is the number of matches of s_r in x. Define the global activity as $\mathbf{a}(x) := \sum_r \mathbf{a}(r, x)$. The probability that the next rule to be applied is r is given by $\mathbf{a}(r, x)/\sum_r \mathbf{a}(r, x)$, and the random time elapsed δt is given by $p(\delta t > T) = \exp(-\mathbf{a}(x)T)$.

Observe that the probability to pick r is 0 iff r has no matches, which seems logical, and likewise the expected time for anything to happen is ∞ iff $\mathbf{a}(x) = 0$.

The above dynamics implements a stochastic version of the mass action law and is often referred to as the 'Gillespie algorithm'. The behaviour of the system will depend both on the reaction rates and the copy numbers, meaning the number of agents of each type defining the system initial state. In our special case these copy numbers will be invariant since we have introduced no rules that consumes or produces an agent. Although we don't have serious quantitative data with which one could constrain our parameters, we can nevertheless make reasonable guesses.

3.2   Choosing Parameters

Let us start with copy numbers. We specify them by annotating the contact map as in Fig. 9. Furthermore, we suppose that all agents are disconnected in the initial state, except for the 400 closed DNA agents which we suppose dimerized with a MeCP2. This is just a convenience since what interests us is the behaviour of the system at steady state and the particulars of the initial state will soon be forgotten -except for the copy numbers which as said are invariant. The 50/1 ratio of Cs to mCs is respected. The other copy numbers are chosen so that the total number of repair agents is about 1% of the number of DNA segments. The true experimental numbers are not known but the proportions should be about right. At any rate, with such a choice repair does not become too easy, as it would if we had more repair agents.

Let us fix (arbitrarily) the deamination rate to $10^{-2}s^{-1}$. This amounts to defining the time units of the model. Since we have roughly $20,000$ DNA agents, one will see about 200 deaminations per time unit, which is 50 times more than in the genome, hence our time currency is worth 50 seconds, and simulations running for 500 such time units (as below §3.3) should make zero mistakes.

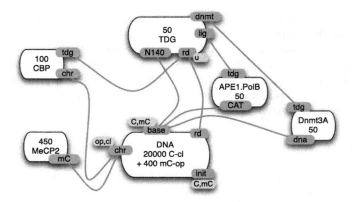

Fig. 9. The initial copy numbers: we suppose all 400 DNA closed agents have an mC base and are dimerized with a MeCP2, the 20000 remaining DNA agents are opened and with a C base; apart from the closed DNAs all agents are disconnected

Regarding the choice of association rates, also known as *on-rates*, eg the rate of the first TDG recognition rule given earlier, we can say the following. In general on-rates are only dependent on the diffusivity of the agents taking part in the interaction, so it seems reasonable to choose them all equal, in the first instance, and we will choose them all equal to 1 in our case. However, something interesting happens here. Since we are working with rules which generate a contact map that allows cyclic bindings, it is possible that in particular matches, or instances, of a given association rule, the association occurs between agents that are already connected with one another. Fig. 10 gives an example. The top most rule is the basic rule for the TDG:APE1.PolB association and various possible instances are given below. In the bottom-most one, our two agents are already connected. In such cases, called sometimes unimolecular or unary instances, obviously the rate is no longer defined by diffusion, and we shall choose these unary on-rates in the $[10^3, 10^5]$ range.

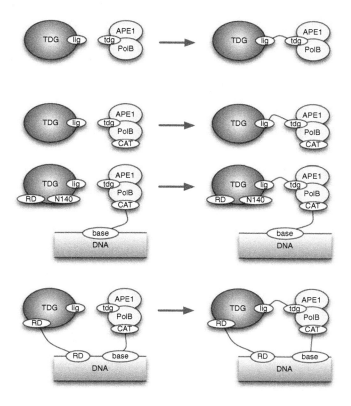

Fig. 10. Refinement of the TDG:APE1.PolB association rule: the top rule is the basic one, the bottom three offer refined and mutually exclusive variants of the former. In the last one the two agents are already connected which makes a unary/unimolecular instance. Given the invariants of the rule set and initial state, these actually cover all possible cases of application of the top rule.

Now what of the off-rates? Contrary to on-rates, these might be much more specific to the actual binding. In the present model we have set all off-rates to 10^{-3}, except for that of the *rd:rd* binding which is known to be a weak binding and set to 1, and that of the *N140:base* binding which is known to be a strong binding and set to 10^{-5}.

Finally there is one key place in the model, namely the Dnmt3A:TDG dissociation, where we modulate the off-rate depending on the context. The reason is the following. The number of *mC*s being much smaller than the number of *C*s, the Dnmt3As will mostly reside with TDGs that are repairing a *C*, ie where they are not needed. Even if we were to make TDG wait for Dnmt3A on the *mC*s -which we are not as explained earlier (§2.2)- this would delay repair and make it less efficient. The trick is to decrease (increase) the dissociation rate of Dnmt3A when bound where it is (not) needed, ie on an *rd*-bound (-free) TDG. This kind of honey pot technique based on rule refinement is analysed in details in Ref. [8]. If Dnmt3A saturates TDG, as is the case with the initial state defined above, it does not make a difference; however, if we suppose we have only a 1/5 ratio of Dnmt3A/TDG and do not use this trick the model performance collapses.

3.3   Results

With our model numerically equipped we can now test its performances. For a repair mechanism there are two clear observables of interest, its accuracy and efficiency. The former measures how often a mistake is made, while the latter measures how long the repair queue is. Let us see if our transient memory model

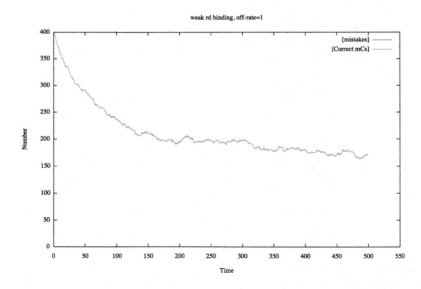

Fig. 11. The curve represents the number of repaired *mC*s (the remainder are being repaired); one observes no mistakes -defined as DNA agents with a *C* base that was methylated (which we can know by looking at the agent *init* site) with a free *rd* site

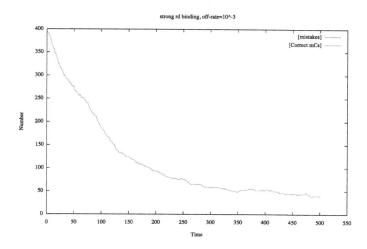

Fig. 12. The refence model perturbed by increasing the *rd* affinity: still no mistakes but the number of repaired *mC*s decreases dramatically

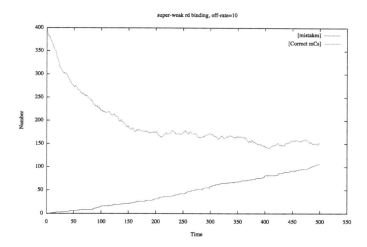

Fig. 13. The refence model perturbed by decreasing the *rd* affinity even further: the number of *mC*s under repair hardly changes in our time window, but the number of mistakes increases steadily

finds the correct trade-off here, as a substantial part of the numerical proof of concept we are looking for consists precisely.

As we can see on Fig. 11, the model does one mistake for the entire duration of this particular stochastic simulation. In general one onbserves less than one mistake. On the other hand the size of the *mC* repair queue stabilizes at about 50% of the *mC* population. Regarding the repair of *C*s, the repair queue is kept well below 1% of the population (not shown). What is remarkable because it is counter-inuitive is that the *rd* affinity is three orders of magnitude weaker than others in the model.

To verify that we have struck the correct trade-off, we can modify the *rd* off-rate. If as intuition would have it, we decrease it, that is to say we increase the affinity of the *rd* binding, then the accuracy does not suffer, but the efficiency is considerably lowered as one can see on Fig. 12 (and the same happens for the repaired *C*s, not shown). If one the other hand one lowers the affinity even more, then mistakes start to accumulate as one sees in Fig. 13.

3.4 Stories (Continued)

We have shown earlier how stories can serve as a useful window into the causal structure of a model. With a numerical model we can put then to further use, by asking for their frequence. For the present model, with its reference parameters, we find that we can classify stories as suffixes of three archetypical stories. One which we have already seen in Fig. 8 occurs about 90% of the time. The other two are shown Fig. 14 which occurs about 9%, and Fig. 15 about 1%. Observe that in both variants, the TDG agent that is responsible for the repair has first to dissociate from another DNA agent before coming to the rescue of the one in point. This hints at a tension in the repair system where the supply in TDG is lower than the demand -a tension of which we have seen the consequences on the optimal affinity of the *rd* domain. In this kind of modelling context, where the just-in-time assembly of complexes is key to the operation of the system, being able to peek in the individual agent trajectories is not only a good way to understand how the rules in a rule set combine, but also offers a way to understand what are the key parameters which will impinge the most on the system behaviour.

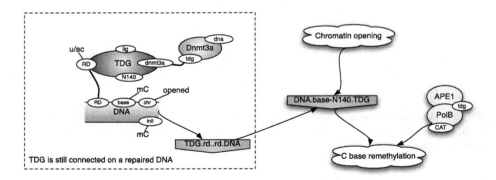

Fig. 14. Another (less frequent) story leading to a *C* remethylation, only the sections that differ from the preceding one (Fig. 8) are shown. One sees that TDG is busy at the outset repairing an *mC*.

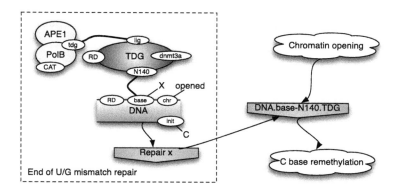

Fig. 15. Another (even less frequent) story leading to the same conclusion where TDG is busy repairing a C

4   Conclusion

To be clear, the model we have considered fails to be realistic in many ways, and it is only one possible model of the system of interest. We have tried to keep rules within the plausible (eg see the discussion at the end of §2.2) but for instance the affinities between TDG and its helper agents APE1:PolB and Dnmt3A is implausibly strong at the moment. Likewise the numbers of copies of agents has little experimental basis. The model also fails to incorporate a lot of the complexities that we know of regarding the biology of TDG and in particular the role of acetylation and sumoylation which is yet to be understood. Nevertheless the somewhat paradoxical conclusion that the rd affinity has to be quite a bit weaker than others is confirmed by experimental data.

This gives some degree of confidence in the basic assumption which one can think of extending in many ways to put other more sophisticated hypotheses to test. For instance, one should consider the resilience of the model to bursts of UG mismatches as are likely to be revealed by the opening of chromatin subsequent to some mC being deaminated. Such repair shocks because of the $50/1$ ratio of Cs to mCs might be difficult to cope with. Other extensions worth pursuing are the competition with the BER (base excision repair) machinery and the potential drift to TA mistakes (as explained briefly in an earlier footnote, §1.1), and/or the interaction with transcriptional mechanisms which might shed some light on transcriptional leakages whereby one sees genes expressed that should presumably be shut in compact chromatin. Indeed the queuing of mCs under repair might allow the opportunistic transcription of hidden genes.

Further, and beyond the particulars of the present biological situation, it is re-assuring to see that using the proper approach, it is actually possible to make way in the modelling of systems where binding figures prominently and combinatori-ally -and which are not well-understood yet. Kappa gives the means and in some sense the imagination to represent and capture numerically assumptions that are very natural (as our transient memory assumption) and difficult to handle otherwise. This suggests that a modelling activity could be succesfully pursued at the same time and in the same stride as experiments.

References

1. Feret, J., Danos, V., Harmer, R., Krivine, J., Fontana, W.: Internal coarse-graining of molecular systems. PNAS (April 2009)
2. Faeder, J.R., Blinov, M.L., Hlavacek, W.S.: Rule-based modeling of biochemical systems with BioNetGen. In: Systems Biology, vol. 500, pp. 113–167. Humana Press (2009)
3. Danos, V., Feret, J., Fontana, W., Harmer, R., Krivine, J.: Rule-based modelling, symmetries, refinements. In: Fisher, J. (ed.) FMSB 2008. LNCS (LNBI), vol. 5054, pp. 103–122. Springer, Heidelberg (2008)
4. Esteller, M.: Cancer epigenomics: Dna methylomes and histone-modification maps. Nat. Rev. Genet. 8(4), 286–298 (2007)
5. Dinant, C., Luijsterburg, M.S., Höfer, T., von Bornstaedt, G., Vermeulen, W., Houtsmuller, A.B., van Driel, R.: Assembly of multiprotein complexes that control genome function. J. Cell Biol. 185(1), 21–26 (2009)
6. Kim, P.M., Lu, L.J., Xia, Y., Gerstein, M.B.: Relating three-dimensional structures to protein networks provides evolutionary insights. Science 314(5807), 1938–1941 (2006)
7. Danos, V., Feret, J., Fontana, W., Krivine, J.: Scalable simulation of cellular signaling networks. In: Shao, Z. (ed.) APLAS 2007. LNCS, vol. 4807, pp. 139–157. Springer, Heidelberg (2007)
8. Danos, V., Feret, J., Fontana, W., Harmer, R., Krivine, J.: Investigation of a biological repair scheme. In: Corne, D.W., Frisco, P., Păun, G., Rozenberg, G., Salomaa, A. (eds.) WMC 2009. LNCS, vol. 5391, pp. 1–12. Springer, Heidelberg (2009)

Component-Based Construction of Real-Time Systems in BIP

Joseph Sifakis

Verimag

BIP is a framework for the component-based construction of real-time systems. It considers that systems can be obtained as the composition of 3-layer components. For a component,

- The lower layer describes its *behavior*, a set of transitions with triggers and actions (atomic state transformations). A trigger consists of an enabling condition on data and a *port* through which synchronization is sought.
- The intermediate level is the set of *interactions* between transitions of the behavior level. An interaction is a set of synchronizing ports and associated actions. Interactions are specified by using *connectors* expressing synchronization constraints on ports.
- The upper level is a set of *priority* rules implementing scheduling policies for interactions.

The framework supports a system construction methodology which is based on a parameterized binary *composition* operator on components. The product of two components consists in composing their corresponding layers, separately. Parameters are used to define new interactions as well as new priorities between the composed components.

Composition of components is defined by operational semantics. Behaviors are transition systems labeled with interactions. Interaction models and priority rules are behavior transformers.

The use of a layered composition operator allows *incremental* construction, that is any compound component can be obtained by successive composition of its constituents.

The *system construction* process in BIP can be considered as a sequence of transformations in a three-dimensional space: Behavior, Interaction, Priority. Elements of the *interaction* × *priority* space characterize the overall *architecture*. A transformation is the result of the superposition of elementary transformations for each dimension. This provides a basis for the study of correct-by-construction system transformations, in particular for the following:

- Architecture transformations allowing preservation of properties of the underlying behavior. Such transformations can provide (sufficient) conditions for *compositionality* and *composability* results.
- Transformations allowing to obtain from a BIP model an observationally equivalent distributed implementation. These involve displacement along the

A. Bouajjani and O. Maler (Eds.): CAV 2009, LNCS 5643, pp. 33–34, 2009.

three coordinates. They consist in replacing multiparty interaction and priorities by protocols based on asynchronous message passing.

The BIP framework has been implemented in a language and a toolset. The BIP language offers primitives and constructs for modeling and composing atomic components described as state machines, extended with data and functions in C. The BIP toolset includes an editor and a compiler for generating from BIP programs, C++ code executable on a dedicated platform. It allows simulation and verification of BIP programs by model checking or by compositional verification techniques for state invariants and deadlock-freedom.

We provide two examples illustrating the use of BIP for modeling and verifying heterogeneous systems: an MPEG encoder, and a hierarchical robotic system.

For further information: `http://www-verimag.imag.fr/~async/bip.html`

Models and Proofs of Protocol Security: A Progress Report

Martín Abadi[1,2], Bruno Blanchet[3,4,5], and Hubert Comon-Lundh[5,6,7]

[1] Microsoft Research, Silicon Valley
[2] University of California, Santa Cruz
[3] CNRS
[4] École Normale Supérieure
[5] INRIA
[6] École Normale Supérieure de Cachan
[7] Research Center for Information Security, Advanced Industrial Science and Technology

Abstract. This paper discusses progress in the verification of security protocols. Focusing on a small, classic example, it stresses the use of program-like representations of protocols, and their automatic analysis in symbolic and computational models.

1 Introduction

As computer security has become a broad, rich field, rigorous models have been developed for many policies and mechanisms. Sometimes these models have been the subject of formal proofs, even automated ones. The goal of this paper is to discuss some of the progress in this direction and some of the problems that remain.

The paper focuses on the study of security protocols, a large, mature, and active area. It aims to offer an introduction and a partial perspective on this area, rather than a comprehensive survey. We explain notations, results, and tools informally, through the description of a basic example: a variant of the classic Wide-mouthed-frog protocol [25]. For this example, we consider specifications and automated proofs in two formalisms. We refer the reader to the research literature for presentations of other formalisms and for precise definitions and theorems, and to a recent tutorial [1] for additional background.

Current research in this area addresses at least three challenges:

1. the treatment of realistic, practical protocols;
2. the analysis of actual implementation code;
3. extending the analysis to refined models, in particular computational models with complexity-theoretic hypotheses on cryptographic functions.

With regard to (1), protocol analysis appears to be catching up with protocol development. In the last few years there have been increasingly thorough analyses of practical protocols. While these analyses remain laborious and difficult, the sophistication and power of the techniques and tools for protocol analysis seem to have grown faster than the complexity of practical protocols. For instance, in the last dozen years, the understanding and formal analysis of SSL and its descendant TLS [30] has progressed

A. Bouajjani and O. Maler (Eds.): CAV 2009, LNCS 5643, pp. 35–49, 2009.

considerably while this protocol has neither changed substantially nor been replaced (e.g., [12,35,42,44]). In this paper we do not discuss (1) further, although we recognize its importance.

Progress on (2) is more recent and still more tentative, but quite encouraging [32, 34]. Moreover, we believe that much further progress is possible using static analyses and type systems, including ones that are not specific to protocol security. This paper concerns (2) in that it deals with protocols written in little programming languages, namely a dialect of the pi calculus [41] and a special-purpose language for writing cryptographic games. It concerns (2) also in that it relies on tools (ProVerif [15, 16, 18] and CryptoVerif [17, 21]) that can be applied to protocols written in a general-purpose programming language such as F♯ (a dialect of ML) [12, 14, 32].

As for (3), models and the corresponding proofs of security can concern several different levels of abstraction. For instance, at a high level, they may deal with secure communication channels as primitive. At a lower level, they may show how these channels are implemented in terms of cryptographic functions, while treating those as "black boxes". An even lower-level model would describe, in detail, how the cryptographic algorithms transform bitstrings. This lower-level model is however not necessarily the final one: we could also take into account such characteristics as timing and power consumption, which some clever attacks may exploit. In this paper we focus on the relation between "black-box" cryptography, in which cryptographic operations are symbolic, and "computational" cryptography, in which these operations are regarded as computations on bitstrings subject to complexity-theoretic assumptions.

The next section introduces our example informally. Section 3 shows how to code it in a dialect of the pi calculus and how to treat it with the tool ProVerif, symbolically. Section 4 gives a computational counterpart to this symbolic analysis via fairly general soundness results that map symbolic guarantees to computational guarantees (e.g., [7, 40, 26]). As an alternative, Section 5 treats the protocol directly in the computational model, with the tool CryptoVerif. Section 6 concludes.

2   An Example, Informally: The Wide-Mouthed-Frog Protocol

The Wide-mouthed-frog (WMF) protocol is a classic, simple method for establishing a secure channel via an authentication server. Mike Burrows originally invented it in order to show that two messages suffice for this task, in the 1980s. It became popular as an example in papers on protocol analysis.

The protocol enables two principals A and B to establish a shared session key K_{AB}. They rely on the help of an authentication server S with which they share keys K_{AS} and K_{BS}, respectively. Informally, the protocol goes roughly as follows:

– First, A generates the session key K_{AB}, and sends A, $\{T_A, B, K_{AB}\}_{K_{AS}}$ to S. Here T_A represents a timestamp, and the braces indicate encryption. It is assumed that clocks are synchronized, and that the encryption not only guarantees secrecy but protects the message from tampering.
– The server S can decrypt this message and check its timeliness. It then sends $\{T_S, A, K_{AB}\}_{K_{BS}}$ to B, where T_S is also a timestamp.
– Finally, B can decrypt this message, check its timeliness, and obtain K_{AB}.

The principals A and B trust that S does not divulge K_{AB} nor use it for its own purposes. They also trust S in other ways—for instance, to check timestamps properly. Defining such trust relations precisely has been one of the important goals of work in this area. Because of this trust, A and B can treat K_{AB} as a shared key. Afterwards, A and B may exchange messages directly under K_{AB}.

This simple example brings up a number of issues. In particular, we may ask what exactly is assumed of timestamps? of cryptographic operations? For instance, it is noteworthy that the protocol relies on A to generate a session key. While this may be acceptable, it is a non-trivial assumption that A can invent good shared secrets; in many other protocols, this important task is left for servers.

Formal analyses of the protocol address these and other questions, with various degrees of explicitness. While early analyses emphasized clock synchronization and A's generation of K_{AB}, those aspects of the protocol seem to be less central, or at least more implicit, in later work. This shift should not be too surprising. As Roger Needham has argued, the assumptions and objectives of security protocols are not uniform, and they have changed over the years [43]. Our analysis, below, focuses on other questions, and in particular on the required properties of cryptographic operations.

3   The WMF Protocol in the Pi Calculus

Specifying the WMF protocol or another protocol can be, to some extent, a simple matter of programming. For each role in the protocol (A, B, or S), one writes code that models the actions of a principal that plays this role. We need not write code for the adversary, which we treat as the environment, and over which we typically have a universal quantification. Similarly, we do not write code for principals that pretend to play a role but do not actually follow the protocol, since those principals can be regarded as part of the adversary.

Note that principals and roles are distinct. Indeed, a principal may play multiple roles, for instance being the initiator A in one session and the interlocutor B in a concurrent session. A role is basically a program, while a principal is a host that may run this program, as well as other programs.

The programs can be written in a variety of ways. We have often used process calculi, and in particular two extensions of the pi calculus: the spi calculus and the applied pi calculus [5, 6].

- The basic pi calculus offers facilities for communication on named channels, for parallel composition, and for generating fresh names, which may represent fresh cryptographic keys. For example, $((\nu k).\overline{c}\langle k \rangle) \mid c(x).\overline{d}\langle x \rangle$ is a process that generates a fresh name k and then sends it on the channel c, in parallel with a process that receives a message on c, with formal name x, then forwards it on d. In this small example, one may think of c and d as public channels on which an attacker may also communicate, for instance intercepting k. More generally, public channels are often represented by free names, not bound by ν.

- The extensions of the pi calculus include both data structures and symbolic representations of cryptographic functions. Tupling, encryption, hashing, signatures, and many of their variants can be accommodated. For instance, classically, $\{M\}_k$ may represent the shared-key encryption of the message M under the key k.

This approach has been followed in modeling many protocols (e.g., [3, 4, 9, 13, 18, 19, 37, 39]). Techniques from the programming-language literature, such as typing, have been employed for proofs, sometimes with substantial extensions or variations; special-purpose techniques have also been developed and exploited, as in the tool ProVerif on which we rely below (e.g., [2, 10, 23, 24, 28, 33, 36]). Research on related formalisms includes many similar themes and methods (e.g., [8, 22, 27, 29, 38, 45]).

Over the last decade, this approach to modeling and proving has evolved and matured considerably. Most noticeably, proof techniques have progressed in their power and sophistication. Partly because of this progress, the specifics of modeling protocols has changed as well.

We use the WMF protocol to illustrate this point. The original paper on the spi calculus [6] contains a description of the WMF protocol (with nonce handshakes rather than timestamps). Below, we give a new description of this protocol. The two descriptions differ on many small but often interesting points. In particular, the new description models probabilistic encryption [31], in which the encryption function has a third parameter that serves for randomizing ciphertexts: $\{M\}_k^r$ represents the encryption of M under k with random component r. This random component ensures that an attacker cannot recognize when two different ciphertexts have the same underlying plaintext. The new description is also crafted so as to be within the realm of application of ProVerif, CryptoVerif, and the general soundness results that map symbolic guarantees to computational guarantees.

The WMF Protocol in the Pi Calculus. We represent principal names by parameters like a and b. The role of A may be executed by any principal a, and the role of B by any principal b. We write k_{as} and k_{bs} for the respective keys shared with the server.

The code for the role of A may be given three parameters: an identity a, an identity b, and a key k_{as}. This code first generates a fresh process id *pid*. Since a may run concurrently several copies of the same program, possibly with the same partner, *pid* is useful in distinguishing the different copies. Next, the code generates a new key k, called K_{AB} in the informal description of Section 2. The code then communicates on a public channel c. It sends a triple that contains *pid*, a, and A. (This message and similar ones below do not appear in the informal description of the protocol but are helpful for enabling the application of computational-soundness results.) It also sends a pair that contains a and the ciphertext $\{\langle c_0, b, k\rangle\}_{k_{as}}^r$. Here r is a freshly generated name, and c_0 is a constant that represents the message type. A distinct constant c_1 will tag the message from S to B. The two tags c_0 and c_1, although rudimentary, serve for avoiding confusion between messages and suffice for the properties that we establish.

$$P_A(a, b, k_{as}) \stackrel{\mathrm{def}}{=} (\nu pid)(\nu k).\bar{c}\langle\langle pid, a, A\rangle\rangle.(\nu r).\bar{c}\langle\langle a, \{\langle c_0, b, k\rangle\}_{k_{as}}^r\rangle\rangle$$

Note that the messages do not specify destinations. Destinations could be included in message headers, but an attacker could change them anyway, so they have no value from the point of view of security.

As a variant, which we adopt, we may wish to quantify over any possible partner b, letting the environment (that is, the attacker) choose b, thus:

$$P_A(a, k_{as}) \stackrel{\text{def}}{=} (\nu pid)(\nu k).\overline{c}\langle\langle pid, a, A\rangle\rangle.$$
$$c(x).\textit{if } \pi_1(x) = pid \textit{ then let } b = \pi_2(x) \textit{ in } (\nu r).\overline{c}\langle\langle a, \{\langle c_0, b, k\rangle\}^r_{k_{as}}\rangle\rangle$$
$$\textit{else } \mathbf{0}$$

Here a receives a message x and performs some computations and tests on x. Specifically, a tries to retrieve the first component of a (supposed) pair using the projection function π_1, then examines the first component to check that the message is intended for this instance. If the projection fails, then the equality test fails as well. If the equality test fails, then the execution stops. (An alternative could be to restart the program or to wait for another message.) In case of success, on the other hand, b is bound to the second component ($\pi_2(x)$) of the message. Otherwise, the execution stops; $\mathbf{0}$ is the null process.

In this presentation we take some liberties—all the i's will be dotted for the ProVerif version of the code, which we describe below. In particular, we omit the axioms for encryption and decryption. We also use a shorthand for pattern matching: we write inputs of the form $c(t)$ when t is a term that can supposedly be decomposed by the principal that receives the message. Such matching tests can be desugared to conditionals in a standard way; variables that occur in the term t are parts of the messages that are not checked and they are bound with a *let* construction. With this notation, we can rewrite P_A as follows:

$$P_A(a, k_{as}) \stackrel{\text{def}}{=} (\nu pid)(\nu k).\overline{c}\langle\langle pid, a, A\rangle\rangle.c(\langle pid, x\rangle).(\nu r).\overline{c}\langle\langle a, \{\langle c_0, x, k\rangle\}^r_{k_{as}}\rangle\rangle$$

Similarly, we specify the process P_B:

$$P_B(a, b, k_{bs}, m) \stackrel{\text{def}}{=} (\nu pid).\overline{c}\langle\langle pid, b, B\rangle\rangle. \ c(\langle pid, x\rangle).$$
$$\textit{let } \langle c_1, a, y\rangle = \textit{decrypt}(x, k_{bs}) \textit{ in } (\nu r).\overline{c}\langle\{m\}^r_y\rangle$$

Here m is an arbitrary message that is supposed to remain secret. According to this code, b sends the secret only to a. However, we may want to enable b to interact with any other principal, sending them an appropriate secret, or nothing at all. In order to model this possibility, we simply show another version of the program in which the final payload is not sent:

$$P^1_B(b, k_{bs}) \stackrel{\text{def}}{=} (\nu pid).\overline{c}\langle\langle pid, b, B\rangle\rangle.c(\langle pid, x\rangle).\textit{let } \langle c_1, z, y\rangle = \textit{decrypt}(x, k_{bs}) \textit{ in } \mathbf{0}$$

Finally, we specify the process P_S:

$$P_S(a, b, k_{as}, k_{bs}) \stackrel{\text{def}}{=} (\nu pid).\overline{c}\langle\langle pid, S\rangle\rangle.c(\langle pid, a, x\rangle).$$
$$\textit{let } \langle c_0, b, y\rangle = \textit{decrypt}(x, k_{as}) \textit{ in } (\nu r).\overline{c}\langle\{\langle c_1, a, y\rangle\}^r_{k_{bs}}\rangle$$

We also consider two variants of P_S in which one of the protocol participants A and B is compromised.

$$P_S^1(a, b, k_{bs}) \stackrel{\text{def}}{=} (\nu pid).\overline{c}\langle\langle pid, S\rangle\rangle.c(\langle pid, k\rangle).c(\langle pid, z, x\rangle).\text{if } z \neq a \wedge z \neq b \text{ then}$$
$$\text{let } \langle c_0, b, y\rangle = decrypt(x, k) \text{ in } (\nu r).\overline{c}\langle\{\langle c_1, z, y\rangle\}_{k_{bs}}^r\rangle$$

$$P_S^2(a, b, k_{as}) \stackrel{\text{def}}{=} (\nu pid).\overline{c}\langle\langle pid, S\rangle\rangle.c(\langle pid, k\rangle).c(\langle pid, a, x\rangle).$$
$$\text{let } \langle c_0, z, y\rangle = decrypt(x, k_{as}) \text{ in}$$
$$\text{if } z \neq a \wedge z \neq b \text{ then } (\nu r).\overline{c}\langle\{\langle c_1, a, y\rangle\}_k^r\rangle$$

We represent a corrupted principal by letting S get its key from the environment. The case in which both A and B are compromised is less interesting, because in that case S can be simulated by the environment entirely. (Similarly, we do not specify corrupted versions of P_A or P_B, because they can be simulated by the environment.)

We assemble these definitions, letting a, b, and the server run any number of copies of their respective programs (for simplicity with a single parameter m):

$$P(m) \stackrel{\text{def}}{=} (\nu k_{as})(\nu k_{bs}).((!P_A(a, k_{as})) \mid (!P_A(b, k_{bs})) \mid$$
$$(!P_B(a, b, k_{as}, m)) \mid (!P_B(b, a, k_{as}, m)) \mid (!P_B(a, a, k_{as}, m)) \mid (!P_B(b, b, k_{bs}, m)) \mid$$
$$(!P_B^1(b, k_{bs})) \mid (!P_B^1(a, k_{as})) \mid$$
$$(!P_S(a, b, k_{as}, k_{bs})) \mid (!P_S(b, a, k_{bs}, k_{as})) \mid$$
$$(!P_S(a, a, k_{as}, k_{as})) \mid (!P_S(b, b, k_{bs}, k_{bs})) \mid$$
$$(!P_S^1(a, b, k_{bs})) \mid (!P_S^1(b, a, k_{as})) \mid (!P_S^2(a, b, k_{as})) \mid (!P_S^2(b, a, k_{bs})))$$

Here ! is the replication operator, so $!P$ behaves like an unbounded number of copies of P in parallel; formally, $!P \equiv P \mid !P$. The names k_{as} and k_{bs} are bound. This binding manifests an important feature of the process calculus: such a construction hides the names, which are not visible outside their scope. The process P therefore expresses that k_{as} and k_{bs} are not a priori known outside, unless they are leaked on a public channel.

The process calculus and ProVerif also allow more compact and more convenient representations of P, as well as many variants and elaborations. We rely on the definitions above partly because we wish to match the conditions of the computational-soundness results. For instance, we avoid the use of functions that link keys to principal names (which are common in ProVerif models, but which appear to be computationally unsound), and also the use of private channels (which may be permitted by ongoing work on computational soundness). As research in this area progresses further, we anticipate that those results will be increasingly flexible and general.

The WMF protocol has several standard security properties. In particular, it preserves the secrecy of the payload m. Formally, this secrecy can be expressed as an observational equivalence: $P(m) \sim P(m')$, for all m and m'. It holds even in the case where m and m' are not atomic names, and it precludes even the leaking of partial information about m and m'. For these reasons, this property is sometimes called "strong secrecy".

As we show below, ProVerif offers one particularly effective method for establishing such security properties. There are others, sometimes relying in part on techniques from the pi calculus (as in [6], for instance).

The WMF Protocol in ProVerif. The WMF protocol can be programmed much as above in the input language of ProVerif. In this language, the encryption $\{m\}_k^r$ is written encrypt(m, k, r). Encryption and decryption are declared in ProVerif by:

fun encrypt$/3$.
reduc decrypt(encrypt$(x, y, r), y) = x$.

which introduces a function symbol encrypt of arity 3 and a function symbol decrypt defined by a rewrite rule decrypt(encrypt$(x, y, r), y) \rightarrow x$, which means that decryption of a ciphertext with the correct key yields the plaintext. Furthermore, we add a function symbol keyeq that allows the adversary to test equality between keys of two ciphertexts:

reduc keyeq(encrypt(x, y, r), encrypt$(x', y, r')) = $ true.

This function symbol models that the encryption scheme is not key-concealing (so the computational-soundness result of Section 4 can be applied without assuming that encryption is key-concealing).

At the level of processes, the input language of ProVerif is an ASCII syntax for the applied pi calculus. For example, the process $P_A(a, k_{as})$ is coded:

let *processAa* =
    new *pid*; **out**(c, (*pid*, a, A)); **in**(c, (= *pid*, *xb*));
    new *Kab*; **new** *r*; **out**(c, (a, encrypt((c0, *xb*, *Kab*), *Kas*, *r*))).

The language uses **new** for ν, **out**(c, m) for $\bar{c}\langle m \rangle$, and **in**(c, m) for $c(m)$. The syntax of patterns is made more explicit, by adding an equality sign (as in $= pid$, for example) when making a comparison with a known value. Other minor departures from the definition of $P_A(a, k_{as})$ above are changes in the identifiers.

The other processes that represent the WMF protocol are coded in a similar way in ProVerif. We therefore omit their ProVerif versions.

ProVerif can establish the security property claimed above, using the technique described in [16]. The proof is fully automatic. For a large class of protocols in which messages are tagged, ProVerif is guaranteed to terminate [20]; our example does not quite fit in this class (in particular, because of the use of inequality tests), but ProVerif does terminate nonetheless. ProVerif can similarly establish security properties of many more complex protocols.

4   Computational Soundness

While formal analysis of protocols has traditionally provided only formal results, like those stated in Section 3, the exact status of those results can be unclear. Do they entail any actual guarantees, or is formal analysis valuable only as a means of identifying assumptions, explaining protocols, and sometimes finding mistakes?

One approach to addressing such questions is to try to map the formal results to a more concrete model via a general theorem. Such a theorem should enable us to leverage high-level notations, proof techniques, and proof tools for obtaining guarantees for large families of protocols. In this section we discuss this approach and how it applies to the WMF protocol.

In the more concrete model, cryptographic operations work on bitstrings, not expressions, and are subject to standard complexity-theoretic assumptions. Names are interpreted as bitstrings—more precisely, ensembles of probability distributions on bitstrings, parameterized by a security parameter η. This interpretation is extended to a mapping from symbolic expressions to bitstrings. The adversary may perform any computation on bitstrings, and not only the basic expected cryptographic operations; the adversary is however constrained to run in (probabilistic) polynomial time with respect to η.

Computational-soundness theorems translate symbolic guarantees to computational guarantees. In particular, a recent computational-soundness theorem [26], on which we rely, roughly says that the symbolic equivalence of two processes implies their computational indistinguishability. In other words, the distinguishing capabilities of a computational attacker are not stronger than the distinguishing capabilities of the symbolic attacker, whose range of operations is much more limited. Of course, these theorems also indicate assumptions, in particular hypotheses on cryptographic operations. Unexpected but necessary hypotheses sometimes surface when one proves soundness theorems.

Assumptions. Specifically, the theorem of [26] requires some assumptions on the encryption scheme:

- IND-CPA security (the standard semantic guarantee for secrecy [31], also called "type-3 security" [7]), and
- INT-CTXT security (an authentication guarantee [11]).

It also requires that:

- the attacker can create a key only using the key-generation algorithm;
- there are no encryption cycles: there is an ordering $<$ on private keys such that, if $k < k'$, then k may appear in the plaintext of a ciphertext encrypted under k', but not the converse;
- finally, it is possible to compute a symbolic representation of any bitstring—this is a "parsing assumption".

The assumptions are far from trivial: IND-CPA is standard, but INT-CTXT is strong, and the inability to create keys without following the key-generation algorithms is quite unusual. These three properties are however necessary for the soundness theorem: if one of these three hypotheses fails, we can find protocols that appear secure symbolically but that are not secure computationally, under some encryption schemes. In fact, under some encryption schemes that do not satisfy INT-CTXT, there are computational attacks on the WMF protocol in particular.

Encryption cycles have attracted a great deal of attention in recent years, in part because of computational-soundness theorems, but they are of independent interest. Their exact status remains a well-known open question.

The parsing assumption is probably not necessary, but eases the proofs.

Application to WMF. Since $P(m) \sim P(m')$ has been proved using ProVerif, we should get some computational indistinguishability guarantee, thanks to the theorem of [26] discussed above. That theorem pertains to a symbolic equivalence relation $\sim_s$ that distinguishes slightly more processes than $\sim$ and ProVerif. For instance, $\sim_s$ distinguishes two symbolic messages whose computational interpretations have distinct lengths, while $\sim$ may not.

This discrepancy illustrates that further work is needed for establishing a perfect match between models. Moreover, the soundness theorems remain hard to establish and they do not yet cover all useful cryptographic primitives, nor all sensible styles for writing protocol code.

The discrepancy might be resolved by refining $\sim$ by introducing functions that, given a ciphertext, reveal the length, structure, or other properties of the underlying plaintext. Such functions could also be incorporated in ProVerif analyses.

For our specific example, more simply, we may require that encryption conceal the length of payloads, and we can weaken $\sim_s$ accordingly. This approach is acceptable for the WMF protocol since its messages can be assumed to have a constant length. In this case, $\sim$ and $\sim_s$ coincide, so the ProVerif verification actually establishes $P(m) \sim_s P(m')$. Moreover, we have proved manually the absence of encryption cycles so, for implementations that satisfy the other assumptions of the computational-soundness theorem, we obtain the desired computational indistinguishability guarantee.

5   The WMF Protocol in CryptoVerif

In this section, we study the WMF protocol using CryptoVerif. In contrast to the approach of Section 4, CryptoVerif works directly in the computational model, and provides proofs by sequences of games, like those constructed manually by cryptographers. In these proofs, one starts from an initial game that represents the protocol under study. This game is then transformed either by relying on security assumptions on cryptographic primitives or by syntactic transformations. These transformations are such that the difference of probability of success of an attack in consecutive games is negligible. The final game is such that the desired security property is obvious from the form of the game. One can then conclude that the security property also holds in the initial game.

The WMF Protocol in CryptoVerif. In order to automate this technique, the games are formalized in a process calculus, as we illustrate on the WMF protocol. Throughout this section, we refer to a and b as honest principals, and we focus on them in writing code. The adversary can play the role of dishonest principals.

The following process P_A models the role of A:

$P_A = !^N c_2(xA : host, xB : host);$ if $xA = $ a $\lor xA = $ b then
   let $KAs = ($if $xA = $ a then Kas else $Kbs)$ in
   new $rKab : keyseed;$ let $Kab : key = \mathsf{kgen}(rKab)$ in
   new $r : seed;$ $\overline{c_3}\langle xA, \mathsf{encrypt}(\mathsf{concat}(\mathsf{c0}, xB, Kab), KAs, r)\rangle$

The process P_A starts with a replication bounded by N, which is assumed to be polynomial in the security parameter: at most N copies of A can be run. Two host names are then received on channel c_2: xA is the name of the host playing the role of A, xB is the name of its interlocutor; xA is required to equal a or b. Then KAs is defined as the key of xA. The protocol proper starts at this point: P_A chooses a fresh key Kab to be shared between xA and xB by generating a random seed $rKab$ (**new** $rKab : keyseed$) and applying the key-generation algorithm kgen. Next, P_A forms the first message, and sends it on channel c_3. The function concat builds the plaintext to be encrypted by concatenating its arguments (a tag, a host name, and a key). After the output on c_3, control returns to the adversary.

Variables are typed. These types simply represent sets of bitstrings, and have no security meaning. They are still necessary in the computational model, in particular when generating random numbers: the random numbers can be drawn from various sets (keys, random seeds, nonces, ...).

The messages are each sent or received on a distinct channel c_j. Furthermore, the replication $!^N$ implicitly defines an index $i \in [1, N]$, and the channel names c_j are in fact abbreviations for $c_j[i]$, so that a distinct channel is used in each copy of the process. Thus, the adversary knows exactly to which process it is talking. Using distinct channel names and replication indices replaces the process identifiers (pid) of the model of Section 3.

The following process P_B represents the role of B:

$P_B = !^N c_8(xB : host)$; **if** $xB =$ a $\vee$ $xB =$ b **then**
　　let $KBs = ($**if** $xB =$ a **then** Kas **else** $Kbs)$ **in** $\overline{c_9}\langle\rangle$;
　　$c_{10}(x : bitstring)$; **let** injbot(concat($=$ c1, xA, kab)) $=$ decrypt(x, KBs) **in**
　　if $xA =$ a $\vee$ $xA =$ b **then**
　　new $r : seed$; $\overline{c_{11}}\langle$encrypt(pad($mpayload$), kab, r)$\rangle$

Similarly to P_A, the process P_B is replicated, and expects as first message its own identity xB; xB is required to equal a or b and KBs is its key. Then a message (normally from the server) is received on channel c_{10}, and P_B decrypts this message. The decryption can succeed or fail. When it succeeds, it returns a normal bitstring; when it fails, it returns $\perp$. The function injbot is the natural injection from bitstrings to bitstrings union $\perp$, so that when injbot(y) $=$ decrypt(x, KBs), the decryption succeeded and its value is y. Next, when the interlocutor xA of xB is honest, the process P_B encrypts the payload $mpayload$ under the shared key kab and sends the ciphertext on channel c_{11}. (The function pad is only a type conversion function, which converts payloads to plaintexts; it leaves the bitstrings unchanged.)

The process P_K is a key-registration process:

$P_K = !^{N_2} c_{12}(h : host, k : key)$;
　　let $Khs : key =$ **if** $h =$ a **then** Kas **else if** $h =$ b **then** Kbs **else** k

All variables defined under replications in CryptoVerif are implicitly arrays indexed by the replication index. So, here, P_K stands for:

$P_K = !^{i \le N_2} c_{12}[i](h[i] : host, k[i] : key)$;
　　let $Khs[i] : key =$ **if** $h[i] =$ a **then** Kas **else if** $h[i] =$ b **then** Kbs **else** $k[i]$

In order to register a key k_1 for host h_1, the adversary sends a pair (h_1, k_1) on channel $c_{12}[i]$ for some i. The host name h_1 is stored in $h[i]$ while the key k_1 is stored in $Khs[i]$, except when h_1 is a or b; in this case, the key Kas or Kbs respectively is stored instead, so that the only keys that can be registered for a and b are Kas and Kbs respectively. In order to retrieve the key for host h', one can then look for an index u' such that $h[u'] = h'$; the key for h' is $Khs[u']$. This is done by the construct **find** $u' \leq N_2$ **suchthat defined**$(Khs[u'], h[u']) \wedge h' = h[u']$ **then** ... $Khs[u']$ ... used below.

The role of the server is specified by the process P_S:

$P_S = !^N c_6(xA : host, x : bitstring);$
  find $uA \leq N_2$ **suchthat defined**$(Khs[uA], h[uA]) \wedge xA = h[uA]$ **then**
  let $KAs = Khs[uA]$ **in**
  let injbot(concat(= c0, $xB, kab)$)) = decrypt(x, KAs) **in**
  find $uB \leq N_2$ **suchthat defined**$(Khs[uB], h[uB]) \wedge xB = h[uB]$ **then**
  let $KBs = Khs[uB]$ **in**
  new $r : seed;$ $\overline{c_7}\langle$encrypt(concat(c1, xA, kab), $KBs, r)\rangle$

The first message of the protocol is received on channel c_6. The variable KAs is set to the key of xA. Then the server decrypts the message with KAs, sets KBs to the key of xB, and finally outputs the second message of the protocol on channel c_7.

The following process P receives two payloads $m0$ and $m1$, chooses a bit $switch$, and sets the payload $mpayload$ to be encrypted by P_B to either $m0$ or $m1$ depending on the value of $switch$. (We will show that the adversary cannot distinguish $switch$ from a fresh random bit, so it cannot distinguish whether the encrypted payload is $m0$ or $m1$.) Next, P generates the keys Kas and Kbs for a and b respectively, using the key-generation algorithm kgen; then it launches processes for the various roles of the protocol and for key registration:

$P = c_{13}(m0 : payload, m1 : payload);$
  new $switch : bool;$ **let** $mpayload : payload = $ test$(switch, m0, m1)$ **in**
  new $rKas : keyseed;$ **let** $Kas : key = $ kgen$(rKas)$ **in**
  new $rKbs : keyseed;$ **let** $Kbs : key = $ kgen$(rKbs)$ **in** $\overline{c_{14}}\langle\rangle; (P_A \mid P_B \mid P_S \mid P_K)$

Here test is defined by test(true, $m0, m1$) = $m0$ and test(false, $m0, m1$) = $m1$.

Assumptions. In addition to these processes, the CryptoVerif model also specifies several hypotheses:

– The encryption scheme is IND-CPA and INT-CTXT.
– The function concat returns bitstrings of constant length. Moreover, concat is injective, and it is possible to compute x, y, z from concat(x, y, z) in polynomial time.
– All payloads have the same length.

We do not assume that the attacker can create a key only using the key-generation algorithm. This contrasts with the assumptions of Section 4, which apply to a large class of protocols, including protocols for which there would be computational attacks without this assumption. Neither do we assume the absence of encryption cycles; however, the success of the game transformation sequence shows that there is a key hierarchy. Finally, we do not have any parsing assumption.

Analysis. With the model presented above, CryptoVerif is not able to complete the proof of the desired properties. Manual inspection of the games computed by CryptoVerif shows that, in P_A, it fails to distinguish automatically the cases in which the key Kab is generated for an honest interlocutor a or b from the cases in which it is generated for a dishonest interlocutor. The code can easily be modified to make this distinction from the start, simply by adding the test "**if** $xB = $ b $\vee$ $xB = $ a **then**" just before the generation of $rKab$ and duplicating the rest of the process P_A. With this modification, the proof of secrecy of *switch* succeeds automatically. That is, the adversary cannot distinguish *switch* from a fresh random bit, so it cannot tell whether the encrypted payload is $m0$ or $m1$.

Additionally, CryptoVerif can also show secrecy properties of the key exchanged between A and B, after removal of the payload message. (We do not present the corresponding process for brevity.) More precisely, CryptoVerif shows that the keys Kab chosen by P_A when xA and xB are honest principals are secret, that is, indistinguishable from fresh independent random keys. However, CryptoVerif cannot show the secrecy of the keys kab received by P_B when xA and xB are honest principals. This failure is not due to a limitation of CryptoVerif, but to an attack: by replaying messages in the protocol, the adversary can force several sessions of B to use the same key kab. Hence, those keys kab may not be independent. CryptoVerif still establishes what we call "one-session secrecy", that is, that each key kab (for xA and xB honest) is indistinguishable from a fresh random key.

The Sequence of Games (Summary). In order to establish the secrecy of *switch*, CryptoVerif successively reduces the original game to simpler games, using the security assumptions. In a first step, it performs syntactic transformations to make explicit all usages of the key Kbs and to replace it with its value kgen($rKbs$). The obtained game is then transformed using the INT-CTXT assumption: CryptoVerif replaces every decryption of a message M under Kbs with a look-up that searches for M among all ciphertexts built by encryption under Kbs. If the ciphertext M is found, the look-up returns the corresponding plaintext; otherwise, decryption fails and the look-up returns $\perp$. If the attacker wins the game before this transformation, then either it wins the new game or, at some point, it has been able to forge an encryption under Kbs. In the latter case, it would break INT-CTXT. Then, CryptoVerif replaces any plaintext M that is encrypted under Kbs with $Z(M)$, a bitstring of the same length as M but consisting only of zeroes. This time, if the attacker wins the game before this transformation, then either it wins the new game or it wins an IND-CPA game.

CryptoVerif performs similar transformations for the key Kas.

At this stage, the key Kab no longer occurs as a plaintext. CryptoVerif now applies the same transformations as above, for this key, and finally replaces all payloads *mpayload* encrypted under Kab with the same plaintext $Z(mpayload)$. The final game is trivial: it cannot be won by an attacker.

6   Conclusion

Model refinements such as those that we discuss in this paper, while numerous and varied, should not be fundamentally surprising. After all, reasoning about software and hardware correctness often employs similar refinements. Furthermore, in any area, models and the corresponding proofs may be incomplete and inaccurate.

Security, however, is different in at least one important respect: an adversary may be doing its best to undermine the validity of the models. This specificity increases the importance of understanding refinements, and the interest of the corresponding theory. Within this domain, we believe that the transition from symbolic to computational models is particularly worthwhile. It can serve for strengthening the foundations of formal analysis, for enabling proofs, and also for indicating implicit hypotheses and subtle flaws.

It remains open to debate whether computational results should be obtained directly, with a tool such as CryptoVerif, or indirectly from symbolic proofs via soundness theorems. Soundness theorems often require more hypotheses: there are situations in which a computational proof can be obtained using CryptoVerif, while the hypotheses of soundness theorems are not met. However, when the hypotheses are satisfied, a symbolic proof suffices, and is generally easier to obtain, often automatically.

At present, both avenues still present challenges. ProVerif, CryptoVerif, and the soundness theorems all still have important limitations. These imply, for instance, that one should be careful in writing protocol specifications—not all equivalent formulations are equally easy to handle. Despite these limitations, as this paper illustrates, the progress to date is substantial.

Acknowledgments

We are grateful to our coauthors Véronique Cortier, Cédric Fournet, Andy Gordon, David Pointcheval, and Phil Rogaway. They are responsible for a good part of the ideas, techniques, and results presented in this paper. This work was partly supported by the ANR project FormaCrypt.

References

1. Abadi, M.: Security protocols: Principles and calculi. In: Aldini, A., Gorrieri, R. (eds.) FOSAD 2007. LNCS, vol. 4677, pp. 1–23. Springer, Heidelberg (2007)
2. Abadi, M., Blanchet, B.: Analyzing security protocols with secrecy types and logic programs. Journal of the ACM 52(1), 102–146 (2005)
3. Abadi, M., Blanchet, B.: Computer-assisted verification of a protocol for certified email. Science of Computer Programming 58(1-2), 3–27 (2005)
4. Abadi, M., Blanchet, B., Fournet, C.: Just Fast Keying in the pi calculus. ACM Transactions on Information and System Security 10(3), 1–59 (2007)
5. Abadi, M., Fournet, C.: Mobile values, new names, and secure communication. In: 28th ACM Symposium on Principles of Programming Languages, pp. 104–115 (2001)
6. Abadi, M., Gordon, A.D.: A calculus for cryptographic protocols: The spi calculus. Information and Computation 148(1), 1–70 (1999); An extended version appeared as Digital Equipment Corporation Systems Research Center report No. 149 (January 1998)
7. Abadi, M., Rogaway, P.: Reconciling two views of cryptography (The computational soundness of formal encryption). Journal of Cryptology 15(2), 103–127 (2002)

8. Amadio, R., Prasad, S.: The game of the name in cryptographic tables. In: Thiagarajan, P.S., Yap, R.H.C. (eds.) ASIAN 1999. LNCS, vol. 1742, pp. 15–27. Springer, Heidelberg (1999)
9. Backes, M., Maffei, M., Unruh, D.: Zero-knowledge in the applied pi-calculus and automated verification of the direct anonymous attestation protocol. In: Proceedings of the 2008 IEEE Symposium on Security and Privacy, pp. 202–215 (2008)
10. Baudet, M.: Sécurité des protocoles cryptographiques: aspects logiques et calculatoires. PhD thesis, Ecole Normale Supérieure de Cachan (2007)
11. Bellare, M., Namprempre, C.: Authenticated encryption: Relations among notions and analysis of the generic composition paradigm. Journal of Cryptology 21(4), 469–491 (2008)
12. Bhargavan, K., Fournet, C., Corin, R., Zalinescu, E.: Cryptographically verified implementations for TLS. In: Proceedings of the 15th ACM Conference on Computer and Communications Security, pp. 459–468 (2008)
13. Bhargavan, K., Fournet, C., Gordon, A.D.: Verifying policy-based security for web services. In: ACM Conference on Computer and Communications Security, pp. 268–277 (2004)
14. Bhargavan, K., Fournet, C., Gordon, A.D.: Verified reference implementations of WS-security protocols. In: Bravetti, M., Núñez, M., Zavattaro, G. (eds.) WS-FM 2006. LNCS, vol. 4184, pp. 88–106. Springer, Heidelberg (2006)
15. Blanchet, B.: An efficient cryptographic protocol verifier based on Prolog rules. In: 14th IEEE Computer Security Foundations Workshop, pp. 82–96 (2001)
16. Blanchet, B.: Automatic proof of strong secrecy for security protocols. In: 2004 IEEE Symposium on Security and Privacy, pp. 86–100 (2004)
17. Blanchet, B.: A computationally sound mechanized prover for security protocols. In: 2006 IEEE Symposium on Security and Privacy, pp. 140–154 (2006)
18. Blanchet, B., Abadi, M., Fournet, C.: Automated verification of selected equivalences for security protocols. Journal of Logic and Algebraic Programming 75(1) (February-March 2008)
19. Blanchet, B., Chaudhuri, A.: Automated formal analysis of a protocol for secure file sharing on untrusted storage. In: 2008 IEEE Symposium on Security and Privacy, pp. 417–431 (2008)
20. Blanchet, B., Podelski, A.: Verification of cryptographic protocols: Tagging enforces termination. In: Gordon, A.D. (ed.) FOSSACS 2003. LNCS, vol. 2620, pp. 136–152. Springer, Heidelberg (2003)
21. Blanchet, B., Pointcheval, D.: Automated security proofs with sequences of games. In: Dwork, C. (ed.) CRYPTO 2006. LNCS, vol. 4117, pp. 537–554. Springer, Heidelberg (2006)
22. Bodei, C.: Security Issues in Process Calculi. PhD thesis, Università di Pisa (January 2000)
23. Boreale, M., Nicola, R.D., Pugliese, R.: Proof techniques for cryptographic processes. SIAM Journal on Computing 31(3), 947–986 (2001)
24. Borgström, J., Briais, S., Nestmann, U.: Symbolic bisimulation in the spi calculus. In: Gardner, P., Yoshida, N. (eds.) CONCUR 2004. LNCS, vol. 3170, pp. 161–176. Springer, Heidelberg (2004)
25. Burrows, M., Abadi, M., Needham, R.: A logic of authentication. Proceedings of the Royal Society of London A 426, 233–271 (1989); A preliminary version appeared as Digital Equipment Corporation Systems Research Center report No. 39 (February 1989)
26. Comon-Lundh, H., Cortier, V.: Computational soundness of observational equivalence. In: Proceedings of the 15th ACM Conference on Computer and Communications Security, pp. 109–118 (2008)
27. Datta, A., Derek, A., Mitchell, J.C., Pavlovic, D.: A derivation system and compositional logic for security protocols. Journal of Computer Security 13(3), 423–482 (2005)
28. Durante, L., Sisto, R., Valenzano, A.: Automatic testing equivalence verification of spi calculus specifications. ACM Transactions on Software Engineering and Methodology 12(2), 222–284 (2003)

29. Focardi, R., Gorrieri, R.: The compositional security checker: A tool for the verification of information flow security properties. IEEE Transactions on Software Engineering 23(9), 550–571 (1997)
30. Freier, A.O., Karlton, P., Kocher, P.C.: The SSL protocol: Version 3.0 (November 1996), http://www.mozilla.org/projects/security/pki/nss/ssl/draft302.txt
31. Goldwasser, S., Micali, S.: Probabilistic encryption. Journal of Computer and System Sciences 28, 270–299 (1984)
32. Gordon, A.D.: Provable implementations of security protocols. In: 21st Annual IEEE Symposium on Logic in Computer Science, pp. 345–346 (2006)
33. Gordon, A.D., Jeffrey, A.: Types and effects for asymmetric cryptographic protocols. In: 15th IEEE Computer Security Foundations Workshop, pp. 77–91 (2002)
34. Goubault-Larrecq, J., Parrennes, F.: Cryptographic protocol analysis on real C code. In: Cousot, R. (ed.) VMCAI 2005. LNCS, vol. 3385, pp. 363–379. Springer, Heidelberg (2005)
35. He, C., Sundararajan, M., Datta, A., Derek, A., Mitchell, J.C.: A modular correctness proof of IEEE 802.11i and TLS. In: Proceedings of the 12th ACM Conference on Computer and Communications Security, pp. 2–15 (2005)
36. Hüttel, H.: Deciding framed bisimilarity. In: 4th International Workshop on Verification of Infinite-State Systems, pp. 1–20 (2002)
37. Kremer, S., Ryan, M.D.: Analysis of an electronic voting protocol in the applied pi calculus. In: Sagiv, M. (ed.) ESOP 2005. LNCS, vol. 3444, pp. 186–200. Springer, Heidelberg (2005)
38. Lowe, G.: Breaking and fixing the Needham-Schroeder public-key protocol using FDR. In: Margaria, T., Steffen, B. (eds.) TACAS 1996. LNCS, vol. 1055, pp. 147–166. Springer, Heidelberg (1996)
39. Lux, K.D., May, M.J., Bhattad, N.L., Gunter, C.A.: WSEmail: Secure internet messaging based on web services. In: ICWS 2005: Proceedings of the IEEE International Conference on Web Services, pp. 75–82 (2005)
40. Micciancio, D., Warinschi, B.: Soundness of formal encryption in the presence of active adversaries. In: Naor, M. (ed.) TCC 2004. LNCS, vol. 2951, pp. 133–151. Springer, Heidelberg (2004)
41. Milner, R., Parrow, J., Walker, D.: A calculus of mobile processes, parts I and II. Information and Computation 100, 1–77 (1992)
42. Morrissey, P., Smart, N.P., Warinschi, B.: A modular security analysis of the TLS handshake protocol. In: Pieprzyk, J. (ed.) ASIACRYPT. LNCS, vol. 5350, pp. 55–73. Springer, Heidelberg (2008)
43. Needham, R.M.: The changing environment for security protocols. IEEE Network 11(3), 12–15 (1997)
44. Paulson, L.C.: Inductive analysis of the internet protocol TLS. ACM Transactions on Information and System Security 2(3), 332–351 (1999)
45. Ramanathan, A., Mitchell, J., Scedrov, A., Teague, V.: Probabilistic bisimulation and equivalence for security analysis of network protocols. In: Walukiewicz, I. (ed.) FOSSACS 2004. LNCS, vol. 2987, pp. 468–483. Springer, Heidelberg (2004)

Predictability vs. Efficiency in the Multicore Era: Fight of Titans or Happy Ever after?

Luca Benini

DEIS Università di Bologna
Luca.benini@unibo.it

In this talk I will give an overview of recent trends in multi-core platforms for embedded computing. The shift toward multicore architectures has been imposed by technology reasons (power consumption and design closure issues in nanometer technology) and not by the "coming of age" of parallel programming models, compilation, analysis and verification environments. Thus, we may be building terascale many-cores architectures that we cannot program efficiently. Even worse, we may not be able to give any guarantees on execution timing, constraints and real time properties of applications. This is a challenge AND an opportunity for the software design and verification community: I will give some views on what is being done, what could be done and what I hope will be done to build efficient and predictable multi-core platforms.

A. Bouajjani and O. Maler (Eds.): CAV 2009, LNCS 5643, p. 50, 2009.
© Springer-Verlag Berlin Heidelberg 2009

SPEED: Symbolic Complexity Bound Analysis
(Invited Talk)

Sumit Gulwani

Microsoft Research, Redmond, USA
sumitg@microsoft.com

Abstract. The SPEED project addresses the problem of computing symbolic computational complexity bounds of procedures in terms of their inputs. We discuss some of the challenges that arise and present various orthogonal/complementary techniques recently developed in the SPEED project for addressing these challenges.

1 Introduction

As processor clock speeds begin to plateau, there is an increasing need to focus on software performance. One of the performance metrics is (worst-case) symbolic computational complexity bounds of procedures (expressed as a function of their inputs). Such automatically generated bounds are useful in early detection of egregious performance problems in large modular codebases that are constantly being changed by multiple developers who make heavy use of code written by others without a good understanding of their implementation complexity. These worst-case bounds also help augment the traditional performance measurement process of profiling, which is only as good as the set of test inputs.

The SPEED project develops static program analysis techniques for computing symbolic computational complexity bounds. Computing such bounds is a technically challenging problem since bounds for even simple sequential programs are usually disjunctive, non-linear, and involve numerical properties of heaps. Sometimes even proving termination is hard in practice, and computing bounds ought to be a harder problem.

This paper briefly describes some techniques that enable existing off-the-shelf linear invariant generation tools to compute non-linear and disjunctive bounds. These techniques include: (i) program transformation (control-flow refinement to transform loops with sophisticated control flow into simpler loops [7]), and (ii) monitor instrumentation (multiple counter variables whose placement is determined dynamically by the analysis [9]). This paper also briefly describes some specialized invariant generation tools (based on abstract interpretation) that enable bound computation. These can compute invariants that describe (i) numerical properties of memory partitions [8], (ii) relationships involving non-linear operators such as logarithm, exponentiation, multiplication, square-root, and Max [6]. These techniques together enable generation of complexity bounds that are usually precise not only in terms of the computational complexity, but also in terms of the constant factors.

A. Bouajjani and O. Maler (Eds.): CAV 2009, LNCS 5643, pp. 51–62, 2009.

The hard part in computing computational complexity bound for a procedure is to compute bounds on the number of iterations of various loops inside that procedure. Given some cost measure for atomic statements, loop iteration bounds can be composed together in an easy manner to obtain procedure bounds (for details, see [9,7].) This paper is thus focused on bounding loop iterations, and is organized by some of the challenges that arise in bounding loop iterations.

2   Loops with Control-Flow

Loops with non-trivial control flow inside them often have (iteration) bounds that are non-linear or disjunctive, i.e., they involve use of the Max operator (which returns the maximum of its arguments). For example, the loop in Figure 1(a) has a disjunctive bound: $100 + \text{Max}(0, m)$, while the loop in Figure 2(a) has a non-linear bound: $n \times (m + 1)$. Such bounds can be computed using one of the following three techniques.

2.1   Single Counter Instrumentation

This technique involves instrumenting a counter i that is initialized to 0 at the beginning of the loop, and is incremented by 1 inside the loop. An invariant generation tool is then used to compute invariants that relate the loop counter i with program variables. Existential elimination of temporary variables (all variables except the counter variable i and the inputs) yields a relation between i and the inputs, from which an upper bound u on i may be read. $\text{Max}(0, u)$ then provides a bound on the number of loop iterations.

For the loop in Figure 1(a), single counter instrumentation results in the loop in Figure 1(b). Bound computation now requires computing the disjunctive inductive invariant $i \leq x + y + 1 \ \wedge \ y \leq \text{Max}(0, m) \ \wedge \ x < 100$ at program point 5 (i.e., at the location immediately before the statement at that point) in Figure 1(b). Existential elimination of temporary variables x and y from this inductive invariant yields the invariant $i \leq 100 + \text{Max}(0, m)$, which implies a bound of $\text{Max}(0, 100 + \text{Max}(0, m)) = 100 + \text{Max}(0, m)$ on the number of loop iterations.

For the loop in Figure 2(a), single counter instrumentation results in the loop in Figure 2(b). Bound computation now requires computing the non-linear inductive invariant $i \leq x \times m + x + y + 1 \ \wedge \ x < n \ \wedge \ y \leq m$ at program point 5 in Figure 2(b). Existential elimination of temporary variables x and y from this inductive invariant yields the invariant $i \leq n \times (m + 1)$, which implies a bound of $n \times (m + 1)$ on the number of loop iterations.

One (semi-automatic) technique to compute such disjunctive and non-linear invariants is to use the numerical abstract domain described in [6]. The numerical abstract domain is parametrized by a base linear arithmetic abstract domain and is constructed by means of two domain lifting operations that extend the base linear arithmetic domain to reason about the max operator and other operators whose semantics is specified using a set of inference rules. One of the

(a)

```
Inputs: int m
x := 0; y := 0;
while (x < 100)
  if (y < m)
    y := y + 1;
  else
    x := x + 1;
```

(b)

```
  Inputs: int m
1 x := 0; y := 0;
2 i := 0;
3 while (x < 100)
4   i := i + 1;
5   if (y < m)
6     y := y + 1;
7   else
8     x := x + 1;
```

(c)

```
  Inputs: int m
1 x := 0; y := 0;
2 i₁ := 0; i₂ := 0;
3 while (x < 100)
4   if (y < m)
5     i₁ := i₁ + 1;
6     y := y + 1;
7   else
8     i₂ := i₂ + 1;
9     x := x + 1;
```

(d)

```
Inputs: int m
x := 0; y := 0;
while (x < 100 ∧ y < m)
  y := y + 1;
while (x < 100 ∧ y ≥ m)
  x := x + 1;
```

Fig. 1. (a) Loop with a disjunctive bound $100 + \texttt{Max}(0, m)$. (b) Single Counter Instrumentation requires computing disjunctive invariants for bound computation. (c) Multiple Counter Instrumentation enables computation of disjunctive bounds using linear invariants on individual counters. (d) Control-flow Refinement enables bound computation by reducing original loop to a code-fragment with simpler loops.

domain lifting operation extends the linear arithmetic domain to represent linear relationships over variables as well as max-expressions (an expression of the form $\texttt{Max}(e_1, \ldots, e_n)$ where e_i's are linear expressions). Another domain lifting operation lifts the abstract domain to represent constraints not only over program variables, but also over expressions from a given finite set of expressions S. The semantics of the operators (such as multiplication, logarithm, etc.) used in constructing expressions in S is specified as a set of inference rules. The abstract domain retains efficiency by treating these expressions just like any other variable, while relying on the inference rules to achieve precision.

2.2 Multiple Counter Instrumentation

This technique (described in [9]) allows for using a less sophisticated invariant generation tool at the cost of using a more sophisticated counter instrumentation scheme. In particular, this technique involves choosing a set of counter variables and for each counter variable selecting the locations to initialize it to 0 and the locations to increment it by 1. The counters and their placement are chosen such that (besides some completeness constraints) a given invariant generation tool can compute bounds on the counter variables at appropriate locations in terms of the procedure inputs. (There is a possibility that no such counter placement is possible, but if there is one, then the algorithm described in Section 4 in [9] will compute one.) The bounds on individual counter variables are then composed together appropriately to obtain a (potentially disjunctive or non-linear) bound on the total number of loop iterations (For details, see Theorem 1 in Section 3 in [9]).

An advantage of this technique is that in most cases (including the loops in Figure 1(a) and Figure 2(a)), it allows use of off-the-shelf linear invariant generation tools to compute disjunctive and non-linear bounds.

Inputs: uint n,m	Inputs: uint n,m	Inputs: uint n,m	Inputs: uint n,m
$x := 0;\ y := 0;$	*1* $x := 0;\ y := 0;$	*1* $x := 0;\ y := 0;$	
while $(x < n)$	*2* $i := 0;$	*2* $i_1 := 0; i_2 := 0;$	Inputs: uint n,m
if $(y < m)$	*3* while $(x < n)$	*3* while $(x < n)$	$x := 0;\ y := 0;$
$y := y + 1;$	*4* $i := i + 1;$	*4* if $(y < m)$	while $(x < n)$
else	*5* if $(y < m)$	*5* $i_1 := i_1 + 1;$	while $(y < m)$
$y := 0;$	*6* $y := y + 1;$	*6* $y := y + 1;$	$y := y + 1;$
$x := x + 1;$	*7* else	*7* else	$y := 0;$
	8 $y := 0;$	*8* $i_2 := i_2 + 1;$	$x := x + 1;$
	9 $x := x + 1;$	*9* $y := 0;$	
		10 $x := x + 1;$	
(a)	(b)	(c)	(d)

Fig. 2. uint denotes an unsigned (non-negative) integer. (a) Loop with a non-linear bound $n \times (m + 1)$. (b) Single Counter Instrumentation requires computing non-linear invariants for bound computation. (c) Multiple Counter Instrumentation enables computation of non-linear bounds using linear invariants on individual counters. (d) Control-flow Refinement enables bound computation by reducing original multi-path loop to a code-fragment in which path-interleaving has been made more explicit.

For the loop in Figure 1(a), the multiple counter instrumentation technique instruments the loop with two counters i_1 and i_2, both of which are initialized to 0 before the loop and are incremented by 1 on either sides of the conditional resulting in the loop shown in Figure 1(b). Now, consider the following (a bit subtle) argument with respect to computing bounds after this instrumentation. (All of this is automated by techniques described in [9].)

- If the then-branch is ever executed, it is executed for at most m iterations. This bound m can be obtained by computing a bound on counter variable i_1 at program point 6, which has been instrumented to count the number of iterations of the then-branch.
- Similarly, if the else-branch is ever executed, it is executed for at most 100 iterations. This bound can be obtained by computing a bound on counter variable i_2 at program point 9, which has been instrumented to count the number of iterations of the else-branch.
- This implies that the total number of loop iterations is bounded by Max $(0, m) + \text{Max}(0, 100) = 100 + \text{Max}(0, m)$.

For the loop in Figure 2(a), the multiple counter instrumentation technique instruments the loop with two counters i_1 and i_2 that are initialized and incremented as shown in Figure 2(c). Now, consider the following argument with respect to computing bounds after this instrumentation.

- The else-branch is executed for at most n iterations. This bound n can be obtained by computing a bound on counter variable i_2 at program point 9, which has been instrumented to count the number of iterations of the else-branch.

- The number of iterations of the then-branch in between any two iterations of the else-branch is bounded by m. This bound can be obtained by computing a bound on counter variable i_1 at program point 6, which is incremented by 1 in the then-branch, but is re-initialized to 0 in the else-branch.
- This implies that the total number of loop iterations is bounded by Max $(0, n) \times (1 + \text{Max}(0, m)) = n \times (m + 1)$.

2.3   Control-Flow Refinement

This technique (described in [7]) allows for using a less sophisticated invariant generation tool, but in a two phase process. The first phase consists of performing *control-flow refinement*, which is a semantics-preserving and bound-preserving transformation on procedures. Specifically, a loop that consists of multiple paths (arising from conditionals) is transformed into a code fragment with one or more simpler loops in which the interleaving of paths is syntactically explicit. For the loops in Figure 1(a) and in Figure 2(a), the control-flow refinement leads to the code-fragments in Figure 1(d) and Figure 2(d) respectively.

The second phase simply consists of performing the analysis on the refined procedure. The code-fragment with transformed loops enables a more precise analysis than would have been possible with the original loop. The additional program points created by refinement allow the invariant generator to store more information. The invariants at related program points (which map to the same program point in the original loop) in the refined code-fragment correspond to a disjunctive invariant at the corresponding program point in the original loop. For the loops in Figure 1(d) and Figure 2(d), the desired bounds can now be easily computed using simple techniques for bound computation such as pattern matching, or single counter instrumentation.

Even though the goals of the multiple counter instrumentation and control-flow refinement techniques are the same (that of enabling bound computation with a less sophisticated invariant generation tool), there are examples for which one of them is preferable than the other. (See the motivating examples in the respective papers [9,7].) An interesting strategy that leverages the power of both techniques would be to use multiple counter instrumentation technique after applying control-flow refinement.

3   Loops in a Nested Context

We now consider the case of a loop nested inside another loop. If our goal is to only prove termination of the outer loop, we can perform the process in a modular fashion: prove that the number of iterations of the outer loop is bounded, and prove that the number of iterations of the inner loop, in between any two iterations of the outer loop, is bounded. However, such a modular scheme would not work well for bound computation since it may often yield conservative bounds, as is illustrated by the example in Figure 3(a). The bound for the inner loop (in terms of the inputs), for each iteration of the outer loop, is n. However,

	Inputs: uint n	Transition System Representation
Inputs: uint n	1 $x := 0;$	
$x := 0;$	2 $i_1 := 0; i_2 := 0;$	$\phi_{\texttt{Next}} : y = y_{\texttt{old}} + 1 \wedge y < n$
while $(x < n \wedge *)$	3 while $(x < n \wedge *)$	$\phi_{\texttt{Init}} : y \geq 0$
$\quad y := x;$	4 $\quad i_1 := i_1 + 1;$	
$\quad$ while $(y < n \wedge *)$	5 $\quad y := x;$	After transformation
$\quad\quad y := y + 1;$	6 $\quad$ while $(y < n \wedge *)$	
$\quad x := y + 1;$	7 $\quad\quad i_2 := i_2 + 1;$	$\phi_{\texttt{Next}} : y \geq y_{\texttt{old}} + 1 \wedge y < n$
	8 $\quad\quad y := y + 1;$	$\phi_{\texttt{Init}} : y \geq 0$
	9 $\quad x := y + 1;$	
(a)	(b)	(c)

Fig. 3. $*$ denotes non-deterministic choice. (a) Nested Loop with a bound of n on the total number of iterations. (b) Counter Instrumentation methodology can be used to compute precise bounds for nested loops by instrumenting counters in an appropriate manner. (c) Transition system of the nested loop in the context of the outer loop, as well as when lifted out of the context of its outer loop. The latter can be used to obtain a precise bound on the total number of loop iterations of the nested loop.

the interesting part to note is that the bound for the total number of iterations of the inner loop is also n. It is quite often the case that the nesting depth of a procedure is not indicative of the precise computational complexity.

Both the counter instrumentation and control-flow refinement techniques introduced in Section 2 can be extended to deal with the challenge of computing precise bounds for loops in a nested context.

Appropriate Counter Instrumentation

The single counter instrumentation methodology can be easily extended to nested loops by using a counter that is incremented by 1 in the nested loop (as before), but is initialized to 0 at the beginning of the procedure (as opposed to immediately before the loop). The idea of multiple counter instrumentation can be similarly extended to address nested loops by having appropriate constraints on the positioning of multiple counters. (For more details, see the notion of a *proof structure* in Section 3 in [9].) In either case, the loop in Figure 3(a) is instrumented as shown in Figure 3(b). The bound of n on the total number of iterations of the nested loop now follows from the inductive invariant $i_2 \leq y \wedge y < n$ at program point 8 in Figure 3(b).

Appropriate Loop Re-structuring

Alternatively, the nested loop can be re-structured as a non-nested loop in a bound-preserving transformation. This is easier illustrated by working with a transition system representation of the loop. A transition system can be described by a relation $\phi_{\texttt{Next}}$ representing relations between loop variables y and their values $y_{\texttt{old}}$ in the previous iteration, and a relation $\phi_{\texttt{Init}}$ representing the initial value of the loop variables.

```
Inputs: bit-vector a
1 b := a;
2 i := 0;
3 while (_BitScanForward(&id1, b))
4     i := i + 1;
      // set all bits before id1
5     b := b | ((1 << id1) − 1);
6     if (_BitScanForward(&id2, ∼ b)) break;
      // reset all bits before id2
7     b := b & (∼ ((1 << id2) − 1));
                    (a)
```

```
Inputs: List of lists of nodes L
e := L.Head();
while (e ≠ null)
    f := e.Head();
    while (f ≠ null)
        f := e.GetNext(f);
    e := L.GetNext(e);
                    (b)
```

Fig. 4. Loops whose bound cannot be expressed using scalar program variables, and instead require reference to quantitative functions of the data-structures over which they iterate. (a) Loop (instrumented with a counter variable i) that iterates over bit-vectors. _BitScanForward returns the bit position of the first set bit in the first parameter (if any, which is signaled by the return value) (b) Loop that iterates over a list of lists.

For the nested loop in Figure 3(a), the transition system representation before and after this transformation is illustrated in Figure 3(c). The interesting part to note is that the relation $y = y_{old} + 1$ is transformed into $y \geq y_{old} + 1$ when we compare any two successive states inside the nested loop, but not necessarily inside the same iteration of the outer loop. (Observe that the value of y increases monotonically inside the nested loop.) The desired precise bound of n for the nested loop can now be easily computed from the transformed transition system (by using simple techniques for bound computation such as pattern matching, or single counter instrumentation.)

The above-mentioned transformation of the transition system can be carried out by making use of *progress invariants* as described in Section 5 in [7].

4   Loops Iterating over Data-Structures

We now consider loops that iterate over data-structures such as lists, trees, bit-vectors, etc. In such cases, it may not be possible to express bounds using only scalar program variables. However, bounds may be expressible in terms of some quantitative functions of these data-structures (such as length of a list, or height of a tree, or number of bits in a bit-vector).

[9] proposes the notion of user-defined quantitative functions, wherein the user specifies the semantics of the quantitative functions by annotating each method of an abstract data-structure with how it may affect the quantitative attributes of the input data-structures, and how it determines the quantitative attributes of the output data-structures. Bounds can then be obtained by computing invariants that relate the instrumented loop counter with the quantitative functions of data-structures. Such invariants can be obtained by using a numerical invariant generation tool that has been extended with support for uninterpreted functions [10] and aliasing.

The loop in Figure 4(a) iterates over a bit-vector by masking out the least significant consecutive chunk of 1s from b in each loop iteration. Bit-vectors have quite a few interesting quantitative functions associated with them. E.g., $\text{Bits}(a)$: total number of bits, $\text{Ones}(a)$: total number of 1 bits, $\text{One}(a)$: position of the least significant 1 bit, etc. Using these quantitative functions, it is possible to express relationships between the instrumented loop counter i and the bit-vectors a and b. In particular, it can be established that $2i \leq 1 + \text{One}(b) - \text{One}(a) \wedge i \leq 1 + \text{Ones}(a) - \text{Ones}(b)$ at program point 5. This implies bounds of both $\text{Ones}(a)$ as well as $(\text{Bits}(a) - \text{One}(a))/2$ on the number of loop iterations.

The loop in Figure 4(b) iterates over a list of lists of nodes. The outer loop iterates over the top-level list, while the inner loop processes all nodes in the nested lists. The iterations of the outer loop are bounded above by the length of the top-level list, while the total iterations of the nested loop are bounded above by the sum of the lengths of all the nested lists. These bounds can be expressed using appropriate quantitative functions $\text{Len}(L)$ and $\text{TotalNodes}(L)$ with the expected semantics. However, computation of these bounds requires inductive invariants that require a few more quantitative functions. (For more details, see Section 5.2 in [9].)

5   Loops with Complex Progress Measure

There are loops with simple control flow (and hence simplification techniques like multiple counter instrumentation or control-flow refinement do not help reduce the complexity of bound computation) that require computing sophisticated invariants for establishing bounds. We discuss below two such classes of invariants.

Invariants That Relate Sizes of Memory Partitions

Consider the BubbleSort procedure shown in Figure 5(a) that sorts an input array A of length n. The algorithm works by repeatedly iterating through the array to be sorted, comparing two items at a time and swapping them if they are in the wrong order (Line 8). The iteration through the array (Loop in lines 6-9) is repeated until no swaps are needed (measured by the **change** boolean variable), which indicates that the array is sorted.

Notice that establishing a bound on the number of iterations of the outer while-loop of this procedure is non-trivial; it is not immediately clear why the outer while-loop even terminates. Note that in each iteration of the while-loop, at least one new element "bubbles" up to its correct position in the array (i.e., it is less than or equal to all of its successors). Hence, the outer while-loop terminates in at most n steps. The set cardinality abstract domain described in [8] can be used to automatically establish this invariant by computing a relationship between the instrumented loop counter i and the number of elements that have been put in the correct position. In particular, the set cardinality analysis computes the invariant that i is less than or equal to the size of the set of the array indices that hold elements at their correct position (provided the parametrized set cardinality analysis is constructed from a set analysis whose base-set constructor can represent such a set).

```
Inputs: integer array A of size n
1 change := true;
2 i := 0;
3 while (change)
4     i := i + 1;
5     change := false;
6     for(x := 0; x < n − 1; x := x + 1)
7         if (A[x] > A[x + 1])
8             Swap(A[x], A[x + 1]);
9             change := true;
```
(a)

```
Inputs: int y0, uint n
x := 0; y := y0;
i := 0;
while (x < n) do
    i := i + 1;
    y := y + 1;
    x := x + y;
```
(b)

Fig. 5. Loops where multiple counter instrumentation and control-flow refinement do not help reduce the complexity of bound computation, and instead sophisticated invariants are required to relate the instrumented counter variable i with program variables. (a) BubbleSort procedure (instrumented with a counter variable i to bound the number of iterations of the outer loop) whose bound computation requires computing numeric invariants over sizes of appropriate memory partitions. (b) Loop (instrumented with a counter variable i) whose bound computation requires computing invariants with non-linear operators, in particular, multiplication and square-root.

Invariants with Non-linear Operators

Consider the loop shown in Figure 5(b) (taken from [3], which uses the principle of second-order differences to establish a lexicographic polyranking function for proving termination). This loop illustrates the importance of using non-linear operators like multiplication and square-root for representing timing bounds as well as computing the invariants required to establish timing bounds. In particular, it is possible to compute a bound of $\sqrt{2n} + \max(0, -2y_0) + 1$ on the counter variable i after establishing the inductive loop invariant $i = y - y_0 \wedge y^2 \leq y_0^2 + 2x$. Such invariants can be computed by the numerical abstract domain [6] briefly described in Section 2.1.

6   Related Work

WCET Analysis: There is a large body of work on estimating worst case execution time (WCET) in the embedded and real-time systems community [20,21]. The WCET research is largely orthogonal, focused on distinguishing between the complexity of different code-paths and low-level modeling of architectural features such as caches, branch prediction, instruction pipelines. For establishing loop bounds, WCET techniques either require user annotation, or use simple techniques based on pattern matching [13] or some relatively simple numerical analysis (e.g., relational linear analysis to compute linear bounds on the delay or timer variables of the system [12], interval analysis based approach [11], symbolic computation of integer points in a polyhedra [14]). These WCET techniques cannot compute precise bounds for several examples considered in this paper.

Termination Techniques: Recently, there have been some new advances in the area of proving termination of loops based on discovering disjunctively well-founded ranking functions [17] or lexicographic polyranking functions [4]. [5,2] have successfully applied the fundamental result of [17] on disjunctively well-founded relations to prove termination of loops in real systems code. It is possible to obtain bounds from certain kind of ranking functions given the initial state at the start of the loop. However, the ranking function abstraction is sometimes too weak to compute precise bounds. In contrast, computation of any (finite) bound for a loop is a proof of its termination.

Symbolic Bound Computation using Recurrence Solving: A common approach to bound analysis has been that of generating recursive equations from programs such that a closed form solution to the recursive equations would provide the desired bounds. The process of generating recursive equations is fairly standard and syntactic; the challenging part lies in finding closed-form solutions. Various techniques have been proposed for finding closed-form solutions such as rewrite rules [15,18], building specialized recurrence solvers using standard mathematical techniques [19], or using existing computer algebra systems. Recently, [1] have proposed a new technique based on computing ranking functions, loop invariants, and partial evaluation to more successfully solve recurrence relations that arise in practice. This recurrence relation approach does not directly address the challenges of dealing with loops with complicated progress measure or loops that iterate over data-structures. It would however be interesting to compare this approach with the techniques mentioned in this paper over numerical loops with non-trivial control-flow and those that occur in a nested context.

7   Conclusion and Future Work

Computing symbolic complexity bounds is a challenging problem, and we have applied a wide variety of static analysis techniques to address some of the involved challenges: new invariant generation tools (for computing invariants that are disjunctive, non-linear, and can express numerical properties of heap partitions), monitor instrumentation (multiple counter instrumentation), program transformation (control-flow refinement), and user annotations (user-defined quantitative functions of data-structures).

The techniques described in this article are applicable for computing bounds of sequential procedures. Computing bounds of procedures in a concurrent setting is a more challenging problem: it requires modeling the scheduler, and bounds would be a function of the number of processors.

It would also be interesting to extend these techniques to compute bounds on other kind of resources (besides time) used by a program, such as memory or network bandwidth, or some user-definable resource [16]. Computing memory bounds is more challenging since unlike time its consumption does not monotonically increase with program execution because of de-allocation.

Acknowledgments.   The SPEED project has received contributions from several colleagues: Trishul Chilimbi, Bhargav Gulavani, Sagar Jain, Eric Koskinen,

Tal Lev-Ami, Krishna Mehra, Mooly Sagiv. We thank the product teams at Microsoft for their assistance with this project. We thank Varun Aggarwala and Aditya Nori for providing useful feedback on a draft of this paper.

References

1. Albert, E., Arenas, P., Genaim, S., Puebla, G.: Automatic inference of upper bounds for recurrence relations in cost analysis. In: Alpuente, M., Vidal, G. (eds.) SAS 2008. LNCS, vol. 5079, pp. 221–237. Springer, Heidelberg (2008)
2. Berdine, J., Chawdhary, A., Cook, B., Distefano, D., O'Hearn, P.: Variance analyses from invariance analyses. In: POPL (2007)
3. Bradley, A., Manna, Z., Sipma, H.: Termination of polynomial programs. In: Cousot, R. (ed.) VMCAI 2005. LNCS, vol. 3385, pp. 113–129. Springer, Heidelberg (2005)
4. Bradley, A.R., Manna, Z., Sipma, H.B.: The polyranking principle. In: Caires, L., Italiano, G.F., Monteiro, L., Palamidessi, C., Yung, M. (eds.) ICALP 2005. LNCS, vol. 3580, pp. 1349–1361. Springer, Heidelberg (2005)
5. Cook, B., Podelski, A., Rybalchenko, A.: Termination proofs for systems code. In: PLDI, pp. 415–426 (2006)
6. Gulavani, B.S., Gulwani, S.: A numerical abstract domain based on expression abstraction and max operator with application in timing analysis. In: Gupta, A., Malik, S. (eds.) CAV 2008. LNCS, vol. 5123, pp. 370–384. Springer, Heidelberg (2008)
7. Gulwani, S., Jain, S., Koskinen, E.: Control-flow refinement and progress invariants for bound analysis. In: PLDI (2009)
8. Gulwani, S., Lev-Ami, T., Sagiv, M.: A combination framework for tracking partition sizes. In: POPL, pp. 239–251 (2009)
9. Gulwani, S., Mehra, K.K., Chilimbi, T.M.: Speed: precise and efficient static estimation of program computational complexity. In: POPL, pp. 127–139 (2009)
10. Gulwani, S., Tiwari, A.: Combining abstract interpreters. In: PLDI, pp. 376–386 (2006)
11. Gustafsson, J., Ermedahl, A., Sandberg, C., Lisper, B.: Automatic derivation of loop bounds and infeasible paths for wcet analysis using abstract execution. In: RTSS, pp. 57–66 (2006)
12. Halbwachs, N., Proy, Y.-E., Roumanoff, P.: Verification of real-time systems using linear relation analysis. FMSD 11(2) (1997)
13. Healy, C.A., Sjodin, M., Rustagi, V., Whalley, D.B., van Engelen, R.: Supporting timing analysis by automatic bounding of loop iterations. Real-Time Systems 18(2/3), 129–156 (2000)
14. Lisper, B.: Fully automatic, parametric worst-case execution time analysis. In: WCET (2003)
15. Métayer, D.L.: Ace: An Automatic Complexity Evaluator. ACM Trans. Program. Lang. Syst. 10(2), 248–266 (1988)
16. Navas, J., Mera, E., López-García, P., Hermenegildo, M.V.: User-definable resource bounds analysis for logic programs. In: Dahl, V., Niemelä, I. (eds.) ICLP 2007. LNCS, vol. 4670, pp. 348–363. Springer, Heidelberg (2007)
17. Podelski, A., Rybalchenko, A.: Transition invariants. In: LICS, pp. 32–41. IEEE, Los Alamitos (2004)
18. Rosendahl, M.: Automatic Complexity Analysis. In: FPCA, pp. 144–156 (1989)

19. Wegbreit, B.: Mechanical Program Analysis. Commun. ACM 18(9), 528–539 (1975)
20. Wilhelm, R., Engblom, J., Ermedahl, A., Holsti, N., Thesing, S., Whalley, D., Bernat, G., Ferdinand, C., Heckmann, R., Mueller, F., Puaut, I., Puschner, P., Staschulat, J., Stenström, P.: The Determination of Worst-Case Execution Times— Overview of the Methods and Survey of Tools. ACM Transactions on Embedded Computing Systems (TECS) (2007)
21. Wilhelm, R., Wachter, B.: Abstract interpretation with applications to timing validation. In: Gupta, A., Malik, S. (eds.) CAV 2008. LNCS, vol. 5123, pp. 22–36. Springer, Heidelberg (2008)

Regression Verification: Proving the Equivalence of Similar Programs
(Invited Talk)

Ofer Strichman

Information Systems Engineering, IE, Technion, Haifa, Israel
ofers@ie.technion.ac.il

The ability to prove equivalence of successive, closely-related versions of a program can be useful for maintaining backward compatibility. This problem has the potential of being easier in practice than functional verification for at least two reasons: First, it circumvents the problem of specifying what the program should do; Second, in many cases it is computationally easier, because it offers various opportunities for abstraction and decomposition that are only relevant in this context.

I will begin the talk by defining six notions of input/output equivalence between programs, and then show Hoare-style proof rules that can be used for proving the equivalence of recursive functions according to these definitions. I will then show a decomposition algorithm that, given a mapping between the recursive functions in the two programs, attempts to reduce the equivalence verification problem into verification of many smaller verification problems corresponding to pairs of mapped functions. Callees of these functions that were already proven equivalent are abstracted with uninterpreted functions. I will conclude the talk by describing a regression verification tool for C programs – built by Benny Godlin – that, based on these rules and decomposition algorithm, was able to prove automatically the equivalence of some nontrivial programs.

The talk is based on [GS08, GS09].

References

[GS08] Godlin, B., Strichman, O.: Inference rules for proving the equivalence of recursive procedures. Acta Informatica 45(6), 403–439 (2008)
[GS09] Godlin, B., Strichman, O.: Regression verification. In: 46th Design Automation Conference (DAC) (2009) (to be published)

A. Bouajjani and O. Maler (Eds.): CAV 2009, LNCS 5643, p. 63, 2009.
© Springer-Verlag Berlin Heidelberg 2009

Symbolic Counter Abstraction
for Concurrent Software[*]

Gérard Basler[1], Michele Mazzucchi[1], Thomas Wahl[1,2], and Daniel Kroening[1,2]

[1] Computer Systems Institute, ETH Zurich, Switzerland
[2] Computing Laboratory, Oxford University, United Kingdom

Abstract. The trend towards multi-core computing has made concurrent software an important target of computer-aided verification. Unfortunately, Model Checkers for such software suffer tremendously from combinatorial state space explosion. We show how to apply *counter abstraction* to real-world concurrent programs to factor out redundancy due to thread replication. The traditional global state representation as a vector of local states is replaced by a vector of thread counters, one per local state. In practice, straightforward implementations of this idea are unfavorably sensitive to the number of local states. We present a novel symbolic exploration algorithm that avoids this problem by carefully scheduling which counters to track at any moment during the search. Our experiments are carried out on Boolean programs, an abstraction promoted by the SLAM project. To our knowledge, this marks the first application of counter abstraction to programs with non-trivial local state spaces, and results in the first scalable Model Checker for concurrent Boolean programs.

1 Introduction

Software Model Checking has been a vibrant branch of research in formal methods for many years. *Predicate abstraction* [1,2] is one of the most prominent approaches in this area, promoted by the success of the SLAM project at Microsoft Research. Instead of tracking the actual values of program variables, the abstraction monitors carefully selected predicates over these variables. Predicate abstraction results in a *Boolean program* [3], i.e., a program using exclusively Boolean variables. Embedded in an automated abstraction-refinement framework [4], verifiers for Boolean programs have been used successfully to increase the reliability of system-level software such as Windows device drivers [5].

Recently, there have been attempts to extend these techniques to the verification of *concurrent* software [6]. The challenge is the classical state space explosion problem: the number of reachable program states grows exponentially with the number of concurrent threads, which renders naive exploration impractical. The authors of [6] conclude that none of the currently available tools is able to handle device drivers of realistic size in the presence of many threads.

---

[*] This research is supported by the EU FP7 STREP MOGENTES (project ID ICT-216679), and by the EPSRC project EP/G026254/1.

A. Bouajjani and O. Maler (Eds.): CAV 2009, LNCS 5643, pp. 64–78, 2009.

One observation that comes to the rescue is that concurrent components of multi-threaded software are often simply *replications* of a template program describing the behavior of a component. The ensuant regularity in the induced system model can be exploited to reduce the verification complexity. One technique towards this goal is *counter abstraction*. The idea is to record the global state of a system as a vector of counters, one per local state, tracking how many of the n components currently reside in the local state. This idea was proposed as a way of achieving *symmetry reduction* for fixed-size systems [7], turning an n-process model of size exponential in n into one of size polynomial in n.

Counter abstraction as proposed in [7] requires conversion of the template program $\mathcal{P}$ into a local-state transition diagram, by identifying a set of local states a component can be in, and translating the program statements into local state changes. Such a conversion is straightforward if there are only few component configurations, such as with certain high-level communication protocols [8]. For concurrent software, however, $\mathcal{P}$ is given in a C-like language, with assignments to variables, branches, loops, etc. A local state is then defined as a valuation of all local variables of a thread. As a result, there are exponentially many local states, measured in the number of local variables. Introducing a counter variable for each local state is impractical but for tiny programs.

In this paper, we present a strategy to solve these complexity problems. Our solution is two-fold. First, we interleave the translation of individual program statements with the Model Checking phase. This has the advantage that the context in which the statement is executed is known; the counters for the source and target local states, which need to be updated, depend on this context. If the translation is performed up-front, one has to embed each statement into all local state contexts where the statement is enabled, which is infeasible for realistic programs. Second, in a global state we keep counters only for those local states that at least one thread resides in. This idea exploits a simple counting argument: given n threads with l conceivable local states each, at most n of the corresponding local state counters are non-zero at any time during execution. Since n is typically much smaller than l, omitting the zero-valued counters results in huge savings: the sensitivity of counter abstraction to the *local state space explosion problem* mentioned in the previous paragraph is reduced from exponential in l to exponential in $\min\{n, l\}$.

Contributions. We present an efficient algorithm for BDD-based symbolic state space exploration of Boolean programs run by a fixed number of parallel threads. The algorithm's primary accomplishment is to curb the local state space explosion problem, the classical bottleneck in implementations of counter abstraction. We demonstrate the effectiveness of our approach on a substantial set of Boolean program benchmarks, generated by two very different CEGAR-based toolkits, SATABS [9] and SLAM. Since symmetry reduction, of which finitary counter abstraction is an instance, has so far been implemented more successfully in explicit-state model checkers, we include an experimental comparison of an explicit-state version of our method against classical explicit-state symmetry reduction, using the well-known MURφ model checker [10].

We believe our algorithm marks a major step towards the solution of an exigent problem in verification today, namely that of Model Checking concurrent software. While the concepts underlying our solution are relatively straightforward, exploiting them in symbolic model checking is not. The succinctness of state space representations that BDDs often permit is paid for by rather rigid data manipulation mechanisms. To the best of our knowledge, our implementation is the first *scalable* approach to counter abstraction in symbolic verification of concurrent software with replicated threads.

Counter abstraction has also been applied in parameterized system verification, using truncated counters, necessarily resulting in an incomplete method (see section on related work). We emphasize that, in this paper, we use the term *counter abstraction* in the sense of **exact** counters. The method we propose can be seen as an "exact abstraction", a notion that is common in symmetry reduction and other bisimulation-preserving reduction methods.

2   Related Work

While the principal idea of using process counters already appeared in early work by Lubachevsky [11], *generic representatives* were suggested by Emerson and Trefler [7] as a means of addressing the complexity of symmetry-reducing symbolically represented systems. The term *counter abstraction* was actually coined in the context of parameterized verification [12]. In contrast to the present work, the counters are cut off at some value c, indicating that *at least* c components currently reside in the corresponding local state.

Local state-space explosion was identified in [13] as the major obstacle to using generic representatives with non-trivial symmetric programs. The paper ameliorates this problem using a static live-variable analysis, and using an approximate but inexpensive local state reachability test. Being heuristic in nature, this work cannot guarantee a reduced complexity of the abstract program.

We are aware of a few significant works that resulted in tools using counter abstraction in symbolic Model Checking: [14], in the context of *virtual symmetry* [15], and [8], for probabilistic models. While valuable in their respective domains, both approaches suffer from a limitation that makes them unsuitable for general software: they are based on a system model (such as the *GSST* of [14]) that describes the process behavior by local state changes and thus require an up-front translation from whatever input language is used. The examples in [14,8] include communication and mutual-exclusion protocols with at most a few dozen local states. The BEACON Model Checker [16] has been applied to a multi-threaded memory management system with 256 local states. In our benchmarks, threads have millions of local states (see section 5).

In [17], 0-1-∞ counter abstraction is applied to predicate-abstracted concurrent C programs for race detection. The counters monitor the states of *context threads*. To avoid local state space explosion, each context thread is simplified to an *abstract control flow automaton* (ACFA). According to [17], the ACFA has at most a few dozen vertices and can thus be explicitly constructed. In contrast, our goal is a general solution for arbitrary predicate abstractions, where we cannot rely on a small number of predicates and, thus, local states. Consequently, our work does not require first building a local state transition diagram.

Compared to canonization-based symmetry reduction approaches such as in MURφ [10] and ZING [18] (explicit-state) or SVISS [19] and RULEBASE [20] (symbolic), the model checking overhead that counter abstraction incurs reduces to translating the program statements into local state counter updates. Sorting local state sequences, or other representative mapping techniques, are implicit in the translation.

Finally, the general problem of symbolically verifying multi-threaded programs has been tackled in many recent publications [21,22, and others]. None of these address the symmetry that concurrent Boolean programs exhibit, although some investigate partial-order based methods [23].

3   Preliminaries

3.1   Boolean Programs

Boolean programs result from applying *predicate abstraction* to general software. All variables are of type Boolean, and track values of predicates over (possibly unbounded) variables of the original program $\mathcal{P}$. To enable sound verification of reachability properties, Boolean programs are constructed to over-approximate the behavior of $\mathcal{P}$. This may permit *spurious* paths, which need to be detected and eliminated, by refining the abstraction using additional predicates.

Several tools exist that translate C code into a Boolean program. Many of the Boolean programs used in our experiments were generated by a front-end of the SATABS model checker, from Linux kernel C code. The code is assumed to be free of recursion and dynamic thread creation.[1] In a preprocessing step, loops and if statements are replaced by nondeterministic gotos and assume statements; function calls are inlined. Figure 1 shows a translation of a fragment of the Apache webserver suite into a Boolean program.

Table 1. Semantics of fundamental Boolean program statements

Syntax	Semantics
$v_1, \ldots, v_n := expr_1, \ldots, expr_n$ $\quad$ constrain $expr_c$	$(expr_c \Rightarrow pc' = pc + 1 \ \wedge \ \forall i \in \{1, \ldots, n\}, v_i' = expr_i \ \wedge$ $\quad same(V \setminus \{v_1, \ldots, v_n\})) \wedge (\neg expr_c \Rightarrow \bot))$
goto $l_1 \ldots, l_n$	$\bigvee_{l \in \{l_1, \cdots, l_n\}} pc' = l \wedge same(V)$

We roughly adopt the Boolean program syntax from [3]; Table 1 defines the valid statements and their semantics. The symbol pc represents the program counter, V the set of program variables. Primes represent the next-state value of variables, and $same(X)$ abbreviates $\bigwedge_{v \in X} v' = v$. Well-formed expressions are

---

[1] Recursion, in particular, renders the concurrent verification problem undecidable, even for Boolean programs. An option is to use overapproximations, as done in [24].

```
      for(i=0;  i < apthr_per_child;  i++) {
        int status = ap_scoreboard_image->servers[child_argno][i].status;

        if (status != SRV_GRACEFUL && status != SRV_DEAD) continue;
        apr_status_t  rv = apr_thread_create(&threads[i], thread_attr,
                                 worker_thread, my_info,pchild);
(a)     if (rv != APR_SUCCESS) {
          ap_log_error(APLOG_MARK, APLOG_ALERT, rv,
                           ap_server_conf, "apthr_create:_error");
          clean_child_exit(CHILDSICK);
        }
        threads_created++;
      }
```

```
      main() begin
        decl i_lt_apthr_per_child, status_eq_SRV_GRACEFUL,
             status_eq_SRV_DEAD, rv_eq_APR_SUCCESS;

        L1: goto L2, L5;
        L2: assume i_lt_apthr_per_child;
            status_eq_SRV_GRACEFUL, status_eq_SRV_DEAD := *, *;
(b)         goto L3,L4;
        L3: assume (!status_eq_GRACEFUL) && (!status_eq_SRV_DEAD);
            i_lt_apthr_per_child := *; goto L1;
        L4: rv_eq_APR_SUCCESS := true;
            skip;
            i_lt_apthr_per_child := *; goto L1;
        L5: assume !i_lt_apthr_per_child;
      end
```

Fig. 1. (a) A C program; (b) a possible translation into a Boolean program

the Boolean closure of constants *true*, *false* and $\star$ (representing either value), and variable identifiers. The constructs assume *expr* and skip are shorthands for $v := v$ constrain *expr* and assume *true*, respectively.

A Boolean program $\mathcal{P}$ induces a *concurrent system* as follows. We define $\mathcal{P}_n := \|\|_{i=1}^n \mathcal{P}$ to be the interleaved parallel composition of n threads executing $\mathcal{P}$. Program $\mathcal{P}_n$ consists of each variable declared *global* in $\mathcal{P}$, and n copies of each variable declared *local* in $\mathcal{P}$. A *state* of $\mathcal{P}_n$ can therefore be described in the form $(g, l_1, \ldots, l_n)$, where vector g is a valuation of the global variables, and l_i stands for the *local state* of thread i; it comprises the value of the program counter pc_i and the valuation of the i-th copy of each local variable. The *thread state* of thread i is the pair (g, l_i). Intuitively, for $i \in \{1, \ldots, n\}$, thread i has full access to the global variables and to the i-th copy of the local variables. It has neither read nor write access to any other local variables. We assume a standard asynchronous execution model for $\mathcal{P}_n$: exactly one thread executes an instruction at any time. A full formalization is given in [24].

3.2 Counter Abstraction

Counter Abstraction can be viewed as a form of symmetry reduction, as follows. *Full symmetry* is the property of a Kripke model $M = (S, R)$ of concurrent components to be invariant under permutations of these components. This invariance is traditionally formalized using permutations acting on component indices. A permutation π on $\{1, \ldots, n\}$ is defined to act on a state $s = (g, l_1, \ldots, l_n)$ by acting on the thread indices, i.e. $\pi(s) = (g, l_{\pi(1)}, \ldots, l_{\pi(n)})$. We extend π to act on a transition (s, t) by acting point-wise on s and t.

Definition 1. *Structure M is **(fully) symmetric** if for all $r \in R$ and all permutations π on $\{1, \ldots, n\}$, $\pi(r) \in R$.*

We observe that a concurrent Boolean program built by *replicating* a template written in the syntax given in section 3.1 is (trivially) symmetric: the syntax does not allow thread identifiers in the program text, which could potentially break symmetry.

From a symmetric M, a reduced *quotient structure* $\overline{M}$ can be constructed using standard existential abstraction. The quotient is based on the *orbit relation* on states, defined as $s \equiv t$ if there exists π such that $\pi(s) = t$. Quotient $\overline{M}$ turns out to be bisimilar to the original model M [25,26]. Thus, verification over M can be replaced by verification over the smaller $\overline{M}$, without loss of precision. In addition, $\overline{M}$ is roughly exponentially smaller than M: the equivalence classes of $\equiv$ collapse up to $n!$ many states of M. Symmetry reduction thus combines two otherwise antagonistic features of abstractions – precision and compression.

Counter abstraction is an alternative formalization of symmetry, namely using process counters. The idea is that two global states are identical up to permutations of the local states of the components exactly if, for every local state L, the same number of components reside in L. To implement this idea, we introduce a counter for each existing local state and translate a transition from local state A to local state B as a decrement of the counter for A and an increment of that for B. With some effort, this translation can actually be performed statically on the text of a symmetric program $\mathcal{P}$, *before* building a Kripke model. The resulting counter-abstracted program $\widehat{\mathcal{P}}$ gives rise to a Kripke structure $\widehat{M}$ whose reachable part is *isomorphic* to that of the traditional quotient $\overline{M}$ and that can be model-checked without further symmetry considerations.

Counter abstraction can be viewed as a translation that turns a state space of potential size l^n (n local states over $\{1, \ldots, l\}$) to one of potential size $(n+1)^l$ (l counters over $\{0, \ldots, n\}$). The technique is thus expected to yield a reduction whenever $n \gg l$. From a theoretical viewpoint, this is the case asymptotically if l is a constant and n is conceptually unbounded. This view does not, however, withstand a practical evaluation, as we shall see in the next section.

4   Symbolic Counter Abstraction

In this section, we present the contribution of this paper, a symbolic algorithm for state space exploration of concurrent Boolean programs that achieves efficiency through counter abstraction. Before we illustrate the data structures used to store system states compactly, and describe our algorithm, we illustrate the problems a naive implementation of counter abstraction will inevitably entail if applied to practical software.

4.1   Classical Counter Abstraction – Merits and Problems

Classical counter abstraction assumes that the behavior of a single process is given as a local state transition diagram. This abstraction level is useful, for instance, in high-level communication protocols implementing some form of N-T-C mutual exclusion. In this case, counter abstraction reduces an n-process Kripke structure of exponential size $\mathcal{O}(3^n)$ to one of low-degree polynomial size $\mathcal{O}(n^3)$. The latter structure can be model-checked for hundreds if not thousands of processes.

This approach is problematic, however, for concurrent *software*, where thread behavior is given in the form of a program that manipulates local variables. The straightforward definition of a local state as a valuation of all thread-local variables is incompatible in practice with the idea of counter abstraction: the number of local states generated is simply too large. Consider again the Boolean program in Figure 1. It declares only four local Boolean variables and the PC with range $\{1, \ldots, 12\}$, giving rise to already $2^4 * 12 = 192$ local states. In applications of the magnitude we consider, concurrent Boolean programs routinely have several dozens of thread-local variables and many dozens of program lines (even after optimizations), resulting in many millions of local states.

Generally, as a result of this *local state explosion* problem, the state space of the counter program is of size **doubly-exponential** in the number v of local variables, namely $\Omega(n^{2^v})$. Our approach to tackling the problem is two-fold:

1. Instead of statically translating each statement s of the input program into counter updates (which would require enumerating the many possible local states in which s is enabled), do the translation *on the fly*. This way we have to execute s only in the narrow context of a *given* and *reachable* local state.
2. Instead of storing the counter values for all local states in a global state, store only the *non-zero* counters. This (obvious) idea exploits the observation that, if $l \gg n$, in every system state most counters are zero.

As a result, the worst-case size of the Kripke structure of the counter-abstracted program is reduced from n^l to $n^{\min\{n,l\}}$, completely **eliminating** the sensitivity to the local state space explosion problem. In the rest of this section, we describe the symbolic state-space exploration algorithm that implements this approach.

4.2   A Compact Symbolic Representation

Resulting from predicate abstractions of C code, Boolean programs make heavy use of data-nondeterminism, in the form of the nondeterministic Boolean value $\star$. Enumerating all possible values an expression involving $\star$ can stand for is infeasible in practice. A better approach is to interpret the value $\star$ symbolically, as the set $\{0, 1\}$. This interpretation is not only compatible with encodings of Boolean programs using BDDs, but can also be combined well with counter abstraction.

Our approach to counter abstraction is to count *sets* of local states represented by propositional formulas, rather than individual local states. Consider 3 threads executing a Boolean program with a single local Boolean variable x, and the global state $s = (\star, \star, \star)$: all threads satisfy $x = \star$. Defining the local state set $B := \{0, 1\}$, we can represent s compactly as the single abstract state characterized by $n_B = 3$, indicating that there are 3 threads whose value for x belongs to B (all other counters are zero).

To formalize our state representation, let L be the set of conceivable local states, i.e., $|L| = l$. An abstract global state takes the form of a set G of valuations of the global variables, followed by a list of pairs of a local state set and a counter:

$$\langle G, (L_1, n_1), \ldots, (L_k, n_k) \rangle \ . \tag{1}$$

In this notation, $L_i \subseteq L$ and $n_i \in \mathbb{N}$. We further maintain the invariants $\sum_{i=1}^{k} n_i = n$ and $n_i \geq 1$. The semantics of this representation is given by the set of concrete states that expression (1) represents, namely the states of the form $(g, l_1, \ldots, l_n)$ such that

(a) $g \in G$, and
(b) there exists a partition $\{I_1, \ldots, I_k\}$ of $\{1, \ldots, n\}$ such that $\qquad$ (2)
    for all $i \in \{1, \ldots, k\}$, $|I_i| = n_i$ and for all $j \in I_i$, $l_j \in L_i$.

That is, an abstract state of the form (1) represents precisely the concrete states in the Cartesian product of valuations of the global variables in G, and valuations of the local variables satisfying the constraint (2) (b). We use separate BDDs to represent the sets G and L_i. Let V_g and V_l denote the sets of shared and local variables in $\mathcal{P}$, respectively, and pc the program counter. We represent the set G using a predicate f over the variables in V_g, and each set L_i using a predicate f_i over the variables in $V_l \cup \{pc\}$.

This representation has a caveat: constraints between global and local variables, such as introduced by an assignment of the form $global := local$, cannot be expressed, since the defining predicates for G and L_i may not refer to variables from *both* V_g and V_l. Clearly, however, Boolean programs can introduce such constraints. Section 4.3 describes how our algorithm addresses this problem.

Intuitively, each pair (L_i, n_i) represents the n_i threads such that the *most precise* information on their local states is that they belong to L_i. For instance, the abstract global state $\langle (x = 0, 3), (x = \star, 4) \rangle$ represents those concrete states where 3 threads satisfy $x = 0$, whereas we have no information on x for the remaining 4 threads. This example also shows that we do not require the sets L_i to be disjoint: forcing the symbolic local $x = 0$ to be merged into the symbolic local state $x = \star$ would imply a loss of information, as the constraint $x = 0$ is more precise.

Traditional approaches that statically counter-abstract the entire input program often use a data structure that can be seen as a special case of (1), namely with $k = l = |L|$. Such implementations do not enforce the invariant $n_i \geq 1$ and thus suffer from the potential redundancy of n_i being 0 for most i.

4.3   Symbolic State Space Exploration

We present a symbolic algorithm for reachability analysis of symmetric Boolean programs for on-the-fly counter abstraction that employs the state representation

---

Algorithm 1. Symbolic counter abstraction algorithm

1: $\mathcal{R} := \{\langle G_0, (L_0, n)\rangle\}$, insert $\langle G_0, (L_0, n)\rangle$ into $\mathcal{W}$ $\quad\quad\quad\quad$ ▷ n threads at location 0
2: **while** $\mathcal{W} \neq \emptyset$ **do**
3: $\quad$ remove $S = \langle G, F\rangle$, with $F = \{(L_1, n_1), \ldots, (L_k, n_k)\}$, from $\mathcal{W}$
4: $\quad$ **for** $i \in \{1, \ldots, k\}$ **do**
5: $\quad\quad$ $T := \langle G, L_i\rangle$ $\quad\quad\quad\quad\quad\quad\quad\quad\quad$ ▷ extract thread state from S
6: $\quad\quad$ **for** $v \in$ all valuations of *SpliceVariables(T)* **do**
7: $\quad\quad\quad$ $T' = \langle G', L'\rangle := \mathsf{Image}(T|_v)$ $\quad\quad$ ▷ compute one image cofactor of T
8: $\quad\quad\quad$ **if** $L' \neq L_i$ **then** $\quad\quad\quad\quad\quad$ ▷ build new system state S' from T'
9: $\quad\quad\quad\quad$ $S' := \langle G', \textsc{UpdateCounters}(F, i, L')\rangle$
10: $\quad\quad\quad\quad$ **if** $S' \notin \mathcal{R}$ **then**
11: $\quad\quad\quad\quad\quad$ $\mathcal{R} := \mathcal{R} \cup S'$ $\quad\quad\quad\quad\quad$ ▷ store S' as reachable, if new
12: $\quad\quad\quad\quad\quad$ insert S' into $\mathcal{W}$

13: **procedure** $\textsc{UpdateCounters}(F, i, L')$
14: $\quad$ let (L_i, n_i) be the i-th pair in F
15: $\quad$ $O := (n_i > 1 \; ? \; \{(L_i, n_i - 1)\} \; : \; \emptyset)$ $\quad\quad$ ▷ determine if L_i is abandoned
16: $\quad$ **if** $\exists j. (L_j, n_j) \in F \wedge L' = L_j$ **then** $\quad$ ▷ update or add a state-counter pair
17: $\quad\quad$ $F' := F \setminus \{(L_i, n_i), (L_j, n_j)\} \cup O \cup \{(L', n_j + 1)\}$
18: $\quad$ **else**
19: $\quad\quad$ $F' := F \setminus \{(L_i, n_i)\} \cup O \cup \{(L', 1)\}$
20: $\quad$ **return** F'

---

described in section 4.2. The input consists of a template program $\mathcal{P}$ and the number n of concurrent threads; the algorithm computes the counter-abstracted set of states reachable from a given set of initial states.

Algorithm 1. expands unexplored system states from a worklist $\mathcal{W}$, initialized to contain the symbolic state that constrains all threads to location 0. The loop in line 4 iterates over all pairs (L_i, n_i) contained in the popped state S. To expand an individual pair, the algorithm first projects it to the ith symbolic thread state.

The next, and crucial, step is to compute the successor thread states induced by the Boolean program (lines 6–7). Recall from the previous section that our Cartesian state representation does not permit constraints between global and local variables, which can, however, be introduced by the program. Consider a global variable a and a local b, and the statement a := b. The concrete thread state (a', b') obtained after executing the statement is characterized by the constraint $a' \equiv b'$. In order to make this constraint expressible, we must treat certain assignments and related statements specially.

Definition 2. *A **splice state** is a symbolic thread state given as a predicate f over the variables in $V_g \cup V_l \cup \{pc\}$ such that*

$$(\exists V_g . f) \; \wedge \; (\exists V_l \exists pc . f) \quad \not\equiv \quad f .$$

*A **splice statement** is a statement s such that there exists a thread state u whose PC points to s and that, when executed on u, results in a splice state. A **splice variable** is a global variable dependent on $\exists V_g . f$.*

A splice statement marks a point where a thread communicates data via the global variables, in a way that constrains its local state with the values of some splice variables. Fortunately, statements with the *potential* to induce such communication can be identified syntactically:

- assignments whose left-hand side is a global variable and the right-hand side expression refers to local variables, or vice versa,
- assignments with a `constrain` clause whose expression refers to both global and local variables, and
- `assume` statements whose expression refers to both global and local variables.

Before executing a splice statement, the current thread state is *split* using Shannon decomposition. Executing the statement on the separate cofactors yields a symbolic successor that can be represented precisely in the form (1). That is, if variable v is the splice variable of the statement in T, denoted by *Splice Variables*$(T) = \{v\}$, we decompose $\mathsf{Image}(T)$ as follows:

$$\mathsf{Image}(T) = \mathsf{Image}(T|_{v=0}) \vee \mathsf{Image}(T|_{v=1}) \, .$$

The price of this expansion is an explosion worst-case exponential in the number of splice variables. However, as we observed in our experiments (see section 5),

1. the percentage of splice statements is relatively small,
2. even within a splice statement, the number of splice variables involved is usually very small (1 or 2),
3. a significant fraction of cofactors encountered during the exploration is actually *unsatisfiable* and does not result in new states.

As a result, the combinatorial explosion never materialized in our experiments.

After the image has been computed for each cofactor, the algorithm constructs the respective system state for it (lines 8–9). The UPDATECOUNTERS function uses the local state part L' of the newly computed thread state to determine the new set of (state,counter) pairs F'. If no more threads reside in the "left" state L_i, its pair is expunged (line 15); if the new local state L' was already present in the system state, its counter n_j is incremented, otherwise the state is added with counter value 1 (lines 16–19).

Finally, the algorithm adds the states encountered for the first time to the set of reachable states, and to the worklist of states to expand (lines 10–12).

Theorem 3. *Let $\mathcal{R}$ be as computed by Algorithm 1. on termination, and let γ be the concretization function for abstract states defined in equation (2). The set $\gamma(\mathcal{R}) = \{\gamma(r) \mid r \in \mathcal{R}\}$ is the set of reachable states of the concurrent system induced by n threads executing the Boolean program $\mathcal{P}$ in parallel.*

The proof of this theorem, and that of the termination of Algorithm 1., follow from (i) the equivalent theorems for classical state space exploration under symmetry using canonical state representatives, and (ii) the isomorphism of the structures over such representatives and the counter representation.

Errors are detected by Algorithm 1. in the form of program locations that contain a violated assertion. We have omitted from the algorithm a description of the standard mechanisms to trace back a reached state to the initial state, in order to obtain error paths. Such a path is, in our case, a sequence of abstract states in the form (1). This abstract trace can be mapped to a concrete trace, by expanding each abstract state to a concrete one according to equation (2), and ensuring that, in the resulting sequence, any state differs from its successor in only one thread. Note that, as our method is exact with respect to the given Boolean program, no spurious reachability results occur.

5   Experimental Evaluation

In addition to the symbolic version of the algorithm, we have also implemented an explicit-state version, both in a tool called BOOM (available at http://www.cprover.org/boom). The symbolic implementation stores the sets G and L_i of global and local variable valuations as individual BDDs, such that the conjunction of G with each L_i forms the thread-visible state T_i. As in most symbolic Model Checkers for software, the program counters are stored in explicit form: this permits partitioning the transition relation and ensures a minimum number of splice tests.

We applied BOOM to over 400 examples from two sources: a set of 208 concurrent Boolean programs generated by SATABS that abstract part of the Linux kernel components (available at http://www.cprover.org/boolean-programs), and a set of 236 Boolean programs generated at Microsoft Research using SLAM. We build a concurrent out of a sequential Boolean program by instantiating n threads that execute the main procedure. All Boolean programs involve communication among threads through global variables. The 444 benchmarks feature, on average, 123 program locations, 21 local variables, and 12 global variables.

We compare the explicit-state implementation to MURφ [10], a mature and popular Model Checker with long-standing support for symmetry reduction. Since other symbolic model checkers did not scale to interesting thread counts (including the few tools with built-in support for symmetry), we compare the symbolic algorithm to a reference implementation in BOOM that ignores the symmetry. On sequential programs, the performance of the reference implementation is similar to that of the Model Checker that ships with SLAM.

The experimental setup is as follows. For each tool and benchmark, we start full reachability analysis with $n = 2$ threads, and increase the thread count until the tool times out; the timeout is set to $720\,\mathrm{s}$ and the memory limit to $12\,\mathrm{GB}$[2].

Figure 2 is a scatter plot of the running times of the explicit-state version of BOOM and of MURφ with symmetry reduction. Since MURφ does not allow data nondeterminism, we replace every occurrence of $\star$ in the input programs randomly by 0 or 1, before passing them to either tool. The resulting programs are converted into MURφ's input language using a MURφ *rule* per statement,

---

[2] The experiments are performed on a 3GHz Intel Xeon machine running the 64-bit variant of Linux 2.6.

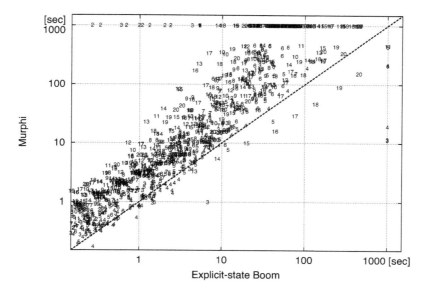

Fig. 2. Running time of explicit-state BOOM vs. MURφ, for various thread counts

guarded by the program counter value. Counter abstraction is faster than MURφ on 94 % of the tests; on 23 %, the improvement is better than one order of magnitude. It completes successfully on a significant number of problems where MURφ times out (19 %). In seven cases (1.2 %), our tool runs out of memory. Note that removing the data nondeterminism simplifies the programs, which is why the explicit-state explorations often terminate for larger thread counts than the symbolic ones.

Figure 3 summarizes the running times of the symbolic counter abstraction implementation in BOOM and the plain symbolic exploration algorithm. The uniform distribution in the upper triangle signifies the improvement in scalability due to counter abstraction. Those tests where traditional Model Checking is faster feature a small number of threads, reflecting the polynomial complexity of counter abstraction; in fact, we can verify many instances for 7 or more threads. Overall, the symbolic counter abstraction tool is faster on 83 % of all tests, and on 96 % of those running three or more threads. Among those, the speed-up is five orders of magnitude and more.

Splice statements do not cause a blow-up in any of the benchmarks. In fact, they amount to less than 12 % of all statements, the average number of splice variables they involve is small (in our benchmarks, mean 2.1, median 1), and each such variable produces two valid cofactors in only 10 % of the cases.

Our implementation of the last step of Algorithm 1. (lines 20–21) uses state merging, a crucial optimization to compact sets of symbolic states. In counter abstraction, two symbolic states can be merged iff a) they differ only in the valuation of the global variables, or b) they differ in the local state of only

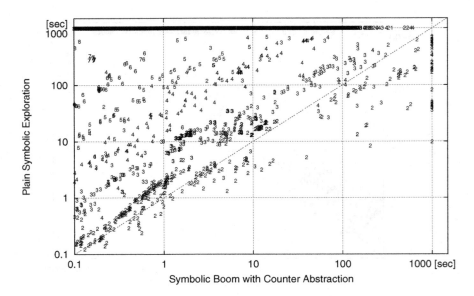

Fig. 3. Running time of symbolic Boom vs. plain exploration, for various thread counts

one thread. These merging rules, albeit apparently strict, provide an average speed-up of 83 % over exploration without merging.

We have also considered global state representations alternative to equation (1). In one implementation, we use a monolithic BDD to represent the global variables and all thread states, along with their counters. In another, we separate the counters from the BDD and keep them explicit, but use a monolithic BDD for all other variables. Both allow us to retain the inter-thread constraints introduced by splice statements, and thus do not require the decomposition step. However, both do require complex manipulations for computing successor states, especially for updating the counters. Moreover, they give rise to very complex BDDs for the set of reachable states, which foils the scalability advantage inherent in counter abstraction. On our benchmarks, the algorithm proposed in Section 4 is at least 30 % faster than all alternatives.

6   Summary

We have presented an algorithm for BDD-based symbolic state space exploration of concurrent Boolean programs, a significant branch of the pressing problem of concurrent software verification. The algorithm draws its efficiency from counter abstraction as a reduction technique, without having to resort to approximation at any time. It is specifically designed to cope with large numbers of local states and thus addresses a classical bottleneck in implementations of counter abstraction. We showed how to avoid the *local state space explosion* problem using a combination of two techniques: 1) interleaving the translation with the state space exploration, and 2) ensuring that only non-zero counters and their corresponding local states are kept in memory.

We have shown experimental results both for an explicit-state and, more importantly, a symbolic implementation. While standard symmetry reduction is employed in tools like MURφ and RULEBASE, we are not aware of a prior implementation of counter abstraction that is efficient on programs other than abstract protocols with relatively few control states. We believe our model checker to be the first with a true potential for scalability in concurrent software verification, due to its polynomial dependence on the thread count n, while incurring little verification time overhead.

An interesting question for future work is the relationship between our work and *partial-order reduction*. The latter is generally viewed as combinable with symmetry reduction for yet better compression. We have preliminary experiments that indicate this is true for our symbolic counter abstraction algorithm as well. We also plan to investigate how our algorithms can be combined with other techniques to curb the local state space explosion problem, such as based on static analysis or approximation (see [13]). Finally, we want to extend our techniques to richer specification languages, especially Boolean programs with dynamic thread creation.

References

1. Graf, S., Saïdi, H.: Construction of abstract state graphs with PVS. In: Grumberg, O. (ed.) CAV 1997. LNCS, vol. 1254. Springer, Heidelberg (1997)
2. Lahiri, S.K., Bryant, R., Cook, B.: A symbolic approach to predicate abstraction. In: Hunt Jr., W.A., Somenzi, F. (eds.) CAV 2003. LNCS, vol. 2725, pp. 141–153. Springer, Heidelberg (2003)
3. Ball, T., Rajamani, S.: Bebop: A symbolic model checker for Boolean programs. In: Model Checking of Software (SPIN) (2000)
4. Kurshan, R.: Computer-Aided Verification of Coordinating Processes. Princeton University Press, Princeton (1995)
5. Ball, T., Bounimova, E., Cook, B., Levin, V., Lichtenberg, J., McGarvey, C., Ondrusek, B., Rajamani, S., Ustuner, A.: Thorough static analysis of device drivers. In: EuroSys. (2006)
6. Witkowski, T., Blanc, N., Kroening, D., Weissenbacher, G.: Model checking concurrent Linux device drivers. In: Automated Software Engineering (ASE) (2007)
7. Emerson, A., Trefler, R.: From asymmetry to full symmetry: New techniques for symmetry reduction in model checking. In: Pierre, L., Kropf, T. (eds.) CHARME 1999. LNCS, vol. 1703, pp. 142–157. Springer, Heidelberg (1999)
8. Donaldson, A., Miller, A.: Symmetry reduction for probabilistic model checking using generic representatives. In: Graf, S., Zhang, W. (eds.) ATVA 2006. LNCS, vol. 4218, pp. 9–23. Springer, Heidelberg (2006)
9. Clarke, E., Kroening, D., Sharygina, N., Yorav, K.: SATABS: SAT-based predicate abstraction for ANSI-C. In: Halbwachs, N., Zuck, L.D. (eds.) TACAS 2005. LNCS, vol. 3440, pp. 570–574. Springer, Heidelberg (2005)
10. Melton, R., Dill, D.: Murφ Annotated Reference Manual, rel. 3.1, http://verify.stanford.edu/dill/murphi.html

78   G. Basler et al.

11. Lubachevsky, B.: An approach to automating the verification of compact parallel coordination programs. Acta Informatica (1984)
12. Pnueli, A., Xu, J., Zuck, L.: Liveness with $(0, 1, \infty)$-counter abstraction. In: Brinksma, E., Larsen, K.G. (eds.) CAV 2002. LNCS, vol. 2404, p. 107. Springer, Heidelberg (2002)
13. Emerson, A., Wahl, T.: Efficient reduction techniques for systems with many components. In: Brazilian Symposium on Formal Methods (SBMF) (2004)
14. Wei, O., Gurfinkel, A., Chechik, M.: Identification and counter abstraction for full virtual symmetry. In: Borrione, D., Paul, W. (eds.) CHARME 2005. LNCS, vol. 3725, pp. 285–300. Springer, Heidelberg (2005)
15. Emerson, A., Havlicek, J., Trefler, R.: Virtual symmetry reduction. In: Logic in Computer Science (LICS) (2000)
16. Ball, T., Chaki, S., Rajamani, S.: Parameterized verification of multithreaded software libraries. In: Margaria, T., Yi, W. (eds.) TACAS 2001. LNCS, vol. 2031, p. 158. Springer, Heidelberg (2001)
17. Henzinger, T., Jhala, R., Majumdar, R.: Race checking by context inference. In: Programming Language Design and Implementation (PLDI) (2004)
18. Andrews, T., Qadeer, S., Rajamani, S., Rehof, J., Xie, Y.: Zing: A model checker for concurrent software. In: Alur, R., Peled, D.A. (eds.) CAV 2004. LNCS, vol. 3114, pp. 484–487. Springer, Heidelberg (2004)
19. Blanc, N., Emerson, A., Wahl, T.: SVISS: Symbolic verification of symmetric systems. In: Ramakrishnan, C.R., Rehof, J. (eds.) TACAS 2008. LNCS, vol. 4963, pp. 459–462. Springer, Heidelberg (2008)
20. Barner, S., Grumberg, O.: Combining symmetry reduction and under-approximation for symbolic model checking. In: Formal Methods in System Design (FMSD) (2005)
21. Cook, B., Kroening, D., Sharygina, N.: Symbolic model checking for asynchronous Boolean programs. In: Godefroid, P. (ed.) SPIN 2005. LNCS, vol. 3639, pp. 75–90. Springer, Heidelberg (2005)
22. Suwimonteerabuth, D., Esparza, J., Schwoon, S.: Symbolic Context-Bounded Analysis of Multithreaded Java Programs. In: Havelund, K., Majumdar, R., Palsberg, J. (eds.) SPIN 2008. LNCS, vol. 5156, pp. 270–287. Springer, Heidelberg (2008)
23. Flanagan, C., Godefroid, P.: Dynamic partial-order reduction for model checking software. In: Principles of Programming Languages (POPL)(2005)
24. Cook, B., Kroening, D., Sharygina, N.: Verification of Boolean programs with unbounded thread creation. Theoretical Computer Science (TCS) (2007)
25. Clarke, E., Enders, R., Filkorn, T., Jha, S.: Exploiting symmetry in temporal logic model checking. In: Formal Methods in System Design (FMSD) (1996)
26. Emerson, A., Sistla, P.: Symmetry and model checking. In: Formal Methods in System Design (FMSD) (1996)

Priority Scheduling of Distributed Systems Based on Model Checking

Ananda Basu[1], Saddek Bensalem[1], Doron Peled[2], and Joseph Sifakis[1]

[1] Centre Equation - VERIMAG, 2 Avenue de Vignate, Gieres, France
[2] Department of Computer Science, Bar Ilan University, Ramat Gan 52900, Israel

Abstract. Priorities are used to control the execution of systems to meet given requirements for optimal use of resources, e.g., by using scheduling policies. For distributed systems, it is hard to find efficient implementations for priorities; because they express constraints on global states, their implementation may incur considerable overhead.

Our method is based on performing model checking for knowledge properties. It allows identifying where the local information of a process is sufficient to schedule the execution of a high priority transition. As a result of the model checking, the program is transformed to react upon the knowledge it has at each point. The transformed version has no priorities, and uses the gathered information and its knowledge to limit the enabledness of transitions so that it matches or approximates the original specification of priorities.

1 Introduction

In a distributed system, it can be quite nontrivial to implement distributed communication; for example, once one process decides that it is willing to communicate with a second process, that communication might not be available anymore, as the second process has meanwhile communicated with a third process. For this reason, concurrent programming languages may restrict the choice of communication. For example, Hoare [7] has initially restricted his programming language CSP to commit to a single output, where choice is still allowed between inputs; overriding this restriction may require some nontrivial algorithms [2,5]. A further implementation complication can, orthogonally, result from imposing priorities between transitions. Separating the design of the system into a transition system and a set of priorities can be a very powerful tool [8], yet quite challenging [1].

Executing transitions according to a priority policy is complicated due to the fact that each process has a limited view of the situation of the rest of the system. Such limited local information can be described as the *knowledge* that processes have at each point of the execution [6,4]. Our solution for implementing priorities is based on running an analysis of the system before it is executed using model checking [3,11]. Specifically, we use model checking for knowledge properties, similar to the algorithms suggested by Van der Meyden in [10]. This analysis checks which processes possess "knowledge" about having a maximal priority transition enabled at the current state.

A. Bouajjani and O. Maler (Eds.): CAV 2009, LNCS 5643, pp. 79–93, 2009.

The information gathered during the model checking stage is used as a basis for a program transformation. It produces a new program without priorities, which implements or at least approximates the prioritized behaviors of the old program. At runtime, processes consult some table, constructed based upon the model checking analysis, that tells them, depending on the current local state, whether a current enabled transition has a maximal priority and thus can be immediately executed. This transformation does not introduce any new executions or deadlocks, and is intended to preserve the linear temporal logic properties [9] of the net.

For states where no process can locally know about having a maximal priority transition, we suggest several options; this includes putting some semi-global observers that can observe the combined situation of several processes, passing additional synchronization messages, or using global variables, to inform the different processes about the situation of their neighbors. Another possibility is to relax the priority policy, and allow a good approximation. The priorities discussed in this paper are inspired by the BIP system (Behavior Interaction Priority) [8].

2   Preliminaries

Definition 1. *A* Petri Net N *is a tuple* (P, T, E, s_0) *where*

- P *is a finite set of* places. *The* states *are defined as* $S = 2^P$.
- T *is a finite set of* transitions.
- $E \subseteq (P \times T) \cup (T \times P)$ *is a bipartite relation between the places and the transition.*
- $s_0 \subseteq P$ *is the* initial state *(hence $s_0 \in S$).*

For a transition $t \in T$, we define the set of input places $^\bullet t$ as $\{p \in P | (p, t) \in E\}$, and *output places* $t^\bullet$ as $\{p \in P | (t, p) \in E\}$. A transition t is *enabled* in a state s if $^\bullet t \subseteq s$ and $t^\bullet \cap s = \emptyset$. A state s is in *deadlock* if there is no enabled transition from it. We denote the fact that t is enabled from s by $s[t\rangle$. A transition t is *fired* (or *executed*) from state s to state s', which is denoted by $s[t\rangle s'$, when t is enabled at s, and, furthermore, $s' = (s \setminus ^\bullet t) \cup t^\bullet$. We extend our notation and denote by $s[t_1 t_2 \ldots t_n\rangle s'$ the fact that there is a sequence of states $s = r_0, r_1, \ldots r_n = s'$ such that $r_i[t_{i+1}\rangle r_{i+1}$.

Definition 2. *Two transitions t_1 and t_2 are* independent *if* $(^\bullet t_1 \cup t_1^\bullet) \cap (^\bullet t_2 \cup t_2^\bullet) = \emptyset$. *Let $I \subset T \times T$ be the* independence *relation. Two transitions are* dependent *if they are not independent.*

Graphically, transitions are represented as lines, places as circles, and the relation E is represented using arrows. In Figure 1, there are places p_1, p_2, ..., p_7 and transitions t_1, t_2, t_3, t_4. We depict a state by putting full circles, called *tokens*, inside the places of that state. In the example in Figure 1, the depicted initial state s_0 is $\{p_1, p_2, p_7\}$. If we fire transition t_1 from the initial state, the tokens from p_1 and p_7 will be removed, and a token will be places in p_3. The transitions that are enabled from the initial state are t_1 and t_2. In the Petri Net of Figure 1, all the transitions are dependent on each other, since they all involve the place p_7. Removing p_7, as in Figure 2, both t_1 and t_3 become independent on both t_2 and t_4.

Definition 3. *An* execution *is a maximal (i.e. it cannot be extended) alternating sequence of states $s_0 t_1 s_1 t_2 s_2 \ldots$ with s_0 the initial state of the Petri Net, such that for each states s_i in the sequence, $s_i[t_{i+1}\rangle s_{i+1}$.*

We denote the executions of a Petri Net N by $exec(N)$. A state is *reachable* in a Petri Net if it appears on at least one of its executions. We denote the reachable states of a Petri Net N by $reach(N)$.

We use places also as state predicates and denote $s \models p_i$ iff $p_i \in s$. This is extended to Boolean combinations in a standard way.

For a state s, we denote by φ_s the formula that is a conjunction of the places that are in s and the negated places that are not in s. Thus, φ_s is satisfied exactly by the state s and no other state. For the Petri Net of Figure 1 we have that the initial state s satisfies $\varphi_s = p_1 \wedge p_2 \wedge \neg p_3 \wedge \neg p_4 \wedge \neg p_5 \wedge \neg p_6 \wedge p_7$. For a set of states $Q \subseteq S$, we can write a *characterizing formula* $\varphi_Q = \bigvee_{s \in Q} \varphi_s$ or use any equivalent propositional formula. We say that a predicate φ is an *invariant* of a Petri Net N if $s \models \varphi$ for each $s \in reach(N)$. As usual in logic, when a formula φ_Q characterizes a set of states Q and a formula $\varphi_{Q'}$ characterizes a set of states Q', then $Q \subseteq Q'$ if and only if $\varphi_Q \rightarrow \varphi_{Q'}$.

Definition 4. *A* process *of a Petri Net N is a subset of the transitions $\pi \subseteq T$ satisfying that for each $t_1, t_2 \in T$, $(t_1, t_2) \notin I$.*

We assume a given set of processes $\mathcal{S}$ that covers all the transitions of the net, i.e., $\bigcup_{\pi \in \mathcal{S}} \pi = T$. A transition can belong to several processes, e.g., when it models a synchronization between processes. Note that there can be multiple ways to define a set of processes for the same Petri Net.

Definition 5. *The* neighborhood *$ngb(\pi)$ of a process π is the set of places $\bigcup_{t \in \pi} ({}^\bullet t \cup t^\bullet)$. For a set of processes Π, $ngb(\Pi) = \bigcup_{\pi \in \Pi} ngb(\pi)$.*

In the rest of this paper, when a formula refers to a set of processes Π, we will often replace writing the singleton process set $\{\pi\}$ by writing π instead. For the Petri Net in Figure 1, there are two executions: $t_1 t_3 t_2 t_4$ and $t_2 t_4 t_1 t_3$. There are two processes: the *left* process $\pi_l = \{t_1, t_3\}$ and the *right* process $\pi_r = \{t_2, t_4\}$. The neighborhood of process π_l is $\{p_1, p_3, p_5, p_7\}$. The place p_7 acts as a semaphore. It can be captured by the execution of t_1 or of t_2, guaranteeing that $\neg(p_3 \wedge p_4)$ is an invariant of the system.

Definition 6. *A* Petri Net with priorities *is a pair $(N, \ll)$, where N is a Petri Net and $\ll$ is a partial order relation among the transitions T of N.*

Definition 7. *A transition t has a* maximal *priority in a state s if $s[t\rangle$ and, furthermore, there is no transition r with $s[r\rangle$ such that $t \ll r$.*

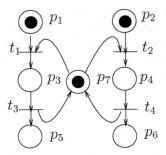

Fig. 1. A (safe) Petri Net

Definition 8. *An execution of a Petri Net with Priorities is a maximal alternating sequence of states and transitions $s_0 t_1 s_1 t_2 s_2 t_3 \ldots$ with s_0 the initial state of the Petri Net. Furthermore, for each state s_i in the sequence it holds that that $s_i[t_{i+1}\rangle s_{i+1}$ for t_{i+1} having maximal priority in s_i.*

To emphasize that the executions take into account the priorities, we sometimes call them *prioritized executions*. We denote the executions of a Prioritized Petri Net $(N, \ll)$ by $priorE(N, \ll)$. The set of states that appear on $priorE(N, \ll)$ will be denoted by $reach(N, \ll)$. The following is a direct consequence of the definitions:

Lemma 1. $priorE(N, \ll) \subseteq exec(N)$ *and* $reach(N, \ll) \subseteq reach(N)$.

The executions of the Petri Net M in Figure 2, when the priorities $t_1 \ll t_4$ and $t_2 \ll t_3$ are not taken into account, include $t_1 t_2 t_3 t_4, t_1 t_3 t_2 t_4, t_2 t_1 t_3 t_4, t_2 t_1 t_4 t_3$, etc. However, when taking the priorities into account, the prioritized executions of M are the same as the executions of the Net N of Figure 1.

Unfortunately, enforcing prioritized executions in a completely distributed way may incur high synchronization overhead [1] or even be impossible. In our example, consider the case where t_1 and t_3 belong to one (left) process π_l, and

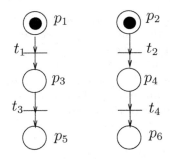

Fig. 2. A Petri Net with Priorities $t_1 \ll t_4, t_2 \ll t_3$

t_2 and t_4 belong to another (right) process π_r, with no interaction between them. Then, the left process π_l, upon having a token in p_1, cannot locally decide whether to execute t_1; the priorities dictate that t_1 can be executed if t_4 is not enabled, since t_1 has a lower priority than t_4. But this information may not be locally available to the left process, which cannot distinguish between the cases where the right process has a token in p_2, p_4 or p_6.

Definition 9. *The* local information *of a set of process Π of a Petri Net N in a state s is $s|_\Pi = s \cap nbg(\Pi)$.*

That is, the local information of Π consists of the restriction of the state to the neighborhood of the transitions of Π. The local information of a process π in a state s plays the role of a *local state* of π in s. However, we prefer to use the term "local information" since neighborhoods of different processes may overlap on some common places rather than partitioning the global states. Thus, in the Petri Net in Figure 1, the local information of the left process in a state s consists of restriction of s to the places $\{p_1, p_3, p_5, p_7\}$. In the initial state, these are $\{p_1, p_7\}$.

Our definition of local information is only one among possible definitions that can be used for modeling the part of the state to which the system is aware at any moment. Consider again the Petri Net of Figure 1. The places p_1, p_3 and p_5 may represent the location counter in the left process. When there is a token in p_1 or p_3, it is reasonable to assume that the existence of a token in place p_7 (the semaphore) is known to the left process. However, it may or may not be true that the left process is aware of the value of the semaphore when the token is at place p_5. This is because at this point, the semaphore may affect the enabledness of the right process (if it has a token in p_2) but would not have an effect on the left process. Thus, a subtle difference in the definition of local information can be used instead. For simplicity, we will continue with the simpler definition above.

Definition 10. *Let $\Pi \subseteq S$ be a set of processes. Define an equivalence relation $\equiv_\Pi \subseteq reach(N) \times reach(N)$ such that $s \equiv_\Pi s'$ when $s|_\pi = s'|_\pi$ for each $\pi \in \Pi$.*

It is easy to see that the enabledness of a transition depends only on the local information of a process that contains it.

Lemma 2. *If $t \in \pi$ and $s \equiv_\pi s'$ then $s[t\rangle$ if and only if $s'[t\rangle$.*

We cannot make a local decision, based on the local information of processes (and sometimes sets of processes), that would guarantee only the prioritized executions in a Prioritized Petri Net $(N, \ll)$. It is possible that there are two states $s, s' \in reach(N)$ such that $s \equiv_\pi s'$, a transition $t \notin \pi$ is a maximal enabled transition in s, but in s' this transition is either not enabled or not maximal among the enabled transitions. This can be easily demonstrated on the Prioritized Petri Net in Figure 2. There, we have that for π_l, $\{p_1, p_2\} \equiv_{\pi_l} \{p_1, p_4\}$. In the state $\{p_1, p_2\}$, t_1 is a maximal priority enabled transition (and so is p_2), while in $\{p_1, p_4\}$, t_1 is not anymore maximal, as we have that $t_1 \ll t_4$, and t_4 is enabled. Since the history of the execution for process π_l is the same in both of the above states, recording the local history, is sufficient for distinguishing between these two cases.

3   Knowledge Based Approach

Although, as we saw in the previous section, we may not be able to decide, based on the local information of a process or a set of processes, whether some enabled transition is maximal with respect to priority, we may be able to exploit some model checking based analysis of the system.

Our first approach for a local or semi-local decision on firing transitions is based on the *knowledge* of processes [4], or of sets of processes. Basically, the knowledge of a process at a given state is the possible combination of reachable states that are consistent with the local information of that process.

Since the set of states is limited to $S = 2^P$ (and the reachable states are a subset of that), we can write formulas characterizing (i.e., satisfied *exactly* by) the states that satisfy various properties as follows, where the propositions of the formula are the places of the Petri Net.

All the reachable states: $\varphi_{reach(N)}$.
The states where transition t is enabled: $\varphi_{en(t)}$.
At least one transition is enabled, i.e., there is no deadlock: $\varphi_{df} = \bigvee_{t \in T} \varphi_{en(t)}$.
The transition t has a maximal priority among all the enabled transitions of
  the system: $\varphi_{max(t)} = \varphi_{en(t)} \wedge \bigwedge_{t \ll r} \neg \varphi_{en(r)}$.
The local information of processes Π at state s: $\varphi_{s|_{\Pi}}$.

We can perform model checking in order to calculate these formulas, and store them in a compact way, e.g., using BDDs.

Definition 11. *The processes Π (jointly) know a (Boolean) property ψ in a state s, denoted $s \models K_{\Pi}\psi$, exactly when for each s' such that $s \equiv_{\Pi} s'$, we have that $s' \models \psi$.*

That is, the processes Π "jointly know" at state s any property that holds for all the reachable states with the same local information that Π have at s. At the moment, the definition of knowledge assumes that the processes do not maintain a log with their history. We henceforth use knowledge formulas combined using Boolean operators with propositions. For a detailed syntactic and semantic description one can refer, e.g., to [4]. We do not define, nor use in this paper the nesting of knowledge operators, e.g., $K_{\Pi_1}(K_{\Pi_2}(\varphi))$, nor the notion of "common" knowledge $C_{\Pi}\varphi$.

Consider the Petri Net in Figure 3, with priorities $t_3 \ll t_5 \ll t_4 \ll t_7$. This Net is an augmentation of the Net in Figure 1. Process π_l now has the additional transition t_6. Process π_r has the same transitions as before (but a bigger neighborhood, as it now includes p_8). We also have a third process $\pi_3 = \{t_5, t_7\}$. Then at any state s with $s|_{\pi_l} = \{p_3\}$ (take, e.g., $s = \{p_2, p_3, p_8\}$), it is impossible that p_4 has a token, because of the mutual exclusion provided by the place p_7. Thus, $s \models K_{\pi_l} \neg p_4$. On the other hand, it is not the case that

$s \models K_{\pi_l} \neg p_{10}$. This follows from the fact that there are two different states $\{p_2, p_3, p_8\}$ and $\{p_2, p_3, p_8, p_{10}\}$, both of them with $s|_{\pi_l} = \{p_3\}$; in the former state p_{10} does not have a token (and t_5 is disabled), while in the latter state, p_{10} has a token (and t_5 is enabled).

The following lemmas follow immediate from the definitions:

Lemma 3. *If $s \models K_\Pi \varphi$ and $s \equiv_\Pi s'$, then $s' \models K_\Pi \varphi$.*

Lemma 4. *The processes Π know ψ at state s exactly when $(\varphi_{reach(N)} \wedge \varphi_{s|_\Pi}) \rightarrow \psi$ is a propositional tautology.*

Now, given a Petri Net with priorities which runs on a distributed architecture, one can perform *model checking* in order to calculate whether $s \models K_\pi \psi$. Note that this is *not* the most space efficient way of checking knowledge properties, since $\varphi_{reach(N)}$ can be exponentially big in the size of the description of the Petri Net. In a (polynomial) space efficient check, we can enumerate all the states s' such that $s \equiv_\pi s'$, check reachability of s' using binary search and, if reachable, check whether $s' \models \psi$.

4 The Supporting Process Policy

The *supporting process policy*, described below, transforms a Prioritized Petri Net $(N, \ll)$ into a priorityless Petri Net N', that implements or at least approximates the priorities of the original net. This transformation augments the states with additional information, and adds conditions for firing the transitions. This is related to the problem of supervisory control [12], where a controller is imposed on a system, restricting transitions from being fired at some of the states. We will identify the states of the transformed version N' with the states of the original version N, since the mapping will only *add* some information to the states; information that will not be addressed by our Boolean formulas. In this way, we will be able to compare between the sets of states of the original and transformed version. In particular, the restriction will imply the following:

$$reach(N') \subseteq reach(N). \tag{1}$$

Note that $reach(N)$ are the reachable states when not taking into account the priorities. We will later relate also the executions of these nets. In particular, the supporting process policy can be classified as having a *disjunctive architecture for decentralized control* [13]. Although the details of the transformation are not given here, it should be clear from the theoretical explanation.

> At a state s, a transition t is *supported by a process π containing t* only if π knows in s about t having a maximal priority (among all the currently enabled transitions of the system), i.e., $s \models K_\pi \varphi_{max(t)}$; a transition can be fired (is enabled) in a state only if, in addition to its previous enabledness condition, at least one of the processes containing it supports it.

Based on Equation (1) and the definition of knowledge, we have the following monotonicity property of knowledge:

Theorem 1. *Given that* $s \models K_{\Pi}\varphi$ *in the original program* N, *(when not taking the priorities into account) then* $s \models K_{\Pi}\varphi$ *also in the transformed version* N'.

This property is important to ensure the maximality of the priority of a transition after the transformation. The knowledge about maximality will be calculated *before* the transformation, and will be used to control the execution of the transitions. Then, we can conclude that the maximality remains also *after* the transformation.

We consider three levels of knowledge of processes related to having a maximally enabled transitions:

φ_1 Each process knows which of its enabled transitions have maximal priorities (among all enabled transitions).

   That is, $\varphi_1 = \bigwedge_{\pi \in \mathcal{S}} \bigwedge_{t \in \pi}(\varphi_{max(t)} \to K_{\pi}\varphi_{\max(t)})$.

φ_2 For each process π, when one of its transitions has a maximal priority, the process knows about at least *one* such transition.

   $\varphi_2 = \bigwedge_{\pi \in \mathcal{S}}((\bigvee_{t \in \pi} \varphi_{max(t)}) \to (\bigvee_{t \in \pi} K_{\pi}\varphi_{\max(t)}))$.

   Note that when all the transitions of each process π are totally ordered, then $\varphi_1 = \varphi_2$.

φ_3 For each state where the system is not in a deadlock, *at least one process* can identify *one* of its transitions that has maximal priority.

   $\varphi_3 = \varphi_{df} \to (\bigvee_{\pi \in \mathcal{S}} \bigvee_{t \in \pi} K_{\pi}\varphi_{\max(t)})$.

Denote the fact that φ is an invariant (i.e., holds in every reachable state) using the usual temporal logic notation $\Box\varphi$ (see [9]). Notice that $\varphi_1 \to \varphi_2$ and $\varphi_2 \to \varphi_3$ hold, hence also $\Box\varphi_1 \to \Box\varphi_2$ and $\Box\varphi_2 \to \Box\varphi_3$. Processes have less knowledge according to φ_2 than according to φ_1, and then even less knowledge if only φ_3 holds.

Definition 12. *Let* $priorS(N, \varphi_i)$ *be the set of executions when transitions are fired according to the supporting process policy when* $\Box\varphi_i$ *holds.*

That is, when $\Box\varphi_1$ holds, the processes support all of their maximal enabled transition. When $\Box\varphi_2$, the processes support at least one of their maximal enabled transition, but not necessarily all of them. When $\Box\varphi_3$ holds, at least one enabled transition will be supported by some process, at each state, preventing deadlocks that did not exist in the prioritized net.

Lemma 5. $priorS(N, \varphi_1) = priorE(N, \ll)$. *Furthermore, for* $i = 2$ *or* $i = 3$, $priorS(N, \varphi_i) \subseteq priorE(N, \ll)$.

This is because when $\Box\varphi_2$ or $\Box\varphi_3$ hold, but $\Box\varphi_1$ does not hold, then some maximally enabled transitions are supported, but some others may not. On the other hand, if $\Box\varphi_1$ holds, the supporting process policy does not limit the firing of maximally enabled transitions.

Advanced note. When $\Box\varphi_1$ holds, our transformation preserves transition fairness (transition justice, respectively) [9]. This is because when a (transformed) transition satisfies its original enabledness condition infinite often (continuously from some point, respectively), then it is also supported infinitely often (continuously from some point, respectively). For a similar argument, $\Box\varphi_2$ guarantees to preserve process fairness (precess justice, respectively); in this case, not all the transitions enabled according to the original enabledness condition are also supported, but at least one per process. Finally, $\Box\varphi_3$ guarantees that no new deadlocks are added.

Implementing the Local Support Policy: The Support Table

We first create a *support table* as follows: We check for each process π, reachable state s and transition $t \in \pi$, whether $s \models K_\pi\varphi_{\max(t)}$. If it holds, we put in the support table at the entry $s|_\pi$ the transitions t that are responsible for satisfying this property. In fact, according to Lemma 3, it is sufficient to check this for a single representative state containing $s|_\pi$ out of each equivalence class of '$\equiv_\pi$'.

Let $\varphi_{support(\pi)}$ denote the disjunction of the formulas $\varphi_{s|_\pi}$ such that the entry $s|_\pi$ is not empty in the support table. It is easy to see from the definition of φ_3 that checking $\Box\varphi_3$ is equivalent to checking the validity of the following Boolean implication:

$$\varphi_{df} \rightarrow \bigvee_{\pi \in \Pi} \varphi_{support(\pi)} \tag{2}$$

This means that at every reachable and non deadlock state, at least one process knows (and hence supports) at least one of its maximal enabled transitions.

Now, if $\Box\varphi_3$ holds, the support table we constructed for checking it can be consulted by the transformed program for implementing the supporting process policy. Each process π is equipped with the entries of this table of the form $s|_\pi$ for reachable s. Before making a transition, a process π consults the entry $s|_\pi$ that corresponds to its current local information, and supports only the transitions that appear in that entry. The transformed program can be represented again as a Petri Net. The construction is simple and the details are not given here for space constraints. The size of the support table is directly proportional to the number of different local information combinations and not to the (sometimes exponentially bigger) size of the state space.

Technically, for Petri Nets, strengthening the enabledness condition means adding input places. Since in Petri Nets the enabledness is a conjunction of places and the added condition for enabledness is disjunctive, we may want to extend the Petri Nets model. Alternatively, we may split transitions, taking into account of the mapping between the new and the original transitions.

Priority Approximation

It is typical that there will be many states where even φ_3 does not hold. That is, processes will not know locally whether one of their transitions is of highest priority.

In the Petri Net of Figure 3, Given the analysis described above, when t_3 is enabled, process π_l knows that t_4 is not enabled. If it also knew that t_5

is not enabled, then, given the above priorities, t_3 would be maximal enabled transitions and will be supported by π_l. However, as shown above, there are two different states were t_3 is enabled, in one of which t_5 is not enabled (this is the first time when t_3 is enabled), and in the other t_5 is enabled (this is the second time). Thus, t_3 cannot be supported by π_l in both states. In the state $\{p_2, p_3, p_8\}$, no transition is supported.

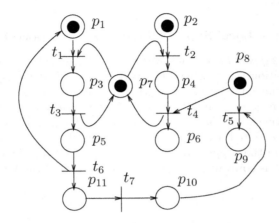

Fig. 3. Petri Net with priorities $t_3 \ll t_5 \ll t_4 \ll t_7$

When $\Box\varphi_3$ does not hold, one can provide various suboptimal solutions, which try to approximate the priority selection, meaning that not at all times the executed transition will be maximal. Consider a nondeadlock state s where $s \not\models \varphi_3$. In this case, the entries $s|_\pi$ are empty for each process π. Under the support policy, in state s, no transition will be supported, hence none will be fired, resulting in a deadlock. A *pessimistic approach* to fix this situation is to add to each empty entry $s|_\pi$ *at least one* of the transitions that are maximal among the enabled transitions of π.

Another possibility, which adds less arbitrary transitions to the support table, but requires more intensive computation, is based on an iterative approach. Select an empty entry $s|_\pi$ in the support table where some transition $t \in \pi$ is enabled and is maximal among the enabled transitions of π. Add t to that entry is sufficient for checking enabledness). Update the formula (2), by adding the disjunct $\varphi_{s|_\pi}$ to $\varphi_{support(\pi)}$. Then recheck Formula (2). Repeat adding transitions to empty entries in the support table until (2) holds. When it holds, it means that for each reachable state, there is a supported enabled transition, preventing new deadlocks.

Synchronizing Processes Approach

When Formula (2) does not hold, and thus also $\Box\varphi_3$, we can combine the knowledge of several processes to make decisions. This can be done by putting a controller that checks the combined local information of multiple processes. We then arrange a support table based on the joint local information of several processes $s|_\Pi$ rather than the local information of single processes $s|_\pi$. This corresponds to replacing π with Π in the formulas φ_1, φ_2 and φ_3. Such controllers may reduce concurrency. However, this is not a problem if the controlled processes are threads, residing anyway in the same processor. It is not clear apriory on which sets of processes we want to put a controller. in order to make their combined knowledge help in deciding the highest priority transition. Model checking under different groupings of processes, controlled and observed together, is then repeated until $\Box\varphi_1$ (or $\Box\varphi_2$ or $\Box\varphi_3$) holds.

Another possibility is the transfer of additional information via messages from one process to another. This also reduces concurrency and increases overhead.

Using Knowledge with Perfect Recall

Knowledge with perfect recall [10] assumes that a process π may keep its own local history, i.e., the sequence of local information sequence (sequence of local states) occurred so far. This may separate different occurrences of the same local information, when they appear at the end of different local histories, allowing to decide on executing a transition even when it was not possible under the previous knowledge definition. For lack of space, we describe the solution based on knowledge with perfect recall briefly and somewhat informally.

Knowledge with perfect recall is defined so that a process *knows some property* φ *at some state s and given some local history* σ, if φ holds for each execution when reaching a state with the same local history σ. In our case, since the system is asynchronous, the processes are not always aware of other processes making moves, unless these moves can affect their own neighborhood (hence their local information). Hence the local history includes only moves by transitions that have some common input or output place with the $ngb(\pi)$. By definition 2, these are the transition that are dependent on some transition in π (this includes all the transitions of π). The properties φ_1, φ_2 and φ_3 can be checked where the knowledge operators refer to knowledge with perfect recall.

An algorithm for model checking knowledge with perfect recall was shown in [10], and our algorithm can be seen as a simplified version of it. For each process π, we construct an automaton representing the entire state space of the system. We keep track of all the possible (global) states Γ that correspond to having some local history. A move from Γ to Γ', corresponds to the execution of any transition t that is dependent on some transition in π. To construct Γ' from Γ, we first take all the states reached from states in Γ by executing t, when t is enabled. Then, we add to this set the states that are obtained by executing any sequence of transitions that are independent of all those in π. The initial state of this automaton contains any state obtained from s_0 by executing a finite number of transitions independent of π. Model checking is possible even though the local histories may be unbounded because the number of such subsets Γ is bounded, and the successor relation between such different subsets, upon firing a transition t, as described above, is fixed.

Instead of the support table, for each process π we have a *support automaton*, representing the subset construction, i.e., the determinization, of the above automaton. At runtime, the execution of each transition dependent on π will cause a move of this automaton (this means access to the support automaton of π with the execution of these transitions, even when they are not in π). If currently the state of the support automaton corresponds to a set of states Γ where a transition $t \in \pi$ is maximally enabled (checking this for the states in Γ was done at the time of performing the transformation), then π currently supports t. Unfortunately, the size of the support automaton, for each process, can be exponential in the size of the state space (reflecting a subset of the states where the current execution can be, given the local history). This gives quite a high overhead to such a transformation. The local histories of the transformed net is a subset of the local histories of the original, priorityless net, providing a result, similar to Theorem 1, that is expressed in terms of knowledge with perfect recall.

Returning to the example in Figure 3, the knowledge with perfect recall can separate the first time when t_3 is enabled from the second time. On the first time, t_5 is not enabled, hence π_l knows that t_3 is a maximal enabled transition, supporting it. On the second time, t_5 is enabled (or first t_7 is enabled and then, due to its priority, will execute and t_5 will become enabled), and π_l does not support t_3. Thus, given knowledge with perfect recall, there is no need to group processes together in order to obtain the knowledge about the maximalty of t_5.

5   Implementation and Experimental Results

We have implemented a prototype engine which performs model checking, creates the process support tables, determines whether the invariant φ_3 holds for the distributed processes, and finally allows for execution of the processes based on their support tables.

For experiments, we used the following example: a train station uses a network of tracks to divert the trains from the point where they enter the station and into an empty platform (we assume that is no preassignment of trains to segments). There are some trains and some track segments. Some of the segments are initial, i.e., where the train first appears when it wishes to enter the station, and some of them final, consisting of actual platforms. When moving from segment r to segment r', a controller for segment r' checks that the segment is empty, and then allows the train to enter. The highest priority trains are TGV trains (Train Grande Vitesse, in our example there is a single TGV train), then there are local trains (two local in our example), and, with least priority, freight trains (a single freight train). There are trains of three speeds. Our Petri Net has the following places:

- $p_{empty-r}$ has a token when the track segment r is empty.
- $p_{k@r}$ train k is at segment r.
- $p_{outside-k}$ train k is not in the vicinity of the station.

There are three types of transitions:

- Progress by train k from segment r to segment r'. Such a transition $t_{r \to r',k}$, has inputs $p_{k@r}$ and $p_{empty-r'}$, and outputs $p_{k@r'}$ and $p_{empty-r}$.
- A new train k is entering the system at segment r. Such a transition $t_{k\ enters-r}$ has inputs $p_{outside-k}$ and $p_{empty-r}$ and one output $p_{k@r}$.
- A train k leaves the station after being on segment (track) r. the input is $p_{k@r}$ and the outputs are $p_{outside-k}$ and $p_{empty-r}$.

Each process π can be a collection of transitions that are related to the same segment. Thus, a transition $t_{r \to r',k}$ is shared between the processes r and r'. Priorities can be assigned according to the train speed (transitions of TGV trains higher than transitions of local trains, and these, in turn have higher transitions than those involving freight trains.

The actual segments structure we used in the experiments is shown in Figure 4

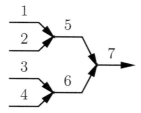

Fig. 4. The actual segments used in the experiments

In order to measure the effect of the approximations, we have considered a penalty, which measures the deviation of the measured behavior from an ideal prioritized behavior. This measure sums up the deviation from selecting a maximal enabled transition at each execution step. If a maximal transition is indeed executed, we add 0. If a second-best transition is selected, e.g., involving a local train when a TGV train is also enabled, we add 1. If all transitions for all types of trains are enabled and a fright train (i.e., with lowest priority) moves, then we add 2. All results are based on random traces of length 100,000 steps (i.e., transitions), and taking the average 10 random traces. We have measured the penalty for the different distributions of the processes. For a worst case estimate of the penalty, we executed the system without considering the priorities. That gave a penalty of 34332, which is considerably higher than the penalties measured when applying approximations, as shown in the results below.

The results obtained for different distribution of the processes are shown in the following table. The global state space of the system consists of 1961 states. This was run on a Pentium-4 PC (Dell GX520) with 1GB RAM, running GNU-linux.

process groups	table size	% table empty	φ_3 holds	penalty
1	1961	0	yes	0
2	1118	0	yes	0
3	219	5.5	no	387
7	126	14.4	no	3891

The "process groups" tells us how many processes are grouped together for calculating the knowledge. When there is only one group, all the processes are grouped together, so the global state is known to all. With 7 groups, each group is a singleton, containing one process; thus the knowledge of multiple processes is not combined. The "table size" shows the number of entries in the knowledge table of the processes. In case of a single process (all transitions in one process), the number of entries in the knowledge table is the same as the total number of states in the system, and the process has complete information with respect to the maximal transitions to be taken from a state (no empty entries). As a result, φ_3 holds, and there is no penalty.

6   Conclusions

Developing concurrent systems is an intricate task. One methodology, which lies behind the BIP system, is to define first the architecture and transitions, and at a later stage add priorities among the transitions. This methodology allows a convenient separation of the design effort. We presented in this paper the idea of using model checking analysis to calculate the local knowledge of the concurrent processes of the system about currently having a maximal priority transition. The result of the model checking is integrated into the program via a data structure that helps the processes to select prioritized transition at each point. Thus, model checking is used to transform the system into a priorityless version that implements the priorities. There are different versions of knowledge, related to the different ways we are allowed to transform the system. For example, the knowledge of each process, at a given time, may depend on including information about the history of computation.

After the analysis, we sometimes identify situations where a process, locally, does not have enough information about having a maximal priority transition. In this case, synchronizing between different processes, reducing the concurrency, is possible; semiglobal observers can coordinate several processes, obtaining joint knowledge of several processes. Another possible solution (not further elaborated here) involves adding coordination messages.

We experimented with an example of a train station, including trains entering the system via a net of segments that divert the trains until they arrive at an available platform.

More generally, we suggest a programming methodology, based on a basic design (in this case, the architecture and the transitions) with added constraints (in this case, priorities). Model checking of knowledge properties is used to lift these added constraints by means of a program transformation. The resulted program behaves in an equivalent way, or approximates the behavior of the basic design with the constraints.

References

1. Basu, A., Bidinger, P., Bozga, M., Sifakis, J.: Distributed Semantics and Implementation for Systems with Interaction and Priority. In: Suzuki, K., Higashino, T., Yasumoto, K., El-Fakih, K. (eds.) FORTE 2008. LNCS, vol. 5048, pp. 116–133. Springer, Heidelberg (2008)
2. Buckley, G.N., Silberschatz, A.: An Effective Implementation for the Generalized Input-Output Construct of CSP. ACM Transactions on Programming Language and Systems 5, 223–235 (1983)
3. Emerson, E.A., Clarke, E.M.: Characterizing Correctness Properties of Parallel Programs using Fixpoints. In: ICALP 1980. LNCS, vol. 85, pp. 169–181. Springer, Heidelberg (1980)
4. Fagin, R., Halpern, J.Y., Moses, Y., Vardi, M.Y.: Reasoning About Knowledge. MIT Press, Cambridge (1995)
5. Francez, N., Rodeh, M.: A Distributed Abstract Data Type Implemented by a Probabilistic Communication Scheme. In: 21st Annual Symposium on Foundations of Computer Science (FOCS), Syracuse, New York, pp. 373–379 (1980)
6. Halpern, J.Y., Zuck, L.D.: A little knowledge goes a long way: knowledge based derivation and correctness proof for a family of protocols. Journal of the ACM 39(3), 449–478 (1992)
7. Hoare, C.A.R.: Communicating Sequential Processes. Communication of the ACM 21, 666–677 (1978)
8. Gößler, G., Sifakis, J.: Priority Systems. In: de Boer, F.S., Bonsangue, M.M., Graf, S., de Roever, W.-P. (eds.) FMCO 2003. LNCS, vol. 3188, pp. 443–466. Springer, Heidelberg (2004)
9. Manna, Z., Pnueli, A.: How to Cook a Temporal Proof System for Your Pet Language. In: POPL 1983, Austin, TX, pp. 141–154 (1983)
10. van der Meyden, R.: Common Knowledge and Update in Finite Environment. Information and Computation 140, 115–157 (1980)
11. Quielle, J.P., Sifakis, J.: Specification and Verification of Concurrent Systems in CESAR. In: 5th International Symposium on Programming, pp. 337–350 (1981)
12. Ramadge, P.J., Wonham, W.M.: Supervisory control of a class of discrete event processes. SIAM Journal on Control and Optimization 25(1), 206–230 (1987)
13. Yoo, T.S., Lafortune, S.: A general architecture for decentralized supervisory control of discrete-event systems. Discrete event dynamic systems, theory & applications 12(3), 335–377 (2002)

Explaining Counterexamples Using Causality[*]

Ilan Beer[1], Shoham Ben-David[2], Hana Chockler[1], Avigail Orni[1], and Richard Trefler[2]

[1] IBM Research
Mount Carmel, Haifa 31905, Israel
{beer,hanac,ornia}@il.ibm.com
[2] David R. Cheriton School of Computer Science
University of Waterloo, Waterloo, Ontario, Canada
{s3bendav,trefler}@cs.uwaterloo.ca

Abstract. When a model does not satisfy a given specification, a counterexample is produced by the model checker to demonstrate the failure. A user must then examine the counterexample trace, in order to visually identify the failure that it demonstrates. If the trace is long, or the specification is complex, finding the failure in the trace becomes a non-trivial task. In this paper, we address the problem of analyzing a counterexample trace and highlighting the failure that it demonstrates. Using the notion of *causality*, introduced by Halpern and Pearl, we formally define a set of causes for the failure of the specification on the given counterexample trace. These causes are marked as red dots and presented to the user as a visual explanation of the failure. We study the complexity of computing the exact set of causes, and provide a polynomial-time algorithm that approximates it. This algorithm is implemented as a feature in the IBM formal verification platform RuleBase PE, where these visual explanations are an integral part of every counterexample trace. Our approach is independent of the tool that produced the counterexample, and can be applied as a light-weight external layer to any model checking tool, or used to explain simulation traces.

1 Introduction

Model checking [9,27] is a method for verifying that a finite-state concurrent system (a *model*) is correct with respect to a given specification. An important feature of model checking tools is their ability to provide, when the specification does not hold in a model, a *counterexample* [10]: a trace that demonstrates the failure of the specification in the model. This allows the user to analyze the failure, understand its source(s), and fix the specification or model accordingly. In many cases, however, the task of understanding the counterexample is challenging, and may require a significant manual effort.

There are different aspects of *understanding* a counterexample. In recent years, the process of finding the source of a bug has attracted significant attention. Many works have approached this problem (see [12,24,14,3,19,20,6,29,32,18,30,31] for a partial list), addressing the question of finding the root cause of the failure in the *model*, and

---

[*] This work was supported in part by the Natural Sciences and Engineering Research Council of Canada.

A. Bouajjani and O. Maler (Eds.): CAV 2009, LNCS 5643, pp. 94–108, 2009.

proposing automatic ways to extract more information about the model, to ease the debugging procedure. Naturally, the algorithms proposed in the above mentioned works involve implementation in a specific tool (for example, the BDD procedure of [24] would not work for a SAT based model checker like those of [19,3]).

We address a different, more basic aspect of understanding a counterexample: the task of finding the failure in the trace itself. To motivate our approach, consider a verification engineer, who is formally verifying a hardware design written by a logic designer. The verification engineer writes a specification — a temporal logic formula — and runs a model checker, in order to check the formula on the design. If the formula fails on the design-under-test (DUT), a counterexample trace is produced and displayed in a trace viewer. The verification engineer does not attempt to debug the DUT implementation (since that is the responsibility of the the logic designer who wrote it). Her goal is to look for some basic information about the manner in which the formula fails on the specific trace. For example, if the formula is a safety property, the first question is *when* the formula fails (at what cycle in the trace). If the formula is a complex combination of several conditions, she needs to know which of these conditions has failed. These basic questions are prerequisites to deeper investigations of the failure.

Answering these questions can be done without any knowledge about the inner workings of the DUT, relying only on the given counterexample and the failed formula. Moreover, even in the given trace, only the signals that appear in the formula are relevant for these basic questions, and any other signals may be ignored. If the failed specification is simple enough, the preliminary analysis can be done manually without much effort. For example, if the failed specification is ERROR *never occurs*, then the user can visually scan the behavior of the signal ERROR in the trace, and find a time point at which ERROR holds, i.e., a place where the Boolean invariant ¬ERROR fails. In practice, however, the Boolean invariant in the specification may be complex, involving multiple signals and Boolean operations between them, in which case the visual scan becomes non-trivial. If the specification involves temporal operators (such as an LTL formula with operators **X** or **U**), then the visual scan becomes even more difficult, since relations between several trace cycles must be considered. This is the point where trace explanations come into play. Explanations show the user the points in the trace that are relevant for the failure, allowing her to focus on these points and ignore other parts of the trace. They are displayed visually in a trace viewer.

We present a method and a tool for explaining the trace itself, without involving the model from which it was extracted. Thus, our approach has the advantage of being light-weight (no size problems are involved, as only one trace is considered at a time) as well as independent: it can be added as an external layer to any model-checking tool, or applied to explanation of simulation traces.

An explanation of a counterexample deals with the question: *what values on the trace cause it to falsify the specification?* Thus, we face the problem of *causality*. The philosophy literature, going back to Hume [23], has long been struggling with the problem of what it means for one event to cause another. We relate the formal definition of causality of Halpern and Pearl [22] to explanations of counterexamples. The definition of causality used in [22], like other definitions of causality in the philosophy literature, is based on *counterfactual dependence*. Event A is said to be a *cause* of event B if, had A not happened (this is the counterfactual condition, since A did in fact happen) then B would not have happened. Unfortunately, this definition does not capture all the subtleties involved with causality. The following story, presented by Hall in [21], demonstrates some of the difficulties in this definition. Suppose that Suzy and Billy both pick up rocks and throw them at a bottle. Suzy's rock gets there first, shattering the bottle. Since both throws are perfectly accurate, Billy's would have shattered the bottle had it not been preempted by Suzy's throw. Thus, according to the counterfactual condition, Suzy's throw is not a cause for shattering the bottle (because if Suzy wouldn't have thrown her rock, the bottle would have been shattered by Billy's throw). Halpern and Pearl deal with this subtlety by, roughly speaking, taking A to be a cause of B if B counterfactually depends on A under some contingency. For example, Suzy's throw is a cause of the bottle shattering because the bottle shattering counterfactually depends on Suzy's throw, under the contingency that Billy doesn't throw.

We adapt the causality definition of Halpern and Pearl from [22] to the analysis of a counterexample trace π with respect to a temporal logic formula φ. We view a trace as a matrix of values, where an entry (i, j) corresponds to the value of variable i at time j. We look for those entries in the matrix that are causes for the first failure of φ on π, according to the definition in [22]. To demonstrate our approach, let us consider the following example.

Example. A transaction begins when START is asserted, and ends when END is asserted. Some unbounded number of time units later, the signal STATUS_VALID is asserted. Our specification requires that a new transaction must not begin before the STATUS_VALID of the previous transaction has arrived and READY is indicated[1]. A counterexample for this specification may look like the computation path π shown in Fig. 1.

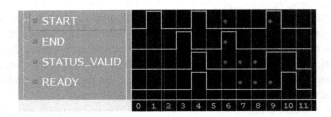

Fig. 1. A counterexample with explanations

In this example, the failure of the specification on the trace is not trivially evident. Our explanations, displayed as *red dots*[2], attract the user's attention to the relevant places, to help in identifying the failure. Note that each dot r is a *cause* of the failure of φ on the trace: switching the value of r would, under some contingency on the

---

[1] The precise specification is slightly more complex, and can be written in LTL as $\mathbf{G}((\neg\text{START} \wedge \neg\text{STATUS\_VALID} \wedge \text{END}) \rightarrow \mathbf{X}[\neg\text{START} \ \mathbf{U} \ (\text{STATUS\_VALID} \wedge \text{READY})])$.

[2] We refer to these explanations as red dots, since this is their characteristic color in Rule-Base PE.

other values, change the value of φ on π. For example, if we switch the value of START in state 9 from 1 to 0, φ would not fail on the given trace anymore (in this case, no contingency on the other values is needed). Thus the matrix entry of the variable START at time 9 is indicated as a cause.

We show that the complexity of detecting an exact causal set is NP-complete, based on the complexity result for causality in binary models (see [17]). We then present an over-approximation algorithm whose complexity is linear in the size of the formula and in the length of the trace. The implementation of this algorithm is a feature in IBM's formal verification platform *RuleBase PE* [28]. We demonstrate that it produces the exact causal set for practical examples.

The rest of the paper is organized as follows. In Section 2 we give definitions. Section 3 is the main section of the paper, where we define causality in counterexamples, analyze the complexity of its computation and provide an efficient over-approximation algorithm to compute a causal set. In Section 4 we discuss the implementation of our algorithm on top of RuleBase PE. We show the graphical visualization used in practice, and present experimental results, demonstrating the usefulness of the method. Section 5 discusses related work, and Section 6 concludes the paper. Due to the lack of space, proofs are omitted from this version, and appear in the technical report [4].

2   Preliminaries

Kripke Structures

Let V be a set of Boolean variables. A *Kripke structure* K over V is a tuple $K = (S, I, R, L)$ where S is a finite set of states, $I \subseteq S$ is the set of initial states, $R \subseteq S \times S$ is a transition relation that must be total, that is, for every state $s \in S$ there is a state $s' \in S$ such that $R(s, s')$. The labeling function $L : S \to 2^V$ labels each state with the set of variables true in that state. We say that $\pi = s_0, s_1, ...$ is a *path* in K if $s_0 \in I$ and $\forall i, (s_i, s_{i+1}) \in R$. We denote $\pi[j..k]$ a sub-path of π, that starts at s_j and ends at state s_k. The concatenation of a finite prefix $\pi[0..k]$ with an infinite path ρ is denoted $(\pi[0..k]) \cdot \rho$. We sometimes use the term "signals" for variables and the term "traces" for paths (as common in the terminology of hardware design).

Linear Temporal Logic (LTL)

Formulas of LTL are built from a set V of Boolean variables and constants **true** and **false** using Boolean operators $\neg$, $\to$, $\wedge$ and $\vee$, and the temporal operators $\mathbf{X}$, $\mathbf{U}$, $\mathbf{W}$, $\mathbf{G}$, $\mathbf{F}$ (see [11] for the definition of LTL semantics). An occurrence of a sub-formula ψ of φ is said to have a *positive polarity* if it appears in φ under an even number of negations, and a *negative polarity* otherwise (note that an antecedent of an implication is considered to be under negation).

3   Causality in Counterexamples

In this section, we define causality in counterexamples based on the definition of causality by Halpern and Pearl [22]. We demonstrate our definitions on several examples, discuss complexity of computing causality in counterexamples, and present a linear-time over-approximation algorithm for computing the set of causes. The original definition of [22] can be found in the appendix.

3.1 Defining Causality in Counterexamples

A *counterexample* to an LTL formula φ in a Kripke structure K is a computation path $\pi = s_0, s_1, \ldots$ such that $\pi \not\models \varphi$. For a state s_i and a variable v, the labeling function L of K maps the pair $\langle s_i, v \rangle$ to $\{0, 1\}$ in a natural way: $L(\langle s_i, v \rangle) = 1$ if $v \in s_i$, and 0 otherwise. For a pair $\langle s, v \rangle$ in π, we denote by $\langle \hat{s}, v \rangle$ the pair that is derived from $\langle s, v \rangle$ by switching the labeling of v in s. Let π be a path, s a state in π and v a variable in the labeling function. We denote $\pi^{\langle \hat{s}, v \rangle}$ the path derived from π by switching the labeling of v in s on π. This definition can be extended for a set of pairs A: we denote $\hat{A}$ the set $\{\langle \hat{s}, v \rangle | \langle s, v \rangle \in A\}$. The path $\pi^{\hat{A}}$ is then derived from π by switching the values of v in s for all pairs $\langle s, v \rangle \in A$. The definition below is needed in the sequel.

Definition 1 (Bottom value). *For a Kripke structure $K = (S, I, R, L)$, a path π in K, and a formula φ, a pair $\langle s, v \rangle$ is said to have a* bottom value *for φ in π, if, for at least one of the occurrences of v in φ, $L(\langle s, v \rangle) = 0$ and v has a* positive *polarity in φ, or $L(\langle s, v \rangle) = 1$ and v has a* negative *polarity in φ.*

Note that while the value of a pair $\langle s, v \rangle$ depends on the computation path π only, determining whether $\langle s, v \rangle$ has a *bottom value* depends also on the polarity of v in φ. Thus, if v appears in multiple polarities in φ, then $\langle s, v \rangle$ has both a bottom value (with respect to one of the occurrences) and a non-bottom value (with respect to a different occurrence) for any state s.

Before we formally define causes in counterexamples we need to deal with one subtlety: the value of φ on finite paths. While computation paths are infinite, it is often possible to determine that $\pi \not\models \varphi$ after a *finite* prefix of the path. Thus, a counterexample produced by a model checker may demonstrate a finite execution path.

In this paper, we use the semantics of LTL model checking on truncated paths as defined by Eisner et al. in [16]. The main advantage of this semantics is that it preserves the complexity of LTL model checking. Since it is quite complicated to explain, instead we present a simpler definition (due to [16]), which coincides with the definition of Eisner et al. on almost all formulas.

Definition 2. *Let $\pi[0..k]$ be a finite path and φ an LTL formula. We say that:*

1. *The value of φ is* **true** *in $\pi[0..k]$ (denoted $\pi[0..k] \models_f \varphi$, where $\models_f$ stands for "finitely models") iff for all infinite computations ρ, we have $\pi[0..k] \cdot \rho \models \varphi$;*
2. *The value of φ is* **false** *in $\pi[0..k]$ (denoted $\pi[0..k] \not\models_f \varphi$, where $\not\models_f$ stands for "finitely falsifies") iff for all infinite computations ρ, we have $\pi[0..k] \cdot \rho \not\models \varphi$;*
3. *The value of φ in π is* **unknown** *(denoted $\pi[0..k]\ ?\ \varphi$) iff there exist two infinite computations ρ_1 and ρ_2 such that $\pi[0..k] \cdot \rho_1 \models \varphi$ and $\pi[0..k] \cdot \rho_2 \not\models \varphi$.*

Let φ be an LTL formula that fails on an infinite path $\pi = s_0, s_1, \ldots$, and let k be the smallest index such that $\pi[0..k] \not\models_f \varphi$. If φ does not fail on any finite prefix of π, we take $k = \infty$ (then $\pi[0..\infty]$ naturally stands for π, and we have $\pi \not\models \varphi$). We can now define the following.

Definition 3 (Criticality in counterexample traces). *A pair $\langle s, v \rangle$ is critical for the failure of φ on $\pi[0..k]$ if $\pi[0..k] \not\models_f \varphi$, but either $\pi^{\langle \hat{s}, v \rangle}[0..k] \models_f \varphi$ or $\pi^{\langle \hat{s}, v \rangle}[0..k] ? \varphi$.*

That is, switching the value of v in s changes the value of φ on $\pi[0..k]$ (to either **true** or **unknown**). As a simple example, consider the formula $\varphi = \mathbf{G}p$, on $\pi = s_0, s_1, s_2$, labeled $p \cdot p \cdot \neg p$. Then, $\pi[0..2] \not\models_f \varphi$, and $\langle s_2, p \rangle$ is critical for this failure, since switching the value of p in state s_2 changes the value of φ on $\pi^{\langle \hat{s}_2, p \rangle}$ to **unknown**.

Definition 4 (Causality in counterexample traces). *A pair $\langle s, v \rangle$ is a cause of the first failure of φ on $\pi[0..k]$ if k is the smallest index such that $\pi[0..k] \not\models_f \varphi$, and there exists a set A of bottom-valued pairs, such that $\langle s, v \rangle \notin A$, and the following hold:*

- *$\pi^{\hat{A}}[0..k] \not\models_f \varphi$, and*
- *$\langle s, v \rangle$ is critical for the failure of φ on $\pi^{\hat{A}}[0..k]$.*

A pair $\langle s, v \rangle$ is defined to be a *cause* for the first failure of φ on π, if it can be made *critical* for this failure by switching the values of some bottom-valued pairs. Note that according to this definition, only bottom-valued pairs can be causes.

Note that a trace π may have more than one failure, as we demonstrate in the examples below. Our experience shows that the first failure is the most interesting one for the user. Also, focusing on one failure naturally reduces the set of causes, and thus makes it easier for the user to understand the explanation.

Examples

1. Consider $\varphi_1 = \mathbf{G}p$ and a path $\pi_1 = s_0, s_1, s_2, s_3, (s_4)^\omega$ labeled as $(p) \cdot (p) \cdot (\neg p) \cdot (\neg p) \cdot (p)^\omega$. The shortest prefix of π_1 on which φ_1 fails is $\pi_1[0..2]$. $\langle s_2, p \rangle$ is critical for the failure of φ on $\pi_1[0..2]$, because changing its value from 0 to 1 changes the value of φ on $\pi_1[0..2]$ from **false** to **unknown**. Also, there are no other bottom-valued pairs in $\pi_1[0..2]$, thus there are no other causes, which indeed meets our intuition.

2. Consider $\varphi_2 = \mathbf{F}p$ and a path $\pi_2 = (s_0)^\omega = (\neg p)^\omega$. The formula φ_2 fails in π_2, yet it does not fail on any finite prefix of π_2. Note that changing the value of any $\langle s_i, p \rangle$ for $i \geq 0$ results in the satisfaction of φ on π, thus all pairs $\{\langle s_i, p \rangle : i \in \mathbb{N}\}$ are critical and hence are causes for the failure of φ_2 on π_2.

3. The following example demonstrates the difference between criticality and causality. Consider $\varphi_3 = \mathbf{G}(a \wedge b \wedge c)$ and a path $\pi_3 = s_0, s_1, s_2, \ldots$ labeled as $(\emptyset)^\omega$ (see Figure 2). The formula φ_3 fails on s_0, however, changing the value of any signal in one state does not change the value of φ_3. There exists, however, a set A of bottom-valued pairs whose change makes the value of a in s_0 critical: $A = \{\langle s_0, b \rangle, \langle s_0, c \rangle\}$. Similarly, $\langle s_0, b \rangle$ and $\langle s_0, c \rangle$ are also causes.

3.2 Complexity of Computing Causality in Counterexamples

The complexity of computing causes for counterexamples follows from the complexity of computing causality in binary causal models defined in [22] (see Section 2).

Lemma 5. *Computing the set of causes for falsification of a linear-time temporal specification on a single trace is NP-complete.*

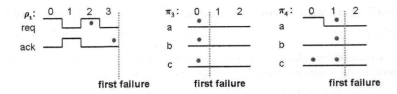

Fig. 2. Counterexample traces

Proof Sketch. Informally, the proof of NP-hardness is based on the reduction from computing causality in binary causal models to computing causality in counterexamples. The problem of computing causality in binary causal models is NP-complete [17]. The reduction from binary causal models to Boolean circuits and from Boolean circuits to model-checking, shown in [8], is based on the automata-theoretic approach to branching-time model checking ([25]), and proves that computing causality in model checking of branching time specifications is NP-complete. On a single trace linear-time and branching temporal logics coincide, and computing the causes for satisfaction is easily reducible to computing the causes for falsification.

The proof of membership in NP is straightforward: given a path π and a formula φ that is falsified on π, the number of pairs $\langle s, v \rangle$ is $|\varphi| \cdot |\pi|$; for a pair $\langle s, v \rangle$, we can nondeterministically choose a set A of bottom-valued pairs; checking whether changing L on S makes $\langle s, v \rangle$ critical for the falsification of φ requires model-checking φ on the modified π twice, and thus can be done in linear time.[3] $\square$

The problem of computing the exact set of causes can be translated into a SAT problem using the reduction from [17], with small changes due to the added semantics of satisfiability on finite paths. However, the natural usage of explanation of a counterexample is in an interactive tool (and indeed this is the approach we use in our implementation), and therefore the computation of causes should be done while the user is waiting. Thus, it is important to make the algorithm as efficient as possible. We describe an efficient approximation algorithm for computing the set of causes in Section 3.3, and its implementation results are shown in Section 4.

3.3 An Approximation Algorithm

The counterexamples we work with have a finite number of states. When representing an infinite path, the counterexample will contain a loop indication, i.e., an indication that the last state in the counterexample is equal to one of the earlier states.

Let φ be a formula, given in negation normal form, and let $\pi[0..k] = s_0, s_1, ..., s_k$ be a non-empty counterexample for it, consisting of a finite number of states and a possible loop indication.

We denote by $\pi[i..k]$ the suffix of $\pi[0..k]$ that starts at s_i. The procedure C below produces $C(\pi[i..k], \psi)$, the approximation of the set of causes for the failure of a

---

[3] Note that the proof of membership in NP relies on model-checking of truncated paths having the same complexity as model-checking of infinite paths [16].

sub-formula ψ on the suffix of $\pi[0..k]$ that starts with s_i. We invoke the procedure C with the arguments $(\pi[0..k], \varphi)$ to produce the set of causes for the failure of φ on $\pi[0..k]$.

If the path $\pi[0..k]$ has a loop indication, the invocation of C is preceded by a pre-processing stage, in which we unwrap the loop $|\varphi| + 1$ times. This gives us a different finite representation, $\pi'[0..k']$ (with $k' \geq k$), for the same infinite path[4]. We then execute $C(\pi'[i..k'], \varphi)$, which returns a set of causes that are pairs in $\pi'[0..k']$. These pairs can then be (optionally) mapped back to pairs in the original representation $\pi[0..k]$, by shifting each index to its corresponding index in the first copy of the loop[5].

During the computation of $C(\pi[i..k], \varphi)$, we use the auxiliary function val, that evaluates sub-formulas of φ on the given path. It returns 0 if the sub-formula fails on the path and 1 otherwise. The computation of val is done in parallel with the computation of the causality set, and relies on recursively computed causality sets for sub-formulas of φ. The value of val is computed as follows:

- $val(\pi[i..k], true) = 1$
- $val(\pi[i..k], false) = 0$
- For any formula $\varphi \notin \{true, false\}$, $val(\pi[i..k], \varphi) = 1$ iff $C(\pi[i..k], \varphi) = \emptyset$

Algorithm 6 (Causality Set). *An over-approximated causality set C for $\pi[i..k]$ and ψ is computed as follows*

- $C(\pi[i..k], true) = C(\pi[i..k], false) = \emptyset$
- $C(\pi[i..k], p) = \begin{cases} \{\langle s_i, p \rangle\} & \textit{if } p \notin L(s_i) \\ \emptyset & \textit{otherwise} \end{cases}$
- $C(\pi[i..k], \neg p) = \begin{cases} \{\langle s_i, p \rangle\} & \textit{if } p \in L(s_i) \\ \emptyset & \textit{otherwise} \end{cases}$
- $C(\pi[i..k], \mathbf{X}\varphi) = \begin{cases} C(\pi[i+1..k], \varphi) & \textit{if } i < k \\ \emptyset & \textit{otherwise} \end{cases}$
- $C(\pi[i..k], \varphi \wedge \psi) = C(\pi[i..k], \varphi) \cup C(\pi[i..k], \psi)$
- $C(\pi[i..k], \varphi \vee \psi) =$
  $\begin{cases} C(\pi[i..k], \varphi) \cup C(\pi[i..k], \psi) & \textit{if } val(\pi[i..k], \varphi) = 0 \textit{ and } val(\pi[i..k], \psi) = 0 \\ \emptyset & \textit{otherwise} \end{cases}$
- $C(\pi[i..k], \mathbf{G}\varphi) =$
  $\begin{cases} C(\pi[i..k], \varphi) & \textit{if } val(\pi[i..k], \varphi) = 0 \\ C(\pi[i+1..k], \mathbf{G}\varphi) & \textit{if } val(\pi[i..k], \varphi) = 1 \textit{ and } i < k \textit{ and } val(\pi[i..k], \mathbf{XG}\varphi) = 0 \\ \emptyset & \textit{otherwise} \end{cases}$
- $C(\pi[i..k], [\varphi \, \mathbf{U} \, \psi]) =$
  $\begin{cases} C(\pi[i..k], \psi) \cup C(\pi[i..k], \varphi) & \textit{if } val(\pi[i..k], \varphi) = 0 \textit{ and } val(\pi[i..k], \psi) = 0 \\ C(\pi[i..k], \psi) & \textit{if } val(\pi[i..k], \varphi) = 1 \textit{ and } val(\pi[i..k], \psi) = 0 \\ & \textit{and } i = k \\ C(\pi[i..k], \psi) \cup C(\pi[i+1..k], [\varphi \, \mathbf{U} \, \psi]) & \textit{if } val(\pi[i..k], \varphi) = 1 \textit{ and } val(\pi[i..k], \psi) = 0 \\ & \textit{and } i < k \textit{ and } val(\pi[i..k], \mathbf{X}[\varphi \, \mathbf{U} \, \psi]) = 0 \\ \emptyset & \textit{otherwise} \end{cases}$

---

[4] It can be shown, by straightforward induction, that φ fails on the finite path with $|\varphi| + 1$ repetitions of the loop iff it fails on the infinite path.

[5] This mapping is necessary for presenting the set of causes graphically on the original path $\pi[0..k]$.

The procedure above recursively computes a set of causes for the given formula φ on the suffix of a counterexample $\pi[i..k]$. At the proposition level, p is considered a cause in the current state if and only if it has a bottom-value in the state. At every level of the recursion, a sub-formula is considered relevant (that is, its exploration can produce causes for falsification of the whole specification) if it has a value of **false** at the current state.

Lemma 7. *The complexity of Algorithm 6 is linear in k and in $|\varphi|$.*

Proof Sketch. The complexity follows from the fact that each subformula ψ of φ is evaluated at most once at each state s_i of the counterexample π. Similarly to global CTL model checking, the decision at each state is made based on the local information.

For paths with a loop, unwrapping the loop $|\varphi| + 1$ times does not add to this complexity, since each subformula ψ is evaluated on a single copy of the loop, based on its depth in φ. □

Theorem 8. *The set of pairs produced by Algorithm 6 for a formula φ on a path π is an over-approximation of the set of causes for φ on π according to Definition 4.*

Proof Sketch. The proof uses the automata-theoretic approach to branching-time model checking[6] introduced in [25], where model checking is reduced to evaluating an AND-OR graph with nodes labeled with pairs ⟨ state s of π, subformula ψ of φ ⟩. The leaves are labeled with ⟨s, l⟩, with l being a literal (variable or its negation), and the root is labeled with ⟨s_0, φ⟩. The values of leaves are determined by the labeling function L, and the value of each inner node is 0 or 1 according to the evaluation of its successors. Since φ fails on π, the value of the root is 0. A path that starts from a bottom-valued leaf, and on the way up visits only nodes with value 0, is called a **failure path**. The proof is based on the following fact: if ⟨s, v⟩ is a cause of failure of φ on π according to Definition 4, then it is a bottom-valued pair and there exists a failure path from the leaf labeled with ⟨s, v⟩ to the root. By examining Algorithm 6, it can be proved that the set of pairs that is the result of the algorithm is exactly the set of bottom-valued leaves from which there exists a failure path to the root. Thus, it contains the exact set of causes. □

We note that not all bottom-valued leaves that have a failure path to the root are causes (otherwise Algorithm 6 would always give accurate results!). In our experience, Algorithm 6 gives accurate results for the majority of real-life examples. As an example of a formula on which Algorithm 6 does not give an accurate result, consider $\varphi_4 = a\,\mathbf{U}\,(b\,\mathbf{U}\,c)$ and a trace $\pi_4 = s_0, s_1, s_2, \ldots$ labeled as $a \cdot (\emptyset)^\omega$ (see Figure 2). The formula φ_4 fails on π_4, and $\pi_4[0..1]$ is the shortest prefix on which it fails. What is the set of causes for failure of φ_4 on $\pi_4[0..1]$? The pair ⟨s_0, a⟩ is not a cause, since it is not bottom-valued. Checking all possible changes of sets of bottom-valued pairs shows that ⟨s_0, b⟩ is not a cause. On the other hand, ⟨s_1, a⟩ and ⟨s_1, b⟩ are causes because changing the value of a in s_1 from 0 to 1 makes φ_4 **unknown** on $\pi_4[0..1]$, and similarly for ⟨s_1, b⟩. The pairs ⟨s_0, c⟩ and ⟨s_1, c⟩ are causes because changing the value of c in either s_0 or s_1 from 0 to 1 changes the value of φ_4 to **true** on $\pi_4[0..1]$. The values of

---

[6] Recall, that on a single trace LTL and CTL coincide.

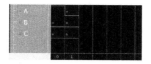

Fig. 3. Counterexample for $a \, \mathbf{U} \, (b \, \mathbf{U} \, c)$

signals in s_2 are not causes because the first failure of φ_4 happens in s_1. The causes are represented graphically as red dots in Figure 2. By examining the algorithm, we can see that on φ_4 and π_4 it outputs the set of pairs that contains, in addition to the exact set of causes, the pair $\langle s_0, b \rangle$. The results of running the implementation of Algorithm 6 on φ_4 are presented in Figure 3.

4   Implementation and Experimental Results

Visual counterexample explanation is an existing feature in RuleBase PE, IBM's formal verification platform. When the formal verification tool displays a counterexample in its trace viewer, it shows trace explanations as red dots at several $\langle position, signal \rangle$ locations on the trace.

The approximation algorithm presented in Section 3.3 is applied to every counterexample produced by the model checker[7]. The algorithm receives the counterexample trace and formula as input, and outputs a set of $\langle position, signal \rangle$ pairs. This set of pairs is passed on to the tool's built-in trace viewer, which displays the red dots at the designated locations.

Users of the formal verification tool may select one or more model-checking engines with which to check each formula. Each engine uses a different model-checking algorithm, as described in [5]. When a formula fails, the engine that finds the failure is also responsible for producing a counterexample trace. Thus, a counterexample viewed by a user may have been generated by any one of the various algorithms. The red dots computation procedure runs independently on any counterexample, and is oblivious to the method by which the trace was obtained.

The red dots are a routine part of the workflow for users. The red dots computation is performed automatically by the tool, behind the scenes, with no user intervention. Displaying the red dots on the trace is also done automatically, every time a user activates the trace viewer. User feedback indicates that red dots are seen as helpful and important, and are relied on as an integral part of trace visualization.

Experimental Results

We ran the RuleBase PE implementation of Algorithm 6 on the following pairs of formulas and counterexamples. These formulas are based on real-world specifications from [1]. In all cases presented below, the output of the approximation algorithm is the exact causality set, according to Definition 4.

---

[7] Commercially available versions of RuleBase PE implement an older version of this algorithm.

1. We consider a formula with a complex Boolean invariant

$\mathbf{G}$ ((STATUS_VALID $\wedge$ ¬LARGE_PACKET_MODE $\wedge$ LONG_FRAME_RECEIVED) $\rightarrow$
((LONG_FRAME_ERROR $\wedge$ ¬STATUS_OK) $\vee$ TRANSFER_STOPPED))

The trace in Figure 4 was produced by a SAT-based BMC engine, which was configured to increase its bound by increments of 20. As a result, the trace is longer than necessary, and the failure does not occur on the last cycle of the trace. The red dots point us to the first failure, at cycle 12. Note that the Boolean invariant also fails at cycle 15, but this later failure is not highlighted. The execution time for the red dots computation on the trace in Figure 4 is less than 1 second. Running with the same formula, but with traces of up to 5000 cycles, gives execution times that are still under 2 seconds.

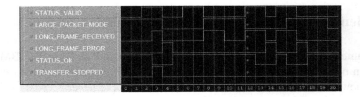

Fig. 4. Counterexample for a Boolean invariant

2. For a liveness property, the model checking engine gives a counterexample with a loop. This is marked by the signal LOOP in the trace viewer, as seen in the trace in Figure 5, which is a counterexample for the formula

$\mathbf{G}$ (P1_ACTIVE $\rightarrow$ $\mathbf{F}$ P2_ACTIVE)

The LOOP signal rises at cycle 9, indicating that the loop starts at that cycle, and that the last cycle (cycle 11) is equal to cycle 9. The point at which the loop begins is marked with a red dot, in addition to the red dots computed by Algorithm 6. The execution time, when running on the trace in Figure 5, is less than 1 second. On a counterexample of 1000 cycles for the same formula, the execution time is less than 2 seconds. For 5000 cycles, the execution time reaches 20 seconds.

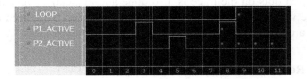

Fig. 5. Counterexample for a liveness property

3. In the introduction, we demonstrated red dot explanations for the formula

$\mathbf{G}$((¬START $\wedge$ ¬STATUS_VALID $\wedge$ END) $\rightarrow$
$\mathbf{X}$[¬START $\mathbf{U}$ (STATUS_VALID $\wedge$ READY)])

This formula contains a combination of temporal operators and Boolean conditions, which makes it difficult to visually identify a failure on the counterexample. The red dots produced by the approximation algorithm are shown in Figure 1. The execution time on the trace in Figure 1 is less than 1 second. For the same formula and a counterexample of 1000 cycles, the execution time is 70 seconds.

5   Related Work

There are several works that tie the definition of causality by Halpern and Pearl to formal verification. Most closely related to our work is the paper by Chockler et. al [8], in which causality and its quantitative measure, responsibility, are viewed as a refinement of coverage in model checking. Causality and responsibility have also been used to improve the refinement techniques of symbolic trajectory evaluation (STE) [7].

As discussed in the introduction, there has been much previous work addressing various aspects of understanding a counterexample. The most relevant to our work is a method that uses *minimal unsatisfiable cores* [13,31][8] to aid in debugging.

We note that minimal unsatisfiable cores differ from our notion of causality in two main aspects. First, a single unsatisfiable core does not give all relevant information for understanding the failure. For example, for the path π_3 in Figure 2 and the specification $\varphi_3 = \mathbf{G}(a \wedge b \wedge c)$, there are three minimal unsatisfiable cores: $\{\langle s_0, a \rangle\}$, $\{\langle s_0, b \rangle\}$, and $\{\langle s_0, c \rangle\}$. None of them gives the full information needed to explain the failure. In contrast, the set of causes is $\{\langle s_0, a \rangle, \langle s_0, b \rangle, \langle s_0, c \rangle\}$, consisting of all pairs that can be made critical for the failure of φ_3 on π_3.

The second difference is that our definition of causality refers to the *first* failure of the formula on the given path. Consider, for example, a specification $\varphi = \mathbf{G}(req \rightarrow \mathbf{X}ack)$ and a trace $\pi = (req) \cdot (ack) \cdot (req) \cdot (req) \cdot (\emptyset)^\omega$ (that is, a trace that is labeled with req in s_0, s_2, and s_3, and with ack in s_1). The minimal unsatisfiable cores in this example are $\{\langle s_2, req \rangle, \langle s_3, ack \rangle\}$ and $\{\langle s_3, req \rangle, \langle s_4, ack \rangle\}$. In contrast, the set of causes for the first failure of φ on π is $\{\langle s_2, req \rangle, \langle s_3, ack \rangle\}$. Unlike the previous example, here the set of causes differs from the union of minimal unsatisfiable cores.

We conjecture that if a given counterexample trace is of minimal length needed to demonstrate the failure, then the *union* of the minimal unsatisfiable cores is equal to the set of causes as defined in this paper. We note though, that computing the union of minimal unsatisfiable cores is a considerably harder task, both in the worst case complexity and in practice, than computing the set of causes directly. Indeed, it is easy to see that the problem of counting the number of all unsatisfiable cores for a given specification and a counterexample trace is complete in $\#P$, similarly to the problem of counting all satisfying assignments to a SAT problem. In practice, extracting several minimal unsatisfiable cores is done sequentially, each time backtracking from the current solution provided by the SAT solver and forcing it to look for a different solution (see, for example, [31]). In contrast, the problem of computing the set of causes is "only" NP-complete, making even the brute-force algorithm feasible for small specifications and

---

[8] An unsatisfiable core of an unsatisfiable CNF formula is a subset of clauses that is in itself unsatisfiable. A minimal unsatisfiable core is an unsatisfiable core such that removing any one of its clauses makes it satisfiable.

short traces. Essentially, computing the union of minimal unsatisfiable cores by computing all unsatisfiable cores separately is an "overkill": it gives us a set of sets, whereas we are only interested in one set - the union.

6   Conclusion and Future Directions

We have shown how the causality definition of Halpern and Pearl [22] can be applied to the task of explaining a counterexample. Our method is implemented as part of the IBM formal verification platform RuleBase PE [28], and it is applied to every counterexample presented by the tool. Experience shows that when visually presented as described in Section 4, the causality information substantially speeds up the time needed for the understanding of a counterexample. Since the causality algorithm is applied to a single counterexample and ignores the model from which it was extracted, no size issues are involved, and the execution time is negligible. An important advantage of our method is the fact that it is independent of the tool that produced the counterexample. When more than one model checking "engine" is invoked to verify a formula, as described in [5], the independence of the causality algorithm is especially important.

The approach presented in this paper defines and (approximately) detects a set of causes for the *first* failure of a formula on a trace. While we believe that this information is the most beneficial for the user, there can be circumstances where the sets of causes for other failures are also desirable. A very small and straightforward enhancement of the algorithm will allow to compute the (approximate) sets of causes of all or a subset of failures of the given counterexample.

As a future work, the relation between causes and unsatisfiable cores should be investigated further. Specifically, a conclusive answer should be provided for the conjecture mentioned in Section 5, about the union of unsatisfiable cores on a trace of minimal length.

In a different direction, it is interesting to see whether there exist subsets of LTL for which the computation of the exact set of causes is polynomial. Natural candidates for being such "easy" sublogics of LTL are the PSL simple subset defined in [15], and the common fragment of LTL and ACTL, called LTL^{det} (see [26]). Finally, we note that our approach, though demonstrated here for LTL specifications, can be applied to other linear temporal logics as well, with slight modifications. This is because our definition of cause holds for any monotonic temporal logic. It will be interesting to see whether it can also be extended to full PSL without significantly increasing its complexity.

Acknowledgments. We thank Cindy Eisner for helpful discussions on the truncated semantics. We thank the anonymous reviewers for important comments.

References

1. Prosyd: Property-Based System Design (2005), http://www.prosyd.org/
2. Armoni, R., Bustan, D., Kupferman, O., Vardi, M.Y.: Resets vs. aborts in linear temporal logic. In: Garavel, H., Hatcliff, J. (eds.) TACAS 2003. LNCS, vol. 2619, pp. 65–80. Springer, Heidelberg (2003)
3. Ball, T., Naik, M., Rajamani, S.: From symptom to cause: Localizing errors in counterexample traces. In: Proc. of POPL, pp. 97–105 (2003)

4. Beer, I., Ben-David, S., Chockler, H., Orni, A., Trefler, R.: Explaining Counterexamples Using Causality. IBM technical report number H-0266, http://domino.watson.ibm.com/library/cyberdig.nsf/Home
5. Ben-David, S., Eisner, C., Geist, D., Wolfsthal, Y.: Model checking at IBM. FMSD 22(2), 101–108 (2003)
6. Chechik, M., Gurfinkel, A.: A framework for counterexample generation and exploration. In: Cerioli, M. (ed.) FASE 2005. LNCS, vol. 3442, pp. 217–233. Springer, Heidelberg (2005)
7. Chockler, H., Grumberg, O., Yadgar, A.: Efficient automatic STE refinement using responsibility. In: Ramakrishnan, C.R., Rehof, J. (eds.) TACAS 2008. LNCS, vol. 4963, pp. 233–248. Springer, Heidelberg (2008)
8. Chockler, H., Halpern, J.Y., Kupferman, O.: What causes a system to satisfy a specification? ACM TOCL 9(3) (2008)
9. Clarke, E., Emerson, E.: Design and synthesis of synchronization skeletons using branching time temporal logic. In: Kozen, D. (ed.) Logic of Programs 1981. LNCS, vol. 131, pp. 52–71. Springer, Heidelberg (1981)
10. Clarke, E., Grumberg, O., McMillan, K., Zhao, X.: Efficient generation of counterexamples and witnesses in symbolic model checking. In: Proc. 32nd DAC, pp. 427–432 (1995)
11. Clarke, E., Grumberg, O., Peled, D.: Model Checking. MIT Press, Cambridge (1999)
12. Copty, F., Irron, A., Weissberg, O., Kropp, N., Kamhi, G.: Efficient debugging in a formal verification environment. In: Margaria, T., Melham, T.F. (eds.) CHARME 2001. LNCS, vol. 2144, pp. 275–292. Springer, Heidelberg (2001)
13. Dershowitz, N., Hanna, Z., Nadel, A.: A scalable algorithm for minimal unsatisfiable core extraction. In: Biere, A., Gomes, C.P. (eds.) SAT 2006. LNCS, vol. 4121, pp. 36–41. Springer, Heidelberg (2006)
14. Dong, Y., Ramakrishnan, C.R., Smolka, S.A.: Model checking and evidence exploration. In: Proc. of ECBS, pp. 214–223 (2003)
15. Eisner, C., Fisman, D.: A Practical Introduction to PSL. Series on Integrated Circuits and Systems (2006)
16. Eisner, C., Fisman, D., Havlicek, J., Lustig, Y., McIsaac, A., Campenhout, D.V.: Reasoning with temporal logic on truncated paths. In: Hunt Jr., W.A., Somenzi, F. (eds.) CAV 2003. LNCS, vol. 2725, pp. 27–39. Springer, Heidelberg (2003)
17. Eiter, T., Lukasiewicz, T.: Complexity results for structure-based causality. In: Proc. 7th IJCAI, pp. 35–40 (2001)
18. Griesmayer, A., Staber, S., Bloem, R.: Automated fault localization for c programs. ENTCS 174(4), 95–111 (2007)
19. Groce, A.: Error explanation with distance metrics. In: Jensen, K., Podelski, A. (eds.) TACAS 2004. LNCS, vol. 2988, pp. 108–122. Springer, Heidelberg (2004)
20. Groce, A., Kroening, D.: Making the most of BMC counterexamples. In: SGSH (July 2004)
21. Hall, N.: Two concepts of causation. Causation and Counterfactuals. MIT Press, Cambridge (2002)
22. Halpern, J., Pearl, J.: Causes and explanations: A structural-model approach — part I: Causes. In: Proc. of 17th UAI, pp. 194–202. Morgan Kaufmann Publishers, San Francisco (2001)
23. Hume, D.: A treatise of human nature. John Noon, London (1939)
24. Jin, H., Ravi, K., Somenzi, F.: Fate and free will in error traces. In: Katoen, J.-P., Stevens, P. (eds.) TACAS 2002. LNCS, vol. 2280, pp. 445–458. Springer, Heidelberg (2002)
25. Kupferman, O., Vardi, M., Wolper, P.: An automata-theoretic approach to branching-time model checking. JACM 47(2), 312–360 (2000)
26. Maidl, M.: The common fragment of CTL and LTL. In: Proc. of FOCS, pp. 643–652 (2000)
27. Queille, J., Sifakis, J.: Specification and verification of concurrent systems in Cesar. In: Dezani-Ciancaglini, M., Montanari, U. (eds.) Programming 1982. LNCS, vol. 137, pp. 337–351. Springer, Heidelberg (1981)

28. RuleBase PE homepage,
    http://www.haifa.il.ibm.com/projects/verification/RB_Homepage
29. Shen, S., Qin, Y., Li, S.: A faster counterexample minization algorithm based on refutation analysis. In: Proc. of DATE, pp. 672–677 (2005)
30. Staber, S., Bloem, R.: Fault localization and correction with QBF. In: Marques-Silva, J., Sakallah, K.A. (eds.) SAT 2007. LNCS, vol. 4501, pp. 355–368. Springer, Heidelberg (2007)
31. Sülflow, A., Fey, G., Bloem, R., Drechsler, R.: Using unsatisfiable cores to debug multiple design errors. In: Proc. of Symp. on VLSI, pp. 77–82 (2008)
32. Wang, C., Yang, Z., Ivancic, F., Gupta, A.: Whodunit? causal analysis for counterexamples. In: Graf, S., Zhang, W. (eds.) ATVA 2006. LNCS, vol. 4218, pp. 82–95. Springer, Heidelberg (2006)

A   Causality Background

The formal definition of causality used in this paper was first introduced in the Artificial Intelligence community in [22]. Our definitions in Section 3 are based on a restricted (and much simpler) version that applies to *binary* causal models, where the range of all variables is binary [17]. We present the definition of a binary causal model below.

Definition 9 (Binary causal model).   *A binary causal model M is a tuple $\langle \mathcal{V}, \mathcal{F} \rangle$, where $\mathcal{V}$ is the set of Boolean variables and $\mathcal{F}$ associates with every variable $X \in \mathcal{V}$ a function F_X that describes how the value of X is determined by the values of all other variables in $\mathcal{V}$. A context $\vec{u}$ is a legal assignment for the variables in $\mathcal{V}$.*

A causal model M is conveniently described by a *causal network*, which is a graph with nodes corresponding to the variables in $\mathcal{V}$ and an edge from a node labeled X to one labeled Y if F_Y depends on the value of X. We restrict our attention to what are called *recursive models*. These are ones whose associated causal network is a directed acyclic graph.

A *causal formula* η is a Boolean formula over the set of variables $\mathcal{V}$. A causal formula η is true or false in a causal model given a context. We write $(M, \vec{u}) \models \eta$ if η is true in M given a context $\vec{u}$. We write $(M, \vec{u}) \models [\vec{Y} \leftarrow \vec{y}](X = x)$ if the variable X has value x in the model M given the context $\vec{u}$ and the assignment $\vec{y}$ to the variables in the set $\vec{Y} \subset \mathcal{V}$.

For the ease of presentation, we borrow from [8] the definition of *criticality* in binary causal models, that captures the notion of counterfactual causal dependence.

Definition 10 (Critical variable [8]).   *Let M be a model, $\vec{u}$ the current context, and η a Boolean formula. Let $(M, \vec{u}) \models \eta$, and X a Boolean variable in M that has the value x in the context $\vec{u}$, and $\bar{x}$ the other possible value (0 or 1). We say that $(X = x)$ is critical for η in $(M, \vec{u})$ iff $(M, \vec{u}) \models (X \leftarrow \neg x)\neg \eta$. That is, changing the value of X to $\neg x$ falsifies η in $(M, \vec{u})$.*

We can now give the definition of a cause in binary causal models from [22,17].

Definition 11 (Cause).   *We say that $X = x$ is a cause of η in $(M, \vec{u})$ if the following conditions hold:*

AC1. $(M, \vec{u}) \models (X = x) \wedge \eta$.
AC2. *There exists a subset $\vec{W}$ of $\mathcal{V}$ with $X \notin \vec{W}$ and some setting $\vec{w}'$ of the variables in $\vec{W}$ such that setting the variables in $\vec{W}$ to the values $\vec{w}'$ makes $(X = x)$ critical for the satisfaction of η.*

Size-Change Termination, Monotonicity Constraints and Ranking Functions

Amir M. Ben-Amram

Academic College of Tel-Aviv Yaffo

Abstract. Size-change termination involves deducing program termination based on the impossibility of infinite descent. To this end we may use a program abstraction in which transitions are described by *monotonicity constraints* over (abstract) variables. When only constraints of the form $x > y'$ and $x \geq y'$ are allowed, we have size-change graphs, for which both theory and practice are now more evolved then for general monotonicity constraints. This work shows that it is possible to transfer some theory from the domain of size-change graphs to the general case, complementing and extending previous work on monotonicity constraints. Significantly, we provide a procedure to construct explicit global ranking functions from monotonicity constraints in singly-exponential time, which is better than what has been published so far even for size-change graphs. We also consider the integer domain, where general monotonicity constraints are essential because the domain is not well-founded.

1 Introduction

This paper is concerned with termination analysis. This is a fundamental and much-studied problem of software verification, certification and transformation. A subproblem of termination analysis is the construction of *global ranking functions*. Such a function is required to decrease in each step of a program (for "step" read basic block, function call, etc, as appropriate); an explicitly presented ranking function whose descent is (relatively) easy to verify is a useful *certificate* for termination and may have other uses, such as running-time analysis.

A structured approach is to break the termination problem for programs into two stages, an *abstraction* of the program and analysis of the abstract program. One benefit of this approach is that the abstract programs may be rather independent of the concrete programming language. Another one is that the termination problem for the abstract programs may be decidable.

Size-change termination (SCT [9]) is such an approach. It views a program as a transition system with states. The abstraction consists in forming a *control-flow graph* for the program, identifying a set of *state variables*, and forming a finite set of *size-change graphs* that are abstractions of the transitions of the program. In essence, a size-change graph is a set of inequalities between variables of the source state and the target state. Thus, the SCT abstraction is an example of a transition system defined by constraints of a particular type. The technique

A. Bouajjani and O. Maler (Eds.): CAV 2009, LNCS 5643, pp. 109–123, 2009.

concentrates on well-founded domains and on the impossibility of infinite descent. Thus, only two types of inequalities were admitted into the constraints in [9]: $x > y'$ (old value of x greater than new value of y) and $x \geq y'$.

Size-change graphs lend themselves to a very natural generalization: Monotonicity Constraints. Here, a transition may be described by any combination of order relations, including equalities as well as strict and non-strict inqualities, and involving any pair of variables from the source state and target state. Thus, it can express a relation among source variables, that applies to states in which the transition may be taken; a relation among the target variables, which applies to states which the transition may produce; and, as in SCT, relations involving a source variable and a target variable, but here equalities can be used, as well as relations like $x \leq x'$, that is, an increase.

The *Monotonicity Constraint Systems* treated in this paper will include another convenience, *state invariants* associated with a point in the control-flow graph. These too are conjunctions of order constraints.

Monotonicity constraint systems generalize the SCT abstraction and are clearly more expressive. It may happen that analysis of a program yields monotonicity constraints which are not size-change graphs; in such a case, simply approximating the constraints by a size-change graph may end up missing the termination proof. Specific examples appear in the next section. It is not surprising, perhaps, that Monotonicity Constraints actually predated the SCT framework—consider the Prolog termination analyses in [5, 10]. But as often happens in science, concentrating on a simplified system that is sufficiently interesting was conductive to research, and thus the formulation of the SCT framework led to a series of interesting discoveries. To pick up some of the salient points:

- The SCT abstraction has a simple semantics, in terms of transition systems.
- It has an appealing combinatorial representation as a set of graphs.
- A termination criterion has been formulated in terms of these graphs (the existence of an infinite descending thread in every infinite multipath [9]).
- This criterion is equivalent to the termination of every model (transition system)—in logical terms, this condition is sound and complete [8, 9].
- Termination of a set of size-change graphs can be effectively decided; while having exponential worst-case time, the method is often usable.
- It has been established that a global ranking function can also be effectively constructed from the size-change graphs. Lee [8] gave the first proof, where the size of the resulting ranking expression is up to triply-exponential. This left open the challenging problem of improving this upper bound. Progress regarding certain special cases is reported in [2].

Which of the desirable features are preserved if we move to the stronger framework of monotonicity constraints? The first contribution of this paper is an answer: *in essence, all of them.*

The second contribution of this paper is an algorithm to verify termination of a monotonicity constraint system while constructing a global ranking function, all in singly-exponential time. Thus, we solve the open problem from [8], and, surprisingly, by tackling a super-problem.

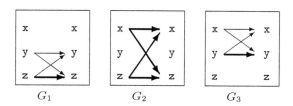

Fig. 1. SCT example with a complex ranking function. There is a single flow-point. Heavy arcs represent strict descent.

To illustrate this result, Figure 1 shows an SCT instance not falling into the classes handled in [2]. A ranking function for this instance, of the kind that we derive in this paper, follows. Its codomain is triples, and it descends lexicographically in every transition.

$$\rho(x,y,z) = \begin{cases} \langle x,y,z \rangle & \text{if} & z < x \leq y \vee y < x \leq z \\ \langle y,y,z \rangle & \text{if} & z < y < x \vee x \leq y \leq z \\ \langle z,y,z \rangle & \text{if} & x \leq z < y \vee y \leq z < x \end{cases}$$

Related Work. An important precursor of this work is [4]. It concentrated on local ranking functions, and made the intriguing observation that the termination test used in [10, 5] is sound and complete for SCT, but incomplete for general monotonicity constraints. It also presented the correct test (see Section 4.3). Even earlier, [7] presented a termination analysis for logic programs in which the correct decision algorithm for monotonicity constraint systems is embedded.

There are many works that target the discovery of relations among variables in a program. Classic examples include [3] for logic programs and [6] for imperative programs. All these techniques can be used to discover monotonicity constraints—none are inherently restricted to size-change graphs.

2   Basic Definitions and Examples

This section introduces monotonicity constraint systems (MCS) and their semantics, and formally relates them to SCT.

A monotonicity constraint system is an abstract program. An abstract program is, essentially, a set of *abstract transitions*. An abstract transition is a relation on (abstract) program states.

When describing program transitions, it is customary to mark the variables in the *resulting* state with primes (e.g., x'). We use S' to denote the primed versions of all variables in a set S. For simplicity, we will name the variables $x_1, \ldots, x_n$ (regardless of what program point we are referring to).

Definition 2.1 (MCS). *A monotonicity constraint system, or MCS, is an abstract program representation that consists of a control-flow graph (CFG), monotonicity constraints and state invariants, all defined below.*

- *A control-flow graph is a directed multigraph over the set F of* flow points.
- *A* monotonicity constraint *or MC is a conjunction of order constraints of the form $x \bowtie y$ where $x, y \in \{x_1, \ldots, x_n, x'_1, \ldots, x'_n\}$, and $\bowtie \in \{>, \geq, =\}$.*
- *Every CFG arc $f \to g$ is associated with a monotonicity constraint G. We write $G : f \to g$.*
- *For each $f \in F$, there is an* invariant I_f, *which is a conjunction of order constraints among the variables.*

The terms "abstract program", "constraint system" and "MCS instance" are used interchangeably, when context permits. The letter $\mathcal{A}$ is usually used to denote such a program; F^A will be its flow-point set. When notions of connectivity are applied to $\mathcal{A}$ (such as, "$\mathcal{A}$ is strongly connected"), they concern the underlying CFG.

Definition 2.2 (constraints as graphs). *The graph representation of $G : f \to g$ is a labeled graph $(X \cup Y, E)$ with the nodes $X = \{x_1, \ldots, x_n\}$ and $Y = X'$ and E includes a labeled arc for each constraint:*

- *For a constraint $x > y$ (respectively $x \geq y$), an arc $x \xrightarrow{\downarrow} y$ ($x \xrightarrow{\overline{\downarrow}} y'$).*
- *For a constraint $x = y$, an edge (undirected arc) $x \to y$ (thus, G is a* mixed graph)[1].

   The labeled arcs are referred to, verbally, as strict *and* non-strict *and the edges are also called* no-change *arcs.*

We remark that the lack of direction in edges is meaningful when we consider paths of size-change arcs. Note also that arcs may connect two source variables, two target variables or a source and a target variable—in any direction.

   Henceforth, we identify a MC with its graph representation: it is a graph and a logical conjunction of constraints at the same time.

Definition 2.3 (semantics). *Let Val be a fixed, infinite well-ordered set. A state of $\mathcal{A}$ (or an abstract state) is $s = (\mathbf{f}, \sigma)$, where $\mathbf{f} \in F^A$ and $\sigma : \{1, \ldots, n\} \to Val$ represents an assignment of values to f's variables. A transition is a pair of states. The truth value of an expression such as $x_1 > x_2$ under σ is defined in the natural way.*

   For $G : f \to g \in \mathcal{A}$, we write $G((f, \sigma) \mapsto (g, \sigma'))$ if all constraints in I_f, I_g and G are satisfied by σ and σ'. In this case, transition $(f, \sigma) \mapsto (g, \sigma')$ is described by G.

   We say that G is unsatisfiable *if it describes no transition.*

   The transition system *associated with $\mathcal{A}$ is the relation $T_{\mathcal{A}}$ defined by*

$$(s, s') \in T_{\mathcal{A}} \iff G(s \mapsto s') \text{ for some } G \in \mathcal{A}.$$

Definition 2.4 (termination). *A* run *of $T_{\mathcal{A}}$ is a (finite or infinite) sequence of states $\tilde{s} = s_0, s_1, s_2 \ldots$ such that for all i, $(s_i, s_{i+1}) \in T_G$. Transition system $T_{\mathcal{A}}$ is* uniformly terminating *if it has no infinite run.*

---

[1] Hopefully, the use of $\to$ to denote both types of arcs will not confuse the reader.

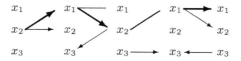

Fig. 2. A multipath

MCS $\mathcal{A}$ is said to be *terminating* if $\mathcal{T}_{\mathcal{A}}$ is uniformly terminating for any choice of *Val*.

Definition 2.5 (size-change graph). *A size-change graph (SCG) is a monotonicity constraint consisting only of relations of the forms $x_i > x'_j$ and $x_i \geq x'_j$.*

An SCT instance *is a MCS where all constraints are size-change graphs and all invariants are trivial.*

Let $P(s, s')$ be any predicate over states s, s', possibly written using variable names, e.g., $x_1 > x_2 \wedge x_2 < x'_2$. We write $G \models P$ if $G(s \mapsto s') \Rightarrow P(s, s')$.

Definition 2.6. *A (global) ranking function for a transition system $\mathcal{T}$ with state space St is a function $\rho : St \rightarrow W$, where W is a well-founded set, that decreases on every transition.*

A ranking function for a MCS $\mathcal{A}$ is a ranking function for $\mathcal{T}_{\mathcal{A}}$. Equivalently, it satisfies $G \models \rho(s) > \rho(s')$ for every $G \in \mathcal{A}$.

Example 2.1 ([4]). Consider an abstract program with a single flow-point f, a trivial invariant, and a single abstract transition G: $x_1 > x'_2 \wedge x_2 \geq x_3 \wedge x'_1 \leq x'_3$.

This system is terminating; a possible proof is to note that the following *ranking function* descends (lexicographically) in every possible transition:

$$f(x_1, x_2, x_3) = \begin{cases} \langle 1, x_1 \rangle \text{ if } x_2 \geq x_3 \\ \langle 0, x_1 \rangle \text{ if } x_2 < x_3. \end{cases}$$

Clearly, G is not a size-change graph. Its best approximation as a size-change graph is $\{x_1 > x'_2\}$ which does not prove termination.

Example 2.2. Change G into $x_2 \geq x_3 \wedge x_3 = x'_3 \wedge x'_2 > x'_3$. Now, termination follows, not from the impossibility of infinite descent, but from the unsatisfiability of $G(s \mapsto s') \wedge G(s' \mapsto s'')$.

We remark that the issue of unsatisfiability never arises with SCT instances.

3   Multipaths, Walks and Termination

Definition 3.1. *A multipath M in $\mathcal{A}$ (an $\mathcal{A}$-multipath) is a finite or infinite sequence of MC graphs $G_1 G_2 \ldots$ that label a (finite or infinite) path in the CFG of $\mathcal{A}$.*

Most often, we view a multipath as the single (finite or infinite) graph obtained by concatenating the sequence of MC graphs, i.e., identifying the target nodes of G_i with the source nodes of G_{i+1} (Figure 2). In this way it can also be seen as a conjunction of constraints on a set of variables which correspond to the nodes of the combined graph.

Thus a multipath is a mixed graph. We will consider walks in this graph; a walk can cross an undirected arc in both directions. Recall also that walks are allowed to repeat nodes and arcs.

Definition 3.2. *A walk that includes a strict arc is said to be* descending. *A walk that includes infinitely many strict arcs is* infinitely descending.

An MCS is size-change terminating *if every infinite multipath has an infinitely descending walk.*

Note that the walk above may actually be a cycle! In this case it is contained in a finite section of the multipath, and, logically, it implies the condition $x > x$ for some variable x. Thus, such a multipath is unsatisfiable and corresponds to no concrete run. If the walk is not a cycle, it indicates an infinite descending chain of values and this contradicts well-foundedness. Thus, we see that if $\mathcal{A}$ is *size-change terminating* it can have no infinite runs. This proves the **if** direction of the next theorem.

Theorem 3.3. *$\mathcal{A}$ is terminating if and only if it is size-change terminating.*

Proof. (**only if**) suppose that $\mathcal{A}$ is not size-change terminating. Hence, an infinite multipath M can be formed, without infinite descent. Consider the infinite set $\mathcal{V}$ of the nodes of M as distinct variables; our aim is to show that there is a choice of *Val* such that these variables can all be assigned while satisfying all the constraints. This assignment will form an infinite run.

In fact, $\mathcal{V}$ itself is partially quasi-ordered by the constraints in M; more precisely, the constraints can be *completed* to a partial quasi-order by including additional inequalities, to satisfy the reflexive axiom $v = v$ for all v, and the various other axioms: $x > y \wedge y \geq z \Rightarrow x > z$, $x \geq y \wedge y \geq x \Rightarrow x = y$,   etc.

The closure ensures transitivity and symmetry of $=$ as well as transitivity of $>$, and the agreement of $\geq$ with $>$ and $=$. The asymmetry of $>$ is guaranteed by the non-existence of a descending cycle.

Moreover, the partial quasi-order is well founded, because of the non-existence of infinite descent in M. Now, let *Val* be $\mathcal{V}/=$, which is a well-founded partial order, and extend the ordering to a total one in an arbitrary way while preserving well-foundedness.   □

The SCT condition [9] is similar to the infinite-descent condition, but only concerns walks that proceed forwards in the multipath. Obviously, with SCT graphs, there are no other walks anyway.

Definition 3.4. *Let $M = G_1 G_2 \ldots$ be a multipath. A thread in M is a walk that only includes arcs in a forward direction ($x_i \to x'_j$). A MCS $\mathcal{A}$ satisfies SCT if every infinite $\mathcal{A}$-multipath has an infinitely descending thread.*

As the examples of Section 1 show, the SCT condition, while clearly a sufficient condition for termination, is not a necessary one with respect to general monotonicity constraint systems.

4   Fully Elaborated Systems and Stability

In this section we describe a procedure that while increasing the size of an abstract program (by duplicating flow points), simplifies its termination proof. In order to express the correctness of a transformation on abstract programs we begin by defining "simulation."

4.1   Simulation

Definition 4.1. *Let T, S be transition systems, with flow-point sets F, F^S respectively, and both having states described by n variables over Val. We say that S simulates T if there is a relation $\phi \subseteq F \times F^S$ and, for all $(f, g) \in \phi$, a bijection $\psi_{f,g} : \{1, \ldots, n\} \to \{1, \ldots, n\}$ such that for every (finite or infinite) state-transition sequence $(f_1, \sigma_1) \mapsto (f_2, \sigma_2) \mapsto (f_3, \sigma_3) \mapsto \ldots$ of T there is a corresponding sequence $(g_1, \sigma_1') \mapsto (g_2, \sigma_2') \mapsto (g_3, \sigma_3') \mapsto \ldots$ of S with $(f_i, g_i) \in \phi$ and $\sigma_i' = \sigma_i \circ (\psi_{f_i, g_i})$.*

Definition 4.2. *We say that an abstract program A simulates an abstract program B if T_A simulates T_B, via mappings ϕ and ψ, as above.*

We say that A simulates B deterministically if for every $f \in F^B$ and assignment σ' satisfying I_f there is a unique $g \in F^A$ with $(f, g) \in \phi$ such that, letting $\sigma' = sigma \circ (\psi_{f,g})$, assignment σ' satisfies I_g.

Briefly, determinism means that the invariants of different A flow-points that simulate a given B flow-point have to be mutually exclusive (for valid states).

4.2   Elaboration

Definition 4.3. *An MCS A is* fully elaborated *if the following conditions hold:*
   (1) Each state invariant fully specifies the relations among all variables. That is, for $i, j \leq n$, one of $x_i = x_j$, $x_i < x_j$ or $x_i > x_j$ is implied by I_f.
   (2) Each size-change graph G is closed under logical consequence (taking the invariants into account). That is, whenever $G((f, \sigma) \mapsto (g, \sigma')) \Rightarrow x \bowtie y$, for $\bowtie \in \{>, \geq, =, \}$, the corresponding arc is included in G.
   (3) No MC in A is unsatisfiable.

In a fully elaborated system, the invariants can be assumed to have the form

$$x_1 \left\{ {< \atop =} \right\} x_2 \left\{ {< \atop =} \right\} \ldots \left\{ {< \atop =} \right\} x_n. \tag{1}$$

In this form, the variables are re-indexed according to the sorted order of their value; this has some convenient consequences. In particular, the closure under logical consequence yields a "downward closure" of the graphs: if $x_i \rightarrow x'_j \in G$ then $x_i \rightarrow x'_k \in G$ for every $k \leq j$, and if $x_i \overset{\downarrow}{\rightarrow} x'_j \in G$ then $x_i \overset{\downarrow}{\rightarrow} x'_k \in G$.

The number of possible orderings of n variables plays a role in the combinatorics of fully elaborated instances. Note that equalities are possible. Therefore, the number of orderings is not $n!$, but a slightly larger number called *the nth ordered Bell number* B_n. An easily proved upper bound is $B_n \leq 2n^{n-1}$. We denote the set of these orderings by Bell_n.

Recall that $f = \tilde{O}(g)$ means that $f = O(g \cdot \log^k g)$ for some constant k. Thus $\tilde{O}(n^n)$ is asymptotically dominated by n^n times a polynomial in n.

Lemma 4.4. *Any MCS $\mathcal{B}$ with n variables at any point, and m flow-points, can be transformed into a fully-elaborated system $\mathcal{A}$, simulating $\mathcal{B}$ deterministically, in $\tilde{O}(mn^n)$ time and space.*

If $\mathcal{B}$ terminates, so does $\mathcal{A}$.

Proof. The algorithm for the transformation follows almost immediately from the definitions: first, for every $f \in F^B$, generate flow-points f_π where π ranges over Bell_n. A mapping $\psi_{f_\pi, f}$ is defined according to the ordering, to satisfy (1). The invariant I_{f_π} is also set to express the chosen ordering.

Next, for every MC $G : f \rightarrow g$ in $\mathcal{B}$, and every pair f_π, g_ϖ, create a size-change graph $G_{\pi,\varpi} : f_\pi \rightarrow g_\varpi$ as follows:

1. For every arc $x \rightarrow y \in G$, include the corresponding arc in $G_{\pi,\varpi}$, according to the variable renaming used in the two $\mathcal{A}$ flow-points.
2. Complete $G_{\pi,\varpi}$ by closure under consequences of the inequalities expressed by the given arcs, I_{f_π} and I_{g_ϖ}. Calculating this closure is easy since it is actually an All-Pairs Shortest-Path problem with weights in the set $\{\downarrow, \top, =\}$. This can be done in polynomial time, at most $O(n^3)$, by a standard algorithm. Note that the algorithm will also find out whether the graph is satisfiable—it only fails to be so if the closure includes a strict self-loop $x > x$.

Unsatisfiable graphs are removed from the constructed system.

If $\mathcal{B}$ terminates, so does $\mathcal{A}$—because every run of $\mathcal{A}$ represents a run of B. $\square$

4.3   Stability

Definition 4.5. *An MC $G : f \rightarrow g$ is stable if it is closed under logical consequence, and, moreover, every relation among variables of state s (respectively, s') implied by $I_f(s) \wedge G(s, s') \wedge I_g(s')$ is already implied by I_f (respectively, I_g).*

MCS $\mathcal{A}$ is stable if all its abstract transitions are.

It is easy to see that a fully elaborated system is stable. Full elaboration can be seen as a brute-force solution; a system can be stabilized by an iterative fixed-point computation, which is likely to end up with fewer than B_n times every flow point. We do not elaborate further on the algorithm in this abstract.

Theorem 4.6. *A stable MCS $\mathcal{A}$ is terminating if and only if it satisfies SCT.*

Proof. If $\mathcal{A}$ satisfies SCT, it is terminating. For the converse direction, Let $M = G_1 G_2 \ldots$ be an infinite $\mathcal{A}$-multipath. We know that it has an infinitely descending walk. We now have two cases, as the walk is either a cycle or extends to infinity. We claim that the first case cannot happen (and leave the proof to the reader; it uses the same ideas as the other case). In the second case, we shall prove that there is an infinitely descending thread.

For unique naming, let the nodes of the multipath be labeled $x[t, i]$ such that $x[t, i]$ is a source node of G_{t+1} representing x_i (and a target node of G_t). The index t is called the time coordinate. The walk is made out of arcs $x[t_k, i_k] \rightarrow x[t_{k+1}, i_{k+1}]$ for $k = k_0, k_0 + 1, \ldots$ Let j_t be the first occurrence of t in the sequence; note that this is well defined for all $t \geq t_{k_0}$. The walk is broken into segments leading from $x[t, i_{j_t}]$ to $x[t + 1, i_{j_{t+1}}]$, of which infinitely many are descending. We claim that each of this segments can be replaced with a single arc, strict when appropriate. This implies that SCT is satisfied.

As there is a walk from $x[t, i_{j_t}]$ to $x[t+1, i_{j_{t+1}}]$, consider the shortest one (the shortest strict one, if appropriate). We claim that it consists of one arc. For if it does not, consider a node $x[t^*, i_{j_{t^*}}]$ of smallest time coordinate that occurs inside the segment (not at its ends). Then consider the two arcs—one that enters that node and one that exits; they must both be in $G_{j_{t^*}+1}$. By consequence closure, there is a single arc (strict if any of the two arcs is) to replace these two arcs. Thus, the presumed shortest walk is not shortest. $\qquad\square$

A decision algorithm. Theorem 4.6 has the immediate consequence of an algorithm to decide MCS termination. Namely, stabilize the system and apply an SCT algorithm. Note that for deciding SCT, we can ignore any "backward" arcs $(x'_j \rightarrow x_i)$, as well as the state invariants, in other words retain just SCT graphs. This observation may possibly be useful in optimizing an implementation, in particular in conjunction with a subsumption test.

Anothe natural expectation is that it would be desirable in practice to avoid full elaboration when possible, as already remarked. The emphasis on "in practice" is due to the fact that when the theoretical worst-case complexity is considered, full elaboration may (somewhat paradoxically) be an improvement, specifically, when the decision procedure used is the closure-based algorithm [9]. The closure set of an SCT instance can reach (at the worst case) a size of $m^2 \, 2^{\Theta(n^2)}$; the closure set of a fully-elaborated system is only $m^2 \, 2^{O(n \log n)}$. However, as the next section will show, once we have fully elaborated the system, there is actually a polynomial-time algorithm that decides termination (and more), so there is no need to do anything as costly as a closure computation.

The decision algorithm for MCS that is embedded in the logic-program analysis of [7] is a "closure type" algorithm similar to the standard algorithm for SCT. It seems that the algorithm can be interpreted as applying the standard SCT algorithm to a stabilized constraint system (disregarding aspects that do not apply to our framework). Yet another similar algorithm is found in [4]. It uses "balancing" which is similar to our stabilization but on a local basis (consistent with the overall local approach of that paper).

5   Constructing a Global Ranking Function

This section describes our ranking-function construction. The general form of the constructed function is a "case expression" which associates tuples of variables and constants with guards. The function evaluates to the value of the tuple whose guard matches the current state. For an example see Section 1.

5.1   Background

We first cite some definitions and results from previous work, specifically [1, 2].

Definition 5.1 (vectors). *For flow-point $f \in F$ and positive integer B, V_f^B is the set of tuples $\mathbf{v}_f = \langle v_1, v_2, \ldots \rangle$ of even length, where every odd position is a variable of f, such that every variable appears once; and every even position is an integer between 0 and B.*

Definition 5.2 (thread preserver). *Given MCS $\mathcal{A}$, a mapping $P : F^{\mathcal{A}} \to \mathcal{P}(\{1, \ldots, n\})$ is called a* thread preserver *of $\mathcal{A}$ if for every $G : f \to g$ in $\mathcal{A}$, it holds that whenever $i \in P(f)$, there is $j \in P(g)$ such that $x_i \to x_j \in G$.*

It is easy to see that the set of thread preservers of $\mathcal{A}$ is closed under union. Hence, there is a unique maximal thread preserver, which we denote by $\mathrm{MTP}(\mathcal{A})$. Given a standard representation of $\mathcal{A}$, $\mathrm{MTP}(\mathcal{A})$ can be found in linear time [1].

Definition 5.3 (complete thread). *A thread in a given multipath is* complete *if it starts at the beginning of the multipath, and is as long as the multipath.*

Lemma 5.4. *If a strongly connected MCS satisfies SCT, every finite multipath includes a complete thread.*

5.2   Preliminaries

The essential idea of the construction is to first fully-elaborate the program, and then process the resulting constraint system. This works, as shown next:

Lemma 5.5. *If $\mathcal{A}$ simulates $\mathcal{B}$ deterministically, any ranking function for $\mathcal{A}$ can be transformed into a ranking function for $\mathcal{B}$.*

Proof. Let ρ be the $\mathcal{A}$ ranking function. The $\mathcal{B}$ ranking function is defined for state (g, σ') as $\rho(f, \sigma)$ where f is the unique point satisfying $(f, g) \in \phi$ and $I_f(\sigma' \circ (\psi_{f,g}^{-1}))$, and $\sigma = \sigma' \circ (\psi_{f,g}^{-1})$. $\square$

Note that, if ρ assigns a unique vector to each flow-point in $\mathcal{A}$, the resulting $\mathcal{B}$ ranking function has just the form described at the beginning of this section.

We assume, henceforth, that $\mathcal{A}$ is a fully-elaborated, terminating constraint system. By Theorem 4.6, $\mathcal{A}$ satisfies SCT, and can be handled as an SCT instance.

Definition 5.6. *A variable x_i is called* thread-safe *at flow-point f if every finite $\mathcal{A}$-multipath, starting at f, includes a complete thread from x_i.*

Lemma 5.7. *Assume that $\mathcal{A}$ is strongly connected. For every f, let $S(f)$ be the set of indices of variables that are thread-safe at f. Then $S(f)$ is not empty for any $f \in F^A$ and S is a thread preserver.*

Proof. Let M be any finite $\mathcal{A}$-multipath starting at f. Observe that since $\mathcal{A}$ satisfies SCT and is strongly connected, there must be a complete thread in M, say starting at x_i. But then x_n can also start a thread (note the downward-closure of fully-elaborated MCs). It follows that $n \in S(f)$.

We now aim to show that S is a thread preserver. Let $i \in S(f)$, and let $G : f \to g$. Every finite multipath M beginning with G has a complete thread that begins with an arc from x_i, say $x_i \to x'_{j_M}$. Let J be the set of all such indices j_M, and $k = \max J$. Then $x_i \to x_k$ is an arc of G, because $k \in J$; and by the downward-closure property one can see that every M has a complete thread beginning with the arc $x_i \to x'_k$. Hence, $k \in S(g)$ and the proof is complete. $\square$

Definition 5.8 (freezer). *Let $C : F^A \to \{1, \ldots, n\}$. Such C is called a freezer for $\mathcal{A}$ if for every $G \in \mathcal{A}$, $G \models x_{C(f)} = x'_{C(g)}$.*

Lemma 5.9. *Suppose that $\mathcal{A}$ is strongly connected, satisfies SCT, and has a freezer C. If for every f, variable $x_{C(f)}$ is ignored, SCT will still be satisfied.*

Proof. Let M be an infinite multipath of $\mathcal{A}$; by the SCT property, M has an infinitely descending thread τ. Observe that C induces one infinite thread ϑ in M, consisting entirely of no-change arcs $x_i \overset{=}{\to} x'_j$; this thread represents a sequence of unchanging data values in any transition sequence described by M, and therefore can have at most finitely many intersections with τ. It follows that M has an infinitely descending thread that avoids the frozen variables. $\square$

Lemma 5.10. *Let $\mathcal{A}$ have thread preserver S, where $S(f) \neq \emptyset$ for all f. For every $f \in F^A$, let $i_f = \min S(f)$. Then every MC $G : f \to g$ includes $x_{i_f} \to x'_{i_g}$.*

Proof. G must have an arc from x_{i_f} to some $x_j \in S(g)$; so by consequence-closure, G includes $x_{i_f} \to x'_{i_g}$. $\square$

5.3   Constructing the Ranking Function

To construct a ranking function for a general MCS, we begin by transforming it into a fully-elaborated $\mathcal{A}$ as described in Lemma 4.4. We then proceed with the construction in an incremental way. To justify the incremental construction, we define a residual transition system and relate it to ranking functions.

Definition 5.11. *Let $\mathcal{T}$ be a transition system with state space St. A quasi-ranking function for $\mathcal{T}$ is a function $\rho : St \to W$, where W is a well-founded set, such that $\rho(s) \geq \rho(s')$ for every $(s, s') \in \mathcal{T}$.*

The residual transition system relative to ρ, denoted $\mathcal{T}/\rho$, includes all (and only) the transitions of $\mathcal{T}$ which do not decrease ρ.

Observe that Lemma 5.10 provides a quasi-ranking function: $\rho(f, \sigma) = \sigma(x_{i_f})$.

The next couple of lemmas are quite trivial but we spell them out because they clarify how a ranking function may be constructed incrementally. We use the notation $v \cdot u$ for concatenation of tuples.

Lemma 5.12. *Assume that ρ is a quasi-ranking function for T, and ρ' a ranking function for T/ρ whose range consists of lexicographically-ordered tuples; then $\rho \cdot \rho'$ is a ranking function for T.*

Lemma 5.13. *Assume that the CFG of A consists of a set $C_1, \ldots, C_k$ of mutually disconnected components (that is, there is no arc from C_i to C_j with $i \neq j$). If for every i, ρ_i is a ranking function for A restricted to C_i, then $\cup_i \rho_i$ is a ranking function for A.*

Lemma 5.14. *Suppose that the CFG of A consists of several strongly connected components (SCCs). Let $C_1, \ldots, C_k$ be a reverse topological ordering of the components. Define a function $\rho(s)$ for $s = (f, \sigma)$ as the index i of the component C_i including f. Then ρ is a quasi-ranking function (with co-domain $[1, k]$) and it is strictly decreasing on every transition represented by an inter-component arc.*

The following algorithm puts all of this together. Note: a CFG whose arc set is empty is called *vacant*. A strongly connected component whose arc set is empty is called *trivial* (it may have connections to other components).

Algorithm 5.1. (ranking function construction for A)

1. List the SCCs of A in reverse-topological order. For each $f \in F^A$, let κ_f be the position of the SCC of f. Form A' by deleting all the inter-component transitions. If A' is vacant, return ρ where $\rho(f, \sigma) = \kappa_f$.
2. For each SCC C, compute the MTP, using the algorithm in [1]. If empty, report failure and exit.
3. For every f, let x_{i_f} be the lowest MTP variable of f.
4. For every graph $G : f \to g$, if it includes $x_{i_f} \xrightarrow{\downarrow} x'_{i_g}$, delete the graph from A'; otherwise, retain the graph but delete (or hide) the node x_{i_f} and incident arcs.
5. For every f, let $\rho(f, \sigma) = \langle \kappa_f, \sigma(x_{i_f}) \rangle$.
6. If A' is now vacant, return ρ. Otherwise, compute a ranking function ρ' recursively for A', and return $\rho \cdot \rho'$.

We claim that the abstract program A', passed to the recursive call, always represents the residual transition system T_A/ρ. This should be clear when we delete graphs that strictly decrease ρ. The less-trivial point is the treatment of graphs G where the MTP arc $x_{i_f} \to x_{i_g}$ is non-strict (Step 4). To obtain the residual system precisely we should have kept x_{i_f} with no-change arcs $x_{i_f} \xrightarrow{=} x_{i_g}$. However, having done so, the variables x_{i_f} for every f become a freezer, and therefore can be dropped (Lemma 5.9).

Dropping the "frozen" variables ensures that these variables will not be used again in ρ'. So in the final tuple $\rho_f \cdot \rho'_f$, each variable will occur at most once.

Finally, the ranking function for the original $\mathcal{A}$ can be obtained according to Lemma 5.5. We summarize the conclusion in a theorem:

Theorem 5.15. *Let $\mathcal{B}$ be a terminating MCS, with m flow-points and n variables per point. There is a ranking function ρ for $\mathcal{B}$ where $\rho_f(\sigma)$ is a case expression with inequality constraints as guards and elements of V_f^m as values. The complexity of construction (as well as the size of the output) is $\tilde{O}(m \cdot n^n)$.*

Even when restricting attention to SCT instances, these results improve upon previous publications. The improvement over [2] is that any positive instance can be handled, and the bound B in V_f^B is reduced from about $m \cdot 2^n$ to m; the improvement over [8] is that in that work, the vectors were possibly doubly exponential in length (as a function of n) and the complexity of the construction was only bounded by a triply exponential function.

6 Monotonicity Constraints over the Integers

In practice, the integers are clearly the predominant domain for the constraints; when they represent the size of a list or tree they are necessarily non-negative, which allows the well-founded model to be used, but it has often been pointed out that in imperative programming languages, in particular, the crucial variables often are of integer type and might be negative (by design or by mistake). With the integer type, monotonicity constraints are still useful: they can prove that in a loop, two values keep approaching each other—which can also be expressed as showing that $x \leq y$ is an invariant and $y - x$ descends. In this section we adapt the ideas of the previous sections to the integer domain. We do not consider the domain of non-negative integers separately but note that by including the constant 0 as a "variable" and indicating its relation to every variable known to be non-negative we reduce the problem to the general integer case.

An intuitive reduction of the integer case to the well-founded case is to create a new variable for every difference $x_i - x_j$ which can be deduced from the MCs to be non-negative, and also deduce relations among these new variables to obtain a constraint system. But this solution may square the number of variables, which is bad because this number is in the exponent of the complexity, and completeness is not obvious(why shouldn't other linear combinations be necessary?). We will tackle the problem directly. Due to space limitations, this part will be rather terse.

6.1 Termination

We begin by formulating a termination condition in combinatorial terms. To this end we generalize the notion of a thread and define an up-thread to be a thread that consists of inverse arcs (so it indicates an ascending chain). A down-thread is an ordinary thread.

Condition S (for Stable MCS). In any infinite multipath (with variables $x[t, i]$ as in Sec. 4.3) there is a up-thread $(x[k, l_k])_{k=k_0,k_0+1,...}$ and a down-thread $(x[k, h_k])_{k=k_0,k_0+1,...}$ such that all the constraints $x[k, l_k] \leq x[k, h_j]$ are present in the corresponding invariants. In addition, at least one of the threads has infinitely many strict arcs.

The condition for a general MCS is similar but uses walks instead of threads.

Condition G (for General MCS). In any infinite multipath (with variables $x[t, i]$) there is an infinite sequence of triples (t_j, l_j, h_j) such that the constraints in the multipath imply: $x[t_j, l_j] \leq x[t_j, h_j]$, $x[t_j, l_j] \leq x[t_{j+1}, l_{j+1}]$ and $x[t_j, h_j] \geq x[t_{j+1}, h_{j+1}]$. In addition, at least one of the walks $(x[t_j, l_j])_{j=1,2,...}$ and $(x[t_j, h_j])_{j=1,2,...}$ has infinitely many strict arcs.

Theorem 6.1. *Conditions* G *and* S *are equivalent for a stable system. Both are sound and complete criteria for termination of the respective transition systems.*

Condition S can be decided by a closure-based algorithm, which is essentially described in [4] (they consider non-negative integers but this difference is trivial).

6.2 Ranking Functions

Consider a fully elaborated system over the integers. If for every pair $x_i \leq x_j$ we create a variable x_{ij} to represent $x_j - x_i$ (as it is non-negative) and we connect such variables with the obvious size-change arcs (if $x_i \leq x'_l$ and $x_j \geq x'_h$ then $x_{ij} \geq x'_{lh}$) then Condition S implies ordinary size-change termination in the new variables. Thus a ranking function exists with such differences as elements of the vectors. Elaborating this system will put n^2 in the exponent. But it turns out that the order relations among the original variables lead to enough information about relations among the differences, that we can apply a version of the algorithm of Section 5. Thus, we can construct a global ranking function in $\tilde{O}(m \cdot n^n)$ time.

A final comment. In principle, we could abstract from the integers and just state the assumption that for any two elements there are only finitely many elements strictly between them. However, this abstraction buys us no generality, as every total order with this property is isomporphic to a subset of the integers.

7 Conclusion

We introduced the MCS abstraction, partly as background to our construction of ranking functions (which was initially developed with size-change graphs in mind), but also in order to explicate the ways in which our knowledge about SCT extends to this more expressive (and practically appealing) framework. This aspect should be seen as a call for further research, involving the application of monotonicity constraints.

The algorithms in this article were aimed at simplicity of presentation and analysis and can certainly be improved, for example by avoiding full elaboration.

For the decision procedure we know that this can be done (by stabilization), but creating practical applications of the procedure is a non-trivial challenge; more so for our ranking-function construction, where full elaboration was directly used in the proof, though it is clear that this does not mean that it is really always necessary.

We should point out that in the worst-case, the exponential behaviour cannot be beaten with this sort of global ranking functions. This is shown in [2], which actually provides a rather tight lower bound as it shows that $n!$ vectors may be needed for programs with n variables. On the bright side, our exponent is tight in that the algorithm is of complexity $m\,2^{O(n\log n)}$, like the lower bound, and unlike the $m^2 \cdot 2^{O(n^2)}$ upper bound of the closure algorithm.

Acknowledgments. The author thanks Chin Soon Lee for inspiration, and the LIPN laboratory at Université Paris 13 for hospitality.

References

[1] Ben-Amram, A.M., Lee, C.S.: Size-change analysis in polynomial time. ACM Transactions on Programming Languages and Systems 29(1) (2007)

[2] Ben-Amram, A.M., Lee, C.S.: Ranking functions for size-change termination II. Logical Methods in Computer Science (to appear, 2009)

[3] Brodsky, A., Sagiv, Y.: Inference of inequality constraints in logic programs. In: Proceedings of the Tenth ACM SIGACT-SIGMOD-SIGART Symposium on Principles of Database Systems (PODS), pp. 227–240. ACM Press, New York (1991)

[4] Codish, M., Lagoon, V., Stuckey, P.J.: Testing for termination with monotonicity constraints. In: Gabbrielli, M., Gupta, G. (eds.) ICLP 2005. LNCS, vol. 3668, pp. 326–340. Springer, Heidelberg (2005)

[5] Codish, M., Taboch, C.: A semantic basis for termination analysis of logic programs. The Journal of Logic Programming 41(1), 103–123 (1999); preliminary (conference) version in LNCS 1298. Springer, Heidelberg (1997)

[6] Cousot, P., Halbwachs, N.: Automatic discovery of linear restraints among variables of a program. In: Conference Record of the Fifth annual ACM Symposium on Principles of Programming Languages, pp. 84–96. ACM, New York (1978)

[7] Dershowitz, N., Lindenstrauss, N., Sagiv, Y., Serebrenik, A.: A general framework for automatic termination analysis of logic programs. Applicable Algebra in Engineering, Communication and Computing 12(1-2), 117–156 (2001)

[8] Lee, C.S.: Ranking functions for size-change termination. ACM Transactions on Programming Languages and Systems (to appear, 2009)

[9] Lee, C.S., Jones, N.D., Ben-Amram, A.M.: The size-change principle for program termination. In: Proceedings of the Twenty-Eigth ACM Symposium on Principles of Programming Languages, vol. 28, pp. 81–92. ACM Press, New York (2001)

[10] Lindenstrauss, N., Sagiv, Y.: Automatic termination analysis of Prolog programs. In: Naish, L. (ed.) Proceedings of the Fourteenth International Conference on Logic Programming, Leuven, Belgium, pp. 64–77. MIT Press, Cambridge (1997)

Linear Functional Fixed-Points

Nikolaj Bjørner and Joe Hendrix

Microsoft, One Microsoft Way, Redmond, WA, 98074, USA

{nbjorner,johendri}@microsoft.com

Abstract. We introduce a logic of functional fixed-points. It is suitable for analyzing heap-manipulating programs and can encode several logics used for program verification with different ways of expressing reachability. While full fixed-point logic remains undecidable, several subsets admit decision procedures. In particular, for the logic of linear functional fixed-points, we develop an abstraction refinement integration of the SMT solver Z3 and a satisfiability checker for propositional linear-time temporal logic. The integration refines the temporal abstraction by generating safety formulas until the temporal abstraction is unsatisfiable or a model for it is also a model for the functional fixed-point formula.

1 Introduction

Software often manipulates heap allocated data structures of finite but potentially unbounded size, such as linked lists, doubly linked lists, and trees. To reason about such structures, invariants about the *reachable* heap contents can be necessary. Logics capable of expressing interesting heap properties often require some form of transitive closure, fixed-points, and/or 2nd-order quantification. As is well known, complete first-order axiomatization of transitive closure is impossible [10], though approximations that suffice for ground validity of some fragments have been formulated. The approximations work directly with theories supported in the same (first-order) setting, but must rely on the capabilities of the generic first-order engine. A different approach is to directly use non-first order logics and rely on specialized decision procedures for these logics. Such specialized decision procedures do not suffice in practice when the invariants also require reasoning in the theories of arithmetic and arrays.

Contributions. This paper analyzes several different fixed-point logic fragments to identify expressive logics that still have good decidability and complexity results. On the practical side, we outline an integration procedure between propositional temporal logic checking and theory solvers.

- We formulate a logic called the *Equational Linear Functional Fixed Point Logic* (or FFP(E) for short). FFP(E) encodes several fixed point logics presented in recent literature on program verification.
- We establish that FFP(E) is PSPACE-complete modulo background theories that are in PSPACE by using a reduction from FFP(E) into propositional linear-time temporal logic. We show that two different extensions are NEXPTIME-hard and undecidable, respectively.

A. Bouajjani and O. Maler (Eds.): CAV 2009, LNCS 5643, pp. 124–139, 2009.
© Springer-Verlag Berlin Heidelberg 2009

– We provide a decision procedure for FFP(E) that combines the SMT solver Z3 with a (symbolic) satisfiability checking of propositional linear time temporal formulas. The proposed integration generalizes the standard abstraction/refinement framework used in SMT solvers. Instead of relying on refining a propositional model, we here refine a propositional linear time model. An early stage prototype of the procedure is available.

The resulting approach can therefore be viewed as a marriage between the flexible axiomatization approach to fixed-points and specialized decision procedures. Our abstraction/refinement framework admits all axiomatizations allowed by other approaches, but furthermore provides a decision procedure for formulas that fall into FFP(E).

Example 1 (A simple example). *We illustrate the use of reachability predicates using a simple example also used in [16]. It exercises transitivity. We use* $\forall x : [a \xrightarrow{f} b].\varphi(x)$ *to say that* $f^n(a) \simeq b$ *for some* n, *and for every* $k < n$ *it is the case that* $\varphi(f^k(a))$.

> **procedure** *INIT-CYCLIC(*head*)*
> $d(head) :=$ true; $curr := f(head)$;
>
>   **invariant** $d(head) \wedge \forall x : [f(head) \xrightarrow{f} curr].d(x)$
>   **while** $curr \neq head$ **do**
> $d(curr) :=$ true
> $curr := f(curr)$
>
>   **ensure** $d(head) \wedge \forall x : [f(head) \xrightarrow{f} head].d(x)$

The invariant and post-condition can be established by verifying properties:

$$\forall x : [f(head) \xrightarrow{f} curr].d(x) \wedge d(curr) \;\rightarrow\; \forall x : [f(head) \xrightarrow{f} f(curr)].d(x)$$

$$head \simeq curr \wedge \forall x : [f(head) \xrightarrow{f} curr].d(x) \;\rightarrow\; \forall x : [f(head) \xrightarrow{f} head].d(x)$$

While these particular properties hardly require the full might of transitive closure reasoning, we are here interested in characterizing the limits of what can be solved in a sufficiently general language with fixed-points.

Related work. We refer to [3] for an extended summary of the extensive related work. An early paper was by Greg Nelson [14], who gave 8 axioms for a ternary reachability predicate. The axioms are sufficient for a verification example, but general completeness with respect to ground validity was left as an open question. Several recent extensions and variants for ground validity have been pursued in [12,9,17,16,8]. These also develop first-order axiomatizations and rely on specialized rewriting or quantifier instantiation engines for their rules. The approach based on first-order axioms is of course quite extensible, as one can throw in useful axioms at will without requiring an encoding into a fixed limited formalism. On the other hand, the approach is only as viable as the strength of the quantifier instantiation heuristics. Balaban et al. [2] use a small model theorem to derive a decision procedure. A different line of work is based on automata-based decision procedures. The PALE system [13] can reason about heap-allocated data structures using weak monadic second-order logic of graph types. The logic of reachable patterns [21] is a decidable and quite expressive logic that combines local reasoning with an extended form of regular expressions. Finally in several practical cases, Separation Logic [18] provides a compelling alternative to reachability predicates.

Paper structure. The rest of this paper is structured as follows. In Section 2, we formally define functional fixed-point logic (FFP), and briefly review results from temporal logic used later in the paper. In Section 3, we study different fragments of FFP to obtain decidability and complexity results. Our main focus in this section is to define linear functional fixed-point logic with equality, FFP(E). We also show that FFP(E) is closed under updates, subsumes several different logics for reasoning about heap invariants, and has a PSPACE-complete satisfiability problem. In Section 4, we describe our reference satisfiability solver for FFP(E) which works by integrating the SMT-based theorem prover Z3 with a decision procedure for propositional LTL. Finally, in Section 5, we summarize our results and discuss ways our results can be extended in future research.

2   Preliminaries

Our results are mainly based on a reduction of FFP fragments into propositional linear-time temporal logic (LTL); and we rely on decision procedures for it. LTL [11] augments propositional logic with the temporal connectives $\mathcal{U}$, $\bigcirc$, $\square$ and $\diamondsuit$. LTL models are represented as an infinite sequence of states σ : $s_0, s_1, s_2, \ldots$, where each state supplies an assignment to propositional atoms. Recall that the operator $\mathcal{U}$ is the least fixed-point solution to the equivalence $A \mathcal{U} B \equiv (B \vee [A \wedge \bigcirc(A \mathcal{U} B)])$, or directly: $A \mathcal{U} B \equiv \mu X . B \vee (A \wedge \bigcirc X)$.

Functional Fixed-point Logic (FFP) extends quantifier-free first-order logic with the fixed-point operator μ to define the least fixed-point of unary predicates. To be more specific, we let x range over bound variables, X ranges over bound unary predicates, f and g range over distinguished unary uninterpreted function symbols, a, b, c, c' range over constant terms, P ranges over unary predicates, R over predicates containing neither bound variables, nor the function symbols f, g. Then the set of formulas φ in FFP are given by the rules:

$$t ::= f(t) \mid g(t) \mid c \mid x \qquad atom ::= X(t) \mid t \simeq t' \mid P(t) \mid R$$

$$A, B, \psi, \psi', \varphi ::= atom \mid \neg\varphi \mid \varphi \vee \varphi \mid \varphi \wedge \varphi \mid (\mu X .\lambda x . \varphi^+[X])(t)$$

where $\varphi^+[\_]$ is a positive context in φ.

The semantics of FFP follows the standard rules for evaluating fixed-point expressions. For example, a model $\mathcal{M}$ over a domain $\mathcal{A}$ satisfies $(\mu X .\lambda x . \varphi[X])(t)$ if $\mathcal{M}(t) \in \bigcap\{\mathcal{B} \subseteq \mathcal{A} \mid \mathcal{M}, [X \mapsto \mathcal{B}] \models \forall x . \varphi[X] \rightarrow X(x)\}$. FFP allows multiple different unary function symbols to be applied to the same bound variables, and allows multiple bound second-order predicates to appear in the same scope.

We will here restrict ourselves to a more modest fragment inspired by Linear Time Temporal Logic (LTL). In this fragment each fixed point expression has the form:

$$\mu X.\lambda x.(B \ \lor \ [A \land X(f(x))]),$$

where A and B are formulas that do not contain X, but may contain x. Intuitively, the function f is used as a next state transition.

Convention 2. *The following shorthands will be used throughout the paper:*

$$(A \ \mathcal{U}_{f,x} \ B)(c) = [\mu X.\lambda x.B \lor [A \land X(f(x))]](c)$$
$$(A \ \mathcal{W}_{f,x} \ B)(c) = \neg(\neg B \ \mathcal{U}_{f,x} \ \neg A \land \neg B)(c) \quad (\square_{f,x} \ B)(c) = \neg((\Diamond_{f,x} \ \neg B)(c))$$
$$\forall x : [a \xrightarrow{f} b].A = (A \ \mathcal{U}_{f,x} \ x \simeq b)(a) \quad (\Diamond_{f,x} \ B)(c) = (\text{true} \ \mathcal{U}_{f,x} \ B)(c)$$
$$\widetilde{\forall} x : [a \xrightarrow{f} b].A = (A \ \mathcal{W}_{f,x} \ x \simeq b)(a) \quad a \xrightarrow{f} b = (\Diamond_{f,x} \ x \simeq b)(a)$$

The connective $\mathcal{W}$ is inspired by the weak until *connective from LTL here, A holds either forever or until B is reached. We also include strong and weak versions for the case when A holds on every value between a and b.*

Convention 3. *The set of subformulas of a formula φ is denoted* SF(φ). *The set of atomic subformulas of φ is denoted* ASF(φ).

We will later establish that formulas in this more modest fragment are in general undecidable, and so we will study various subsets of it. Of particular utility is restricting the number of free variables that a formula may contain. We say that a formula φ is *linear* if each subformula $\psi \in$ SF(φ) has at most one free variable. As an example, the formula stating that c reaches an infinite number of elements, $(\square_{f,x} (\square_{f,y} \ y \not\simeq x) (f(x))) (c)$, is not a linear formula, because $y \not\simeq x$ has two free variables.

Normal forms of linear formulas. When a formula is linear, we can rename the variables in the formula to achieve a normal form which we use to simplify later exposition. Specifically, we give the same name to variables bound in nested quantifiers, while giving different names to variables bound in unrelated contexts. We are going to unfold fixed-points incrementally. In this context it is going to be useful to have an anchor on the bound variables. Therefore, for each top-level application of $(\varphi \ \mathcal{U}_{f,x} \ \psi)(t)$ we can introduce a fresh constant x that has the same name as the bound variable x, replace t by the variable, and add the constraint that $x \simeq t$. Thus, for instance

$$[x \not\simeq a \ \mathcal{U}_{f,x} \ P(x) \land (y \not\simeq b \ \mathcal{U}_{f,y} \ \neg P(y))(x)](c) \land (\Diamond_{g,x} \ x \simeq b)(c)$$

is converted into

$$[x \not\simeq a \ \mathcal{U}_{f,x} \ P(x) \land (x \not\simeq b \ \mathcal{U}_{f,x} \ \neg P(x))(x)](x) \land x \simeq c$$
$$\land (\Diamond_{g,y} \ y \simeq b)(y) \land y \simeq c.$$

This transformation allows us to distinguish variables occurring in unrelated fixed-point expressions while identifying variables occurring in related sub-expressions.

Atomic formulas containing unbound variables are called *flexible*; otherwise, they are called *rigid* atoms. For example $x \simeq c$ and $ff(x) \simeq x$ are flexible atoms, while $c \simeq f(c')$ and $P(f(c))$ are rigid atomic formulas.

We will use a shorthand $\textcircled{f}$ for distributing an application f over all free variables. For example, $\textcircled{f}(x \simeq f(x) \land \textcircled{f}(\psi \, \mathcal{U}_{f,x} \, \psi')(x))$ is short for $(f(x) \simeq f(f(x)) \land (\psi \, \mathcal{U}_{f,x} \, \psi')(f(f(x))))$.

3   Complexity Results for FFP Logics

We will here introduce various variants of FFP and summarize relevant complexity results. Fig. 1 summarizes how the examined fragments relate to each other in terms of generality. 2FFP(E) is the fragment of linear FFP allowing at most two functions f and g to be nested inside fixed-point operators. FFP(NL) does not allow nesting of functions inside fixpoint operators, but does allow non-linear subformulas. We will show that satisfiability of 2FFP(E) is undecidable while satisfiability of FFP(NL) is NEXPTIME-hard. FFP(E) is the linear fragment of FFP(NL), and FFP(PL) is the purely propositional fragment of FFP(E).

3.1   FFP(PL)

We first study the propositional fragment of FFP, called FFP(PL). It corresponds very closely to linear time temporal logic, the only real difference is that the temporal subformulas refer to an explicit *anchor*, as a constant.

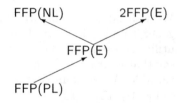

Fig. 1. Relative expressiveness of the FFP fragments

Formulas in FFP(PL) have the form:

$$\varphi ::= P(t) \mid R \mid \varphi \land \varphi \mid \neg\varphi \mid (\varphi \, \mathcal{U}_{f,x} \, \varphi)(t)$$
$$t ::= f^n(x) \mid f^n(c)$$

where x is a variable, $f^n(x)$ is the n-time application of f to x, c is an arbitrary *rigid* term (without variables), P is a unary predicate, and R is a relation using only rigid terms.

FFP(PL) is formulated to be very similar to propositional LTL. It is indeed very straightforward to translate formulas from LTL to FFP(PL) and to translate formulas from FFP(PL) into equisatisfiable formulas in LTL. The correspondence can be used to establish:

Theorem 4. FFP(PL) *is PSPACE complete.*

Proof (Sketch). We can embed LTL into FFP(PL) using transformations, such as $\Diamond \bigcirc P \mapsto (\Diamond_{f,x} P(f(x)))(x)$. Conversely, we can translate FFP(PL) formulas into LTL by dropping the explicit variable references and annotating predicates based on the context they appear, e.g.,

$$(\Diamond_{f,y} P(y))(d) \mapsto \Diamond P_d \quad \text{and} \quad (P(x) \, \mathcal{U}_{f,x} \, Q(f(x)))(ff(c)) \mapsto \bigcirc\bigcirc(P_c \, \mathcal{U} \bigcirc Q_c).$$

By reusing results from [19], we can take advantage of the reduction to LTL and obtain a few results on NP-complete subsets "for free". For instance, Sistla and Clarke show that linear-time temporal logic using only the operators $\square$ and $\lozenge$ is NP-complete, and so is the case if formulas are in positive normal form using $\lozenge$ and $\bigcirc$. The corresponding FFP(PL) subsets are therefore also NP-complete.

3.2   FFP(E)

We will now consider an extension of FFP(PL) by admitting equality predicates on terms containing bound variables. The resulting logic is called FFP(E). In contrast to FFP(PL), the embedding into LTL is less straightforward, since the equalities interact in an essential way with the models for the propositional temporal abstraction. Formulas in FFP(E) extend FFP(PL) by admitting atomic formulas that are equalities between terms containing variables, constants, and distinguished functions used in fixed-points. We use f and g to refer to the distinguished functions. For simplicity we will assume that formulas in FFP(E) use just two functions f and g in the fixed-points. The generalization to multiple functions is simple.

The operators $\widehat{f}$ and $\widehat{g}$ are used to limit the number possible equality predicates to consider. We also admit terms where the distinguished functions f and g are applied to a constant. Thus, formulas of FFP(E) are of the form:

$$\varphi, \varphi' ::= f^n(x) \simeq x \mid g^n(x) \simeq x \mid c \simeq f(c') \mid c \simeq g(c') \mid \widehat{g}\varphi \mid \widehat{f}\varphi \mid x \simeq c \mid c \simeq c'$$
$$\mid P(x) \mid R \mid \neg\varphi \mid \varphi \vee \varphi' \mid \varphi \wedge \varphi' \mid (\varphi \, \mathcal{U}_{f,x} \, \varphi')(x) \mid (\varphi \, \mathcal{U}_{g,x} \, \varphi')(x)$$

such that the formulas φ and φ' in $(\varphi \, \mathcal{U}_{f,x} \, \varphi')(x)$ contain at most one free variable, which is x. So we require every bound variable to appear linearly.

We furthermore restrict applications of f and g so that they do not appear together in the same flexible formula. Specifically, for each subformula $(\varphi \, \mathcal{U}_{f,x} \, \varphi')(t)$, g may not appear in φ or φ'. A similar condition is also required where the roles of f and g are exchanged. Thus,

$$(\lozenge_{f,x} \, x \simeq a)(c) \wedge (\lozenge_{g,y} \, y \simeq b)(c)$$

is a legal formula in FFP(E), but

$$(\lozenge_{f,x} \, x \simeq a)(c) \wedge (\lozenge_{g,y} \, \widehat{f}(y \simeq b))(c)$$

is not, because both f and g are used on the same variable y. In general, this restriction is necessary to ensure our complexity result in Theorem 10. However, when g does not directly refer to the same variable x, one can introduce fresh rigid predicates to normalize the formula into an equisatisfiable formula with this restricted form. For example,

$$(\lozenge_{f,x} \, x = c \wedge (\square_{g,x} \, P(x))(b))(a)$$

can be expressed as the equisatisfiable formula

$$(\lozenge_{f,x} \, x = c \wedge r)(a) \wedge (r \iff (\square_{g,x} \, P(x))(b)).$$

It is not hard to see that we can build all combinations of equality predicates using one variable x, the function f and up to two constants c and c' using the base cases $f^n(x) \simeq x$, $x \simeq c$, $c \simeq f(c')$, $c \simeq c'$ and the operator $\textcircled{f}\psi$. For example $\varphi[f(c) \simeq ff(c'), f(x) \simeq c]$ is equisatisfiable to the formula $c_1 \simeq f(c) \wedge c_2 \simeq f(c') \wedge \varphi[c_1 \simeq f(c_2), \textcircled{f}(x \simeq c)]$. We will use the operator $\textcircled{f}$ in two ways: in a *temporal view* and a *ground view*. In the temporal view, we do not normalize the formula with respect to the definition of $\textcircled{f}$; the use of $\textcircled{f}$ is essential for bridging FFP(E) with LTL. In the ground view, we distribute $\textcircled{f}$ over the free variables such that $\textcircled{f}$ gets eliminated.

Even very small examples can show how the interaction between equalities makes checking the satisfiability of FFP(E) more complex. For example, the following unsatisfiable formula illustrates how distinct constants can not be as easily partitioned as was done in FFP(PL):

$$(\Diamond_{f,x} \, x \simeq c \wedge \textcircled{f}P(x)) \, (a) \wedge (\Diamond_{f,x} \, x \simeq c \wedge \neg \textcircled{f}P(x)) \, (b).$$

The first conjunct implies that $P(f(c))$, but the second required $\neg P(f(c))$, although $P(f(c))$ does not directly appear in the formulas.

To illustrate how equalities and predicates may interact, consider the formula:

$$(\Diamond_{f,x} \, x \simeq f^3(x)) \, (a) \wedge (\Diamond_{f,x} \, x \simeq f^2(x)) \, (a) \wedge (\Box_{f,x} (\textcircled{f}P(x) \iff \neg P(x))) \, (a)$$

The first two conjuncts require that $f^{i+3}(a) = f^i(a)$ and $f^{j+2}(a) = f^j(a)$ for some i and j in $\mathbb{N}$. Collectively, this implies that $f(f^k(a)) = f^k(a)$ for $k \geq \min(i, j)$. Conversely, the third clause requires that the value of P changes at each dereference, and consequently, $f(f^k(a))$ cannot equal $f^k(a)$.

Expressivity of FFP(E). We make a case that the FFP(E) logic is quite general and expressive. It subsumes several (but not all) logics recently proposed for reasoning about heaps. We summarize some of the properties that can be expressed in FFP by encoding logics from the literature on verification of heap manipulating programs.

Example 5 (Transitive Closure of f). *Suppose we let $f^*(a, b)$ mean that there is a sequence of 0 or more applications of f to a that produces an element b. That is, $f^*(a, b) \equiv \exists n \, . \, f^n(a) \simeq b$. This can be easily represented:*

$$f^*(a, b) \equiv (\Diamond_{f,x} \, x \simeq b) \, (a) \equiv a \xrightarrow{f} b$$

Example 6 (Reachability Invariants [14]). *Nelson introduced a ternary predicate $u \xrightarrow[w]{f} v$ which indicates that u reaches v without going through w. It can be used to verify a program that computes the union of two sets represented as doubly linked lists, and can be expressed in FFP(E) as: $u \xrightarrow[w]{f} v \equiv (x \not\simeq w \, \mathcal{U} \,_{f,x} \, x \simeq v) \, (u)$.*

Example 7 (Well-Founded Reachability [7]). *Lahiri and Qadeer use blocking set predicates BS to identify distinguished elements in potentially cyclic data structures.Blocking sets generalize Nelson's blocking variable.Under the assumption that every node eventually reaches a blocker, they can define the program* *verification-friendly functions and predicates:* FFP(E) *allows formulating these predicates directly:*

$$B(u) \simeq v \;\equiv\; (\neg BS(x)\; \mathcal{U}_{f,x}\; x \simeq v)\,(u) \wedge BS(v)$$
$$R(u,v) \;\equiv\; (\neg BS(f(x))\; \mathcal{U}_{f,x}\; x \simeq v)\,(u)$$

Example 8 (btwn$_f$ **[16]**). *The dual to Nelson's reachability predicate is the predicate* btwn$_f(a,b,c)$ *which requires b is visited before c. It is versatile for a wide range of program verification cases, and can be defined as:*

$$\text{btwn}_f(a,b,c) \equiv (x \not\simeq c\; \mathcal{U}_{f,x}\; x \simeq b)\,(a) \wedge b \xrightarrow{f} c$$

FFP(E) is also closed under the weakest-precondition predicate transformer, when a pointwise update is made to the function f:

Proposition 9. FFP(E) *is closed under pointwise functional updates. As we show in [3]: if* $\varphi[f]$ *is in* FFP(E)*, then for constants* u *and* v*, the formula* $\varphi[\lambda y.\text{if } y \simeq u \text{ then } v \text{ else } f(y)]$ *can also be expressed in* FFP(E)*.*

Theorem 10. *The satisfiability problem of* FFP(E) *is PSPACE-complete.*

Proof (Sketch [3]). We reduce FFP(E) to LTL, and use the PSPACE-completeness result from [19]. The reductions follow 3 transformations Tableau, Erase, and Embed:

$$\varphi \xrightarrow{\quad\text{Tableau}\quad} Tab(\varphi) \xrightarrow{\quad\text{Erase}\quad} \varphi_{PTL} \xrightarrow{\quad\text{Embed}\quad} \varphi_{PTL*}$$

Each of the transformations can be done in polynomial time and space, with the last transformation being the most expensive, requiring quadratic space.

Tableau. The tableau normal form [11] of a formula φ is a conjunction of the form:

$$Tab(\varphi):\; \lceil \varphi \rceil \wedge Next \wedge Inv \wedge \bigwedge_{F \in \mathcal{F}} \Box \Diamond F$$

where $\lceil \varphi \rceil$ replaces the top-most occurrences of $\bigcirc$ and $\mathcal{U}_{f,x}$ subformulas by fresh auxiliary propositional variables, *Next* encodes an accessibility relation over the original and auxiliary propositional variables, *Inv* is a state invariant that ensures that the interpretation of temporal connectives is consistent on every state; and the set $\mathcal{F}$ contains the set of acceptance conditions:

$$\lceil (\psi\; \mathcal{U}_{f,x}\; \psi') \rceil(x) \;\rightarrow\; \lceil \psi' \rceil \text{ for each } (\psi\; \mathcal{U}_{f,x}\; \psi')\,(x) \in \text{SF}(\varphi).$$

Erase. The propositional erasure converts an FFP(E) formula φ into an LTL formula φ_{PTL} by using the transformations:

$$((\psi\; \mathcal{U}_{f,x}\; \psi')\,(x))_{PTL} = \psi_{PTL}\; \mathcal{U}\; \psi'_{PTL} \quad \text{and} \quad (\bigcirc\psi)_{PTL} = \bigcirc\psi_{PTL}.$$

Embed. The heart of the reduction is to add a sufficient set of axioms such that the LTL formula is equisatisfiable with the FFP(E) formula. The formula φ_{PTL*} is obtained by enumerating the atomic subformulas of φ and adding the conjunctions, whenever there are atomic formulas matching the pre-conditions of the implications:

$$x \simeq c \;\Rightarrow\; \bigcirc\, (x \not\simeq c \; \mathcal{W} \; F) \quad F \in \mathcal{F}(x) \tag{1}$$

$$f^n(x) \simeq x \Rightarrow (\ell(x) \leftrightarrow \bigcirc^n \ell(x)) \tag{2}$$

$$f^n(x) \simeq x \wedge f^m(x) \simeq x \;\Rightarrow\; f^{\gcd(m,n)}(x) \simeq x \tag{3}$$

$$f^n(x) \not\simeq x \wedge x \simeq c \;\Rightarrow\; \bigcirc^n (x \not\simeq c) \tag{4}$$

$$f^n(x) \not\simeq x \wedge f^m(x) \simeq x \;\Rightarrow\; f^{n-m}(x) \not\simeq x \quad n > m \tag{5}$$

$$f^n(x) \simeq x \Rightarrow \bigcirc(f^n(x) \simeq x) \tag{6}$$

$$x \simeq c \wedge \ell(x) \;\Rightarrow\; R_{\ell,c} \tag{7}$$

$$x \simeq c \;\Rightarrow\; (x \simeq c' \;\leftrightarrow\; c \simeq c') \tag{8}$$

$$c \simeq f(c') \wedge x \simeq c' \;\Rightarrow\; \bigcirc(x \simeq c) \tag{9}$$

$$x_{f,c} \simeq c \wedge (R_{\ell c} \;\rightarrow\; \ell(x_{f,c})) \tag{10}$$

$$\square E - taut \tag{11}$$

Let us motivate the conditions a bit. The condition (1) ensures that all acceptance conditions mentioning x are visited between two anchor states where x is equal to a constant anchor c. It can still be the case that f is periodic on x, but x is not constrained to be a constant; conditions (2), (3), and (6) handle such cases and enforce that once f is periodic it remains so, it satisfies congruence closure over the period, and that states are identical after n steps. Conditions (4) and (5) ensure that the state literals are consistent with disequalities $f^n(x) \not\simeq x$. The last set of invariants (11) are the set of tautologies needed to axiomatize the theory of equality for the rigid predicates. They are the counterpart to the axioms (7)–(9) which are used to axiomatize the theory of equality inside temporal subformulas. The conditions (7) and (10) are used to force evaluations after each constant anchor to be consistent across different variables. They use the rigid predicate $R_{\ell,c}$, which is introduced for every literal $\ell(x)$ and constant c. Suppose that one state s_1 requires the variable x to satisfy $x \simeq c$. Another state s_2 requires a different variable y to satisfy $y \simeq c$. These states must satisfy the same literals $\ell(x)$ respectively $\ell(y)$. To ensure that also the states following s_1 and s_2 evaluate the same literals in tandem we use condition (10) which uses the new variable $x_{f,c}$ and will involve all literals associated with x and y, and any other variable that anchors with c.

Let us assume that the variables are x, y, z. To extract a model $\mathcal{M}$ of φ from an LTL model $\sigma = s_1, s_2, s_3 \ldots$ of φ_{PTL*}, we partition each state $s_i \in \sigma$ into $s_i(x)$, $s_i(y)$, and $s_i(z)$. The state $s_i(x)$ contains all the assignments to the atomic subformulas using the variable x. For each variable x, there are 3 cases to consider: (1) $x \simeq c$ appears in both $s_i(x)$ and $s_j(x)$ for some indices $i < j$ but $x \simeq c$ is not in any other state before $s_j(x)$. (2) $f^n(x) \simeq x$ appears in some state $s_j(x)$, but not in any earlier states; and (3) neither cases (1) or (2) apply and consequently each equality $x \simeq c$ appears in at most one state in σ.

In the first case, we add fresh elements $a_1, \ldots, a_{j-1}$, set $f(a_k) = a_{k+1}$ for $k < j - 1$, set $f(a_{j-1}) = a_i$, and assign predicates based on the assignments to the states $s_1(x), \ldots, s_{j-1}$. We are guaranteed acceptance conditions are satisfied by the axioms (1). In the second case, we add fresh elements $a_1, \ldots, a_{i+n-1}$, and assign f and the predicates in the obvious way, with $f(a_{i+n-1}) = a_i$. We are guaranteed consistency by the axioms (2)–(6). In the final case, we add an infinite sequence of fresh elements $a_1, a_2, \ldots$.

3.3   Extensions to FFP(E)

In this section, we analyze the complexity of two extensions to FFP(E).

FFP(NL) is the fragment of FFP that admits only a single function symbol f with fixed-point expressions, but allows different bound variables to appear together in the same scope. We can reduce FFP(NL) to monadic second order logic by translating each fixed-point expression $(\mu R.\lambda x.C[R])t$ into an equivalent second-order expression $(\forall Z)\,(\forall x.Z(x) \iff C[Z](x)) \implies Z(t)$.

Both weak and strong monadic second-order logic with a single function symbol is decidable [4] (Corollary 7.2.11 and 7.2.12). So FFP(NL) logic is decidable. The second-order theory of one unary function is on the other hand not elementary recursive. It does not necessarily follow that FFP(NL) is non-elementary as well, but we establish in [3] that FFP(NL) is at least NEXPTIME-hard. Our proof is inspired by a similar construction for LRP [21], and reduces the NEXPTIME-complete problem of deciding whether a tiling problem $\mathcal{T}$ admits a tiling compatible with $\mathcal{T}$ on a square grid of size $2^n \times 2^n$.

FFP(NL) does not enjoy the finite model property. For example:

Proposition 11. *The sentence* $(\square_{f,x} (\square_{f,y} x \not\simeq y) (f(x)))\,(c)$ *is satisfiable by an infinite model, but unsatisfiable for finite models.*

In [3], we use this result to show that FFP(NL) is incomparable with the *Logic of Reachable Patterns (LRP)* [21]. LRP allows reasoning backwards along edges, and consequently can specify properties that FFP(NL) cannot. However, LRP has the finite model theory whereas by Prop. 11, FFP(NL) does not. We are not aware of any matching lower and upper bounds on the complexity of FFP(NL), neither do we know if the weak theory (that only admits finite models) of FFP(NL) is any easier than full FFP(NL).

We also consider the fragment of FFP where multiple function symbols are allowed to be associated with the temporal connectives and we are allowed to nest different functions over the variables. We call this fragment 2FFP(E). Among other things, this logic allows us to encode arbitrarily large grids. For example, we can express that functions f and g commute over all nodes reachable from a given constant c

$$(\square_{f,x} [\square_{g,y} f(g(y)) \simeq g(f(y))]x)\,(c)$$

We show in [3] that the satisfiability problem for this logic is undecidable. The proof uses a commonly used reduction from tiling problems. It is very similar to results in [6,21].

4   SMT Solver Integration

This section describes how Theorem 10 can be used to provide a decision procedure for FFP(E) together with a background theory $\mathcal{T}$. The theorem suggests a direct embedding of FFP(E) into LTL, but this is not always necessary, and we here examine how intermediary steps can be used. The approach we will present is analogous to how SAT solvers may be combined with decision procedures, except, instead of extracting conflict clauses for a propositional SAT solver, we extract temporal safety formulas to refine a propositional LTL abstraction.

4.1   FFP and Theories

Our formulation of FFP(E) uses auxiliary constants a, b, c but does not say whether there are any additional constraints on the constants. This is a convenient simplification for presenting FFP(E), but we would like integrating FFP(E) with other theories, such as the theories $\mathcal{T}$ of arrays and linear arithmetic. These theories can directly be combined in a Nelson-Oppen [15] framework of signature disjoint, stably infinite theories. In this setting FFP(E) can treat subterms that use symbols from other theories as constants. The theory EUF of uninterpreted theories is half-way built into FFP(E) because it relies on congruence closure over unary functions. SMT solvers most commonly provide general purpose congruence closure decision procedures, and these can be used directly for the unary functions used in the FFP(E) fragment.

We here observe that the Nelson-Oppen combination result can also be used for FFP(E). Formally, FFP(E) is not a first-order theory, yet it can still satisfy the conditions for a Nelson-Oppen combination: First, FFP(E) is stably infinite. In other words, if a formula φ over FFP(E) has a model, it has a model of any larger cardinality. This follows because the evaluation of φ only depends on values of the original auxiliary constants a, b, c, their forward closure under a fixed set of unary functions f, g, and the values of unary predicates (P, Q) over the closure. The original model will already fix their interpretation. Second, we will assume that the unary predicates and functions used for FFP(E) formulas are not used in other theories. This restriction is required for completeness. For example, the combination result does not apply to the formula $(\Box_{f,x} \, read(x) \leq read(f(x))) \, (a)$ which uses arithmetical relation $\leq$ and the shared function $read$.

To summarize, we have:

Theorem 12. *Let φ be a formula over FFP(E) $+ \mathcal{T}$, where $\mathcal{T}$ is stably infinite decidable theory whose signature is disjoint from the unary functions and predicates used by FFP(E). Then satisfiability of φ is decidable.*

Proof (Sketch). (1) We first *purify* φ to create a conjunction $\varphi_{\mathsf{FFP(E)}} \wedge \varphi_{\mathcal{T}}$, such that $\varphi_{\mathsf{FFP(E)}}$ uses only the vocabulary from $\mathsf{FFP(E)}$, and $\varphi_{\mathcal{T}}$ uses only the vocabulary from $\mathcal{T}$. The two conjuncts may share constants $a, b, c, \dots$ (2) Then apply Theorem 10 to $\varphi_{\mathsf{FFP(E)}}$ to obtain φ_{PTL*}. (3) Create the conjunction φ_{Frame} comprising of the frame conditions $\Box(a \simeq b) \vee \Box(a \not\simeq b)$ for each pair of constants a, b that occur in both conjuncts. The resulting formula $\varphi_{PTL*} \wedge \varphi_{\mathcal{T}} \wedge \varphi_{Frame}$ is equisatisfiable with φ. Furthermore, since $\mathsf{FFP(E)}$ is stably infinite we can reconstruct the Nelson-Oppen combination result and observe that it is satisfiable iff there is a propositional LTL model σ for $\varphi_{PTL*} \wedge \varphi_{Frame}$ and model $\mathcal{M}$ for $\varphi_{\mathcal{T}}$, such that $\sigma \models a \simeq b$ iff $\mathcal{M} \models a \simeq b$ for each pair of shared variables a, b.

4.2   Abstraction/Refinement Solver Combinations

The proof of Theorem 12 could suggest applying the transformations from Theorem 10 eagerly. The drawback is that a potential quadratic number of new formulas are created in the process. We will therefore develop a method that integrates with an SMT solver, such as Z3 [5], in a more incremental way. The integration is a bit similar to how state-of-the-art SAT solving techniques are used in SMT solvers: The SAT solver treats each interpreted atom in a formula as a propositional atom. It provides propositional models that assign each atom to *true* or *false*. We will use s to refer to a propositional model, and it will be represented as the set of atomic formulas that are true in the propositional model. A propositional model s of a formula φ corresponds to a conjunction of literals:

$$L := \bigwedge_{a \in \mathrm{ASF}(\varphi), a \in s} a \ \wedge \bigwedge_{a \in \mathrm{ASF}(\varphi), a \notin s} \neg a$$

The theory solvers check the propositional models for $\mathcal{T}$ consistency. If the conjunction is $\mathcal{T}$-unsatisfiable, then there is a minimal subset $L' \subseteq L$ such that $\mathcal{T} \wedge L'$ is inconsistent. The SAT solver can in exchange learn the clause $\neg L'$ and has to search for a propositional model that avoids L'.

An incremental integration of a solver for LTL with a $\mathcal{T}$ solver is a simple generalization. Instead of refining a propositional model s, we here refine a propositional temporal model σ that is generated by a propositional LTL solver.

1. *Purify*: From the original formula φ create the purified and separated conjunction $\varphi_{\mathsf{FFP(E)}} \wedge \varphi_{\mathcal{T}}$.
2. *Erase*: Create a temporal abstraction φ_{PTL} from $\varphi_{\mathsf{FFP(E)}}$. This formula does not contain the embedding axioms.
3. *Incremental Embed*: If φ_{PTL} has a temporal model σ, then check (a) that each state is consistent with $\varphi_{\mathcal{T}}$, (b) that σ evalutes rigid subformulas to

In the limit, this procedure produces $\varphi_{PTL*} \wedge \varphi_{Frame}$. On the other hand, it allows first adding partial constraints that increase the complexity of checking propositional temporal satisfiability only incrementally. It also allows interposing partial checks on σ that result in a modest cost for the LTL checking phase.

Example 13 (Neighbor consistency). *Suppose the model σ contains the sequence of states $s_0, s_1, \ldots$, and suppose that s_0 contains the state assignment $c \simeq f(c') \wedge x \simeq c' \wedge \neg P(c)$, and s_1 contains the state assignment $P(x)$. The states cannot be neighbors because the conjunction*

$$c \simeq f(c') \wedge x \simeq c' \wedge \neg P(c) \wedge \textcircled{\tiny\textit{f}} P(x) \;\equiv\; c \simeq f(c') \wedge x \simeq c' \wedge \neg P(c) \wedge P(f(x))$$

is contradictory. To rule out this case, it suffices to add the safety formula

$$c \simeq f(c') \wedge x \simeq c' \wedge \neg P(c) \;\Rightarrow\; \neg \bigcirc P(x),$$

or equivalently strengthen the accessiblity relation Next.

Example 14 (Cross-state consistency). *The two states s_1 and s_2 are contradictory if s_1 entails the assignment $P(x) \wedge x \simeq c$ and state s_2 entails the assignment $\neg P(y) \wedge y \simeq c$ for potentially different variables x and y. Such a situation is ruled out if we apply safety condition (7) for every pair of variables x, y, and every literal $\ell(x)$, but cross-state consistency checking will also capture this case. The resulting safety condition is in this case*

$$\square \neg (P(x) \wedge x \simeq c) \;\vee\; \square \neg (\neg P(y) \wedge y \simeq c)$$

A set of relevant tests are in order of their overhead:

State consistency: Each state can be checked for consistency in isolation. If the state is not $\mathcal{T}$ consistent, we can constrain the LTL abstraction by adding an invariant to rule out the inconsistent state. The saturation condition E-taut is contained in the state consistency check.

Cross-state consistency: The conjunction of states can be checked for consistency. If the conjunction is inconsistent, then generate a disjunction of invariants to rule out the inconsistent combination of states. This check requires creating fresh copies of variables so that their evaluation is not fixed across states. Cross-state consistency implies state consistency, but requires checking a larger formulas.

Neighbor consistency: Each pair of consecutive states s_i, s_{i+1} can be checked for relative consistency. In contrast to cross-state consistency, we only need one copy of the variables; the occurrences of the variable x in s_{i+1} is replaced by $f(x)$. If some pair of states is found to not be consecutive, one can add an additional safety constraint. The safety constraint does not increase the set of states reachable in the temporal tableau. Neighbor and cross-state consistency can be used to enforce the frame condition φ_{Frame}.

Saturation consistency: In the spirit of approaches based on first-order encodings of fixed-point logics [8,12,16] we can saturate φ_{FFP} using a first-order approximation. In the context of $\mathsf{FFP(E)}$, we can enforce some properties of $\mathcal{U}$ by instantiating the axiom:

$$\forall x \; . \; \lceil(\psi \; \mathcal{U}_{f,x} \; \psi')\rceil(x) \; \leftrightarrow \; \psi' \vee (\psi \wedge \lceil(\psi \; \mathcal{U}_{f,x} \; \psi')\rceil(f(x))).$$

There are two ways to instantiate this axiom in a way that avoids indefinite unfoldings. The first is to instantiate it whenever there is a ground subformula in $\varphi_{\mathsf{FFP(E)}}$ congruent to $\lceil(\psi \; \mathcal{U}_{f,x} \; \psi')\rceil(f(t))$ for some t. The second is to instantiate it when both $f(t)$ and $\lceil(\psi \; \mathcal{U}_{f,x} \; \psi')\rceil(t)$ appear in $\varphi_{\mathsf{FFP(E)}}$. The Z3 solver allows controlling such instantiations using so called E-matching on patterns. Note that saturation consistency can in some cases completely replace all other checks. This is the case when there is a complete axiomatization for ground queries using quantifiers, as in [8].

Embedding consistency: Finally, the auxiliary axioms (1)-(11) required for a full embedding can be added lazily by only adding axioms that are violated by the current model.

5   Conclusions and Future Work

In this paper, we have introduced several ground first-order logics with fixed-points, and shown how satisfiability for the functional fixed-point logic with equality $\mathsf{FFP(E)}$ can be reduced to checking satisfiability of linear-time temporal formulas. Furthermore, we have developed and implemented an abstraction/refinement framework that integrates an LTL solver with an SMT solver to efficiently solve $\mathsf{FFP(E)}$ satisfiability problems directly.

Our choice of LTL as the target is a matter of convenience that was useful for identifying NP-complete subsets of $\mathsf{FFP(PL)}$ in Section 3.1. We suspect that one can extend those techniques to identify fragments of $\mathsf{FFP(E)}$ with an NP-complete decision problem. Our reduction to $\mathsf{FFP(E)}$ satisfiability checking was reduced to checking satisfiability of tableau normal forms. It is well-known that the tableau construction captures more than LTL; it also allows for handling formulas in the extended temporal logic, ETL [20]. In ETL, we can for instance express $\forall n \geq 0.P(f^{2n}(a))$. It is expressible as $(\nu X \lambda x.X(ff(x)) \wedge P(x))(a)$, but does not correspond to a formula in $\mathsf{FFP(E)}$. Nevertheless, the satisfiability of such formulas can be checked using the same apparatus developed in this paper.

While simple extensions of $\mathsf{FFP(E)}$ are undecidable, there are decidable classes of formulas that can be formulated using functional fixed-points, yet they cannot be formulated in $\mathsf{FFP(E)}$. For example [8] studies a fragment based on the predicate $\forall x : [a \xrightarrow{f} b].\varphi$ that allows multiple functions and variables to interact. Among other things, their predicate allows one to specify the formula

$$\forall x : [a \xrightarrow{f} nil]. \left(x = nil \vee \forall y : [f(x) \xrightarrow{f} nil].y \not\simeq x \right)$$

which states that the elements in the list from a to nil are distinct. The formula refers simultaneously to multiple dereference functions. The reduction to LTL does not work when there are multiple bound variables: The LTL reduction requires that at most one variable is affected in the tableau state transitions. We are investigating whether *freeze* quantifiers, which were developed in the context of real-time temporal logic [1] can be applied. We thank the reviewers, Sergio Mera and Margus Veanes for valuable feedback.

References

1. Alur, R., Henzinger, T.A.: A really temporal logic. J. ACM 41(1), 181–204 (1994)
2. Balaban, I., Pnueli, A., Zuck, L.D.: Shape analysis of single-parent heaps. In: Cook, B., Podelski, A. (eds.) VMCAI 2007. LNCS, vol. 4349, pp. 91–105. Springer, Heidelberg (2007)
3. Bjørner, N., Hendrix, J.: Linear functional fixed-points. Technical Report MSR-TR-2009-8, Microsoft Research (2009)
4. Börger, E., Grädel, Gurevich: The Classical Decision Problem. Springer, Heidelberg (1996)
5. de Moura, L., Bjørner, N.: Z3: An Efficient SMT Solver. In: Ramakrishnan, C.R., Rehof, J. (eds.) TACAS 2008. LNCS, vol. 4963, pp. 337–340. Springer, Heidelberg (2008)
6. Immerman, N., Rabinovich, A.M., Reps, T.W., Sagiv, S., Yorsh, G.: The boundary between decidability and undecidability for transitive-closure logics. In: Marcinkowski, J., Tarlecki, A. (eds.) CSL 2004. LNCS, vol. 3210, pp. 160–174. Springer, Heidelberg (2004)
7. Lahiri, S.K., Qadeer, S.: Verifying properties of well-founded linked lists. In: Principles of Programming Languages (POPL 2006), pp. 115–126 (2006)
8. Lahiri, S.K., Qadeer, S.: Back to the future: revisiting precise program verification using SMT solvers. In: POPL, pp. 171–182. ACM, New York (2008)
9. Lev-Ami, T., Immerman, N., Reps, T.W., Sagiv, S., Srivastava, S., Yorsh, G.: Simulating reachability using first-order logic with applications to verification of linked data structures. In: Nieuwenhuis, R. (ed.) CADE 2005. LNCS, vol. 3632, pp. 99–115. Springer, Heidelberg (2005)
10. Libkin, L.: Elements of Finite Model Theory. Springer, Heidelberg (2004)
11. Manna, Z., Pnueli, A.: Temporal Verification of Reactive Systems: Safety. Springer, Heidelberg (1995)
12. McPeak, S., Necula, G.C.: Data structure specifications via local equality axioms. In: Etessami, K., Rajamani, S.K. (eds.) CAV 2005. LNCS, vol. 3576, pp. 476–490. Springer, Heidelberg (2005)
13. Møller, A., Schwartzbach, M.I.: The pointer assertion logic engine. In: Programming Language Design and Implementation (PLDI 2001), pp. 221–231 (2001)
14. Nelson, G.: Verifying Reachability Invariants of Linked Structures. In: Principles of Programming Languages (POPL 1983), pp. 38–47 (1983)
15. Nelson, G., Oppen, D.C.: Simplification by cooperating decision procedures. ACM Transactions on Programming Languages and Systems 1(2), 245–257 (1979)
16. Rakamarić, Z., Bingham, J., Hu, A.J.: An inference-rule-based decision procedure for verification of heap-manipulating programs with mutable data and cyclic data structures. In: Cook, B., Podelski, A. (eds.) VMCAI 2007. LNCS, vol. 4349, pp. 106–121. Springer, Heidelberg (2007)

17. Ranise, S., Zarba, C.G.: A Theory of Singly-Linked Lists and its Extensible Decision Procedure. In: SEFM 2006, pp. 206–215 (2006)
18. Reynolds, J.C.: Separation logic: A logic for shared mutable data structures. In: 17th LICS, pp. 55–74. IEEE Computer Society, Los Alamitos (2002)
19. Sistla, A.P., Clarke, E.M.: The complexity of propositional linear temporal logics. J. ACM 32(3), 733–749 (1985)
20. Wolper, P.: Specification and synthesis of communicating processes using an extended temporal logic. In: POPL, pp. 20–33 (1982)
21. Yorsh, G., Rabinovich, A.M., Sagiv, S., Meyer, A., Bouajjani, A.: A logic of reachable patterns in linked data-structures. In: Aceto, L., Ingólfsdóttir, A. (eds.) FOSSACS 2006. LNCS, vol. 3921, pp. 94–110. Springer, Heidelberg (2006)

Better Quality in Synthesis through Quantitative Objectives*

Roderick Bloem[1], Krishnendu Chatterjee[2],
Thomas A. Henzinger[3], and Barbara Jobstmann[3]

[1] Graz University of Technology
[2] IST Austria
[3] EPFL

Abstract. Most specification languages express only qualitative constraints. However, among two implementations that satisfy a given specification, one may be preferred to another. For example, if a specification asks that every request is followed by a response, one may prefer an implementation that generates responses quickly but does not generate unnecessary responses. We use quantitative properties to measure the "goodness" of an implementation. Using games with corresponding quantitative objectives, we can synthesize "optimal" implementations, which are preferred among the set of possible implementations that satisfy a given specification.

In particular, we show how automata with lexicographic mean-payoff conditions can be used to express many interesting quantitative properties for reactive systems. In this framework, the synthesis of optimal implementations requires the solution of lexicographic mean-payoff games (for safety requirements), and the solution of games with both lexicographic mean-payoff and parity objectives (for liveness requirements). We present algorithms for solving both kinds of novel graph games.

1 Introduction

Traditional specifications are Boolean: an implementation satisfies a specification, or it does not. This Manichean view is not entirely satisfactory: There are usually many different ways to satisfy a specification, and we may prefer one implementation over another. This is especially important when we automatically synthesize implementations from a specification, because we have no other way to enforce these preferences. In this paper, we add a quantitative aspect to system specification, imposing a preference order on the implementations that satisfy the qualitative part of the specification. Then, we present synthesis algorithms that construct, from a given specification with both qualitative and quantitative aspects, an implementation that (i) satisfies the qualitative aspect and (ii) is optimal or near-optimal with respect to the quantitative aspect. Along the way,

---

* This research was supported by the Swiss National Science Foundation (Indo-Swiss Research Program and NCCR MICS) and the European Union projects COMBEST and COCONUT.

A. Bouajjani and O. Maler (Eds.): CAV 2009, LNCS 5643, pp. 140–156, 2009.

we introduce and solve graph games with new kinds of objectives, namely, lexicographic mean-payoff objectives and the combination of parity and lexicographic mean-payoff objectives.

Suppose we want to specify an arbiter for a shared resource. For each client i, the arbiter has an input r_i (request access) and an output g_i (access granted). A first attempt at a specification in LTL may be $\bigwedge_i \mathsf{G}(r_i \to \mathsf{F}\, g_i) \wedge \mathsf{G} \bigwedge_i \bigwedge_{j \neq i} (\neg g_i \vee \neg g_j)$. (All requests are granted eventually and two grants never occur simultaneously.) This specification is too weak: An implementation that raises all g_i signals in a round-robin fashion satisfies the specification but is probably undesired. The unwanted behaviors can be ruled out by adding the requirements $\bigwedge_i \mathsf{G}(g_i \to \mathsf{X}(\neg g_i \,\mathsf{W}\, r_i)) \wedge \bigwedge_i \neg g_i \,\mathsf{W}\, r_i$. (No second grant before a request.)

Such Boolean requirements to rule out trivial but undesirable implementations have several drawbacks: (i) they are easy to forget and difficult to get right (often leading to unrealizable specifications) and, perhaps more importantly, (ii) they constrain implementations unnecessarily, by giving up the abstract quality of a clean specification. In our example, we would rather say that the implementation should produce "as few unnecessary grants as possible" (where a grant g_i is unnecessary if there is no outstanding request r_i). We will add a quantitative aspect to specifications which allows us to say that. Specifically, we will assign a real-valued reward to each behavior, and the more unnecessary grants, the lower the reward.

A second reason that the arbiter specification may give rise to undesirable implementations is that it may wait arbitrarily long before producing a grant. Requiring that grants come within a fixed number of steps instead of "eventually" is not robust, because it depends on the step size of the implementation and the number of clients. Rather, we assign a lower reward to executions with larger distances between a request and corresponding grant. If we use rewards both for punishing unnecessary grants and for punishing late grants, then these two rewards need to be combined. This leads us to consider tuples of costs that are ordered lexicographically. We define the quantitative aspect of a specification using *lexicographic mean-payoff automata*, which assign a tuple of costs to each transition. The cost of an infinite run is obtained by taking, for each component of the tuple, the long-run average of all transition costs. Such automata can be used to specify both "produce as few unnecessary grants as possible" and "produce grants as quickly as possible," and combinations thereof.

If the qualitative aspect of the specification is a safety property, then synthesis requires the solution of *lexicographic mean-payoff games*, for which we can synthesize optimal solutions. (The objective is to minimize the cost of an infinite run lexicographically.) If the qualitative aspect is a liveness property, then we obtain *lexicographic mean-payoff parity games*, which must additionally satisfy a parity objective. We present the solution of these games in this paper. We show that lexicographic mean-payoff games are determined for memoryless strategies and can be decided in NP ∩ coNP, but that in general optimal strategies for lexicographic mean-payoff parity games require infinite memory. We prove, however, that for any given real vector $\varepsilon > \mathbf{0}$, there exists a finite-state strategy that ensures a value within ε of the optimal value. This allows us to synthesize ε-optimal implementations, for any ε. The complexity class of the optimal synthesis problem is NP.

Related work. There are several formalisms for quantitative specifications in the literature [2,5,6,7,8,11,12,15,16,20]; most of these works (other than [2,8,11]) do not consider mean-payoff specifications and none of these works focus on how quantitative specifications can be used to obtain better implementations for the synthesis problem. Several notions of metrics have been proposed in the literature for probabilistic systems and games [13,14]; these metrics provide a measure that indicates how close are two systems with respect to all temporal properties expressible in a logic; whereas our work compares how good an implementation is with respect to a given specification. The work [10] considers non-zero-sum games with lexicographic ordering on the payoff profiles, but to the best of our knowledge, the lexicographic quantitative objective we consider for games has not been studied before.

2   Examples

After giving necessary definitions, we illustrate with several examples how quantitative constraints can be a useful measure for the quality of an implementation.

Alphabets, vectors, and lexicographic order. Let $\mathcal{I}$ and $\mathcal{O}$ be finite sets of *input* and *output signals*, respectively. We define the *input alphabet* $\Sigma_I = 2^{\mathcal{I}}$ and the *output alphabet* $\Sigma_O = 2^{\mathcal{O}}$. The joint alphabet Σ is defined as $\Sigma = 2^{\mathcal{I} \cup \mathcal{O}}$. Let $\mathbb{R}^d$ be the set of real vectors of dimension d with the usual lexicographic order.

Mealy machines. A *Mealy machine* is a tuple $M = \langle Q, q_0, \delta \rangle$, where Q is a finite set of states, $q_0 \in Q$ is the initial state, and $\delta \subseteq Q \times \Sigma_I \times \Sigma_O \times Q$ is a set of labeled edges. We require that the machine is *input enabled* and *deterministic*: $\forall q \in Q . \forall i \in \Sigma_I$, there exists a unique $o \in \Sigma_O$ and a unique $q' \in Q$ such that $\langle q, i, o, q' \rangle \in \delta$. Each input word $i = i_0 i_1 \cdots \in \Sigma_I{}^{\omega}$ has a unique *run* $q_0 i_0 o_0 q_1 i_1 o_1 \ldots$ such that $\forall k \geq 0 . \langle q_k, i_k, o_k, q_{k+1} \rangle \in \delta$. The corresponding *I/O word* is $i_0 \cup o_0, i_1 \cup o_1, \cdots \in \Sigma^{\omega}$. The *language* of M, denoted by L_M, is the set of all I/O words of the machine. Given a language $L \subseteq \Sigma^{\omega}$, we say a Mealy machine M *implements* L if $L_M \subseteq L$.

Quantitative languages. A *quantitative language [8]* over Σ is a function $L : \Sigma^{\omega} \to V$ that associates to each word in Σ^{ω} a *value* from V, where $V \subset \mathbb{R}^d$ has a least element. Words with a higher value are more desirable than those with a lower value. In the remainder, we view an ordinary, *qualitative* language as a quantitative language that maps words in L to true $(= 1)$ and words not in L to false $(= 0)$. We often use a pair $\langle L, L' \rangle$ of a qualitative language L and a quantitative language $L' : \Sigma^{\omega} \to V$ as specification, where L has higher priority than L'. We can also view $\langle L, L' \rangle$ as quantitative language with $\langle L, L' \rangle(w) = \mathbf{0}$ if $L(w) = 0$, and $\langle L, L' \rangle(w) = L'(w) - v_{\perp} + \mathbf{1}$ otherwise, where $v_{\perp}$ is the minimal value in V. (Adding constant factors does not change the order between words).

We extend the definition of value to Mealy machines. As in verification and synthesis of qualitative languages, we take the worst-case behavior of the Mealy machine as a measure. Given a quantitative language L over Σ, the *value* of a Mealy machine M, denoted by $L(M)$, is $\inf_{w \in L_M} L(w)$.

Lexicographic mean-payoff automata. We use lexicographic mean-payoff automata to describe quantitative languages. In lexicographic mean-payoff automata each edge is mapped to a reward. The automaton associates a run with a word and assigns to the word the average reward of the edges taken (as in mean-payoff games [17]). Unlike in mean-payoff games, rewards are vectors.

Formally, a *lexicographic mean-payoff automaton* of dimension d over Σ is a tuple $A = \langle \langle S, s_0, E \rangle, \boldsymbol{r} \rangle$, where S is a set of states, $E \subseteq S \times \Sigma \times S$ is a labeled set of edges, $s_0 \in S$ is the initial state, and $\boldsymbol{r} : E \to \mathbb{N}^d$ is a reward function that maps edges to d-vectors of natural numbers. Note that all rewards are non-negative. We assume that the automaton is complete and deterministic: for each s and σ there is exactly one s' such that $\langle s, \sigma, s' \rangle \in E$. A word $w = w_0 w_1 \cdots \in \Sigma^\omega$ has a unique run $\rho(w) = s_0 e_0 s_1 e_1 \ldots$ such that $s_i \in S$ and $e_i = \langle s_i, w_i, s_{i+1} \rangle \in E$ for all $i \geq 0$. The *lexicographic mean payoff* $LM(\rho)$ of a run ρ is defined as $LM(\rho) = \liminf_{n \to \infty} \frac{1}{n} \sum_{i=0}^n \boldsymbol{r}(e_i)$. The automaton defines a quantitative language with domain $\mathbb{R}^d$ by associating to every word w the value $L_A(w) = LM(\rho(w))$.

If the dimension of A is 1 and the range of L_A is $\{0, 1\}$ then, per definition, L_A defines a qualitative language. We say that A is a *safety automaton* if it defines a qualitative language and there is no path from an edge with reward 0 to an edge with reward > 0. Safety automata define safety languages [1]. Note that in general, ω-regular languages and languages expressible with mean-payoff automata are incomparable [8].

Example 1. Let us consider a specification of an arbiter with one client. In the following, we use r, $\bar{r}$, g, and $\bar{g}$ to represent that r or g are set to **true** and **false**, respectively and $\top$ to indicate that a signal can take either value. A slash separates input and output.

Take the specification $\varphi = \mathsf{G}(r \to g \vee \mathsf{X} g)$: every request is granted within two steps. The corresponding language L_φ maps a word $w = w_0 w_1, \ldots$ to **true** iff for every position i in w, if $r \in w_i$, then $g \in w_i \cup w_{i+1}$. Fig. 1 shows three implementations for L_φ. Machine M_1 asserts g continuously independent of r, M_2 responds to each request with a grant but keeps g low otherwise, and M_3 delays its response if possible.

We use a quantitative specification to state that we prefer an implementation that avoids unnecessary grants. Fig. 2 shows two mean-payoff automata, A_1 and A_2 that define rewards for the behavior of an implementation. Note that we have summarized edges using Boolean algebra. For instance, an arc labeled g in the figure corresponds to the edges labeled rg and $\bar{r}g$. Automata A_1 and A_2 define quantitative languages that distinguish words by the frequency of grants and the condition under which they appear. Specification A_1 defines a reward of 1 except when a grant is given; A_2 only withholds a reward when a grant is given unnecessarily. Consider the words $w_1 = (rg, \bar{r}\bar{g})^\omega$ and $w_2 = (r\bar{g}, \bar{r}g, \bar{r}g)^\omega$.

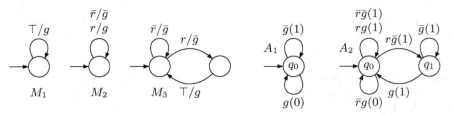

Fig. 1. Three Mealy machines that implement $\mathsf{G}(r \rightarrow g \vee \mathsf{X} g)$

Fig. 2. Two specifications that provide different ways of charging for grants

Specification A_1 defines the rewards $L_{A_1}(w_1) = 1/2$, and $L_{A_1}(w_2) = 1/3$. For A_2, we get $L_{A_2}(w_1) = 1$ and $L_{A_2}(w_2) = 2/3$. Both specifications are meaningful but they express different preferences, which leads to different results for verification and synthesis, as discussed in Section 4.

Recall the three implementations in Fig. 1. Each of them implements L_φ. For A_1, input r^ω gives the lowest reward. The values corresponding to the input/output word of M_1, M_2, and M_3 are 0, 0, and 1/2, respectively. Thus, A_1 prefers the last implementation. The values of the implementations for A_2 are minimal when the input is $\bar{r}^\omega$; they are 0, 1, and 1, respectively. Thus, A_2 prefers the last two implementations, but does not distinguish between them.

Example 2. Assume we want to specify an arbiter for two clients that answers requests within three steps. Simultaneous grants are forbidden. Formally, we have $\varphi = \bigwedge_{i \in \{1,2\}} \mathsf{G}(r_i \rightarrow \bigvee_{t \in \{0,1,2\}} \mathsf{X}^t g_i) \wedge \mathsf{G}(\neg g_1 \vee \neg g_2)$. We want grants to come as quickly as possible. Fig. 3 shows a mean-payoff automaton A_3 that rewards rapid replies to Client 1. Suppose we want to do the same for Client 2. One option is to construct a similar automaton A_3' for Client 2 and to add the two resulting quantitative languages. This results in a quantitative language $L_{A_3} + L_{A_3'}$ that treats the clients equally. Suppose instead that we want to give Client 1 priority. In that case, we can construct a lexicographic mean-payoff automaton that maps a word w to a tuple $\langle s_1(w), s_2(w) \rangle$, where the first and second elements correspond to the payoff for Clients 1 and 2, resp. Part of this automaton, A_4, is shown in Fig. 3.

Automaton A_3 distinguishes words with respect to the maximal average distance between request and grant. For instance, $L_{A_3}((r_1 g_1, \bar{r}_1 \bar{g}_1)^\omega) = 1$ and $L_{A_3}((r_1 \bar{g}_1, \bar{r}_1 g_1)^\omega) = 1/2$. Automaton A_4 associates a vector to every word. For instance, $L_{A_4}((r_1 g_1 r_2 \bar{g}_2, \bar{r}_1 \bar{g}_1 \bar{r}_2 g_2)^\omega) = 1/2 \cdot (\langle 1, 0 \rangle + \langle 1, 1 \rangle) = \langle 1, 1/2 \rangle$, which makes it preferable to the word $(r_1 \bar{g}_1 r_2 g_2, \bar{r}_1 g_1 \bar{r}_2 \bar{g}_2)^\omega$, which has value $\langle 1/2, 1 \rangle$. This is what we expect: the first word gives priority to requests from Client 1, while the second gives priority to Client 2.

Example 3. Let us consider the liveness specification $\varphi = \mathsf{G}(r \rightarrow \mathsf{F} g)$ saying that every request must be granted eventually. This languages can usefully be combined with A_3, stating that grants must come quickly. It can also be combined with A_1 from Fig. 2 stating that grants should occur as infrequently as possible. A Mealy machine may emit a grant every k ticks, which gives a reward

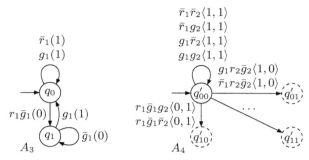

Fig. 3. A specification that rewards quick grants for a request from Client 1, and a specification that rewards quick grants for both clients, while giving priority to Client 1

of $1 - 1/k$. Thus, there is an infinite chain of ever-better machines. There is no Mealy machine, however, that obtains the limit reward of 1. This can only be achieved by an implementation with infinite memory, for instance one that answers requests only in cycle 2^k for all k [9].

3   Lexicographic Mean-Payoff (Parity) Games

We show how to solve lexicographic mean-payoff games and lexicographic mean-payoff parity games, which we will need in Section 4 to solve the synthesis problem for quantitative specifications.

3.1   Notation and Known Results

Game graphs and plays. A *game graph* over the alphabet Σ is a tuple $G = \langle S, s_0, E \rangle$ consisting of a finite set of states S, partitioned into S_1 and S_2, representing the states of Player 1 and Player 2, an initial state $s_0 \in S$, and a finite set of labeled edges $E \subseteq S \times \Sigma \times S$. We require that the labeling is deterministic, i.e., if $\langle s, \sigma, t \rangle, \langle s, \sigma, t' \rangle \in E$, then $t = t'$. We write $\bar{E} = \{\langle s, t \rangle \mid \exists \sigma \in \Sigma : \langle s, \sigma, t \rangle \in E\}$. At S_1 states, Player 1 decides the successor state and at S_2 states, Player 2 decides the successor states. We assume that $\forall s \in S . \exists t \in S . \langle s, t \rangle \in \bar{E}$. A *play* $\rho = \rho_0 \rho_1 \cdots \in S^\omega$ is an infinite sequence of states such that for all $i \geq 0$ we have $\langle \rho_i, \rho_{i+1} \rangle \in \bar{E}$. We denote the set of all plays by Ω.

The labels and the initial state are not relevant in this section. They are used later to establish the connection between specifications, games, and Mealy machines. They also allow us to view automata as games with a single player.

Strategies. Given a game graph $G = \langle S, s_0, E \rangle$, a *strategy for Player 1* is a function $\pi_1 : S^* S_1 \rightarrow S$ such that $\forall s_0 \ldots s_i \in S^* S_1$ we have $\langle s_i, \pi_1(s_0 s_1 \ldots s_i) \rangle \in \bar{E}$. A Player-2 strategy is defined similarly. We denote the set of all Player-p strategies by Π_p. The *outcome* $\rho(\pi_1, \pi_2, s)$ of π_1 and π_2 on G starting at s is the unique play $\rho = \rho_0 \rho_1 \ldots$ such that for all $i \geq 0$, if $\rho_i \in S_p$, then $\rho_{i+1} = \pi_p(\rho_0 \ldots \rho_i)$ and $\rho_0 = s$.

A strategy $\pi_p \in \Pi_p$ is memoryless if for any two sequences $\sigma = s_0 \ldots s_i \in S^* S_p$ and $\sigma' = s'_0 \ldots s'_{i'} \in S^* S_p$ such that $s_i = s'_{i'}$, we have $\pi_p(\sigma) = \pi_p(\sigma')$. We represent a memoryless strategy π_p simply as a function from S_p to S. A strategy is a *finite-memory strategy* if it needs only finite memory of the past, consisting of a finite-state machine that keeps track of the history of the play. The strategy chooses a move depending on the state of the machine and the location in the game. Strategies that are not finite-memory are called *infinite-memory strategies*.

Quantitative and qualitative objectives. We consider different objectives for the players. A *quantitative* objective f is a function $f : \Omega \to \mathbb{R}^d$ that assigns a vector of reals as reward to every play. We consider complementary objectives for the two players; i.e., if the objective for Player 1 is f, then the objective for Player 2 is $-f$. The goal of each player is to maximize her objective. Note that Player 2 tries to minimize f by maximizing the complementary $-f$. An objective $f : \Omega \to \{0, \pm 1\}$ that maps to the set $\{0, 1\}$ (or $\{0, -1\}$) is per definition a *qualitative objective*. Given a qualitative objective $f : \Omega \to V$ we say a play $\rho \in \Omega$ is *winning for Player 1* if $f(\rho) = \max(V)$ holds, otherwise the play is *winning for Player 2*.

Value. Given an objective f, the *Player-1 value of a state s for a strategy π_1* is the minimal value Player 1 achieves using π_1 against all Player-2 strategies, i.e., $\mathcal{V}_1(f, s, \pi_1) = \inf_{\pi_2 \in \Pi_2} f(\rho(\pi_1, \pi_2, s))$. The *Player-1 value of a state s* is the maximal value Player-1 can ensure from state s, i.e., $\mathcal{V}_1(f, s) = \sup_{\pi_1 \in \Pi_1} \mathcal{V}_1(f, s, \pi_1)$. Player-2 values are defined analogously. If $\mathcal{V}_1(f, s) + \mathcal{V}_2(-f, s) = 0$ for all s, then the game is *determined* and we call $\mathcal{V}_1(f, s)$ the *value of s*.

Optimal, ε-optimal, and winning strategies. Given an objective f and a vector $\varepsilon \geq \mathbf{0}$, a Player-1 strategy π_1 is *Player-1 ε-optimal from a state s* if $\mathcal{V}_1(f, s, \pi_1) \geq \mathcal{V}_1(f, s) - \varepsilon$. If π_1 is $\mathbf{0}$-optimal from s, then we call π_1 *optimal from s*. Optimality for Player-2 strategies is defined analogously. If $f : \Omega \to V$ is a qualitative objective, a strategy π_1 is *winning for Player 1* from s if $\mathcal{V}_1(f, s, \pi_1) = \max(V)$.

We now define various objectives.

Parity objectives. A *parity objective* consists of a *priority function* $p : S \to \{0, 1, \ldots, k\}$ that maps every state in S to a number (called *priority*) between 0 and k. We denote by $|p|$ the maximal priority (i.e., $|p| = k$). The objective function P of Player 1 maps a play ρ to 1 if the smallest priority visited infinitely often is even, otherwise ρ is mapped to 0.

Lexicographic mean-payoff objectives. A *lexicographic mean-payoff objective* consists of a *reward function* $\mathbf{r} : E \to \mathbb{N}^d$ that maps every edge in G to a d-vector (called *reward*) of natural numbers. We define $|\mathbf{r}| = \prod_{1 \leq i \leq d} \max_{e \in E} r_i(e)$, where $r_i(e)$ is the i-component of $\mathbf{r}(e)$. The objective function of Player 1 for a play ρ is the lexicographic mean payoff $LM_{\mathbf{r}}(\rho) = \liminf_{n \to \infty} \frac{1}{n} \sum_{i=0}^{n} \mathbf{r}(\langle \rho_i, \rho_{i+1} \rangle)$. If $d = 1$, then $LM_{\mathbf{r}}(\rho)$ is the *mean payoff* [17] and we refer to it as $M_{\mathbf{r}}(\rho)$.

Lexicographic mean-payoff parity objectives. A *lexicographic mean-payoff parity objective* has a priority function $p : S \to \{0, 1, \ldots, k\}$ and a reward function $r : E \to \mathbb{N}^d$. The *lexicographic mean-payoff parity value* $LMP_r(\rho)$ for Player 1 of a play ρ is the lexicographic mean-payoff $LM_r(\rho)$ if ρ is winning for the parity objective (i.e., $P_p(\rho) = 1$), else the payoff is -1. If $d = 1$, then $LMP_{r,p}(\rho)$ defines the *mean-payoff parity value* [9] and we write $MP_{r,p}(\rho)$. If p or r are clear from the context, we omit them.

Games and automata. A *game* is a tuple $\mathcal{G} = \langle G, f \rangle$ consisting of a game graph $G = \langle S, s_0, E \rangle$ and an objective f. An *automaton* is a game with only one player, i.e., $S = S_1$. We name games and automata after their objectives.

3.2   Lexicographic Mean-Payoff Games

In this section, we prove that memoryless strategies are sufficient for lexicographic mean-payoff games and we present an algorithm to decide these games by a reduction to simple mean-payoff games. We first present the solution of lexicographic mean-payoff games with a reward function with two components, and then extend it to d-dimensional reward functions. Consider a lexicographic mean-payoff game $\mathcal{G}_{LM} = \langle \langle S, s_0, E \rangle, r \rangle$, where $r = \langle r_1, r_2 \rangle$ consists of two reward functions.

Memoryless strategies suffice. We show that memoryless strategies suffice by a reduction to a finite cycle forming game. Let us assume we have solved the mean-payoff game with respect to the reward function r_1. Consider a *value class* of r_1, i.e., a set of states having the same value with respect to r_1. It is not possible for Player 1 to move to a higher value class, and Player 1 will never choose an edge to a lower value class. Similarly, Player 2 does not have edges to a lower value class and will never choose edges to a higher value class. Thus, we can consider the sub-game for a value class.

Consider a value class of value ℓ and the sub-game induced by the value class. We now play the following finite-cycle forming game: Player 1 and Player 2 choose edges until a cycle C is formed. The payoff for the game is as follows: (1) If the mean-payoff value of the cycle C for r_1 is greater than ℓ, then Player 1 gets reward $|r_2| + 1$. (2) If the mean-payoff value of the cycle C for r_1 is smaller than ℓ, then Player 1 gets reward -1. (3) If the mean-payoff value of the cycle C for r_1 is exactly ℓ, then Player 1 gets the mean-payoff value for reward r_2 of the cycle C.

Lemma 1. The value of Player 1 for any state in the finite-cycle forming game is (i) strictly greater than -1 and (ii) strictly less than $|r_2| + 1$.

Lemma 2. Both players have memoryless optimal strategy in the finite-cycle forming game.

Proof. The result can be obtained from the result of Björklund et al. [3]. From Theorem 5.1 and the comment in Section 7.2 it follows that in any finite-cycle forming game in which the outcome depends only on the vertices that appear in the cycle (modulo cyclic permutations) we have that memoryless optimal strategies exist for both players. Our finite-cycle forming game satisfies the conditions.   □

Lemma 3. *The following assertions hold.*

1. *If the value of the finite-cycle forming game is β at a state s, then the value of the lexicographic mean-payoff game is $\langle \ell, \beta \rangle$ at s.*
2. *A memoryless optimal strategy of the finite-cycle forming game is optimal for the lexicographic mean-payoff game.*

The proof can be found in [4].

Reduction to mean-payoff games. We now sketch a reduction of lexicographic mean-payoff games to mean-payoff games for optimal strategies. We reduce the reward function $r = \langle r_1, r_2 \rangle$ to a single reward function r^*. We ensure that if the mean-payoff difference of two cycles C_1 and C_2 for reward r_1 is positive, then the difference in reward assigned by r^* exceeds the largest possible difference in the mean-payoff for reward r_2. Consider two cycles C_1 of length n_1 and C_2 of length n_2, such that the sum of the r_1 rewards of C_i is α_i. Since all rewards are integral, $|\frac{\alpha_1}{n_1} - \frac{\alpha_2}{n_2}| > 0$ implies $|\frac{\alpha_1}{n_1} - \frac{\alpha_2}{n_2}| \geq \frac{1}{n_1 \cdot n_2}$. Hence we multiply the r_1 rewards by $m = |S|^2 \cdot |r_2| + 1$ to obtain $r^* = m \cdot r_1 + r_2$. This ensures that if the mean-payoff difference of two cycles C_1 and C_2 for reward r_1 is positive, then the difference exceeds the difference in the mean-payoff for reward r_2. Observe that we restrict our attention to cycles only since we have already proven that optimal memoryless strategies exist.

We can easily extend this reduction to reduce lexicographic mean-payoff games with arbitrarily many reward functions to mean-payoff games. The following theorem follows from this reduction in combination with known results for mean payoff parity games [17,21].

Theorem 1 (Lexicographic mean-payoff games). *For all lexicographic mean-payoff games $\mathcal{G}_{LM} = \langle \langle S, s_0, E \rangle, r \rangle$, the following assertions hold.*

1. *(Determinacy.) For all states $s \in S$, $\mathcal{V}_1(LMP, s) + \mathcal{V}_2(-LMP, s) = \mathbf{0}$.*
2. *(Memoryless optimal strategies.) Both players have memoryless optimal strategies from every state $s \in S$.*
3. *(Complexity). Whether the lexicographic mean-payoff value vector at a state $s \in S$ is at least a rational value vector $\mathbf{v}$ can be decided in NP ∩ coNP.*
4. *(Algorithms). The lexicographic mean-payoff value vector for all states can be computed in time $O(|S|^{2d+3} \cdot |E| \cdot |r|)$.*

3.3   Lexicographic Mean-Payoff Parity Games

Lexicographic mean-payoff parity games are a natural lexicographic extension of mean-payoff parity games [9]. The algorithmic solution for mean-payoff parity games is a recursive algorithm, where each recursive step requires the solution of a parity objective and a mean-payoff objective. The key correctness argument of the algorithm relies on the existence of memoryless optimal strategies for parity

and mean-payoff objectives. Since memoryless optimal strategies exist for lexicographic mean-payoff games, the solution of mean-payoff parity games extends
to lexicographic mean-payoff parity games: in each recursive step, we replace the
mean-payoff objective by a lexicographic mean-payoff objective. Thus, we have
the following result.

Theorem 2 (Lexicographic mean-payoff parity games). *For all lexico-
graphic mean-payoff parity games* $\mathcal{G}_{LMP} = \langle\langle S, s_0, E\rangle, \boldsymbol{r}, p\rangle$, *the following assertions hold.*

1. *(Determinacy).* $\mathcal{V}_1(LMP, s) + \mathcal{V}_2(-LMP, s) = \boldsymbol{0}$ *for all state* $s \in S$.
2. *(Optimal strategies). Optimal strategies for Player 1 exist but may require
   infinite memory; finite-memory optimal strategies exist for Player 2.*
3. *(Complexity). Whether the value at a state* $s \in S$ *is at least the vector* $\boldsymbol{v}$ *can
   be decided in coNP.*
4. *(Algorithms). The value for all states can be computed in time* $O\big(|S|^{|p|} \cdot
   (\min\{|S|^{\frac{|p|}{3}} \cdot |E|, |S|^{O(\sqrt{S})}\} + |S|^{2d+3} \cdot |E| \cdot |\boldsymbol{r}|)\big)$.

In the following, we prove two properties of mean-payoff parity games that are
interesting for synthesis. For simplicity, we present the results for mean-payoff
parity games. The results extend to lexicographic mean-payoff parity games as in
Theorem 2. First, we show that the algorithm of [9] can be adapted to compute
finite-memory strategies that are ε-optimal. Then, we show that Player 1 has
a finite-memory optimal strategy if and only if she has a memoryless optimal
strategy.

Finite-memory ε-optimal strategy. In mean-payoff parity games, though
optimal strategies require infinite memory for Player 1, there is a finite-memory
ε-optimal strategy for every $\varepsilon > 0$. The proof of this claim is obtained by a
more detailed analysis of the optimal strategy construction of [9]. The optimal
strategy constructed in [9] for Player 1 can be intuitively described as follows.
The strategy is played in rounds, and each round has three phases: (a) playing
a memoryless optimal mean-payoff strategy; (b) playing a strategy in a sub-
game; (c) playing a memoryless attractor strategy to reach a desired priority.
Then the strategy proceeds to the next round. The length of the first phase
is monotonically increasing in the number of rounds, and it requires infinite
memory to count the rounds. Given an $\varepsilon > 0$, we can fix a bound on the number
of steps in the first phase that ensures a payoff within ε of the optimal value.
Hence, a finite-memory strategy can be obtained.

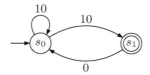

Fig. 4. Game in which the optimal strategy requires infinite memory

We illustrate the idea with an example. Consider the example shown in Fig. 4 where we have a game graph where all states belong to Player 1. The goal of Player 1 is to maximize the mean-payoff while ensuring that state s_1 is visited infinitely often. An optimal strategy is as follows: the game starts in round 1. In each round i, the edge $s_0 \to s_0$ is chosen i times, then the edge $s_0 \to s_1$ is chosen once, and then the game proceeds to round $i + 1$. Any optimal strategy in the game shown requires infinite memory. However, given $\varepsilon > 0$, in every round the edge $s_0 \to s_0$ can be chosen a fixed number K times such that $K > \frac{10}{\varepsilon} - 2$. Then the payoff is $\frac{10 \cdot K + 10}{K + 2} = 10 - \frac{10}{K+2} \geq 10 - \varepsilon$ (since $K > \frac{10}{\varepsilon} - 2$); which is within ε of the value. It may also be noted that given $\varepsilon > 0$, the finite-memory optimal strategy can be obtained as follows. We apply the recursive algorithm to solve the game to obtain two memoryless strategies: one for the mean-payoff strategy and other for the attractor strategy. We then specify the bound (depending on ε) on the number of steps for the mean-payoff strategy for each phase (this requires an additional $O(\frac{1}{\varepsilon})$ time for the strategy description after the recursive algorithm).

Theorem 3. *For all lexicographic mean-payoff parity games and for all $\varepsilon > 0$, there exists a finite-memory ε-optimal strategy for Player 1. Given $\varepsilon > 0$, a finite-memory ε-optimal strategy can be constructed in time $O(|S|^{|p|} \cdot |E|^{2d+6} \cdot |r| + \frac{1}{\varepsilon})$.*

Optimal finite-memory and memoryless strategies. Consider a mean-payoff parity game $\mathcal{G} = \langle \langle S, s_0, E \rangle, r, p \rangle$. Our goal is to show that if there is a finite-memory optimal strategy for Player 1, then there is a memoryless optimal strategy for Player 1. Suppose there is a finite-memory optimal strategy $\widehat{\pi}_1$ for Player 1. Consider the finite graph $\widehat{\mathcal{G}}$ obtained by fixing the strategy $\widehat{\pi}_1$. ($\widehat{\mathcal{G}}$ is obtained as the synchronous product of the given game graph and finite-state strategy automaton for $\widehat{\pi}_1$.) For a state $s \in S$, consider any cycle $\widehat{C}$ in $\widehat{\mathcal{G}}$ that is reachable from $\langle s, q_0 \rangle$ (where q_0 is the initial memory location) and $\widehat{C}$ is executed to ensure that Player 1 does not achieve a payoff greater than the value of the game from s. We denote by $\widehat{C}|_{\mathcal{G}}$ the sequence of states in $\mathcal{G}$ that appear in $\widehat{C}$. We call a cycle C of $\mathcal{G}$ that appears in $\widehat{C}|_{\mathcal{G}}$ a *component cycle of* $\widehat{C}$. We have the following properties about the cycle $\widehat{C}$ and its component cycles.

1. $\min(p(\widehat{C}|_{\mathcal{G}}))$ is even.
2. Suppose there is a component cycle C of $\widehat{C}$ such that the average of the rewards of C is greater than the average of the rewards of $\widehat{C}$. If Player 2 fixes a finite-memory strategy that corresponds to the execution of cycle $\widehat{C}$, then an infinite-memory strategy can be played by Player 1 that pumps the cycle C longer and longer to ensure a payoff that is equal to the average of the weights of C. The infinite memory strategy ensures that all states in $\widehat{C}|_{\mathcal{G}}$ are visited infinitely often, but the long-run average of the rewards is the average of the rewards of C. This would imply that for the cycle $\widehat{C}$, Player 1 can switch to an infinite-memory strategy and ensure a better payoff.
3. If there is component cycle C of $\widehat{C}$ such that $\min(p(C)) > \min(p(\widehat{C}|_{\mathcal{G}}))$, then the cycle segment of C can be ignored from $\widehat{C}$ without affecting the payoff.

4. Suppose we have two component cycles C_1 and C_2 in $\widehat{C}$ such that $\min(p(C_1)) = \min(p(C_2)) = \min(p(\widehat{C}|_{\mathcal{G}}))$, then one of the cycles can be ignored without affecting the payoff.

It follows from above that if the finite-memory strategy $\widehat{\pi}_1$ is an optimal one, then it can be reduced to a strategy π_1' such that if Player 2 fixes a finite-memory counter-optimal strategy π_2, then every cycle C in the finite graph obtained from fixing π_1' and π_2 is also a cycle in the original game graph. Since finite-memory optimal strategies exist for Player 2, a correspondence of the value of the game and the value of the following finite-cycle forming game can be established. The finite-cycle forming game is played on $\mathcal{G}$ and the game stops when a cycle C is formed, and the payoff is as follows: if $\min(p(C))$ is even, then the payoff for Player 1 is the average of the weights of the C, otherwise the payoff for Player 1 is -1. The existence of pure memoryless optimal strategy in the finite-cycle forming game can be obtained from the results of Björklund et al. [3]. This concludes the proof of the following theorem.

Theorem 4. *For all lexicographic mean-payoff parity games, if Player 1 has a finite-memory optimal strategy, then she has a memoryless optimal strategy.*

It follows from Theorem 4 that the decision whether there is a finite-memory optimal strategy for Player 1 is in NP. The NP procedure goes as follows: we guess the value v_0 of state s_0 and verify that the value at s_0 is no more than v_0. We can decide in coNP whether the value at a state is at least v, for $v \in \mathbb{Q}$. Thus, we can decide in NP whether the value at state s_0 is no more than v_0 (as it is the complement). Then, we guess a memoryless optimal strategy for Player 1 and verify (in polynomial time) that the value is at least v_0 given the strategy.

4   Quantitative Verification and Synthesis

We are interested in the verification and the synthesis problem for quantitative specifications given by a lexicographic mean-payoff (parity) automaton. In the following simple lemma we establish that these automata also suffice to express qualitative properties.

Lemma 4. *Let $A = \langle G, p \rangle$ be a deterministic parity automaton and let $A' = \langle G', r \rangle$ be a lexicographic mean-payoff automaton. We can construct a lexicographic mean-payoff parity automaton $A \times A' = \langle G \times G', r, p \rangle$, where $G \times G'$ is the product graph of G and G' such that for any word w and associated run ρ, $LMP_{A \times A'}(\rho) = -1$ if the run of w is lost in A, and $LM_{A'}(\rho')$ otherwise, where ρ' is the projection of ρ on G'.*

Note that $\langle L_A, L_{A'} \rangle = L_{A \times A'} + 1$, assuming that $\inf_{w \in \Sigma^\omega} L_{A'}(w) = 0$. If A is a safety automaton, the language $\langle L_A, L_{A'} \rangle$ can be presented by a lexicographic mean-payoff automaton (see Example 4). Thus, lexicographic mean-payoff automata suffice to express both a quantitative aspect and a safety aspect of a

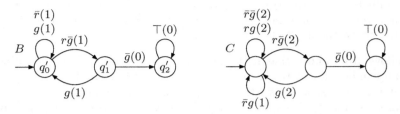

Fig. 5. Safety automaton B for $\mathsf{G}(r \to g \vee \mathsf{X} g)$ and automaton C for $\langle L_B, L_{A_2} \rangle$

specification. Lexicographic mean-payoff parity automata can be used to introduce a quantitative aspect to liveness specifications and thus to the usual linear-time temporal logics.

Example 4. Let us resume Example 1. Fig. 5 shows a safety automaton B for the specification $\mathsf{G}(r \to g \vee \mathsf{X} g)$. It also shows the mean-payoff automaton C for $\langle L_B, L_{A_2} \rangle$. (See Fig. 2 for the definition of A_2.)

4.1 Quantitative Verification

We now consider the verification problem for quantitative specifications. For qualitative specifications, the verification problem is whether an implementation satisfies the specification for all inputs. For quantitative specifications, the problem generalizes to the question if an implementation can achieve a given value independent of the inputs.

Let $A = \langle \langle S, s_0, E \rangle, r, p \rangle$ be a lexicographic mean-payoff parity automaton and let $M = \langle Q, q_0, \delta \rangle$ be a Mealy machine. The *quantitative verification problem* is to determine $L_A(M)$. The corresponding decision problem is whether $L_A(M) \geq c$ for a given cutoff value c. Clearly, verification of qualitative languages is a special case in which the cutoff value is 1.

Theorem 5. *The value $L_A(M)$ can be computed in time $O(|S| \cdot |Q| \cdot |E| \cdot |\delta| \cdot d \cdot \lg(|Q| \cdot |\delta| \cdot |r|))$.*

Proof. We reduce the lexicographic mean-payoff parity automata to a mean-payoff parity automaton A' using the reduction stated in Section 3.2 and build the product automaton of A' and M. Then, we check if it contains a cycle that is not accepted by the parity algorithm [19]. If so, we return $-\mathbf{1}$. If not, in the second step we find the minimal mean-weight cycle [18].

Example 5. In Example 1, we computed the values of Implementations M_1, M_2, and M_3 (Fig. 1) for the specifications A_1 and A_2 given in Fig. 2. Specification A_1 requires the number of grants to be minimal. Under this specification, M_3 is preferable to both other implementations because it only produces half as much grants in the worst case. Unfortunately, A_1 treats a grant the same way regardless of whether a request occurred. Thus, this specification does not

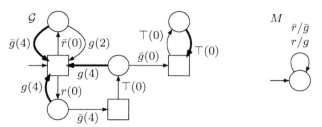

Fig. 6. A game (optimal strategy shown in bold) and corresponding Mealy machine

distinguish between M_1 and M_2. Specification A_2 only punishes "unnecessary" grants, which means that A_2 prefers M_2 and M_3 to M_1.

A preference between the eagerness of M_2 and the laziness of M_3 can be resolved in either direction. For instance, if we combine the two quantitative languages using addition, lazy implementations are preferred.

4.2   Quantitative Synthesis

In this section, we show how to automatically construct an implementation from a quantitative specification given by a lexicographic mean-payoff (parity) automaton. First, we show the connection between automata and games, and between strategies and Mealy machines, so that we can use the theory from Sections 3 to perform synthesis. Then, we define different notions of synthesis and give their complexity bounds.

We will show the polynomial conversions of an automata to a game and of a strategy to a Mealy machines using an example.

Example 6. Fig. 6(left) shows the game $\mathcal{G}$ corresponding to the automaton C shown in Fig. 5. Note: The alphabet 2^{AP} has been split into an input alphabet 2^{I} controlled by Player 2 (squares) and an output alphabet 2^{O} controlled by Player 1 (circles). Accordingly, each edge e of C is split into two edges e_2 and e_1; the reward of e_2 is zero and the reward of e_2 is double the reward of e. It should be clear that with the appropriate mapping between runs, the payoff remains the same. Because we want a Mealy machine, the input player makes the first move.

The figure also shows an optimal strategy (bold edges) for $\mathcal{G}$ with payoff 2. The right side of the figure shows the Mealy machine M corresponding to the strategy. It is constructed by a straightforward collection of inputs and chosen outputs. It is easily verified that $L_C(M) = 2$.

Definition 1. *Let L be a quantitative language and let $\mathbf{c} \in \mathbb{R}^d$ be a cutoff value. We say that L is $\mathbf{c}$-realizable if there is a Mealy machine M such that $L(M) \geq \mathbf{c}$. We say that L is* limit-$\mathbf{c}$-realizable *if for all $\varepsilon > 0$ there is a Mealy machine M such that $L(M) + \varepsilon \geq \mathbf{c}$.*

Suppose the supremum of $L(M)$ over all Mealy machines M exists, and denote it by $\mathbf{c}^*$. We call L realizable (limit-realizable) *if L is $\mathbf{c}^*$-realizable (limit-$\mathbf{c}^*$-realizable). A Mealy machine M with value $L(M) \geq \mathbf{c}^*$ $(L(M) + \varepsilon \geq \mathbf{c}^*)$ is called* optimal *(ε-optimal, resp.).*

Clearly, realizability implies limit-realizability. Note that by the definition of supremum, L is limit-c^*-realizable iff c^* is defined. Note also that realizability for qualitative languages corresponds to realizability with cutoff 1. Synthesis is the process of constructing an optimal (ε-optimal) Mealy machine. Note that for a cutoff value c, if L is c-realizable, then we have that $L(M) \geq c$ for any optimal Mealy machine M. If L is limit-c-realizable, then $L(M_\varepsilon) + \varepsilon \geq c$ holds for any ε-optimal Mealy machine M_ε.

Example 7. We have already seen an example of a realizable specification expressed as a mean-payoff automaton (See Figs. 2 and 5 and Example 4.) Example 3 shows a language that is only limit-realizable.

For the combination of safety and quantitative specifications, we have Theorem 6.

Theorem 6. *Let $A = \langle\langle S, s_0, E\rangle, r\rangle$ be a lexicographic mean-payoff automaton of dimension d, and let c be a cutoff value. The following assertions hold.*

1. *L_A is realizable (hence limit-realizable); L_A is c-realizable iff L_A is limit-c-realizable.*
2. *c-realizability (and by (1) limit-c-realizability) of L_A are decidable in NP $\cap$ coNP.*
3. *An optimal Mealy machine can be constructed in time $O(|E|^{4d+6} \cdot |r|)$.*

The first results follow from the existence of memoryless optimal strategies for lexicographic mean-payoff games. The second and third results follows from the complexity and algorithms of solving these games. (See Theorem 1.) For liveness, we have the following result.

Theorem 7. *Let $A = \langle\langle S, s_0, E\rangle, r, p\rangle$ be a lexicographic mean-payoff parity automaton of dimension d and let c be a cutoff value. The following assertions hold.*

1. *L_A is limit-realizable, but it may not be realizable; limit-c-realizability of L_A does not imply c-realizability.*
2. *Realizability and c-realizability of L_A are decidable in NP, and limit-c-realizability of L_A is decidable in coNP.*
3. *For $\varepsilon > 0$, an ε-optimal Mealy machine can be constructed in time $O(|S|^{|p|} \cdot |E|^{4d+6} \cdot |r| + \frac{1}{\varepsilon})$. If L_A is realizable, then an optimal Mealy machine can be constructed in time $O(|S|^{|p|} \cdot |E|^{4d+6} \cdot |r|)$.*

Explanation. Following Theorem 4, realizability and c-realizability can be computed in NP. We have that L_A is limit-c-realizable iff c is not higher than the value of the initial state, which can be decided in coNP. (Theorem 2.) Limit-realizability follows from Theorem 3.

Example 8. In Example 3 we discussed the specification $\varphi = \mathsf{G}(r \rightarrow \mathsf{F}\, g)$. In combination with the quantitative language given by A_3 in Fig. 3, this specification is optimally realizable by a finite implementation: implementations M_1 and M_2 from Fig. 1 are two examples. The combination of φ and the quantitative language given by A_1 in Fig. 2 only yields a specification that is optimally limit-realizable. Automaton A_1 prefers as few as possible requests. An implementation that is optimal within $1/k$ could simply give a request every k cycles. It may not be useful to require that something happens as infrequently as possible in the context of liveness specifications. Instead, more subtle approaches are necessary; in this case we could require that *unnecessary* grants occur as little as possible. (Cf. A_2 in Fig. 2.)

5 Conclusions and Future Work

We introduced a measure for the "goodness" of an implementation by adding quantitative objectives to a qualitative specification. Our quantitative objectives are mean-payoff objectives, which are combined lexicographically. Mean-payoff objectives are relatively standard and, as we demonstrated, sufficiently expressive for our purposes. Other choices, such as discounted objectives [12], are possible as well. These give rise to different expressive powers for specification languages [8].

Finally, we have taken the worst-case view that the quantitative value of an implementation is the worst reward of all runs that the implementation may produce. There are several alternatives. For instance, one could take the average-case view of assigning to an implementation some expected value of the cost taken over all possible runs, perhaps relative to a given input distribution. Another option may be to compute admissible strategies. It can be shown that such strategies do not exist for all mean-payoff games, but they may exist for an interesting subset of these games.

References

1. Alpern, B., Schneider, F.B.: Defining liveness. Information Processing Letters (1985)
2. Alur, R., Degorre, A., Maler, O., Weiss, G.: On omega-languages defined by mean-payoff conditions. In: de Alfaro, L. (ed.) FOSSACS 2009. LNCS, vol. 5504, pp. 333–347. Springer, Heidelberg (2009)
3. Björklund, H., Sandberg, S., Vorobyov, S.: Memoryless determinacy of parity and mean payoff games: a simple proof. Theor. Comput. Sci. (2004)
4. Bloem, R., Chatterjee, K., Henzinger, T.A., Jobstmannn, B.: Better quality in synthesis through quantitative objectives. CoRR, abs/0904.2638 (2009)
5. Chakrabarti, A., Chatterjee, K., Henzinger, T.A., Kupferman, O., Majumdar, R.: Verifying quantitative properties using bound functions. In: Borrione, D., Paul, W. (eds.) CHARME 2005. LNCS, vol. 3725, pp. 50–64. Springer, Heidelberg (2005)
6. Chakrabarti, A., de Alfaro, L., Henzinger, T.A., Stoelinga, M.: Resource interfaces. In: Alur, R., Lee, I. (eds.) EMSOFT 2003. LNCS, vol. 2855, pp. 117–133. Springer, Heidelberg (2003)
7. Chatterjee, K., de Alfaro, L., Faella, M., Henzinger, T.A., Majumdar, R., Stoelinga, M.: Compositional quantitative reasoning. In: QEST, pp. 179–188. IEEE Computer Society Press, Los Alamitos (2006)
8. Chatterjee, K., Doyen, L., Henzinger, T.A.: Quantitative languages. In: Kaminski, M., Martini, S. (eds.) CSL 2008. LNCS, vol. 5213, pp. 385–400. Springer, Heidelberg (2008)

9. Chatterjee, K., Henzinger, T.A., Jurdzinski, M.: Mean-payoff parity games. In: Annual Symposium on Logic in Computer Science (LICS) (2005)
10. Chatterjee, K., Henzinger, T.A., Jurdziński, M.: Games with secure equilibria. In: LICS 2004, pp. 160–169. IEEE, Los Alamitos (2004)
11. de Alfaro, L.: How to specify and verify the long-run average behavior of probabilistic systems. In: LICS 1998, pp. 454–465. IEEE Computer Society Press, Los Alamitos (1998)
12. de Alfaro, L., Henzinger, T.A., Majumdar, R.: Discounting the future in systems theory. In: Baeten, J.C.M., Lenstra, J.K., Parrow, J., Woeginger, G.J. (eds.) ICALP 2003. LNCS, vol. 2719. Springer, Heidelberg (2003)
13. de Alfaro, L., Majumdar, R., Raman, V., Stoelinga, M.: Game relations and metrics. In: LICS, pp. 99–108. IEEE Computer Society Press, Los Alamitos (2007)
14. Desharnais, J., Gupta, V., Jagadeesan, R., Panangaden, P.: Metrics for labelled Markov systems. In: Baeten, J.C.M., Mauw, S. (eds.) CONCUR 1999. LNCS, vol. 1664, pp. 258–273. Springer, Heidelberg (1999)
15. Droste, M., Gastin, P.: Weighted automata and weighted logics. Theoretical Computer Science 380, 69–86 (2007)
16. Droste, M., Kuich, W., Rahonis, G.: Multi-valued MSO logics over words and trees. Fundamenta Informaticae 84, 305–327 (2008)
17. Ehrenfeucht, A., Mycielski, J.: Positional strategies for mean payoff games. International Journal of Game Theory (1979)
18. Karp, R.M.: A characterization of the minimum cycle mean of a digraph. Discrete Mathematics (1978)
19. King, V., Kupferman, O., Vardi, M.Y.: On the complexity of parity word automata. In: Honsell, F., Miculan, M. (eds.) FOSSACS 2001. LNCS, vol. 2030, p. 276. Springer, Heidelberg (2001)
20. Kupferman, O., Lustig, Y.: Lattice automata. In: Cook, B., Podelski, A. (eds.) VMCAI 2007. LNCS, vol. 4349, pp. 199–213. Springer, Heidelberg (2007)
21. Zwick, U., Paterson, M.: The complexity of mean payoff games on graphs. Theoretical Computer Science (1996)

Automatic Verification of Integer Array Programs[*]

Marius Bozga[1], Peter Habermehl[2], Radu Iosif[1], Filip Konečný[1,3], and Tomáš Vojnar[3]

[1] VERIMAG, CNRS, 2 av. de Vignate, 38610 Gières, France
{bozga,iosif}@imag.fr
[2] LIAFA, University Paris 7, Case 7014, 75205 Paris 13, France
haberm@liafa.jussieu.fr
[3] FIT BUT, Božetěchova 2, 61266, Brno, Czech Republic
{ikonecny,vojnar}@fit.vutbr.cz

Abstract. We provide a verification technique for a class of programs working on *integer arrays* of finite, but not a priori bounded length. We use the logic of integer arrays **SIL** [13] to specify pre- and post-conditions of programs and their parts. Effects of non-looping parts of code are computed syntactically on the level of **SIL**. Loop pre-conditions derived during the computation in **SIL** are converted into counter automata (CA). Loops are automatically translated—purely on the syntactical level—to transducers. Pre-condition CA and transducers are composed, and the composition over-approximated by flat automata with difference bound constraints, which are next converted back into **SIL** formulae, thus inferring post-conditions of the loops. Finally, validity of post-conditions specified by the user in **SIL** may be checked as entailment is decidable for **SIL**.

1 Introduction

Arrays are an important data structure in all common programming languages. Automatic verification of programs using arrays is a difficult task since they are of a finite, but often not a priori fixed length, and, moreover, their contents may be unbounded too. Nevertheless, various approaches for automatic verification of programs with arrays have recently been proposed.

In this paper, we consider programs over integer arrays with assignments, conditional statements, and *non-nested* while loops. Our verification technique is based on a combination of the logic of integer arrays **SIL** [13], used for expressing pre-/post-conditions of programs and their parts, and *counter automata* (CA) and *transducers*, into which we translate both **SIL** formulae and program loops in order to be able to compute the effect of loops and to be able to check entailment.

SIL (Single Index Logic) allows one to describe properties over arrays of integers and scalar variables. **SIL** uses difference bound constraints to compare array elements situated within a window of a constant size. For instance, the formula $(\forall i.0 \leq i \leq n_1 - 1 \rightarrow b[i] \geq 0) \wedge (\forall i.0 \leq i \leq n_2 - 1 \rightarrow c[i] < 0)$ describes a post-condition of a program partitioning an array a into an array b containing its positive elements and an array c containing its negative elements. **SIL** formulae are interpreted over program

---

[*] This work was supported by the French project RNTL AVERILES, the Czech Science Foundation (projects 102/07/0322, 102/09/H042), the Barrande project MEB 020840, and the Czech Ministry of Education by the project MSM 0021630528.

A. Bouajjani and O. Maler (Eds.): CAV 2009, LNCS 5643, pp. 157–172, 2009.

states assigning integers to scalar variables and finite sequences of integers to array variables. As already proved in [13], the set of models of an $\exists^*\forall^*$-**SIL** formula corresponds naturally to the set of traces of a *flat* CA with loops labelled by difference bound constraints. This entails decidability of the satisfiability problem for $\exists^*\forall^*$-**SIL**.

In this paper we take a novel perspective on the connection between $\exists^*\forall^*$-**SIL** and CA, allowing to benefit from the advantages of both formalisms. Indeed, the logic is useful to express human-readable pre-/post-conditions of programs and their parts, and to compute the post-image of (non-looping) program statements symbolically. On the other hand, automata are suitable for expressing the effects of program loops.

In particular, given an $\exists^*\forall^*$-**SIL** formula, we can easily compute the strongest post-condition of an assignment or a conditional statement in the same fragment of the logic. Upon reaching a program loop, we then translate the $\exists^*\forall^*$-**SIL** formula φ describing the set of states at the beginning of the loop into a CA A_φ encoding its set of models. Next, to characterise the effect of a loop L, we translate it—purely syntactically—into a *transducer* T_L, i.e., a CA describing the input/output relation on scalars and array elements implemented by L. The post-condition of L is then obtained by composing T_L with A_φ. The result of the composition is a CA $B_{\varphi,L}$ representing the *exact* set of states after *any number* of iterations of L. Finally, we translate $B_{\varphi,L}$ back into $\exists^*\forall^*$-**SIL**, obtaining a post-condition of L w.r.t. φ. However, due to the fact that counter automata are more expressive than $\exists^*\forall^*$-**SIL**, this final step involves a (refinable) *abstraction*. We first generate a *flat* CA that over-approximates the set of traces of $B_{\varphi,L}$, and then translate the flat CA back into $\exists^*\forall^*$-**SIL**.

Our approach thus generates automatically a *human-readable post-condition* for each program loop, giving the end-user some insight of what the program is doing. Moreover, as these post-conditions are expressed in a decidable logic, they can be used to check entailment of user-specified post-conditions given in the same logic.

We validate our approach by successfully and fully algorithmically verifying several array-manipulating programs, like splitting of an array into positive and negative elements, rotating an array, inserting into a sorted array, etc. Some of the steps were done manually as we have not yet implemented all of the techniques—a full implementation that will allow us to do more examples is underway.

Due to space reasons, we skip below some details of the techniques and their proofs, which are deferred to [4].

Related Work. The area of automated verification of programs with arrays and/or synthesising loop invariants for such programs has recently received a lot of attention. For instance, [1,2,8,12,16,18] build on templates of universally quantified loop invariants and/or atomic predicates provided by the user. The form of the sought invariants is then based on these templates. Inferring the invariants is tackled by various approaches, such as predicate abstraction using predicates with Skolem constants [8], constraint-based invariant synthesis [1,2], or predicate abstraction combined with interpolation-based refinement [16].

In [20], an interpolating saturation prover is used for deriving invariants from finite unfoldings of loops. In the very recent work of [17], loop invariants are synthesised by first deriving scalar invariants, combining them with various predefined first-order array axioms, and finally using a saturation prover for generating the loop invariants on arrays.

This approach can generate invariants containing quantifier alternation. A disadvantage is that, unlike our approach, the method does not take into account loop preconditions, which are sometimes necessary to find reasonable invariants. Also, the method does not generate invariants in a decidable logical fragment, in general.

Another approach, based on abstract interpretation, was used in [11]. Here, arrays are suitably partitioned, and summary properties of the array segments are tracked. The partitioning is based on heuristics related to tracking the position of index variables. These heuristics, however, sometimes fail, and human guidance is needed. The approach was recently improved in [15] by using better partitioning heuristics and relational abstract domains to keep track of the relations of the particular array slices.

Recently, several works have proposed decidable logics capable of expressing complex properties of arrays [3,6,9,10,21]. In general, these logics lack the capability of universally relating two successive elements of arrays, which is allowed in our previous work [13,14]. Moreover, the logics of [3,6,9,10,21] do not give direct means of automatically dealing with program loops, and hence, verifying programs with arrays. In this work, we provide a fully algorithmic verification technique that uses the decidable logic of [13]. Unlike many other works, we do not synthesise loop invariants, but directly post-conditions of loops with respect to given preconditions, using a two-way automata-logic connection that we establish.

2   Preliminaries

For a set A, we denote by A^* the set of finite sequences of elements from A. For such a sequence $\sigma \in A^*$, we denote by $|\sigma|$ its length, and by σ_i the element at position i, for $0 \le i < |\sigma|$. We denote by $\mathbb{N}$ the set of natural numbers, and by $\mathbb{Z}$ the set of integers. For a function $f : A \to B$ and a set $S \subseteq A$, we denote by $f \downarrow_S$ the restriction of f to S. This notation is naturally lifted to sets, pairs or sequences of functions.

Given a formula φ, we denote by $FV(\varphi)$ the set of its free variables. If we denote a formula as $\varphi(x_1, ..., x_n)$, we assume $FV(\varphi) \subseteq \{x_1, ..., x_n\}$. For $\varphi(x_1, ..., x_n)$, we denote by $\varphi[t_1/x_1, ..., t_n/x_n]$ the formula which is obtained from φ by replacing each free occurrence of $x_1, ..., x_n$ by the terms $t_1, ..., t_n$, respectively. Moreover, we denote by $\varphi[t/x_1, ..., x_n]$ the formula that arises from φ when all free occurrences of all the variables $x_1, ..., x_n$ are replaced by the same term t. Given a formula φ and a valuation v of its free variables, we write $v \models \varphi$ if by replacing each free variable x of φ with $v(x)$ we obtain a valid formula. By $\models \varphi$ we denote the fact that φ is valid.

A *difference bound constraint* (DBC) is a conjunction of inequalities of the forms (1) $x - y \le c$, (2) $x \le c$, or (3) $x \ge c$, where $c \in \mathbb{Z}$ is a constant. We denote by $\top$ (true) the empty DBC.

A *counter automaton* (CA) is a tuple $A = \langle X, Q, I, \to, F \rangle$, where: X is a finite set of counters ranging over $\mathbb{Z}$, Q is a finite set of control states, $I \subseteq Q$ is a set of initial states, $\to$ is a transition relation given by a set of rules $q \xrightarrow{\varphi(X,X')} q'$ where φ is an arithmetic formula relating current values of counters X to their future values $X' = \{x' \mid x \in X\}$, and $F \subseteq Q$ is a set of final states.

A *configuration* of a CA A is a pair $\langle q, \mathbf{v} \rangle$ where $q \in Q$ is a control state, and $\mathbf{v}: X \to \mathbb{Z}$ is a valuation of the counters in X. For a configuration $c = \langle q, \mathbf{v} \rangle$, we designate by $val(c) = \mathbf{v}$ the valuation of the counters in c. A configuration $\langle q', \mathbf{v}' \rangle$ is an *immediate successor* of $\langle q, \mathbf{v} \rangle$ if and only if A has a transition rule $q \xrightarrow{\varphi(X, X')} q'$ such that $\mathbf{v} \cup \mathbf{v}' \models \varphi$. Given two control states $q, q' \in Q$, a *run* of A from q to q' is a finite sequence of configurations $c_1 c_2 \ldots c_n$ with $c_1 = \langle q, \mathbf{v} \rangle$, $c_n = \langle q', \mathbf{v}' \rangle$ for some valuations $\mathbf{v}, \mathbf{v}': X \to \mathbb{Z}$, and c_{i+1} is an immediate successor of c_i, for all $1 \leq i < n$. Let $\mathcal{R}(A)$ denote the set of runs of A from some initial state $q_0 \in I$ to some final state $q_f \in F$, and $Tr(A) = \{val(c_1) val(c_2) \ldots val(c_n) \mid c_1 c_2 \ldots c_n \in \mathcal{R}(A)\}$ be its set of *traces*.

For two counter automata $A_i = \langle X_i, Q_i, I_i, \to_i, F_i \rangle$, $i = 1, 2$ we define the *product automaton* as $A_1 \otimes A_2 = \langle X_1 \cup X_2, Q_1 \times Q_2, I_1 \times I_2, \to, F_1 \times F_2 \rangle$, where $\langle q_1, q_2 \rangle \xrightarrow{\varphi} \langle q_1', q_2' \rangle$ if and only if $q_1 \xrightarrow{\varphi_1}_1 q_1'$, $q_2 \xrightarrow{\varphi_2}_2 q_2'$ and $\models \varphi \leftrightarrow \varphi_1 \wedge \varphi_2$. We have that, for all sequences $\sigma \in Tr(A_1 \otimes A_2)$, $\sigma \downarrow_{X_1} \in Tr(A_1)$ and $\sigma \downarrow_{X_2} \in Tr(A_2)$, and vice versa.

3   Counter Automata as Recognisers of States and Transitions

In the rest of this section, let $\mathbf{a} = \{a_1, a_2, \ldots, a_k\}$ be a set of *array variables*, and $\mathbf{b} = \{b_1, b_2, \ldots, b_m\}$ be a set of *scalar variables*. A *state* $\langle \alpha, \iota \rangle$ is a pair of valuations $\alpha: \mathbf{a} \to \mathbb{Z}^*$, and $\iota: \mathbf{b} \to \mathbb{Z}$. For simplicity, we assume that $|\alpha(a_1)| = |\alpha(a_2)| = \ldots = |\alpha(a_k)| > 0$, and denote by $|\alpha|$ the size of the arrays in the state.

In the following, let X be a set of counters that is partitioned into *value counters* $\mathbf{x} = \{x_1, x_2, \ldots, x_k\}$, *index counters* $\mathbf{i} = \{i_1, i_2, \ldots, i_k\}$, *parameters* $\mathbf{p} = \{p_1, p_2, \ldots, p_m\}$, and *working counters* $\mathbf{w}$. Notice that $\mathbf{a}$ is in a 1:1 correspondence with both $\mathbf{x}$ and $\mathbf{i}$, and that $\mathbf{b}$ is in a 1:1 correspondence with $\mathbf{p}$.

Definition 1. *Let $\langle \alpha, \iota \rangle$ be a state. A sequence $\sigma \in (X \to \mathbb{Z})^*$ is said to be* consistent *with $\langle \alpha, \iota \rangle$, denoted $\sigma \vdash \langle \alpha, \iota \rangle$ if and only if, for all $1 \leq p \leq k$, and all $1 \leq r \leq m$:*

1. *for all $q \in \mathbb{N}$ with $0 \leq q < |\sigma|$, we have $0 \leq \sigma_q(i_p) \leq |\alpha|$,*
2. *for all $q, r \in \mathbb{N}$ with $0 \leq q < r < |\sigma|$, we have $\sigma_q(i_p) \leq \sigma_r(i_p)$,*
3. *for all $s \in \mathbb{N}$ with $0 \leq s \leq |\alpha|$, there exists $0 \leq q < |\sigma|$ such that $\sigma_q(i_p) = s$,*
4. *for all $q \in \mathbb{N}$ with $0 \leq q < |\sigma|$, if $\sigma_q(i_p) = s < |\alpha|$, then $\sigma_q(x_p) = \alpha(a_p)_s$,*
5. *for all $q \in \mathbb{N}$ with $0 \leq q < |\sigma|$, we have $\sigma_q(p_r) = \iota(b_r)$.*

Intuitively, a run of a CA represents the contents of a single array by traversing all of its entries in one move from the left to the right. The contents of multiple arrays is represented by arbitrarily interleaving the traversals of the different arrays. From this point of view, for a run to correspond to some state (i.e., to be *consistent* with it), it must be the case that each index counter either keeps its value or grows at each step of the run (point 2 of Def. 1) while visiting each entry within the array (points 1 and 3 of Def. 1).[1] The value of a certain entry of an array a_p is coded by the value that

---

[1] In fact, each index counter reaches the value $|\alpha|$ which is by one more than what is needed to traverse an array with entries $0, \ldots, |\alpha| - 1$. The reason is technical, related to the composition with transducers representing program loops (which produce array entries with a delay of one step and hence need the extra index value to produce the last array entry) as will become clear later. Note that the entry at position $|\alpha|$ is left unconstrained.

the array counter x_p has when the index counter i_p contains the position of the given entry (point 4 of Def. 1). Finally, values of scalar variables are encoded by values of the appropriate parameter counters which stay constant within a run (point 5 of Def. 1).

A CA is said to be *state consistent* if and only if for every trace $\sigma \in Tr(A)$, there exists a (unique) state $\langle \alpha, \iota \rangle$ such that $\sigma \vdash \langle \alpha, \iota \rangle$. We denote $\Sigma(A) = \{\langle \alpha, \iota \rangle \mid \exists \sigma \in Tr(A) . \sigma \vdash \langle \alpha, \iota \rangle\}$ the set of states recognised by a CA.

A consequence of Definition 1 is that, in between two adjacent positions of a trace, in a state-consistent CA, the index counters never increase by more than one. Consequently, each transition whose relation is non-deterministic w.r.t. an index counter can be split into two transitions: an *idle* (no change) and a *tick* (increment by one). In the following, we will silently assume that each transition of a state-consistent CA is either idle or tick w.r.t. a given index counter.

For any set $U = \{u_1, ..., u_n\}$, let us denote $U^i = \{u_1^i, ..., u_n^i\}$ and $U^o = \{u_1^o, ..., u_n^o\}$. If $s = \langle \alpha, \iota \rangle$ and $t = \langle \beta, \kappa \rangle$ are two states such that $|\alpha| = |\beta|$, the pair $\langle s, t \rangle$ is referred to as a *transition*. A CA $T = \langle X, Q, I, \rightarrow, F \rangle$ is said to be a *transducer* iff its set of counters X is partitioned into: *input counters* $\mathbf{x}^i$ and *output counters* $\mathbf{x}^o$, where $\mathbf{x} = \{x_1, x_2, \ldots, x_k\}$, *index counters* $\mathbf{i} = \{i_1, i_2, \ldots, i_k\}$, *input parameters* $\mathbf{p}^i$ and *output parameters* $\mathbf{p}^o$, where $\mathbf{p} = \{p_1, p_2, \ldots, p_m\}$, and *working counters* $\mathbf{w}$.

Definition 2. *A sequence $\sigma \in (X \rightarrow \mathbb{Z})^*$ is said to be* consistent *with a transition $\langle s, t \rangle$, where $s = \langle \alpha, \iota \rangle$ and $t = \langle \beta, \kappa \rangle$, denoted $\sigma \vdash \langle s, t \rangle$ if and only if, for all $1 \leq p \leq k$ and all $1 \leq r \leq m$:*

1. *for all $q \in \mathbb{N}$ with $0 \leq q < |\sigma|$, we have $0 \leq \sigma_q(i_p) \leq |\alpha|$,*
2. *for all $q, r \in \mathbb{N}$ with $0 \leq q < r < |\sigma|$, we have $\sigma_q(i_p) \leq \sigma_r(i_p)$,*
3. *for all $s \in \mathbb{N}$ with $0 \leq s \leq |\alpha|$, there exists $0 \leq q < |\sigma|$ such that $\sigma_q(i_p) = s$,*
4. *for all $q \in \mathbb{N}$ with $0 \leq q < |\sigma|$, if $\sigma_q(i_p) = s < |\alpha|$, then $\sigma_q(x_p^i) = \alpha(a_p)_s$,*
5. *for all $q \in \mathbb{N}$ with $0 \leq q < |\sigma|$, if $\sigma_q(i_p) = s > 0$, then $\sigma_q(x_p^o) = \beta(a_p)_{s-1}$,*
6. *for all $q \in \mathbb{N}$ with $0 \leq q < |\sigma|$, we have $\sigma_q(p_r^i) = \iota(b_r)$ and $\sigma(p_r^o) = \kappa(b_r)$.*

The intuition behind the way the transducers represent transitions of programs with arrays is very similar to the way we use counter automata to represent states of such programs—the transducers just have input as well as output counters whose values in runs describe the corresponding input and output states. Note that the definition of transducers is such that the output values occur with a delay of exactly one step w.r.t. the corresponding input (cf. point 5 in Def. 2).[2]

A transducer T is said to be *transition consistent* iff for every trace $\sigma \in Tr(T)$ there exists a transition $\langle s, t \rangle$ such that $\sigma \vdash \langle s, t \rangle$. We denote $\Theta(T) = \{\langle s, t \rangle \mid \exists \sigma \in Tr(T) . \sigma \vdash \langle s, t \rangle\}$ the set of transitions recognised by a transducer.

Dependencies between Index Counters. Counter automata and transducers can represent one array in more than one way, which poses problems when composing them. For instance, the array $a = \{0 \mapsto 4, 1 \mapsto 3, 2 \mapsto 2\}$ may be encoded, e.g., by the runs

---

[2] The intuition is that it takes the transducer one step to compute the output value, once it reads the input. It is possible to define a completely synchronous transducer, we, however, prefer this definition for technical reasons related to the translation of program loops into transducers.

$(0,4),(0,4),(1,3),(2,2),(2,2)$ and $(0,4),(1,3),(1,3),(2,2)$, where the first elements of the pairs are the values taken by the index counters, and the second elements are the values taken by the value counters corresponding to a. To obtain a sufficient criterion that guarantees that a CA and a transducer can be composed, meaning that they share a common representation of arrays, we introduce a notion of *dependence*. Intuitively, we call two or more index counters *dependent* if they increase at the same moments in all possible runs of a CA or transducer.

For the rest of this section, let $X \subset \mathbf{i}$ be a fixed set of index counters. A *dependency* δ is a conjunction of equalities between elements belonging X. For a sequence of valuations $\sigma \in (X \to \mathbb{Z})^*$, we denote $\sigma \models \delta$ if and only if $\sigma_l \models \delta$, for all $0 \le l < |\sigma|$.

For a dependency δ, we denote $[\![\delta]\!] = \{\sigma \in (X \to \mathbb{Z})^* \mid$ there exists a state s such that $\sigma \vdash s$ and $\sigma \models \delta\}$, i.e., the set of all sequences that correspond to an array and that satisfy δ. A dependency δ_1 is said to be *stronger* than another dependency δ_2, denoted $\delta_1 \to \delta_2$, if and only if the first order logic entailment between δ_1 and δ_2 is valid. Note that $\delta_1 \to \delta_2$ if and only if $[\![\delta_1]\!] \subseteq [\![\delta_2]\!]$. If $\delta_1 \to \delta_2$ and $\delta_2 \to \delta_1$, we write $\delta_1 \leftrightarrow \delta_2$. For a state consistent counter automaton (transition consistent transducer) A, we denote by $\Delta(A)$ the strongest dependency δ such that $Tr(A) \subseteq [\![\delta]\!]$.

Definition 3. *A CA $A = \langle \mathbf{x}, Q, I, \to, F \rangle$, where $\mathbf{x} \subseteq X$, is said to be* state-complete *if and only if for all states $s \in \Sigma(A)$, and each sequence $\sigma \in (X \to \mathbb{Z})^*$, such that $\sigma \vdash s$ and $\sigma \models \Delta(A)$, we have $\sigma \in Tr(A)$.*

Intuitively, an automaton A is state-complete if it represents any state $s \in \Sigma(A)$ in all possible ways w.r.t. the strongest dependency relation on its index counters.

Composing Counter Automata with Transducers. For a counter automaton A and a transducer T, $\Sigma(A)$ represents a set of states, whereas $\Theta(T)$ is a transition relation. A natural question is whether the post-image of $\Sigma(A)$ via the relation $\Theta(T)$ can be represented by a CA, and whether this automaton can be effectively built from A and T.

Theorem 1. *If A is a state-consistent and state-complete counter automaton with value counters $\mathbf{x} = \{x_1, ..., x_k\}$, index counters $\mathbf{i} = \{i_1, ..., i_k\}$, and parameters $\mathbf{p} = \{p_1, ..., p_m\}$, and T is a transducer with input (output) counters $\mathbf{x}^i$ ($\mathbf{x}^o$), index counters $\mathbf{i}$, and input (output) parameters $\mathbf{p}^i$ ($\mathbf{p}^o$) such that $\Delta(T)[\mathbf{x}/\mathbf{x}^i] \to \Delta(A)$, then one can build a state-consistent counter automaton B, such that $\Sigma(B) = \{t \mid \exists s \in \Sigma(A) . \langle s, t \rangle \in \Theta(T)\}$, and, moreover $\Delta(B) \to \Delta(T)[\mathbf{x}/\mathbf{x}^i]$.*

4   Singly Indexed Logic

We consider three types of variables. The *scalar variables* $b, b_1, b_2, ... \in BVar$ appear in the bounds that define the intervals in which some array property is required to hold and within constraints on non-array data variables. The *index variables* $i, i_1, i_2, ... \in IVar$ and *array variables* $a, a_1, a_2, ... \in AVar$ are used in array terms. The sets $BVar$, $IVar$, and $AVar$ are assumed to be pairwise disjoint.

Fig. 1 shows the syntax of the Single Index Logic **SIL**. We use the symbol $\top$ to denote the boolean value *true*. In the following, we will write $i < f$ instead of $i \le f - 1$,

$n, m, p \ldots \in \mathbb{Z}$	integer constants	$i, j, i_1, i_2, \ldots \in IVar$	index variables
$b, b_1, b_2, \ldots \in BVar$	scalar variables	$a, a_1, a_2, \ldots \in AVar$	array variables
ϕ	Presburger constraints	$\sim \quad \in \{\leq, \geq\}$	

$$
\begin{aligned}
B &:= n \mid b + n & \text{array-bound terms} \\
G &:= \top \mid B \leq i \leq B \mid G \wedge G \mid G \vee G & \text{guard expressions} \\
V &:= a[i+n] \sim B \mid a_1[i+n] - a_2[i+m] \sim p \mid i - a[i+n] \sim m \mid V \wedge V & \text{value expressions} \\
F &:= \forall i . G \rightarrow V \mid \phi(B_1, B_2, \ldots, B_n) \mid \neg F \mid F \wedge F & \text{formulae}
\end{aligned}
$$

Fig. 1. Syntax of the Single Index Logic

$i = f$ instead of $f \leq i \leq f$, $\varphi_1 \vee \varphi_2$ instead of $\neg(\neg\varphi_1 \wedge \neg\varphi_2)$, and $\forall i . \upsilon(i)$ instead of $\forall i . \top \rightarrow \upsilon(i)$. If $B_1(b_1), \ldots, B_n(b_n)$ are bound terms with free variables $b_1, \ldots, b_n \in BVar$, respectively, we write any Presburger formula φ on terms $a_1[B_1], \ldots, a_n[B_n]$ as a shorthand for $(\bigwedge_{k=1}^{n} \forall j . j = B_k \rightarrow a_k[j] = b'_k) \wedge \varphi[b'_1/a_1[B_1], \ldots, b'_n/a_n[B_n]]$, where $b'_1, \ldots, b'_n$ are fresh scalar variables.

The semantics of a formula φ is defined in terms of the forcing relation $\langle \alpha, \iota \rangle \models \varphi$ between states and formulae. In particular, $\langle \alpha, \iota \rangle \models \forall i . \gamma(i, \mathbf{b}) \rightarrow \upsilon(i, \mathbf{a}, \mathbf{b})$ if and only if, for all values n in the set $\bigcap\{[-m, |\alpha| - m - 1] \mid a[i + m] \text{ occurs in } \upsilon\}$, if $\iota \models \gamma[n/i]$, then also $\iota \cup \alpha \models \upsilon[n/i]$. Intuitively, the value expression γ should hold only for those indices that do not generate out of bounds array references.

We denote $[\![\varphi]\!] = \{\langle \alpha, \iota \rangle \mid \langle \alpha, \iota \rangle \models \varphi\}$. The *satisfiability problem* asks, for a given formula φ, whether $[\![\varphi]\!] \stackrel{?}{=} \emptyset$. We say that an automaton A and a **SIL** formula φ *correspond* if and only if $\Sigma(A) = [\![\varphi]\!]$.

The $\exists^*\forall^*$ fragment of **SIL** is the set of SIL formulae which, when written in prenex normal form, have the quantifier prefix of the form $\exists i_1 \ldots \exists i_n \forall j_1 \ldots \forall j_m$. As shown in [13] (for a slightly more complex syntax), the $\exists^*\forall^*$ fragment of **SIL** is equivalent to the set of existentially quantified boolean combinations of (1) Presburger constraints on scalar variables $\mathbf{b}$, and (2) array properties of the form $\forall i . \gamma(i, \mathbf{b}) \rightarrow \upsilon(i, \mathbf{b}, \mathbf{a})$.

Theorem 2 ([13]). *The satisfiability problem is decidable for the $\exists^*\forall^*$ fragment of* **SIL**.

Below, we establish a two-way connection between $\exists^*\forall^*$-**SIL** and counter automata. Namely, we show how loop pre-conditions written in $\exists^*\forall^*$-**SIL** can be translated to CA in a way suitable for their further composition with transducers representing program loops (for this reason the translation differs from [13]). Then, we show how $\exists^*\forall^*$-**SIL** formulae can be derived from the CA that we obtain as the product of loop transducers and pre-condition CA.

4.1 From $\exists^*\forall^*$-**SIL** to Counter Automata

Given a pre-condition φ expressed in $\exists^*\forall^*$-**SIL**, we build a corresponding counter automaton A, i.e., $\Sigma(A) = [\![\varphi]\!]$. Without loosing generality, we will assume that the pre-condition is satisfiable (which can be effectively checked due to Theorem 2).

For the rest of this section, let us fix a set of array variables $\mathbf{a} = \{a_1, a_2, \ldots, a_k\}$ and a set of scalar variables $\mathbf{b} = \{b_1, b_2, \ldots, b_m\}$. As shown in [13], each $\exists^*\forall^*$-**SIL** formula can be equivalently written as a boolean combination of two kinds of formulae:

(i) array properties of the form $\forall i \cdot f \leq i \leq g \rightarrow \upsilon$, where f and g are bound terms, and υ is either: (1) $a_p[i] \sim B$, (2) $i - a_p[i] \sim n$, or (3) $a_p[i] - a_q[i+1] \sim n$, where $\sim \in \{\leq, \geq\}$, $1 \leq p, q \leq k$, $n \in \mathbb{Z}$, and B is a bound term.

(ii) Presburger constraints on scalar variables $\mathbf{b}$.

Let us now fix a (normalised) pre-condition formula $\varphi(\mathbf{a}, \mathbf{b})$ of $\exists^* \forall^*$-**SIL**. By pushing negation inwards (using DeMorgan's laws) and eliminating it from Presburger constraints on scalar variables, we obtain a boolean combination of formulae of the forms (i) or (ii) above, where *only array properties may occur negated*.

W.l.o.g., we consider only pre-condition formulae without disjunctions.[3] For such formulae φ, we build CA A_φ with index counters $\mathbf{i} = \{i_1, i_2, ..., i_k\}$, value counters $\mathbf{x} = \{x_1, x_2, ..., x_k\}$, and parameters $\mathbf{p} = \{p_1, p_2, ..., p_m\}$, corresponding to the scalars $\mathbf{b}$.

For a term or formula f, we denote by $\overline{f}$ the term or formula obtained from f by replacing each b_q by p_q, $1 \leq q \leq m$, respectively. The construction of A_φ is defined recursively on the structure of φ:

- If $\varphi = \psi_1 \wedge \psi_2$, then $A_\varphi = A_{\psi_1} \otimes A_{\psi_2}$.
- If φ is a Presburger constraint on $\mathbf{b}$, then $A_\varphi = \langle X, Q, \{q_i\}, \rightarrow, \{q_f\} \rangle$ where:
  - $X = \{p_q \mid b_q \in FV(\varphi) \cap BVar, 1 \leq q \leq m\}$,
  - $Q = \{q_i, q_f\}$,
  - $q_i \xrightarrow{\overline{\varphi} \wedge \bigwedge_{x \in X} x' = x} q_f$ and $q_f \xrightarrow{\bigwedge_{x \in X} x' = x} q_f$.
- For φ being $\forall i \cdot f \leq i \leq g \rightarrow \upsilon$, A_φ and $A_{\neg\varphi}$ have states $Q = \{q_i, q_1, q_2, q_3, q_f\}$, with q_i and q_f being the initial and final states, respectively. Intuitively, the automaton waits in q_1 increasing its index counters until the lower bound f is reached, then moves to q_2 and checks the value constraint υ until the upper bound g is reached. Finally, the control moves to q_3 and the automaton scans the rest of the array until the end. In each state, the automaton can also non-deterministically choose to idle, which is needed to ensure state-completeness when making a product of such CA. For υ of type (1) and (2), the automaton has one index (i_p) and value (x_p) counters, while for υ of type (3), there are two dependent index (i_p, i_q) and value (x_p, x_q) counters. The full definitions of A_φ and $A_{\neg\varphi}$ are given in [4], for space reasons.

We aim now at computing the strongest dependency $\Delta(A_\varphi)$ between the index counters of A_φ, and, moreover, at showing that A_φ is state-complete (cf. Definition 3). Since A_φ is defined inductively, on the structure of φ, $\Delta(A_\varphi)$ can also be computed inductively. Let $\delta(\varphi)$ be the formula defined as follows:

- $\delta(\varphi) = \top$ if φ is a Presburger constraint on $\mathbf{b}$,
- for $\varphi \equiv \forall i \cdot f \leq i \leq g \rightarrow \upsilon$, $\delta(\varphi) \triangleq \delta(\neg\varphi) \triangleq \begin{cases} \top & \text{if } \upsilon \text{ is } a_p[i] \sim B \text{ or } i - a_p[i] \sim n, \\ i_p = i_q & \text{if } \upsilon \text{ is } a_p[i] - a_q[i+1] \sim n, \end{cases}$
- $\delta(\varphi_1 \wedge \varphi_2) = \delta(\varphi_1) \wedge \delta(\varphi_2)$.

Theorem 3. *Given a satisfiable $\exists^* \forall^*$-**SIL** formula φ, the following hold for the CA A_φ defined above: (1) A_φ is state consistent, (2) A_φ is state complete, (3) A_φ and φ correspond, and (4) $\delta(A_\varphi) \leftrightarrow \Delta(A_\varphi)$.*

---

[3] Given a formula containing disjunctions, we put it in DNF and check each disjunct separately.

4.2   From Counter Automata to $\exists^*\forall^*$-SIL

The purpose of this section is to establish a dual connection, from counter automata to the $\exists^*\forall^*$ fragment of **SIL**. Since obviously, counter automata are much more expressive than $\exists^*\forall^*$-**SIL**, our first concern is to abstract a given state-consistent CA A by a set of *restricted* CA $\mathcal{A}_1^K, \mathcal{A}_2^K, \ldots, \mathcal{A}_n^K$, such that $\Sigma(A) \subseteq \bigcap_{i=1}^n \Sigma(\mathcal{A}_i^K)$, and for each $\mathcal{A}_i^K$, $1 \leq i \leq n$, to generate an $\exists^*\forall^*$-**SIL** formula φ_i that corresponds to it. As a result, we obtain a formula $\varphi_A = \bigwedge_{i=1}^n \varphi_i$ such that $\Sigma(A) \subseteq [\![\varphi_A]\!]$.

Let $\rho(X, X')$ be a relation on a given set of integer variables X, and $I(X)$ be a predicate defining a subset of $\mathbb{Z}^k$. We denote by $\rho(I) = \{X' \mid \exists X \in I . \langle X, X'\rangle \in R\}$ the image of I via R, and we let $\rho \wedge I = \{\langle X, X'\rangle \in \rho \mid X \in I\}$. By ρ^n, we denote the n-times relational composition $\rho \circ \rho \circ \ldots \circ \rho$, $\rho^* = \bigvee_{n \geq 0} \rho^n$ is the reflexive and transitive closure of ρ, and $\top$ is the entire domain $\mathbb{Z}^k$. If ρ is a difference bound constraint, then ρ^n is also a difference bound constraint, for a fixed constant $n > 0$, and ρ^* is a Presburger definable relation [7,5] (but not necessarily a difference bound constraint).

Let $\mathcal{D}(\rho)$ denote the strongest (in the logical sense) difference bound relation D s.t. $\rho \subseteq D$. If ρ is Presburger definable, $\mathcal{D}(\rho)$ can be effectively computed[4], and, moreover, if ρ is a finite union of n difference bound relations, this takes $O(n \times 4k^2)$ time[5], where k is the number of free variables in ρ.

We now define the restricted class of CA, called *flat counter automata with difference bound constraints* (FCADBC) into which we abstract the given CA. A *control path* in a CA A is a finite sequence $q_1 q_2 \ldots q_n$ of control states such that, for all $1 \leq i < n$, there exists a transition rule $q_i \xrightarrow{\varphi_i} q_{i+1}$. A *cycle* is a control path starting and ending in the same control state. An *elementary cycle* is a cycle in which each state appears only once, except for the first one, which appears both at the beginning and at the end. A CA is said to be *flat* (FCA) iff each control state belongs to at most one elementary cycle. An FCA such that every relation labelling a transition occurring in an elementary cycle is a DBC, and the other relations are Presburger constraints, is called an FCADBC.

With these notations, we define the *K-unfolding* of a one-state self-loop CA $A_\rho = \langle X, \{q\}, \{q\}, q \xrightarrow{\rho} q, \{q\}\rangle$ as the FCADBC $A_\rho^K = \langle X, Q_\rho^K, \{q_1\}, \rightarrow_\rho^K, Q_\rho^K\rangle$, where $Q_\rho^K = \{q_1, q_2, \ldots, q_K\}$ and $\rightarrow_\rho^K$ is defined such that $q_i \xrightarrow{\rho} q_{i+1}$, $1 \leq i < K$, and $q_K \xrightarrow{\rho^K(\top) \wedge \rho} q_K$. The *K-abstraction* of A_ρ, denoted $\mathcal{A}_\rho^K$ (cf. Fig. 2), is obtained from A_ρ^K by replacing the transition rule $q_K \xrightarrow{\rho^K(\top) \wedge \rho} q_K$ with the difference bound rule $q_K \xrightarrow{\mathcal{D}(\rho^K(\top) \wedge \rho)} q_K$. Intuitively, the information gathered by unfolding the *concrete* relation K times prior to the abstraction on the loop $q_K \rightarrow q_K$, allows to tighten the abstraction, according to the K parameter. Notice that the $\mathcal{A}_\rho^K$ abstraction of a relation ρ is an FCADBC with exactly one initial state, one self-loop, and all states final. The following lemma proves that the abstraction is sound, and that it can be refined, by increasing K.

Lemma 1. *Given a relation* $\rho(X, X')$ *on* $X = \{x_1, \ldots, x_k\}$, *the following facts hold:* (1) $Tr(A_\rho) = Tr(A_\rho^K) \subseteq Tr(\mathcal{A}_\rho^K)$, *for all* $K > 0$, *and* (2) $Tr(\mathcal{A}_\rho^{K_2}) \subseteq Tr(\mathcal{A}_\rho^{K_1})$ *if* $K_1 \leq K_2$.

---

[4] $\mathcal{D}(\rho)$ can be computed by finding the unique minimal assignment $\nu : \{z_{ij} \mid 1 \leq i, j \leq k\} \rightarrow \mathbb{Z}$ that satisfies the Presburger formula $\phi(\mathbf{z}) : \forall X \forall X' . \rho(X, X') \rightarrow \bigwedge_{x_i, x_j \in X \cup X'} x_i - x_j \leq z_{ij}$.

[5] If $\rho = \rho_1 \vee \rho_2 \vee \ldots \vee \rho_n$, and each ρ_i is represented by a $(2k)^2$-matrix M_i, $\mathcal{D}(\rho)$ is given by the pointwise maximum among all matrices M_i, $1 \leq i \leq n$.

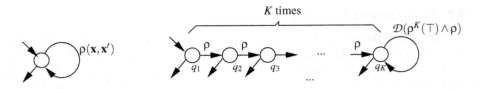

Fig. 2. K-abstraction of a relation

For the rest of this section, assume a set of arrays $\mathbf{a} = \{a_1, a_2, \ldots, a_k\}$ and a set of scalars $\mathbf{b} = \{b_1, b_2, \ldots, b_m\}$. At this point, we can describe an abstraction for counter automata that yields from an arbitrary state-consistent CA A, a set of state-consistent FCADBC $\mathcal{A}_1^K, \mathcal{A}_2^K, \ldots, \mathcal{A}_n^K$, whose intersection of sets of recognised states is a superset of the original one, i.e., $\Sigma(A) \subseteq \bigcap_{i=1}^n \Sigma(\mathcal{A}_i^K)$. Let A be a state-consistent CA with counters X partitioned into value counters $\mathbf{x} = \{x_1, \ldots, x_k\}$, index counters $\mathbf{i} = \{i_1, \ldots, i_k\}$, parameters $\mathbf{p} = \{p_1, \ldots, p_m\}$ and working counters $\mathbf{w}$. We assume that the only actions on an index counter $i \in \mathbf{i}$ are *tick* ($i' = i + 1$) and *idle* ($i' = i$), which is sufficient for the CA that we generate from **SIL** or loops.

The main idea behind the abstraction method is to keep the idle relations separate from ticks. Notice that, by combining (i.e., taking the union of) idle and tick transitions, we obtain non-deterministic relations (w.r.t. index counters) that may break the state-consistency requirement imposed on the abstract counter automata. Hence, the first step is to eliminate the idle transitions.

Let δ be an over-approximation of the dependency $\Delta(A)$, i.e., $\Delta(A) \to \delta$. In particular, if A was obtained as in Theorem 1, by composing a pre-condition automaton with a transducer T, and if we dispose of an over-approximation δ of $\Delta(T)$, i.e., $\Delta(T) \to \delta$, we have that $\Delta(A) \to \delta$, cf. Theorem 1—any over-approximation of the transducer's dependency is an over-approximation of the dependency for the post-image CA.

The dependency δ induces an equivalence relation on index counters: for all $i, j \in \mathbf{i}$, $i \simeq_\delta j$ iff $\delta \to i = j$. This relation partitions $\mathbf{i}$ into n equivalence classes $[i_{s_1}], [i_{s_2}], \ldots, [i_{s_n}]$, where $1 \leq s_1, s_2, \ldots, s_n \leq k$. Let us consider n identical copies of A: $A_1, A_2, \ldots, A_n$. Each copy A_j will be abstracted *w.r.t. the corresponding* $\simeq_\delta$-*equivalence class* $[i_{s_j}]$ into $\mathcal{A}_j^K$ obtained as in Fig. 2. Thus we obtain $\Sigma(A) \subseteq \bigcap_{j=1}^n \Sigma(\mathcal{A}_j^K)$, by Lemma 1.

We describe now the abstraction of the A_j copy of A into $\mathcal{A}_j^K$. W.l.o.g., we assume that the control flow graph of A_j consists of one strongly connected component (SCC)—otherwise we separately replace each (non-trivial) SCC by a flat CA obtained as described below. Out of the set of relations $\mathcal{R}_{A_j}$ that label transitions of A_j, let $\upsilon_1^j, \ldots, \upsilon_p^j$ be the set of *idle* relations w.r.t. $[i_{s_j}]$, i.e., $\upsilon_t^j \to \bigwedge_{i \in [i_{s_j}]} i' = i$, $1 \leq t \leq p$, and $\theta_1^j, \ldots, \theta_q^j$ be the set of *tick* relations w.r.t. $[i_{s_j}]$, i.e., $\theta_t^j \to \bigwedge_{i \in [i_{s_j}]} i' = i + 1$, $1 \leq t \leq q$. Note that since we consider index counters belonging to the same $\simeq_\delta$-equivalence class, they either all idle or all tick, hence $\{\upsilon_1^j, \ldots, \upsilon_p^j\}$ and $\{\theta_1^j, \ldots, \theta_q^j\}$ form a partition of $\mathcal{R}_{A_j}$.

Let $\Upsilon_j = \mathcal{D}(\bigvee_{t=1}^p \upsilon_t^j)$ be the best difference bound relation that approximates the idle part of A_j, and Υ_j^* be its reflexive and transitive closure[6]. Let $\Theta_j = \bigvee_{t=1}^q \mathcal{D}(\Upsilon_j^*) \circ \theta_t^j$, and

---

[6] Since Υ_j is a difference bound relation, by [7,5], we have that Υ_j^* is Presburger definable.

let A_{Θ_j} be the one-state self-loop automaton whose transition is labelled by Θ_j, and $\mathcal{A}_j^K$ be the K-abstraction of A_{Θ_j} (cf. Fig. 2). It is to be noticed that the abstraction replaces a state-consistent FCA with a single SCC by a set of state-consistent FCADBC *with one self-loop*. The soundness of the abstraction is proved in the following:

Lemma 2. *Given a state-consistent CA A with index counters* $\mathbf{i}$ *and a dependency* δ *s.t.* $\Delta(A) \rightarrow \delta$, *let* $[i_{s_1}], [i_{s_2}], \ldots, [i_{s_n}]$ *be the partition of* $\mathbf{i}$ *into* $\simeq_\delta$-*equivalence classes. Then each* $\mathcal{A}_i^K$, $1 \leq i \leq n$ *is state-consistent, and* $\Sigma(A) \subseteq \bigcap_{i=1}^n \Sigma(\mathcal{A}_i^K)$, *for any* $K \geq 0$.

The next step is to build, for each FCADBC $\mathcal{A}_i^K$, $1 \leq i \leq n$, an $\exists^*\forall^*$-**SIL** formula φ_i such that $\Sigma(\mathcal{A}_i^K) = [\![\varphi_i]\!]$, for all $1 \leq i \leq n$, and, finally, let $\varphi_A = \bigwedge_{i=1}^n \varphi_i$ be the needed formula. The generation of the formulae builds on that we are dealing with CA of the form depicted in the right of Fig. 2.[7]

For a relation $\varphi(X, X')$, $X = \mathbf{x} \cup \mathbf{p}$, let $\mathcal{T}_i(\varphi)$ be the **SIL** formula obtained by replacing (1) each unprimed value counter $x_s \in FV(\varphi) \cap \mathbf{x}$ by $a_s[i]$, (2) each primed value counter $x_s' \in FV(\varphi) \cap \mathbf{x}'$ by $a_s[i+1]$, and (3) each parameter $p_r \in FV(\varphi) \cap \mathbf{p}$ by b_r, for $1 \leq s \leq k$, $1 \leq r \leq m$.

For the rest, fix an automaton $\mathcal{A}_j^K$ of the form from Fig. 2 for some $1 \leq j \leq n$, and let $q_p \xrightarrow{\rho} q_{p+1}$, $1 \leq p < K$, be its sequential part, and $q_K \xrightarrow{\lambda} q_K$ its self-loop. Let $[i_{s_j}] = \{i_{t_1}, i_{t_2}, \ldots, i_{t_q}\}$ be the set of relevant index counters for $\mathcal{A}_j^K$, and let $\mathbf{x}_r = \mathbf{x} \setminus \{x_{t_1}, \ldots, x_{t_q}\}$ be the set of redundant value counters. With these notations, the desired formula is defined as $\varphi_j = (\bigvee_{l=1}^{K-1} \tau(l)) \vee (\exists b \,.\, b \geq 0 \wedge \tau(K) \wedge \omega(b))$, where:

$$\tau(l): \bigwedge_{s=0}^{l-1} \mathcal{T}_s(\exists \mathbf{i}, \mathbf{x}_r, \mathbf{x}_r', \mathbf{w}. \, \rho) \qquad \omega(b): (\forall i \,.\, K \leq j < K+b \rightarrow \mathcal{T}_i(\exists \mathbf{i}, \mathbf{x}_r, \mathbf{x}_r', \mathbf{w}. \, \lambda)) \wedge$$
$$\mathcal{T}_0(\exists \mathbf{i}, \mathbf{x}, \mathbf{x}', \mathbf{w}. \, \lambda^b[K/i_{t_1}, \ldots, i_{t_q}][K+b-1/i_{t_1}', \ldots, i_{t_q}'])$$

Here, $b \in BVar$ is a fresh scalar denoting the number of times the self-loop $q_K \xrightarrow{\lambda} q_K$ is iterated. λ^b denotes the formula defining the b-times composition of λ with itself.[8]

Intuitively, $\tau(l)$ describes arrays corresponding to runs of $\mathcal{A}_j^K$ from q_1 to q_l, for some $1 \leq l \leq K$, without iterating the self-loop $q_K \xrightarrow{\lambda} q_K$, while $\omega(b)$ describes the arrays corresponding to runs going through the self-loop b times. The second conjunct of $\omega(b)$ uses the closed form of the b-th iteration of λ, denoted λ^b, in order to capture the possible relations between b and the scalar variables $\mathbf{b}$ corresponding to the parameters $\mathbf{p}$ in λ, created by iterating the self-loop.

Theorem 4. *Given a state-consistent CA A with index counters* $\mathbf{i}$ *and given a dependency* δ *such that* $\Delta(A) \rightarrow \delta$, *we have* $\Sigma(A) \subseteq [\![\varphi_A]\!]$, *where:*

- $\varphi_A = \bigwedge_{i=1}^n \varphi_i$, *where* φ_i *is the formula corresponding to* $\mathcal{A}_i^K$, *for all* $1 \leq i \leq n$, *and*
- $\mathcal{A}_1^K, \mathcal{A}_2^K, \ldots, \mathcal{A}_n^K$ *are the K-abstractions corresponding to the equivalence classes induced by* δ *on* $\mathbf{i}$.

---

[7] In case we start from a CA with more SCCs, we get a CA with a DAG-shaped control flow interconnecting components of the form depicted in Fig. 2 after the abstraction. Such a CA may be converted to **SIL** by describing each component by a formula as above, parameterised by its beginning and final index values, and then connecting such formulae by conjunctions within particular control branches and taking a disjunction of the formulae derived for the particular branches. Due to lack of space, we give this construction in detail in [4] only.

[8] Since λ is difference bound relation, λ^b can be defined by a Presburger formula [7,5].

5   Array Manipulating Programs

We consider programs consisting of assignments, conditional statements, and non-nested while loops in the form shown in Fig. 4, working over arrays $AVar$ and scalar variables $BVar$ (for a formal syntax, see [4]). In a loop, we assume a 1:1 correspondence between the set of arrays $AVar$ and the set of indices $IVar$. In other words, each array is associated exactly

$b \in BVar, a \in AVar, i \in IVar, n \in \mathbb{Z}, c \in \mathbb{N}$

$ASGN ::= LHS = RHS$
$LHS \ \ ::= b \mid a[i+c]$
$TRM \ ::= LHS \mid i$
$RHS \ ::= TRM \mid -TRM \mid TRM+n$
$CND \ ::= CND \ \&\& \ CND \mid RHS \leq RHS$

Fig. 3. Assignments and conditions

one index variable. Each index $i \in IVar$ is initialised at the beginning of a loop using an expression of the form $b + n$ where $b \in BVar$ and $n \in \mathbb{Z}$. The indices are local to the loop. The body $S_1^l;...;S_{n_l}^l;$ of each loop branch consists of zero or more assignments followed by a single index increment statement $\mathtt{incr}(I)$, $I \subseteq IVar$. The syntax of the assignments and boolean expressions used in conditional statements is shown in Fig. 3. We consider a simple syntax to make the presentation of the proposed techniques easier: various more complex features can be handled by straightforwardly extending the techniques described below.

A *state of a program* is a pair $\langle l, s \rangle$ where l is a line of the program and s is a state $\langle \alpha, \iota \rangle$ defined as in Section 3. The semantics of program statements is the usual one (e.g., [19]). For simplicity of the further constructions, we assume that no *out-of-bound array references* occur in the programs—such situations are considered in [4].

Considering the program statements given in Fig. 3, we have developed a strongest post-condition calculus for the $\exists^*\forall^*$-**SIL** fragment. This calculus captures the semantics of the assignments and conditionals, and is used to deal with the sequential parts of the program (the blocks of statements outside the loops). It is also shown that $\exists^*\forall^*$-**SIL** is closed for strongest post-conditions. Full details are given in [4].

5.1   From Loops to Counter Automata

Given a loop L starting at control line l, such that l' is the control line immediately following L, we denote by $\Theta_L = \{\langle s,t \rangle \mid$ there is a run of L from $\langle l,s \rangle$ to $\langle l',t \rangle\}$ the transition relation induced by L.[9] We define the *loop dependency* δ_L as the conjunction of equalities $i_p = i_q$, $i_p, i_q \in IVar$, where (1) $e_p \equiv e_q$ where e_1 and e_2 are the expressions initialising i_p and i_q and (2) for each branch of L finished by an index increment statement $\mathtt{incr}(I)$, $i_p \in I \iff i_q \in I$. The equivalence relation $\simeq_{\delta_L}$ on index counters is defined as before: $i_p \simeq_{\delta_L} i_q$ iff $\models \delta_L \to i_p = i_q$.

Assume that we are given a loop L as in Fig. 4 with $AVar = \{a_1,...,a_k\}$, $IVar = \{i_1,...,i_k\}$, and $BVar = \{b_1,...,b_m\}$ being the sets of array, index,

$while_{a_1:i_1=e_1,...,a_k:i_k=e_k}$ (C)
$if \ (C_1) \ S_1^1;...;S_{n_1}^1;$
$else \ if \ (C_2) \ S_1^2;...;S_{n_2}^2;$
$...$
$else \ if \ (C_{h-1}) \ S_1^{h-1};...;S_{n_{h-1}}^{h-1};$
$else \ S_1^h;...;S_{n_h}^h;$

Fig. 4. A while loop

---

[9] Note that we ignore non-terminating runs of the loop in case there are some—our concern is not to check termination of the loop, but correctness of terminating runs of the loop.

and scalar variables, respectively. Let $I_1, I_2, \ldots, I_n \subseteq IVar$ be the partition of $IVar$ into equivalence classes, induced by $\simeq_{\delta_L}$. For E being a condition, assignment, index increment, or an entire loop, we define $d_E : AVar \to \mathbb{N} \cup \{\bot\}$ as $d_E(a) = max\{c \mid a[i+c] \text{ occurs in } E\}$ provided a is used in E, and $d_E(a) = \bot$ otherwise. The transducer $T_L = \langle X, Q, \{q_0\}, \to, \{q_{fin}\}\rangle$, corresponding to the program loop L, is defined below:

- $X = \{x_r^i, x_r^o, i_r \mid 1 \leq r \leq k\} \cup \{w_{r,l}^i \mid 1 \leq r \leq k, 1 \leq l \leq d_L(a_r)\} \cup \{w_{r,l}^o \mid 1 \leq r \leq k, 0 \leq l \leq d_L(a_r)\} \cup \{p_r^i, p_r^o, w_r \mid 1 \leq r \leq m\} \cup \{w_N\}$ where $x_r^{i/o}$, $1 \leq r \leq k$, are input/output array counters, $p_r^{i/o}$, $1 \leq r \leq k$, are parameters storing input/output scalar values, and w_r, $1 \leq r \leq m$, are working counters used for the manipulation of arrays and scalars (w_N stores the common length of arrays).
- $Q = \{q_0, q_{pre}, q_{loop}, q_{suf}, q_{fin}\} \cup \{q_r^l \mid 1 \leq l \leq h, 0 \leq r < n_l\}$.
- The transition rules of T_L are the following. We assume an implicit constraint $x' = x$ for each counter $x \in X$ such that x' does not appear explicitly:
  - $q_0 \xrightarrow{\varphi} q_{pre}$, $\varphi = \bigwedge_{1 \leq r \leq m}(w_r = p_r^i) \wedge w_N > 0 \wedge \bigwedge_{1 \leq r \leq k}(i_r = 0 \wedge x_r^i = w_{r,0}^o) \wedge \bigwedge_{\substack{1 \leq r \leq k \\ 1 \leq l \leq d_L(a_r)}}(w_{r,l}^i = w_{r,l}^o)$ (the counters are initialised).
  - For each $\simeq_{\delta_L}$-equivalence class I_j, $1 \leq j \leq n$, $q_{pre} \xrightarrow{\varphi} q_{pre}$ with $\varphi = \bigwedge_{1 \leq r \leq k}(i_r < \xi(e_r)) \wedge \xi(incr(I))$ (T_L copies the initial parts of the arrays untouched by L).
  - $q_{pre} \xrightarrow{\varphi} q_{loop}$, $\varphi = \bigwedge_{1 \leq r \leq k} i_r = \xi(e_r)$ (T_L starts simulating L).
  - For each $1 \leq l \leq h$, $q_{loop} \xrightarrow{\varphi} q_0^l$, $\varphi = \xi(C) \wedge \bigwedge_{1 \leq r < l}(\neg\xi(C_r)) \wedge \xi(C_l)$ where $C_h = \top$ (T_L chooses the loop branch to be simulated).
  - For each $1 \leq l \leq h$, $1 \leq r \leq n_l$, $q_{r-1}^l \xrightarrow{\xi(S_r^l)} q$ where $q = q_r^l$ if $r < n_l$, and $q = q_{loop}$ otherwise (the automaton simulates one branch of the loop).
  - $q_{loop} \xrightarrow{\varphi} q_{suf}$, $\varphi = \neg\xi(C) \wedge \bigwedge_{1 \leq r \leq m}(w_r = p_r^o)$ (T_L finished the simulation of the actual execution of L).
  - For each $\simeq_{\delta_L}$-equivalence class I_j, $1 \leq j \leq n$, and $i_r \in I_j$, $q_{suf} \xrightarrow{\varphi} q_{suf}$, $\varphi = i_r < w_N \wedge \xi(incr(I_j))$ (copy the array suffixes untouched by the loop).
  - $q_{suf} \xrightarrow{\varphi} q_{fin}$, $\varphi = \bigwedge_{1 \leq r \leq k} i_r = w_N$ (all arrays are entirely processed).

The syntactical transformation ξ of assignments and conditions preserves the structure of these expressions, but replaces each b_r by the counter w_r and each $a_r[i_r + c]$ by $w_{r,c}^o$ for $b_r \in BVar$, $a_r \in AVar$, $i_r \in IVar$, and $c \in \mathbb{N}$. On the left-hand sides of the assignments, future values of the counters are used (cf. [4]). For increment statements we define, for all $i_r \in IVar$:

- $\xi(incr(i_r)) : x_r^{i'} = w_{r,1}^i \wedge \bigwedge_{1 < l \leq d_L(a_r)} w_{r,l-1}^{i'} = w_{r,l}^i \wedge x_r^{o'} = w_{r,0}^o \wedge \bigwedge_{0 < l \leq d_L(a_r)} w_{r,l-1}^{o'} = w_{r,l}^o \wedge w_{r,d_L(a_r)}^{i'} = w_{r,d_L(a_r)}^o \wedge i_r' = i_r + 1$, if $d_L(a_r) > 0$,
- $\xi(incr(i_r)) : x_r^{i'} = w_{r,0}^{o'} \wedge x_r^{o'} = w_{r,0}^o \wedge i_r' = i_r + 1$, if $d_L(a_r) = 0$.

For the increment of a set of indices, we extend this definition pointwise.

The main idea of the construction is the following. T_L preserves the exact sequences of operations done on arrays and scalars in L, but performs them on suitably chosen counters instead, exploiting the fact that the program always accesses the arrays through a bounded window only, which is moving from the left to right. The contents of this window is stored in the working counters. The values stored in these counters are shifted among the counters at each increment step. In particular, the initial value of an array cell $a_r[l]$ is stored in $w^o_{r,d_L(a_r)}$ for $d_L(a_r) > 0$ (the case of $d_L(a_r) = 0$ is just a bit simpler). This value can then be accessed and/or modified via $w^o_{r,q}$ where $q \in \{d_L(a_r),...,0\}$ in the iterations $l - d_L(a_r),...,l$, respectively, due to copying $w^o_{r,q}$ into $w^o_{r,q-1}$ whenever simulating $incr(i_r)$ for $q > 0$. At the same time, the initial value of $a_r[l]$ is stored in $w^i_{r,d_L(a_r)}$, which is then copied into $w^i_{r,q}$ for $q \in \{d_L(a_r) - 1,...,1\}$ and finally into x^i_r, which happens exactly when i_r reaches the value l. Within the simulation of the next $incr(i_r)$ statement, the final value of $a_r[l]$ appears in x^o_r, which is exactly in accordance with how a transducer expresses a change in a certain cell of an array (cf. Def. 2).

Note also that the value of the index counters i_r is correctly initialised via evaluating the appropriate initialising expressions e_r, it is increased at the same positions of the runs in both the loop L and the transducer T_L, and it is tested within the same conditions. Moreover, the construction takes care of appropriately processing the array cells which are accessed less than the maximum possible number of times (i.e., less than $\delta_L(a_r)+1$-times) by (1) "copying" from the input x^i_r counters to the output x^o_r counters the values of all the array cells skipped at the beginning of the array by the loop, (2) by appropriately setting the initial values of all the working array counters before simulating the first iteration of the loop, and (3) by finishing the pass through the entire array even when the simulated loop does not pass it entirely.

The scalar variables are handled in a correct way too: Their input value is recorded in the p^i_r counters, this value is initially copied into the working counters w_r which are modified throughout the run of the transducer by the same operations as the appropriate program variables, and, at the end, the transducer checks whether the p^o_r counters contain the right output value of these variables.

Finally, as for what concerns the dependencies, note that all the arrays whose indices are dependent in the loop (meaning that these indices are advanced in exactly the same loop branches and are initialised in the same way) are processed at the same time in the initial and final steps of the transducers (when the transducer is in the control states q_{pre} or q_{suf}). Within the control paths leading from q_{loop} to q_{loop}, indices of such arrays are advanced at the same time as these paths directly correspond to the branches of the loop. Hence, the working counters of these arrays have always the same value, which is, however, not necessarily the case for the other arrays.

It is thus easy to see that we can formulate the correctness of the translation as captured by the following Theorem.

Theorem 5. *Given a program loop L, the following hold: (1) T_L is a transition-consistent transducer, (2) $\Theta(L) = \Theta(T_L)$, and (3) $\Delta(T_L) \to \delta_L$.*

The last point of Theorem 5 ensures that δ_L is a safe over-approximation of the dependency between the index counters of T_L. This over-approximation is used in Theorem 1 to check whether the post-image of a pre-condition automaton A can be effectively computed, by checking $\delta_T \to \Delta(A)$. In order to meet requirements of Theorem 1, one can extend T_L in a straightforward way to copy from the input to the output all the arrays and integer variables which appear in the program but not in L.

6   Examples

In order to validate our approach, we have performed proof-of-concept experiments with several programs handling integer arrays. Table 1 reports the size of the derived post-image automata (i.e., the CA representing the set of states after the main program loop) in numbers of *control states* and *counters*. The automata were slightly optimised using simple, lightweight static techniques (eliminating useless counters, compacting sequences of idling transitions with the first tick transition, eliminating clearly infeasible transitions). The result sizes give a hint on the simplicity and compactness of the obtained automata. As our prototype implementation is not completed to date, we have performed several steps of the translation into counter automata and back manually. The details of the experiments are given in [4].

The init example is the classical initialisation of an array with zeros. The partition example copies the positive elements of an array *a* into another array *b*, and the negative ones into *c*. The insert example inserts an element on its corresponding position in a sorted array. The rotate example takes an array and rotates it by one position to the left. For all examples from Table 1, a human-readable post-condition describing the expected effect of the program has been inferred by our method.

Table 1. Examples

program	control states	counters
init	4	8
partition	4	24
insert	7	19
rotate	4	15

7   Conclusion

In this paper, we have developed a new method for the verification of programs with integer arrays based on a novel combination of logic and counter automata. We use a logic of integer arrays to express pre- and post-conditions of programs and their parts, and counter automata and transducers to represent the effect of loops and to decide entailments. We have successfully validated our method on a set of experiments. A full implementation of our technique, which will allow us to do more experiments, is currently under way. In the future, we are, e.g., planning to investigate possibilities of using more static analyses to further shrink the size of the generated automata, optimisations to be used when computing transitive closures needed within the translation from CA to **SIL**, adjusted for the typical scenarios that happen in our setting, etc.

References

1. Beyer, D., Henzinger, T.A., Majumdar, R., Rybalchenko, A.: Invariant Synthesis for Combined Theories. In: Cook, B., Podelski, A. (eds.) VMCAI 2007. LNCS, vol. 4349, pp. 378–394. Springer, Heidelberg (2007)
2. Beyer, D., Henzinger, T.A., Majumdar, R., Rybalchenko, A.: Path Invariants. In: Proc. of PLDI 2007, ACM SIGPLAN (2007)
3. Bouajjani, A., Habermehl, P., Jurski, Y., Sighireanu, M.: Rewriting Systems with Data: A Framework for Reasoning about Systems with Unbounded Structures over Infinite Data Domains. In: Csuhaj-Varjú, E., Ésik, Z. (eds.) FCT 2007. LNCS, vol. 4639, pp. 1–22. Springer, Heidelberg (2007)

4. Bozga, M., Habermehl, P., Iosif, R., Konečný, F., Vojnar, T.: Automatic Verification of Integer Array Programs. Technical Report TR-2009-2, Verimag, Grenoble, France (2009)
5. Bozga, M., Iosif, R., Lakhnech, Y.: Flat Parametric Counter Automata. In: Bugliesi, M., Preneel, B., Sassone, V., Wegener, I. (eds.) ICALP 2006. LNCS, vol. 4052, pp. 577–588. Springer, Heidelberg (2006)
6. Bradley, A.R., Manna, Z., Sipma, H.B.: What's Decidable About Arrays? In: Emerson, E.A., Namjoshi, K.S. (eds.) VMCAI 2006. LNCS, vol. 3855, pp. 427–442. Springer, Heidelberg (2006)
7. Comon, H., Jurski, Y.: Multiple Counters Automata, Safety Analysis and Presburger Arithmetic. In: Y. Vardi, M. (ed.) CAV 1998. LNCS, vol. 1427. Springer, Heidelberg (1998)
8. Flanagan, C., Qadeer, S.: Predicate Abstraction for Software Verification. In: Proc. of POPL 2002. ACM, New York (2002)
9. Ghilardi, S., Nicolini, E., Ranise, S., Zucchelli, D.: Decision Procedures for Extensions of the Theory of Arrays. Annals of Mathematics and Artificial Intelligence 50 (2007)
10. Ghilardi, S., Nicolini, E., Ranise, S., Zucchelli, D.: Towards SMT Model Checking of Array-based Systems. In: Armando, A., Baumgartner, P., Dowek, G. (eds.) IJCAR 2008. LNCS, vol. 5195, pp. 67–82. Springer, Heidelberg (2008)
11. Gopan, D., Reps, T.W., Sagiv, S.: A Framework for Numeric Analysis of Array Operations. In: POPL 2005. ACM, New York (2005)
12. Gulwani, S., McCloskey, B., Tiwari, A.: Lifting Abstract Interpreters to Quantified Logical Domains. In: POPL 2008. ACM, New York (2008)
13. Habermehl, P., Iosif, R., Vojnar, T.: A Logic of Singly Indexed Arrays. In: Cervesato, I., Veith, H., Voronkov, A. (eds.) LPAR 2008. LNCS (LNAI), vol. 5330, pp. 558–573. Springer, Heidelberg (2008)
14. Habermehl, P., Iosif, R., Vojnar, T.: What Else is Decidable about Integer Arrays? In: Amadio, R. (ed.) FOSSACS 2008. LNCS, vol. 4962, pp. 474–489. Springer, Heidelberg (2008)
15. Halbwachs, N., Péron, M.: Discovering Properties about Arrays in Simple Programs. In: Proc. of PLDI 2008. ACM, New York (2008)
16. Jhala, R., McMillan, K.: Array Abstractions from Proofs. In: Damm, W., Hermanns, H. (eds.) CAV 2007. LNCS, vol. 4590, pp. 193–206. Springer, Heidelberg (2007)
17. Kovács, L., Voronkov, A.: Finding Loop Invariants for Programs over Arrays Using a Theorem Prover. In: Chechik, M., Wirsing, M. (eds.) FASE 2009. LNCS, vol. 5503, pp. 470–486. Springer, Heidelberg (2009)
18. Lahiri, S.K., Bryant, R.E.: Indexed Predicate Discovery for Unbounded System Verification. In: Alur, R., Peled, D.A. (eds.) CAV 2004. LNCS, vol. 3114, pp. 135–147. Springer, Heidelberg (2004)
19. Manna, Z., Pnueli, A.: The Temporal Logic of Reactive and Concurrent Systems. Springer, Heidelberg (1992)
20. McMillan, K.: Quantified Invariant Generation Using an Interpolating Saturation Prover. In: Ramakrishnan, C.R., Rehof, J. (eds.) TACAS 2008. LNCS, vol. 4963, pp. 413–427. Springer, Heidelberg (2008)
21. Stump, A., Barrett, C.W., Dill, D.L., Levitt, J.R.: A Decision Procedure for an Extensional Theory of Arrays. In: Proc. of LICS 2001. IEEE Computer Society, Los Alamitos (2001)

Automated Analysis of Java Methods for Confidentiality*

Pavol Černý and Rajeev Alur

University of Pennsylvania
{cernyp,alur}@cis.upenn.edu

Abstract. We address the problem of analyzing programs such as J2ME midlets for mobile devices, where a central correctness requirement concerns confidentiality of data that the user wants to keep secret. Existing software model checking tools analyze individual program executions, and are not applicable to checking confidentiality properties that require reasoning about equivalence among executions. We develop an automated analysis technique for such properties. We show that both over- and under- approximation is needed for sound analysis. Given a program and a confidentiality requirement, our technique produces a formula that is satisfiable if the requirement holds. We evaluate the approach by analyzing bytecode of a set of Java (J2ME) methods.

1 Introduction

Security properties based on information flow, such as confidentiality, are increasingly becoming a concern in software development [28]. This motivates research in verification techniques for establishing that a given program preserves confidentiality of sensitive information. The main problem we consider is how to prove that an attacker cannot infer user-specified secrets based on observed behavior. A specific application context consists of Java midlets. Midlets are third-party programs designed to enhance features of mobile devices. These programs can access data on the phone and send messages. The security requirement is that the information is revealed only selectively, and in particular, no confidential information is leaked.

Informally, a property f over the program variables is said to be *confidential* if the adversary cannot infer the truth of f based on the observed behavior of the program at runtime and the knowledge of the source code of the program. Formal definition of confidentiality (as well as of other information flow properties) relies on a notion of observational equivalence of traces. More precisely, a property f is conditionally confidential with respect to a property g if for every execution r for which the property g holds, there exists another execution r' such that r and r' disagree on the truth of f, but are equivalent according to the observer. Two executions are equivalent to the observer, if they produce

* This research was partially supported by NSF grants CNS 0524059 and CPA 0541149.

A. Bouajjani and O. Maler (Eds.): CAV 2009, LNCS 5643, pp. 173–187, 2009.

the same sequence of observations (observations can be, for example, outputs or inputs of the program).

Software model checkers have made great progress in recent years, having become efficient and used in practice. Existing tools (such as SLAM [7] and BLAST [20]) are designed for checking linear-time properties of programs, and are based on abstraction, symbolic state-space traversal, and counter-example guided abstraction refinement. These tools cannot be used for verifying confidentiality properties. The reasons are two-fold. First, conditional confidentiality is not a property of a single execution, and in fact, it is not specifiable in μ-calculus, which is more expressive than the specification languages of these tools. Second, the definition of conditional confidentiality involves both universal and existential quantifiers. Therefore, abstraction based solely on over-approximation (or solely on under-approximation) is not sufficient for checking conditional confidentiality. More precisely, let us consider two programs P1 and P2, such that P1 is an over-approximation of P2, that is, the set of executions of P2 is included in the set of executions of P1. The fact that conditional confidentiality holds for P1 does not imply that conditional confidentiality holds for P2 (and vice-versa).

We focus on methods written in a subset of Java that contains booleans, integers, on which we allow linear arithmetic, as well as data from an unbounded domain D equipped with only equality tests. Furthermore, the programs can have arrays, which are *a priori* unbounded in length and whose elements are from D. For example, in the application domain of interest, J2ME midlets, the data domain D models strings (representing names or phone numbers), and the array might contain a phone book or a list of events. Our technique currently does not handle method calls. (In practice, midlet methods call methods from a small set of APIs. The effect of these methods has been hard-coded into the tool. In a future version, we plan to allow specification of these methods using pre-/post-conditions.)

Our method proceeds in two steps. First, we compute a formula φ that is valid if the conditional confidentiality requirement holds. In order to do so, we need to consider both an over- and an under-approximation of reachable states for every program location. We use user-specified invariants for over-approximation. In all the examples we considered, the invariants that were used are simple enough, and could have been discovered by existing techniques for automatic invariant generation [17,24,27]. The under-approximation is specified by a bound on the number of loop iterations and a bound on the size of the array.

Second, we develop a method for deciding the validity of the obtained formulas, which involves both universal and existential quantifiers. We leverage the restrictions on the program expressions, as well as the specific form of the obtained formulas, to devise a decision method based on using an existing SMT solver. The restriction on the program expressions used is the fact that the domain D (over which the universal quantification takes place) has only equality tests. Therefore given a formula φ, it is possible to produce an equivalent formula φ' where the universal quantification takes place over a bounded domain.

As φ' can then be seen as a boolean combination of existential formulas with no free variables, its validity can be decided using an SMT solver.

We confirmed feasibility of our solution by checking conditional confidentiality for methods from J2ME midlets and the core Java library. Our tool CONAN uses WALA [2] library to process Java bytecode and the Yices [14] solver to decide the resulting formulas. The running times for the methods we analyzed were all under two seconds. The size of the methods we analyzed was small, with the largest one having little over 100 lines. We show that this is typical for midlets by presenting statistics for lines of code per method for 20 most downloaded open source midlets.

2   Motivating Example

J2ME midlets have legitimate reasons to access data on the mobile device (such as the list of contacts or a phone book), and a legitimate reason to send outgoing messages. Therefore an access control mechanism that would prevent the programs from performing either of these tasks would be too restrictive. Thus there is a question of how to ensure that a given (possibly malicious) midlet does not leak confidential information. For instance, the recently released report [23] describes several attack vectors through which a malicious midlet can stealthily release private data through connections such as text messages, emails, or http requests. In this application context, we focus on verification, rather than bug finding, as the goal is to certify that the midlet does not leak a secret, and thus is safe to run on a mobile device.

The J2ME security model uses the concept of *protection domains* (see MIDP specification [3]). A protection domain is associated with permissions for security-sensitive APIs. Midlets that need more privileges have to be either signed by a certificate from a trusted certification authority (CA) or registered with the manufacturer of the device; depending on the policy of the vendor. The source code of the midlets is not analyzed, the registration serves only to enable the possibility of tracking the harmful midlets and their authors. A verification tool would be very useful in this context, because it could be used for guaranteeing that registered midlets do not leak confidential information.

We will use a simplified version of the EventSharingMidlet from a J2ME manual [1] as an example. The example uses a security-sensitive PIM[1] API. It allows accessing the native data (e.g. the phone book) of the phone. For this API, a confidentiality requirement might be that phone numbers in the phone book should not be leaked. EventSharingMidlet allows the user to plan an event and send information about it to contacts in her phone book. The core of the midlet is in Figure 1. The property to be kept secret for the example is whether a particular string, say "555-55" is in the phone book. Let us denote it by *secret*. We want to verify that the attacker cannot infer whether the *secret* holds or not based on her knowledge of the program and observation of the outputs (in this case, the variable `message`). Note that the outgoing message does depend on the

---

[1] Personal information management. See https://java.sun.com/javame/index.jsp

```
//get the phone number
number = phoneBook.
          elementAt(selected);
//test if the number is valid
if ((number == null)
        || (number ==  "")) {
  //output error
} else {
  String message = inputMessage();
  //send a message to the receiver
  sendMessage(number,message);
}
}
```

```
...
if ((number == null)
        || (number ==  "")) {
  //output error
} else {
  if (contains(phoneBook,''555-55'')) {
    String message = inputMessage();
    //send a message to the receiver
    sendMessage(number,message);
  }
}
```

Fig. 1. EventSharingMidlet

Fig. 2. EventSharingMidlet (malicious version)

variable **phoneBook** (via the control-flow dependency). However, in this case, the answer is that the attacker cannot infer whether the *secret* holds or not. Now let us consider the case when midlet is malicious as in the Figure 2. The attacker inserted a test on whether the number "555-55" is in the phone book. Now if a message (any message) is sent, the attacker can infer that the *secret* holds.

3   Related Work

Model-checking for confidentiality. The definition of conditional confidentiality we use in this work is similar to notions in [18] based on logics of knowledge with perfect recall. Verification of this type confidentiality properties has been studied recently [4,30] for finite state systems. The problem of checking confidentiality is shown to be PSPACE-complete. We focus here on extending this line of research to verification of confidentiality for software. Traditional software verification is not directly applicable to this problem. The reason is that conditional confidentiality cannot be expressed in branching-time temporal logics, such as μ-calculus [5]. Furthermore, abstractions based solely on over-approximations or solely on under-approximations are not sufficient for checking conditional confidentiality. Frameworks for three-valued abstractions of modal transition systems ([13],[15]) combine over- and under-approximations, but the logics studied in this context (μ-calculus or less expressive logics) cannot express the conditional confidentiality requirement.

Opacity. The definition of conditional confidentiality we use is related to [8]. The main difference is that the notion of confidentiality we consider here is conditional (with the secret specified by a property f and the condition specified by a property g), whereas opacity is not. If we set g to be true, then the confidentiality notion used in this paper corresponds exactly to the property f being final-opaque under a static observation function, in the terminology of [8].

Language-based security. Noninterference is a security property often used to ensure confidentiality. Informally, it can be described as follows: "if two input states share the same values of low variables then the behaviors of the program executed from these states are indistinguishable by the observer". See [25] for a survey of the research on noninterference and [22] for a Java-based programming language with a type systems that supports information flow control based on noninterference.

Noninterference is too strong for the specification of confidentiality for the example in Figure 1. (The reason is, briefly, that the variable **number** depends on the variable **message** via control flow.) The definition of confidentiality we presented in this paper can be seen as a relaxation of noninterference. It is relaxed by allowing the user to specify which predicate(s) should stay secret; noninterference requires that *all* properties of high variables stay secret. It is well-known that the noninterference requirement needs to be relaxed in various contexts. See [26] for a survey of methods for defining such relaxations via declassification. In this context, the main benefit of our approach is automation, as our method allows verification of existing programs without requiring annotations by the programmer.

It is known that possibilistic noninterference is not preserved when nondeterministic choices are eliminated. This is the case also for conditional confidentiality. (It is also the reason why considering only over-approximation is not sufficient for sound analysis.)

Static analysis. Program analysis for (variants of) noninterference has been examined in literature. The approaches that have been considered include slicing [29] or using a logic for information flow [6]. These methods conservatively approximate noninterference, and thus would not certify valid midlets. It is possible to relax these requirements by using e.g. escape-hatch expressions [6]. It would be interesting to see if these ideas can be used to develop a specification-driven automated method for checking confidentiality. Decidability of some of the variants of noninterference for WHILE-programs is shown in [11]. Dam and Giambagi [12] introduce a notion of *admissible* information flow, allowing a finer grained control. Admissible information flow is a relaxation of noninterference, where the programmer can specify which specific data dependencies are allowed. The information required from the programmer are quite complex however (a set of relabellings) and it is not straightforward to see how this method can be automated.

Probabilistic notions of confidentiality. We have presented a possibilistic definition of confidentiality. Probabilistic definitions have been examined in the literature (see e.g. [16,31]). We chose a possibilistic one for two reasons: first, a probabilistic definition could not be applied without making (artificial) assumptions about the probability distribution on inputs, and second, common midlets do not use randomization (so a security measure might be to reject programs that use randomization). However, there are settings where a probabilistic definitions would be appropriate, and the question on how to extend the analysis method to a probabilistic definition is left for future work.

4   Formalizing Confidentiality

We consider methods in a subset of Java that contains boolean variables, integer variables, data variables, and array variables. Data variables are variables ranging over an infinite domain D equipped with equality. The domain D models any domain, but we restrict the programs to use only equality tests on data variables. The length of the arrays is unbounded, and their elements come from the domain D.

Integer expressions IE are defined by the following grammar:

IE ::= s | i | IE OP IE,

where s is a constant, i is a variable, and OP is in $+, -$. Data expressions DE are of the form

DE :: = c | v | A[IE],

where c is a constant, v is a data variable and A is an array. Note that there is no arithmetic on data expressions. The only way to access the data domain is through equality tests. Boolean expressions are defined by the following grammar:

```
B :: =    true | b | B and B | not B
     | IE = IE | IE < IE
     | DE = DE
```

We do not restrict the intra-procedural control structures. We do not allow procedure calls. In what follows, the programs are assumed to be annotated with assignments to a history variable hist. The variable is of type list and it stores the sequence that the observer can see. The first command of a program initializes hist to the empty list. Where the other annotations with an assignment to hist are placed depends on a particular security model. If an observer can see every change of the value of a variable, then every command that can change the value of the variable is annotated with an assignment to hist. If an observer sees only values sent via a particular API, the calls to this API are annotated. For example, a call of a method send(d) which sends a message (visible to the observer) containing the value of variable d, is annotated by a command that appends the value of d to the variable hist (hist := append(hist,d)). Let us emphasize that this annotation is not program-specific, and can be done automatically (and is done automatically by our tool). In what follows, we will assume that hist contains of a list of values from the data domain D. (The definition and the analysis can be extended to capture also boolean values being visible.)

We will now formalize what an observer can infer based on his or her observations. Let us fix a program P. A *state* of P is a valuation of its variables. Given

```
result = -1; i = 0;
while (i < n) {
  if (A[i]==key) { result=A[i]; }
  i++;
}
hist := append(hist,result);
```

Fig. 3. Program `ArraySearch`

a program location l, the set R_l denotes a set of states that are reachable at l. An *observation* is a sequence of data values d_i, where d_i is in D. It represents what the observer sees during an execution of the program. Let e be the exit location of the program (we assume there is a unique exit location). Let *secret* and *cond* be predicates over states of the program.

Definition 1. *Let h be an observation, let s_0, s_1, s_2 be states. The predicate secret is confidential w.r.t. the condition cond if and only if*

$$\forall h(\exists s_0 : s_0 \in R_e \wedge s_0 \models cond \wedge s_0[\mathtt{hist}] = h) \Rightarrow$$
$$(\exists s_1 : s_1 \in R_e \wedge s_1 \models secret \wedge s_1[\mathtt{hist}] = h \wedge \qquad (1)$$
$$\exists s_2 : s_2 \in R_e \wedge s_2 \not\models secret \wedge s_2[\mathtt{hist}] = h)$$

We rephrase the definition in order to convey the intuition behind it. We say that a program execution (a sequence of states) produces a observation h if $s[\mathtt{hist}] = h$, where s is the last state of the execution. Two executions are equivalent iff they produce the same observation. This notion of equivalence captures when the observer cannot distinguish between two executions. Let us call a observation h feasible, if there exists a a state s in R_e, such that $s[\mathtt{hist}] = h$. Intuitively, the definition says that for all feasible observations h, if there exists a execution for which the condition *cond* holds, then there exists an equivalent execution for which *secret* holds, and an equivalent execution for which $\neg secret$ holds. Therefore the definition ensures that the observer cannot infer whether *secret* holds or not.

Remark. This definition can be expressed in the logic CTL$\approx$ introduced in [4] for specification of information flow properties.

Example. Let us consider the program `ArraySearch` in Figure 3 to illustrate the definition and to show why we need the conditional definition. The program takes an array and an integer `key` as an input. It scans through the array to find if there is an element whose value is equal to `key`, and if so, returns this element. The secret we would like to protect is whether the array contains 7. We therefore define *secret* to be $\exists i : A[i] = 7$. Now let us consider the observations the observer sees. Such a observation contains a single number, the final value of `result`. If the observer sees the value 7, he or she can conclude that 7 is in the array. Therefore confidentiality does not hold. However, the program should preserve confidentiality as long as `key` is not equal to 7. Thus we set *cond* to be

key $\neq 7$. In this case, it is easy to see that confidentiality is preserved. Intuitively, by observing the final value of the **result**, the observer only knows that this value is in the array. If the size of the array is at least 2, the observer does not know whether 7 is or is not in the array. As the size of the array is unknown to the observer, we can conclude that the confidentiality of the secret is preserved. (Note however, that if the observer knows that the size of the array is 1, the confidentiality of *secret* does not hold. If the final value of **result** is not equal to -1, and is not equal to 7, then the observer can infer that the array does not contain 7.)

5   Analysis of Programs for Conditional Confidentiality

We consider Definition 1 of conditional confidentiality and we show that one needs to compute both over- and under- approximation. If only one of these techniques is used, it is not possible to get a sound approximation of the confidentiality property. The reason is, at a high level, that the definition involves both universal and existential quantification over the set of executions of the program. More precisely, recall that as explained in Section 3, the definition requires that for all feasible observations h, if there exists a execution t_1 for which the condition *cond* holds, then there exists an equivalent execution t_2 for which *secret* holds, and an equivalent execution t_3 for which $\neg secret$ holds. If we use only over-approximation, that is, a technique that makes the set of executions larger, we might find an execution t_2 or t_3 as required, even though it is not an execution of the original program. Such analysis is thus unsound. If we use under-approximation, some feasible observations might become infeasible. An analysis on the under-approximation would tell us nothing about such observations. It is not difficult to construct a concrete example where reasoning only about the under-approximation would be unsound.

We thus need to consider over- and under-approximations of sets R_e. Let R_e^+ be an over-approximation of R_e, that is, $R_e \subseteq R_e^+$. Similarly, let R_e^- be an under-approximation R_e^-, that is, $R_e \supseteq R_e^-$.

Using the sets R_e^+ and R_e^-, we can approximate conditional confidentiality as follows:

$$\forall h (\exists s_0 : s_0 \in R_e^+ \land s_0 \models cond \land s_0[\text{hist}] = h) \Rightarrow$$
$$(\exists s_1 : s_1 \in R_e^- \land s_1 \models secret \land s_1[\text{hist}] = h \land \qquad (2)$$
$$\exists s_2 : s_2 \in R_e^- \land s_2 \not\models secret \land s_2[\text{hist}] = h)$$

The formula (2) soundly approximates conditional confidentiality, as expressed by the following lemma.

Lemma 1. *If the formula (2) holds, then secret is confidential w.r.t cond.*

We will now show how, given a program and the predicates *secret* and *cond* specified as logical formulae, we can derive a logical formula expressing the formula (2). We will use the following logic.

Logic $\mathcal{L}$. The formulas of $\mathcal{L}$ will use boolean, integer, data and array variables (similarly to the expressions defined in Section 4). The definition of integer and data expressions will be the same as well. The grammar defining the boolean formulas is:

```
BL ::=   true | b | BL | BL | not BL
      | IE = IE | IE < IE | DE = DE
      | ∃ b: BL | ∃ i: BL | ∃ v: BL
```

The difference between the formulas in $\mathcal{L}$ and the boolean expressions in the programs we consider is that in $\mathcal{L}$ we allow quantification in the logic.

Weakest precondition. We will need the notion of the weakest precondition computation (see e.g. [32]). Given a program P and a formula φ, $WP(P, \varphi)$ is the weakest formula that guarantees that if P terminates, it terminates in a state in which F holds. The main property we require for the logic is that it should be closed under the weakest precondition of *loop-free* programs, that is, for any $\mathcal{L}$-formula φ and any loop-free program P, $WP(P, \varphi)$ is in $\mathcal{L}$. Given the restrictions on expressions in the language, it is easy to show that this requirement holds.

Over-approximation R_e^+. Let us consider the antecedent of the formula (2), i.e. ($\exists s_0 : s_0 \in R_e^+ \land s_0 \models cond \land s_0[\text{hist}] = h$). We need to obtain an $\mathcal{L}$ formula characterizing this requirement, given that *cond* is an $\mathcal{L}$ formula. Given an $\mathcal{L}$ formula ψ that characterizes R_e^+, we obtain the desired characterization as $\varphi^+ \equiv \exists pv : \psi \land cond \land \text{hist} = h$. Note that the free formulas in ψ and *cond* range over the program variables, and the notation $\exists pv : F$ (for a formula F) is a shorthand for saying that all program variables are existentially quantified.

The formula ψ that characterizes the set of reachable states at a program location can be either provided by the user or computed by standard methods of abstract interpretation [9], using a standard abstract domain (e.g. octagons [21], polyhedra [10]) Recently, such techniques have been extended for discovering disjunctive invariants (see [17,24,27]). These latter techniques would be needed to discover the invariants needed for the examples we present in Section 6.

Under-approximation R_e^-. The under-approximation is obtained by loop unrolling. More precisely, all loops are unrolled a fixed number of times (k) and the program is thus transformed to a loop-free program P'. For example, each occurrence of `while B { C }` in a program is replaced by k conditional statements `if B then C;` followed by `assume (not B)`. The command `assume B` ensures that B holds. If it is not the case, the execution fails. Let P' be a program obtained by this transformation. Let R_e' be the set of reachable states obtained for P'. It is straightforward to prove that $R_e' \subseteq R_e$.

We are interested in characterizing the requirement (from the consequent of formula (2)): $\exists s_1 : s_1 \in R_e^- \land s_1 \models secret \land s_1[\text{hist}] = h$ by a $\mathcal{L}$-formula φ_1^-. It is computed using the weakest precondition computation on the program P' as follows: $\varphi_1^- \equiv \exists pv : WP(P', \text{hist} = h \land secret)$. Similarly, φ_2^- is defined as $\exists pv : WP(P', \text{hist} = h \land \neg secret)$.

Computing confidentiality. We can now check if confidentiality holds using the following formula:

$$\forall h : (\exists pv : \psi \wedge cond \wedge \mathtt{hist} = h) \Rightarrow$$
$$(\exists pv : WP(P', \mathtt{hist} = h \wedge secret) \wedge \tag{3}$$
$$\exists pv : WP(P', \mathtt{hist} = h \wedge \neg secret))$$

As formulas (2) and (3) are equivalent, we can use Lemma 1 to prove the following:

Lemma 2. *If the formula (3) holds, then secret is confidential w.r.t cond.*

5.1 Deciding Validity of the Confidentiality Formula

In this section, we describe a method for deciding the confidentiality formula (3). The method is based on satisfiability modulo theories (SMT) solving.

Restrictions on cond and secret. First we identify some restrictions on the predicates *cond* and *secret*. The restriction on *cond* is that we will consider only existential formulas. The predicate *secret* appears in the formula (3) also under negation, therefore we restrict it not to use quantification. Note that for some examples, the property *secret* contains a quantification on the array indices. This is the case for the ArraySearch example discussed in Section 3. In such cases, the under-approximation uses also a bound on the size of the array, thus making the quantification to be effectively over a bounded set.

The $\mathcal{L}$-formula (3) has one quantifier alternation (taking into account the restrictions above). Here we show how such a formula can be decided using an SMT solver. In order to simplify the presentation, in this section we will suppose the observation h in the confidentiality formula consists of only one data value d (and not of a sequence of values from D). The results in this section, as well as their proofs, can be easily extended to the general case.

Let us first suppose that we have an existential formula $\varrho(h)$ (in the logic $\mathcal{L}$) with one free data variable h. Let D be an infinite set, let C be the finite set of values interpreting in D the constants that appear in $\varrho(h)$. For an element d of D, we write $d \models \varrho$ if ϱ holds when h is interpreted as d.

We show that the formula ϱ cannot distinguish between two values d and d', if d and d' are not in C.

Lemma 3. *For all $d, d' \in D$, if $d \notin C$ and $d' \notin C$, then $d \models \varrho \leftrightarrow d' \models \varrho$.*

Intuitively, the lemma holds, because the formula ϱ can only compare the value of h to constants in C or to other existentially quantified data variables. The proof proceeds by structural induction on the formula ϱ.

Lemma 3 suggests a method for deciding whether $\forall h : \varrho$ holds: First, check whether $\varrho(c)$ holds for all constants in C, and second, check whether $\varrho(c)$ and for one value not in C. Note that as C is finite and D infinite, there must exist an element of D not in C.

The following lemma shows that this method can be extended to the confidentiality formula (3). Let C' be $C \cup \{d\}$, where d is in D, but not in C.

Lemma 4. *Let ψ be a formula: $\forall h : \varphi_0(h) \rightarrow (\varphi_1(h) \wedge \varphi_2(h))$, where φ_0, φ_1, φ_2 are existential formulas with one free data variable h. Then ψ is equivalent to $\bigwedge_{c \in C'} \psi_c$, where ψ_c is $\varphi_0(c) \rightarrow (\varphi_1(c) \wedge \varphi_2(c))$.*

The proof uses Lemma 3 for all of φ_0, φ_1 and φ_2.

Let us now consider the resulting formula $\bigwedge_{c \in C'} \psi_c$. Each ψ_c has the form $\varphi_0(c) \rightarrow (\varphi_1(c) \wedge \varphi_2(c))$, where $\varphi_0(c)$, $\varphi_1(c)$, and $\varphi_2(c)$ are existential formulas without free variables. Therefore we can check satisfiability of each of these formulas separately, and then combine the results appropriately (i.e. if $\varphi_0(c)$ is satisfiable, then both $\varphi_1(c)$ and $\varphi_2(c)$ have to be satisfiable).

We have thus leveraged the fact that the only operation on the data domain is equality to devise a decision method based on SMT checking for the confidentiality formula (2).

Example. Let us consider the `ArraySearch` example presented in Section 3. Recall that we considered the predicate *secret* to be $\exists i : A[i] = 7$ and the condition *cond* to be `key` $\neq 7$. Recall also that the observer might either see an empty observation, or a observation containing a single number, the final value of `result`.

For the over-approximation, we will need an invariant asserting that (`result` = `key` or `result` = -1). The formula φ^+ will thus be: $\varphi^+ \equiv ((\text{result} = -1) \vee (\text{result} = \text{key})) \wedge (\text{key} \neq 7) \wedge \text{result} = h$.

The under-approximation will be specified by a number of unrollings and the size of the array. We choose 2 in both cases. We then compute φ_1^- using the weakest precondition computation $\exists s_1 : WP(P, \text{hist} = h \wedge \exists i : A[i] = 7)$ and φ_2^- as $\exists s_2 : WP(P, \text{hist} = h \wedge \neg\exists i : A[i] = 7)$.

The formula characterizing confidentiality becomes:

$$\forall h : (\exists s : ((\text{result} = -1) \vee (\text{result} = \text{key})) \wedge (\text{result} = h) \wedge (\text{key} \neq 7)) \Rightarrow$$
$$(\varphi_1^- \wedge \varphi_2^-)$$

The formulas contains two constants from the data domain -1 (appeared in the program) and the value 7 (appeared in *cond* and *secret*). We also need to consider one value that is different for these constants. We can pick for example the value 1. For -1 (1) the formula says that if the observer sees the value, he or she cannot infer whether 7 is in the array and are easily proven. For 7, the antecedent of the formula is false (as the purpose of the condition was to exclude 7 from consideration), thus the formula is proven.

6 Experiments

We have performed experiments in order to confirm that the proposed method is feasible in the sense that the formulas produced can be decided by existing tools in reasonable time. The experiments were performed on methods of J2ME classes and classes from the core Java library on a computer with a 2.8Ghz processor and 2GB of RAM.

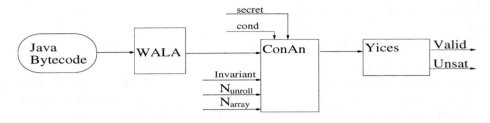

Fig. 4. Toolchain

We have implemented a prototype tool called ConAn (for CONfidentiality ANalysis). It takes as input a program in Java bytecode, a secret, a condition, and parameters specifying the over- and under- approximation to be used.

The complete toolchain is shown in Figure 4. The WALA [2] library is used to process the bytecode. The ConAn tool then performs the analysis on an intermediate representation called WALA IR. The IR represents a method's instructions in a language close to JVM bytecode, but in an SSA-based language which eliminates the stack abstraction. The IR organizes instructions in a control-flow graph of basic blocks. The tool analyzes a fragment of the IR subject to the same restrictions on expressions as described in Section 3. The methods call methods from a small set of APIs such as the PIM API mentioned in Section 2. The effect of these methods has been hard-coded into the tool. In a future version, we plan to allow specification of these methods using pre-/post-conditions. Furthermore, the programs we examined use iterators (with operations such as `hasNext` and `Next` to iterate over data structures). The effect of these methods was also hard-coded using iteration over arrays.

As shown in Figure 4, the ConAn tool takes as input a specification for the over-approximation (in the form of the invariant) and the specification of the under-approximation (in the form of the number of loop unrollings to consider and a bound on the size of the array). The tool Yices [14] is used for deciding satisfiability of the resulting formulas.

We briefly describe the examples we considered and report on the performance of the tool. Table 1 contains, for each example, the number of lines of code, the running time of the tool, and the result, i.e. whether the formula was satisfiable (and confidentiality preserved) or unsatisfiable (i.e. no conclusion possible). Note that the running times presented in the table do not include the running time of the translation from bytecode to the WALA IR format. It includes only the running time of the analysis in ConAn, and the time taken by the Yices tool to decide the satisfiability of the formulas.

In all cases the secret is a fact about the array. We used the predicate $\exists i : A[i] = 7$ as the secret. The condition *cond* is specified for each example separately. The over-approximation was specified via an invariant, and the under-approximation was specified via the number of loop unrollings (as shown in Table 1) and the bound on the size of the array (chosen to be 2 in all of the examples). The observation visible to the observer is defined by either the

Table 1. Experimental evaluation

	project / class	Method Name	# of lines in Java	unroll	running time (s)	result
1	Vector	elementAt	6	1	0.18	valid
2	EventSharing	SendEvent	122	2	1.83	valid
3	EventSharing	SendEvent (bug)	126	2	1.80	unsat
4		find	9	1	0.31	unsat
5		find	9	2	0.34	valid
6	Funambol/Contact	getContact	13	2	0.32	valid
7	Blackchat/ICQContact	getContactByReference	23	2	0.24	valid
8	password	check	9	2	0.22	valid

message(s) the program send out, or the values the functions return. The latter is useful for modular verification of programs that access a data structure via a call to the analyzed functions and subsequently send messages depending on the returned value.

Example 1 is from the class Vector, whose method elementAt is similar to `ArrayAccess` example from Section 4. Examples 2 and 3 are from a J2ME example called EventSharingMidlet. This is the example described in Section 2. We considered both the correct version and a version with an artificially introduced bug as in Example 2. This example is taken from [1].

Examples 4 and 5 are versions of the `ArraySearch` example from Section 4. For Example 4, we used only one unrolling of the loop. The tool did not prove that the secret is not leaked. Increasing the number of unrollings to two (Example 5) helped; the confidentiality was proved in this case.

Example 6 from the class Contact found in the Funambol library scans the phonebook obtained via a call to PIM API to find an element corresponding to a key. Example 7 is similar to Example 6. Example 8 is a version of the classical password checking example - an array is scanned and if the name/password pair matches, the function returns 1. The results show that no password is leaked. Example 8 is taken from [19].

Discussion. All Java methods we considered are small in size. For these programs, the running times were in tens of seconds. The experiments succeeded in showing that our approach is feasible for relatively short Java methods. We argue that this shows that our methods is suitable for the intended application, certification of J2ME midlets. Firstly, J2ME midlets are rather small in size. We surveyed 20 of the most popular[2] midlet applications. We used the tool LOCC[3] to calculate for each of this midlets the average number N_a as well as maximal number N_m of lines of code per method. Over all of these programs, the average of the N_a numbers was 15, the maximum of the N_a numbers was 25. The average of the N_m numbers was 206, the maximum of the N_m numbers was 857. These data confirm that the

---

[2] The criterion was the number of downloads from sourceforge.net
[3] http://csdl.ics.hawaii.edu/Tools/LOCC/

size of methods in J2ME midlets is small, and our methods are directly applicable to average-sized method. Secondly, for each midlet we reported on in Table 1 we analyzed the methods that are key from the point of view of preserving secrecy, i.e. the methods that access the data structure for which the secret should hold, or methods that send messages. Therefore we believe that a pre-processing phase using program slicing followed by our techniques would enable our tool to analyze most of the methods of midlets.

7   Conclusions

We have presented a verification technique and a tool for checking confidentiality for programs. The proposed verification method analyzes a program (from a syntactically restricted class) to produce logical formula that characterizes the confidentiality requirement. The resulting formulas can be discharged by using existing SMT tools. We demonstrated the feasibility of our approach on illustrative Java methods from the intended application domain, J2ME midlets.

We have shown that both over- and under- approximation are necessary for sound analysis of confidentiality requirements. Therefore an interesting question for future research is how to develop a counter-example guided abstraction refinement for this problem. Furthermore, there are other specific application domains where confidentiality specification is useful. An example of such an application are implementations of payment protocols.

References

1. JavaTM ME Developer's Library 2.0, http://www.forum.nokia.com
2. WALA - Watson libraries for analyses, http://wala.sourceforge.net
3. JSR 118 Expert Group. Mobile Information Device Profile for J2ME 2.1 (2007)
4. Alur, R., Černý, P., Chaudhuri, S.: Model checking on trees with path equivalences. In: Grumberg, O., Huth, M. (eds.) TACAS 2007. LNCS, vol. 4424, pp. 664–678. Springer, Heidelberg (2007)
5. Alur, R., Černý, P., Zdancewic, S.: Preserving secrecy under refinement. In: Bugliesi, M., Preneel, B., Sassone, V., Wegener, I. (eds.) ICALP 2006. LNCS, vol. 4052, pp. 107–118. Springer, Heidelberg (2006)
6. Amtoft, T., Banerjee, A.: Verification condition generation for conditional information flow. In: Proc. of FMSE 2007, pp. 2–11 (2007)
7. Ball, T., Rajamani, S.: The SLAM project: debugging system software via static analysis. In: Proc. POPL 2002, pp. 1–3 (2002)
8. Bryans, J., Koutny, M., Mazaré, L., Ryan, P.: Opacity generalised to transition systems. Int. J. Inf. Sec. 7(6), 421–435 (2008)
9. Cousot, P., Cousot, R.: Abstract interpretation: a unified lattice model for static analysis of programs by construction or approximation of fixpoints. In: Proc. of POPL 1977, Los Angeles, California, pp. 238–252 (1977)
10. Cousot, P., Halbwachs, N.: Automatic discovery of linear restraints among variables of a program. In: Proc. of POPL 1978, pp. 84–97 (1978)
11. Dam, M.: Decidability and proof systems for language-based noninterference relations. In: POPL 2006, pp. 67–78 (2006)

12. Dam, M., Giambiagi, P.: Confidentiality for mobile code: The case of a simple payment protocol. In: Proc. of CSFW 2000, pp. 233–244 (2000)
13. Dams, D., Gerth, R., Grumberg, O.: Abstract interpretation of reactive systems. ACM Trans. Program. Lang. Syst. 19(2), 253–291 (1997)
14. Dutertre, B., de Moura, L.: A fast linear-arithmetic solver for DPLL(T). In: Ball, T., Jones, R.B. (eds.) CAV 2006. LNCS, vol. 4144, pp. 81–94. Springer, Heidelberg (2006)
15. Godefroid, P., Huth, M., Jagadeesan, R.: Abstraction-based model checking using modal transition systems. In: Larsen, K.G., Nielsen, M. (eds.) CONCUR 2001. LNCS, vol. 2154, pp. 426–440. Springer, Heidelberg (2001)
16. Gray, J.: Probabilistic interference. In: Proc. of SP 1990, pp. 170–179 (1990)
17. Gulavani, B., Rajamani, S.: Counterexample driven refinement for abstract interpretation. In: Hermanns, H., Palsberg, J. (eds.) TACAS 2006. LNCS, vol. 3920, pp. 474–488. Springer, Heidelberg (2006)
18. Halpern, J., O'Neill, K.: Secrecy in multiagent systems. In: Proc. of CSFW 2002, pp. 32–46 (2002)
19. Hammer, C., Krinke, J., Nodes, F.: Intransitive noninterference in dependence graphs. In: Proc. of ISoLA 2006, pp. 136–145 (2006)
20. Henzinger, T., Jhala, R., Majumdar, R., Necula, G., Sutre, G., Weimer, W.: Temporal-safety proofs for systems code. In: Brinksma, E., Larsen, K.G. (eds.) CAV 2002. LNCS, vol. 2404, pp. 526–538. Springer, Heidelberg (2002)
21. Miné, A.: The octagon abstract domain. Higher-Order and Symbolic Computation 19, 31–100 (2006)
22. Myers, A.: JFlow: Practical mostly-static information flow control. In: Proc. of POPL 1999, pp. 228–241 (1999)
23. O'Connor, J.: Attack surface analysis of Blackberry devices. White Paper: Symantec security response (2007)
24. Popeea, C., Chin, W.: Inferring disjunctive postconditions. In: Okada, M., Satoh, I. (eds.) ASIAN 2006. LNCS, vol. 4435, pp. 331–345. Springer, Heidelberg (2006)
25. Sabelfeld, A., Myers, A.: Language-based information-flow security. IEEE Journal on Selected Areas in Communications 21(1), 5–19 (2003)
26. Sabelfeld, A., Sands, D.: Dimensions and principles of declassification. In: CSFW 2005, pp. 255–269 (2005)
27. Sankaranarayanan, S., Ivancic, F., Shlyakhter, I., Gupta, A.: Static analysis in disjunctive numerical domains. In: Yi, K. (ed.) SAS 2006. LNCS, vol. 4134, pp. 3–17. Springer, Heidelberg (2006)
28. Schneider, F. (ed.): Trust in Cyberspace. National Academy Press (1999)
29. Snelting, G., Robschink, T., Krinke, J.: Efficient path conditions in dependence graphs for software safety analysis. ACM Trans. Softw. Eng. Methodol. 15(4), 410–457 (2006)
30. van der Meyden, R., Zhang, C.: Algorithmic verification of noninterference properties. Electr. Notes Theor. Comput. Sci. 168, 61–75 (2007)
31. Volpano, D., Smith, G.: Probabilistic noninterference in a concurrent language. Journal of Computer Security 7(1) (1999)
32. Winskel, G.: The formal semantics of programming languages: An Introduction. MIT Press, Cambridge (1993)

Requirements Validation for Hybrid Systems*

Alessandro Cimatti, Marco Roveri, and Stefano Tonetta

Fondazione Bruno Kessler (FBK-irst), Trento, Italy

Abstract. The importance of requirements for the whole development flow calls for strong validation techniques based on formal methods. In the case of discrete systems, some approaches based on temporal logic satisfiability are gaining increasing momentum. However, in many real-world domains (e.g. railways signaling), the requirements constrain the temporal evolution of both discrete and continuous variables. These hybrid domains pose substantial problems: on one side, a continuous domain requires very expressive formal languages; on the other side, the resulting expressiveness results in highly intractable problems.

In this paper, we address the problem of requirements validation for real-world hybrid domains, and present two main contributions. First, we propose the HRELTL logic, that extends the Linear-time Temporal Logic with Regular Expressions (RELTL) with hybrid aspects. Second, we show that the satisfiability problem for the linear fragment can be reduced to an equi-satisfiable problem for RELTL. This makes it possible to use automatic (albeit incomplete) techniques based on Bounded Model Checking and on Satisfiability Modulo Theory.

The choice of the language is inspired by and validated within a project funded by the European Railway Agency, on the formalization and validation of the European Train Control System specifications. The activity showed that most of requirements can be formalized into HRELTL, and an experimental evaluation confirmed the practicality of the analyses.

1 Introduction

Requirements analysis is a fundamental step in the development process of software and system design. In fact, flaws and ambiguities in the requirements can lead to the development of correct systems that do not do what they were supposed to. This is often unacceptable, especially in safety-critical domains, and calls for strong tools for requirements validation based on formal techniques. The problem of requirements validation is significantly different from traditional formal verification, where a system model (the entity under analysis) is compared against a set of requirements (formalized as properties in a temporal logic), which are assumed to be "golden". In requirements validation, on the contrary, there is no system to be analyzed (yet), and the requirements themselves are the entity under analysis.

Formal methods for requirements validation are being devoted increasing interest [1,13,16,28]. In such approaches, referred to as *property-based*, the requirements are represented as statements in some temporal logics. This allows to retain a correspondence between the informal requirements and the formal statement, and gives the

---

* The first and second authors are supported by the European Commission (FP7-2007-IST-1-217069 COCONUT). The third author is supported by the Provincia Autonoma di Trento (project ANACONDA).

A. Bouajjani and O. Maler (Eds.): CAV 2009, LNCS 5643, pp. 188–203, 2009.

ability to reason at the level of abstraction of the requirements engineer. Typical analysis functionalities include the ability to check whether the specification is consistent, whether it is strict enough to rule out some undesirable behaviors, and whether it is weak enough not to rule out some desirable scenarios. These analysis functionalities can in turn be obtained by reduction to temporal logics satisfiability [28].

Property-based approaches have been typically applied in digital domains, where the requirements are intended to specify a set of behaviors over discrete variables, and the wealth of results and tools in temporal logic and model checking provides a substantial technological basis. However, in many real-world domains (e.g. railways, space, industrial control), the requirements are intended to constrain the evolution over time of a combination of discrete and continuous variables. Hybrid domains pose substantial problems: on the one side, a continuous domain requires very expressive formal languages; on the other side, the high expressiveness leads to highly intractable problems.

In this paper, we address the problem of requirements validation in such hybrid domains by making two main contributions.

First, we define a suitable *logic for the representation of requirements in hybrid domains*. The logic, called Hybrid Linear Temporal Logic with Regular Expressions (HRELTL), is interpreted over hybrid traces. This allows to evaluate constraints on continuous evolutions as well as discrete changes. The basic atoms (predicates) of the logic include continuous variables and their derivatives over time, and are interpreted both over time points and over open time intervals.[1] The semantics relies on the fact that each open interval of a hybrid trace can be split if it does not have a uniform evaluation of predicates in the temporal formulas under analysis (cf. [14,27]), and that the formulas satisfy properties of sample invariance and finite variability [14]. The logic encompasses regular expressions and linear-time operators, and suitable choices have been made to interpret the "next" operator and regular expressions over the open time intervals, and the derivative of continuous variables over the time points.

Second, we define a *translation method for automated verification*. The translation encodes satisfiability problems for the linear fragment of HRELTL into an equi-satisfiable problem in a logic over discrete traces. The restrictions of the linear fragment guarantee that if the formula is satisfiable, there exists a piecewise-linear solution. We exploit the linearity of the predicates with regard to the continuous variables to encode the continuity of the function into quantifier-free constraints. We can therefore compile the resulting formula into a fair transition system and use it to solve the satisfiability and the model checking problem with an automata-theoretic approach. We apply infinite-state model checking techniques to verify the language emptiness of the resulting fair transition system.

Our work has been inspired by and applied within a project funded by the European Railway Agency (http://www.era.europa.eu). The aim of the project was to develop a methodology supported by a tool for the validation of requirements in railway domains. Within the project, we collaborated with domain experts in a team that tackled the formalization of substantial fragments of the European Train Control System (ETCS) specification. With regard to the hybrid aspects of ETCS requirements, the

---

[1] This is known to be a nontrivial issue: see for instance [27,14,23] for a discussion on which type of intervals and hybrid traces must be considered.

formalization and the validation were based on the language and techniques described in this paper, and were successfully applied by the domain experts.

2   Motivating Application Domain

The ETCS specification is a set of requirements related to the automatic supervision of the location and speed performed by the train on-board system. The system is intended to be progressively installed on all European trains in order to guarantee the interoperability with the track-side system which are currently governed by national rules. ETCS specifies how the train should behave in the proximity of the target location. In particular, the Chapter 3 of the System Requirement Specification (SRS) [15] describes how trains move on a line and periodically receive a so-called Movement Authority (MA). The MA consists of a set of sections and a series of timeout that define some deadlines of the authorization to move in each section while a number of curves limit the speed of the train approaching the end of the MA (see Fig. 1). The specific curves are not defined by ETCS, but only constrained by high-level requirements (*"The algorithm for their calculation is an implementation matter"* SRS Sec. 3.13.4.1). Moreover, when the trains pass some limit, particular actions must be taken on board: e.g. when the train passes the end of the MA the "train trip" must be started.

The ETCS specification poses demanding requisites to the formal methods adopted for its validation. First, the adopted formalism shall be able to capture the meaning of the requirements. Second, the formalism shall be as simple as possible to be used by non-experts in formal methods: the requirements are usually ambiguous English sentences that only an expert in the domain can formalize and validate.

In this context, a model-based approach is not natural. First, designing a hybrid system that captures all behaviors allowed by the requirements requires to consider all possible intricate combinations of timeout values, locations where to reset the timers, speed limits for given locations. Second, these are not parameters of the system but variables that change their value at discrete steps. Finally, in a model-based approach it is hard to maintain the link between a requirement and its formal counterpart in the model.

A property-based approach to requirements validation relies on the availability of an expressive temporal logic, so that each informal statement has a formal counterpart with similar structure. A natural choice are formulas in Linear-time Temporal Logic

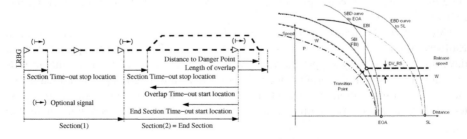

Fig. 1. Structure of an MA (left) and a speed monitoring curve (right) [15]

(LTL) [26] extended with Regular Expressions (RELTL) [6], because temporal formulas often resemble their informal counterpart. This is of paramount importance when experts in the application domain have the task of disambiguating and formalizing the requirements. For instance, a complex statement such as *"The train trip shall issue an emergency brake command, which shall not be revoked until the train has reached standstill and the driver has acknowledged the trip"* SRS Sec. 3.13.8.2 can be formalized into $\mathbf{G}$ $(train\_trip \rightarrow (emergency\_brake$ $\mathbf{U}$ $(train\_speed = 0 \wedge ack\_trip)))$.

In order to deal with an application domain such as ETCS, first, we need to model the dynamic of continuous variables, such as position, speed, time elapse, and timers, in a way that is reasonably accurate from the physical point of view. For example, we expect that a train can not move forward and reach a location without passing over all intermediate positions. Second, we must be able to express properties of continuous variables over time intervals. This poses problems of the satisfiability of formulas like $(pos \leq P$ $\mathbf{U}$ $pos > P)$ or $(speed > 0$ $\mathbf{U}$ $speed = 0)$. The first formula is satisfiable only if we consider left-open intervals, while the second one is satisfiable only if we consider left-closed intervals (see [23]). Considering time points (closed singular intervals) and open intervals is enough fine grained to represent all kinds of intervals.

Last, we need to be able to intermix continuous evolution and discrete steps, intuitively modeling "instantaneous" changes in the status of modes and control procedures. For example, the requirement *"The End Section timer shall be started on-board when the train passes the End Section timer start location"* (SRS Sec. 3.8.4.1.1) demands to interrupt the continuous progress of the train for resetting a timer.

3   Hybrid Traces

Let V be the finite disjoint union of the sets of variables V_D (with a discrete evolution) and V_C (with a continuous evolution) with values over the Reals.[2] A state s is an assignment to the variables of V ($s : V \rightarrow \mathbb{R}$). We write Σ for the set of states. Let $f : \mathbb{R} \rightarrow \Sigma$ be a function describing a continuous evolution. We define the projection of f over a variable v, written f^v, as $f^v(t) \doteq f(t)(v)$. We say that a function $f : \mathbb{R} \rightarrow \mathbb{R}$ is piecewise analytic iff there exists a sequence of adjacent intervals $J_0, J_1, \ldots \subseteq \mathbb{R}$ and a sequence of analytic functions $h_0, h_1, \ldots$ such that $\cup_i J_i = \mathbb{R}$, and for all $i \in \mathbb{N}$, $f(t) = h_i(t)$ for all $t \in J_i$. Note that, if f is piecewise analytic, the left and right derivatives exist in all points. We denote with $\dot{f}$ the derivative of a real function f, with $\dot{f}(t)_-$ and $\dot{f}(t)_+$ the left and the right derivatives respectively of f in t. Let I be an interval of $\mathbb{R}$ or $\mathbb{N}$; we denote with $le(I)$ and $ue(I)$ the lower and upper endpoints of I, respectively. We denote with $\mathbb{R}^+$ the set of non-negative real numbers.

Hybrid traces describe the evolution of variables in every point of time. Such evolution is allowed to have a countable number of discontinuous points corresponding to changes in the discrete part of the model. These points are usually called *discrete steps*, while we refer to the period of time between two discrete steps as *continuous evolution*.

Definition 1 (Hybrid   Trace). *A   hybrid   trace   over V is   a   sequence* $\langle \overline{f}, \overline{I} \rangle \doteq \langle f_0, I_0 \rangle, \langle f_1, I_1 \rangle, \langle f_2, I_2 \rangle, \ldots$ *such that, for all $i \in \mathbb{N}$,*

---

[2] In practice, we consider also Boolean and Integer variables with a discrete evolution, but we ignore them to simplify the presentation.

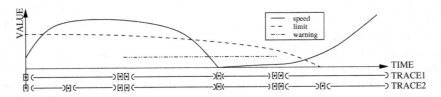

Fig. 2. Possible evolution of two continuous variables (*speed* and *limit*) and a discrete variable (*warning*), and two possible hybrid traces that represent it. TRACE2 is a refinement of TRACE1.

- *either I_i is an open interval ($I_i = (t, t')$ for some $t, t' \in \mathbb{R}^+$, $t < t'$) or is a singular interval ($I_i = [t, t]$ for some $t \in \mathbb{R}^+$);*
- *the intervals are adjacent, i.e. $ue(I_i) = le(I_{i+1})$;*
- *the intervals cover $\mathbb{R}^+$: $\bigcup_{i \in \mathbb{N}} I_i = \mathbb{R}^+$ (thus $I_0 = [0, 0]$);*
- *$f_i : \mathbb{R} \to \Sigma$ is a function such that, for all $v \in V_C$, f_i^v is continuous and piecewise analytic, and for all $v \in V_D$, f_i^v is constant;*
- *if $I_i = (t, t')$ then $f_i(t) = f_{i-1}(t)$, $f_i(t') = f_{i+1}(t')$.*

Typically, the f_i are required to be smooth. Since observable events may occur during a continuous evolution, we wish that a predicate over the continuous variable changes its truth value only a finite number of times in a bounded interval. For this reason, we require the analyticity of functions (see similar assumptions in [14]). At the same time, we weaken the condition of smoothness allowing discontinuity in the derivatives also during a continuous evolution. This allows to observe the value of functions and their derivatives without the need to break the continuous evolution with discrete steps not required by the specification.

Fig. 2 shows the evolution of two continuous variables (*speed* and *limit*) and a discrete variable (*warning*). The evolution presents two discrete steps and three continuous evolutions. The figure shows two possible traces, respectively with 10 and 14 intervals. In the second continuous evolution the function associated to *speed* is continuous but not derivable in all points.

Some predicate over the variables in V may evaluate to true only in particular points of a continuous evolution. Therefore, it is important to sample the evolution in particular time points. We say that a trace is a sampling refinement of another one if it has been obtained by splitting an open interval into two parts by adding a sampling point in the middle [14]. In Fig. 2, TRACE2 refines TRACE1 by exposing two more points.

Definition 2 (Partitioning Function [14]). *A partitioning function μ is a sequence $\mu_0, \mu_1, \mu_2, \dots$ of non-empty, adjacent and disjoint intervals of $\mathbb{N}$ partitioning $\mathbb{N}$. Formally, $\bigcup_{i \in \mathbb{N}} \mu_i = \mathbb{N}$ and $ue(\mu_i) = le(\mu_{i+1}) - 1$.*

Definition 3 (Trace Sampling Refinement [14]). *A hybrid trace $\langle \overline{f}', \overline{I}' \rangle$ is a sampling refinement of $\langle \overline{f}, \overline{I} \rangle$ by the partitioning μ (denoted with $\langle \overline{f}', \overline{I}' \rangle \preceq^\mu \langle \overline{f}, \overline{I} \rangle$) iff, for all $i \in \mathbb{N}$, $I_i = \bigcup_{j \in \mu_i} I'_j$ and, for all $j \in \mu_i$, $f'_j = f_i$.*

4 A Temporal Logic for Hybrid Traces

In this section we define HRELTL, i.e. linear temporal logic extended with regular expressions equipped to deal with hybrid traces. The language is presented in a general form with real arithmetic predicates without details on the syntax and the semantics of the real functions. It is indeed possible that some requirements need such expressiveness to be faithfully represented. A linear sub-case is then presented for which we have a discretization that produces equi-satisfiable formulas.

Syntax. If v is a variable we denote with $\text{NEXT}(v)$ the value of v after a discrete step and with $\text{DER}(v)$ the derivative of v. If V is the set of variables, we denote with V_{next} the set of next variables and with V_{der} the set of derivatives. HRELTL is built over a set of basic atoms, that are real arithmetic predicates over $V \cup V_{next}$, or over $V \cup V_{der}$.[3] We denote with $PRED$ the set of predicates, with p a generic predicate, with p_{curr} a predicate over V only, with p_{next} a predicate over V and V_{next}, and with p_{der} a predicate over V and V_{der}. We denote with $\overline{p}$ the predicate obtained from p by replacing $<$ with $\geq$, $>$ with $\leq$, $=$ with $\neq$ and vice versa. We denote with $p_{\bowtie}$ the predicate obtained from p by substituting the top-level operator with $\bowtie$, for $\bowtie \in \{<, >, =, \leq, \geq, \neq\}$.

The subset $PRED_{la}$ of $PRED$ over *linear arithmetic* constraints consists of the predicates in one of the following forms

- $a_0 + a_1 v_1 + a_2 v_2 + \cdots + a_n v_n \bowtie 0$ where $v_1, \ldots, v_n \in V_C$, $a_0, \ldots, a_n$ are arithmetic predicates over variables in V_D, and $\bowtie \in \{<, >, =, \leq, \geq, \neq\}$.
- $a_0 + a_1 \dot{v} \bowtie 0$ where $v \in V_C$, a_0, a_1 are arithmetic predicates over variables in V_D, and $\bowtie \in \{<, >, =, \leq, \geq, \neq\}$.

Example 1. $x \leq y + z$, $\text{NEXT}(x) = 0$, $\text{DER}(x) \leq d$ are in $PRED$. The first two predicates are also in $PRED_{la}$, while the third one is in $PRED_{la}$ only if d is a discrete variable.

We remark that, the class of predicates generalizes the class of constraints used for linear hybrid automata [2,20]; in particular, we replace constants with discrete (dense-domain) variables.

The HRELTL is defined by combining extended regular expressions (SEREs) and temporal operators from LTL. The *linear fragment* of HRELTL is defined by considering only predicates in $PRED_{la}$.

Definition 4 (SERE syntax). *If $p \in PRED$, r, r_1 and r_2 are SEREs, then:*

- *p is a SERE;*
- *ϵ is a SERE;*
- *$r[*]$, $r_1 ; r_2$, $r_1 : r_2$, $r_1 \mid r_2$, and r_1 && r_2 are SEREs.*

Definition 5 (HRELTL syntax). *If $p \in PRED$, ϕ, ϕ_1 and ϕ_2 are HRELTL formulas, and r is a SERE, then:*

- *p is a HRELTL formula;*

---

[3] In practice, we consider also predicates with next variables and derivatives, and derivatives after a discrete step, but we ignore this extensions to simplify the presentation.

– $\neg\phi_1$, $\phi_1 \wedge \phi_2$, $\mathbf{X}\ \phi_1$, $\phi_1\ \mathbf{U}\ \phi_2$ *are HRELTL formulas;*
– $r \Diamond\!\!\rightarrow \phi$ *is an HRELTL formula.*

We use standard abbreviations for $\vee$, $\rightarrow$, $\mathbf{G}$, $\mathbf{F}$, and $\mapsto$ (see, e.g., [11]).

Example 2. $\mathbf{G}\ (warning = 1 \rightarrow (warning = 1\ \mathbf{U}\ speed \leq limit))$ is in HRELTL.

Semantics. Some choices underlie the definition of the semantics in order to guarantee that the satisfaction of a formula by a hybrid trace does not depend on the sampling of continuous evolutions, rather it depends only on the discrete steps and on the shape of the functions that describe the continuous evolutions (*sampling invariance* [14]). Other choices have been taken to make the formalization of requirements more natural. For example, predicates including next variables can be true only in discrete steps.

Definition 6 (PRED semantics)

– $\langle \overline{f}, \overline{I}\rangle, i \models p_{curr}$ *iff, for all $t \in I_i$, p_{curr} evaluates to true when v is equal to $f_i^v(t)$, denoted with $f_i(t) \models p$;*
– $\langle \overline{f}, \overline{I}\rangle, i \models p_{next}$ *iff there is a discrete step between i and $i + 1$, i.e. $I_i = I_{i+1} = [t, t]$, and p_{next} evaluates to true when v is equal to $f_i^v(t)$ and NEXT(v) to $f_{i+1}^v(t)$, denoted with $f_i(t), f_{i+1}(t) \models p_{next}$;*
– $\langle \overline{f}, \overline{I}\rangle, i \models p_{der}$ *iff, for all $t \in I_i$, p_{der} evaluates to true both when v is equal to $f_i^v(t)$ and DER(v) to $\dot{f}_i^v(t)_+$, and when v is equal to $f_i^v(t)$ and DER(v) to $\dot{f}_i^v(t)_-$, denoted with $f_i(t), \dot{f}_i(t)_+ \models p_{der}$ and $f_i(t), \dot{f}_i(t)_- \models p_{der}$ (when $\dot{f}_i(t)$ is defined this means that $f_i(t), \dot{f}_i(t) \models p_{der}$).*

Note that, for all $i \in \mathbb{N}$, f_i is defined on all reals, and thus the left and right derivatives are defined in all points of I_i.

In order to ensure sample invariance, the predicates inside a SERE can be true over a sequence of more than one moment. This is different from the standard discrete approach, where they are usually true only if evaluated on just one state. Moreover, we require that if a sequence satisfies the concatenation or repetition of two SEREs, the sequence must contain a discrete step.

Definition 7 (SERE semantics)

– $\langle \overline{f}, \overline{I}\rangle, i, j \models p$ *iff, for all k, $i \leq k < j$, there is no discrete step at k ($I_k \neq I_{k+1}$), and, for all k, $i \leq k \leq j$, $\langle \overline{f}, \overline{I}\rangle, k \models p$;*
– $\langle \overline{f}, \overline{I}\rangle, i, j \models \epsilon$ *iff $i > j$;*
– $\langle \overline{f}, \overline{I}\rangle, i, j \models r[^*]$ *iff $i > j$, or $\langle \overline{f}, \overline{I}\rangle, i, j \models r$, or there exists a discrete step at k ($I_k = I_{k+1}$), $i \leq k < j$, such that $\langle \overline{f}, \overline{I}\rangle, i, k \models r$, $\langle \overline{f}, \overline{I}\rangle, k + 1, j \models r[^*]$;*
– $\langle \overline{f}, \overline{I}\rangle, i, j \models r_1 ; r_2$ *iff $\langle \overline{f}, \overline{I}\rangle, i, j \models r_1$, $\langle \overline{f}, \overline{I}\rangle, j + 1, j \models r_2$ (i.e., r_2 accepts the empty word), or; $\langle \overline{f}, \overline{I}\rangle, i, i - 1 \models r_1$, $\langle \overline{f}, \overline{I}\rangle, i, j \models r_2$ (i.e., r_1 accepts the empty word), or there exists a discrete step at k ($I_k = I_{k+1}$), $i \leq k < j$, such that $\langle \overline{f}, \overline{I}\rangle, i, k \models r_1$, $\langle \overline{f}, \overline{I}\rangle, k + 1, j \models r_2$;*
– $\langle \overline{f}, \overline{I}\rangle, i, j \models r_1 : r_2$ *iff there exists a discrete step at k ($I_k = I_{k+1}$), $i \leq k \leq j$, such that $\langle \overline{f}, \overline{I}\rangle, i, k \models r_1$, $\langle \overline{f}, \overline{I}\rangle, k, j \models r_2$;*
– $\langle \overline{f}, \overline{I}\rangle, i, j \models r_1 \mid r_2$ *iff $\langle \overline{f}, \overline{I}\rangle, i, j \models r_1$ or $\langle \overline{f}, \overline{I}\rangle, i, j \models r_2$;*
– $\langle \overline{f}, \overline{I}\rangle, i, j \models r_1$ **&&** r_2 *iff $\langle \overline{f}, \overline{I}\rangle, i, j \models r_1$ and $\langle \overline{f}, \overline{I}\rangle, i, j \models r_2$.*

Definition 8 (HRELTL semantics)

- $\langle \overline{f}, \overline{I} \rangle, i \models p$ *iff* $\langle \overline{f}, \overline{I} \rangle, i \models p$;
- $\langle \overline{f}, \overline{I} \rangle, i \models \neg\phi$ *iff* $\langle \overline{f}, \overline{I} \rangle, i \not\models \phi$;
- $\langle \overline{f}, \overline{I} \rangle, i \models \phi \wedge \psi$ *iff* $\langle \overline{f}, \overline{I} \rangle, i \models \phi$ *and* $\langle \overline{f}, \overline{I} \rangle, i \models \psi$;
- $\langle \overline{f}, \overline{I} \rangle, i \models \mathbf{X}\,\phi$ *iff there is a discrete step at i ($I_i = I_{i+1}$), and* $\langle \overline{f}, \overline{I} \rangle, i + 1 \models \phi$;
- $\langle \overline{f}, \overline{I} \rangle, i \models \phi \mathbf{U}\, \psi$ *iff, for some $j \geq i$,* $\langle \overline{f}, \overline{I} \rangle, j \models \psi$ *and, for all $i \leq k < j$,* $\langle \overline{f}, \overline{I} \rangle, k \models \phi$;
- $\langle \overline{f}, \overline{I} \rangle, i \models r \Diamond\!\!\rightarrow \phi$ *iff, there exists a discrete step at $j \geq i$ ($I_j = I_{j+1}$) such that* $\langle \overline{f}, \overline{I} \rangle, i, j \models r$, *and* $\langle \overline{f}, \overline{I} \rangle, j \models \phi$.

Definition 9 (Ground Hybrid Trace [14]). *A hybrid trace $\langle \overline{f}, \overline{I} \rangle$ is a ground hybrid trace for a predicate p iff the interpretation of p is constant throughout every open interval: if $I_i = (t, t')$ then either $\langle \overline{f}, \overline{I} \rangle, i \models p$ or $\langle \overline{f}, \overline{I} \rangle, i \models \overline{p}$. A hybrid trace $\langle \overline{f}, \overline{I} \rangle$ is a ground hybrid trace for a formula ϕ iff it is ground for all predicates of ϕ.*

Given an HRELTL formula ϕ, and a hybrid trace $\langle \overline{f}, \overline{I} \rangle$ ground for ϕ, we say that $\langle \overline{f}, \overline{I} \rangle \models \phi$ iff $\langle \overline{f}, \overline{I} \rangle, 0 \models \phi$.

Given an HRELTL formula ϕ, and any hybrid trace $\langle \overline{f}, \overline{I} \rangle$, we say that $\langle \overline{f}, \overline{I} \rangle \models \phi$ iff there exists a sampling refinement $\langle \overline{f}', \overline{I}' \rangle$ of $\langle \overline{f}, \overline{I} \rangle$ such that $\langle \overline{f}', \overline{I}' \rangle$ is ground for ϕ and $\langle \overline{f}', \overline{I}' \rangle \models \phi$.

For example, the hybrid traces depicted in Fig. 2 satisfy the formula of Example 2.

The following theorems guarantee that the semantics is well defined. (We refer the reader to [12] for the proofs.)

Theorem 1 (Finite variability). *Given a formula ϕ, for every hybrid trace $\langle \overline{f}, \overline{I} \rangle$ there exists another hybrid trace $\langle \overline{f}', \overline{I}' \rangle$ which is a sampling refinement of $\langle \overline{f}, \overline{I} \rangle$ and ground for ϕ.*

Theorem 2 (Sample invariance). *If $\langle \overline{f}', \overline{I}' \rangle$ is a sampling refinement of $\langle \overline{f}, \overline{I} \rangle$, then the two hybrid traces satisfy the same formulas.*

Note that we can encode the reachability problem for linear hybrid automata into the satisfiability problem of a linear HRELTL formula. Despite the undecidability of the satisfiability problem, we provide automatic techniques to look for satisfying hybrid traces, by constructing an equi-satisfiable discrete problem.

5 Reduction to Discrete Semantics

RELTL is the temporal logic that combines LTL with regular expressions and constitutes the core of many specification languages. Here, we refer to a first-order version of RELTL with real arithmetic predicates. RELTL syntax can be seen as a subset of HRELTL where predicates are allowed to include only current and next variables, but not derivatives.

RELTL formulas are interpreted over discrete traces. A discrete trace is a sequence of states $\sigma = s_0, s_1, s_2, \ldots$ with $s_i \in \Sigma$ for all $i \in \mathbb{N}$. The semantics for RELTL is analogue to the one of HRELTL but restricted to discrete steps only. We refer the reader to [12] for more details.

Encoding Hybrid RELTL into Discrete RELTL. We now present a translation of formulas of the linear fragment of HRELTL into equi-satisfiable formulas of RELTL. In the rest of this document we assume that formulas contain only predicates in $PRED_{la}$.

We introduce two Real variables δ_t and ζ respectively to track the time elapsing between two consecutive steps, and to enforce the non-Zeno property (i.e. to guarantee that time diverges). We introduce a Boolean variable ι that tracks if the current state samples a singular interval or an open interval.

We define a formula ψ_ι that encodes the possible evolution of δ_t and ι:

$$\psi_\iota := \iota \wedge \zeta > 0 \qquad\qquad\qquad\qquad\qquad\qquad\qquad\qquad \wedge$$
$$\mathbf{G}\,((\iota \wedge \delta_t = 0 \wedge \mathbf{X}\,(\iota)) \vee (\iota \wedge \delta_t > 0 \wedge \mathbf{X}\,(\neg\iota)) \vee (\neg\iota \wedge \delta_t > 0 \wedge \mathbf{X}\,(\iota)))\,\wedge$$
$$\mathbf{G}\,(\text{NEXT}(\zeta) = \zeta) \qquad\qquad\qquad\qquad\qquad\qquad\qquad\qquad\qquad \wedge \quad (1)$$
$$\mathbf{G}\,\mathbf{F}\,\delta_t \geq \zeta.$$

In particular, we force to have a discrete step, which is characterized by two consecutive singular intervals, if and only if $\delta_t = 0$.

For every continuous variable $v \in V_C$ we introduce the Real variable $\dot{v}_l$ and $\dot{v}_r$ that track the left and right derivative of v. We define a formula ψ_{DER} that encodes the relation among continuous variables and their derivatives:

$$\psi_{\text{DER}} := \bigwedge_{v \in V_C} ((\delta_t > 0 \wedge \iota) \to (\text{NEXT}(v) - v) = (\delta_t \times \text{NEXT}(\dot{v}_l)))\,\wedge$$
$$((\delta_t > 0 \wedge \neg\iota) \to (\text{NEXT}(v) - v) = (\delta_t \times \dot{v}_r)). \qquad\qquad (2)$$

The equation says that, before a point that samples an open interval, the evolution is tracked with the value of left derivative assigned in the sampling point, while afterwards, the evolution is tracked with the right derivative in the same point.

We define a formula ψ_{PRED_ϕ}, being $PRED_\phi$ the set of predicates occurring in ϕ without next variables and derivatives, that encodes the continuous evolution of the predicates.

$$\psi_{PRED_\phi} := (\delta_t > 0 \wedge \iota) \quad\to \bigwedge_{p \in PRED_\phi} \text{NEXT}(p_=) \to p_= \qquad\qquad \wedge$$
$$(\delta_t > 0 \wedge \neg\iota) \to \bigwedge_{p \in PRED_\phi} p_= \to \text{NEXT}(p_=) \qquad\qquad \wedge \quad (3)$$
$$\delta_t > 0 \qquad\qquad \to \bigwedge_{p \in PRED_\phi} ((p_< \to \neg\mathbf{X}\,p_>) \wedge (p_> \to \neg\mathbf{X}\,p_<)).$$

The first two conjuncts encode that if $p_=$ holds in an open interval, then $p_=$ holds in the immediately adjacent singular intervals too. The third conjuncts encodes that if $p_<$ holds we cannot move to an immediately following state where $p_>$ holds (and vice versa) without passing through a state where $p_=$ holds.

We define ψ_{V_D} to encode that discrete variables do not change value during a continuous evolution:

$$\psi_{V_D} := \delta_t > 0 \to (\bigwedge_{v \in V_d} (\text{NEXT}(v) = v)). \qquad\qquad (4)$$

Finally, we define the partial translation $\tau'(\phi)$ recursively over ϕ. The translation τ'_a of predicates is defined as:

– $\tau'_a(p_{curr}) = p_{curr}$;
– $\tau'_a(p_{next}) = (\delta_t = 0) \wedge p_{next}$;
– $\tau'_a(p_{der}) = p_{der}[\dot{v}_l/\text{DER}(v)] \wedge p_{der}[\dot{v}_r/\text{DER}(v)])$.

Where, $p[v'/v]$ is predicate p where every occurrence of v is replaced with v'.

The translation τ'_r of SEREs is defined as:

– $\tau'_r(p) = (\delta_t > 0 \wedge \tau'_a(p))[\mathbf{*}]\,;\,\tau'_a(p);$[4]

---

[4] This has the effect that $\tau'_r(p_{next}) = \tau'_a(p_{next}) = (\delta_t = 0 \wedge p_{next})$.

- $\tau'_r(\epsilon) = \epsilon$;
- $\tau'_r(r[\boldsymbol{*}]) = \epsilon \mid \{\tau'_r(r) : \delta_t = 0\}[\boldsymbol{*}] ; \tau'_r(r)$;
- $\tau'_r(r_1 ; r_2) = \{\{\epsilon \ \boldsymbol{\&\&} \ \tau'_r(r_1)\} ; \tau'_r(r_2)\} \mid \{\tau'_r(r_1) ; \{\epsilon \ \boldsymbol{\&\&} \ \tau'_r(r_2)\}\} \mid \{\{\tau'_r(r_1) : \delta_t = 0\} ; \{\tau'_r(r_2) : \top\}\}$;
- $\tau'_r(r_1 : r_2) = \tau'_r(r_1) : \delta_t = 0 : \tau'_r(r_2)$;
- $\tau'_r(r_1 \mid r_2) = \tau'_r(r_1) \mid \tau'_r(r_2)$;
- $\tau'_r(r_1 \ \boldsymbol{\&\&} \ r_2) = \tau'_r(r_1) \ \boldsymbol{\&\&} \ \tau'_r(r_2)$.

The translation τ' of HRELTL is defined as:

- $\tau'(p) = \tau'_a(p)$;
- $\tau'(\neg\phi_1) = \neg\tau'(\phi_1)$;
- $\tau'(\phi_1 \wedge \phi_2) = \tau'(\phi_1) \wedge \tau'(\phi_2)$;
- $\tau'(\mathbf{X} \ \phi_1) = \delta_t = 0 \wedge \mathbf{X} \ \tau'(\phi_1)$;
- $\tau'(\phi_1 \ \mathbf{U} \ \phi_2) = \tau'(\phi_1) \ \mathbf{U} \ \tau'(\phi_2)$;
- $\tau'(r \diamondsuit\!\!\rightarrow \phi) = \{\tau'_r(r) : \delta_t = 0\} \diamondsuit\!\!\rightarrow \tau'(\phi)$.

Thus, the translation τ for a generic HRELTL formula is defined as:

$$\tau(\phi) := \psi_\iota \wedge \psi_{\mathrm{DER}} \wedge \psi_{PRED_\phi} \wedge \psi_{V_D} \wedge \tau'(\phi). \tag{5}$$

Remark 1. If ϕ contains only quantifier-free predicates then also $\tau(\phi)$ is quantifier-free. In general, the predicates in $\tau(\phi)$ are non linear. ϕ may contain non linear predicates, even in the case ϕ is in the linear fragment of HRELTL, since it may contain polynomials over discrete variables or multiplications of a continuous variable with discrete variables. Moreover, Equation 2 introduces quadratic equations. Finally, note that if ϕ does not contain SEREs, then the translation is linear in the size of ϕ.

We now define a mapping from the hybrid traces of ϕ to the discrete traces of $\tau(\phi)$, and vice versa. Without loss of generality, we assume that the hybrid trace does not have discontinuous points in the derivatives in the open intervals.

Definition 10. *Given a hybrid trace $\langle \overline{f}, \overline{I} \rangle$, the discrete trace $\sigma = \Omega(\langle \overline{f}, \overline{I} \rangle)$ is defined as follows: for all $i \in \mathbb{N}$,*

- $t_i = t$ *if if* $I_i = [t, t]$, *and* $t_i = (t + t')/2$ *if* $I_i = (t, t')$;
- $s_i(v) = f_i^v(t_i)$;
- *if* $I_i = (t, t')$, $s_i(\dot{v}_l) = (f_i^v(t_i) - f_i^v(t_{i-1}))/(t_i - t_{i-1})$ *and* $s_i(\dot{v}_r) = (f_i^v(t_{i+1}) - f_i^v(t_i))/(t_{i+1} - t_i)$; *if* $I_i = [t, t]$ *then* $s_i(\dot{v}_l) = \dot{f}_i^v(t)_-$ *and* $s_i(\dot{v}_r) = \dot{f}_i^v(t)_+$;
- $s_i(\iota) = \top$ *if* $I_i = [t, t]$, *and* $s_i(\iota) = \bot$ *if* $I_i = (t, t')$;
- $s_i(\delta_t) = t_{i+1} - t_i$;
- $s_i(\zeta) = \alpha$, *such that for all* $i \in \mathbb{N}$, *there exists* $j \geq i$ *such that* $t_{i+1} - t_i \geq \alpha$ *(such α exists for the Cauchy's condition on the divergent sequence $\{t_i\}_{i \in \mathbb{N}}$).*

We then define the mapping in the opposite direction.

Definition 11. *Given a discrete trace σ, the hybrid trace $\langle \overline{f}, \overline{I} \rangle = \Upsilon(\sigma)$ is defined as follows: for all $i \in \mathbb{N}$,*

- $t_i = \sum_{0 \leq j < i-1} s_j(\delta_t)$,

- if $s_i(\iota) = \top$ then $I_i = [t_i, t_i]$ else $I_i = (t_{i-1}, t_{i+1})$,
- if $s_i(\delta_t) > 0$ then f_i is the piecewise linear function defined as $f_i^v(t) = s_i(v) - s_i(\dot{v}_l) \times (t_i - t)$ if $t \le t_i$ and as $f_i^v(t) = s_i(v) + s_i(\dot{v}_r) \times (t - t_i)$ if $t > t_i$.

Theorem 3 (Equi-satisfiability). *If $\langle \overline{f}, \overline{I} \rangle$ is ground for ϕ and $\langle \overline{f}, \overline{I} \rangle \models \phi$, then $\Omega(\langle \overline{f}, \overline{I} \rangle) \models \tau(\phi)$. If σ is a discrete trace such that $\sigma \models \tau(\phi)$, then $\Upsilon(\sigma) \models \phi$ and $\Upsilon(\sigma)$ is ground for ϕ. Thus ϕ and $\tau(\phi)$ are equi-satisfiable.*

For the proofs we refer the reader to [12].

6   Fair Transition Systems and Language Emptiness

Fair Transition Systems (FTS) [26] are a symbolic representation of infinite-state systems. First-order formulas are used to represent the initial set of states I, the transition relation T, and each fairness condition $\psi \in F$.

To check the satisfiability of an RELTL formula ϕ with first-order constraints we build a fair transition system S_ϕ and we check whether the language accepted by S_ϕ is not empty with standard techniques. For the compilation of the RELTL formula S_ϕ into an equivalent FTS S_ϕ we rely on the works described in [11,10].

The language non-emptiness check for the FTS S_ϕ is performed by looking for a lasso-shape trace of length up to a given bound. We encode this trace into an SMT formula using a standard Bounded Model Checking (BMC) encoding and we submit it to a suitable SMT solver. This procedure is incomplete from two point of views: first, we are performing BMC limiting the number of different transitions in the trace; second, unlike the Boolean case, we cannot guarantee that if there is no lasso-shape trace does not exist an infinite trace satisfying the model (since a real variable may be forced to increase forever). Nevertheless, we find the procedure extremely efficient in the framework of requirements validation.

The BMC encoding allows us to perform some optimizations. First, as we are considering a lasso-shape path, the Cauchy condition for the non-Zeno property can be reduced to $\mathbf{G} \, \mathbf{F} \, \delta_t > 0$ and no extra variables are needed. Second, whenever we have a variable whose value is forced to remain the same in all moments, we can remove such constraint and use a unique copy of the variable in the encoding.

The definition of HRELTL restricts the predicates that occur in the formula to linear function in the continuous variables in order to allow the translation to the discrete case. Nevertheless, we may have non-linear functions in the whole set of variables (including discrete variables). Moreover, the translation introduces non-linear predicates to encode the relation of a variable with its derivatives.

We aim at solving the BMC problem with an SMT solver for linear arithmetics over Reals. To this purpose, first, we assume that the input formula does not contain non-linear constraints; second, we approximate (2) with linear constraints. Suppose $\mathrm{DER}(v)$ is compared with constants $c_1, \dots, c_n$ in the formula, we replace the non-linear equations of (2) that are in the form $\mathrm{NEXT}(v) - v = h \times \delta_t$ with:

$$\bigwedge_{1 \le i \le n} (h < c_i \leftrightarrow \mathrm{NEXT}(v) - v < c_i \times \delta_t \quad \wedge$$
$$h = c_i \leftrightarrow \mathrm{NEXT}(v) - v = c_i \times \delta_t \quad \wedge \qquad (6)$$
$$h > c_i \leftrightarrow \mathrm{NEXT}(v) - v > c_i \times \delta_t))).$$

7   Practical Experience

The HRELTL language has been evaluated in a real-world project that aims at formalizing and validating the ETCS specification. The project is in response to the ERA tender ERA/2007/ERTMS/OP/01 ("Feasibility study for the formal specification of ETCS functions"), awarded to a consortium composed by RINA SpA, Fondazione Bruno Kessler, and Dr. Graband and Partner GmbH (see http://www.era.europa.eu/public/core/ertms/Pages/Feasibility_Study.aspx for further information on the project). The language used within the project is actually a superset of HRELTL that encompasses first-order constructs to represent classes of objects and their relationships. The extension enriches the representation power of the discrete part of the specification, and therefore it is orthogonal to the hybrid aspects of the language. The techniques used to handle objects and first-order constraints are described in [10].

We implemented the translation from linear HRELTL to RELTL in an extended version of the NuSMV [9] model checker that interfaces with the MathSAT [5] SMT solver. For an RELTL formula ϕ, we use NuSMV to compile ϕ into an equivalent FTS S_ϕ. Then, we check the language non-emptiness of S_ϕ by submitting the corresponding BMC problem to the MathSAT SMT solver.

We ran the experiments on a 2.20GHz Intel Core2 Duo Laptop equipped with 2GB of memory running Linux version 2.6.24. All the data and binaries necessary to reproduce the results here presented are available at http://es.fbk.eu/people/tonetta/tests/cav09/.

We extracted from the fragment of the ETCS specification a set of requirements that falls in HRELTL and that are relevant for their hybrid aspects. This resulted in a case study consisting of 83 HRELTL formulas, with 15 continuous variables, of which three are timers and two are stop watches. An excerpt of the ETCS specification in HRELTL format is reported in [12].

We first checked whether the specification is consistent, i.e. if it is satisfiable (SAT). Then, we validated the formalization with 3 different scenarios (SCEN_{1,2,3}), checking the satisfiability of the conjunction of the specification with a formula that represents some assumptions on the evolution of the variables. In all cases, the tool generated a trace proving the satisfiability of the formulas. We then asked the tool to generate witness traces of different increasing lengths k (10, 20, and 30 respectively). We obtained the results reported in Fig. 3(a). In the table we report also the size, in terms of number of variables and number of fairness conditions of the FTS we submit to underlying verification tool. (We use $\#r, \#b, \#f$ with the meaning, r Real variables, b Boolean variables, and f fairness conditions.) Fig. 3(b) also reports some curves that we can extract from the trace generated by the tool. These curves are the same that are manually depicted in ETCS (Fig. 1(b)). The fact that the automated generated traces resemble the ones inserted in the requirements document makes us more confident that the requirements captures what the designers have in mind.

8   Related Work

To the best of our knowledge, this is the first attempt to generalize requirements validation to the case of hybrid domains.

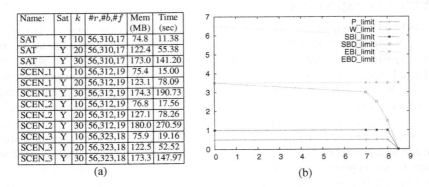

Name:	Sat	k	#r,#b,#f	Mem (MB)	Time (sec)
SAT	Y	10	56,310,17	74.8	11.38
SAT	Y	20	56,310,17	122.4	55.38
SAT	Y	30	56,310,17	173.0	141.20
SCEN_1	Y	10	56,312,19	75.4	15.00
SCEN_1	Y	20	56,312,19	123.1	78.09
SCEN_1	Y	30	56,312,19	174.3	190.73
SCEN_2	Y	10	56,312,19	76.8	17.56
SCEN_2	Y	20	56,312,19	127.1	78.26
SCEN_2	Y	30	56,312,19	180.0	270.59
SCEN_3	Y	10	56,323,18	75.9	19.16
SCEN_3	Y	20	56,323,18	122.5	52.52
SCEN_3	Y	30	56,323,18	173.3	147.97

(a)   (b)

Fig. 3. The results of the experimental evaluation

The work most closed to the current paper is described in [14], where LTL with continuous and hybrid semantics is compared with the discrete semantics. It is proved that a positive answer to the model checking problem and to the validity problem with the discrete semantics implies a positive answer to the corresponding problem in the continuous semantics. The properties of finite variability and sampling invariance are introduced. Notably, the hybrid semantics of the logic relies on the hybrid traces accepted by a hybrid system (while our definition is independent).

Besides [14], our work is also inspired by the ones of [23,24,27]. [24,27] face the problem of the observability of predicates during continuous evolutions, and define phase transition systems, which are a symbolic version of hybrid automata. [23] formally defines a continuous semantics for LTL without next operator and derivatives. In all these works, there is no attempt to solve the satisfiability problem for LTL with the continuous semantics.

Many logics have been introduced to describe properties of timed systems (see [3,4] for a survey), but none of them can force the continuity of functions, because the semantics is discrete, though in some cases even a dense time domain is considered. Hybrid systems [27,20] assume that some functions are continuous but the logic used to express the properties is discrete.

In [18,22], a translation from dense time to discrete time is proposed for a particular class of specifications, but only discrete semantics is considered. In [30], the discretization of hybrid systems is obtained with an over-approximation, while our translation produces an equi-satisfiable discrete formula.

In [19], a framework for specifying requirements of hybrid systems is proposed. However, the techniques are model based, and the requirements are formalized in a tabular notation, which can be seen as a symbolic representation of an automaton.

In [29], a hybrid dynamic logic is proposed for the verification of hybrid systems and it was used to prove safety properties for ETCS. The approach is still model-based since the description of the system implementation is embedded in the logical formula. The regular expression operations are used to define hybrid programs, that represent the hybrid systems. Properties of hybrid programs are expressed with the modalities of first-order dynamic logic. As in RELTL, we use regular expressions with a linear semantics. Moreover, the constraints on the continuous evolution are part of the requirements rather than the system description. As explained in Sec. 2, our approach to the validation of ETCS specifications is property-based.

In [2,20], linear hybrid automata are defined and a symbolic procedure is proposed to check their emptiness. Besides the different property-based approach that we propose, our techniques differ in the following points. First, instead of a finite set of states, the discrete modes are represented by the infinite (uncountable) set of assignments to the discrete variables. Second, instead of fix-point computations where the image is based on the quantifier elimination in the theory of Reals, we propose a BMC-based approach with a quantifier-free encoding (this is accomplished by forcing each step to move in a convex region). Related to the encoding of invariants that hold in a continuous evolution, also [31] faces the problem of concave conditions, and splits concave time conditions into convex segments. The condition (3) of our translation has the purpose to split the trace into convex regions in an analogue way.

In [25], a continuous semantics to a temporal logic which does not consider next operators and derivatives is presented. The paper addresses the problem of monitoring temporal properties of circuits with continuous signals.

On a different line of research, Duration Calculus (DC) [7] specifies requirements of real-time systems with predicates over the integrals of Boolean functions over finite intervals of time. Extensions of DC such as Extended Duration Calculus [8] can specify properties over continuous and differentiable functions. DC has been used to specify properties for ETCS [17]. Similarly to DC, Hybrid Temporal Logic (HTL) [21] uses the "chop" operator to express the temporal succession and can express temporal constraints on the derivatives of dynamic functions. Both DC and HTL interpret formulas over intervals of time (rather than infinite sequences of intervals). On the contrary, HRELTL is based on RELTL, which has been consolidated as specification language at the industrial level. HRELTL has the advantage to allow the reuse of requirements analysis techniques for RELTL.

9   Conclusions and Future Work

In this paper, we tackled the problem of validating requirements for hybrid systems. We defined a new logic HRELTL, that allows to predicate over properties of hybrid traces. Then, we showed that the satisfiability for the linear fragment of HRELTL can be reduced to an equi-satisfiable problem for RELTL over discrete traces. HRELTL was used for modeling in a real-world project aiming at the validation of a subset of the ETCS specification. The validation showed that the temporal requirements of ETCS can be formalized with HRELTL, and the experimental evaluation we carried out showed the practicality of the analysis, based on the use of SMT techniques.

As future work, we will enhance the scalability of the satisfiability procedure, by means of incrementality, lemmas on demand, and abstraction-refinement techniques. We will also consider alternative ways to deal with nonlinear constraints.

References

1. The PROSYD project on property-based system design (2007),
   http://www.prosyd.org
2. Alur, R., Courcoubetis, C., Henzinger, T.A., Ho, P.-H.: Hybrid Automata: An Algorithmic
   Approach to the Specification and Verification of Hybrid Systems. In: Hybrid Systems, pp.
   209–229 (1992)
3. Alur, R., Henzinger, T.A.: Logics and Models of Real Time: A Survey (1992)
4. Alur, R., Henzinger, T.A.: Real-Time Logics: Complexity and Expressiveness. Inf. Comput. 104(1), 35–77 (1993)
5. Bruttomesso, R., Cimatti, A., Franzén, A., Griggio, A., Sebastiani, R.: The MathSAT 4 SMT
   Solver. In: Gupta, A., Malik, S. (eds.) CAV 2008. LNCS, vol. 5123, pp. 299–303. Springer,
   Heidelberg (2008)
6. Bustan, D., Flaisher, A., Grumberg, O., Kupferman, O., Vardi, M.Y.: Regular vacuity. In:
   Borrione, D., Paul, W. (eds.) CHARME 2005. LNCS, vol. 3725, pp. 191–206. Springer,
   Heidelberg (2005)
7. Chaochen, Z., Hoare, C.A.R., Ravn, A.P.: A calculus of durations. Inf. Process. Lett. 40(5),
   269–276 (1991)
8. Chaochen, Z., Ravn, A.P., Hansen, M.R.: An extended duration calculus for hybrid real-time
   systems. In: Hybrid Systems, pp. 36–59 (1992)
9. Cimatti, A., Clarke, E.M., Giunchiglia, F., Roveri, M.: NuSMV: a new Symbolic Model
   Verifier. In: Halbwachs, N., Peled, D.A. (eds.) CAV 1999. LNCS, vol. 1633, pp. 495–499.
   Springer, Heidelberg (1999)
10. Cimatti, A., Roveri, M., Susi, A., Tonetta, S.: Object models with temporal constraints. In:
    SEFM 2008, pp. 249–258. IEEE Press, Los Alamitos (2008)
11. Cimatti, A., Roveri, M., Tonetta, S.: Symbolic Compilation of PSL. IEEE Trans. on CAD of
    Integrated Circuits and Systems 27(10), 1737–1750 (2008)
12. Cimatti, A., Roveri, M., Tonetta, S.: Requirements Validation for Hybrid Systems. Technical
    Report 200904002, FBK, Extended version of CAV 2009 (2009)
13. Claessen, K.: A coverage analysis for safety property lists. In: FMCAD, pp. 139–145. IEEE,
    Los Alamitos (2007)
14. de Alfaro, L., Manna, Z.: Verification in Continuous Time by Discrete Reasoning. In: Alagar,
    V.S., Nivat, M. (eds.) AMAST 1995. LNCS, vol. 936, pp. 292–306. Springer, Heidelberg
    (1995)
15. ERTMS/ETCS — Baseline 3: System Requirements Specifications. SUBSET-026-1, i3.0.0
    (2008), http://www.era.europa.eu/core/ertms/Pages/
    FirstETCSSRS300.aspx
16. Eveking, H., Braun, M., Schickel, M., Schweikert, M., Nimbler, V.: Multi-level assertion-
    based design. In: MEMOCODE, pp. 85–86. IEEE, Los Alamitos (2007)
17. Faber, J., Meyer, R.: Model checking data-dependent real-time properties of the european
    train control system. In: FMCAD, pp. 76–77 (2006)
18. Furia, C.A., Pradella, M., Rossi, M.: Automated Verification of Dense-Time MTL Specifi-
    cations Via Discrete-Time Approximation. In: Cuellar, J., Maibaum, T., Sere, K. (eds.) FM
    2008. LNCS, vol. 5014, pp. 132–147. Springer, Heidelberg (2008)
19. Heitmeyer, C.L.: Requirements Specifications for Hybrid Systems. In: Hybrid Systems, pp.
    304–314 (1995)
20. Henzinger, T.A.: The Theory of Hybrid Automata. In: LICS, pp. 278–292 (1996)
21. Henzinger, T.A., Manna, Z., Pnueli, A.: Towards refining temporal specifications into hybrid
    systems. In: Hybrid systems, pp. 60–76 (1992)
22. Henzinger, T.A., Manna, Z., Pnueli, A.: What Good Are Digital Clocks? In: Kuich, W. (ed.)
    ICALP 1992. LNCS, vol. 623, pp. 545–558. Springer, Heidelberg (1992)

23. Kapur, A.: Interval and point-based approaches to hybrid system verification. PhD thesis, Stanford, CA, USA (1998)
24. Maler, O., Manna, Z., Pnueli, A.: From Timed to Hybrid Systems. In: REX Workshop, pp. 447–484 (1991)
25. Maler, O., Nickovic, D., Pnueli, A.: Checking Temporal Properties of Discrete, Timed and Continuous Behaviors. In: Pillars of Computer Science, pp. 475–505 (2008)
26. Manna, Z., Pnueli, A.: The Temporal Logic of Reactive and Concurrent Systems: Specification. Springer, Heidelberg (1992)
27. Manna, Z., Pnueli, A.: Verifying Hybrid Systems. In: Hybrid Systems, pp. 4–35 (1992)
28. Pill, I., Semprini, S., Cavada, R., Roveri, M., Bloem, R., Cimatti, A.: Formal analysis of hardware requirements. In: DAC, pp. 821–826 (2006)
29. Platzer, A.: Differential dynamic logic for verifying parametric hybrid systems. In: Olivetti, N. (ed.) TABLEAUX 2007. LNCS, vol. 4548, pp. 216–232. Springer, Heidelberg (2007)
30. Tiwari, A.: Abstractions for hybrid systems. Formal Methods in System Design 32(1), 57–83 (2008)
31. Wang, F.: Time-Progress Evaluation for Dense-Time Automata with Concave Path Conditions. In: ATVA, pp. 258–273 (2008)

Towards Performance Prediction of Compositional Models in Industrial GALS Designs

Nicolas Coste[1,2], Holger Hermanns[1,3],
Etienne Lantreibecq[2], and Wendelin Serwe[1]

[1] INRIA Grenoble – Rhône-Alpes, VASY project team
[2] STMicroelectronics Grenoble
[3] Universität des Saarlandes

Abstract. Systems and Networks on Chips (NoCs) are a prime design focus of many hardware manufacturers. In addition to functional verification, which is a difficult necessity, the chip designers are facing extremely demanding performance prediction challenges, such as the need to estimate the latency of memory accesses over the NoC. This paper attacks this problem in the setting of designing globally asynchronous, locally synchronous systems (GALS). We describe foundations and applications of a combination of compositional modeling, model checking, and Markov process theory, to arrive at a viable approach to compute performance quantities directly on industrial, functionally verified GALS models.

1 Introduction and Motivation

Systems and networks on chip (NoC) are becoming more complex. Because mono-clocked designs are reaching their limits, globally asynchronous, locally synchronous (GALS) designs with multiple locally synchronous clock domains are prevalent in many hardware design labs. Due to high masking and production costs, their functional verification is a major concern, and concurrency phenomena pose additional challenges for the designers.

A complex NoC may be functionally verified but still not compliant with its targeted performances. Similar observations are well-known in the networked distributed systems community [12], but three difficulties characterize the NoC domain: *(i)* functionality and performance are much more deeply intertwined, *(ii)* prototype costs are prohibitive in the hardware domain, and *(iii)* isolated components are not available for physical experimentation or post-design tuning.

Therefore it is imperative to carry out performance evaluation as early as possible, i.e., on system models before having first prototypes, and even before having precise descriptions of the architecture. Until now, industrial performance evaluation of architectural specifications have been very approximative and based on back-of-the-envelope (or spreadsheet) calculations and sometimes rough simulations. This notoriously results in over-dimensioned communication networks. Therefore, STMicroelectronics is investigating a sound methodology

A. Bouajjani and O. Maler (Eds.): CAV 2009, LNCS 5643, pp. 204–218, 2009.

to integrate performance evaluation and functional verification, which fits into their established design flow. This paper is a result of these activities.

Of specific interest are performance results concerning system utilization, latency, and throughput. For instance, one may want to study the utilization of a FIFO queue, the latency between entry and exit of a shared resource part, or the throughput of an operation. In this paper, we focus on the study of latencies. Notice that throughput problems can be seen as latency problems: the average throughput corresponds to the inverse of the average latency.

In a GALS design, hardware delays local to a single synchronous clock domain are discrete and can be precisely expressed as a number of clock steps. Generalizing the expression of a delay to a discrete probability distribution allows one to incorporate cumulative effects of system parts that are outside the scope of — but interfering with — the current model (e.g., arbitration strategies, memory latencies). In this way probabilities enter the modeling as an abstraction aid, possibly also to represent drifts between different clock domains. Figure 1 shows an example distribution, where a delay takes either one, two, or three steps. Modeling delays in this way, performance measures can be obtained by analyzing the underlying stochastic process, often a Markov chain (MC).

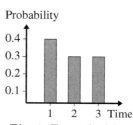

Fig. 1. Example delay

Due to the inherent complexity of asynchronous designs, existing functional verification approaches (mostly based on simulation) require long execution times to ensure sufficient coverage. Therefore formal methods are being applied to ensure functional correctness and detect errors. STMicroelectronics currently invests in the use of LOTOS [6] to formally model and validate their designs.

Performance evaluation studies for the same system usually require the development of another model. To avoid the cost of two different formal models, and to allow for joint considerations, we are working on a compositional approach allowing designers to enrich the available functional models with probabilistic time information. After first experiments with interactive Markov chains [4] the architects urged us to develop a synchronous variant with similar properties, and the result is presented in this paper. In our analysis so far, we are focusing on studying latencies of network components. As a matter of fact, though the notion of latency is often used in practical investigations, it turned out to be difficult to make that notion precise in a probabilistic timed setting. We define it as a Cesáro limit over the distribution of time elapsing between pairs of events.

In summary, the genuine contributions of this paper are: *(i)* the formalization of latency distributions on Markov chains, *(ii)* a compositional approach using a single model for functional verification and performance evaluation in a probabilistic discrete time setting, and *(iii)* the illustration of this approach on an industrial case study.

The remainder of this paper is organized as follows: Section 2 formally defines latency distributions of MC. Section 3 introduces the model of interactive probabilistic chains (IPCs). Section 4 describes how to extract latency distributions from an IPC via transformation to a MC. Section 5 reports on an industrial case study. Section 6 presents related work. Finally, Section 7 presents our conclusions.

2   Latency Distribution of Markov Chains

This section discusses latency distributions for time-homogeneous discrete time Markov chains (MC). After recalling the definition of an MC, we define the latency as a random variable denoting the number of time steps to reach a set of states from another set. Finally, we present how to compute latency distributions.

2.1   Markov Chains and Latencies

Definition 1. *A Markov chain is a tuple $\langle C, P, \hat{c} \rangle$ where C is a countable set of states, $P : C \times C \to [0,1]$ is a matrix of transition probabilities that satisfies $\sum_{c' \in C} P(c, c') = 1$ for all $c \in C$, and $\hat{c} \in C$ is a unique initial state.*

For a given MC $M = \langle C, P, \hat{c} \rangle$, $Paths(c)$ denotes the set of infinite paths starting in $c \in C$ where an infinite path is an infinite sequence $\sigma = c_0, c_1, c_2, \ldots$ satisfying $P(c_t, c_{t+1}) > 0$ for all $t \in \mathbb{N}$. A prefix $c_0, \ldots, c_n$ of an infinite path σ is called finite path, and in this case we write $\sigma = c_0, \ldots, c_n \cdot \star$.

For each state $c \in C$, a unique probability measure Pr^c is induced via the sigma-algebra generated from the finite prefixes of the paths in $Paths(c)$, by the cylinder set construction:

$$\mathsf{Pr}^c \{ \sigma \in Paths(c) \mid \sigma = c_0, \ldots, c_t \cdot \star \} = \prod_{0 \leq i < t} P(c_i, c_{i+1})$$

Applying this construction to the initial state $\hat{c}$ leads to the usual discrete-time stochastic process $X = \langle X_t, t \in \mathbb{N} \rangle$ associated with M, where the random variable X_t denotes the state occupied at time t. We write Pr instead of $\mathsf{Pr}^{\hat{c}}$, and use X^c for the stochastic process induced by $\langle C, P, c \rangle$, i.e., the MC where the initial state is c instead of $\hat{c}$.

In this work we focus on evaluating the latency of a NoC. To make this notion precise we identify two sets of states α and ω. The latency then corresponds to the number of time-steps required to reach a state in ω from a state in α. This is a time dependent quantity, since it may differ for different start times.

We include the case where α and ω are not disjoint: For a state $c \in \alpha \cap \omega$, one may imagine two possibilities to define the latency: either as zero or as the number of steps to reach ω after at least one step. We chose the latter approach, since the former seems irrelevant in practice: studying latencies is interesting only for operations incurring a non-zero delay, and it will become apparent in Sect. 4 that the case $\alpha \cap \omega$ is indeed a relevant one.

The time-dependent latency between states in α and ω will be defined in two steps: first, we introduce a notion of observation corresponding to the number time steps required to reach (from the current state) a state in ω. In a second step, we incorporate the set α. We fix a chain $M = \langle C, P, \hat{c} \rangle$ in the sequel.

Definition 2. *Let $O_{t_0}(\omega)$ be the random variable describing the number of steps, starting from time point t_0, before the first observation of a state in ω, defined as $O_{t_0}(\omega) = \min\{t \mid t > 0 \wedge X_{t_0+t} \in \omega\}$.*

The minimum over an empty set is defined to be ∞, which corresponds to the situation where a state of ω is never reached from X_{t_0}. If we consider the above definition for a different initial state c and thus X^c, we write $O_{t_0}^c(\omega)$.

For each time point t_0, we now define the latency to be $O_{t_0}(\omega)$ under the assumption that the chain currently resides in a state of α. In other words, the latency is defined as the number of time-steps between a state of α (start state) and a state of ω (stop state).

Definition 3. *The time-dependent latency $L_{t_0}(\alpha, \omega)$ from α to ω at time point t_0 is $L_{t_0}(\alpha, \omega) = O_{t_0}(\omega)$ if $X_{t_0} \in \alpha$ and 0 otherwise.*

When designing a system it is natural to look for the long-run behavior of the system, such as to take out the influence of initialization effects. One is thus usually interested not only in the time-dependent latency, but also in the latency perceived in the steady state equilibrium, thus the steady-state latency. We use the Cesáro limit construction to avoid periodicity considerations.

Definition 4. *The latency $L(\alpha, \omega)$ from α to ω is*

$$L(\alpha, \omega) = \lim_{t \to \infty} \frac{1}{t} \sum_{t_0=0}^{t} L_{t_0}(\alpha, \omega)$$

The Cesáro limit always exists for time-homogeneous MCs. The standard steady state limit $\lim_{t \to \infty} L_t(\alpha, \omega)$ may not exist, but agrees with the Cesáro limit if it does.

2.2 Computing Latencies

We now discuss how to calculate the above measures for a given MC $\langle C, P, \hat{c} \rangle$.

Lemma 1. *For $t \in \mathbb{N}_{>0}$ the distribution of $O_{t_0}(\omega)$ is given by*

$$\Pr\big(O_{t_0}(\omega) = t\big) = \sum_{c \in \omega} \Pr\big(X_{t_0+t} = c \wedge (\forall i \in \{1, \dots, t-1\}) \, X_{t_0+i} \notin \omega\big)$$

The probability distribution of the latency $L_{t_0}(\alpha, \omega)$ can be derived from the probability distribution of $O_{t_0}(\omega)$. We only consider nonzero time points.

Lemma 2. *For all $t > 0$, the distribution of $L_{t_0}(\alpha, \omega)$ is given by:*

$$\Pr\big(L_{t_0}(\alpha, \omega) = t\big) = \sum_{c_b \in \alpha} \Pr\big(X_{t_0} = c_b \mid X_{t_0} \in \alpha\big) \, \Pr\big(O_{t_0}(\omega) = t \mid X_{t_0} = c_b\big)$$

$$= \sum_{c_b \in \alpha} \Pr\big(X_{t_0} = c_b \mid X_{t_0} \in \alpha\big) \, \Pr\big(O_0^{c_b}(\omega) = t\big)$$

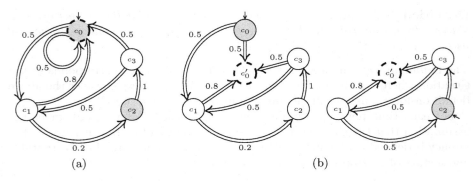

Fig. 2. Example of an MC and extracted sub-chains

The last equality is justified by the fact that in a time-homogeneous MC, each time point is a renewal point, and thus the probability of $O_{t_0}(\omega)$ is independent from the time t_0, if we fix a start state c_b. Therefore, we can compute it as $\Pr(O_0^{c_b}(\omega) = t)$. This, in turn, can be computed by considering the sub-chain consisting of all paths in $Paths(c_b)$.

Lemma 3. *For each state $c \in \alpha$, we have:*

$$\Pr\left(O_0^c(\omega) = t\right) = \sum_{\sigma \in Paths(c)} \Pr^c \left\{ \sigma \,\middle|\, \begin{array}{l} \sigma = c_0, \ldots, c_t \cdot \star \wedge c_t \in \omega \wedge \\ (\forall i \in \{1, \ldots, t-1\}) \; c_i \notin \omega \end{array} \right\}$$

The function associating $\Pr(O_0^{c_b}(\omega) = t)$ to each value of t is the distribution of the time to reach a state in ω given that the initial state is $c_b \in \alpha$. For our MC M, let $M^c(\omega)$ be the sub-chain spanning of all finite paths of M starting in c and ending at the first occurrence of a state $c' \in \omega$. By Lemma 3, the probability to reach an absorbing state of $M^c(\omega)$ in t time steps equals $\Pr(O_0^c(\omega) = t)$.

Example 1. For the MC of Fig. 2(a) and sets $\alpha = \{c_0, c_2\}$ (depicted as filled states) and $\omega = \{c_0\}$ (depicted with a dashed border), the two sub-chains $M^{c_0}(\omega)$ and $M^{c_2}(\omega)$ are shown in Fig. 2(b).

Now consider $L(\{c_b\}, \omega)$, the latency if starting in $c_b \in \alpha$. Since $\{c_b\}$ is a singleton, we have by Lemma 2 that $\Pr(L(\{c_b\}, \omega) = t) = \Pr(O_0^{c_b}(\omega) = t)$. Hence, this latency is time-independent and can be computed by reachability analysis of the absorbing states of $M^{c_b}(\omega)$. On the other hand, the probability of residing in a state $c_b \in \alpha$ under the assumption that M is in some state in α is a time-dependent quantity.

Lemma 4. *For each state $c_b \in \alpha$, we have:*

$$\Pr(X_{t_0} = c_b \mid X_{t_0} \in \alpha) = \frac{\Pr(X_{t_0} = c_b)}{\sum_{c \in \alpha} \Pr(X_{t_0} = c)}$$

The probability distribution of the steady-state latency $L(\alpha, \omega)$ (Def. 4) can now be computed using long-run averages of the states in M (steady-state may not exist, but if it does, it agrees with long-run average if existing). Let $\pi(c)$ denote the long run fraction of time spent in state $c \in C$. In vector-matrix notation, vector π is the unique probability distribution satisfying $\pi P = \pi$ (which always exists).

Lemma 5

$$\Pr\big(L(\alpha, \omega) = t\big) = \sum_{c_b \in \alpha} \frac{\pi(c_b)}{\sum_{c \in \alpha} \pi(c)} \ \Pr\big(L(\{c_b\}, \omega) = t\big)$$

The factor $\pi(c_b) / \sum_{c \in \alpha} \pi(c)$ is a normalization of the steady state probability of c_b over the set of states α. Consequently, the distribution of the latency $L(\alpha, \omega)$ is the sum of the normalized steady state probabilities of states of α, weighted by the distributions of the latencies starting in the states of α.

Example 2. For the MC chain shown in Fig. 2(a), with $\alpha = \{c_0, c_2\}$ (depicted as filled states) and $\omega = \{c_0\}$ (depicted with a dashed border), the latency distributions computed from the two extracted sub-chains starting in c_0 and c_2 shown in Fig. 2(b) are shown in Fig. 3. The distribution of $L(\alpha, \omega)$ (hashed bars on Fig. 3) is the sum of the normalized steady state probabilities of c_0 (9/10) and c_2 (1/10) weighted by those distributions.

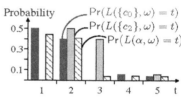

Fig. 3. Latency distributions

3 Compositional Modeling Approach

In this section, we introduce a compositional modeling approach merging functional and timed aspects, using probabilistic discrete-time distributions.

3.1 Interactive Probabilistic Chain

Our aim is to enable performance evaluation by enriching an existing formal model with timing information, following an approach similar to interactive Markov chains [4]. For the purpose of this paper, we use a probabilistic process calculus using the set of actions $\mathcal{A}$ (including the internal action τ). We assume that actions are taken instantaneously, and that every probabilistic choice takes exactly one time step.

A behavior is described using the following grammar (with $A \subset \mathcal{A} \setminus \{\tau\}$):

$$B ::= \delta \mid a \, ; B \mid \sum_i p_i :: B_i \mid B_1 \, [] \, B_2 \mid B_1 \, |[A]| \, B_2 \mid \text{hide } A \text{ in } B \mid \widetilde{B}$$

The operators will be referred to as: termination (δ), sequential composition (;), probabilistic choice ($\sum$, with the constraint $\sum_i p_i = 1$), non-deterministic choice ([]), LOTOS-style parallel composition with synchronization set ($|[A]|$), hiding of actions (hide A in $\cdots$), and process calls. A possibly recursive process is defined by a rule of the form $\widetilde{B} = B$. We write $\mathcal{B}$ to denote the set of all B.

$$\overline{\delta \xRightarrow{1} \delta} \qquad \overline{a;B \xrightarrow{a} B} \qquad \overline{a;B \xRightarrow{1} a;B} \qquad \overline{\textstyle\sum_i p_i :: B_i \xRightarrow{p_i} B_i}$$

$$\dfrac{B_1 \xrightarrow{a} B_1'}{B_1[]B_2 \xrightarrow{a} B_1'} \qquad \dfrac{B_2 \xrightarrow{a} B_2'}{B_1[]B_2 \xrightarrow{a} B_2'} \qquad \dfrac{B_1 \xRightarrow{p_1} B_1' \quad B_2 \xRightarrow{p_2} B_2'}{B_1[]B_2 \xRightarrow{p_1\,p_2} B_1'[]B_2'}$$

$$\dfrac{B_1 \xrightarrow{a} B_1' \quad a \notin A}{B_1|[A]|B_2 \xrightarrow{a} B_1'|[A]|B_2} \qquad \dfrac{B_2 \xrightarrow{a} B_2' \quad a \notin A}{B_1|[A]|B_2 \xrightarrow{a} B_1|[A]|B_2'} \qquad \dfrac{B_1 \xrightarrow{a} B_1' \quad B_2 \xrightarrow{a} B_2' \quad a \in A}{B_1|[A]|B_2 \xrightarrow{a} B_1'|[A]|B_2'}$$

$$\dfrac{B_1 \xRightarrow{p_1} B_1' \quad B_2 \xRightarrow{p_2} B_2'}{B_1|[A]|B_2 \xRightarrow{p_1\,p_2} B_1'|[A]|B_2'} \qquad \dfrac{\widetilde{B}=B \quad B \xrightarrow{a} B'}{\widetilde{B} \xrightarrow{a} B'} \qquad \dfrac{\widetilde{B}=B \quad B \xRightarrow{p} B'}{\widetilde{B} \xRightarrow{p} B'}$$

Fig. 4. Operational semantics of the modeling language

Example 3. Consider the four processes $\widetilde{B}_1$, $\widetilde{B}_2$, $\widetilde{B}_3$, and $\widetilde{B}_4$, defined over the set of actions $\mathcal{A} = \{a_1, a_2, \tau\}$ by:

$$\widetilde{B}_1 = a_1 ; \widetilde{B}_2 \qquad \widetilde{B}_2 = \sum \begin{matrix} 0.5 :: \widetilde{B}_3 \\ 0.5 :: \widetilde{B}_4 \end{matrix} \qquad \widetilde{B}_3 = a_2 ; \widetilde{B}_1 \qquad \widetilde{B}_4 = \sum \begin{matrix} 0.8 :: \widetilde{B}_3 \\ 0.2 :: \left(a_1 ; \sum 1 :: \widetilde{B}_2\right) \end{matrix}$$

The semantics of this language is defined in a structured operational semantics style as a probabilistic extension of a labeled transition system, called Interactive Probabilistic Chain (IPC).

Definition 5. *An IPC is a quintuple $D = \langle S, \mathcal{A}, \longrightarrow, \Longrightarrow, \hat{s} \rangle$ where S is a finite set of states, $\mathcal{A}$ is a finite set of actions including the internal action τ, $\longrightarrow \subset S \times \mathcal{A} \times S$ is a set of interactive transitions, $\Longrightarrow \subset S \times]0,1] \times S \to \mathbb{N}$ is a multi-set of probabilistic transitions, and $\hat{s} \in S$ is the initial state.*

We write $\mathcal{D}$ to denote the set of all IPCs over $\mathcal{A}$.

Definition 6. *The operational semantics of a behavior B_0 over the set of actions $\mathcal{A}$ is defined as the IPC $D = \langle \mathcal{B}, \mathcal{A}, \longrightarrow, \Longrightarrow, B_0 \rangle$ where $\longrightarrow$ and $\Longrightarrow$ are defined by the inference rules of Fig. 4.*

The third rule expresses the *arbitrary waiting* property: a process may be blocked waiting for a synchronization that is arbitrarily long (even infinitely) while still letting time advance. All these rules are partly inspired by Hansson [3], and as a whole enforce that time advances synchronously and that it may always advance.

We also require the property of *minimal delay* or *maximal progress* [9]: a process cannot delay an internal transition. In other words, if we have a probabilistic transition in competition with a τ-transition, the probabilistic transition incurs a time-step, while the τ-transition is possible immediately and will not be delayed. So a τ-transition has precedence over any probabilistic transition. However, this is not integrated into the semantics, but is taken care of by the bisimulation equivalences we are defining below.

Example 4. The IPC corresponding to Example 3 is shown in Fig. 5(a).

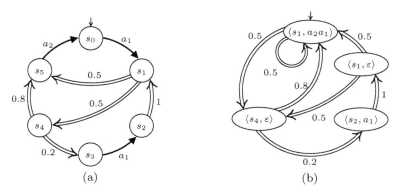

Fig. 5. Example of an IPC and its associated MC

3.2   Probabilistic Bisimulations

For a regular expression e over $\mathcal{A}$, let $s_0 \xrightarrow{e} s_n$ denote that there exists a sequence
of transitions $s_0 \xrightarrow{a_1} \ldots \xrightarrow{a_n} s_n$ where $a_1 \ldots a_n$ is a word in the language over $\mathcal{A}$
defined by e. We define a predicate $\gamma_0(s, a, S')$ which holds if and only if there is
an $s' \in S'$ such that $s \xrightarrow{a} s'$. Moreover, we define a function $\gamma_P : S \times 2^S \mapsto [0, 1]$,
that cumulates the probability of reaching a set of states S' from a single state
s, by $\gamma_P(s, S') = \sum_{(n,p) \in M(s,S')} n\, p$, where $M(s, S')$ is the largest set satisfying
$(n', p') \in M(s, S')$ if and only if $|\{s \xrightarrow{p'} s' \mid s' \in S'\}| = n'$. We use $s \xnrightarrow{\tau}$ to
abbreviate $\neg\gamma_0(s, \tau, \mathcal{D})$. Finally, we write $\mathcal{D}/_E$ to denote the set of equivalence
classes of $\mathcal{D}$ with respect to relation E. These ingredients are needed to define
bisimulations along the lines of [5,8].

Definition 7. *Strong probabilistic bisimulation equivalence ($\sim$) is the coarsest
equivalence relation on $\mathcal{D}$ such that $s_1 \sim s_2$ implies for all $a \in \mathcal{A}$ and all $C \in \mathcal{D}/_\sim$:*

- $\gamma_0(s_1, a, C) \;\Rightarrow\; \gamma_0(s_2, a, C)$,
- $s_1 \xnrightarrow{\tau} \;\Rightarrow\; (\, s_2 \xnrightarrow{\tau} \;\wedge\; \gamma_P(s_1, C) = \gamma_P(s_2, C) \,)$.

When relating MCs and IPCs, we need to abstract from internal computation.
Thus, we use a weaker notion of equivalence, branching bisimulation, here lifted
to IPC [5,14].

Definition 8. *Branching probabilistic bisimulation equivalence ($\approx$) is the coarsest equivalence relation on $\mathcal{D}$ such that $s_1 \approx s_2$ implies for all $a \in \mathcal{A}$ and all
$C \in \mathcal{D}/_\approx$:*

- $\gamma_0(s_1, a, C) \;\Rightarrow\; \left((\exists s_2')\; s_2 \xrightarrow{\tau^*} s_2' \wedge s_1 \approx s_2' \wedge \gamma_0(s_2', a, C)\right) \vee (a, s_2) \in \{\tau\} \times C$,
- $s_1 \xnrightarrow{\tau} \;\Rightarrow\; \left((\exists s_2' \xnrightarrow{\tau})\; s_2 \xrightarrow{\tau^*} s_2' \wedge s_1 \approx s_2' \wedge \gamma_P(s_1, C) = \gamma_P(s_2', C)\right)$.

Strong and branching bisimulation equivalence enjoy all the usual properties of
bisimulation-style relations. In particular, branching probabilistic bisimulation

is a congruence with respect to the parallel composition operator. This is exploited in our model construction process, where we replace components of a large system by equivalent, but smaller ones. In addition, strong and branching bisimulation equivalence preserve the probabilistic behavior, in the sense that whenever two IPCs s_1, s_2 are equivalent, then for each resolution of the nondeterminism in s_1 there is a resolution of the nondeterminism in s_2 (and vice versa) such that the resulting MCs have the same transient and steady-state behavior, if one only looks at probabilities of the equivalence classes. The relation between determinized IPC and MC is the topic of the following section.

4   Performance Analysis of a Deterministic IPC

In general, an IPC is a non-deterministic object, and non-determinism is an essential aid in building interacting systems from components. The resulting system however often shows deterministic behavior modulo branching bisimulation equivalence. Indeed, abstracting from all functional information (i.e., renaming them into τ) and minimizing with respect to branching bisimulation equivalence, *always* yields a deterministic system, though a very simple one, namely a single state with a probabilistic transition with probability 1. This is a trivial MC, and, of course, not very a insightful one. We will describe below how we keep precisely the information needed. Though this is only a partial solution, we focus in the analysis on deterministic non-zeno IPCs (dIPCs), and discuss the general case towards the end of this section.

Definition 9. *A deterministic IPC is an IPC* $\langle S, \mathcal{A}, \longrightarrow, \Longrightarrow, \hat{s} \rangle$ *satisfying:*

$$(\forall s, s', s'' \in S, a, a' \in \mathcal{A}) \quad (s \xrightarrow{a} s') \wedge (s \xrightarrow{a'} s'') \text{ implies } (s' = s'') \wedge (a = a')$$

$$(\forall s, s' \in S, a \in \mathcal{A}) \quad (s \xrightarrow{a} s') \text{ implies } (\exists s'', s''' \in S, w \in \mathcal{A}^*) \; s' \xrightarrow{w} s'' \xRightarrow{p} s'''$$

The above conditions guarantee that only finite, linear sequences of interactive transitions appear in a dIPC. When analyzing a complete system, we consider it *closed*, not interacting with the environment. Under this assumption, the maximal progress property generalizes to all actions, and is called *urgency* [9].

Definition 10. *An IPC* $D = \langle S, \mathcal{A}, \longrightarrow, \Longrightarrow, \hat{s} \rangle$ *is said to be urgency-cut iff*

$$(\forall s, s' \in S, a \in \mathcal{A}) \quad s \xrightarrow{a} s' \text{ implies } (\not\exists s'' \in S) \; s \xRightarrow{p} s''$$

Example 5. The IPC shown in Fig. 5(a) is deterministic and urgency-cut.

We apply the urgency property by moving from a dIPC to the largest urgency-cut dIPC contained therein. Transforming the resulting dIPC into an MC must allow us to keep information about some of the interactive transitions. To this end, we enrich states of the MC with a word (over $\mathcal{A}$) representing the (possibly empty) sequence of actions executed since the last time step, i.e., last probabilistic transition. We let ε stand for the empty word, representing two successive probabilistic transitions.

Definition 11. *Let* $D = \langle S, \mathcal{A}, \longrightarrow, \Longrightarrow, \hat{s} \rangle$ *be an urgency-cut dIPC over* $\mathcal{A}$. *Let* k *be the length of the longest sequence of interactive transitions in* D. *The associated MC* $M(D) = \langle C, P, \langle \hat{s}, \varepsilon \rangle \rangle$ *is given by:*

- $C = \{ s \in R(D) \mid (\exists s')\, s \overset{p}{\Longrightarrow} s' \} \times \mathcal{A}^{\leq k}$, *where* $R(D)$ *is the set of reachable states in* D, *and* $\mathcal{A}^{\leq k} = \{ w \mid w \in \mathcal{A}^* \wedge length(w) \leq k \}$.
- $P(\langle s, w \rangle, \langle s', w' \rangle) = \sum_{\{ i \mid (\exists s'')\, s \overset{p_i}{\Longrightarrow} s'' \overset{w'}{\longrightarrow} s' \}} p_i$

Notice that the transition probabilities from a state $\langle s, w \rangle$ to a state $\langle s', w' \rangle$ are accumulated from all possibilities to move from IPC state s — after one time step — to IPC state s' according to interactive transitions forming the word w'. The urgency cut ensures that in each state either one can spend time or one can engage in interactive actions, but not both.

Example 6. Consider the IPC D of Example 4. The associated MC $M(D)$ is shown in Fig. 5(b) and corresponds to the one of Example 1.

4.1 Computing Latency Distribution for dIPC

For a dIPC D, we define a latency $L_{IPC}(\mathsf{start}, \mathsf{stop})$ as the number of time steps between an action start (beginning of the latency) and stop (end of the latency). Considering the sets of states where a transition start (respectively stop) is possible, we can define the latency using the MC $M(D)$ and Def. 4.

Definition 12. *Let* $D = \langle S, \mathcal{A}, \longrightarrow, \Longrightarrow, \hat{s} \rangle$ *be a dIPC. The latency between two actions* $\mathsf{start}, \mathsf{stop} \in \mathcal{A}$ *is defined on the associated MC* $M(D)$:

$$L_{IPC}(\mathsf{start}, \mathsf{stop}) = L(\alpha, \omega)$$

where $\alpha = \{ \langle s, w \rangle \mid w = (A')^*.\mathsf{start}.\mathcal{A}^* \}$, $\omega = \{ \langle s, w \rangle \mid w = (A')^*.\mathsf{stop}.\mathcal{A}^* \}$, *and* $A' = \mathcal{A} \setminus \{ \mathsf{start}, \mathsf{stop} \}$.

Notice that, similar to the definitions of Sect. 2, Def. 12 does not consider zero-latencies, i.e., a start followed by an stop in the same time step. Indeed, for each state $c = \langle s, w \rangle$ of $M(D)$ with w of the form $(A')^*.\mathsf{start}.\mathcal{A}^*.\mathsf{stop}.\mathcal{A}^*$, we have $c \notin \omega$. However, for each state $c' = \langle s, w \rangle$ of $M(D)$ with w of the form $(A')^*.\mathsf{stop}.\mathcal{A}^*.\mathsf{start}.\mathcal{A}^*$, we have $c' \in \alpha \cap \omega$: this allows to take into account latencies that follow each other immediately.

Example 7. Consider the dIPC and its associated MC of Fig. 5. We are interested in the latency between actions a_1 and a_2. The associated MC with sets $\alpha = \{ \langle s_1, a_2 a_1 \rangle, \langle s_2, a_1 \rangle \}$ and $\omega = \{ \langle s_1, a_1 a_2 \rangle \}$ is identical to the MC of Fig. 2(a) with sets α and ω respectively depicted as filled states and dashed border states.

The restriction to dIPCs is a partial solution. But that does not mean that we cannot make use of the non-deterministic language constructs (choice, interleaving parallel composition) in our modeling. In practice, we construct an IPC using the non-deterministic constructs to let the systemcomponents interact as intended.

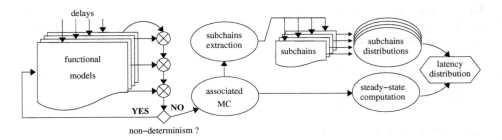

Fig. 6. Performance Evaluation Flow

Once the specification is complete, we identify the **start** and **stop** actions, and regard any other action as τ. We then move to the branching bisimulation quotient. In many cases this quotient is deterministic. The reason is that, intuitively, the nondeterministic branches are confluent up to branching bisimulation. In this case we can proceed with the resulting dIPC as suggested above. Otherwise, we need to (manually) refine the model, in order to resolve that non-determinism. This approach to handling nondeterminism via a quotient construction is akin to the one used in IMC modeling via CTMCs [4].

4.2 Implementation Considerations

Following these ideas, we implemented the flow depicted in Fig. 6 to compute the distribution of a latency between two actions **start** and **stop** of a system consisting of several sub-components.

First, functional models of sub-components of our system are enriched with delays, modeled as discrete-time probabilistic distributions. The sub-components are then composed according to the semantic rules given in Sect. 3.1 to get an IPC (the state space of which is minimized wrt branching bisimulation using the **bcg_min** tool of the CADP toolbox [2]). Before computing performance results, we ensure the IPC is deterministic. The associated MC is generated from the dIPC according to Def. 11.

Thus, an implementable way to compute the distribution of the latency $L_{IPC}(\text{start}, \text{stop})$ is provided by Def. 12 and Lemma 5. For each state $c_b \in \alpha$ (where α is defined according to Def. 12): on one hand, the distribution of the latency $L(\{c_b\}, \alpha)$ can be obtained by extracting the sub-chain $M^{c_b}(\omega)$ and computing the distribution of the number of time steps needed to reach an absorbing state; on the other hand, steady state (actually long-run average) analysis yields $\pi(c_b)/\sum_{c \in \alpha} \pi(c)$. The distribution of the latency $L_{IPC}(\text{start}, \text{stop})$ is then computed as the weighted sum given by Lemma 5.

5   Case Study: The xSTream Architecture

In the context of the Multival project [1], we investigated the xSTream architecture. xSTream is a multiprocessor data-flow architecture for high-performance

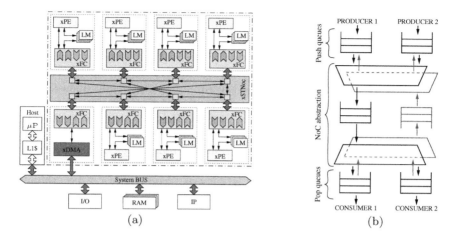

Fig. 7. xSTream architecture and the model of two parallel streams

embedded multimedia streaming applications designed at STMicroelectronics. xSTream supports stream-oriented programming, where an application performs several computation steps, called *filters*, on a stream of data. Each filter is mapped to a *processing element* (xPE) (i.e., a processor with some local memory), communicating over a *NoC* (xSTNoc). Several filters might be mapped to a single processing element according to its workload. To absorb traffic bursts, each processing element is linked to the NoC through buffering hardware queues for input flows (called *pop queues*) and for output flows (called *push queues*). A *flow controller* (xFC) manages the different push and pop queues for each processing element. The xSTream architecture is depicted on Fig. 7(a).

Operations on xSTream queues are blocking: a Push operation (insertion of an element in a queue) is blocked until there is a free place and a Pop operation (removal of an element from a queue) is blocked until an element is available. A queue stores its elements either in its dedicated hardware or in a *backlog* (LM) (i.e., the memory of the processing element) — the latter being much less efficient. Due to xSTream specific operations on these hardware queues, they are significantly more complex than standard FIFO queues: Each of them has between 1300 and 2400 states, for a capacity of up to three elements.

We focussed on the interaction between pairs of xSTream queues. Therefore, we developed a LOTOS [6] model of two parallel streams between two processing elements using two shared queues as an abstraction of the NoC, according to the virtual channel concept as defined in xSTream. This model is depicted on Fig. 7(b). This application scenario (two consumer-producer pairs) is not unrealistic, since xSTream is targeted at streaming applications.

Using the CADP toolbox [2], we analyzed the correct functioning of the model, highlighting some issues. For example, an under-specification concerning a credit protocol has been found. This protocol aims to avoid deadlocks in the NoC and was claimed optional by architects. Analysis of our model showed that it was mandatory. This protocol ensures that a push queue does not send more elements than there are free places in the corresponding pop queue. It is based on counters local to queues and a stream from pop queues to push queues (opposite to data streams, see Fig. 7(b)) used to update the counters according to a defined threshold. As this protocol adds communication, it may influence performance.

The LOTOS model is composed of several sub-components: queues, a NoC abstraction, network interfaces between queues and NoC. Performance evaluation of this kind of system depends on applications running on it. We added producers and consumers for modeling these applications. The sub-components have been enriched with delays for insertion and removal of elements in queues and delays modeling the application.

We focus on the study of the mean latency of a Pop operation, i.e., the mean time needed to get an element from the pop queue. The study of the distribution of the Pop operation latency could give us more information concerning bounds and borderline behaviors. In this case-study, we only consider mean values which can be (and have been) confirmed by simulation.

The Pop operation latency has a theoretical lower bound corresponding to the time physically needed to access the pop queue's head. In the case of an empty pop queue, the Pop operation is blocked until an element is available. In a streaming application, the mean duration of a Pop operation should be close to its minimum value. Indeed, queues are dedicated to absorb traffic variations, and to hide communication latencies. A mean duration of a Pop operation that is much greater than its minimum value indicates that pop queues are often in a starvation context and do not fulfill their task.

Using our prototypical tool-chain, we performed three experiments varying the applications (production and consumption rates) and the credit protocol threshold. The first two experiments use the worst possible threshold (i.e., a threshold equal to the pop queue size): hence the push queue is often blocked (it has no more credit left). Experiments (a) and (a') differ in the delay between the generation and consumption of two packets: Exp. (a) uses the distribution shown in Fig. 1, whereas Exp. (a') uses a similar distribution, but with higher mean value. Experiment (b) differs from Exp. (a) by using a larger pop queue and a threshold strictly smaller than the pop queue size. For all three experiments, the delay to insert an element in the pop queue was abstracted by a probabilistic distribution: insertion of an element took either one time step (insertion in the queue) or five time steps (insertion in the backlog). Figure 8(a) gives the sizes of IPCs and MCs, and Fig. 8(b) shows the mean latency of the three experiments for different probability values to insert in the backlog.

Experiments (a) and (a') are similar: the throughput of applications has indeed no real influence on the Pop operation latency. However, using the worst case for the threshold impacts the Pop latency (its theoretical lower bound is 1.5 packets every time step on average). Experiment (b) confirms that using a lower threshold reduces the latency. Finally, for all experiments, we see that the lower the probability to insert in the backlog, the better the performance.

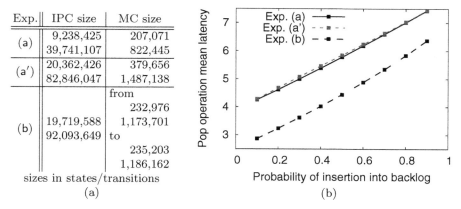

Exp.	IPC size	MC size
(a)	9,238,425	207,071
	39,741,107	822,445
(a')	20,362,426	379,656
	82,846,047	1,487,138
(b)	19,719,588	from 232,976 / 1,173,701
	92,093,649	to 235,203 / 1,186,162

sizes in states/transitions

(a)   (b)

Fig. 8. Experimental results

The results are showing trends that one would indeed expect for a single pair of queues. But it is not obvious that these trends are actually observed for a system consisting of two pairs of queues sharing the same virtual channels. Thus, the results confirm the architectural choices.

6 Related Work

There is a plethora of probabilistic process calculi around in the literature [7], none of which served our purposes, because we needed a synchronous time model as in ATP [10], which incorporates probabilistic branching. The calculus is most inspired by the alternating model of Hansson [3]. For this model a branching bisimulation has been studied in [13], which is similar in spirit to ours, but can amalgamate sequences of probabilistic steps. This is not compatible with our setting where probabilistic steps are time steps.

Our maximal progress and compositionality considerations are akin to those in IMC [4]. One might consider IPC as the discrete time analogon of IMC, and indeed we are re-using for IPC the IMC branching bisimulation minimizer of CADP.

Looking superficially at the example case one may think of (discrete time) queueing networks and related models as a possible alternative. However, standard queueing networks are usually too abstract to incorporate the complex behavior of the circuit. If one indeed invests in extending the queueing network setting to incorporate this hardware behavior, there seems to be no obvious advantage over the approach presented by us.

7 Conclusion

The industrial practitioners are asking for new recipes to study the performance of SoCs and NoCs. In this paper we introduced interactive probabilistic chains to enable compositional modeling, functional verification, and performance evaluation, the latter via a translation into Markov chains. This is a partial solution approach, because in general the resulting model is a Markov decision process. We applied this approach to compute latencies in an industrial case study.

Though the theory is solid and prototype tool support is available, a lot remains to be achieved before the issue of model-based performance evaluation can be closed. As a concrete future challenge, we need to improve the efficiency of our prototypical performance evaluation flow, and we plan to apply it to further examples and performance measures. We are also thinking of combining it with simulative approaches. It appears possible to extend our analysis approach to the general IPC setting, because the principal algorithmic building blocks, working on Markov decision processes, are known [11].

References

1. Coste, N., Garavel, H., Hermanns, H., Hersemeule, R., Thonnart, Y., Zidouni, M.: Quantitative evaluation in embedded system design: Validation of multiprocessor multithreaded architectures. In: DATE (March 2008)
2. Garavel, H., Lang, F., Mateescu, R., Serwe, W.: CADP 2006: A toolbox for the construction and analysis of distributed processes. In: Damm, W., Hermanns, H. (eds.) CAV 2007. LNCS, vol. 4590, pp. 158–163. Springer, Heidelberg (2007)
3. Hansson, H.A.: Time and Probability in Formal Design of Distributed Systems. Elsevier Science, Amsterdam (1994)
4. Hermanns, H. (ed.): Interactive Markov Chains. LNCS, vol. 2428. Springer, Heidelberg (2002)
5. Hermanns, H., Lohrey, M.: Priority and maximal progress are completely axiomatisable (extended abstract). In: Sangiorgi, D., de Simone, R. (eds.) CONCUR 1998. LNCS, vol. 1466, pp. 237–252. Springer, Heidelberg (1998)
6. ISO/IEC. LOTOS — a formal description technique based on the temporal ordering of observational behaviour. International Standard 8807 (1989)
7. Jonsson, B., Yi, W., Larsen, K.G.: Probabilistic Extensions of Process Algebras, ch. 11, pp. 685–710. North Holland, Amsterdam (2001)
8. Larsen, K.G., Skou, A.: Compositional verification of probabilistic processes. In: Cleaveland, W.R. (ed.) CONCUR 1992. LNCS, vol. 630, pp. 456–471. Springer, Heidelberg (1992)
9. Nicollin, X., Sifakis, J.: An overview and synthesis on timed process algebras. In: Larsen, K.G., Skou, A. (eds.) CAV 1991. LNCS, vol. 575, pp. 376–398. Springer, Heidelberg (1992)
10. Nicollin, X., Sifakis, J.: The algebra of timed processes ATP: Theory and application. Information and Computation 114(1), 131–178 (1994)
11. Puterman, M.L.: Markov Decision Processes. Wiley, Chichester (1994)
12. Swartz, K.L., Cottrell, R.L., Dart, M.: Adventures in the evolution of a high-bandwidth network for central servers. In: LISA. USENIX (1994)
13. Trčka, N., Georgievska, S.: Branching bisimulation congruence for probabilistic systems. In: QAPL 2008. Electronic Notes in Theoretical Computer Science, vol. 220, pp. 129–143 (2008)
14. van Glabbeek, R.J., Weijland, W.P.: Branching time and abstraction in bisimulation semantics (extended abstract). In: IFIP congress, pp. 613–618 (1989)

Image Computation for Polynomial Dynamical Systems Using the Bernstein Expansion

Thao Dang and David Salinas

Verimag,
2 avenue de Vignate, 38610 Gières, France

Abstract. This paper is concerned with the problem of computing the image of a set by a polynomial function. Such image computations constitute a crucial component in typical tools for set-based analysis of hybrid systems and embedded software with polynomial dynamics, which found applications in various engineering domains. One typical example is the computation of all states reachable from a given set in one step by a continuous dynamics described by a differential or difference equation. We propose a new algorithm for over-approximating such images based on the Bernstein expansion of polynomial functions. The images are stored using template polyhedra. Using a prototype implementation, the performance of the algorithm was demonstrated on two practical systems as well as a number of randomly generated examples.

1 Introduction

Hybrid systems, that is, systems exhibiting both continuous and discrete dynamics, have been an active research domain, thanks to their numerous applications in chemical process control, avionics, robotics, and most recently molecular biology. Due to the safety critical features of many such applications, formal analysis is a topic of particular interest. A major component in any verification algorithm for hybrid systems is an efficient method to compute the reachable sets of their continuous dynamics described by differential or difference equations. Well-known properties of affine systems and other simpler systems can be exploited to design relatively efficient methods[1]. A recently-developed method can handle continuous systems of 100 and more variables [11]. Nevertheless, non-linear systems are much more difficult to analyze.

In this work, we address the following image computation problem: given a set in $\mathbb{R}^n$, compute its image by a polynomial. This problem typically arises when we deal with a dynamical system of the form $x(k + 1) = \pi(x(k))$ where π is a multivariate polynomial. Such a dynamical system could result from a numerical approximation of a continuous or hybrid system. Many existing reachability computation methods for continuous systems can be seen as an extension of numerical integration. For reachability analysis which requires considering all

---

[1] The hybrid systems reachability computation literature is vast. The reader is referred to the recent proceedings of the conferences HSCC.

A. Bouajjani and O. Maler (Eds.): CAV 2009, LNCS 5643, pp. 219–232, 2009.

possible solutions (for example, due to non-determinism in initial conditions), one has to solve the above equation with sets, that is $x(k)$ and $x(k + 1)$ in the equation are subsets of $\mathbb{R}^n$ (while they are points if we only need a single solution, as in numerical integration). In addition, similar equations can arise in embedded control systems, such as some physical system controlled by a computer program, which is the implementation of some continuous (or possibly hybrid) controller using appropriate discretization.

Another reason for our interest in the image computation problem for polynomials is that such systems can be used to model a variety of physical phenomena in engineering, economy and bio-chemical networks. This problem was previously considered in [4], where a method using Bézier techniques from Computer Aided Geometric Design (CAGD) was proposed. The drawback of this method is that it requires expensive convex-hull and triangulation computation, which restricts its application to systems of dimensions not higher than 3, 4. The essence of the new method we propose in this paper can be summarized as follows. Using a special class of polyhedra together with optimization, we are able to reduce the complexity of the required polyhedral manipulation. Furthermore, by exploiting the Bernstein expansion, we only need to solve linear programming problems instead of polynomial optimization problems.

Our method is similar to a number of existing methods for continuous and hybrid systems in the use of linear approximation. Its novelty resides in the efficient way of computing linear approximations. Indeed, a common method to approximate a non-linear function by a piecewise linear one, as in the hybridization approach [1] for hybrid systems, requires non-linear optimization. Indeed, the work presented in this paper follows the approach using template polyhedra and optimization for hybrid systems with continuous dynamics proposed in [21].

Besides constrained global optimization, other important applications of the Bernstein expansion include various control problems [7] (in particular, robust control). The approximation of the range of a multivariate polynomial over a box is also used in program analysis and optimization (for example [3,23]). In the hybrid systems verification, polynomial optimization is used to compute barrier certificates [18]. Algebraic properties of polynomials are used to compute polynomial invariants [24] and to study the computability of image computation in [17].

The paper is organized as follows. In Section 2 we introduce the notions of template polyhedra and the Bernstein expansion. We then formally state our problem and describe an optimization-based solution. In order to transform the polynomial optimization problem to a linear programming problem, a method for computing bound functions is presented. We then describe an algorithm summarizing the main steps of our method. Some experimental results, in particular the analysis of a control and a biological systems, are reported in Section 4.

2   Preliminaries

Notation. Let $\mathbb{R}$ denote the set of reals. Throughout the paper, vectors are often written using bold letters. Exceptionally, scalar elements of multi-indices, introduced later, are written using bold letters. Given a vector $\mathbf{x}$, x_i denotes its ith component. Capital letters, such as A, B, X, Y, denote matrices or sets. If A is a matrix, A^i denotes the ith row of A. An affine function is thus represented as $\mathbf{c}^T\mathbf{x} + \mathbf{d}$.

We use B_u to denote the unit box $B_u = [0,1]^n$. We use π to denote a vector of n functions such that for all $i \in \{1,\ldots,n\}$, π_i is an n-variate polynomial of the form $\pi_i : \mathbb{R}^n \to \mathbb{R}$. In the remainder of the paper, we sometimes refer to π simply as "a polynomial".

To discuss the Bernstein expansion, we use multi-indices of the form $\mathbf{i} = (\mathbf{i}_1,\ldots,\mathbf{i}_n)$ where each $\mathbf{i}_j$ is a non-negative integer. Given two multi-indices $\mathbf{i}$ and $\mathbf{w}$, we write $\mathbf{i} \leq \mathbf{w}$ if for all $j \in \{1,\ldots,n\}$, $\mathbf{i}_j \leq \mathbf{w}_j$. Also, we write $\frac{\mathbf{i}}{\mathbf{w}}$ for $(\frac{\mathbf{i}_1}{\mathbf{w}_1},\ldots,\frac{\mathbf{i}_n}{\mathbf{w}_n})$ and $\binom{\mathbf{i}}{\mathbf{w}}$ for $\binom{\mathbf{i}_1}{\mathbf{w}_1}\binom{\mathbf{i}_2}{\mathbf{w}_2}\ldots\binom{\mathbf{i}_n}{\mathbf{w}_n}$.

Template polyhedra. A convex polyhedron is a conjunction of a finite number of linear inequalities described as $A\mathbf{x} \leq \mathbf{b}$, where A is a $m \times n$ matrix, $\mathbf{b}$ is a column vector of size m. Template polyhedra are commonly used in static analysis of programs for computing invariants (see for example [19]). The reader is referred to [19] for a thorough description of template polyhedra.

A template is a set of linear functions over $\mathbf{x} = (x_1,\ldots,x_n)$. We denote a template by an $m \times n$ matrix H, such that each row H^i corresponds to the linear function $H^i\mathbf{x}$. Given such a template H and a real-valued vector $\mathbf{d} \in \mathbb{R}^m$, a template polyhedron is defined by considering the conjunction of the linear inequalities of the form $\bigwedge_{i=1,\ldots,m} H^i\mathbf{x} \leq d_i$. We denote this polyhedron by $\langle H, \mathbf{d}\rangle$.

By changing the values of the elements of $\mathbf{d}$, one can define a family of template polyhedra corresponding to the template H. We call $\mathbf{d}$ a *polyhedral coefficient vector*. Given $\mathbf{d}, \mathbf{d}' \in \mathbb{R}^m$, if $\forall i \in \{1,\ldots,m\} : d_i \leq d_i'$, we write $\mathbf{d} \preceq \mathbf{d}'$. Given an $m \times n$ template H and two polyhedral coefficient vectors $\mathbf{d}, \mathbf{d}' \in \mathbb{R}^m$, if $\mathbf{d} \preceq \mathbf{d}'$ then the inclusion relation $\langle H, \mathbf{d}\rangle \subseteq \langle H, \mathbf{d}'\rangle$ holds, and we say that $\langle H, \mathbf{d}\rangle$ is not larger than $\langle H, \mathbf{d}'\rangle$.

The advantage of template polyhedra over general convex polyhedra is that the Boolean operations (union, intersection) and common geometric operations can be performed more efficiently [19].

Bernstein expansion. We consider an n-variate polynomial $\pi : \mathbb{R}^n \to \mathbb{R}^n$ defined as: $\pi(\mathbf{x}) = \sum_{\mathbf{i}\in I_\mathbf{w}} \mathbf{a}_\mathbf{i}\mathbf{x}^\mathbf{i}$ where $\mathbf{x}^\mathbf{i} = x_1^{\mathbf{i}_1}\ldots x_n^{\mathbf{i}_n}$, $\mathbf{a}_\mathbf{i}$ is a vector in $\mathbb{R}^n$; $\mathbf{i}$ and $\mathbf{w}$ are two multi-indices of size n such that $\mathbf{i} \leq \mathbf{w}$; $I_\mathbf{w}$ is the set of all multi-indices $\mathbf{i} \leq \mathbf{w}$, that is $I_\mathbf{w} = \{\mathbf{i} \mid \mathbf{i} \leq \mathbf{w}\}$. The multi-index $\mathbf{w}$ is called the *degree* of π.

Given a set $X \subset \mathbb{R}^n$, *the image of X by π*, denoted by $\pi(X)$, is defined as follows: $\pi(X) = \{(\pi_1(\mathbf{x}),\ldots,\pi_n(\mathbf{x})) \mid \mathbf{x} \in \mathbb{R}^n\}$.

In order to explain the Bernstein expansion of the polynomial π, we first introduce Bernstein polynomials. For $\mathbf{x} = (x_1,\ldots,x_n) \in \mathbb{R}^n$, the $\mathbf{i}^{th}$ Bernstein polynomial of degree $\mathbf{w}$ is: $\mathcal{B}_{\mathbf{w},\mathbf{i}}(\mathbf{x}) = \beta_{\mathbf{w}_1,\mathbf{i}_1}(x_1)\ldots\beta_{\mathbf{w}_n,\mathbf{i}_n}(x_n)$ where for a real number y, $\beta_{\mathbf{w}_j,\mathbf{i}_j}(y) = \binom{\mathbf{w}_j}{\mathbf{i}_j}y^{\mathbf{i}_j}(1-y)^{\mathbf{w}_j-\mathbf{i}_j}$. Then, for all $\mathbf{x} \in B_u = [0,1]^n$, π can be written using the Bernstein expansion as follows: $\pi(\mathbf{x}) = \sum_{\mathbf{i}\in I_\mathbf{w}} \mathbf{b}_\mathbf{i}\mathcal{B}_{\mathbf{w},\mathbf{i}}(\mathbf{x})$ where for each $\mathbf{i} \in I_\mathbf{w}$ the Bernstein coefficient $\mathbf{b}_\mathbf{i}$ is:

$$\mathbf{b_i} = \sum_{\mathbf{j} \le \mathbf{i}} \frac{\binom{i}{j}}{\binom{w}{j}} \mathbf{a_j}. \tag{1}$$

The following property of the Bernstein coefficients is of interest. The above enclosure yields: $\forall \mathbf{x} \in B_u : \pi(\mathbf{x}) \in \square(\{\mathbf{b_i} \mid \mathbf{i} \in I_{\mathbf{w}}\})$ where $\square$ denotes the bounding box of a point set.

Let us return to the main problem of the paper, which is computing the image of a set by a polynomial. Using the above convex-hull property, we can use the coefficients of the Bernstein expansion to over-approximate the image of the unit box B_u by the polynomial π. To compute the image of a general convex polyhedron, one can over-approximate the polyhedron by a box and then transform it to the unit box via some affine transformation. A similar idea, which involves using the coefficients of the Bézier simplex representation, was used in [4] to compute the image of a convex polyhedron. However, the convex-hull computation is expensive especially in high dimensions, which poses a major problem in continuous and hybrid systems verification approaches using polyhedral representations.

In this work, we propose a new method which can avoid complex convex-hull operations over general convex polyhedra as follows. First, we use template polyhedra to over-approximate the images. Second, the problem of computing such template polyhedra can be formulated as a polynomial optimization problem. This optimization problem is computationally difficult, despite recent progress in the development of methods and tools for polynomial programming (see for example [25,13,6] and references therein). We therefore seek their affine bound functions for polynomials, in order to transform the polynomial optimization problem to a linear programming one, which can be solved more efficiently (in polynomial time) using well-developed techniques, such as Simplex [8] and interior point techniques [2]. Indeed, the above-described Bernstein expansion is used to compute these affine bound functions. This is discussed in the next section.

Bound functions. To compute bound functions, we employ the method using the Bernstein expansion, published in [8,9,10]. Finding convex lower bound functions for polynomials is a problem of great interest, especially in global optimization. It is important to note that the method described in this section only works for the case where the variable domain is the unit box B_u. We however want to compute the images of more general sets, in particular polyhedra. An extension of this method to such cases will be developed in Section 3.2.

A simple affine lower bound function is a constant function, which can be deduced from the property of the Bernstein expansion mentioned in Section 2: $x_i \le \min\{\mathbf{b_i} \mid \mathbf{i} \in I_{\mathbf{w}}\} = \mathbf{b_{i^0}} = \mathbf{b^0}$. The main idea of the method is as follows. We first compute the affine lower bound function whose corresponding hyperplane passes through this control point $\mathbf{b^0}$. Then, we aditionally determine $(n-1)$ hyperplanes passing through n other control points. This allows us to construct a sequence of n affine lower bound functions $l_0, l_1, \ldots l_n$. We end up with l_n, a function whose corresponding hyperplane passes through a lower facet of the convex hull spanned by these control points. A detailed description of the algorithm can be found in [5]. Note that we can easily compute upper bound functions of π by computing the lower bound functions for $(-\pi)$ using this method and then multiply each resulting function by (-1).

3 Image Approximation Using Template Polyhedra

We want to use a template polyhedron $\langle H, \mathbf{d} \rangle$ to over-approximate the image of a polyhedron P by the polynomial π. The template matrix H, which is of size $m \times n$ is assumed to be given; the polyhedral coefficient vector $\mathbf{d} \in \mathbb{R}^m$ is however unknown. The question is thus to find $\mathbf{d}$ such that

$$\pi(P) \subseteq \langle H, \mathbf{d} \rangle. \tag{2}$$

It is not hard to see that the following condition is sufficient for (2) to hold: $\forall \mathbf{x} \in P : H\pi(\mathbf{x}) \leq \mathbf{d}$. Therefore, to determine $\mathbf{d}$, one can formulate the following optimization problem:

$$\forall i \in \{1, \ldots, m\}, d_i = \max(\Sigma_{k=1}^n H_k^i \pi_k(\mathbf{x})) \text{ subj. to } \mathbf{x} \in P. \tag{3}$$

where H^i is the ith row of the matrix H and H_k^i is its kth element. Note that the above functions to optimize are polynomials. As mentioned earlier, polynomial optimization is expensive. Our solution is to bound these functions with affine functions, in order to transform the above optimization problem to a linear programming one. This is formalized as follows.

3.1 Optimization-Based Solution

In Section 2 we discussed lower bound functions for polynomials. Note that these bound functions are valid only when the variables $\mathbf{x}$ are inside the unit box B_u. To consider more general domains, we introduce the following definition.

Definition 1 (Upper and lower bound functions). *Given $f : \mathbb{R}^n \to \mathbb{R}$, the function $\upsilon : \mathbb{R}^n \to \mathbb{R}$ is called an upper bound function of f w.r.t. a set $X \subset \mathbb{R}^n$ if $\forall \mathbf{x} \in X : f(\mathbf{x}) \leq \upsilon(\mathbf{x})$. A lower bound function can be defined similarly.*

The following property of upper and lower bound functions is easy to prove.

Lemma 1. *Given $X, Y \subseteq \mathbb{R}^n$ s.t. $Y \subseteq X$, if υ is an upper (lower) bound function of f w.r.t. X, then υ is an upper (lower) bound function of f w.r.t. Y.*

For each $k \in \{1, \ldots, m\}$, let $u_k(\mathbf{x})$ and $l_k(\mathbf{x})$ respectively be an upper bound function and a lower bound function of $\pi_k(\mathbf{x})$ w.r.t. a bounded polyhedron $P \subset \mathbb{R}^n$. We consider the following optimization problem:

$$\forall i \in \{1, \ldots, m\}, d_i = \Sigma_{k=1}^n H_k^i \omega_k. \tag{4}$$

where the term $H_k^i \omega_k$ is defined as follows:

- If the element $H_k^i > 0$, $H_k^i \omega_k = H_k^i \max u_k(\mathbf{x})$ subj. to $\mathbf{x} \in P$;
- If the element $H_k^i \leq 0$, $H_k^i \omega_k = H_k^i \min l_k(\mathbf{x})$ subj. to $\mathbf{x} \in P$.

The following lemma is a direct result of (4).

Lemma 2. *If* $\mathbf{d} \in \mathbb{R}^m$ *satisfies (4), then* $\pi(P) \subseteq \langle H, \mathbf{d} \rangle$.

Proof. It is indeed not hard to see that the solution d_i of the optimization problems (4) is greater than or equal to the solution of (3). Hence, if $\mathbf{d}$ satisfies (4), then $\forall i \in \{1, \ldots, m\}$ $\forall \mathbf{x} \in P : \Sigma_{k=1}^n H_k^i \pi_k(\mathbf{x}) \leq d_i$. This implies that $\forall \mathbf{x} \in P : H\pi(\mathbf{x}) \leq \mathbf{d}$, that is the image $\pi(P)$ is included in $\langle H, \mathbf{d} \rangle$. □

We remark that if all the bound functions in (4) are affine and P is a bounded convex polyhedron, $\mathbf{d}$ can be computed by solving at most $2n$ linear programming problems. It remains now to find the affine bound functions u_k and l_k for π w.r.t. a polyhedron P, which is the problem we tackle in the next section.

3.2   Computing Affine Bound Functions over Polyhedral Domains

As mentioned earlier, the method to compute affine bound functions for polynomials in Section 2 can be applied only when the function domain is a unit box, anchored at the origin. The reason is that the expression of the control points of the Bernstein expansion in (1) is only valid for this unit box. If we over-approximate P with a box B, it is then possible to derive a formula expressing the Bernstein coefficients of π over B. However, this formula is complex and its representation and evaluation can become expensive.

We alternatively consider the composition of the polynomial π with an affine transformation τ that maps the unit box B_u to B. The functions resulting from this composition are still polynomials, for which we can compute their bound functions over the unit box. This is explained more formally in the following.

Let B be the bounding box of the polyhedron P, that is, the smallest box that includes P. The composition $\gamma = (\pi \ o \ \tau)$ is defined as $\gamma(\mathbf{x}) = \pi(\tau(\mathbf{x}))$. The functions τ and γ can be computed symbolically, which will be discussed later.

Lemma 3. *Let* $\gamma = \pi \ o \ \tau$. *Then,* $\pi(P) \subseteq \gamma(B_u)$.

Proof. By the definition of the composition γ, $\gamma(B_u) = \{\pi(\tau(\mathbf{x})) \mid \mathbf{x} \in B_u\}$. Additionally, $\tau(B_u) = B$. Therefore, $\gamma(B_u) = \pi(B)$. Since the polyhedron P is included in its bounding box B, we thus obtain $\pi(P) \subseteq \pi(B) = \gamma(B_u)$. □

We remark that the above proof is still valid for any affine function τ. This means that instead of an axis-aligned bounding box, we can over-approximate P more precisely with an oriented (i.e. non-axis-aligned) bounding box. This can be done using the following method.

3.3   Computing an Oriented Bounding Box

The directions of an oriented bounding box can be computed using Principal Component Analysis [14]. We first choose a set $S = \{\mathbf{s}^1, \mathbf{s}^2, \ldots, \mathbf{s}^m\}$ of m points[2]

---

[2] By abuse of notation we use m to denote both the number of template constraints and the number of points here.

in the polyhedron P, such that $m \geq n$. We defer a discussion on how this point set is selected to the end of this section. PCA is used to find an orthogonal basis that best represents the point set S. More concretely, we use $\bar{\mathbf{s}}$ to be the mean of S, that is $\bar{\mathbf{s}} = \frac{1}{m} \sum_{i=1}^{m} \mathbf{s}^i$ and we denote $\tilde{\mathbf{s}}_{i,j} = \mathbf{s}_i^j - \bar{\mathbf{s}}_i$. For two points $\mathbf{s}^i$ and $\mathbf{s}^j$ in S, the covariance of their translated points is: $cov(\mathbf{s}_i, \mathbf{s}_j) = \frac{1}{m-1} \sum_{k=1}^{m} \tilde{\mathbf{s}}_{k,i} \tilde{\mathbf{s}}_{k,j}$. Then, we define the co-variance matrix C such that the element $C_{ij} = cov(\mathbf{s}^i, \mathbf{s}^j)$. The n largest singular values of C provide the orientation of the bounding box. More concretely, since C is symetric, by singular value decomposition, we have $C = U \Lambda U^T$ where Λ is the matrix of singular values. The axes of the bounding box are hence determined by the first n columns of the matrix U, and its centroid is $\bar{\mathbf{s}}$.

We now discuss how to select the set S. When the vertices of P are available, we can include them in the set. However, if P is given as a template polyhedron, this requires computing the vertices which is expensive. Moreover, using only the vertices, when their distribution do not represent the geometric form of the polyhedron, may cause a large approximation error, since the resulting principal directions are not the ones along which the points inside P are mostly distributed. To remedy this, we sample points inside P as follows. First, we compute an axis-aligned bounding box of P (this can be done by solving $2n$ linear programming problems). We then uniformly sample points inside this bounding box and keep only the points that satisfy the constraints of P. Uniform sampling on the boundary of P in general enables a better precision. More detail on this can be found in [5].

3.4   Image Computation Algorithm

The following algorithm summarizes the main steps of our method for over-approximating the image of a bounded polyhedron $P \subset \mathbb{R}^n$ by the polynomial π. The templates are an input of the algorithm. In the current implementation of the algorithm, the templates can be fixed by the user, or the templates forming regular sets are used.

Algorithm 1. Over-approximating $\pi(P)$

/* Inputs: convex polyhedron P, polynomial π, templates H */
$B = PCA(P)$ /* Compute an oriented bounding box */
$\tau = UnitBoxMap(B)$ /* Compute the function mapping the unit box B_u to B */
$\gamma = \pi \, o \, \tau$
$(u, l) = BoundFunctions(\gamma)$ /* Compute the affine bound functions */
$\bar{\mathbf{d}} = PolyApp(u, l, H)$ /* Compute the coefficient vector $\mathbf{d}$ */
$Q = \langle H, \bar{\mathbf{d}} \rangle$ /* Form the template polyhedron and return it */
Return(Q)

The role of the procedure PCA is to compute an oriented bounding box B that encloses P. The procedure $UnitBoxMap$ is then used to determine the affine function τ that maps the unit box B_u at the origin to B. This affine function is composed with the polynomial π, the result of which is the polynomials γ. The affine lower and upper bound functions l and u of γ are then computed, using the Bernstein expansion. The function *PolyApp* determines the polyhedral coefficient vector $\mathbf{d}$ by solving the linear programs in (4) with u, l and the optimization domain is B_u. The polyhedral coefficient vector $\mathbf{d}$ are then used to define a template polyhedron Q, which is the result to be returned.

Based on the analysis so far, we can state the correctness of Algorithm 1.

Theorem 1. *Let $\langle H, \bar{\mathbf{d}} \rangle$ be the template polyhedron returned by Algorithm 1. Then $\pi(P) \subseteq \langle H, \bar{\mathbf{d}} \rangle$.*

We remark that u and l are upper and lower bound functions of γ with respect to B_u. It is not hard to see that $\tau^{-1}(P) \subseteq B_u$ where τ^{-1} is the inverse of τ. Using the property of bound functions, u and l are also bound functions of γ with respect to $\tau^{-1}(P)$. Hence, if we solve the optimization problem over the domain $\tau^{-1}(P)$ (which is often smaller than B_u), using Lemma 2, the resulting polyhedron is still an over-approximation of $\pi(P)$. This remark can be used to obtain more accurate results.

Approximation errors and Complexity. We finish this section by briefly discussing the precision and complexity of our method. A more detailed analysis can be found in [5]. The approximation errors are caused by the use of bound functions, the bounding box approximation and template polyhedra.

It can be proven that in one dimensional cases, the error between the bound functions and the original polynomial is quadratic in the length of box domains. This quadratic convergence seems to hold for higher dimensional cases in practice, as shown in [9]. We conjecture that there exists a subdivision method of the box B which allows a quadratic convergence of the error. This subdivision method is similar to the one used for finding roots of a polynomial with quadratic convergence [16].

On the other hand, a polyhedron can be approximated by a set of non-overlapping oriented boxes with arbitrarily small error. Then, for each box, we compute a bounding function, with which we then compute a coefficient for each template. Finally, for each template, we take the largest coefficient to define the template polyhedron. Since the boxes are smaller, the bounding functions are more precise, we can thus improve the coefficients as much as desired.

Concerning the error inherent to the approximation by template polyhedra, it can be controlled by fine-tuning the number of template constraints. If using this method with a sufficient number of templates to assure the same precision as the convex hull in our previous Bézier method [4], then the convergence of both methods are quadratic. However the Bezier method requires expensive convex-hull and triangulation operations, and geometric complexity of resulting sets may grow step after step. Combining template polyhedra and bounding functions allows a good accuracy-cost compromise.

We now discuss the complexity of our algorithm. Let each polynomial π_i be written as $\pi_i = \sum_{\mathbf{j} \in I_i} a_{\mathbf{j}}^i \mathbf{x}^{\mathbf{j}}$ where each $a_{\mathbf{j}}^i \neq 0$. We denote by $\#(\pi_i)$ the number of such monomials in π_i, *i.e.* the cardinality of I_i. Let K be the maximal number of monomials in each π_i, that is $K = \max_{i \in \{1,...,n\}} \#(\pi_i)$.

First, we remark that the computation of the bound functions and PCA only requires manipulating matrices and linear equations. Additionally, linear programming with n variables and m constraints can be solved in polynomial time $O((mn)^{3.5})$.

The proofs of the following results can be found in [5]. The complexity of the computation of the bound functions is $\mathcal{O}(n^4 + Kn^5)$. The complexity of the computation of an affine function τ mapping the unit box to an oriented box is $\mathcal{O}(nn^{3.5})$ (due to n LP problems). The approximation using a template polyhedron requires solving $2n$ LP problems over the unit box and has thus the complexity $\mathcal{O}(2n(2nn)^{3.5})$ (see (4)).

The exponentiel factor in the complexity of our algorithm comes from the composition of π and an affine transformation τ. Let us suppose that we use a simple composition algorithm whose complexity depends on the number of monomials[3]. The following theorem shows some cases for which our algorithm has a polynomial time complexity.

Theorem 2. *If π and τ satisfy two conditions:*

$$(1) \; \forall i \in \{1, \dots, n\} : \sum_{\mathbf{j} \in I_i} \sum_{k=1}^{n} \mathbf{j}_k = O(ln(n))$$

$$(2) \; \forall i \in \{1, \dots, n\} \#(\tau_i) \leq 2$$

then the composition $\pi \circ \tau$ has in total $\mathcal{O}(Kn^3)$ monomials, thus the computation of $\pi \circ \tau$ can be done in $\mathcal{O}(Kn^3)$.

The proof of this can be found in [5]. Note that if we use axis-aligned bounding boxes, each component of τ always have 2 terms, and the second condition of the theorem are satisfied. However, this polynomial time complexity w.r.t. the dimension may not hold if we use oriented bounding boxes to over-approximate the reachable sets before mapping them to the unit box. Indeed, in this case each component of τ may have more than 2 terms.

Concerning the complexity w.r.t. the number of iterations, if the number of template constraints is constant, we can prove that the complexity depends linearly on the number of iterations (see more in [5]).

4   Experimental Results

We have implemented our method in a prototype tool using the template polyhedral library developed by S. Sankaranarayanan [20] and the library **lpsolve** for linear programming. In the following, we demonstrate the method with two examples: a control system (modelled as a hybrid system) and a biological system (modelled as a continuous system). The time efficiency of the tool is also evaluated by considering using a number of randomly generated polynomials.

---

[3] Advanced composition algorithms, *e.g.* [22], can achieve a better complexity.

A control system. The control system we consider is the Duffing oscillator [15,6]. Its continuous-time dynamics is described by $\ddot{y}(t) + 2\zeta\dot{y}(t) + y(t) + y(t)^3 = u(t)$, where $y \in \mathbb{R}$ is the state variable and $u \in \mathbb{R}$ is the control input. The damping coefficient $\zeta = 0.3$. In [6], using a forward difference approximation with a sampling period $h = 0.05$, this system is approximated by the following discrete-time model: $x_1(k+1) = x_1(k) + hx_2(k)$, $x_2(k+1) = -hx_1(k) + (1 - 2\zeta h)x_2(k) + hu)k) - hx_1(k)^3$.

In [6], an optimal predictive control law $u(k)$ was computed by solving a parametric polynomial optimization problem. In Figure 4 one can see the phase portrait of the system under this control law and without it (i.e. $\forall k ge0 \, u(k) = 0$) is shown . We model this control law by the following switching law with 3 modes: $u(k) = 0.5k$ if $0 \le k \le 10$, $u(k) = 5 - 0.5(k - 10)/3$ if $10 < k \le 40$, and $u(k) = 0$ if $k > 40$. The controlled system is thus modelled as a hybrid automaton with 3 discrete modes. The result obtained using our tool on this system is shown in Figure 4, which is coherent with the phase portrait in [6]. The initial set is a ball with radius $1e - 04$. The number of template constraints is 100. In addition to the reachable set after 120 steps (computed after $3s$), in Figure 4, we also illustrate the approximation error by visualizing the template polyhedron after the first step and a cloud of exact points (obtained by sampling the initial set and applying the polynomial to the sampled points).

A biological system. The second example is the well-known Michaelis-Menten enzyme kinetics [12], where E is the concentration of an enzyme that combines with a substrate S to form an enzyme substrate complex ES. In the next step, the complex can be dissociated into E and S or it can further proceed to form a product P.

This pathway kinetics can be described by the following ODEs where x_1, x_2, x_3 and x_4 are the concentrations of S, E, ES and P: $\dot{x}_1 = -\theta_1 x_1 x_2 + \theta_2 x_3$,

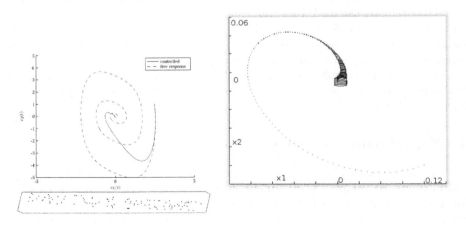

Fig. 1. The Duffing oscillator: phase portrait, the reachable set, and the reachable set after the first step

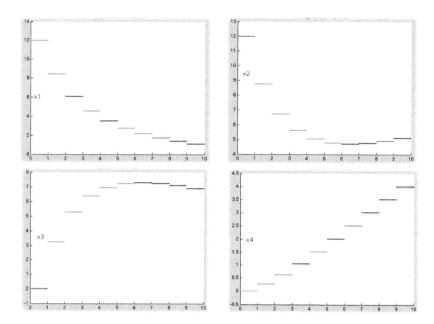

Fig. 2. Michaelis-Menten enzyme kinetics. The evolution of the reachable set after 10 steps.

$\dot{x}_2 = -\theta_1 x_1 x_2 + (\theta_2 + \theta_3) x_3$, $\dot{x}_3 = \theta_1 x_1 x_2 + (\theta_2 + \theta_3) x_3$, $\dot{x}_4 = \theta_3 x_3$. Using a second order Runge Kutta discretization with time step 0.3, we obtain

$$\pi_1(\mathbf{x}) = x_1 - 0.053838 x_1 x_2 + 0.001458 x_1^2 x_2 + 0.001458 x_1 x_2^2 - 3.9366e - 5.x_1^2 x_2^2$$
$$+0.005775 x_3 - 0.002025 x_1 x_3 - 0.000162 x_2 x_3 + 5.9049e - 5 x_1 x_2 x_3 - 6.075e - 6 x_3^2$$

$$\pi_2(\mathbf{x}) = x_2 - 0.051975 x_1 x_2 + 0.001458 x_1^2 x_2 + 0.001458 x_1 x_2^2 - 3.9366e - 5 x_1^2 x_2^2 + 0.0721875 x_3$$
$$-0.002025 x_1 x_3 - 0.000162 x_2 x_3 + 5.9049e - 5 x_1 x_2 x_3 - 6.075e - 6 x_3^2$$

$$\pi_3(\mathbf{x}) = 0.051975 x_1 x_2 - 0.001458.x1^2 x_2 - 0.001458 x_1 x_2^2 + 3.9366e - 5 x1^2 x_2^2$$
$$+0.927812 x_3 + 0.002025 x_1 x_3 + 0.000162 x_2 x_3 - 5.9049e - 5 x_1 x_2 x_3 + 6.075e - 6 x_3^2$$

$$\pi_4(\mathbf{x}) = 0.001863 x_1 x_2 + 0.0664125 x_3 + x_4.$$

The reachable set computed for all the initial states inside a ball centered at $(12, 12, 0, 0)$ with radius $1e - 0.4$ is shown in Figure 2. The number of template constraints is 60. In order to compare with the result in [12], the figures depict the evolution of each variable for the first 10 steps (the horizontal axis is time). In the vertical axis, the minimal and maximal values of the variables are shown. This result is conherent with the simulation result in [12]. The computation time for 20 steps is $3.7s$.

Randomly generated systems. In order to evaluate the performance of our method, we tested it on a number of randomly generated polynomials in various dimensions and maximal degrees (the maximal degree is the largest degree for

dim	degree	nb steps	time (s)	nb constraints = 5 x dim
2	2	1	0.02 s	10
2	2	10	0.18 s	
2	2	100	1.82 s	
2	3	1	0.01 s	
2	3	10	0.32 s	
2	3	100	1.98 s	
3	2	1	0.01 s	15
3	2	10	0.37 s	
3	2	100	3.64 s	
3	3	1	0.02 s	
3	3	10	0.3 s	
3	3	100	3.84 s	
4	2	1	0.03 s	20
4	2	10	0.6 s	
4	2	100	6.64 s	
4	3	1	0.06 s	
4	3	10	0.67 s	
4	3	100	6.41 s	

Fig. 3. Computation time for randomly generated polynomial systems

dim	degree	nb steps	time (s)	nb constraints = 5 x dim
5	2	1	0.12 s	25
5	2	10	1.02 s	
5	2	100	10.2 s	
5	3	1	0.37 s	
5	3	10	1.22 s	
5	3	100	10.74 s	
6	2	1	0.61 s	30
6	2	10	2.01 s	
6	2	100	16.85 s	
6	3	1	3.99 s	
6	3	10	42.47s	
6	3	100	400.30s	
7	2	1	4.11 s	35
7	2	10	60.12s	
7	2	100	568.35s	
7	3	1	30.01s	
7	3	10	345.68s	
7	3	100	3856.4s	

Fig. 4. Computation time for randomly generated polynomial systems

all variables). For a fixed dimension and degree, we generated different examples to estimate an average computation time. In the current implementation, polynomial composition is done symbolically, and we do not yet exploit the possibility of sparsity of polynomials (in terms of the number of monomials). The computation time shown in Figures 3-4 does not include the time for polynomial composition. Note that the computation time for 7-variate polynomials of degree 3 is significant, because the randomly generated polynomials have a large number of monomials; however, practical systems often have a much smaller number of monomials. As expected, the computation time does not grows linearly w.r.t.

the number of steps. This can be explained by the use of template polyhedra where the number of constraints can be chosen according to required precisions and thus control better the complexity of the polyhedral operations, compared to general convex polyhedra. Indeed, when using general polyhedra, the operations such as convex hull may increase their geometric complexity (roughly described by the number of vertices and constraints).

Conclusion. In this paper we propose a new method to compute images of polynomials. This method combines the ideas from optimization and the Bernstein expansion. This result can be readily applicable to solve the reachability analysis problem for hybrid systems with polynomial continuous dynamics.

The performance of the method was demonstrated on a number of randomly generated examples, which shows an improvement in efficiency compared to our previously developed method using Bézier techniques [4]. These encouraging results also show an important advantage of the method: thanks to the use of template polyhedra as a symbolic set representations, the complexity and precision of the method are more controllable than those using general polyhedra.

There are a number interesting directions to explore. Indeed, different tools from geometric modeling could be exploited to improve the efficiency of the method. For example, polynomial composition can be done for sparse polynomials more efficiently using the blossoming technique [22]. In addition to more experimentation on other hybrid systems case studies, we intend to explore a new application domain, which is verification of embedded control software. In fact, multivariate polynomials arise in many situations when analyzing programs that are automatically generated from practical embedded controllers.

Acknowledgement. We would like to thank S. Sankaranarayanan, F. Ivancic and O. Maler for inspiring us and for their valuable collaboration.

References

1. Asarin, E., Dang, T., Girard, A.: Hybridization methods for the analysis of nonlinear systems. Acta Informatica 43(7), 451–476 (2007)
2. Boyd, S., Vandenberghe, S.: Convex optimization. Cambridge Uni. Press, Cambridge (2004)
3. Clauss, F., Yu, C.I.: Application of symbolic approach to the Bernstein expansion for program analysis and optimization. Program. Comput. Softw. 30(3), 164–172 (2004)
4. Dang, T.: Approximate reachability computation for polynomial systems. In: Hespanha, J.P., Tiwari, A. (eds.) HSCC 2006. LNCS, vol. 3927, pp. 138–152. Springer, Heidelberg (2006)
5. Dang, T., Salinas, D.: Computing set images of polynomias. Technical report, VERIMAG (June 2008)
6. Fotiou, I.A., Rostalski, P., Parrilo, P.A., Morari, M.: Parametric optimization and optimal control using algebraic geometriy methods. Int. Journal of Control 79(11), 1340–1358 (2006)
7. Garloff, J.: Application of Bernstein expansion to the solution of control problems. University of Girona, pp. 421–430 (1999)

8. Garloff, J., Jansson, C., Smith, A.P.: Lower bound functions for polynomials. Journal of Computational and Applied Mathematics 157, 207–225 (2003)
9. Garloff, J., Smith, A.P.: An improved method for the computation of affine lower bound functions for polynomials. In: Frontiers in Global Optimization. Series Nonconvex Optimization and Its Applications. Kluwer Academic Publ., Dordrecht (2004)
10. Garloff, J., Smith, A.P.: A comparison of methods for the computation of affine lower bound functions for polynomials. In: Jermann, C., Neumaier, A., Sam, D. (eds.) COCOS 2003. LNCS, vol. 3478, pp. 71–85. Springer, Heidelberg (2005)
11. Girard, A., Le Guernic, C., Maler, O.: Efficient Computation of Reachable Sets of Linear Time-Invariant Systems with Inputs. In: Hespanha, J.P., Tiwari, A. (eds.) HSCC 2006. LNCS, vol. 3927, pp. 257–271. Springer, Heidelberg (2006)
12. He, F., Yeung, L.F., Brown, M.: Discrete-time model representation for biochemical pathway systems. IAENG Int. Journal of Computer Science 34(1) (2007)
13. Henrion, D., Lasserre, J.B.: Gloptipoly: Global optimization over polynomials with matlab and sedumi. In: Proceedings of CDC (2002)
14. Jolliffe, I.T.: Principal Component Analysis. Springer, Heidelberg (2002)
15. Jordan, D.W., Smith, P.: Nonlinear Ordinary Differential Equations. Oxford Applied Mathematics and Computer Science. Oxford Uni. Press, Oxford (1987)
16. Mourrain, B., Pavone, J.P.: Subdivision methods for solving polynomial equations. Technical report, INRIA Research report, 5658 (August. 2005)
17. Platzer, A., Clarke, E.M.: The Image Computation Problem in Hybrid Systems Model Checking. In: Bemporad, A., Bicchi, A., Buttazzo, G. (eds.) HSCC 2007. LNCS, vol. 4416, pp. 473–486. Springer, Heidelberg (2007)
18. Prajna, S., Jadbabaie, A.: Safety verification of hybrid systems using barrier certificates. In: Alur, R., Pappas, G.J. (eds.) HSCC 2004. LNCS, vol. 2993, pp. 477–492. Springer, Heidelberg (2004)
19. Sankaranarayanan, S., Sipma, H., Manna, Z.: Scalable analysis of linear systems using mathematical programming. In: Cousot, R. (ed.) VMCAI 2005. LNCS, vol. 3385, pp. 25–41. Springer, Heidelberg (2005)
20. Sankaranarayanan, S.: Mathematical analysis of programs. Technical report, Standford, PhD thesis (2005)
21. Sankaranarayanan, S., Dang, T., Ivancic, F.: Symbolic Model Checking of Hybrid Systems using Template Polyhedra. In: Ramakrishnan, C.R., Rehof, J. (eds.) TACAS 2008. LNCS, vol. 4963, pp. 188–202. Springer, Heidelberg (2008)
22. Seidel, H.-P.: Polar forms and triangular B-spline surfaces. In: Blossoming: The New Polar-Form Approach to Spline Curves and Surfaces, SIGGRAPH 1991 (1991)
23. Tchoupaeva, I.: A symbolic approach to Bernstein expansion for program analysis and optimization. In: Duesterwald, E. (ed.) CC 2004. LNCS, vol. 2985, pp. 120–133. Springer, Heidelberg (2004)
24. Tiwari, A., Khanna, G.: Nonlinear systems: Approximating reach sets. In: Alur, R., Pappas, G.J. (eds.) HSCC 2004. LNCS, vol. 2993, pp. 600–614. Springer, Heidelberg (2004)
25. Vandenberghe, S., Boyd, S.: Semidefinite programming. SIAM Review 38(1), 49–95 (1996)

Cuts from Proofs:
A Complete and Practical Technique for Solving Linear Inequalities over Integers*

Isil Dillig**, Thomas Dillig, and Alex Aiken

Department of Computer Science
Stanford University
{isil,tdillig,aiken}@cs.stanford.edu

Abstract. We propose a novel, sound, and complete Simplex-based algorithm for solving linear inequalities over integers. Our algorithm, which can be viewed as a semantic generalization of the *branch-and-bound* technique, systematically discovers and excludes entire subspaces of the solution space containing no integer points. Our main insight is that by focusing on the *defining constraints* of a vertex, we can compute a *proof of unsatisfiability* for the intersection of the defining constraints and use this proof to systematically exclude subspaces of the feasible region with no integer points. We show experimentally that our technique significantly outperforms the top four competitors in the QF-LIA category of the SMT-COMP '08 when solving linear inequalities over integers.

1 Introduction

A quantifier-free system of linear inequalities over integers is defined by $Ax \leq b$ where A is an $m \times n$ matrix with only integer entries, and b is a vector in Z^n. This system has a solution if and only if there exists a vector $x^* \in Z^n$ that satisfies $Ax^* \leq b$. Determining the satisfiability of such a system of inequalities is a recurring theme in program analysis and verification. For example, array dependence analysis, buffer overrun analysis, and integer overflow checking all rely on solving linear inequalities over integers [1,2]. Similarly, linear integer inequalities arise in RTL datapath and symbolic timing verification [3,4]. For this reason, many modern SMT solvers incorporate a dedicated linear arithmetic module for solving this important subclass of constraints [5,6,7,8,9].

While practical algorithms, such as Simplex, exist for solving linear inequalities over the reals [10], solving linear inequalities over integers is known to be an NP-complete problem, and existing algorithms do not scale well in practice. There are three main approaches for solving linear inequalities over integers. One approach first solves the *LP-relaxation* of the problem to obtain a rational solution and adds additional constraints until either an integer solution is

---

* This work was supported by grants from NSF and DARPA (CCF-0430378, CNS-0716695).

** Supported by the Stanford Graduate Fellowship.

A. Bouajjani and O. Maler (Eds.): CAV 2009, LNCS 5643, pp. 233–247, 2009.

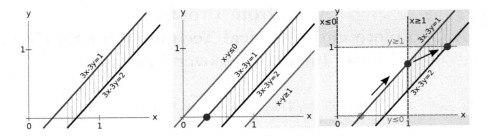

Fig. 1. (a) The projection of Equation 1 onto the xy plane. (b) The green lines indicate the closest lines parallel to the proof of unsatisfiability; the red point marks the solution of the LP-relaxation. (c) Branch-and-bound first adds the planes $x = 0$ and $x = 1$, then the planes $y = 0$ and $y = 1$, and continues to add planes parallel to the coordinate axes.

found or the LP-relaxation becomes infeasible. The second approach is based on the Omega Test, an extension of the Fourier-Motzkin variable elimination for integers [2]. Yet a third class of algorithms utilize finite-automata theory [11].

The algorithm presented in this paper falls into the first class of techniques described above. Existing algorithms in this class include *branch-and-bound*, *Gomory's cutting planes* method, or a combination of both, known as *branch-and-cut* [12]. Branch-and-bound searches for an integer solution by solving the two subproblems $Ax \leq b \cup \{x_i \leq \lfloor f_i \rfloor\}$ and $Ax \leq b \cup \{x_i \geq \lceil f_i \rceil\}$ when the LP-relaxation yields a solution with fractional component f_i. The original problem has a solution if at least one of the subproblems has an integer solution. Even though upper and lower bounds can be computed for each variable to guarantee termination, this technique is often intractably slow on its own. Gomory's cutting planes method computes *valid inequalities* that exclude the current fractional solution without excluding feasible integer points from the solution space. Unfortunately, this technique has also proven to be impractical on its own and is often only used in conjunction with branch-and-bound [13].

All of these techniques suffer from a common weakness: While they exclude the current fractional assignment from the solution space, they make no systematic effort to exclude the cause of this fractional assignment. In particular, if the solution of the LP-relaxation lies at the intersection of n planes defined by the initial set of inequalities, and $k \leq n$ of these planes have an intersection that contains no integer points, then it is desirable to exclude at least this entire $n-k$ dimensional subspace. The key insight underlying our approach is to systematically discover and exclude exactly this $n-k$ dimensional subspace rather than individual points that lie on this space. To be concrete, consider the following system with no integer solutions:

$$
\begin{aligned}
-3x + 3y + z &\leq -1 \\
3x - 3y + z &\leq 2 \\
z &= 0
\end{aligned}
\tag{1}
$$

The projection of this system onto the xy plane is shown in Figure 1(a). Suppose the LP-relaxation of the problem yields the fractional assignment $(x, y, z) = (\frac{1}{3}, 0, 0)$. The planes

$$\begin{aligned} z &= 0 \\ -3x + 3y + z &= -1 \end{aligned} \qquad (2)$$

are the *defining constraints* of this vertex because the point $(\frac{1}{3}, 0, 0)$ lies at the intersection I of these planes. Since I contains no integer points, we would like to exclude exactly I from the solution space. Our technique discovers such intersections with no integer points by computing *proofs of unsatisfiability* for the defining constraints. A proof of unsatisfiability is a single equality that (i) has no integer solutions and (ii) is implied by the defining constraints. In our example, a proof of unsatisfiability for I is $-3x + 3y + 3z = -1$ since it has no integer solutions and is implied by Equation 2. Such proofs can be obtained from the *Hermite normal form* of the matrix representing the defining constraints.

Once we discover a proof of unsatisfiability, our algorithm proceeds as a semantic generalization of branch-and-bound. In particular, instead of branching on a fractional component of the solution, our technique branches around the proof of unsatisfiability, if one exists. In our example, once we discover the equation $-3x + 3y + 3z = -1$ as a proof of unsatisfiability, we construct two new subproblems:

$$\begin{array}{ll} \begin{aligned} -3x + 3y + z &\leq -1 \\ 3x - 3y + z &\leq 2 \\ z &= 0 \\ -x + y + z &\leq -1 \end{aligned} & \qquad \begin{aligned} -3x + 3y + z &\leq -1 \\ 3x - 3y + z &\leq 2 \\ z &= 0 \\ -x + y + z &\geq 0 \end{aligned} \end{array}$$

where $-x + y + z = -1$ and $-x + y + z = 0$ are the closest planes parallel to and on either side of $-3x + 3y + 3z = -1$ containing integer points. As Figure 1(b) illustrates, neither of these systems have a real-valued solution, and we immediately determine the initial system to be unsatisfiable. In contrast, as shown Figure 1(c), branch-and-bound only adds planes parallel to the coordinate axes, repeatedly yielding points that lie on either $3x - 3y = 1$ or $3x - 3y = 2$, neither of which contains integer points. On the other hand, Gomory's cutting planes technique first derives the valid inequality $y \geq 1$ before eventually adding a cut that makes the LP-relaxation infeasible. Unfortunately, this technique becomes much less effective in identifying the cause of unsatisfiability in higher-dimensions.

In this paper, we make the following key contributions:

- We propose a novel, sound, and complete algorithm for solving linear inequalities over integers that systematically excludes subspaces of the feasible region containing no integer points.
- We argue that by focusing on the defining constraints of a vertex, we can quickly home in on the right "cuts" derived from proofs of unsatisfiability of the defining constraints.
- We present a semantic generalization of the branch-and-bound algorithm that utilizes the proofs of unsatisfiability of the defining constraints.

- We show experimentally that the proposed technique significantly outperforms existing state-of-the art solvers, usually by orders of magnitude. Specifically, we compare Mistral, an implementation of our algorithm, with the top four competitors (by score) in the QF-LIA category of SMT-COMP '08 for solving linear inequalities over integers.
- Our algorithm is easy to implement and does not require extensive tuning to make it perform well in practice. We believe it can be profitably incorporated into existing SMT solvers that reason about linear arithmetic over integers.

2   Technical Background

2.1   Polyhedra, Faces, and Facets

In this section, we review a few standard definitions from polyhedral theory. The interested reader can refer to [13] for an in-depth discussion.

Definition 1. (Convex Polyhedron) *The set of (real-valued) solutions satisfying $Ax \leq b$ describes a convex polyhedron P. The dimension $dim(P)$ of P is one less than the maximal number of affinely independent points in P.*

Definition 2. (Valid Inequality) *An inequality $\pi x \leq \pi_0$ defined by some row vector π and a constant π_0 is a valid inequality for a polyhedron P if it is satisfied by all points in P.*

Definition 3. (Faces and Facets) *F is a face of polyhedron P if $F = \{x \in P : \pi x = \pi_0\}$ for some valid inequality $\pi x \leq \pi_0$. A facet is a face of dimension $dim(P) - 1$.*

In Figure 2, polyhedron P has dimension 2 because there exist exactly 3 affinely independent points in P. The equation $ax + by \leq c$ is a valid inequality since all points in P satisfy this inequality. The point F is a face with dimension 0 since it is the intersection of P with the valid inequality represented by the dashed line. The line segment G is a facet of P since it is a face of dimension 1.

2.2   Linear Diophantine Equations

Definition 4. (Linear Diophantine Equation) *A linear equation of the form $\sum a_i x_i = c$ is diophantine if all coefficients a_i are integers and c is an integer.*

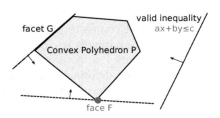

Fig. 2. A convex polyhedron of dimension 2

We state the following well-known result [13]:

Lemma 1. *A linear diophantine equation $\sum a_i x_i = c$ has a solution if and only if c is an integral multiple of the greatest common divisor $gcd(a_1, \ldots, a_n)$.*

Example 1. The equation $3x + 6y = 1$ has no integer solutions since 1 is not evenly divisible by $3 = gcd(3, 6)$. However, $3x + 6y = 9$ has integer solutions.

Corollary 1. *Let E be a plane defined by $\sum a_i x_i = c$ with no integer solutions and let $g = gcd(a_1, \ldots, a_n)$. Then, the two closest planes parallel to and on either side of E containing integer points are $\lfloor E \rfloor$ and $\lceil E \rceil$, given by $\sum \frac{a_i}{g} x_i = \lfloor c/g \rfloor$ and $\sum \frac{a_i}{g} x_i = \lceil c/g \rceil$ respectively.*

This corollary follows immediately from Lemma 1 and implies that there are no integer points between E and $\lfloor E \rfloor$ as well as between E and $\lceil E \rceil$.

2.3   Proofs of Unsatisfiability and the Hermite Normal Form

Given a system $Ax = b$ of linear diophantine equations, we can determine in polynomial time whether this system has any integer solutions using the *Hermite normal form* of A.[1]

Definition 5. (HNF) *An $m \times m$ integer matrix H is said to be in Hermite normal form (HNF) if (i) H is lower triangular, (ii) $h_{ii} > 0$ for $0 \leq i < m$, and (iii) $h_{ij} \leq 0$ and $|h_{ij}| < h_{ii}$ for $i > j$.[2]*

It can be shown that the Hermite normal form for any $m \times n$ matrix A with $\text{rank}(A) = m$ always exists and is unique. Another important property of the Hermite normal form is that if H is the HNF of A, then $H^{-1}A$ is integral. The following lemma is well-known [13]:

Lemma 2. (Proof of Unsatisfiability) *The system $Ax = b$ has an integer solution if and only if $H^{-1}b \in Z^m$. If $Ax = b$ has no integer solutions, there exists a row vector r_i of the matrix $H^{-1}A$ such that the corresponding entry $\frac{n_i}{d_i}$ of $H^{-1}b$ is not an integer. We call the linear diophantine equation $d_i r_i x = n_i$ with no integer solutions a proof of unsatisfiability of $Ax = b$.*

If the equation $d_i r_i x = n_i$ is a proof of unsatisfiability of $Ax = b$, then it is implied by the original system and does not have integer solutions.

Example 2. Consider the defining constraints from the example in Section 1:

$$z = \quad 0$$
$$-3x + 3y + z = -1$$

---

[1] While it is possible to determine the satisfiability of a system of linear diophantine equalities in polynomial time, determining the satisfiability of a system of linear integer *inequalities* is NP-complete.

[2] There is no agreement in the literature on the exact definition of the Hermite Normal Form. The one given here follows the definition in [13].

Here, we have:

$$A = \begin{bmatrix} 0 & 0 & 1 \\ -3 & 3 & 1 \end{bmatrix} \quad b = \begin{bmatrix} 0 \\ -1 \end{bmatrix} \quad H = \begin{bmatrix} 1 & 0 \\ -2 & 3 \end{bmatrix} \quad H^{-1}A = \begin{bmatrix} 0 & 0 & 1 \\ -1 & 1 & 1 \end{bmatrix} \quad H^{-1}b = \begin{bmatrix} 0 \\ -\frac{1}{3} \end{bmatrix}$$

This system does not have an integer solution because $H^{-1}b$ contains a fractional component, and the equation $-3x + 3y + 3z = -1$ is a proof of unsatisfiability for this system.

3   The Cuts-from-Proofs Algorithm

In this section, we present our algorithm for determining the satisfiability of the system $Ax \leq b$ over integers. In the presentation of the algorithm, we assume that there is a procedure lp_solve that determines the satisfiability of $Ax \leq b$ over the reals, and if satisfiable returns a vertex v at an extreme point of the polyhedron induced by $Ax \leq b$. This assumption is fulfilled by standard algorithms for linear programming, such as Simplex [10].

Definition 6. (Defining Constraint) *An inequality $\pi x \leq \pi_0$ is a defining constraint of vertex v of the polyhedron induced by $Ax \leq b$ if v satisfies the equality $\pi v = \pi_0$ where π is a row of A and π_0 is the corresponding entry in b.*

With slight abuse of terminology, we call $\pi x = \pi_0$ a defining constraint whenever $\pi x \leq \pi_0$ is a defining constraint.

3.1   Algorithm

Let A be the initial $m \times n$ matrix and let a_{max} be the entry with the maximum absolute value in A. Then, choose any α such that $\alpha \geq n \cdot |a_{max}|$.

1. Invoke lp_solve. If the result is unsatisfiable, return unsatisfiable. Otherwise, if vertex v returned by lp_solve is integral, return v.
2. Identify the defining constraints $A'x' \leq b'$ of v.
3. Determine if the system $A'x' = b'$ has any integer solutions, and, if not, obtain a proof of unsatisfiability as described in Section 2.3.[3]
4. There are two cases:
   Case 1: (Conventional branch-and-bound) If a proof of unsatisfiability does not exist (i.e., $A'x' = b'$ has integer solutions) or if the proof of unsatisfiability contains a coefficient greater than $\alpha \cdot gcd(a_1, \ldots, a_n)$, pick a fractional component f_i of v and solve the two subproblems:

$$\begin{array}{ll} Ax \leq b & \quad Ax \leq b \\ v_i \leq \lfloor f_i \rfloor & \quad -v_i \leq -\lceil f_i \rceil \end{array}$$

   Case 2: (Branch around proof of unsatisfiability) Otherwise, consider the proof of unsatisfiability $\Sigma a_i x_i = c_i$ of $A'x' = b'$. Let $\lfloor E \rfloor$ be $\Sigma \frac{a_i}{g} x_i \leq$

---

[3] If A' does not have full rank, drop redundant rows of A' before computing the Hermite normal form.

$\lfloor c_i/g \rfloor$ and let $\lceil E \rceil$ be $\Sigma \frac{a_i}{g} x_i \geq \lceil c_i/g \rceil$ where $g = gcd(a_1, \ldots, a_n)$ as described in Section 2.2. Solve the two subproblems:

$$S_1 = \{Ax \leq b \cup \lfloor E \rfloor\} \qquad S_2 = \{Ax \leq b \cup \lceil E \rceil\}$$

3.2   Discussion of the Algorithm

In the above algorithm, if lp_solve yields a fractional assignment, then either the intersection of the defining constraints does not have an integer solution or the defining constraints do have an integer solution but lp_solve did not pick an integer assignment. In the latter case, we simply perform conventional branch-and-bound around any fractional component of the assignment to find an integer point on this intersection. On the other hand, if the defining constraints do not admit an integer solution, the algorithm obtains a proof of unsatisfiability with maximum coefficient less than α, if one exists, and constructs two subproblems that exclude this intersection without missing any integer points in the solution space. The constant α ensures that case 2 in step 4 of the algorithm is invoked a finite number of times and guarantees that there is a minimum bound on the volume excluded from the polyhedron at each step of the algorithm. (See Section 3.3 for the relevance of α for termination.)

Excluding the proof of unsatisfiability guarantees that the intersection of the defining constraints is no longer in the polyhedra defined by either of the two subproblems. However, there may exist a strict subset of these defining constraints whose intersection contains no integer points but is not excluded from the solution space of the two subproblems. The following example illustrates such a situation.

Example 3. Consider the defining constraints $x + y \leq 1$ and $2x - 2y \leq 1$. Using Hermite normal forms to compute a proof of unsatisfiability for the system

$$\begin{aligned} x + y &= 1 \\ 2x - 2y &= 1 \end{aligned}$$

yields $4x = 3$. While $4x = 3$ is a proof of unsatisfiability for the intersection of $x + y = 1$ and $2x - 2y = 1$, the strict subset $2x - 2y = 1$ has a proof of unsatisfiability on its own (namely itself), and it is not implied by $4x = 3$.

As this example illustrates, the proof of unsatisfiability of a set of constraints does not necessarily imply the proof of unsatisfiability of any subset of these constraints. At first glance, this seems problematic because if the intersection of any subset of the defining constraints contains no integer solutions, we would prefer excluding this larger subspace represented by the smaller set of constraints. Fortunately, as stated by Lemma 5, the algorithm will discover and exclude this higher-dimensional intersection in a finite number of steps. We first prove the following helper lemmas:

Lemma 3. *Let* $C = \begin{bmatrix} A \\ B \end{bmatrix}$ *be an* $m \times n$ *matrix composed of* A *and* B, *and let*

$\mathrm{HNF}(C) = \begin{bmatrix} H_A & 0 \\ X & Y \end{bmatrix}$. *Then,* $\mathrm{HNF}(A) = H_A$.

Proof. Our proof uses the HNF construction outlined in [13]. Let i be a row that the algorithm is currently working on and let i' be another row such that $i' < i$. Then, by construction, any entry $c_{i'j}$ where $j > i'$ is 0. Since any column operation performed while processing row i adds a multiple of column $k \geq i$ to another column, entry $c_{i'k}$ must be 0. Thus, any column operation is idempotent on row i'.

Using blockwise inversion to invert $HNF(C)$, it can be easily shown that:

$$HNF(C)^{-1} = \begin{bmatrix} H_A^{-1} & 0 \\ -Y^{-1}XH_A^{-1} & Y^{-1} \end{bmatrix}$$

Thus, it is easy to see that $HNF(C)^{-1}C = HNF(C)^{-1}b'$ implies $HNF(A)^{-1}A = HNF(A)^{-1}b$ if b' is obtained by adding entries to the bottom of b. This is the case because both $HNF(C)^{-1}$ and $HNF(A)^{-1}$ are lower triangular matrices. Intuitively, this result states that if $Ax = b$ has a proof of unsatisfiability, we cannot "lose" this proof by adding extra rows at the bottom of A.

Example 4. Consider the constraints from Example 2. Suppose we add the additional constraint $x = 1$ at the bottom of matrix A. Then, we obtain:

$$A = \begin{bmatrix} 0 & 0 & 1 \\ -3 & 3 & 1 \\ 1 & 0 & 0 \end{bmatrix} \quad b = \begin{bmatrix} 0 \\ -1 \\ 1 \end{bmatrix} \quad H = \begin{bmatrix} 1 & 0 & 0 \\ -2 & 3 & 0 \\ 0 & 0 & 1 \end{bmatrix} \quad H^{-1}A = \begin{bmatrix} 0 & 0 & 1 \\ -1 & 1 & 1 \\ 1 & 0 & 0 \end{bmatrix} \quad H^{-1}b = \begin{bmatrix} 0 \\ -\frac{1}{3} \\ 1 \end{bmatrix}$$

Clearly, $-3x + 3y + 3z = -1$ is still obtained as a proof of unsatisfiability from the second row of $H^{-1}A = H^{-1}b$.

Lemma 4. *Consider any proof of unsatisfiability* $\Sigma a_i x_i = c$ *of any subset of the initial system* $Ax \leq b$. *Then,* $\forall i.|a_i| \leq \alpha \cdot \gcd(a_1, \ldots, a_n)$.

Proof. The coefficients a_i are obtained from the matrix $H^{-1}A'$ where A' is a matrix whose rows are a subset of those of A. Recall from basic linear algebra $H^{-1} = \frac{1}{det(H)} adj(H)$ where $adj(H)$ is the classical adjoint of H. It is known that the infinity norm of $adj(H)$ is bound by

$$||adj(H)|| \leq det(H)$$

where $||A||$ is defined as $max_{ij}|a_{ij}|$ [14]. Hence any coefficient c in H^{-1} satisfies $|c| \leq 1$, and the entries in $H^{-1}A'$ are therefore bound by $\alpha = n \cdot |a_{max}|$. Since the proof of unsatisfiability is some row of $H^{-1}A'$ multiplied by some $d_i > 1$, $d_i \leq \gcd(a_1, \ldots, a_n)$. Thus, any coefficient in the proof of unsatisfiability is bound by $\alpha \cdot \gcd(a_1, \ldots, a_n)$.

Using the above lemmas, we can now show the following result:

Lemma 5. *Let F be a k-dimensional face without integer points of the initial polyhedron P with $dim(P) = d$. Suppose* lp_solve *repeatedly returns vertices that lie on this face. The algorithm will exclude F from P in a finite number of steps.*

Proof. Every time lp_solve yields a vertex that lies on F, the algorithm excludes at least one of the currently defining constraints. At some point, when lp_solve returns a vertex on F, its defining constraints will be exactly the $d - k$ of the original constraints defining F, along with new constraints that were added to the bottom of the matrix. By Lemma 3, the additional constraints preserve the proof of unsatisfiability of the original $d - k$ constraints. Furthermore, by Lemma 4, this proof of unsatisfiability will have coefficients with absolute value of at most $\alpha \cdot gcd(a_1, \ldots, a_n)$. Thus, the algorithm will obtain a proof of unsatisfiability for F and exclude all of F from the solution space.

As Lemma 5 elucidates, the Cuts-from-Proofs algorithm discovers any relevant face without integer points on a demand-driven basis without explicitly considering all possible subsets of the initial set of inequalities. This allows the algorithm to add exactly the relevant cuts while staying computationally tractable in practice.

3.3 Soundness and Completeness

It is easy to see that the algorithm given above is correct because it never excludes integer points in the solution space. For arguing termination, we can assume, as standard, that the polyheron P is finite; if it is not, one can compute maximum and minimum bounds on each variable without affecting the satisfiability of the original problem (see, for example [12,5]). The key observation is that the volume we cut off the polyhedron cannot become infinitesimally small over time as we add more cuts. To see this, observe that there is a finite set of normal vectors N for the planes added by the Cuts-from-Proofs algorithm. Clearly, this holds for planes added by case 1 of step 4 since all such planes are parallel to one of the coordinate planes. This fact also holds for planes added in case 2 of step 4 since the coefficients of the normal vectors must be less than or equal to α. Since the set N of normal vectors is finite, the algorithm will either terminate or, at some point, it will have to add planes parallel to already existing ones. The following lemma states that these parallel planes are at least some minimal distance ϵ apart:

Lemma 6. (Progress) *Let E be a plane added by the Cuts-from-Proofs algorithm and let E' be another plane parallel to E, also added by the algorithm. Then, E and E' are at least some minimum distance $\epsilon > 0$ apart.*

Proof. Let E be defined by $\mathbf{n} \cdot \mathbf{x} = c_1$ and E' be defined by $\mathbf{n} \cdot \mathbf{x} = c_2$. Since c_1 and c_2 are integers and $c_1 \neq c_2$, E and E' are a minimum $d = 1/\sqrt{n_1^2 + \ldots + n_k^2}$ apart. Since there are a finite number of non-parallel planes added by the algorithm, choose ϵ to be the minimum such d.

Let $n \in N$ be any normal vector along which the algorithm must eventually cut. Because P is finite, there is a finite distance δ we can move along n through P. Since the distance we move along n is at least ϵ, the algorithm can cut perpendicular to n at most δ/ϵ times. Hence, the algorithm must terminate.

4   Implementation

In Section 4.1, we first discuss improvements over the basic algorithm presented in Section 3; then, in Section 4.2, we discuss the details of our implementation.

4.1   Improvements and Empirical Observations

An improvement over the basic algorithm described in Section 3 can be achieved by selectively choosing the proofs of unsatisfiability that the algorithm branches on. In particular, recall from Lemma 5 that if lp_solve repeatedly returns vertices on the same face with no integer points, the algorithm will also repeatedly obtain the same proof of unsatisfiability. Thus, in practice, it is beneficial to delay branching on a proof until the same proof is obtained at least twice. This can be achieved by using case 1 in step 4 of the algorithm instead of case 2 each time a new proof is discovered. Since few of these proofs appear repeatedly, this easy modification often allows the algorithm to exclude only the highest-dimensional intersection with no integer points without having to branch around additional intermediate proofs. In our experience, this optimization can improve running time up to a factor of 3 on some examples.

An important empirical observation about the algorithm is that the overwhelming majority ($> 99\%$) of the proofs of unsatisfiability do not result in true branching. In practice, one of the planes parallel to the proof of unsatisfiability often turns out to be a valid inequality, while the other parallel plane lies outside the feasible region, making its LP-relaxation immediately unsatisfiable. Thus, in practice, the algorithm only branches around fractional components of an assignment.

4.2   Implementation Details

Our implementation of the Cuts-from-Proofs algorithm is written in C++ and consists of approximately 5000 lines of code, including modules to perform various matrix operations as well as support for infinite precision arithmetic. The Cuts-from-Proofs algorithm is a key component of the Mistral constraint solver, which implements the decision procedure for the combined theory of integer linear arithmetic and uninterpreted functions. Mistral is used in the Compass program analysis system (under development) to solve large real-world constraints that arise from modeling contents of unbounded data structures, such as arrays and linked lists.

Our Simplex implementation, used as the lp_solve procedure in the Cuts-from-Proofs algorithm, uses *Bland's rule* for pivot selection [12]. Mistral utilizes a custom-built infinite precision arithmetic library based on the GNU MP Bignum Library (GMP) [15]. Our library performs computation natively on 64-bit values until an overflow is detected, and then switches to GNU bignums. If no overflow is detected, our implementation results in less than 25% slow down over native word-level arithmetic. We also found the selective use of hand-coded SIMD instructions to improve performance of Simplex by approximately a factor of 2.

Our implementation for Hermite normal form conversion is based on the algorithm given in [16]. This algorithm uses the modulo reduction technique of [17] to control the number of required bits in any intermediate computation. In practice, the Hermite normal form conversion takes less than 5% of the overall running time and is not a bottleneck.

The implementation of the core Cuts-from-Proofs algorithm takes only about 250 lines of C++ code and does not require any features beyond what is discussed in this paper. In our implementation, α was chosen to be $10n \cdot |a_{max}|$, and we have not observed the coefficients in the computed proofs of unsatisfiability to exceed this limit. In practice, the coefficients stay reasonably small.

5   Experimental Results

To evaluate the effectiveness of the Cuts-from-Proofs algorithm, we compared Mistral with the four leading competitors (by score) in the QF-LIA category of SMT-COMP '08, namely Yices 1.0.16, Z3.2, MathSAT 4.2, and CVC3 1.5 obtained from [18]. We did not compare Mistral against (mixed) integer linear programming tools specialized for optimization problems. Existing tools such as GLPK [19], lp-solve [20], and CPLEX [21] all use floating point numbers instead of infinite precision arithmetic and yield unsound results for determining satisfiability even on small systems due to rounding errors. Furthermore, we did not use the QF-LIA benchmarks from SMT-COMP because they contain arbitrary boolean combinations of linear integer inequalities and equalities, making them unsuitable for comparing different algorithms to solve integer linear programs. The full set of test inputs and running times for each tool is available from http://www.stanford.edu/~isil/benchmarks.tar.gz. All experiments were performed on an 8 core 2.66 GHz Xeon workstation with 24 GB of memory. (All the tools, including Mistral, are single-threaded applications.) Each tool was given a maximum running time of 1200 seconds as well as 4 GB of memory. Any run exceeding the time or memory limit was aborted and marked as failure. If a run was aborted, its running time was assumed to be 1200 seconds for computing average running times.

In the experiments, presented in Figure 3, we randomly generated more than 500 systems of linear inequalities, containing between 10 and 45 variables and between 15 and 50 inequalities per system with a fixed maximum coefficient size of 5. Figure 3a plots the number of variables against the average running time over all sizes of constraints, ranging from 15 to 50. As is evident from this figure, the Cuts-from-Proofs algorithm results in a dramatic improvement over all existing tools. For instance, for 25 variables, Yices, Mistral's closest

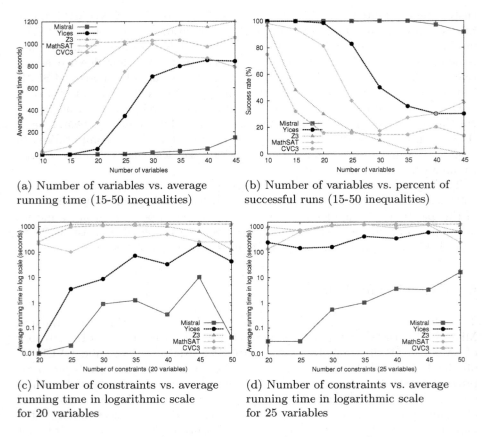

(a) Number of variables vs. average running time (15-50 inequalities)

(b) Number of variables vs. percent of successful runs (15-50 inequalities)

(c) Number of constraints vs. average running time in logarithmic scale for 20 variables

(d) Number of constraints vs. average running time in logarithmic scale for 25 variables

Fig. 3. Experimental Results (fixed coefficient)

competitor, takes on average 347 seconds while Mistral takes only 3.45 seconds. This trend is even more pronounced in Figure 3b, which plots number of variables against the percentage of successful runs. For example, for 35 variables, Yices has a success rate of 36% while Mistral successfully completes 100% of its runs, taking an average of only 28.11 seconds.

Figures 3c and 3d plot the number of inequalities per system against average running time on a logarithmic scale for 20 and 25 variables, respectively. We chose not to present detailed breakouts for larger numbers of variables since such systems trigger time-out rates over 50% for all tools other than Mistral. These graphs demonstrate that the Cuts-from-Proofs algorithm reliably performs significantly, and usually at least an order of magnitude, better than any of the other tools, regardless of the number of inequalities per system.

To evaluate the sensitivity of different algorithms to maximum coefficient size, we also compared the running time of different tools for coefficients ranging from 10 to 100 for systems with 10 variables and 20 inequalities. As shown in

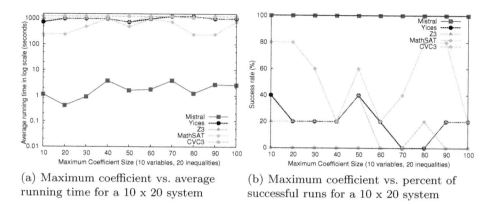

(a) Maximum coefficient vs. average running time for a 10 x 20 system

(b) Maximum coefficient vs. percent of successful runs for a 10 x 20 system

Fig. 4. Experimental Results (fixed dimensions)

Figure 4, Mistral is less sensitive to coefficient size than the other tools. For example, for maximum coefficient 50, Mistral's closest competitor, MathSAT, takes an average of 482 seconds with a success rate of 60% while Mistral takes an average of 1.6 seconds with a 100% success rate.

Among the tools we compared, Yices and Z3 use a Simplex-based branch-and-cut approach, while CVC3 implements the Omega test. MathSAT mainly uses a Simplex-based algorithm augmented with the Omega test as a fallback mechanism. In our experience, one of the main differences between Simplex-based and Omega test based algorithms is that the former run out of time, while the latter run out of memory. On average, Simplex-based tools seem to perform better than tools using the Omega test.

We believe these experimental results demonstrate that the Cuts-from-Proofs algorithm outperforms leading implementations of existing techniques by orders of magnitude and significantly increases the size and complexity of integer linear programs that can be solved. Furthermore, our algorithm is easy to implement and does not require extensive tuning to make it perform well. We believe that the Cuts-from-Proofs algorithm can be profitably incorporated into existing SMT solvers that integrate the theory of linear integer arithmetic.

6   Related Work

As discussed in Section 1, there are three major approaches for solving linear inequalities over integers. LP-based approaches include branch-and-bound, Gomory's cutting planes method, and various combinations of the two [12,13]. The cutting planes method derives valid inequalities from the final Simplex tableau. More abstractly, a Gomory cut can be viewed as the proof of unsatisfiability of a single inequality obtained from a linear combination of the original set of inequalities. This is in contrast with our Cuts-from-Proofs algorithm which obtains a proof from the set of defining constraints, rather than from a single inequality in the final Simplex tableau. Unfortunately, the number of cuts added by Gomory's cutting planes technique is usually very large, and few of these cuts ultimately prove helpful in obtaining an integer solution [12]. Branch-and-cut techniques that combine branch-and-bound and variations on cutting planes techniques have proven more successful and are used by many state-of-the-art SMT solvers [5,6,8]. However, the algorithm proposed in this paper significantly outperforms leading implementations of the branch-and-cut technique.

Another technique for solving linear integer inequalities is the Omega test, an extension of the Fourier-Motzkin variable elimination for integers [2]. A drawback of this approach is that it can consume gigabytes of memory even on moderately sized inputs, causing it to perform worse in practice than Simplex-based techniques. A third approach for solving linear arithmetic over integers is based on finite automata theory [11]. Unfortunately, while complete, automata-based approaches perform significantly worse than all of the aforementioned techniques. The authors are not aware of any tools based on this approach that are currently under active development.

Hermite normal forms are a well-studied topic in number theory, and efficient polynomial-time algorithms exist for computing Hermite normal forms [14,16]. Their application to solving systems of linear diophantine equations is discussed, for example, in [12,13]. Jain et al. study the application of Hermite normal forms to computing interpolants of systems of linear diophantine equalities and disequalities [22]. We adopt the term "proof of unsatisfiability" from the literature on Craig interpolation.

7   Conclusion

We have presented a novel, sound, and complete algorithm called Cuts-from-Proofs for solving linear inequalities over integers and demonstrated experimentally that this algorithm significantly outperforms leading implementations of existing approaches.

Acknowledgements

We would like to thank the anonymous reviewers for their insightful comments and feedback. We would also like to thank David Dill for his useful suggestions and Suhabe Bugrara for his comments on a draft of this paper.

References

1. Cousot, P., Halbwachs, N.: Automatic discovery of linear restraints among variables of a program, pp. 84–97. ACM Press, New York (1978)
2. Pugh, W.: The omega test: A fast and practical integer programming algorithm for dependence analysis. Communications of the ACM (1992)
3. Brinkmann, R., Drechsler, R.: RTL-datapath verification using integer linear programming. In: VLSI Design, pp. 741–746 (2002)

4. Amon, T., Borriello, G., Hu, T., Liu, J.: Symbolic timing verification of timing diagrams using presburger formulas. In: DAC 1997: Proceedings of the 34th annual conference on Design automation, pp. 226–231. ACM, New York (1997)
5. Dutertre, B., De Moura, L.: The yices SMT solver. Technical report, SRI International (2006)
6. De Moura, L., Bjørner, N.: Z3: An efficient SMT solver. In: Ramakrishnan, C.R., Rehof, J. (eds.) TACAS 2008. LNCS, vol. 4963, pp. 337–340. Springer, Heidelberg (2008)
7. Barrett, C., Tinelli, C.: CVC3. In: Damm, W., Hermanns, H. (eds.) CAV 2007. LNCS, vol. 4590, pp. 298–302. Springer, Heidelberg (2007)
8. Bruttomesso, R., Cimatti, A., Franzén, A., Griggio, A., Sebastiani, R.: The mathsat 4 SMT solver. In: Gupta, A., Malik, S. (eds.) CAV 2008. LNCS, vol. 5123, pp. 299–303. Springer, Heidelberg (2008)
9. Bofill, M., Nieuwenhuis, R., Oliveras, A., Rodríguez-Carbonell, E., Rubio, A.: The barcelogic SMT solver. In: Gupta, A., Malik, S. (eds.) CAV 2008. LNCS, vol. 5123, pp. 294–298. Springer, Heidelberg (2008)
10. Dantzig, G.: Linear Programming and Extensions. Princeton University Press, Princeton (1963)
11. Ganesh, V., Berezin, S., Dill, D.: Deciding presburger arithmetic by model checking and comparisons with other methods. In: Aagaard, M.D., O'Leary, J.W. (eds.) FMCAD 2002. LNCS, vol. 2517, pp. 171–186. Springer, Heidelberg (2002)
12. Schrijver, A.: Theory of Linear and Integer Programming. J. Wiley & Sons, Chichester (1986)
13. Nemhauser, G.L., Wolsey, L.: Integer and Combinatorial Optimization. John Wiley & Sons, Chichester (1988)
14. Storjohann, A., Labahn, G.: Asymptotically fast computation of hermite normal forms of integer matrices. In: Proc. Int'l. Symp. on Symbolic and Algebraic Computation: ISSAC 1996, pp. 259–266. ACM Press, New York (1996)
15. http://gmplib.org/: Gnu mp bignum library
16. Cohen, H.: A Course in Computational Algebraic Number Theory. Graduate Texts in Mathematics. Springer, Heidelberg (1993)
17. Domich, P., Kannan, R., Trotter, J.L.: Hermite normal form computation using modulo determinant arithmetic. Mathematics of Operations Research 12(1), 50–59 (1987)
18. http://www.smtcomp.org: Smt-comp 2008
19. http://www.gnu.org/software/glpk/: Glpk (gnu linear programming kit)
20. http://lpsolve.sourceforge.net/5.5/: lp_solve reference guide
21. http://www.ilog.com/products/cplex/: Cplex
22. Jain, H., Clarke, E., Grumberg, O.: Efficient craig interpolation for linear diophantine (dis)equations and linear modular equations. In: Gupta, A., Malik, S. (eds.) CAV 2008. LNCS, vol. 5123, pp. 254–267. Springer, Heidelberg (2008)
23. Golub, G.H., Van Loan, C.F.: Matrix Computations. JHU Press (1996)

Meta-analysis for Atomicity Violations under Nested Locking

Azadeh Farzan[1], P. Madhusudan[2], and Francesco Sorrentino[2]

[1] University of Toronto
[2] Univ. of Illinois at Urbana-Champaign

Abstract. We study the problem of determining, given a run of a concurrent program, whether there is any alternate execution of it that violates atomicity, where atomicity is defined using marked blocks of local runs. We show that if a concurrent program adopts *nested locking*, the problem of predicting atomicity violations is efficiently solvable, without exploring all interleavings. In particular, for the case of atomicity violations involving only two threads and a single variable, which covers many of the atomicity errors reported in bug databases, we exhibit efficient algorithms that work in time that is *linear* in the length of the runs, and quadratic in the number of threads. Moreover, we report on an implementation of this algorithm, and show experimentally that it scales well for benchmark concurrent programs and is effective in predicting a large number of atomicity violations even from a single run.

1 Introduction

The multicore revolution is transforming computer science. The fact that individual processors may not get any faster, and the only way software can gain speed is to exploit concurrent executions on multiple processor cores, has created a need to update all disciplines within computer science (algorithms, data structures, programming languages, software engineering, architecture, operating systems, testing, verification, etc.) to adapt themselves to concurrency.

The motivation of this paper is to study problems in testing concurrent programs. Testing, which is the primary technique used in the industry to assure correctness of software, is fundamentally challenged for concurrent programs because of the *interleaving explosion problem*. Given a concurrent program P and a *single* test input i to it, there are a multitude of interleaved executions on i. This grows exponentially with the number of cores, making a systematic exploration of all executions on the test infeasible.

One way to tackle this problem is to choose (wisely) a subset of interleaved executions to test. The CHESS project at Microsoft research is one such tool, which systematically explores all interleavings that involve only k context-switches (for a small fixed k), banking on the intuition that most errors manifest themselves within a few context switches. IBM's ConTest tool also explores schedules that are more likely to have data races, deadlocks, etc.

A. Bouajjani and O. Maler (Eds.): CAV 2009, LNCS 5643, pp. 248–262, 2009.

In the line of work we pursue, we have chosen the class of executions that *violate atomicity* as a candidate for selecting schedules. A programmer writing a procedure often wants uninterfered access to certain shared data that will enable him/her to reason about the procedure locally. The programmer often puts together concurrency control mechanisms to ensure atomicity, often by taking locks on the data accessed. This is however extremely error-prone: errors occur if not all the required locks for the data are acquired, non-uniform ordering of locking can cause deadlocks, and naive ways of locking can inhibit concurrency, which force programmers to invent intricate ways to achieve concurrency and correctness at the same time. Recent studies of concurrency errors [11] show that a majority of errors (69%) are atomicity violations. This motivates our choice in selecting executions that violate atomicity as the criterion for choosing interleavings to execute.

In this paper, we tackle a key problem towards this goal: given an execution of a concurrent program on a test input, say ρ, we pose the meta-analysis problem of efficiently checking whether there is an alternate scheduling of the events in ρ that violates atomicity.

Notice that this is much more complex than *monitoring* problem, which checks, given a particular execution ρ, whether ρ itself violates atomicity. We examined the monitoring problem in work reported in CAV last year [3], where we showed that it is efficiently solvable using *streaming* algorithms that take space independent of the length of the executions. The recent tool Velodrome [6] also considers only the simpler monitoring problem, and not the meta-analysis problem we consider in this paper.

In recent work [4], we have studied the meta-analysis problem for atomicity, and shown that when all synchronization actions in the execution are *ignored*, efficient algorithms that work in time *linear* in n (where n is the length of the execution) are feasible. However, we also showed that if the locking synchronization between threads is taken into account, an algorithm that is linear in n is *unlikely* to exist using complexity-theoretic arguments.

The main result of this paper is to show that when the program uses only *nested locking* (i.e. when threads release locks in the reverse order of how they acquired them), we can build algorithms that effectively analyze *all* interleavings for basic atomicity violations in time that is *linear* in the length of the execution.

Our goal in this work is also to find an efficient scalable practical algorithm for analyzing executions for atomicity violations. Consequently, we study atomicity violations caused by two threads accessing one variable only. More precisely, we define atomicity using *serializability*. We look for *minimal serializability* violations which are those caused by two threads and one variable only; i.e. we look for threads T and T', where there are two events e_1 and e_2 that access a variable v in a single transaction of T, and there is an action in thread T' that happens in between the events e_1 and e_2, and is conflicting with both e_1 and e_2.

In our experience in studying concurrency bugs, we have found that many atomicity violations are caused due to such patterns of interaction. The recent study of concurrency bugs by Lu et al. [11] in fact found that 96% of concurrency errors involved only two threads, and 66% of (non-deadlock) concurrency errors involved only one variable. The restriction of atomicity errors involving only two threads and one variable makes our algorithm feasible in practice.

Our main result is to show that given a run ρ of length n where threads synchronize using nested locking, we can predict whether any of the many interleavings (which can be exponential in n) has a minimal serializability violation in time linear in n, linear in the number of global variables, and quadratic in the number of threads. Our algorithm is *compositional*: it works first locally on each individual thread, extracting information called *profiles* that depend only on the set of locks and variables, and is independent of n. Then, in a second phase, we combine the profiles obtained from the different threads to check whether there is an interleaved run that violates atomicity.

Our algorithm is derived by reducing the meta-analysis of minimal atomicity violations to the problem of pairwise reachability of two threads. We then use a beautiful result by Kahlon et al. [9] to solve the latter problem for threads with nested locking compositionally, using lock-sets and acquisition histories.

We have also implemented our meta-analysis algorithm for atomicity in a tool.[1] By transforming concurrent programs so that they can be monitored, we extract concurrent executions on test inputs, and use our algorithm to find atomicity violations. In these examples, the length of the executions are extremely long (some have about 11 million events), and any algorithm that runs even in time quadratic in n would not scale. We show, through experiments, that our linear algorithm scales well to these long executions, and accurately predicts a large number of atomicity violations even from a single run.

Related Work. Apart from the related work discussed above, *atomicity violations based on serializability* have been suggested to be effective in finding concurrency bugs in many works [5,7,17,18,19]. Lipton transactions have been used to find atomicity violations in programs [5,7,8,10]. In [2], we proposed a slightly different notion of atomicity called *causal atomicity*; the violations we find in this paper can also be seen as causal atomicity violations.

The run-time *monitoring* for atomicity violations is well-studied [3,6]. Note that here the problem is to simply observe a run and check whether that particular run (and only that run) is atomic. The work in [13] defines *access interleaving invariants*, which are certain patterns of access interactions on variables, learns the intended specifications using tests, and monitors runs to find errors. A variant of dynamic two-phase locking algorithm [12] for detection of serializability violations is used in the atomicity monitoring tool developed in [19].

Turning to predictive analysis, there are two main streams of work that are relevant. In papers [17,18], Wang and Stoller study the prediction of runs that violate serializability from a single run. Under the assumptions of deadlock-freedom and nested locking, they show precise algorithms that can handle serializability violations involving *at most two transactions* (not threads). They also give heuristic incomplete algorithms for checking arbitrary runs. In contrast, we focus on *minimal* serializability here, and check for violations involving

---

[1] All experimental data can be found at http://www.cs.uiuc.edu/~madhu/cav09/

two *threads* that could involve a large number of transactions. The approach in [17] uses a structure which grows quadratically with the size of the observed run, and therefore has limited scalability. Our algorithm uses space independent of the size of the observed run, and time linear in the observed run, and scales well. Predicting alternate executions from a single run are also studied in a series of papers by Rosu et al. [1,14]. While these tools can also predict runs that can violate atomicity, their prediction model is tuned towards *explicitly* generating alternate runs, which can then be subject to atomicity analysis. In sharp contrast, the results we present here search the exponential space of alternate interleavings efficiently, without enumerating them. However, the accuracy and feasibility of prediction in the above papers are better as the algorithm is aware of the static structure of the programs and other control dependencies.

2   Modeling Executions of Concurrent Programs

Notation. For any alphabet A, and any word $w \in A^\star$, let $w[i]$ ($1 \le i \le |w|$) denote the letter in the i'th position of w, and $w[i,j]$ denote the substring $w[i]w[i+1]\ldots w[j]$ of w. For $w \in A^\star$ and $B \subseteq A$, let $w|_B$ denote the word w projected to the letters in B.

Transactions and Schedules. A program consists of a set of threads that run concurrently. Each thread executes a series of *transactions*. A transaction is a sequence of *actions*; each action can be a read or a write to a (global) variable, or a synchronization action.

We assume an infinite set of thread identifiers $\mathcal{T} = \{T_1, T_2, \ldots, \}$. We also assume an infinite set of entity names (or just entities) $\mathcal{X} = \{x_1, x_2, \ldots, \ldots\}$ that the threads can access. The set of actions that a thread T can perform on a set of entities $X \subseteq \mathcal{X}$ is defined as $\Sigma_{T,X} = \{T{:}{\triangleright}, T{:}{\triangleleft}\} \cup \{T{:}\mathrm{read}(x), T{:}\mathrm{write}(x) \mid x \in X\}$. Actions $T{:}\mathrm{read}(x)$ and $T{:}\mathrm{write}(x)$ correspond to thread T reading and writing to entity x, while $T{:}{\triangleright}$ and $T{:}{\triangleleft}$ correspond to the beginning and the end of transaction blocks in thread T.

Define $\Sigma_X = \bigcup_{T \in \mathcal{T}} \Sigma_{T,X}$ (actions on entities X by all threads), $\Sigma_T = \bigcup_{X \in \mathcal{X}} \Sigma_{T,X}$ (actions by thread T on all entities), and $\Sigma = \bigcup_{X \in \mathcal{X}, T \in \mathcal{T}} \Sigma_{T,X}$ (all actions).

For a word $w \subseteq \Sigma^\star$, let $w|_T$ be a shorthand notation for $w|_{\Sigma_T}$, which includes only the actions of thread T from w. The following defines the notion of observable behaviors on the global variables of a concurrent program, which we call a *schedule*.

Let $\mathit{Tran}_{T,\mathcal{X}} = (T{:}{\triangleright}) \cdot \{T{:}\mathrm{read}(x), T{:}\mathrm{write}(x) \mid x \in \mathcal{X}\}^\star \cdot (T{:}{\triangleleft})$. A *transaction* tr of a thread T is a word in $\mathit{Tran}_{T,\mathcal{X}}$. Let $\mathit{Tran}_T = (\mathit{Tran}_{T,\mathcal{X}})^\star$ denote the set of all possible sequences of transactions for a thread T, and let Tran denote the set of all possible transaction sequences.

Definition 1. *A schedule over a set of threads $\mathcal{T}$ and entities $\mathcal{X}$ is a word $\sigma \in (\Sigma_{\mathcal{T},\mathcal{X}})^\star$ such that for each $T \in \mathcal{T}$, $\sigma|_T$ belongs to Tran_T. Let $\mathit{Sched}_{\mathcal{T},\mathcal{X}}$ denote the set of all schedules over threads $\mathcal{T}$ and entities $\mathcal{X}$.*

In other words, a schedule is a sequence of actions such that its projection to any thread T is a word divided into a sequence of transactions, where each transaction begins with $T{:}{\rhd}$, is followed by a set of reads and writes, and ends with $T{:}{\lhd}$.

When we refer to two particular actions $\sigma[i]$ and $\sigma[j]$ in σ, we say they *belong to the same transaction* if they are actions of the same thread T, and they are in the same transaction block in $\sigma|_T$: i.e. if there is some T such that $\sigma[i], \sigma[j] \in \mathcal{A}_T$, and there is no i', $i < i' < j$ such that $\sigma[i'] = T{:}{\lhd}$.

Concurrent executions with lock-synchronization.

Let us now define *executions* of concurrent programs that synchronize using (nested) locks. An *execution* is more detailed than a *schedule* in that it also contains the synchronization actions a program performs. In this paper, we limit the synchronization actions to acquires and releases of global locks.

Let us fix a set of global locks $\mathcal{L}$. For a thread $T \in \mathcal{T}$ and a set of locks $L \subseteq \mathcal{L}$, define the set of lock-actions of T on L by $\Pi_{L,T} = \{T{:}acquire(l), T{:}release(l) \mid l \in L\}$. Let $\Pi_L = \bigcup_{T \in \mathcal{T}} \Pi_{L,T}$, and $\Pi_T = \Pi_{\mathcal{L},T}$, and finally $\Pi = \bigcup_{T \in \mathcal{T}} \Pi_T$.

A word $\gamma \in \Pi^\star$ is *lock-valid* if it respects the semantics of the locking mechanism; formally, for every $l \in \mathcal{L}$, $\gamma|_{\Pi_{\{l\}}}$ is a prefix of $\left[\bigcup_{T \in \mathcal{T}} (T{:}acquire(l) \ T{:}release(l)) \right]^\star$.

A global execution over the set $\mathcal{L}$ is a *finite* word $\rho \in (\Sigma \cup \Pi_\mathcal{L})^\star$ such that (a) for any thread T, $\rho|_\Sigma$ is a schedule and (b) $\rho|_{\Pi_\mathcal{L}}$ is lock-valid.

In other words, a global execution is a finite sequence of actions, involving a finite set of threads accessing a finite set of variables, along with acquisitions and releases of locks, such that the sequence projected to any thread forms a sequence of transactions, and the sequence respects the locking mechanism.

We will often handle *local executions* as well, which are executions of individual threads. Formally, **a local set of executions over the set $\mathcal{L}$ is a set** $\{\alpha_t\}_{t \in \mathcal{T}}$, where for each thread T, $\alpha_T \in \left(\Sigma_{\{T,\mathcal{X}\}} \cup \Pi_\mathcal{L} \right)^\star$. Note that a global execution ρ naturally defines a set of local executions $\{\rho_T\}_{T \in \mathcal{T}}$.

An event in a set of local executions $\{\rho_T\}_{T \in \mathcal{T}}$ is a pair (T, i) where $T \in \mathcal{T}$ and $1 \le i \le |\rho_T|$. In other words, an event is a particular action that one of the threads executes, indexed by its local timestamp.

Let ρ be a global execution, and $e = (T, i)$ be an event in $\{\rho_T\}_{T \in \mathcal{T}}$. Then we say that the j'th action $(1 \le j \le |\rho|)$ in ρ *is the event* e (or, $Event(\rho[j]) = e = (T, i))$, if $\rho[j] = T{:}a$ (for some action a) and $\rho_T[1, i] = \rho[1, j]|_T$. In other words, the event $e = (T, i)$ appears at the position j in ρ in the particular interleaving of the threads that constitutes ρ. Conversely, for any event e in $\{\rho_T\}_{T \in \mathcal{T}}$, let $Occur(e, \rho)$ denote the (unique) j $(1 \le j \le |\rho|)$ such that the j'th action in ρ is the event e, i.e $Event(\rho[j]) = e$. Therefore, we have $Event(\rho[Occur(e, \rho)]) = e$, and $Occur(Event(\rho[j])) = j$.

A (global) execution ρ over $\mathcal{L}$ is said to respect *nested-locking* if there is no thread T and two locks l and l' such that $\rho|_{\Pi_{\{l,l'\},\{T\}}}$ has a contiguous subsequence $T{:}acquire(l)T{:}acquire(l')T{:}release(l)$. In other words, an execution respects nested-locking if each thread releases locks strictly in the reverse order in which they were acquired.

Finally, for any execution ρ, the schedule defined by ρ is the word obtained by removing the locking-events from it: $Sched(\rho) = \rho|_{\Sigma}$.

The prediction model.   Given an execution ρ over a set of locks $\mathcal{L}$, we would like to *infer* other executions ρ' from ρ. This prediction model we consider is defined as follows. An execution ρ' belongs to the inferred set of ρ iff ρ'_T is a prefix of ρ_T, for every thread T. (Of course, ρ' is lock-valid by the merit of being an execution.)

In other words, we infer executions from ρ by projecting ρ to each thread to obtain local executions, and combining these local executions into a global execution ρ' in any interleaved fashion that respects the synchronization mechanism. Let $Infer(\rho)$ denote the set of executions inferred from ρ.

Notice that our prediction model is an *abstraction* of the problem of finding alternate runs that violate atomicity in the concrete program, and is quite optimistic: it recombines executions in any manner that respects the locking constraints. Of course, these executions may not be valid/feasible in the original program (this could happen if the threads communicate using other mechanisms; for example, if a thread writes a particular value to a global variable based on which another thread chooses an execution path, an execution that switches these events may not be feasible). The choice of a simple abstract prediction model is *deliberate*: while we could build more accurate models, we believe that having a simple prediction model can yield faster algorithms. Since we can in any case try to execute a predicted interleaving that violates atomicity and check whether it is feasible, this will not contribute to the final false positives in a testing scenario.

Deadlock freedom.   We say that an execution ρ is deadlock-free if no run inferred from ρ deadlocks. Formally, ρ is *deadlock-free* if for every $\rho' \in Infer(\rho)$, there is a $\rho'' \in Infer(\rho)$ such that ρ' is a prefix of ρ'' and $|\rho| = |\rho''|$ (i.e. any partial execution inferred from ρ can be completed to another that executes all the actions of ρ). Note that deadlock freedom is defined abstractly by combining events of the execution, and not on the concrete program. See the end of Section 3 for a discussion on deadlock freedom.

Defining atomicity through serializability.   We now define atomicity as the notion of *conflict serializability*. Define the *dependency* relation D as a symmetric relation defined over the events in Σ, which captures the dependency between (a) two events accessing the same entity, where one of them is a write, and (b) any two events of the same thread, i.e.,

$$D = \{(T_1{:}a_1, T_2{:}a_2) \mid T_1 = T_2 \text{ and } a_1, a_2 \in A \cup \{\triangleright, \triangleleft\} \text{ or}$$
$$\exists x \in \mathcal{X} \text{ such that } (a_1 = \text{read}(x) \text{ and } a_2 = \text{write}(x)) \text{ or}$$
$$(a_1 = \text{write}(x) \text{ and } a_2 = \text{read}(x)) \text{ or } (a_1 = \text{write}(x) \text{ and } a_2 = \text{write}(x))\}$$

Definition 2 (Equivalence of schedules). *The equivalence of schedules is defined as the* smallest *equivalence relation* $\sim \subseteq Sched \times Sched$ *such that: if* $\sigma = \rho ab\rho', \sigma' = \rho ba\rho' \in Sched$ *with* $(a, b) \notin D$, *then* $\sigma \sim \sigma'$.

It is easy to see that the above notion is well-defined. Two schedules are considered equivalent if we can derive one schedule from the other by iteratively swapping consecutive independent actions in the schedule.

We call a schedule σ *serial* if all the transactions in it occur sequentially: formally, for every i, if $\sigma[i] = T{:}a$ where $T \in \mathcal{T}$ and $a \in A$, then there is some $j < i$ such that $T[i] = T{:}\triangleright$ and every $j < j' < i$ is such that $\sigma[j'] \in A_T$. In other words, the schedule is made up of a sequence of complete transactions from different threads, interleaved at boundaries only.

Definition 3. *A schedule is* serializable *(or atomic) if it has an equivalent serial schedule. That is, σ is a serializable schedule if there is a serial schedule σ' such that $\sigma \sim \sigma'$.*

2.1 Serializability Violations Involving Two Threads and one Variable

While the above defines the general notion of serializability, in this paper we confine ourselves to checking a more restricted notion called *minimally serializable*; a schedule is minimally serializable if there are no serializability violations that involve two threads and a single variable only. More precisely,

Definition 4. *A schedule σ is* minimally serializable *(or minimally atomic) if for every pair of threads (T, T') and every entity $x \in \mathcal{X}$, the schedule $\sigma|_{\Sigma_{\{T,T'\},\{x\}}}$ is serializable. An execution ρ is minimally serializable if the schedule corresponding to it, $Sched(\rho)$, is minimally serializable.*

We can now define the precise problem we consider in this paper:

[Problem of meta-analysis of executions for minimal serializability:]

Given: A finite deadlock-free execution ρ over a set of threads, entities and locks.

Problem: Is there any execution $\rho' \in Infer(\rho)$ that is not minimally serializable?

First, note that an execution ρ' is not minimally serializable iff there exist two threads T and T' such that ρ' projected to T and T' is not serializable. Even for a fixed T and T', there are a large number of interleavings possible (in fact, exponential in $|\rho|$), making an explicit search over interleavings infeasible.

A better way of solving the above problem is to build an automaton that generates all possible interleavings of two threads T and T', and *intersect* it with another automaton that detects atomicity violations [3]. The state of this automaton is represented by a triple (x, y, π) where x tracks the position in the first thread, y tracks the position of the second thread, and $\pi : \mathcal{L} \to \{\bot, T, T'\}$ tracks the thread that holds each lock ($\bot$ denoting the lock is free). Alternatively, we can view this as a *dynamic programming* solution, where we track, for each pair (x, y), the state of the monitor on them.

Though the above algorithm does not explicitly enumerate all interleavings, it works in time $O(n^2)$ (where $n = |\rho|$). Since n, the length of the given run, can be extremely large (millions of events in our benchmarks), an algorithm that runs in time quadratic in n simply will not scale in practice.

The goal of this paper is to find an algorithm that solves the above problem in time *linear* in n (and linear in the number of entities, and quadratic in the number of threads). Note that this means that we do not explore all interleavings explicitly, and yet predict atomicity violations. Our scheme is in fact *compositional*; we extract a finite amount of information from each local execution in linear time, and combine this information to predict minimal atomicity violations.

3 Meta-analysis of Runs for Minimal Serializability

In this section, we present the main result of this paper: the basis for an algorithm that solves the meta-analysis problem for minimal serializability in time linear in the length of the given run. We will show how meta-analysis for minimal serializability can be reduced to the *global reachability problem* for two threads, which in turn can be compositionally and efficiently solved for nested-locking programs. The results obtained in this section will be used to formulate our algorithm in Section 4.

The first observation is that only three events are relevant in finding a violation of minimal serializability; we need to observe two events e_1 and e_2 from a *single transaction* of a thread T and an event f from another thread T' such that e_1 and f are dependent and e_2 and f are dependent. Moreover, and crucially, there should exist an execution in which f occurs after e_1, and e_2 occurs after f. The figure on the right describes this pattern, and the following lemma captures this property:

Lemma 1. *Let ρ be a global execution, and let $\{\rho_T\}_{T\in\mathcal{T}}$ be the set of local executions corresponding to it. Infer(ρ) contains a minimally non-serializable run iff there exists two different threads T and T', an entity $x \in \mathcal{X}$, and $\rho' \in$ Infer$(\rho|_{\Sigma_{\{T,T'\},\{x\}}})$ such that there are (read or write) events e_1, e_2, f of $\{\rho_T\}_{T\in\mathcal{T}}$ where*

- $Occur(e_1, \rho') < Occur(f, \rho') < Occur(e_2, \rho')$
- e_1 *and* e_2 *are events of thread T, and f is an event of thread T'*
- e_1 *and* e_2 *belong to the same transaction,*
- $e_1 \ D \ f \ D \ e_2$.

While we can find candidate events e_1 and e_2 from thread T and a candidate event f from T' by *individually* examining the local runs of T and T', the main problem is in ensuring the condition that we can find an inferred run where e_1 occurs before f and f occurs before e_2. This is hard as the threads synchronize using (nested) locks which needs to be respected by the inferred run. In fact, for threads communicating using general locking, our results in [3] show that it is highly unlikely to avoid considering the two thread runs in tandem, which involves $O(n^2)$ time.

Let us first show the following lemma that reduces checking whether three events e_1, f, and e_2 are executable in that order, to global reachability of two threads (this lemma has nothing to do with atomicity violations).

Lemma 2. *Let ρ be a deadlock-free execution, and let T, T' be two threads with $T \neq T'$. Let e_1, e_2, f be (read or write) events in $\{\rho_T\}_{T \in \mathcal{T}}$ such that $e_1 = (T, i_1)$ and $e_2 = (T, i_2)$ are events of thread T with $i_1 < i_2$, and f is an event of thread T'. Then, there is an execution $\rho' \in Infer(\rho)$ such that $Occur(e_1, \rho') < Occur(f, \rho') < Occur(e_2, \rho')$*

if, and only if,

there is an execution $\rho'' \in Infer(\rho)$ such that

- *e_1 occurs in ρ'' and e_2 does not occur in ρ'', and*
- *f occurs in ρ'', and in fact f is the last event of T' that occurs in ρ''.*

Intuitively, the above lemma says the following: fix an execution ρ, and three events e_1, e_2, f in it such that events e_1 and e_2 belong to the same transaction (and thread) and event f belongs to a different thread. Then, we can find a run inferred from ρ that executes event e_1 followed by event f followed by event e_2 if, and only if, we can find an (incomplete) inferred run that executes events e_1 of thread T (and possibly later events), but does not execute e_2, and executes precisely up to event f in thread T'. This is depicted in the figure on the right.

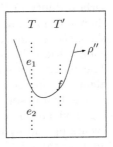

The above lemma is useful as it reduces finding a series of three events to the simpler global reachability question of a set of pairs of positions in the two threads.

Pairwise reachability. Our final hammer in solving the problem relies on a beautiful result by Kahlon et al. [9] that argues that global reachability of two threads communicating via nested locks is effectively and *compositionally* solvable by extracting locking information from the two threads in terms of *acquisition histories.*

Let ρ be an execution and let $\{\rho_T\}_{T \in \mathcal{T}}$ be its set of local executions. Consider ρ_T (for any T). The *lock-set held after ρ_T* is the set of all locks T holds: $LockSet(\rho_T) = \{l \in \mathcal{L} \mid \exists i.\rho_T[i] = T{:}acquire(l)$ and there is no $j > i$ and $\rho_T[j] = T{:}release(l)\}$.

The *acquisition history* of ρ_T records, for each lock l held by T at the end of ρ_T, the set of locks that T acquired (and possibly released) after the last acquisition of the lock l. Formally, the acquisition history of ρ_T, $AH(\rho_T) : LockSet(\rho_T) \rightarrow 2^{\mathcal{L}}$, where $AH(l)$ is the set of all locks $l' \in \mathcal{L}$ such that $\exists i.\rho_T[i] = T{:}acquire(l)$ and there is no $j > i$ such that $\rho_T[j] = T{:}release(l)$ and $\exists k > i.\rho_T[k] = T{:}acquire(l')$.

Two acquisition histories AH and AH' are said to be *compatible* if there do not exist two locks l and l' such that $l' \in AH(l)$ and $l \in AH(l')$. The following is a direct consequence of a result by Kahlon et al. [9], which says that there is an execution that ends with event e in one thread and event f in the other thread, if, and only if, the acquisition histories at e and f are compatible.

Lemma 3 (Kahlon et al. [9]). *Let ρ be an execution, let $\{\rho_T\}_{T \in \mathcal{T}}$ be its set of local executions, and let T and T' be two different threads. Let $e = (T, i)$ be an event of thread T and $f = (T', j)$ be an event of thread T' of these local executions.*

There is a run $\rho' \in Infer(\rho)$ such that e and f occur in ρ', and further, $\rho'_T = \rho_T[1, i]$ and $\rho'_{T'} = \rho_{T'}[1, j]$

if, and only if,

$Lockset(\rho_T[1, i]) \cap Lockset(\rho_{T'}[1, j]) = \emptyset$, and the acquisition history of $\rho_T[1, i]$ and the acquisition history of $\rho_{T'}[1, j]$ are compatible.   □

We have reduced checking of serializability to pairwise reachability, which is solvable compositionally by computing the acquisition histories from each thread, and checking them for compatibility. We summarize this in the following:

Theorem 1. *Let ρ be a deadlock-free global execution. A minimally non-serializable execution can be inferred from ρ iff there exists two different threads T and T' and an entity $x \in \mathcal{X}$, and there are events $e_1 = (T, i), e_2 = (T, i'), f = (T', j)$ of $\{\rho_T\}_{T \in \mathcal{T}}$ such that*

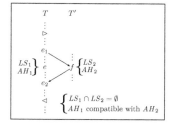

- *e_1 and e_2 belong to the same transaction,*
- *$e_1 \mathrel{D} f \mathrel{D} e_2$,*
- *There is an event $e = (T, i'')$ of $\{\rho_T\}_{T \in \mathcal{T}}$ such that $i \le i'' < i'$ and the acquisition histories of $\rho_T[1, i'']$ and $\rho_{T'}[1, j]$ are compatible.*

On the assumption of deadlock freedom. Deadlock freedom is a strong assumption. Note that a deadlocking inferred run may not be feasible in the concrete program. We use the deadlock-free assumption to ensure that the partial run (containing e_1 and f) can be completed to a full run where e_2 occurs. We can remove the assumption of deadlock freedom and build a more sophisticated algorithm (using locksets and *backward* acquisition histories) that ensures that e_2 is also executed; however, this complicates the algorithm considerably, and we have chosen not to implement it for practical reasons. In the benchmarks that we experiment with, all partial runs could be completed to full runs.

Actually, under the assumption of deadlock freedom, checking compatibility of acquisition histories is redundant, as it suffices to check if locksets are disjoint. However, we check compatibility of acquisition histories in order not to rely on the assumption of deadlock freedom to generate the events e_1 and f.

4   The Meta-analysis Algorithm for Minimal Serializability

Given a set of local executions $\{\rho_T\}_{T \in \mathcal{T}}$ with nested locking, Theorem 1 allows us to engineer an efficient algorithm to predict an interleaving of them that violates minimal serializability.

The aim is to find three events e_1, e_2, and f, where e_1 and e_2 occur in the same transaction in a thread T, f occurs in a different thread T', with $e_1 D f D e_2$, and further, find an event e between e_1 and e_2 (e is allowed to be e_1 but not to be e_2) such that the locksets of e and f are disjoint, and their acquisition histories are compatible.

The algorithm is divided into two phases. In the first phase, it gathers the lockset and acquisition histories of all possible witnesses e and all possible witnesses f; this is done by examining the events of each thread *individually*. In the second phase, we test the compatibility of the locksets and acquisition histories of every pair of witnesses e and f in different threads.

Let us fix an entity $x \in \mathcal{X}$. We divide our work into finding two patterns: one where e_1 and e_2 are writes to x and f is a read of x, and the other where e_1 and e_2 are accesses (read/write) to x and f is a write to x. This clearly covers all cases of minimal serializability violations— the former covers violations $e_1 - f - e_2$ of the form $Write-Read-Write$, while the latter covers those of the form $Read-Write-Read$, $Read-Write-Write$, $Write-Write-Read$ and $Write-Write-Write$.

Phase I. In the first phase, for each thread T and each entity x, the algorithm gathers witnesses in four lists: $R[T, x]$, $W[T, x]$, $WW[T, x]$ and $AA[T, x]$. Intuitively, the sets $R[T, x]$ and $W[T, x]$ gather witnesses of events of thread T that read and write to x, respectively, for each lockset and acquisition history pair, in order to witness the event f in our pattern.

The set $WW[T, x]$ gathers all witnesses e that are sandwiched between two write-events to x that occur in the same transaction of thread T, keeping only one representative witness for each lockset and acquisition history pair. Similarly $AA[T, x]$ gathers witnesses e sandwiched between any two accesses of thread T to x that occur in the same transaction.

The algorithm gathers the witnesses by processing the execution in a single pass. It continually updates the lockset and acquisition history, adding events to the various witness sets, making sure that no set has multiple events with the same lockset and acquisition history. Note that the computation of $WW[T, x]$ and $AA[T, x]$ sets need care due to the fact that events e recorded must be validated by a later occurrence of the relevant event e_2.

Note that phase I considers every event at most once, in one pass, in a streaming fashion, and hence runs in time linear in the length of the execution.

Phase II. In the second phase, the algorithm checks whether there are pairs of compatible witnesses that were collected in the first phase. More precisely, we check whether, for any entity x, and for any pair of threads T and T', there is an event $e \in WW[T, x]$ and an event $f \in R[T', x]$ that have disjoint locksets and compatible acquisition histories. Similarly, we also check whether there is an event $e \in AA[T, x]$ and an event $f \in W[T', x]$ that have disjoint locksets and compatible acquisition histories. The existence of any such pair of events would mean (by Theorem 1) that there is a minimal serializability violation.

```
1 for each entity x ∈ X do
2    for each T, T' in T such that T ≠ T' do
3       for each (e, LS, AH) in WW[T, X] do
4          for each (f, LS', AH') in R[t, x] do
5             if (LS ∩ LS' = ∅  ∧  AH and AH' are compatible) then
6                Report minimal serializability violation found;
7 end
```

Fig. 1. Phase II for R-WW patterns

For example, the algorithm runs the procedure in Figure 1 for finding the violations using the R and WW sets (the procedure using the W and AA sets is similar):

Note that phase II runs in time $O(t^2.v.ah^2)$ where t is the number of threads, v is the number of entities accessed, and ah is the total number of disjoint acquisition histories of events in the thread. Note that this is *independent* of the length of the execution (Phase I summarized the events in the execution, and Phase II does not consider the run again). The compatibility check for acquisition histories can be done in time linear in the size of the acquisition histories (however, our current implementation is quadratic.).

The quadratic dependence on the number of threads is understandable as we consider serializability violation between all pairs of threads. The linear dependence on x is very important for scalability as the number of entities accessed can be very large on typical runs. The number of different acquisition histories, in theory, can be large $(O(2^{l^2})$, where the execution uses l locks)— however, in practice, there tend to be very few distinct acquisition histories that get manifested, and hence is not a bottleneck (see the next section for details).

Though we record violations only in terms of the two witnesses e and f, we can actually recover a precise execution that shows the atomicity violation. This run can be obtained using the locksets and acquisition histories of e and f (using the method prescribed by Kahlon et al. [9]), and may in fact involve several context switches $(O(l)$ of them, if there are l locks) to execute the atomicity violation. However, this replay of an exact run that violates atomicity is involved, and has not been implemented.

5   Implementation and Experiments

We have implemented the meta-analysis algorithm to look for minimal serializability violations in the set of executions inferred from a single execution of a concurrent program. Note that though the real problem is to find alternate executions of a concurrent program that violate minimal serializability, we have, in this paper, adopted a simple prediction model, according to which we find alternate runs. The algorithm that we implement (as detailed in the previous sections) is sound and complete with respect to our prediction model, but clearly not with respect to the concrete model. In particular, the alternate schedules that we report may not be feasible in the concrete model. We could, of course, try to schedule them and see if they are feasible; however, this is a complex engineering task that is out of the scope of this paper. Preliminary analysis of the runs found in our experiments, however, suggest that most executions are indeed feasible in the concrete program (see below).

Note that our algorithm computes only one representative violation for each pair of threads, each entity, each pair of events with a compatible set of locksets and acquisition histories, and each pattern of violation (R-W-R and A-R-A). The current implementation does not find all multiplicities of these serializability violations. Note that our algorithm guarantees to report at least one minimal serializability violation, if violations at all exist. The tool can also be easily modified to enumerate all possible violations. More specifically, after the second phase of the algorithm, all the *interesting acquisition histories* are known, so one can use this information and the original execution to generate all violations without significant performance cost.

We evaluated the algorithms on a benchmark suite of six concurrent Java programs that use `synchronized` blocks and methods as means of synchronization (note that using synchronized blocks automatically ensures nested locking, and is one of the reasons why nested locking programs are common). They include `raytracer` from the Java Grande multithreaded benchmarks [15], `elevator`, `tsp`, and `hedc` from [16], and `Vector` and `HashTable` from Java libraries. `elevator` simulates multiple lifts in a building, `tsp` solves the traveling salesman problem in parallel for a given input map, `raytracer` renders a frame of an arrangement of spheres from a given view point, `hedc` is a web-crawler, and `Vector` and `HashTable` are Java libraries that respectively implement the concurrent vector and the concurrent hashtable data structures.

Since *recurrent* locks (multiple acquisitions of the same lock by the same thread) are typical in Java, the tool is tuned to handle them by ignoring all the subsequent acquisitions of the same lock by the same thread. One can easily verify that this approach maintains well-nestedness of locks and (hence) the correctness of the main theorem of the paper.

We investigated the other concurrent benchmarks in the Java Grande suite, but they either had no synchronization, or used *barriers* as their synchronization mechanism, and hence were not good candidates for testing our analysis method.

Executions were extracted by (manually) instrumenting programs to output accesses to entities and synchronization events at runtime. We have a simple *escape analysis* unit that excludes from the execution all accesses to thread-local entities. We then run the meta-analysis algorithm on these output files off-line. The algorithm can be implemented as an online algorithm as well (as Phase I can be implemented online), but the current implementation works off-line.

Table 1 presents the results of our evaluation. We ran each benchmark with different input parameters, such as number of threads and input files. For each program, we report in the table the number of lines of code (LOC) (appears below the program names), number of threads used in the execution, the number of *truly shared* entities between threads, the number of locks, the number of transactions, and the length of the global execution (number of events). The table presents the results of the meta-analysis of the generated executions; in particular, we report how many inferred executions with minimal serializability violations were found

Table 1. Running Results (K=1000; M=1000000)

Application (LOC)	Threads	Entities	Locks	Events	Trans	Time (s)	Violations WRW	RWR /RWW WWR /WWW
elevator (566)	3	32	8	9K	140	0.09s	0	4
	5	32	8	29K	423	0.27s	0	4
	5	200	50	78K	273	26.23s	8	12
raytracer (1537)	10	1	10	86	10	0.03s	0	90
	20	1	20	160	20	0.02s	0	380
	40	1	40	320	40	0.16s	0	1560
hedc (2165)	10	6	2	176	10	0.03s	20	4
	10	6	2	132	10	0.03s	12	5
tsp (794)	3	30	2	97	5	0.03s	0	0
	8	50	2	18K	10	0.53s	0	0
	5	140	2	1.4M	17	1.55s	16	248
	10	140	2	2.5M	31	2.51s	36	339
	20	1510	2	11M	106	12.58s	171	1609
stack (1400)	2	4	2	105	2	0.07s	0	194
vector (1281)	2	4	2	107	2	0.08s	0	144

for the two classes of patterns (these correspond to possible alternate executions we could schedule in a testing scenario). Note that the cause for the somewhat large number of violations reported for some benchmarks is that a single problem in the program could manifest itself in several inferred violations. For example, one wrongly synchronized method for the class Vector causes many violations, one for each time it is executed in parallel with (almost) every other method in the class.

The executions were obtained using various machines (2-core and 4-core); the analysis of the executions were performed on a 2.16 Ghz Intel Core2 Duo laptop with 2 GB of memory running MacOS 10.5.

Our results clearly illustrate the tremendous impact of using an algorithm that runs in time linear in the length of the execution. There are examples of long executions for the tsp benchmark for which the algorithm finds the violations very quickly. For example, in the setting with 20 threads and more then 11 million events, the algorithm finds 1780 violations in less than 13 seconds. The only exception is elevator with 50 locks. However, we noticed that for this example, the time is almost entirely spent in the compatibility check between two acquisition histories. Unfortunately, the compatibility check is not implemented optimally in the current version of the tool (as we need indexed dictionaries, etc. to do so); we believe that an optimized version of this procedure will considerably speed up our algorithm.

In the case of Java libraries Vector and Stack, the experiments were set to run each pair of the library methods concurrently as two threads. These experiments include many small executions (a few hundred, involving two threads, four entities, and two locks), in which many atomicity violations are found which are actually related to subtle concurrency errors in quite a few of these library methods. The numbers reported in Table 1 represent average values over these executions, while the violations are the *total* number of violations found.

Though checking whether alternate schedules found by the tool are actually feasible in the concrete program is beyond the scope of this paper, preliminary results suggest that many are feasible (e.g. `raytracer` has all schedules feasible, `hedc` has 16/24 and 12/17 schedules feasible).

Acknowledgements. This work was partially funded by NSF CAREER Award CCF 0747041 and by the Universal Parallel Computing Research Center at the University of Illinois at Urbana-Champaign (a center sponsored by Intel Corporation and Microsoft Corporation).

References

1. Chen, F., Serbanuta, T.F., Rosu, G.: Jpredictor: a predictive runtime analysis tool for java. In: ICSE, pp. 221–230 (2008)
2. Farzan, A., Madhusudan, P.: Causal atomicity. In: Ball, T., Jones, R.B. (eds.) CAV 2006. LNCS, vol. 4144, pp. 315–328. Springer, Heidelberg (2006)
3. Farzan, A., Madhusudan, P.: Monitoring atomicity in concurrent programs. In: Gupta, A., Malik, S. (eds.) CAV 2008. LNCS, vol. 5123, pp. 52–65. Springer, Heidelberg (2008)
4. Farzan, A., Madhusudan, P.: The complexity of predicting atomicity violations. In: Kowalewski, S., Philippou, A. (eds.) TACAS 2009. LNCS, vol. 5505, pp. 155–169. Springer, Heidelberg (2009)
5. Flanagan, C., Freund, S.N.: Atomizer: a dynamic atomicity checker for multi-threaded programs. In: POPL, pp. 256–267 (2004)
6. Flanagan, C., Freund, S.N., Yi, J.: Velodrome: a sound and complete dynamic atomicity checker for multithreaded programs. In: PLDI, pp. 293–303 (2008)
7. Flanagan, C., Qadeer, S.: A type and effect system for atomicity. In: PLDI, pp. 338–349 (2003)
8. Hatcliff, J., Robby, Dwyer, M.: Verifying atomicity specifications for concurrent object-oriented software using model-checking. In: Steffen, B., Levi, G. (eds.) VMCAI 2004. LNCS, vol. 2937, pp. 175–190. Springer, Heidelberg (2004)
9. Kahlon, V., Ivancic, F., Gupta, A.: Reasoning about threads communicating via locks. In: Etessami, K., Rajamani, S.K. (eds.) CAV 2005. LNCS, vol. 3576, pp. 505–518. Springer, Heidelberg (2005)
10. Lipton, R.J.: Reduction: a method of proving properties of parallel programs. Commun. ACM 18(12), 717–721 (1975)
11. Lu, S., Park, S., Seo, E., Zhou, Y.: Learning from mistakes: a comprehensive study on real world concurrency bug characteristics. In: Proc. ASPLOS (2008)
12. Papadimitriou, C.: The theory of database concurrency control. Computer Science Press, Inc., New York (1986)
13. Tucek, S.J., Qin, F., Zhou, Y.: Avio: detecting atomicity violations via access interleaving invariants. In: ASPLOS, pp. 37–48 (2006)
14. Sen, K., Rosu, G., Agha, G.: Online efficient predictive safety analysis of multi-threaded programs. STTT 8(3), 248–260 (2006)
15. Java Grande Benchmark Suite, http://www.javagrande.org/
16. von Praun, C., Gross, T.R.: Object race detection. SIGPLAN Not. 36(11), 70–82 (2001)
17. Wang, L., Stoller, S.D.: Accurate and efficient runtime detection of atomicity errors in concurrent programs. In: PPoPP, pp. 137–146 (2006)
18. Wang, L., Stoller, S.D.: Runtime analysis of atomicity for multi-threaded programs. IEEE Transactions on Software Engineering 32, 93–110 (2006)
19. Xu, M., Bodík, R., Hill, M.D.: A serializability violation detector for shared-memory server programs. SIGPLAN Not. 40(6), 1–14 (2005)

An Antichain Algorithm for LTL Realizability[*]

Emmanuel Filiot, Naiyong Jin, and Jean-François Raskin

CS, Faculty of Sciences
Université Libre de Bruxelles (U.L.B.), Belgium

Abstract. In this paper, we study the structure of underlying automata based constructions for solving the LTL realizability and synthesis problem. We show how to reduce the LTL realizability problem to a game with an observer that checks that the game visits a bounded number of times accepting states of a universal co-Büchi word automaton. We show that such an observer can be made deterministic and that this deterministic observer has a nice structure which can be exploited by an incremental algorithm that manipulates antichains of game positions. We have implemented this new algorithm and our first results are very encouraging.

1 Introduction

Automata theory has revealed very elegant for solving verification and synthesis problems. A large body of results in computer aided verification can be phrased and solved in this framework. Tools that use those results have been successfully used in industrial context, see [16] for an example. Nevertheless, there is still plenty of research to do and new theory to develop in order to obtain more efficient algorithms able to handle larger or broader classes of practical examples. Recently, we and other authors have shown in [4,5,6,14,21] that several automata-based constructions enjoy structural properties that can be exploited to improve algorithms on automata. For example, in [6] we show how to solve more efficiently the language inclusion problem for nondeterministic Büchi automata by exploiting a partial-order that exists on the state spaces of subset constructions used to solve this problem. Other structural properties have been additionally exploited in [7]. In this paper, we pursue this line of research and revisit the automata-based approach to LTL realizability and synthesis. Although LTL realizability is 2ExpTime-Complete, we show that there are also automata structures equipped with adequate partial-orders that can be exploited to obtain a more practical decision procedure for it.

The realizability problem for an LTL formula ϕ is best seen as a game between two players [13]. Each of the players is controlling a subset of the set P of propositions on which the LTL formula ϕ is constructed. The set of propositions P is partitioned into I the set of *input signals* that are controlled by "Player input" (the environment, also called Player I), and O the set of *output signals* that are controlled by "Player output"

---

[*] Work supported by the projects: (*i*) Quasimodo: "Quantitative System Properties in Model-Driven-Design of Embedded Systems", http://www.quasimodo.aau.dk, (*ii*) Gasics: "Games for Analysis and Synthesis of Interactive Computational Systems", http://www.ulb.ac.be/di/gasics/, and (*iii*) Moves: "Fundamental Issues in Modelling, Verification and Evolution of Software", http://moves.ulb.ac.be, a PAI program funded by the Federal Belgian Government.

A. Bouajjani and O. Maler (Eds.): CAV 2009, LNCS 5643, pp. 263–277, 2009.

(the controller, also called Player O). The realizability game is played in turns. Player O is the protagonist, she wants to satisfy the formula ϕ, while Player I is the antagonist as he wants to falsify the formula ϕ. Player O starts by giving a subset o_0 of propositions[1], Player I responds by giving a subset of propositions i_0, then Player O gives o_1 and Player I responds by i_1, and so on. This game lasts forever and the outcome of the game is the infinite word $w = (i_0 \cup o_0)(i_1 \cup o_1)(i_2 \cup o_2) \cdots \in (2^P)^\omega$. We say that Player O wins if the resulting infinite word w is a model of ϕ. This problem is central when dealing with specifications for reactive systems. In that context, the signals of the environment being uncontrollable, unrealizable specifications are useless as they can not be implemented. The LTL realizability problem has been studied starting from the end of the eighties with the seminal works by Pnueli and Rosner [13], and Abadi, Lamport and Wolper [1]. The 2EXPTIME lower bound was established in [15].[2]

The classical automata-based solution to LTL synthesis can be summarized as follows. Given an LTL formula ϕ, construct a nondeterministic Büchi automaton A_ϕ that accepts all models of ϕ, transform A_ϕ into a deterministic Rabin automaton B using Safra's determinization procedure [18], and use B as an observer in a turn-based two-player game. Unfortunately, this theoretically elegant procedure has turn out to be very difficult to implement. Indeed, Safra's determinization procedure generates very complex state spaces: states are colored trees of subsets of states of the original automaton. No nice symbolic data-structure is known to handle such state spaces. Moreover, the game to solve as the last step (on a potentially doubly-exponential state-space) is a Rabin game, and this problem is known to be NP complete[3].

This situation has triggered further research for alternative procedures. Most notably, Kupferman and Vardi in [10] have recently proposed procedures that avoid the determinization step and so the Safra's construction[4]. In particular, they reduce the LTL realizability problem to the emptiness of a Universal Co-Büchi Tree automaton (UCT). They show how to test emptiness of a UCT by translation to an alternating weak Büchi tree automaton, again translated into a non-deterministic Büchi tree automaton for which testing emptiness is easy. All these steps have been implemented and optimized in several ways by Jobstmann and Bloem in a tool called Lily [9].

In this paper, we propose a different and more direct Safraless decision procedure for the LTL realizability and synthesis problem and we identify structural properties that allow us to define an antichain algorithm in the line of our previous works. We highlight differences with [10,9] in Section 5. Our procedure uses Universal Co-Büchi Word automaton, UCW. Those automata have the following simple nice property. If a Moore machine M with m states defines a language included into the language defined by a UCW with n states, then obviously every run on the words generated by M contains at most $2mn$ accepting states. As a consequence a Moore machine that enforces a language defined by a UCW also enforces a stronger requirement defined by the same automaton where the acceptance condition is strengthened to a so called $2mn$-bounded one: "a run is accepting if it passes at most $2mn$ times by an accepting state". Using the

---

[1] Technically, we could have started with Player I, for modeling reason it is conservative to start with Player O.

[2] Older works also consider the realizability problem but for more expressive and computationally intractable formalisms, see [20].

[3] Instead of Rabin automata, Parity automata can also be used [12]. Nevertheless, there are no known polynomial time algorithm to solve parity games.

[4] As a consequence, they call their new procedures *Safraless* procedures. Nevertheless they use the result by Safra in their proof of correctness.

result by Safra, we know that the size of a Moore machine that realizes a language defined by a UCW can be bounded. This gives a reduction from the general problem to the problem of the realizability of a k-bounded UCW specification. Contrarily to general UCW specifications, k-bounded UCW specifications can easily be made deterministic and, most importantly the underlying deterministic automaton is always equipped with a partial-order on states that can be used to efficiently manipulate its state space using our antichain method. We have implemented this new antichain algorithm in a tool called Acacia and our experiments show promising results. Indeed, even without further optimizations, Acacia outperforms Lily.

The rest of this paper is organized as follows. In Section 2, we recall definitions. In Section 3, we show how to reduce the LTL realizability problem to the realizability of a k-bounded UCW specification. In Section 4, we show structural properties of the deterministic structure that we obtain from the k-bounded UCW specification and study antichains for manipulating sets of states of this deterministic structure. In Section 5, we report on preliminary experiments using our antichain algorithm for synthesis and compare them to the results obtained by using the tool Lily [9]. In Section 6, we draw conclusions and identify future works.

2   LTL and Realizability Problem

*Linear Temporal Logic (*LTL*).* The formulas of LTL are defined over a set of atomic propositions P. The syntax is given by the grammar:

$$\phi ::= p \mid \phi \vee \phi \mid \neg\phi \mid \mathcal{X}\phi \mid \phi \mathcal{U}\phi \qquad p \in P$$

The notations true, false, $\phi_1 \wedge \phi_2$, $\Diamond\phi$ and $\Box\phi$ are defined as usual. In particular, $\Diamond\phi = \text{true}\,\mathcal{U}\phi$ and $\Box\phi = \neg\Diamond\neg\phi$. LTL formulas ϕ are interpreted on infinite words $w = \sigma_0\sigma_1\sigma_2\cdots \in (2^P)^\omega$ via a satisfaction relation $w \models \phi$ inductively defined as follows: (i) $w \models p$ if $p \in \sigma_0$, (ii) $w \models \phi_1 \vee \phi_2$ if $w \models \phi_1$ or $w \models \phi_2$, (iii) $w \models \neg\phi$ if $w \not\models \phi$, (iv) $w \models \mathcal{X}\phi$ if $\sigma_1\sigma_2\ldots \models \phi$, and (v) $w \models \phi_1\mathcal{U}\phi_2$ if there is $n \geq 0$ such that $\sigma_n\sigma_{n+1}\cdots \models \phi_2$ and for all $0 \leq i < n$, $\sigma_i\sigma_{i+1}\ldots \models \phi_1$.

LTL *Realizability and Synthesis.* As recalled in the introduction, the realizability problem for LTL is best seen as a game between two players. Each of the players is controlling a subset of the set P of propositions on which the LTL formula is constructed. Accordingly, unless otherwise stated, we partition the set of propositions P into I the set of *input signals* that are controlled by "Player input" (the environment, also called Player I), and O the set of *output signals* that are controlled by "Player output" (the controller, also called Player O). It is also useful to associate this partition of P with the three following alphabets: $\Sigma = 2^P$, $\Sigma_I = 2^I$, and $\Sigma_O = 2^O$. We denote by $\varnothing$ the empty set. The realizability game is played in turns. Player O starts by giving a subset o_0 of propositions, Player I responds by giving a subset of propositions i_0, then Player O gives o_1 and Player I responds by i_1, and so on. This game lasts forever and the output of the game is the infinite word $(i_0 \cup o_0)(i_1 \cup o_1)(i_2 \cup o_2)\cdots \in \Sigma^\omega$. The players play according to strategies. A strategy for Player O is a (total) mapping $\lambda_O : (\Sigma_O\Sigma_I)^* \to \Sigma_O$ while a strategy for Player I is a (total) mapping $\lambda_I : \Sigma_O(\Sigma_I\Sigma_O)^* \to \Sigma_I$. The outcome of the strategies λ_O and λ_I is the word $\text{outcome}(\lambda_O, \lambda_I) = (o_0 \cup i_0)(o_1 \cup i_1)\ldots$ such that for all $j \geq 0$, $o_j = \lambda_O(o_0 i_0 \ldots o_{j-1} i_{j-1})$ and $i_j = \lambda_I(o_0 i_0 \ldots o_{j-1} i_{j-1} o_j)$. In particular, $o_0 = \lambda_O(\epsilon)$ and $i_0 = \lambda_I(o_0)$.

We can now define the realizability problem. Given an LTL formula ϕ (the specification), the *realizability problem* is to decide whether there exists a strategy λ_O of Player O such that for all strategies λ_I of Player I, outcome$(\lambda_O, \lambda_I) \models \phi$. If such a strategy exists, we say that the specification ϕ is *realizable*. If an LTL specification is realizable, there exists a finite-state strategy that realizes it [13]. The *synthesis problem* is to find a finite-state strategy that realizes the LTL specification.

E.g., let $I = \{q\}$, $O = \{p\}$ and $\psi = p\,\mathcal{U}q$. The formula ψ is not realizable. As q is controlled by the environment, he can decide to leave it always false and the outcome does not satisfy ϕ. However $\Diamond q \rightarrow (p\mathcal{U}q)$ is realizable. The assumption $\Diamond q$ states that q will hold at some point, and ensures the controller wins if it always asserts p.

Infinite Word Automata. An *infinite word automaton* over the finite alphabet Σ is a tuple $A = (\Sigma, Q, q_0, \alpha, \delta)$ where Q is a finite set of states, $q_0 \in Q$ is the initial state, $\alpha \subseteq Q$ is a set of final states and $\delta \subseteq Q \times \Sigma \times Q$ is a transition relation. For all $q \in Q$ and all $\sigma \in \Sigma$, we let $\delta(q, \sigma) = \{q' \mid (q, \sigma, q') \in \delta\}$. We let $|A| = |Q| + |\delta|$ be the size of A. We say that A is *deterministic* if $\forall q \in Q \cdot \forall \sigma \in \Sigma \cdot |\delta(q, \sigma)| \leq 1$. It is *complete* if $\forall q \in Q \cdot \forall \sigma \in \Sigma \cdot \delta(q, \sigma) \neq \varnothing$. In this paper, unless otherwise stated, the automata are complete. A *run* of A on a word $w = \sigma_0 \sigma_1 \cdots \in \Sigma^\omega$ is an infinite sequence of states $\rho = \rho_0 \rho_1 \cdots \in Q^\omega$ such that $\rho_0 = q_0$ and $\forall i \geq 0 \cdot q_{i+1} \in \delta(q_i, \rho_i)$. We denote by Runs$_A(w)$ the set of runs of A on w. We denote by Visit(ρ, q) the number of times the state q occurs along the run ρ. We consider three acceptance conditions (a.c.) for infinite word automata. A word w is accepted by A if (depending on the a.c.):

Non-deterministic Büchi : $\exists \rho \in$ Runs$_A(w) \cdot \exists q \in \alpha \cdot$ Visit$(\rho, q) = \infty$
Universal Co-Büchi   : $\forall \rho \in$ Runs$_A(w) \cdot \forall q \in \alpha \cdot$ Visit$(\rho, q) < \infty$
Universal K-Co-Büchi : $\forall \rho \in$ Runs$_A(w) \cdot \forall q \in \alpha \cdot$ Visit$(\rho, q) \leq K$

The set of words accepted by A with the non-deterministic Büchi a.c. is denoted by $L_b(A)$, and with this a.c. in mind, we say that A is a non-deterministic Büchi word automaton, NBW for short. Similarly, we denote respectively by $L_{uc}(A)$ and $L_{uc,K}(A)$ the set of words accepted by A with the universal co-Büchi and universal K-co-Büchi a.c. respectively. With those interpretations, we say that A is a universal co-Büchi automaton (UCW) and that (A, K) is a universal K-co-Büchi automaton (UKCW) respectively. By duality, we have clearly $L_b(A) = \overline{L_{uc}(A)}$, for any infinite word automaton A. Finally, note that for any $0 \leq K_1 \leq K_2$, we have that $L_{uc,K_1}(A) \subseteq L_{uc,K_2}(A) \subseteq L_{uc}(A)$.

Infinite automata and LTL. It is well-known (see for instance [19]) that NBWs subsume LTL in the sense that for all LTL formula ϕ, there is an NBW A_ϕ (possibly exponentially larger) such that $L_b(A_\phi) = \{w \mid w \models \phi\}$. Similarly, by duality it is straightforward to associate an equivalent UCW with any LTL formula ϕ: take $A_{\neg\phi}$ with the universal co-Büchi a.c., so $L_{uc}(A_{\neg\phi}) = \overline{L_b(A_{\neg\phi})} = L_b(A_\phi) = \{w \mid w \models \phi\}$.

To reflect the game point of view of the realizability problem, we introduce the notion of turn-based automata to define the specification. A *turn-based automaton* A over the input alphabet Σ_I and the output alphabet Σ_O is a tuple $A = (\Sigma_I, \Sigma_O, Q_I, Q_O, q_0, \alpha, \delta_I, \delta_O)$ where Q_I, Q_O are finite sets of input and output states respectively, $q_0 \in Q_O$ is the initial state, $\alpha \subseteq Q_I \cup Q_O$ is the set of final states, and $\delta_I \subseteq Q_I \times \Sigma_I \times Q_O$, $\delta_O \subseteq Q_O \times \Sigma_O \times Q_I$ are the input and output transition relations respectively. It is *complete* if for all $q_I \in Q_I$, and all $\sigma_I \in \Sigma_I$, $\delta_I(q_I, \sigma_I) \neq \varnothing$, and for all $q_O \in Q_O$ and all $\sigma_O \in \Sigma_O$, $\delta_O(q_O, \sigma_O) \neq \varnothing$. As for usual automata, in this paper we assume that

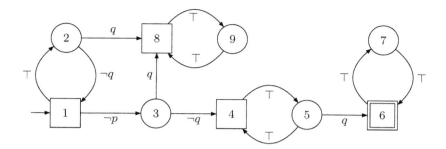

Fig. 1. tbUCW for $\Diamond q \to (p \mathcal{U} q)$ where $I = \{q\}$ and $O = \{p\}$

turn-based automata are always complete. Turn-based automata A still run on words from Σ^ω as follows: a run on a word $w = (o_0 \cup i_0)(o_1 \cup i_1) \cdots \in \Sigma^\omega$ is a word $\rho = \rho_0 \rho_1 \cdots \in (Q_O Q_I)^\omega$ such that $\rho_0 = q_0$ and for all $j \geq 0$, $(\rho_{2j}, o_j, \rho_{2j+1}) \in \delta_O$ and $(\rho_{2j+1}, i_j, \rho_{2j+2}) \in \delta_I$. All the acceptance conditions considered in this paper carry over to turn-based automata. Turn-based automata with acceptance conditions C are denoted by tbC, e.g. tbNBW. Every UCW (resp. NBW) with state set Q and transition set Δ is equivalent to a tbUCW (resp. tbNBW) with $|Q| + |\Delta|$ states: the new set of states is $Q \cup \Delta$, final states remain the same, and each transition $r = q \xrightarrow{\sigma_o \cup \sigma_i} q' \in \Delta$ where $\sigma_o \in \Sigma_O$ and $\sigma_i \in \Sigma_I$ is split into a transition $q \xrightarrow{\sigma_o} r$ and a transition $r \xrightarrow{\sigma_i} q'$.

Moore Machines. LTL realizability is equivalent to LTL realizability by a finite-state strategy [13]. We use Moore machines to represent finite-state strategies. A *Moore machine* M with input alphabet Σ_I and output alphabet Σ_O is a tuple $(\Sigma_I, \Sigma_O, Q_M, q_0, \delta_M, g_M)$ where Q_M is a finite set of states with initial state q_0, $\delta_M : Q_M \times \Sigma_I \to Q_M$ is a (total) transition function, and $g_M : Q \to \Sigma_O$ is a (total) output function. We extend δ_M to $\delta_M^* : \Sigma_I^* \to Q_M$ inductively as follows: $\delta_M^*(\epsilon) = q_0$ and $\delta_M^*(u\sigma) = \delta_M(\delta_M^*(u), \sigma)$. The language of M, denoted by $L(M)$, is the set of words $w = (o_0 \cup i_0)(o_1 \cup i_1) \cdots \in \Sigma_P^\omega$ such that for all $j \geq 0$, $\delta_M^*(i_0 \ldots i_{j-1})$ is defined and $o_j = g_M(\delta_M^*(i_0 \ldots i_{j-1}))$. In particular, $o_0 = g_M(\delta_M^*(\epsilon)) = g_M(q_0)$. The size of a Moore machine is defined similarly as the size of an automaton.

Thanks to previous remarks, the LTL realizability problem reduces to decide, given a tbUCW A over inputs Σ_I and outputs Σ_O, whether there is a non-empty Moore machine M such that $L(M) \subseteq L_{uc}(A)$. In this case we say that A is realizable. In our implementation, the tbUCW is equivalent to an LTL formula given as input and is constructed by using *Wring* [19].

Running example. A tbUCW A equivalent to $\Diamond q \to (p \mathcal{U} q)$ is depicted in Fig. 1. Output states $Q_O = \{1, 4, 6, 8\}$ are depicted by squares and input states $Q_I = \{2, 3, 5, 7, 9\}$ by circles. In the transitions, $\top$ stands for the sets Σ_I or Σ_O, depending on the context, $\neg q$ (resp. $\neg p$) stands for the sets that do not contain q (resp. p), i.e. the empty set. One can see that starting from state 1, if the controller does not assert p and next the environment does not assert q, then the run is in state 4. From this state, whatever the controller does, if the environment asserts q, then the controller loses, as state 6 will be visited infinitely often. A strategy for the controller is to assert p all the time, therefore the runs will loop in states 1 and 2 until the environment asserts q. Afterwards the runs will loop in states 8 and 9, which are non-final.

3   Reduction to a UKCW Objective

In this section, we reduce the realizability problem with a specification given by a turn-based universal co-Büchi automaton (tbUCW) to a specification given by a turn-based universal K-co-Büchi automaton (tbUKCW). Then we reduce this new problem to an infinite turn-based two-player game with a safety winning condition. This is done via an easy determinization of tbUKCWs (which produces a deterministic tbUKCW). To solve this game efficiently, we propose an antichain-based algorithm in Section 4.

Lemma 1. *Let A be a* tbUCW *over inputs Σ_I and outputs Σ_O with n states, and M be a Moore machine over inputs Σ_I and outputs Σ_O with m states. Then $L(M) \subseteq L_{uc}(A)$ iff $L(M) \subseteq L_{uc,2mn}(A)$.*

Proof. The back direction is obvious since $L_{uc,k}(A) \subseteq L_{uc}(A)$ for all $k \in \mathbb{N}$. We sketch the forth direction. Informally, the infinite paths of M starting from the initial state define words that are accepted by A. Therefore in the product of M and A, there is no cycle visiting an accepting state of A, which allows one to bound the number of visited final states by the number of states in the product.   □

The following result is proved in Th. 4.3 of [10], as a small model property of universal co-Büchi tree automata. We also prove it here for the sake of self-containdness.

Lemma 2. *Given a realizable* tbUCW *A over inputs Σ_I and outputs Σ_O with n states, there exists a non-empty Moore machine with at most $n^{2n+2} + 1$ states that realizes it.*

Proof. We sketch the proof. In the first step, we show by using Safra's determinization of NBWs that A is equivalent to a turn-based deterministic and complete parity automaton A^d. By using a result of [12], we can assume that A^d has at most $m := 2n^{2n+2} + 2$ states. We then view A^d has a turn-based two-player parity game $G(A^d)$ (with at most m states) such that A^d (or equivalently A) is realizable iff Player O has a winning strategy in $G(A^d)$. It is known that parity games admit memoryless strategies [8]. Therefore if A^d is realizable, there exists a strategy for Player O in $G(A^d)$ that can be obtained by removing all but one outgoing edge per Player O's state. We can finally transform this strategy into a Moore machine with at most $n^{2n+2} + 1$ states that realizes A^d (and A).□

The following theorem states that we can reduce the realizability of a tbUCW specification to the realizability of a tbUKCW specification.

Theorem 1. *Let A be a* tbUCW *over Σ_I, Σ_O with n states and $K = 2n(n^{2n+2} + 1)$. Then A is realizable iff (A, K) is realizable.*

Proof. If A is realizable, by Lem. 2, there is a non-empty Moore machine M with m states ($m \leq n^{2n+2} + 1$) realizing A. Thus $L(M) \subseteq L_{uc}(A)$ and by Lem. 1, it is equivalent to $L(M) \subseteq L_{uc,2mn}(A)$. We can conclude since $L_{uc,2mn}(A) \subseteq L_{uc,K}(A)$ ($2mn \leq K$). The converse is obvious as $L_{uc,K}(A) \subseteq L_{uc}(A)$.   □

In the first part of this section, we reduced the tbUCW realizability problem to the tbUKCW realizability problem. In the next part, we reduce this new problem to a safety game. It is based on the determinization of tbUKCWs into complete turn-based deterministic 0-Co-Büchi automata, which can also be viewed as safety games.

Safety Game. Turn-based two-player games are played on game arenas by two players, Player I and Player O. A *game arena* is a tuple $G = (S_O, S_I, s_0, T)$ where S_I, S_O are disjoint sets of player states (S_I for Player I and S_O for Player O), $s_0 \in S_O$ is the initial state, and $T \subseteq S_O \times S_I \cup S_I \times S_O$ is the transition relation. A *finite play* on G of length n is a finite word $\pi = \pi_0 \pi_1 \ldots \pi_n \in (S_O \cup S_I)^*$ such that $\pi_0 = s_0$ and for all $i = 0, \ldots, n - 1$, $(\pi_i, \pi_{i+1}) \in T$. Infinite plays are defined similarly. Note that all infinite plays belong to $(S_O S_I)^\omega$. A *winning condition* W is a subset of $(S_O S_I)^\omega$. A play π is won by Player O if $\pi \in W$, otherwise it is won by Player I. A *strategy* λ_i for Player i ($i \in \{I, O\}$) is a mapping that maps any finite play whose last state s is in S_i to a state s' such that $(s, s') \in T$. The *outcome* of a strategy λ_i of Player i is the set $\mathsf{Outcome}_G(\lambda_i)$ of infinite plays $\pi = \pi_0 \pi_1 \pi_2 \cdots \in (S_O S_I)^\omega$ such that for all $j \geq 0$, if $\pi_j \in S_i$, then $\pi_{j+1} = \lambda_i(\pi_0, \ldots, \pi_j)$. We consider the safety winning condition. It is given by a subset of states denoted by safe. A strategy λ_i for Player i is *winning* if $\mathsf{Outcome}_G(\lambda_i) \subseteq \mathsf{safe}^\omega$. We sometimes write $(S_O, S_I, s_0, T, \mathsf{safe})$ to denote the game G with safety condition safe. Finally, a strategy λ_i for Player i is winning in the game G *from a state* $s \in S_O \cup S_I$ if it is winning in (S_O, S_I, s, T).

Determinization of UKCW. Let A be a tbUKCW $(\Sigma_O, \Sigma_I, Q_O, Q_I, q_0, \alpha, \Delta_O, \Delta_I)$ with $K \in \mathbb{N}$. We let $Q = Q_O \cup Q_I$ and $\Delta = \Delta_O \cup \Delta_I$. It is easy to construct an equivalent complete turn-based deterministic 0-co-Büchi automaton $\det(A, K)$. Intuitively, it suffices to extend the usual subset construction with counters, for all $q \in Q$, that count (up to $K + 1$) the maximal number of accepting states which have been visited by runs ending up in q. We set the counter of a state q to -1 when no run on the prefix read so far ends up in q. The final states are the sets in which a state has its counter greater than K. For any $n \in \mathbb{N}$, $[n]$ denotes the set $\{-1, 0, 1, \ldots, n\}$. Formally, we let $\det(A, K) = (\Sigma_O, \Sigma_I, \mathcal{F}_O, \mathcal{F}_I, F_0, \alpha', \delta_O, \delta_I)$ where:

$$
\begin{aligned}
\mathcal{F}_O &= \{F \mid F \text{ is a mapping from } Q_O \text{ to } [K + 1]\} \\
\mathcal{F}_I &= \{F \mid F \text{ is a mapping from } Q_I \text{ to } [K + 1]\} \\
F_0 &= q \in Q_O \mapsto \begin{cases} -1 & \text{if } q \neq q_0 \\ (q_0 \in \alpha) & \text{otherwise} \end{cases} \\
\alpha' &= \{F \in \mathcal{F}_I \cup \mathcal{F}_O \mid \exists q, F(q) > K\} \\
\mathsf{succ}(F, \sigma) &= q \mapsto \max\{\min(K + 1, F(p) + (q \in \alpha)) \mid q \in \Delta(p, \sigma), F(p) \neq -1\} \\
\delta_O &= \mathsf{succ}|_{\mathcal{F}_O \times \Sigma_O} \qquad \delta_I = \mathsf{succ}|_{\mathcal{F}_I \times \Sigma_I}
\end{aligned}
$$

where $\max \emptyset = -1$, and $(q \in \alpha) = 1$ if q is in α, and 0 otherwise. The automaton $\det(A, K)$ has the following properties:

Proposition 1. *Let A be a* tbUCW *and $K \in \mathbb{N}$. Then $\det(A, K)$ is deterministic, complete, and $L_{uc,0}(\det(A, K)) = L_{uc,K}(A)$.*

Reduction to a Safety game. Finally, we define the game $G(A, K)$ as follows: it is $\det(A, K)$ where input states are viewed as Player I's states and output states as Player O's states. Transition labels can be ignored since $\det(A, K)$ is deterministic. Formally, $G(A, K) = (\mathcal{F}_O, \mathcal{F}_I, F_0, T, \mathsf{safe})$ where $\mathsf{safe} = \mathcal{F} \backslash \alpha'$ and $T = \{(F, F') \mid \exists \sigma \in \Sigma_O \cup \Sigma_I, F' = \mathsf{succ}(F, \sigma)\}$. As an obvious consequence of Th. 1 and Prop. 1, we get:.

Theorem 2 (Reduction to a safety game). *Let A be a* tbUCW *over inputs Σ_I and outputs Σ_O with n states ($n > 0$), and let $K = 2n(n^{2n+2} + 1)$. The specification A is realizable iff Player O has a winning strategy in the game $G(A, K)$.*

4   Antichain-Based Symbolic Algorithm

A fixpoint algorithm. In the previous section, we have shown how to reduce the realizability problem to a safety game. Symbolic algorithms for solving safety games are constructed using the so-called controllable predecessor operator, see [8] for details. Let $A = (\Sigma_O, \Sigma_I, Q_O, Q_I, q_0, \alpha, \Delta_O, \Delta_I)$ be a tbUCW with n states, $K = 2n(n^{2n+2}+1)$ and $G(A, K) = (\mathcal{F}_O, \mathcal{F}_I, F_0, T, \text{safe})$ be the two-player turn-based safety game defined in the previous section. Remind that $\Delta = \Delta_O \cup \Delta_I$ and let $\mathcal{F} = \mathcal{F}_O \cup \mathcal{F}_I$. In our case, the controllable predecessor operator is based on the two following monotonic functions over $2^{\mathcal{F}}$:

$$\mathsf{Pre}_I : 2^{\mathcal{F}_O} \to 2^{\mathcal{F}_I}$$
$$S \mapsto \{F \in \mathcal{F}_I \mid \forall F' \in \mathcal{F}_O, (F, F') \in T \implies F' \in S\} \cap \mathsf{safe}$$

$$\mathsf{Pre}_O : 2^{\mathcal{F}_I} \to 2^{\mathcal{F}_O}$$
$$S \mapsto \{F \in \mathcal{F}_O \mid \exists F' \in \mathcal{F}_I, (F, F') \in T\} \cap \mathsf{safe}$$

Let $\mathsf{CPre} = \mathsf{Pre}_O \circ \mathsf{Pre}_I$ (CPre stands for "controllable predecessors"). The function CPre is monotonic over the complete lattice $(2^{\mathcal{F}_O}, \subseteq)$, and so it has a greatest fixed point that we denote by CPre^*.

Theorem 3. *The set of states from which Player O has a winning strategy in $G(A, K)$ is equal to CPre^*.*

In particular, by Th. 2, $F_0 \in \mathsf{CPre}^*$ iff the specification A is realizable. To compute CPre^*, we consider the following $\subseteq$-descending chain: $S_0 = \mathcal{F}$, and for $i \geq 0$ $S_{i+1} = \mathsf{CPre}(S_i) \cap S_i$, until $S_{k+1} = S_k$.

Ordering of game configurations. We define the relation $\preceq \subseteq \mathcal{F}_I \times \mathcal{F}_I \cup \mathcal{F}_O \times \mathcal{F}_O$ by $F \preceq F'$ iff $\forall q, F(q) \leq F'(q)$. It is clear that $\preceq$ is a partial order. Intuitively, if Player O can win from F' then she can also win from all $F \preceq F'$. Formally, $\preceq$ is a game simulation relation in the terminology of [3].

Closed sets and antichains. A set $S \subseteq \mathcal{F}$ is *closed for* $\preceq$, if $\forall F \in S \cdot \forall F' \preceq F \cdot F' \in S$. We usually omit references to $\preceq$ if clear from the context. Let S_1 and S_2 be two closed sets, then $S_1 \cap S_2$ and $S_1 \cup S_2$ are closed. Furthermore, the image of a closed set S by the functions $\mathsf{Pre}_I, \mathsf{Pre}_O$, and CPre are closed sets:

Lemma 3. *For all closed sets $S_1, S_2 \subseteq \mathcal{F}_I$, $S_3 \subseteq \mathcal{F}_O$, the sets $\mathsf{Pre}_O(S_1)$, $\mathsf{CPre}(S_2)$, and $\mathsf{Pre}_I(S_3)$ are closed.*

As a consequence, all the sets manipulated by the symbolic algorithm above are closed sets. We next show how to represent and manipulates those sets efficiently.

The *closure* of a set $S \subseteq \mathcal{F}$, denoted by $\downarrow S$, is the set $S' = \{F' \in \mathcal{F} \mid \exists F \in S \cdot F' \preceq F\}$. Note that for all closed sets $S \subseteq \mathcal{F}$, $\downarrow S = S$. A set $L \subseteq \mathcal{F}$ is an *antichain* if all elements of L are incomparable for $\preceq$. Let $S \subseteq \mathcal{F}$, we denote by $\lceil S \rceil$ the set of maximal elements of S, that is $\lceil S \rceil = \{F \in S \mid \nexists F' \in S \cdot F' \neq F \land F \preceq F'\}$, it is an antichain. If S is closed then $\downarrow \lceil S \rceil = S$, i.e. antichains are *canonical representations* for closed sets. Next, we show that antichains are a compact and efficient representation to manipulate closed sets in $\mathcal{F}$. We start with the algorithms for union, intersection, inclusion and membership. Since the size of a state $F \in \mathcal{F}$ is in practice much smaller than the number of elements in the antichains, we consider that comparing two states is in constant time.

Proposition 2. *Let $L_1, L_2 \subseteq \mathcal{F}$ be two antichains and $F \in \mathcal{F}$, then (i) $\downarrow L_1 \cup \downarrow L_2 = \downarrow \lceil L_1 \cup L_2 \rceil$, this antichain can be computed in time $O((|L_1| + |L_2|)^2)$ and its size is bounded by $|L_1| + |L_2|$, (ii) $\downarrow L_1 \cap \downarrow L_2 = \downarrow \lceil L_1 \sqcap L_2 \rceil$, where $F_1 \sqcap F_2 : q \mapsto \min(F_1(q), F_2(q))$, this antichain can be computed in time $O(|L_1|^2 \times |L_2|^2)$ and its size is bounded by $|L_1| \times |L_2|$, (iii) $\downarrow L_1 \subseteq \downarrow L_2$ iff $\forall F_1 \in L_1 \cdot \exists F_2 \in L_2 \cdot F_1 \preceq F_2$, which can be established in time $O(|L_1| \times |L_2|)$, (iv) $F \in \downarrow L_1$ can be established in time $O(|L_1|)$.*

Let us now turn to the computation of controllable predecessors. Let $F \in \mathcal{F}$, and $\sigma \in \Sigma_I \cup \Sigma_O$. We denote by $\Omega(F, \sigma) \in \mathcal{F}$ the function defined by:

$$\Omega(F, \sigma) : q \in Q \mapsto \min\{\max(-1, F(q') - (q' \in \alpha)) \mid (q, \sigma, q') \in \delta\}$$

Note that since A is complete, the argument of min is a non-empty set. The function Ω is not the inverse of the function succ, as succ has no inverse in general. Indeed, it might be the case that a state $F \in \mathcal{F}$ has no predecessors or has more than one predecessor H such that $\text{succ}(H, \sigma) = F$. However, we prove the following:

Proposition 3. *For all $F, F' \in \mathcal{F} \cap \text{safe}$, and all $\sigma \in \Sigma_I \cup \Sigma_O$,*

(i) $F \preceq F' \implies \Omega(F, \sigma) \preceq \Omega(F', \sigma)$ $\quad(iii)$ $F \preceq \Omega(\text{succ}(F, \sigma), \sigma)$
(ii) $F \preceq F' \implies \text{succ}(F, \sigma) \preceq \text{succ}(F', \sigma)$ $\quad(iv)$ $\text{succ}(\Omega(F, \sigma), \sigma) \preceq F$

For all $S \subseteq \mathcal{F}$ and $\sigma \in \Sigma_I \cup \Sigma_O$, we denote by $\text{Pre}(S, \sigma) = \{F \mid \text{succ}(F, \sigma) \in S\}$ the set of predecessors of S. The set of predecessors of a closed set $\downarrow F$ is closed and has a unique maximal element $\Omega(F, \sigma)$:

Lemma 4. *For all $F \in \mathcal{F} \cap \text{safe}$ and $\sigma \in \Sigma_I \cup \Sigma_O$, $\text{Pre}(\downarrow F, \sigma) = \downarrow \Omega(F, \sigma)$.*

Proof. Let $H \in \text{Pre}(\downarrow F, \sigma)$. Hence $\text{succ}(H, \sigma) \preceq F$. By Prop. $3(i)$, we have $\Omega(\text{succ}(H, \sigma), \sigma) \preceq \Omega(F, \sigma)$, from which we get $H \preceq \Omega(F, \sigma)$, by Prop. $3(iii)$. Conversely, let $H \preceq \Omega(F, \sigma)$. By Prop. $3(ii)$, $\text{succ}(H, \sigma) \preceq \text{succ}(\Omega(F, \sigma), \sigma)$. Since by Prop. $3(iv)$, $\text{succ}(\Omega(F, \sigma), \sigma) \preceq F$, we get $\text{succ}(H, \sigma) \preceq F$. $\qquad\square$

We can now use the previous result to compute the controllable predecessors:

Proposition 4. *Let A be a tbUKCW. Given two antichains L_1, L_2 such that $L_1 \subseteq \mathcal{F}_I \cap \text{safe}$ and $L_2 \subseteq \mathcal{F}_O \cap \text{safe}$:*

$$\text{Pre}_O(\downarrow L_1) = \bigcup\nolimits_{\sigma \in \Sigma_O} \text{Pre}(\downarrow L_1, \sigma) = \bigcup\nolimits_{\sigma \in \Sigma_O} \downarrow\{\Omega(F, \sigma) \mid F \in L_1\}$$
$$\text{Pre}_I(\downarrow L_2) = \bigcap\nolimits_{\sigma \in \Sigma_I} \text{Pre}(\downarrow L_2, \sigma) = \bigcap\nolimits_{\sigma \in \Sigma_I} \downarrow\{\Omega(F, \sigma) \mid F \in L_2\}$$

$\text{Pre}_O(\downarrow L_1)$ can be computed in time $O(|\Sigma_O| \times |A| \times |L_1|)$, and $\text{Pre}_I(\downarrow L_2)$ can be computed in time $O((|A| \times |L_2|)^{|\Sigma_I|})$.

As stated in the previous proposition, the complexity of our algorithm for computing the Pre_I is worst-case exponential. We establish as a corollary of the next proposition that this is unavoidable unless $P=NP$. Given a graph $G = (V, E)$, a set of vertices W is independent iff no pairs of elements in W are linked by an edge in E. We denote by $\text{IND}(G) = \{W \subseteq V \mid \forall \{v, v'\} \in E \cdot v \notin W \vee v' \notin W\}$ the set of independent sets in G. The problem "independent set" asks given a graph $G = (V, E)$ and an integer $0 \le k \le |V|$, if there exists an independent set in G of size larger than k. It is known to be NP-complete.

Proposition 5. *Given a graph* $G = (V, E)$, *we can construct in deterministic polynomial time a* UKCW A, *with* $K = 0$, *and an antichain* L *such that* $\mathsf{IND}(G) = \downarrow$ $\mathsf{Pre}_I(\mathsf{Pre}_O(\mathsf{Pre}_O((L))))$.

Corollary 1. *There is no polynomial time algorithm to compute the* Pre_I *operation on antichains unless* $P = NP$.

Note that this negative result is not a weakness of antichains. Indeed, it is easy to see from the proofs of those results that any algorithm based on a data structure that is able to represent compactly the set of subsets of a given set has this property.

Incremental Algorithm. In practice, for checking the existence of a winning strategy for Player O in the safety game, we rely on an incremental approach. We use the following property of UKCWs: for all $K_1, K_2 \cdot 0 \leq K_1 \leq K_2 \cdot L_{uc,L_1}(A) \subseteq L_{uc,K_2}(A) \subseteq L_{uc}(A)$. So, the following theorem which is a direct consequence of the previous property allows us to test the existence of strategies for increasing values of K:

Theorem 4. *For all* tbUCWs A, *for all* $K \geq 0$, *if Player* O *has a winning strategy in the game* $G(A, K)$ *then the specification defined by* A *is realizable.*

Unrealizable Specifications. The incremental algorithm is not reasonable to test unrealizability. Indeed, with this algorithm it is necessary to reach the bound $2n(n^{2n+2} + 1)$ to conclude for unrealizability. To obtain a more practical algorithm, we rely on the determinacy of ω-regular games (a corollary of the general result by Martin [11]).

Theorem 5. *For all* LTL *formulas* ϕ, *either* (i) *there exists a Player* O's *strategy* λ_O *s.t. for all Player* I's *strategies* λ_I, $\mathsf{outcome}(\lambda_O, \lambda_I) \models \phi$, *or there exists a Player* I's *strategy* λ_I *s.t. for all Player* O's *strategies* λ_O, $\mathsf{outcome}(\lambda_O, \lambda_I) \models \neg\phi$.

So, when an LTL specification ϕ is not realizable for Player O, it means that $\neg\phi$ is realizable for Player I. To avoid in practice the enumeration of values for K up to $2n(n^{2n+2} + 1)$, we propose the following algorithm. First, given the LTL formula ϕ, we construct two UCWs: one that accepts all the models of ϕ, denoted by A_ϕ, and one that accepts all the models of $\neg\phi$, denoted by $A_{\neg\phi}$. Then we check realizability by Player O of ϕ, and in parallel realizability by Player I of $\neg\phi$, incrementing the value of K. When one of the two processes stops, we know if ϕ is realizable or not. In practice, we will see that either ϕ is realizable for Player O for a small value of K or $\neg\phi$ is realizable for Player I for a small value of K.

Synthesis. If a UCW A is realizable, it is easy to extract from the greatest fixpoint computation a Moore machine that realizes it. Let $\Pi_I \subseteq \mathcal{F}_I \cap \mathsf{safe}$ and $\Pi_O \subseteq \mathcal{F}_O \cap \mathsf{safe}$ be the two sets obtained by the greatest fixpoint computation. In particular, Π_I and Π_O are downward-closed and $\mathsf{Pre}_O(\Pi_I) = \Pi_O$, $\mathsf{Pre}_I(\Pi_O) = \Pi_I$. By definition of Pre_O, for all $F \in \lceil\Pi_O\rceil$, there exists $\sigma_F \in \Sigma$ such that $\mathsf{succ}(F, \sigma_F) \in \Pi_I$, and this σ_F can be computed. From this we can extract a Moore machine whose set of states is $\lceil\Pi_O\rceil$, the output function maps any state $F \in \lceil\Pi_O\rceil$ to σ_F, and the transition function, when reading some $\sigma \in \Sigma_I$, maps F to a state $F' \in \lceil\Pi_O\rceil$ such that $\mathsf{succ}(\mathsf{succ}(F, \sigma_F), \sigma) \preceq F'$ (it exists by definition of the fixpoint and by monotonicity of succ). The initial state is some state $F \in \lceil\Pi_O\rceil$ such that $F_0 \preceq F$ (it exists if the specification is realizable). Let M be this Moore machine. For any word w accepted by M, it is clear that w is also accepted by $\det(A, K)$, as succ is monotonic and $\Pi_O \subseteq \mathsf{safe}$. Therefore $L(M) \subseteq L_{uc,0}(\det(A, K)) = L_{uc,K}(A) \subseteq L_{uc}(A)$.

Example. We apply the antichain algorithm on the tbUCW depicted in Fig. 1, with $K = 1$. Remember that $I = \{q\}$ and $O = \{p\}$, so that $\Sigma_I = \{\varnothing, \{q\}\}$ and $\Sigma_O = \{\varnothing, \{p\}\}$. For space reasons, we cannot give the whole fixpoint computation. We starts with the safe state in $G(A, K)$ for Player O, i.e. the constant function from Q_O to 1 denoted by $F_1 = (1 \mapsto 1, 4 \mapsto 1, 6 \mapsto 1, 8 \mapsto 1)$. It represents the set $\downarrow F_1$. Then we compute $\lceil \mathsf{Pre}_I(\downarrow F_1) \rceil \cap \mathsf{safe} = \lceil \downarrow$

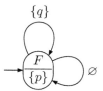

Fig. 2. Moore machine

$\Omega(F_1, \{q\}) \cap \downarrow \Omega(F_1, \varnothing) \rceil \cap \mathsf{safe}$. We have $\Omega(F_1, \{q\}) = (2 \mapsto 1, 3 \mapsto 1, 5 \mapsto 0, 7 \mapsto 0, 9 \mapsto 1)$ and $\Omega(F_1, \varnothing) = (2 \mapsto 1, 3 \mapsto 1, 5 \mapsto 1, 7 \mapsto 0, 9 \mapsto 1)$. Therefore $\lceil \mathsf{Pre}_I(\downarrow F_1) \rceil = \{F_2 := (2 \mapsto 1, 3 \mapsto 1, 5 \mapsto 0, 7 \mapsto 0, 9 \mapsto 1)\}$. Then we have $\Omega(F_2, \{p\}) = \Omega(F_2, \varnothing) = (1 \mapsto 1, 4 \mapsto 0, 6 \mapsto 0, 8 \mapsto 1)$. Therefore $\lceil \mathsf{Pre}_O(\downarrow F_2) \rceil \cap \mathsf{safe} = \lceil \mathsf{CPre}(\{F_1\}) \rceil \cap \mathsf{safe} = \{(1 \mapsto 1, 4 \mapsto 0, 6 \mapsto 0, 8 \mapsto 1)\}$. At the end of the computation, we get the fixpoint $\downarrow \{F := (1 \mapsto 1, 4 \mapsto -1, 6 \mapsto -1, 8 \mapsto 1)\}$. Since the initial state F_0 is in $\downarrow F$, Player O has a winning strategy and the formula is realizable. Fig. 2 shows a Moore machine obtained from the fixpoint computation.

5   Performance Evaluation

In this section, we briefly present our implementation Acacia and compare it to Lily [9]. More information can be found online [2]. Acacia is a prototype implementation of our antichain algorithm for LTL realizability and synthesis. To achieve a fair comparison, Acacia is written in Perl as Lily. Given an LTL formula and a partition of its propositions into inputs and outputs, Acacia tests realizability of the formula. If it is realizable, it outputs a Moore machine representing a winning strategy for the output player[5], otherwise it outputs a winning strategy for the input player. As Lily, Acacia runs in two steps. The first step builds a tbUCW for the formula, and the second step checks realizability of the automaton. As Lily, we borrow the LTL-to-tbUCW construction procedure from *Wring* [19] and adopt the automaton optimizations from Lily, so that we can exclude the influence of automata construction to the performance comparison between Acacia and Lily[6].

We carried out experiments on a Linux platform with a 2.1GHz CPU and 2GB of memory. We compared Acacia and Lily on the test suite included in Lily, and on other examples derived from Lily's examples, as detailed in the sequel. As shown in the previous section (Th. 5), realizability or unrealizability tests are slightly different, as we test unrealizability by testing the realizability by the environment of the negation of the specification. In the experiments, depending on whether the formula is realizable or not, we only report the results for the realizability or unrealizability tests. In practice, those two tests should be run in parallel.

Results. Tables 1 and 2 report on the results of the tests for unrealizable and realizable examples respectively. In those tables, **Column *formula size*** gives the size of the

---

[5] Note that the correctness of this Moore machine can be automatically verified by model-checking tools if desired.

[6] In Lily, this first step produces universal co-Büchi tree automata over Σ_O-labeled Σ_I-trees, which can easily be seen as tbUCWs over inputs Σ_I and outputs Σ_O. Although the two models are close, we introduced tbUCWs for the sake of clarity (as all our developments are done on construction for word automata).

Table 1. Performance comparison for unrealizability test

		Lily			Acacia					
	formula size	tbUCW St./Tr.	tbUCW Time(s)	Check Time(s)	tbUCW St./Tr.	tbUCW Time(s)	K	No. Iter.	max{|Pre$_I$|}/ max{|Pre$_O$|}	Check Time(s)
1	28	∅	0.17	0.01	6/27	0.24	1	1	1/1	0.00
2	28	∅	0.17	0.01	18/101	1.89	3	6	1/1	0.05
4	38	18/56	3.53	1.13	23/121	3.16	2	8	3/4	0.14
11	12	∅	1.32	0.04	3/10	0.07	0	1	1/1	0.00
22.1	24	5/9	0.18	0.09	22/126	4.97	1	5	2/2	0.05
22.2	23	4/14	0.32	0.11	23/126	4.85	1	4	1/1	0.04
22.3	29	5/15	0.36	0.11	23/130	6.25	1	5	2/2	0.06
22.4	37	6/34	2.48	0.18	26/137	6.47	1	10	12/10	0.38

formulas (number of atomic propositions and connectives). **Column tbUCW *St./Tr.*** gives the number of states and transitions of the tbUCWs transformed from LTL formula. One may encounter ∅ when Lily's tbUCW optimization procedure concludes the language emptiness of the tbUCW. **Column tbUCW *Time(s)*** gives the time (in seconds) spent on building up the tbUCWs. For realizability tests, Lily and Acacia construct the same tbUCW, while for unrealizability tests, they are different (as shown in Section 4, we use the tbUCW corresponding to the negation of the formula). **Column *Rank*** gives the maximal rank used by Lily when trying to transform the tbUCW to an alternating weak tree automaton. *Rank* is a complexity measure for Lily. **Column *Check Time(s)*** gives the time (in seconds) spent in realizability checking. If the language of a tbUCW is proved to be empty during the optimization stage, Lily will directly conclude for unrealizability. **Column *K*** reports the minimal K for which Acacia was able to conclude realizability of the tbUKCW. Usually, K is small for realizable specifications. **Column *No. Iter.*** gives the number of iterations to compute the fixpoint. **Column** $max\{|Pre_I|\}/max\{|Pre_O|\}$ reports on the maximal sizes of the antichains obtained during the fixpoint computation when applying Pre$_I$ and Pre$_O$ respectively.

Comments. Lily's test suite includes examples 1 to 23. Except examples 1, 2, 4, and 11, they are all realizable. Table 2 shows, except demo 16, Acacia performs much better than Lily in realizability tests. For unrealizability tests, if we do not take into account the time for tbUCW construction, Acacia performs better as well. In the test suite, demo 3 describes a scheduler. We have taken a scalability test by introducing more clients. In Table 2, from 3.4 to 3.6, when the number of clients reached 4, Lily ran over-time (> 3600 seconds). However, Acacia managed in finishing the check within the time bound. One can weaken/strengthen a specification by removing/appending environment assumptions and controller assertions. We have carried out a diagnostic test based on demo 22. In the test cases from 22.3 to 22.9, the environment assumptions are getting stronger and stronger. The specifications turn out to be realizable after the case 22.5. A controller with a stronger environment shall be easier to realize. The data in Table 2, from 22.5 to 22.9, confirm this. For unrealizability check, in Table 1 from 22.1 to 22.4, both tools spent more time on case 22.4 than on case 22.3. However, Acacia turns out to be better for *Check Time*. Finally, we can see that the bottleneck for examples 22.1 to 22.9, as well as for examples 20 to 22, is the time spent to construct the automaton. With regards to this concern, the improvement in time complexity compared to Lily is less impressive. However, it was not expected that this first step of the algorithm (constructing the NBW for the LTL formula) would have been the bottleneck

Table 2. Performance comparison for realizability test

		Lily			Acacia			
	formula size	tbUCW St./Tr.	tbUCW Time(s)	Rank	Check Time(s)	K Iter.	No.	max{|Pre$_O$|}/ max{|Pre$_I$|}	Check Time(s)
3	34	10/28	0.97	1	0.30	0	2	2/2	0.00
5	44	13/47	1.53	1	0.65	0	2	2/2	0.01
6	49	19/63	3.19	1	0.91	0	3	3/3	0.03
7	50	11/34	1.42	1	0.31	0	2	2/2	0.01
8	7	3/6	0.07	1	0.02	0	1	1/1	0.00
9	22	5/10	0.33	1	0.03	1	6	3/2	0.01
10	13	7/21	0.63	1	0.10	0	1	1/1	0.00
12	14	8/26	0.35	1	0.07	0	1	1/1	0.00
13	11	3/4	0.02	1	0.01	1	3	2/1	0.00
14	21	5/13	0.26	1	0.07	1	4	3/3	0.01
15	31	6/16	0.24	1	0.11	2	9	9/13	0.08
16	56	8/26	0.57	1	1.45	3	16	64/104	7.89
17	37	6/20	0.40	1	0.31	2	12	8/7	0.10
18	63	8/31	0.92	1	2.35	2	12	19/19	0.89
19	32	7/17	0.75	3	4.05	2	12	5/5	0.03
20	72	25/198	7.03	1	0.99	0	3	1/1	0.04
21	119	13/72	15.61	1	1.88	0	4	25/13	0.40
22	62	19/115	25.28	1	1.21	1	7	4/7	0.10
23	19	7/12	0.47	1	0.04	2	2	2/1	0.00
3.1	34	10/28	1.09	1	0.31	0	2	2/2	0.01
3.2	63	18/80	2.60	1	7.70	0	2	4/4	0.07
3.3	92	26/200	2.60	1	554.99	0	2	8/8	0.65
3.4	121	34/480	7.59	-	> 3600	0	2	16/16	8.46
3.5	150	42/1128	12.46	-	> 3600	0	2	32/32	138.18
3.6	179	50/2608	22.76	-	> 3600	1	2	64/64	2080.63
22.5	41	7/38	4.17	1	0.50	2	19	4/6	0.12
22.6	62	19/115	21.20	1	1.52	1	7	4/7	0.11
22.7	56	13/75	7.51	1	0.73	1	6	3/4	0.05
22.8	51	10/50	3.82	1	0.43	1	5	2/3	0.03
22.9	47	7/29	1.46	1	0.33	1	5	2/3	0.02

of the approach. Indeed, the problem is 2EXPTIME-COMPLETE, while the automata construction is in EXPTIME, and in [13], the forseen bottleneck is clearly the second step that relies on Safra's determinization.

As a conclusion, the experiments show that the antichain algorithm is a very promising approach to LTL synthesis. Although the formulas are still rather small, the results validate the relevance of the method. Indeed, without any further optimization, the results outperform Lily. We think that our algorithm is a step towards the realization of a tool that can handle specifications of practical interest.

Comparison with Kupferman-Vardi's Approach (implemented in Lily*).* In [10], the authors give a Safraless procedure for LTL synthesis. It is a three steps algorithm: (i) transform an LTL formula into a universal co-Büchi tree automaton (UCT) A that accepts the winning strategies of the controller, (ii) transform A into an alternating weak tree automaton B (AWT) such that $L(B) \neq \varnothing$ iff $L(A) \neq \varnothing$, (iii) transform B into an equivalent Büchi tree automaton C (NBT) and test its emptiness. This latter problem can be seen as solving a game with a Büchi objective. This approach differs from our approach in the following points. First, in [10], the author somehow reduce the realizability problem to a game with a *Büchi objective*, while our approach reduces it to a game with a *safety objective*. Second, our approach allows one to define a natural partial order on states that can be exploited by an antichain algorithm, which is not obvious in the approach of [10]. Finally, in [10], states of AWT are equipped with unique ranks that partition the set of states into layers. States which share the same rank are either all accepting or all non-accepting. The transition function allows one to stay in the same layer or to go in a layer with lower rank. A run is accepting if it gets stuck in a non-accepting layer. While our notion of counters looks similar to ranks, it is different. Indeed, the notion of rank does not constraint the runs to visit accepting states a bounded number of times (bounded by a constant). This is why a Büchi acceptance condition is needed, while counting the number of visited accepting states allows us to define a safety acceptance condition. However, we conjecture that when our approach concludes for realizability with bound k, the algorithm of [10] can conclude for realizability with a maximal rank linearly bounded by k. The converse is not true, we can define a class of examples where the maximal rank needed by [10] is 1 while our approach necessarily needs to visit at least an exponential number of accepting states. This is because the ranks does not count the number of accepting states, but counts somehow the number of finite sequences of accepting states of a certain type. We think that it is an interesting question for future research to see how the two methods can benefit from each other, and to formally prove the conjecture above.

6   Summary

This paper described a novel Safraless approach to LTL realizability and synthesis, based on universal K-Co-Büchi word automata. These automata can be easily determinized, and enjoy a structure that allowed us to define an antichain algorithm for LTL realizability, implemented in the tool Acacia. The results are very promising, as Acacia outperforms the existing tool Lily without any further optimizations (apart from antichains) while Lily uses clever optimizations to make the Vardi and Kupferman algorithm practical. Note that our approach also applies to any logic which can be translated into a UCW, and in particular, any logic closed by negation which can be translated into an NBW[7].

We plan to optimize Acacia in several ways. First, as the construction of the nondeterministic automaton from the LTL formula is currently the bottleneck of our approach, we would like to translate LTL formulas (in linear time) into alternating word automata, and then to UCW by applying the Miyano-Hayashi (MH) construction [17] implicitly as in [6,21]. The difficulty here is to find an adequate symbolic representation of counting functions for the implicit MH state space. Second, we would like to study how a compositional approach to realizability could apply to specifications which are large conjunctions of (small) sub-specifications.

Acknowledgments. We are grateful to the referees for their valuable comments and we warmly thank Laurent Doyen for his helpful remarks.

---

[7] Note also that any ω-regular specification can be expressed as a UCW, as a consequence our method is applicable to all such objective.

References

1. Abadi, M., Lamport, L., Wolper, P.: Realizable and unrealizable specifications of reactive systems. In: Ausiello, G., Dezani-Ciancaglini, M., Ronchi Della Rocca, S. (eds.) ICALP 1989. LNCS, vol. 372, pp. 1–17. Springer, Heidelberg (1989)
2. Acacia (2009), http://www.antichains.be
3. Alur, R., Henzinger, T.A., Kupferman, O., Vardi, M.Y.: Alternating refinement relations. In: Sangiorgi, D., de Simone, R. (eds.) CONCUR 1998. LNCS, vol. 1466, pp. 163–178. Springer, Heidelberg (1998)
4. Bouajjani, A., Habermehl, P., Holík, L., Touili, T., Vojnar, T.: Antichain-based universality and inclusion testing over nondeterministic finite tree automata. In: CIAA, pp. 57–67 (2008)
5. De Wulf, M., Doyen, L., Henzinger, T.A., Raskin, J.-F.: Antichains: A new algorithm for checking universality of finite automata. In: Ball, T., Jones, R.B. (eds.) CAV 2006. LNCS, vol. 4144, pp. 17–30. Springer, Heidelberg (2006)
6. Doyen, L., Raskin, J.-F.: Improved algorithms for the automata-based approach to model-checking. In: Grumberg, O., Huth, M. (eds.) TACAS 2007. LNCS, vol. 4424, pp. 451–465. Springer, Heidelberg (2007)
7. Fogarty, S., Vardi, M.: Buechi complementation and size-change termination. In: Kowalewski, S., Philippou, A. (eds.) TACAS 2009. LNCS, vol. 5505, pp. 16–30. Springer, Heidelberg (2009)
8. Grädel, E., Thomas, W., Wilke, T. (eds.): Automata, Logics, and Infinite Games. LNCS, vol. 2500. Springer, Heidelberg (2002)
9. Jobstmann, B., Bloem, R.: Optimizations for LTL synthesis. In: FMCAD, pp. 117–124. IEEE Computer Society, Los Alamitos (2006)
10. Kupferman, O., Vardi, M.Y.: Safraless decision procedures. In: FOCS: IEEE Symposium on Foundations of Computer Science (FOCS) (2005)
11. Martin, D.: Borel determinacy. Annals of Mathematics 102, 363–371 (1975)
12. Piterman, N.: From nondeterministic büchi and streett automata to deterministic parity automata. Logical Methods in Computer Science 3(3) (2007)
13. Pnueli, A., Rosner, R.: On the synthesis of a reactive module. In: ACM Symposium on Principles of Programming Languages (POPL). ACM, New York (1989)
14. Raskin, J.-F., Chatterjee, K., Doyen, L., Henzinger, T.A.: Algorithms for omega-regular games with imperfect information. Logical Methods in Computer Science 3(3) (2007)
15. Rosner, R.: Modular synthesis of reactive systems. Ph.d. dissertation, Weizmann Institute of Science (1992)
16. Ruys, T.C., Holzmann, G.J.: Advanced SPIN Tutorial. In: Graf, S., Mounier, L. (eds.) SPIN 2004. LNCS, vol. 2989, pp. 304–305. Springer, Heidelberg (2004)
17. Miyano, S., Hayashi, T.: Alternating automata on ω-words. Theoretical Computer Science 32, 321–330 (1984)
18. Safra, S.: On the complexity of ω automata. In: FOCS, pp. 319–327 (1988)
19. Somenzi, F., Bloem, R.: Efficient büchi automata from LTL formulae. In: Emerson, E.A., Sistla, A.P. (eds.) CAV 2000. LNCS, vol. 1855. Springer, Heidelberg (2000)
20. Thomas, W.: Church's problem and a tour through automata theory. In: Avron, A., Dershowitz, N., Rabinovich, A. (eds.) Pillars of Computer Science. LNCS, vol. 4800, pp. 635–655. Springer, Heidelberg (2008)
21. De Wulf, M., Doyen, L., Maquet, N., Raskin, J.-F.: Antichains: Alternative algorithms for LTL satisfiability and model-checking. In: Ramakrishnan, C.R., Rehof, J. (eds.) TACAS 2008. LNCS, vol. 4963, pp. 63–77. Springer, Heidelberg (2008)

On Extending Bounded Proofs to Inductive Proofs

Oded Fuhrmann and Shlomo Hoory

IBM Haifa Research Lab
{odedf,shlomoh}@il.ibm.com

Abstract. We propose a method for extending a bounded resolution proof to an unbounded inductive proof. More specifically, given a resolution proof that a state machine beginning at an initial state satisfies some property at cycle k, we show that the existence of a Δ-invariant cut implies that the property holds for cycles $k+\Delta$, $k+2\Delta$, etc. We suggest a linear algorithm for identifying such Δ-extendible proofs and develop the required theory for covering all cycles by Δ-extendible proofs. To expose Δ-invariant cuts, we develop an efficient proof manipulation algorithm that rearranges the proof by the natural temporal order. We demonstrate the applicability of our techniques on a few real-life examples.

Keywords: Formal verification, resolution proofs, extending proofs, proof simplification.

1 Introduction

One of the main focal points of formal verification is proving bounded and unbounded safety properties. Namely, given a non-deterministic finite state machine, one would like to know whether all states reachable from an initial state set I comply with a specifying property S. The bounded problem asks if the above holds for a specific cycle k, while the unbounded problem asks if the property holds for all non-negative values of k. An efficient algorithm to either problem seems hopeless, since the problems are NP-complete and PSPACE-complete, respectively [SC85].

The safety problem has attracted a significant amount of research due to its practical importance. The common state-of-the-art technology for solving this problem is based on an invocation of a DPLL-based SAT solver. Various SAT-based approaches have been suggested over the last decade, such as SAT-based BMC [BCCZ99], k-induction [SSS00], interpolation [McM03], and proof-based abstraction refinement [LWS03]. These solutions utilize the fact that, given a SAT query, any modern solver returns either a satisfying assignment or a resolution-based refutation that no such assignment exists (see [ZM03b]).

In this work, we propose a method for extending the proof that a property holds at cycle k to an infinite number of cycles[1]. The method consists of an

---

[1] An interesting reference in this context is [SK97] in which a method for sequential equivalence based on unwinding of the circuit combined with learning is presented.

A. Bouajjani and O. Maler (Eds.): CAV 2009, LNCS 5643, pp. 278–290, 2009.

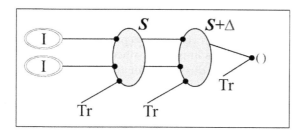

Fig. 1. Δ-extendible proof: The gray Δ-invariant cut separates the root from the encircled Init axioms and is sufficient to prove its Δ shift, possibly using Transition Relation Axioms

efficient algorithm that can be added on top of a standard BMC platform, as an extra post-processing stage for the generated proofs. When successful, our algorithm declares that the proof for the property at cycle k is Δ-extendible, implying the property at cycles $k + i\Delta$, for all positive integers i.

A proof is Δ-extendible if it contains a Δ-invariant cut. That is, a set of proof nodes S that separates the Init axioms from the consequence of the proof, and that implies its forward shift by Δ cycles. This is demonstrated in Figure 1. One should note that $\Delta = 1$ implies that the property holds for all cycles starting at k. However, the problem of covering all cycles when $\Delta > 1$ requires careful treatment.

We mention, for the reader acquainted with Interpolation Theory [McM03] that the Δ-invariant cut defined above is an interpolant. This is implied by the fact that it partitions the proof into two disjoint sets of clauses (A, B), where A includes the cut. This special interpolant, in conjunction with transition relation constraints, implies the same interpolant shifted Δ cycles. The interested reader is referred to [FH09] for an example of a Δ-extendible proof where the classical interpolant computation [McM03] leads to a spurious solution.

As might be expected, looking for a Δ-invariant cut in a messy computer generated proof is rather naive. We suggest an algorithm for preprocessing the proof to reveal Δ-invariant cuts. The algorithm consists of two components. The novel component reorders the proof by increasing cycle number from its axioms to the final consequent clause. The second component is the double pivot simplification, which was introduced in [BIFH$^+$08]. Such an algorithm may be of interest in its own right for any other application using resolution proofs, such as building better interpolants [JM05] and minimizing resolution proofs [GKS08, ZM03a]. We emphasize that both preprocessing components, as well as the detection of Δ-extendible cuts are efficient in that they amount to a linear pass of the proof, though their success is not guaranteed.

The experimental results of this work include a few examples taken from the IBM internal benchmark suite. Starting with the smallest benchmark problems, our technique solved the first three problems, but failed on the fourth. For each example, our algorithm was given a sequence of SAT solver generated proofs, where the k'th proof implied the property at cycle k. For the first three examples, our algorithm deduced the property for all k, where two extensions had $\Delta = 2$, which amounted to covering the even and odd values of k by two separate proofs. In all successful examples preprocessing was paramount. Reporting the negative result for the fourth example is important since it exposes the weak sides of our method and points to possible directions for future research.

The rest of the paper is organized as follows: In Section 2, we give an example for our method and introduce the necessary notation. In Section 3, we show how to extend proofs by Δ-invariant cuts, present an algorithm for finding such a cut, and discuss the problem of covering all cycles when $\Delta > 1$. In Section 4, we present the proof reorder algorithm. Section 5 deals with the experimental results, and Section 6 concludes.

2   A Motivating Example, and Some Notation

2.1   Preliminaries and Notations

A literal is a Boolean variable or its negation, and a clause is a set of literals. We say that a clause is satisfied if at least one of its literals is assigned true. Given two clauses c_1, c_2 and a variable p s.t. $p \in c_1$ and $-p \in c_2$ their resolution is defined as $res_p(c_1, c_2) := (c_1 \cup c_2) \setminus \{p, -p\}$ and the variable p is called the resolution pivot. A proof $\mathcal{P}(A, R)$ is a directed acyclic graph on the nodes $A \cup R$ corresponding to axioms and resolution nodes. An *axiom node* $n \in A$ holds a clause field $n.C$. A *resolution node* $n \in R$ holds the clause field $n.C$, two references to other nodes $n.L, n.R$, and the pivot literal $n.Piv$. The edges of the dag are $(n.L, n)$ and $(n.R, n)$ for all $n \in R$. The fields $n.C$ and $n.Piv$ are defined so that $n.C = res_{n.Piv}(n.L.C, n.R.C)$ for all $n \in R$. We use the notation $S_1 \vdash_{\mathcal{P}} S_2$ when the proof $\mathcal{P}(A, R)$ with $A \subseteq S_1$ proves a set of clauses $S_2 \subseteq \{n.C \text{ for } n \in A \cup R\}$. If S_2 consists of a single clause, we call it the consequence of $\mathcal{P}$ and the node of the clause the root, $root(\mathcal{P})$.[2]

We assume that the finite state machine has an n bit state $(v_1, \ldots, v_n)$, where v_i is a binary state signal and v_i^j represents the state signal v_i at cycle j. The set $\{v_i^j\}_{i,j}$ is the problem variables. The cycle shift operator $(\cdot)_\Delta$ shifts its argument by Δ cycles forward, and is defined on variables, literals, clauses, etc. For example, $(\{-v_1^5, v_2^3\})_3 = \{-v_1^8, v_2^6\}$. A model M for a state machine is a pair of sets of clauses (M_I, M_{Tr}) describing the Init and Transition Relation constraints encoded into clauses (see [BCCZ99, Tse68]). The set M_I describes the initial constraints, while M_{Tr} describes the transition relation of the underlying state machine. We assume that M_I is finite and that M_{Tr} is the closure under the cycle shift operator of a finite clause set $base(M_{Tr})$. The negation of the property at cycle k is encoded as the clauses $M_{\overline{Spec_k}}$. We will usually assume that $M_{\overline{Spec_k}}$ consists of the single literal $-s^k$. By the notation above, $M \vdash_{\mathcal{P}} s^k$ states that $\mathcal{P}$ proves that the property holds at cycle k.

---

[2] In the sequel, we abuse notation and identify a set of proof nodes with their clauses.

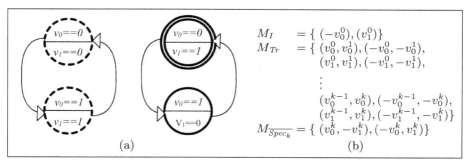

$$M_I = \{ (-v_0^0), (v_1^0) \}$$
$$M_{Tr} = \{ (v_0^0, v_0^1), (-v_0^0, -v_0^1),$$
$$(v_1^0, v_1^1), (-v_1^0, -v_1^1),$$
$$\vdots$$
$$(v_0^{k-1}, v_0^k), (-v_0^{k-1}, -v_0^k),$$
$$(v_1^{k-1}, v_1^k), (-v_1^{k-1}, -v_1^k) \}$$
$$M_{\overline{Spec_k}} = \{ (v_0^k, -v_1^k), (-v_0^k, v_1^k) \}$$

Fig. 2. A state machine: (a) represented as a state diagram, (b) encoded as CNF

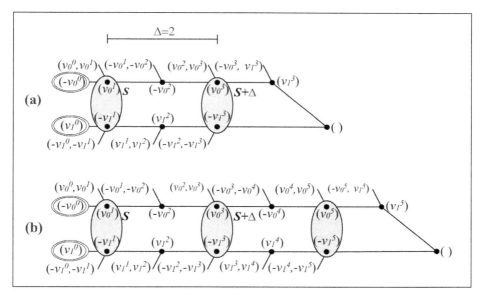

Fig. 3. (a) A proof that $Spec$ holds at cycle 3 for the state machine of Figure 2a, where S is a 2-invariant cut, (b) an extension of the proof, using the invariant S, showing that $Spec$ holds at cycle 5

2.2   An Example

Consider the state machine described in Figure 2a. Its state is described by two binary state variables v_1 and v_2, yielding a state space of size 4. The single initial state, (double encircled) is $(v_0 = 0, v_1 = 1)$, while the states violating the specified property $\overline{Spec} = \{(v_0 = 0, v_1 = 0), (v_0 = 1, v_1 = 1)\}$ are dashed. It is visually apparent that no "unsafe" finite path exists.

In the bounded variant of the above problem one would like to know if there is a finite path of length k from an init state to $\overline{Spec}$. The model of the problem, which is given in Figure 2b, is passed to a SAT solver that checks if there exists a satisfying assignment for all given clauses. As expected, since the problem has no satisfying assignment, the solver supplies us with a refutation showing that the state machine encoded in Figure 2b conforms with the given *Spec* at cycle k. An example for such proof when $k = 3$ is given in Figure 3a. The essence of this paper is that such a proof can be extended to all odd $k \geq 3$. This is demonstrated by a proof for $k = 5$ (see Figure 3b). This extension is possible since there is a grayed 2-invariant cut. In the following section we address this topic rigorously.

3   Proof Extension

Given a proof for the spec at cycle k, one would like to extend it to other cycles in a similar manner to the familiar inductive proof process. The following definition and theorem give a sufficient condition for achieving this.

Definition 1 (Δ-invariant cut). *Let $\mathcal{P}$ be a resolution proof for s^k from $M_I \cup M_{Tr}$. Then, a set of proof nodes S is a Δ-invariant cut if (a) all paths in $\mathcal{P}$ from an I axiom to $root(\mathcal{P})$ go through S, and (b) $S \cup M_{Tr} \vdash (S)_\Delta$. A Δ-extendible proof is a proof with a Δ-invariant cut.*

Theorem 1 (Proof Extension Theorem). *If there is a Δ-extendible proof for s^k, then there is a Δ-extendible proof for $s^{k+\Delta}$.*

Corollary 1 (Inductive extension). *If there is a Δ-extendible proof for the spec at cycle k, then the spec holds for all cycles $k, k + \Delta, k + 2\Delta, \ldots$.*

Proof (of Theorem 1). We first mention the composition of implication: If $M_1 \underset{\mathcal{P}_a}{\vdash} M_2$ and $M_2 \cup M_1 \underset{\mathcal{P}_b}{\vdash} M_3$ then $M_1 \underset{\mathcal{P}_b \circ \mathcal{P}_a}{\vdash} M_3$, where the proof $\mathcal{P}_b \circ \mathcal{P}_a$ is obtained by taking disjoint copies of $\mathcal{P}_a$ and $\mathcal{P}_b$, and identifying the M_2 axiom nodes of $\mathcal{P}_b$ with the corresponding nodes in $\mathcal{P}_a$. One should note that M_2 is a cut between M_1 and M_3 in the resulting proof.

Given some proof $\mathcal{P}$ for s^k with a Δ-invariant cut S:

(1) $M_I \cup M_{Tr} \underset{\mathcal{P}_1}{\vdash} S$ since S is a set of proof nodes

(2) $M_{Tr} \cup S \underset{\mathcal{P}_2}{\vdash} (S)_\Delta$ since S is Δ-invariant

(3) $M_{Tr} \cup S \underset{\mathcal{P}_3}{\vdash} s^k$ since S is a cut

(4) $M_I \cup M_{Tr} \underset{\mathcal{P}_2 \circ \mathcal{P}_1}{\vdash} (S)_\Delta$ by composition of (1),(2)

(5) $M_{Tr} \cup (S)_\Delta \underset{(\mathcal{P}_3)_\Delta}{\vdash} s^{k+\Delta}$ (3) shifted forward by Δ cycles

(6) $M_I \cup M_{Tr} \underset{(\mathcal{P}_3)_\Delta \circ \mathcal{P}_2 \circ \mathcal{P}_1}{\vdash} s^{k+\Delta}$ by composition of (2),(5).

Therefore, $\mathcal{P}' = (\mathcal{P}_3)_\Delta \circ \mathcal{P}_2 \circ \mathcal{P}_1$ is a proof for the spec at cycle $k + \Delta$. It remains to show that S is a Δ-invariant cut for $\mathcal{P}'$. Indeed, S is a cut between $\mathcal{P}_1$ and $(\mathcal{P}_3)_\Delta \circ \mathcal{P}_2$ as observed earlier. Also, $S \cup M_{Tr} \vdash (S)_\Delta$ since S is a Δ-invariant cut for $\mathcal{P}$. This completes the proof of the theorem.   □

Let us recall that the main objective of this work is to prove that the spec holds at all cycles. In view of Theorem 1, the obvious approach is as follows: As long as the spec is not known to hold at all cycles, ask the SAT solver to prove the spec for the smallest unknown cycle, analyze the proof hoping to find a Δ-invariant cut for some Δ, and declare that the spec holds for the appropriate set of cycles. The following two algorithms `ProofExtension` and `AnalayzeProof` make the above framework precise.

Algorithm 1. `ProofExtension`

Input: Models M_I, M_{Tr}, and the spec signal s
Output: Fail at k or Passed

1. $U \leftarrow \{0, 1, 2, \ldots\}$
2. While $U \neq \emptyset$
3. $k \leftarrow \min(U)$
4. $(res, \mathcal{P}) \leftarrow$ `SatSolve`(k)
5.   If $res ==$ **SAT**
6.   Return Fail at k
7.   Else
8. $\Delta \leftarrow$ `AnalayzeProof`$(\mathcal{P}, k)$
9. $U \leftarrow U \setminus \{k, k+\Delta, k+2\Delta, \ldots\}$
10. Return Passed

Algorithm 2. `AnalyzeProof`

Input: A proof $\mathcal{P}$ proving the spec at cycle k
Output: The smallest Δ for which $\mathcal{P}$ is Δ-extendible

1. For Δ in $\{1, \ldots, k\}$
2.   If `DeltaExtendible`$(\mathcal{P}, \Delta)$
3.   Return Δ
4. Return 0

One should note that there are two problems with the complete realization of the plan. The first is the infinite set of uncovered cycles U used by Algorithm `ProofExtension`. The second and more substantial problem is that of checking if a proof is Δ-extendible. We discuss the two problems in the following subsections.

3.1 Dealing with an Infinite Set

Consider the infinite set U of uncovered cycles used by Algorithm 1. After m iterations, the covered cycles are described by m pairs of numbers (k_i, Δ_i) for $i = 1, \ldots, m$, where (k_i, Δ_i) is the value of (k, Δ) at the end of the i'th iteration. Each such pair (k, Δ) represents an arithmetic progression $k, k+\Delta, k+2\Delta, \ldots$, where for $\Delta = 0$ the progression reduces to a single number k. Although the required query for the minimal uncovered cycle in U seems to demand searching an infinite set, we show that it suffices to search among a finite number of candidate. These candidates are $k_m + 1, k_m + 2, \ldots, k_m + L$, where L is the least common multiple (lcm) of the non-zero integers in $\Delta_1, \ldots, \Delta_m$. The algorithm and correctness lemma are stated next. One should note that the efficiency of the algorithm depends on L, which can conceivably be large. However the largest value we have encountered in practice is $L = 2$, as shown in the experimental section.

Algorithm 3. FindFirstUncovered

Input: A sequence (k_i, Δ_i) for $i = 1, \ldots, m$ supplied by Algorithm 1
Output: The smallest uncovered cycle, or ∞ if no such cycle

1.   Let L be the lcm of the non-zero integers in $\Delta_1, \ldots, \Delta_m$
2.   For c in $\{k_m + 1, k_m + 2, \ldots, k_m + L\}$
3.   Mark c as uncovered
4.   For i in $\{1, \ldots, m\}$
5.   If $\Delta_i > 0$ and $(c \equiv k_i \mod \Delta_i)$
6.   Mark c as covered
7.   Return the minimal uncovered c or ∞ if no such c

Lemma 1. *Algorithm* FindFirstUncovered *is correct when supplied with* (k_i, Δ_i) *pairs from Algorithm 1.*

3.2   Detecting Δ-Extendible Proofs

We suggest a naive algorithm DeltaExtendible that identifies a subset of the Δ-Extendible proofs. The algorithm performs DFS on the proof DAG starting from the root, backtracking when it reaches an axiom, a previously visited node, or a clause whose forward shift by Δ cycles was already visited. The algorithm returns true, if no init axiom was reached. The correctness of the algorithm follows from the fact that when it returns true, one can construct a Δ-invariant cut for the proof. The cut is just the set of all nodes n where the DFS backtracked because $(n.C).\Delta$ was already visited. The correctness of the algorithm is stated in Lemma 2 below.

Algorithm DeltaExtendible can be implemented efficiently, since it consists of a linear pass over the proof, where the maintenance and queries to the set of previously visited clauses V is performed in logarithmic time to the number of proof nodes. Further optimization can be achieved by ignoring nodes that are not tagged by init (i.e. that no init axiom was used in their proof). Another question that should be raised is about the best order of visiting proof nodes, which can be any topological order from root to axioms. It is not difficult to construct synthetic Δ-extendible proofs that are recognized by one order, but not by another. This direction of work requires more research.

Algorithm 4. `DeltaExtendible`

Input: A proof $\mathcal{P}$ proving the spec at cycle k, and a shift Δ
Output: If true, then $\mathcal{P}$ is Δ-Extendible

1. Mark all proof nodes as unvisited
2. Let $V \leftarrow \emptyset$
3. Return `RecDeltaExtendible`$(root(\mathcal{P}), \Delta, V)$

Algorithm 5. `RecDeltaExtendible`

Input: A proof node n, a shift Δ, and a reference to a set of clauses V

1. If (n is marked visited) or ($n \in M_{Tr}$) or $(n.C)_\Delta \in V$
2.   Return True
3. Else if $n \in M_I$
4.   Return False
5. Else
6.   Mark n visited
7.   Let $V \leftarrow V \cup \{n.C\}$
8.   Return `RecDeltaExtendible`$(n.L, \Delta, V)$
            and `RecDeltaExtendible`$(n.R, \Delta, V)$

Lemma 2. *If* `DeltaExtendible`$(root(\mathcal{P}), \Delta)$ *returns true then $\mathcal{P}$ is Δ-extendible.*

4   Proof Reordering

The proof extension algorithm described in the previous section implicitly assumes that a significant portion of the proofs generated by the SAT solver satisfy the necessary conditions of Theorem 1. As might be expected, our experiments indicate that this assumption is overly optimistic in practice. The obvious way to proceed is *preprocessing*. This section explores a few preprocessing algorithms that can be applied to real-life proofs. The techniques explored in this section use the *double pivot* simplification method, (see [BIFH+08]). Double pivot simplification identifies cases where the same pivot variable was used more than once on a path from the root to an axiom and attempts to eliminate them.

4.1   On Combs and Order

Proofs generated by industrial SAT solvers tend to have special properties that may be exploited. In particular, such proofs consist of proof segments representing the derivation of conflict clauses, which are paths with internal nodes of out-degree one. We call such a proof segment *a comb*. Since combs are relatively isolated proof segments, and since many combs have a significant size, it is natural to try and optimize combs.

Formally, a comb $\overline{C}$ in the proof P is a directed path $(n_1, n_2, \ldots, n_k)$ in the DAG of P such that outdegree$(n_i) = 1$ for all $i < k$. For ease of exposition, we always consider left handed combs where $n_{i+1}.L = n_i$ for all i. The comb resolves the clauses $c_0 = n_1.L.C, c_1 = n_1.R.C, c_2 = n_2.R.C, \ldots, c_k = n_k.R.C$ to obtain $n_k.C$. Since the actual nodes used by the comb are immaterial to the exposition, we denote $\overline{C} = (c_0, c_1, \ldots, c_k)$, and $res(\overline{C}) = n_k.C$. The support of a comb, $supp(\overline{C}) = \{c_0, c_1, \ldots, c_k\}$, is its unordered set of clauses.

We attempt to optimize a comb by rearranging its clauses so that pivots are ordered by their cycle number whenever possible. The following example demonstrates the power of this technique. It can be easily verified that the resulting comb satisfies the condition of Theorem 1. Consider the model:

$$M_I = \{\{x^0\}, \{y^0\}\}$$
$$base(M_{Tr}) = \{\{-x^0, -y^0, x^1\}, \{-y^0, y^1\}, \{-x^0, -y^0, s^0\}\}$$
$$M_{\overline{Spec_k}} = \{-s^k\}.$$

The comb in Figure 4a proves that the spec holds at cycle 4. Rearranging the comb results in significantly shorter clauses as can be seen in Figure 4b. In fact, extending this example to a comb proving s^n yields clauses of width $\Theta(n)$ before rearranging, and $\Theta(1)$ after. Moreover, the rearranged comb satisfies the requirements of Theorem 1 while the original comb did not. It is interesting to compare the rather synthetic example with real-life results, as depicted in Figures 4, 6 respectively. In the next subsection, we describe the theoretical and algorithmic framework needed for reordering combs.

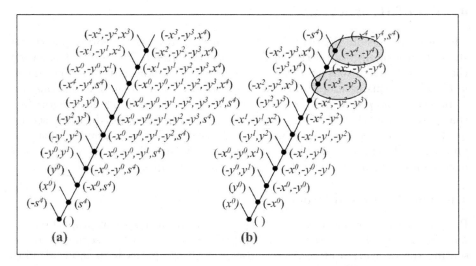

Fig. 4. A comb before and after proof reordering according to literals cycles

4.2 The CombReorder Algorithm

This subsection is devoted to the development of the CombReorder algorithm for comb optimization. As the name indicates, the algorithm attempts to permute the input clauses of each comb to sort the comb pivots by their cycle. We assume that combs are double pivot free, i.e., that all pivot variables used along a comb are distinct, and that no pivot variable occurs in the comb's consequent clause. The CombReorder algorithm is incorporated into the following high-level algorithm:

Algorithm 6. ReorderProof

1.   Repeat
2.   Eliminate double pivots
3.   Apply CombReorder to all combs
4.   Until stable

The double pivot elimination step is demonstrated in Figure 5. Note that this procedure may strengthen the consequent clause of the comb from c to $c' \subsetneq c$, which may lead to further simplification of the proof beyond the scope of the comb. The essential property satisfied by the double pivot elimination step is stated in Lemma 3. See [BIFH$^+$08] for a proof and for a full description of the simplification algorithm.

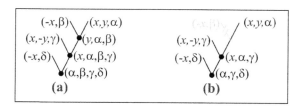

Fig. 5. Double Pivot on x enables resolution trimming

Lemma 3 (Double pivot elimination [BIFH$^+$08]). *Any comb $\overline{C}$ with a double pivot can be converted into a double pivot free comb $\overline{C'}$ where $supp(\overline{C'}) \subsetneq supp(\overline{C})$ and $res(\overline{C'}) \subseteq res(\overline{C})$.*

Our next step is the observation that any algorithm for optimizing a double pivot free comb $\overline{C}$ may restrict its attention to double pivot free reordering of $\overline{C}$. These are the only combs that yield the best possible consequent clause $res(\overline{C})$, as stated in the next Lemma:

Lemma 4. *Let $\overline{C}$ be a double pivot free comb. Then: (a) if $\overline{C'}$ is a double pivot free comb with $supp(\overline{C'}) = supp(\overline{C})$ then the two combs prove the same result, and (b) the result of any other comb $\overline{C'}$ with $supp(\overline{C'}) \subseteq supp(\overline{C})$ is not stronger or equal to the result of $\overline{C}$, i.e. $res(\overline{C'}) \setminus res(\overline{C})$ is not empty.*

Consider the following non-deterministic reordering algorithm for the given set of clauses C. The algorithm constructs a comb starting from its last resolution.In each iteration it picks a unit clause relative to the current consequent clause c. Theorem 2 states that all legal orders are feasible outputs of the algorithm, and that the choices made by the algorithm can always be completed to a legal comb without any need to backtrack.

Algorithm 7. `CombReorder`

Input: A set of clauses C and a clause c
Output: A valid comb proving c from C with the comb's clauses
        listed in reverse order

1.   While $|C| > 1$
2.   Choose a clause $c' \in C$ such that $c' \setminus c = \{u\}$ for some u
3.   Output c'
4.   Let $c := c \cup \{-u\}$, $C := C \setminus c'$
5.   Output the single clause c' remaining in C

Theorem 2. *Given a double pivot free comb $\overline{C}$, the following properties hold for runs of* `CombReorder` *on input $C = supp(\overline{C})$ and $c = res(\overline{C})$: (a) There is always at least one choice at step 2 regardless of the previous choices made by the algorithm. (b) Any comb generated by the algorithm is a valid double pivot free comb proving c. (c) The* `CombReorder` *algorithm can generate any double pivot free comb with support C.*

The final step needed to make `CombReorder` a deterministic algorithm is a method for choosing the clause c' at step 2. We suggest a greedy rule that chooses c' to maximize $|u|$ under some predetermined variable order, where $|u|$ denotes the variable of the literal u. We suggest two lexicographic orders on the variables, where variables are first ordered by *increasing or decreasing cycle number*, and then by their base, which is given some fixed arbitrary order. The effectiveness of this greedy reordering heuristic is demonstrated both on the synthetic example (see Figure 4) and on real life examples in the next section.

The proofs of Lemma 4 and of Theorem 2 were omitted for lack of space.

5   Experimental Results

We present here four examples taken from the IBM internal benchmark suite, where the proof extension algorithm (Algorithm 1) was able to solve the first three. The proofs were constructed by Mage, IBM's state-of-the-art DPLL-based SAT solver. The following table gives some statistics on the examples and their solution. For each solved example, the fifth column gives the first value of k for which the proof for spec cycle k was extended. As can be seen, for two of the examples extension was done with $\Delta = 2$, which means that one proof was extended to all even spec cycles, and another to all odd cycles. One more interesting fact is that all successful examples were solved by finding a Δ-invariant cut consisting of a single proof node.

Example	FFs	Inputs	Logic elements	Solved at k	Comb order
a	78	94	1128	11	increasing
b	225	174	7252	37 odd, 42 even	decreasing
c	387	170	4913	35 odd, 36 even	decreasing
d	133	89	993	not solved	—

In all the above examples, applying the `CombReorder` algorithm was required for the detection of a Δ-invariant cut. It's interesting to note the significance `CombReorder` has on various proof parameters, where one specific parameter for which visualization is especially effective is the clause width $|n_i.C|$ along the longest comb from init to root. We present in Figure 6 the before and after graph for each of the three examples. In (a), the clause width has decreased and a periodic behavior has emerged. In (b), the improvement in clause width is more dramatic, especially if ignoring the first 200 clauses that can be attributed to an init effect. In (c), the effect is most dramatic from the start.

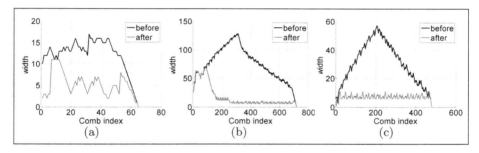

Fig. 6. Width of resolved clause as a function of the clause index

Finally, it's worth noting that the problem with the failed fourth example is the existence of a very wide clause in the proof. For $k = 30$, it consists of 61 literals with cycles ranging from 3 to k. It turns out that this wide clause enters the proof close to the init axioms, and that it takes most of the proof to resolve its literals. The effect of this problem is that Δ-shifted clauses are unlikely to appear later on in the proof, causing Algorithm 4 to fail.

6   Conclusion

This work presents a method for extracting a Δ-invariant cut from a bounded proof of unsatisfiability. We show that such an invariant may be sufficient in extending a bounded proof to an unbounded one. A natural continuation of this work would be to extract weaker invariants to enhance the traditional BMC flow. Effective extraction of invariants relies on the periodic nature of a proof. Thus an essential future component for any method's success is to tune a SAT solver to create cleaner, more structured refutations. A source of optimism is that the natural proof for many real-life problems is periodic by nature.

Acknowledgments. Thanks to Karen Yorav for reviewing the paper drafts, and to Tatyana Veksler and Ofer Strichman for many enlightening talks.

References

[BCCZ99]   Biere, A., Cimatti, A., Clarke, E.M., Zhu, Y.: Symbolic model checking without BDDS. In: Cleaveland, W.R. (ed.) TACAS 1999. LNCS, vol. 1579, pp. 193–207. Springer, Heidelberg (1999)

[BIFH+08]   Bar-Ilan, O., Fuhrmann, O., Hoory, S., Shacham, O., Strichman, O.: Linear-time reductions of resolution proofs. In: Chockler, H., Hu, A.J. (eds.) HVC 2008. LNCS, vol. 5394, pp. 114–128. Springer, Heidelberg (2008)

[FH09]   Fuhrman, O., Hoory, S.: An Example of a Δ-extendible Proof with a Spurious Interpolant. Technical Report H-0265, IBM Haifa Research Lab (2009)

[GKS08]   Gershman, R., Koifman, M., Strichman, O.: An approach for extracting a small unsatisfiable core. Form. Methods Syst. Des. 33(1-3), 1–27 (2008)

[JM05]   Jhala, R., McMillan, K.L.: Interpolant-based transition relation approximation. In: Etessami, K., Rajamani, S.K. (eds.) CAV 2005. LNCS, vol. 3576, pp. 39–51. Springer, Heidelberg (2005)

[LWS03]   Li, B., Wang, C., Somenzi, F.: A satisfiability-based approach to abstraction refinement in model checking. Electr. Notes Theor. Comput. Sci. 89(4) (2003)

[McM03]   McMillan, K.L.: Interpolation and SAT-based model checking. In: Hunt Jr., W.A., Somenzi, F. (eds.) CAV 2003. LNCS, vol. 2725, pp. 1–13. Springer, Heidelberg (2003)

[SC85]   Sistla, A.P., Clarke, E.M.: The complexity of propositional linear temporal logic. Journal ACM 32, 733–749 (1985)

[SK97]   Stoffel, D., Kunz, W.: Record & play: a structural fixed point iteration for sequential circuit verification. In: ICCAD 1997: Proceedings of the 1997 IEEE/ACM international conference on Computer-Aided Design, Washington, DC, USA, pp. 394–399. IEEE Computer Society, Los Alamitos (1997)

[SSS00]   Sheeran, M., Singh, S., Stålmarck, G.: Checking safety properties using induction and a sat-solver. In: Johnson, S.D., Hunt Jr., W.A. (eds.) FMCAD 2000. LNCS, vol. 1954, pp. 108–125. Springer, Heidelberg (2000)

[Tse68]   Tseitin, G.S.: On the complexity of derivations in the propositional calculus. Studies in Mathematics and Mathematical Logic Part II, 115–125 (1968)

[ZM03a]   Zhang, L., Malik, S.: Extracting small unsatisfiable cores from unsatisfiable boolean formula. In: Giunchiglia, E., Tacchella, A. (eds.) SAT 2003. LNCS, vol. 2919. Springer, Heidelberg (2004)

[ZM03b]   Zhang, L., Malik, S.: Validating sat solvers using an independent resolution-based checker: Practical implementations and other applications. In: DATE 2003: Proceedings of the conference on Design, Automation and Test in Europe, Washington, DC, USA, p. 10880. IEEE Computer Society, Los Alamitos (2003)

Games through Nested Fixpoints

Thomas Martin Gawlitza and Helmut Seidl

TU München, Institut für Informatik, I2, 85748 München, Germany

Abstract. In this paper we consider two-player zero-sum payoff games on finite graphs, both in the deterministic as well as in the stochastic setting. In the deterministic setting, we consider total-payoff games which have been introduced as a refinement of mean-payoff games [10, 18]. In the stochastic setting, our class is a turn-based variant of liminf-payoff games [4, 15, 16]. In both settings, we provide a non-trivial characterization of the values through nested fixpoint equations. The characterization of the values of liminf-payoff games moreover shows that solving liminf-payoff games is polynomial-time reducible to solving stochastic parity games. We construct practical algorithms for solving the occurring nested fixpoint equations based on strategy iteration. As a corollary we obtain that solving deterministic total-payoff games and solving stochastic liminf-payoff games is in $\mathbf{UP} \cap \mathbf{co-UP}$.

1 Introduction

We consider two-player zero-sum payoff games on finite graphs without sinks. The goal of the maximizer (called $\vee$-player) is to maximize the outcome (his payoff) of the play whereas the goal of the minimizer (called $\wedge$-player) is to minimize this value (his losing). We consider both deterministic and stochastic games. In the stochastic setting there additionally exists a probabilistic player who makes decisions randomly.

In the deterministic setting we consider *total-payoff* games, where the payoff is the long-term minimal value of the sum of all immediate rewards. This means that, if $r_1, r_2, r_3 \cdots$ denotes the sequence of the immediate rewards of a play, then the total reward is $\lim \inf_{k \to \infty} \sum_{i=1}^{k} r_i$. This natural criterion has been suggested by Gimbert and Zielonka in [10], where they prove that both players have positional optimal strategies.

Total-payoff games can be considered as a refinement of *mean-payoff games* (cf. e.g. [6, 19]). Mean-payoff games are payoff games where the outcome of a play is given as the *limiting average* of the immediate rewards. For the same game, the mean-payoff is positive iff the total-payoff is ∞; likewise, the mean-payoff is negative iff the total-payoff is $-\infty$. The refinement concerns games where the mean-payoff is 0. For these, the total-payoff is finite and thus allows to differentiate more precisely between games.

Many algorithms have been proposed for solving mean-payoff games (e.g. [1, 11, 17, 19]). While it is still not known whether mean-payoff games can be solved in polynomial time, it at least has been shown that the corresponding decision problem, i.e., deciding whether the $\vee$-player can enforce a positive outcome, is in $\mathbf{UP} \cap \mathbf{co} - \mathbf{UP}$. Much less is known about total-payoff games.

One contribution of this paper therefore is a method for computing the values and positional optimal strategies for total-payoff games. For this, we provide a polynomial-time reduction to *hierarchical systems of simple integer equations* as introduced in [8].

A. Bouajjani and O. Maler (Eds.): CAV 2009, LNCS 5643, pp. 291–305, 2009.

The hierarchical system utilized for the reduction consists of a greatest fixpoint subsystem which is nested inside a least fixpoint system. This reduction allows to compute the values of total-payoff games by means of the strategy improvement algorithm for the corresponding hierarchical system as presented in [8].

Deterministic total-payoff games can be generalized to stochastic total-payoff games, where the objective is to maximize the expected long-term minimal value of the sum of all immediate rewards. The immediate generalization of deterministic total-payoff games to stochastic total-payoff games is problematic, if both $-\infty$ and ∞ are possible rewards with positive probabilities. Here it is possible to restrict the considerations to stochastic total-payoff games, where the payoff for every play is finite. This allows to model the realistic situation, where each player has an initial amount of money and can go bankrupt. These games can be reduced to *stochastic liminf-payoff games* by encoding the currently accumulated rewards into the positions (cf. [15]).

In stochastic liminf-payoff games an immediate reward is assigned to each position and the payoff for a play is the least immediate reward that occurs infinitely often. These games are more general than they appear at first sight. Stochastic liminf-payoff games have been studied by Maitra and Sudderth in the more general concurrent setting with infinitely many positions [15, 16]. In particular, they show that concurrent stochastic liminf-payoff games have a value and that this value can be expressed through a transfinite iteration. Recently, Chatterjee and Henzinger showed that stochastic liminf-payoff games can be solved in **NP** ∩ **co−NP** [4]. This result is obtained by providing polynomial-time algorithms for both 1-player cases, using the fact that these games are positionally determined. A practical algorithm for the 2-player case is not provided.

In this paper we present a practical method for computing the values and positional optimal strategies for liminf-payoff games which consists of a reduction to a class of nested fixpoint equation systems. The resulting algorithm is a strategy improvement algorithm. As a corollary we obtain that solving liminf-payoff games is in fact in **UP** ∩ **co−UP**. As a consequence of the provided characterization we moreover get that liminf-payoff games are polynomial-time reducible to stochastic parity games.

The technical contribution of this paper consists of a practical algorithm for solving *hierarchical systems of stochastic equations*. These are generalizations of hierarchical systems of simple integer equations as considered in [8]. The latter hierarchical systems are equivalent the quantitative μ-calculus introduced in [7]. In a hierarchical equation system least and greatest fixpoint computations are nested as in the μ-calculus. In this paper we use the nesting in order to describe the values of both deterministic total-payoff games and stochastic liminf-payoff games.

Omitted proofs can be found in the corresponding technical report.

2   Definitions

As usual, $\mathbb{N}$, $\mathbb{Z}$, $\mathbb{Q}$ and $\mathbb{R}$ denote the set of natural numbers, the set of integers, the set of rational numbers and the set of real numbers, respectively. We assume $0 \in \mathbb{N}$ and we denote $\mathbb{N} \setminus \{0\}$ by $\mathbb{N}_{>0}$. We set $\overline{\mathbb{Z}} := \mathbb{Z} \cup \{-\infty, \infty\}$, $\overline{\mathbb{Q}} := \mathbb{Q} \cup \{-\infty, \infty\}$ and $\overline{\mathbb{R}} := \mathbb{R} \cup \{-\infty, \infty\}$. We use a uniform cost measure where we count arithmetic operations and memory accesses for $\mathcal{O}(1)$. The size of a data structure S in the uniform cost measure will be denoted by $\|S\|$. An algorithm is called *uniform* iff its running time w.r.t. the uniform cost measure only depends on the size of the input in the uniform cost measure, i.e., the running time does not depend on the sizes of the occurring numbers. Given a binary relation $R \subseteq A \times B$ and a subset $A' \subseteq A$, we write $A'R$ for the set $\{b \in B \mid \exists a \in A' : (a, b) \in R\}$.

Game Graphs. A *(stochastic) game graph* is a tuple $G = (P_\vee, P_\wedge, P_+, \delta, E)$ with the following properties: The sets $P_\vee, P_\wedge$ and P_+ are pair-wise disjoint sets of positions which are controlled by the $\vee$-player, the $\wedge$-player, and the probabilistic player, respectively. We always write P for the set $P_\vee \cup P_\wedge \cup P_+$ of all positions. The set $E \subseteq P^2$ is the set of *moves*, where we claim that $\{p\}E \neq \emptyset$ holds for all $p \in P$, i.e., the graph (P, E) has no sinks. The mapping $\delta : P_+ \to P \to [0, 1]$ assigns a probability distribution $\delta(p)$ with $\sum_{p' \in \{p\}E} \delta(p)(p') = 1$ to each probabilistic position $p \in P_+$, i.e., $\delta(p)(p')$ denotes the probability for p' being the next position assuming that p is the current position. For convenience, we assume that $\{p' \mid \delta(p)(p') > 0\} = \{p\}E$ holds for every $p \in P_+$. A game graph G is called deterministic iff $|\{p\}E| = 1$ holds for all $p \in P_+$. It is called 0-*player* game graph iff $|\{p\}E| = 1$ holds for all $p \in P_\vee \cup P_\wedge$.

Plays and Histories. An infinite word $\mathbf{p} = p_1 p_2 p_3 \cdots$ over the alphabet P with $p_i E p_{i+1}$ for all $i \in \mathbb{N}_{>0}$ is called a *play in* G. The set of all plays in G is denoted by $\mathbf{P}^\omega(G)$. The set of all plays in G starting at position $p \in P$ is denoted by $\mathbf{P}^\omega(G, p)$. A non-empty, finite word $\mathbf{h}$ is called *play prefix (or history) of* $\mathbf{p} \in \mathbf{P}^\omega(G)$ iff there exists some $\mathbf{p}' \in \mathbf{P}^\omega(G)$ such that $\mathbf{p} = \mathbf{hp}'$ holds. The set of all play prefixes of $\mathbf{p}$ is denoted by $\mathbf{P}^*(\mathbf{p})$ and we set $\mathbf{P}^*(G) := \bigcup_{\mathbf{p} \in \mathbf{P}^\omega(G)} \mathbf{P}^*(\mathbf{p})$ and $\mathbf{P}^*(G, p) := \bigcup_{\mathbf{p} \in \mathbf{P}^\omega(G, p)} \mathbf{P}^*(\mathbf{p})$.

Strategies. A function $\sigma : \mathbf{P}^*(G) \cap P^* P_\vee \to P \to [0, 1]$ is called *(mixed)* $\vee$*-strategy for* G iff $\sigma(\mathbf{hp})$ is a probability distribution with $\{p' \in P \mid \sigma(\mathbf{hp})(p') > 0\} \subseteq \{p\}E$ for all $\mathbf{hp} \in \mathbf{P}^*(G) \cap P^* P_\vee$. Mixed $\wedge$-strategies are defined dually. We denote the set of all mixed $\vee$-strategies and all mixed $\wedge$-strategies by $\overline{\Sigma}_G$ and $\overline{\Pi}_G$, respectively. A $\vee$-strategy σ is called *pure* iff, for every $\mathbf{hp} \in \mathbf{P}^*(G) \cap P^* P_\vee$, $\sigma(\mathbf{hp})$ is a Dirac measure, i.e., it holds $|\{p' \in P \mid \sigma(\mathbf{hp})(p') > 0\}| = 1$. Pure $\wedge$-strategies are defined dually. A pure $\vee$-strategy σ for G is called *(pure and) positional* iff $\sigma(\mathbf{p}p) = \sigma(\mathbf{p}'p)$ holds for all $\mathbf{p}p, \mathbf{p}'p \in \mathbf{P}^*(G) \cap P^* P_\vee$. We identify a positional $\vee$-strategy σ for G with a function which maps a position $p \in P_\vee$ to some position $\sigma(p) \in \{p\}E$. Positional $\wedge$-strategies are defined dually. We denote the set of all positional $\vee$-strategies (resp. positional $\wedge$-strategies) for G by Σ_G (resp. Π_G). We omit the subscript G, whenever it is clear from the context. For a positional $\vee$-strategy $\sigma \in \Sigma$, we write $G(\sigma)$ for the game graph that is obtained from G by removing all moves that are not used whenever the $\vee$-player plays consistent with σ. For a positional $\wedge$-strategy $\pi \in \Pi$, $G(\pi)$ is defined dually.

After fixing a starting position p, a $\vee$-strategy σ and a $\wedge$-strategy π, a probability measure $\mathbb{P}_{G,p,\sigma,\pi}$ on $\mathbf{P}^\omega(G, p)$ is defined as usual, i.e., for a given measurable set A of plays, $\mathbb{P}_{G,p,\sigma,\pi}(A)$ denotes the probability that a play which starts at position p and is played according to the strategies σ and π is in the set A. In a *deterministic* game graph, after fixing a starting position p, a pure $\vee$-strategy σ, and a pure $\wedge$-strategy π, there exists exactly one play which can be played from p according to the strategies σ and π. We denote this play by $\mathbf{play}(G, p, \sigma, \pi)$.

Payoff functions. We assign a *payoff* $U(\mathbf{p})$ to each play $\mathbf{p} \in \mathbf{P}^\omega(G)$ due to a measurable *payoff function* U. A pair $\mathcal{G} = (G, U)$ is called a *payoff game*. We set $\mathcal{G}(\sigma) := (G(\sigma), U)$ for all $\sigma \in \Sigma$ and $\mathcal{G}(\pi) := (G(\pi), U)$ for all $\pi \in \Pi$.

Values. For a payoff game $\mathcal{G} = (G, U)$ we denote the expectation of U under the probability measure $\mathbb{P}_{G,p,\sigma,\pi}$ by $\langle\!\langle p \rangle\!\rangle_{\mathcal{G},\sigma,\pi}$. For $p \in P$, $\sigma \in \overline{\Sigma}$, and $\pi \in \overline{\Pi}$ we set:

$$\langle\!\langle p \rangle\!\rangle_{\mathcal{G},\sigma} := \inf_{\pi \in \overline{\Pi}} \langle\!\langle p \rangle\!\rangle_{\mathcal{G},\sigma,\pi} \qquad \langle\!\langle p \rangle\!\rangle_{\mathcal{G}}^\vee := \sup_{\sigma \in \overline{\Sigma}} \langle\!\langle p \rangle\!\rangle_{\mathcal{G},\sigma}$$
$$\langle\!\langle p \rangle\!\rangle_{\mathcal{G},\pi} := \sup_{\sigma \in \overline{\Sigma}} \langle\!\langle p \rangle\!\rangle_{\mathcal{G},\sigma,\pi} \qquad \langle\!\langle p \rangle\!\rangle_{\mathcal{G}}^\wedge := \inf_{\pi \in \overline{\Pi}} \langle\!\langle p \rangle\!\rangle_{\mathcal{G},\pi}$$

$\langle\!\langle p \rangle\!\rangle_{\mathcal{G}}^\vee$ and $\langle\!\langle p \rangle\!\rangle_{\mathcal{G}}^\wedge$ are called the *lower* and the *upper value* of $\mathcal{G}$ at position p, respectively. The payoff game $\mathcal{G}$ is called *determined* iff $\langle\!\langle p \rangle\!\rangle_{\mathcal{G}}^\vee = \langle\!\langle p \rangle\!\rangle_{\mathcal{G}}^\wedge$ holds for all positions p. In this case we simply denote the *value* $\langle\!\langle p \rangle\!\rangle_{\mathcal{G}}^\vee = \langle\!\langle p \rangle\!\rangle_{\mathcal{G}}^\wedge$ of $\mathcal{G}$ at p by $\langle\!\langle p \rangle\!\rangle_{\mathcal{G}}$. We omit the subscript $\mathcal{G}$, whenever it is clear from the context. Let $\mathcal{C}$ be a class of payoff games. Deciding whether, for a given payoff game $\mathcal{G} \in \mathcal{C}$, a given position p, and a given value $x \in \overline{\mathbb{R}}$, $\langle\!\langle p \rangle\!\rangle_{\mathcal{G}} \geq x$ holds, is called the *quantitative decision problem* for $\mathcal{C}$.

Optimal Strategies. A $\vee$-strategy σ is called *optimal* iff $\langle\!\langle p \rangle\!\rangle_{\mathcal{G},\sigma} = \langle\!\langle p \rangle\!\rangle_{\mathcal{G}}^\vee$ holds for all positions p. Accordingly, a $\wedge$-strategy π is called *optimal* iff $\langle\!\langle p \rangle\!\rangle_{\mathcal{G},\pi} = \langle\!\langle p \rangle\!\rangle_{\mathcal{G}}^\wedge$ holds for all positions p. A payoff game $\mathcal{G}$ is called *positionally determined* iff it is determined and there exist positional optimal strategies for both players.

Mean-payoff function. Let $c : E \to \mathbb{R}$ be a real-valued function that assigns an immediate payoff to every move. The mean-payoff function U_c^{mp} is defined by

$$U_c^{\mathrm{mp}}(\mathbf{p}) := \liminf_{k \to \infty} \frac{1}{k-1} \sum_{i=1}^{k-1} c(p_i, p_{i+1}), \qquad \mathbf{p} = p_1 p_2 \cdots \in \mathbf{P}^\omega(G)$$

The pair $\mathcal{G} = (G, U_c^{\mathrm{mp}})$ is called *mean-payoff* game and is for simplicity identified with the pair (G, c). Mean-payoff games are widely studied (e.g. [6, 19]).

Example 1. For the mean-payoff game $\mathcal{G} = (G, c)$ in figure 1 it holds $U_c^{\mathrm{mp}}(a(bc)^\omega) = U_c^{\mathrm{mp}}(a(de)^\omega) = 0$. Moreover, it holds $U_c^{\mathrm{mp}}((bc)^\omega) = U_c^{\mathrm{mp}}((cb)^\omega) = 0$. $\qquad\square$

Total-payoff function. Let $c : E \to \mathbb{R}$ be a real-valued function that assigns an immediate payoff to every move. The total-payoff function U_c^{tp} is defined by

$$U_c^{\mathrm{tp}}(\mathbf{p}) := \liminf_{k \to \infty} \sum_{i=1}^{k-1} c(p_i, p_{i+1}), \qquad \mathbf{p} = p_1 p_2 \cdots \in \mathbf{P}^\omega(G)$$

The pair $\mathcal{G} = (G, U_c^{\mathrm{tp}})$ is called *total-payoff* game and is for simplicity identified with the pair (G, c).

We only consider the total-payoff function in the deterministic context, because otherwise the expectation may be undefined. This is the case, whenever the payoff is $-\infty$ with some positive probability as well as ∞ with some positive probability. Motivated by applications in economics [18], Gimbert and Zielonka introduced this total-payoff function in [10]. This payoff function is very natural, since it basically just sums up all occurring immediate payoffs. Since this sum may be undefined, it associates to a play $\mathbf{p}$ the most pessimistic long-term total reward of $\mathbf{p}$ from the $\vee$-player's perspective. The following example shows that the total-payoff function allows to differentiate more precisely between plays, whenever the mean-payoff is 0.

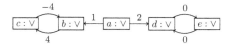

Fig. 1. A Payoff Game

Example 2. For the total-payoff game $\mathcal{G} = (G, c)$ in figure 1 it hold $U_c^{\text{tp}}(a(bc)^\omega) = 1$ and $U_c^{\text{tp}}(a(de)^\omega) = 2$. Thus, the $\vee$-player should prefer the play $a(de)^\omega$. Moreover, the payoff may depend on the starting position. In the example we have $U_c^{\text{tp}}((bc)^\omega) = 0$ and $U_c^{\text{tp}}((cb)^\omega) = -4$.   □

Liminf-payoff function. Let $r : P \to \mathbb{R}$ be a real-valued function that assigns an immediate payoff to every position. The liminf-payoff function $U_r^{\text{lim inf}}$ is defined by

$$U_r^{\text{lim inf}}(\mathbf{p}) := \liminf_{i \to \infty} r(p_i), \qquad \mathbf{p} = p_1 p_2 \cdots \in \mathbf{P}^\omega(G)$$

The pair $\mathcal{G} = (G, U_r^{\text{lim inf}})$ is called *liminf-payoff* game and is for simplicity identified with the pair (G, r). Limsup-payoff games are defined dually. We only consider liminf-payoff games, since every limsup-payoff game can be transformed in an equivalent liminf-payoff game by negating the immediate payoff function r and switching the roles of the two players (cf. [4]).

Liminf-payoff games are more general than it may appear at first sight. Some classes of games on graphs where the decision at a current position only depends on the value achieved so far can be encoded into liminf-payoff games, provided that only finitely different values are possible (cf. [15]). In particular variants of stochastic total-payoff games, where each player starts with an initial amount of money and can go bankrupt, can be expressed using liminf-payoff games.

Parity-payoff function. Let $r : P \to \mathbb{N}_{>0}$ be a function that assigns a rank to every position. The parity-payoff function U_r^{parity} is defined by

$$U_r^{\text{parity}}(\mathbf{p}) := \begin{cases} 0 & \text{if } \liminf_{i \to \infty} r(p_i) \text{ is odd} \\ 1 & \text{if } \liminf_{i \to \infty} r(p_i) \text{ is even} \end{cases}, \qquad \mathbf{p} = p_1 p_2 \cdots \in \mathbf{P}^\omega(G)$$

The pair $\mathcal{G} = (G, U_r^{\text{parity}})$ is called (stochastic) *parity* game and is for simplicity identified with the pair (G, r). Recently, Chatterjee et al. showed that stochastic parity games can be solved using a strategy improvement algorithm [5, 2]. Moreover, computing the values of stochastic parity games is polynomial-time reducible to computing the values of stochastic mean-payoff games [3].

Lemma 1 (**[2,4,6,9,10,14]**). *Liminf-payoff games, Mean-payoff games, parity games, and deterministic total-payoff games are positionally determined.*   □

3   Hierarchical Systems of Stochastic Equations

In this section we introduce *hierarchical systems of stochastic equations*, discuss elementary properties, and show how to solve these hierarchical systems using a strategy improvement algorithm. Hierarchical systems of stochastic equations are a generalization of hierarchical systems of simple integer equations (studied in [8]).

Assume that a fixed set $\mathbf{X}$ of variables is given. *Rational expressions* are specified by the abstract grammar

$$e ::= q \mid \mathbf{x} \mid e_1 + e_2 \mid t \cdot e \mid e_1 \vee e_2 \mid e_1 \wedge e_2,$$

where $q \in \overline{\mathbb{Q}}$, $t \in \mathbb{Q}_{>0}$, $\mathbf{x} \in \mathbf{X}$, and e, e_1, e_2 are rational expressions. The operator $t\cdot$ has highest precedence, followed by $+$, $\wedge$ and finally $\vee$ which has lowest precedence. We also use the operators $+$, $\vee$ and $\wedge$ as k-ary operators. An element $q \in \overline{\mathbb{Q}}$ is identified with the nullary function that returns q. An equation $\mathbf{x} = e$ is called *rational equation* iff e is a rational expression.

A *system* $\mathcal{E}$ of equations is a finite set $\{\mathbf{x}_1 = e_1, \ldots, \mathbf{x}_n = e_n\}$ of equations where $\mathbf{x}_1, \ldots, \mathbf{x}_n$ are pairwise distinct. We denote the set $\{\mathbf{x}_1, \ldots, \mathbf{x}_n\}$ of variables occurring in $\mathcal{E}$ by $\mathbf{X}_\mathcal{E}$. We drop the subscript, whenever it is clear from the context. The set of subexpressions occurring in right-hand sides of $\mathcal{E}$ is denoted by $\mathcal{S}(\mathcal{E})$ and $\|\mathcal{E}\|$ denotes $|\mathcal{S}(\mathcal{E})|$. An expression e or an equation $\mathbf{x} = e$ is called *disjunctive* (resp. *conjunctive*) iff e does not contain $\wedge$-operators (resp. $\vee$-operators). It is called *basic* iff e does neither contain $\wedge$- nor $\vee$-operators.

A $\vee$-*strategy* σ (resp. $\wedge$-*strategy* π) for $\mathcal{E}$ is a function that maps every expression $e_1 \vee \cdots \vee e_k$ (resp. $e_1 \wedge \cdots \wedge e_k$) occurring in $\mathcal{E}$ to one of the immediate subexpressions e_j. We denote the set of all $\vee$-strategies (resp. $\wedge$-strategies) for $\mathcal{E}$ by $\Sigma_\mathcal{E}$ (resp. $\Pi_\mathcal{E}$). We drop subscripts, whenever they are clear from the context. For $\sigma \in \Sigma$ the expression $e\sigma$ is defined by

$$(e_1 \vee \cdots \vee e_k)\sigma := (\sigma(e_1 \vee \cdots \vee e_k))\sigma, \qquad (f(e_1, \ldots, e_k))\sigma := f(e_1\sigma, \ldots, e_k\sigma),$$

where $f \neq \vee$ is some operator. Finally, we set $\mathcal{E}(\sigma) := \{\mathbf{x} = e\sigma \mid \mathbf{x} = e \in \mathcal{E}\}$. The definitions of $e\pi$ and $\mathcal{E}(\pi)$ for a $\wedge$-strategy π are dual.

The set $\mathbf{X} \to \overline{\mathbb{R}}$ of all *variable assignments* is a complete lattice. We denote the least upper and the greatest lower bound of a set X by $\bigvee X$ and $\bigwedge X$, respectively. For a *variable assignment* ρ an expression e is mapped to a value $[\![e]\!]\rho$ by setting $[\![\mathbf{x}]\!]\rho := \rho(\mathbf{x})$ and $[\![f(e_1, \ldots, e_k)]\!]\rho := f([\![e_1]\!]\rho, \ldots, [\![e_k]\!]\rho)$, where $\mathbf{x} \in \mathbf{X}$, f is a k-ary operator, for instance $+$, and $e_1, \ldots, e_k$ are expressions.

A *basic* rational expression e is called *stochastic* iff it is of the form

$$q + t_1 \cdot \mathbf{x}_1 + \cdots + t_k \cdot \mathbf{x}_k,$$

where $q \in \overline{\mathbb{Q}}$, $k \in \mathbb{N}$, $\mathbf{x}_1, \ldots, \mathbf{x}_k$ are pair-wise distinct variables, $t_1, \ldots, t_k \in \mathbb{Q}_{>0}$, and $t_1 + \cdots + t_k \leq 1$. A rational expression e is called *stochastic* iff $e\sigma\pi$ is stochastic for every $\vee$-strategy σ and every $\wedge$-strategy π. An equation $\mathbf{x} = e$ is called *stochastic* iff e is stochastic.

We define the unary operator $[\![\mathcal{E}]\!]$ by setting $([\![\mathcal{E}]\!]\rho)(\mathbf{x}) := [\![e]\!]\rho$ for $\mathbf{x} = e \in \mathcal{E}$. A solution (resp. pre-solution, resp. post-solution) is a variable assignment ρ such that $\rho = [\![\mathcal{E}]\!]\rho$ (resp. $\rho \leq [\![\mathcal{E}]\!]\rho$, resp. $\rho \geq [\![\mathcal{E}]\!]\rho$) holds. The set of solutions (resp. pre-solutions, resp. post-solutions) is denoted by $\mathbf{Sol}(\mathcal{E})$ (resp. $\mathbf{PreSol}(\mathcal{E})$, resp. $\mathbf{PostSol}(\mathcal{E})$).

A *hierarchical* system $\mathcal{H} = (\mathcal{E}, r)$ of stochastic equations consists of a system $\mathcal{E}$ of stochastic equations and a rank function r mapping the variables $\mathbf{x}$ of $\mathcal{E}$ to natural numbers $r(\mathbf{x}) \in \{1, \ldots, d\}, d \in \mathbb{N}_{>0}$. The canonical solution $\mathbf{CanSol}(\mathcal{H})$ of $\mathcal{H}$ is a particular solution of $\mathcal{E}$ which is characterized by r. In order to define it formally, let, for $j \in \{1, \ldots, d\}$ and $\bowtie \in \{=, <, >, \leq, \geq\}$, $\mathbf{X}_{\bowtie j} := \{\mathbf{x} \in \mathbf{X} \mid r(\mathbf{x}) \bowtie j\}$. Then the equations $\mathbf{x} = e$ of $\mathcal{E}$ with $\mathbf{x} \in \mathbf{X}_{\geq j}$ define a monotonic mapping $[\![\mathcal{E}, r]\!]_j$ from the set $\mathbf{X}_{<j} \to \overline{\mathbb{R}}$ of variable assignments with domain $\mathbf{X}_{<j}$ into the set $\mathbf{X}_{\geq j} \to \overline{\mathbb{R}}$ of variable assignments with domain $\mathbf{X}_{\geq j}$ as follows: We set $[\![\mathcal{E}, r]\!]_{d+1}\rho := \{\}$ for all ρ. Assume that j is odd. Given the mapping $[\![\mathcal{E}, r]\!]_{j+1}$, the mapping $[\![\mathcal{E}, r]\!]_j$ is inductively defined by

$$[\![\mathcal{E}, r]\!]_j\, \rho := \rho^* + [\![\mathcal{E}, r]\!]_{j+1}(\rho + \rho^*),$$

where $\rho : \mathbf{X}_{<j} \to \overline{\mathbb{R}}$ is a variable assignment and $\rho^* : \mathbf{X}_{=j} \to \overline{\mathbb{R}}$ is the *least* variable assignment such that

$$\rho^*(\mathbf{x}) = [\![e]\!](\rho + \rho^* + [\![\mathcal{E}, r]\!]_{j+1}(\rho + \rho^*))$$

holds for all equations $\mathbf{x} = e \in \mathcal{E}$ with $\mathbf{x} \in \mathbf{X}_{=j}$. Here, the operator $+$ denotes combination of two variable assignments with disjoint domains. The case where j is even, i.e., corresponds to a greatest solution is defined dually. Finally, the *canonical solution* is defined by

$$\mathbf{CanSol}(\mathcal{E}, r) := [\![\mathcal{E}, r]\!]_1\{\},$$

where $\{\}$ denotes the variable assignment with empty domain. The existence of a canonical solution is ensured by Knaster-Tarski's fixpoint theorem, since all used operators are monotone. For convenience, we denote an equation $\mathbf{x} = e$ with $r(\mathbf{x})$ odd by $\mu : \mathbf{x} = e$ and with $r(\mathbf{x})$ even by $\nu : \mathbf{x} = e$. Equations of lower ranks will be written above equations of higher rank.

Example 3. Consider the following hierarchical system $\mathcal{H} = (\mathcal{E}, r)$:

$$\begin{array}{ll}
\mu : \mathbf{b}_1 = 0 \vee (2 + \mathbf{x}_2 \vee 1 + \mathbf{x}_3) & \mu : \mathbf{b}_2 = 0 \vee \frac{1}{3} \cdot (-2 + \mathbf{x}_3) + \frac{2}{3} \cdot (1 + \mathbf{x}_4) \\
\mu : \mathbf{b}_3 = 0 \vee 2 + \mathbf{x}_2 & \mu : \mathbf{b}_4 = 0 \vee -1 + \mathbf{x}_2 \\
\nu : \mathbf{x}_1 = \mathbf{b}_1 \wedge (2 + \mathbf{x}_2 \vee 1 + \mathbf{x}_3) & \nu : \mathbf{x}_2 = \mathbf{b}_2 \wedge \frac{1}{3} \cdot (-2 + \mathbf{x}_3) + \frac{2}{3} \cdot (1 + \mathbf{x}_4) \\
\nu : \mathbf{x}_3 = \mathbf{b}_3 \wedge 2 + \mathbf{x}_2 & \nu : \mathbf{x}_4 = \mathbf{b}_4 \wedge -1 + \mathbf{x}_2
\end{array}$$

Thereby, r is given by $r(\mathbf{b}_i) = 1$ and $r(\mathbf{x}_i) = 2$ for all i. It holds $\mathbf{CanSol}(\mathcal{H}) = \{\mathbf{b}_1 \mapsto 1, \mathbf{b}_2 \mapsto 0, \mathbf{b}_3 \mapsto 0, \mathbf{b}_4 \mapsto 0, \mathbf{x}_1 \mapsto 1, \mathbf{x}_2 \mapsto -2, \mathbf{x}_3 \mapsto 0, \mathbf{x}_4 \mapsto -3\}$.   □

We only consider hierarchical systems $\mathcal{H} = (\mathcal{E}, r)$ with *finite* canonical solutions. A variable assignment $\rho : \mathbf{X} \to \overline{\mathbb{R}}$ is called *finite* iff $-\infty < \rho(\mathbf{x}) < \infty$ holds for all $\mathbf{x} \in \mathbf{X}$. In order to make finite solutions *unique*, we introduce the lattice

$$\mathbb{R}_d := \mathbb{R} \times (-1)^1 \cdot \mathbb{R}_{\geq 0} \times (-1)^2 \cdot \mathbb{R}_{\geq 0} \times \cdots \times (-1)^d \cdot \mathbb{R}_{\geq 0},$$

which is lexicographically linear ordered (for instance: $(2, -3, 5) < (2, -2, 1)$). The same idea is also used in [8]. Finally, we set $\overline{\mathbb{R}}_d := \mathbb{R}_d \cup \{-\infty, \infty\}$, where $-\infty$ and ∞ is the least and the greatest element, respectively. We define:

$$(x, y_1, \ldots, y_d) + (x', y_1', \ldots, y_d') := (x + x', y_1 + y_1', \ldots, y_d + y_d')$$
$$t \cdot (x, y_1, \ldots, y_d) := (t \cdot x, t \cdot y_1, \ldots, t \cdot y_d)$$

where $(x, y_1, \ldots, y_d), (x', y_1', \ldots, y_d') \in \mathbb{R}_d$ and $t \in \mathbb{R}$. As usual, we set $-\infty + \infty :=$ $-\infty$. With these definitions the usual commutativity, associativity and distributivity laws hold, i.e., for instance $t \cdot (x_1 \vee x_2) = t \cdot x_1 \vee t \cdot x_2$ holds for all $t \in \mathbb{R}_{>0}, x_1, x_2 \in \mathbb{R}_d$.

We call the analogon to stochastic equations (resp. stochastic expressions), where constants are from $\overline{\mathbb{R}}_d$, *stochastic equations over* $\overline{\mathbb{R}}_d$ (resp. *stochastic expressions over* $\overline{\mathbb{R}}_d$). Since $\overline{\mathbb{R}}_d$ is not a complete lattice, Knaster-Tarski's fixpoint theorem cannot be applied. Nevertheless, every system $\mathcal{E}$ of stochastic equations over $\overline{\mathbb{R}}_d$ has a least and a greatest solution, which we denote by $\mu[\![\mathcal{E}]\!]$ and $\nu[\![\mathcal{E}]\!]$, respectively.

Lemma 2. *Every system $\mathcal{E}$ of stochastic equations over $\overline{\mathbb{R}}_d$ has a least solution $\mu[\![\mathcal{E}]\!] =$ $\bigwedge \mathbf{PostSol}(\mathcal{E})$ and a greatest solution $\nu[\![\mathcal{E}]\!] = \bigvee \mathbf{PreSol}(\mathcal{E})$.* $\qquad\square$

Given a stochastic expression e, we define the stochastic expression $e^{\sharp}$ over $\overline{\mathbb{R}}_d$ as the expression obtained from e by replacing every constant $x \in \mathbb{R}$ occurring in e with the constant $(x, 0, \ldots, 0) \in \mathbb{R}_d$, i.e., $x^{\sharp} := (x, 0, \ldots, 0)$, $-\infty^{\sharp} := -\infty^{\sharp}$, $\infty^{\sharp} := \infty^{\sharp}$, $\mathbf{x}^{\sharp} :=$ $\mathbf{x}$, $(e_1 + e_2)^{\sharp} := e_1^{\sharp} + e_2^{\sharp}$, $(t \cdot e)^{\sharp} := t \cdot e^{\sharp}$, $(e_1 \wedge e_2)^{\sharp} := e_1^{\sharp} \wedge e_2^{\sharp}$, and $(e_1 \vee e_2)^{\sharp} := e_1^{\sharp} \vee e_2^{\sharp}$, where $x \in \mathbb{Q}$, $\mathbf{x} \in \mathbf{X}$, $t \in \mathbb{Q}_{>0}$, and e, e_1, e_2 are expressions. For $j \in \{1, \ldots, d\}$ we set $\mathbf{1}_j := (0, \delta_{1j} \cdot (-1)^1, \delta_{2j} \cdot (-1)^2, \ldots, \delta_{dj} \cdot (-1)^d)$. Thereby δ denotes the Kronecker delta, i.e., δ_{ij} equals 1 if $i = j$ and 0 otherwise. For a hierarchical system $\mathcal{H} = (\mathcal{E}, r)$ of stochastic equations we define the system $\mathcal{E}^{r\sharp}$ of stochastic equations over $\overline{\mathbb{R}}_d$ by $\mathcal{E}^{r\sharp} := \{\mathbf{x} = \mathbf{1}_{r(\mathbf{x})} + e^{\sharp} \mid \mathbf{x} = e \in \mathcal{E}\}$.

We define mappings α and β by $\alpha(-\infty) := -\infty$, $\alpha(\infty) := \infty$, $\alpha(x, y_1, \ldots, y_d) :=$ x, $\beta(-\infty) := \beta(\infty) := (0, \ldots, 0)$, and $\beta(x, y_1, \ldots, y_d) := (y_1, \ldots, y_d)$ for all $(x, y_1, \ldots, y_d) \in \mathbb{R}_d$. For a basic stochastic expression e over $\overline{\mathbb{R}}_d$, we define $W(e)$ by $W(x) := \beta(x)$, $W(\mathbf{x}) := (0, \ldots, 0)$, $W(e_1 + e_2) := W(e_1) + W(e_2)$, and $W(t \cdot e) := t \cdot W(e)$, where $x \in \overline{\mathbb{R}}_d$, $\mathbf{x} \in \mathbf{X}$, $t \in \mathbb{R}_{>0}$, and e, e_1, e_2 are expressions. We call e *non-zero* iff $\mathbf{Vars}(e) = \emptyset$ or $W(e) \neq (0, \ldots, 0)$. A stochastic expression e (resp. stochastic equation $\mathbf{x} = e$) over $\overline{\mathbb{R}}_d$ is finally called *non-zero* iff $e\sigma\pi$ is non-zero for every $\vee$-strategy σ and every $\wedge$-strategy π. A non-zero expression e remains non-zero if one rewrites it using commutativity, associativity, and distributivity. Note that $\mathcal{E}^{r\sharp}$ is non-zero. We have:

Lemma 3. 1. *Every system $\mathcal{E}$ of non-zero stochastic equations over $\overline{\mathbb{R}}_d$ has at most one finite solution ρ. If ρ exists, then its size is polynomial in the size of $\mathcal{E}$.*
   2. *Let $\mathcal{H} = (\mathcal{E}, r)$ be a hierarchical system of stochastic equations. Assume that the canonical solution $\mathbf{CanSol}(\mathcal{H})$ of $\mathcal{H}$ is finite. The non-zero system $\mathcal{E}^{r\sharp}$ has exactly one finite solution ρ and it holds $\alpha \circ \rho = \mathbf{CanSol}(\mathcal{H})$.* $\qquad\square$

Example 4. Consider again the hierarchical system $\mathcal{H} = (\mathcal{E}, r)$ of stochastic equations from example 3. The system $\mathcal{E}^{r\sharp}$ of non-zero stochastic equations over $\overline{\mathbb{R}}_d$ is given by:

$$\mathbf{b}_1 = (0, -1, 0) + ((0, 0, 0) \vee ((2, 0, 0) + \mathbf{x}_2 \vee (1, 0, 0) + \mathbf{x}_3))$$
$$\mathbf{b}_2 = (0, -1, 0) + ((0, 0, 0) \vee \tfrac{1}{3} \cdot ((-2, 0, 0) + \mathbf{x}_3) + \tfrac{2}{3} \cdot ((1, 0, 0) + \mathbf{x}_4))$$
$$\mathbf{b}_3 = (0, -1, 0) + ((0, 0, 0) \vee (2, 0, 0) + \mathbf{x}_2)$$
$$\mathbf{b}_4 = (0, -1, 0) + ((0, 0, 0) \vee (-1, 0, 0) + \mathbf{x}_2)$$
$$\mathbf{x}_1 = (0, 0, 1) + (\mathbf{b}_1 \wedge ((2, 0, 0) + \mathbf{x}_2 \vee (1, 0, 0) + \mathbf{x}_3))$$
$$\mathbf{x}_2 = (0, 0, 1) + (\mathbf{b}_2 \wedge \tfrac{1}{3} \cdot ((-2, 0, 0) + \mathbf{x}_3) + \tfrac{2}{3} \cdot ((1, 0, 0) + \mathbf{x}_4))$$
$$\mathbf{x}_3 = (0, 0, 1) + (\mathbf{b}_3 \wedge (2, 0, 0) + \mathbf{x}_2)$$
$$\mathbf{x}_4 = (0, 0, 1) + (\mathbf{b}_4 \wedge (-1, 0, 0) + \mathbf{x}_2)$$

The unique finite solution ρ of $\mathcal{E}^{r\sharp}$ is given by $\rho(\mathbf{b}_1) = (1, -2, 1)$, $\rho(\mathbf{b}_2) = (0, -1, 0)$, $\rho(\mathbf{b}_3) = (0, -1, 0)$, $\rho(\mathbf{b}_4) = (0, -1, 0)$, $\rho(\mathbf{x}_1) = (1, -2, 2)$, $\rho(\mathbf{x}_2) = (-2, -1, 6)$, $\rho(\mathbf{x}_3) = (0, -1, 1)$, $\rho(\mathbf{x}_4) = (-3, -1, 7)$. Lemma 3 implies $\mathbf{CanSol}(\mathcal{H}) = \alpha \circ \rho$. $\square$

An equation $\mathbf{x} = e$ is called *bounded* iff e is of the form $e' \wedge b \vee a$ with $-\infty < a, b < \infty$. A system $\mathcal{E}$ of equations is called *bounded* iff every equation of $\mathcal{E}$ is bounded. A bounded system $\mathcal{E}$ of non-zero stochastic equations over $\overline{\mathbb{R}}_d$ has exactly one solution $\rho^\sharp$. The problem of deciding, whether, for a given bounded system $\mathcal{E}$ of non-zero stochastic equations over $\overline{\mathbb{R}}_d$, a given variable $\mathbf{x}$, and a given $x \in \overline{\mathbb{R}}_d$, $\rho^\sharp(\mathbf{x}) \geq x$ holds, is called the quantitative decision problem for bounded systems of non-zero stochastic equations over $\overline{\mathbb{R}}_d$. Thereby $\rho^\sharp$ denotes the unique solution of $\mathcal{E}$. Since by lemma 3 the size of $\rho^\sharp$ is polynomial in the size of $\mathcal{E}$, the uniqueness of $\rho^\sharp$ implies that the quantitative decision problem is in $\mathbf{UP} \cap \mathbf{co{-}UP}$.

We use a strategy improvement algorithm for computing the unique solution $\rho^\sharp$ of a bounded system $\mathcal{E}$ of non-zero stochastic equations over $\overline{\mathbb{R}}_d$. Given a $\vee$-strategy σ and a pre-solution ρ, we say that a $\vee$-strategy σ' is an *improvement* of σ w.r.t. ρ iff $[\![\mathcal{E}(\sigma')]\!]\rho > [\![\mathcal{E}(\sigma)]\!]\rho$ holds. Assuming that $\rho \in \mathbf{PreSol}(\mathcal{E}) \setminus \mathbf{Sol}(\mathcal{E})$ holds, an improvement σ' of σ w.r.t. ρ can be computed in time $\mathcal{O}(\|\mathcal{E}\|)$ (w.r.t. the uniform cost measure). For instance one can choose σ' such that, for every expression $e = e_1 \vee \cdots \vee e_k$ occurring in $\mathcal{E}$, $\sigma'(e) = e_j$ only holds, if $[\![e_j]\!]\rho = [\![e]\!]\rho$ holds (known as *all profitable switches*). The definitions for $\wedge$-strategies are dual.

Our method for computing $\rho^\sharp$ starts with an arbitrary $\vee$-strategy σ_0 such that $\mathcal{E}(\sigma_0)$ has a unique finite solution ρ_0. The $\vee$-strategy which select a for every right-hand side $e \wedge b \vee a$ can be used for this purpose. Assume that, after the i-th step, σ_i is a $\vee$-strategy such that $\mathcal{E}(\sigma_i)$ has a unique finite solution $\rho_i < \rho^\sharp$. Let σ_{i+1} be an improvement of σ_i w.r.t. ρ_i. By Lemmas 2 and 3, it follows that $\mathcal{E}(\sigma_{i+1})$ has a unique finite solution ρ_{i+1} and it holds $\rho_i \leq \rho_{i+1} \leq \rho^\sharp$. Since ρ_i is not a solution of $\mathcal{E}(\sigma_{i+1})$, it follows $\rho_i < \rho_{i+1} \leq \rho^\sharp$. Thus $\rho_0, \rho_1, \ldots$ is strictly increasing until the unique solution $\rho^\sharp$ of $\mathcal{E}$ is reached. This must happen at the latest after iterating over all $\vee$-strategies.

Analogously, the unique finite solution ρ_i of the non-zero system $\mathcal{E}(\sigma_i)$ of stochastic equations over $\overline{\mathbb{R}}_d$ can also be computed by iterating over at most all $\wedge$-strategies for $\mathcal{E}(\sigma_i)$. Every $\wedge$-strategy π considered during this process leads to a non-zero system of *basic* stochastic equations over $\overline{\mathbb{R}}_d$ with a unique finite solution, which, according to the following lemma, can be computed using an arbitrary algorithm for solving linear equation systems.

Lemma 4. *Let $\mathcal{E}$ be a system of basic non-zero stochastic equations over $\overline{\mathbb{R}}_d$ with a unique finite solution ρ. For $i \in \{1, \ldots, d\}$ we set $\beta_i(x, y_1, \ldots, y_d) := y_i$ for $(x, y_1, \ldots, y_d) \in \mathbb{R}_d$ and $\beta_i(c) = c$ for $c \in \{-\infty, \infty\}$. For $\gamma \in \{\alpha, \beta_1, \ldots, \beta_d\}$ we denote the system of stochastic equations obtained from $\mathcal{E}$ by replacing every constant c occurring in $\mathcal{E}$ with $\gamma(c)$ by $\gamma(\mathcal{E})$. The following assertions hold:*

1. *The system $\gamma(\mathcal{E})$ has a unique finite solution ρ_γ for all $\gamma \in \{\alpha, \beta_1, \ldots, \beta_d\}$.*
2. *It holds $\rho(\mathbf{x}) = (\rho_\alpha(\mathbf{x}), \rho_{\beta_1}(\mathbf{x}), \ldots, \rho_{\beta_d}(\mathbf{x}))$ for all $\mathbf{x} \in \mathbf{X}$.* $\square$

As a consequence of the above lemma, the unique solution of a system $\mathcal{E}$ of basic non-zero stochastic equations over $\overline{\mathbb{R}}_d$, provided that it exists, can be computed in time $\mathcal{O}(d \cdot (|\mathbf{X}|^3 + \|\mathcal{E}\|))$ (w.r.t. the uniform cost measure). Moreover, if $\mathcal{E}$ is a system of basic non-zero *simple integer* equations over $\overline{\mathbb{R}}_d$ (see [8]), then this can be done in time $\mathcal{O}(d \cdot (|\mathbf{X}| + \|\mathcal{E}\|))$ (w.r.t. the uniform cost measure), since there are no cyclic variable dependencies.

We have shown that $\rho^\sharp$ can be computed using a strategy improvement algorithm which needs at most $\mathcal{O}(|\Sigma| \cdot |\Pi| \cdot d \cdot (|\mathbf{X}|^3 + \|\mathcal{E}\|))$ arithmetic operations. The numbers $|\Sigma|$ and $|\Pi|$ are exponential in the size of $\mathcal{E}$. However, it is not clear, whether there exist instances for which super-polynomial many strategy improvement steps are necessary.

Observe that all steps of the above procedure can be done in polynomial time. Summarizing, we have the following main result:

Lemma 5. *The unique solution of a bounded system $\mathcal{E}$ of non-zero stochastic equations over $\overline{\mathbb{R}}_d$ can be computed in time $|\Sigma| \cdot |\Pi| \cdot \mathcal{O}(d \cdot (|\mathbf{X}|^3 + \|\mathcal{E}\|))$ (w.r.t. the uniform cost measure) using a strategy improvement algorithm. The quantitative decision problem for bounded systems of non-zero stochastic equations over $\overline{\mathbb{R}}_d$ is in $\mathbf{UP} \cap \mathbf{co-UP}$.* □

A hierarchical system $\mathcal{H} = (\mathcal{E}, r)$ is called *bounded* iff $\mathcal{E}$ is bounded. The problem of deciding, whether, for a given bounded hierarchical system of stochastic equations $\mathcal{H} = (\mathcal{E}, r)$, a given $\mathbf{x} \in \mathbf{X}$, and a given $x \in \overline{\mathbb{R}}$, $\mathbf{CanSol}(\mathcal{H})(\mathbf{x}) \geq x$ holds, is called the quantitative decision problem for bounded hierarchical systems of stochastic equations.

We finally want to compute the canonical solution $\mathbf{CanSol}(\mathcal{H})$ of a bounded hierarchical system $\mathcal{H} = (\mathcal{E}, r)$ of stochastic equations. By Lemma 3, it suffices to compute the *unique* solution of the bounded system $\mathcal{E}^{r\sharp}$ which can be done according to Lemma 5. Thus, we obtain:

Theorem 1. *The canonical solution of a bounded hierarchical system $\mathcal{H} = (\mathcal{E}, r)$ of stochastic equations can be computed in time $|\Sigma| \cdot |\Pi| \cdot \mathcal{O}(d \cdot (|\mathbf{X}|^3 + \|\mathcal{E}\|))$ (w.r.t. the uniform cost measure) using a strategy improvement algorithm, where $d = \max r(\mathbf{X})$ is the highest occurring rank. The quantitative decision problem for bounded hierarchical systems of stochastic equations is in $\mathbf{UP} \cap \mathbf{co-UP}$.* □

If a hierarchical system $\mathcal{H} = (\mathcal{E}, r)$ of stochastic equations is not bounded but has a finite canonical solution $\mathbf{CanSol}(\mathcal{H})$, then it is nevertheless possible to compute $\mathbf{CanSol}(\mathcal{H})$ using the developed techniques. For that, one first computes a bound $B(\mathcal{E})$ such that $|\mathbf{CanSol}(\mathcal{H})(\mathbf{x})| \leq B(\mathcal{E})$ holds for all $\mathbf{x} \in \mathbf{X}$. Then one solves the hierarchical system $(\mathcal{E} \wedge B(\mathcal{E}) \vee -B(\mathcal{E}), r)$ instead of $\mathcal{H}$, where $\mathcal{E} \wedge B(\mathcal{E}) \vee -B(\mathcal{E}) := \{\mathbf{x} = e \wedge B(\mathcal{E}) \vee -B(\mathcal{E}) \mid \mathbf{x} = e \in \mathcal{E}\}$. An adequate bound $B(\mathcal{E})$ can be computed in polynomial time. Moreover, there will be obvious bounds to the absolute values of the components of the canonical solutions in the applications in the following sections.

4   Solving Deterministic Total-Payoff Games

A lower complexity bound. In a first step we establish a lower complexity bound for deterministic total-payoff games by reducing deterministic mean-payoff games to deterministic total-payoff games. The quantitative decision problem for mean-payoff games is in $\mathbf{UP} \cap \mathbf{co-UP}$ [13], but, despite of many attempts for finding polynomial algorithms, not known to be in $\mathbf{P}$. Let $\mathcal{G} = (G, c)$ be a deterministic mean-payoff game, where we w.l.o.g. assume that all immediate rewards are from $\mathbb{Z}$, i.e., it holds $c(E) \subseteq \mathbb{Z}$.

Lemma 6. *For all positions $p \in P$ and all $x \in \mathbb{R}$ it holds:*

$$\langle\!\langle p \rangle\!\rangle_{(G,U_c^{\mathrm{mp}})} \begin{cases} < x & \text{if } \langle\!\langle p \rangle\!\rangle_{(G,U_{c-x}^{\mathrm{tp}})} = -\infty \\ = x & \text{if } \langle\!\langle p \rangle\!\rangle_{(G,U_{c-x}^{\mathrm{tp}})} \in \mathbb{R} \\ > x & \text{if } \langle\!\langle p \rangle\!\rangle_{(G,U_{c-x}^{\mathrm{tp}})} = \infty. \end{cases}$$

$\square$

By lemma 6 the quantitative decision problem for mean-payoff games is polynomial-time reducible to the problem of computing the values of total-payoff games. Since the problem of computing the values of mean-payoff games is polynomial-time reducible to the quantitative decision problem for mean-payoff games we finally get:

Theorem 2. *Computing the values of deterministic mean-payoff games is polynomial-time reducible to computing the values of deterministic total-payoff games.* $\square$

Computing the values. Our next goal is to compute the values of deterministic total-payoff games. We do this through *hierarchical systems of stochastic equations*. Since stochastic expressions like $\frac{1}{2}e_1 + \frac{1}{2}e_2$ are ruled out, we only need *hierarchical systems of simple integer equations* as considered in [8].

Let $\mathcal{G} = (G, c)$ be a deterministic total-payoff game where we w.l.o.g. assume that $P_+ = \emptyset$ holds. For every Position $p \in P$ we define the expression $e_{\mathcal{G},p}$ by

$$e_{\mathcal{G},p} := \begin{cases} \bigvee_{p' \in \{p\}E} c(p,p') + \mathbf{x}_{p'} & \text{if } p \in P_\vee \\ \bigwedge_{p' \in \{p\}E} c(p,p') + \mathbf{x}_{p'} & \text{if } p \in P_\wedge. \end{cases}$$

Finally, we define, for $b \in \mathbb{N}$, the hierarchical system $\mathcal{H}_{\mathcal{G},b} = (\mathcal{E}_{\mathcal{G},b}, r_{\mathcal{G}})$ by

$$\mathcal{E}_{\mathcal{G},b} := \{\mathbf{b}_p = (0 \vee e_{\mathcal{G},p}) \wedge 2b + 1, \ \mathbf{x}_p = (\mathbf{b}_p \wedge e_{\mathcal{G},p}) \vee -2b - 1 \mid p \in P\}$$

and $r_{\mathcal{G}} := \{\mathbf{b}_p \mapsto 1, \ \mathbf{x}_p \mapsto 2 \mid p \in P\}$. We set $B(\mathcal{G}) := \sum_{m \in E} |c(m)|$, $\mathcal{E}_{\mathcal{G}} := \mathcal{E}_{\mathcal{G},B(\mathcal{G})}$, and $\mathcal{H}_{\mathcal{G}} := (\mathcal{E}_{\mathcal{G}}, r_{\mathcal{G}})$.

Thus $\mathcal{H}_{\mathcal{G}}$ is a hierarchical system, where the variables $\mathbf{x}_p$ ($p \in P$) live within the scope of the variables $\mathbf{b}_p$ ($p \in P$). Moreover, the $\mathbf{x}_p$'s ($p \in P$) are "greatest" whereas the $\mathbf{b}_p$'s ($p \in P$) are "least fixpoint variables". Intuitively, we are searching for the greatest values for the $\mathbf{x}_p$'s ($p \in P$) under the least possible bounds $\mathbf{b}_p$'s ($p \in P$) that are greater than or equal to 0. We illustrate the reduction by an example:

Example 5 (The Reduction). Let $\mathcal{G}$ be the deterministic total-payoff game shown in figure 1. The system $\mathcal{E}_{\mathcal{G},11}$ of simple integer equations is given by:

$$\begin{aligned}
\mathbf{b}_a &= (0 \vee (1 + \mathbf{x}_b \vee 2 + \mathbf{x}_d)) \wedge 23 & \mathbf{x}_a &= (\mathbf{b}_a \wedge (1 + \mathbf{x}_b \vee 2 + \mathbf{x}_d)) \vee -23 \\
\mathbf{b}_b &= (0 \vee 4 + \mathbf{x}_c) \wedge 23 & \mathbf{x}_b &= (\mathbf{b}_b \wedge 4 + \mathbf{x}_c) \vee -23 \\
\mathbf{b}_c &= (0 \vee -4 + \mathbf{x}_b) \wedge 23 & \mathbf{x}_c &= (\mathbf{b}_c \wedge -4 + \mathbf{x}_b) \vee -23 \\
\mathbf{b}_d &= (0 \vee \mathbf{x}_e) \wedge 23 & \mathbf{x}_d &= (\mathbf{b}_d \wedge \mathbf{x}_e) \vee -23 \\
\mathbf{b}_e &= (0 \vee \mathbf{x}_d) \wedge 23 & \mathbf{x}_e &= (\mathbf{b}_e \wedge \mathbf{x}_d) \vee -23 \,.
\end{aligned}$$

Together with the rank function $r_{\mathcal{G}}$ defined by $r_{\mathcal{G}}(\mathbf{b}_a) = r_{\mathcal{G}}(\mathbf{b}_b) = r_{\mathcal{G}}(\mathbf{b}_c) = r_{\mathcal{G}}(\mathbf{b}_d) = r_{\mathcal{G}}(\mathbf{b}_e) = 1$ and $r_{\mathcal{G}}(\mathbf{x}_a) = r_{\mathcal{G}}(\mathbf{x}_b) = r_{\mathcal{G}}(\mathbf{x}_c) = r_{\mathcal{G}}(\mathbf{x}_d) = r_{\mathcal{G}}(\mathbf{x}_e) = 2$ we have given the hierarchical system $\mathcal{H}_{\mathcal{G},11} = (\mathcal{E}_{\mathcal{G},11}, r_{\mathcal{G}})$. Then $\mathbf{CanSol}(\mathcal{H}_{\mathcal{G},11}) = \{\mathbf{b}_a \mapsto 2, \mathbf{b}_b \mapsto 0, \mathbf{b}_c \mapsto 0, \mathbf{b}_d \mapsto 0, \mathbf{b}_e \mapsto 0, \mathbf{x}_a \mapsto 2, \mathbf{x}_b \mapsto 0, \mathbf{x}_c \mapsto -4, \mathbf{x}_d \mapsto 0, \mathbf{x}_e \mapsto 0\}$. $\square$

In order to show that the values of a total-payoff game $\mathcal{G}$ are given by the canonical solution of the hierarchical system $\mathcal{H}_\mathcal{G}$, we first show this result for the case that no player has choices. In order to simplify notations, for $b \in \mathbb{N}$, we set

$$v_b(x) := \begin{cases} -\infty & \text{if } x < -b \\ x & \text{if } b \leq x \leq b \\ \infty & \text{if } x > b \end{cases}, \quad x \in \overline{\mathbb{R}}.$$

Lemma 7. *Let* $\mathcal{G} = (G, c)$ *be a 0-player deterministic total-payoff game and* $b \geq B(\mathcal{G})$. *It holds* $\langle\!\langle p \rangle\!\rangle = v_b(\mathbf{CanSol}(\mathcal{H}_{\mathcal{G},b})(\mathbf{x}_p))$ *for all* $p \in P$. $\square$

In order to generalize the statement of the above lemma, we show that (in a certain sense) there exist positional optimal strategies for the hierarchical system $\mathcal{H}_{\mathcal{G},b}$:

Lemma 8. *Let* $\mathcal{G}$ *be a deterministic total-payoff game and* $b \in \mathbb{N}$. *It hold*

1. $\mathbf{CanSol}(\mathcal{H}_{\mathcal{G},b}) = \max_{\sigma \in \Sigma} \mathbf{CanSol}(\mathcal{H}_{\mathcal{G}(\sigma),b})$ *and*
2. $\mathbf{CanSol}(\mathcal{H}_{\mathcal{G},b}) = \min_{\pi \in \Pi} \mathbf{CanSol}(\mathcal{H}_{\mathcal{G}(\pi),b})$.

Proof. We only show statement 1. Statement 2 can be shown analogously. By monotonicity it holds $\mathbf{CanSol}(\mathcal{H}_{\mathcal{G}(\sigma),b}) \leq \mathbf{CanSol}(\mathcal{H}_{\mathcal{G},b})$ for all $\sigma \in \Sigma$. It remains to show that there exists some $\sigma \in \Sigma$ such that $\mathbf{CanSol}(\mathcal{H}_{\mathcal{G}(\sigma),b}) = \mathbf{CanSol}(\mathcal{H}_{\mathcal{G},b})$ holds. Since by lemma 3 $\mathcal{E}^{rg\sharp}_{\mathcal{G},b}$ has a unique finite solution $\rho^\sharp$, there exists a $\sigma \in \Sigma$ such that $\rho^\sharp$ is the unique finite solution of the system $\mathcal{E}^{rg\sharp}_{\mathcal{G}(\sigma),b}$. Thus lemma 3 gives us that $\mathbf{CanSol}(\mathcal{H}_{\mathcal{G}(\sigma),b}) = \alpha \circ \rho^\sharp = \mathbf{CanSol}(\mathcal{H}_{\mathcal{G},b})$ holds. $\square$

We now prove our main result for deterministic total-payoff games:

Lemma 9. *Let* $b \geq B(\mathcal{G})$. *It holds* $\langle\!\langle p \rangle\!\rangle = v_b(\mathbf{CanSol}(\mathcal{H}_{\mathcal{G},b})(\mathbf{x}_p))$ *for every* $p \in P$.

Proof. For every $p \in P$, it holds

$$\begin{aligned}
\langle\!\langle p \rangle\!\rangle_\mathcal{G} &= \max_{\sigma \in \Sigma} \min_{\pi \in \Pi} \langle\!\langle p \rangle\!\rangle_{\mathcal{G}(\sigma)(\pi)} && \text{(Lemma 1)} \\
&= \max_{\sigma \in \Sigma} \min_{\pi \in \Pi} v_b(\mathbf{CanSol}(\mathcal{H}_{\mathcal{G}(\sigma)(\pi),b})(\mathbf{x}_p)) && \text{(Lemma 7)} \\
&= v_b(\max_{\sigma \in \Sigma} \min_{\pi \in \Pi} (\mathbf{CanSol}(\mathcal{H}_{\mathcal{G}(\sigma)(\pi),b})(\mathbf{x}_p))) && \\
&= v_b(\mathbf{CanSol}(\mathcal{H}_{\mathcal{G},b})(\mathbf{x}_p)) && \text{(Lemma 8).}\quad\square
\end{aligned}$$

We additionally want to compute positional optimal strategies. By lemma 3 $\mathcal{E}^{rg\sharp}_\mathcal{G}$ has a unique finite solution $\rho^\sharp$ and it holds $\mathbf{CanSol}(\mathcal{H}_\mathcal{G}) = \alpha \circ \rho^\sharp$. The unique finite solution can be computed using lemma 5. A $\vee$-strategy σ and a $\wedge$-strategy π such that $\rho^\sharp$ is a solution and thus the unique finite solution of $\mathcal{E}^{rg\sharp}_{\mathcal{G}(\sigma),B(\mathcal{G})}$ and $\mathcal{E}^{rg\sharp}_{\mathcal{G}(\pi),B(\mathcal{G})}$ can then be computed in linear time. Thus, it holds $\mathbf{CanSol}(\mathcal{H}_{\mathcal{G}(\sigma),B(\mathcal{G})}) = \mathbf{CanSol}(\mathcal{H}_\mathcal{G}) = \mathbf{CanSol}(\mathcal{H}_{\mathcal{G}(\pi),B(\mathcal{G})})$ which (by lemma 9) implies $\langle\!\langle \cdot \rangle\!\rangle_{\mathcal{G}(\sigma)} = \langle\!\langle \cdot \rangle\!\rangle_\mathcal{G} = \langle\!\langle \cdot \rangle\!\rangle_{\mathcal{G}(\pi)}$. Thus, σ and π are positional optimal strategies. Summarizing, we have shown:

Theorem 3. *Let* $\mathcal{G}$ *be a deterministic total-payoff game. The values and positional optimal strategies for both players can be computed using a strategy improvement algorithm. Each inner strategy improvement step can be done in time* $\mathcal{O}(\|\mathcal{G}\|)$ *(w.r.t. the uniform cost measure). The quantitative decision problem is in* $\mathbf{UP} \cap \mathbf{co-UP}$. $\square$

Additionally one can show that the strategy improvement algorithm presented in section 3 needs only polynomial time for solving deterministic 1-player total-payoff games.

5 Solving Stochastic Liminf-Payoff Games

In this section we characterize the values of a liminf-payoff game $\mathcal{G} = (G, r)$ by a hierarchical system of stochastic equations. Firstly, observe that the values fulfill the *optimality equations*, i.e., $\langle\!\langle p \rangle\!\rangle = \bigvee_{p' \in \{p\}E} \langle\!\langle p' \rangle\!\rangle$ for all $p \in P_\vee$, $\langle\!\langle p \rangle\!\rangle = \bigwedge_{p' \in \{p\}E} \langle\!\langle p' \rangle\!\rangle$ for all $p \in P_\wedge$, and $\langle\!\langle p \rangle\!\rangle = \sum_{p' \in \{p\}E} \delta(p)(p') \cdot \langle\!\langle p' \rangle\!\rangle$ for all $p \in P_+$. The optimality equations, however, do not have unique solutions. In order to obtain the desired solution, we define the hierarchical system $\mathcal{H}_\mathcal{G} = (\mathcal{E}_\mathcal{G}, r_\mathcal{G})$ by

$$\mathcal{E}_\mathcal{G} := \{ \mathbf{b}_p = r(p) \vee e_{\mathcal{G},p}, \ \mathbf{x}_p = \mathbf{b}_p \wedge e_{\mathcal{G},p} \mid p \in P \}$$

and $r_\mathcal{G}(\mathbf{b}_p) := 1$, $r_\mathcal{G}(\mathbf{x}_p) := 2$ for all $p \in P$, where

$$e_{\mathcal{G},p} := \begin{cases} \bigvee_{p' \in \{p\}E} \mathbf{x}_{p'} & \text{if } p \in P_\vee \\ \bigwedge_{p' \in \{p\}E} \mathbf{x}_{p'} & \text{if } p \in P_\wedge \\ \sum_{p' \in \{p\}E} \delta(p)(p') \cdot \mathbf{x}_{p'} & \text{if } p \in P_+ \end{cases}, \qquad p \in P.$$

Analogously to lemma 8 we find:

Lemma 10. *Let $\mathcal{G}$ be a stochastic liminf-payoff game. It hold*
1. $\mathbf{CanSol}(\mathcal{H}_\mathcal{G}) = \max_{\sigma \in \Sigma} \mathbf{CanSol}(\mathcal{H}_{\mathcal{G}(\sigma)})$ *and*
2. $\mathbf{CanSol}(\mathcal{H}_\mathcal{G}) = \min_{\pi \in \Pi} \mathbf{CanSol}(\mathcal{H}_{\mathcal{G}(\pi)})$. □

Finally, we can show the correctness of our reduction. Because of Lemma 1 and 10, we only have to consider the 0-player case. There the interesting situation is within an end-component, i.e., a strongly connected component without out-going edges. In such a component every position is visited infinitely often. Thus, the value of every position in such a component is equal to the minimal immediate payoff within the component. By induction one can show that this corresponds to the canonical solution of the hierarchical system $\mathcal{H}_\mathcal{G}$. Since the canonical solution solves the optimality equations and there exists exactly one solution of the optimality equations where the values of all positions in end-components are fixed, we finally obtain the following lemma:

Lemma 11. *It holds* $\langle\!\langle p \rangle\!\rangle = \mathbf{CanSol}(\mathcal{H}_\mathcal{G})(\mathbf{x}_p)$ *for every position* $p \in P$. □

We want to compute positional optimal strategies. By lemma 3 $\mathcal{E}_\mathcal{G}^{r_\mathcal{G}\sharp}$ has a unique finite solution $\rho^\sharp$ and it holds $\mathbf{CanSol}(\mathcal{H}_\mathcal{G}) = \alpha \circ \rho^\sharp$. The unique finite solution can be computed using lemma 5. A $\vee$-strategy σ and a $\wedge$-strategy π such that $\rho^\sharp$ is a solution and thus the unique finite solution of $\mathcal{E}_{\mathcal{G}(\sigma)}^{r_\mathcal{G}\sharp}$ and $\mathcal{E}_{\mathcal{G}(\pi)}^{r_\mathcal{G}\sharp}$ can then be computed in time $\mathcal{O}(\|\mathcal{G}\|)$ (w.r.t. the uniform cost measure). Thus, it holds $\mathbf{CanSol}(\mathcal{H}_{\mathcal{G}(\sigma)}) = \mathbf{CanSol}(\mathcal{H}_\mathcal{G}) = \mathbf{CanSol}(\mathcal{H}_{\mathcal{G}(\pi)})$ which (by lemma 11) implies $\langle\!\langle \cdot \rangle\!\rangle_{\mathcal{G}(\sigma)} = \langle\!\langle \cdot \rangle\!\rangle_\mathcal{G} = \langle\!\langle \cdot \rangle\!\rangle_{\mathcal{G}(\pi)}$. Thus, σ and π are positional optimal strategies. Summarizing, we have shown:

Theorem 4. *Let $\mathcal{G}$ be a stochastic liminf-payoff game. The values and positional optimal strategies for both players can be computed using a strategy improvement algorithm. Each inner strategy improvement step can be done in time $\mathcal{O}(|P|^3)$ (w.r.t. the uniform cost measure). The quantitative decision problem is in $\mathbf{UP} \cap \mathbf{co{-}UP}$.* □

It is not clear whether the strategy improvement algorithm presented in section 3 needs only polynomial time for solving deterministic 1-player total-payoff games.

6   Solving Stochastic Parity Games

In this section we characterize the values of a stochastic parity game $\mathcal{G} = (G, r)$. For that, we define the hierarchical system $\mathcal{H}_{\mathcal{G}} = (\mathcal{E}_{\mathcal{G}}, r_{\mathcal{G}})$ of stochastic equations by $\mathcal{E}_{\mathcal{G}} := \{\mathbf{x}_p = e_{\mathcal{G},p} \wedge 1 \vee 0 \mid p \in P\}$ and $r_{\mathcal{G}}(\mathbf{x}_p) := r(p)$, $p \in P$. Thereby, the expression $e_{\mathcal{G},p}$ is defined as in section 5. We get:

Lemma 12. *For every position $p \in P$ it holds $\langle\!\langle p \rangle\!\rangle = \mathbf{CanSol}(\mathcal{H}_{\mathcal{G}})(\mathbf{x}_p)$.* $\qquad\square$

Since lemma 10 holds also for stochastic parity games (with the definition of $\mathcal{H}_{\mathcal{G}}$ given in this section), one can use the strategy improvement algorithm presented in section 3 for computing the values and positional optimal strategies. This is literally the same as for liminf-payoff games. We get:

Theorem 6.1 *Let $\mathcal{G}$ be a stochastic parity game. The values and positional optimal strategies for both players can be computed using a strategy improvement algorithm. Each inner strategy improvement step can be done in time $\mathcal{O}(|P|^3)$ (w.r.t. the uniform cost measure). The quantitative decision problem is in $\mathbf{UP} \cap \mathbf{co-UP}$.* $\qquad\square$

Finally, we show that computing the values of stochastic parity games is at least as hard as computing the values of stochastic liminf-payoff games. The values of a stochastic liminf-payoff game $\mathcal{G}$ can (by lemma 11) be characterized by the hierarchical system $\mathcal{H}_{\mathcal{G}}$ of equations (see the definition in section 5). Let us assume that $r(P) \subseteq [0, 1]$ holds. This precondition can be achieved in polynomial time by shifting and scaling r. Now one can set up a stochastic parity game $\overline{\mathcal{G}}$ such that the hierarchical system $\mathcal{H}_{\overline{\mathcal{G}}}$ (see the definition in this section) which characterizes the values of $\overline{\mathcal{G}}$, and the hierarchical system $\mathcal{H}_{\mathcal{G}}$ have the same canonical solution (besides additional variables). Thus, using lemma 11 and lemma 12 we obtain the following result:

Theorem 6.2 *Computing the values of stochastic liminf-payoff games is polynomial-time reducible to computing the values of stochastic parity games with at most 2 different ranks.* $\qquad\square$

Stochastic parity games are polynomial-time reducible to stochastic mean-payoff games [3]. The latter are polynomial-time equivalent to simple stochastic games [12]. Since stochastic liminf-payoff games generalize simple stochastic games, computing the values of stochastic liminf-payoff games is in fact polynomial-time equivalent to computing the values of stochastic parity games.

7   Conclusion

We introduced hierarchical systems of stochastic equations and presented a practical algorithm for solving bounded hierarchical systems of stochastic equations. The obtained results could be applied to deterministic total-payoff games and stochastic liminf-payoff games. We showed how to compute the values of as well as optimal strategies for these games through a reduction to hierarchical systems of stochastic equations — which results in practical strategy improvement algorithms. In the deterministic case, the 1-player games can be solved in polynomial time. We also proved that the quantitative decision problems for theses games are in $UP \cap co-UP$. As a by-product we obtained that the problem of computing the values of stochastic liminf-payoff games is polynomial-time reducible to the problem of computing the values of stochastic parity games.

References

1. Björklund, H., Vorobyov, S.G.: A combinatorial strongly subexponential strategy improvement algorithm for mean payoff games. Discrete Applied Mathematics (2007)
2. Chatterjee, K., Henzinger, T.A.: Strategy improvement and randomized subexponential algorithms for stochastic parity games. In: Durand, B., Thomas, W. (eds.) STACS 2006. LNCS, vol. 3884, pp. 512–523. Springer, Heidelberg (2006)
3. Chatterjee, K., Henzinger, T.A.: Reduction of stochastic parity to stochastic mean-payoff games. Inf. Process. Lett. 106(1), 1–7 (2008)
4. Chatterjee, K., Henzinger, T.A.: Probabilistic systems with limsup and liminf objectives. ILC (to appear, 2009)
5. Chatterjee, K., Jurdzinski, M., Henzinger, T.A.: Quantitative stochastic parity games. In: SODA, pp. 121–130 (2004)
6. Ehrenfeucht, A., Mycielski, J.: Positional strategies for mean payoff games. IJGT 8, 109–113 (1979)
7. Fischer, D., Grädel, E., Kaiser, L.: Model checking games for the quantitative μ-calculus. In: STACS, pp. 301–312 (2008)
8. Gawlitza, T., Seidl, H.: Computing game values for crash games. In: Namjoshi, K.S., Yoneda, T., Higashino, T., Okamura, Y. (eds.) ATVA 2007. LNCS, vol. 4762, pp. 177–191. Springer, Heidelberg (2007)
9. Gillette, D.: Stochastic games with zero stop probabilities. In: Contributions to the Theory of Games III, vol. 39, pp. 179–187. Princeton University Press, Princeton (1957)
10. Gimbert, H., Zielonka, W.: When can you play positionally? In: Fiala, J., Koubek, V., Kratochvíl, J. (eds.) MFCS 2004. LNCS, vol. 3153, pp. 686–697. Springer, Heidelberg (2004)
11. Gurvich, V., Karzanov, A., Khachiyan, L.: Cyclic games and an algorithm to find minimax cycle means in directed graphs. U.S.S.R. Computational Mathematics and Mathematical Physics 28(5), 85–91 (1988)
12. Gurvich, V., Miltersen, P.B.: On the computational complexity of solving stochastic mean-payoff games. CoRR, abs/0812.0486 (2008)
13. Jurdzinski, M.: Deciding the winner in parity games is in $UP \cap co - UP$. Inf. Process. Lett. 68(3), 119–124 (1998)
14. Liggett, T.M., Lippman, S.A.: Stochastic games with perfect information and time average payoff. SIAM Review 11, 604–607 (1969)
15. Maitra, A., Sudderth, W.: An operator solution of stochastic games. Israel Journal of Mathematics 78, 33–49 (1992)
16. Maitra, A., Sudderth, W.: Borel stochastic games with limsup payoff. Annals of Probability 21, 861–885 (1993)
17. Pisaruk, N.: Mean cost cyclical games. Mathematics of Operations Research 24(4), 817–828 (1999)
18. Thuijsman, F., Vrieze, O.: Total reward stochastic games and sensitive average reward strategies. Journal of Optimazation Theory and Applications 98 (1998)
19. Zwick, U., Paterson, M.: The Complexity of Mean Payoff Games on Graphs. Theoretical Computer Science (TCS) 158(1,2), 343–359 (1996)

Complete Instantiation for Quantified Formulas in Satisfiabiliby Modulo Theories

Yeting Ge[1] and Leonardo de Moura[2]

[1] Department of Computer Science, New York University, NY, NY 10012, USA
yeting@cs.nyu.edu
[2] Microsoft Research, One Microsoft Way, Redmond, WA 98052, USA
leonardo@microsoft.com

Abstract. Quantifier reasoning in Satisfiability Modulo Theories (SMT) is a long-standing challenge. The practical method employed in modern SMT solvers is to instantiate quantified formulas based on heuristics, which is not refutationally complete even for pure first-order logic. We present several decidable fragments of first order logic modulo theories. We show how to construct models for satisfiable formulas in these fragments. For richer undecidable fragments, we discuss conditions under which our procedure is refutationally complete. We also describe useful heuristics based on model checking for prioritizing or avoiding instantiations.

1 Introduction

Applications in software verification have benefited greatly from recent advances in automated reasoning. Applications in this field often require determining the satisfiability of first-order formulas with respect to some background theories. Satisfiability Modulo Theories (SMT) solvers have proven highly scalable, efficient and suitable for integrated theory reasoning. Most SMT solvers are restricted to ground formulas. However, for numerous applications in software verification, quantifiers are needed. For example, quantifiers are convenient for capturing frame conditions over loops, summarizing auxiliary invariants over heaps, and for supplying axioms of theories that are not already equipped with decision procedures for ground formulas.

Quantifier reasoning in SMT is a long-standing challenge. Because most quantified SMT formulas contain both interpreted and uninterpreted symbols, it is difficult to have a general decision procedure for quantifiers in SMT. For example, there is no sound and complete procedure for first-order logic formulas of linear arithmetic with uninterpreted function symbols [1]. Some SMT solvers [2,3] integrate the superposition calculus with ground decision procedures. These solvers are refutationally complete for pure first-order logic with equality, but do not provide any guarantee when other interpreted symbols appear in quantified formulas. Several first-order calculi have been proposed based on the idea of theory resolution [4]. These calculi provide nice theoretical results, yet no efficient implementations, because the computation of theory unifiers is too expensive or impossible for

A. Bouajjani and O. Maler (Eds.): CAV 2009, LNCS 5643, pp. 306–320, 2009.
© Springer-Verlag Berlin Heidelberg 2009

background theories of interest. In general, it is inefficient to use general first-order theorem prover to check the satisfiability of SMT formulas when the background theory does not have a finite axiomatization (e.g., arithmetic).

Most state-of-the-art SMT solvers with support for quantifiers use heuristic quantifier instantiation [5,6,7,3] for incorporating quantifier reasoning with ground decision procedures. A well known heuristic instantiation-based approach is the E-matching algorithm introduced by the Simplify theorem prover [8]. Although heuristic instantiation is relatively effective for some software verification applications [9,10], it suffers from several problems: it is not refutationally complete for first-order logic, hints (triggers) are usually required, it is sensitive to the syntactic structure of the formula, and it fails to prove formulas that can be easily discharged by saturation-based provers.

Instantiation-based approaches are attractive because SMT solvers have efficient ground decision procedures for many useful theories. For some fragments of first order logic modulo theories, we have complete decision procedures based on quantifier instantiation. We call this type of decision procedure complete instantiation.

In this paper, we investigate several decidable fragments of first-order logic modulo theories. The new fragments subsume well-known fragments such as the Bernays-Schönfinkel class, stratified vocabularies for many-sorted logic [11], and the Array Property Fragment [12]. We also consider richer fragments which are not decidable, and we discuss conditions under which our procedure is refutationally complete. The proposed decision procedures can be directly used to prove complex quantified array properties. Arrays are common in most programming languages and provide a natural model for memories. Decision procedures for array theories are of great interest for verification applications. Our approach is also suitable for formulas coming from verification of parameterized systems, and the axiomatization application specific theories (e.g., the axiomatization of the Spec# type system based on the theory of partial orders).

In software verification, models of satisfiable verification conditions are of great interest because they usually suggest potential errors. Therefore, we also show how to construct models for satisfiable quantified formulas in these fragments. On the implementation side, we describe useful heuristics based on model checking for prioritizing or avoiding instantiations.

The ground terms used for instantiating quantified formulas come from the least solution of systems of set constraints. We first consider a fragment in which quantified variables only occur as arguments of uninterpreted function (predicate) symbols. Then, we introduce more fragments, by relaxing some restrictions and by augmenting the system of constraints. We give examples to illustrate the usefulness of these fragments as well.

2   Background

We will assume the usual notions and terminology of first order logic and model theory. Let Σ be a *signature* consisting of a set of *function* and *predicate* symbols.

Each function symbol f is associated with a non-negative integer, the *arity* of f, denoted by $arity(f)$. We call 0-arity function symbols *constant* symbols, and usually denote them by a, b, c and d. We use f, g, h to denote non-constant function symbols, and x_1, x_2, x_3,... to denote variables. We use t, r, s to denote arbitrary terms. An f-application is a term of the form $f(t_1, \ldots, t_n)$. We call an *atomic formula* a formula of the form $p(t_1, \ldots, t_n)$, where p is a predicate symbol. A *literal* is an atomic formula or the negation of one. A *clause* is a disjunction $l_1 \vee \ldots \vee l_n$ of literals. A *CNF formula* is a conjunction $C_1 \wedge \ldots \wedge C_n$ of clauses. We use C_i to denote the i-th clause in a CNF formula. Without loss of generality, we assume every formula that is being checked for satisfiability is in CNF, and any variable in a clause C is universally quantified. We also assume that existentially quantified variables were eliminated using *Skolemization*. For instance, the formula $\forall x \colon \exists y \colon \neg p(x) \vee q(y)$ is converted into the equisatisfiable formula $\forall x \colon \neg p(x) \vee q(f_y(x))$, where f_y is a fresh function symbol. We will write CNF formulas replacing the $\wedge$ connectives by commas. We use $C[x_1, \ldots, x_n]$ to denote a clause that may contain variables x_1, ..., x_n, and a similar notation $t[x_1, \ldots, x_n]$ is defined for a term t. Where there is no confusion, we denote $C[x_1, \ldots, x_n]$ by $C[\overline{x}]$ and $t[x_1, \ldots, x_n]$ by $t[\overline{x}]$. In the rest of this paper, the difference between functions and predicates is trivial, and we will thus only discuss functions except at a few places.

A first order Σ-theory T is a set of deductively closed Σ-sentences. Interpreted symbols are those symbols whose interpretation is restricted to the models of a certain theory T, whereas free or uninterpreted symbols are those symbols not in Σ. In this paper we assume the usual interpreted symbols for equality, linear arithmetic and bit-vectors. We use $\simeq$ to denote the interpreted predicate symbol for equality.

A Σ-structure M consists of a non-empty universe $|M|$ and an interpretation for variables and symbols in Σ. For each symbol f in Σ, the interpretation of f is denoted by $M(f)$. For a function symbol f with $arity(f) = n$, the interpretation $M(f)$ is a total n-ary function on $|M|$. For each predicate symbol p with $arity(p) = n$, $M(p)$ is a subset of $|M|^n$. For a variable x, $M(x)$ is an element in $|M|$. The interpretation of an arbitrary term t is denoted by $M[\![t]\!]$ and defined as: $M[\![m]\!] = M(m)$ for constant or variable m, and $M[\![f(t_1, \ldots, t_n)]\!] = M(f)(M[\![t_1]\!], \ldots, M[\![t_n]\!])$. If S is a set of terms, $M(S)$ means the set $\{M(t) \mid t \in S\}$.

We use $M\{x \mapsto v\}$ to denote a structure where the variable symbol x is interpreted as v, $v \in |M|$, and all other variables, function and predicate symbols have the same interpretation as in M. That is $M\{x \mapsto v\}(x) = v$. $M\{\overline{x} \mapsto \overline{v}\}$ denotes $M\{x_1 \mapsto v_1\}\{x_2 \mapsto v_2\} \ldots \{x_n \mapsto v_n\}$.

Satisfaction $M \models \phi$ is defined as usual. In particular, given atomic formula $p(t_1, \ldots, t_n)$, $M \models p(t_1, \ldots, t_n)$ if and only if $(M[\![t_1]\!], \ldots, M[\![t_n]\!]) \in M(p)$. Given a vector $\overline{x}$ of n variables, $M \models C[\overline{x}]$ if for all $\overline{v} \in |M|^n$ there is a literal l in $C[\overline{x}]$ such that $M\{\overline{x} \mapsto \overline{v}\} \models l$. M is a model for a formula F if $M \models F$. A formula is *satisfiable* if and only if it has a model. A formula F is satisfiable modulo theory

T if there is a model for $\{F\} \cup T$. A formula F is satisfiable modulo a class Ω of intended structures if there is a M in Ω that is a model for F.

3   Essentially Uninterpreted Formulas

Given a theory T, we say a formula F is *essentially uninterpreted* if any variable in F appears only as an argument of uninterpreted function or predicate symbols.

Example 1 (essentially uninterpreted clause). In the following example, the symbols $+$ and $\leq$ are interpreted by the theory of arithmetic, and a, b, f, g, h and p are uninterpreted symbols.

$$f(g(x_1) + a) \leq h(x_1) \vee p(f(x_1) + b, x_2)$$

We show that every essentially uninterpreted formula F is equisatisfiable to a (potentially infinite) set of ground formulas F^*. For that purpose, let us introduce some additional notational conventions. For a term $t[x_1, \ldots, x_n]$, $t[r_1, \ldots, r_n]$ is the result of simultaneously substituting r_i for x_i $(1 \leq i \leq n)$ in t. When S_i $(1 \leq i \leq n)$ are sets, we shall write $t[S_1, \ldots, S_n]$ for $\{t[r_1, \ldots, r_n] \mid r_1 \in S_1, \ldots, r_n \in S_n\}$. For a clause C, $C[r_1, \ldots, r_n]$ and $C[S_1, \ldots, S_n]$ are defined in the obvious way, where r_i are ground terms and S_i are sets of ground terms. For each variable x_i in every C_k, we introduce a set $S_{k,i}$. For each uninterpreted function symbol f with arity n, we introduce the sets $A_{f,1}, \ldots, A_{f,n}$. We obtain the sets $S_{k,i}$ and $A_{f,j}$ as the least solution to a system of set constraints Δ_F induced by F. The constraints in Δ_F describe relationships between sets of terms. We follow the set constraint conventions also used in [13]. We generate Δ_F using the following rules based on the occurrences $f(\bar{s})$ of uninterpreted function symbols in F.

j-th argument of f in C_k	*Set constraint*
a ground term t	$t \in A_{f,j}$
$t[x_1, \ldots, x_n]$	$t[S_{k,1}, \ldots, S_{k,n}] \subseteq A_{f,j}$
x_i	$S_{k,i} = A_{f,j}$

Informally, the first two rules capture the *relevant domain*, a set of ground terms, of an uninterpreted function symbol f. The first says that any ground argument of an f-application in F is relevant, and the second says the *relevant domain* of a function symbol f may be increased when we instantiate a non-ground clause containing f. In the second rule, we are implicitly assuming t is a non ground term. The last rule states that it is sufficient to instantiate x_i using terms of the *relevant domain*. Without loss of generality, we assume the least solution of Δ_F contains only non-empty sets of terms. We can always add extra constraints of the form $a \in S$ to Δ_F to force S to be non-empty. Since we are discussing essentially uninterpreted formulas, for each $S_{k,i}$ there must be a equation $S_{k,i} = A_{f,j}$ in Δ_F. Intuitively, $A_{f,j}$ contains all ground terms that can be the j-th argument of f, and $S_{k,i}$ is the set of ground terms that can appear in the place of x_i in C_k. To illustrate the construction of Δ_F, consider the following example.

Example 2 (Δ_F construction). Let F be the following four clauses.

$$g(x_1, x_2) \simeq 0 \vee h(x_2) \simeq 0,$$
$$g(f(x_1), b) + 1 \le f(x_1),$$
$$h(b) \simeq 1, \quad f(a) \simeq 0$$

Δ_F is:

$$S_{1,1} = A_{g,1}, \quad S_{1,2} = A_{g,2}, \quad S_{1,2} = A_{h,1}$$
$$S_{2,1} = A_{f,1}, \quad b \in A_{g,2}, \quad f(S_{2,1}) \subseteq A_{g,1}$$
$$b \in A_{h,1}, \quad a \in A_{f,1}$$

The least solution of Δ_F is $S_{1,1} = A_{g,1} = \{f(a)\}$, $S_{1,2} = A_{g,2} = A_{h,1} = \{b\}$, $S_{2,1} = A_{f,1} = \{a\}$.

Now we define F^* as the set of ground clauses $\{C_k[S_{k,1}, \ldots, S_{k,m}] \mid C_k \text{ in } F\}$. That is, F^* is obtained by instantiating clauses with ground terms from $S_{k,i}$. For the above example, F^* is

$$g(f(a), b) \simeq 0 \vee h(b) \simeq 0, \quad g(f(a), b) + 1 \le f(a), \quad h(b) \simeq 1, \quad f(a) \simeq 0$$

Proposition 1. *For every ground term $f(\ldots, t_j, \ldots)$ in F^*, where t_j is the j-th argument and f is uninterpreted, t_j is in $A_{f,j}$.*

Suppose F^* has a model M, for each $A_{f,j}$, we define a projection function $\pi_{f,j}$ on $|M|$ such that $\pi_{f,j}(v) \in M(A_{f,j})$ and $\pi_{f,j}(v) = v$ when $v \in M(A_{f,j})$. The projection functions essentially map the domain of f to its relevant subset. Similarly we define a projection function $\pi_{k,i}$ for each $S_{k,i}$ and require $\pi_{k,i} = \pi_{f,j}$ if $S_{k,i} = A_{f,j}$ appears in Δ_F.

The functions $\pi_{f,j}$ and $\pi_{k,i}$ are well-defined because we assume the least solution of Δ_F contains only non-empty sets of terms. We use $\pi_k(\overline{v})$ to denote the tuple $\langle \pi_{k,1}(v_1), \ldots, \pi_{k,m}(v_m) \rangle$.

Suppose F^* has a model M, we construct a model M^π for F. In other words, if F^* is satisfiable, so is F. We say M^π is a π-*extension* of M if $|M^\pi| = |M|$, $M^\pi(a) = M(a)$ for every constant a, $M^\pi(f) = M(f)$ for every interpreted function symbol f, and $M^\pi(f)(v_1, \ldots, v_n) = M(f)(\pi_{f,1}(v_1), \ldots, \pi_{f,n}(v_n))$ for every uninterpreted function symbol f.

Lemma 1. *For every ground term t in F^*, $M[\![t]\!] = M^\pi[\![t]\!]$.*

Proof. (Sketch)[1] By induction on the complexity of t. The proof is based on the observation that $M[\![s_i]\!] \in M(A_{f,i})$ whenever s_i is the i-th argument of an uninterpreted function symbol f in the set F^*.

Lemma 1 implies that M^π is also a model of F^* if M is. Now, let us show that M^π is also a model for F.

---

[1] The full proofs for the proof sketches in this paper can be found at [14] (http://research.microsoft.com/~{}leonardo/citr09.pdf)

Lemma 2. *For every term $t[\overline{x}]$ in clause C_k, where $t[\overline{x}]$ is not a variable, we have that for all tuples of $\overline{v}$, $M^\pi\{\overline{x} \mapsto \overline{v}\}[\![t[\overline{x}]]\!] = M\{\overline{x} \mapsto \pi_k(\overline{v})\}[\![t[\overline{x}]]\!]$.*

Proof. (Sketch) By induction on the complexity of t. The only interesting case is when t is $f(\overline{s})$, and f is an uninterpreted symbol. Then, it suffices to show that $\pi_{f,j}(M^\pi\{\overline{x} \mapsto \overline{v}\}[\![s_j[\overline{x}]]\!]) = M\{\overline{x} \mapsto \pi_k(\overline{v})\}[\![s_j[\overline{x}]]\!]$, for each s_j in $\overline{s}$. We consider three cases: $s_j[\overline{x}]$ is ground, a variable, or a composite non-ground term. The first case follows from Lemma 1. The second is based on the observation that $\pi_{k,i} = \pi_{f,j}$ whenever x_i is the j-th argument of some f in a clause C_k. The final case follows from the induction hypothesis, and the fact that Δ_F contains the constraint $s_j[S_{k,1}, \ldots, S_{k,m}] \subseteq A_{f,j}$.

Theorem 1. *F and F^* are equisatisfiable.*

Proof. If F^* is unsatisfiable, then so is F, since F^* is the conjunction of ground instances of F. Suppose that F^* is satisfiable, but F is not. Let M be a model for F^* and M^π be its π-extension. Since F is unsatisfiable, there is a clause $C_k[\overline{x}]$ in F such that for some $\overline{v}$, $M^\pi\{\overline{x} \mapsto \overline{v}\} \not\models C_k[\overline{x}]$. By Lemma 2, $M\{\overline{x} \mapsto \pi_k(\overline{v})\} \not\models C_k[\overline{x}]$. Let $\overline{v}$ be the tuple $\langle v_1, \ldots, v_m \rangle$, then for every $\pi_{k,i}(v_i)$ in $\pi_k(\overline{v})$, there is some ground term r_j in $S_{k,j}$ such that $M[\![r_j]\!] = \pi_{k,j}(v_j)$. Thus, $M\{\overline{x} \mapsto \pi_k(\overline{v})\} \models C_k[\overline{x}]$ if and only if $M \models C_k[\overline{r}]$, and consequently $M \not\models C_k[\overline{r}]$, contradicting the assumption that F^* is satisfiable since $C_k[\overline{r}]$ is in F^*.

We say a formula F is in the *finite essentially uninterpreted fragment* (FEU) if every $S_{k,i}$ is finite in the least solution of Δ_F. A system Δ_F is *stratified* if there is a function *level* from set variables into natural numbers such that for each constraint $S_{k,j} = A_{f,i}$, $level(S_{k,j}) = level(A_{f,i})$, and for each constraint $t[S_{k,1}, \ldots, S_{k,n}] \subseteq A_{f,j}$, $level(A_{f,j}) < level(S_{k,i})$, for all $i = 1, \ldots, n$.

Proposition 2. *The least solution of Δ_F is finite if and only if Δ_F is stratified.*

By proposition 2, a formula F is in the FEU fragment if and only if Δ_F is stratified. Theorem 1 suggests a simple decision procedure for the formulas in the FEU fragment. We just generate F^* and check its satisfiability using a SMT solver such as Z3 [3]. The decidability problem for FEU-formulas is NEXPTIME-hard, because F^* is finite for any formula in the Bernays-Schönfinkel (EPR) class. The EPR class comprise of formulas of the form $\forall \overline{x} \colon \varphi(\overline{x})$, where $\varphi(\overline{x})$ is a quantifier-free formula with relations, equality, constants, but without non constant function symbols. The size of F^* is at most doubly exponential in the size of F. The first exponential blowup is caused by the construction of the least solution of Δ_F. For example, assume Δ_F contains the following constraints:

$$a \in S_1, \ b \in S_1, \ f_1(S_1, S_1) \subseteq S_2, \ f_2(S_2, S_2) \subseteq S_3, \ \ldots, \ f_n(S_n, S_n) \subseteq S_{n+1}$$

The second exponential blowup is caused by the instantiation of the clauses $C_k[\overline{x}]$.

Compactness. The least solution of Δ_F is infinite if some $S_{k,i}$ in the least solution of Δ_F is infinite. If Δ_F is infinite, then F^* is an infinite set of ground clauses. Therefore, a tempting possibility is to assume a refutationally complete procedure can be devised by using the Compactness Theorem for first-order logic. The Compactness Theorem says that for any unsatisfiable set of first-order formulas F, there is a finite subset F' that is also unsatisfiable. In this paper, we are interested in the satisfiability of a Σ'-formula F modulo a Σ-theory T, where the signature Σ' includes Σ. Then, in principle, the satisfiability of F modulo T is equivalent to the satisfiability of $F \cup T$ in pure first-order logic, and the Compactness Theorem can be applied to $F \cup T$. This approach can be used to handle useful background theories such as: algebraic/real closed fields and finite size bit-vectors. However, in practice, we are also interested in checking the satisfiability of F modulo a class Ω of intended structures. Before continuing, let us introduce some notational conventions. Let Σ' be any signature including Σ. An expansion M' to Σ' of a Σ-structure M is a Σ'-structure that has the same universe as M, and agrees with M on the interpretation of the symbols in Σ. We denote by $Exp_{\Sigma'}(T)$ the class of all Σ'-structures that are expansions of the Σ-structure T. Note that Theorem 1 guarantees that F and F^* are equisatisfiable modulo a class $Exp_{\Sigma'}(T)$ of intended structures, because M and M^π only differ on the interpretation of symbols that are in Σ' but not in Σ. Thus, if M is in $Exp_{\Sigma'}(T)$, then so is M^π. A Σ-theory $Th(\Omega)$ for a class Ω of Σ-structures is the set of all Σ-sentences ϕ such that $M \models \phi$ for every M in Ω. Now, consider the following example:

Example 3 (Nonstandard models of arithmetic). Let Σ be the signature $(0, 1, +, -, <)$. Let $\mathcal{Z}$ be the structure that interprets these symbols in the usual way over the integers. Let Σ' be the signature $(0, 1, +, -, <, f)$. Now, let us check the satisfiability of the following set of Σ'-clauses F modulo the background theory $Th(\mathcal{Z})$.

$$f(x_1) < f(f(x_1)), \ f(x_1) < a, \ 1 < f(0)$$

By Theorem 1, these three clauses are equisatisfiable to the set of ground clauses $F^* = \{f(0) < f^2(0), f^2(0) < f^3(0), \ldots, f(0) < a, f^2(0) < a, \ldots, 1 < f(0)\}$ modulo $Th(\mathcal{Z})$. Since, every finite subset of $F^* \cup Th(\mathcal{Z})$ is satisfiable, then by compactness $F^* \cup Th(\mathcal{Z})$ is satisfiable. This is counterintuitive, since clause $f(x_1) < f(f(x_1))$ implies that the range of any interpretation of f contains infinite strictly increasing chains $M(f)(v) < M(f)^2(v) < \ldots < M(f)^n(v) < \ldots$, and clause $f(x_1) < a$ says there is a value $M(a)$ greater than any value in the range of $M(f)$. The problem here is that $Th(\mathcal{Z})$ has nonstandard models. Now suppose we want to check the satisfiability of F modulo the class of structures $Exp_{\Sigma'}(\mathcal{Z})$. F^* is still equisatisfiable to F modulo $Exp_{\Sigma'}(\mathcal{Z})$, but we cannot apply the Compactness Theorem. Therefore, if F^* is infinite, the procedures described in this paper are not refutationally complete for satisfiability modulo $Exp_{\Sigma'}(\mathcal{Z})$. Note also that Theorem 1 does not hold if the background theory is $Th(Exp_{\Sigma'}(\mathcal{Z}))$ because this theory restricts the interpretations of the function symbols in $\Sigma' \setminus \Sigma$. For instance, it contains a sentence stating that if f is a strictly increasing function, then the range of f does not have a supremum.

From hereafter, we only consider the problem of checking the satisfiability of F modulo a theory T, instead of satisfiability modulo a class Ω of intended structures. Therefore, if F^* is unsatisfiable, there is a finite subset of F^* that is also unsatisfiable. Given a fair enumeration of F^*, we obtain a refutationally complete procedure. By fair, we mean a sequence $F^1 \subseteq F^2 \subseteq \ldots F^i \subseteq \ldots \subseteq F^*$, where each F^i is a finite set, and for each clause C in F^* there is an n such that C is in F^n. A fair enumeration of F^* can be obtained by performing a fair enumeration of the least solution of the system Δ_F. It is not difficult to generate such enumeration [14]. For each $S_{k,i}$ in Δ_F, we have a sequence $S_{k,i}^0 \subseteq S_{k,i}^1 \subseteq S_{k,i}^2 \subseteq \ldots \subseteq S_{k,i}$, where each $S_{k,i}^j$ is finite, and for each t in $S_{k,i}$, there is an n such that t is in $S_{k,i}^n$. Note that these sequences are finite when Δ_F is stratified.

4   Almost Uninterpreted Formulas

In an essentially uninterpreted formula, a variable x can only be the argument of uninterpreted function and predicate symbols. In this section, we present many extensions of the framework described so far. The first trivial extension is to use *destructive equality resolution* (DER) as a preprocessing step. In DER, the clause $\neg(x \simeq t) \vee C[x]$ is simplified to $C[t]$, when x does not occur in t. From hereafter, all proposed extensions come equipped with new rules for generating constraints for Δ_F. As before, the idea is to show that a formula F in the extended fragment is equisatisfiable to a set of ground formulas F^*. Moreover, if the least solution of Δ_F is finite, the satisfiability of F can be determined in finite time.

Arithmetical literals. First, let us consider literals of the form $\neg(x_i \leq x_j)$, $\neg(x_i \leq t)$, $\neg(t \leq x_i)$, and $x_i \simeq t$, where t is a ground term. The literal $x_i \simeq t$ is in the new fragment only if x_i ranges over integers. We say these literals are *arithmetical*. Positive literals of the form $x_i \leq t$ can be rewritten into $\neg(t+1 \leq x_i)$ if x_i ranges over integers. In order to support arithmetical literals, we use the following additional rules to generate the system Δ_F.

Literal of C_k	Set constraint
$\neg(x_i \leq x_j)$	$S_{k,i} = S_{k,j}$
$\neg(x_i \leq t), \neg(t \leq x_i)$	$t \in S_{k,i}$
$x_i \simeq t$	$\{t+1, t-1\} \subseteq S_{k,i}$

We say a formula F is *almost uninterpreted* if any variable in F appears as an argument of an arithmetical literal, or as an argument of uninterpreted function or predicate symbols. To handle almost uninterpreted formulas, we define a new projection function $\pi_{k,i}$. With a small abuse of notation, we use $v_1 \leq v_2$ to denote $(v_1, v_2) \in M(\leq)$, and $v_1 > v_2$ to denote $(v_1, v_2) \notin M(\leq)$. Then, $\pi_{k,i}(v) = v_1$ such that $v_1 \in M(S_{k,i})$, and either $v_1 \leq v$ and for all $v_2 \in M(S_{k,i})$, $v_2 \leq v_1$ or $v_2 > v$; or $v_1 > v$ and for all $v_2 \in M(S_{k,i})$, $v_1 \leq v_2$. As before, $\pi_{k,i} = \pi_{f,j}$ if $S_{k,i} = A_{f,j}$ appears in Δ_F. We remark that the range of $\pi_{k,i}$ is equal to $M(S_{k,i})$, and $\pi_{k,i}(v) = v$ for any $v \in M(S_{k,i})$. Thus, the proof of Lemma 2 is not affected.

Proposition 3. *The projection functions $\pi_{k,j}$ defined above are monotonic. That is, for all v_1 and v_2 in $|M|$, $v_1 \leq v_2$ implies $\pi_{k,j}(v_1) \leq \pi_{k,j}(v_2)$.*

Theorem 2. *F and F^* are equisatisfiable.*

Proof. It suffices to show that for each arithmetical literal $l[\overline{x}]$, if $M^\pi\{\overline{x} \mapsto \overline{v}\} \not\models l[\overline{x}]$ then $M\{\overline{x} \mapsto \pi_k(\overline{v})\} \not\models l[\overline{x}]$. This is an immediate consequence of Proposition 3, and the fact that $\pi_{k,i} = \pi_{k,j}$ when $l[\overline{x}]$ is of the form $\neg(x_i \leq x_j)$. The rest of the proof is identical to the proof of Theorem 1.

Example 4 (Stratified Arrays). The fragment described in this section can decide the following set of satisfiable clauses. In this example, f should be viewed as an array of pointers, and h as a heap from pointers to values, h' is the heap h after an update at position a with value b. The first clause states that the array f is sorted in the range $[0, n]$. If we replace c with a, the example becomes unsatisfiable.

$$\neg(0 \leq x_1) \vee \neg(x_1 \leq x_2) \vee \neg(x_2 \leq n) \vee h(f(x_1)) \leq h(f(x_2)),$$
$$\neg(0 \leq x_1) \vee \neg(x_1 \leq n) \vee f(x_1) \not\simeq c,$$
$$\neg(x_1 \simeq a) \vee h'(x_1) \simeq h(x_1), \quad h'(a) = b$$
$$0 \leq i, \quad i \leq j, \quad j \leq n, \quad h'(f(i)) > h'(f(j))$$

Offsets. We now consider terms of the form $f(\ldots, x_i + r, \ldots)$, where r is a ground term. For this extension, we use the following additional rule:

j-th argument of f in C_k	*Set constraint*
$x_i + r$	$S_{k,i} + r \subseteq A_{f,j}, \quad A_{f,j} + (-r) \subseteq S_{k,i}$

Without this additional rule, it is not possible, for instance, to detect the unsatisfiability of $\{p(f(x + 1)), \neg p(f(a))\}$. The set $S + r$ is defined as the set of ground terms $\{t \oplus r \mid t \in S\}$, where $t \oplus r$ creates a term equivalent to $t + r$ modulo the simplification rules: $(x + y) + (-y) \rightsquigarrow x$, and $(x + (-y)) + y \rightsquigarrow x$. For example, $(t + (-r)) \oplus r = t$. These simplifications prevent Δ_F from being trivially infinite. Again, with a small abuse of notation, we use $v_1 + v_2$ to denote $M(+)(v_1, v_2)$. Similarly, $v_1 - v_2$ denotes $M(-)(v_1, v_2)$. For this extension, we use the same projection functions used for handling arithmetical literals.

Proposition 4. *If $x_i + r$ is the j-th argument of a term $f(\overline{s})$ in clause C_k, then for all $v \in |M|$, $v \in M(A_{f,j})$ if and only if $v - M[\![r]\!] \in M(S_{k,i})$.*

The proof of Lemma 2 has to be updated, since $x_i + r$ can be the argument of an f-application. For this extra case, it suffices to show that $\pi_{f,j}(v_i + M[\![r]\!]) = \pi_{k,i}(v_i) + M[\![r]\!]$. This equality follows from Proposition 4, and from the definition of the projection functions [14].

Example 5 (Shifting). The following clause states that the segment $[2, n + 2]$ of the array f is equal to the segment $[0, n]$ of the array g.

$$\neg(0 \leq x_1) \vee \neg(x_1 \leq n) \vee f(x_1 + 2) \simeq g(x_1)$$

Similarly, we can add support for literals of the form $\neg(x_i \leq x_j + r)$. The idea is to include the constraints $S_{k,i} + (-r) \subseteq S_{k,j}$, and $S_{k,j} + r \subseteq S_{k,i}$, for each literal $\neg(x_i \leq x_j + r)$ in a clause C_k.

4.1   Many-Sorted First-Order Logic

Sorts naturally arise in SMT applications and in some cases sort information significantly simplifies the problem. SMT solvers such as CVC3 [15] and Z3 [16] have support for sorts. We say a sort σ is uninterpreted if it is not in the signature of the background theory. We use $\simeq_\sigma$ to denote the equality predicate for elements of sort σ. Given a formula F in many-sorted logic, we can support any literal using the equality predicate $\simeq_\sigma$, when σ is an uninterpreted sort. The basic idea is to axiomatize the equality predicate $\simeq_\sigma$, and treat it as an uninterpreted predicate symbol. That is, we add the clauses EQ_σ asserting that $\simeq_\sigma$ is reflexive, symmetric, transitive, and congruent. This is a standard technique used in saturation-based provers that do not have built-in support for equality. The previous theorems asserting the equisatisfiability of F and F^* can be easily adapted to the many-sorted case. In practice, we do not really need to add the clauses EQ_σ, since any SMT solver has built-in support for equality. It is sufficient to add to Δ_F any constraints that are induced by EQ_σ. We denote by $dom_{f,j}$ the sort of the j-th argument of f. We introduce the auxiliary set S_σ in Δ_F. Intuitively, S_σ contains the ground terms of sort σ. We use the following additional rules to generate Δ_F.

argument of $\simeq_\sigma$ in C_k	*Set constraint*
x_i	$S_{k,i} = S_\sigma$
$t[x_1, \ldots, x_n]$	$t[S_{k,1}, \ldots, S_{k,n}] \subseteq S_\sigma$

Sort declaration	*Set constraint*
$dom_{f,j} = \sigma$	$A_{f,j} = S_\sigma$

For example, now we can handle the anti-symmetry axiom used in the axiomatization of the *subtype* relation in ESC/Java [10]: $\neg subtype(x_1, x_2) \vee \neg subtype(x_2, x_1) \vee x_1 \simeq_\sigma x_2$. From hereafter, we suppress the σ in $\simeq_\sigma$.

5   Macros and Pseudo-Macros

In practice, many formulas contain non-ground clauses that can be seen as *macro definitions*. These clauses have the following form: $g(\overline{x}) \simeq t[\overline{x}]$, where g does not occur in $t[\overline{x}]$. For example, the macro $g(x_1) \simeq x_1 + c$ is not in any of the fragments described so far. The simplest way to handle a macro $g(\overline{x}) \simeq t[\overline{x}]$ is to remove it from F, and replace every term of the form $g(\overline{s})$ with $t[\overline{s}]$. Clearly, the resultant formula is equisatisfiable to F. More generally, we say g is a *pseudo-macro* defined by the non-ground clauses $D_g = \{C_1[\overline{x}], \ldots, C_n[\overline{x}]\}$ if all clauses in D_g contain $g(\overline{x})$, and are trivially satisfied (i.e., are equivalent to *true*) by replacing $g(\overline{x})$ with a term $t_g[\overline{x}]$.

Example 6 (Pseudo-Macro). The function symbol g is a pseudo-macro in the following example. Note that replacing $g(x_1)$ with 0 trivially satisfies the first two clauses.

$$g(x_1) \geq 0 \vee f(g(x_1)) \simeq x_1, \quad g(x_1) \geq 0 \vee h(g(x_1)) \leq g(x_1), \quad g(a) < 0$$

Many different heuristics may be used to find pseudo-macros. For example, it is clear that g is a pseudo-macro if $D_g = \{C_1[\overline{x}] \vee g(\overline{x}) \bowtie t_g[\overline{x}], \ldots, C_n[\overline{x}] \vee g(\overline{x}) \bowtie t_g[\overline{x}]\}$, where $\bowtie$ is $\simeq$, $\leq$, or $\geq$. From hereafter, we assume some heuristic was used to select the pseudo-macros g, their definitions D_g, and the terms $t_g[\overline{x}]$. We now describe how to incorporate pseudo-macros in our framework. A clause C is *regular* if C is not in any set D_g. First we observe that a pseudo-macro g may occur in regular clauses C if none of its arguments is a variable. Intuitively, a pseudo-macro g is treated as an interpreted function symbol in regular clauses. The rules for generating constraints from regular clauses are unchanged. For clauses $C_k[\overline{x}]$ in D_g, we use slightly different rules. The main difference is the rule for a variable x_i occurring as an argument of f.

x_i is an argument of f in C_k	Set constraint
$f = g$	$S_{k,i} = A_{f,j}$
$f \neq g$	$S_{k,i} \subseteq A_{f,j}$

The construction of M^π is also slightly modified. If g is a pseudo-macro, then $M^\pi(g)$ is defined in the following way

$$M^\pi(g)(\overline{v}) = M[\![g(\overline{s})]\!] \qquad \text{if } g(\overline{s}) \in F^*, \text{ and } M[\![\overline{s}]\!] = \overline{v}$$
$$= M\{\overline{x} \mapsto \overline{v}\}[\![t_g[\overline{x}]]\!] \quad \text{otherwise}$$

The proof that F and F^* are still equisatisfiable, when F contains pseudo-macros, is a direct consequence of Theorem 1 and the definition above.

6   Implementation

Some of the ideas described in this paper were already implemented in the Z3 theorem prover submitted to the SMT 2008 competition[2]. The extensions for many-sorted logic, and pseudo-macros defined by multiple clauses were not implemented yet.

We would like to make it clear that Z3's performance is not a consequence of the theory or heuristics described on this paper. On the other hand, the techniques proposed here increased Z3's precision. For example, Z3 was the only theorem prover in the competition that produced the correct answers for satisfiable problems in the divisions for quantified formulas. Z3 detected that 33 benchmarks with quantifiers were satisfiable; 3 of them were *Almost Uninterpreted Formulas* (AUF), and 30 were AUF+*pseudo-macros*.

---

[2] http://www.smtcomp.org

For some applications, it is desirable not only to know whether a formula is satisfiable, but also, what a satisfying model is. In general, it is very challenging to capture the structure of an arbitrary first-order model. We have a more modest goal: we only want to describe models for the decidable fragments described in this paper. We also propose a heuristic to minimize the number of instantiations. The basic idea is to use "candidate" models to guide quantifier instantiation. A similar idea is used in the theorem prover Equinox [17] for pure first-order logic.

Model representation. Assume T is a Σ-theory, Σ' includes the signature Σ, and F is a set of Σ'-clauses. In our implementation, a "model" is essentially a function that maps a Σ-structure $\mathcal{T}$ that satisfies T, into an expanded Σ'-structure M that satisfies $T \cup F$. Our "models" also come equipped with a set of formulas R that restricts the class of Σ-structures that satisfy T. If T is the empty theory, then R is just a cardinality constraint on the size of the universe. When needed, we use fresh constant symbols $k_1, \ldots, k_n$ to name the elements in $|M|$. We also use R to restrict the interpretation of under-specified interpreted function symbols such as: division and modulo [14]. In our implementation, the interpretation of an uninterpreted symbol s in $\Sigma' \setminus \Sigma$ is an expression $I_s[\overline{x}]$, which contains only interpreted symbols and the fresh constants $k_1, \ldots, k_n$. For uninterpreted constants c, $I_c[\overline{x}]$ is a ground term I_c, and $M[\![c]\!] = \mathcal{T}[\![I_c]\!]$. When I_c is ground we say it is a *value*. For uninterpreted function and predicate symbols, the term $I_s[\overline{x}]$ should be viewed as a *lambda expression*, where for all $\overline{v}$ in $|M|^n$, $M(f)(\overline{v}) = \mathcal{T}\{\overline{x} \mapsto \overline{v}\}[\![I_f[\overline{x}]\!]]$. We assume the construct $ite(\phi, t_1, t_2)$ (the if-then-else construct for terms) is available in our language.

Example 7 (Model representation). Let F be the following four clauses.

$$\neg(5 \leq x_1) \vee f(x_1) < 0, \quad f(a) \simeq 0, \quad f(b) \simeq 1, \quad a < 2$$

These clauses are satisfiable, and Z3 generates the following model.

$$a \mapsto 0, \quad b \mapsto 2, \quad f \mapsto ite(x_1 < 2, 0, ite(x_1 < 5, 1, -1))$$

Note that SMT solvers can be used to model check any clause $C_k[\overline{x}]$ in F. Let $C_k^I[\overline{x}]$ be the clause obtained from $C_k[\overline{x}]$ by replacing any term $f(\overline{s})$ with $I_f[\overline{s}]$, when f is uninterpreted. Thus, a model satisfies $C_k[\overline{x}]$ if and only if $R \wedge \neg C_k^I[\overline{w}]$ is unsatisfiable, where $\overline{w}$ is a tuple of fresh constant symbols. For example, in the previous example, the first clause is satisfied by the model above because the following formula is unsatisfiable.

$$5 \leq w_1 \wedge \neg(ite(w_1 < 2, 0, ite(w_1 < 5, 1, -1)) < 0)$$

It is straightforward to construct the term I_c for uninterpreted constants. For uninterpreted function symbols, we construct $I_f[\overline{x}]$ based on the definition of $M^\pi(f)$ using the *ite* construct.

We say M^n is a *candidate model* for F if it is a model for a finite subset F^n of F^*. The set of ground terms $A_{f,j}^n$ contains all j-th arguments of terms $f(\overline{s})$ in F^n. The *candidate interpretation* $I_f[\overline{x}]$ for f is defined using the set $A_{f,i}^n$ instead of the set $A_{f,i}$. If $A_{f,i}^n$ is empty, then $I_f[\overline{x}] = t_f[\overline{x}]$ if f is a pseudo-macro, and $I_f[\overline{x}]$ is an arbitrary constant function otherwise.

Model-based quantifier instantiation (MBQI). Let $t_1 \prec_{k,j} t_2$ be a total order on the terms in $S_{k,j}$ such that $t_1 \prec_{k,j} t_2$ whenever there is an n such that $t_1 \in S_{k,j}^n$ and $t_2 \notin S_{k,j}^n$. Let $\pi_{k,j}^{-1}(v_j, M)$ be a function that maps a value v_j to the least (with respect to $\prec_{k,j}$) ground term r_j in $S_{k,j}$ such that $\pi_{k,j}(v_j) = M[\![r_j]\!]$. As before, we use $\pi_k^{-1}(\overline{v}, M)$ to denote the tuple $\langle \pi_{k,1}^{-1}(v_1, M), \ldots, \pi_{k,n}^{-1}(v_n, M) \rangle$. Instead of generating the fair enumeration of F^*, we guide quantifier instantiation using the model checking procedure described above, and the following procedure.

$\varphi :=$ set of ground clauses in F
loop
    if φ is unsatisfiable **return** unsat
    create the candidate model M^n
    ok := true
    foreach non-ground clause $C_k[\overline{x}]$ in F
        create $C_k^I[\overline{w}]$ using M^n
        if $R \wedge \neg C_k^I[\overline{w}]$ is satisfiable
            let M_k be the model for $R \wedge \neg C_k^I[\overline{w}]$, **and** $\overline{v}$ be $M_k(\overline{w})$.
            $\varphi := \varphi \cup C_k[\pi_k^{-1}(\overline{v}, M^n)]$
            ok := false
    if ok **return** sat

Heuristics. Heuristic quantifier instantiation based on E-matching generates a subset of the instances in F^*. An advantage of E-matching is that it can be used incrementally. In [5,3] it was observed that incremental and eager quantifier instantiation (EQI) is more efficient, in software verification benchmarks, than lazy quantifier instantiation (LQI). In this way, MBQI does not substitute E-matching in Z3, but complements it. MBQI increases the number of benchmarks that Z3 can solve. The prototype of Z3 submitted to SMT-COMP'08 still uses E-matching, and only applies MBQI after a candidate model is produced. In SMT-COMP'08, 22 benchmarks were proved to be unsatisfiable by Z3 using MBQI, and a prover solely based on e-matching would fail on these benchmarks. Another important heuristic used is relevancy propagation [3]. Relevancy propagation keeps track of which truth assignments are essential for determining satisfiability of a formula. Only terms that are marked as relevant are considered for E-matching and constructing candidate models.

7   Related Work

The fragment that contains arithmetical literals and the associated projection functions resemble much in spirit the array property fragment and its projection function proposed in [12], which is the original motivation for this paper. It is obvious that our fragments subsume the array property fragment, since we support nested array reads, offsets on indices, and pseudo-macros. As proved in [12], nested array reads and offsets on indices will in general make the formula undecidable. However, we show that for certain cases containing nested array reads and offsets, a complete decision procedure is possible as long as the set F^* is finite. In [18] a logic called LIA is proposed, in which modulo equalities, difference constraints, and non-nested array reads are allowed. The decidability of LIA is proved by employing a customized counter Büchi automata. Compared with LIA, our fragments allow propositional combination of any theory constraints and nested array reads. For certain cases containing offsets on array indices, our procedure will result in an infinite set of instantiations, while a decision procedure of LIA will terminate.

In [19,20,11] procedures based on stratified vocabularies are presented. These procedures are in the context of many-sorted logic. A vocabulary is stratified if there is a function *level* from sorts to naturals, and for every function $f \colon \sigma_1 \times \ldots \times \sigma_n \to \sigma$, $level(\sigma) < level(\sigma_i)$. Our method can decide a broader class of problems. For example, these methods fail if there is a single function $f \colon \sigma \to \sigma$, and cannot handle simple examples such as $f(x) = b \land f(a) = a$. In [21] local theories and local extensions are studied; they propose a complete instantiation procedure for certain types of quantified formulas. One major difference is that our method can provide models for satisfiable cases.

In our approach, if T is the empty theory, then Theorem 1 can be viewed as a frugal version of the standard Herbrand theorem, and the universe does not necessarily become infinite in the presence of function symbols.

8   Conclusion

We proposed several new useful fragments of first order logic modulo theories that have complete instantiation. We showed how to construct models for satisfiable formulas in these fragments. We also described undecidable fragments and discussed the conditions under which a refutationally complete procedure exists. We discussed the difference between a theory as a deductively closed set of sentences, and as a class of intended structures. We used model-based quantifier instantiation to prioritize quantifier instantiation. Some of ideas in this paper have been implemented in Z3 2.0. In the last SMT competition, Z3 was the only prover that solved satisfiable quantified formulas. Future work includes investigation of more heuristics to prioritize instantiations, and more decidable fragments. For instance, our approach cannot handle a clause containing the term $f(x_1 + x_2)$, where x_1 and x_2 are universally quantified variables.

Acknowledgments. We'd like to thank Tom Ball, Clark Barrett, Margus Veanes, Cesare Tinelli, and the anonymous reviewers for reading early drafts of this paper, and providing helpful feedback.

References

1. Halpern, J.Y.: Presburger Arithmetic with unary predicates is Π_1^1 Complete. Journal of Symbolic Logic 56, 637–642 (1991)
2. Deharbe, D., Ranise, S.: Satisfiability solving for software verification. International Journal on Software Tools Technology Transfer (2008) (to appear)

3. de Moura, L.M., Bjørner, N.: Efficient E-Matching for SMT Solvers. In: Pfenning, F. (ed.) CADE 2007. LNCS (LNAI), vol. 4603, pp. 167–182. Springer, Heidelberg (2007)

4. Stickel, M.E.: Automated deduction by theory resolution. Journal of Automated Reasoning 1, 333–355 (1985)

5. Ge, Y., Barrett, C., Tinelli, C.: Solving quantified verification conditions using satisfiability modulo theories. In: Pfenning, F. (ed.) CADE 2007. LNCS (LNAI), vol. 4603, pp. 167–182. Springer, Heidelberg (2007)

6. Flanagan, C., Joshi, R., Saxe, J.B.: Theorem proving using lazy proof explication. In: Hunt Jr., W.A., Somenzi, F. (eds.) CAV 2003. LNCS, vol. 2725, pp. 355–367. Springer, Heidelberg (2003)

7. Dutertre, B., de Moura, L.: A fast linear-arithmetic solver for DPLL(T). In: Ball, T., Jones, R.B. (eds.) CAV 2006. LNCS, vol. 4144, pp. 81–94. Springer, Heidelberg (2006)

8. Detlefs, D., Nelson, G., Saxe, J.B.: Simplify: a theorem prover for program checking. J. ACM 52 (2005)

9. Barnett, M., Chang, B.Y.E., DeLine, R., Jacobs, B., Leino, K.R.M.: Boogie: A modular reusable verifier for object-oriented programs. In: de Boer, F.S., Bonsangue, M.M., Graf, S., de Roever, W.-P. (eds.) FMCO 2005. LNCS, vol. 4111, pp. 364–387. Springer, Heidelberg (2006)

10. Flanagan, C., Leino, K.R.M., Lillibridge, M., Nelson, G., Saxe, J.B., Stata, R.: Extended static checking for java. In: PLDI 2002. ACM, New York (2002)

11. Abadi, A., Rabinovich, A., Sagiv, M.: Decidable fragments of many-sorted logic. In: Dershowitz, N., Voronkov, A. (eds.) LPAR 2007. LNCS, vol. 4790, pp. 17–31. Springer, Heidelberg (2007)

12. Bradley, A.R., Manna, Z., Sipma, H.B.: What's decidable about arrays? In: Emerson, E.A., Namjoshi, K.S. (eds.) VMCAI 2006. LNCS, vol. 3855, pp. 427–442. Springer, Heidelberg (2005)

13. Aiken, A.: Set Constraints: Results, Applications, and Future Directions. In: Second Workshop on the Principles and Practice of Constraint Programming (1994)

14. Ge, Y., de Moura, L.: Complete instantiation for quantified SMT formulas. Technical report, Microsoft Research (2009)

15. Barrett, C., Tinelli, C.: CVC3. In: Damm, W., Hermanns, H. (eds.) CAV 2007. LNCS, vol. 4590, pp. 298–302. Springer, Heidelberg (2007)

16. de Moura, L., Bjørner, N.: Z3: An Efficient SMT Solver. In: Ramakrishnan, C.R., Rehof, J. (eds.) TACAS 2008. LNCS, vol. 4963, pp. 337–340. Springer, Heidelberg (2008)

17. Claessen, K.: Equinox, a new theorem prover for full first-order logic with equality. Presentation at Dagstuhl Seminar 05431 on Deduction and Applications (2005)

18. Habermehl, P., Iosif, R., Vojnar, T.: What else is decidable about integer arrays? In: Amadio, R. (ed.) FOSSACS 2008. LNCS, vol. 4962, pp. 474–489. Springer, Heidelberg (2008)

19. Fontaine, P., Gribomont, E.P.: Decidability of invariant validation for paramaterized systems. In: Garavel, H., Hatcliff, J. (eds.) TACAS 2003. LNCS, vol. 2619, pp. 97–112. Springer, Heidelberg (2003)

20. Arons, T., Pnueli, A., Ruah, S., Xu, J., Zuck, L.D.: Parameterized verification with automatically computed inductive assertions. In: Berry, G., Comon, H., Finkel, A. (eds.) CAV 2001. LNCS, vol. 2102, p. 221. Springer, Heidelberg (2001)

21. Ihlemann, C., Jacobs, S., Sofronie-Stokkermans, V.: On local reasoning in verification. In: Ramakrishnan, C.R., Rehof, J. (eds.) TACAS 2008. LNCS, vol. 4963, pp. 265–281. Springer, Heidelberg (2008)

Software Transactional Memory on Relaxed Memory Models*

Rachid Guerraoui, Thomas A. Henzinger, and Vasu Singh

EPFL, Switzerland

Abstract. Pseudo-code descriptions of STMs assume sequentially consistent program execution and atomicity of high-level STM operations like read, write, and commit. These assumptions are often violated in realistic settings, as STM implementations run on relaxed memory models, with the atomicity of operations as provided by the hardware. This paper presents the first approach to verify STMs under relaxed memory models with atomicity of 32 bit loads and stores, and read-modify-write operations. We present RML, a new high-level language for expressing concurrent algorithms with a hardware-level atomicity of instructions, and whose semantics is parametrized by various relaxed memory models. We then present our tool, FOIL, which takes as input the RML description of an STM algorithm and the description of a memory model, and automatically determines the locations of fences, which if inserted, ensure the correctness of the STM algorithm under the given memory model. We use FOIL to verify DSTM, TL2, and McRT STM under the memory models of sequential consistency, total store order, partial store order, and relaxed memory order.

1 Introduction

Software transactional memory (STM) [11,19] is now widely accepted as a concurrent programming model. STM allows the programmer to think in terms of coarse-grained code blocks that appear to be executed atomically, and at the same time, yields a high level of parallelism. The algorithm underlying an STM is non-trivial, precisely because it simplifies the task of the programmer by encapsulating the difficulty of synchronization and recovery. Various correctness criteria have been proposed for STM algorithms. One criterion, popular for its relevance to the STM designers, is opacity [8]. Opacity is motivated by the fact that in STMs, observing inconsistent state by even an aborted transaction can lead to unexpected side effects. Opacity builds upon strict serializability [17], a correctness property used for database transactions. Strict serializability requires that the committed transactions appear to be executed in a serial order, consistent with the order of non-overlapping transactions. Opacity further requires that even aborted transactions appear to be executed in a serial order.

Previous attempts at formally verifying the correctness of STMs [3,6,7] with respect to different correctness criteria assumed that high-level transactional commands like start, read, write, commit, and abort execute atomically and in a sequentially consistent manner. Verification of an STM at this level of abstraction leaves much room for

* This research was supported by the Swiss National Science Foundation.

A. Bouajjani and O. Maler (Eds.): CAV 2009, LNCS 5643, pp. 321–336, 2009.
© Springer-Verlag Berlin Heidelberg 2009

```
txCommit :    ...
              update global timestamp ts
              for each variable v in write set
              update value of v
              ...
```

```
txRead :      ...
              t₁ := ts
              if (t₁ ≠ t₂) then abort
              read value of v
              t₂ := ts
              if (t₁ ≠ t₂) then abort
```

Fig. 1. Code fragments of commit and read procedures of a timestamp-based STM

errors in a realistic setting. This is because the actual hardware on which STMs run supports a finer-grained degree of atomicity: in practice, the set of atomic instructions rather corresponds to *load, store,* and *read-modify-write.* Furthermore, compilers and processors assume relaxed memory models [1] and are notorious for playing tricks to optimize performance, e.g., by reversing the order of instructions to different addresses. Typically, STM designers use *fences* to ensure a strict ordering of memory operations. As fences hurt performance, STM designers want to use fences only when necessary for correctness.

To illustrate some of the issues, consider the code fragments of the commit and the read procedures of a typical timestamp-based STM like TL2 [4] in Figure 1. Assume that at the start of a transaction, t_1 and t_2 are set to the global timestamp ts. The commit procedure updates the timestamp ts before it updates the variables in the write set. The read procedure first reads the timestamp, followed by the read of the variable, followed by a second read of the timestamp. The read is successful only if the two timestamps are equal. A crucial question is, given the memory model, which fences are required to keep the STM correct. On a memory model like sequential consistency [12] or total store order [20], the code fragment in Figure 1 is correct without fences. On the other hand, on memory models that relax store order, like partial store order [20], we need to add a *store fence* after the timestamp update in the commit procedure. For even more relaxed memory models that may swap independent loads, like relaxed memory order [20], as well as the Java memory model [16], we need more fences, namely, *load fences* in the read procedure. But the question is how many? Do we need to ensure that the read of v is between the two reads of ts, and thus put two fences? The answer is no. To ensure correctness, we just need one fence and guarantee that the second read of ts comes after the read of v.

Devising a verification technique to model check STM algorithms assuming relaxed memory models and hardware-level atomicity is challenging. A first challenge is to devise a precise and unified formalism in which the STM implementations can be expressed. A second challenge is to cope with the non-determinism explosion. Not surprisingly, when compared to verifying an STM at a high-level atomic alphabet, the level of non-determinism to be dealt with at hardware-level atomicity under a relaxed memory model is much higher. For example, the implementation of DSTM [10] with 2 threads and 2 variables generates 1,000 states with a high-level atomic alphabet [6] and 1,200,000 states with a low-level one, even on a sequentially consistent memory model. A relaxed memory model further increases the state space.

This paper takes up the challenge of bridging the gap between STM descriptions in the literature and their real implementations on actual hardware. We start by presenting a formalism to express memory models as a function of hardware memory instructions, that is, loads and stores to 32 bit words. We describe various relaxed memory models, such as total store order (TSO), partial store order (PSO), and relaxed memory order (RMO) in our formalism. The reason for choosing these memory models is to capture different levels of relaxations allowed by different multiprocessors. Unlike earlier formalisms [3,6] used for verification, our formalism can be used to express and check the correctness of STMs with both update semantics: direct (eager) and deferred (lazy). Then, we present a new language, RML (*Relaxed Memory Language*), with a hardware-level of atomicity, whose semantics is parametrized by various relaxed memory models. At last, we describe a new tool, FOIL (a fencing weapon), to verify the opacity of three different STM algorithms, DSTM, TL2, and McRT STM, under different memory models. We choose these STMs as they represent three different and important trends in STM design. DSTM is obstruction-free (does not use locks), TL2 is a lock-based STM with deferred-update semantics, and McRT STM is a lock-based STM with direct-update semantics. While we choose opacity as the correctness criterion, using FOIL we can also verify other correctness properties such as strict serializability that can be specified in our formalism.

FOIL proves the opacity of the considered STM algorithms under sequential consistency and TSO. As the original STM algorithms have no fences, FOIL generates counterexamples to opacity for the STMs under further relaxed memory models (PSO and RMO), and automatically inserts fences within the RML description of the STM algorithms which are required (depending upon the memory model) to ensure opacity. We observe that FOIL inserts fences in a pragmatic manner, as all fences it inserts match those in the manually optimized official implementations of the considered STMs. Our verification leads to an interesting observation that many STMs are sensitive to the order of loads and stores, but neither to the order of a store followed by a load, nor to store buffering. Thus, while all STM algorithms we consider need fences for opacity under PSO and RMO, they are indeed opaque under TSO without any fences.

2 Framework

We first present a general formalism to express hardware memory instructions and memory models. Then, we formalize the correctness of STMs at the level of hardware instructions.

Memory instructions. Let $Addr$ be a set of memory addresses. Let I be the set of *memory instructions* that are executed atomically by the hardware. We define the set I as follows, where $a \in Addr$:

$$I ::= \langle \text{load } a \rangle \mid \langle \text{store } a \rangle \mid \langle \text{cas } a \rangle$$

We use the $\langle \text{cas } a \rangle$ instruction as a generic read-modify-write instruction.

Memory models. Memory models [1] specify the behavior of memory instructions to shared memory in a multiprocessor setting. For example, the memory model *sequential consistency* specifies that a multiprocessor executes the instructions of a thread in program order. On the other hand, the memory model *total store order* specifies that a multiprocessor may relax the order of a store followed by a load to a different address, by delaying stores using a store buffer. In principle, a memory model offers a tradeoff between transparency to the programmer and flexibility to the hardware to optimize performance. Sequential consistency is the most stringent memory model, and thus the most intuitive to the programmer. But, most of the available multiprocessors do not support sequential consistency for reasons of performance. We present a formalism to express relaxed memory models.

A *memory model* is a function $M : I \times I \rightarrow \{N, E, Y\}$. For all instructions $i, j \in I$, when i is immediately followed by j, we have: (i) if $M(i, j) = N$, then M imposes a strict order between i and j, (ii) if $M(i, j) = E$, then M allows to eliminate the instruction j, (iii) if $M(i, j) = Y$, then M allows to reorder i and j. The case (ii) allows us to model store load forwarding using store buffers, and case (iii) allows us to model reordering of instructions. Thus, our formalism can capture many of the hardware memory models. But, our formalism cannot capture some common compiler optimizations like irrelevant read elimination, and thus disallows many software memory models (like the Java memory model [16]). We specify different memory models in our framework. These memory models are chosen to illustrate different levels of relaxations generally provided by the hardware.

1. Sequential consistency does not allow any pair of instructions to be reordered. *Sequential consistency* [12] is specified by the memory model M_{sc}. We have $M_{sc}(i, j) = N$ for all instructions $i, j \in I$.

2. Total store order (TSO) relaxes the order of a store followed by a load to a different address. But, the order of stores cannot be reordered. TSO allows a load which follows a store to the same address to be eliminated. TSO [20] is given by the memory model M_{tso} such that for all memory instructions $i, j \in I$, (i) if $i = \langle \text{store } a \rangle$ and $j = \langle \text{load } a' \rangle$ such that $a \neq a'$, then $M_{tso}(i, j) = Y$, (ii) if $i \in \{\langle \text{store } a \rangle, \langle \text{cas } a \rangle\}$ and $j = \langle \text{load } a \rangle$, then $M_{tso}(i, j) = E$, (iii) else $M_{tso}(i, j) = N$.

3. Partial store order (PSO) is similar to TSO, but further relaxes the order of stores. PSO [20] is specified by M_{pso}, such that for all memory instructions $i, j \in I$, (i) if $i = \langle \text{store } a \rangle$ and $j \in \{\langle \text{load } a' \rangle, \langle \text{store } a' \rangle, \langle \text{cas } a' \rangle\}$ such that $a \neq a'$, then $M_{pso}(i, j) = Y$, (ii) if $i \in \{\langle \text{store } a \rangle, \langle \text{cas } a \rangle\}$ and $j = \langle \text{load } a \rangle$, then $M_{pso}(i, j) = E$, (iii) else $M_{pso}(i, j) = N$.

4. Relaxed memory order (RMO) relaxes the order of instructions even more than PSO, by allowing to reorder loads to different addresses too. RMO [20] is specified by M_{rmo}, such that for all memory instructions $i, j \in I$, (i) if $i \in \{\langle \text{load } a \rangle, \langle \text{store } a \rangle, \langle \text{cas } a \rangle\}$ and $j \in \{\langle \text{load } a' \rangle, \langle \text{store } a' \rangle, \langle \text{cas } a' \rangle\}$ such that $a \neq a'$, then $M_{rmo}(i, j) = Y$, (ii) if $i \in \{\langle \text{store } a \rangle, \langle \text{cas } a \rangle\}$ and $j = \langle \text{load } a \rangle$, then $M_{rmo}(i, j) = E$, (iii) else $M_{rmo}(i, j) = N$.

Example. Figure 2 illustrates a concurrent program with two threads that distinguishes between the different memory models in terms of the possible outcomes. Outcome O_1 is allowed by M_{sc}, while other outcomes are not. Outcomes O_1 and O_2 are allowed by M_{tso}. Outcomes $O_1, O_2,$ and O_3 are allowed by M_{pso}. All outcomes $O_1, O_2, O_3,$ and O_4 are allowed by M_{rmo}.

Transactional programs. Let V be a set of *transactional variables*. Let T be a set of *threads*. Let the set C of *commands* be $(\{\text{read}, \text{write}\} \times V) \cup \{\text{xend}\}$. These commands

Initially : $x_1 = y_1 = x_2 = y_2 = 0$	
Thread 1	Thread 2
$x_1 := 1$	$x_2 := 1$
$y_1 := 1$	$y_2 := 1$
$r_1 := y_2$	$r_2 := y_1$
$r_3 := x_2$	$r_4 := x_1$
$x_1 := 2$	$x_2 := 2$

$O_1 : r_1 = 1, r_2 = 1, r_3 = 1, r_4 = 1$
$O_2 : r_1 = 0, r_2 = 0, r_3 = 0, r_4 = 0$
$O_3 : r_1 = 1, r_2 = 1, r_3 = 0, r_4 = 0$
$O_4 : r_1 = 1, r_2 = 1, r_3 = 2, r_4 = 2$

Fig. 2. A concurrent program with some possible outcomes on different memory models

correspond to a read or write of a transactional variable, and to a transaction end. Depending upon the underlying TM, the execution of these commands may correspond to a sequence of hardware memory instructions. For example, a read of a transactional variable may require to check the consistency of the variable by first reading a version number. Similarly, a transaction end may require to copy many variables from a thread-local buffer to global memory. Moreover, the semantics of the write and the xend commands depend on the underlying STM. For example, a (write, v) command does not alter the value of v in a deferred-update STM, whereas it does in a direct-update STM.

We restrict ourselves to purely transactional code, that is, every operation is part of some transaction. We consider transactional programs as our basic sequential unit of computation. We express transactional programs as infinite binary trees on commands, which makes the representation independent of specific control flow statements, such as exceptions for handling aborts of transactions. For every command of a thread, we define two successor commands, one if the command is successfully executed, and another if the command fails due to an abort of the transaction. Note that this definition allows us to capture different retry mechanisms of TMs, e.g., retry the same transaction until it succeeds, or try another transaction after an abort. We use a set of transactional programs to define a multithreaded transactional program. A *transactional program* θ on V is an infinite binary tree $\theta : \mathbb{B}^* \to C$. A *multithreaded transactional program* $prog = \langle \theta^1 \dots \theta^n \rangle$ on V is a tuple of transactional programs on V. Let *Progs* be the set of all multithreaded transactional programs.

STM correctness. An STM is characterized by the set of histories (sequences of memory instructions) the STM produces for a given transactional program. In order to reason about the correctness of STMs, the history must contain, apart from the sequence of memory instructions that capture the loads and stores to transactional variables in the program, the following information: (i) when transactions finish (captured with commit and abort instructions), (ii) when read and write commands finish (captured with rfin and wfin instructions), and (iii) rollback of stores to transactional variables in V (captured with rollback a). We define $\hat{I} = I_V \cup (\text{rollback} \times V) \cup \{\text{rfin}, \text{wfin}, \text{commit}, \text{abort}\}$, where $I_V \subseteq I$ is the set of memory instructions to the transactional variables V.

Let $O = \hat{I} \times T$ be the set of *operations*. A *history* $h \in O^*$ is a finite sequence of operations. An STM takes as input a transactional program and, depending upon the memory model, produces a set of histories. Formally, a *software transactional memory* is a function $\Gamma : Progs \times \mathbf{M} \to 2^{O^*}$.

A *correctness property* π is a subset of O^*. It is natural to require that an STM is correct for *all* programs on a *specific* memory model. This is because an STM may be optimized for performance for a specific memory model, while it could be incorrect on weaker models. That is, different implementation versions may be designed for different memory models. An STM Γ is *correct* for a property π under a memory model M if for all programs $prog \in Progs$, we have $\Gamma(prog, M) \subseteq \pi$.

Opacity. We consider opacity [8] as the correctness (safety) requirement of transactional memories. Opacity builds upon the property of strict serializability [17], which requires that the order of conflicting operations from committing transactions is preserved, and the order of non-overlapping transactions is preserved. Opacity, in addition to strict serializability, requires that even aborting transactions do not read inconsistent values. The motivation behind the stricter requirement for aborting transactions in opacity is that in STMs, inconsistent reads may have unexpected side effects, like infinite loops, or array bound violations. Most of the STMs [4,10,18] in the literature are designed to satisfy opacity. However, there do exist STMs that ensure just strict serializability (for example, a variant to McRT STM), and use exception handling to deal with inconsistent reads.

Given a history $h \in O^*$, we define the *thread projection* $h|_t$ of h on thread $t \in T$ as the subsequence of h consisting of all operations op in h such that $op \in \hat{I} \times \{t\}$. Given a thread projection $h|_t = op_0 \ldots op_m$ of a history h on thread t, an operation op_i is *finishing in* $h|_t$ if op_i is a commit or an abort. An operation op_i is *initiating in* $h|_t$ if op_i is the first operation in $h|_t$, or the previous operation op_{i-1} is a finishing statement. Given a thread projection $h|_t$ of a history h on thread t, a consecutive subsequence $x = op_0 \ldots op_m$ of $h|_t$ is a *transaction* of thread t in h if (i) op_0 is initiating in $h|_t$, and (ii) op_m is either finishing in $h|_t$, or op_m is the last operation in $h|_t$, and (iii) no other operation in x is finishing in $h|_t$. The transaction x is *committing* in h if op_m is a commit. The transaction x is *aborting* in h if op_m is an abort. Otherwise, the transaction x is *unfinished* in h. We say that a load of a transaction variable by thread t is *used* in a history h if the load is immediately succeeded by an rfin statement in $h|_t$. Given a history h, we define $usedloads(h)$ as the longest subsequence of h such that all loads of transaction variables in $usedloads(h)$ are used. Given a history h and two transactions x and y in h (possibly of different threads), we say that x *precedes* y in h, written as $x <_h y$, if the last operation of x occurs before the first operation of y in h. A history h is *sequential* if for every pair x, y of transactions in h, either $x <_h y$ or $y <_h x$. An operation op_1 of transaction x and an operation op_2 of transaction y (where x is different from y) *conflict* in a history h if (i) op_1 is a load, store, or a rollback instruction to some transactional variable v and (ii) op_2 is a store or rollback instruction to v.

A history $h = op_0 \ldots op_m$ is *strictly equivalent* to a history h' if (i) for every thread $t \in T$, we have $h|_t = h'|_t$, and (ii) for every pair op_i, op_j of operations in h, if op_i and op_j conflict and $i < j$, then op_i occurs before op_j in h', and (iii) for every pair x, y of transactions in h, where x is a finished transaction, if $x <_h y$, then it is not the case that $y <_{h'} x$. We define *opacity* as the set of histories h such that there exists a sequential history h', where h' is strictly equivalent to $usedloads(h)$. We specify correctness properties using transition systems called TM specifications [7].

$l ::= lv \mid la[idx] \qquad g ::= gv \mid ga[idx] \qquad e ::= f(l,\ldots,l,idx,\ldots,idx) \qquad c ::= f(idx,\ldots,idx)$

$mem\_stmt ::= \ g := e \mid l := g \mid l := e \ \mid idx := c \mid l := \mathsf{cas}(g,e,e) \mid \mathsf{rollback} \ g := e$

$tm\_stmt ::= \mathsf{rfin} \mid \mathsf{wfin} \mid \mathsf{commit} \mid \mathsf{abort} \qquad\qquad\qquad fence ::= \mathsf{stfence} \mid \mathsf{ldfence}$

$p ::= \ mem\_stmt \ \mid \ tm\_stmt \ \mid fence \ \mid \ p \ ; \ p \ \mid \ \mathbf{if} \ e \ \mathbf{then} \ p \ \mathbf{else} \ p \ \mid \ \mathbf{while} \ e \ \mathbf{do} \ p$

Fig. 3. The syntax of RML

TM specifications. A *TM specification* is a 3-tuple $\langle Q, q_{init}, \delta \rangle$, where Q is a set of states, q_{init} is the initial state, and $\delta : Q \times O \rightarrow Q$ is a transition function. A history $op_0 \ldots op_m$ is a *run* of the TM specification if there exist states $q_0 \ldots q_{m+1}$ in Q such that $q_0 = q_{init}$ and for all i such that $0 \leq i \leq m$, we have $(q_i, op_i, q_{i+1}) \in \delta$. The *language L* of a TM specification is the set of all runs of the TM specification. A *TM specification* Σ defines a correctness property π if $L(\Sigma) = \pi$. A TM specification for opacity at a coarse-grained alphabet of read, write, commit, and abort statements was developed [7]. To verify the STM algorithms at the low-level atomicity, we build a new TM specification for opacity with the alphabet O. The new TM specification is about 30 times the size of the TM specification for the coarse-grained alphabet, and has about 70,000 states.

3   The RML Language

We introduce a high-level language, RML, to express STM algorithms with hardware-level atomicity on relaxed memory models. The key idea behind the design of RML is to have a semantics parametrized by the underlying memory model. To capture a relaxed memory model, RML defers a statement until the statement is forced to execute due to a fence, and RML reorders or eliminates deferred statements according to the memory model. We describe below the syntax and semantics of RML.

Syntax. To describe STM algorithms in RML, we use local and global integer-valued locations, which are either variables or arrays. We also have a set of array index variables. The syntax of RML is given in Figure 3. A memory statement (denoted by mem_stmt) in RML models an instruction that executes atomically on the hardware. It can, for instance, be a store or a load of a global variable. Moreover, the TM specific statements are denoted by tm_stmt, and fence statements are denoted by $fence$. Let S_M be the set of memory statements, S_{tm} be the set of TM specific statements, and S_F be the set of fence statements in RML. Let P be the set of RML programs.

Semantics. Let G and L be the set of global and local addresses respectively. Let Idx be the set of index variables. Let $q : G \cup L \cup Idx \rightarrow \mathbb{N}$ be a *state* of the global and local addresses and the index variables. Let Q be the set of all states. Note that the syntax of RML is defined in a way that the value of an index variable idx may not depend on a global variable. Given a global location g and a valuation q, we write $[\![g]\!]_q \in G$ to denote the global address represented by g in state q. Similarly, we write $[\![l]\!]_q \in L$ to denote the local address represented by a local location l in state q.

Let $\gamma : S_M \times Q \rightarrow I \cup \{\mathsf{skip}\}$ be a mapping function for memory statements, which for a given memory statement and a state, gives the generated hardware instruction. For example, we have $\gamma(g := e, q) = \langle \text{store } [\![g]\!]_q \rangle$ in state q, as the statement $g := e$ causes a store to the global address represented by g in state q. The statement rollback $g := e$ is physically a store instruction, as a rollback undoes the effect of a previous store instruction. We define a *local-variables* function *lvars* such that given an expression e and a state q, $lvars(e, q)$ is the smallest set of local addresses in L such that if the location l appears in e, then the address $[\![l]\!]_q \in lvars(e, q)$. We define a *write-locals* function $lw : S \times Q \rightarrow 2^L$ and a *read-locals* function $lr : S \times Q \rightarrow 2^L$ to obtain the written and read local addresses in a statement respectively. Table 1 gives the formal definitions of the functions γ, lw, and lr. Moreover, we define a mapping function $\gamma_{tm} : S_{tm} \rightarrow S_F \cup \{\text{skip}\}$, which maps the TM specific statements to fence statements. To avoid instructions of two transactions from the same thread to interleave with each other, we define $\gamma_{tm}(\text{commit}) = \gamma_{tm}(\text{abort}) = \text{stfence}$. Moreover, to ensure that during the read of a global variable, the variable is loaded before the read is declared as finished, we define $\gamma_{tm}(\text{rfin}) = \text{ldfence}$. We define $\gamma_{tm}(\text{wfin}) = \text{skip}$.

We now describe when two memory statements can be reordered in a given state under a given memory model. Let $R : S_M \times S_M \times Q \times \mathbf{M} \rightarrow \{true, false\}$ be a *reordering* function such that $R(s_1, s_2, q, M) = true$ if the following conditions hold: (i) $M(\gamma(s_1, q), \gamma(s_2, q)) = Y$, (ii) $lw(s_1, q) \cap lr(s_2, q) = \emptyset$, (iii) $lw(s_1, q) \cap lw(s_2, q) = \emptyset$, and (iv) $lr(s_1, q) \cap lw(s_2, q) = \emptyset$. Here, the first condition restricts reorderings to those allowed by the memory model, and the remaining conditions check for data dependence between the statements. To defer memory statements and execute them in as many ways as possible, we define a model-dependent enqueue function. This function takes as input the current state, the current sequence of deferred statements, a statement to defer, and a memory model, and produces the set of new possible sequences of deferred statements. We define the *enqueue* function $Enq : S_M^* \times S_M \times Q \times \mathbf{M} \rightarrow 2^{S^*}$ such that given a sequence $d = s_1 \ldots s_n$ of memory statements, a statement s, a state q, and a memory model M, $Enq(d, s, q, M)$ is the largest set such that (i) $s_1 \ldots s_k \cdot s \cdot s_{k+1} \ldots s_n \in Enq(d, s, q, M)$ if for all i such that $k < i < n$, we have $R(s_i, s, q, M) = true$, and (ii) if s is of the form $l := g$, then $s_1 \ldots s_k \cdot (l := e) \cdot s_{k+1} \ldots s_n \in Enq(d, s, q, M)$ if for all i with $k < i < n$, we have $R(s_i, s, q, M) = true$, and $M(\gamma(s_k, q), \gamma(s, q)) = E$ where (a) if s_k is $g := f$, then $e = f$, (b) if s_k is $m := g$ or $m := \text{cas}(g, e_1, e_2)$, then $e = m$. Note that the definition of the reordering function restricts the reordering of control and data-dependent statements. Thus, we cannot capture memory models like Alpha, which allows to reorder data-dependent loads. Similarly, the enqueue function restricts the elimination of only load instructions. While this is sufficient to model many hardware memory models, we cannot capture coalesced stores or redundant store elimination.

Given a program p and a sequence d of deferred statements, we define a predicate *allowDequeue*(d, p) to be *true* if (i) p is of the form $\{\textbf{while } e \textbf{ do } p_1 \mid p_1 \in P\}$ or $\{\textbf{if } e \textbf{ then } p_1 \textbf{ else } p_2 \mid p_1, p_2 \in P\}$, and there exists a memory statement s in d such that $lw(s, q) \cap lvars(e, q) \neq \emptyset$, or (ii) p is a store fence and there exists a statement s of the form $g := l$ in d, or (iii) p is a load fence and there exists a statement s of the form $l := g$ in d. Figure 4 describes the operational semantics of a program in RML parametrized by the underlying memory model.

Table 1. Formal definitions of the functions γ, lw, and lr for a statement s in a state q

Statement s	$\gamma(s, q)$	$lw(s, q)$	$lr(s, q)$
$g := e$	$\langle \text{store } [\![g]\!]_q \rangle$	$\emptyset$	$lvars(e, q)$
$l := g$	$\langle \text{load } [\![g]\!]_q \rangle$	$\{[\![l]\!]_q\}$	$\emptyset$
$l := e$	skip	$\{[\![l]\!]_q\}$	$lvars(e, q)$
$l := \text{cas}(g, e_1, e_2)$	$\langle \text{cas } [\![g]\!]_q \rangle$	$\{[\![l]\!]_q\}$	$lvars(e_1, q) \cup lvars(e_2, q)$
$\text{rollback } g := e$	$\langle \text{store } [\![g]\!]_q \rangle$	$\emptyset$	$lvars(e, q)$
$idx := c$	skip	$\emptyset$	$\emptyset$

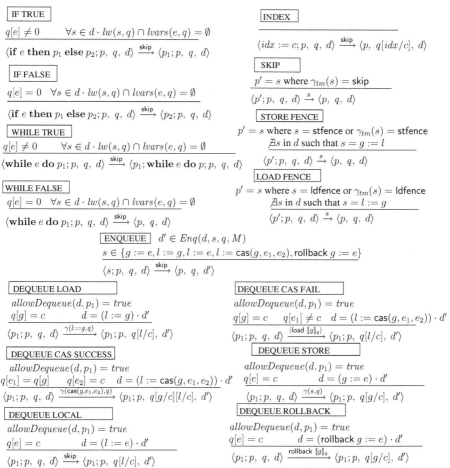

Fig. 4. The operational semantics of RML

STM algorithms in RML. A state of a thread carries the information of the program currently being executed, the valuation of the local variables, the deferred statements of the thread, and the location of the transactional program. A *thread-local state* z_l^t

of thread t is the tuple $\langle p^t, q_L^t, D^t, loc^t \rangle$, where p^t is the current RML program being executed by thread t, $q_L^t : L \cup Idx \rightarrow \mathbb{N}$ is the valuation of the local and index variables of thread t, D^t is the deferred statements of thread t, and $loc^t \in \mathbb{B}^*$ is the location of the transactional program θ^t. A *state* z of an STM algorithm with T threads is given by $\langle q_G, z_l^1 \ldots z_l^T \rangle$, where $q_G : G \rightarrow \mathbb{N}$ is the valuation of the global variables of the STM algorithm, and z_l^t is the thread-local state of thread t for $1 \leq t \leq T$. An STM algorithm A is a 4-tuple $\langle p_r, p_w, p_e, z_{init} \rangle$, where p_r, p_w, and p_e are RML programs, and z_{init} is the initial state of the STM algorithm. Moreover, we define a function $\alpha : C \rightarrow P$ that maps a transactional command to an RML program, such that $\alpha((\text{read}, k)) = (v := k; p_r)$, $\alpha((\text{write}, k)) = (v := k; p_w)$, and $\alpha(\text{xend}) = p_e$.

Language of an STM algorithm. Let a *scheduler* σ on T be a function $\sigma : \mathbb{N} \rightarrow T$. Given a scheduler σ, a transactional program *prog*, and a memory model M, a *run* of an STM algorithm A is a sequence $\langle z_0, i_0 \rangle, \ldots \langle z_n, i_n \rangle$ such that $z_0 = z_{init}$, and for all j such that $0 \leq j < n$, if $z_j = \langle q_G, z_l^1 \ldots z_l^T \rangle$ and $z_{j+1} = \langle q_G', z_l'^1 \ldots z_l'^T \rangle$, then (i) $\langle p, q_G \cup q_L, D \rangle \xrightarrow{i_{j+1}} \langle p', q_G' \cup q_L', D' \rangle$ is a step of RML with memory model M, and (ii) for all threads $t \neq \sigma(j)$, we have $z_l'^t = z_l^t$, and (iii) for thread $t = \sigma(j)$, we have $z_l'^t = \langle p'', q_L', D' \rangle$, where (a) if $i_{j+1} \in \{\text{rfin}, \text{wfin}, \text{commit}\}$, then $p'' = \alpha(\theta(loc \cdot 1))$, (b) else if $i_{j+1} = \text{abort}$, then $p'' = \alpha(\theta(loc \cdot 0))$, (c) else $p'' = p'$. A run $\langle z_{init}, i_0 \rangle, \ldots, \langle z_n, i_n \rangle$ of an STM algorithm A produces a history h such that h is the longest subsequence of operations in $i_1 \ldots i_n$. The *language* $L(A, M)$ of an STM algorithm A under a memory model M is the set of all histories h where there exists a multi-threaded transactional program *prog* and a scheduler σ such that h can be produced by A on *prog* with σ under M. An STM algorithm A is safe for property π under a memory model M if every history in the language of A under M is included in π.

We describe an STM algorithm by p_r, p_w, and p_e programs, and a set of global and a set of local variables, along with their initial values. As an example of an STM algorithm expressed in RML, we present the TL2 algorithm. Similar descriptions can be obtained for DSTM and McRT STM. DSTM is an obstruction-free STM that does not use locks for controlling concurrency. McRT STM is a lock-based direct-update STM.

TL2 algorithm in RML. Transactional locking II (TL2) is an STM algorithm, which is highly popular for its good performance. It is a deferred-update STM, and uses locks to ensure safety. Figure 5 shows four RML programs: p_r (read), p_w (write), p_e (end), and p_a (abort). The program p_a can be called from within p_r, p_w, and p_e. We use the notation $own[V]$ to denote that own is an array of size V. The global variables are $own[V]$, $ver[V]$, $g[V]$, and clk. The local variables are $rs[V]$, $ws[V]$, $lver[V]$, $localclk$, c, and l. The index variables are u and v. *self* denotes the thread number of the executing thread.

Structural properties of STMs. As STMs provide a programmer with a flexible programming paradigm, an STM can involve an arbitrary number of concurrent threads and variables. Thus, an STM algorithm may have an unbounded number of states (corresponding to state of every variable for every thread), where every state has an unbounded number of transitions (corresponding to read or write for every variable). A common technique in checking correctness of arbitrarily sized systems lies in exploiting the inherent symmetry of the system [5,9]. Guerraoui et al. [6] presented a set of four

```
01  program p_a :                                 08  l := 0;
02  u := 0;                                        09  while l < localclk do
03  while u < V do                                 10    l := cas(clk, localclk, localclk + 1);
04    u := u + 1;                                  11    localclk := localclk + 1
05    if own[u] = self then own[u] := 0;          12  u := 0;
06  rs[u] := 0; ws[u] := 0                         13  while u < V do
07  abort                                          14    u := u + 1;
                                                   15    if rs[u] = 1 then
01  program p_r :                                  16      rs[u] := 0;
02  if localclk = 0 then localclk := clk;          17      l := own[u];
03  if ws[v] = 0 then                              18      c := ver[u];
04    l := own[v];                                 19      if c ≠ lver[u] then p_a
05    if l ≠ 0 then p_a                            20      if l ≠ 0 then p_a
06    l := g[v];                                   21  u := 0;
07    lver[v] := ver[v];                           22  while u < V do
08    if localclk ≠ lver[v] then p_a               23    u := u + 1;
09    rs[v] := 1;                                  24    if ws[u] = 1 then
10  rfin                                           25      ver[u] := localclk;
                                                   26      g[u] := l;
01  program p_w :                                  27  u := 0;
02  ws[v] := 1;                                    28  while u < V do
03  wfin                                           29    u := u + 1;
                                                   30    if ws[u] = 1 then
01  program p_e :                                  31      own[u] := 0;
02  u := 0;                                        32      ws[u] := 0;
03  while u < V do                                 33  commit
04    u := u + 1;
05    if (ws[u] = 1) then
06      l := cas(own[ws[u]], 0, self);
07      if l ≠ self then p_a
```

Fig. 5. TL2 algorithm in RML

structural properties of STMs for the alphabet of read, write, commit, and abort commands for deferred-update STMs. The authors subsequently verified these properties by hand for different STMs. These structural properties allowed the authors to reduce the problem of verification of an unbounded number of threads and variables to the problem of verification for two threads and two variables. With slight modifications to two of the four properties, the structural properties can be adapted to our framework for both, deferred and direct-update STMs. The properties P2 (*thread symmetry*) and P3 (*variable projection*) are independent of the level of atomicity and the relaxations of the memory model. Thus, these two properties can be directly used in our framework. The property P1, *transactional projection*, originally [6] stated that aborting and pending transactions have no influence on committing transactions, and can thus be projected away. This holds for deferred-update STMs as an aborted transaction does not write to any variable v of the transactional program. In direct-update STMs, an aborting transaction may write a value to a variable, but that value is not read if the transaction aborts. Thus, aborted transactions can still be projected away. On the other hand, pending transactions can be projected away in a coarse grained alphabet [6], but not in our fine-grained alphabet due to the fact that a pending transaction may be in the process of committing values to memory. Furthermore, we generalize P4, the *monotonicity* property, to handle any number of pending transactions, as opposed to just one pending transaction in the original property [6]. Note that although this generalization is possible for opacity, it cannot be extended to some weaker properties, like strict serializability.

We proved manually that all considered STM algorithms, DSTM, TL2, and McRT STM, satisfy the four structural properties. This allows us to extend the reduction theorem [6] to our framework.

4   The FOIL Tool

We developed a stateful explicit-state model checker, FOIL, that takes as input the RML description of an STM algorithm A, a memory model M, and a correctness property π, and checks whether A is correct for π under the memory model M. FOIL uses the RML semantics with respect to the memory model M to compute the state space of the STM algorithm A, and checks inclusion within the correctness property π. FOIL builds on the fly, the product of the transition system for A and the TM specification for π. If an STM algorithm A is not opaque for a memory model M, FOIL automatically inserts fences within the RML representation of A in order to make A opaque. FOIL succeeds if it is indeed possible to make A opaque solely with the use of fences. In this case, FOIL reports a possible set of missing fences. FOIL fails if inserting fences cannot make A opaque. In this case, FOIL produces a shortest counterexample to opacity under sequential consistency.[1] We implemented FOIL in OCaml. We used FOIL to check the opacity of DSTM, TL2, and McRT STM under different memory models.

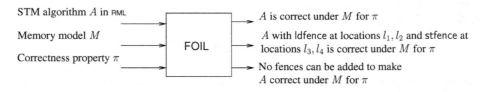

Fig. 6. Inputs and examples of possible outputs of FOIL

Results under sequential consistency. We first model check the STM algorithms for opacity on a sequentially consistent memory model. We find that all of DSTM, TL2, and McRT STM are opaque. The state space obtained for these STM algorithms is large as it covers every possible interleaving, where the level of atomicity is that of the hardware. Table 2 lists the number of states of different STM algorithms with the verification results under sequential consistency. The usefulness of FOIL is demonstrated by the size of state spaces it can handle.

Results under relaxed memory models. Next, we model check the STM algorithms on the following relaxed memory models: TSO, PSO, and RMO. We find that none

---

[1] Note that if an STM algorithm A cannot be made opaque with fences under some memory model M, then A is not opaque even under sequential consistency.

Table 2. Time for checking the opacity of STM algorithms under sequential consistency on a 2.8 GHz PC with 2 GB RAM. The time is divided into time t_g needed to generate the language of the STM algorithm from the RML description, and time t_i needed to check inclusion within the property of opacity.

STM algorithm A	Number of states	A is opaque?	t_g	t_i
DSTM	1239503	Yes	$212s$	$2.3s$
TL2	2431181	Yes	$471s$	$5.1s$
McRT STM	1756115	Yes	$319s$	$3.9s$

Table 3. Counterexamples generated for opacity, and the type and location of fences required to remove all counterexamples on different relaxed memory models. Instead of the exact location, we list here only the RML program in which the fence has to be introduced.

STM	TSO	PSO	RMO
DSTM	No fences	w_1, stfence: p_e	w_1, stfence: p_e
TL2	No fences	w_1, stfence: p_e	w_1, stfence: p_e
			w_3, ldfence: p_e
			w_4, ldfence: p_r
McRT STM	No fences	w_2, stfence: p_a	w_2, stfence: p_a

Counterexamples

$w_1 : (\langle \text{load } v_1 \rangle, t_1), (\langle \text{rfin} \rangle, t_1), (\langle \text{store } v_1 \rangle, t_2), (\langle \text{store } v_1 \rangle, t_1)$

$w_2 : (\langle \text{store } v_1 \rangle, t_1), (\langle \text{load } v_2 \rangle, t_2), (\langle \text{rfin} \rangle, t_2), (\langle \text{load } v_1 \rangle, t_2), (\langle \text{rfin} \rangle, t_2), (\langle \text{rollback } v_1 \rangle, t_1)$

$w_3 : (\langle \text{load } v_1 \rangle, t_1), (\langle \text{rfin} \rangle, t_1), (\langle \text{load } v_2 \rangle, t_2), (\langle \text{rfin} \rangle, t_2), (\langle \text{store } v_1 \rangle, t_2), (\langle \text{store } v_2 \rangle, t_1)$

$w_4 : (\langle \text{load } v_1 \rangle, t_1), (\langle \text{rfin} \rangle, t_1), (\langle \text{store } v_1 \rangle, t_2), (\langle \text{load } v_1 \rangle, t_1), (\langle \text{rfin} \rangle, t_1)$

of the STM algorithms is opaque for PSO and RMO. FOIL gives counterexamples to opacity. We let FOIL insert fences automatically until the STM algorithms are opaque under different memory models. Table 3 lists the number and location of fences inserted by FOIL to make the various STM algorithms opaque under various memory models. Note that the counterexamples shown in the table are projected to the loads, stores, and rollbacks of the transactional variables, and rfin instructions. We omit the original long counterexamples (containing for example, a sequence of loads and stores of locks and version numbers) for brevity. We give the exact locations of fences for the RML description of TL2 from Figure 5. FOIL discovers that a store fence is needed after the label 26 of p_e under the memory model PSO. Similarly, for RMO, FOIL finds that three fences are needed: one store fence after label 26 in p_e, and two load fences, one after label 17 in p_e and one after label 06 in p_r.

Currently, STM designers use intuition to place fences, as lack of fences risks correctness, and too many fences hamper performance. As FOIL takes as input a memory model, it makes it easy to customize an STM implementation according to the relaxations allowed by the memory model. Although FOIL is not guaranteed to put the minimal number of fences, we found that FOIL indeed inserts the same fences as those in the official STM implementations.

On the need of fences. We note that reordering a store followed by a load, and reading own write early (due to store buffers) does not create a problem in the STMs we have studied. This is evident from the fact that all STMs are correct under the TSO memory model without any fences. On the other hand, relaxing the order of stores or loads can be disastrous for the correctness of an STM. This is because most STMs use version numbers or locks to control access. For example, a reading thread first checks that the variable is unlocked and then reads the variable. A writing thread first updates the variable and then unlocks it. Reversing the order of writes or reads renders the STM incorrect.

5   Related Work

Cohen et al. [3] model checked STMs applied to programs with a small number of threads and variables. They studied safety properties in situations where transactional code has to interact with non-transactional accesses. Guerraoui et al. [6,7] presented specifications for strict serializability and opacity in STM algorithms and model checked various STMs. All these verification techniques in STMs assumed sequentially consistent execution and the atomicity of STM operations like read, write, and commit. The only work that has looked into relaxed memory models in conjunction with transactional memories focused on the testing of TM implementations [15]. We believe that, as with any other concurrent program, it is difficult to eliminate subtle bugs in STM implementations solely with testing.

Our RML language was inspired by +CAL [13], a language for writing and model checking concurrent algorithms. +CAL assumes sequentially consistent behavior, and the notion of an atomic step does not coincide with a hardware atomic step.

There has also been research in guaranteeing sequential consistency under various relaxed memory models [14]. However, conservatively putting fences into STM implementations to guarantee sequential consistency would badly hurt STM performance. STM programmers put fences only where necessary. Also closely related to our work is the CheckFence tool [2], a verifier for concurrent C programs on relaxed memory models. The tool requires as input a bounded test program (a finite sequence of operations) for a concurrent data type and uses a SAT solver to check the consistency and introduce fences where needed. We use the structural properties of STMs which allow us to consider a maximal program on two threads and two variables in order to generalize the result to all programs with any number of threads and variables. Moreover, we model the correctness problem as a relation between transition systems.

6   Conclusion

This paper contributes to bridging the gap between reasoning about the correctness of STMs as described in the literature, typically in high-level pseudo-code assuming a coarse-grained atomicity and sequential consistency, and the correctness of STM implementations on actual multiprocessors. We first presented a formalism to express STMs and their correctness properties at the hardware level of atomicity under relaxed memory models. The formalism is general and encompasses both deferred-update and direct-update STM schemes. We illustrated our formalism by specifying common STMs such as DSTM, TL2, and McRT STM; memory models such as total store order (TSO), partial store order (PSO), and relaxed memory order (RMO); and correctness criteria such as opacity. We then presented a tool, FOIL, to automatically check the correctness of STMs under fine-grained hardware atomicity and relaxed memory models. FOIL can automatically insert load and store fences where necessary in the STM algorithm description, in order to make the STMs correct under various relaxed memory models. We plan to extend our work to more complicated software memory models, such as Java [16], which further relax the order of memory instructions.

References

1. Adve, S.V., Gharachorloo, K.: Shared memory consistency models: A tutorial. IEEE Computer 29(12), 66–76 (1996)
2. Burckhardt, S., Alur, R., Martin, M.M.K.: CheckFence: Checking consistency of concurrent data types on relaxed memory models. In: PLDI, pp. 12–21. ACM, New York (2007)
3. Cohen, A., Pnueli, A., Zuck, L.D.: Mechanical verification of transactional memories with non-transactional memory accesses. In: Gupta, A., Malik, S. (eds.) CAV 2008. LNCS, vol. 5123, pp. 121–134. Springer, Heidelberg (2008)
4. Dice, D., Shalev, O., Shavit, N.: Transactional locking II. In: Dolev, S. (ed.) DISC 2006. LNCS, vol. 4167, pp. 194–208. Springer, Heidelberg (2006)
5. Emerson, E.A., Sistla, A.P.: Symmetry and model checking. In: Formal Methods in System Design, pp. 105–131 (1996)
6. Guerraoui, R., Henzinger, T.A., Jobstmann, B., Singh, V.: Model checking transactional memories. In: PLDI, pp. 372–382. ACM, New York (2008)
7. Guerraoui, R., Henzinger, T.A., Singh, V.: Nondeterminism and completeness in transactional memories. In: van Breugel, F., Chechik, M. (eds.) CONCUR 2008. LNCS, vol. 5201, pp. 21–35. Springer, Heidelberg (2008)
8. Guerraoui, R., Kapalka, M.: On the correctness of transactional memory. In: PPoPP, pp. 175–184. ACM, New York (2008)
9. Henzinger, T.A., Qadeer, S., Rajamani, S.K.: Verifying sequential consistency on shared-memory multiprocessor systems. In: Halbwachs, N., Peled, D.A. (eds.) CAV 1999. LNCS, vol. 1633, pp. 301–315. Springer, Heidelberg (1999)
10. Herlihy, M., Luchangco, V., Moir, M., Scherer, W.N.: Software transactional memory for dynamic-sized data structures. In: PODC, pp. 92–101. ACM, New York (2003)
11. Herlihy, M., Moss, J.E.B.: Transactional memory: Architectural support for lock-free data structures. In: ISCA, pp. 289–300. ACM, New York (1993)
12. Lamport, L.: How to make a multiprocessor computer that correctly executes multiprocess programs. IEEE Trans. Computers 28(9), 690–691 (1979)
13. Lamport, L.: The $^+$CAL algorithm language. In: Najm, E., Pradat-Peyre, J.-F., Donzeau-Gouge, V.V. (eds.) FORTE 2006. LNCS, vol. 4229, p. 23. Springer, Heidelberg (2006)
14. Lee, J., Padua, D.A.: Hiding relaxed memory consistency with a compiler. IEEE Trans. Computers 50(8), 824–833 (2001)
15. Manovit, C., Hangal, S., Chafi, H., McDonald, A., Kozyrakis, C., Olukotun, K.: Testing implementations of transactional memory. In: PACT, pp. 134–143 (2006)
16. Manson, J., Pugh, W., Adve, S.V.: The Java memory model. In: POPL, pp. 378–391. ACM, New York (2005)
17. Papadimitriou, C.H.: The serializability of concurrent database updates. Journal of the ACM 26(4) (1979)

18. Saha, B., Adl-Tabatabai, A., Hudson, R.L., Minh, C.C., Hertzberg, B.: McRT-STM: A high performance software transactional memory system for a multi-core runtime. In: PPOPP, pp. 187–197. ACM, New York (2006)
19. Shavit, N., Touitou, D.: Software transactional memory. In: PODC, pp. 204–213. ACM, New York (1995)
20. Weaver, D., Germond, T. (eds.): The SPARC Architecture Manual (version 9). Prentice-Hall, Inc., Englewood Cliffs (1994)

Sliding Window Abstraction for Infinite Markov Chains*

Thomas A. Henzinger[1], Maria Mateescu[1], and Verena Wolf[1,2]

[1] EPFL, Switzerland
[2] Saarland University, Germany

Abstract. We present an on-the-fly abstraction technique for infinite-state continuous-time Markov chains. We consider Markov chains that are specified by a finite set of transition classes. Such models naturally represent biochemical reactions and therefore play an important role in the stochastic modeling of biological systems. We approximate the transient probability distributions at various time instances by solving a sequence of dynamically constructed abstract models, each depending on the previous one. Each abstract model is a finite Markov chain that represents the behavior of the original, infinite chain during a specific time interval. Our approach provides complete information about probability distributions, not just about individual parameters like the mean. The error of each abstraction can be computed, and the precision of the abstraction refined when desired. We implemented the algorithm and demonstrate its usefulness and efficiency on several case studies from systems biology.

1 Introduction

We present a new abstraction technique for infinite-state continuous-time Markov chains (CTMCs) that are specified by a finite set of transition classes. Such models naturally represent biochemical reactions and therefore play an important role in the stochastic modeling of inter- and intracellular processes. A *state* is a vector $x \in \mathbb{N}_0^n$ whose dimension n is the number of chemical species, and whose components (the state variables) represent the number of molecules of each species. The analysis of Markov models reveals the biological role of intrinsic noise in gene-network structures, which has received much attention in systems biology [35,44]. The method of choice has been Monte Carlo simulation. This is because standard numerical solution algorithms for CTMCs do not apply to infinite-state systems, whereas upper bounds for the state variables are rarely known, and even if they are known, the algorithms suffer from a "curse of dimensionality," i.e., state explosion. The usual measure of interest is the full probability distribution of state variables at various time instances. Repeated simulation, however, while useful to give some information about individual state parameters such as means and variances, is too expensive to obtain more information about probability distributions [12].

In the context of systems biology, the computation of event probabilities is important for several reasons. First, cellular process may decide probabilistically between several

---

* The research has been partially funded by the Swiss National Science Foundation under grant 205321-111840.

A. Bouajjani and O. Maler (Eds.): CAV 2009, LNCS 5643, pp. 337–352, 2009.

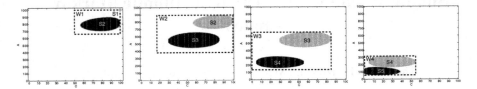

Fig. 1. Sliding window method. In each iteration step, the window W_j captures the set S_j of states where the significant part of the probability mass is located initially (light gray), the set S_{j+1} of states that are reached after a time step (dark gray), and the states that are visited in between.

possibilities, e.g., in the case of developmental switches [4,21,39]. In order to verify, falsify, or refine the mathematical model based on experimental data, the likelihood for each of these possibilities has to be calculated. But also full distributions are of interest, such as the distribution of switching delays [30], the distribution of the time of DNA replication initiation at different origins [34], and the distribution of gene expression products [46]. Finally, many parameter estimation methods require the computation of the posterior distribution because means and variances do not provide enough information to calibrate parameters [22].

If the populations of certain chemical species are large, then the discrete structure of model renders its analysis difficult. However, their effect on the system's variance may be small, and if this is the case, they can be approximated assuming a continuous deterministic change, and it would be better to use continuous-state approximations such as the Langevin approach [25]. For species with small populations, however, a continuous approximation is not appropriate and other approximation techniques are necessary to reduce the computational effort of the analysis.

We propose a new numerical solution algorithm that approximates the desired probability distributions by solving a sequence of dynamically constructed abstract models. Each abstract model is a finite CTMC that represents the behavior of the original, infinite CTMC during a specific time interval. In each step, we construct geometric boundaries in the original state space which encompass the states where most of the probability mass is located. These boundaries form a "window" that moves through the infinite state space. The state space of each abstract model is formed by the finitely many states inside the window, together with a single absorbing state that represents all of the infinitely many states outside the window. In subsequent time intervals, the window movement follows the direction in which the probability mass moves; see Fig. 1. In each step, the initial conditions are given by a probability vector (whose support is shown in light gray); then an abstract model is constructed (whose state space is depicted by the dashed rectangle), and solved to obtain the next vector (dark gray).

Our approach works well if during each time interval, most of the probability mass is concentrated on a tractable subset of the states. Often real-world systems, such as a biological process, have this property, while, for instance, a random-walk model will become intractable after a certain time period, because the probability mass will be distributed uniformly on the entire infinite state space. We can compute the error of each abstract model, and refine the precision of the abstraction when desired, by enlarging the window (as usual, there is a trade-off between precision and cost of the analysis).

To demonstrate the effectiveness of our approach, we have implemented the algorithm and applied it successfully to several examples from systems biology. The experimental results show that our method allows for an efficient analysis while providing high accuracy. The two most complex examples that we consider are infinite in three dimensions and describe networks of at least seven chemical reactions. It is difficult to find comparison data, because these examples are beyond the scope of what has been handled in other work on solving CTMCs.

Related work. Various abstraction techniques for Markov chains with *finite* state spaces have been developed during the last years [10,11,26,28]. Infinite-state Markov chains with *discrete time* have been considered in the context of probabilistic lossy-channel systems [1,2,3,38] and probabilistic pushdown systems [13,14,15,27]. In the infinite-state continuous-time setting, model-checking algorithms for quasi-birth-death processes and Jackson queuing networks have been studied by Remke [40], where the underlying Markov chains are highly structured and represent special cases of CTMCs defined by transition classes. The closest work to ours is the model-checking algorithm for infinite-state CTMCs by Zhang et al. [47]. Depending on the desired precision, their algorithm simply explores the reachable states up to a finite path depth. In contrast, our approach takes into account the direction into which the probability mass moves, and constructs a sequence of abstract models "on-the-fly," during the verification process. Similar approaches have also been used in the context of biochemical reaction networks. Similar to [47], Munsky et al. [32] explore models up to a specified finite path depth, whereas Burrage et al. [7] consider a finite projection that is doubled if necessary. The latter method, however, requires a priori knowledge about the direction and spread of the probability mass.

2 Transition Class Models

Our approach builds on a high-level modeling formalism, called *Transition Class Models* (TCMs), which provides a functional description of structured Markov chains with countably infinite state spaces. TCMs have been used in queuing theory [43] and recently for stochastic models of coupled chemical reactions [41]. We consider a dynamical system with a countable set S of states.

Definition 1. *A transition class C is a triple (G, u, α) with a guard set $G \subset S$, an update function $u : G \to S$, and a rate function $\alpha : G \to \mathbb{R}_{>0}$. A transition class model (TCM) is a pair $(y, \{C_1, \ldots, C_k\})$, where $y \in S$ is an initial state and $\{C_1, \ldots, C_k\}$ is a finite set of transition classes.*

The guard set G contains all states x in which a transition of class C is possible, and $u(x)$ is the target state of the transition. Each C-transition has an associated rate $\alpha(x)$ that depends on the current state x.

Example 1. We consider a simple birth-death process with $S = \mathbb{N}_0$, $y = 0$, and two transition classes $C_b = (G_b, u_b, \alpha_b)$ and $C_d = (G_d, u_d, \alpha_d)$. A birth event increments the value of the state variable by 1 at a constant rate $\lambda > 0$, whereas a death event decrements it by 1 at a constant rate $\mu > 0$. Formally, for all $x \in S$, we define $G_b = S$, $u_b(x) = x + 1$, $\alpha_b(x) = \lambda$, $G_d = \{x \in S \mid x > 0\}$, $u_d(x) = x - 1$, and $\alpha_d(x) = \mu$.

In practice, we can usually express the sets G by a finite number of constraints on the state variables of the system, and u and α by elementary arithmetic functions.

Stochastic Semantics. For a given TCM $M = (y, \{C_1, \ldots, C_k\})$ we derive a continuous-time Markov chain (CTMC) $(X(t), t \geq 0)$ with state space S. Let $i \in \{1, \ldots, k\}$ and $C_i = (G_i, u_i, \alpha_i)$. We define the probability of a transition of type C_i, occurring within an infinitesimal time interval $[t, t + dt)$, by

$$Pr\left(X(t + dt) = u_i(x) \mid X(t) = x\right) = \alpha_i(x) \cdot dt \tag{1}$$

for all $x \in G_i$. We call $\alpha_i(x)$ the *rate* of the transition $x \rightarrow u_i(x)$. Note that the transition probability in Eq. 1 does not depend on t but only on the length of the interval. Moreover, as $(X(t), t \geq 0)$ possesses the Markov property, the above probability does not depend on the states visited before time t. Since y is the initial state of M, we have $Pr\left(X(0) = y\right) = 1$, and, for $x \in S$, we define the probability that the process is in state x at time t by

$$p^{(t)}(x) = Pr\left(X(t) = x \mid X(0) = y\right). \tag{2}$$

In the sequel, a matrix description of the transition probabilities is more advantageous. To simplify our presentation, for all i, we extend the domain of both α_i and u_i to S and set $\alpha_i(x) = 0$ if $x \notin G_i$. Let $Q : S \times S \rightarrow \mathbb{R}$ be the function that calculates the transition rate of each pair (x, x') of states with $x \neq x'$, that is[1],

$$Q(x, x') = \sum_{i : u_i(x) = x'} \alpha_i(x). \tag{3}$$

As for the diagonal of the matrix, we set $Q(x, x) = -\sum_{x' \neq x} Q(x, x')$. By assuming a fixed enumeration of S, we can regard Q as a matrix, called *generator matrix* of $(X(t), t \geq 0)$, and describe the evolution of the system by the *Kolmogorov differential equation* [?]

$$\frac{dp^{(t)}}{dt} = p^{(t)} \cdot Q. \tag{4}$$

We write $\mathbf{1}_y$ for the column vector with zeros everywhere except at state y, where it is one. By $(\cdot)^T$ we denote matrix transposition. If we assume that the initial condition of the system is $p^{(0)} = (\mathbf{1}_y)^T$ and $(X(t), t \geq 0)$ is a regular Markov chain [?] then Eq. 4 has the unique solution

$$p^{(t)} = p^{(0)} \cdot \exp(Qt). \tag{5}$$

Assume that $|S| < \infty$. Then $\exp(Qt) = \sum_{i=0}^{\infty} (Qt)^i / i!$ and, for all $t \geq 0$, $(\exp(Qt))_{x,z}$ is the probability to reach state z from x after t time units. Analytic solutions for the function $p^{(t)}$ can only be derived for special cases. If the underlying graph of the CTMC is acyclic, a closed-form expression for $p^{(t)}(x)$ can be calculated using the recursive scheme of the ACE algorithm [29]. In general, finding the state probabilities as a symbolic function of t is not possible.

---

[1] Note that the stochastic semantics ignores self-loops, because they do not have any effect on the probabilities $p^{(t)}(x)$.

Numerical solutions of the differential equation in Eq. 4 usually exploit the following property. If we split the time interval $[0, t)$ into r intervals $[t_0, t_1), \ldots, [t_{r-1}, t_r)$ with $t_0 < \ldots < t_r$, and $t_0 = 0$, $t_r = t$, then Eq. 5 can be rewritten as

$$
\begin{aligned}
\boldsymbol{p}^{(t_r)} &= \boldsymbol{p}^{(t_0)} \cdot \exp(Qt_r) \\
&= \boldsymbol{p}^{(t_0)} \cdot \exp(Q(t_1 - t_0)) \cdot \exp(Q(t_2 - t_1)) \cdot \ldots \cdot \exp(Q(t_r - t_{r-1})) \\
&= \qquad\qquad \boldsymbol{p}^{(t_1)} \cdot \ \exp(Q(t_2 - t_1)) \cdot \ldots \cdot \exp(Q(t_r - t_{r-1})) \quad (6) \\
&\ \vdots \qquad\qquad\qquad\quad \ddots \qquad\qquad\quad \vdots \\
&= \qquad\qquad\qquad\quad \boldsymbol{p}^{(t_{r-1})} \qquad \cdot \quad \exp(Q(t_r - t_{r-1})).
\end{aligned}
$$

This yields an iterative scheme for the system of differential equations given by Eq. 4. However, numerical solution approaches suffer from the fact that even if upper bounds on the state variables of the system are known, the size of the (truncated) state space is still too large for an efficient solution. We present a way to combat this problem by constructing and analyzing abstract models that approximate the behavior of the infinite-state Markov chain during each interval.

Biochemical Reaction Networks. We illustrate our approach by presenting transition class models of cellular chemical systems. According to the theory of *stochastic chemical kinetics* [16], a network of chemical reactions can be modeled as a CTMC. We consider a system of n different types of molecules and assume that molecules collide randomly and may undergo chemical reactions. If we assume further that the reaction volume (e.g., a cell) has a fixed size and temperature, as well as that the system is well-stirred, a state of the system is given by the numbers of molecules of each type. Hence, the state space S consists of n-dimensional vectors $(x_1, \ldots, x_n) \in \mathbb{N}_0^n$. The different types of reactions are usually specified by means of *stochiometric equations*. For instance, $A + B \to C$ means that if a molecule of type A hits a molecules of type B, they may form a complex molecule C. We call the molecule types that are consumed by a reaction *reactants*; in the above example, A and B are reactants. Each reaction type can be described by a transition class, and for a class $C = (G, u, \alpha)$, the guard G contains the states in which enough reactants are available. The update function u specifies how many molecules of each type are produced and how many are consumed by the reaction. Thus, u is of the form $u(x) = x + v$ where $v \in \mathbb{Z}^n$. Recall that the probability of a transition of class C_i occurring in the next infinitesimal time interval of length dt is $\alpha_i(x) \cdot dt$. For a stochastic kinetic analysis, $\alpha_i(x)$ is the product of a constant and the number of distinct combinations of reactants. This ensures that a chemical reaction is more likely to happen if many reactants are available.

Example 2. We consider a simple transition class model for transcription of a gene into messenger RNA (mRNA), and subsequent translation of the latter into proteins [45]. An illustration is given in Fig. 2. This reaction network involves three chemical species, namely, gene, mRNA, and protein. As always only a single copy of the gene exists, a state of the system is uniquely determined by the number of mRNA and protein molecules. Therefore, $S = \mathbb{N}_0^2$ and a state is a pair $(x_R, x_P) \in S$. We assume that initially there are no mRNA molecules and no proteins in the system, i.e., $y = (0, 0)$. Four types of reactions occur in the system. Let $i \in \{1, \ldots, 4\}$ and $C_i = (G_i, u_i, \alpha_i)$

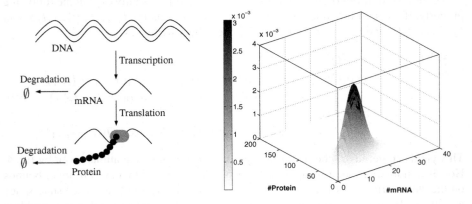

Fig. 2. Transcription of a gene into mRNA and subsequent translation into a protein

Fig. 3. Probability distribution of the gene expression network at $t = 1000$

be the transition class that describes the i-th reaction type. We first define the guard sets $G_1, \ldots, G_4$ and the update functions $u_1, \ldots, u_4$.

- Transition class C_1 models gene transcription. If a C_1-transition occurs, the number of mRNA molecules increases by 1. Thus, $u_1(x_R, x_P) = (x_R + 1, x_P)$. This transition class is possible in all states, i.e., $G_1 = S$.
- We represent the translation of mRNA into protein by C_2. A C_2-transition is only possible if there is at least one mRNA molecule in the system. We set $G_2 = \{(x_R, x_P) \in S \mid x_R > 0\}$ and $u_2(x_R, x_P) = (x_R, x_P + 1)$. Note that in this case mRNA is a reactant that is not consumed.
- Both mRNA and protein molecules can degrade, which is modeled by C_3 and C_4. Hence, $G_3 = G_2$, $G_4 = \{(x_R, x_P) \in S \mid x_P > 0\}$, $u_3(x_R, x_P) = (x_R - 1, x_P)$, and $u_4(x_R, x_P) = (x_R, x_P - 1)$.

Let $c_1, c_2, c_3, c_4 in \mathbb{R}_{>0}$ be constants. Gene transcription happens at the constant rate $\alpha_1(x_R, x_P) = c_1$, as only one reactant molecule (the gene) is available. The translation rate depends linearly on the number of mRNA molecules. Therefore, $\alpha_2(x_R, x_P) = c_2 \cdot x_R$. Finally, for degradation, we set $\alpha_3(x_R, x_P) = c_3 \cdot x_R$ and $\alpha_4(x_R, x_P) = c_4 \cdot x_P$.

Fig. 3 shows the probability distribution $p^{(t)}$ of the underlying Markov chain after $t = 1000$ seconds. The parameters are chosen as $c_1 = 0.05$, $c_2 = 0.0058$, $c_3 = 0.0029$, and $c_4 = 10^{-4}$, where c_3 and c_4 correspond to a half-life of 4 minutes for mRNA and 2 hours for the protein [45]. Most of the probability mass concentrates on the part of the state space where $5 \leq x_R \leq 30$ and $25 \leq x_P \leq 110$ and, in a 3D-plot, it forms a steep "hill" whose top represents the states with the highest probability. Note that *every* state in the infinite set S has a non-zero probability at all time points $t > 0$, because the underlying graph of the Markov chain is strongly connected. As time passes, the hill moves through the state space until the distribution reaches its steady-state.

Input:	TCM $(y, \{C_1, \ldots, C_k\})$, $t_1, \ldots, t_r$ with $0 < t_1 < \ldots < t_r$.
Output:	Approximations $\hat{p}^{(t_1)}, \ldots, \hat{p}^{(t_r)}$ and error ϵ.

1   Initialize $W_0 = \{y\}$, $p(y) = 1$, and $\epsilon = 0$.
2   **for** $j \in \{1, \ldots, r\}$ **do**
3   Set $h_j = t_j - t_{j-1}$.
4   Compute W_j depending on p, $C_1, \ldots, C_k$, and h_j.
5   Construct generator Q_j of the abstract model based on $C_1, \ldots, C_k$ and W_j.
6   Set $q(x) = \begin{cases} p(x) & \text{if } x \in W_{j-1} \cap W_j, \\ \sum_{x \in W_{j-1} \backslash W_j} p(x) & \text{if } x = x_f, \\ 0 & \text{otherwise.} \end{cases}$
7   Compute $p = q \cdot \exp(Q_j h_j)$.
8   Set $\hat{p}^{(t_j)}(x) = p(x)$ for $x \in W_j$ and $\hat{p}^{(t_j)}(x) = 0$ otherwise.
9   Set $\epsilon = \epsilon + p(x_f)$;
10 **end**

Algorithm 1. The basic steps of the approximate solution of the Markov chain

3   Abstraction of TCMs

Our approach is based on the observation that a Markov chain describing a certain real-world system often has the following property. After starting with probability 1 in the initial state y, the probability mass does not distribute uniformly in S, such as, for instance, in the case of a random walk. Instead, at each point in time, most of the probability mass distributes among a finite, relatively small number of states. This set of states changes as time progresses, but it never exceeds a certain size. Often, the states with "significant" probability are located at the same part of the state space, as illustrated in Fig. 3.

Let $(y, \{C_1, \ldots, C_k\})$ be a TCM and let $p^{(t)}$ be the probability distribution of the associated CTMC. We propose an abstraction technique for the computation of $p^{(t)}$ that proceeds in an iterative fashion. We divide the time interval $[0, t)$ into r intervals as in Eq. 6 and approximate $p^{(t_1)}, \ldots, p^{(t_r)}$ by considering a sequence of r abstractions of the Markov chain under study. Let $j \in \{1, \ldots, r\}$. In the j-th step, we construct, on-the-fly, a finite Markov chain for the system behavior during the interval $[t_{j-1}, t_j)$ from the transition class description. The state space of the j-th abstract model is the set W_j of states where most of the probability mass is located during $[t_{j-1}, t_j)$. We refer to this set as a *window*. The remaining states are collapsed into a single absorbing state x_f, i.e., a state that cannot be left.

3.1   Algorithm

Alg. 1 describes an iterative method to approximate $p^{(t_1)}, \ldots, p^{(t_r)}$ by vectors $\hat{p}^{(t_1)}$, $\ldots, \hat{p}^{(t_r)}$. We start with probability 1 in the initial state y (line 1). In line 4, we compute the window W_j such that most of the probability mass remains within W_j during the next h_j time units. In line 5, we construct the generator matrix of the abstract model (the finite Markov chain with state space $W_j \cup \{x_f\}$). We define the initial distribution of the abstract model in line 6 and calculate its solution in line 7. The approximation $\hat{p}^{(t_j)}$ of $p^{(t_j)}$ is then defined in line 8. Finally, in line 9, we add the approximation error to ϵ. A detailed error analysis is given below. Note that after the j-th loop $\epsilon = 1 - \sum_{x \in W_j} p(x)$, that is, in each loop, the probability of being in x_f may increase. Thus,

$$\sum_{x \in S} \hat{p}^{(t_1)} \leq \cdots \leq \sum_{x \in S} \hat{p}^{(t_r)}.$$

The general idea of this abstraction approach is apparent from Fig. 3, but the main difficulty is to find the states that can be neglected in step j (line 4). In Section 3.2, we explain how to predict the direction and spread of the probability mass during $[t_{j-1}, t_j)$.

Let $\epsilon > 0$. For an interval $[t, t + h)$, we define the size $m(\epsilon, t, h)$ of the set of significant states as the smallest number for which there exists $W \subset S$, $|W| = m(\epsilon, t, h)$ such that

$$P\left(X(t') \in W, t' \in [t, t + h)\right) \geq 1 - \epsilon. \tag{7}$$

The value $m(\epsilon, t, h)$ indicates how strongly the probability mass spreads out on S during $[t, t + h)$. Consider, for instance, a random walk on the non-negative integer lattice in the plane that starts in $(0, 0)$ [33]. Between each pair of neighbor states there is a transition with rate 1. For $h > 0$, the value $m(\epsilon, t, h)$ approaches infinity as $t \to \infty$. As opposed to the random walk example, in many systems $m(\epsilon, t, h)$ is a manageable number of states, even if ϵ is small and t is large (or tends to infinity). Consider, for instance, Ex. 2 and assume that $h = 500$, $\epsilon = 10^{-6}$. For each interval $[t, t + h) \subset [0, \infty)$, $m(\epsilon, t, h)$ does not exceed 20000 states. Alg. 1 works well if $m(\epsilon, t_{j-1}, h_j)$ is a manageable number of states for all j. Note that, in particular, cellular usually follow a small number of trends, that is, the quantitative outcomes of a biological experiments can usually be classified within a small number of different categories. Thus, our approach is well suited for TCMs of biological systems.

Construction of the Abstract Model. For $j \in \{1, \ldots, r\}$, let W_j be such that

$$P\left(X(h) \in W_j, h \in [t_{j-1}, t_j)\right) \geq 1 - \epsilon_j \tag{8}$$

where $\epsilon_j > 0$ is the approximation error of the j-th step. Note that Eq. 8 implies that $W_j \cap W_{j+1} \neq \emptyset$, because the intersection of two successive windows must contain those states that have a high probability at time t_j. It is far too costly to construct the *smallest* set with this property. Instead, we propose a cheap construction of a set W_j with a hyper-rectangular shape. We will outline the construction in Section 3.2. The abstract Markov chain of the j-th step has the finite state space $W_j \cup \{x_f\}$, where x_f represents all states $x \in S \setminus W_j$. The transitions of the abstract model are given by the transition classes of the original model except that all transitions of states at the boundary lead to x_f. Formally, for each class $C = (G, u, \alpha)$ of the infinite-state Markov chain $(X(t), t \geq 0)$, we define $C' = (G', u', \alpha')$ such that $G' = G \cap W_j$,

$$u'(x) = \begin{cases} u(x) & \text{if } u(x) \in W_j, \\ x_f & \text{otherwise,} \end{cases}$$

and $\alpha'(x) = \alpha(x)$ for all $x \in G'$. Thus, we consider an (extended) subgraph of the one underlying $(X(t), t \geq 0)$, with vertexes set W_j, and all edges leading from W_j to $S \setminus W_j$ redirected to the extension x_f. Note that no transitions are possible from x_f. We will see that x_f can be used to calculate the approximation error as it captures the probability mass that leaves W_j.

Error Analysis. Recall that if Q is the generator matrix of the original Markov chain (cf. Eq. 3), $\exp(Qh_j)$ is the transition probability matrix for time step h_j. Let Q_j be the generator matrix of the abstract Markov chain constructed in the j-th step (see Alg. 1, line 5). For $x, z \in W_j$, we use the approximation

$$
\begin{aligned}
(\exp(Qh_j))_{x,z} &= P\left(X(t_j) = z \mid X(t_{j-1}) = x\right) \\
&\approx P\left(X(t_j) = z \wedge X(h) \in W_j, h \in (t_{j-1}, t_j) \mid X(t_{j-1}) = x\right) \quad (9) \\
&= (\exp(Q_j h_j))_{x,z}.
\end{aligned}
$$

in line 5 of Alg. 1. Thus, we ignore the probability to reach z from x after h_j time units by leaving W_j at least once.

For the error analysis, we assume that the vector q_j of size $|W_j| + 1$ is such that $q_j(x) = p^{(t_{j-1})}(x)$ if $x \in W_j$. This is true for $j = 1$ and for $j > 1$ we replace $p^{(t_{j-1})}(x)$ by $\hat{p}^{(t_{j-1})}(x)$ in Alg. 1. In line 7 and 8, we define $\hat{p}^{(t_j)}(z) = (q_j \cdot \exp(Q_j h_j))_z$ for $z \in W_j$. Thus,

$$
\begin{aligned}
\hat{p}^{(t_j)}(z) &= (q_j \cdot \exp(Q_j h_j))_z \\
&= \sum_{x \in W_j} p^{(t_{j-1})}(x) \left(\exp(Q_j h_j)\right)_{x,z} \\
&\approx \sum_{x \in W_j} p^{(t_{j-1})}(x) \left(\exp(Q h_j)\right)_{x,z} \\
&= \sum_{x \in W_j} P\left(X(t_{j-1}) = x\right) \cdot P\left(X(t_j) = z \mid X(t_{j-1}) = x\right) \\
&\approx \sum_{x \in S} P\left(X(t_{j-1}) = x\right) \cdot P\left(X(t_j) = z \mid X(t_{j-1}) = x\right) \\
&= P\left(X(t_j) = z\right) = p^{(t_j)}(z).
\end{aligned}
\quad (10)
$$

The first approximation is due to Eq. 9. The second approximation comes from the fact that we ignore the probability of not being in W_j at time t_{j-1}. In both cases we use an underapproximation. By setting $\hat{p}^{(t_j)}(z) = 0$ if $z \notin W_j$, we obtain $\hat{p}^{(t_j)}(z) \le p^{(t_j)}(z)$ for all $z \in S$. Overall, we use three approximations, where probability is "lost" namely,

(a) the probability that is lost due to the approximation given by Eq. 9,
(b) the probability of not starting in W_j at time t_{j-1} (second approximation in Eq. 10),
(c) the probability of leaving W_j during $[t_{j-1}, t_j)$ (which arises due to the approximation $p^{(t_j)}(z) \approx 0$ if $z \notin W_j$).

It is easy to see that, if the probability of being in W_j during $[t_{j-1}, t_j)$ is at least $1 - \epsilon_j$ (see Eq. 8), then all three errors are at most ϵ_j. Thus, $||p^{(t_j)} - \hat{p}^{(t_j)}||_1 \le \epsilon_j$. Note that the entry $p(x_f)$ that is computed in line 7 of Alg. 1 contains all three approximation errors (a), (b), (c). After the termination of the for loop, ϵ contains the total approximation error, which is at most $\epsilon_1 + \ldots + \epsilon_r$.

Numerical Solution Methods. For the solution step in line 7 of Alg. 1, we apply a numerical method to compute the matrix exponential. If Q_j is small then the matrix exponential can be computed efficiently using, for instance, Padé approximation [5,31]. If the size of Q_j is large but Q_j is sparse then iterative methods perform better, such as uniformization [17,24], approximations in the Krylov subspace [37], or numerical integration [18,19].

3.2 Window Construction

Let us now focus on the construction of the set W_j in line 7 of Algorithm 1 (see also Eq. 8). Recall that this requires the prediction of the size and location of the probability mass during $[t_{j-1}, t_j)$. For arbitrary transition class models, a cheap prediction of the future behavior of the process is not possible as the transition classes may describe any kind of "unsystematic" behavior. However, many systems have certain linearity properties, which allow for an efficient approximation of the future behavior of the process. Consider a transition class $C_m = (G_m, u_m, \alpha_m)$, and assume that the successor $u_m(x)$ of a state $x \in G_m$ is computed as $u_m(x) = x + v_m$, where $v_m \in \mathbb{Z}^n$ is a constant change vector. In many applications, a discrete state variable represents the number of instances of a certain system component type, which is incremented or decremented by a small amount. For instance, in the case of biochemical reaction networks, $v_m \in \{-2, -1, \ldots, 2\}^n$, because a reaction changes the population vectors of the chemical species by an amount of at most two. Any reaction that requires the collision of more than two molecules is usually modeled as a sequence of several reactions. For the rate function α_m, we assume that the relative difference $|\alpha_m(x) - \alpha_m(u(x))|/\alpha_m(x)$ is small for all $x \in G_m$. This is the case if, for instance, α_m is linear or at most quadratic in the state variables. According to stochastic chemical kinetics, this assumption is adequate for biochemical reaction networks, because the rate of a reaction is proportional to the number of distinct combinations of reactants. Finally, we assume that the sets G_m can be represented as intersections of half planes of S. Again, this assumption holds for biochemical reaction networks, as G_m refers to the availability of reactant molecules.

The conditions stated above ensure that we can derive geometric boundaries for the window W_j. More precisely, in line 4 of Alg. 1 we can construct an n-dimensional hyper-rectangular W_j such that the left hand of Eq. 8 is close to one. Intuitively, the boundaries of W_j describe upper and lower bounds on the state variables $x_1, \ldots, x_n$. Consider, for instance, Fig. 3 and recall that the initial state of the process is $y = (0, 0)$. For the rectangle $W = \{(x_R, x_P) \in S \mid 0 \le x_R \le 30, 0 \le x_P \le 120\}$, we have $P(X(t) \in W, t \in [0, 1000)) \approx 0.99$.

For the construction of W_j, we use a technique that considers only the "worst case" behavior of the Markov chain during $[t_{j-1}, t_j)$ and is therefore cheap compared to the solution of the abstract model. The random variable $\alpha_m(X(t))$ represents the rate of transition type C_m at time t. We can assume that during a small time interval of length Δ, $\alpha_m(X(t+h))$ is constant, with $0 \le h \le \Delta$. If x is the current state then the number of C_m-transition within the next Δ time units is Poisson distributed with parameter $\alpha_m(x) \cdot \Delta$ [?]. We can approximate this number by the expectation $\alpha_m(x) \cdot \Delta$ of the Poisson distribution. As we are interested in an upper and lower bound, we additionally consider the standard deviation $\sqrt{\alpha_m(x) \cdot \Delta}$ of the Poisson distribution. Thus, in the worst case, the number of transitions of type C_m is

- at least $\kappa_m^-(x, \Delta) = \max(0, \alpha_m(x) \cdot \Delta - \sqrt{\alpha_m(x) \cdot \Delta})$,
- at most $\kappa_m^+(x, \Delta) = \alpha_m(x) \cdot \Delta + \sqrt{\alpha_m(x) \cdot \Delta}$

Note that if, for instance, $\alpha_m(x) \cdot \Delta = 1$, then we have a confidence of 91.97% that the real number of transitions lies in the interval

$$\left[\alpha_m(x) \cdot \Delta - \sqrt{\alpha_m(x) \cdot \Delta}, \alpha_m(x) \cdot \Delta + \sqrt{\alpha_m(x) \cdot \Delta} \right].$$

Let $\kappa_m \in \{\kappa_m^+, \kappa_m^-\}$ and $x^{(0)} = x$. For $l = 0, 1, \ldots$, the iteration

$$x^{(l+1)} = x^{(l)} + \sum_{m=1}^{k} v_m \cdot \kappa_m(x^{(l)}, \Delta) \tag{11}$$

yields worst-case approximations of $X(t+\Delta), X(t+2\Delta), \ldots$ under the condition that $X(t) = x$. Note that $x^{(l)} \in \mathbb{R}_{\geq 0}^n$. For functions α_m that grow extremely fast in the state variables, the iteration may yield bad approximations since it is based on the assumption that the rates are constant during a small interval. In the context of biochemical reaction networks, the linearity properties mentioned above are fulfilled and Eq. 11 yields adequate approximations. The bounds $b_d^+(x)$ and $b_d^-(x)$ for dimension $d \in \{1, \ldots, n\}$ are given by the minimal and maximal values during the iteration. More precisely, $b_d^+(x) = \lceil \max_l x_d^{(l)} \rceil$ and $b_d^-(x) = \lfloor \min_l x_d^{(l)} \rfloor$, where $x^{(l)} = (x_1^{(l)}, \ldots, x_n^{(l)})$.

In order to construct W_j, we do not consider *all* combinations $\{\kappa_1^+, \kappa_1^-\} \times \ldots \times \{\kappa_k^+, \kappa_k^-\}$ in Eq. 11. We choose only those combinations that do not treat preferentially transition types leading to opposite directions in the state space. Consider, for instance, Ex. 2 with $x = (5, 50)$ and $\Delta = 10$. If we assume that more reactions of type C_1 and C_2 happen (than on average) and fewer of C_3 and C_4, we get $\kappa_1^+(x, \Delta) = c_1 \cdot 10 + \sqrt{c_1 \cdot 10} = 1.2$, $\kappa_2^+(x, \Delta) = c_2 \cdot 10 \cdot 5 + \sqrt{c_2 \cdot 10 \cdot 5} = 0.83$, $\kappa_3^-(x, \Delta) = \max(0, c_3 \cdot 10 \cdot 5 - \sqrt{c_3 \cdot 10 \cdot 5}) = 0$, $\kappa_4^-(x, \Delta) = \max(0, c_4 \cdot 10 \cdot 50 - \sqrt{c_4 \cdot 10 \cdot 50}) = 0$. This means that the number of protein and mRNA molecules increases and $x^{(1)} = (6.2, 50.83)$. We do not consider the combinations that contain both κ_1^+ and κ_3^+. As C_1 equates C_3 and vice versa, these combinations do not result in extreme values of the state variables. For each dimension, we can identify two combinations that yield minimal and maximal values by examining the vector field of the transition classes. We refer to a chosen combination as a *branch* and fix for each transition class C_m a choice $\kappa_m = \kappa_m^+$ or $\kappa_m = \kappa_m^-$ for all l.

For the construction of W_j, we first need to define the significant set of states at time t_{j-1}. A very precise method would require sorting of the vector $\hat{p}^{(t_{j-1})}(x)$, which we find far too expensive. Therefore, we opt for a simpler solution where we define the set $S_j = \{x \in S \mid \hat{p}^{(t_{j-1})}(x) > \delta\}$ of states significant at time t_{j-1}. Here, $\delta > 0$ is a small constant that is several orders of magnitude smaller than the desired precision. For our experimental results, we used $\delta = 10^{-10}$ and decreased this value during the iteration if $\sum_{x \notin S_j} \hat{p}^{(t_{j-1})}(x)$ exceeded our desired precision. For each branch, we carry out the iteration in Eq. 11 for $\lceil h_j/\Delta \rceil$ steps with 10 different initial states randomly chosen from S_j. This yields a cheap approximation of the behavior of the process during the interval $[0, h_j)$. For dimension d, let b_d^+ and b_d^- denote the bounds that we obtain by merging the bounds of each branch and each randomly chosen state. We set

$$W_j = S_j \cup \{x = (x_1, \ldots, x_n) \in S \mid b_d^- \leq x_d \leq b_d^+, 1 \leq d \leq n\}.$$

We choose the time steps Δ in the order of the expected residence time of the current state such that the assumption of $\alpha_m(X(t))$ being constant is reasonable.

The boundaries of the window become rough if h_j is large. Therefore, for the experimental results in Section 4, we choose h_j dynamically. During the iterative computation of the bounds b_d^+ and b_d^-, we compute the size of the current window W_j. We stop the iteration if $|W_j|$ exceeds twice the size of S_j but not before W_j has reached a minimal size of 5000 states. By doing so, we induce a sliding of the window, which is forced to move from its previous location. It is, of course, always possible to choose a smaller value for h_j if the distribution at a specific time instant $t < t_{j-1} + h_j$ is of interest.

Precision. If the approximation error ϵ in Alg. 1 exceeds the desired error threshold, the window construction can be repeated using a larger window W_j. This may happen if the confidence of the estimated interval $[\kappa_m^-(x, \Delta), \kappa_m^+(x, \Delta)]$ for the number of transitions of type m is not large enough. In this case, the approximation $\hat{p}^{(t_j)}$ can be used to determine where to expand W_j. Several heuristics for the window expansion are possible. The smooth distribution of the probability mass, however, suggests to expand only those boundaries of W_j where states with a high probability are located.

4   Experimental Results

We implemented Alg. 1 in C++ and run experiments on a 3.16 GHz Intel Linux PC with 6 GB of RAM. We consider various examples and present our results in Table 1. For the parameters, we used values from literature. We provide a detailed description of the parameters and branches that we used for the gene expression example (cf. Ex. 2). For the parameter details of the remaining examples, we refer to [23].

First we applied our method to finite examples and those we found analyzed in the literature (Examples 1-3). We then considered significantly larger examples (Examples 4-6). The examples studied in [47,32] are much simpler than the ones presented here. These approaches explore the reachable states up to a certain depth, which yields large spaces that contain many states with a very small probability. For instance, in the case of Ex. 2 the path depth is proportional to the expected number of protein molecules (see also Fig. 3). The states reachable within this fixed number of steps always include states with a high number of mRNA molecules although their probability is very small. In contrast, with our method, we achieve a similar accuracy while using windows that are much smaller. We are therefore able to handle more complex examples.

The enzyme reaction is a prototype of a stiff model and has 5151 states. The crystallization example is also finite but has 5499981 reachable states. To the best of our knowledge, the crystallization, the gene expression, and the virus example have not yet been solved numerically by others. Goutsias model and the enzyme reaction have been considered by Burrage et al. [7], but as already stated, their method requires additional knowledge about the direction and spread of the probability mass.

For the gene expression example, we choose $y = (0, 0)$, a time horizon of $t = 10000$, and rate constants $c_1 = 0.05$, $c_2 = 0.0058$, $c_3 = 0.0029$, and $c_4 = 10^{-4}$, where c_3 and c_4 correspond to a half-life of 4 minutes for mRNA and 2 hours for the protein [45]. We use four branches for the iteration given by Eq. 11. We maximize the number of mRNA molecules by choosing κ_1^+ and κ_3^- and minimize it with κ_1^- and κ_3^+. Transition classes C_2 and C_4 are irrelevant for this species. We maximize the number of proteins by choosing κ_1^+, κ_2^+, κ_3^-, and κ_4^-. The number of proteins becomes minimal with κ_1^-, κ_2^-, κ_3^+, and κ_4^+.

In Table 1, the column *ref.* refers to the literature where the example has been presented. Column *#dim* lists the number of dimensions of the set of reachable states. Note that this is not equal to the number of chemical species since certain conservation laws

Table 1. Experimental results of the sliding window method

name	ref.	#dim	#classes	infinite	mean $|W_j|$	running time	%constr.	error	steps
enzyme reaction	[7]	2	3	no	1437	15 sec	6	1×10^{-5}	4
crystallization	[20]	2	2	no	47229	8907 sec	30	2×10^{-7}	5175
protein synthesis	[47]	1	4	yes	179	2 sec	< 1	2×10^{-8}	8
gene expression	[45]	2	4	yes	32404	107 sec	39	2×10^{-5}	87
Goutsias model	[7]	3	10	yes	710204	25593 sec	6	9×10^{-6}	54
Virus model	[6]	3	7	yes	1092441	27850 sec	9	6×10^{-6}	51

may hold[2] or the copy number of some species can never exceed a small value. Column *#classes* refers to the number of transition classes, and column *infinite* indicates whether the model has an infinite number of states or not. In column *mean $|W_j|$* we list the mean size of the windows that we considered during the iteration. The running times of the sliding window method are given in the column *running times* and *%constr.* refers to the percentage of time used for the construction of the window boundaries and the generator matrices Q_j. For the computation of the matrix exponential (compare line 7 of Alg. 1) we used the uniformization method [24,17]. The column *error* in Table 1 refers to the total approximation error of our method. The column *steps* in Table 1 gives the number r of steps in Alg. 1. For each example, the method yields accurate results. We never had to recompute $\hat{p}^{(t_j)}$ because too much probability was lost. The numerical solution of the abstract models takes most of the running time whereas the window construction takes less than 40% of the running time. Since the memory requirements of the sliding window method are not excessive as it is the case for other methods, we are able to numerically approximate the solution of complex models that have not been solved before.

5   Conclusion

The sliding window method is a new approach to analyze infinite-state continuous-time Markov chains. The method applies in particular to Markov chains that arise from networks of biochemical reactions. It is therefore a promising approach for the analysis of cellular stochasticity, which has become increasingly important in recent years.

We approximate the probability distributions of the infinite Markov chain at various time instances by solving a sequence of dynamically constructed finite Markov chains. The abstract models can be solved with any existing numerical algorithm for finite Markov chains. Moreover, it is possible to combine our approach with other techniques, such as time scale separation methods [20,36,8].

We demonstrated the effectiveness of our method with a number of experiments. The results show that we can solve more complex systems than previous approaches in acceptable time.

---

[2] For instance, in the case of complex formation the number of complex molecules is uniquely determined by the initial populations and the remaining number of complex components.

As further enhancements, we plan to develop a steady-state detection mechanism, which allows us to compute the steady-state distribution if the location and size of the window becomes stable. Moreover, we plan to investigate a splitting of the windows, which will be particularly useful for multistable systems.

References

1. Abdulla, P., Baier, C., Iyer, S., Jonsson, B.: Reasoning about probabilistic lossy channel systems. In: Palamidessi, C. (ed.) CONCUR 2000. LNCS, vol. 1877, pp. 320–333. Springer, Heidelberg (2000)
2. Abdulla, P., Bertrand, N., Rabinovich, A., Schnoebelen, P.: Verification of probabilistic systems with faulty communication. Inf. Comput. 202(2), 141–165 (2005)
3. Abdulla, P., Henda, N.B., Mayr, R.: Verifying infinite Markov chains with a finite attractor or the global coarseness property. In: Proc. LICS 2005, pp. 127–136. IEEE Computer Society, Los Alamitos (2005)
4. Arkin, A., Ross, J., McAdams, H.H.: Stochastic kinetic analysis of developmental pathway bifurcation in phage λ-infected escherichia coli cells. Genetics 149, 1633–1648 (1998)
5. Baker, G.A.: The essentials of Padé approximants. Academic Press, New York (1975)
6. De Boer, R.: Theoretical Fysiology. Online Lecture Notes (2006)
7. Burrage, K., Hegland, M., Macnamara, F., Sidje, B.: A Krylov-based finite state projection algorithm for solving the chemical master equation arising in the discrete modelling of biological systems. In: Proc. of the Markov 150th Anniversary Conference, pp. 21–38. Boson Books (2006)
8. Busch, H., Sandmann, W., Wolf, V.: A numerical aggregation algorithm for the enzyme-catalyzed substrate conversion. In: Priami, C. (ed.) CMSB 2006. LNCS (LNBI), vol. 4210, pp. 298–311. Springer, Heidelberg (2006)
9. Çinlar, E.: Introduction to Stochastic Processes. Prentice-Hall, Englewood Cliffs (1975)
10. D'Argenio, P., Jeannet, B., Jensen, H., Larsen, K.: Reachability analysis of probabilistic systems by successive refinements. In: de Luca, L., Gilmore, S. (eds.) PROBMIV 2001, PAPM-PROBMIV 2001, and PAPM 2001. LNCS, vol. 2165, pp. 39–56. Springer, Heidelberg (2001)
11. de Alfaro, L., Pritam, R.: Magnifying-lens abstraction for Markov decision processes. In: Damm, W., Hermanns, H. (eds.) CAV 2007. LNCS, vol. 4590, pp. 325–338. Springer, Heidelberg (2007)
12. Didier, F., Henzinger, T.A., Mateescu, M., Wolf, V.: Approximation of event probabilities in noisy cellular processes. Technical Report MTC-REPORT-2009-002, EPF Lausanne, Switzerland (2009), http://infoscience.epfl.ch/record/135535
13. Esparza, J., Etessami, K.: Verifying probabilistic procedural programs. In: Lodaya, K., Mahajan, M. (eds.) FSTTCS 2004. LNCS, vol. 3328, pp. 16–31. Springer, Heidelberg (2004)
14. Esparza, J., Kucera, A., Mayr, R.: Model checking probabilistic pushdown automata. In: Proc. LICS 2004, pp. 12–21. IEEE Computer Society, Los Alamitos (2004)
15. Etessami, K., Yannakakis, M.: Algorithmic verification of recursive probabilistic state machines. In: Halbwachs, N., Zuck, L.D. (eds.) TACAS 2005. LNCS, vol. 3440, pp. 253–270. Springer, Heidelberg (2005)
16. Gillespie, D.T.: Markov Processes. Academic Press, New York (1992)
17. Gross, D., Miller, D.: The randomization technique as a modeling tool and solution procedure for transient Markov processes. Operations Research 32(2), 926–944 (1984)
18. Hairer, E., Norsett, S., Wanner, G.: Solving Ordinary Differential Equations I: Nonstiff Problems. Springer, Heidelberg (2008)

19. Hairer, E., Wanner, G.: Solving Ordinary Differential Equations II. Stiff and Differential-Algebraic Problems. Springer, Heidelberg (2004)
20. Haseltine, E., Rawlings, J.: Approximate simulation of coupled fast and slow reactions for stochastic chemical kinetics. The Journal of Chemical Physics 117(15), 6959–6969 (2002)
21. Hasty, J., Pradines, J., Dolnik, M., Collins, J.J.: Noise-based switches and amplifiers for gene expression. PNAS 97, 2075 (2000)
22. Henderson, D.A., Boys, R.J., Proctor, C.J., Wilkinson, D.J.: Linking systems biology models to data: a stochastic kinetic model of p53 oscillations. In: O'Hagan, A., West, M. (eds.) Handbook of Applied Bayesian Analysis, Oxford University Press, Oxford (2009)
23. Henzinger, T.A., Mateescu, M., Wolf, V.: Sliding window abstraction for infinite Markov chains. Technical Report MTC-REPORT-2009-003, EPF Lausanne, Switzerland (2009), http://infoscience.epfl.ch/record/135537
24. Jensen, A.: Markoff chains as an aid in the study of Markoff processes. Skandinavisk Aktuarietidskrift 36, 87–91 (1953)
25. van Kampen, N.G.: Stochastic Processes in Physics and Chemistry, 3rd edn. Elsevier, Amsterdam (2007)
26. Katoen, J.-P., Klink, D., Leucker, M., Wolf, V.: Three-valued abstraction for continuous-time Markov chains. In: Damm, W., Hermanns, H. (eds.) CAV 2007. LNCS, vol. 4590, pp. 316–329. Springer, Heidelberg (2007)
27. Kucera, A.: Methods for quantitative analysis of probabilistic pushdown automata. Electr. Notes Theor. Comput. Sci. 149(1), 3–15 (2006)
28. Kwiatkowska, M., Norman, G., Parker, D.: Game-based abstraction for Markov decision processes. In: QEST, pp. 157–166. IEEE CS Press, Los Alamitos (2006)
29. Marie, R.A., Reibman, A.L., Trivedi, K.S.: Transient analysis of acyclic Markov chains. Perform. Eval. 7(3), 175–194 (1987)
30. McAdams, H.H., Arkin, A.: Stochastic mechanisms in gene expression. Proceedings of the National Academy of Science 94, 814–819 (1997)
31. Moler, C., Van Loan, C.: Nineteen dubious ways to compute the exponential of a matrix, twenty-five years later. SIAM Review 45(1), 3–49 (2003)
32. Munsky, B., Khammash, M.: The finite state projection algorithm for the solution of the chemical master equation. J. Chem. Phys. 124, 44144 (2006)
33. Norris, J.: Markov Chains, 1st edn. Cambridge University Press, Cambridge (1999)
34. Patel, P., Arcangioli, B., Baker, S., Bensimon, A., Rhind, N.: DNA replication origins fire stochastically in fission yeast. Mol. Biol. Cell 17, 308–316 (2006)
35. Paulsson, J.: Summing up the noise in gene networks. Nature 427(6973), 415–418 (2004)
36. Peles, S., Munsky, B., Khammash, M.: Reduction and solution of the chemical master equation using time scale separation and finite state projection. J. Chem. Phys. 125, 204104 (2006)
37. Philippe, B., Sidje, R.: Transient solutions of Markov processes by Krylov subspaces. In: Proc. International Workshop on the Numerical Solution of Markov Chains, pp. 95–119. Kluwer Academic Publishers, Dordrecht (1995)
38. Rabinovich, A.: Quantitative analysis of probabilistic lossy channel systems. Inf. Comput. 204(5), 713–740 (2006)
39. Rao, C., Wolf, D., Arkin, A.: Control, exploitation and tolerance of intracellular noise. Nature 420(6912), 231–237 (2002)
40. Remke, A.: Model Checking Structured Infinite Markov Chains. PhD thesis (2008)
41. Sandmann, W., Wolf, V.: A computational stochastic modeling formalism for biological networks. Enformatika Transactions on Engineering, Computing and Technology 14, 132–137 (2006)
42. Stewart, W.J.: Introduction to the Numerical Solution of Markov Chains. Princeton University Press, Princeton (1995)

43. Strelen, C.: Approximate disaggregation-aggregation solutions for general queueing networks. In: Society for Computer Simulation, pp. 773–778 (1997)
44. Swain, P.S., Elowitz, M.B., Siggia, E.D.: Intrinsic and extrinsic contributions to stochasticity in gene expression. Proceedings of the National Academy of Science, USA 99(20), 12795–12800 (2002)
45. Thattai, M., van Oudenaarden, A.: Intrinsic noise in gene regulatory networks. PNAS 98(15), 8614–8619 (2001)
46. Warmflash, A., Dinner, A.: Signatures of combinatorial regulation in intrinsic biological noise. PNAS 105(45), 17262–17267 (2008)
47. Zhang, L., Hermanns, H., Moritz Hahn, E., Wachter, B.: Time-bounded model checking of infinite-state continuous-time Markov chains. In: ACSD, China (2008)

Centaur Technology Media Unit Verification
Case Study: Floating-Point Addition

Warren A. Hunt Jr. and Sol Swords

Centaur Technology
7600C North Capitol of Texas Hwy
Austin, TX 78731
{hunt,sswords}@centtech.com

Abstract. We have verified floating-point addition/subtraction instructions for the media unit from Centaur's 64-bit, X86-compatible microprocessor. This unit implements over one hundred instructions, with the most complex being floating-point addition/subtraction. This media unit can add/subtract four pairs of floating-point numbers every clock cycle with an industry-leading two-cycle latency.

Using the ACL2 theorem proving system, we model the media unit by translating its Verilog design into an HDL that we have deeply embedded in the ACL2 logic. We specify the addition/subtraction instructions as integer-based ACL2 functions. Using a combination of AIG- and BDD-based symbolic simulation, case splitting, and theorem proving, we produce a mechanically checked theorem in ACL2 for each instruction examined stating that the hardware model yields the same result as the instruction specification.

In pursuit of these verifications, we implemented a formal HDL and symbolic simulation framework, including formally verified BDD and AIG operators, within the ACL2 theorem proving system. The HDL includes an extensible interpreter capable of performing concrete and symbolic simulations as well as non-functional analyses. We know of no other symbolic simulation-based floating-point verification that is performed within a single formal system and produces a theorem in that system without relying on unverified external tools.

1 Introduction

Media units in contemporary microprocessors contain sophisticated implementations to provide low-latency arithmetic operations. We have used the ACL2 theorem-proving system [1] to mechanically verify a number of media instructions for Centaur's X86-compatible, 64-bit CN microprocessor; this unit implements over 100 of the SSE media instructions and X87 addition and subtraction. The most complex instructions we verified are the packed addition/subtraction instructions; it is these instructions that are the focus of this paper.

Floating-point addition/subtraction implementations must precisely contend with a variety of numeric input conditions: normal, denormal, zero, infinity, quiet not-a-number (QNaN), and signaling not-a-number (SNaN). If the inputs can be added, they first are aligned, then the addition or subtraction and rounding

A. Bouajjani and O. Maler (Eds.): CAV 2009, LNCS 5643, pp. 353–367, 2009.

occurs, and finally the result flags are calculated and set.The result produced itself may be any of the six types just mentioned except for an SNaN. When performing packed (with multiple operand pairs) addition/subtraction, the computation of the result flags involves merging the flag results for all input pairs. Note that there is essentially no difference between addition and subtraction: an addition operation may effectively be a subtraction because one of the inputs represents a negative number. For the remainder of this paper we will only write addition, but the reader should always keep in mind that a subtraction may occur.

Our tool flow involves translating the Verilog representation of the entire media unit to our formally defined HDL [2]. This process captures Centaur's design as an ACL2 constant that we interpret with our ACL2-based HDL simulator. Our HDL simulator can be used to symbolically simulate the formal circuit description; we use a combination of theorem proving and equivalence checking to prove that the circuit's outputs are equivalent to an integer-level specification of floating-point operations. Separately, we have verified that our integer-level specification actually implements IEEE floating-point addition [3]; this proof is not discussed here.

Our formally defined HDL is a deep-embedding of the EMOD HDL [4] inside of the ACL2 logic. We have defined a function that determines whether a module has a well-formed syntax, and we have also defined an interpreter that gives meaning to such modules. Our EMOD interpreter provides multiple interpretations, thus a module can be evaluated with either a two-valued (Boolean) logic or a four-valued logic. In addition, the EMOD interpreter can compute dependencies and estimate circuit delays; the EMOD interpreter has an input parameter that allows a user to specify which evaluation mechanism to use. We are not aware of any other verification of a commercial floating-point design using such a deep-embedding approach. This approach reduces the risk of translation errors, as it is possible to perform co-simulation between Verilog and EMOD to ensure the veracity of the translation. We can also translate the design as represented in the EMOD language back to Verilog.

We begin by describing Centaur's media unit and the process by which we capture this unit's design in our HDL. Once we have a formal representation of the media unit, we perform symbolic simulation to produce a set of equations that represent the operation of the media unit. We then refine these equations given that we want to verify three sizes of addition operations, and then use parametrization and equivalence checking to prove that the media unit can add four 32-bit pairs, two 64-bit pairs, or one 80-bit pair of numbers. This yields a theorem for each instruction stating the equivalence of its hardware implementation (as interpreted in our HDL) with its specification function. We close by relating our efforts to previous work and describing how our effort is unique.

2   Centaur CN's Media Unit

Our effort is focused on Centaur's 64-bit CN processor shown in Figs. 1 and 2. The CN family of processors is compliant with AMD and Intel's 64-bit

Fig. 1. Die Plot of Centaur CN

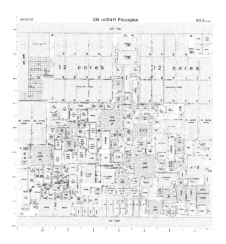

Fig. 2. Floor Plan of Centaur CN

processors, and its implementation supports almost 40 operating systems and four hypervisors. The Centaur CN media unit handles X87 and SSE instructions. The **fadd** unit, a major component of the media unit, itself implements single, double, and extended floating-point addition and subtraction, both scalar and packed; floating-point to integer conversions and integer to floating-point conversions; SSE logical and integer operations; and other operations. Our investigation was focused on the two-cycle latency floating-point addition instructions of the **fadd** unit; we believe that this design is the lowest clock-cycle latency floating-point implementation presently available.

The Centaur media unit is part of the execution cluster; operands and instructions are provided to this unit by the instruction scheduler. Logical operation results are available in one clock cycle while floating-point addition, subtraction, and conversions are available in two cycles. The lower-left-hand corner of the die contains the media unit; the relevant parts can be seen in Fig. 3. Multiple 128-bit inputs and outputs are provided and this unit can forward results internally so operations may be chained.

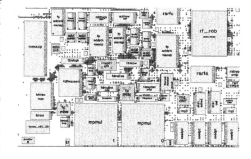

Fig. 3. Floorplan of CN Media Unit

The **fadd** RTL-level design is composed of 680 modules, which we convert from Verilog into our **EMOD** hardware description language; it is this **EMOD** form of Centaur's design that we subject to analysis. The physical implementation is composed of 432,322 transistors, almost evenly split between PMOS and NMOS devices. This represents less than 5% of the total transistors in the implementation, but its 33,700 line Verilog description represents more than 6% of the CN design specification. The **fadd** unit has 374 output signals and 1074 inputs including 26 clock inputs. Multiple inputs representing the same clock are used in order to manage power usage.

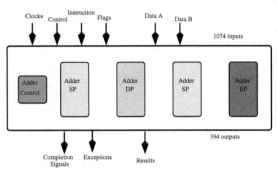

Fig. 4. Adder Units Inside of **fadd**

The **fadd** unit is composed of four adders: two 32-bit units, one 64-bit unit, and one 80-bit unit (see Fig. 4). When a 32-bit packed addition is requested, all four units are used, and the 64-bit and 80-bit adders each take 32-bit operands and produce a 32-bit results. When a 64-bit packed addition is requested, the 64-bit and 80-bit adders each take 64-bit operands and produce a 64-bit result. The **fadd** unit can only add one pair 80-bit operands per clock cycle. Other combinations are possible when a memory-resident operand is added to a register-resident, X87-style, 80-bit operand; the **fadd** unit also manages such X87-mode, mixed-size addition requests.

The critical speed path through **fadd** is the floating-point addition logic. There are multiple paths through the addition logic that operate in parallel. The relevant path for a particular pair of operands is determined by characteristics such as the operand types (NaN, zero, denormal, etc.) and their sign and exponent bits, and the result from that path is selected as the result of the addition.

Floating-point numbers are composed of three parts: a sign, a mantissa, and an exponent. Floating-point addition operands are identified as numbers, either normal, denormal or infinity, or as non-numbers (NaNs), either quiet (QNaN) or signaling (SNaN). Any NaN operand produces a QNaN result but may also cause an exception.

In addition to the floating-point operands, the setting of the floating-point control flags must be considered when adding. For instance, the flush-to-zero (FTZ) flag indicates that when a denormal result is internally produced, zero should be stored. Producing result flags is complicated by flag priority and the interaction of flag settings with input mask settings when performing packed operations. For example, when one pair of operands would produce an invalid exception and another pair would produce a denormal exception, the denormal flag is only set when the invalid exception is masked.

Floating-point addition proceeds in steps. First, several special cases are detected. If a NaN operand is identified, then a NaN result is produced. Infinite operands also require special consideration, as does the case where both input operands are either zero or denormal with the denormals-are-zero control flag set. If none of these cases hold, the mantissas of the two operands are shifted relative to one another as determined by the difference in their exponents, and the shifted mantissas are added or subtracted as appropriate and rounded according to the rounding mode specified by the control flags. Finally, the correct exponent for the rounded result is calculated and is examined to determine whether an overflow or underflow occurred.

3   Verification Method

As shown in Fig. 5, our verification methodology compares the result of symbolic simulations of an instruction specification and a translation of the **fadd** unit's Verilog design into our EMOD hardware description language. By running an AIG-based symbolic simulation of the **fadd** model using the EMOD symbolic simulator, we represent the outputs of the **fadd** unit as fully general functions of the inputs using AIGs as the Boolean function representation. We then specialize these functions by setting input control bits to values appropriate for the desired instruction. In order to compare these functions with those produced by the specification, we then convert these AIGs into BDDs.

In order to make this feasible, we use case splitting via BDD parametrization [5,6] to restrict the analysis to subsets of the input space. This allows us to choose a BDD variable ordering specially for each input subset, which is essential to avoid blowup due to adding mantissas composed of poorly aligned BDD variables. For each case split, we run a symbolic simulation of the instruction specification and an AIG-to-BDD conversion of the specialized AIGs for the instruction. Checking that corresponding BDDs from these results are equal shows that the **fadd** unit operates identically to the specification function on the subset

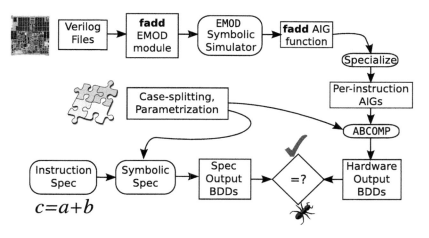

Fig. 5. Verification Method

of the input space covered case split; otherwise, we can generate counterexamples by analyzing the differences in the outputs.

In the following subsections we will describe in more detail the case-splitting mechanism, the process of translating the Verilog design into an EMOD description, and the methods of symbolic simulation used for the **fadd** unit model and the instruction specification.

3.1   Case-Splitting and Parametrization

A major obstacle to symbolic simulation of floating-point adders is a BDD blowup that occurs due to a non-constant shift of the operand mantissas based on the difference in their exponents. By choosing case-splitting boundaries appropriately, the shift amount can be reduced to a constant. The strategy for choosing these boundaries is documented by others [5, 7, 8, 9], and we believe it to be reusable for new designs.

In total, we split into 138 cases for single, 298 for double, and 858 for extended precision. Most of these cases cover input subsets over which the exponent difference of the two operands is constant and either all input vectors are effective additions or all are effective subtractions. Exponent differences greater than the maximum shift amount are considered as a block. Special inputs such as NaNs and infinities are considered separately. For performance reasons, we use a finer-grained case-split for extended precision than for single or double precision.

For each case split, we restrict the simulation coverage to the chosen subset of the input space using BDD parametrization. This generates a symbolic input vector (a BDD for each input bit) that covers exactly and only the appropriate set of inputs; we describe BDD parametrization in more detail in Sec. 4.3. Each such symbolic input vector is used in both an AIG-to-BDD conversion and a symbolic simulation of the specification. The BDD variable ordering is chosen specifically for each case split, thereby reducing the overall size of the intermediate BDDs. No knowledge of the design was used to determine the case-splitting approach.

3.2   Symbolic Simulation of the Hardware Model

The object we actually consider for verification is a representation of Centaur's Verilog description of the **fadd** unit. This object is created by translating Verilog to the EMOD language by way of a parser and translator written in ACL2 [2]. The Verilog to EMOD translator parses the Verilog design and performs a synthesis step resulting in a gate-level model that is then directly translated into the EMOD language.

Our translator targets a limited subset of Verilog, mainly related to register-transfer-level constructs like gate and submodule instances and arrays, continuous assignments, and very limited "always" blocks for modeling latches and flops. This allows translation of most of the 550,000 lines of Verilog used to describe the full Centaur design. Transistor-level constructs are not supported. Certain other Verilog features, such as strings, real variables, hierarchical identifiers, and multi-dimensional arrays are not supported, but in some of these cases we may be able to extend the translator.

To obtain formulas representing the outputs of the **fadd** unit in terms of its primary inputs, we use the EMOD simulator to perform an AIG-based symbolic simulation of the **fadd** model. We use a four-valued logic in this simulation, in which each signal may take values 1 (true), 0 (false), X (unknown), or Z (floating). This is encoded using two AIGs (onset and offset) per signal. The Boolean values taken by each AIG determine the value taken by the signal as in Fig. 6.

In this simulation, all bits of the initial state are set to unknown (X) values and the onsets and offsets of all non-clock inputs are assigned to unique Boolean variables at each cycle, so that every input signal but the clocks can take any of the four values. This results in a fully general formula for each output in terms of the inputs at each clock cycle.

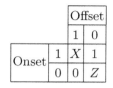

Fig. 6.

Many of the primary inputs of the **fadd** unit are either irrelevant to the operation of the addition instructions or must be set to exact values in order for the addition instruction to occur. We therefore restrict the fully-general output formulas by setting control signals to the values required for an instruction and setting irrelevant signals to unknown (X) input values. This reduces the number of variables present in these functions and keeps our result as general as possible. Constant propagation with these specified values restricts the AIGs to formulas in terms of only the operand and status register inputs, which are the same as the inputs to the specification function. In fact, our verification results in a proof that the Boolean functions represented by these specialized AIGs are equivalent to the output bits of the instruction specification.

As the final step in symbolically simulating the **fadd** unit, for each case split, we derive from the specialized AIGs a set of BDDs that express the **fadd** unit results for input vectors covered by the case. To do this, we assign to each bit of the operands and status register the corresponding BDD constructed by the parametrization for the case split. We then use the AIG/BDD composition procedure AIG2BDD described in Sec. 4.4 to produce BDDs representing the primary outputs. AIG2BDD avoids computing certain intermediate-value BDDs that are irrelevant to the final output, which helps to solve some BDD size explosions. This AIG-to-BDD conversion concludes the symbolic simulation flow on the hardware side; the resulting BDDs may then be compared to the results from the symbolic simulation of the instruction specification.

3.3   Symbolic Simulation of Specification

The specification for each instruction is an ACL2 function that takes integers representing the operands and the control register and produces integers representing the result and the flag register. It is defined in terms of word-level primitives such as shift, bitwise AND, plus and minus. It is optimized for symbolic simulation performance rather than referential clarity; however, it has separately been proven equivalent to a high-level, rational arithmetic-based specification of the IEEE floating-point standard [10]. Additionally, it has been tested against floating-point instructions running on Intel and AMD CPUs on many millions of input operand pairs, including a test suite designed to detect floating-point corner-cases [11] as well as random tests.

We use the GL symbolic execution framework [12] for ACL2 in order to perform the symbolic simulation of the specification. The GL framework contains a routine that apples a code transform to the definition of an ACL2 user function to produce a BDD-based symbolic simulator function and proves that the symbolic simulator results reflect the behavior of the original function. The symbolic simulator function operates on data structures that use BDDs to symbolically represent Booleans and lists of BDDs to symbolically represent two's-complement integers.

To symbolically simulate the specification function, we use the GL code transform to produce such a symbolic simulator function. For each case split, we use BDDs resulting from parametrization to construct symbolic integer data structures representing the operands and the status register. We run the symbolic simulator function on these inputs, obtaining symbolic integer data structures representing the result and flag register. BDDs extracted from these data structures (representing individual bits of the result and flag register) can be compared with the BDDs obtained by symbolically simulating the hardware model on the same case split.

3.4   Comparison of Specification to Hardware Model

For each case split in which the results from the symbolic simulations of the specification and the hardware model are equal, this serves to prove that for any concrete input vector drawn from the coverage set of the case, a simulation of the **fadd** model will produce the same result as the instruction specification. If the results are not equal, we can generate a counterexample by finding a satisfying assignment for the XOR of two corresponding output BDDs.

To prove the top-level theorem that the **fadd** unit produces the same result as the specification for all legal concrete inputs, we must also prove that the union of all such input subsets covers the entire set of legal inputs. For each case split, we produce a BDD representing the indicator function of the coverage set (the function which is true on inputs that are elements of the set and false on inputs that are not.) As in [8], the OR of all such BDDs is shown to be implied by the indicator function BDD of the set of legal inputs; therefore, if an input vector is legal then it is in one or more of the coverage sets of the case split.

4   Mechanisms Used to Achieve the Verification

4.1   EMOD Symbolic Simulator

The EMOD interpreter is capable of running various simulations and analyses on a hardware model; examples include concrete-value simulations in two- or four-value mode, symbolic simulations in two- or four-value mode using AIGs or BDDs as the Boolean function representations, and delay and dependency

```
(defm *half-adder-module*
  '(:i (a b)
    :o (sum carry)
    :occs
    ((:u o0 :o (sum)   :op ,*xor2* :i (a b))
     (:u o1 :o (carry) :op ,*and2* :i (a b)))))

(defm  *one-bit-cntr*
  '(:i (c-in reset-)
    :o (out c)
    :occs
    ((:u o2 :o out         :op ,*ff* :i (sum-reset))
     (:u o0 :o (sum c)     :op ,*half-adder-module* :i (c-in out))
     (:u o1 :o (sum-reset) :op ,*and2* :i (sum reset-)))))
```

Fig. 7. EMOD examples

analyses. The interpreter can also easily be extended with new analyses. The language supports multiple clocks with different timing behavior, clock gating, and both latch- and flip-flop-based sequential designs as well as implicitly clocked finite state machines. Its language for representing hardware models is a hierarchical, gate-level HDL. A hardware model in the EMOD language is either a primitive module (such as basic logic gates, latches and flip-flops), or a hierarchically defined module, containing a list of submodules and a description of their interconnections. The semantics of primitive modules are built into the EMOD interpreter, whereas hierarchical modules are simulated by recursively simulating submodules.

A pair of small example modules, ***half-adder-module*** and ***one-bit-cntr***, are shown in Fig. 7. Both are hierarchically defined since they each have a list of occurrences labelled :occs. Connectivity between submodules, inputs, and outputs is defined by the :i (input) and :o (output) fields of the modules and the occurrences. We translate the RTL design of the **fadd** unit into this format for our analysis.

A novel feature of our approach is that we can actually print the theorem we are checking; thus, we have an explicit, circuit-model representation that includes all of the original hierarchy, annotations, and wire names. This is different than all other approaches of which we are aware; for instance, Forte reads Intel design descriptions and builds a FSM in the Forte tool memory image. Our representation allows us to search the design using database-like commands to inspect our representation of Centaur's design; this explicit representation also enables easy tool construction for users as they can write ACL2 programs to investigate the design in a manner of their choosing.

4.2 BDDs and AIGs

BDDs and AIGs both are data objects that represent Boolean-valued functions of Boolean variables. We have defined evaluators for both BDDs and AIGs in

ACL2. The BDD (resp. AIG) evaluator, given a BDD (AIG) and an assignment of Boolean values to the relevant variables, produces the Boolean value of the function it represents at that variable assignment. The BDD and AIG evaluators accept different formats for the variable assignment argument: the BDD evaluator expects a list of Booleans that correspond positionally to the variables at the levels of the BDDs, whereas the AIG evaluator expects a list of key/value pairs associating the primary inputs of the AIG with their Boolean values. Here, for brevity, we use the notation $\langle x \rangle_{\mathrm{bdd}}(env)$ or $\langle x \rangle_{\mathrm{aig}}(env)$ for the evaluation of x with variable assignment env. We use the same notation when x is a list to denote the mapping of $\langle \_ \rangle_{\mathrm{bdd}}(env)$ over the elements of x.

The BDD and AIG logical operators are defined in the ACL2 logic and proven correct relative to the evaluator functions. For example, the following theorem shows the correctness of the BDD AND operator (written $\wedge_{\mathrm{bdd}}$); similar theorems are proven for every basic BDD and AIG operator such as NOT, OR, XOR, and ITE:

$$\langle a \wedge_{\mathrm{bdd}} b \rangle_{\mathrm{bdd}}(env) = \langle a \rangle_{\mathrm{bdd}}(env) \wedge \langle b \rangle_{\mathrm{bdd}}(env)$$

4.3   Parametrization

BDD parametrization is also implemented in ACL2. The parametrization algorithm is described in [5]; we describe its interface here. Assume that a hardware model has n input bits. To run a symbolic simulation over all 2^n possible input vectors, one possible set of symbolic inputs is n distinct BDD variables – say, $\boldsymbol{v} = [v_0, \ldots, v_{n-1}]$. This provides complete coverage because $\langle \boldsymbol{v} \rangle_{\mathrm{bdd}}(env)$ may equal any list of n Booleans. (In fact, if env has length n, then $\langle \boldsymbol{v} \rangle_{\mathrm{bdd}}(env) = env$.) However, to avoid BDD blowups, we wish to run symbolic simulations that each cover only a subset of the well-formed inputs. For each such case, we first represent the desired coverage set as a BDD p, so that an input vector $\boldsymbol{w}$ is in the coverage set if and only if $\langle p \rangle_{\mathrm{bdd}}(\boldsymbol{w})$. To do this, we parametrize $\boldsymbol{v}$ by predicate p and use the resulting BDDs $\boldsymbol{v}_p$ as the symbolic inputs. The following theorems hold of the parametrization transform and have been proved in ACL2:

$$\forall \boldsymbol{w} \; . \; \langle p \rangle_{\mathrm{bdd}}(\langle \boldsymbol{v}_p \rangle_{\mathrm{bdd}}(\boldsymbol{w}))$$

and, assuming $\boldsymbol{u}$ is a list of n Booleans,

$$\langle p \rangle_{\mathrm{bdd}}(\boldsymbol{u}) \Rightarrow \exists \boldsymbol{u}'.\langle \boldsymbol{v}_p \rangle_{\mathrm{bdd}}(\boldsymbol{u}') = \boldsymbol{u}.$$

The first property shows that the parametrized BDDs always evaluate to a list of Booleans that satisfies p; therefore, a concrete input vector is only covered by a symbolic simulation of $\boldsymbol{v}_p$ if it satisfies p. The second property shows that any input vector that does satisfy p will be covered by such a symbolic simulation.

It can be nontrivial to produce "by hand" a BDD p that correctly represents a particular subset of the input space. Instead, we define an ACL2 function that determines whether or not a pair of input operands is in a particular desired subset. We then run the GL code transform to produce a symbolic analogue for this function. Running this symbolic simulator on (unparametrized) symbolic inputs yields a symbolic Boolean value (represented as a BDD) that exactly represents the accepted subset of the inputs.

4.4 AIG-to-BDD Translation

In the symbolic simulation process for the **fadd** unit, we obtain AIGs representing the outputs as a function of the primary inputs and subsequently assign parametrized input BDDs to each primary input, computing BDDs representing the function composition of the AIG with the input BDDs. A straightforward (but inefficient) method to obtain this composition is an algorithm that recursively computes the BDD corresponding to each AIG node: at a primary input, look up the assigned BDD; at an AND node, compute the BDD AND of the BDDs corresponding to the child nodes; at a NOT node, compute the BDD NOT of the BDD corresponding to the negated node. This method proves to be impractical for our purpose; we describe here the algorithm `AIG2BDD` that we use instead.

To improve the efficiency of the straightforward recursive algorithm, one necessary modification is to memoize it so as to traverse the AIG as a DAG (without examining the same node twice) rather than as a tree: due to multiple fanouts in the hardware model, most AIGs produced would take time exponential in the logic depth if traversed as a tree. The second important improvement is to attempt to avoid computing the full BDD translation of nodes that are not relevant to the primary outputs. For example, if there is a multiplexor present in the circuit and, for the current parametrized subset of the inputs, the selector is always set to 1, then the value of the unselected input is irrelevant unless it has another fanout that is relevant. In AIGs, such irrelevant branches appear as fanins to ANDs in which the other fanin is unconditionally false. More generally, an AND of two child AIGs a and b can be reduced to a if it can be shown that $a \Rightarrow b$ (though the most common occurrence of this is when a is unconditionally false.) The `AIG2BDD` algorithm applies in iterative stages two methods that can each detect certain of these situations without fully translating b to a BDD. In both methods, we calculate exact BDD translations for nodes until some node's translation exceeds a BDD size limit. We replace the oversized BDD with a new representation that loses some information but allows the computation to continue while avoiding blowup. When the primary outputs are computed, we check to see whether or not they are exact BDD translations. If so, we are done; if not, we increase the size limit and try again. During each iteration of the translation, we check each AND node for an irrelevnant branch; if a branch is irrelevant it is removed from the AIG so that it will be ignored in subsequent iterations. We use the weaker of the two methods first with small size limits, then switch to the stronger method at a larger size limit.

In the weaker method, the translated value of each AIG node is two BDDs that are upper and lower bounds for its exact BDD translation, in the sense that the lower-bound BDD implies the exact BDD and the exact BDD implies the upper-bound BDD. If the upper and lower bound BDDs for a node are equal, then each is the exact BDD translation for the node. When a BDD larger than the size limit is produced, it is thrown away and the constant-*true* and constant-*false* BDDs are instead used for its upper and lower bounds. If an AND node $a \wedge b$ is encountered for which the upper bound for a implies the lower bound for b, then we have $a \Rightarrow b$; therefore we may replace the AND node with a. Thus using the weak method we can, for example, replace an AIG representing $a \wedge (a \vee b)$ with a as long as the BDD translation of a is known exactly, without computing the exact translation for b.

In the stronger method, instead of approximating BDDs by an upper and lower bound, fresh BDD variables are introduced to replace oversized BDDs. (We necessarily take care that these variables are not reused.) The BDD associated with a node is its exact translation if it references only the variables used in the primary input assignments. This catches certain additional pruning opportunities that the weaker method might miss, such as $b \neq (a \neq b) \rightarrow a$.

These two AIG-to-BDD translation methods, as well as the combined method AIG2BDD that uses both in stages, have been proven in ACL2 to be equivalent, when they produce an exact result, to the straightforward AIG-to-BDD translation algorithm described above.

When symbolically simulating the **fadd** unit, using input parameterization in conjunction with the AIG2BDD procedure works around the problem that BDD variable orderings that are efficient for one execution path are inefficient for another. Input parametrization allows cases where one execution path is selected to be analyzed separately from cases where others are used. However, a naive method of building BDDs from the hardware model might still construct the BDDs of the intermediate signals produced by multiple paths, leading to blowups. The AIG2BDD procedure ensures that unused paths do not cause a blowup.

5   Results of Verification

Our floating-point addition verification was performed using a machine with four Intel Xeon X7350 processors running at 2.93 GHz with 128 GB of system memory. However, each of our verification runs is a single-threaded procedure, and we limit our memory usage to 35GB for each process so that we can run single, double, and extended-precision verifications concurrently on this machine without swapping. The symbolic simulations run in 8 minutes 40 seconds for single precision, 36 minutes for double precision, and 48 minutes for extended precision. Proof scripts required to complete the three theorems take an additional 10 minutes of real time when using multiple processors, totalling 25 minutes of CPU time. The process of reading the Verilog design into ACL2, which is done as part of a process that additionally reads in a number of other units, takes about 17 minutes. In total it takes about 75 minutes of real time (125 minutes of CPU time) to reread the design from Verilog sources and complete verifications of all three instructions.

We found two design flaws in the media unit during our verification process, which began after the floating-point addition instructions had been thoroughly checked using a testing-based methodology. The first bug was a timing anomaly affecting SSE addition instructions, which we found during our initial investigation of the media unit. Later, a bug in the extended precision instruction was detected by symbolic simulation. This bug affected a total of four pairs of input operands out of the 2^{160} possible, producing a denormal result of twice the correct magnitude. Because of the small number of inputs affected, it is unlikely that random testing would have encountered the bug; directed testing had also not detected it. Both bugs have been fixed in the current design.

6   Related Work

Several groups have completed floating-point addition and other related verifications. We differ from previous verifications in that we obtained our result using verified automated methods within a general-purpose theorem prover, and in that we base our verification on a formally defined HDL operating on a data representation mechanically translated from the RTL design.

An AMD floating-point addition design was verified using ACL2. It was proven to comply with the primary requirement of the IEEE 754 floating-point addition specification, namely that the result of the addition operation must equal the result obtained by performing the addition at infinite precision and subsequently rounding to the required precision [13]. The design was represented in ACL2 by mechanically translating the RTL design into ACL2 functions. A top-level function representing the full addition unit was proven to always compute a result satisfying the specification. This theorem was proved in ACL2 by the usual method of mechanical theorem proving, wherein numerous human-crafted lemmas are proven until they suffice to prove the final theorem. A drawback to this method is that even small changes to the RTL design may require the proof script to be updated. We avoid this pitfall by using a symbolic simulation-based methodology. Our method also differs in that we use a deep embedding scheme, translating the RTL design to be verified into a data object in an HDL rather than a set of special-purpose functions.

Among bit-level symbolic simulation-based floating-point addition verifications, many have used a similar case-splitting and BDD parametrization scheme as ours [5,9,7,14]. The symbolic simulation frameworks used in all of these verifications, including the symbolic trajectory evaluation implementation in Intel's Forte prover, are themselves unverified programs. Similarly, the floating-point verification described in [8] uses the SMV model checker and a separate argument that its case-split provides full coverage. In order to obtain more confidence in our results, we construct our symbolic simulation mechanisms within the theorem prover and prove that they yield sound results. Combining tool verifications with the results of our symbolic simulations yields a theorem showing that the instruction implementation equals its specification.

7 Observations

Working in an industrial environment forced us to be able to respond to design changes quickly. Every night, we run our Verilog translator on the entire 550,000 lines of Verilog that comprise the Centaur CN and produce output for all of the Verilog that we can translate. We build a new copy of ACL2 with our EMOD representation of the design already included so when we sit down in the morning, we are ready to work with the current version of the design. Also, each night, we re-run every verification that has been done to date to make sure that recent changes are safe.

Our major challenges involved getting our toolsuite to be sufficiently robust, getting the specification correct, dealing with the complicated clocking and power-saving schemes employed, and creating a suitable circuit input environment for the 1074 inputs. It is difficult for us to provide a meaningful labor estimate for this verification because we were developing the translator, flow, our tools, our understanding of floating-point arithmetic, and specification style simultaneously. Now, we could check another IEEE-compatible floating-point design in the time it would take us to understand the clocking and input requirements. Centaur will certainly be using this methodology in the future; it is much faster, cheaper, and more thorough than non-exhaustive simulation.

The improvements in ACL2 that permitted this verification will be included in future ACL2 releases. The specifics of Centaur's two-cycle, floating-point design are considered proprietary. We plan to publish our ACL2-checked proof that our integer-level specification is equal to our IEEE floating-point specification; this level of proof is similar to work by Harrison [15].

8 Conclusion

The verification of Centaur CN floating-point addition instructions was performed through a combination of theorem proving, symbolic simulation, and equivalence checking. Centaur's CN media unit has an industry-leading, two-cycle latency, which complicates the implementation. Our efforts resulted in the discovery of two flaws that had escaped extensive simulation; these flaws have been corrected in Centaur's current design. In contrast to other floating-point adder verifications, our hardware model is represented by deep embedding in an extensible formal HDL with an interpreter written in ACL2. Furthermore, we programmed and verified our symbolic simulation procedures inside the ACL2 theorem prover, allowing us to obtain an ACL2 theorem stating the equivalence between each instruction's execution on the hardware model and its specification.

Acknowledgements

We would like to acknowledge the support of Centaur Technology, Inc., and ForrestHunt, Inc. We would also like to thank Bob Boyer for development of much of the technology behind `EMOD` and the BDD package, Terry Parks for developing a very detailed floating-point addition specification, and Jared Davis for authoring our Verilog-to-E translator.

References

1. Kaufmann, M., Moore, J.S., Boyer, R.S.: ACL2 version 3.4 (2009), `http://www.cs.utexas.edu/~moore/acl2/`
2. Davis, J.: VL Verilog translator (unpublished)
3. Krug, R.: Correctness proof of ACL2 floating-point addition specification (unpublished)
4. Hunt Jr., W.A., Swords, S.: Use of the E language. In: Hardware design and Functional Languages (2009)
5. Aagaard, M.D., Jones, R.B., Seger, C.J.H.: Formal verification using parametric representations of boolean constraints. In: Proceedings of the 36th Design Automation Conference, pp. 402–407 (1999)
6. Jones, R.B.: Symbolic Simulation Methods for Industrial Formal Verification. Kluwer Academic Publishers, Dordrecht (2002)
7. Jacobi, C., Weber, K., Paruthi, V., Baumgartner, J.: Automatic formal verification of fused-multiply-add FPUs. In: Proceedings of Design, Automation and Test in Europe, vol. 2, pp. 1298–1303 (2005)
8. Chen, Y., Bryant, R.E.: Verification of floating-point adders. In: Y. Vardi, M. (ed.) CAV 1998. LNCS, vol. 1427. Springer, Heidelberg (1998)
9. Seger, C.J.H., Jones, R.B., O'Leary, J.W., Melham, T., Aagaard, M.D., Barrett, C., Syme, D.: An industrially effective environment for formal hardware verification. IEEE Transactions on Computer-Aided Design of Integrated Circuits and Systems 24(9), 1381 (2005)
10. IEEE Computer Society: IEEE Standard for Floating-Point Arithmetic. IEEE std 754^{TM}-2008 edn. (2008)
11. University of California at Berkeley, Department of Electrical Engineering and Computer Science, Industrial Liaison Program: A compact test suite for P754 arithmetic – version 2.0
12. Boyer, R.S., Warren, A., Hunt, J.: Symbolic simulation in ACL2. In: Proceedings of the Eighth International Workshop on the ACL2 Theorem Prover and its Applications (2009)
13. Russinoff, D.: A case study in formal verification of Register-Transfer logic with ACL2: the floating point adder of the AMD Athlon (TM) processor. In: Johnson, S.D., Hunt Jr., W.A. (eds.) FMCAD 2000. LNCS, vol. 1954, pp. 3–36. Springer, Heidelberg (2000)
14. Slobodová, A.: Challenges for formal verification in industrial setting. In: Brim, L., Haverkort, B.R., Leucker, M., van de Pol, J. (eds.) FMICS 2006 and PDMC 2006. LNCS, vol. 4346, pp. 1–22. Springer, Heidelberg (2007)
15. Harrison, J.: Floating-point verification using theorem proving. In: Bernardo, M., Cimatti, A. (eds.) SFM 2006. LNCS, vol. 3965, pp. 211–242. Springer, Heidelberg (2006)

Incremental Instance Generation
in Local Reasoning

Swen Jacobs

Max-Planck-Institut für Informatik, Campus E1.4, Saarbrücken, Germany
sjacobs@mpi-inf.mpg.de

Abstract. Many verification approaches use SMT solvers in some form, and are limited by their incomplete handling of quantified formulas. Local reasoning allows to handle SMT problems involving a certain class of universally quantified formulas in a complete way by instantiation to a finite set of ground formulas. We present a method to generate these instances incrementally, in order to provide a more efficient way of solving these satisfiability problems. The incremental instantiation is guided semantically, inspired by the instance generation approach to first-order theorem proving. Our method is sound and complete, and terminates on both satisfiable and unsatisfiable input after generating a subset of the instances needed in standard local reasoning. Experimental results show that for a large class of examples the incremental approach is substantially more efficient than eager generation of all instances.

1 Introduction

SMT solvers are widely used tools in software verification today. One of the big challenges for current SMT solvers [11] is to handle quantified formulas, e.g. in order to make statements over potentially unbounded data structures. Current approaches to solve problems involving quantifiers [6] are usually refinements of the heuristical instantiation introduced with the Simplify prover [3]. A drawback of these approaches is that completeness is sacrificed: even for unsatisfiable problems, termination cannot be guaranteed.

Local reasoning [12] provides a decision procedure for SMT problems containing quantified formulas, provided they satisfy a locality property with respect to the base theory. For example, axioms specifying monotonicity or injectivity fall into this class, allowing us to specify sortedness or uniqueness of elements in an unbounded array. In local reasoning, these axioms are instantiated to a finite set of ground instances, which grows with the number of ground terms appearing in the given problem. For large problems, generating all instances at once may become inefficient, especially in verification problems where unsatisfiability often only depends on a relatively small part of the formula.

We introduce a method to generate the needed instances incrementally, in a systematical way that allows termination without generating the full set of instances in both the satisfiable and unsatisfiable case, while preserving completeness. The idea is based on the instantiation-based theorem proving methods introduced by Ganzinger and Korovin [5]: we keep a candidate model which

A. Bouajjani and O. Maler (Eds.): CAV 2009, LNCS 5643, pp. 368–382, 2009.

satisfies the ground part of the current problem, and only add instances that evolve this candidate model, either strengthening or refuting it.

This paper is organized as follows: in Section 2 we introduce the logical terminology used throughout this paper, as well as the basics of local reasoning. In Section 3, we introduce our approach, together with proofs of correctness. This approach is refined in Section 4, resulting in broader applicability. In Section 5, we evaluate experimental results, comparing different approaches to local reasoning. We conclude the paper with remarks on related and ongoing work.

2 Local Reasoning and Terminology

This section introduces necessary terminology and gives a short introduction to local reasoning. For a more detailed description, including theoretical background, we refer to Sofronie-Stokkermans et al. [12,9,8].

2.1 Logical Prerequisites

We use the usual symbols, notation and terminology of sorted first-order logic with standard definitions.

Formulas and instances. We use x, y to denote variables, a, b, c, d for constants and f as non-constant function symbol. L will denote literals, C and D clauses, and F formulas. We consider all formulas to be in clausal normal form, represented as a set of clauses, where all variables in a clause are implicitly universally quantified. Clauses are called *axioms* if they contain variables, *ground clauses* otherwise. We denote sets of axioms by $\mathcal{K}$, sets of ground clauses by G.

If F is a formula and σ a substitution, then $F\sigma$ is an *instance* of F. If F_2 is an instance of F_1, then F_1 is a *generalization* of F_2. A *variable renaming* is an injective substitution mapping variables to variables. Two formulas F_1 and F_2 are *variants* of each other if there is a variable renaming σ such that $F_1\sigma = F_2$. For a formula F, let $\mathsf{st}(F)$ be the set of ground subterms appearing in F.

Theories and models. Consider a signature $\Pi = (S, \Sigma, \mathsf{Pred})$, where S is a set of sorts, Σ is a set of function symbols and Pred a set of predicate symbols (with given arities). A Π-*structure* assigns concrete, non-empty sets of elements to all sorts $s \in S$ and concrete valuations to every $f \in \Sigma$ and $P \in \mathsf{Pred}$, according to their arity. A *theory* $\mathcal{T}$ can be defined by a set of axioms or a set of models. A given Π-structure M is a *model* of a theory $\mathcal{T}$ iff every axiom of $\mathcal{T}$ is satisfied by M. If a formula F is true in all models of $\mathcal{T}$, we write $\models_{\mathcal{T}} F$. A formula F_2 is a *consequence* of F_1 (modulo $\mathcal{T}$), written $F_1 \models_{\mathcal{T}} F_2$, if F_2 is true in every model of $\mathcal{T}$ which also satisfies F_1. If no model of $\mathcal{T}$ satisfies F, we write $F \models_{\mathcal{T}} \Box$, where $\Box$ represents the empty clause. Validity (modulo $\mathcal{T}$) of a formula F in a Π-structure M is depicted by $M \models_{\mathcal{T}} F$.

The *Herbrand base* $\mathcal{H}$ of Π is the set of all ground atoms over the signature. A *Herbrand interpretation* of Π is a set of literals $\mathcal{I}$ which contains for every atom $A \in \mathcal{H}$ either A or $\neg A$. A set of literals $\mathcal{L} \subseteq \mathcal{I}$ is a *partial Herbrand interpretation* of Π. A (partial) Herbrand interpretation $\mathcal{L}$ is a (partial) *Herbrand model* of a set of clauses F if $\mathcal{L}$ contains at least one of the literals from each clause in F.

2.2   Reasoning in Local Theory Extensions

Hierarchic reasoning in local theory extensions, or in short: *local reasoning*, has been introduced by Sofronie-Stokkermans [12]. The approach is based on earlier results by Givan and McAllester [7] and Ganzinger [4]. In this section we present the method, which allows us to solve satisfiability problems in local extensions of decidable background theories.

Local theory extensions. Consider a background theory T with signature $\Pi_0 = (S, \Sigma_0, \mathsf{Pred})$. In the following, we will allow formulas which are not restricted to this signature, but may contain additional function (and constant) symbols given by a set Σ_1. If F and G are formulas in the signature $\Pi = (S, \Sigma_0 \cup \Sigma_1, \mathsf{Pred})$, we will reason in T^{Σ_1}, the extension of T with free function symbols from Σ_1. Whenever Σ_1 is clear from the context, we will write $F \models_T G$ instead of $F \models_{T^{\Sigma_1}} G$.

A *theory extension* of a base theory T is given by a set $\mathcal{K}$ of axioms with a set of additional function symbols Σ_1, and denoted by $T \subseteq T \cup \mathcal{K}$. We will use $T \cup \mathcal{K}$ to denote the *extended theory*, which treats symbols from Σ_1 according to the axioms in $\mathcal{K}$. For non-constant function symbols $f \in \Sigma_1$, f is called an *extension symbol*, terms $f(t)$ are *extension terms*. Note that $F \models_{T \cup \mathcal{K}} G$ iff $\mathcal{K} \cup F \models_T G$.

In the following, we only consider theory extensions $T \subseteq T \cup \mathcal{K}$ such that every $C \in \mathcal{K}$ is Σ_1-*linear*: all extension terms in C which contain the same variable are syntactically equal, and no extension term in C contains two occurrences of the same variable.[1] Furthermore, we require that all variables in a clause $C \in \mathcal{K}$ have at least one occurrence in an extension term.

For a set G of ground clauses (in signature Π, but possibly with additional constant symbols), and a Σ_1-linear set of axioms $\mathcal{K}$, let

$$\mathcal{K}[G] = \{C\sigma \mid C \in \mathcal{K} \text{ and } f(t)\sigma \in \mathsf{st}(G) \text{ for each extension subterm } f(t) \text{ of } C\}.$$

For the fragment we consider, an extension $T \subseteq T \cup \mathcal{K}$ is *local* if it satisfies condition (Loc):

(Loc)   For every set G of ground clauses, $G \models_{T \cup \mathcal{K}} \square \Leftrightarrow \mathcal{K}[G] \cup G \models_T \square$,

where by our convention from above $\models_T$ means $\models_{T^{\Sigma_1}}$, with Σ_1 containing the additional function and constant symbols from $\mathcal{K}$ and G.

Examples. In previous papers [12,9,8], several theory extensions have been proved to be local.[2] We want to mention a few of them which satisfy our additional restriction and are interesting in a verification context:

- *monotone functions* over several theories with a partial or total ordering,
- *strictly monotone functions*, if additionally the codomain is densely ordered,

---

[1] This restriction is needed to prove locality of an extension and is also used throughout previous papers [12,8].

[2] The proof is done by hand and requires to show that certain partial models can be embedded into total models.

— *injective functions*, if domain and codomain allow them,
— sets of *guarded boundedness* conditions of the form

$$\phi_i(\overline{x}) \rightarrow s_i(\overline{x}) \leq f(\overline{x}) \leq t_i(\overline{x}),$$

where the ϕ_i are mutually exclusive formulas in the base theory and the s_i, t_i are terms in the base theory such that $\phi_i(\overline{x}) \rightarrow s_i(\overline{x}) \leq t_i(\overline{x})$ for all $i, \overline{x}$ (where $\overline{x}$ is the vector of all variables occurring in the given clause).

Hierarchic reasoning in local theory extensions. Let $\mathcal{T} \subseteq \mathcal{T} \cup \mathcal{K}$ be a local theory extension. Satisfiability of a set G of ground clauses modulo the extended theory $\mathcal{T} \cup \mathcal{K}$ can be checked in the following way (for details and the general approach cf. [12]):

By the locality condition, $G \models_{\mathcal{T} \cup \mathcal{K}} \square$ iff $\mathcal{K}[G] \cup G \models_{\mathcal{T}} \square$. Note that because in every clause in $\mathcal{K}$, all variables occur in extension terms, $\mathcal{K}[G]$ is a set of ground clauses. As everything is ground, extension functions can now be treated as free functions. Thus, we can check $\mathcal{K}[G] \cup G \models_{\mathcal{T}} \square$ with any SMT solver which supports the base theory $\mathcal{T}$ plus uninterpreted functions (EUF).

Example 1. Suppose $\mathcal{T}$ is any theory with a partial ordering (like real or integer arithmetic) and we consider its extension with a monotone function f, i.e.

$$\mathcal{K} = \{x \leq y \rightarrow f(x) \leq f(y)\}.$$

We want to check whether the following ground goal G is satisfiable with respect to the extended theory $\mathcal{T} \cup \mathcal{K}$:

$$G = \{\ a \leq b,\ \neg(f(a) \leq f(b))\ \}.$$

By locality of the extension $\mathcal{T} \subseteq \mathcal{T} \cup \mathcal{K}$, we know that

$$G \models_{\mathcal{T} \cup \mathcal{K}} \square \ \Leftrightarrow\ \mathcal{K}[G] \cup G \models_{\mathcal{T}} \square,$$

where $\mathcal{K}[G] = \{\ a \leq a \rightarrow f(a) \leq f(a),\quad a \leq b \rightarrow f(a) \leq f(b)$
$$b \leq a \rightarrow f(b) \leq f(a),\quad b \leq b \rightarrow f(b) \leq f(b)\ \}.$$

$\mathcal{K}[G] \cup G \models_{\mathcal{T}} \square$ can be checked with any prover for SMT(EUF $\cup\, \mathcal{T}$).

Chains of extensions. If we have an extension $\mathcal{K}$ which is not local wrt. the base theory, we may still be able to treat it within the local reasoning framework:

Suppose we have the case that $\mathcal{T} \subseteq \mathcal{T} \cup \mathcal{K}_1 \cup \mathcal{K}_2$ is not a local extension, but both $\mathcal{T} \subseteq \mathcal{T} \cup \mathcal{K}_1$ and $\mathcal{T} \cup \mathcal{K}_1 \subseteq \mathcal{T} \cup \mathcal{K}_1 \cup \mathcal{K}_2$ are local extensions. This means we can extend the base theory $\mathcal{T}$ to the extended theory $\mathcal{T} \cup \mathcal{K}_1 \cup \mathcal{K}_2$ in two steps, and use the local reasoning procedure repeatedly to reduce a ground goal from $\mathcal{T} \cup \mathcal{K}_1 \cup \mathcal{K}_2$ to $\mathcal{T} \cup \mathcal{K}_1$ and then to $\mathcal{T}$. This approach can be generalized to an arbitrary number of steps. We call such a repeated extension a *chain of extensions*, and will have a more detailed look at reasoning in chains of extensions in Section 4.

3   An Incremental Approach to Local Reasoning

In the last section we have introduced *local reasoning*, which provides a decision procedure for satisfiability problems in local extensions of theories. Given unlimited resources, the procedure is guaranteed to terminate. As in practice neither time nor space are unlimited, we are looking for more efficient methods for local reasoning. In Section 3.1, we introduce *local instance generation*, a method which generates instances of local axioms incrementally, in a semantically guided way inspired by the instance generation approach of Ganzinger and Korovin [5]. In Section 3.2, we give examples how local reasoning can benefit from this approach, and in Section 3.3 we prove correctness of the method.

3.1   Local Instance Generation (LIG)

We present the procedure LIG, which solves the satisfiability problem of a ground formula G in an extended theory $T \cup K$ by interleaving ground satisfiability checks with instantiation of axioms from K. For ground reasoning we use a blackbox SMT solver, which should allow incremental addition of constraints and must be able to generate models for satisfiable input.

Proof procedure. We keep working sets K of axioms and G of ground clauses. Define a selection function sel on K so that for every $C \in K$, $\mathsf{sel}(C)$ is the literal $L \in C$ which contains the highest number of variables, preferably so that variables occur below extension symbols. This selection is chosen in order to enforce fast instantiation to the ground level, as explained below. Then, the following two steps are repeated until termination:

(1) Ground satisfiability check. We give G to an SMT solver. If $G \models_T \square$, then the procedure terminates and states unsatisfiability of the input. Otherwise, obtain a model M such that $M \models_T G$. From M, compute a partial Herbrand model $\mathcal{M}$ of G.

(2) Instance generation. Instances are generated according to the following inference rule:

$$LIG \qquad \frac{(L_1 \vee D_1) \ \cdots \ (L_n \vee D_n) \mid \mathcal{M}}{(L_1 \vee D_1)\sigma \ \cdots \ (L_n \vee D_n)\sigma}$$

where:
(i) the $L_i \vee D_i$ are (variants of) clauses from K with $\mathsf{sel}(L_i \vee D_i) = L_i$,
(ii) σ is a substitution such that all $L_i\sigma$ are ground literals,
(iii) all clauses $(L_i \vee D_i)\sigma$ are generalizations of clauses in $K[\mathcal{M}]$, and
(iv) $\{L_i\sigma\}_{1 \le i \le n} \cup \mathcal{M} \models_T \square$

Note that several variants of a clause $C \in K$ may be instantiated in one inference. Ground clauses $(L_i \vee D_i)\sigma$ are added to G, axioms (if any) are added to K. If all inferences based on a given selection sel and model $\mathcal{M}$ only produce variants of clauses in K and G, we call the pair (K, G) *saturated* under LIG. If (K, G) is saturated under LIG, the procedure terminates and states satisfiability of the input. Otherwise, define sel on new axioms as described above and return to **(1)**.

Finding substitutions. Side conditions (ii) and (iii) allow to restrict the search for substitutions to a finite set. The following lemma shows how side condition (iii) can be ensured.

Lemma 1. *Let* $\{(L_1 \vee D_1), \ldots, (L_n \vee D_n)\}$ *and* $\mathcal{M}$ *be premises of an LIG-inference. For* $1 \leq i \leq n$, *let* $\mathsf{sel}(L_i \vee D_i) = L_i$, *and let* $\mathcal{L}_i$ *be a set of literals such that* $\mathcal{L}_i \subseteq (L_i \vee D_i)$, *and all variables from* $(L_i \vee D_i)$ *appear in extension terms in* $\mathcal{L}_i$. *Then, for any substitution* σ *which satisfies condition* (ii) *of the LIG inference rule, the following two are equivalent:*

(1) σ *satisfies condition* (iii) *of the LIG inference rule.*
(2) σ *is such that all ground extension terms in* $\mathcal{L}_i\sigma$ *are in* $\mathsf{st}(\mathcal{M})$.

Proof. Suppose (1) holds. Then by (iii), all $(L_i \vee D_i)\sigma$ are generalizations of clauses in $\mathcal{K}[\mathcal{M}]$, which means they are either in $\mathcal{K}[\mathcal{M}]$ or they can be instantiated to a clause in $\mathcal{K}[\mathcal{M}]$. In any way, by definition of $\mathcal{K}[G]$, they can only contain ground extension terms that are in $\mathsf{st}(\mathcal{M})$. Thus, this holds also for every subset of every $(L_i \vee D_i)\sigma$, implying (2).

Now suppose (2) holds. Because $\mathcal{K}$ is Σ_1-linear, for every $(L_i \vee D_i)$, all extension terms containing the same variable are syntactically equal. As $\mathcal{L}_i$ contains all variables in extension terms, all non-ground extension terms in $(L_i \vee D_i) \setminus \mathcal{L}_i$ must be equal to some term in $\mathcal{L}_i$. As all ground extension terms in $\mathcal{L}_i\sigma$ are in $\mathsf{st}(\mathcal{M})$, so must be all ground extension terms in $(L_i \vee D_i)\sigma$. By definition of $\mathcal{K}[\mathcal{M}]$, every $(L_i \vee D_i)\sigma$ is a generalization of a clause in $\mathcal{K}[\mathcal{M}]$, satisfying (iii).□

The lemma suggests that in order to ensure condition (iii) of the inference rule, we may watch for every clause $C \in \mathcal{K}$ a set of literals $\mathcal{L} \subseteq C$ such that in $\mathcal{L}$, all variables from C occur in extension terms. Together with condition (ii), we then only need to consider substitutions σ mapping variables of $\mathsf{sel}(C)$ to ground terms such that all ground extension terms in $\mathcal{L}\sigma$ are in $\mathsf{st}(\mathcal{M})$.

Special cases. The following special cases make the search for a substitution easier, and justify our definition of sel on $\mathcal{K}$. For any $C \in \mathcal{K}$:

- if all variables from C occur in $\mathsf{sel}(C)$, then any conclusion $C\sigma$ of an LIG-inference will be ground.
- if furthermore all variables appear below extension terms in $\mathsf{sel}(C)$, then it is sufficient to consider $\mathcal{L} = \{\mathsf{sel}(C)\}$.

Unsatisfiable cores. In order to minimize the number of generated instances, one can eliminate premises (and conclusions) of an inference which are not needed to satisfy condition (iv) of the LIG rule. If $\{L_i\sigma\}_{1 \leq i \leq n} \cup \mathcal{M} \models_{\mathcal{T}} \Box$, then a decision procedure for $\mathcal{T}$ can be used to compute an *unsatisfiable core* of $\{L_i\sigma\}_{1 \leq i \leq n}$ with respect to $\mathcal{M}$, i.e. a small subset $\mathcal{L} \subseteq \{L_i\sigma\}_{1 \leq i \leq n}$ such that $\mathcal{L} \cup \mathcal{M} \models_{\mathcal{T}} \Box$. If we drop premises and conclusions which do not contain a literal $L_i \in \mathcal{L}$, we still have a valid LIG inference.

3.2   Examples: Behaviour of *LIG*

In the following examples, we compare the different approaches to local reasoning. We will call the standard method from Section 2.2 *eager instantiation*, the incremental method without unsatisfiable cores *LIG*, and with unsatisfiable cores LIG_{uc}. For all examples, consider the same background theory and extension as in Example 1, i.e. T has a partial ordering and $K = \{\ x \leq y \rightarrow f(x) \leq f(y)\ \}$.

Example 2. Let $G = \{\ a \leq b,\ \neg(f(a) \leq f(b))\ \}$. Then, as seen in Example 1, eager instantiation generates a set of clauses $K[G]$, with $|K[G]| = 4$.

When using *LIG*, we have $\mathsf{sel}(K) = \{\ f(x) \leq f(y)\ \}$ and $M = G$ (as we only have unit clauses in G). To satisfy the side conditions of the *LIG* rule, we search for a substitution instantiating one or several variants of $f(x) \leq f(y)$ such that the resulting ground instances are unsatisfiable together with M, and the resulting extension terms (starting with f) already appear in M.

In the worst case *LIG* considers the whole set $L = \mathsf{sel}(K)[G]$, containing 4 instances of the literal $f(x) \leq f(y)$. As $L \cup M$ is unsatisfiable, *LIG* produces exactly the same instances as before.

LIG_{uc} searches for an unsatisfiable core in L and will probably find out that already $\{\ f(a) \leq f(b)\ \} \cup M$ is unsatisfiable. Thus, it will produce $a \leq b \rightarrow f(a) \leq f(b)$ with its first inference and add it to G, which makes G unsatisfiable.

We can see that because of the missing boolean structure in G, the *LIG* rule does not reduce the number of instances. However, the additional effort of computing an unsatisfiable core pays off: we produce exactly the one instance which is needed to show unsatisfiability of $K[G] \cup G$.

The following example shows that the effect of the incremental methods grows with the amount of boolean structure in G and of information that does not contribute to the proof of unsatisfiability.

Example 3. Let G consist of the ground clauses

(C_i) $\qquad a_i \leq b_i \vee c_i \leq d_i$, $\qquad$ for $1 \leq i \leq n$

(D_i) $\quad f(a_i) \leq f(b_i) \vee f(c_i) \leq f(d_i)$, $\quad$ for $1 \leq i \leq n$

(E) $\quad \neg(a_1 \leq b_1) \vee \neg(f(a_1) \leq f(b_1))$

(F) $\quad \neg(c_1 \leq d_1) \vee \neg(f(c_1) \leq f(d_1))$

For any n, this set of clauses is unsatisfiable, because the set $\{C_1, D_1, E, F\}$ is already unsatisfiable in $T \cup K$. The instances of the monotonicity axiom needed to prove this are $a_1 \leq b_1 \rightarrow f(a_1) \leq f(b_1)$ and $c_1 \leq d_1 \rightarrow f(c_1) \leq f(d_1)$. Let us compare how the different approaches to local reasoning treat this problem:

The eager approach generates $K[G]$, which consists of all instances of the monotonicity axiom with all combinations of substituting x and y with the constants a_i, b_i, c_i, d_i, i.e. $|K[G]| = (4n)^2$, and then checks satisfiability.

In *LIG*, $\mathsf{sel}(K)$ is as above, and M may contain an arbitrary literal out of each clause, except for C_1, D_1, E and F. The dependencies between these imply that either $f(a_1) \leq f(b_1)$ and $\neg(f(c_1) \leq f(d_1))$ are in M, or $\neg(f(a_1) \leq f(b_1))$ and

$f(c_1) \leq f(d_1)$. From the other D_i, we have $n-1$ different literals in $\mathcal{M}$, each with 2 extension terms that do not appear elsewhere. Thus, $\mathsf{st}(\mathcal{M})$ contains $2n + 2$ extension terms and in search for a substitution we generate a set $\mathcal{L}$ containing $(2n+2)^2$ instances of the literal $f(x) \leq f(y)$. $\mathcal{L}$ is unsatisfiable and LIG may produce all $(2n + 2)^2$ corresponding clause instances. Since $f(a_1), f(b_1), f(c_1), f(d_1)$ are all in $\mathsf{st}(\mathcal{M})$, among these instances are $a_1 \leq b_1 \rightarrow f(a_1) \leq f(b_1)$ and $c_1 \leq d_1 \rightarrow f(c_1) \leq f(d_1)$, which makes G unsatisfiable after the inference.

In LIG_{uc}, we compute an unsatisfiable core of $\mathcal{L}$ with respect to $\mathcal{M}$. As $\mathcal{M}$ must contain either $\neg(f(a_1) \leq f(b_1))$ or $\neg(f(c_1) \leq f(d_1))$, we can find that either $f(a_1) \leq f(b_1)$ or $f(c_1) \leq f(d_1)$ are unsatisfiable cores. After adding the corresponding instance of the axiom, the problem is still satisfiable, and the new model must contain exactly those literals from C_1, D_1, E and F which were not in $\mathcal{M}$ before. Assume that the other literals in $\mathcal{M}$ do not change unnecessarily. Then, $\mathsf{st}(\mathcal{M})$ and our set $\mathcal{L}$ of literals will be the same as in the first inference. Now, the unsatisfiable core consists again of one of the two literals $f(a_1) \leq f(b_1)$ or $f(c_1) \leq f(d_1)$, namely the one that was not chosen before. The generated instance is exactly the one which makes G unsatisfiable.

Thus, LIG proves $G \models_{\mathcal{T} \cup \mathcal{K}} \square$ by generating $(2n + 2)^2$ instances in one step, and LIG_{uc} needs to generate only 2 instances in 2 steps. Recall that in contrast to this, eager instantiation generates $(4n)^2$ instances.

Finally, we give an example how LIG and LIG_{uc} can not only prove unsatisfiability, but also generate models for satisfiable problems incrementally.

Example 4. Consider a modified version of Example 3: let $\mathcal{K}$ be as before, and remove clause F from G, which makes the problem satisfiable for all n. We will show how the different approaches generate a model for $|\mathcal{K}[G]|$.

In the eager approach, $\mathcal{K}[G]$ is generated completely and the search for a model is left to the SMT solver.

In LIG, the SMT solver generates a model $\mathcal{M}$ for G. We can distinguish two cases: either (i) the second literal of E is not in $\mathcal{M}$, or (ii) it is. In case (i), LIG will not generate any instances, since $\mathcal{M}$ only contains positive literals with extension symbols, i.e. no set of instantiations of $\mathsf{sel}(\mathcal{K}) = \{f(x) \leq f(y)\}$ can be unsatisfiable with respect to $\mathcal{M}$. In case (ii), LIG will find out that $\mathsf{sel}(\mathcal{K})[\mathcal{M}]$ is unsatisfiable with respect to $\mathcal{M}$, and generate $(2n + 1)^2$ axiom instances. After this, LIG calls the SMT solver for a new model of $G \cup \mathcal{K}[\mathcal{M}]$. The procedure above is repeated until we get back a model which does not include the second literal of E, or until the set of instances is saturated with respect to the model, i.e. all axiom instances that can be generated have already been generated.

In LIG_{uc}, we can make the same case distinction. In case (i) we detect satisfiability immediately, in case (ii) we will find out that $f(a_1) \leq f(b_1)$ is already unsatisfiable with respect to $\mathcal{M}$, and generate $a_1 \leq b_1 \rightarrow f(a_1) \leq f(b_1)$. After that, the SMT solver is called again, and we can apply the same case distinction for the new model: in case (i), we cannot generate any instances, and in case (ii) the only instance we can generate is $a_1 \leq b_1 \rightarrow f(a_1) \leq f(b_1)$, which we have already generated. Thus, the set of instances is saturated.

We see that in this case the benefit of LIG may become smaller than before, since termination depends very much on the models supplied by the SMT solver. For LIG_{uc} however, we can still guarantee termination after two iterations and generation of a single axiom instance.

3.3   Correctness of LIG

In the following, we show that LIG is sound, complete and terminating. An LIG-*derivation* is a sequence of tuples $(\mathcal{K}^0, G^0) \vdash (\mathcal{K}^1, G^1) \vdash \ldots \vdash (\mathcal{K}^n, G^n)$ such that G^0 is a set of ground clauses, $\mathcal{K}^0$ is a local extension of the background theory $\mathcal{T}$, and for $0 \leq i \leq n-1$, G^i is $\mathcal{T}$-satisfiable and $(\mathcal{K}^{i+1}, G^{i+1})$ is the result of an LIG-inference on $(\mathcal{K}^i, G^i)$.

Theorem 1 (Soundness). *Let* $(\mathcal{K}^0, G^0) \vdash (\mathcal{K}^1, G^1) \vdash \ldots \vdash (\mathcal{K}^n, G^n)$ *be an LIG-derivation. If* $G^n \models_{\mathcal{T}} \square$, *then* $\mathcal{K}^0 \cup G^0 \models_{\mathcal{T}} \square$.

Proof. All elements of G^n are instances of clauses in $\mathcal{K}^0 \cup G^0$. Thus, their unsatisfiability implies unsatisfiability of $\mathcal{K}^0 \cup G^0$. $\square$

For the proof of completeness we need the following definition: Let $\mathcal{F}$ be a set of formulas. F_1 is a *most specific generalization of F_2 with respect to $\mathcal{F}$* if F_1 is a generalization of F_2 and there is no $F_3 \in \mathcal{F}$ which is both a non-variant instance of F_1 and a generalization of F_2.

Theorem 2 (Completeness). *Let* $(\mathcal{K}^0, G^0) \vdash (\mathcal{K}^1, G^1) \vdash \ldots \vdash (\mathcal{K}^n, G^n)$ *be an LIG-derivation. If* G^n *is $\mathcal{T}$-satisfiable and* $(\mathcal{K}^n, G^n)$ *is saturated under LIG with respect to a given selection function* sel *and a partial Herbrand model* $\mathcal{M}$, *then* G^0 *is* $(\mathcal{T} \cup \mathcal{K}^0)$*-satisfiable.*

Proof. Let $\mathcal{K}^0, G^0, \mathcal{K}^n, G^n$, sel and $\mathcal{M}$ as defined above. $\mathcal{M}$ is a partial Herbrand model of G^n, where $G^n \subseteq \mathcal{K}^0[G^0] \cup G^0$. We extend $\mathcal{M}$ to a total Herbrand model of $\mathcal{K}^0[G^0] \cup G^0$ in the following way: for every $C_i \in (\mathcal{K}^0[G^0] \cup G^0) \setminus G^n$ we can find a non-ground clause $D_i \in \mathcal{K}^n$ s.t. $D_i\sigma_i = C_i$ and D_i is a most specific generalization of C_i wrt. $\mathcal{K}^n$. For every such C_i, we add sel$(D_i)\sigma_i$ to $\mathcal{M}$, i.e. the resulting set of literals $\mathcal{M}'$ contains at least one literal from each clause in $\mathcal{K}^0[G^0] \cup G^0$. Furthermore, $\mathcal{M}'$ cannot be contradictory: if this was the case, we would have an LIG inference with the D_i and $\mathcal{M}$ as premises, producing the C_i or generalizations thereof. As the D_i were chosen to be most specific generalizations of the C_i wrt. $\mathcal{K}^n$, the produced instances are neither in G^n nor $\mathcal{K}^n$, thus contradicting our assumption that $(\mathcal{K}^n, G^n)$ is saturated under LIG wrt. sel and $\mathcal{M}$.[3] As $\mathcal{M}'$ is not contradictory and contains one literal out of each clause in $\mathcal{K}^0[G^0] \cup G^0$, $\mathcal{M}'$ is a partial Herbrand model of $\mathcal{K}^0[G^0] \cup G^0$. By locality, G^0 is $(\mathcal{T} \cup \mathcal{K}^0)$-satisfiable iff $\mathcal{K}^0[G^0] \cup G^0$ is $\mathcal{T}$-satisfiable. $\square$

---

[3] If unsatisfiable cores are used, the argument is the same except that only a subset of the D_i are used as premises — but since $\mathcal{M}$ was not contradictory before, at least one of the D_i has to be instantiated to a new instance.

Theorem 3 (Termination). *For any input $(\mathcal{K}^0, G^0)$ (where $\mathcal{K}^0$ and G^0 are as defined above), LIG terminates after a finite number of inferences.*

Proof. *LIG*-inferences produce only clauses which are both instances of clauses in $\mathcal{K}$ and generalizations of clauses in $\mathcal{K}[\mathcal{M}]$, where for every sel, $\mathcal{K}[\mathcal{M}] \subseteq \mathcal{K}[G]$. For a given input $(\mathcal{K}, G)$, only finitely many clauses are both instances of clauses in $\mathcal{K}$ and generalizations of clauses in $\mathcal{K}[G]$, and thus there are only finitely many possible *LIG*-inferences.   □

4   Chains of Local Theory Extensions

In Section 2.2, we mentioned that local extensions of theories can be serialized, i.e. an extended theory can be extended again. This approach is especially useful in the context of verification [9], but it requires a more sophisticated approach to incremental generation than one-time extensions. Section 4.1 introduces some terminology for reasoning in chains of extensions. In Section 4.2 we show how *LIG* can be extended to chains of extensions, followed by examples (Section 4.3) and a correctness argument (Section 4.4).

4.1   Hierarchic Reasoning in Chains of Extensions

Consider a base theory $\mathcal{T}_0$ and a number of clause sets $\mathcal{K}_1, \ldots, \mathcal{K}_m$. For $j = 0, \ldots, m-1$, let $\mathcal{T}_{j+1} = \mathcal{T}_j \cup \mathcal{K}_{j+1}$ and assume that $\mathcal{T}_j \subseteq \mathcal{T}_{j+1}$ is a local extension. Then, for every extension, we can use local reasoning to reduce a given ground goal G from theory $\mathcal{T}_j$ to theory $\mathcal{T}_{j-1}$:

$$G \models_{\mathcal{T}_j} \Box \Leftrightarrow \mathcal{K}_j[G] \cup G \models_{\mathcal{T}_{j-1}} \Box.$$

If we define

$$\begin{aligned}
G_m &= G \\
G_{j-1} &= \mathcal{K}_j[G_j] \cup G_j \ (\text{for } 1 \leq j \leq m),
\end{aligned}$$

then $G \models_{\mathcal{T}_m} \Box \Leftrightarrow G_0 \models_{\mathcal{T}_0} \Box$.

For incremental generation we cannot use the given *LIG* procedure, as that would require for every reduction from $\mathcal{T}_j$ to $\mathcal{T}_{j-1}$ an SMT procedure for $\mathcal{T}_{j-1}$ to already exist. On the other hand, reasoning in chains of extensions can benefit very much from incremental generation of instances, since the ground goal G_j grows polynomially with every reduction. Therefore, we supply a more sophisticated method *LIG** that can treat several extensions at once.

4.2   Chain-Local Instance Generation (*LIG**)

We present the procedure *LIG**, which solves the satisfiability problem of a ground goal G in a repeatedly extended theory $\mathcal{T} \cup \mathcal{K}_1 \cup \ldots \cup \mathcal{K}_n$, and differs from *LIG* mainly in two points: First, for m successive extensions, axioms need to be kept in m different sets. Second, the search space is restricted to the sets of instances G_j defined above.

Proof procedure. For a given input $(\mathcal{K}_1, \ldots, \mathcal{K}_m, G)$, LIG^* keeps axioms from the different extensions and ground clauses in separate sets. The selection function sel is defined as in LIG, except that we have different extension symbols for each $\mathcal{K}_j$. For every j, $\mathsf{sel}(\mathcal{K}_j)$ consists of the literals with the highest number of variables, preferably below extension symbols of $\mathcal{K}_j$. Then, the following two steps are repeated until termination:

(1) Ground satisfiability check. We give G to an SMT solver. If $G \models_{\mathcal{T}_0} \Box$, then the procedure terminates and returns unsatisfiable. Otherwise, the solver returns a model M such that $M \models_{\mathcal{T}_0} G$. As before, generate from M a partial Herbrand model $\mathcal{M}$ of G.

(2) Instance generation. Define the following sets of literals:

$$\mathcal{L}_{m+1} = \mathcal{M}$$
$$\mathcal{L}_j = \mathsf{sel}(\mathcal{K}_j)[\textstyle\bigcup_{j<k\leq m+1} \mathcal{L}_k] \text{ (for } 1 \leq j \leq m)$$

Then, instances are generated according to the following rule:

$$LIG^* \quad \frac{(L_1 \vee D_1) \ \cdots \ (L_n \vee D_n) \mid \mathcal{M}}{(L_1 \vee D_1)\sigma \ \cdots \ (L_n \vee D_n)\sigma}$$

where:
  (i) the $L_i \vee D_i$ are (variants of) clauses from $\mathcal{K}_1 \cup \ldots \cup \mathcal{K}_m$ with $\mathsf{sel}(L_i \vee D_i) = L_i$,
  (ii) σ is a substitution such that all $L_i\sigma$ are ground literals,
  (iii) if $(L_i \vee D_i) \in \mathcal{K}_j$, then $(L_i \vee D_i)\sigma$ is a generalization of a clause in $\mathcal{K}_j[\bigcup_{j<k\leq m+1} \mathcal{L}_k]$, and
  (iv) $\{L_i\sigma\}_{1\leq i\leq n} \cup \mathcal{M} \models_{\mathcal{T}} \Box$

Again, several variants of an axiom may be instantiated in one inference. Ground clauses are added to G, non-ground instances $C\sigma$ with $C \in \mathcal{K}_j$ are added to $\mathcal{K}_j$. The notion of saturation applies as before. If $(\mathcal{K}_1, \ldots, \mathcal{K}_n, G)$ is saturated under LIG^*, the procedure terminates and states satisfiability of the input. Otherwise, define sel on new axioms as described above and return to **(1)**.

Search for substitutions. The remarks we made for LIG apply analogously: for every axiom C, we can watch a set of literals $\mathcal{L} \subseteq C$ to ensure conditions (ii) and (iii) of the inference rule. Then, we only need to consider those substitutions σ which map variables of $\mathsf{sel}(C)$ to ground terms such that resulting ground extension terms (in the extension $\mathcal{K}_j \supseteq C$) in $\mathcal{L}\sigma$ are in $\mathsf{st}(\mathcal{L}_j)$. We omit a proof of this property, which is a straightforward lifting of the proof of Lemma 1.

Special cases, unsatisfiable cores. The special cases apply as before, except that axioms $C\sigma$ have to be added to the set $\mathcal{K}_j$ which contains C. Also, unsatisfiable cores can be computed as before.

4.3   Examples: Applications of LIG^*

In previous work on verification of parametric systems [9] we introduced typical applications of LIG^*. Due to space restrictions, we can only sketch the idea here.

Example 5. Local axioms can be used to model parameterized systems by using sets of guarded boundedness axioms (see Section 2.2) as update rules. Consider a system were a function f is used to model the current state of the system (e.g., the contents of a data structure), and updates are defined by

$$\text{update} = \{\phi_i(\overline{x}) \rightarrow s_i(\overline{x}) \le f'(\overline{x}) \le t_i(\overline{x}) \mid 1 \le i \le n\},$$

i.e. f' is used to model the state of the system after the update. A desired invariant of such a system may be that f is sorted, i.e. if the monotonicity axiom for f ($\text{Mon}(f)$) holds before an update, it should also hold for f' after the update. To prove this, one can show that $\text{Mon}(f) \cup \text{update} \cup \neg\text{Mon}(f') \models_{\mathcal{T}_0} \Box$ by using locality of the first extension $\mathcal{T}_0 \subseteq \mathcal{T}_0 \cup \text{Mon}(f)$ and the second extension $\mathcal{T}_0 \cup \text{Mon}(f) \subseteq \mathcal{T}_0 \cup \text{Mon}(f) \cup \text{update}$.

Example 6. If the safety property of a system is not inductive, we may resort to bounded model checking (BMC). Consider a system where an update can be expressed as a local theory extension, and this extension can be repeated (after proper renaming of extension symbols) in order to model successive updates. Then, LIG^* can be used to prove safety of the system for m steps by proving

$$\text{init} \wedge \text{update}_1 \wedge \dots \wedge \text{update}_m \wedge \neg\text{safe} \models_{\mathcal{T}_0} \Box,$$

where init is the initial condition of the system, update gives the update rules (with subscript i for the ith step), and safe gives the safety condition.

Since eager instantiation will blow up the ground goal polynomially in each extension, we should benefit a lot from an incremental approach.

4.4   Correctness of LIG^*

In the following we state that LIG^* is sound, complete, and terminating. Detailed proofs are omitted due to space restrictions. They are straightforward liftings of the corresponding proofs in Section 3.3, with $\mathcal{K}_1 \cup \dots \cup \mathcal{K}_m$ replacing $\mathcal{K}$, G_0 replacing $\mathcal{K}[G]$, and with $\mathcal{L} = \bigcup_{1 \le j \le m+1} \mathcal{L}_j$.

Consider a base theory $\mathcal{T}_0$ and successively extended theories $\mathcal{T}_{j+1} = \mathcal{T}_j \cup \mathcal{K}_{j+1}^0$. An LIG^*-*derivation* is a sequence of tuples $(\mathcal{K}_1^0, \dots, \mathcal{K}_m^0, G^0) \vdash \dots \vdash (\mathcal{K}_1^n, \dots, \mathcal{K}_m^n, G^n)$ such that for $0 \le j \le m-1$, $\mathcal{T}_j \subseteq \mathcal{T}_j \cup \mathcal{K}_{j+1}^0$ is a local theory extension, and for $0 \le i \le m-1$, G^i is $\mathcal{T}_0$-satisfiable and $(\mathcal{K}_1^{i+1}, \dots, \mathcal{K}_m^{i+1}, G^{i+1})$ is the result of an LIG^*-inference on $(\mathcal{K}_1^i, \dots, \mathcal{K}_m^i, G^i)$.

Theorem 4 (Soundness). *Let* $(\mathcal{K}_1^0, \dots, \mathcal{K}_m^0, G^0) \vdash \dots \vdash (\mathcal{K}_1^n, \dots, \mathcal{K}_m^n, G^n)$ *be an* LIG^*-*derivation. If* $G^n \models_{\mathcal{T}_0} \Box$, *then* $G^0 \models_{\mathcal{T}_m} \Box$.

Theorem 5 (Completeness). *Let* $(\mathcal{K}_1^0, \dots, \mathcal{K}_m^0, G^0) \vdash \dots \vdash (\mathcal{K}_1^n, \dots, \mathcal{K}_m^n, G^n)$ *be an* LIG^*-*derivation. If* G^n *is* $\mathcal{T}_0$-*satisfiable and* $(\mathcal{K}_1^n, \dots, \mathcal{K}_m^n, G^n)$ *is saturated* *under LIG* with respect to a given selection function* sel *and a Herbrand model* $\mathcal{M}$ *of* G^n, *then* G^0 *is* $\mathcal{T}_m$-*satisfiable.*

Theorem 6 (Termination). *For any input* $(\mathcal{K}_1^0, \ldots, \mathcal{K}_m^0, G^0)$ *(with the* $\mathcal{K}_i^0$ *and* G^0 *as defined above), LIG* terminates after a finite number of inferences.*

5   Experimental Results

We implemented the incremental approaches on top of an existing OCaml implementation of the eager approach, with Z3 [2] as our blackbox SMT solver. We tested our implementation on four sets of benchmarks:[4]

In Figure 1 (a) we see runtimes of all three approaches on the parameterized problem from Example 3. The incremental approaches outperform the eager instantiation substantially, while LIG_{uc} is a bit slower than LIG. Figure 1 (b) shows runtimes for Example 4: here, LIG_{uc} is significantly faster than LIG.

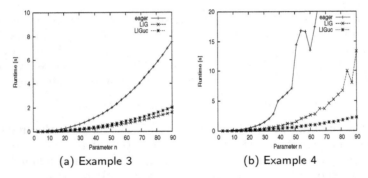

(a) Example 3   (b) Example 4

Fig. 1. Runtime comparison of the three approaches on parameterized example

In Figure 2, we see runtimes of LIG and the eager approach on a set of verification benchmarks taken from the QF_UFLIA/wisas section of SMT-LIB.[5] We checked satisfiability when the background theory assumes one of the functions to be either monotone or injective. All of the problems turned out to be unsatisfiable in both of the extended theories. Figure 2 (a) compares performance of the two approaches for the subset of originally satisfiable problems. In the diagram, a point above the diagonal means that LIG is faster than eager instantiation on a given problem, and vice versa for points below the diagonal. We can see that LIG is faster on allmost all of the problems.

For the set of all benchmarks from the QF_UFLIA/wisas section of SMT-LIB, we had mixed results (see Figure 2 (b)): although LIG is faster on the vast majority, there are some problems for which it needs much longer than the eager

---

[4] The implementation of LIG_{uc} is still preliminary, therefore it is only included in two of the four comparisons below.

[5] These were originally benchmarks of the Wisconsin Safety Analyzer.

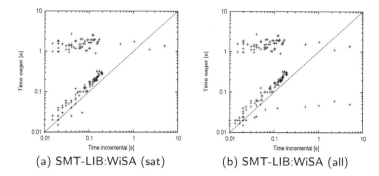

(a) SMT-LIB:WiSA (sat)   (b) SMT-LIB:WiSA (all)

Fig. 2. Runtime comparison of LIG and eager approach on verification problems

method. It turned out that these problems are already unsatisfiable without the additional axioms, but proving unsatisfiability of the original problem was much harder than proving unsatisfiability after adding a few hundred axiom instances.

6   Conclusions and Future Work

We have introduced incremental procedures for reasoning in local theory extensions and chains of local extensions. We have shown that our methods are decision procedures and generate less instances than the standard approach. Experimental results indicate that already LIG, which always takes maximal inferences, is considerably more efficient than eager instantiation. LIG_{uc}, taking minimal inferences, can outperform LIG at least for satisfiable problems.

In part, our approach resembles quantifier handling in SMT procedures. This holds specifically for the matching of extension terms in watched literals to ground terms in the model. The main differences are our additional semantic condition for instantiation, and matching modulo equality in SMT solvers, in contrast to our syntactical matching. It would be interesting to check whether we could benefit somehow from using E-matching instead of syntactical matching.

A similar approach of generating instances incrementally, guided by a candidate model, has been followed by Veanes et al. [13] in context of bounded reachability analysis. Although not explained in much detail, they seem to use an even stronger semantic condition: only instances which contradict the current candidate model are generated. Furthermore, their search for substitutions is guided by all ground terms appearing in the problem, where our approach takes into account only the terms in the candidate model.

An extension of our work in this paper would be to consider more general notions of locality. In previous work, we have shown that both the array property fragment of Bradley et al. [1] and the pointer data structures of McPeak and Necula [10] can be expressed as Ψ-local extensions [8]. Thus, extending our approach to Ψ-locality would give us an incremental procedure for these fragments.

Acknowledgments. Thanks to the German Research Council (DFG) for financial support of this work as part of the Transregional Collaborative Research Center "Automatic Verification and Analysis of Complex Systems" (SFB/TR 14 AVACS, see www.avacs.org for more information). Many thanks also to Viorica Sofronie-Stokkermans for our fruitful discussions, and to Leonardo de Moura for supporting the integration of Z3 and answering many questions.

References

1. Bradley, A.R., Manna, Z., Sipma, H.B.: What's decidable about arrays? In: Emerson, E.A., Namjoshi, K.S. (eds.) VMCAI 2006. LNCS, vol. 3855, pp. 427–442. Springer, Heidelberg (2005)
2. de Moura, L., Bjørner, N.: Z3: An Efficient SMT Solver. In: Ramakrishnan, C.R., Rehof, J. (eds.) TACAS 2008. LNCS, vol. 4963, pp. 337–340. Springer, Heidelberg (2008)
3. Detlefs, D., Nelson, G., Saxe, J.B.: Simplify: a theorem prover for program checking. Journal of the ACM 52(3), 365–473 (2005)
4. Ganzinger, H.: Relating semantic and proof-theoretic concepts for polynomial time decidability of uniform word problems. In: 16th IEEE Symposium on Logic in Computer Science, pp. 81–92. IEEE Computer Society Press, New York (2001)
5. Ganzinger, H., Korovin, K.: Theory instantiation. In: Hermann, M., Voronkov, A. (eds.) LPAR 2006. LNCS, vol. 4246, pp. 497–511. Springer, Heidelberg (2006)
6. Ge, Y., Barrett, C., Tinelli, C.: Solving Quantified Verification Conditions Using Satisfiability Modulo Theories. In: Pfenning, F. (ed.) CADE 2007. LNCS (LNAI), vol. 4603, pp. 167–182. Springer, Heidelberg (2007)
7. Givan, R., McAllester, D.: Polynomial-time computation via local inference relations. ACM Transactions on Computational Logic 3(4), 521–541 (2002)
8. Ihlemann, C., Jacobs, S., Sofronie-Stokkermans, V.: On local reasoning in verification. In: Ramakrishnan, C.R., Rehof, J. (eds.) TACAS 2008. LNCS, vol. 4963, pp. 265–281. Springer, Heidelberg (2008)
9. Jacobs, S., Sofronie-Stokkermans, V.: Applications of Hierarchical Reasoning in the Verification of Complex Systems. In: Fourth Workshop on Pragmatics of Decision Procedures in Automated Reasoning. ENTCS, vol. 174(8), pp. 39–54. Elsevier, Amsterdam (2007)
10. McPeak, S., Necula, G.C.: Data structure specifications via local equality axioms. In: Etessami, K., Rajamani, S.K. (eds.) CAV 2005. LNCS, vol. 3576, pp. 476–490. Springer, Heidelberg (2005)
11. Nieuwenhuis, R., Oliveras, A., Rodriguez-Carbonell, E., Rubio, A.: Challenges in Satisfiability Modulo Theories. In: Baader, F. (ed.) RTA 2007. LNCS, vol. 4533, pp. 2–18. Springer, Heidelberg (2007)
12. Sofronie-Stokkermans, V.: Hierarchic reasoning in local theory extensions. In: Nieuwenhuis, R. (ed.) CADE 2005. LNCS (LNAI), vol. 3632, pp. 219–234. Springer, Heidelberg (2005)
13. Veanes, M., Bjørner, N., Raschke, A.: An SMT Approach to Bounded Reachability Analysis of Model Programs. In: Suzuki, K., Higashino, T., Yasumoto, K., El-Fakih, K. (eds.) FORTE 2008. LNCS, vol. 5048, pp. 53–68. Springer, Heidelberg (2008)

Quantifier Elimination via Functional Composition

Jie-Hong R. Jiang

Department of Electrical Engineering / Graduate Institute of Electronics Engineering
National Taiwan University, Taipei 10617, Taiwan
jhjiang@cc.ee.ntu.edu.tw

Abstract. This paper poses the following basic question: Given a quantified Boolean formula $\exists x.\varphi$, what should a function/formula f be such that substituting f for x in φ yields a logically equivalent quantifier-free formula? Its answer leads to a solution to quantifier elimination in the Boolean domain, alternative to the conventional approach based on formula expansion. Such a composite function can be effectively derived using symbolic techniques and further simplified for practical applications. In particular, we explore Craig interpolation for scalable computation. This compositional approach to quantifier elimination is analyzably superior to the conventional one under certain practical assumptions. Experiments demonstrate the scalability of the approach. Several large problem instances unsolvable before can now be resolved effectively. A generalization to first-order logic characterizes a composite function's complete flexibility, which awaits further exploitation to simplify quantifier elimination beyond the propositional case.

1 Introduction

Quantifier elimination is a way of transforming a formula with quantifiers to an equivalent one without quantifiers. Eliminating quantified variables often yields desirable reduction of some sort, and applies to constraint solving, e.g., Gauss elimination for solving systems of linear equations, Fourier-Motzkin elimination for systems of linear inequalities, cylindrical algebraic decomposition [4,2] for systems of polynomial inequalities, and so on. It plays important roles in computation theory, mathematical logic, mathematical programming, scientific computing, and other fields. Its applications are pervasive and profound. This paper is concerned about quantifier elimination in propositional logic as well as first-order logic.

Quantifier elimination in propositional logic augmented with quantifiers over propositional variables is a well-studied subject. There are several approaches to this problem:

Formula expansion. A conventional approach to quantifier elimination is based on formula expansion, $\exists x.\varphi = \varphi[x/0] \vee \varphi[x/1]$, where formula φ is expanded under all truth assignments on x by substituting 0 and 1 for x in φ. Binary

A. Bouajjani and O. Maler (Eds.): CAV 2009, LNCS 5643, pp. 383–397, 2009.

decision diagrams (BDDs), and-inverter graphs (AIGs), and other data structures for Boolean function representation and manipulation can be adopted for the computation. BDDs tended to be a popular approach to such computation, the so-called image computation [3]. BDD-based computation however has its intrinsic memory-explosion limitation. On the other hand, recent progress in AIG packages [14,13] has made AIG-based quantification a viable alternative to BDD-based one. For example, AIGs have been directly used in unbounded model checking [17]. Our approach to quantifier elimination also uses AIGs extensively.

Normal-form conversion. Eliminating the existential (respectively universal) quantifier of formula $\exists x.\varphi$ (respectively $\forall x.\varphi$) is easy[1] when φ is in disjunctive normal form (DNF) (respectively conjunctive normal form (CNF)). Thereby the normal-form conversion between CNF and DNF can be exploited for quantifier elimination, as was suggested in [15] in application to unbounded model checking.

Satisfiability solving. Using a decision procedure, the quantifier-free equivalent of $\exists x.\varphi$ can be generated by searching through all satisfying assignments to the non-quantified variables. By collecting these satisfying assignments, one can construct an equivalent quantifier-free formula. A detailed exposition of this method can be found, e.g., in [7] and the references therein.

Despite these existing approaches, there is not a single best one to quantifier elimination for all problem instances. Different approaches may have their own strengths and weaknesses.

This paper adds to the above list a new item, a compositional approach to quantifier elimination, which is by nature closer to the formula-expansion approach. We ask, given a quantified Boolean formula $\exists x.\varphi$, what should a function/formula f be such that substituting f for x in φ, denoted as $\varphi[x/f]$, yields a logically equivalent quantifier-free formula. This paper characterizes the complete flexibility of such a composite function f. Furthermore, an effective and scalable derivation of f with reasonable quality is proposed using Craig interpolation. An analysis shows that, under the sparsity assumption of φ (which is common in certain practical applications), the new compositional approach is superior to the conventional one based on formula expansion. Practical experience suggests that the new approach often yields much more compact AIGs than the conventional one when the sparsity condition holds. Several problem instances that suffer from exponential blow-up by formula expansion are effectively resolvable by functional composition.

Quantifier elimination in first-order logic is much more complicated and relatively less explored. In fact, exhaustive formula expansion does not work in first-order logic as variables can take on infinite values. Moreover, not every

---

[1] When φ is in DNF and CNF, respectively, removing every appearance of literals x, $\neg x$ and the so-induced illegal logic connectives from φ yields a quantifier-free equivalent of $\exists x.\varphi$ and $\forall x.\varphi$, respectively. So the computation is achievable in linear time and the size of the resultant quantifier-free formula is non-increasing compared to that of φ.

first-order theory allows quantifier elimination. One of the earliest attempts at quantifier elimination in first-order logic is Tarski's work [21], where the first quantifier-elimination procedure of real closed fields was demonstrated. Since then, algorithmic improvements have been achieved, see, e.g., [4,2]. Also quantifier elimination has been shown possible in other first-order theories, such as term algebras, Presburger arithmetic, and other theories [20].

Extending the results of propositional logic, this paper characterizes the complete flexibility of composite functions for quantifier elimination in first-order logic. Unlike most prior efforts, which gave concrete quantifier-elimination procedures for some specific theories, we rather present a generic viewpoint and show the potential usefulness of the complete flexibility in simplifying quantifier elimination.

One of the common practices to quantifier elimination of first-order theories is based on the principle of *virtual substitution* with *elimination sets* [23]. To eliminate a quantifier, a finite set of solution terms with their validity conditions is identified for substitution. Our characterized complete flexibility may be exploited to reduce elimination sets.

This paper is organized as follows. After preliminaries are given in Section 2, Section 3 presents the main results on quantifier elimination in propositional logic. Section 4 extends the results to first-order logic. Experimental results and discussions are given in Section 5. Section 6 compares our results with some related work. Finally, Section 7 concludes this paper and outlines future work.

2   Preliminaries

Predicate logic. We closely follow the definitions and notation of [6] about first-order logic. A *first-order language* may consist of logical symbols (including parentheses, sentential connectives, variables, and the (optional) equality symbol) and parameters (including quantifier symbols, constant symbols, predicate symbols, and function symbols). Given a language, *terms* are finite expressions representing names of objects, whereas *(well-formed) formulas* are finite expressions representing assertions about objects. Given a formula, variables not in the scope of any quantifier are called *free variables*, otherwise *bound variables*. Formulas without free variables are called *sentences*.

As a notational convention, substituting a term t for some variable x in a formula φ is denoted as $\varphi[x/t]$. We say that t is *substitutable* for x in φ if every variable y in t is not captured by some quantifier $\forall y$ or $\exists y$ in φ. Substitutability can be achieved through proper renaming of bound variables. By writing $\varphi[x/t]$, this paper assumes that t is substitutable for x in φ.

A *structure* (or called an *interpretation*) $\mathfrak{A}$ of some first-order language $\mathcal{L}$ is a tuple specifying the *domain* (or *universe*), denoted $|\mathfrak{A}|$, of the variables, and associating the constant, predicate, and function symbols with meanings. A sentence σ of $\mathcal{L}$ is true in structure $\mathfrak{A}$ is denoted as $\models_{\mathfrak{A}} \sigma$.

Propositional logic can be seen as a special case of first-order logic, where functions and predicates are interchangeable, so are terms and formulas. Also there is a unique structure $\mathfrak{B}$ with $|\mathfrak{B}| = \{0, 1\}$. In propositional logic, the *positive* and *negative cofactors* of formula φ with respect to variable x are $\varphi[x/1]$ and $\varphi[x/0]$, respectively.

Propositional satisfiability and Craig interpolation. A brief introduction to SAT solving and circuit-to-CNF conversion, essential to our development, can be found in [16]. To introduce terminology and convention for later use, we restate the following theorem.

Theorem 1 (Craig Interpolation Theorem). *[5]*
Given two Boolean formulas ϕ_A and ϕ_B, with $\phi_A \wedge \phi_B$ unsatisfiable, then there exists a Boolean formula ψ_A referring only to the common variables of ϕ_A and ϕ_B such that $\phi_A \rightarrow \psi_A$ and $\psi_A \wedge \phi_B$ remains unsatisfiable.

The Boolean formula ψ_A is referred to as the *interpolant* of ϕ_A with respect to ϕ_B. Modern SAT solvers can be extended to construct interpolants from resolution refutations [16]. In the sequel, we shall assume that Boolean functions, circuits, and interpolants are represented using AIGs, which can be converted to CNF formulas in polynomial time.

3   Propositional Logic

In this section we consider quantifier elimination of propositional logic augmented with quantifiers over propositional variables.

3.1   Composability for Quantifier Elimination

Putting propositional logic in the context of first-order logic, we note that it has a unique structure/interpretation. Under this unique structure, terms, functions, predicates, and formulas all coincide. This simplicity is crucial to the following development for propositional logic, and will become apparent when we encounter first-order logic.

Theorem 2. *A quantified Boolean formula $\exists y.\varphi(\boldsymbol{x}, y)$ is logically equivalent to the quantifier-free formula $\varphi(\boldsymbol{x}, f(\boldsymbol{x}))$ for some function $f : \mathbb{B}^n \rightarrow \mathbb{B}$ if and only if every pair $a \in \mathbb{B}^n, b \in \mathbb{B}$ with $f(a) = b$ satisfies $\varphi(a, b) \vee \forall y.\neg\varphi(a, y)$.*

Proof. ($\Longrightarrow$) For $f(a) = b$, then $\varphi(a, f(a)) = \varphi(a, b)$. If $\varphi(a, b)$ is true, then $\exists y.\varphi(a, y)$ is true. On the other hand, if $\neg\varphi(a, b)$ is true, then $\neg\exists y.\varphi(a, y)$ is true due to the logical equivalence between $\varphi(\boldsymbol{x}, f(\boldsymbol{x}))$ and $\exists y.\varphi(\boldsymbol{x}, y)$. Hence every pair $a \in \mathbb{B}^n, b \in \mathbb{B}$ with $f(a) = b$ satisfies $\varphi(a, b) \vee \forall y.\neg\varphi(a, y)$.

($\Longleftarrow$) For the sake of contradiction, assume $\exists y.\varphi(\boldsymbol{x}, y)$ and $\varphi(\boldsymbol{x}, f(\boldsymbol{x}))$ are not logically equivalent. Then there exists some $a \in \mathbb{B}^n$ such that $\neg\exists y.\varphi(a, y) \wedge \varphi(a, f(a))$ or $\exists y.\varphi(a, y) \wedge \neg\varphi(a, f(a))$. The former is trivially unsatisfiable; the latter contradicts with the premise, $\varphi(a, f(a)) \vee \forall y.\neg\varphi(a, y)$.   ∎

In essence the above theorem answers the following question: Given a quantified Boolean formula $\exists y.\varphi(\boldsymbol{x}, y)$, what should a function f be such that the composition $\varphi(\boldsymbol{x}, f(\boldsymbol{x}))$ equals $\exists y.\varphi$? It also implies the existence of such a function.

Proposition 1. *Given a quantified Boolean formula $\exists y.\varphi(\boldsymbol{x}, y)$, there always exists a function $f(\boldsymbol{x})$ such that $\exists y.\varphi(\boldsymbol{x}, y) = \varphi(\boldsymbol{x}, f(\boldsymbol{x}))$.*

Proof. The proposition follows from the fact that, for every $a \in \mathbb{B}^n$, there always exists some $b \in \mathbb{B}$ such that $\varphi(a, b) = 1$ if $\exists y.\varphi(a, y)$ is true. ∎

The following proposition characterizes the complete flexibility of a composite function for quantifier elimination.

Proposition 2. *The equality $\exists y.\varphi(\boldsymbol{x}, y) = \varphi(\boldsymbol{x}, f(\boldsymbol{x}))$ holds if and only if the composite function f satisfies $(\neg\varphi[y/0] \wedge \varphi[y/1]) \to f$ and $f \to \neg(\neg\varphi[y/1] \wedge \varphi[y/0])$. That is, $\neg\varphi[y/0] \wedge \varphi[y/1]$ and $\neg\varphi[y/1] \wedge \varphi[y/0]$ are the tightest onset and offset of f, respectively.*

Proof. There are four possible valuations of $\varphi(a, 0)$ and $\varphi(a, 1)$ for every $a \in \mathbb{B}^n$.

For $(\varphi(a, 0), \varphi(a, 1)) = (0, 0)$, a is a don't-care minterm of f because $\varphi(a, f(a)) = 0$ independent of the value of $f(a)$.

For $(\varphi(a, 0), \varphi(a, 1)) = (0, 1)$, a is an onset minterm of f because $\exists y.\varphi(a, y)$ is true and $f(a) = 1$ is the only way to make $\varphi(a, f(a))$ true.

For $(\varphi(a, 0), \varphi(a, 1)) = (1, 0)$, a is an offset minterm of f for reason similar to that of case $(0, 1)$.

For $(\varphi(a, 0), \varphi(a, 1)) = (1, 1)$, a is a don't-care minterm of f for reason similar to that of case $(0, 0)$.

Hence $\neg\varphi[y/0] \wedge \varphi[y/1]$ and $\neg\varphi[y/1] \wedge \varphi[y/0]$ are the tightest onset and offset of f, respectively. ∎

Therefore the composite function f can be minimized using the don't-care condition $(\varphi[y/1] \wedge \varphi[y/0]) \vee (\neg\varphi[y/1] \wedge \neg\varphi[y/0])$.

Since universal quantification can be converted to existential quantification by the equality $\forall x.\varphi = \neg\exists x.\neg\varphi$, the compositional approach can be used in general quantifier elimination of quantified Boolean formulas (QBFs). The quantifiers of a QBF can be removed from inside out.

3.2 Interpolation of Composite Function

By Proposition 2, the composite function f can be obtained using symbolic methods. Finding a simple implementation of f under the don't-care flexibility hopefully makes $\varphi(\boldsymbol{x}, f(\boldsymbol{x}))$ simple and facilitates quantifier elimination. We exploit Craig interpolation for scalable computation. It relies on the following proposition, whose correctness is immediate by Theorem 1.

Proposition 3. *The interpolant with respect to*

$$\phi_A = \neg\varphi[y/0] \wedge \varphi[y/1] \quad and \tag{1}$$

$$\phi_B = \neg\varphi[y/1] \wedge \varphi[y/0] \tag{2}$$

is a valid implementation of a composite function f satisfying $\exists y.\varphi = \varphi[y/f]$.

Interpolation can be seen as a way to derive simple functions as long as the don't-care set is reasonably large. When the don't-care set is large, proving the unsatisfiability of $\phi_A \wedge \phi_B$ is easy and the corresponding refutation proof is simple. So the interpolant size (in term of AIG nodes) is likely to be small.

3.3   Analysis of Applicability

We compare expansion- and composition-based quantifier-elimination procedures assuming that AIGs are the underlying data structure. The AIG sizes of $\varphi[y/0] \vee \varphi[y/1]$ and $\varphi[y/f(\boldsymbol{x})]$ are analyzed.

The AIGs of $\varphi[y/0]$ and $\varphi[y/1]$ are obtained from φ through constant propagation. From practical experience, the sizes of $\varphi[y/0]$ and $\varphi[y/1]$ are rarely reduced much, especially for large AIGs. It is possible to apply aggressive minimization using don't cares. Specifically, in building $\varphi[y/0] \vee \varphi[y/1]$, $\varphi[y/0]$ can be used as the don't-care condition to minimize $\varphi[y/1]$, or vice versa (but simultaneous minimization of $\varphi[y/0]$ and $\varphi[y/1]$ is forbidden). For instance, in minimizing $\varphi[y/1]$ using don't-care condition $\varphi[y/0]$, the optimization is constrained by

$$\phi_A = \varphi[y/1] \wedge \neg\varphi[y/0] \text{ and} \tag{3}$$
$$\phi_B = \neg\varphi[y/1] \wedge \neg\varphi[y/0] \tag{4}$$

being the tightest onset and offset, respectively. Notice that interpolation or other symbolic techniques can be applied here to extract a function, say f', hopefully simpler than $\varphi[y/1]$. So $\varphi[y/0] \vee f'$ can be simpler than $\varphi[y/0] \vee \varphi[y/1]$ for quantifier elimination. (With interpolation, such simplification however was not empirically observed in our experiments. It may be due to the small size of the don't-care set, which results in ineffective interpolation.)[2]

Observe that Equations (1) and (3) are identical, whereas Equations (2) and (4) differ only in the second term. This slight difference in fact makes substantial impact on interpolation. When φ is a sparse function (with relatively few onset minterms), $\varphi[y/0]$ is very likely a sparse function as well. In this case, the offset corresponding to ϕ_B of Equation (2) is much smaller than that of Equation (4). Accordingly, proving the unsatisfiability of $\phi_A \wedge \phi_B$ of Equations (1) and (2) is easier to establish than that of Equations (3) and (4). The derived interpolant with respect to Equations (1) and (2) can be much smaller. On the contrary, for dense function φ the derived interpolant with respect to Equations (3) and (4) can be smaller.

The above sparsity condition commonly holds in practical applications. For instance, the transition relation built up from a set of transition functions of a sequential system appears to be sparse. In fact, the more the transition functions are, the sparser the transition relation is. Under this sparsity assumption, quantifier elimination using functional composition is superior to that using formula expansion.

By a qualitative comparison, expansion- and composition-based quantifier-elimination methods show different characteristics:

---

[2] Practical experience suggests that the size of an interpolant can be sensitive to the amount of don't cares. It was observed that, for a function f, the AIG size of the interpolant of $\phi_A = f$ and $\phi_B = \neg f$ (i.e., interpolation without don't cares) is typically much (e.g., two orders of magnitude) larger than that of f. Therefore, quantifier elimination of $\exists \boldsymbol{y}.\varphi(\boldsymbol{x}, \boldsymbol{y})$ by interpolating $\phi_A = \varphi(\boldsymbol{x}, \boldsymbol{y})$ and $\phi_B = \neg\exists \boldsymbol{y}.\varphi(\boldsymbol{x}, \boldsymbol{y})$ is ineffective.

Manipulation complexity. The former requires cofactoring and disjunction
operations; the latter requires interpolation (which invokes SAT solving)
and composition operations. In addition to the above operations, for both
methods AIG minimization also plays an important role in the entire quantification effort.

Circuit level. The circuit depth of a resultant AIG is shallower for the former
and deeper for the latter. On the other hand, the circuit width of a resultant
AIG is thicker for the former and thinner for the latter.

Circuit size. The AIG resulted from the former is often larger than that of
the latter in certain applications. This phenomenon can be related to the
sparsity assumption and due to the amount of achieved logic sharing.

3.4   Application to Circuit Optimization

In addition to quantifier elimination, a potential application of (the "if"-part of)
Theorem 2 is to reduce circuit levels. Consider a circuit C implementing some
function $f(X)$. Suppose t is an intermediate signal in the circuit with function
$g(X)$ and $f(X) = h(X, t) = h(X, g(X))$. If $g(X)$ satisfies Theorem 2, then the
circuit can be reexpressed by $h[t/0] \vee h[t/1]$, whose circuit level can be potentially
smaller than that of $h[t/g(X)]$.

4   Predicate Logic

We study quantifier elimination in predicate logic with the following principle.

Proposition 4. *Given a language $\mathcal{L}$ in predicate logic and a structure $\mathfrak{A}$, then*

$$\models_{\mathfrak{A}} \forall \boldsymbol{x}.(\exists y.\varphi(\boldsymbol{x}, y) = \exists F.\varphi(\boldsymbol{x}, F(\boldsymbol{x}))),$$

where φ is a formula, F is an n-place function symbol, and $\boldsymbol{x} = (x_1, \ldots, x_n)$ and
y are variable symbols of $\mathcal{L}$.

Proof. By the axiom of choice, such a function can be obtained by letting $f(a) = b$ for every a with some b satisfying $\varphi(a, b)$ or some arbitrary b if $\forall y.\neg\varphi(a, y)$. ∎

Note that the above proof characterizes the complete flexibility of the composite
function in predicate logic.

The equality of Proposition 4 suggests an equivalence-preserving transformation (with respect to some structure), and should be distinguished from the
satisfiability-preserving Skolemization [18] of

$$\forall \boldsymbol{x}, \exists y.\varphi(\boldsymbol{x}, y) \models = \mid \exists F, \forall \boldsymbol{x}.\varphi(\boldsymbol{x}, F\boldsymbol{x}).$$

Unlike propositional logic, the nice coincidence of terms, functions, predicates,
and formulas no longer holds in predicate logic. In fact all of them are distinct.
Terms are built up from constant symbols, variables, and function symbols. They
represent names of objects and should be distinguished from functions. Substituting terms for variables is legitimate, but substituting functions or formulas for

variables is not. Quantifier elimination through substitution is achievable only when a function can be conditionally expressed by a finite set of terms. Therefore quantifier elimination by exhaustive formula expansion does not work in predicate logic. Different from propositional logic, a function in predicate logic may not be always expressible with a single term, and sometimes not even finitely expressible. With these differences in mind, we generalize Theorem 2 in the context of predicate logic as Theorems 3 and 4.

Theorem 3. *Given a first-order language $\mathcal{L}$ and a structure $\mathfrak{A}$, if a formula $\exists y.\varphi(\boldsymbol{x}, y)$ is equivalent to*

$$\varphi[y_i/t_f] = \varphi(\boldsymbol{x}, t_f),$$

by substituting for y some term t_f (finitely expressible in the language) that represents $f(\boldsymbol{x})$ for some function $f : |\mathfrak{A}|^n \rightarrow |\mathfrak{A}|$, then $\varphi(a, b) \vee \neg\exists y.\varphi(a, y)$ is satisfied for any $a \in |\mathfrak{A}|^n, b \in |\mathfrak{A}|$ with $f(a) = b$.

Unlike the necessary and sufficient condition of Theorem 2, the converse of Theorem 3 is not true because in general the composite function f may not be finitely expressible in the language. For finitely expressible f, however, the converse holds by Theorem 4.

Theorem 4. *Given a formula $\varphi(\boldsymbol{x}, y)$ of some first-order language $\mathcal{L}$ and a structure $\mathfrak{A}$, if a function $f : |\mathfrak{A}|^n \rightarrow |\mathfrak{A}|$ with $f(a) = b$ satisfying $\varphi(a, b) \vee \neg\exists y.\varphi(a, y)$ is finitely expressible in the language with*

$$f = \begin{cases} f_1 & \text{if } \gamma_1 \\ \quad \vdots \\ f_m & \text{if } \gamma_m \end{cases}$$

such that each f_i can be expressed with some term t_{f_i}, where guard γ_i is the predicate defining the applicability of f_i over $|\mathfrak{A}|^n$, then the quantified formula $\exists y.\varphi(\boldsymbol{x}, y)$ is equivalent to

$$\bigvee_i \gamma_i \wedge \varphi(\boldsymbol{x}, t_{f_i}).$$

The above theorems can be applied for universal quantifier elimination by $\forall x.\varphi = \neg\exists x.\neg\varphi$, and thus work for nested quantifier elimination.

With the following examples, we illustrate the usefulness of the complete flexibility of a composite function to simplify quantifier elimination.

Example 1. Consider the first-order language $\mathcal{L}_G$ with equality, 1-place function symbol S, 2-place predicate symbol R. Let structure $\mathfrak{A} = (\{0, \ldots, 4\}; S$ (successor function modulo 5), $R = \{(0,0), (1,1), (2,2), (3,3), (0,1), (0,2), (1,3), (3,0), (4,1)\})$. The graph induced by the structure $\mathfrak{A}$ is shown in Figure 1, where every element of the universe $\{0, \ldots, 4\}$ is represented as a vertex, and every $(u, v) \in R$ is represented as a directed edge from u to v. Let φ be

$$\exists y.((y \neq x) \wedge R(x, y) \wedge R(y, y)).$$

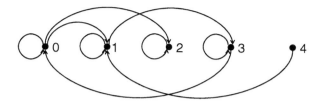

Fig. 1. Graph defined by the first-order language $\mathcal{L}_G$

Then the (x, y)-values satisfying $((y \neq x) \wedge R(x, y) \wedge R(y, y))$ have the property that vertex x connects to a different vertex y that has a self-loop. So (x, y)-values are as follows.

x	y
0	1, 2
1	3
2	∅
3	0
4	1

By Theorem 4, a solution function f can be as follows.

x	$f(x)$
0	2
1	3
2	4
3	0
4	1

In this case, f can be expressed in terms of S as $f(x) = S(S(x))$. So φ can be transformed into the equivalent quantifier-free formula

$$(S(S(x)) \neq x) \wedge R(x, S(S(x))) \wedge R(S(S(x)), S(S(x))).$$

Example 2. Consider the following formula φ in the language of number theory under structure $\mathfrak{N} = (\mathbb{N}; 0, S, S^{-1}, <, +, \cdot, E)$, where S^{-1} is the inverse of the successor function S with $S^{-1}(0) = 0$.

$$(S(0) < x) \wedge (x < y) \wedge (\forall a, \forall b.(y = a \cdot b \rightarrow (a = S(0) \vee b = S(0)))$$
$$\rightarrow \forall a, \forall b.(x = a \cdot b \rightarrow (a = S(0) \vee b = S(0))))$$

φ asserts that x is greater than 1, y is greater than x, and, if y is prime, then x is prime. By the property of Mersenne numbers, the quantification of $\exists y.\varphi$ can be eliminated by substituting $2^x - 1$, shorthand for $S^{-1}(S(S(0))Ex)$, for y in φ as

$$(S(0) < x) \wedge (x < (2^x - 1)) \wedge (\forall a, \forall b.((2^x - 1) = a \cdot b \rightarrow (a = S(0) \vee b = S(0)))$$
$$\rightarrow \forall a, \forall b.(x = a \cdot b \rightarrow (a = S(0) \vee b = S(0)))),$$

which can be further simplified to

$$(S(0) < x) \land (\forall a, \forall b.((2^x - 1) = a \cdot b \rightarrow (a = S(0) \lor b = S(0)))$$
$$\rightarrow \forall a, \forall b.(x = a \cdot b \rightarrow (a = S(0) \lor b = S(0)))).$$

Example 3. Consider the following first-order formula over real closed fields. (The notation and symbols are used in the conventional arithmetic sense.)

$$\exists x.(a \cdot x^2 + c = 0) \tag{5}$$

Let

$$f(a, c) = \begin{cases} \sqrt{-c/a} & \text{if } c/a < 0 \text{ or } c/a = 0 \\ 0 & \text{if } 0 < c/a \end{cases}.$$

(For $0 < c/a$, the value of $f(a, c)$ can be arbitrary and is set to 0.) Quantifier elimination by substituting $f(a, c)$ for x in Equation (5) yields

$$((c/a < 0 \lor c/a = 0) \land a \cdot (\sqrt{-c/a})^2 + c = 0) \lor (0 < c/a \land a \cdot 0^2 + c = 0),$$

which can be simplified to $c/a < 0 \lor c/a = 0$. Alternatively, let

$$f(a, c) = \sqrt{\sqrt{(-c/a)^2}}.$$

The corresponding quantifier-free formula becomes

$$a \cdot \left(\sqrt{\sqrt{(-c/a)^2}} \right)^2 + c = 0.$$

As this paper focuses on the characterization of the complete flexibility of a composite function, how to effectively exploit such flexibility in simplifying quantifier elimination in predicate logic remains an open problem. In fact interpolation is not directly extensible to generate composite functions due to the difference between formulas and functions in predicate logic.

5   Experimental Results

The proposed compositional approach to quantifier elimination was implemented in the ABC package [1]; the experiments were conducted on a Linux machine with Xeon 3.4GHz CPU and 6Gb RAM.

We showed the effectiveness of quantifier elimination by constructing the transition relations of circuits taken from ISCAS and ITC benchmark suites. In the transition relation of a circuit, its primary-input variables were existentially quantified.

Despite recent advances in AIG packages, it was observed that AIG minimization may not be effective when AIG sizes reach tens of thousands of nodes. Hence it is beneficial to perform AIG minimization whenever possible before the sizes get too large to be reduced. So in the experiments AIGs were constantly minimized throughout the computation. Specifically, for expansion-based quantification, minimization was applied after the disjunction of two cofactored circuits; for composition-based quantification, minimization was applied before circuit-to-CNF conversion for SAT solving, at interpolant simplification, and after functional composition.[3]

As quantification scheduling is crucial to the scalability of quantifier elimination, we adopted a simple strategy: By imposing a postponement threshold (the percentage of AIG-size increase due to quantification), variables whose corresponding quantifications result in substantial increase in AIG sizes (exceeding the postponement threshold) are deferred. This threshold is lifted gradually in the iterative computation until all quantifiers are eliminated. In the following experiments, the threshold starts at and increases by 10%. The same scheduling strategy is applied for both expansion- and composition-based quantifications.

Table 1 compares the two quantification methods based on formula expansion (denoted QE-EXP) and functional composition (denoted QE-CMP), where an entry with "—" indicates data unavailable due to time-out at the limit of 90000 seconds. The smaller number of every corresponding pair of AIG sizes (circuit depths) between QE-EXP and QE-CMP is highlighted in bold. The ratio shown in the table is calculated under the exclusion of the 5 unsolvable circuits of QE-EXP.

As can be seen from Columns 5 and 9 of Table 1, QE-CMP is much more scalable than QE-EXP. The AIG sizes of QE-CMP after quantification are typically much smaller than or comparable to those of QE-EXP. Apart from the 5 unsolvable circuits of QE-EXP, s991 is an extreme, where the final AIG size of QE-CMP is 3 orders of magnitude smaller than that of QE-EXP. On the other hand, circuit s1196 is an exception, where the result of QE-CMP is 6 times larger than that of QE-EXP due to the failure to derive reasonable-sized interpolants. Despite the effectiveness of QE-CMP, there are still cases b14, ..., b22 of the ITC benchmark circuits (not shown in Table 1) unsolvable by either of QE-EXP and QE-CMP. In these cases, the unsatisfiability of $\phi_A \wedge \phi_B$ is hard to establish. Even if an interpolation succeeds, the corresponding interpolant is too large to be useful. Further breakthroughs are needed to overcome these limitations.

In addition to circuit sizes, we examine the effects of QE-EXP and QE-CMP on circuit depths. Columns 6 and 10 of Table 1 show the characteristics of both methods. Compared to Column 4, the transition relations before quantifier elimination, QE-EXP yielded circuits with comparable logic levels as shown in Column 6, whereas QE-CMP produced circuits with many more logic levels as shown in Column 10. QE-EXP (respectively QE-CMP) can be seen in a sense as quantification with restricted (respectively unrestricted) increase in logic levels. QE-EXP and QE-CMP are analogous to two-level and multi-level logic minimization, respectively. QE-CMP therefore can potentially achieve more logic sharing and generate smaller circuits. Since logic-level increase is not immaterial

---

[3] A synthesis script of commands `ifraig`, `rewrite`, `refactor`, `balance`, `rewrite`, `refactor`, `balance` of ABC was applied for AIG minimization.

Table 1. Quantifier elimination with formula expansion and functional composition

circuit	(#in, #reg, #n, #l)	rel before QE		QE-Exp				QE-Cmp			
		#n	#l	#n	#l	time	mem	#n	#l	time	mem
prolog	(36, 136, 1656, 26)	1474	29	—	—	—	—	**1088**	**31**	6.27	38.0
s1196	(14, 18, 529, 24)	548	22	**3473**	**21**	5.15	37.3	21881	2532	123.15	37.3
s1269	(18, 37, 569, 35)	622	37	31005	39	59.24	37.5	**1694**	**116**	41.05	37.5
s13207.1	(62, 638, 8027, 59)	5272	45	—	—	—	—	**4741**	**44**	50.60	40.6
s1423	(17, 74, 657, 59)	757	63	17619	59	25.45	38.1	**3142**	**452**	6.19	38.1
s1488	(8, 6, 653, 17)	686	19	1269	21	2.90	38.1	**515**	**48**	3.82	38.1
s1494	(8, 6, 647, 17)	696	20	1261	21	2.98	38.1	**607**	**42**	2.54	38.1
s1512	(29, 57, 780, 30)	697	28	1187	24	2.64	37.7	**823**	**53**	3.78	37.7
s15850.1	(77, 534, 9786, 82)	5679	57	—	—	—	—	**180597**	**14247**	49409.27	427.4
s208.1	(10, 8, 104, 11)	103	14	65	**11**	0.08	37.4	**49**	12	0.06	37.4
s298	(3, 14, 119, 9)	157	15	**117**	**12**	0.08	37.4	122	**12**	0.23	37.4
s3271	(26, 116, 1573, 28)	1565	32	**1549**	**29**	3.08	38.0	1604	62	7.11	38.0
s3330	(40, 132, 1789, 29)	1434	29	—	—	—	—	**1029**	**28**	6.37	38.0
s3384	(43, 183, 1702, 60)	1801	63	1307	58	6.94	38.3	**1276**	**58**	17.29	38.3
s344	(9, 15, 160, 20)	164	19	**140**	**19**	0.33	37.1	155	**19**	0.81	37.1
s349	(9, 15, 161, 20)	168	19	**140**	**19**	0.26	37.5	155	**19**	0.82	37.5
s382	(3, 21, 158, 9)	220	19	**179**	**16**	0.10	37.7	189	**16**	0.27	37.7
s38417	(28, 1636, 22397, 47)	15762	44	**15705**	**40**	44.79	48.7	18865	106	149.13	46.8
s38584.1	(38, 1426, 19407, 56)	18094	48	57105	45	1382.97	71.4	**38089**	**1362**	268.94	46.0
s386	(7, 6, 159, 11)	189	15	217	16	0.62	37.8	**166**	**25**	0.48	37.8
s400	(3, 21, 162, 9)	228	20	**180**	**16**	0.13	37.7	190	**16**	0.27	37.7
s420.1	(18, 16, 218, 13)	223	17	137	19	0.03	37.4	**105**	**20**	0.05	37.4
s444	(3, 21, 181, 11)	234	19	**179**	**16**	0.09	37.6	191	**16**	0.24	37.6
s499	(1, 22, 152, 12)	274	25	**299**	**17**	0.10	37.4	368	31	0.22	37.4
s510	(19, 6, 211, 12)	236	16	431	21	1.08	37.7	**177**	**13**	1.49	37.7
s526	(3, 21, 193, 9)	284	16	**188**	17	0.09	37.6	210	**14**	0.27	37.6
s5378	(35, 164, 2779, 25)	1995	25	957759	43	63744.28	49.1	**37072**	**2602**	415.18	38.5
s635	(2, 32, 286, 127)	317	42	312	**35**	0.21	37.6	**280**	42	0.28	37.6
s641	(35, 19, 379, 74)	221	30	1202	**18**	4.5	37.5	**277**	27	5.82	37.5
s6669	(83, 239, 3148, 93)	3218	90	—	—	—	—	**2428**	**79**	68.58	39.0
s713	(35, 19, 393, 74)	235	30	1060	**18**	5.36	37.5	**324**	39	3.88	37.5
s820	(18, 5, 289, 10)	364	19	1821	19	3.71	37.9	**460**	49	2.85	37.9
s832	(18, 5, 287, 10)	374	19	1579	20	3.25	37.9	**419**	**37**	2.77	37.9
s838.1	(34, 32, 446, 17)	463	22	281	35	0.04	37.7	**217**	**36**	0.08	37.7
s9234.1	(36, 211, 5597, 58)	2790	44	109835	45	955.24	39.2	**18898**	**653**	119.83	39.2
s938	(34, 32, 446, 17)	463	22	281	35	0.10	37.4	**217**	**36**	0.08	37.4
s967	(16, 29, 394, 14)	483	20	9020	**27**	13.05	37.3	**2159**	244	12.58	37.3
s991	(65, 19, 519, 59)	372	46	3227475	41	32425.76	90.7	**1287**	**124**	33.57	37.8
sbc	(41, 27, 1023, 22)	764	21	39023	31	72.07	38.0	**2300**	213	21.41	38.0
b01	(2, 5, 42, 6)	59	11	**61**	**11**	0.23	37.2	75	19	0.26	37.2
b02	(1, 4, 23, 5)	36	9	**40**	**9**	0.02	37.3	**40**	12	0.07	37.3
b03	(4, 30, 127, 10)	247	17	247	**16**	0.14	37.6	**239**	**16**	0.34	37.6
b04	(11, 66, 660, 28)	809	32	33633	46	50.24	38.2	**5271**	302	9.83	38.2
b05	(1, 34, 963, 55)	965	39	552	37	0.06	38.1	**512**	**35**	0.13	38.1
b06	(2, 9, 46, 5)	77	10	**80**	**9**	0.11	37.4	92	17	0.29	37.4
b07	(1, 49, 391, 31)	560	35	661	28	0.14	37.6	**566**	**27**	0.13	37.6
b08	(9, 21, 153, 16)	238	27	212	18	0.29	37.7	**205**	**18**	0.77	37.7
b09	(1, 28, 141, 9)	247	19	**237**	17	0.03	37.6	**237**	17	0.08	37.6
b10	(11, 17, 178, 12)	247	17	1510	26	2.12	37.6	**353**	26	1.23	37.6
b11	(7, 31, 732, 34)	734	35	618	**25**	0.50	37.9	**590**	**25**	0.96	37.9
b12	(5, 121, 952, 19)	1485	26	**1740**	**24**	0.65	38.3	1908	41	2.21	38.3
b13	(10, 53, 299, 20)	472	20	435	**16**	0.49	37.6	**423**	**16**	1.15	37.6
ratio				1.000	1.000	1.000	1.000	0.036	8.064	0.013	0.952

"#in": number of primary inputs; "#reg": number of registers; "#n": number of AIG nodes; "#l": AIG circuit depth; "time": CPU time (sec); "mem": memory (Mb)

in every application, in this case heavy logic synthesis, e.g., with collapse operation, can be adopted to reduce logic levels. On the other hand, these extreme characteristics about logic levels might hint at the potential reduction power of the proposed optimization method discussed in Section 3.4.

The proposed method can be easily integrated into the framework of unbounded model checking as suggested in [17]. Our preliminary experiments on reachability analysis suggested that sparsity is an important factor for QE-CMP to be effective. Without taking advantage of sparsity in reachability analysis, QE-CMP may not be as good as QE-EXP. How to enforce sparsity in reachability analysis using QE-CMP remains to be done.

6   Prior Work

Propositional logic. There have been intensive efforts on BDD-based image computation based on the principle of formula expansion, e.g., [22], and efforts on SAT-based computation with solution enumeration, e.g., [7]. The closest to ours, however, is AIG-based formula expansion [17].

This paper proposes a compositional approach to quantifier elimination. The complete flexibility of the composite function is characterized. Although symbolic techniques, such as BDDs, can be applied, we use SAT solving and Craig interpolation for scalable derivation of the composite function.

Craig interpolation was adopted in [16] to approximate image computation and in [8] to approximate transition relation. This paper uses interpolation to compute exact image and exact transition relation.

Under the virtual substitution principle of [23], quantifier elimination by formula expansion can be considered as virtual substitution with two terms [19]; quantifier elimination by functional composition can be considered as virtual substitution with a single term.

Predicate logic. When generalized to predicate logic, our composite function is similar to the Skolem function [18] with the following differences: Firstly, the former is used for quantifier elimination with term substitution, whereas the latter is used to rewrite formulas in Skolem normal form using Skolem function symbols. Secondly, quantifier elimination with composite functions is structure-specific (i.e., with respect to some structure/interpretation), whereas normal form conversion with Skolem functions is structure-independent (i.e., universal to all structures/interpretations). Thirdly, quantifier elimination with composite functions is equivalence preserving, whereas normal form conversion with Skolem functions is only satisfiability preserving.

Under predicate logic, our quantifier elimination is similar to virtual substitution [23] with the following differences: In virtual substitution, a finite elimination set of terms is identified for quantifier elimination. The notion of composite functions is not explicit in [23]. Our emphasis, on the other hand, is on the characterization of the complete flexibility of composite functions. In eliminating a quantified variable, a single composite function is characterized, rather than a set of terms of the underlying language. We do not address how to represent a composite function by terms, but suggest the usefulness of flexibility in reducing elimination sets.

7   Conclusions and Future Work

We have presented a compositional approach to quantifier elimination. The complete flexibility of composite functions was characterized; Craig interpolation was exploited for effective computation. Experiments showed promising results on extending the capacity of quantifier elimination when the sparsity assumption holds. For first-order logic, our results may shed light on elimination-set minimization as motivated by the examples of Section 4.

As this paper just showed the first step, much work remains to be done. The effectiveness of our method on unbounded model checking and on circuit optimization suggested in Section 3.4 needs further investigation. Quantification scheduling under the new compositional approach awaits improvement. Moreover, a hybrid approach to quantifier elimination by combining the expansion- and composition-based methods may be pursued to keep both AIG sizes and depths small. We anticipate applications of the new quantification method in scalable logic synthesis, where Craig interpolation is evidently gaining importance [10,9,11,12].

Acknowledgments

This work was supported in part by NSC grants 95-2218-E-002-064-MY3 and 96-2221-E-002-278-MY3.

References

1. Berkeley Logic Synthesis and Verification Group. ABC: A System for Sequential Synthesis and Verification (2005), http://www.eecs.berkeley.edu/~alanmi/abc/
2. Caviness, B.F., Johnson, J.R. (eds.): Quantifier Elimination and Cylindrical Algebraic Decomposition. Springer, Heidelberg (1998)
3. Coudert, O., Madre, J.C.: A unified framework for the formal verification of sequential circuits. In: Proc. Int'l. Conf. Computer-Aided Design, pp. 126–129 (1990)
4. Collins, G.E.: Quantifier elimination for real closed fields by cylindrical algebraic decomposition. In: Brakhage, H. (ed.) GI-Fachtagung 1975. LNCS, vol. 33, pp. 134–183. Springer, Heidelberg (1975)
5. Craig, W.: Linear reasoning: A new form of the Herbrand-Gentzen theorem. J. Symbolic Logic 22(3), 250–268 (1957)
6. Enderton, H.B.: A Mathematical Introduction to Logic, 2nd edn. Academic Press, London (2000)
7. Ganai, M., Gupta, A., Ashar, P.: Efficient SAT-based unbounded symbolic model checking using circuit cofactoring. In: Proc. Int'l. Conf. Computer-Aided Design, pp. 510–517 (2004)
8. Jhala, R., McMillan, K.: Interpolant-based transition relation approximation. In: Etessami, K., Rajamani, S.K. (eds.) CAV 2005. LNCS, vol. 3576, pp. 39–51. Springer, Heidelberg (2005)
9. Lee, R.-R., Jiang, J.-H.R., Hung, W.-L.: Bi-decomposing large Boolean functions via interpolation and satisfiability solving. In: Proc. Design Automation Conf., pp. 636–641 (2008)
10. Lee, C.-C., Jiang, J.-H.R., Huang, C.-Y., Mishchenko, A.: Scalable exploration of functional dependency by interpolation and incremental SAT solving. In: Proc. Int'l. Conf. on Computer-Aided Design, pp. 227–233 (2007)

11. Lin, H.-P., Jiang, J.-H.R., Lee, R.-R.: To SAT or not to SAT: Ashenhurst decomposition in a large scale. In: Proc. Int'l. Conf. Computer-Aided Design, pp. 32–37 (2008)
12. Mishchenko, A., Brayton, R.K., Jiang, J.-H.R., Jang, S.: Scalable don't-care-based logic optimization and resynthesis. In: Proc. Int'l. Symp. on Field Programmable Gate Arrays, pp. 151–160 (2009)
13. Mishchenko, A., Chatterjee, S., Brayton, R.K.: DAG-aware AIG rewriting: A fresh look at combinational logic synthesis. In: Proc. Design Automation Conference, pp. 532–536 (2006)
14. Mishchenko, A., Chatterjee, S., Jiang, J.-H.R., Brayton, R.K.: FRAIGs: A unifying representation for logic synthesis and verification. Technical Report, EECS Dept., UC Berkeley (2005)
15. McMillan, K.: Applying SAT methods in unbounded symbolic model checking. In: Brinksma, E., Larsen, K.G. (eds.) CAV 2002. LNCS, vol. 2404, pp. 250–264. Springer, Heidelberg (2002)
16. McMillan, K.: Interpolation and SAT-based model checking. In: Hunt Jr., W.A., Somenzi, F. (eds.) CAV 2003. LNCS, vol. 2725, pp. 1–13. Springer, Heidelberg (2003)
17. Pigorsch, F., Scholl, C., Disch, S.: Advanced unbounded model checking based on AIGs, BDD sweeping, and quantifier scheduling. In: Proc. Formal Methods on Computer Aided Design, pp. 89–96 (2006)
18. Skolem, T.: Uber die mathematische Logik. Norsk. Mat. Tidsk. 10, 125–142 (1928); Translation in From Frege to Gödel, A Source Book in Mathematical Logic, J. van Heijenoort. Harvard Univ. Press (1967)
19. Seidl, A., Sturm, T.: Boolean quantification in a first-order context. In: Proc. Int'l. Workshop on Computer Algebra in Scientific Computing, pp. 329–345 (2003)
20. Sturm, T.: New domains for applied quantifier elimination. In: Proc. Int'l. Workshop on Computer Algebra in Scientific Computing, pp. 295–301 (2006)
21. Tarski, A.: A Decision Method for Elementary Algebra and Geometry. University of California Press, Berkeley (1951)
22. Touati, H., Savoj, H., Lin, B., Brayton, R.K., Sangiovanni-Vincentelli, A.: Implicit enumeration of finite state machines using BDDs. In: Proc. Int'l. Conf. on Computer-Aided Design, pp. 130–133 (1990)
23. Weispfenning, V.: The complexity of linear problems in fields. Journal of Symbolic Computation 5, 3–27 (1988)

Monotonic Partial Order Reduction: An Optimal Symbolic Partial Order Reduction Technique

Vineet Kahlon, Chao Wang, and Aarti Gupta

NEC Laboratories America
4 Independence Way, Princeton, NJ 08540, USA

Abstract. We present a new technique called *Monotonic Partial Order Reduction (MPOR)* that effectively combines dynamic partial order reduction with symbolic state space exploration for model checking concurrent software. Our technique hinges on a new characterization of partial orders defined by computations of a concurrent program in terms of *quasi-monotonic sequences* of thread-ids. This characterization, which is of independent interest, can be used both for explicit or symbolic model checking. For symbolic model checking, MPOR works by adding constraints to allow automatic pruning of redundant interleavings in a SAT/SMT solver based search by restricting the interleavings explored to the set of quasi-monotonic sequences. Quasi-monotonicity guarantees both soundness (all necessary interleavings are explored) and optimality (no redundant interleaving is explored) and is, to the best of our knowledge, the only known optimal symbolic POR technique.

1 Introduction

Verification of concurrent programs is a hard problem. A key reason for this is the behavioral complexity resulting from the large number of interleavings of transitions of different threads. In explicit-state model checking, partial order reduction (POR) techniques [6, 14, 16] have, therefore, been developed to exploit the equivalence of interleavings of independent transitions in order to reduce the search space. Since computing the precise dependency relation between transitions may be as hard as the verification problem itself, existing POR methods often use a conservative statically computed approximation. Dynamic [5] and Cartesian [9] partial order reduction obviate the need to apply static analysis *a priori* by detecting collisions (data dependencies) on-the-fly. These methods can, in general, achieve better reduction due to more accurate collision detection. However, applying these POR methods (which were designed for explicit state space search) to symbolic model checking is a non-trivial task.

A major strength of symbolic state space exploration methods [2] is that *property dependent* and *data dependent* search space reduction is automatically exploited inside modern SAT or SMT (Satisfiability Modulo Theory) solvers, through the addition of conflict clauses and non-chronological backtracking [15]. Symbolic methods are often more efficient in reasoning about variables with large domains. However, combining classic POR methods (e.g., those based on persistent-sets [7]) with symbolic algorithms has proven to be difficult [1, 3, 8, 10, 12]. The difficulty arises from the fact that symbolic methods implicitly manipulate large *sets of states* as opposed to manipulating

A. Bouajjani and O. Maler (Eds.): CAV 2009, LNCS 5643, pp. 398–413, 2009.

states individually. Capturing and exploiting transitions that are dynamically independent with respect to a *set of states* is much harder than for individual states.

Consider the example program from [17] shown in Fig. 1 comprised of two concurrent threads accessing a global array $a[\,]$. It is hard to determine statically whether transitions t_A, t_B in thread T_1 are dependent with t_α, t_β in T_2. Similarly, without knowing the points-to locations of p and q, we cannot decide whether t_C and t_γ are dependent or not. This renders POR methods relying on a static computation of conflicts non-optimal. Indeed, when $i \neq j$ holds in some executions, t_A, t_B and t_α, t_β become independent, meaning that the two sequences $t_A; t_B; t_\alpha; t_\beta; t_C; t_\gamma$; and $t_\alpha; t_\beta; t_A; t_B; t_C; t_\gamma$; are equivalent. However, none of the existing symbolic partial order reduction methods [1, 3, 8, 10, 12] takes advantage of such information. Among explicit-state POR methods, dynamic partial order reduction [5] and Cartesian partial order reduction [9] are able to achieve some reduction by detecting conflicts on-the-fly; in any individual state s, the values of i and j (as well as p and q) are fully determined, allowing us to detect conflicts accurately. However, it is not clear how to directly apply these techniques to symbolic model checking, where conflict detection is performed with respect to a set of states. Missing out on these kind of partial-order reductions can be costly since the symbolic model checker needs to exhaustively search among the reduced set of execution sequences.

T_1		T_2	
i = foo() ;		j = bar() ;	
...		...	
A	a[i] = 10 ;	α	a[j] = 50 ;
B	a[i] = a[i]+20;	β	a[j] = a[j]+100;
C	*p = a[j] ;	γ	*q = a[i] ;

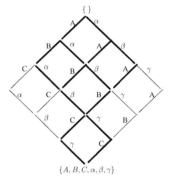

Fig. 1. t_A, t_B are independent with t_α, t_β when $i \neq j$; t_C is independent with t_γ when $(i \neq j) \wedge (p \neq q)$

Fig. 2. The lattice of interleavings

Recently, a new technique called Peephole Partial Order Reduction (PPOR) [17] has been proposed that allows partial order reduction to be integrated with symbolic state space exploration techniques. The key idea behind PPOR is to place constraints on which processes can be scheduled to execute in the next two steps starting at each global state. If in a global state, transitions tr and tr' such that $tid(tr) < tid(tr')$, where tid denotes thread-id, are enabled and independent then tr' cannot execute immediately before tr. It was shown that PPOR is optimal for programs with two threads but non-optimal for programs with more than two. The reason is that in order to achieve optimality for programs with more than two threads, we might need to track dependency chains involving many processes. These chains, which could be spread out over an entire computation, are hard to capture via local scheduling constraints.

We present a new technique called *Monotonic Partial Order Reduction (MPOR)* that exploits a new characterization of partial orders defined by computations of a given concurrent program in terms of *quasi-monotonic sequences* of thread-ids. This characterization, which is of independent interest, can be used both for explicit or symbolic model checking. In this paper, we show that restricting the interleavings explored to the set of quasi-monotonic sequences guarantees both soundness (all necessary interleavings are explored) and optimality (no redundant interleaving is explored). This is accomplished by proving that for each computation there exists a quasi-monotonic sequence that is Mazurkiewicz equivalent[1] [13] to it, and that no two quasi-monotonic sequences can be Mazurkiewicz equivalent. The key intuition behind quasi-monotonicity is that if all transitions enabled at a global state are independent then we need to explore just one interleaving. We choose this interleaving to be the one in which transitions are executed in increasing (monotonic) order of their thread-ids. If, however, some of the transitions enabled at a global state are dependent than we need to explore interleavings that may violate this *natural* monotonic order. In that case, we allow an out-of-order-execution, viz., a transition tr with larger thread-id than that of transition tr' to execute before tr' only if there exists a *dependency chain* from tr to tr', i.e., a sequence of transitions from tr to tr' wherein adjacent transitions are pairwise dependent. Such sequences are called quasi-monotonic.

Note that although our monotonic POR method has the same goal as classic POR methods [6, 14, 16, 5, 9], it does not correspond directly to any existing method. In particular, it is not a symbolic implementation of any of these explicit-state methods. Importantly, our method is optimal for programs with arbitrarily many threads, which, to the best of our knowledge, is not guaranteed by any of the existing symbolic POR techniques [1, 12, 8, 3, 10, 17]. Finally, the proposed encoding scheme is well suited for symbolic search using SAT/SMT solvers.

To summarize, our main contributions are: (1) the notion of quasi-monotonic sequences, which isolates a unique representative for each partial order resulting from the computations of the given program; (2) a new partial order reduction that adds constraints to ensure quasi-monotonicity, along with a symbolic formulation; and (3) the guarantee of removal of all redundant interleavings for programs with an arbitrary number of threads.

2   Classical Partial Order Reduction

We start by reviewing standard notions from classical partial order reduction (POR) [11, 7]. Let T_i ($1 \leq i \leq N$) be a thread with the set $trans_i$ of transitions. Let $trans = \bigcup_{i=1}^{N} trans_i$ be the set of all transitions. Let V_i be the set of local variables of thread T_i, and V_{global} the set of global variables of the given concurrent program. For $t_1 \in trans_i$, we denote the thread-id, i.e., i, by $tid(t_1)$, and denote the enabling condition by en_{t_1}. If t_1 is a transition in T_i from control locations loc_1 to loc_2 and is guarded by $cond$, then en_{t_1} is defined as $(pc_i = loc_1) \wedge cond$. Here $pc_i \in V_i$ is a special variable representing

---

[1] Intuitively, two computations x and y are said to be Mazurkiewicz equivalent if x can be obtained from y by repeatedly permuting adjacent pairs of independent transitions, and vice versa.

the thread program counter. Let S be the set of global states of the given program. A state $s \in S$ is a valuation of all local and global variables. For two states $s, s' \in S$, $s \xrightarrow{t_1} s'$ denotes a state transition by applying t_1, and $s \xrightarrow{t_i \ldots t_j} s'$ denotes a sequence of state transitions.

2.1 Independence Relation

Partial-order reduction exploits the fact that computations of concurrent programs are partial orders on operations of threads on communication objects. Thus instead of exploring all interleavings that realize these partial orders it suffices to explore just a few (ideally just one for each partial order). Interleavings which are equivalent, i.e., realize the same partial order, are characterized using the notion of an independence relation over the transitions of threads constituting the given concurrent program.

Definition 1 (Independence Relation [11, 7]). *$R \subseteq trans \times trans$ is an independence relation iff for each $\langle t_1, t_2 \rangle \in R$ the following two properties hold for all $s \in S$:*

1. *if t_1 is enabled in s and $s \xrightarrow{t_1} s'$, then t_2 is enabled in s iff t_2 is enabled in s'; and*
2. *if t_1, t_2 are enabled in s, there is a unique state s' such that $s \xrightarrow{t_1 t_2} s'$ and $s \xrightarrow{t_2 t_1} s'$.*

In other words, independent transitions can neither disable nor enable each other, and enabled independent transitions commute. As pointed out in [6], this definition has been mainly of semantic use, since it is not practical to check the above two properties for all states to determine which transitions are independent. Instead, traditional collision detection, i.e., identification of dependent transitions, often uses conservative but easy-to-check sufficient conditions. These checks, which are typically carried out statically, over-approximate the collisions leading to exploration of more interleavings than are necessary. Consider, for example, the transitions $t_1 : a[i] = e_1$ and $t_2 : a[j] = e_2$. When $i \neq j$, t_1 and t_2 are independent. However since it is hard to determine statically whether $a[i]$ and $a[j]$ refer to the same array element, t_1 and t_2 are considered (statically) dependent irrespective of the values of i and j. This results in the exploration of more interleavings than are necessary. Such techniques are therefore not guaranteed to be optimal.

In the *conditional* dependence relation [11, 7], which is a refinement of the dependence relation, two transitions are defined as independent with respect to a state $s \in S$ (as opposed to for all states $s \in S$). This extension is geared towards explicit-state model checking, in which persistent sets are computed for individual states. A persistent set at state s is a subset of the enabled transitions that need to be explored from s. A transition is added to the persistent set if it may conflict with a future operation of another thread. The main difficulty in persistent set computation lies in detecting future collisions with enough precision due to which these classic definitions of independence are not well suited for symbolic search.

3 Optimal Partial Order Reduction

We formulate a new characterization of partial order reduction in terms of quasi monotonic sequences that is easy to incorporate in both explicit and symbolic methods for

```
T1 () {                    T2 () {                    T3 () {
    c1:  sh = 1;               c2:  sh = sh';             c3:  sh'  = 2;
}                          }                          }
```

Fig. 3. An Example Program

state space search. To motivate our technique, we consider a simple concurrent program P comprised of three threads T_1, T_2 and T_3 shown in figure 3. Suppose that, to start with P is in the global state (c_1, c_2, c_3) with thread T_i at location c_i (for simplicity, we show only the control locations and not the values of the variables in each global state). Our goal is to add constraints on-the-fly during model checking that restrict the set of interleavings explored in a way such that all necessary interleavings are explored and no two interleavings explored are Mazurkiewicz equivalent. Let t_i denote the program statement at location c_i of thread T_i, respectively. In the global state $s = (c_1, c_2, c_3)$, we see that transitions t_1 and t_2 are dependent as are t_2 and t_3. However, t_1 and t_3 are independent with each other. Since t_1 and t_2 are dependent with each other, we need to explore interleavings wherein t_1 is executed before t_2, and vice versa.

For convenience, given transitions t and t' executed along a computation x of the given program, we write $t <_x t'$ to denote that t is executed before t' along x. Note that the same thread statement (say within a program loop) may be executed multiple times along a computation. Each execution is considered a different transition. Then, using the new notation, we can rephrase the scheduling constraints imposed by dependent transitions as follows: since t_1 and t_2 are dependent transitions, we need to explore interleavings along which $t_1 < t_2$ and those along which $t_2 < t_1$. Similarly, we need to explore interleavings along which $t_2 < t_3$, and vice versa. However, since t_1 and t_3 are independent we need to avoid exploring both relative orderings of these transitions wherever possible.

Let the thread-id of transition tr executed by thread T_i, denoted by $tid(tr)$, be i. In general, one would expect that for independent transitions tr and tr' we need not explore interleavings along which $tr < tr'$ as well as those along which $tr' < tr$ and it suffices to pick one relative order, say, $tr < tr'$, where $tid(tr) < tid(tr')$, i.e., force pairwise independent transitions to execute in increasing order of their thread-ids. However, going back to our example, we see that the transitivity of '$<$', might result in ordering constraints on the independent transitions t_1 and t_3 that force us to explore both relative orderings of the two transitions. Indeed, the ordering constraints $t_3 < t_2$ and $t_2 < t_1$ imply that $t_3 < t_1$. On the other hand, the constraints $t_1 < t_2$ and $t_2 < t_3$ imply that $t_1 < t_3$. Looking at the constraints $t_3 < t_2$ and $t_2 < t_1$ from another perspective, we see that t_3 needs to be executed before t_1 because there is a sequence of transitions from t_3 to t_1 (in this case t_3, t_2, t_1) wherein adjacent transitions are pairwise dependent. Thus given a pair of independent transitions tr and tr' such that $tid(tr) < tid(tr')$, a modification to the previous strategy would be to explore an interleaving wherein $tr' < tr$ only if there is a sequence of transitions from tr' to tr wherein adjacent transitions are pairwise dependent, i.e., force independent transitions to execute in increasing order of their thread-ids as long as there are no dependency constraints arising from the transitivity of '$<$' that force an *out-of-order* execution.

This strategy, however, might lead to unsatisfiable scheduling constraints. To see that we consider a new example program with a global state (c_1, c_2, c_3, c_4), where for each i, local transition t_i of T_i is enabled. Suppose that t_1 are t_4 dependent only with each other, as are t_2 and t_3. Consider the set of interleavings satisfying $t_4 < t_1$ and $t_3 < t_2$. Using the facts that (i) $tid(t_1) < tid(t_3)$, and (ii) there cannot be a sequence of transitions leading from t_3 to t_1 wherein adjacent transitions are pairwise dependent, by the above strategy we would execute t_1 before t_3 leading to the interleaving t_4, t_1, t_3, t_2. However, since t_2 and t_4 are independent, and there is no sequence of transitions from t_4 to t_2 wherein adjacent transitions are pairwise dependent, t_2 must be executed before t_4. This rules out the above interleaving. Using a similar reasoning, one can show that the above strategy will, in fact, rule out all interleavings where $t_4 < t_1$ and $t_3 < t_2$. Essentially, this happens because thread-ids of processes in groups of dependent transitions have opposing orders. In our case, the groups t_1, t_4 and t_2, t_3 of mutually dependent transitions are such that $tid(t_1) < tid(t_2)$ but $tid(t_4) > tid(t_3)$.

Our strategy to handle the above problem, is to start scheduling the transitions in increasing order of their thread-ids while taking into account the scheduling constraints imposed by the dependencies. Thus in the above example, suppose that we want to explore interleavings satisfying $t_4 < t_1$ and $t_3 < t_2$. Then we start by first trying to schedule t_1. However, since $t_4 < t_1$, we have to schedule t_4 before t_1. Moreover, since there are no scheduling restrictions (even via transitivity) on t_2 and t_3, vis-a-vis t_1 and t_4, and since $tid(t_2) > tid(t_1)$ and $tid(t_3) > tid(t_1)$, we schedule both t_2 and t_3 to execute after t_1. Thus we constrain all interleavings satisfying $t_4 < t_1$ and $t_3 < t_2$ to start with the sequence t_4, t_1. Next we try to schedule the transition with the lowest thread-id that has not yet been scheduled, i.e., t_2. However, since $t_3 < t_2$, we must schedule t_3 first and then t_2 resulting in the unique interleaving $t_4 t_1 t_3 t_2$.

In general, for independent transitions t and t', where $tid(t) < tid(t')$, we allow t' to be executed before t only if there is a sequence of transitions $t_0, t_1, ..., t_k$, wherein $t_0 = t'$, each pair of adjacent transitions is dependent, and either $t_k = t$ or $tid(t_k) < tid(t)$. This leads to the key concept of a *dependency chain*.

Definition 2 (Dependency Chain). *Let t and t' be transitions executed along a computation x such that $t <_x t'$. A dependency chain along x starting at t is a (sub-)sequence of transitions $tr_{i_0}, ..., tr_{i_k}$ executed along x, where (a) $i_0 < i_1 < ... < i_k$, (b) for each $j \in [0..k-1]$, tr_{i_j} is dependent with $tr_{i_{j+1}}$, and (c) there does not exist a transition executed along x between tr_{i_j} and $tr_{i_{j+1}}$ that is dependent with tr_{i_j}.*

We use $t \Rightarrow_x t'$ to denote the fact that there is a dependency chain from t to t' along x. Then our strategy can be re-phrased as follow: for independent transitions t and t', where $tid(t) < tid(t')$, we allow t' to be executed before t only if either (i) $t' \Rightarrow_x t$, or (ii) there exists transition t'', where $tid(t'') < tid(t)$, $t' <_x t'' <_x t$ and $t' \Rightarrow_x t''$. This leads to the notion of a *quasi-monotonic sequence*.

Definition 3 (Quasi-Monotonic Computation). *A computation x is said to be quasi-monotonic if and only if for each pair of transitions tr and tr' such that $tr' <_x tr$ we have $tid(tr') > tid(tr)$ only if either (i) $tr' \Rightarrow_x tr$, or (ii) there exists a transition tr'' such that $tid(tr'') < tid(tr)$, $tr' \Rightarrow_x tr''$ and $tr' <_x tr'' <_x tr$.*

MPOR Strategy. *Restrict the interleavings explored to the set of all quasi-monotonic computations.*

We now show the following:

   Soundness., i.e., all necessary interleavings are explored.

   Optimality. i.e., no two interleavings explored are Mazurkiewicz equivalent.

For soundness, we show the following result.

Theorem 1. (Soundness). *For each computation π there exists a quasi-monotonic interleaving that is Mazurkiewicz equivalent to π.*

Proof. The proof is by induction on the length n of π. For the base case, i.e., $n = 1$, the path π comprises only of one state and is therefore trivially quasi-monotonic.

For the induction step, we assume that the result holds for all paths of length less than or equal to k. Consider a path π of length $k + 1$. Write π as $\pi = \rho.tr$, where ρ is the prefix of π of length k and tr is the last transition executed along π. By the induction hypothesis, these exists a quasi-monotonic path ρ' that is Mazurkiewicz equivalent to ρ. Set $\pi' = \rho'.tr$. Let $\pi' = tr_0...tr_{k-1}tr$. Note that we have represented π' in terms of the sequence of transitions executed along it as opposed to the states occurring along it. Thus here tr_i represents the $(i + 1)$st transition executed along π'. Let $tr' = tr_j$ be the last transition executed along ρ' such that $tid(tr') \leq tid(tr)$. Define $T_{dc} = \{tr_l \mid l \in [j + 1, k - 1] \text{ and } tr_l \Rightarrow_{\pi'} tr\}$ and $T_{nc} = \{tr_l \mid l \in [j + 1, k - 1] \text{ and } tr_l \notin T_{dc}\}$.

Let $\rho'' = tr_0...tr_j.\nu.tr.\zeta$, where ν is the sequence of all transitions in T_{dc} listed in the relative order in which they were executed along π'. Similarly, let ζ be the sequence of transitions of T_{nc} listed in the relative order in which they were executed along π'. We claim that ρ'' is Mazurkiewicz equivalent to π'. Indeed, the effect of our transformation on π' is to migrate the execution of transitions of T_{nc} rightwards. The only way ρ'' cannot be Mazurkiewicz equivalent to ρ' is if there exist transitions $t \in T_{nc}$ and $t' \in T_{dc} \cup \{tr\}$ such that t and t' are dependent. However in that case we can show that $t \in T_{dc}$ contradicting our assumption that $t \in T_{nc}$. Indeed, the only case where we cannot move the transition $t \in T_{nc}$ to the right is if there exists a transition $t' \in T_{dc} \cup \{tr\}$ fired after t along ρ' such that t' is dependent with t. Since $t' \in T_{dc} \cup \{tr\}$, by definition of T_{dc}, $t' \Rightarrow_{\pi'} tr$. However, since t is dependent with t', we have that $t \Rightarrow_{\pi'} tr$ and so $t \in T_{dc}$.

Set $\pi'' = tr_0...tr_j.\nu'.tr.\zeta'$, where ν' and ζ' are quasi-monotonic computations that are Mazurkiewicz equivalent to ν and ζ, respectively. The existence of ν' and ζ' follows from the induction hypothesis. Clearly π'' is a valid computation.

All we need to show now is that π'' is quasi-monotonic. If possible, suppose that there exists a pair of transitions t and t' such that $tid(t') > tid(t)$ that violate quasi monotonicity. We now carry out a case analysis. Note that since $tr_0, ..., tr_j$ is quasi-monotonic, t and t' cannot both occur along $tr_0, ..., tr_j$. Thus there are two main cases to be considered: (1) t' occurs along $tr_0, ..., tr_j$ and t along $\nu'.tr.\zeta'$, and (2) t' and t both occur along $\nu'.tr.\zeta'$.

First assume that t' and t occur along $tr_0..., tr_j$ and $\nu'.tr.\zeta'$, respectively. We start by observing that from the definition of j it follows that all transitions executed along ν' and ζ' have thread-id greater than $tid(tr) \geq tid(tr_j)$. Thus $tid(t) \geq tid(tr_j)$, and so $tid(t') > tid(t) \geq tid(tr_j)$. Since $tr_0, ..., tr_j$ is quasi-monotonic, either (i) $t' \Rightarrow_{tr_0...tr_j}$

tr_j, or (ii) there exist a transition tr_p, where $p \in [0..j]$, such that $t' \Rightarrow_{tr_0...tr_j} tr_p$ and $tid(tr_p) < tid(tr_j)$. If $tr_p \Rightarrow_{\pi''} t$ then from $t' \Rightarrow_{tr_0...tr_j} tr_p$ it follows that $t' \Rightarrow_{\pi''} t$ and so t and t' do not violate quasi-monotonicity. If, on the other hand, $tr_p \not\Rightarrow_{\pi''} t$ we observe that $tid(tr_p) < tid(tr_j) \leq tid(t)$. Also since $t' \Rightarrow_{tr_0...tr_j} tr_p$ implies that $t' \Rightarrow_{\pi''} tr_p$, we again see that t and t' do not constitute a violation.

Next we consider case 2, i.e., both t and t' occur along $\nu'.tr.\zeta'$. Note that since by our construction, (i) ν' and ζ' are quasi-monotonic, and (ii) there is a dependency chain from each transition occurring along ν' to tr, a violation could occur only if t' occurs along $\nu'.tr$ and t along ζ'. Since t occurs along ζ', we have $tid(t) > tid(tr)$. Moreover, since t occurs along ν', there is a dependency chain from t' to tr (note that since ν and ν' are Mazurkiewicz equivalent they have the same dependency chains). Thus t and t' satisfy the quasi-monotonicity property thereby contradicting our assumption that π'' is not quasi-monotonic. This completes the induction step and proves the result.   □

For optimality, we show the following result.

Theorem 2. (Optimality). *No two computations explored are Mazurkiewicz equivalent.*

Proof. We prove by contradiction. Assume that π, π' are two different quasi-monotonic sequences which are (Mazurkiewicz) equivalent. By definition, π and π' have the same set of transitions, i.e., π' is a permutation of π. Let $tr_1 = \pi'_i$ be the first transition along π' that is swapped to be π_j, where $i \neq j$, along π. Let $tr_0 = \pi_i$. Note that $i < j$, else the minimality of i will be contradicted. Then π and π' share a common prefix up to i (Fig. 4). For definiteness, we assume that $tid(tr_1) < tid(tr_0)$, the other case where $tid(tr_1) > tid(tr_0)$ being handled similarly.

Since π and π' are Mazurkiewicz equivalent and the relative order of execution of tr_0 and tr_1 is different along the two paths, tr_0 and tr_1 must be independent. Since $tid(tr_1) < tid(tr_0)$ and π is quasi-monotonic, there must exist a transition tr_2, such that $tr_0 <_\pi tr_2 <_\pi tr_1$, $tid(tr_2) < tid(tr_1)$ and $tr_0 \Rightarrow_\pi tr_2$ (note that there cannot exist a dependency chain from tr_0 to tr_1 else π and π' will not be Mazurkiewicz equivalent). In Fig. 4, the circle on the square bracket corresponding to tr_2 along π indicates that tr_2 lies between tr_0 and tr_1 along π.

Since all adjacent transitions along a dependency chain are, by definition, dependent, the relative ordering of the execution of transitions along any dependency chain must be the same along both π and π' as they are Mazurkiewicz equivalent. It follows then that $tr_0 <_{\pi'} tr_2$. Since $tr_1 <_{\pi'} tr_0$, we have $tr_1 <_{\pi'} tr_2$. Furthermore, it cannot be the case that $tr_1 \Rightarrow_{\pi'} tr_2$ else to preserve Mazurkiewicz equivalence it must be the case that $tr_1 \Rightarrow_\pi tr_2$ and so $tr_1 <_\pi tr_2$ leading to a contradiction. Therefore, since π' is quasi-monotonic and $tid(tr_2) < tid(tr_1)$, there must exist a transition tr_3, such that $tr_1 <_{\pi'} tr_3 <_{\pi'} tr_2$, $tid(tr_3) < tid(tr_2)$ and $tr_1 \Rightarrow_{\pi'} tr_3$. Again as before since $tr_1 \Rightarrow_{\pi'} tr_3$, we have $tr_1 \Rightarrow_\pi tr_3$. Thus $tr_1 <_\pi tr_3$. Since $tr_2 <_\pi tr_1$, we have $tr_2 <_\pi tr_3$. But $tid(tr_3) < tid(tr_2)$ and we can repeat the above argument. Thus continuing the above process we can obtain a sequence $tr_0, tr_1, ..., tr_k$ of transitions such that $tid(tr_k) < tid(tr_{k-1}) < ... < tid(tr_1) < tid(tr_0)$ and

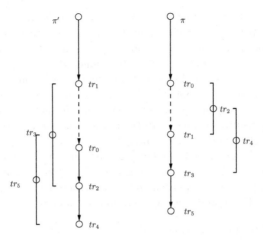

Fig. 4. Dependency Chains

1. for each $i \in [0..k-2]$, $tr_i \Rightarrow tr_{i+2}$ ($tr_i \Rightarrow_\pi tr_{i+2}$ and $tr_i \Rightarrow_{\pi'} tr_{i+2}$)
2. for each $i \in [1..k/2]$, $tr_{2i} <_\pi tr_{2i-1}$
3. for each $i \in [0..k/2]$, $tr_{2i+1} <_{\pi'} tr_{2i}$.

Since the thread-ids of the transitions tr_i form a strictly descending sequence, there exists a sequence of transitions of maximum length satisfying the above properties. Assume now that the above sequence is, in fact, maximal. We consider two cases. First assume that k is even. Then there is dependency chain (property 1) from tr_{k-2} to tr_k along π'. Thus tr_k is executed after tr_{k-2} along both π and π' and so $tr_{k-2} <_{\pi'} tr_k$. Also, by property 3, $tr_{k-1} <_{\pi'} tr_{k-2}$. By combining the above facts, we have $tr_{k-1} <_{\pi'} tr_{k-2} <_{\pi'} tr_k$. Note also that $tid(tr_k) < tid(tr_{k-1})$. Thus by quasi-monotonicity of π' either (i) there exists a dependency chain from tr_{k-1} to tr_k, or (ii) there exists a transition tr_{k+1} such that $tr_{k-1} \Rightarrow tr_{k+1}$ and $tr_{k-1} <_{\pi'} tr_{k+1} <_{\pi'} < tr_k$. The second case cannot happen as it would violate the maximality of the sequence $\{tr_i\}$. Thus $tr_{k-1} \Rightarrow tr_k$ which implies that $tr_{k-1} <_\pi tr_k$ (as dependency chains are preserved across Mazurkiewicz equivalent sequences). However by property 2, $tr_k <_\pi tr_{k-1}$ which is absurd. This contradicts our initial assumption that there exist two different Mazurkiewicz equivalent quasi-monotonic sequences. The other case where k is odd can be handled similarly. This completes the proof.   □

4   Implementation

4.1   Bounded Model Checking (BMC)

We start by reviewing the basics of SMT/SAT-based bounded model checking. Given a multi-threaded program and a reachability property, BMC can check the property on all execution paths of the program up to a fixed depth K. For each step $0 \le k \le K$, BMC builds a formula Ψ such that Ψ *is satisfiable iff there exists a length-k execution that* *violates the property.* The formula is denoted $\Psi = \Phi \wedge \Phi_{prop}$, where Φ represents all possible executions of the program up to k steps and Φ_{prop} is the constraint indicating violation of the property (see [2] for more details about Φ_{prop}). In the following, we focus on the formulation of Φ.

Let $V = V_{global} \cup \bigcup V_i$, where V_{global} is the set of global variables and V_i the set of local variables of T_i. For all local (global) program variables, we add a state variable for V_i (V_{global}). Array and pointer accesses need special handling. For an array access $a[i]$, we add separate variables for the index i and for the content $a[i]$. Similarly, for a pointer access $*p$, we maintain separate state variables for $(*p)$ and p. We add a pc_i variable for each thread T_i to represent its current program counter. To model nondeterminism in the scheduler, we add a variable sel whose domain is the set of thread indices $\{1, 2, \ldots, N\}$. A transition in T_i is executed only when $sel = i$.

At every time frame, we add a fresh copy of the set of state variables. Let $v^i \in V^i$ denote the copy of $v \in V$ at the i-th time frame. To represent all possible length-k interleavings, we first encode the transition relations of individual threads and the scheduler, and unfold the composed system exactly k time frames.

$$\Phi := I(V^0) \wedge \bigwedge_{i=0}^{k} (SCH(V^i) \wedge \bigwedge_{j=1}^{N} TR_j(V^i, V^{i+1}))$$

where $I(V^0)$ represents the set of initial states, SCH represents the constraint on the scheduler, and TR_j represents the transition relation of thread T_j. Without any partial order reduction, $SCH(V^i) := true$, which means that sel takes all possible values at every step. This default SCH considers all possible interleavings. Partial order reduction can be implemented by adding constraints to SCH to remove redundant interleavings.

We now consider the formulation of TR_j. Let $VS_j = V_{global} \cup V_j$ denote the set of variables visible to T_j. At the i-th time frame, for each $t \in trans_j$ (a transition between control locations loc_1 and loc_2), we create tr_t^i. If t is an assignment $v := e$, then $tr_t^i :=$

$$pc_j^i = loc_1 \wedge pc_j^{i+1} = loc_2 \wedge v^{i+1} = e^i \wedge (VS_j^{i+1} \setminus v^{i+1}) = (VS_j^i \setminus v^i) \ .$$

If t is a branching statement $assume(c)$, as in $\texttt{if(c)}$, then $tr_t^i :=$

$$pc_j^i = loc_1 \wedge pc_j^{i+1} = loc_2 \wedge c^i \wedge VS_j^{i+1} = VS_j^i.$$

Overall, TR_j^i is defined as follows:

$$TR_j^i := \left(sel^i = j \wedge \bigvee_{t \in trans_j} tr_t^i \right) \vee (sel^i \neq j \wedge V_j^{i+1} = V_j^i)$$

The second term says that if T_j is not selected, variables in V_j do not change values.

4.2   Encoding MPOR

In order to implement our technique, we need to track dependency chains in a space efficient manner. Towards that end, the following result is crucial.

Theorem 3. *Let transitions tr and tr' executed by processes T_i and T_j, respectively, along a computation x, constitute a violation of quasi-monotonicity. Suppose that $tr' <_x tr$ and $tid(tr') > tid(tr)$. Then any transition tr'' executed by T_j such that $tr' <_x tr'' <_x tr$ also constitutes a violation of quasi-monotonicity with respect to tr.*

Proof. If possible, suppose that the pair of transitions tr'' and tr do not constitute a violation of quasi-monotonicity. Since $tid(tr'') > tid(tr)$ and $tr'' <_x tr$, either (1) there is a dependency chain from tr'' to tr, or (2) there exists tr''' such that (a) $tr'' <_x tr''' <_x tr$, (b) $tid(tr''') < tid(tr)$, and (c) there is a dependency chain from tr'' to tr'''. However, since all transitions belonging to the same thread are dependent with each other, we see that tr' is dependent with tr''. Thus any dependency chain starting at tr'' can be extended backwards to start at tr'. As a result we have that either (1) there is a dependency chain from tr' to tr, or (2) there exists tr''' such that (a) $tr' <_x tr''' <_x tr$, (b) $tid(tr''') < tid(tr)$, and (c) there is a dependency chain from tr' to tr'''. However, in that case transitions tr' and tr do not violate quasi-monotonicity, leading to a contradiction.   □

Theorem 3 implies that if there is a violation of quasi-monotonicity involving transitions tr and tr' executed by threads T_i and T_j, respectively, such that $tid(tr') > tid(tr)$, then there is also a violation between tr and the last transition executed by T_j before tr along the given computation. This leads to the important observation that in order to ensure that a computation π is quasi-monotonic, we need to track dependency chains only from the last transition executed by each process along π and not from every transition.

Tracking Dependency Chains. To formulate our MPOR encoding, we first show how to track dependency chains. Towards that end, for each pair of threads T_i and T_j, we introduce a new variable DC_{ij} defined as follows.

Definition 4. $DC_{il}(k)$ *is 1 or -1 accordingly as there is a dependency chain or not, respectively, from the last transition executed by T_i to the last transition executed by T_l up to time step k. If no transition has been executed by T_i till time step k, $DC_{il} = 0$.*

Updating DC_{ij}. If at time step k thread T_i is executing transition tr, then for each thread T_l, we check whether the last transition executed by T_l is dependent with tr. To track that we introduce the dependency variables DEP_{li} defined below.

Definition 5. $DEP_{li}(k)$ *is true or false accordingly as the transition being executed by thread T_i at time step k is dependent with the last transition executed by T_l, or not. Note that $DEP_{ii}(k)$ is always true (due to control conflict).*

If $DEP_{li}(k) = true$ and if $DC_{jl}(k-1) = 1$, i.e., there is a dependency chain from the last transition executed by T_j to the last transition executed by T_l, then this dependency chain can be extended to the last transition executed by T_i, i.e., tr. In that case, we set $DC_{ji}(k) = 1$. Also, since we track dependency chains only from the last transition executed by each thread, the dependency chain corresponding to T_i needs to start afresh and so we set $DC_{ij}(k) = -1$ for all $j \neq i$. To sum up, the updates are as follows.

$$DC_{ii}(k) = 1$$
$$DC_{ij}(k) = -1 \qquad\qquad\qquad\qquad \text{when } j \neq i$$
$$DC_{ji}(k) = 0 \qquad\qquad\qquad\qquad \text{when } j \neq i \text{ and } DC_{jj}(k-1) = 0$$
$$DC_{ji}(k) = \bigvee_{l=1}^{n}(DC_{jl}(k-1) = 1 \wedge DEP_{li}(k)) \text{ when } j \neq i \text{ and } DC_{jj}(k-1) \neq 0$$
$$DC_{pq}(k) = DC_{pq}(k-1) \qquad\qquad\qquad \text{when } p \neq i \text{ and } q \neq i$$

Scheduling Constraint. Next we introduce the scheduling constraints variables S_i, where $S_i(k)$ is *true* or *false* based on whether thread T_i can be scheduled to execute or not, respectively, at time step k in order to ensure quasi-monotonicity. Then we conjoin the following constraint to SCH (see subsection 4.1):

$$\bigwedge_{i=1}^{n}(sel^k = i \Rightarrow S_i(k))$$

We encode $S_i(k)$ (where $1 \leq i \leq n$) as follows:
$S_i(0) = true$ and
for $k > 0$, $S_i(k) = \bigwedge_{j>i}(DC_{ji}(k) \neq -1 \vee \bigvee_{l<i}(DC_{jl}(k-1) = 1))$

In the above formula, $DC_{ji}(k) \neq -1$ encodes the condition that either a transition by thread T_j, where $j > i$, hasn't been executed up to time k, i.e., $DC_{ji}(k) = 0$, or if it has then there is a dependency chain from the last transition executed by T_j to the transition of T_i enabled at time step k, i.e., $DC_{ji}(k) = 1$. If these two cases do not hold and there exists a transition tr' executed by T_j before the transition tr of T_i enabled at time step k, then in order for quasi-monotonicity to hold, there must exist a transition tr'' executed by thread T_l, where $l < i$, after tr' and before tr such that there is a dependency chain from tr' to tr'' which is encoded via the condition $\bigvee_{l<i}(DC_{jl}(k-1) = 1)$.

Encoding DEP. The decoupling of the encoding of the dependency constraints (via the *DEP* variables) from the encoding of quasi-monotonicity has the advantage that it affords us the flexibility to incorporate various notions of dependencies based on the application at hand. These include dependencies arising out of synchronization primitives, memory consistency models like sequential consistency, etc. For our implementation, we have, for now, used only dependencies arising out of shared variable accesses the encoding of which is given below.

We define the following set of variables for each thread T_i:

- $pWV_i(k)$, $pRV_i(k)$, $pR^2V_i(k)$ denote the Write-Variable and Read-Variables of the last transition executed by T_i before step k. For simplicity, we assume that each assignment has at most three operands: a write variable occurring on the left hand side of the assignment, i.e., $pWV_i(k)$ and up to two read variables occurring on the right hand side of the assignment, i.e., $pRV_i(k)$ and $pR^2V_i(k)$.
- $wv_i(k)$, $wr_i(k)$, $r^2v_i(k)$ denote the Write-Variable and Read-Variables of the transition executed by T_i at step k.

We encode $DEP_{ij}(k)$ as follows,

$$DEP_{ij}(k) = (\ pWV_i(k) = wv_i(k) \wedge pWV_i(k) \neq 0 \vee$$
$$pWV_i(k) = rv_i(k) \wedge pWV_i(k) \neq 0 \vee$$
$$pWV_i(k) = r^2v_i(k) \wedge pWV_i(k) \neq 0 \vee$$
$$pRV_i(k) = wv_i(k) \wedge wv_i(k) \neq 0 \vee$$
$$pR^2V_i(k) = wv_i(k) \wedge wv_i(k) \neq 0)$$

Read and Write Variables. Let $t_1, \ldots, t_n \in trans_i$ be the set of transitions of T_i, and $t_1.writeVar$ be the Write-Variable of the transition t_1. Moreover, $en_{t_i}(V^k)$ equals *true* or *false* accordingly as t_i is enabled at time step k or not, respectively.

– We encode $wv_i(k)$ as follows

$$wv_i(k) = (sel^k = i \wedge en_{t_1}(V^k))\ ?\ t_1.writeVar\ :$$
$$(sel^k = i \wedge en_{t_2}(V^k))\ ?\ t_2.writeVar\ :$$
$$\cdots$$
$$(sel^k = i \wedge en_{t_n}(V^k))\ ?\ t_n.writeVar\ :\ 0$$

– We encode $pWV_i(k+1)$ as follows (with $pWV_i(0) = 0$)

$$pWV_i(k+1) = (sel^k = i \wedge en_{t_1}(V^k))\ ?\ t_1.writeVar\ :$$
$$(sel^k = i \wedge en_{t_2}(V^k))\ ?\ t_2.writeVar\ :$$
$$\cdots$$
$$(sel^k = i \wedge en_{t_n}(V^k))\ ?\ t_n.writeVar\ :\ pWV_i(k)$$

Important Optimization. Note that the last encoding requires an if-then-else chain of length $|trans_i|$. However, we need to detect dependencies only between transitions of threads which access shared objects (as all internal transitions following a shared object access can be executed in one atomic step). Thus, $trans_i$ would now denote the number of transitions of T_i accessing only shared objects which typically is a small fraction of the total number of transitions of T_i.

5   Experiments

We have implemented the optimal POR methods in an SMT-based bounded model checker using the Yices SMT solver [4]. The experiments were performed with two variants of the optimal POR reduction and a baseline BMC algorithm with no POR. The two variants represent different tradeoffs between the encoding overhead and the amount of achievable reduction. The first one is *PPOR* [17], in which the quasi monotonicity constraints are collected only within a window of two consecutive time frames (and so the reduction is not optimal). The second one is *MPOR*, in which the entire set of quasi-monotonicity constraints are added to ensure quasi monotonicity (the reduction is optimal). Our experiments were conducted on a workstation with 2.8 GHz Xeon processor and 4GB memory running Red Hat Linux 7.2.

We use a parameterized version of *dining philosophers* as our test example. The dining philosopher model we used can guarantee the absence of deadlocks. Each philosopher

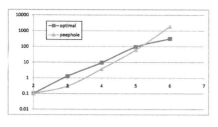

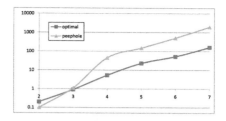

(a) With SAT instances (property 'pa')   (b) With UNSAT instances (property 'pb')

Fig. 5. Comparing runtime performance of (optimal) MPOR and (peephole) PPOR

has its own local state variables, and threads communicate through a shared array of chop-sticks. When accessing the global array, threads may have conflicts (data dependency). The first property (pa) we checked is whether all philosophers can eat simultaneously (the answer is no). The second property (pb) is whether it is possible to reach a state in which all philosophers have eaten at least once (the answer is yes).

We set the number of philosophers (threads) to 2, 3, . . ., and compared the runtime performance of the three methods. The results are given in Fig. 5. The x-axis represents unroll depth. The y-axis is the BMC runtime in seconds, and is in logarithmic scale. The number of variable decisions and conflicts of the SMT solver look similar to the runtime curves and are, therefore, omitted for brevity. When comparing the sizes of the SMT formulae, we found that those produced by the optimal POR encoding typically are twice as large as the plain BMC instances, and those produced by the PPOR encoding are slightly larger than the plain BMC instances.

The detailed results are given in Table 1. In Table 1, Columns 1-3 show the name of the examples, the number of BMC unrolling steps, and whether the property is true or

Table 1. Comparing PPOR, MPOR and plain BMC

Test Program			Total CPU Time (s)			#Conflicts (k)			#Decisions (k)		
name	steps	prop	none	MPOR	PPOR	none	MPOR	PPOR	none	MPOR	PPOR
phil2-pa	15	unsat	0.2	0.2	**0.1**	1	1	1	1	1	0
phil3-pa	22	unsat	18.2	**0.9**	1.1	17	1	1	23	2	3
phil4-pa	29	unsat	49.6	**5.3**	44.9	39	3	27	53	8	41
phil5-pa	36	unsat	76.3	**22.9**	148.6	48	6	53	69	17	82
phil6-pa	43	unsat	98.4	**52.3**	504.4	56	12	92	84	30	147
phil7-pa	50	unsat	502.3	**161.6**	> 1h	161	16	-	238	48	-
phil2-pb	15	sat	0.1	0.1	**0.1**	1	1	1	1	1	0
phil3-pb	22	sat	1.5	1.3	**0.3**	2	1	1	4	4	1
phil4-pb	29	sat	18.3	9.5	**3.8**	12	3	3	17	11	6
phil5-pb	36	sat	195.5	94.7	**61.7**	44	9	16	61	26	31
phil6-pb	43	sat	>1h	**315.4**	2283	-	16	122	-	52	200
phil7-pb	50	sat	>1h	**1218**	> 1h	-	31	-	-	85	-

not. Columns 4-6 report the runtime of the three methods. Columns 7-9 and Columns 10-12 report the number of backtracks and the number of decisions of the SMT solver.

In general, adding more SAT constraints involves a tradeoff between the state space pruned and the additional overhead in processing these constraints. However, the results in Fig. 5 indicate that the reduction achieved by MPOR more than outweighs its encoding overhead. For programs with two threads, PPOR always outperforms MPOR. This is because PPOR is also optimal for two threads, and it has a significantly smaller encoding overhead. However, as the number of threads increases, percentage-wise, more and more redundant interleavings elude the PPOR constraints. As is shown in Fig. 1, for more than four threads, the overhead of PPOR constraints outweighs the benefit (runtime becomes longer than MPOR).

6   Conclusions

We have presented a monotonic partial order reduction method for model checking concurrent systems, based on the new notion of quasi-monotonic sequences. We have also presented a concise symbolic encoding of quasi-monotonic sequences which is well suited for use in SMT/SAT solvers. Finally, our new method is guaranteed optimal, i.e., removes all redundant interleavings.

References

[1] Alur, R., Brayton, R.K., Henzinger, T.A., Qadeer, S., Rajamani, S.K.: Partial-order reduction in symbolic state-space exploration. Formal Methods in System Design 18(2), 97–116 (2001)

[2] Biere, A., Cimatti, A., Clarke, E., Zhu, Y.: Symbolic model checking without BDDs. In: Cleaveland, W.R. (ed.) TACAS 1999. LNCS, vol. 1579, p. 193. Springer, Heidelberg (1999)

[3] Cook, B., Kroening, D., Sharygina, N.: Symbolic model checking for asynchronous boolean programs. In: Godefroid, P. (ed.) SPIN 2005. LNCS, vol. 3639, pp. 75–90. Springer, Heidelberg (2005)

[4] Dutertre, B., de Moura, L.: A fast linear-arithmetic solver for dpll(t). In: Ball, T., Jones, R.B. (eds.) CAV 2006. LNCS, vol. 4144, pp. 81–94. Springer, Heidelberg (2006)

[5] Flanagan, C., Godefroid, P.: Dynamic partial-order reduction for model checking software. In: Principles of programming languages (POPL 2005), pp. 110–121 (2005)

[6] Godefroid, P.: Partial-Order Methods for the Verification of Concurrent Systems - An Approach to the State-Explosion Problem. Springer, Heidelberg (1996)

[7] Godefroid, P., Pirottin, D.: Refining dependencies improves partial-order verification methods. In: Courcoubetis, C. (ed.) CAV 1993. LNCS, vol. 697, pp. 438–449. Springer, Heidelberg (1993)

[8] Grumberg, O., Lerda, F., Strichman, O., Theobald, M.: Proof-guided underapproximation-widening for multi-process systems. In: POPL (2005)

[9] Gueta, G., Flanagan, C., Yahav, E., Sagiv, M.: Cartesian partial-order reduction. In: Bošnački, D., Edelkamp, S. (eds.) SPIN 2007. LNCS, vol. 4595, pp. 95–112. Springer, Heidelberg (2007)

[10] Kahlon, V., Gupta, A., Sinha, N.: Symbolic model checking of concurrent programs using partial orders and on-the-fly transactions. In: Ball, T., Jones, R.B. (eds.) CAV 2006. LNCS, vol. 4144, pp. 286–299. Springer, Heidelberg (2006)

[11] Katz, S., Peled, D.: Defining conditional independence using collapses. Theor. Comput. Sci. 101(2), 337–359 (1992)

[12] Lerda, F., Sinha, N., Theobald, M.: Symbolic model checking of software. Electr. Notes Theor. Comput. Sci. 89(3) (2003)

[13] Mazurkiewicz, A.W.: Trace theory. In: Brauer, W., Reisig, W., Rozenberg, G. (eds.) APN 1986. LNCS, vol. 255, pp. 279–324. Springer, Heidelberg (1987)

[14] Peled, D.: All from one, one for all: on model checking using representatives. In: Courcoubetis, C. (ed.) CAV 1993. LNCS, vol. 697. Springer, Heidelberg (1993)

[15] Silva, J.P.M., Sakallah, K.A.: Grasp—a new search algorithm for satisfiability. In: International Conference on Computer-Aided Design, San Jose, CA (1996)

[16] Valmari, A.: Stubborn sets for reduced state space generation. In: Rozenberg, G. (ed.) APN 1990. LNCS, vol. 483, pp. 491–515. Springer, Heidelberg (1991)

[17] Wang, C., Yang, Z., Kahlon, V., Gupta, A.: Peephole partial order reduction. In: Ramakrishnan, C.R., Rehof, J. (eds.) TACAS 2008. LNCS, vol. 4963, pp. 382–396. Springer, Heidelberg (2008)

Replacing Testing with Formal Verification in Intel® Core™ i7 Processor Execution Engine Validation

Roope Kaivola, Rajnish Ghughal, Naren Narasimhan, Amber Telfer,
Jesse Whittemore, Sudhindra Pandav, Anna Slobodová, Christopher Taylor,
Vladimir Frolov, Erik Reeber, and Armaghan Naik

Intel Corporation, JF4-451, 2111 NE 25th Avenue, Hillsboro, OR 97124, USA

Abstract. Formal verification of arithmetic datapaths has been part of the established methodology for most Intel processor designs over the last years, usually in the role of supplementing more traditional coverage oriented testing activities. For the recent Intel® Core™ i7 design we took a step further and used formal verification as the primary validation vehicle for the core execution cluster, the component responsible for the functional behaviour of all microinstructions. We applied symbolic simulation based formal verification techniques for full datapath, control and state validation for the cluster, and dropped coverage driven testing entirely. The project, involving some twenty person years of verification work, is one of the most ambitious formal verification efforts in the hardware industry to date. Our experiences show that under the right circumstances, full formal verification of a design component is a feasible, industrially viable and competitive validation approach.

1 Introduction

Most Intel processors launched over the last ten years have contained formally verified components. This is hardly surprising, as their reliability is crucial, and the cost of correcting problems can be very high. Formal verification has been applied to a range of design components or features: low-level protocols, register renaming, arithmetic units, microarchitecture descriptions etc. [19,4]. In an industrial product development setting, formal verification is a tool, one among others, and it competes with traditional testing and simulation. Usually testing can produce initial results much faster than formal verification, and in our view the value of formal verification primarily comes from its ability to cover every possible behaviour. In most of the cases where formal verification has been applied, its role has been that of a supplementary verification method on top of a full-fledged simulation based dynamic validation effort.

The single most sustained formal verification effort has been made in the area of arithmetic, in particular floating point datapaths. In this area verification methods have reached sufficient maturity that they have now been routinely applied for a series of design projects [17,3,13,21,6], and expanded to cover the full datapath functionality of the Execution Cluster EXE, a top-level component of a core responsible for the functional behaviour of all microinstructions. In the current paper we discuss further expansion of this work on Intel® Core™ i7 design [1]. For this project, we used formal verification as the primary validation vehicle for the execution cluster, including full

A. Bouajjani and O. Maler (Eds.): CAV 2009, LNCS 5643, pp. 414–429, 2009.

datapath, control and state validation, and dropped most usual RTL simulation and all coverage driven simulation validation for the cluster. To give a flavour of the magnitude of the work, Intel Core i7 design implements over 2700 distinct microinstructions.

Most of the particular verification techniques we applied are already documented in literature [3,12,13,15], and our goal here is to discuss the overall programme and the factors that allowed us to be succesful in mostly replacing testing by verification. We believe that the effort is an important step forward in the industrial application of formal verification, At the time of writing this paper, Intel Core i7 is Intel's flagship, top of the line processor. We used formal verification as the main pre-silicon validation vehicle for a large, crucial component of the design in the actual development project, providing results that were competitive with traditional testing-based methods in timeliness and validation cost, and at least comparable if not superior in quality - the execution cluster had the lowest number of issues escaping to silicon for any cluster of the design.

Our methodology has gradually emerged over several years of work on large verification tasks. On a philosophical level, we approach verification as program construction, by emphasizing the role of the human verifier over automation. Technically most of our work is based on symbolic simulation. This works particularly well for self-contained pipelines, such as processor execution units. In fact, the vast majority of execution units inside an Intel microprocessor can be completely verified with direct symbolic simulation. Direct symbolic simulation does not fare quite so well when the amount of interdependence between pipelines increase, as is typically the case in verification of control logic. To extend symbolic simulation to such feedback-intensive verification problems, we use inductive invariants written by a human verifier. The concreteness of the computation steps in the approach allows a verifier to locate and analyze computational problems and devise a strategy around them if and when capacity issues arise. This is a very common scenario in practice, and in our experience one of the key issues regarding the practical usability of a verification tool. Building the verification method on the intuitively tangible ideas of symbolic simulation and invariants also allows us to communicate the work easily to designers, and to draw on their insights.

In the rest of the paper, we will first look briefly at Intel IA-32 processor structure, the execution cluster, Intel Core i7 design, and a typical processor design and validation flow. We will then outline execution cluster verification in past projects and Intel Core i7, and discuss the challenges, advantages and drawbacks of applying formal verification in a live development project. In Section 7, we will touch on the basic technologies enabling our work, and in Section 8 describe different aspects of the Intel Core i7 execution cluster verification effort: datapath, control and state verification.

2 Intel IA-32 Processor Structure

Intel IA-32 processor architecture has evolved gradually over the years. Typically a new IA-32 design project is intended to maintain functional backwards compatibility with the earlier designs while providing improvements along different axes: collections of new instructions (e.g. MMX™, SSE, SSE2 etc.), new capabilities (e.g. 64-bit address support, vPro™ technology), improved performance (clock frequency, throughput, power), or design adjustments to meet side conditions set by a new manufacturing process. Components from earlier designs are often reused in later projects, especially for proliferations but also for entirely new microarchitectures like NetBurst® or Core™. A typical single-core IA-32 processor consists of the following major design components called clusters [9]:

- The *front end cluster FEC* fetches and decodes architectural instructions, translates them to microinstructions and computes branch predictions. For example, a simple instruction with a memory source operand typically maps to a memory load microinstruction and a computation microinstruction, and a complex instruction, such as FCOS (Cosine) to a microprogram.
- The *out-of-order cluster OOO* receives streams of microinstructions from the front end, keeps track of dependencies between them, schedules ready-to-execute microinstructions for execution, takes care of branch misprediction and event recovery, retires completed instructions and updates architectural state.
- The *execution cluster EXE* carries out data computations for all microinstructions. The EXE cluster usually also performs memory address calculations and determines and signals branch mispredictions.
- The *memory cluster MEC* interacts with the front end and execution clusters when they need memory accesses, contains first levels of caches and interfaces with the external environment of the processor, e.g. the main memory or external bus.

In a multi-core design like Intel Core i7 [1], a single processor contains several cores and logic for communication and arbitration between different cores and the environment of the processor such as memory or external bus. Some of the logic that would exist in MEC in a single core design may be pushed to the logic outside the cores in a multi-core design. A register-transfer level (RTL) description of a cluster in System Verilog usually contains a few hundred thousand lines of code. While not a physical entity like the above, microcode is also a major design component, the complexity of which is comparable to that of the clusters.

In this paper we discuss the validation of the execution cluster EXE of the Intel Core i7 design. This cluster consists of the following units:

- The *integer execution unit IEU* contains logic for plain integer and miscellaneous other operations (e.g. control register access)
- The *SIMD integer unit SIU* (single instruction multiple data) contains logic for packed integer operations (MMX and SSE)
- The *floating point unit FPU* implements plain and packed floating point operations such as FDIV, FMUL, FADD etc.
- The *address generation unit AGU* performs address calculations and access checks for memory accesses as well as miscellaneous memory-related operations.
- The *jump execution unit JEU* implements jump operations and determines and signals branch mispredictions.
- The *memory interface unit MIU* receives load data from and passes store data to memory cluster, maintains store forwarding buffers, performs various datatype conversions, and takes care of data bypassing

Intel Core i7 EXE cluster implements over 2700 distinct microinstructions, and supports simultaneous multi-threading (SMT), which allows two independent threads to run simultaneously on the core.

3   Intel Processor Design and Validation Flow

A processor design project implementing a new microarchitecture typically involves a team of over 500 engineers over a time-line of 2 to 3 years [5]. The pre-silicon development effort can be divided into two roughly equal stages:

– *front end development*, which focuses on architecture, RTL and functionality, and
– *execution stage*, which focuses more on timing and physical design.

Pre-silicon development culminates in *tape-out*, the moment the design database is considered healthy enough to be sent to a fabrication plant for the first samples to be produced. After tape-out usually about 9-12 months of post-silicon development work is required to obtain a production-quality design [5].

Organizationally validation forms a separate organization within the product development team. Validation is an ongoing activity throughout the development effort. Pre-silicon validation starts at the same time as the design, and often design and validation are racing to add new design features and the infrastructure to validate them. Pre-silicon validation goes through three stages:

– *Design exercise* checks for basic functionality of design with 'easy' stimulus
– *Stress testing* checks for corner-case functionality by selections of 'hard' stimuli
– *Coverage testing* attempts to hit coverage goals through biased random stimulus

The goal of the pre-silicon validation effort is to tape out a product that is healthy enough to enable post-silicon development and validation. Typically the first silicon is able to boot an operating system and run at least some meaningful software content.

The standard approach for pre-silicon validation is register-transfer level (RTL) simulation. These dynamic validation activities take place at two levels of granularity:

– *Cluster simulation* concentrates on validating each cluster in isolation, in the context of a cluster test environment (CTE). CTE is a test bench approximating the interface of the rest of the design towards the cluster under test. Cluster simulation provides better controllability and is significantly faster than full chip simulation. It is the primary vehicle for pre-silicon validation.
– *Full chip simulation* targets the validation of the entire design. It is especially useful in analysis of multi-cluster protocols, and essentially checks whether the design faithfully implements the IA-32 architecture.

Both cluster and full chip simulation compare the observed behaviour of the design against a reference model. For full-chip simulation the reference model is an architecture level IA-32 simulator. For each cluster, the reference model is purpose-built - for the execution cluster EXE the reference model consists of a microcode simulator, which specifies the intended behaviour of each microinstruction, and a collection of ad-hoc checkers. The register-transfer level description is connected downwards to schematics with formal equivalence verification (FEV) tools.

The main workhorse of the pre-silicon dynamic validation effort is coverage-driven testing. Essentially in this testing methodology validators enumerate all different interesting scenarios they can think of for the design under test, and attempt to hit all of these by random or biased random stimulus, with the implicit intention that in the process they also hit most of the interesting scenarios they did not happen to think of. The methodology is very powerful in practice and results in remarkably clean designs, as long as interesting scenarios are carefully identified and the temptation to manually select the stimulus to hit a particular case avoided. However, in many cases no amount of testing provides certainty: a single dyadic extended-precision (80-bit) floating point instruction has 2^{160} possible source data combinations. Hitting coverage goals can also be very hard – usually for any given coverage goal, there is a point well below 100% after which additional coverage becomes exceedingly hard to gain.

After tape-out, post-silicon validation tries to identify any functional issues pre-silicon validation may have missed. It also serves at the ultimate reality check: not all electrical and physical phenomena can always be modelled accurately beforehand, and the actual behaviour of the circuit may diverge from the logical description. Testing the actual silicon instead of simulation makes any debug work much harder, as we lose visibility of and control over internal state. However, the silicon is much faster than any simulation. For example, a typical Core i7 pre-silicon full-chip simulation runs at 2-3Hz, whereas the launch frequency of the processor was 2.66GHz. This means that the total number of all pre-silicon simulation cycles on a large server farm amounts to no more than a few minutes of run time on a single actual processor.

4   Execution Cluster Verification – A Retrospective

While exploratory formal verification initiatives are carried out by members of Intel research laboratories, in the product development context formal verification is commonly done by a separate dedicated group within the validation team of the product development organization. In most projects, formal verification is viewed as a complementary activity alleviating possible shortcomings of dynamic validation in select target areas, with dynamic validation forming the backbone of the validation effort.

In a project, there is a spectrum of different usage models for formal verification. It can be used for a one-off effort for establishing the basic soundness of some particular feature, as a periodical activity validating and re-validating a design after major modifications, or as a part of regular regression suite preventing the introduction of faulty code into the design database. Most register transfer level verification work is done on models that are automatically compiled from RTL source code, essentially at gate level. The code, written by circuit designers, is usually highly optimized using knowledge about expected operating constraints, often to the degree that it is "almost wrong". Formal verification has often little influence over design style or decisions.

The single most sustained formal verification programme within Intel has been carried out in the area of floating-point and arithmetic datapath verification. In fact, most Intel processors over the last ten years have had formally verified floating-point datapaths. The work discussed in the current paper builds on and extends this body of work.

The earliest concerted floating-point verification effort in Intel was carried out on the Pentium® Pro design [17]. The goal of the effort was full formal verification of all floating-point datapaths of the design, and it was done using the forte toolset, symbolic trajectory evaluation (STE) and a word-level model checking tool. The verification effort was essentially a one-off research project, establishing the basic feasibility of such verification of an industrial-scale design. After the original project, the verification code was regressed to verify the changes in proliferation projects.

The first processor design where formal verification of floating point and other arithmetic datapaths was done within the product development organization was the Pentium® 4 project. The effort was also based on the forte toolset and symbolic trajectory evaluation, but used mainstream BDD manipulation techniques, decompositions and theorem proving instead of word-level tools. Some of the verification efforts on the more complex operations, such as division and multiplication, are reported in [12,13,15] The verification code was maintained throughout the original Pentium 4 project and all its proliferations with regular, though occasionally infrequent regressions, and many parts of the code have lived on in other projects.

The Pentium 4 EXE formal verification effort consolidated some of our verification methodology and introduced a number of technical improvements. For the first time, formal verification was carried out in the level of the entire EXE cluster, instead of individual units. This turns out to be important in practice, as clusters are the lowest level of granularity for which there are clean, well-documented interfaces and on which dynamic validation works, which facilitates comparisons and reviews between formal and dynamic validation content. During the Pentium 4 project we also started to validate assumptions used in formal verification against test traces, by translating FV assumptions to DV checkers, first manually and later automatically.

The Intel® Core™ 2 processor design project extended the range of formal verification from floating-point and other high-complexity, high-risk datapaths to almost all datapaths in the EXE cluster [6]. This project was also the first to combine formal verification and dynamic validation efforts in a single team, and reduce the amount of testing in areas covered by the formal approach. As with Pentium 4, the effort was based on forte toolset and standard BDD manipulation utilities, and the verification code was maintained and regressed throughout the project and for proliferations.

5   Execution Cluster Verification for Intel Core i7

During the early stages of Intel Core i7 development, EXE cluster validation was separated into two teams, formal verification and dynamic validation, according to traditional lines. However, during the front end development stage, reflecting the success of the previous EXE cluster formal verification initiatives, a decision was reached to wind down the dynamic validation activities and reduce cluster test environment (CTE) development. Considering the usual stages of validation, dynamic validation was used extensively for the early design exercise, a moderate amount of stress testing was done, and coverage driven testing was dropped entirely. In certain areas where verification work was delayed, dynamic validation was used as a temporary back-up olution.

To account for the more prominent role of formal verification, the scope of the Intel Core i7 EXE formal verification effort was expanded to include full control, state and bypass verification in addition to the already standard datapath verification - see Section 8 for more discussion. We spent significant effort in software engineering the verification code in a way that would help code maintenance over a live, continuously evolving design and ease reusability for future projects. At the time of the design tape-out, all datapath and control verification was completed. Some bypass work and most of state verification took place after initial tape-out, prior to the design reaching production quality. At any given time, five to eight persons were working on the project, and the total amount of work was about twenty person years. The size of the team was comparable to a typical testing-based cluster validation team, perhaps slightly on the high side.

To provide timely feedback and to prevent bugs from slipping into the continuously changing design, existing verification code was routinely run on all new design models. Nightly regression runs consisting of a representative selection of verification sessions were responsible for catching most of the design issues, and weekly regressions carrying out a complete re-verification the rest. The computational effort to carry out the regressions was a fraction of the amount of cycles needed for a usual simulation-based regression suite. To check the soundness of external assumptions used in the formal verification activity, all assumptions were automatically translated to checkers that were piggybacking on full-chip RTL simulation test runs. This was an extremely useful activity and resulted in many assumption refinements.

The verification effort found a variety of issues in different aspects of the design. However, the success of validation is often measured not by what it finds but by what it misses, and it is probably instructive to look at the issues the verification effort failed to find. In the end, we missed three bugs that escaped to silicon and needed to be fixed prior to achieving production quality:

– When writeback of 64-bit MMX data from SIU is bypassed to a floating point store, an event was signaled incorrectly for negative infinity data.
– When two simultaneous broadcasts of cs.l bit ("Code Segment is in 64-bit mode") happen on different threads, one of the broadcast values ends up being stored in a register for both threads, and the broadcast value for the other thread is dropped.
– The EXE cluster produces the #GP (General Protection) fault instead of #SS (Stack Segment) fault for descriptor loads that cross the canonical boundary.

The first of these escaped due to an incomplete formal specification for the floating point store consuming the bypassed data. In its original form it was treating the eventing condition as a don't-care. The second problem was caused by formal verification work not having been done yet on the failing piece of logic before tape-out. In the third case, the EXE cluster correctly implemented a micro-architectural protocol between EXE and MEC, but the protocol itself failed to yield the expected architectural result. While not zero, this was the lowest number of bugs escaping to silicon for any cluster.

Furthermore, during the pre-silicon stage two other issues went undetected by the formal verification effort, but were caught in full chip testing:

– Packed floating point precision flag was incorrectly raised for precise unmasked underflows.
– Certain floating point constant ROM reads corrupted the result flags of a subsequent floating point compare operation.

The first of these was caused by both the RTL code and the formal specification inheriting material from an earlier project, and missing an intended design change between the projects, and the second by the fact that the control verification work that would have identified the unintended interference between the operations had not been done yet at the time. To summarize, out of the five misses, three could be attributed to an incorrect formal specification, and two to formal verification work not being completed early enough. The positive side of this is that there were no issues that would have fallen through the cracks because of failures in our methodology.

6   Formal Verification Value Proposition

The conventional wisdom about formal verification in industrial context is easy to spell out. Simulation yields partial results quickly and progresses reliably in a linear fashion, although reaching full coverage is very hard, and completeness unattainable. Formal verification, on the other hand, while in principle holding the promise of completeness, is in practice woefully capacity constrained and either slow or downright unable to produce meaningful results. Although a caricature, we feel this view is not altogether unjustified. To better understand the barriers of more wide-spread application of formal verification in industry, at least from an Intel perspective, let us look briefly at some possible application models for formal verification:

- FV may be applied to the fundamental algorithms,
- FV may be applied as an extra layer of protection,
- FV may be mixed with dynamic simulation on the same design, or
- FV may replace simulation as the primary validation approach.

In the first usage model, formal and dynamic validation do not directly overlap. Usually, dynamic validation cannot start until an implementation has been coded, and validation of the underlying algorithms is done only by inspection and reviews. Recent forays into such early microarchitecture validation in Intel [4] have been very encouraging.

As discussed above, much of Intel's formal verification work has historically followed the second usage model, where formal verification is done on top of a full dynamic validation effort. There are several pragmatic problems in this approach. First, if dynamic validation is done diligently, it will find most of the bugs, and thereby get most of the credit. Secondly, the few remaining bugs are likely to be in extreme corners of the design, and formal verification will look at these only if a very thorough and costly effort is made to cover all aspects of the design. This means that doing a little formal verification will not find any new issues, and doing a thorough effort only a few, in both cases leading to a perceived low return on investment. The areas where projects have routinely chosen to do formal verification have then been limited to those where an uncaught problem would be so visible and costly that the extra effort of doing formal verification can be justified. As a positive exception, SAT-based bounded model checking has been very successfully used as a bug-hunting tool in targeted areas.

The third usage model, mixing formal and dynamic techniques on validating a single design area, sounds appealing at face value. However, the following fundamental problem makes it hard to offset the dynamic validation effort by formal verification. The coverage-based validation paradigm is based on the identification of all interesting aspects of the design and the sets of interesting cases for all these aspects, with the expectation that once we gain coverage for most of these, we will have also exercised those aspects of the design we failed to account for in the process. Now, even if some aspects of the design are formally verified, we will still need to identify and gain coverage for them in order to give us confidence that we are also reaching the unaccounted parts of the design. Therefore, formal verification gives little or no reduction in simulation effort. A practical implication of this problem is also that it is hard to gradually offset dynamic validation by formal verification.

Consider then the fourth usage model, replacing dynamic simulation by formal verification. In our view, in to be successful, formal verification needs to

- work at the same level of design granularity as simulation
- address all the aspects of the design simulation does,
- relate to the surrounding simulation-based collateral, and
- provide timely feedback about the changing design.

The timeliness aspect merits some more discussion. A common complaint regarding formal verification in project context is "FV is usually late". In many situations this is caused by the FV computational complexity problem simply being too hard. If verifiers need to first solve a research problem, it is little wonder that they are unable to produce quick feedback or put together meaningful schedules. In our opinion, the key aspect in alleviating this problem is a collection of "FV recipes", tried-and-tested strategies for solving certain classes of problems. These allow the verifiers either to identify a computational strategy, or to flag a verification task as being of unknown complexity. A difficulty in producing timely feedback may also come just from lack of collateral. In our context, dynamic validation is usually able to draw on material from earlier projects. If formal verification needs to implement comparable material from scratch, it starts off with a handicap. While there may be good reasons for slow progress of FV work, we cannot see that it would step beyond a secondary role without timely results.

There were a number of factors enabling the effort discussed in the current paper. First of all, the choice of symbolic simulation as the primitive verification approach allowed us to work on cluster-size design objects. Secondly, symbolic simulation directly supported main datapath verification tasks, and combined with inductive invariants allowed us to address control and state verification, as well. Thirdly, the background of previous execution cluster verification projects had given us a wealth of experience, existing verification recipes and directly re-usable code, allowing us to progress quickly with many verification tasks. Fourthly, through the translation of FV assumption to simulation checkers, we were also able to relate our work to the existing dynamic validation collateral and get feedback from it.

The issues our validation effort missed can be traced back to failures to meet the requirements above. Two bugs were related to timeliness - our control and bypass verification efforts were running late, as we were hashing out methodology and doing the actual verification at the same time. The other three bugs were cases of validation against an incorrect specification. Mechanical checking of specifications against the simulation reference model would have likely identified at least two of these.

To be an effective verification engineer in our environment, one needs to have both an understanding of the design and the FV technologies. In our experience, the two systematically hardest problems the team members faced were the analysis of BDD behaviour in a computation, and the identification of hardware invariants – both of these skills are still something of a black art.

Looking forward, replicating the work reported here for subsequent projects has been considerably easier. The methodology and infrastructure for the complete effort is in place, the verification code is engineered to support reuse and be robust in the face of design changes, and a variety of strategies and guidelines have been obtained from practical experience. We are already seeing very effective early validation results from future projects - our hope is that the methodology will allow us to arrive at a logically clean design faster than before, and this way allow for faster design convergence.

We believe that the programme discussed in the current paper shows that in areas where a verifier can concentrate on verification, instead of solving verification research problems, the effort to carry out formal verification is comparable to thorough coverage-based validation. Such an effort is not easy, and existing verification collateral, in the form of verifier experience, reusable code or verification recipes, is likely to be needed to enable timely results. In areas where these circumstances exist, the choice of whether to do or not to do formal verification is in the end a risk tolerance question. On the one hand, formal verification can provide complete design coverage, on the other a formal verification based validation programme is going to involve more unknowns than a traditional testing based one.

7   Technical Framework

Technically our verification work is carried out in the Forte verification framework, originally built on top of the Voss system [8]. The interface language to Forte is *reFLect*, a lazy, strongly-typed functional language in the ML family [18]. Most of our verification code is written in reFLect: specifications, whether they are functional specifications or relational constraints, verification facilities, analysis routines etc. The execution of a verification task in our framework amounts to the evaluation of a reFLect program. Let us next briefly touch on a collection of aspects of the framework that have been key enablers for our work: symbolic evaluation of terms, symbolic trajectory evaluation, weakening techniques, parametric substitutions, relational STE and reflection.

Binary decision diagrams are first-class objects in the forte framework. In fact, in the reFLect language the type Bool includes not just the constants T and F, but arbitrary BDD's. For verification purposes, a very important feature of the language is that it allows *symbolic evaluation* of objects containing BDD's. For example, consider the following code:

```
let a = variable "a"; let b = variable "b"; let c = variable "c";
let moo = a => [ F, F, b ] | [ F, T, c ];
```

where 'variable' is a function that generates a BDD variable, $x \Rightarrow y|z$ means if-then-else, and $[\ldots]$ is used to build tuples. When evaluated, 'moo' yields $[F, \neg a, a \wedge b \vee \neg a \wedge c]$. The symbolic evaluation capability allows us to use arbitrary reFLect code when writing specifications and then use the evaluation mechanism of the language for determining satisfaction of a specification for all possible assignments to symbolic variables.

The forte framework directly supports *symbolic simulation* on circuit models through symbolic trajectory evaluation (STE) [20] as a built-in function. Symbolic simulation is based on traditional notions of digital circuit simulation, but the value of a signal in simulation can either by a constant (T or F) or a symbolic expression representing the conditions under which the signal is T. Trajectory evaluation extends the normal Boolean logic to a quaternary logic, with the value X denoting lack of information, i.e. the signal could be either T or F, and the value $\top$ denoting contradictory information. It carries out circuit simulation with quaternary values starting from a maximally unconstrained start state. In the current work we use STE to symbolically simulate the circuit and trace the values of relevant signals. A single STE simulation is best viewed as an over-approximation of the class of all actual Boolean traces of the circuit agreeing with the stimuli driving the STE simulation: If we manage to verify a Boolean property on the STE simulation, we can deduce that it also holds for all circuit traces.

The computational effort required for an STE simulation is often reduced by the technique of *weakening*, in which the simulated value of a given circuit node at a given time is replaced with the undefined value X. In explicit weakening, the user manually defines the weakening points, and in dynamic weakening any BDD that is larger than a user given threshold is automatically replaced with the undefined value X. We also use more sophisticated automated techniques using causal fan-in information from a circuit trace to determine weakening points. The automated weakening techniques solve most circuit simulation capacity problems without need for human intervention.

Parametric substitution is a technique for reducing symbolic evaluation complexity when we are interested in the result of the evaluation only under a given set of constraints [10]. It is an algorithm that takes a Boolean condition A, and computes a substitution list $v/B = [(v_1, B_1), (v_2, B_2), \ldots]$, which associates each variable v_i occurring in A with a BDD B_i on a set of fresh variables such that the range of the functions B_i is exactly the range of assignments to v_i's that satisfy A. For example, if we want to evaluate an implication $A \Rightarrow C$, we can compute the substitution v/B, apply it to C, and check whether $C' = T$ for the resulting C'. In general, parametric substitution allow us to evaluate a term only in scenarios where the parametrized constraint holds: If C contains a subterm $A => D|E$, in C' the corresponding term will be $T => D'|E'$, and we will never need to evaluate E'. We often use parametric substitutions together with case splitting to bring down the complexity of a problem C by decomposing it into a number of cases $A_1, \ldots, A_n$, and then consider each case A_i separately, parameterizing A_i to ease the computation of C.

In the work discussed in the current paper, we access STE through a layer called *relational STE* or rSTE, a package built around STE to support relational specifications. Effectively, rSTE is a tool allowing us to check whether one list of constraints ("the input constraints"), implies another list of constraints ("the output constraints") over all traces of the circuit. Most common computational complexity reduction techniques, including weakening, parametric substitution etc. are made easily accessible to the user as rSTE options. It also provides sophisticated debug support, breakpoints etc. to enable users to quickly focus on usual verification problems. For the verification of the implication between input and output constraints, we use the tool discussed in [11].

Finally, the *reflection* mechanism allows terms in the reFLect language to be used as objects in the language itself [7]. We use it for sanity check traversals, and to reason about proof decompositions in the theorem prover Goaled [16].

8   Intel Core i7 EXE Verification Effort

8.1   High-Level EXE Model

The structure of our verification work is motivated by a generic abstract model of the execution cluster EXE. This model has a set of *abstract microinstructions*. These may be executed in EXE through a number of *schedule ports*. An instruction scheduled on a particular port will execute in an *execution unit*, and write the result back through a *writeback port* after a *latency*, which depends on the instruction. The set of implemented instructions, the collection of schedule and writeback ports and execution units and the mapping of instructions to ports, execution units and latencies is left open at the level of the generic model and is fixed by every individual design. The abstract cluster model has a number of *state components*, which an instruction may read or update synchronously. Our abstract EXE model does not model memory or caches, allowing us to avoid all the related intricacies. In a real design, EXE accesses memory through the memory cluster MEC, but for the purposes of EXE verification, it suffices for us to model the interactions at the EXE-MEC interface only: the load and store addresses and store data EXE sends to, and the load data EXE receives from MEC.

Much of our work on building the Cluster Verification Environment (CVE) for EXE is proof engineering [13] and software engineering to create a standard, uniform methodology for writing specifications and carrying out verification tasks. The aim of the effort is to support reuse and code maintenance over a constantly changing design, and separate common and project-specific parts to allow shared code to be written only once. We use reFLect user-defined record-like datatypes to enforce structure. For example, all functional micro-instruction specifications are mappings from an abstract type of source data to an abstract type of writeback data. The CVE collects all verification code to a single common directory structure.

8.2   Datapath Verification

Datapath verification is the most important part of our programme. Much of the effort is related to formally specifying the intended behaviour of the over 2700 individual microinstructions. On the one hand, this is a formidable task - the informal specifications of IA-32 architectural instructions take two volumes [2]. On the other, the existence of written specifications as a starting point was very helpful. The formal specifications taking most effort were typically those for auxiliary micro-architectural operations without direct architectural counterparts, which were often lacking in precise documentation. The largest systematic problem in microinstruction specification was the determination of don't-care spaces. Often the architectural specification might explicitly leave an aspect undefined, but the de-facto micro-architectural specification required for backwards compatibility would be stricter. Particular complications included:

- IEEE floating point arithmetic with micro-architectural variations in FPU
- the microarchitecture mixing with the architecture complicates the IA-32 memory addressing mechanism in AGU, already non-trivial due to its gradual evolution over a long history

- mispredicted branch signalling and recovery protocol interacts with the jump operation datapath in JEU
- mispredicted branch and event recovery protocols interact with control register operations datapath in IEU
- some of MIU functionality is intermingled with the bypass network, which made it hard to determine clean verification task boundaries

In the time-frame of the Core i7 work, the formal specifications of the micro-operations were essentially stand-alone, and some of the missed bugs were caused by incorrect specifications. To reduce this risk, we are currently examining ways to more closely link the formal specifications with the C++ specifications used by dynamic validation.

We verified separately for each micro-operation op and for each port p on which the operation op may be scheduled that the following holds for all circuit traces:

$$D(p,op) \land DE(p,op) \land DI(p,op) \Rightarrow (wb(p) = spec(op,src(p)))$$

Where D, DE and DI are sets of basic constraints, environment constraints and internal constraints for operation op on port p, respectively, src and wb refer to the source data and write-back results in the circuit trace, and $spec$ is the formal specification for the operation op. In reality the specification target is not strict equality, but may include partially undefined don't-care results etc. In the actual verification work we would routinely refine the specification and discover missing environment assumptions, augmenting DE and DI, until either the verification succeeded, or we had identified a design issue. We also translated all environment assumptions DE and DI to simulation checkers that were routinely run on full-chip simulation traces. This activity was extremely useful in weeding out incorrect or overly restrictive assumptions.

Most micro-operations could be verified with direct symbolic simulation using a reasonably straightforward variable ordering, with the following exceptions:

- The FADD family of operations uses a case split and parametric substitution strategy, as discussed in [3,21].
- The FMUL, IMUL and PMUL families of multiplication operations need a sequential decomposition as in [15,21].
- The FDIV, FSQRT and IDIV families of operations need an iterative sequential decomposition as in [12,13].
- Intel Core i7 added a collection of SSE4 instructions for accelerated string and text processing, e.g. for faster XML parsing. The verification of these require advanced parametric substitution strategies and sequential decomposition.
- The PSADBW and MPSADBW operations (sum of absolute differences) require a case split and parametric substitution strategy.
- Most AGU operations require the use of symbolic indexing to deal with complexity caused by segment register file (SRF) reads.

For a self-contained example of a related datapath verification task, see [22].

8.3   Control and Bypass Verification

The datapath verification above uses collections of internal constraints DI as assumptions. The first goal of the control verification is to establish these, by strengthening them to an inductive invariant I, and showing for every operation op and relevant schedule port p:

$$D(p,op) \land DE(p,op) \land I \land IE \Rightarrow DI(o,op)$$

Here D and DE are sets of basic and external constraints for op, I is the global control invariant for the design, and IE is an external control invariant on circuit inputs. The second goal is then to show that I indeed is an inductive invariant, i.e. that I holds at the end of the circuit initialization sequence and is inductive. The techniques used to establish this are discussed in [11,14].

The global control invariant for the Core i7 EXE cluster contains roughly 800 individual components. This large number reflects the aggressive clock gating the design uses to conserve power. Many internal circuit restrictions that would automatically propagate from an existing environment assumption were all circuit clocks toggling continuously will need to be established via an inductive invariant when we do not know whether all the relevant clocks will toggle or not.

In the datapath verification, we usually sample source data at the inputs of the execution unit where the microinstruction is executed. The task of the *bypass verification* is then to show that the data at the execution unit inputs is either the properly bypassed result data of an earlier operation, or the value received by the cluster from a register file read, depending on the bypass control inputs. The primary challenges in the bypass verification were the identification of the relevant micro-architectural invariants, and the management of the sheer number of different possible bypass scenarios.

8.4   State Verification

The abstract EXE model has a number of state components. The primary register file does not reside inside the cluster in Core i7, but there is a variety of auxiliary registers, for example the segment register file, floating point control word file etc. In CVE, each state component is annotated with a specification of which instructions are allowed to read or update it, and under which constraints. The verification of an update to a state component by an instruction is done in the context of the datapath proof for that instruction. The inverse, verification of the claim that the value of a state component does not change when there is no updating instruction is done as a separate verification task we call *state stability proof*. The validation of these typically involves new control invariant clauses added to the global invariant I.

In the abstract EXE model, all access to state data is synchronous. All instructions reading a state component do so at a fixed offset relative to their start time, and if they update the state components, the update takes place exactly one cycle after the read so that any subsequent operation reading the component will get the updated value. In reality, an operation often takes several cycles longer to update a state component than to read it. However, to guarantee consistency, we require that when an update happens, no reader should access the state component before the value is actually updated. We call the verification of this restriction the *state sequential consistency proof*. Usually the restriction follows from external scheduling constraints. The necessity of articulating these constraints explicitly to carry out the sequential consistency proof has the upside that the constraints can then be translated to simulation checkers and used to identify scheduling violations, for example due to insufficient synchronization in microcode.

Acknowledgments

We would like to thank Tom Schubert, Blair Milburn and Bob Bentley for the opportunity to carry out this work, Jim Grundy and Eran Talmor for reFLect support and enhancements throughout the project, John O'Leary for Goaled support, Brad Kelly and Evgeny Semenov for their CTE work, and Michael Bair and Kyle Dirks for their healthy scepticism towards the initiative.

References

1. First the Tick, Now the Tock: Next Generation Intel® Microarchitecture (Nehalem) Intel Corp., http://www.intel.com/technology/architecture-silicon/next-gen/whitepaper.pdf
2. IA-32 Intel® Architecture Software Developer's Manual, Vol. 2A and 2B. Intel Corp.
3. Aagaard, M.D., Jones, R.B., Melhan, T.F., O'Leary, J.W., Seger, C.-J.H.: A methodology for large-scale hardware verification. In: Johnson, S.D., Hunt Jr., W.A. (eds.) FMCAD 2000. LNCS, vol. 1954, pp. 263–282. Springer, Heidelberg (2000)
4. Beers, R.: Pre-RTL formal verification: an Intel experience. In: DAC 2008: Proc. of the 45th annual conf. on Design automation, pp. 806–811. ACM, New York (2008)
5. Bentley, B.: Validating a modern microprocessor. In: Etessami, K., Rajamani, S.K. (eds.) CAV 2005. LNCS, vol. 3576, pp. 2–4. Springer, Heidelberg (2005)
6. Flaisher, A., Gluska, A., Singerman, E.: Case study: Integrating FV and DV in the verification of the Intel Core™2 Duo microprocessor. In: FMCAD, Formal Methods in Computer-Aided Design, pp. 192–195 (2007)
7. Grundy, J., Melhan, T., O'Leary, J.: A reflective functional language for hardware design and theorem proving. Journal of Functional Programming 16(2), 157–196 (2006)
8. Hazelhurst, S., Seger, C.-J.H.: Symbolic trajectory evaluation. In: Kropf, T. (ed.) Formal Hardware Verification. LNCS, vol. 1287, pp. 3–78. Springer, Heidelberg (1997)
9. Hinton, G., Sager, D., Upton, M., Boggs, D., Carmean, D., Kyker, A., Roussel, P.: The microarchitecture of the Pentium® 4 processor. Intel. Technology Journal Q1 (February 2001)
10. Jones, R.B.: Symbolic Simulation Methods for Industrial Formal Verification. Kluwer Academic Publishers, Dordrecht (2002)
11. Kaivola, R.: Formal verification of Pentium® 4 components with symbolic simulation and inductive invariants. In: Etessami, K., Rajamani, S.K. (eds.) CAV 2005. LNCS, vol. 3576, pp. 170–184. Springer, Heidelberg (2005)
12. Kaivola, R., Aagaard, M.D.: Divider circuit verification with model checking and theorem proving. In: Aagaard, M.D., Harrison, J. (eds.) TPHOLs 2000. LNCS, vol. 1869, pp. 338–355. Springer, Heidelberg (2000)
13. Kaivola, R., Kohatsu, K.: Proof engineering in the large: formal verification of Pentium® 4 floating-point divider. Int'l J. on Software Tools for Technology Transfer 4, 323–334 (2003)
14. Kaivola, R., Naik, A.: Formal verification of high-level conformance with symbolic simulation. In: HLDVT, High-Level Design Validation and Test, pp. 153–159 (2005)
15. Kaivola, R., Narasimhan, N.: Formal verification of the Pentium® 4 floating-point multiplier. In: DATE, Design, Automation and Test in Europe, pp. 20–27 (2002)
16. O'Leary, J.: Using a reflective functional language for hardware verification and theorem proving. In: Third Workshop on Applied Semantics (APPSEM 2005), September 12–15, 2005, pp. 12–15 (2005)

17. O'Leary, J.W., Zhao, X., Gerth, R., Seger, C.-J.H.: Formally verifying IEEE compliance of floating-point hardware. Intel. Technology Journal Q1 (Feburary 1999)
18. Paulson, L.: ML for the Working Programmer. Cambridge University Press, Cambridge (1996)
19. Schubert, T.: High level formal verification of next-generation microprocessors. In: DAC 2003: Proceedings of the 40th conference on Design automation, pp. 1–6. ACM Press, New York (2003)
20. Seger, C.-J.H., Bryant, R.E.: Formal verification by symbolic evaluation of partially-ordered trajectories. Formal Methods in System Design 6(2), 147–189 (1995)
21. Slobodova, A.: Challenges for formal verification in industrial setting. In: Brim, L., Haverkort, B.R., Leucker, M., van de Pol, J. (eds.) FMICS 2006 and PDMC 2006. LNCS, vol. 4346, pp. 1–22. Springer, Heidelberg (2007)
22. Slobodova, A.: Formal verification of hardware support for advanced encryption standard. In: FMCAD, Formal Methods in Computer-Aided Design, pp. 61–64 (2008)

Generating and Analyzing Symbolic Traces of Simulink/Stateflow Models

Aditya Kanade[1] and Rajeev Alur[1], Franjo Ivančić[2], S. Ramesh[3],
Sriram Sankaranarayanan[2], and K.C. Shashidhar[3]

[1] University of Pennsylvania
[2] NEC Laboratories America
[3] GM India Science Lab

Abstract. We present a methodology and a toolkit for improving simulation coverage of Simulink/Stateflow models of hybrid systems using symbolic analysis of simulation traces. We propose a novel instrumentation scheme that allows the simulation engine of Simulink/Stateflow to output, along with the concrete simulation trace, the symbolic transformers needed for our analysis. Given a simulation trace, along with the symbolic transformers, our analysis computes a set of initial states that would lead to traces with the same sequence of discrete components at each step of the simulation. Such an analysis relies critically on the use of convex polyhedra to represent sets of states. However, the exponential complexity of the polyhedral operations implies that the performance of the analysis would degrade rapidly with the increasing size of the model and the simulation traces. We propose a new representation, called the *bounded vertex representation*, which allows us to perform under-approximate computations while fixing the complexity of the representation *a priori*. Using this representation we achieve a trade-off between the complexity of the symbolic computation and the quality of the under-approximation. We demonstrate the benefits of our approach over existing simulation and verification methods with case studies.

1 Introduction

Simulink/Stateflow[1] (SL/SF) models are currently the de-facto standard in the model-based development of real-time, embedded systems. They are widely used in many domains, including automotive and avionics. Simulink models are constructed by interconnecting blocks representing operations such as *gain*, *addition*, *multiplexors*, *lookup tables*, and *integrators*. Stateflow charts specify the control in the form of concurrent and hierarchical finite state machines that interact with the Simulink model. Together, they provide a powerful modeling framework that enables the development, testing, and rapid prototyping of control software, supported by automated code generation techniques.

The critical nature of the software developed with these models calls for the use of formal design verification tools. However, there are many challenges for

---

[1] Simulink and Stateflow are trademarks of The MathWorks Inc.

A. Bouajjani and O. Maler (Eds.): CAV 2009, LNCS 5643, pp. 430–445, 2009.

the construction of such verification tools. First of all, the semantics of these models is loosely defined in terms of a simulation engine. The lack of clearly specified semantics makes the construction of formal tools hard. Secondly, these models incorporate both the discrete state changes due to the Stateflow charts and the continuous evolution of the state due to the presence of blocks such as *integrators*. Hybrid automata [3] and related formulations are ideal for representing these models. However, the task of model-level translation from SL/SF to hybrid automata is difficult to automate.

In this paper, we present an approach for systematic exploration of distinct behaviors of SL/SF models. Our approach provides practical solutions to some of the key challenges using a novel approach to the problem of deciphering the semantics of these models. Rather than translating these models statically into hybrid automata [2] or Lustre programs [34], our approach performs an on-the-fly translation by instrumenting Simulink blocks and Stateflow transitions with *callback functions*. During numerical simulation, a callback function is called whenever the corresponding block is evaluated. The callback functions construct the symbolic transformer of the simulation step. An appropriate composition of these transformers gives us the *symbolic trace* of the simulation.

Given the concrete and symbolic traces of a k-step simulation starting from an initial model state m, our analysis constructs a set M of states that are *equivalent* to m up to the given simulation length k. Two model states m and m' are equivalent if they yield the same sequence of discrete components at each step of simulation. Systematic exploration of the model's behaviors is obtained by repeating simulation starting from an initial state outside the set M.

The performance of such analyses depends critically on the choice of a representation for sets of continuous states. While the representation of convex polyhedra as linear constraints with arbitrary coefficients [10] is expressive, it suffers from worst-case exponential time complexity. Various restrictions have been proposed to achieve tradeoff between precision and tractability. The typical restrictions include axis-parallel constraints (e.g. intervals [9]), difference constraints (e.g. octagons [23] and octahedra [7]), or an arbitrary but fixed set of linear constraints (e.g. template polyhedra [27]).

While most of these representations are designed for over-approximations, our approach requires under-approximations of state-sets to eliminate only redundant simulations. We therefore design an under-approximate *bounded vertex representation* of polyhedra using a set of direction vectors. The size of this representation is fixed by the number of direction vectors used to compute such a representation. As a result, the time and space complexity of the analysis can be controlled, allowing analysis of longer simulations for larger system models. This representation can potentially be useful to improve precision of over-approximate analyses, detect valid counter-examples, and in controller synthesis methods.

We have implemented our approach using model instrumentation and the bounded vertex representation of polyhedra for SL/SF models with *linear blocks*. The model instrumentation is implemented using the Simulink runtime API [31] and operations over the bounded vertex representation are performed using the GNU Linear Programming Kit (GLPK) [18].

We illustrate the benefits of our approach on three case studies: a Simulink demo model from The MathWorks [1] and two instances of the room heating benchmark [12]. These models use several commonly used modeling features of SL/SF including hierarchical and concurrent Stateflow charts and lookup tables. Nevertheless, the symbolic traces generated by our instrumentation technique accurately capture the simulation semantics of these models. The experimental results indicate that the test cases generated by our tool successfully exercise distinct discrete mode switchings of these models, leading to better temporal coverage of model behaviors. Further, the use of the bounded vertex representation leads to scalable analysis. While most of the verification tools [5, 13, 21, 30] for hybrid systems are limited to systems with up to 10 continuous variables, the small runtime of our analysis on a case study with 10 continuous variables suggests that our technique can handle systems with large number of variables. We also compare our tool with Reactis [8, 25] and with random testing on a case study. The test cases generated by our tool explore significantly large number of inequivalent simulation behaviors than both Reactis and random testing.

Related work. Bisimulation metrics and expansion functions provide a mechanism of identifying states whose continuous trajectories stay close in space and time [11,17,22]. However, these techniques require transition guards to be planar and are not suitable for the case studies considered in this paper.

Our recent work on analysis of SL/SF models [4] also considers the problem of temporal coverage but requires static translation from SL/SF models to hybrid automata. The runtime technique of symbolic trace generation presented in this paper overcomes this drawback, enabling automated analysis of large and complex models. Further, the use of convex polyhedra may limit the scalability of the earlier approach. The algorithm presented in this paper exploits the scalability of linear programming solvers in under-approximate computations. Some related approaches that combine concrete and symbolic executions with constraint solving have been explored in software testing [19,29].

There are many commercial and in-house tools for testing SL/SF models [14, 25, 28, 32, 35] which aim at structural coverage of model elements. These tools combine randomization with constraint solving techniques to generate test cases. Our notion of temporal coverage captures the simulation behaviors of models instead of structural properties (like blocks and branches) of model designs.

In hybrid systems verification, convex polyhedra are widely used to represent sets of states [5, 13, 16, 20, 21, 30]. However, the scalability of verification tools is limited by the worst-case exponential complexity of polyhedral operations. Restricted forms of polyhedra [5,6,15,26,33] have been designed for over-approximate computations. Our approach proposes the use of bounded vertex representations as under-approximations of sets of states. The bounded vertex representation bears some similarities to zonotopes [15,16] but it need not be symmetric about a central vertex and computes under-approximations.

2   Discrete-Time Simulations of Simulink/Stateflow

An SL/SF model of an embedded system defines time-dependent mathematical relationships between the inputs, internal state variables, and outputs of the system. These models are represented graphically as dataflow diagrams of interconnected blocks. Simulink provides a diverse family of continuous, discrete, and logical building blocks. Stateflow complements these design features with concurrent and hierarchical state machines called Stateflow charts that are used for specifying discrete mode control logic.

2.1   Single-Step Concrete and Symbolic Simulation Semantics

The SL/SF models are simulated on numerical data to generate concrete executions. The MathWorks simulation engine evaluates the blocks in a given model at discrete time steps. Each block has an associated sampling time which specifies the period at which the block is evaluated. Sampling times of the individual blocks are used to determine the *simulation time step* $h \in \mathbb{R}_+$ of the overall model, so that the model is evaluated every h time units. For simplicity, we assume that the sampling time of each block equals the simulation time step h.

Each block in a model represents a mathematical function. For example, an *integrator block* represents assignment to a *continuous state variable* of the model such that the time derivative of its output equals the value of its input. The output is computed by means of numerical integration. The precision of the integration can be controlled by choosing an integration routine and the simulation time step. We consider (explicit) fixed-step integration routines.

A *continuous state* $s \in \mathbb{R}^n$ of an SL/SF model consists of a valuation of the continuous state variables in the model. A *discrete state* $q \in Q$ of an SL/SF model consists of the set of *active states* in a Stateflow chart of the model along with the various choices of the conditional blocks in the model. Q denotes the set of discrete states of the model. The *model state* of an SL/SF model is denoted by $m = (q, s) \in M$ where $M = Q \times \mathbb{R}^n$.

For the numerical simulation, we fix an integration routine $\mathbb{S}$ and a simulation time step h. An SL/SF model defines a function $f : M \to M$. The inputs to the model are fixed at the beginning of a simulation run. A *concrete simulation step* of an SL/SF model applies the function f to a model state (q, s) to yield a model state (q', s') as shown in Figure 1(a). The transition between discrete states consists of a change in the choices of the conditional blocks and the transitions of the Stateflow charts. The transition between continuous states consists of an assignment to the continuous state variables. The function f is deterministic but it is defined *operationally* according to an evaluation order of the blocks in the model determined by the MathWorks simulation engine.

In order to overcome the opacity in the evaluation order semantics of SL/SF, we augment the concrete simulations of SL/SF models with symbolic simulations by instrumenting the model with callback functions. Our method discovers the function f defined by the model incrementally. The symbolic simulation emits the description of f applicable in each simulation step. A *concrete and symbolic*

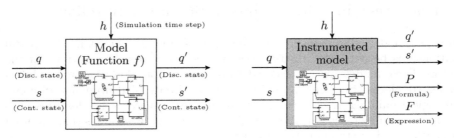

(a) Concrete simulation step   (b) Concrete and symbolic simulation step

Fig. 1. Single-step concrete and symbolic simulation semantics of SL/SF models

simulation step of the instrumented SL/SF model maps a model state (q, s) to a tuple (q', s', P, F) where $(q', s') = f(q, s)$, P is a quantifier-free formula and F is an expression over the continuous state variables. The simulation step of the instrumented model is shown in Figure 1(b). The symbolic transformers (P, F) generated by the simulation step satisfy the following properties: $[\![P]\!](s) = true$, $s' = [\![F]\!](s)$, and for all $v \in \mathbb{R}^n$, if $[\![P]\!](v) = true$ then $f(q, v) = (q', [\![F]\!](v))$.

2.2   Automated Instrumentation of Simulink/Stateflow Models

The ability to symbolically simulate SL/SF models presents many possibilities for automated analysis. It is however challenging due to their complex semantics. Factors such as concurrency and hierarchy in Stateflow charts, triggered or conditional subsystems, and virtual blocks complicate the semantics.

In this section, we present a technique that enables symbolic simulation of SL/SF models. It involves two steps: manual implementation of callback functions for the block types in the SL/SF language and automated technique of composing the callback functions through instrumentation of models.

Manual implementation of callback functions. For each block type T in a given model, we implement a callback function f_T that encodes the semantics of the block type T. The callback function for a block of type T takes a symbolic transformer (P_i, F_i) for each input port i of the block and generates a symbolic transformer (P'_j, F'_j) for each output port j of the block. For example, if (P_1, F_1) and (P_2, F_2) are the symbolic transformers of the inputs to a *sum block* then the symbolic transformer of the output is $(P_1 \wedge P_2, F_1 + F_2)$.

If a block type is conditional then we use the concrete input values to determine which conditional branch is being executed to generate corresponding symbolic transformer. Consider a *relational operator block* with relational operator $<=$. Suppose (P_1, F_1) and (P_2, F_2) are the input symbolic transformers. If the concrete input values satisfy the relation then the symbolic transformer of the output is $(F_1 \leq F_2 \wedge P_1 \wedge P_2, 1)$ otherwise it is $(F_1 > F_2 \wedge P_1 \wedge P_2, 0)$.

The symbolic transformer for a *constant block* with constant value c is $(true, c)$. If the constant block corresponds to a continuous variable x_i of the

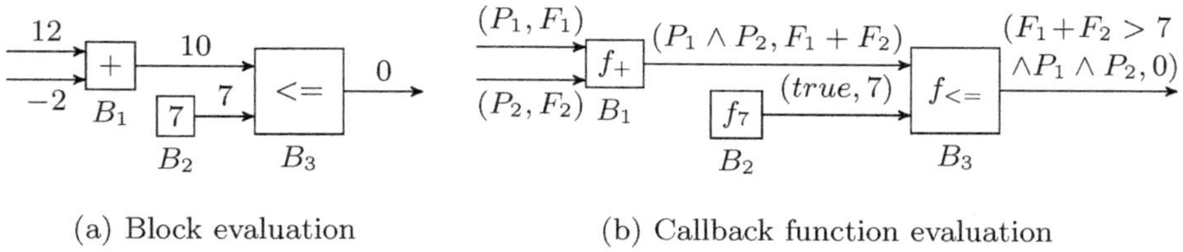

(a) Block evaluation   (b) Callback function evaluation

Fig. 2. Block-level compositional semantics

model then the symbolic transformer is $(true, x_i)$. An *integrator block* always corresponds to some continuous variable of the model. If it represents a variable x_i then the output symbolic transformer is $(P_1, \mathbb{S}(x_i, h, F_1))$ where (P_1, F_1) is the input symbolic transformer, h is the simulation time step, and $\mathbb{S}(x_i, h, F_1)$ is the expression for the numerical integration. For the Euler solver, the expression is $x_i + hF_1$.

Automated composition of callback functions. For every block B of type T in the model, we attach the callback function f_T with it. During simulation, the callback function of a block is evaluated immediately after the output of the block is computed by Simulink and before the next block is executed.

Consider Figure 2(a) which shows three inter-connected blocks and a valuation to the inter-connections during a simulation step. We use *the Simulink block runtime API* to access block data, such as block inputs and outputs, and parameters, during simulation. The key part of our scheme is to correctly access symbolic transformers of the blocks connected to the input of a given block. The inter-connections between blocks can be identified programmatically through the 'PortConnectivity' parameter of each block. This allows us to compose the callback functions of the individual blocks in a model as shown in Figure 2(b).

The block evaluation order determined by the MathWorks simulation engine is guided by data dependencies between the blocks so that a block is evaluated only after its inputs are computed. The technique of callback functions works with any valid block evaluation order. For instance, $\langle B_1, B_2, B_3 \rangle$ and $\langle B_2, B_1, B_3 \rangle$ are the valid block evaluation orders for the model in Figure 2. The callback functions f_+, f_7, and $f_{<=}$ are also evaluated in the order chosen by the simulator.

The presence of virtual blocks and enabled, triggered, or conditional subsystems requires special care. For instance, a virtual block (e.g. an *inport*) cannot be attached a callback function because it is compiled away before simulation. For a block whose input port is attached to a virtual block, we need to walk the inter-connections to find the correct non-virtual input block.

The callback function for a Stateflow chart uses *the Stateflow API* to access the elements of the chart. We annotate the transitions of a Stateflow chart to monitor which transitions are taken in a simulation step. The guards on these transitions are used for generating the corresponding symbolic transformers for the simulation step. We check consistency of symbolic transformers with the corresponding concrete simulation values by evaluating the transformers independently in MATLAB and matching the output with the concrete values.

Limitations. Our current implementation is restricted to linear transformers. While we support several block types and their configuration settings, the library of callback functions that we built is not complete, given the rich set of modeling features that Simulink provides. Most of these limitations can be overcome by means of simple extensions to the basic scheme proposed here. We assume that there are no local variables and functions in Stateflow charts and that all the output variables take discrete values. While we handle many commonly used Stateflow features including hierarchy and concurrency, extension to advanced features such as recursive broadcasts and completion semantics is future work.

3   Under-Approximations of Convex Polyhedra

Polyhedra form a natural representation of sets of continuous states. However, the worst-case exponential complexity of polyhedral operations limits the scalability of analysis tools. Several restricted forms of domains support efficient over-approximate computations. Since the goal of our analysis is to eliminate redundant simulations, it requires exact or under-approximate computations.

We now present a novel representation of polyhedra for under-approximate computations. The representation called, the *bounded vertex representation*, consists of a finite number, say k, of vectors where k is bounded *a priori*. The polyhedron represented by these vectors is their convex hull. In other words, the vectors form the vertices of the polyhedron. The rapid increase in the number of vertices with repeated operations affects the performance of an iterative analysis. The approach of working with a bounded number of vertices overcomes this bottleneck. In our analysis, the under-approximation of the set of states equivalent to a given state s should contain the state s itself to ensure that s is not chosen as an initial state subsequently. Therefore, given a vector v in a polyhedron P, the under-approximation of P with respect to v should contain v itself.

3.1   Bounded Vertex Representation

Consider the polyhedron $P \subseteq \mathbb{R}^n$ shown in Figure 3(a) (for $n = 2$) and a vector $v \in P$. An under-approximation of P can be obtained by selecting a collection $U = [u_1, \ldots, u_4]$ of vectors from the vertex set of P. To obtain these vertices, we pick a collection $C = [c_1, \ldots, c_4]$ of vectors and maximize the objective functions $c_i^T x$ over the polyhedron P where x is the $n \times 1$ vector of real valued variables. For instance, Figure 3(a) shows the vertices obtained by selecting c_i parallel to positive and negative axes of the 2-dimensional space. While the intersection of the half-spaces $c_i^T x \leq c_i^T u_i$ gives an over-approximation (bounding box) of P, the convex hull of the vertices u_i gives an under-approximation. We denote the convex hull of a collection U of vectors by $\mathrm{CH}(U)$. However, the given vector $v \in P$ may not belong to the convex hull of U as shown in Figure 3(a).

Another under-approximation of P is shown in Figure 3(b). It is formed with respect to the vector v by extending rays starting from v along the directions given by vectors in $D = [d_1, d_2, -d_1, -d_2]$ where d_1 and d_2 are axis-parallel. Let

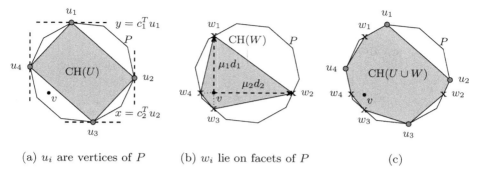

(a) u_i are vertices of P (b) w_i lie on facets of P (c)

Fig. 3. Under-approximations of a polyhedron P with respect to a vector $v \in P$

$W = [w_1, \ldots, w_4]$ be the collection of vectors that lie at the intersection of these rays $v + \mu_i d_i$, where $\mu_i \in \mathbb{R}^+$ are the scaling factors, and facets of the polyhedron. The convex hull of W is a subset of P. If there are at least two direction vectors $d_i, d_j \in D$ such that $d_i = -d_j$, the vector v is guaranteed to belong to CH(W).

While the collection W ensures that the vector v is included in the under-approximation, the collection U is potentially useful in obtaining a better under-approximation. The under-approximation given by the union $U \cup W$ of the two collections U and W is shown in Figure 3(c). We combine these two observations to define the bounded vertex representation of P.

Consider two collections $C = [c_1, \ldots, c_m]$ and $D = [d_1, \ldots, d_r]$ of $n \times 1$ real vectors, called the *coefficient* and *direction* vectors respectively. We require that there exist at least two vectors $d_i, d_j \in D$ such that $d_i = -d_j$. Given C and D, the *bounded vertex representation* (BVR) of a convex polyhedron $P \subseteq \mathbb{R}^n$ with respect to a vector $v \in P$ consists of a collection $V = U \cup W$ where $U = [u_1, \ldots, u_m]$ and $W = [w_1, \ldots, w_r]$ of vectors, called *vertices*, such that

1. The vector u_i, $i \in [1, m]$, maximizes the function $c_i^T x$ over P and
2. The vector $w_i = v + \mu_i d_i, i \in [1, r]$, where $\mu_i = \max\{\lambda \geq 0 \mid w_i = v + \lambda d_i \in P\}$.

A bounded vertex representation V of a polyhedron $P \subseteq \mathbb{R}^n$ with respect to a vector $v \in P$ satisfies the following properties: CH(V) $\subseteq P$ (under-approximation) and $v \in$ CH(V) (membership).

3.2   Computing Bounded Vertex Representations

In the following discussion, we consider collections $C = [c_1, \ldots, c_m]$ and $D = [d_1, \ldots, d_r]$ of coefficient and direction vectors.

Construction. We define a procedure BVR(A, b, v, C, D) to compute a bounded representation $V = U \cup W$ of a convex polyhedron $P = \{x : Ax \leq b\}$ with respect to a vector $v \in P$ using linear programming (LP). For each $c_i \in C$, the vertex $u_i \in U$ is computed by maximizing the linear objective function $c_i^T x$ over P.

$$u_i = \text{maximize } c_i^T x \text{ subject to } Ax \leq b \tag{1}$$

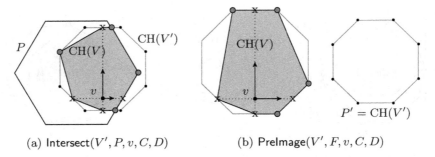

(a) Intersect(V', P, v, C, D) (b) PreImage(V', F, v, C, D)

Fig. 4. Operations on the bounded vertex representation

An optimal solution to a linear objective function over a convex polyhedron occurs at a vertex of the polyhedron. A vector u_i is thus a vertex of the polyhedron P. The optima with respect to $c_i^T x$ may not be unique but, given a deterministic LP solver, the set U is uniquely defined.

For each direction vector $d_i \in D$, the procedure BVR maximizes a scalar variable μ such that $v + \mu\, d_i \in P$.

$$\mu_i = \text{maximize } \mu \text{ subject to } (A\, d_i)\, \mu \leq (b - Av) \wedge \mu \geq 0 \qquad (2)$$

The vector $w_i \in W$ is obtained from the optimal value μ_i as: $w_i = v + \mu_i\, d_i$.

Intersection. We define a procedure Intersect(V', P, v, C, D) that takes as input a bounded vertex representation V', a convex polyhedron $P = \{x\colon Ax \leq b\}$, and $v \in P \cap \text{CH}(V')$. It computes a bounded vertex representation $V = U \cup W$ of the intersection of P and $\text{CH}(V')$ with respect to the vector v.

Let $|V'| = k$. For convenience, we treat the collection V' as $k \times n$ matrix. The vertices in V' form the rows of the matrices. Let $R_{(V')}$ be the constraint representation of $\text{CH}(V')$ using a $k \times 1$ vector λ of real-valued auxiliary variables. Informally, R represents vectors x and λ such that $x \in \text{CH}(V')$ and λ are multipliers that certify the membership of x.

$$R_{(V')}(x, \lambda) : \ x = V'^T \lambda \wedge \lambda \geq \mathbf{0} \ \wedge \ \mathbf{1}^T \cdot \lambda = 1$$

A vertex $u_i \in U$ is computed by solving the following linear program:

$$u_i = \text{maximize } c_i^T x \text{ subject to } Ax \leq b \ \wedge \ R_{(V')}(x, \lambda)$$

Consider Figure 4(a) as an example where $|C| = 4$ and $|D| = 4$. The vectors in V' are shown as small black dots. The vectors in the set U are shown as small gray circles and are vertices of $P \cap \text{CH}(V')$. A vector $w_i \in W$ is obtained by solving the following linear program:

$$\mu_i = \text{maximize } \mu \text{ subject to } x = v + \mu\, d_i \wedge Ax \leq b \ \wedge \ R_{(V')}(x, \lambda) \ \wedge \ \mu \geq 0$$

The optimal solution for x directly yields the required element w_i of the collection W. In Figure 4(a), the vectors in the set W are shown as 'x's.

Preimages of Affine Functions. We define a procedure $\mathsf{PreImage}(V', F, v, C, D)$ that takes as input a bounded vertex representation V', an affine function $F(x) = Ax + b$, and a vector v such that $F(v) \in \mathrm{CH}(V')$. It computes a bounded vertex representation $V = U \cup W$ of the preimage of $\mathrm{CH}(V')$ under F with respect to v. For each $c_i \in C$, the following LP is solved to yield $u_i \in U$:

$$u_i = \text{maximize } c_i^T x \text{ subject to } x' = Ax + b \ \wedge \ R_{(V')}(x', \lambda)$$

Similarly, each direction vector $d_i \in D$ yields an element $w_i = v + \mu_i d_i \in W$:

$$\mu_i = \text{maximize } \mu \text{ subject to } x = v + \mu\, d_i \ \wedge \ x' = Ax + b \ \wedge \ R_{(V')}(x', \lambda) \wedge \ \mu \geq 0$$

Figure 4(b) illustrates the preimage computation using BVR.

Complexity. Consider bounded vertex representations $V = U \cup W$ where $|U| = m$ and $|V| = r$. The construction of a BVR of a polyhedron $P \subseteq \mathbb{R}^n$ involves solving m LP instances in n variables and r LP instances in a single variable. The intersection and preimage operations involve solving m instances in $(m + r + n)$ variables and r instances in $(m + r + 1)$ variables. Each LP instance can be solved in time polynomial in the number of variables.

We have implemented BVR using the GNU linear programming kit (GLPK). We present preliminary evaluation of BVR in the context of a case study with 10 continuous variables in Section 5.

4   Symbolic Analysis of Simulation Traces

The SL/SF models are typically analyzed through numerical simulation. However, the usual practice of random testing does not guarantee coverage of all the model behaviors. In this section, we propose an automated testing technique to systematically explore distinct behaviors of SL/SF models. Our technique is based on an analysis of simulation traces of the model.

Consider an SL/SF model instrumented for symbolic simulation (Section 2). We fix a simulation framework $\langle \mathbb{S}, h, k \rangle$ where $\mathbb{S}$ is the integration routine, h is the simulation time step, and $k > 0$ is the bound on the number of simulation steps. The *concrete trace* of the simulation of the model starting from an initial model state (q_1, s_1) is $\langle (q_1, s_1), \ldots, (q_{k+1}, s_{k+1}) \rangle$ where (q_i, s_i) and (q_{i+1}, s_{i+1}) are the model states before and after the ith simulation step, for $i \in [1, k]$. The *symbolic trace* of the simulation is a sequence $\langle (P_1, F_1) \ldots (P_k, F_k) \rangle$ where (P_i, F_i) is the symbolic transformer of the ith simulation step. We consider models with linear transformers, that is, P_i is a conjunction of linear predicates over the continuous state variables of the model and F_i is a linear transformation of the state variables. During a simulation step, the blocks in the model are evaluated in a deterministic order chosen by the MathWorks simulation engine. Thus, the choice of the initial model state completely determines the simulation trace of the model. Presently, we do not allow time-varying inputs to the models.

Algorithm 1. Iterative preimage computation

Input :
1. A k-step concrete simulation trace $\langle (q_1, s_1), \ldots, (q_{k+1}, s_{k+1}) \rangle$
2. A k-step symbolic simulation trace $\langle (P_1, F_1), \ldots, (P_k, F_k) \rangle$
3. A polyhedron $X = \{x \colon Ax \leq b\}$ of the continuous state-space of the model
4. Collections $C = [c_1, \ldots, c_m]$ and $D = [d_1, \ldots, d_r]$ of coefficients and directions

Output: A BVR V such that for all $s \in \mathrm{CH}(V)$, $(q_1, s) \equiv_k (q_1, s_1)$

1   $V := \mathsf{BVR}(A, b, s_{k+1}, C, D)$
2   **for** $i := k;\ \ i > 0;\ \ i := i - 1$ **do**
3     $V' := \mathsf{Preimage}(V, F_i, s_i, C, D)$
4     $V := \mathsf{Intersect}(V', P_i, s_i, C, D)$
5   **return** V

We propose the notion of *equivalence of states* to improve effectiveness of simulation-based analysis. If two states are equivalent, it is sufficient to simulation the model from only one of them and search for different model behaviors starting with states that are not equivalent to the already chosen one.

Definition 1. *Consider an* SL/SF *model SL with a simulation framework* $\langle \mathbb{S}, h, k \rangle$. *Two model states* (q, s) *and* (q', s') *are* equivalent up to k *simulation steps, denoted by* $(q, s) \equiv_k (q', s')$, *if the discrete components of the concrete traces starting from them agree at each step of the simulation.*

Note that the notion of equivalence is valid even for models which do not have any Stateflow chart because the discrete component of a model state also consists of the outcomes of the conditional blocks in the model (Section 2.1).

Our overall testing technique proceeds as follows. We choose an initial state (q_1, s_1) and simulate the model for k steps. Using the concrete and symbolic traces of the simulation, we infer the set of states that are equivalent to (q_1, s_1) up to k steps. Even with a single simulation, we can thus declare a non-trivial set of model states as covered. Below we discuss the algorithm for computation of equivalent states. The initial model state for the next simulation is then chosen randomly from outside the covered region.

Algorithm. Given the concrete trace $\langle (q_1, s_1), \ldots, (q_{k+1}, s_{k+1}) \rangle$ and the symbolic trace $\langle (P_1, F_1), \ldots, (P_k, F_k) \rangle$ of a k-step simulation of an SL/SF model, Algorithm 1 computes the bounded vertex representation V of the set of continuous states equivalent to s_1. Thus, for each continuous state $s \in \mathrm{CH}(V)$, (q_1, s) is equivalent to (q_1, s_1) up to k simulation steps.

Let V_{i+1} be the bounded vertex representation at the beginning of an iteration with the loop counter equal to i (Lines 1–1). Initially, V_{k+1} is the BVR of the continuous state-space X of the model (Line 1). The loop body computes the intersection of the convex polyhedron P_i and the preimage of $\mathrm{CH}(V_{i+1})$ under the function F_i, where (P_i, F_i) is the symbolic transformer of the ith simulation step. The bounded vertex representation V_i is the under-approximation of the intersection. The symbolic operations are computed as defined in Section 3 using an LP solver. The number of vertices in the bounded vertex representations is bounded by the number of coefficient and direction vectors chosen as input to the algorithm. For each $i \in [1, k+1]$, $|V_i| = m + r$ where $m = |C|$ and $r = |D|$.

Performance optimizations. The quality of the result in the iterative analysis of long simulation runs may reduce due to successive under-approximations. We achieve a tradeoff between runtime and quality of under-approximations by reducing the number of preimage computations. We select a parameter called the *width of preimage computation*. If w is the width then we perform a preimage computation at every wth simulation step instead of every step. For example, if $w = 2$ and the symbolic trace is $\langle (P_1, F_1), \dots, (P_{2k}, F_{2k}) \rangle$ then the symbolic transformer for the ith preimage computation is (P'_i, F'_i) where $P'_i = P_j \wedge P_{j+1}[F_j(x)/x]$, $F'_i = F_{j+1} \circ F_j$, and $j = 2k - 2i + 1$. The expression $e[y/x]$ denotes substitution of y for x in e and $G \circ H$ is the function composition. The number of variables in a preimage computation (a linear program) is independent of the width but the number of constraints is proportional to the width.

The quality of an under-approximate bounded vertex representation can be improved by selecting more coefficient and direction vectors but at higher computational cost. In Section 5, we discuss the effect of varying these parameters on performance of the algorithm and quality of analysis results.

5   Experimental Results

We evaluated our model instrumentation and analysis tool on the following case studies: a Simulink demo model (VCC) from The MathWorks [1] and two instances, with 3 and 10 continuous state variables, of a parametrized hybrid systems verification benchmark (RHB) [12]. Figure 5 shows their characteristics. The VCC model uses many modeling features of SL/SF including hierarchical and concurrent Stateflow and lookup tables. RHB{10} models a system with 4 heaters that can be distributed among 10 rooms. Each heater can be either on or off. The number of discrete states is $\binom{10}{4} \cdot 2^4$. The runtime technique of symbolic trace generation enables analysis of such large models.

An instrumented model is simulated from a randomly chosen initial state (q, s) and a set of states equivalent to (q, s) up to 100 simulation steps is computed. The initial state for the next simulation is chosen from outside the states covered in all the preceding simulations. Figure 6 summarizes the test results. For VCC, over

Model	Variables	SL blocks	SL conn.	SF states	SF trans.	Discrete states	State-space
VCC	2	75	83	12	28	106	$[172, 373]^2$
RHB{3}	3	33	42	1	18	12	$[16.5, 23]^3$
RHB{10}	10	33	42	1	18	3360	$[15, 23]^{10}$

Fig. 5. Characteristics of the case studies

Model	Total simulations	BVR size	Width	Avg. constraints per simulation	Inequivalent simulations	Avg. analysis time per simulation(sec.)
VCC	592	8	10	1170	575 (97%)	0.1697
RHB{3}	957	10	10	500	531 (55%)	0.1503
RHB{10}	324	24	50	1292	298 (92%)	7.1514

Fig. 6. Analysis results for the case studies: Total runtime is 1 hour for each case study

97% initial states chosen by our tool explore inequivalent simulation traces, each exhibiting distinct discrete mode switches. The tool however cannot eliminate all equivalent initial states because of the use of under-approximations in the analysis and the presence of disjunctive guards in the models, as can be seen for the results on RHB{3} and RHB{10} models. The small runtime of our analysis for RHB{10} suggests that our technique of using the bounded vertex representation can scale to systems with large number of variables.

We compared effectiveness of our tool with Reactis [25, 8] and with random testing for the VCC model on 100 test cases generated by these tools individually. Given the model, Reactis selects test inputs at different simulation steps. We treat the test inputs generated by Reactis as distinct initial states and also choose a set of initial states by random sampling. Our tool successfully explores 96 inequivalent simulations as compared to 56 by Reactis and 73 by random testing as summarized in Figure 7. The last 4 columns report the typical structural coverage metric as percentages of the total number of conditions, decisions, modified condition/decision (MC/DC), and lookup table rows covered by the tools.

We evaluate the effect of various parameters to the analysis algorithm in the context of the RHB{10} case study. The quality of under-approximations and the computational cost can be balanced by varying the size of the bounded vertex representation and the width of preimage computation. Figure 8 shows the relative growth in computation time and coverage with increasing BVR size and width. The coverage plots show the percentage of the volume of the entire initial continuous state-space covered by a single simulation. The volumes are estimated using the MATLAB interface to the QuickHull algorithm [24]. While the number of variables is independent of the width, the number of constraints for a preimage computation increases with the width. The number of calls to the LP solver increase for decreasing widths. For small widths, the cost of calls to the LP solver may slow down the analysis as shown in Figure 8(b).

Tool	Inequivalent simulations	Conditions	Decisions	MC/DC	Lookup table rows
Our tool	96	58	84	16	29
Reactis	56	55	86	17	30
Random	73	58	84	16	29

Fig. 7. Comparison with Reactis and random testing on 100 step simulations

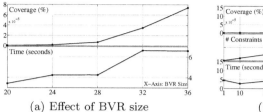
(a) Effect of BVR size

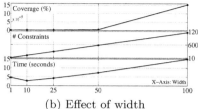
(b) Effect of width

Fig. 8. Results are measured for the RHB{10} model and are averages over 10 runs of 100 simulation steps each. In (a), the width is 25; and in (b), the size of BVR is 24.

6   Conclusions

We have presented an analysis technique for systematic exploration of distinct behaviors of SL/SF models. The completely automated analysis of SL/SF models is made possible via symbolic trace generation using model instrumentation. Through the use of under-approximate bounded vertex representation, we can analyze models with large number of continuous variables. We have demonstrated the benefits of our approach with case studies, including a model that has 10 continuous variables. Our current implementation covers many SL/SF modeling features and extending it is future work.

Acknowledgments. The work by authors at University of Pennsylvania was partially supported by NSF award CNS 0524059 and a grant from General Motors.

References

1. Simulink demos, `http://www.mathworks.com/products/simulink/demos.html`
2. Agrawal, A., Simon, G., Karsai, G.: Semantic translation of Simulink/Stateflow models to hybrid automata using graph transformations. ENTCS 109, 43–56 (2004)
3. Alur, R., Courcoubetis, C., Halbwachs, N., Henzinger, T.A., Ho, P., Nicollin, X., Olivero, A., Sifakis, J., Yovine, S.: The algorithmic analysis of hybrid systems. Theoretical Computer Science 138, 3–34 (1995)
4. Alur, R., Kanade, A., Ramesh, S., Shashidhar, K.C.: Symbolic analysis for improving simulation coverage of Simulink/Stateflow models. In: EMSOFT, pp. 89–98 (2008)
5. Asarin, E., Dang, T., Maler, O.: The d/dt tool for verification of hybrid systems. In: Brinksma, E., Larsen, K.G. (eds.) CAV 2002. LNCS, vol. 2404, pp. 365–370. Springer, Heidelberg (2002)
6. Bournez, O., Maler, O., Pnueli, A.: Orthogonal polyhedra: Representation and computation. In: Vaandrager, F.W., van Schuppen, J.H. (eds.) HSCC 1999. LNCS, vol. 1569, pp. 46–60. Springer, Heidelberg (1999)
7. Clarisó, R., Cortadella, J.: The octahedron abstract domain. Science of Computer Programming 64(1), 115–139 (2007)

8. Cleaveland, R., Smolka, S.A., Sims, S.: An instrumentation-based approach to controller model validation. In: Broy, M., Krüger, I.H., Meisinger, M. (eds.) ASWSD 2006. LNCS, vol. 4922, pp. 84–97. Springer, Heidelberg (2008)
9. Cousot, P., Cousot, R.: Static determination of dynamic properties of programs. In: Proc. of the Second International Symp. on Programming, pp. 106–130 (1976)
10. Cousot, P., Halbwachs, N.: Automatic discovery of linear restraints among variables of a program. In: POPL, pp. 84–96 (1978)
11. Donzé, A., Maler, O.: Systematic simulation using sensitivity analysis. In: Bemporad, A., Bicchi, A., Buttazzo, G. (eds.) HSCC 2007. LNCS, vol. 4416, pp. 174–189. Springer, Heidelberg (2007)
12. Fehnker, A., Ivancic, F.: Benchmarks for hybrid systems verification. In: Alur, R., Pappas, G.J. (eds.) HSCC 2004. LNCS, vol. 2993, pp. 326–341. Springer, Heidelberg (2004)
13. Frehse, G.: PHAVer: Algorithmic verification of hybrid systems past HyTech. In: Tomlin, C.J., Greenstreet, M.R. (eds.) HSCC 2002. LNCS, vol. 2289, pp. 258–273. Springer, Heidelberg (2005)
14. Gadkari, A.A., Yeolekar, A., Suresh, J., Ramesh, S., Mohalik, S., Shashidhar, K.C.: AutoMOTGen: Automatic Model Oriented Test Generator for Embedded Control Systems. In: Gupta, A., Malik, S. (eds.) CAV 2008. LNCS, vol. 5123, pp. 204–208. Springer, Heidelberg (2008)
15. Girard, A.: Reachability of uncertain linear systems using zonotopes. In: Morari, M., Thiele, L. (eds.) HSCC 2005. LNCS, vol. 3414, pp. 291–305. Springer, Heidelberg (2005)
16. Girard, A., Guernic, C.L.: Zonotope/hyperplane intersection for hybrid systems reachability analysis. In: Egerstedt, M., Mishra, B. (eds.) HSCC 2008. LNCS, vol. 4981, pp. 215–228. Springer, Heidelberg (2008)
17. Girard, A., Pappas, G.J.: Verification using simulation. In: Hespanha, J.P., Tiwari, A. (eds.) HSCC 2006. LNCS, vol. 3927, pp. 272–286. Springer, Heidelberg (2006)
18. GLPK (GNU Linear Programming Kit), http://www.gnu.org/software/glpk/
19. Godefroid, P., Klarlund, N., Sen, K.: DART: directed automated random testing. In: PLDI, pp. 213–223 (2005)
20. Halbwachs, N., Proy, Y.E., Roumanoff, P.: Verification of real-time systems using linear relation analysis. Form. Meth. in Sys. Design 11(2), 157–185 (1997)
21. Henzinger, T.A., Ho, P.: HyTech: The Cornell hybrid technology tool. In: Antsaklis, P.J., Kohn, W., Nerode, A., Sastry, S.S. (eds.) HS 1994. LNCS, vol. 999, pp. 265–293. Springer, Heidelberg (1995)
22. Agung Julius, A., Fainekos, G.E., Anand, M., Lee, I., Pappas, G.J.: Robust test generation and coverage for hybrid systems. In: Bemporad, A., Bicchi, A., Buttazzo, G. (eds.) HSCC 2007. LNCS, vol. 4416, pp. 329–342. Springer, Heidelberg (2007)
23. Miné, A.: The octagon abstract domain. In: WCRE, p. 310 (2001)
24. Implementation of Qhull, http://www.qhull.org
25. Reactis, Reactive Systems, Inc., http://www.reactive-systems.com
26. Sankaranarayanan, S., Dang, T., Ivancic, F.: Symbolic model checking of hybrid systems using template polyhedra. In: Ramakrishnan, C.R., Rehof, J. (eds.) TACAS 2008. LNCS, vol. 4963, pp. 188–202. Springer, Heidelberg (2008)
27. Sankaranarayanan, S., Sipma, H.B., Manna, Z.: Scalable analysis of linear systems using mathematical programming. In: Cousot, R. (ed.) VMCAI 2005. LNCS, vol. 3385, pp. 25–41. Springer, Heidelberg (2005)
28. Simulink Design Verifier, The Mathworks, Inc.,
http://www.mathworks.com/products/sldesignverifier

29. Sen, K., Marinov, D., Agha, G.: CUTE: a concolic unit testing engine for C. In: FSE, pp. 263–272 (2005)
30. Silva, B.I., Richeson, K., Krogh, B.H., Chutinan, A.: Modeling and verifying hybrid dynamic systems using CheckMate. In: ADPM (2000)
31. Simulink Reference, The Mathworks, Inc., `http://www.mathworks.com`
32. Safety Test Builder, TNI-Software,
    `http://www.tni-software.com/en/produits/safetytestbuilder`
33. Stursberg, O., Krogh, B.H.: Efficient representation and computation of reachable sets for hybrid systems. In: Maler, O., Pnueli, A. (eds.) HSCC 2003. LNCS, vol. 2623, pp. 482–497. Springer, Heidelberg (2003)
34. Tripakis, S., Sofronis, C., Caspi, P., Curic, A.: Translating discrete-time Simulink to Lustre. ACM Trans. Embedded Comput. Syst. 4(4), 779–818 (2005)
35. T-VEC Tester, T-VEC Technologies, Inc.,
    `http://www.t-vec.com/solutions/simulink.php`

A Markov Chain Monte Carlo Sampler for Mixed Boolean/Integer Constraints

Nathan Kitchen[1] and Andreas Kuehlmann[1,2]

[1] University of California, Berkeley, CA, USA
[2] Cadence Research Labs, Berkeley, CA, USA

Abstract. We describe a Markov chain Monte Carlo (MCMC)-based algorithm for sampling solutions to mixed Boolean/integer constraint problems. The focus of this work differs in two points from traditional SAT Modulo Theory (SMT) solvers, which are aimed at deciding whether a given set of constraints is satisfiable: First, our approach targets constraint problems that have a large solution space and thus are relatively easy to satisfy, and second, it aims at efficiently producing a large number of samples with a given (e.g. uniform) distribution over the solution space. Our work is motivated by the need for such samplers in constrained random simulation for hardware verification, where the set of valid input stimuli is specified by a "testbench" using declarative constraints. MCMC sampling is commonly applied in statistics and numerical computation. We discuss how an MCMC sampler can be adapted for the given application, specifically, how to deal with non-connected solution spaces, efficiently process equality and disequality constraints, handle state-dependent constraints, and avoid correlation of consecutive samples. We present a set of experiments to analyze the performance of the proposed approach.

1 Introduction

Simulating design models for random input sequences and comparing their responses with the expected behavior has become common practice in functional hardware verification. A "testbench" that encapsulates the design model and is executed (or "simulated") with it specifies the valid input sequences and expected design behavior. In their early days, testbenches were written in imperative programming languages such as C or C++, and they specified explicitly the process of generating input stimuli. They supported nondeterminism through the use of random number generators (e.g. `rand()`) for generating data or choosing alternative generation paths. However, with increasingly complex constraints, such an unstructured approach quickly became unworkable. First, in the absence of a concise means to encode complex constraints, the inputs can easily be under- or over-constrained, resulting in spurious verification failures or uncovered input stimuli. Second, the ad-hoc use of random number generators for diversifying the stimuli makes it impossible to ensure a "good" distribution over the solution space. This can dramatically decrease the verification coverage and increase the required lengths of simulation runs.

A. Bouajjani and O. Maler (Eds.): CAV 2009, LNCS 5643, pp. 446–461, 2009.
© Springer-Verlag Berlin Heidelberg 2009

The need for a more concise constraint specification led to the use of declarative languages such as e [1] or SystemVerilog [2]. However, since declarative constraints are not directly executable, an online constraint solver is required to generate the stimuli. Since the testbench can have an internal state and the constraints may depend on it or the state of the design itself (e.g., to produce specific data during the different phases of a communication protocol), the solver must run in lockstep with the simulator to generate stimuli that correspond to the current state. There are two key requirements on constraint solvers that are geared for this application domain: First, the solver must be fast to avoid becoming a performance bottleneck; in practice not more than 20-30% of the overall verification runtime should be spent solving the input constraints. Second, the distribution of the generated stimuli must be well defined. In the absence of user-specified biases or knowledge of the design's state space, the generated stimuli should be distributed uniformly over the entire set of solutions.

The focus of this work is on sampling from constraints over Boolean and bounded-domain integers. We assume that the constraint formula is given in conjunctive normal form (CNF) where the clause literals are either Boolean or predicates over integer variables using linear or multilinear arithmetic; as predicates we support equality, inequality, and disequality. We note that, unlike decision procedures for word-level hardware verification, we do not require the support of bit-vector arithmetic. This is because testbench specifications typically do not rely on the side effects of two's-complement encoding or overflow as is often the case in hardware models. Operations on individual bits of the integer variables can be handled by full or partial bit-blasting the corresponding terms.

In this paper, we extend our work on MCMC sampling [3] into a new and more robust approach. After summarizing the overall approach in Section 2, we address specific challenges in Section 3, including a new approach to handle non-connected solution spaces, how to process constraint inputs used for expressing stimuli dependency on the design state, the handling of equality and disequality constraints, and how to avoid correlation between consecutive samples. In Section 4 we provide experiments that evaluate the performance of the proposed sampler on various benchmarks.

2   Preliminaries and Related Work

2.1   Mixed Boolean/Integer Constraints

Let $\hat{x} = (\hat{x}_1, \ldots, \hat{x}_{\hat{m}})$ and $x = (x_1, \ldots, x_m); \hat{x}_i, x_i \in \mathbb{B}$ be Boolean input and output variables, respectively, and $\hat{y} = (\hat{y}_1, \ldots, \hat{y}_{\hat{n}})$ and $y = (y_1, \ldots, y_n); \hat{y}_i, y_i \in \mathbb{Z}$ be integer input and output variables, respectively. The predicate $\varphi(\hat{x}, \hat{y}, x, y)$ specifies the constraints on the outputs (x, y) for given inputs $(\hat{x}, \hat{y})$. In a practical verification setting, φ is given in a declarative form in the testbench; the $\hat{x}$ and $\hat{y}$ are constraint inputs projected from the current state of the design under test and the x and y are the stimuli to be produced for simulating the design. Figure 1 gives a simplified view of such a verification setup.

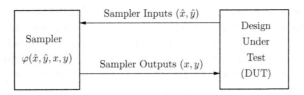

Fig. 1. Simplified view of a hardware design verification setup

For a given assignment to $(\hat{x}, \hat{y})$, we denote by $\Phi(\hat{x}, \hat{y})$ the set of solutions for φ, i.e., $\Phi(\hat{x}, \hat{y}) = \{(x, y) \mid \varphi(\hat{x}, \hat{y}, x, y) = 1\}$. Let $d(x, y | \hat{x}, \hat{y})$ be the desired distribution function for the samples (x, y) specified in the testbench. When sampling φ for a stream of inputs $((\hat{x}^1, \hat{y}^1), \ldots, (\hat{x}^s, \hat{y}^s))$, we want a sequence of solutions $S = ((x^1, y^1), \ldots, (x^s, y^s))$ with $(x^i, y^i) \in \Phi(\hat{x}^i, \hat{y}^i)$ that obeys this distribution; i.e., each sample in the sequence is chosen independently of the other samples and with probability proportional to its distribution value:

$$\forall(x^i, y^i) : \Pr((x^i, y^i) = (x, y)) \;=\; \frac{d(x, y | \hat{x}^i, \hat{y}^i)}{\sum_{(x,y) \in \Phi(\hat{x}^i, \hat{y}^i)} d(x, y | \hat{x}^i, \hat{y}^i)}$$

where $\Pr(A)$ denotes the probability of event A.

For this work, we assume that the constraints are specified as a CNF formula with the following grammar:

$$formula : clause \mid formula \wedge clause$$
$$clause : literal \mid clause \vee literal$$
$$literal : BooleanIdentifier \mid \neg BooleanIdentifier \mid$$
$$(\; expression \; rel \; Constant \;)$$
$$rel : \leq \mid \geq \mid = \mid \neq$$
$$expression : term \mid expression \; + \; expression$$
$$term : Constant \mid term * IntegerIdentifier$$

We note that for predicates on integers, strict inequalities $<$ ($>$) can be handled by using non-strict inequalities $\leq$ ($\geq$) and decrementing (incrementing) the constant on the right-hand side by one.

A contemporary approach to solve the constraint satisfaction problem given in the above form would be a SAT Modulo Theory (SMT) solver (see [4,5] for an overview) combining propositional logic with the theory of integers. Applying the latest advances of DPLL SAT solvers, these algorithms enumerate variable assignments over the Boolean space and dynamically instantiate integer constraint problems which are then solved with a specialized theory solver. The problem with using a DPLL-style method for stimulus generation is that it does not produce a good distribution of solutions. Although randomness can be introduced into such an approach (e.g., by modifying the decision heuristic to choose random initial assignments for literals), the distribution is difficult to control.

We refer to [3] for a detailed discussion of a DPLL-style sampler for Boolean constraints, including experiments demonstrating the distribution problems.

2.2   Markov Chain Monte Carlo Methods

MCMC methods are widely used in the statistics, computational physics, and computational biology communities for sampling from complex distributions. Instead of generating each sample independently, these methods take as samples the successive states visited in a simulation of a Markov chain [6]. If the Markov state transitions are set up appropriately (such that all states are always reachable), the distribution of states converges over time to a unique stationary distribution. MCMC methods provide a basis for solving constraints randomly with a well-defined, useful distribution. Although adaptations for practical use can violate the requirements of the MCMC theory and thus distort the distribution, in practice we find that the distortion is usually small.

Metropolis Sampling. One of the most commonly used MCMC algorithms is Metropolis sampling [7]. The Metropolis algorithm implements the Markov state transitions in terms of a target stationary distribution d. It is not necessary for d to be a normalized probability distribution, which is useful in our setting where the number of solutions is generally not known a priori.

In the Metropolis algorithm, a state transition begins with the generation of a proposed new state $\tilde{s}^{(t+1)}$ at random from the current state $s^{(t)}$. The state $\tilde{s}^{(t+1)}$ is then accepted as the new state $s^{(t+1)}$ with probability α:

$$\alpha = \min\left\{1, \frac{d(\tilde{s}^{(t+1)})}{d(s^{(t)})}\right\}$$

If $\tilde{s}^{(t+1)}$ is not accepted, the new state is taken as $s^{(t+1)} = s^{(t)}$.

In order for the state distribution to converge to d, the Metropolis algorithm requires that the proposal distribution be symmetric, i.e., $q(s'|s) = q(s|s')$, where $q(s'|s)$ is the probability of proposing a move to s' given current state s. A generalization of the algorithm known as Metropolis-Hastings [8] relaxes this restriction and uses an adjusted acceptance probability:

$$\alpha = \min\left\{1, \frac{d(\tilde{s}^{(t+1)})}{d(s^{(t)})} \frac{q(s^{(t)}|s^{(t+1)})}{q(s^{(t+1)}|s^{(t)})}\right\}$$

For simplicity in the remainder of this paper we use the name "Metropolis algorithm" to refer to this generalization and omit the "Hastings" qualification.

The particular choice of proposal distribution $q(s'|s)$ does not affect the correctness of the Metropolis algorithm (as long as the reachability requirement is satisfied), but it does determine how fast samples are generated and the rate at which the distribution converges. If the proposed moves are small, then the number of moves needed to cross the sample space is large, and the distribution converges slowly. On the other hand, if large moves are proposed without taking

---

Algorithm 1. MIXED BOOLEAN/INTEGER SAMPLER

1: {Given: formula $\varphi(x, y)$; parameter p_{ls}}
2: $(x, y) :=$ random assignment
3: **loop**
4:    $(x, y) :=$ METROPOLISMOVE(x, y)
5:    **while** $\neg\varphi(x, y)$ **do**
6:       **with** probability p_{ls} **do**
7:          $(x, y) :=$ LOCALSEARCHMOVE(x, y)
8:       **else**
9:          $(x, y) :=$ METROPOLISMOVE(x, y)
10:    output (x, y)

---

into account the target distribution, the probability of rejection can be high, so that moves to new states are infrequent and convergence is still slow.

One proposal method that allows efficient large moves with a rejection rate of zero is Gibbs sampling [9,10]. In this approach, a move consists of changing only a single variable's value, which is sampled from the target distribution, conditioned on the current values of the remaining variables:

$$q(s'|s) = \begin{cases} d(s_i'|s \setminus s_i) & \text{if } s' \setminus s_i' = s \setminus s_i \\ 0 & \text{otherwise} \end{cases}$$

MCMC Sampling with Constraints. One challenge that arises when applying the Metropolis algorithm to sampling with constraints is the requirement that each solution be reachable from every other. In general, moves that can be proposed efficiently, such as Gibbs moves, do not fully connect the solution space. This problem can be addressed by allowing moves to invalid states and using a target distribution $\tilde{d}$ that favors solutions, such as $\tilde{d}(s) = d(s)e^{-U(s)}$ where $U(s)$ is the number of clauses unsatisfied under s.

In theory, this is sufficient for the state distribution to converge. However, in practice it can take too long to reach a solution from an invalid state. In our previous work [3], we strengthened the solving power of an MCMC sampler by interleaving the Metropolis moves with iterations of a local-search solver [11]. This approach was inspired by SAMPLESAT [12], which applies it to purely Boolean constraints. Since the local-search moves do not use the Metropolis acceptance rule, they distort the stationary distribution away from the target distribution; however, the distortion is usually small in practice.

Our approach from [3] for the specific case of uniform sampling with constraints is outlined in Algorithms 1., 2., and 3.. Algorithm 1. is the main sampling loop. Algorithms 2 and 3 are the Metropolis and local-search moves, respectively. Both types of moves use a subroutine PROPOSE(y_k, x, y), which samples a new value for one variable y_k similarly to Gibbs sampling.

PROPOSE constructs proposal distributions as a combination of indicator functions for individual integer relations; the structure of the combination is isomorphic to the structure of the clauses: Let $\{C_i'\}$ be a projection of the clauses $\{C_i\}$

Algorithm 2. METROPOLISMOVE
1: {Given: assignment $(x, y) = (x_1, \ldots, x_m; y_1, \ldots, y_n)$; temperature T}
2: select variable v from $\{x_1, \ldots, x_m, y_1, \ldots, y_n\}$ uniformly at random
3: **if** v is Boolean x_k **then**
4:     $(x', y') := (x_1, \ldots, x_{k-1}, \neg x_k, x_{k+1} \ldots, x_m; y)$
5:     $Q := 1$
6: **else** {v is integer y_k}
7:     $(x', y') :=$ PROPOSE(y_k, x, y)
8:     $Q := q(y|y')q(y'|y)^{-1}$
9: $U := \#$ clauses unsatisfied under (x, y)
10: $U' := \#$ clauses unsatisfied under (x', y')
11: $p := \min\{1, Q\, e^{-(U'-U)/T}\}$
12: **with probability** p **do**
13:     **return** (x', y')
14: **else**
15:     **return** (x, y)

Algorithm 3. LOCALSEARCHMOVE
1: {Given: formula φ; assignment $(x, y) = (x_1, \ldots, x_m; y_1, \ldots, y_n)$}
2: select unsatisfied clause $C_i \in \varphi$ uniformly at random
3: **for each** literal $l_j \in C_i$ **do**
4:     **if** l_j is Boolean x_k or $\neg x_k$ **then**
5:         $(x^j, y^j) := (x_1, \ldots, x_{k-1}, \neg x_k, x_{k+1} \ldots, x_m; y)$
6:     **else** {l_j is integer relation R}
7:         select $y_k \in$ SUPPORT(R) uniformly at random
8:         $(x^j, y^j) :=$ PROPOSE(y_k, x, y)
9:     $U^j := \#$ clauses unsatisfied under (x^j, y^j)
10: $j^* := \arg\min_j U^j$
11: **return** (x^{j^*}, y^{j^*})

---

onto the current assignments of x and $y \setminus y_k$, so they are constraints on y'_k only. Then the proposal distribution q is

$$q(y'_k | x, y \setminus y_k) = \min_{C'_i} \max_{R_{ij} \in C'_i} d(x, y'_k, y \setminus y_k)\, \sigma_{R_{ij}}(y'_k) \qquad (1)$$

where $\sigma_R(y'_k)$ is a "soft" indicator that decays exponentially in the invalid range. The indicator for $R \Leftrightarrow y_k \leq c$ ($y'_k \geq c$), with softness parameter r, is given by:

$$\sigma_R(y'_k) = \begin{cases} 1 & \text{if } y'_k \leq c \quad (y'_k \geq c) \\ e^{-|y'_k - c|/r} & \text{otherwise} \end{cases} \qquad (2)$$

The min and max in (1) are isomorphic to $\wedge$ and $\vee$, respectively, in φ. We refer to this type of proposal distribution as *Gibbs-style*, since it resembles a relaxed form of Gibbs sampling; in the limit as $r \to 0$, it *is* Gibbs sampling.

3   Challenges in Practical Verification

3.1   Non-connected Solution Spaces

The solution spaces for constraints used in verification often consist of multiple components that are not connected by single-variable moves; that is, the sampler must change multiple variables in order to move between components. Sometimes the non-connectedness is due to the presence of equality constraints, for which we use special handling as described in Section 3.2. For other cases we use the approach described in Section 2.2: We allow moves to invalid states and use local-search moves to bring the sampler more quickly back to a solution. We refer to the extra moves from invalid states as *recovery moves* (lines 5–9 in Algorithm 1.).

Both the time for recovery and the ability to move effectively between solution-space components are affected by the choice of proposal distribution. In our previous work, we used the Gibbs-style distribution described in Section 2.2. This type of distribution usually works well for quick recovery, since it strongly favors valid states, but it puts low probability on moves through wide gaps to other components.

To move more easily between widely separated components, we propose a new proposal distribution based on the number of unsatisfied clauses rather than the distance from satisfying values. For this we define the *cost* function $U(y'_k)$, which gives for each value of y'_k the number of clauses not satisfied by the assignment $(x, y \setminus y_k, y'_k)$. $U(y'_k)$ is easily computed from the intervals for y'_k that satisfy the integer relations. To construct the proposal distribution $q(y'_k | x, y \setminus y_k)$ we first sample a cost u from the range of $U(y'_k)$ with probability proportional to $e^{-u/T}$, where T is a temperature parameter. Then we sample a value for y'_k from the set $\{\tilde{y}_k : U(\tilde{y}_k) = u\}$.

In our experiments, we found cases where recovery moves using Gibbs-style proposal distributions succeeded while cost-based proposals failed, and vice versa. Therefore, in our new algorithm we use both types, selecting one of them at random in each move, for greater robustness than our previous work.

3.2   Equality Constraints

An equality constraint can be expressed by and handled as a pair of inequality constraints. However, generic MCMC sampling with equality is inefficient because any change of state requires moving through invalid states. On the other hand, equality constraints can be viewed as reducing the dimensionality of the problem, which we exploit in the approach described below.

General Case. For simplicity, we focus the following discussion on the integers y and omit the Boolean variables x and inputs $\hat{x}$ and $\hat{y}$. This does not result in any loss of generality; in fact, the same arguments hold equivalently for the Boolean variables x. For a constraint formula φ, if there exists a variable $y_i \in y$ and a function $f_i(y \setminus y_i)$ such that:

$$\varphi(y) \Rightarrow y_i = f_i(y \setminus y_i)$$

then the dimensionality of the sampling problem can be reduced by 1. That is, we can simply sample the quantified formula $\exists y_i.\varphi$ over the variables $y \setminus y_i$ and determine at each step the value of y_i by evaluating f_i.

Theorem 1. *If* $\varphi(y) \Rightarrow y_i = f_i(y \setminus y_i)$ *then sampling* φ *is equivalent to sampling* $\exists y_i.\varphi$ *for* $y^t \setminus y_i^t$ *and completing each sample with* $y_i^t = f_i(y^t \setminus y_i^t)$.

Proof. First, we need to show that the solution space has not changed, that is, $(\varphi(y) \Rightarrow y_i = f_i(y \setminus y_i)) \Rightarrow (\varphi(y) \Leftrightarrow (\exists y_i.\varphi(y) \wedge y_i = f_i(y \setminus y_i)))$. Let D_i be the domain of y_i, then $\varphi(y) \Leftrightarrow \bigvee_{\tilde{y}_i \in D_i}(\varphi(y_1, \ldots, \tilde{y}_i, \ldots, y_n) \wedge (\tilde{y}_i = y_i))$ and $\exists y_i.\varphi(y) \Leftrightarrow \bigvee_{\tilde{y}_i \in D_i} \varphi(y_1, \ldots, \tilde{y}_i, \ldots, y_n)$. The condition $\varphi(y) \Rightarrow y_i = f_i(y \setminus y_i)$ implies that only one disjunct for the quantified expression will evaluate to true, specifically the one for $\tilde{y}_i = f_i(y_1, \ldots, y_{i-1}, y_{i+1}, \ldots, y_n)$. The required equivalence is established when y_i is restricted to this value by conjoining the quantified expression with $y_i = f_i(y_1, \ldots, y_{i-1}, y_{i+1}, \ldots, y_n)$.

Second, we need to show that the distribution has not changed. For this, we notice that each satisfying assignment to the variables $y \setminus y_i$ has a unique value assignment to the y_i. Therefore, $\Pr(y) = \Pr(y \setminus y_i)$. $\square$

This theorem shows that if we can extract dependent variables from φ by either syntactical or functional analysis, we can reduce the dimensionality of the problem and thus increase the efficiency for the solver. This applies for Boolean variables as well as the integer variables. In this context, we handle a specific case of linear equality constraints, which are common in practical applications.

Linear Equality Constraints. In the common case where equality constraints are linear, computing the quantified formula $\exists y_{i_1}, \ldots, y_{i_k}.\varphi(y)$ for dependent variables $y_{i_1}, \ldots, y_{i_k}$ is straightforward because it is equivalent to solving each inequality simultaneously with the equations. However, the set of dependent variables and relevant equations is, in general, not unique. In the following we describe how we select the variables and equations.

Assume that we selected variable y_k for the next PROPOSE step in line 7 of Algorithm 2. or line 8 of Algorithm 3. First we describe the case where each equality constraint E_i with y_k in its support is the only literal in its clause. Each such equation has only one solution for y_k as long as the values of $y \setminus y_k$ are held fixed. In order to generate moves to solutions with other values of y_k, we must allow a simultaneous change to at least one other variable in each E_i. These variables whose values change in the same move are the *dependent* variables.

In the general case, each dependent variable may be constrained by other equations that do not have y_k in their support. An additional dependent variable must be chosen for each of these equations, and so on. Different choices of the initial dependent variables may lead to different sets of equations to solve. In our approach we select the variables randomly; if the resulting system of equations does not have a unique solution we fall back to a single-variable move.

Algorithm 4. outlines our procedure for selecting dependent variables and equations. Note that equations are taken from a priority queue which is ordered

---

Algorithm 4. SELECTION OF DEPENDENT VARIABLES

1: {Given: primary sampling variable y_k; equations $\{E_i\}$}
2: $Y := \{\}$ {dependent variables}
3: $F := \{\}$ {dependency equations}
4: $Q := ()$ {priority queue sorted by increasing $|\text{SUPPORT}(E_i)|$}
5: $y_j := y_k$
6: **loop**
7:     **for** E_i such that $y_j \in \text{SUPPORT}(E_i)$ and $E_i \notin Q$ **do**
8:        insert E_i in Q
9:     **if** $|Q| = 0$ **then**
10:       **return** (Y, F)
11:     pop E_i from Q
12:     $V := \text{SUPPORT}(E_i) \setminus \{y_j\} \setminus Y$
13:     **if** $|V| > 0$ **then**
14:       select new y_j from V uniformly at random
15:       $Y := Y \cup \{y_j\}$
16:       $F := F \cup \{E_i\}$

---

by increasing size of support (see line 4). This strategy reduces the likelihood that all the variables in an equation's support have already been selected by the time it is processed.

After collecting the dependent variables and dependency equations, we solve these equations simultaneously with each inequality on y_k in order to get transformed bounds for y_k. We combine these bounds to construct a proposal distribution for y_k as described in Section 3.1. After sampling a new value for y_k, we substitute it into the collected equations and solve them to obtain new values for the dependent variables.

Example 1. A two-dimensional problem is established by the following inequalities and equality constraint:

$$
\begin{aligned}
(\ \ y_1 - \ \ y_2 &\geq -2\ ) \wedge \\
(\ \ y_1 + \ \ y_2 &\leq 32\ ) \wedge \\
(\ \ y_1 + \ \ y_2 &\geq 17\ ) \wedge \\
(\ \ y_1 - 4y_2 &\leq \ \ 1\ ) \wedge \\
(\ 2y_1 - \ \ y_2 &= 16\ )
\end{aligned}
$$

Let $s^{(t)} = (13, 10)$ be the current Markov chain state and assume that we select y_1 as the primary sampling variable; y_2 is the only possible dependent variable. Solving the equation with each of the four inequalities gives the following transformed bounds for y_1:

$$y_1 \leq 18 \qquad y_1 \leq 16 \qquad y_1 \geq 11 \qquad y_1 \geq 9$$

leading to the sampling range $11 \leq y_1^{(t+1)} \leq 16$. After sampling $y_1^{(t+1)}$, the value for $y_2^{(t+1)}$ is computed from the equality constraint, i.e., $y_2 = 2y_1 - 16$. Note that if y_2 is selected as the primary sampling variable and an odd value is chosen for it, no integer solution exists for y_1. In this case the nearest integer state is taken. Even though this state is invalid it does not break the algorithm; it will either be rejected in the Metropolis acceptance rule or be handled by recovery moves.

Disjunctions of Equations. When a clause contains an equality constraint and another constraint that shares support with it, the dependencies between variables may not be well defined. For example, suppose that the primary sampling variable is y_1 and one of the clauses is $(y_1 + y_2 = a) \lor (y_1 - y_3 \geq b)$. If $y_1 + y_2 = a$ is enforced, then y_2 is dependent on y_1, but if $y_1 - y_3 \geq b$ is enforced, then this clause requires no dependent variable. The dependency between y_1 and y_2 holds only for possible values of y_1 that do not satisfy $y_1 - y_3 \geq b$.

We handle this case by distributing such clauses over the rest of the formula, thus creating a disjunction of formulas where the dependencies in each sub-formula are well defined, e.g.:

$$(E_1 \lor E_2) \land (I_1 \lor I_2) \quad \Rightarrow \quad (E_1 \land (I_1 \lor I_2)) \lor (E_2 \land (I_1 \lor I_2))$$

for equations E_1, E_2 and inequalities I_1, I_2. We construct the proposal distributions for the disjuncts by solving each inequality simultaneously with the equations in its disjunct (e.g., I_1 with E_1, etc.) and combining the transformed inequalities as described in Section 2.2 or Section 3.1. For Gibbs-style proposals we take the pointwise maximum of the distributions for the sub-formulas as the overall distribution for the primary sampling variable. For cost-based proposals we take the pointwise minimum of the cost functions for the sub-formulas and construct the distribution from this composite cost function as in Section 3.1.

The number of sub-formulas may be exponential in the number of clauses, so we impose a bound on the number of them that we use. If the total number exceeds the bound, we select a random subset to use.

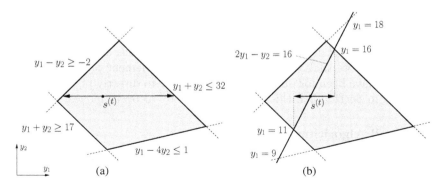

Fig. 2. Illustration of handling equality constraints for Example 1: (a) sampling range for y_1 to produce state $s^{(t+1)}$ without equality constraint, (b) sampling range with equality constraint

3.3   Disequality Constraints

A disequality constraint $g(y) \neq 0$ can be translated into a pair of inequalities $g(y) < 0 \lor g(y) > 0$. However, when a disequality appears in a clause with an equation, this transformation forces distribution of the disjunction as described in the previous section, creating more instances for the equation solver. To avoid this, we ignore disequality constraints while constructing proposal distributions. If the proposed next state violates the disequality, the violation is counted in the evaluation for the Metropolis acceptance rule and the move may be rejected.

3.4   Input-Dependent Constraints

As described in Section 2.1, constraints may be dependent on input variables $\hat{x}$, $\hat{y}$ coming from the state of the design under test. In practice, state-dependency is applied to select between different sets of constraints. When input values change, the current assignment may be far from a solution. In our MCMC framework, we utilize the the recovery moves to guide the search back into valid space.

Our practical observation is that state-dependency does not trigger a large amount of jumping between disjoint solution spaces. However, in theory it can cause distorted distributions. When the inputs move frequently between values with very different solution sets, the distribution can be distorted. The solutions that are closest (in number of moves) to the previous solution set will be sampled more often. This is because we do not use the Hastings rule in recovery moves.

3.5   Serial Correlation

A fundamental property of Markov-chain-based sampling is the high correlation of consecutive states. Since for verification purposes consecutive stimuli must not be correlated, the generated state sequence cannot be applied directly as stimuli. Instead, we apply a *mixing pool* to cache the generated states and randomly shuffle them before the next move. The mixing pool is implemented as a simple array of memory and shuffling is obtained inexpensively by a memory read and write. In addition to mixing, subsampling can be applied to de-correlate samples. For this, a fixed number of Markov chain state transitions are executed at each sampling step. Note that when accessing a random element of the mixing pool its state may have been for different inputs. Similar to directly processing inputs as described in Section 3.4, this case is handled by recovery moves.

3.6   Overall Algorithm

Algorithm 5. shows the complete flow for the proposed sampling approach. It includes the initialization of the mixing pool (lines 4–6), input processing (line 8), actual sampling (lines 10–12), and mixing (lines 9 and 13).

Algorithm 5. MCMC STIMULUS GENERATOR

1: {Given: formula $\varphi(x, y)$; parameters p_{ls}, K; mixing pool $(s_P^1, \ldots, s_P^M)$}
2: $(x, y) :=$ random assignment
3: $(\hat{x}, \hat{y}) :=$ random assignment
4: **for** $i := 1$ to M **do** {fill mixing pool}
5:    $(x, y) :=$ METROPOLISMOVE(x, y)
6:    $s_P^i := (x, y)$
7: **loop** {generate samples}
8:    $(\hat{x}, \hat{y}) :=$ READINPUTS()
9:    select $i \in \{1, \ldots, M\}$ uniformly at random
10:    **for** $k := 1$ to K **do** {subsample}
11:      $(x, y) :=$ METROPOLISMOVE(s_P^i)
12:      recovery: see lines 5–9 in Algorithm 1.
13:    $s_P^i := (x, y)$
14:    output (x, y)

---

4 Experimental Results

We have implemented our MCMC-based stimulus generation algorithm. In this section we analyze its performance on benchmarks designed to illustrate practical challenges arising in verification.

As we stated in Section 3.1, the Gibbs-style proposal distributions that we proposed in [3] are not effective for moving between disconnected components of solution spaces that are separated by wide multidimensional gaps. For this reason we introduced a new type of proposal distribution based on the number of unsatisfied clauses (the cost). To test the effectiveness of the cost-based distributions in moving between disconnected solution regions, we generated two groups of constraint sets. The solution sets for the benchmarks in the first group consist of two squares of width 8 separated by distance D: $0 \leq y_1, y_2 < 16 + D$, $(y_1 < 8 \wedge y_2 < 8) \vee (y_1 \geq 8 + D \wedge y_2 \geq 8 + D)$. We generated 100 000 solutions for each of $D = 0, 1, 2, 4, 8, \ldots, 2^{14}$ and for each type of proposal distribution. We disabled local-search moves to avoid distortion of the basic Metropolis distribution. Figure 3(a) shows the relative frequencies of transitions between the regions that we observed, i.e., the frequencies with which consecutive solutions were from different regions. The transition frequencies are constant with increasing distance for cost-based proposal distributions and decrease quickly to zero for Gibbs-style proposals. A combination of both proposal types gives intermediate transition frequencies.

The second group of benchmarks has solution regions at the corners of n-dimensional simplices for $n = 2, 3, 4, 5, 10, 15, \ldots, 100$, with 100 instances for each value of n. The constraints have the form $0 \leq a_i y_i \leq b$, $\sum_i a_i y_i \leq b$, $\bigvee_i (y_i \geq c_i)$. We generated the benchmarks randomly, constraining the parameters $\{a_i\}, \{c_i\}$ so that the solution regions would not be connected. For each benchmark we sampled 100 000 solutions for each type of proposal distribution. Figure 3(b) shows the relative frequencies of transitions between regions. The

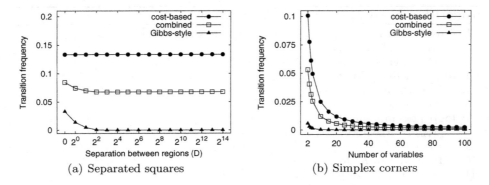

(a) Separated squares   (b) Simplex corners

Fig. 3. Frequencies of transitions between regions for different types of proposal distributions. Parameters: $T = 1$, $r = 1$, $K = 1$, $M = 1$; for (a) $p_{ls} = 0$; for (b) $p_{ls} = 0.5$.

sampler moved between regions much more often when using cost-based proposal distributions than when using Gibbs-style proposals. Even for the cost-based proposals, the transition frequency decreases rapidly with the number of variables; this fits with the fact that the average probability of an invalid value decreases exponentially as the average cost increases linearly.

The results from these first benchmarks demonstrate that cost-based proposal distributions are more effective for moving between disconnected regions than Gibbs-style proposals, especially when the regions are widely separated.

To test the effectiveness of the mixing pool at reducing serial correlation, we generated benchmarks with solution spaces consisting of a narrow space between oblique hyperplanes: $-c \le y_i \le c$, $-b \le \sum_i a_i y_i \le b$, $b = \frac{c}{10}$. We generated 100 instances with each of 4, 16, and 64 variables and sampled 10 000 solutions for each instance with mixing pool sizes $1, 2, 4, \ldots, 256$. Figure 4(a) shows the autocorrelation of the solutions, computed as an average of the autocorrelation

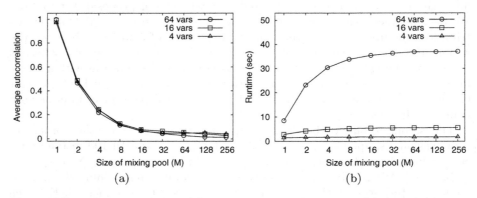

(a)   (b)

Fig. 4. Effect of mixing pool on (a) average autocorrelation and (b) average runtime in seconds. Parameters: $p_{ls} = 0.5$, $T = 1$, $r = 1$, $K = 1$.

for each variable. The correlation decreases quickly as the size of the mixing pool increases, showing the effectiveness of our mixing approach.

Figure 4(b) shows the average runtimes of the instances for each mixing pool size M. The scaling of runtime with the number of variables for $M = 1$ is expected, since each benchmark has constraints with all the variables in their support and these constraints are evaluated for every move. However, the trend of the runtimes for the 64-variable benchmarks requires further explanation. The rapid rise for small values of M and the disproportionately long runtimes in general are likely due to cache misses. This suggests a strategy for improving runtime: Subsample with a longer period and use a smaller mixing pool. Subsampling on the same position in the pool gives higher cache hit rates than mixing but reduces serial correlation similarly.

5 Other Work

There are several works in the area of stimulus generation for constrained random simulation. The authors of [13] use BDDs to representing the constraints and then apply a random walk from the root to the 1-leaf for producing samples. Although this approach can guarantee a uniform or other desired distribution, BDDs often blow up for practical problems. For example, many testbenches use multiplication operations on data variables, which BDDs cannot handle for larger bitwidths. In general, all bit-level sampling algorithm, including the work presented in [14] and SampleSat [12], require to bit-blast the constraints and thus lose the word-level structure and its information for efficient sampling.

Word-level samplers take advantage of the higher-level structure of the given formulas to quickly produce stimuli. Interval-propagation-based sampling [15] combines random variable assignment, iterative interval refinement, and backtracking on mixed bit- and word-level constraints. Although it is efficient for most practical constraints, the interval propagation scheme produces stimuli with skewed distributions, which in the worst case, can have exponential error. A number of other, specialized stimulus generators [16,17,18] utilize specific domain knowledge for constraint specification and solving.

The work closest to ours is presented in [19]. Similar to our approach, the authors propose the use of an MCMC sampler to generate stimuli for software verification. The sampler is placed in a feedback loop to learn a good biasing from the observed design coverage. In contrast to our work, this paper applies a bare-bones Metropolis-Hasting sampler and does not address the specific challenges present in large-scale practical verification as discussed here. The work in [20] discusses sampling from disconnected spaces; however, it focuses on the confidence level of the resulting distribution and is mainly of theoretical interest.

6 Conclusions

We presented an MCMC-based sampler for generating stimuli for hardware verification, although the same approach can also be applied for verifying software.

The focus of this work was on making an MCMC approach work for large-scale, practical applications. Although MCMC methods provide a solid theoretical foundation for sampling with a desired distribution, a naive implementation would not perform well and would be impractical. We showed how an MCMC-based approach can be adapted to deal with non-connected solution spaces, efficiently process equality and disequality constraints, handle state-dependent constraints, and avoid correlation of consecutive samples. Our future work is focused on a concurrent design of an MCMC sampler that exploits the probabilistic nature of the approach to maximally benefit from parallel execution.

References

1. Iman, S., Joshi, S.: The e Hardware Verification Language. Kluwer Academic, Norwell (2004)
2. Sutherland, S., Davidmann, S., Flake, P.: SystemVerilog for Design: A guide to using SystemVerilog for hardware design and modeling. Kluwer Academic Publisher, Norwell (2003)
3. Kitchen, N., Kuehlmann, A.: Stimulus generation for constrained random simulation. In: IEEE/ACM Int'l Conf. on CAD, pp. 258–265 (November 2007)
4. Sebastiani, R.: Lazy satisfiability modulo theories. Journal on Satisfiability, Boolean Modeling and Computation (JSAT) 3, 141–224 (2007)
5. Kroening, D., Strichman, O.: Decision Procedures. Springer, Heidelberg
6. Brémaud, P.: Markov Chains: Gibbs fields, Monte Carlo Simulation, and Queues. Texts in Applied Mathematics, vol. 31. Springer, New York (1999)
7. Metropolis, N., Rosenbluth, A.W., Rosenbluth, M.N., Teller, A.H., Teller, E.: Equations of state calculations by fast computing machines. J. Chem. Phys. 21, 1087–1092 (1953)
8. Hastings, W.K.: Monte Carlo sampling methods using Markov chains and their applications. Biometrika 57, 97–109 (1970)
9. Geman, S., Geman, D.: Stochastic relaxation, Gibbs distributions, and the Bayesian restoration of images. IEEE Trans. Pattern Analysis and Machine Intelligence 6(6), 721–741 (1984)
10. Gelfand, A.E., Smith, A.F.M.: Sampling-based approaches to calculating marginal densities. J. Amer. Statist. Assoc. 85(410), 398–409 (1990)
11. Selman, B., Kautz, H.A., Cohen, B.: Local search strategies for satisfiability testing. In: Trick, M., Johnson, D.S. (eds.) Proc. 2nd DIMACS Challenge on Cliques, Providence RI (1993)
12. Wei, W., Erenrich, J., Selman, B.: Towards efficient sampling: Exploiting random walk strategies. In: Proc. Nat'l Conf. Artificial Intelligence, pp. 670–676 (July 2004)
13. Yuan, J., Shultz, K., Pixley, C., Miller, H., Aziz, A.: Modeling design constraints and biasing in simulation using BDDs. In: Digest Tech. Papers IEEE/ACM Int'l Conf. Computer-Aided Design, pp. 584–589 (November 1999)
14. Kim, H., Jin, H., Ravi, K., Spacek, P., Pierce, J., Kurshan, B., Somenzi, F.: Application of formal word-level analysis to constrained random simulation. In: Gupta, A., Malik, S. (eds.) CAV 2008. LNCS, vol. 5123, pp. 487–490. Springer, Heidelberg (2008)
15. Iyer, M.A.: RACE: A word-level ATPG-based constraints solver system for smart random simulation. In: IEEE International Test Conference (ITC), Charlotte, NC, United States, pp. 299–308 (September 2003)

16. Chandra, A., Iyengar, V., Jameson, D., Jawalekar, R., Nair, I., Rosen, B., Mullen, M., Yoon, J., Armoni, R., Geist, D., Wolfsthal, Y.: AVPGEN— a test generator for architectural verification. IEEE Trans. Very Large Scale Int. 3(2), 188–200 (1995)
17. Shimizu, K., Dill, D.L.: Deriving a simulation input generator and a coverage metric from a formal specification. In: Proc. 39th Design Automation Conf., New Orleans, LA, United States, pp. 801–806 (June 2002)
18. Mihail, M., Papadimitriou, C.H.: On the random walk method for protocol testing. In: Computer Aided Verification. LNCS, pp. 132–141. Springer, Heidelberg (1994)
19. Sankaranarayanan, S., Chang, R.M., Jiang, G., Ivancic, F.: State space exploration using feedback constraint generation and Monte-Carlo sampling. In: Proc. ESEC-FSE 2007: – 6th joint meeting of the European Software Engineering Conference and the ACM SIGSOFT Symposium on the Foundations of Software Engineering, pp. 321–330. ACM, New York (2007)
20. Bandyopadhyay, A., Aldous, D.J.: How to combine fast heuristic Markov chain Monte Carlo with slow exact sampling. Electronic Communications in Probability 6, 79–89 (2001)

Generalizing DPLL to Richer Logics

Kenneth L. McMillan[1], Andreas Kuehlmann[1], and Mooly Sagiv[2]

[1] Cadence Research Labs
[2] Tel Aviv University

Abstract. The DPLL approach to the Boolean satisfiability problem (SAT) is a combination of search for a satisfying assignment and logical deduction, in which each process guides the other. We show that this approach can be generalized to a richer class of theories. In particular, we present an alternative to lazy SMT solvers, in which DPLL is used only to find propositionally satisfying assignments, whose feasibility is checked by a separate theory solver. Here, DPLL is applied directly to the theory. We search in the space of theory structures (for example, numerical assignments) rather than propositional assignments. This makes it possible to use conflict in model search to guide deduction in the theory, much in the way that it guides propositional resolution in DPLL. Some experiments using linear rational arithmetic demonstrate the potential advantages of the approach.

1 Introduction

Many modern Boolean satisfiability (SAT) solvers use an approach known as DPLL that is in some sense a fusion of the exhaustive resolution approach of Davis and Putnam [8] and the backtracking search approach of Davis Logeman and Loveland [7]. In DPLL, these two approaches are tightly coupled in a way that helps to focus the search on relevant decisions and the resolution on relevant deductions. When the search reaches a conflict (a point from which no further progress can be made) a new clause is deduced by resolution. This new clause guides the search away from the conflict and allows it to continue. By focusing deduction only on the points where model search fails, we avoid an explosion of irrelevant deductions. We also gain a measure of the relevance of variables which allows us to focus search decisions.

In this paper, we provide a highly abstract view of this process that generalizes to richer languages, such as linear arithmetic. We start with a theory (a set of sentences in a given logic for which we wish to find a model) and a logical structure which is proposed as a model of the theory. For example, in the case of SAT, a theory is a set of clauses over some propositional atoms, and a structure is a Boolean assignment to those atoms. Two processes then proceed alternately:

- A *model search* process attempts to mutate the structure in a way that will make it, in a well-defined sense, closer to being a model.
- A *refutation* process attempts to deduce new sentences that will make the structure, in a well-defined sense, closer to being refuted.

A. Bouajjani and O. Maler (Eds.): CAV 2009, LNCS 5643, pp. 462–476, 2009.

The refutation process is only triggered when the model search process can no longer make progress (is in conflict). Thus, failure of model search guides deduction. Conversely, by adding a new sentence that must be satisfied, deduction guides model search. We will refer to this general proof search strategy as *general* DPLL, or GDPLL.

Related work. The prevalent method of applying DPLL to non-Boolean theories is the lazy SMT solver [2]. In this approach, a Boolean SAT solver is combined with a *theory solver*. The SAT solver sees atomic formulas of the theory as propositional variables, and attempts to construct a propositionally satisfying assignment. The theory solver refutes these attempts by adding clauses that are tautologies of the theory. In the simplest case, these are "blocking clauses", built from existing atoms, and representing partial truth assignments that are infeasible in the theory. A more sophisticated solver may add clauses containing new atoms, perhaps representing instances of proof rules that can be used to refute a given assignment [10]. This is referred to as "theory learning".

A potential weakness of this approach is that the theory solver has no effective means of choosing between the many possible refutations of a given truth assignment. Nonetheless, as we will see, this choice can have an exponential effect on performance of the solver. Theory deduction in lazy SMT solvers occurs only in response to satisfying propositional assignments (or partial assignments) rather than as a response to a conflict in the model search process. Thus, there is very limited relevance feedback for deductions in the theory, as compared to propositional deduction. In the general DPLL approach, we search not in the Boolean space, but in the space of structures of the theory. These may be, for example, numeric assignments or first-order structures. This allows the general DPLL mechanism to choose relevant deductions in the theory based on conflict in model search, just as DPLL does in the propositional case.

After submitting this work, we were made aware of unpublished work of Scott Cotton along similar lines [6]. This independent work also contains the basic ideas of searching in the space of numerical structures, using theory deduction to resolve conflicts.

Outline. In the next section, we introduce the concepts of GDPLL, using the example of quantifier-free linear rational arithmetic (QFLRA). We present some experiments with a prototype implementation. Section 3 then presents the general framework.

2 Linear Rational Arithmetic

The abstract framework of GDPLL will be more easily understood if we begin with a concrete instance of it. We will take as our logical language the formulas of quantifier-free linear rational arithmetic (QFLRA) in clausal form. A sentence (or clause) in this logic is a disjunction of linear constraints, each of which is of the form $c_0 \bowtie c_1 x_1 + \cdots c_n x_n$, where c_i is a rational constant, x_i is a rational variable, and $\bowtie$ is either $\leq$ or $<$. We don't require negation, because $\neg(x \leq y)$ can be expressed as $y < x$. For clarity, we will often write constraints with variables on both sides of $\bowtie$, but it should be understood that this is a shorthand for a constraint in the normalized form above.

A *structure* for QFLRA is just an assignment of rational values to the variables. A structure is a *model* of a set of clauses S if it satisfies every clause in S according to the usual semantics of arithmetic.

A variable x_i *occurs* in a constraint if its coefficient c_i in that constraint is non-zero, and it occurs in a clause if it occurs in any constraint of the clause. A constraint or clause in which no variable occurs is equivalent to either TRUE or FALSE. We will not distinguish between a clause equivalent to FALSE and the constant FALSE. We also drop redundant literals without comment.

A variable is *lower-bounded* by a constraint if its coefficient is positive, and *upper-bounded* if it is negative. It is lower-bounded (upper-bounded) by a clause if lower-bounded (upper-bounded) by any constraint in the clause.

An *interval* is a connected subset of the rational line $\mathcal{Q}$. We will express intervals using the standard notation, as a pair of possibly infinite lower and upper bounds with a square bracket indicating a closed end and a round bracket an open end. Thus, for example, $(-\infty, 5]$ is the set $\{r \in \mathcal{Q} \mid r \leq 5\}$.

Given a structure A and a clause s, we will say the *feasible set* for variable x_i, denoted $\text{feas}(A, s, x_i)$, is the set of rational numbers r such that $A\langle r/x_i \rangle$ satisfies s. For example, given the assignment $(a = 0, b = 0, c = 0)$ and the clause $(a + 5 \leq b)$, the feasible set for b is the rational interval $[5, \infty)$. The feasible set for variable c is the empty set, since we cannot make the constraint true by plugging in any value for c.

2.1   Algorithm

The algorithm in Figure 1 searches for a model of a set of clauses by assigning feasible values to variables in some chosen order. This is similar to DPLL except that the values are rational rather than Boolean. When we reach a situation in which some variable has no feasible value, we are in *conflict*. We resolve the conflict by performing a deduction step. This introduces a new clause that guides us away from the conflict. Again, this is similar to DPLL, except that we will require a richer proof calculus. As we discuss the algorithm, we will use a running example, in which the set S consists of the clauses $(a < b)$, $(a < c)$, $(b < d \lor c < d)$ and $(d < a)$. Our initial structure A_0 will be $(a = 0, b = 0, c = 0, d = 0)$.

Let $\sqsubset$ be a fixed total order on the variables. In our example, we will put the variables in alphabetical order, so that $a \sqsubset b \sqsubset c \sqsubset d$. Relative to this order, a variable x_i *dominates* a clause s if x_i is the maximal variable occurring in s, according to $\sqsubset$. For example, the variable c dominates the clause $(a < c)$. The subset of S dominated by x_i will be denoted $\text{domin}(S, x_i)$. In our example, $\text{domin}(S, c) = \{(a < c)\}$.

The *ordered* feasible set for x_i, denoted $\text{feas}_\sqsubset(A, S, x_i)$, is the *intersection* of the feasible sets for x_i over the clauses dominated by x_i, that is,

$$\text{feas}_\sqsubset(A, S, x_i) = \cap \{\text{feas}(A, s, x_i) \mid s \in \text{domin}(S, x_i)\}$$

Algorithm: GDPLLQFLRA
Input: a set S of clauses of QFLRA
Output: a satisfying assignment for S, or UNSAT

> Let $\sqsubset$ be some total order on $x_1 \ldots x_n$
> Let A be a structure of QFLRA
> **repeat**
> > if $A \models S$ return A
> > if FALSE $\in S$ return UNSAT
> > let x_i be the least variable w.r.t. $\sqsubset$ such that $A(x_i) \notin \text{feas}_\sqsubset(A, S, x_i)$
> > if $\text{feas}_\sqsubset(A, S, x_i)$ is not empty
> > > choose $r \in \text{feas}_\sqsubset(A, S, x_i)$ and set $A \leftarrow A\langle r/x_i \rangle$
> > else if there exists strictly compatible (s, s') in $\text{minim}_\sqsubset(A, S, x_i)$
> > > set $S \leftarrow S \cup \{\text{shad}_{x_i}(s, s')\}$
> > else *abort*

Fig. 1. Decision procedure for QFLRA

In our example, $\text{feas}_\sqsubset(A_0, S, c) = (0, \infty)$ and $\text{feas}_\sqsubset(A_0, S, d) = \emptyset$ (since no value of d can satisfy both $(b < d \vee c < d)$ and $d < a$). We will say that a variable x_i is *correct* if $A(x_i) \in \text{feas}_\sqsubset(A, S, x_i)$ and *incorrect* otherwise.

The algorithm of Figure 1 executes a loop so long as A is not a model of clause set S and S does not contain the clause FALSE (in which case there is no model). In this loop, we choose the least incorrect variable x_i. In our example, this variable is b, since its feasible set is $(0, \infty)$ and its initial value is $A_0(b) = 0$. If the feasible set of x_i is not empty, we correct x_i by assigning it some value in its feasible set. This step corresponds to making a "decision" in DPLL. In our example, we can choose any value for b greater than zero, say, $A_1(b) = 1$. Notice that the mutation of x_i cannot, by definition, modify the feasible sets of any variables less than x_i. Therefore, by this mutation, we are in some sense making progress towards a satisfying assignment. In our example, we would proceed to set $A_2(c) = 1$. At this point, the least incorrect variable is d, whose feasible set is empty. We say that d is in conflict.

When we reach a variable x_i whose feasible set is empty, we resolve the conflict by choosing two clauses s_1 and s_2 from the set dominated by x_i and combining them to deduce a new clause. The feasible set for x_i defined by this new clause is the intersection of the feasible sets defined by s_1 and s_2. This is precisely what happens in DPLL when we use a resolution step to learn a "conflict clause". That is, for some Boolean variable x_i, we have one clause whose feasible set for x_i is $\{$TRUE$\}$ (it implies x_i in the current assignment) and one whose feasible set is $\{$FALSE$\}$ (it implies $\neg x_i$ in the current assignment). We resolve these two clauses to obtain a learned clause whose feasible set is the empty set (it is false in the current assignment).

In the case of QFLRA, the deduction step is a bit more subtle, again because the variables are rational rather than Boolean. To resolve a conflict, we will use a deduction rule we call the *shadow rule*. If a pair of clauses (s_1, s_2) is *compatible*, in a sense we will define shortly, this rule produces a new clause whose feasible set for x_i is the intersection of the feasible sets for s_1 and s_2.

The shadow rule. The shadow rule is shown in Figure 2. To express transitivity of inequality with both strict and non-strict inequalities, we use the notation $\bowtie\bowtie'$, where $\bowtie$ and $\bowtie'$ are $<$ or $\leq$. This stands for $\leq$ if both $\bowtie$ and $\bowtie'$ are $\leq$ and $<$ otherwise. Thus if $x \bowtie y$ and $y \bowtie' z$, then $x \bowtie\bowtie' z$, for all four choices of strict and non-strict comparisons. Given this, and using distributivity of conjunction over disjunction, the shadow rule is easily shown to be sound. The side conditions of the rule are not needed for soundness. Rather, they restrict deduction so that, from any ordered pair of premises, for any given variable x_i, exactly one conclusion can be deduced. To derive this conclusion from a pair (s, s') of clauses, we gather all the lower-bounding constraints from s, and rewrite then in the form $l_j \bowtie_j x_i$. Similarly, we rewrite all the upper-bounding constraints of s' in the form $x_i \bowtie'_{j'} u_{j'}$. In our example, applying the shadow to the clauses $(b < d \vee c < d)$ and $(d < a)$, on variable d, yields $(b < a \vee c < a)$.

We will denote the clause resulting from application of the shadow rule $\text{shad}_{x_i}(s, s')$.

$$\frac{C \vee l_1 \bowtie_1 x_i \vee \cdots \vee l_m \bowtie_m x_i \qquad \qquad x_i \text{ not occurs in } l_{1\ldots m}, u_{1\ldots m'}}{C' \vee x_i \bowtie'_1 u_1 \vee \cdots \vee x_i \bowtie'_{m'} u_{m'} \qquad \qquad C \text{ does not lower-bound } x_i}{C \vee C' \vee \bigvee_{j=1\ldots m} \bigvee_{j'=1\ldots m'} (l_j \bowtie_j\bowtie'_{j'} u_{j'}) \qquad \qquad C' \text{ does not upper-bound } x_i}$$

Fig. 2. The shadow rule

In our search algorithm, we apply the shadow rule only to pairs of clauses (s, s') that are *compatible* at A. To define this notion, we begin with a corresponding definition on intervals. Given two intervals I and I', let $\text{glue}(I, I')$ be the interval that takes its lower bound from I and its upper bound from I'. For example, $\text{glue}((-\infty, 5), [-1, 3]) = (-\infty, 3]$. Note that this operator is not commutative, and is not the convex hull operator. An ordered pair of intervals I, I' is *compatible* if $\text{glue}(I, I') = I \cup I'$. Examples of compatible pairs are $(-\infty, 0), [0, \infty)$ and $(3, 5], (4, 7]$. Incompatible examples are $(-\infty, 0), (0, \infty)$ and $(4, 5], (3, 7]$.

Now, for any structure A, clause s and variable x_i, the feasible set $\text{feas}(A, s, x_i)$ is the complement of an interval that we will call the *forbidden interval*, denoted $\text{fbd}(A, s, x_i)$. For example, for structure $(a = 0, b = 0, c = 0)$ and clause $(c + 5 < a \vee b \leq c)$ the forbidden interval for c is $[-5, 0)$. In effect, the shadow rule applies the glue operator to the forbidden intervals of two clauses. We say a pair of clauses is compatible when their forbidden intervals are compatible:

Definition 1. *Given structure A and clauses s, s' dominated by variable x_i, the pair (s, s') is compatible when the pair of intervals $\text{fbd}(A, s, x_i), \text{fbd}(A, s', x_i)$ is compatible. It is strictly compatible when, further, $\text{fbd}(A, s, x_i) \neq \text{fbd}(A, s', x_i)$.*

Since taking the union of the forbidden intervals corresponds to taking the intersection of the feasible sets, we have the following theorem:

Theorem 1. *For any QFLRA structure A and compatible pair of clauses (s, s') of QFLRA, and any variable x_i:*

$$\text{feas}(A, \text{shad}_{x_i}(s, s'), x_i) = \text{feas}(A, s, x_i) \cap \text{feas}(A, s', x_i)$$

Proof sketch. Let I and I' be the forbidden intervals of s and s' respectively. We can show that the forbidden interval of $\text{shad}_{x_i}(s, s')$ is $\text{glue}(I, I')$. Since (s, s') is compatible, this is $I \cup I'$, which gives us the theorem by DeMorgans's laws. $\square$

Our search procedure places one additional restriction on deductions. We say a clause in $s \in S$ is *minimal* for a given variable x_i, if there is no other clause $t \in S$ such that $\text{feas}(A, S, t) \subset \text{feas}(A, S, s)$. We denote the set of such minimal clauses $\text{minim}_\sqsubset(A, S, x_i)$. By restricting deduction to minimal clauses, we avoid repetition of deductions.

With these provisos, our algorithm is a decision procedure for QFLRA. Partial correctness is trivial, since a result can only be returned in case A is a satisfying assignment, or we have deduced FALSE. It remains only to argue that the procedure terminates (without aborting). We postpone this until we have introduced the general framework.

To complete our example, recall our structure A_2 is $(a = 0, b = 1, c = 1, d = 0)$ and we have just deduced $(b < a \vee c < a)$. Now c is the least incorrect variable. The clause $(a < c)$ has forbidden interval $(-\infty, 0]$ while $(b < a \vee c < a)$ has $[0, \infty)$. These are strictly compatible, so we apply the shadow rule to obtain $(b < a \vee 0 < 0)$. We can ignore the second constraint, since it equivalent to FALSE. Now we find that the feasible set for b is empty, and we apply the shadow rule to $(a < b)$ and $(b < a)$, obtaining $(0 < 0)$. Since this is equivalent to FALSE, we report UNSAT.

2.2 Discussion

In our instantiation of GDPLL for linear arithmetic, we can observe several significant differences with respect to the lazy SMT approach. First, notice that GDPLL searches in the space of assignments to rational variables, while lazy SMT searches in the space of Boolean assignments to atoms. Second, theory deduction in GDPLL is performed only in response to conflict in the model search, just as in propositional DPLL. In lazy SMT, theory deduction occurs in response to *satisfying* Boolean assignments (or partial assignments). Third, GDPLL applies *proof rules* of the theory, while lazy SMT uses only *axioms* generated by the theory solver. While the lazy theory solver generates only tautologies of the theory, our procedure never deduces tautologies. Every clause we generate derives from original problem clauses and is false in some structure (the one generating the conflict). In lazy SMT, Boolean and theory reasoning are deliberately separated. The theory solver cannot resolve problem clauses, because it never sees them. In GDPLL, there is no such separation.

From a heuristic point of view, we will argue that the Boolean assignments generated by the SAT solver in lazy SMT provide inadequate guidance to the theory solver as to which of many possible refutations is preferred. In principle, for any deduction performed using our shadow rule, a theory solver could provide a sufficient set of axioms to allow the SAT solver to reproduce the conclusion by a sequence of resolution steps. In practice, lazy SMT lacks the heuristic guidance needed to produce this result.

A simple example will serve to illustrate this point. We consider a class of "diamond formulas", that are hard for most existing solvers based on lazy SMT [15]. Our running example above is a diamond formula for $N = 1$. Figure 3 depicts the general case. In the graph, an arrow represents a $<$ constraint between variables, and a dashed line between arrows indicates disjunction of constraints.

Our GDPLL procedure can show unsatisfiability of these formulas in a number steps linear in N, the number of diamonds. Figure 3 shows the deduction sequence for any N for the variable order $a_0, b_0, c_0, a_1, b_1, c_1, \ldots$. It turns out that this result is not particularly sensitive to variable order. For example, the order $a_0, \ldots, a_n, b_0, \ldots, b_{n-1}, c_0, \ldots, c_{n-1}$ also yields a linear number of steps. Notice how deterministic this procedure is. Once the variable order is chosen, the sequence of deductions is fixed. The conflicts in model search tell us precisely which deductions to perform.

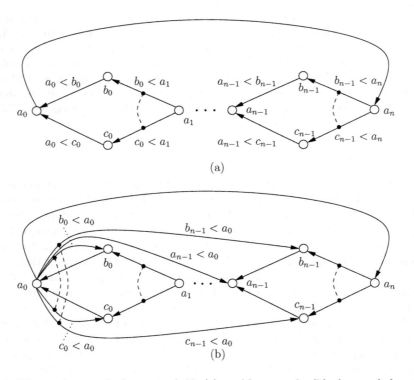

Fig. 3. Diamond example for general N: (a) problem graph, (b) clauses deduced by GDPLL, by repeating these three steps: (1) $(b_{i-1} < a_i \lor c_{i-1} < a_i), (a_i < a_0) \vdash (b_{i-1} < a_0 \lor c_{i-1} < a_0)$, followed by (2) $(b_{i-1} < a_0 \lor c_{i-1} < a_0), (a_{i-1} < c_{i-1}) \vdash (b_{i-1} < a_0 \lor a_{i-1} < a_0)$ and (3) $(b_{i-1} < a_0 \lor a_{i-1} < a_0), (a_{i-1} < b_{i-1}) \vdash (a_{i-1} < a_0)$

Now consider the lazy SMT approach. The difficulty with diamond formulas for lazy SMT is that a sequence of N diamonds contains 2^N infeasible cycles. Suppose, for example, that the theory solver can only generate blocking clauses. Each such clause eliminates exactly one of the infeasible cycles, so 2^N calls to the theory solver are needed. This is true even if theory propagation [11] is used. This problem can be solved in principle by having the theory solver introduce new atoms into the SAT solver. For example, new equality literals are commonly introduced when using Nelson-Oppen style theory combinations [4]. This can also be done through *theory learning*, which introduces tautologies containing fresh atoms [10]. A lazy SMT solver could handle the diamonds efficiently if the theory solver were to inject, for example, all the atoms of form $a_i < a_0$, $b_i < a_0$ and $c_i < a_0$ into the SAT solver. In practice, though, we must choose these atoms without generating an explosion of irrelevant ones. A Boolean assignment, by itself, does not give us enough information to make this choice. In fact, as we will observe shortly, all of the applicable solvers from the 2008 SMT competition [1] are exponential on diamond formulas.

This problem has sparked some research effort. For example, in the Dynamic Predicate Learning method [16], Wang, Gupta and Ganai apply transitivity to difference logic predicates (a subset of LRA). They use frequency of occurrence in blocking clauses as a selection criterion, with a fixed threshold of 200 occurrences, and other *ad hoc* criteria. While this heuristic is sufficient to handle diamond formulas, the method applies only to difference logic, and is not shown to be effective in general (for other than diamond formulas). Despite some progress [13], the problem of effective theory learning in QFLRA still appears to be open.

We note that there may be many other methods that can handle the diamond formulas efficiently. We use this example only to illustrate the heuristic difficulties faced by a lazy SMT solver, and to show how searching in the space of numerical assignments avoids these difficulties.

We also note that the "shadow rule" we used for QFLRA is only one of many possibilities. For example, the LASCA proof calculus [14] has three proof rules that deal with inequalities. By combining these rules, we can generate many conclusions whose feasible set is the intersection of the feasible sets of the premises. Thus, while we say that deduction in GDPLL is *guided* by conflict, it is not always fully determined, as it was in the example above.

Finally, there are some related proof methods that should be mentioned. Exhaustive methods, such as Fourier-Motzkin elimination use no heuristic guidance whatever, and simply perform all possible deductions. Eager variable elimination [9] uses resolution steps to simplify the formula in a pre-processing step. This method can also be used with GDPLL. There are methods that use models generated by theory solvers to guide the lazy SMT approach [4,12]. They do not address the issues discussed above. The method DPLL(⊔) makes some of the Boolean structure of the problem visible to the theory solver, allowing it to produce joins of facts deducible along different search paths [3]. This method attacks the problem of lack of guidance in theory learning, while maintaining the basic lazy SMT framework. There are also eager SMT approaches [2] that encode the formula into an equisatisfiable Boolean SAT formula. This has the advantage of fully exploiting DPLL principles, but the disadvantage that the encodings can be extremely large.

2.3   Experiments

To evaluate the performance potential of GDPLL and to illustrate the difference between our search approach and existing SMT solvers, we performed two experiments using a prototype implementation of the linear arithmetic decision procedure using GDPLL. All experiments were performed on a server with 32 GB of main memory, using one CPU of a 4-processor Opteron machine, running at 2.587 GHz with 1 MB of cache.

For our experiments, we use a very simple static variable ordering heuristic. Boolean SAT solvers generally base their initial variable ordering on the number of occurrences of each variable. However, in the case of QFLRA we can also exploit the numerical relationships between variables. We construct a directed graph in which the vertices are variables, and an edge (x, y) occurs when there is a unit constraint, such as $x < y$, in which is upper-bounding for x and lower-bounding for y (thus, increasing x may force us to increase y). We use a DFS-based heuristic that orders the nodes of this graph, attempting to reduce the number of back edges in the graph. Intuitively, this reduces the number of times that a variable will have to be updated because its predecessor is updated.

In the first experiment we confirmed our conjecture of the solver's performance for the diamond example described in Section 2.2. For this, we run the GDPLL solver on diamond structures shown in Figure 3 for sizes N ranging from 1 to 25. We also run six solvers that participated in the 2008 SMT competition and can handle rational difference logic (QF_RDL). We applied a timeout of 500 seconds to all runs. Figure 4 provides the results. As shown, the GDPLL implementation solves all the diamond problems in a negligible amount of time whereas all other solvers demonstrate an exponential run time in N.

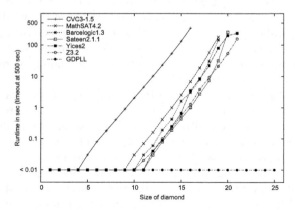

Fig. 4. Run time comparison for the diamond structure for our solver "GDPLL" and 6 solvers from SMT-COMP'08

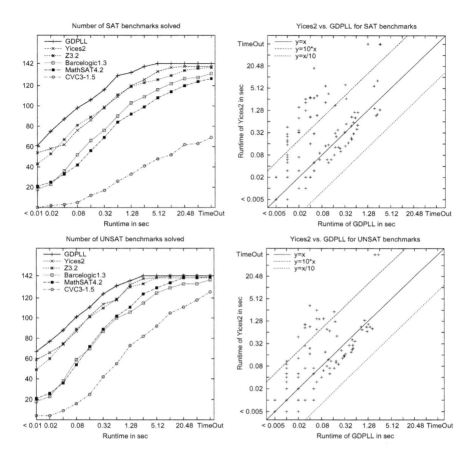

Fig. 5. Solver statistics for synthesized timing analysis problems for 142 ISCAS circuit comparing GDPLL with 5 solvers from SMT-COMP'08 and detailed comparison of GDPLL with Yices2 (Timeout at 81.9 sec)

In the second experiment we evaluated the solver's performance for a simplified circuit timing analysis problem. For this we generated timing constraints from 142 ISCAS benchmarks using simple gate delays. We also modeled the fact that the delay of a CMOS gate increases if the two latest inputs arrive at approximately the same time. As an example, suppose the arrival times of a two-input gate are denoted by t_1, t_2 and t_o for the two inputs and for the output, respectively. The following inequalities model the described timing behavior of that gate:

$$(t_o \geq t_1 + \delta_{small}) \wedge$$
$$(t_o \geq t_2 + \delta_{small}) \wedge$$
$$((t_1 > t_2) \vee (t_o \geq t_1 + \delta_{large})) \wedge$$
$$((t_2 > t_1) \vee (t_o \geq t_2 + \delta_{large}))$$

For each benchmark circuit we generate the timing constraints for all gates and added for every output an additional constraint, requiring that its arrival time be less or equal than its precomputed arrival time for the SAT case and strictly less for the UNSAT case. Figure 5 shows the run time comparison for the SAT and UNSAT cases. For the SMT-COMP'08 solvers, we excluded the Sateen solver because it reported "unknown" for all problems. For the other solvers, we recorded all correct results produced within the given time limit of 82.9 sec. As shown, GDPLL outperforms all solvers by a significant margin. In the right part of the figure, we show a scatter plot comparing the run times of our implementation with Yices2, the best performing solver on this benchmark among the SMT-COMP'08 participants. The points lying below the diagonal show that the constant factors of our preliminary implementation are not as good as the highly tuned Yices2. However, in some cases, Yices2 is two orders of magnitude slower; in five cases Yices2 was not able to solve the problem within the time limit of 82.9 sec, though our solver handled all cases in less than 2.8s. We conjecture that in these cases, a large number of timing paths in these circuits had to be individually refuted by blocking clauses.

We do not claim based on these results that GDPLL is superior in any way to other methods. In particular, we were not able to perform comparisons on the standard SMTLIB benchmarks because our implementation currently does not support Boolean variables. Moreover, the question of variable ordering heuristics needs to be addressed in a more general way. Nonetheless, we do feel that these results demonstrate that GDPLL has different performance characteristics from lazy SMT, and that the use of model search to drive theory deduction can be an effective heuristic.

3   General DPLL

We now introduce a framework for GDPLL that abstracts away from particular logics. This framework can be used as a proof search and model search strategy for a range of logics and proof calculi, provided certain general conditions are met.

Let $\mathcal{L}$ be a logical language, that is, a set of sentences. A subset of $\mathcal{L}$ is a *theory*. We assume a set of logical *structures* $\mathcal{A}$. The semantics of $\mathcal{L}$ is defined by the relation $\models$, and we write $A \models s$, when $A \in \mathcal{A}$ is a model of $s \in \mathcal{L}$ (alternatively, A satisfies s, or s is true in A). We allow the use of non-standard structures and semantics, provided $A \models s$ implies that s is satisfiable in the standard semantics. In particular, we may use a three-valued semantics, so that possibly $A \not\models a$ and $A \not\models \neg a$. We assume that $\mathcal{L}$ contains a sentence FALSE that has no models (in the standard semantics).

We think of GDPLL as a search process. The state of our search is a pair (S, A), where S is a set of sentences and A a structure. The search goal is to reach a state in which $A \models S$. As in any search, we require a *heuristic*, that is, some measure of progress toward reaching the goal. We will define this in terms of a partial order $\succ$ on search states. That is, if $(S, A) \succ (S', A')$, then in some heuristic sense, state (S', A') is closer to the goal.

while $A \not\models S$ and $\mathrm{FALSE} \notin S$ do
$$\left\{ \begin{array}{c} 1) \text{ set } A \leftarrow A', \text{ where } A \rhd A' \text{ and } (S, A) \succ (S, A') \\ \text{or} \\ 2) \text{ set } S \leftarrow S', \text{ where } S' = S \cup \{s\}, \ S \vdash s \text{ and } (S, A) \prec (S', A) \end{array} \right\}$$

Fig. 6. The GDPLL algorithm

Our moves in the search space are defined by a *mutation relation* $\rhd$ and a *deduction relation* $\vdash$. The former is a relation on structures. If $A \rhd A'$, we can move from A to A'. The latter allows us to add sentences to S. That is, if $S \vdash s$, where s is a sentence, then we may add s to S. Of course, we require that $\vdash$ is sound, in the sense that $S \vdash s$ implies $S \models s$. In our search process, we only perform mutations in the downward direction of $\succ$. To move from (S, A) to (S, A'), where $A \rhd A'$, we require $(S, A) \succ (S', A')$. When we reach a "local minimum", in which no mutation can move us downward, we say we are in conflict. We escape the local minimum by deducing a new sentence s, such that addition of s moves us *upward* in $\succ$. Intuitively, we have learned new information about the problem which has refined our heuristic.

This general algorithm is depicted in Figure 6. It starts with an initial theory S and an arbitrary initial structure A. It repeatedly performs either a model search step (1) or a deduction step (2). In a model search step, we mutate A to some A', moving downward in $\succ$. In a deduction step, we deduce a new sentence s, moving upward in $\succ$. This process continues until either A is a model of S, or the sentence FALSE is deduced.

Correctness. We would like to argue that this is a decision procedure for $\mathcal{L}$. Partial correctness is trivial, since the procedure only terminates with a model of S or a deduction of FALSE. It remains only to guarantee termination. For this, we require three key conditions:

- Progress: there are no infinite chains $(S, A_1) \succ (S, A_2) \succ \cdots$.
- Boundedness: the deductive closure of any finite S under $\vdash$ is finite.
- Deadlock freedom: in any state (S, A), such that $A \not\models S$ and $\mathrm{FALSE} \notin S$, either a model search step or a deduction step is possible.

Theorem 2. *Given progress, boundedness and deadlock freedom, the GDPLL algorithm terminates.*

Proof sketch. The progress condition guarantees that we cannot execute model search steps infinitely. If we execute model search steps only, we eventually reach a state where no model search step is possible. By deadlock freedom, a deduction step must be possible in this state. Thus, if we we do not terminate, we must execute a deduction step infinitely often. However, this is a contradiction, since each deduction step must add a sentence to S and S is contained in the finite deductive closure of the initial S.   □

Note that is also possible to modify the heuristic order $\succ$ during execution of GDPLL, provided we do this only a bounded number of times between deductions. This can model dynamic ordering heuristics in DPLL. Also, note that this general framework allows many heuristically useless instantiations. In the extreme, $\triangleright$ could allow mutation to any structure, and $\vdash$ could deduce FALSE in one step from every inconsistent S. The key in practice is to define a search space in which mutation and deduction are tractable and not overly non-deterministic.

Instantiation for QFLRA. To illustrate these concepts, consider instantiating the general algorithm for QFLRA. In this case, a mutation changes the value of one rational variable, and the deduction relation is defined by the shadow rule. Our heuristic $\succ$ puts a priority on correcting the least incorrect variable according to the fixed variable order $\sqsubseteq$. Given two states (S, A) and (S', A') whose least incorrect variables are x_i and $x_{i'}$ respectively, we say that $(S, A) \succ (S', A')$ when $x_i \sqsubset x_{i'}$. That is, we make progress when we increase the least incorrect variable. In case of a tie, when $x_i = x_{i'}$, we will say $(S, A) \succ (S', A')$ iff $\mathrm{domin}(S, x_i) \subset \mathrm{domin}(S', x_i)$. Intuitively, more constraints on x_i make the problem harder to solve (though there are actually many equivalent ways we could define this).

Now consider the three properties needed for termination. Progress is easily guaranteed, since a mutation must increase the least incorrect variable and this cannot be done infinitely.

Boundedness is a property of the shadow rule. We will refer to an instance of the shadow rule as *ordered*, with respect to our total order $\sqsubseteq$ on variables, if the same variable x_i dominates both premises. Note that our algorithm only applies the shadow rule to clauses s and s' dominated by x_i, so we use only ordered instances.

Lemma 1. *For any total order $\sqsubseteq$ on variables, the ordered shadow rule is bounded.*

Proof sketch. Consider the set of constraints C occurring in a finite set S of clauses. The ordered shadow rule can only create a new constraint by applying transitivity, eliminating the highest variable. Since there can be no infinite chains of such deductions, the set of constraints generated from S is finite. Since every deduced clause is a disjunction over this finite set, the deductive closure of S is finite.   □

To show deadlock-freedom, we rely on the following property of intervals:

Lemma 2. *For any finite set $\mathcal{I}$ of intervals, such that $\cup \mathcal{I} = \mathcal{Q}$, either $\mathcal{Q} \in \mathcal{I}$, or $\mathcal{I}$ contains a strictly compatible pair.*

If we cannot execute a model search step, it is because the feasible set of some variable x_i is empty. This means that the forbidden intervals of $\mathrm{minim}_{\sqsubseteq}(A, S, x_i)$ cover the real line. By the above lemma, these intervals must contain a strictly compatible pair (s, s'). By applying the shadow rule to the corresponding clauses, we obtain a new clause t with strictly smaller feasible set than s, s'. If the feasible set of t for x_i is empty, then $A \not\models t$ and x_i does not occur in t. Thus we have reduced the least incorrect variable. Otherwise, minimality of s and s' implies that t is not already present in S, thus we increase $\text{domin}(S, x_i)$. In either case we move up in the heuristic order $\succ$, making this a legal deduction step.

It follows that this instantiation of GDPLL terminates. Since every step of our original algorithm GDPLLQFLRA can be simulated by this instantiation, we can show:

Theorem 3. GDPLLQFLRA *terminates (without aborting) for all inputs.*

Finally, we note that, unlike in the Boolean case, we cannot change the variable order arbitrarily during execution of the solver because the unordered shadow rule is not bounded. In fact, it is easy to construct cases in which regularly changing the order leads to non-termination. For this reason, care will be needed in developing dynamic variable ordering strategies for QFLRA without sacrificing termination.

4   Conclusion

An essential feature of DPLL algorithms for SAT is the interaction of model search and proof. In DPLL, we focus a very prolific deduction system (resolution) by using conflict in model search as a guide. The resulting deduced clauses in turn guide the model search away from the conflict. We have attempted to generalize the DPLL procedure in a way that preserves this essential feature, while extending it to non-propositional theories. We have seen that GDPLL applies to linear arithmetic, allowing us to search in the space of numerical assignments instead of Boolean assignments. It allows us to use the DPLL approach to focus arithmetic deduction as well as propositional deduction. This may provide a significant advantage over the lazy SMT approach, which lacks heuristic guidance in learning theory facts. We saw, for example, that the ability to use model search to guide deduction allows us to avoid an exponential explosion of Boolean combinations that the lazy SMT solvers we tested incurred for diamond formulas. We noted that GDPLL is not simply a special case of theory learning in lazy SMT. In GDPLL, deduction occurs only in response to conflicts, while in lazy SMT, theory deduction occurs in response to satisfying assignments. In lazy SMT, the theory solver generates only tautologies, while in GDPLL, tautologies are never deduced.

We would like to stress that our purpose is not to create a more efficient arithmetic solver, but rather a general framework to allow the DPLL approach to guide reasoning in a broad range of theories. For example, we have implemented versions of GDPLL for quantifier-free equality with uninterpreted functions and quantified first-order logic without equality. There remains considerable work to be done to create practical solvers, however. For example, the linear arithmetic approach we describe uses a static variable order. It is likely to be more efficient to order the variables dynamically as is done in a SAT solver. Variable ordering heuristics in the style of VSIDS are needed. It is also theoretically possible to make an integer linear arithmetic (QFLIA) solver in this style, for example using GDPLL to guide Cooper's method [5]. However, it is unclear whether such a solver would be efficient, and there seem to be many possible approaches to integer arithmetic. There remains also the question of combining theories, for example combining arithmetic with uninterpreted functions. The GDPLL model also suggests a wide space of alternative SAT implementations, including possible parallel SAT. We have not explored these possibilities.

References

1. Barrett, C., Deters, M., Oliveras, A., Stump, A.: Design and results of the 4th annual satisfiability modulo theories competition, SMT-COMP 2008 (2008) (to appear)
2. Barrett, C., Sebastiani, R., Seshia, S., Tinelli, C.: Satisfiability modulo theories. In: Biere, A., Heule, M., van Maaren, H., Walsh, T. (eds.) Handbook of Satisfiability, ch. 8. IOS Press, Amsterdam (2009)
3. Bjørner, N., Dutertre, B., de Moura, L.: Accelerating lemma learning using joins - DPPL(⊔). In: LPAR (2008)
4. Bozzano, M., Bruttomesso, R., Cimatti, A., Junttila, T.A., Ranise, S., van Rossum, P., Sebastiani, R.: Efficient satisfiability modulo theories via delayed theory combination. In: Etessami, K., Rajamani, S.K. (eds.) CAV 2005. LNCS, vol. 3576, pp. 335–349. Springer, Heidelberg (2005)
5. Cooper, D.C.: Theorem proving in arithmetic without multiplication. Machine Intelligence 7, 91–99 (1972)
6. Cotton, S.: Algebraic satisfiability solving. Personal communication (2009)
7. Davis, M., Logemann, G., Loveland, D.: A machine program for theorem proving. Communications of the ACM 5(7), 394–397 (1962)
8. Davis, M., Putnam, H.: A computing procedure for quantification theory. Journal of the ACM 7(3), 201–215 (1960)
9. Een, N., Biere, A.: Effective preprocessing in SAT through variable and clause elimination. In: Bacchus, F., Walsh, T. (eds.) SAT 2005. LNCS, vol. 3569, pp. 61–75. Springer, Heidelberg (2005)
10. Flanagan, C., Joshi, R., Ou, X., Saxe, J.B.: Theorem proving using lazy proof explication. In: Hunt Jr., W.A., Somenzi, F. (eds.) CAV 2003. LNCS, vol. 2725, pp. 355–367. Springer, Heidelberg (2003)
11. Ganzinger, H., Hagen, G., Nieuwenhuis, R., Oliveras, A., Tinelli, C.: DPLL(T): Fast decision procedures. In: Alur, R., Peled, D.A. (eds.) CAV 2004. LNCS, vol. 3114, pp. 175–188. Springer, Heidelberg (2004)
12. Goldwasser, D., Strichman, O., Fine, S.: A theory-based decision heuristic for DPLL(T). In: FMCAD, pp. 1–8 (2008)
13. Koppensteiner, P., Veith, H.: A novel SAT procedure for linear real arithmetic. In: PDPAR (2005)
14. Korovin, K., Voronkov, A.: Integrating linear arithmetic into superposition calculus. In: Duparc, J., Henzinger, T.A. (eds.) CSL 2007. LNCS, vol. 4646, pp. 223–237. Springer, Heidelberg (2007)
15. Strichman, O., Seshia, S.A., Bryant, R.E.: Deciding separation formulas with sat. In: Brinksma, E., Larsen, K.G. (eds.) CAV 2002. LNCS, vol. 2404, pp. 209–222. Springer, Heidelberg (2002)
16. Wang, C., Gupta, A., Ganai, M.K.: Predicate learning and selective theory deduction for a difference logic solver. In: DAC, pp. 235–240 (2006)

Reducing Context-Bounded Concurrent Reachability to Sequential Reachability[*]

Salvatore La Torre[1], P. Madhusudan[2], and Gennaro Parlato[1,2]

[1] Università degli Studi di Salerno, Italy
[2] University of Illinois at Urbana-Champaign, USA

Abstract. We give a translation from concurrent programs to sequential programs that reduces the context-bounded reachability problem in the concurrent program to a reachability problem in the sequential one. The translation has two salient features: (a) the sequential program tracks, at any time, the local state of only one thread (though it does track multiple copies of shared variables), and (b) all reachable states of the sequential program correspond to reachable states of the concurrent program.

We also implement our transformation in the setting of concurrent recursive programs with finite data domains, and show that the resulting sequential program can be model-checked efficiently using existing recursive sequential program reachability tools.

1   Introduction

Analysis of concurrent programs is an important problem that is difficult for a variety of reasons. The explosion in the number of interleavings between threads is one problem, and the explosion in the state-space needed to keep track of the combined states of each thread is another. For instance, even checking reachability of n parallel systems, each modeled as a *finite-state* transition system (with some form of communication) is solvable only in time exponential in n, as there are exponentially many global configurations which are feasible.

In this paper, we consider the problem of translating concurrent programs to sequential programs, which reduces the reachability problem for the former to that for the latter. The motivation behind such a translation is to use the fairly sophisticated sequential analysis tools to analyze concurrent programs. For instance, this has been proposed in this same volume by Lahiri, Qadeer, and Rakamarić [5], in order to apply deductive verification tools based on SMT solvers to verify concurrent C programs.

A translation of the above kind is of course always possible— given a concurrent program, we can build a sequential program that simply simulates its (global) behavior. However, such a sequential interpreter would track the entire global state of the concurrent program, which involves keeping the local state of each thread. Our aim is to provide a translation that avoids this extreme blow-up

---

[*] This work was partially funded by NSF CAREER Award CCF 0747041, by the MIUR grants ex-60% 2007-2008, and FARB 2009 Università degli Studi di Salerno (Italy).

A. Bouajjani and O. Maler (Eds.): CAV 2009, LNCS 5643, pp. 477–492, 2009.

in state-space, and build a sequential program that tracks, at any point, the local state of only one thread of the concurrent program. However, such a translation is not always feasible.

A restricted reachability for concurrent programs has emerged in the last few years, mainly motivated from testing concurrent programs and model-checking finite-state models of them, called *context-bounded reachability*, wherein we ask whether an error state is reachable within k context-switches, for a fixed k. This was first suggested by Qadeer and Wu [11], and has several appealing features.

First, it has been argued that bounded context-switching is a natural restriction as most concurrency related errors manifest themselves within a few context-switches. Musuvathi and Qadeer have, for example, experimentally shown that a few context-switches explores a vast space of reachable configurations [9].

Second, when we deal with concurrent programs where variables range over finite domains (obtained either by restricting the domain or using some form of abstraction such as predicate abstraction), we obtain essentially concurrent pushdown systems, which have an undecidable reachability problem. However, it turns out, mainly due to results of [10], that the bounded context-switching reachability problem is decidable.

Finally, and perhaps most importantly, when one examines why context-bounded reachability is decidable for concurrent programs over finite data domains, the primary reason is that we can *compositionally* analyze the program, examining each thread *separately* and combining the results. This compositional reasoning hence involves searching a state-space where at any point only the local state of a single thread is tracked.

In [6], Lal and Reps propose a transformation of concurrent programs to sequential programs that reduces context-bounded reachability in the former to reachability in the latter. This translation exploits compositional arguments underlying the decidability proofs to construct a sequential program that tracks, at any point, the local state of one thread, the shared state, as well as k copies of the shared state (corresponding to the shared state at the k context-switches). This translation is appealing when the local state is complex (in particular, when the local state has a stack to model recursive control), and the shared state is comparably less complex.

The translation proposed by Lal and Reps, however, does not permit a *lazy* analysis: the sequential program *guesses* in advance the valuations of shared variables $g_1, \ldots, g_k$ at the context-switches, and verifies each thread locally against this guess. Hence, the sequential program unnecessarily explores unreachable states of the concurrent program (as the guessed g_i's may not be reachable).

In our opinion, a transformation that results in a lazy analysis (one which explores only reachable states) is highly desirable; for example, in model-checking, it can drastically reduce the size of the state-space that needs to be explored. In fact, Lal and Reps [6] do give direct lazy analysis algorithms for finite-state programs, and our recent work in [4] also provides a direct fixed-point algorithm for lazy analysis. However, a transformation from concurrent programs to sequential programs that preserves laziness was not known.

Contributions. In this paper, we show a lazy translation: given a concurrent program and a bound k, we show how it can be transformed to a sequential program, such that reachability within k context-switches in the concurrent program reduces to reachability in the sequential one. Moreover, the salient feature of the translation is that the reachable states of the sequential program correspond to reachable states of the concurrent program, and hence is, in our opinion, a more faithful representation of the sequential program. The main idea behind our reduction is to have the sequential program *calling individual threads multiple times from scratch* in order to recompute the local states at context-switches.

We also implement an eager translation and our lazy translation for concurrent programs over finite data-domains (a.k.a. concurrent Boolean programs). This results in sequential programs over a finite data-domain, which can be model-checked using existing tools. Our implementations of the translations are available online[1]. We show that our laziness-preserving transformation outperforms eager transformations on a class of multithreaded Bluetooth driver examples (the original programs and the transformed ones are also available online).

The paper is organized as follows: Section 2 gives a high-level and intuitive description of our eager and lazy translations; Section 3 formally defines the class of sequential and concurrent programs; Section 4 describes the eager translation (which is mainly adapted from ideas in [6]); the laziness-preserving translation is presented in Section 5; Section 6 reports on our implementation and experiments for Boolean programs; and Section 7 concludes with some future directions.

Related Work. Bounded context-switching reachability was introduced in [11]: the KISS project implemented reachability within two context-switches and found data-race errors in device drivers; interestingly, it also reduced the problem to sequential reachability (the reduction is simple for two switches). Decidability of context-bounded analysis for concurrent recursive Boolean programs was established in [10] using automata theoretic methods. There have been a number of analysis algorithms and implementations of context-bounded reachability problems: [13] implement the automata-theoretic solution symbolically, [6] propose an algorithm to compute the reachable states lazily, and the work in [4] implements symbolic fixed-point based solutions for lazy reachability. Bounded context-switching has also been exploited in other contexts: the tool CHESS [8] explores bounded context-switching interleavings to test concurrent programs, and bounded context-switching for systems with heaps [1], systems communicating using queues [3], and weighted pushdown systems [7] have been proposed.

Bounded context-switches vs bounded rounds. Lal and Reps [6], apart from giving a transformation for eager analysis, also make a technical improvement: by using only k extra sets of shared variables, we can explore all the state space reachable in k round-robin rounds (which is larger than that reached in k context-switches).

In both our transformations, we have considered bounded context-switching reachability, and not bounded round-robin reachability (this is why our eager transformation is slightly different from that of [6]). The reason is that we see no

---

[1] At http://www.cs.uiuc.edu/~madhu/getafix/cbp2bp

efficient way of transforming programs using only $O(k)$ sets of global variables that effects a *lazy-transformation*. While we do know of such a translation, this requires calling each thread too many times (exponentially) many times, which we believe will not work well in practice. This translation is out of the scope of this paper, and the problem of coming up with a more efficient translation for bounded rounds reachability is an open problem.

2   From Concurrent to Sequential Programs

In this section, we briefly sketch two translation schemes from concurrent to sequential programs which preserve reachability up to a fixed number of context-switches. The transformations work for general programs (even when the domain of variables is not bounded), except that they assume that the state of shared variables is known, and can be replicated and compared against each other.

Of course, there is a simple translation of concurrent programs to sequential programs that keeps the entire global configuration of the program. However, our aim here is to build a sequential program that keeps only the local state of a single thread at any time (though we allow some copies of shared states). In particular, when applied to concurrent recursive programs over *finite data-domains*, the translation will should yield a sequential recursive program over a finite data-domain; this would reduce concurrent context-bounded reachability on finite domains to reachability of sequential programs over finite domains, which is a decidable problem.

We consider concurrent programs with a *fixed* number of threads that communicate with each other using shared variables. Each thread is a sequential program (with possibly recursive procedures). A state is thus given by the values of the shared variables and the local state of each thread. A computation of a concurrent program is a sequence of contexts, where in each context a single thread has control.

For ease of presentation let us first consider the case of a concurrent program with only two threads T_1 and T_2. Also, instead of describing the transformation, we take one particular path in the concurrent program, and describe how the corresponding sequential program will discover it.

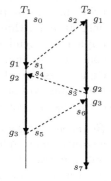

Consider a sample computation whose control flow at the thread level is shown on the right. It starts in a state s_0 with the control in T_1, then at a state s_1 switches the control to T_2 at state s_2, then locally executes T_2 till it reaches the state s_3, and then switches to T_1 again at state s_4, and so on. In a simple sequential simulation of this computation, while we execute instructions of T_2, say from s_2, we need to remember the local component of thread T_1 in state s_1, in order to compute the switch from s_3 to s_4. This can be very expensive. In the case of finite data domains, where threads have recursive procedures and we would like to build a sequential program also over a finite data domain, this is in fact *impossible*, as it involves keeping the unbounded call-stack of T_1 at s_1. Schemes for translation to sequential programs hence need to explore this run in a different manner, where only the local state of one process is kept at any given point.

The two translation schemes we present in the rest of this section do not store the local states of more than one thread, but will store k valuations of shared variables, which intuitively correspond to the value of shared variables at context-switches. In the computation sketched above, if g is the set of shared variables, we denote by g_1 the value of the shared variables at the first context-switch from T_1 to T_2, i.e., the value of shared variables at states s_1 and s_2. Similarly, let g_2 be the value at the next context-switch back to T_1 (i.e., at states s_3 and s_4), and g_3 the value at the last context-switch back to T_2 (i.e., at states s_5 and s_6).

The eager and lazy translations differ in the way they compute the values of these shared variables at the context-switches: the eager approach *nondeterministically* guesses them right at the beginning, while the lazy approach computes them dynamically.

The eager approach. In the eager approach, we guess the values g_1, g_2, g_3 at the beginning (non-deterministically). Then, we process thread T_1 completely, handling both segments of its run (s_0 to s_1 and s_4 to s_5), and then erase the local state and proceed to process the two segments of thread T_2 (s_2 to s_3 and s_6 to s_7). Note that each thread is processed only once.

More precisely, after guessing g_1, g_2 and g_3, we start to compute in T_1 the first context. At any point where the shared variables match the guessed value g_1, we allow a "jump" where the global variables are rewritten to g_2, and we proceed in T_1 computing the *third* context, till we reach g_3. Note that across the "jump" above (from s_1 to s_4), the local state of thread T_1 is preserved. Hence the call to thread T_1 verifies that there is a run which can reach shared-variable-state g_1, jump to g_2, and proceed to reach g_3.

Next, we erase the local state of T_1 and proceed to process thread T_2 from its initial local states with the shared variables assigned with g_1. We then continue till we reach a state with shared-variable valuation g_2, jump to g_3 preserving local state, and continue the computation of the fourth context in T_2.

Intuitively, the guessed values g_1, g_2, g_3 allow the stitching of the two execution segments that have been executed in the two threads. However, since the tuple of values of the shared variables is guessed, they may not correspond to reachable states of the concurrent program, and hence may lead to exploring the individual threads on unreachable regions of the state-space.

The lazy approach. In the lazy approach, we start computing T_1 in the first context from an initial global state. At any point of the execution, we can choose nondeterministically to switch context, in which case we store the value of the shared variables in g_1 and terminate the thread (thereby *losing* its local state).

Then, we execute T_2 in the second context, starting from a local initial state and shared variables initialized with g_1. At any point of the execution, we can choose nondeterministically to switch context, in which case we store in g_2 the value of the shared variables and terminate the thread (again losing the local state).

We then would like to start executing T_1 (i.e., from s_4) in the third context, but since we had lost its local state, we need to recompute it. Thus, starting from an initial global state, we execute T_1 until we reach a state matching g_1 on the shared variables. (Notice that this may be an *entirely* different local state than the one we explored in the first context! However, as we show, this does not affect correctness.)

At such a point, we allow the thread to replace the value of the shared variables with g_2, and proceed to execute T_1 to compute the third context (from s_4 to s_5). Again, at any point, we can decide nondeterministically to switch context, in which case we store the value of the shared variables in g_3, and end thread T_1.

Finally, we move to execute T_2 in the fourth context. As we did for T_1, we need to restart thread T_2 from its initial state to recompute the local state at the beginning of the fourth context (i.e. at s_3 or s_6). Thus, we simulate T_2 with shared variables initialized to g_1, wait for it to reach a state with shared variables matching g_2, non-deterministically choose to assign the global variables with g_3, and proceed to compute the fourth context (from s_6 to s_7). Again, the local state produced on this new invocation of thread T_2 may be entirely different, and yet the states discovered in the fourth context are indeed reachable.

In contrast to the eager approach, the values of g_1, g_2, g_3 are computed dynamically, and thus are guaranteed to be reachable by the concurrent program. This can be sometimes a huge advantage as large (and complex) portions of the state space are spared from analysis. More importantly, we believe that this is a more faithful representation of the concurrent program. On the other hand, it is true that this approach executes each context several times (at most $k/2$ times).

Generalization to multiple threads. Consider now a concurrent program with n threads $T_1, \ldots, T_n$ and a fixed integer $k > 0$. Let the variables g_i ($i = 1, \ldots, k$) hold the valuation of the shared variables at the i-th context-switch, and let the variables t_i ($i = 0, \ldots, k$) hold the index of the thread that has control in the $(i + 1)$-th context.

In the eager approach, we start guessing non-deterministically both tuples $g_1, \ldots, g_k$ and $t_0, \ldots, t_k$. Then, we run each thread T_i, for $i = 1, \ldots, n$, through all the contexts where it has the control (i.e., all contexts j such that $t_j = i$) and in doing this we check that the context-switches happen at states that match the values of the shared variables in the tuple $g_1, \ldots, g_k$.

In the lazy approach, the thread scheduling $t_0, \ldots, t_k$ is determined nondeterministically as and when the context-switches happen, and each g_i is computed by executing the thread T_j which has the control in the context i (i.e., such that $j = t_i$) through all the contexts in which it had control up until context i. As in the previous approach, when re-executing the thread in the previously computed contexts, we check that the context-switches happen at states that match the values of the shared variables in the already computed tuple $g_1, \ldots, g_{i-1}$.

3   Concurrent Programs

Sequential recursive programs. Let us fix the syntax of a simple *sequential* programming language with variables ranging over only the integer and Boolean domains, and with explicit syntax for nondeterminism, (recursive) function calls, and tuples of return values.

The transformations in this paper require that we can cache the shared variables, and copy and compare them, and the notation is far simpler when we do not have complex or dynamically allocated structures. Handling domains of types other than integers is straightforward, but we will stick to integers for simplicity.

Programs are described by the following grammar:

$$
\begin{array}{ll}
\langle pgm \rangle & ::= \langle gvar\text{-}decl \rangle\,;\ \langle proc\text{-}list \rangle \\
\langle gvar\text{-}decl \rangle & ::= \texttt{decl int } x \mid \texttt{decl bool } x \mid \langle gvar\text{-}decl \rangle\,;\ \langle gvar\text{-}decl \rangle \\
\langle proc\text{-}list \rangle & ::= \langle proc \rangle\ \langle proc\text{-}list \rangle \mid \langle proc \rangle \\
\langle proc \rangle & ::= f^{h,m}\,(x_1, \ldots, x_h)\ \texttt{begin}\ \langle lvar\text{-}decl \rangle\,;\ \langle stmt \rangle\ \texttt{end} \\
\langle lvar\text{-}decl \rangle & ::= \texttt{decl int } x \mid \texttt{decl bool } x \mid \langle lvar\text{-}decl \rangle\,;\ \langle lvar\text{-}decl \rangle \\
\langle stmt \rangle & ::= \langle stmt \rangle\,;\ \langle stmt \rangle \mid \texttt{skip} \mid \langle assign \rangle \mid \texttt{assume}(\langle b\text{-}expr \rangle)\mid \\
& \quad\ \ \texttt{call } f^{h,0}(x_1, \ldots, x_h)\quad \mid\quad \texttt{return } x_1, \ldots, x_m \mid \\
& \quad\ \ \texttt{if } (\langle b\text{-}expr \rangle)\ \texttt{then}\ \langle stmt \rangle\ \texttt{else}\ \langle stmt \rangle\ \texttt{fi} \mid \\
& \quad\ \ \texttt{while } (\langle b\text{-}expr \rangle)\ \texttt{do}\ \langle stmt \rangle\ \texttt{od} \\
\langle assign \rangle & ::= x_1, \ldots, x_m\ \texttt{:=}\ \langle expr \rangle_1, \ldots, \langle expr \rangle_m \mid \\
& \quad\ \ x_1, \ldots, x_m\ \texttt{:=}\ f^{h,m}(y_1, \ldots, y_h) \\
\langle expr \rangle & ::= x \mid c \mid \langle b\text{-}expr \rangle \\
\langle b\text{-}expr \rangle & ::= T \mid F \mid * \mid x \mid \neg \langle b\text{-}expr \rangle \mid \langle b\text{-}expr \rangle \vee \langle b\text{-}expr \rangle
\end{array}
$$

In the above, x, x_i, y_i are from a set of variable names Var, c is any integer constant, and $f^{h,m}$ denotes a function with h formal parameters and m return values. Some of the functions $f^{h,m}$ may be interpreted to have existing functionality, such as integer addition or library functions, in which case their code is not given and we assume they happen atomically.

A program has a global variable declaration followed by a list of functions. Each function is a declaration of local variables followed by a sequence of statements, where statements can be tuple assignments, calls to functions (call-by-value) that take in multiple parameters and return multiple values, conditional statements, while-loops, or return statements. Expressions can be integer constants, variables or Boolean expressions. Boolean expressions can be true, false, or non-deterministically true or false ($*$), and can be combined using standard Boolean operations. Functions that do not return any values are called using the `call` statement. We also assume that the program type-checks with respect to the integer and Boolean types.

We will assume several obvious restrictions on the above syntax: global variables and local variables are assumed to be disjoint; formal parameters are local variables; the body of a function $f^{h,m}$ has only variables that are either globally declared, locally declared, or a formal parameter; a return statement in the body of $f^{h,m}$ is of the form `return` $x_1, \ldots, x_m$ or simply `return` (in the latter case arbitrary values will be returned).

Let us also assume that there is a function `main`, which is the function where the program starts, and that there are no calls to this function in the code of P.

The semantics is the obvious one: a configuration of a program consists of a *stack* which stores the history of positions at which calls were made, along with valuations for local variables, and the top of the stack contains the local and global valuations, and a pointer to the current statement being executed.

The *reachability problem* asks whether a particular statement in the program marked using a special label *Target* is reachable.

Concurrent programs. A *concurrent program* is a finite set of recursive programs running in parallel and sharing some (global) variables.

Formally, the syntax of concurrent programs is defined by extending the syntax of sequential recursive programs with the following rules:

$$
\begin{aligned}
\langle conc\text{-}pgm \rangle &::= \langle svar\text{-}decl \rangle;\ \langle init \rangle\ \langle pgm\text{-}list \rangle \\
\langle svar\text{-}decl \rangle &::= \texttt{decl int } x \mid \texttt{decl bool } x \mid \langle svar\text{-}decl \rangle;\ \langle svar\text{-}decl \rangle \\
\langle init \rangle &::= \langle proc \rangle \\
\langle pgm\text{-}list \rangle &::= \langle pgm \rangle\ \langle pgm\text{-}list \rangle \mid \langle pgm \rangle
\end{aligned}
$$

Let $\mathcal{P}$ be a concurrent program formed by the sequential programs $P_1, \ldots, P_n$ (where $n > 0$). Each program P_i has its own global and local variables, and also has access to variables that are shared with the other component programs. Let us assume that each concurrent program has a function $\texttt{init}$ where the shared variables are initialized (corresponding to the *init* construct in the above abstract syntax). Let us further assume that the function $\texttt{main}$ of each component program P_i is named $\texttt{thread}_i$.

The behavioral semantics of $\mathcal{P}$ is obtained by interleaving the behaviors of $P_1, \ldots, P_n$. At the beginning of any computation the shared variables are set according to function $\texttt{init}$. At any point of a computation, only one of the programs is *active*. Therefore, a *state* of $\mathcal{P}$ is denoted by a tuple $(i, u_S, \overline{u}_1, \ldots, \overline{u}_n)$ where P_i is the currently active program, u_S is a valuation of the shared variables and $\overline{u}_j$ is a state of P_j for $j = 1, \ldots, n$. From such a state the computation of $\mathcal{P}$ can evolve either according to the local behavior of P_i or by switching to another program P_j, which then becomes the new active program. A maximal consecutive part of a computation visiting only states where the same program P_i is active is called a *context*.

The *reachability problem for concurrent programs* asks whether a particular statement in the program marked using a special label *Target* is reachable. The *reachability problem for concurrent programs under a context-switch bound k*, for $k \geq 1$, asks whether *Target* is reachable within k context-switches.

Example 1. Figure 1 illustrates a simple concurrent program with two component programs starting at $\texttt{thread}_1$ and $\texttt{thread}_2$ respectively, and five shared variables $test, x_1, \ldots, x_4$, all over the Boolean domain. Function $\texttt{init}$ assigns the initial value to the shared variable $test$ and leaves all the others unassigned. Function $\texttt{thread}_1$ simply assigns all variables $x_1, \ldots, x_4$ to false, and then sets $test$ to true. Function $\texttt{thread}_2$ halts if $test$ is false. Otherwise, it will loop forever by nondeterministically choosing either to swap x_1 and x_2, or to shift the bits $x_1, \ldots, x_4$ circularly. The instruction labeled with *Target* is never reached on

```
decl bool test,x₁, x₂, x₃, x₄;              void thread₂() begin
                                               assume(test);
void init() begin                              while(T) do
  test := F;                                      if (*) then
  return;                                           x₁, x₂, x₃, x₄ := x₂, x₁, x₄, x₃;
end                                              else
                                                  x₁, x₂, x₃, x₄ := x₂, x₃, x₄, x₁;
                                                fi
void thread₁() begin                            od
  x₁, x₂, x₃, x₄ := F, F, F, F;              Target: skip;
  test := T;                                   return;
  return;                                    end
end
```

Fig. 1. The concurrent program *permutation*

any computation. thread_2 eventually computes (on various runs) all the permutations of the bits stored in $x_1, \ldots, x_4$. Note that, since these variables are set to false by thread_1, the reachable state-space at the while-loop has only the valuation $\langle x_1 = F, x_2 = F, x_3 = F, x_4 = F \rangle$. □

4   Translation Scheme: The Eager Approach

In this section, we give a detailed description of the translation of a concurrent program $\mathcal{P}$ with target program counter pc under a context-switching bound k to a sequential program using the eager approach (denoted $\text{Eager}_k(\mathcal{P}, pc)$), and argue its correctness.

Besides the variables in $\mathcal{P}$, the sequential program $\text{Eager}_k(\mathcal{P}, pc)$ will have extra global variable tuples $g_1, \ldots, g_k$ and $t_0, \ldots, t_k$, as described in Section 2. We add also the following control variables: a variable t to keep the index of the active component program, a variable cx to keep the current context number, a Boolean variable *terminate* to interrupt the execution of a program component, and a Boolean variable *goal* which gets set to true when the target pc of $\mathcal{P}$ is reached.

The sequential program $\text{Eager}_k(\mathcal{P}, pc)$ is composed of: two new functions **main** and *contextSwitch* that are shown in Figure 2, and for every function P of $\mathcal{P}$, a function P^e which is a transformation of P.

In Figure 2, we use $nextContext(cx, t, t_0, \ldots, t_k)$ to denote a function that computes the index of the first context in which P_t is active after cx, if any, and $k + 1$, otherwise. Formally, $nextContext(cx, t, t_0, \ldots, t_k)$ is the value i such that either $t_i = t$ and $t_j \neq t$ for all j s.t. $cx < j < i$, or $i = k + 1$ and $t_j \neq t$ for all $j > cx$. Clearly, such an index can be computed with a few lines of code. We also use $firstContext(t, t_0, \ldots, t_k)$ to compute the first context in which P_t is active in the computation.

Let g: shared variables of $\mathcal{P}$;   Let $g_1, \ldots, g_k$ be k copies of g;
`decl int` $cx, t, t_0, \ldots, t_k$;   `decl bool` $goal, terminate$;

```
void main( )                              void contextSwitch( )
begin                                     begin
  goal := F;                                if (cx = k) then
  assume(⋀ᵏᵢ₌₀(0 < tᵢ ≤ n));                  terminate := T;
  for(i := 1; i ≤ n; i + +) do              else
    t := i;                                   assume(g = g_{cx+1});
    cx := firstContext(t, t₀, ..., tₖ);       cx := nextContext(cx, t, t₀, ..., tₖ);
    if (cx ≤ k) then                          if (cx ≤ k) then g := g_{cx};
      if (cx = 0) then init( );               else terminate := T; fi
      else  g := g_{cx}; fi                  fi
      terminate := F;                       return;
      call thread^e_{t_{cx}}( );          end
    fi
  od
  assume(goal);
  Target: skip;
  return;
end
```

Fig. 2. Functions `main` and *contextSwitch* of the program $\text{Eager}_k(\mathcal{P}, pc)$

Each function P^e is obtained from the corresponding function P of $\mathcal{P}$ by a simple transformation. We first interleave the statements of P with the lines of control code $\mathcal{C}$ shown in Figure 3. More precisely, we rewrite the

```
if (terminate) then return;
else
      if (*) then call contextSwitch( ); fi
      if (terminate) then return; fi
fi
```

Fig. 3. Control code

statements of P according to the following rules ($\mathcal{E}$ is an arbitrary Boolean expression, $\mathcal{S}_1$ and $\mathcal{S}_2$ are arbitrary statements, and $\mathcal{S}$ is a basic statement of the kind `assign` or `skip` or `assume` or `call`):

- $\tau[\mathcal{S}_1; \mathcal{S}_2] = \tau[\mathcal{S}_1]; \tau[\mathcal{S}_2]$
- $\tau[\mathcal{S}] = \mathcal{S}; \mathcal{C}$
- $\tau[\text{return } x_1, \ldots, x_m] = \text{return } x_1, \ldots, x_m$
- $\tau[\text{while } (\mathcal{E}) \text{ do } \mathcal{S}_1 \text{ od}] = \text{while } (\mathcal{E}) \text{ do } \mathcal{C}; \tau[\mathcal{S}_1] \text{ od}$
- $\tau[\text{if } (\mathcal{E}) \text{ then } \mathcal{S}_1 \text{ else } \mathcal{S}_2 \text{ fi}] = \text{if } (\mathcal{E}) \text{ then } \mathcal{C}; \tau[\mathcal{S}_1] \text{ else } \mathcal{C}; \tau[\mathcal{S}_2] \text{ fi}$

Actually, we can optimize the above translation by inserting control code only after statements that read or write a shared variable, or calls to a function.

Next, we insert "`assume(F);`" before each return statement of the functions `thread`$_i$ for $i = 1, \ldots, n$; this prevents `thread`$_i$ from returning to `main` after executing to completion. Finally, we insert "$goal{:=}T$;" right before the statement labeled with the target program counter pc.

The general behavior of $\text{Eager}_k(\mathcal{P}, pc)$ is as follows.

Procedure **main** works as a driver program that calls each component program P_i in turn at most once. After checking that $t_0, \ldots, t_n$ all contains valid indices of component programs (i.e., $1 \leq t_i \leq n$ holds for each t_i), for each component program P_i, $i = 1, \ldots, n$, control variables t and cx are assigned respectively with the current component index (i.e., i) and the first context at which the current component is active if any (according to the scheduling of components given by $t_0, \ldots, t_n$). If there is no such context, the next component program is processed. Otherwise, the shared variables are consistently assigned with the initial values (given by **init**, if the current context is the first one, or by g_{cx} otherwise), and **thread**$_i^e$ is called.

Once called, a component program must run through all the contexts in which it is active and report if the target pc is reached by setting $goal$ to true. This is ensured by the control code inserted in each function.

Unless the variable $terminate$ holds true, after each step of the original program, it is possible (nondeterministically) to call the function $contextSwitch$. In each such call, the computation proceeds by trying to make a context-switch. In case there are no more contexts in which the current program is active, the function sets $terminate$ to true and returns. Otherwise, the shared variables are assigned with the guessed values for the next context where the current program is active and $contextSwitch$ returns.

Observe that the **if**-statements checking the value of $terminate$ in the control code ensure that in case $terminate$ is set to true in $contextSwitch$, the control returns from all the calls stored in the call stack up to the **main** function. Since $terminate$ is set to true only when there are no more contexts to run for the current component program, it is correct to interrupt the execution of the current component program and return to **main** so that the next component program (if any) can be executed.

Also, observe that the added "**assume**(F);" statement halts any computation that would have reached a return statement in each function **thread**$_i^e$. Therefore, a call to any **thread**$_i^e$ returns if and only if all the contexts in which P_i is active have been successfully executed (i.e., $terminate$ is set to true).

When all programs have successfully terminated we check the variable $goal$, and if it holds true, then the label $Target$ is reached, else the program halts.

Note that if the guessed tuples $g_1, \ldots, g_k$ and $t_0, \ldots, t_k$ do not correspond to an actual computation of $\mathcal{P}$ then there will be at least one component program P_i, with $1 \leq i \leq n$, that cannot match the sequence $g_1, \ldots, g_k$ and thus the call to **thread**$_i^e$ will not return.

From the above arguments, we conclude that a program counter pc is reachable within k context-switches in a computation of $\mathcal{P}$ if and only if $Target$ in **main** is reachable in a computation of $Eager_k(\mathcal{P}, pc)$. Therefore,

Theorem 1. *Given an integer $k \geq 0$, a concurrent program $\mathcal{P}$ and a program counter pc, pc is reachable in $\mathcal{P}$ within at most k context-switches if and only if $Target$ is reachable in $Eager_k(\mathcal{P}, pc)$.*

5   Translation Scheme: The Lazy Approach

We now detail the description of the translation of a concurrent program $\mathcal{P}$ under a context-switching bound k to a sequential program using the lazy approach (denoted $\text{Lazy}_k(\mathcal{P})$), and argue its correctness.

The structure of $\text{Lazy}_k(\mathcal{P})$ is similar to that of $\text{Eager}_k(\mathcal{P},pc)$. We keep all the variables we used earlier except for t and $goal$ which are not needed here. Also, besides variable cx, we need a second global variable, ic, to store a context number (from 1 to k). Recall that for each context c we need to run the component program P_i that is active in c through all the contexts c' in which P_i was active, from the first context through context c. We use cx to store the context c and ic to keep track of the context c' in the above computation.

In $\text{Lazy}_k(\mathcal{P})$ each function P of $\mathcal{P}$ is translated to a function P^l which is similar P^e in Section 4, except that here we do not need to set the global variable $goal$ when the target program counter is reached. The remaining functions are **main** and *contextSwitch*, which are significantly different from those described in Section 4, and are given in Figure 4.

For each context cx, function **main** iteratively: (1) chooses the component program P_i which is active in context cx, (2) determines the first context ic in which P_i is active starting from context 0 through context cx, (3) assigns the shared variables consistent with ic (i.e., if $ic = 0$ then the shared variables are assigned by function **init**, otherwise they are assigned with the values they have at the context-switch ic), and (4) calls function $\mathbf{thread}_i^l$.

In **main**, the call to function $\mathbf{thread}_i^l$ executes the component program P_i^l through all the contexts in which it is active, from the first one up to cx. In fact,

Let g: shared variables of $\mathcal{P}$;   *Let $g_1, \ldots, g_k$: be k copies of g*
`decl int` $cx, ic, t_0, \ldots, t_k$;   `decl bool` *terminate*;

```
void main( )
begin
   cx := 0;
   while(cx ≤ k) do
      assume(1 ≤ t_cx ≤ n);
      ic := firstContext(t_cx, t_0, ..., t_cx);
      if (ic = 0) then
         init();
      else
         g := g_ic;
      fi
      terminate := F;
      call thread^l_{t_cx} ();
      cx := cx + 1;
   od
end
```

```
void contextSwitch( )
begin
   if (ic = cx) then
      terminate := T;
      if (cx < k) then g_{cx+1} := g; fi
   else
      if (g = g_{ic+1}) then
         ic := nextContext(ic, t_ic, t_0, ..., t_cx);
         g := g_ic;
      fi
   fi
end
```

Fig. 4. Functions **main** and *contextSwitch* of the program $\text{Lazy}_k(\mathcal{P})$

when $\texttt{thread}_i^l$ is called the computation of P_i^l starts at the beginning of context ic (which is set to the first context where P_i^l is active). After any step of P_i^l, it is possible to call $contextSwitch$ ($terminate$ is set to false before calling $\texttt{thread}_i^l$ in function $\texttt{main}$) and then perform a context-switch if possible.

In function $contextSwitch$, if $ic < cx$, we check if it is possible to perform a context-switch by determining if the current value of the shared variables matches the stored value for the next context-switch. If so, the next context c in which P_i is active is computed and the shared variables are assigned with the value at the beginning of context c (i.e., with g_c). Observe that since we know that P_i is active in cx, there will always be such a context c.

From the last observation, we also have that if $ic < cx$ does not hold then $ic = cx$ must hold. Thus, in the remaining case, i.e. $ic = cx$, it is possible to make a context-switch at any point. This is correct, since we are executing P_i in context cx, which is newly added before making this call to $\texttt{thread}_i^l$ in $\texttt{main}$, and thus we have no requirements to match. When context-switching in this case, we only need to store the values of the shared variables in g_{cx+1} (if we are not yet in the last context k) and flag that this call to $\texttt{thread}_i^l$ has terminated by setting $terminate$ to true.

From the above observations, any computation π of $\mathcal{P}$ can be executed step-by-step by program $\text{Lazy}_k(\mathcal{P})$, and thus if π visits a program counter pc, the corresponding computation of $\text{Lazy}_k(\mathcal{P})$ will also visit pc.

Now consider any computation π of $\text{Lazy}_k(\mathcal{P})$ which successfully terminates (i.e., the return statement of function $\texttt{main}$ is reached). Recall that by construction each function $\texttt{thread}_i^l$ has a statement "$\texttt{assume}(F)$" guarding each return statement from the original function $\texttt{thread}_i$. Thus, as in the case of the eager approach construction, the only way for a call to $\texttt{thread}_i^l$ to return is by setting the variable $terminate$ to true.

From all the above observations, all calls to each $\texttt{thread}_i^l$ made from $\texttt{main}$ return if and only if the computed sequence $g_1, \ldots, g_k$ is matched by a computation of $\mathcal{P}$. Therefore, for each computation π of $\text{Lazy}_k(\mathcal{P})$ which successfully terminates and which visits a program counter pc of $\mathcal{P}$ there is a corresponding computation π' of $\mathcal{P}$ which visits pc. Hence,

Theorem 2. *Given an integer $k \geq 0$, a concurrent program $\mathcal{P}$ and a program counter pc, pc is reachable in $\mathcal{P}$ within at most k context-switches if and only if pc is reachable in $\text{Lazy}_k(\mathcal{P})$.*

6   Experiments

Boolean programs. Boolean programs are programs where the data-domain is only Boolean. Since the data-domain is finite, Boolean programs can be subject to *decidable model-checking* for analyzing reachability. In particular, it is well known that sequential Boolean programs have a decidable reachability problem, and that for concurrent Boolean programs, reachability is undecidable (due to multiple stacks). However, it has also been shown that reachability problem for concurrent Boolean programs under a context-switching bound is decidable.

Context switches	1-adder, 1-stopper			2-adders, 1-stopper			1-adder, 2-stoppers			2-adders, 2-stoppers		
		Eager	Lazy		Eager	Lazy		Eager	Lazy		Eager	Lazy
1	N	0.1	0.1	N	0.2	0.1	N	0.1	0.1	N	0.2	0.1
2	N	0.3	0.2	N	0.9	0.8	N	0.7	0.9	N	1.6	2.0
3	N	43.3	1.4	N	135.9	6.3	Y	70.1	0.4	Y	177.6	0.8
4	N	73.6	5.5	Y	1601.0	2.6	Y	597.2	2.9	Y	out of mem.	7.5
5	N	930.0	20.2	Y	-	18.0	Y	-	14.0	Y	out of mem.	66.5
6	N	-	66.8	Y	-	122.9	Y	-	66.1	Y	out of mem.	535.9

Fig. 5. Experimental results on the Bluetooth driver example. Times are expressed in seconds, "-" denotes timeout in 30 minutes and Y/N denote if the target is reachable.

Translation for Boolean programs. We have implemented both the eager and lazy translations described in the previous sections for Boolean programs, in order to reduce the reachability of concurrent Boolean programs under a context-switching bound to the (decidable) problem of sequential Boolean program reachability. We then subject the sequential program to the reachability model-checker Moped [2]. Our goal is to show the applicability of the translations, and in showing that, the lazy translation can outperform the eager one; we show this on a class of Bluetooth driver examples.

The first concurrent program we consider illustrates the difference between the eager and the lazy analysis; we consider the *permutation* example with 16-bits (a four-bit version of this program is shown in Figure 1). Initially, only $thread_1$ can evolve as $thread_2$ is blocked on its first statement. $thread_1$ sets all 16-bits to false and, before returning, sets *test* to true. Now, $thread_2$ can take over and goes into an infinite loop in which the bits are shuffled producing sooner or later all permutations of the

Context switches	permutation 16-bits		
		Eager	Lazy
1	N	6.97	0.1
2	N	194.7	1.0
3	N	out of mem.	122.5

Table 1. Experiments of *permutation* program with 16 bits. Times are expressed in seconds

16-bits. Since all the bits are set to false, only one permutation of the 16-bits is possible in the execution. The table with the experiments for *permutation* is reported in Table 1. As it is evident, the eager version simply fails after a few context-switches. In the eager approach all the global variables are guessed at the beginning and all the threads are executed on the guesses. Therefore this does not prevent $thread_2$ to work on arbitrary values of $x_1, \ldots, x_{16}$ and hence ends up exploring a large and complex state-space (storing all permutations requires large BDDs). The lazy version on the other hand only considers reachable states and hence works well on this example.

The second set of experiments is related to a concurrent boolean program modeling a Windows NT Bluetooth driver [11]. Figure 5 depicts the experimental results. This driver has two types of threads: stoppers and adders. A stopper calls a stopping procedure to halt the driver, while an adder calls a procedure to perform I/O in the driver. The I/O is successfully handled if the driver is not stopped, and an error state is reached otherwise. The pending I/O requests to the driver are maintained in a counter which is modeled with five bits in our Boolean model of the program.

We have considered four different configurations, by considering one or two adders, and one or two stoppers. We translated the corresponding concurrent programs both with the lazy and eager version of our translator allowing up to six context-switches, and run Moped on them. As from Figure 5, the lazy scheme performs a lot better than the eager one, and the performance gap between them increases with the increase in the number of context-switches.

7   Future Directions

There are two interesting future directions we see. One is to see whether using the lazy translation scheme presented here in the context of deductive verification of concurrent C programs as done in [5] leads to more efficient analysis. Second, it would be interesting to see whether the scheme proposed here can be extended to more general concurrent programs with dynamic and unbounded thread creation.

References

1. Bouajjani, A., Fratani, S., Qadeer, S.: Context-bounded analysis of multithreaded programs with dynamic linked structures. In: Damm, W., Hermanns, H. (eds.) CAV 2007. LNCS, vol. 4590, pp. 207–220. Springer, Heidelberg (2007)
2. Esparza, J., Schwoon, S.: A BDD-based model checker for recursive programs. In: Berry, G., Comon, H., Finkel, A. (eds.) CAV 2001. LNCS, vol. 2102, pp. 324–336. Springer, Heidelberg (2001)
3. La Torre, S., Madhusudan, P., Parlato, G.: Context-bounded analysis of concurrent queue systems. In: Ramakrishnan, C.R., Rehof, J. (eds.) TACAS 2008. LNCS, vol. 4963, pp. 299–314. Springer, Heidelberg (2008)
4. La Torre, S., Madhusudan, P., Parlato, G.: Analyzing recursive programs using a fixed-point calculus. In: PLDI (2009)
5. Lahiri, S.K., Qadeer, S., Rakamarić, Z.: Static and Precise Detection of Concurrency Errors in Systems Code using SMT solvers. In: Bouajjani, A., Maler, O. (eds.) CAV 2009. LNCS, vol. 5643, pp. 509–524. Springer, Heidelberg (2009)
6. Lal, A., Reps, T.W.: Reducing concurrent analysis under a context bound to sequential analysis. In: Gupta, A., Malik, S. (eds.) CAV 2008. LNCS, vol. 5123, pp. 37–51. Springer, Heidelberg (2008)
7. Lal, A., Touili, T., Kidd, N., Reps, T.W.: Interprocedural analysis of concurrent programs under a context bound. In: Ramakrishnan, C.R., Rehof, J. (eds.) TACAS 2008. LNCS, vol. 4963, pp. 282–298. Springer, Heidelberg (2008)
8. Musuvathi, M., Qadeer, S.: Chess: Systematic stress testing of concurrent software. In: Puebla, G. (ed.) LOPSTR 2006. LNCS, vol. 4407, pp. 15–16. Springer, Heidelberg (2007)
9. Musuvathi, M., Qadeer, S.: Iterative context bounding for systematic testing of multithreaded programs. In: PLDI, pp. 446–455. ACM, New York (2007)
10. Qadeer, S., Rehof, J.: Context-bounded model checking of concurrent software. In: Halbwachs, N., Zuck, L.D. (eds.) TACAS 2005. LNCS, vol. 3440, pp. 93–107. Springer, Heidelberg (2005)

11. Qadeer, S., Wu, D.: Kiss: keep it simple and sequential. In: PLDI, pp. 14–24. ACM, New York (2004)
12. Ramalingam, G.: Context-sensitive synchronization-sensitive analysis is undecidable. ACM Trans. Program. Lang. Syst. 22(2), 416–430 (2000)
13. Suwimonteerabuth, D., Esparza, J., Schwoon, S.: Symbolic context-bounded analysis of multithreaded java programs. In: Havelund, K., Majumdar, R., Palsberg, J. (eds.) SPIN 2008. LNCS, vol. 5156, pp. 270–287. Springer, Heidelberg (2008)

Intra-module Inference

Shuvendu K. Lahiri[1], Shaz Qadeer[1], Juan P. Galeotti[2], Jan W. Voung[3],
and Thomas Wies[4]

[1] Microsoft Research
[2] University of Buenos Aires
[3] University of California, San Diego
[4] École Polytechnique Fédérale de Lausanne

Abstract. Contract-based property checkers hold the potential for precise, scalable, and incremental reasoning. However, it is difficult to apply such checkers to large program modules because they require programmers to provide detailed contracts, including an interface specification, module invariants, and internal specifications. We argue that given a suitably rich assertion language, modest effort suffices to document the interface specification and the module invariants. However, the burden of providing internal specifications is still significant and remains a deterrent to the use of contract-based checkers. Therefore, we consider the problem of *intra-module inference*, which aims to infer annotations for internal procedures and loops, given the interface specification and the module invariants. We provide simple and scalable techniques to search for a broad class of desired internal annotations, comprising quantifiers and Boolean connectives, guided by the module specification. We have validated our ideas by building a prototype verifier and using it to verify several properties on Windows device drivers with zero false alarms and small annotation overhead. These drivers are complex; they contain thousands of lines and use dynamic data structures such as linked lists and arrays. Our technique significantly improves the soundness, precision, and coverage of verification of these programs compared to earlier techniques.

1   Introduction

Program verification is an undecidable problem, which makes it impossible to build automated and precise program verifiers. In the last few decades, research in static analysis and program verification has attempted to improve the precision and scalability of program verification tools without requiring significant user input. Most existing tools for verifying properties of software fall under two extremes: push-button tools based on model checking [7] and abstract interpretation [9] that have little room for user guidance, or contract-based verifiers such as ESC/Java [14] and Spec# [5] that require the user to specify all the contracts.

Contract-based property checkers hold the potential for precise, scalable, and incremental reasoning. However, it is difficult to apply such checkers to large program modules because they require programmers to provide detailed contracts.

A. Bouajjani and O. Maler (Eds.): CAV 2009, LNCS 5643, pp. 493–508, 2009.

These contracts include an interface specification (preconditions and postconditions for public procedures), module invariants, and internal specifications (loop invariants, preconditions, and postconditions for internal procedures). Manually providing such contracts is infeasible for large modules that typically contain thousands of lines and hundreds of procedures. Operating systems modules such as device drivers, file systems, and memory managers are typically large and consequently remain outside the scope of existing verification techniques.

We argue that given a suitably rich assertion language, modest effort suffices to document the interface specification and the module invariants. This is fortunate because these specifications are the most useful for documentation and program understanding. While the interface specification documents the client's view, the module invariants provide the central argument for establishing the interface specification and other desirable properties of the module. However, the burden of providing internal specifications is still significant and remains a deterrent to the use of contract-based checkers. Therefore, we solve the problem of *intra-module inference*. Given a module with an interface specification, module invariants, and a property to be proved, we infer annotations on loops and internal procedures guided by the provided specifications.

In this work, we demonstrate how to synthesize a broad class of internal annotations containing quantifiers and Boolean structure, in a scalable fashion, guided by the module invariants. Our inference method generates a set of *candidate annotations* using an idea of *exception sets*, and then searches for annotations within the candidate pool using the scalable Houdini algorithm [13]. We formalize our ideas in terms of a general and extensible annotation language comprising *type-state assertions*. The type-state of a pointer can be static or can depend on runtime attributes such as the runtime type of a pointer, values of object fields, and membership (or non-membership) in heap-allocated data structures [22].

We have validated our ideas by building a prototype verifier and using it to verify several properties on Windows device drivers with zero false alarms and small annotation overhead. These drivers are complex; they contain thousands of lines and use dynamic data structures such as linked lists and arrays. We show that proving even simple type-state properties may require tracking typestates related to linked lists and non-trivial aliasing constraints in the module invariants. We then demonstrate how our inference technique is able to infer almost all internal annotations. Our technique significantly improves the soundness, precision and coverage of verification of these programs compared to earlier techniques applied on these programs (see Section 6 for related work).

Our experience leads us to the following conclusions:

1. Having the programmer specify the module invariants and the tool infer the internal annotations is a useful tradeoff in the quest for automated program verifiers that can check general properties with high precision. Given only the property to be proved, inferring the module invariants automatically with reasonable cost seems unlikely because the required invariant may depend on sophisticated type-state abstractions absent from the property. Inference of

internal annotations guided by the structure of the module invariants seems more amenable to cost-effective automation.

2. Searching for internal annotations guided by user-specified module invariants discovers annotations that are understandable by a programmer, unlike intermediate assertions of static analysis tools that can only be understood by machines. This attribute is important if a tool attempts to aid program documentation and incremental checking, in addition to finding bugs.

2   Motivating Example

In this section, we show the module invariants and internal annotations required to verify properties of a real-life Windows device driver kbdclass. We focus on checking the absence of the following *double-free property*: a pointer of type DEVICE_OBJECT that is deleted with a call to IoDeleteDevice was allocated via a prior call to IoCreateDevice, and an object is not deleted twice. The purpose of this section is to show that the module invariants required to check this property can be expressed succinctly over a set of suitable type-states with a relatively low annotation burden. On the other hand, it is non-trivial to arrive at the relevant invariants mechanically starting from the property of interest, as they contain type-state abstractions, quantifiers and Boolean structure.

2.1   Module Invariants

Module invariants are a set of assertions that are preserved by the public procedures of a module and are strong enough to prove the property of interest. Figure 2 shows the module invariants required to prove the double-free property on kbdclass. Each of these invariants either specifies a property on all pointers satisfying a dynamic type-state, or the type-state of a global variable. In this section, we will explain these invariants with respect to the kbdclass module.

Allocation type-states and aliasing invariants. We use the mutable sets MyDevObj and MyDevExtn to model the allocation (in IoCreateDevice) and deletion (in IoDeleteDevice) of DEVICE_OBJECT pointers in kbdclass. The structure of a device object and a device extension are described below (ignore the field of type PLIST_ENTRY for now):

```
typedef struct _DEVICE_OBJECT{      typedef struct _DEVICE_EXTENSION{
    void *DeviceExtension;              PLIST_ENTRY    Link;
    ...                                 PDEVICE_OBJECT Self;
}                                       ...
DEVICE_OBJECT, *PDEVICE_OBJECT;     }
                                    DEVICE_EXTENSION, *PDEVICE_EXTENSION;
```

Intuitively, each call to IoCreateDevice adds a pointer u to MyDevObj and a pointer v to MyDevExtn, setting u->DeviceExtension to v at the same time. Conversely, when a pointer u is passed to IoDeleteDevice, it removes u from MyDevObj and u->DeviceExtension from MyDevExtn. The aliasing constraints

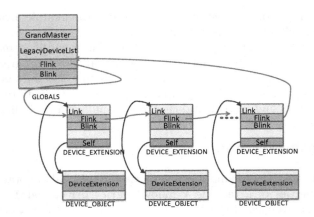

Fig. 1. Data structures in `kbdclass`

between the fields `Self` and `DeviceExtension` (see Figure 1) are captured by
invariants 1 and 2.

Now, consider the public method `KeyboardPnP` in the `kbdclass` module:

```
requires (DeviceObject ∈ MyDevObj)
NTSTATUS KeyboardPnP(PDEVICE_OBJECT DeviceObject, PIRP Irp){
    ...
    data = (PDEVICE_EXTENSION) DeviceObject->DeviceExtension;
    ...
    case IRP_MN_REMOVE_DEVICE: IoDeleteDevice (data->Self);
    ...
}
```

When the request `IRP_MN_REMOVE_DEVICE` is passed in the `Irp` parameter,
the procedure deletes the device object `DeviceObject`. The kernel ensures that
`KeyboardPnP` is only invoked on a device object that was previously allocated by
a call to `IoCreateDevice` in this module. This property is reflected in the precondition given in the **requires** annotation. However, note that `IoDeleteDevice` is
invoked on `DeviceObject->DeviceExtension->Self` — it is typical of device
drivers to extract the device extension from the device object at the beginning
and then use the device extension for the rest of the routine. This is safe because
`DeviceObject->DeviceExtension->Self` is identical to `DeviceObject`, a fact
provided by the module invariant 1 in Figure 2.

Type-state for list membership. The `kbdclass` module also contains a global
structure variable `Globals` of type `GLOBALS` as shown below:

```
typedef struct _GLOBALS{              typedef struct _LIST_ENTRY{
    LIST_ENTRY  LegacyDeviceList;         PLIST_ENTRY Flink;
    PDEVICE_EXTENSION GrandMaster;        PLIST_ENTRY Blink;
    ...                               } LIST_ENTRY, *PLIST_ENTRY;
} GLOBALS;
```

$$\forall x \in \text{MyDevObj} : \text{x->DeviceExtension->Self} = x \qquad (1)$$
$$\forall y \in \text{MyDevExtn} : \text{y->Self->DeviceExtension} = y \qquad (2)$$
$$\forall x \in \text{MyDevObj} : \text{x->DeviceExtension} \in \text{MyDevExtn} \qquad (3)$$
$$\forall y \in \text{MyDevExtn} : \text{y->Self} \in \text{MyDevObj} \qquad (4)$$
$$\forall z \in \text{GL\_LIST} : z = \text{HD} \lor \text{ENCL}(z) \in \text{MyDevExtn} \qquad (5)$$
$$\text{HD} \in \text{GL\_LIST} \qquad (6)$$
$$\text{Globals.GrandMaster} \neq 0 \implies \text{Globals.GrandMaster} \in \text{MyDevExtn} \qquad (7)$$
$$\&\text{Globals.GrandMaster->Link} \notin \text{GL\_LIST} \qquad (8)$$

Fig. 2. Module invariants for checking double-free property on kbdclass. ENCL(x) is a macro for CONTAINING_RECORD(x, DEVICE_EXTENSION, Link).

The GLOBALS structure contains a pointer to a device extension in GrandMaster, and the head of a list of device extensions in LegacyDeviceList. The LIST_ENTRY structure contains forward and backward links for a linked list; fields of this type represent the head (LegacyDeviceList in GLOBALS) as well as the links (Link in DEVICE_EXTENSION) in a list (refer to Figure 1).

Now consider the public procedure KeyboardClassUnload which deletes all the device objects present in the driver, before unloading the driver.

```
VOID KeyboardClassUnload(PDRIVER_OBJECT DriverObject){
    ...
    // Delete all of our legacy devices
    for (entry = Globals.LegacyDeviceList.Flink;
         entry != &Globals.LegacyDeviceList;){
        PDEVICE_EXTENSION data =
                CONTAINING_RECORD (entry, DEVICE_EXTENSION, Link);
        RemoveEntryList (&data->Link);
        entry = entry->Flink;
        ...
        IoDeleteDevice(data->Self);
    }

    // Delete the grandmaster if it exists
    if (Globals.GrandMaster) {
        data = Globals.GrandMaster;
        Globals.GrandMaster = NULL;
        ...
        IoDeleteDevice(data->Self);
    }
}
```

The loop in the procedure iterates over the list Globals.LegacyDeviceList using the iterator variable entry. The macro CONTAINING_RECORD is used to obtain the enclosing structure given the address of an internal field, and is defined as:

```
#define CONTAINING_RECORD(x, T, f) ((T *)((int)(x) - (int)(&((T
*)0)->f)))
```

For each iteration, `data` points to the enclosing `DEVICE_EXTENSION` structure of `entry`. This `entry` is removed from the list by `RemoveEntryList` and freed by the call to `IoDeleteDevice` on `data->Self`. Finally, the device object in `Globals.GrandMaster` is freed, after the loop terminates.

We argue about the safety of these operations in the remainder of this section. First, we define two macros that are used in the definition of the module invariants in Figure 2, to refer to the linked list in `Globals.LegacyDeviceList`:

```
#define HD        &Globals.LegacyDeviceList
#define GL_LIST   Btwn(Flink, HD->Flink, HD)
```

Here `HD` denotes the dummy head of the linked list and `GL_LIST` denotes the pointers in the linked list. The set constructor $Btwn(f, x, y)$ [20] denotes the set of pointers $\{x, x\text{->}f, x\text{->}f\text{->}f, \ldots, y\}$ when x reaches y using f, or $\{\}$ otherwise.

1. We need to specify that for each entry `z` of the list apart from the dummy head `HD`, the pointer `CONTAINING_RECORD(z, DEVICE_EXTENSION, Link)` is a `MyDevExtn` pointer. This is specified in invariant 5. Invariant 6 denotes that the set is non-empty. Notice that invariant 5 corresponds to a type-state invariant, where the type-state is determined by membership in a data structure.
2. For any `MyDevExtn` pointer x, `x->Self` should be a `MyDevObj` pointer, to enable the call to `IoDeleteDevice` to succeed (invariant 4).
3. Furthermore, we need to ensure that `IoDeleteDevice` is not invoked on the same device object pointer in two different iterations of the loop. This can happen if $x\text{->}\text{Self} = y\text{->}\text{Self}$, where x and y correspond to the values of `data` in two different loop iterations. This can be prevented by requiring that any `MyDevExtn` pointer x satisfies $x\text{->}\text{Self->DeviceExtension} = x$ (invariant 2).
4. Finally, invariant 7 ensures that `Globals.GrandMaster` is a valid device extension and invariant 8 ensures that `Globals.GrandMaster` is not present in the `GL_LIST`, and therefore `Globals.GrandMaster->Self` was not freed in the loop.

2.2   Internal Annotations

Let us now look at some of the annotations required on the internal procedures to verify the absence of the double-free property modularly. In the ideal case, the module invariants would act as the necessary preconditions, postconditions and loop invariants for all the procedures. However, these invariants can be temporarily broken due to *allocation* of new objects satisfying a given type-state or *mutation* of fields in objects. For instance, many invariants on the global state (invariants 5, 7, 8) do not hold on internal procedures and loops called within the initialization procedure of the module. For `kbdclass`, most of the internal annotations *in addition* to the module invariants can be categorized into one of the following:

Module invariant exceptions. In the procedure `KeyboardClassUnload` below, a device object `*ClassDeviceObject` is initialized after being created by `IoCreateDevice`.

```
NTSTATUS KbdCreateClassObject(..., PDEVICE_OBJECT
*ClassDeviceObject) {
    ...
    status = IoCreateDevice(..., ClassDeviceObject);
    ...
    deviceExtension =
            (PDEVICE_EXTENSION) (*ClassDeviceObject)->DeviceExtension;
    deviceExtension->Self =  *ClassDeviceObject;
    ...
}
```

Any procedure call between the call to `IoCreateDevice` and the setting of `Self` would violate the invariant 1. In this case, the type-state invariant 1 holds for all pointers with the *exception* of `*ClassDeviceObject`.

Type-states of pointers and their fields. We have to propagate the type-states of pointers available from preconditions of public procedures to internal procedures to utilize the type-state invariants. In another case, we need the loop invariant `entry` $\in$ `GL_LIST` for the loop in `KeyboardClassUnload` (described in Section 2.1); it describes the type-state of the local variable `entry`.

Modifies clauses. In the absence of any annotation about the *side-effect* (or *modifies set*), a procedure havocs (scrambles) all the globals the fields and type-states of pointers in the heap. Modifies annotations are needed to provide precise updates to the relevant fields and type-states.

Conditional annotations. Sometimes the annotations in each of above categories need to be guarded by some conditions (e.g. return value, flags in some parameters). The procedure `KbdCreateClassObject` (encountered earlier in this section) creates and returns a `MyDevObj` pointer through the out-parameter `*ClassDeviceObject`, *only* when the return value is non-negative.

In the remainder of the paper, we formalize the notion of *type-states* (Section 3), and provide mechanisms to generate internal annotations guided by the module invariants (Section 4), and finally evaluate our technique on a set of real-world device drivers (Section 5).

3   Type-State Assertions

In this section, we formally define a *type-state* and *type-state assertions* that comprise our annotation language. A *type-state* is a set of pointers, and the type-state of a pointer is determined by membership or exclusion from the set. Type-states are a generalization of static types in a program and are useful

$$\phi \in Formula \quad ::= \quad \forall \mathtt{x} \in S : \ \phi \mid \psi$$
$$\psi \in BFormula ::= \quad t \in S \mid t \leq t \mid \neg\psi \mid \psi \vee \psi$$
$$t \in Expr \qquad ::= \quad \mathtt{x} \mid t\texttt{->f} \mid \texttt{\&}t \mid *t$$
$$S \in SetExpr \quad ::= \quad \{\} \mid \mathtt{int} \mid S \cup S \mid S \setminus S \mid \mathtt{Btwn(f}, t, t) \mid \mathtt{Array}(t, t, t) \mid \ldots$$

Fig. 3. Grammar for type-state invariants. Here f refers to a program field. The top-level invariant is of the form ϕ, S is a set expression, and int is the set of all integers. We require that x not appear in S in the formula $\forall \mathtt{x} \in S : \ \phi$.

for two purposes: (a) for establishing non-aliasing between pointers belonging to disjoint type-states, and (b) to state a property about a set of pointers satisfying a type-state.

The language of type-states is extensible by the user and includes the following:

1. **Static.** The static types in programs correspond to immutable type-states.
2. **Dynamic.** Some type-states are mutable at runtime. For example, the type-state MyDevObj is mutated by calls to IoCreateDevice and IoDeleteDevice.
3. **Membership in data structures.** As we have seen, we often need to distinguish pointers based on their membership in a list (e.g., GL_LIST), a tree or an array. We use set constructors to refer to all elements of a list between two pointers (Btwn) or all elements in the range between two pointers or integers [6].

Often, there are interesting sub-typing relationships among type-states. For example, the type-state MyDevObj is a subtype of PDEVICE_OBJECT.

Figure 3 shows the recursive structure of a type-state assertion. *Formula* represents a top-level assertion, that can either be a quantified type-state assertion, or a *BFormula*. A *BFormula* represents a Boolean combination over type-states and arithmetic relations over terms; *Expr* represents the various pointer terms that can be constructed from a variable x. The vocabulary of type-states *SetExpr* is extensible by the user. Here $\mathtt{Array}(a, s, n) \doteq \{a + s * i \mid 0 \leq i < n \}$ is the set constructor for all pointers in an array of size n starting at a, where each entry has a size of s bytes.

The quantified assertions represent *type-state invariants* which state a property for all pointers satisfying a given type-state; examples of such an assertion are invariants 1 and 5 in Figure 2. Quantifier-free assertions are used to describe type-states of variables or their fields; invariants 7 and 8 are examples of it. Type-state invariants can be nested: the following invariant establishes the parent-child relationship for all elements in a list:

$$\forall \mathtt{x} \in \mathtt{TypeA} : \ \forall \mathtt{y} \in \mathtt{Btwn(Flink, x->first, NULL)} : \ \mathtt{y->parent} = \mathtt{x}$$

4   Generating Internal Annotations

Given the interface specification and the module invariants, the next step is to infer the internal annotations. There are two broad classes of annotations that need to be inferred for modular verification—assertions and modifies clauses. Assertions include loop invariants and preconditions and postconditions on internal procedures.

As we illustrated in Section 2, sound verification of real-world modules requires module invariants to contain quantifiers and Boolean connectives. Automatic inference of such annotations is challenging and existing procedures for constructing quantified invariants with Boolean structure is limited to relatively small programs [15,19,17,24]. In this section, we demonstrate the use of *exception sets* to synthesize a broad class of internal annotations containing quantifiers and Boolean structure, in a scalable fashion guided by the module invariants.

We use the Houdini [13] algorithm for inferring the internal annotations of a module decorated with module invariants. The algorithm is simple yet scalable: the algorithm takes as input a set of candidate annotations for the internal procedures and outputs the largest subset of the candidate annotations that is mutually consistent. The algorithm initially assumes all the candidate annotations and then greedily removes an annotation that does not hold during a modular verification step — the process terminates when the set of annotations is consistent or empty. Although this can be seen as solving a restricted case of the predicate abstraction problem (often called *monomial* predicate abstraction), the restricted nature of the problem makes it scalable. For example, when the complexity of deciding formulas in the assertion logic is **Co-NP** complete, the complexity of the predicate abstraction problem is **PSPACE** complete, whereas the complexity of monomial predicate abstraction is **Co-NP** complete [21].

The main challenge in using Houdini is to generate enough candidate annotations to capture a broad class of internal invariants containing quantifiers and Boolean connectives. In the next two sections, we illustrate the use of exception sets to generate candidate annotations for assertions (Section 4.1) and modifies clauses (Section 4.2) guided by the module invariants. We conclude the section with some description of conditional annotations that our approach does not capture currently (Section 4.3).

4.1   Candidate Assertions

We have found the following kinds of assertions suitable for populating the candidate pool for preconditions, postconditions, and loop invariants.

Type-states of pointers. The various type-states mentioned in the module invariants and the interface specification signify the relevant attributes of pointers that should be tracked. For every well-typed path expression in scope and for each relevant type-state, we introduce a candidate assertion stating that the path expression is in the type-state. The declared types of variables and fields are of great value in reducing the set of pointers to check for membership in a given type-state. These candidate facts are important for instantiating the universally-quantified type-state invariants in the module invariants.

Module invariant exceptions. Consider a module invariant $\forall \mathbf{x} \in S : \psi(\mathbf{x})$ which specifies some property $\psi(x)$ holds for all pointers x satisfying S. Such an assertion could be broken at a few pointers, which we call *module invariant exceptions*. We guess that this can happen only for the sets of pointers $\Theta_1, \Theta_2, \ldots, \Theta_k$. We can generate the following candidate assertions:

$$\forall x \in S : \ x \in \Theta_1 \vee \ldots \vee x \in \Theta_k \vee \psi(x)$$
$$\forall x \in \Theta_1 : \ \psi(x)$$
$$\ldots$$
$$\forall x \in \Theta_k : \ \psi(x)$$

Assuming the different sets $\Theta_1, \ldots, \Theta_k$ are pairwise disjoint, the above candidate assertions allow us to capture the *tighest* exception to the module invariant in terms of the input sets. For instance, if the module invariant holds, then all the candidate assertions hold. On the other hand, if the exceptions to the module invariant cannot be captured in the input sets, then the first assertion would fail. When a set $\Theta_i \doteq \{\theta_i\}$ is a singleton, then the quantified fact $\forall x \in \Theta_i : \ \psi(x)$ can be simplied to $\psi(\theta_i)$.

Example 1. Consider a simple example with the following module invariant in the "steady state" (recall the set constructor `Array` from Section 3):

$$\forall x \in \text{Array}(a, 4, n) : \ x\text{->}d = 42$$

For a loop that initializes the array, the loop invariant is a combination of a module invariant exception and a type-state assertion on the pointer `iter`, where `iter` is the iterator over the array.

$$\forall x \in \text{Array}(a, 4, n) : \ x \in \text{Array}(a, 4, n) \setminus \text{Array}(a, 4, \text{iter}) \vee x\text{->}d = 42$$
$$\text{iter} \in \text{Array}(0, 1, n + 1)$$

The exception set in this example is $\text{Array}(a, 4, n) \setminus \text{Array}(a, 4, \text{iter})$.

4.2   Candidate Modifies Clauses

A *candidate* modifies annotation for a field **F** looks as follows:

$$\text{modifies F } \Theta_1$$
$$\ldots$$
$$\text{modifies F } \Theta_k$$

This is an annotation that specifies that **F** is possibly modified only at pointers in the set $\bigcup_{1 \leq i \leq k} \Theta_i$. These annotations relate the state of **F** at entry and exit from a procedure, or at entry and the beginning of an arbitrary iteration of a loop. Modifies annotations are crucial for tracking the side-effect of a procedure or a loop on the heap.

We model the memory as a collection of maps, one for each type and each field [8]. Notice that the modifies annotation simply says that the sets Θ_i are exceptions to the assertion stating that the map **F** is preserved at all pointers! Hence, we use an almost identical strategy as the module invariant exceptions. If the user provides the above modifies annotations as candidates, we generate the following candidate annotations:

$$\forall x \in \text{int} : \ x \in \Theta_1 \lor \dots \lor x \in \Theta_k \lor F(x) = \text{old}(F)(x)$$
$$\forall x \in \Theta_1 : \ F(x) = \text{old}(F)(x)$$
$$\dots$$
$$\forall x \in \Theta_k : \ F(x) = \text{old}(F)(x)$$

Here `old(F)` refers to the value of the map `F` at the pre-state (either at the entry of a procedure or a loop). For singleton $\Theta_i = \{\theta_i\}$, the quantified assertions can be simplified to $F(\theta_i) = \text{old}(F)(\theta_i)$.

The modifies clauses for mutable type-states (such as `MyDevExtn`) are dealt with similarly.

4.3   Conditional Annotations

In some cases, the above candidate assertions may need to be guarded by the type-states of a few pointers. For example, the type-state of a pointer might depend on the type-state of the return variable and/or some flag in the parameters. In other cases, different type-states of a pointer may be correlated (e.g., invariant 7 in Figure 2). We currently require the user to provide the conditional annotations.

5   Implementation and Results

We have implemented a prototype tool for the problem of intra-module inference. The input to the tool is a module (a single compilation unit) written in C, along with the specifications of external procedures that are called from the module, and the interface specifications for the public procedures. The user then describes a set of module invariants (similar to Figure 2) for the module. Our tool generates a set of candidate annotations and infers the internal annotations over them using the Houdini algorithm.

Generation of the candidate annotations from the module invariants requires providing a set of pointers at procedure and loop boundaries. These pointers form parts of type-state assertions or exception sets for module invariants and modifies clauses. Pointers can range over the variables (procedure parameters, globals) in scope and field dereferences over them. However, manually specifying the pointers for each procedure and loop can be cumbersome. To relieve this burden, we provide *patterns* that match against the variables in scope at procedure and loop boundaries to generate actual pointer expressions. For example, to generate pointers of type `PDEVICE_EXTENSION`, we provide a pattern to match against variables of type `PDEVICE_EXTENSION`, or `DeviceExtension` fields of `PDEVICE_OBJECT` variables.

We use `HAVOC` to translate [8] an annotated C program into an intermediate language `BoogiePL` [12] and use the `Boogie` [4] verification condition generator to translate a `BoogiePL` program into an logical formula. We use an efficient implementation of the Houdini algorithm [13] using the Satisfiability Modulo Theory (SMT) solver `Z3` [11].

5.1   Benchmarks

We have evaluated our prototype on 4 sample device driver modules in the Windows operating system. These drivers are distributed with the Windows Driver Development Kit (DDK) [1]. Among these drivers, kbdclass is a class driver for keyboard devices installed in a system, mouclass is a class driver for all mouse devices installed in a system, flpydisk is a class floppy driver, and mouser is a serial mouse driver. The size and complexity of the drivers are mentioned in Figure 4.

Example	LOC	# Pr	# Pub	# Loops
kbdclass	7242	51	28	20
mouclass	6857	50	27	18
flpydisk	6771	35	11	24
mouser	7415	67	27	12

Example	Module Inv		Infrd	Manual			Time	
	Type	Glob		Pr	Cond	Oth	Inf	Chk
kbdclass-df	5	3	1476	3	1	2	480	190
kbdclass-all	6	3	1591	3	4	2	818	228
mouclass-df	5	3	1391	3	1	2	491	185
mouclass-all	6	3	1502	3	4	2	892	273
flpydisk-df	4	0	1355	0	0	0	632	129
flpydisk-all	5	0	1431	0	0	0	827	167
mouser-df	4	0	1608	0	0	0	571	126
mouser-all	5	0	1774	2	0	2	224	124

Fig. 4. Benchmarks and results: "df" extensions check double-free and "all" checks both the double-free and lock-usage property. "Module Inv" is the number of module invariants, and comprises of type-state invariants ("Type") type-state assertions on globals ("Glob"). "Infrd" and "Manual" represent sizes of inferred, and manual annotations. "Pr" is the number of procedures manually annotated. The manual annotations are broken up into conditional ("Cond") or others ("Oth"). "Time" is the runtime in seconds — "Inf" is the time for inference, and "Chk" is the time to check the annotated program.

For each driver, we check two properties:

1. The *double-free* property, as illustrated in Section 2.
2. The *lock-usage* property, as described below.

The lock-usage property states that all KSPINLOCK locks alternate between *acquired* and *released* states by calls to KeAcquireSpinLock and KeReleaseSpinLock respectively, after the lock has been initialized into the released state by a call to KeInitializeSpinLock. We use a mutable type-state Released to capture the state of a lock; this type-state is modified by these Ke*SpinLock procedures.

Since these locks appear as fields of device extensions, we also augmented the module invariants with the following invariant:

$$\forall x \in \texttt{MyDevExtn}: \bigwedge_i \texttt{Released} \ (\& \ x\texttt{->lock}_i) \qquad (L)$$

where $\texttt{lock}_i$ is the name of the ith field of type KSPINLOCK. This invariant signifies that at entry and exit from a module, the locks in the module are released.

5.2   Results

Figure 4 summarizes the results of our experiments. The experiments were performed on a 2.4GHz machine running Windows with 2GB of memory. For each driver, we first check the double free property (`-df` extension) and then check both the properties (`-all` extension). For checking the `-all` properties, the additional type-state invariant ("Type") in the module invariant column refers to the invariant L described for the locks. Since `flpydisk` and `mouser` do not have any global variables relevant to the properties, their module invariants do not require any type-state assertions on the globals.

The results show that our technique is able to infer most of the internal annotations — the number of manual annotations is small. Besides, the number of inferred annotation is much larger than the set of module invariants, thereby justifying the intra-module inference problem. Finally, our inference technique is scalable; the time taken to generate the inferred annotations ("Inf") is of the same order as the time taken to check the final set of annotations ("Chk"). A distributed implementation of the algorithm would further reduce the time.

We have already seen that the burden of writing the module invariants is low, and these annotations are quite succinct. In fact, most of the module invariants for `MyDevObj` and `MyDevExtn` are reusable across all drivers of a given class, modulo renaming of fields. This further amortizes the annotation effort across a class of drivers, and also provides module invariants that drivers of a given class should document and export.

Some internal annotations still had to be provided manually. For `kbdclass`, most of the manual annotations were on a procedure `KbdCreateClassObject` which is a wrapper around `IoCreateDevice` with partial initialization of some of the fields. These annotations were guarded postconditions, where the guard is a predicate on the return value signifying successful device creation. More such annotations were needed for checking the lock-usage property, as only a subset of the locks were initialized in the procedure violating the module invariant L temporarily on some locks. The other manual annotations required for this module included the loop invariant `entry` $\in$ `GL_LIST` for the `KeyboardClassUnload`.[1] For `mouser`, the additional annotations for checking both the properties come from the need to specify preconditions on the objects of asynchronous procedure calls that are never called directly — these procedures get enqueued along with their input argument (a `DEVICE_EXTENSION` object), and can fire later. For these procedures, we had to specify that the argument satisfied the type-state `MyDevExtn`.

For `mouser`, Figure 4 shows a surprising result: the runtime of the inference component of `mouser-all` is substantially smaller than `mouser-df`, even though the latter checks only one property. Recall that the verification of `mouser-all` required extra manully-provided preconditions on asynchronous procedure calls. Even though the verification of `mouser-df` did not require these preconditions, their absence caused many candidate annotations to be refuted in Houdini and thus the algorithm took longer to converge.

The verification of `kbdclass` and `mouclass` relies on an assumption that has not been mechanically verified. These drivers have linked lists of two different

---

[1] This loop invariant matches our template for candidate assertions, but our tool currently does not support instrumenting local variables. Therefore, the user has to provide loop invariants involving local variables.

types, DEVICE_EXTENSION and IRP, that use the same underlying Flink field. We assume that linked lists of these two types are disjoint. We have verified this assumption manually, and are currently working on verifying it mechanically.

6 Related Work

In this work, we have shown how to extend the precise reasoning performed by modular checkers to large modules in systems code with small annotation overhead. We have shown that verification of simple type-state properties may need invariants about type-states and data structures that can be best specified by users at the level of a module. In this section, we briefly compare with related work on checking type state properties on large modules.

Automated software verification tools for simple type-state properties (e.g. lock-usage, resource leaks) are largely based on predicate abstraction [16] (e.g. SLAM [3], BLAST [18]), data-flow analysis (e.g. ESP [10], Saturn [2]) and more recently on interpolants [23]. Most of these approaches lose precision when the analysis requires complex type-state invariants in the presence of open modules or unbounded heap, as shown in Figure 2, resulting in false alarms. Existing automated tools deal with this problem in two ways. First, post processing of the set of warnings is done to heuristically report a subset of warnings whereby real bugs may be hidden. Second, a *harness* is created that nondeterministically calls a public procedure after initializing the heap with a small number of objects, thus avoiding the need to specify quantified invariants on an unbounded set of heap objects. Both of these approaches reduce false alarms by sacrificing soundness.

Tools based on abstract interpretation [9] have been specialized to perform *shape analysis* [25] for systems code. These tools have specialized abstractions to deal with recursive data structures. Recent work using separation logic has been shown to scale to realistic device drivers [26]. However, such tools cannot be used for checking generic type-state properties without building specialized abstract domains. Unlike our method, these tools do not allow the specification and verification of the module invariants.

Verification of object-oriented programs makes heavy use of class or module invariants [4]. However, the focus on annotation inference and automation is secondary — these techniques are primarily focused on scalability of *inter module* analysis, where each module has manageable complexity. However, for OS modules with several hundred and possibly thousands of internal procedures, the problem of intra-module inference is crucial for utilizing module invariants. The work on HOB [22] is closest in spirit to our work, where a combination of user-specified type-state annotations and inference is used to verify non-trivial programs; however unlike our approach the inference does not leverage the module invariants.

Acknowledgments

We wish to thank Aditya Nori, Julien Vanegue, and the anonymous reviewers for their detailed comments.

References

1. Windows Driver Kit,
   http://www.microsoft.com/whdc/devtools/wdk/default.mspx
2. Aiken, A., Bugrara, S., Dillig, I., Dillig, T., Hackett, B., Hawkins, P.: An overview
   of the Saturn project. In: Program Analysis for Software Tools and Engineering
   (PASTE 2007), pp. 43–48. ACM, New York (2007)
3. Ball, T., Majumdar, R., Millstein, T., Rajamani, S.K.: Automatic predicate abstraction of C programs. In: Programming Language Design and Implementation
   (PLDI 2001), pp. 203–213 (2001)
4. Barnett, M., Leino, K.R.M.: Weakest-precondition of unstructured programs. In:
   Program Analysis For Software Tools and Engineering (PASTE 2005), pp. 82–87.
   ACM, New York (2005)
5. Barnett, M., Leino, K.R.M., Schulte, W.: The Spec# programming system: An
   overview. In: Barthe, G., Burdy, L., Huisman, M., Lanet, J.-L., Muntean, T. (eds.)
   CASSIS 2004. LNCS, vol. 3362, pp. 49–69. Springer, Heidelberg (2005)
6. Chatterjee, S., Lahiri, S.K., Qadeer, S., Rakamarić, Z.: A reachability predicate
   for analyzing low-level software. In: Grumberg, O., Huth, M. (eds.) TACAS 2007.
   LNCS, vol. 4424, pp. 19–33. Springer, Heidelberg (2007)
7. Clarke, E.M., Grumberg, O., Peled, D.A.: Model Checking. MIT Press, Cambridge
   (2000)
8. Condit, J., Hackett, B., Lahiri, S.K., Qadeer, S.: Unifying type checking and property checking for low-level code. In: Principles of Programming Languages (POPL
   2009), pp. 302–314 (2009)
9. Cousot, P., Cousot, R.: Abstract interpretation: A unified lattice model for the
   static analysis of programs by construction or approximation of fixpoints. In: Symposium on Principles of Programming Languages (POPL 1977), pp. 238–252. ACM
   Press, New York (1977)
10. Das, M., Lerner, S., Seigle, M.: ESP: Path-sensitive program verification in polyno-
    mial time. In: Programming Language Design and Implementation (PLDI 2002),
    pp. 57–68 (2002)
11. de Moura, L., Bjorner, N.: Efficient incremental e-matching for SMT solvers. In:
    Pfenning, F. (ed.) CADE 2007. LNCS, vol. 4603, pp. 183–198. Springer, Heidelberg
    (2007)
12. DeLine, R., Leino, K.R.M.: BoogiePL: A typed procedural language for checking
    object-oriented programs. Technical Report MSR-TR-2005-70, Microsoft Research
    (2005)
13. Flanagan, C., Leino, K.R.M.: Houdini, an annotation assistant for ESC/Java. In:
    Oliveira, J.N., Zave, P. (eds.) FME 2001. LNCS, vol. 2021, pp. 500–517. Springer,
    Heidelberg (2001)
14. Flanagan, C., Leino, K.R.M., Lillibridge, M., Nelson, G., Saxe, J.B., Stata, R.:
    Extended static checking for Java. In: Programming Language Design and Imple-
    mentation (PLDI 2002), pp. 234–245 (2002)
15. Flanagan, C., Qadeer, S.: Predicate abstraction for software verification. In: Prin-
    ciples of Programming Languages (POPL 2002), pp. 191–202. ACM Press, New
    York (2002)
16. Graf, S., Saïdi, H.: Construction of abstract state graphs with PVS. In: Grumberg,
    O. (ed.) CAV 1997. LNCS, vol. 1254, pp. 72–83. Springer, Heidelberg (1997)
17. Gulwani, S., McCloskey, B., Tiwari, A.: Lifting abstract interpreters to quantified
    logical domains. In: Principles of Programming Languages (POPL 2008), pp. 235–
    246 (2008)

18. Henzinger, T.A., Jhala, R., Majumdar, R., Sutre, G.: Lazy abstraction. In: Principles of Programming Languages (POPL 2002), pp. 58–70 (2002)
19. Lahiri, S.K., Bryant, R.E.: Constructing quantified invariants via predicate abstraction. In: Steffen, B., Levi, G. (eds.) VMCAI 2004. LNCS, vol. 2937, pp. 267–281. Springer, Heidelberg (2004)
20. Lahiri, S.K., Qadeer, S.: Back to the future: revisiting precise program verification using SMT solvers. In: Principles of Programming Languages (POPL 2008), pp. 171–182 (2008)
21. Lahiri, S.K., Qadeer, S.: Complexity and algorithms for monomial and clausal predicate abstraction. Technical Report MSR-TR-2009-2012, Microsoft Research (2009)
22. Lam, P., Kuncak, V., Rinard, M.C.: Generalized typestate checking for data structure consistency. In: Cousot, R. (ed.) VMCAI 2005. LNCS, vol. 3385, pp. 430–447. Springer, Heidelberg (2005)
23. McMillan, K.L.: Lazy abstraction with interpolants. In: Ball, T., Jones, R.B. (eds.) CAV 2006. LNCS, vol. 4144, pp. 123–136. Springer, Heidelberg (2006)
24. McMillan, K.L.: Quantified invariant generation using an interpolating saturation prover. In: Ramakrishnan, C.R., Rehof, J. (eds.) TACAS 2008. LNCS, vol. 4963, pp. 413–427. Springer, Heidelberg (2008)
25. Sagiv, S., Reps, T.W., Wilhelm, R.: Solving shape-analysis problems in languages with destructive updating. ACM Transactions on Programming Languages and Systems (TOPLAS 1998) 20(1), 1–50 (1998)
26. Yang, H., Lee, O., Berdine, J., Calcagno, C., Cook, B., Distefano, D., O'Hearn, P.W.: Scalable shape analysis for systems code. In: Gupta, A., Malik, S. (eds.) CAV 2008. LNCS, vol. 5123, pp. 385–398. Springer, Heidelberg (2008)

Static and Precise Detection of Concurrency Errors in Systems Code Using SMT Solvers[*]

Shuvendu K. Lahiri[1], Shaz Qadeer[1], and Zvonimir Rakamarić[2]

[1] Microsoft Research, Redmond, WA, USA
{shuvendu,qadeer}@microsoft.com
[2] Department of Computer Science, University of British Columbia, Canada
zrakamar@cs.ubc.ca

Abstract. Context-bounded analysis is an attractive approach to verification of concurrent programs. Bounding the number of contexts executed per thread not only reduces the asymptotic complexity, but also the complexity increases gradually from checking a purely sequential program.

Lal and Reps [14] provided a method for reducing the context-bounded verification of a concurrent boolean program to the verification of a sequential boolean program, thereby allowing sequential reasoning to be employed for verifying concurrent programs. In this work, we adapt the encoding to work for systems programs written in C with the heap and accompanying low-level operations such as pointer arithmetic and casts. Our approach is completely automatic: we use a verification condition generator and SMT solvers, instead of a boolean model checker, in order to avoid manual extraction of boolean programs and false alarms introduced by the abstraction. We demonstrate the use of *field slicing* for improving the scalability and (in some cases) coverage of our checking. We evaluate our tool STORM on a set of real-world Windows device drivers, and has discovered a bug that could not be detected by extensive application of previous tools.

1 Introduction

Context-bounded analysis is an attractive approach to verification of concurrent programs. This approach advocates analyzing all executions of a concurrent program in which the number of contexts executed per thread is bounded by a given constant K. Bounding the number of contexts executed per thread reduces the asymptotic complexity of checking concurrent programs: while reachability analysis of concurrent boolean programs is undecidable, the same analysis under a context-bound is NP-complete [15,18]. Moreover, there is ample empirical evidence that synchronization errors, such as data races and atomicity violations, are manifested in concurrent executions with small number of context switches [16,19]. These two properties together make context-bounded analysis an effective approach for finding concurrency errors. At the same time, context-bounding provides for a useful trade-off between the cost and coverage of verification.

---

[*] This work was supported by a Microsoft Research Graduate Fellowship.

A. Bouajjani and O. Maler (Eds.): CAV 2009, LNCS 5643, pp. 509–524, 2009.
© Springer-Verlag Berlin Heidelberg 2009

In this work, we apply context-bounded verification to concurrent C programs such as those found in low-level systems code. In order to deal with the complexity of low-level concurrent C programs, we take a three-step approach. First, we eliminate all the complexities of C, such as dynamic memory allocation, pointer arithmetic, casts, etc. by compiling into the Boogie programming language (BoogiePL) [9], a simple procedural language with scalar and map data types. Thus, we obtain a concurrent BoogiePL program from a concurrent C program. Second, we eliminate the complexity of concurrency by appealing to the recent method of Lal and Reps [14] for reducing context-bounded verification of a concurrent boolean program to the verification of a sequential boolean program. By adapting this method to the setting of concurrent BoogiePL programs, we are able to construct a sequential BoogiePL program that captures all behaviors of the concurrent BoogiePL program (and therefore of the original C program as well) up to the context-bound. Third, we generate a verification condition from the sequential BoogiePL program and check it using a Satisfiability Modulo Theories (SMT) solver [8].

In order to scale our verification to realistic C programs, we introduce the idea of *field slicing*. The main insight is that the verification of a given property typically depends only on a small number of fields in the data structures of the program. Our algorithm partitions the set of fields into *tracked* and *untracked* fields; we only track accesses to the tracked fields and abstract away accesses to the untracked fields. This approach not only reduces the complexity of sequential code being checked, but also allows us to soundly drop context-switches from the program points where only untracked fields are accessed. Our approach is similar to localization-reduction [13], but adapted to work with arrays. We present an algorithm for refining the set of tracked fields based on the counterexample-guided-abstraction-refinement (CEGAR) loop, starting with the fields in the property of interest. Our refinement algorithm is effective; on a number of examples it discovered the field abstraction that was carefully picked by a manual inspection of the program.

We implemented our ideas in a prototype tool called STORM. We applied STORM on several real-life Windows device drivers that operate in a highly concurrent setting, and we clearly demonstrate its usability and scalability. Furthermore, we assess the effect of code size, number of contexts, and number of places where a context-switch could happen on STORM's performance. In the process, we found a bug in one of the drivers that could not be detected by extensive application of previous tools. The bug was confirmed and fixed by the driver developers.

2   Translation

In earlier work, Lal and Reps [14] presented a mechanism for transforming a multi-threaded program operating on scalar variables into a sequential program, with a fixed context-bound. In this section, we show the main steps to transform a multithreaded program written in C into a sequential program, using Lal and Reps method. The input C programs support pointers, dynamic memory allocation, unbounded arrays, and low-level operations such as casts and pointer arithmetic that are prevalent in systems software. Our translation is performed in two steps:

$$
\begin{array}{ll}
Locs & l ::= *e \mid e \rightarrow f \\
Expr & e ::= x \mid n \mid l \mid \&l \mid e_1 \text{ op } e_2 \mid e_1 \oplus_n e_2
\end{array}
$$

$$
Command\ c ::= \texttt{skip} \mid c_1 ; c_2 \mid x := e \mid l := e \mid \texttt{if } e \texttt{ then } c \mid \texttt{while } e \texttt{ do } c
$$

Fig. 1. A simplified subset of C

$$
\begin{array}{ll}
E(x) & = x \\
E(n) & = n \\
E(e \rightarrow f) & = \mathrm{Mem}^f[E(e) + \mathit{Offset}(f)] \\
E(*(e : \tau)) & = \mathrm{Mem}^\tau[E(e)] \\
E(\&e \rightarrow f) & = E(e) + \mathit{Offset}(f) \\
E(\&*e) & = E(e) \\
E(e_1 \text{ op } e_2) & = E(e_1) \text{ op } E(e_2) \\
E(e_1 \oplus_n e_2) & = E(e_1) + n * E(e_2)
\end{array}
\qquad
\begin{array}{ll}
C(\texttt{skip}) & = \texttt{skip} \\
C(c_1 ; c_2) & = C(c_1) ; C(c_2) \\
C(x := e) & = x := E(e); \\
C(l := e) & = E(l) := E(e); \\
C(\texttt{if } e \texttt{ then } c) & = \texttt{if } E(e) \texttt{ then } C(c) \\
C(\texttt{while } e \texttt{ do } c) & = \texttt{while } E(e) \texttt{ do } C(c)
\end{array}
$$

Fig. 2. Translation from C into BoogiePL

1. Translate a multithreaded C program into a multithreaded BoogiePL program using the HAVOC tool [3]. The resultant BoogiePL program contains scalars and maps, and operations on them. The translation compiles away the complexities of C programs related to pointers, dynamic memory allocation, casts, and pointer arithmetic.
2. Translate the multithreaded BoogiePL program into a sequential BoogiePL program, for a fixed context-bound. We show how to extend Lal and Reps method to deal with programs with maps or arrays.

In the next two subsections, we describe these two steps in details.

2.1   Translating from C into BoogiePL

We present a translation of a simplified subset of C into BoogiePL programs. The translation is similar to the one presented earlier [6]; the main difference lies in splitting the C heap into multiple maps corresponding to different fields and types in the program, by assuming a *field-safe* C program — the field-safety can be justified formally in HAVOC and we explain it in this section.

Figure 1 shows a simplified subset of C for illustrating the translation from C into BoogiePL. We assume that the input program is well-typed in the original C type system. Furthermore, all structures, global variables, and local variables whose address can be taken are allocated on the heap. The field names are assumed to be unique and $\mathit{Offset}(f)$ provides the offset of a field f in its enclosing structure. For this presentation, we do not show how we handle nested structures and unions. The tool supports all the features of C programming language and details of the translation can be found in earlier work [6]. In the figure, *Locs* denotes the set of heap expressions that can be used or assigned to, and *Expr* denotes the set of C expressions. The expressions include variables (x), constants (n), *Locs* and their addresses, binary operations (such as $\leq$), and pointer arithmetic $\oplus_n$ over n-byte pointers. The language contains skip, sequential composition, assignments, conditional statements, and loops.

Figure 2 shows our translation from C into BoogiePL. Initially, ignore the superscript to Mem and assume there is a single Mem map. We represent the C heap using the map Mem : int $\rightarrow$ int that maps an address to a value. The operator $E(e)$ describes the translation of a C expression e. We use $e : \tau$ to denote that τ is the static type of e. Addresses of fields and pointer arithmetic are compiled away in terms of arithmetic operations. Finally, a dereference is translated as a lookup into the Mem map. The operator $C(c)$ translates a C statement into BoogiePL and is self-explanatory. Assignments to heap expressions result in updates to the Mem map.

The benefit of the translation with a single map Mem is that it does not rely on the types and the type-safety of a C program. However, the lack of types can make disambiguating locations in the heap difficult. For example, the following assertion cannot be proved without knowledge about the layout of the pointers x and y:

```
x->f = 1; y->g = 0; assert(x->f == 1);
```

To disambiguate heap locations, we had earlier proposed the use of a map Type : int $\rightarrow$ type that maintains a "type" with each location in the heap [6]. A global quantified *type-safety invariant* relating the contents of Mem and Type is asserted after every update to the heap; the assertion ensures that the runtime type of a pointer corresponds to its static type. The type safety invariant helps disambiguate pointers and fields of different types, such as the pointers &x->f and &y->g in the example above.

Although the scheme described above provides an accurate memory model for C, using the type invariant while checking other properties is computationally expensive as this invariant makes use of quantifiers. Therefore, we have adopted the following strategy that provides a way for a separation of concerns. We split the Mem map into a set of maps where there is a map Mem^f for each (word-valued) field f and Mem$^\tau$ for each pointer type τ, and use the translation shown in Figure 2. We then add assertions for each memory dereference as follows: for a dereference $e \rightarrow f$ in a statement, we assert Type$[E(e) + \mathit{Offset}(f)] = f$, and for a dereference $*e$, we assert Type$[E(e)] = \tau$. These assertions are checked during the type-checking phase. If the assertions can be proved by the type-safety checker in HAVOC or other orthogonal techniques [21], we say that the resultant program is *field-safe* with respect to our choice of memory splits. This allows us to have a high-level (Java-like) view of the C heap while proving the concurrency related properties, without sacrificing soundness. Besides, as we show in the next section, the ability to split the C heap into independent maps allows us to perform scalable bug detection using SMT solvers.

The type-safety checker may fail to prove the introduced assertions in programs that take the address of fields in structures and dereference them directly, as in the following example:

```
x->f = 1; int *y = &x->f ; *y = 0; assert(x->f == 0);
```

In this case, the pointers y and &x->f are aliased and the type-safety checker would complain. To get around this problem, the user can specify that the maps for field f and type int* should be unified into a single map.[1]

2.2   Eliminating Concurrency under a Context-Bound

The previous section showed how to convert a concurrent C program into a concurrent BoogiePL program. In this section, we show how to reduce a concurrent BoogiePL program into a sequential BoogiePL program while capturing all behaviors within a context-bound, i.e. within a certain number of contexts per thread [14].

For the rest of this section, we fix the number of threads in the input program to a positive number n and the context-bound to a positive number K. Note that the number of possible context-switches in that case is $n * K - 1$. Without loss of generality, we assume that the input concurrent program is provided as a collection of procedures containing $n + 1$ distinguished procedures *Init*, T_1, ..., T_n, each of which takes no parameters and returns no value. The concurrent program is then given by $P \triangleq Init(); (T_1() || \cdots || T_n())$. Our goal is to create a sequential program Q that captures all behaviors of P up to the context-bound K. More precisely, Q will capture all round-robin schedules of P starting from thread T_1 in which each thread can execute at most K times. Each thread is allowed to stutter in each turn, thereby enabling Q to model even those schedules that are not round-robin.

The global store of the concurrent C program is captured in the BoogiePL program as a collection of global maps from integers to integers, as described in the previous section. We assume that the program has been transformed so that every statement either reads (into a local variable) or writes (from a local variable) a global map at a single index, and that the condition for every branch depends entirely on local variables. We will also assume that each such read or write to the global memory executes atomically. To model synchronization constructs, the grain of atomicity can be explicitly increased by encapsulating statements inside an atomic block. For example, the acquire operation on a lock stored at the address a is modeled using a global map variable *Lock* and a local scalar variable *tmp* as follows:

$$\text{atomic } \{ \ tmp := Lock[a]; \ \text{assume } tmp = 0; \ Lock[a] := 1; \ \}$$

Finally, we assume that assertions in the program are modeled using a special global boolean variable *error* that is set to true whenever the condition in the assert statement evaluates to false.

To convert the concurrent program P into the semantically-equivalent sequential program Q, we introduce several extra global variables. First, we introduce a global variable k to keep track of the number of contexts executed by each thread. Second, for each global map G, we introduce $K - 1$ new symbolic map constants named V_2^G to V_K^G. Finally, we replace each global map G with K new global maps named G_1 to G_K. Intuitively, the sequential program Q mimics a concurrent execution of P as follows.

---

[1] In our examples from Section 4.1, we only had to unify three fields in the **serial** driver. HAVOC automatically issued field-safety warnings, and we introduced three annotations to merge the fields (no code changes are required).

First, each map G_i is initialized to the arbitrary symbolic constant V_i^G for all $2 \leq i \leq K$. The initialization procedure *Init* runs using the global map G_1 (with an arbitrary initial value) and initializes it. Then, the procedure T_1 starts executing using the global map G_1. Context switches in T_1 are simulated by a sequence of $K - 1$ nondeterministic choices. The i-th such choice enforces that the program stops using the map G_i and starts using the map G_{i+1}. Then, each of T_2 to T_n is executed sequentially one after another under the same policy. Note that when T_{j+1} starts executing on the map G_i, the value of this map is not arbitrary; rather, its value is left there by T_j when it made its i-th context switch. Finally, when T_n has finished executing, we ensure that the final value of map G_i is equated to V_{i+1}^G, which was the arbitrary initial value of the map G_{i+1} at the beginning of the $i + 1$-th context of T_1.

We capture the intuition described above by performing the following transformations in sequence:

1. Replace each statement of the form $tmp := G[a]$ with

$$
\begin{aligned}
&\text{atomic } \{ \\
&\quad \text{if } (k = 1) \; tmp := G_1[a] \\
&\quad \text{elsif } (k = 2) \; tmp := G_2[a] \\
&\quad \ldots \\
&\quad \text{else } tmp := G_K[a] \\
&\}
\end{aligned}
$$

and each statement of the form $G[a] := tmp$ with

$$
\begin{aligned}
&\text{atomic } \{ \\
&\quad \text{if } (k = 1) \; G_1[a] := tmp \\
&\quad \text{elsif } (k = 2) \; G_2[a] := tmp \\
&\quad \ldots \\
&\quad \text{else } G_K[a] := tmp \\
&\}
\end{aligned}
$$

2. After each atomic statement that is not within the lexical scope of another atomic statement, insert a call to procedure *Schedule* with the following specification:

$$
\begin{aligned}
&\text{modifies } k \\
&\text{ensures } old(k) \leq k \wedge k \leq K \\
&\text{exsures true} \\
&\text{void } Schedule(\text{void});
\end{aligned}
$$

Here, exsures true means that *Schedule* may terminate either normally or exceptionally; under normal termination, k is incremented by an arbitrary amount but remains within the context-bound K. The possibility of incrementing k by more than one allows the introduction of stuttering into the round-robin schedules. The possibility of exceptional termination allows a thread to stop executing at any point. The raised exception is caught by handlers (as shown below) that wrap the invocation of each T_i. We assume that *Init* does not share any code with the threads and we do not add a call to *Schedule* to any of the procedures called from *Init*.

For each procedure f, let the procedure obtained by the transformation above be denoted by f'. Let us assume that there is a single map variable G in the original program. The sequential program Q is then defined to be as follows:

$$G_2 := V_2^G; \ \ldots; \ G_K := V_K^G;$$
$$Init();$$
$$error := false; \ k := 1;$$
$$\text{try } \{ \ Schedule(); \ T_1'() \ \} \text{ finally } k := 1;$$
$$\ldots$$
$$\text{try } \{ \ Schedule(); \ T_n'() \ \} \text{ finally } k := 1;$$
$$\text{assume } G_1 = V_2^G; \ \ldots; \ \text{assume } G_{K-1} = V_K^G;$$
$$\text{assert } \neg error$$

Note that all constraints involving the symbolic map constants are *assumed* equalities. These equalities can be handled by the select-update theory of arrays without requiring the axiom of extensionality. Consequently, these constraints do not present any impediment to the use of an off-the-shelf SMT solver. The transformed program contains control flow due to exceptions which can be easily compiled away if the underlying verification-condition generator does not understand it. Furthermore, since the transformed program is sequential, the verification-condition generator can ignore the atomic annotations in the code.

3 Field Slicing

Once we have the sequential BoogiePL program generated from the multithreaded C program, the next step is to try to verify the program using BOOGIE. BOOGIE performs precise reasoning across loop-free and call-free code, but needs loop invariants and procedure contracts to deal with loops and procedure calls modularly. In order to have an automatic tool, we inline procedures and unroll loops (with some exception discussed later).[2] Since recursion is rare in system programs, inlining procedures is acceptable; however, the size of inlined procedures can be very large. Our initial attempt at verifying these inlined programs did not succeed. On the other hand, we may lose coverage when we unroll loops a fixed number of times. In this section, we illustrate the use of a simple *field slicing* technique to achieve scalability when checking large inlined call-free programs without sacrificing precision; in some cases, our method enables us to avoid unrolling loops and therefore obtain greater coverage.

3.1 Abstraction with Tracked Fields

The high-level idea of this section is fairly simple: our translation of C programs described in Section 2.1 uses a map Mem^f for dereferencing a field f, and a map Mem^τ for dereferencing pointers of type τ. We assume that the input C program has been proven *field-safe* for this split, i.e. the type checker has verified the assertions about the Type map as described earlier. We guess a subset of these fields and types as *relevant* and slice the program with respect to these fields. If the abstracted program can

---

[2] Inference of loop invariants and procedure contracts is an important area of future work.

be proved correct, then we have proved the correctness of the sequential BoogiePL program. Otherwise, we have to *refine* the set of relevant fields and try again. While proving the abstracted program, we can skip loops (without the need to unroll them) that do not modify any of the relevant fields.

In this section, we formalize how we perform the slicing with respect to a set of fields, while in the next section we show how to refine the set of fields we track. Let us define the operation $\texttt{Abstract}(P, F)$ that takes a BoogiePL program P generated in the last section and a set of fields F, and performs the following operations:

1. For any field $g \notin F$, translate the writes $\text{Mem}_i^g[e] := tmp$ for all $1 \leq i \leq K$ as skip.
2. For any field $g \notin F$, translate the reads $tmp := \text{Mem}_i^g[e]$ for all $1 \leq i \leq K$ as havoc tmp, which scrambles the value of tmp.
3. Finally, remove the call to *Schedule* that was inserted after the atomic section for a read or write from a field $g \notin F$.

It is easy to see that the first two steps are property-preserving, i.e. they do not result in missed bugs. Since statements such as havoc tmp and skip do not access any global state, context switches after them will not introduce any extra behavior. Consequently, the trailing calls to *Schedule* can be removed, thereby eliminating a significant number of redundant context switches.

In addition to reducing code size and eliminating context switches, checking the abstraction $\texttt{Abstract}(P, F)$ has another benefit. It enables us to create simple summaries for loops whose body does not contain any reads or writes from F. The summary leaves the memory maps unchanged and puts nondeterministic values into the local variables modified by the loop. This simple heuristic for creating loop summaries is precise enough for our examples: it worked for 5 out of a total of 15 loops in our benchmarks from Section 4.1.

Both of these factors improve the scalability of our approach and improve coverage by not requiring every loop to be unrolled. In particular, we can avoid the problem with unrolling loops whose exit condition does not depend on any input values (e.g. a loop that goes from 1 to 100) — for such loops any unrolling less than 100 times would block the execution after the loop.

3.2   Refining Tracked Fields

In this section, we provide an algorithm for inferring the set of relevant fields that affect the property being checked. Our inference algorithm is a variant of the counterexample-guided abstraction refinement (CEGAR) framework [5,13]. Figure 3 gives the pseudocode for the algorithm. The algorithm takes a program P and checks if the assertion in the program holds. We start with initializing *trackedFields* with an empty set, and then we add fields to the set based on the analysis of counterexamples. The outer loop in lines 3 to 26 refines *trackedFields* from a single abstract counterexample *absErrTrace* obtained by checking the abstract program A. If the abstract program A is not correct, we concretize the abstract counterexample trace *absErrTrace* and check if the trace is spurious. If the trace is not spurious, then we have a true error in line 23. The operation $\texttt{Concretize}$ simply restores the reads and writes of fields that were abstracted away (we do not add the context switches back, although adding them would not break the

Input: Program P
Output: Program P checked or error trace
 1: $allFields \leftarrow$ all fields in P
 2: $trackedFields \leftarrow \emptyset$
 3: **loop**
 4:     $A \leftarrow \texttt{Abstract}(P, trackedFields)$
 5:     $(checked, absErrTrace) \leftarrow \texttt{Check}(A)$
 6:     **if** $checked = $ **true then**
 7:         **return** CHECKED
 8:     **else**
 9:         $concTrace \leftarrow \texttt{Concretize}(P, absErrTrace)$
10:         $checked \leftarrow \texttt{Check}(concTrace)$
11:         **if** $checked = $ **true then**
12:             $F \leftarrow allFields$
13:             **for all** $f \in allFields$ **do**
14:                 $absTrace \leftarrow \texttt{Abstract}(concTrace, trackedFields \cup F \setminus \{f\})$
15:                 $checked \leftarrow \texttt{Check}(absTrace)$
16:                 **if** $checked = $ **true then**
17:                     $F \leftarrow F \setminus \{f\}$
18:                 **else**
19:                     $trackedFields \leftarrow trackedFields \cup \{f\}$
20:                 **end if**
21:             **end for**
22:         **else**
23:             **return** BUG$(concTrace)$
24:         **end if**
25:     **end if**
26: **end loop**

Fig. 3. Algorithm for tracked fields refinement based on the CEGAR loop

algorithm). The inner loop in lines 13 to 21 greedily finds a minimal set of fields from *allFields* such that abstracting them would result in a spurious counterexample. Those fields are added to *trackedFields* and the outer loop is iterated again. Since each iteration of the inner loop increases the size of *trackedFields* and the total number of fields is finite, the algorithm terminates.

4   Implementation and Results

In this section, we describe our prototype implementation STORM, and our experience with applying the tool on several real-life benchmarks. As described earlier, STORM first uses HAVOC to translate a multithreaded C program along with a set of relevant fields into a multithreaded BoogiePL program (Section 2.1), then reduces it to a sequential BoogiePL program (Section 2.2), and finally uses BOOGIE to check the sequential program. The BOOGIE verifier [2] generates a verification condition from the BoogiePL description, and uses the SMT solver Z3 [8] to check the resulting verification condition.

Table 1. Windows device drivers used in the experiments. "LOC" is the bare number of lines of code in the scenarios we check, excluding whitespaces, comments, variable and function declarations, etc.; "Routine" lists the dispatch routines we checked; "#F" gives the total number of fields; "#T" is the number of threads in the checked scenario; "Scenario" shows the concurrent scenario being checked, i.e. which driver routines are executed concurrently as threads (D – dispatch routine, CA – cancel routine, CP – completion routine, DPC – deferred procedure call).

Driver	LOC	Routine	#F	#T	Scenario
daytona	105	ioctl	53	2	D | CA
mqueue	494	read write ioctl	72	4	D | CA | CP | DPC
usbsamp	644	read write ioctl	113	3	D | CA | CP
usbsamp_fix	643	read write ioctl	113	3	D | CA | CP
serial	1089	read write	214	3	D | CA | DPC

4.1 Benchmarks

We evaluated STORM on a set of real-world Windows device driver benchmarks. Table 1 lists the device drivers used in our experiments and the corresponding driver dispatch routines we checked. It also provides their size, total number of fields, number of threads, and the scenario in which they are checked. STORM found a bug in the usbsamp driver (see Section 4.3) and usbsamp_fix is the fixed version of the example.

We implemented a common harness for putting device drivers through different concurrent scenarios. Each driver is checked in a scenario possibly involving concurrently executing driver dispatch routines, driver request cancellation and completion routines, and deferred procedure calls (column "Scenario" in Table 1). The number of threads and the complexity of a scenario depend on the given driver's capabilities. For example, for the usbsamp driver, the harness executes a dispatch, cancel, and completion routine in three threads. Apart from providing a particular scenario, our harness also models synchronization provided by the device driver framework, as well as synchronization primitives, such as locks, that are used for driver-specific synchronization.

STORM has the ability to check any user-specified safety property. In our experiments, we checked the *use-after-free* property for the IRP (*IO Request Packet*) data structure used by the device drivers. A driver may complete and free an IRP it receives by calling a request completion routine (e.g. WdfRequestComplete in Figure 4), and must not access an IRP object once it has been completed. To check this property, we introduced assertions via automatic instrumentation before each access to an IRP object; our examples have up to a hundred of such assertions. Typically, drivers access and may complete the same request in multiple routines executing concurrently. To satisfy our crucial *use-after-free* property, the code must follow the proper and often complex synchronization protocol. Bugs often manifest only in highly concurrent

Table 2. Varying the number of contexts per thread

Example	Routine	# of contexts per thread				
		1	2	3	4	5
daytona	ioctl	3.4	3.8	4.2	4.5	5.6
mqueue	read	62.1	161.5	236.2	173.0	212.4
	write	48.6	113.4	171.2	177.4	192.3
	ioctl	120.6	198.6	204.7	176.1	199.9
usbsamp	read	17.9	37.7	65.8	66.8	85.2
	write	17.8	48.8	52.3	74.3	109.7
	ioctl	4.4	5.0	5.1	5.3	5.4
usbsamp_fix	read	16.9	28.2	38.6	46.7	47.5
	write	18.1	32.2	46.9	52.5	63.6
	ioctl	4.8	4.7	5.1	5.1	5.2
serial	read	36.5	95.4	103.4	240.5	281.4
	write	37.3	164.3	100.8	233.0	649.8

scenarios; consequently, this property is difficult to check with static analysis tools for sequential programs.

4.2 Evaluation

Our empirical evaluation of STORM consists of two sets of experiments. In the first one (Table 2 and Table 3), we run STORM on the benchmarks described in the previous section using manually provided fixed set of tracked fields. We assess the scalability of STORM with respect to code size, number of threads, number of contexts, and number of locations where a context switch could potentially happen. In the second set of experiments (Table 4), instead of using manually provided tracked fields, we determine the usability of our tracked fields refinement algorithm by using it to completely automatically check our benchmark drivers. All experiments were conducted on an Intel Pentium D at 2.8GHz running Windows XP, and all runtimes are in seconds.

Table 2 shows the result of varying the number of contexts per thread from 1 (sequential case) to 5. We managed to successfully check all of our benchmarks with up to 5 contexts per thread, which clearly demonstrates the scalability of our approach. In the process, our tool discovered a bug in the usbsamp driver (details can be found in Section 4.3).

Table 3 demonstrates how the runtimes vary with the number of places in the code where a context switch can be introduced. For the usbsamp example that has a bug, removing the context switches results in the bug not being discovered. The runtime decreases as the number of context-switch locations decreases. This observation justifies that removing context switches during field slicing is important for scalability.

Table 4 describes the results of applying the abstraction-refinement algorithm from Section 3 to discover the set of relevant fields and completely automatically check the examples. Using the refinement algorithm, we were always able to obtain a set of relevant fields that is just a small fraction of the set of all fields and that closely matches the set of manual fields that we used previously. Most of the runtime is actually spent in

Table 3. Varying the number of locations where a context switch could happen. The number of contexts per thread is fixed to 2. "CS" represents the total number of places where a context switch could happen. The examples where we missed the `usbsamp` bug because of randomly (unsoundly) removing context switch locations are marked with *.

Example	Routine	#CS	% of switches removed			
			0	40	80	100
`daytona`	`ioctl`	26	3.9	3.7	3.6	3.5
`mqueue`	`read`	201	161.1	121.3	112.1	57.8
	`write`	198	112.7	101.5	100.6	25.2
	`ioctl`	202	197.7	192.8	168.5	73.1
`usbsamp`	`read`	90	37.7	42.2	*22.6	*17.9
	`write`	90	48.9	37.7	*22.7	*18.9
	`ioctl`	22	5.0	4.8	4.5	4.4
`usbsamp_fix`	`read`	89	28.2	25.9	22.6	17.0
	`write`	89	32.2	28.2	22.5	16.5
	`ioctl`	21	4.7	4.7	4.5	4.3
`serial`	`read`	307	95.4	92.7	66.3	47.6
	`write`	309	164.8	120.2	94.3	29.7

Table 4. Results of the tracked fields refinement algorithm. "#F" gives the total number of fields; "#MF" is the number of manually provided tracked fields; "#AF" denotes the number of tracked fields generated by the refinement algorithm; "#IT" is the number of CEGAR loop iterations; "Time" is the total running time.

Example	Routine	#F	#MF	#AF	#IT	Time(s)
`daytona`	`ioctl`	53	3	3	3	244.3
`mqueue`	`read`	72	7	9	9	3446.3
	`write`			8	8	3010.0
	`ioctl`			9	9	3635.6
`usbsamp_fix`	`read`	113	1	3	3	4382.4
	`write`			4	4	2079.2
	`ioctl`			0	0	21.7
`serial`	`read`	214	5	5	5	3013.7
	`write`			4	3	1729.4

scripts to perform the abstraction, and can be significantly reduced. Without the use of field slicing, STORM was unable to run on large examples. For example, even checking the `mqueue` `read` routine with only two contexts does not terminate in one hour if we do not use field slicing.

4.3 Bug Found

By applying STORM on the Windows device drivers listed in Table 1, we found a concurrency bug in the `usbsamp` driver. We reported the bug, and driver developers confirmed and fixed it. Figure 4 illustrates the bug with a simplified code excerpt from the

```
 1 // Thread T1
 2 VOID UsbSamp_EvtIoRead(
 3     WDFQUEUE    Queue,
 4     WDFREQUEST  Request,
 5     size_t      Length
 6   ) {
 7   ...
 8   WdfRequestMarkCancelable(
 9     Request, UsbSamp_EvtRequestCancel);
10   ... // SWITCH 1: T1->T2
11   WdfRequestComplete(Request, status);
12   ... // SWITCH 3: T1->T2
13 }
```

```
 1 // Thread T2
 2 VOID UsbSamp_EvtRequestCancel(
 3     WDFREQUEST Request
 4   ) {
 5   PREQUEST_CONTEXT rwContext;
 6   ... // SWITCH 2: T2->T1
 7   rwContext =
 8     GetRequestContext(Request);
 9   ...
10 }
```

Fig. 4. Simplified version of the code illustrating the concurrency bug STORM found in the usbsamp example. Places where context switches happen when the bug occurs are marked with SWITCH.

driver. It contains two routines, the UsbSamp_EvtIoRead dispatch routine and the UsbSamp_EvtRequestCancel cancellation routine. The routines get executed by threads T1 and T2, respectively. The example proceeds as follows:

1. Thread T1 starts executing on a request Request, while thread T2 is blocked since cancellation for Request has not been enabled.
2. T1 enables cancellation and sets the cancellation routine with the call to the driver framework routine WdfRequestMarkCancelable on line 8. Then the context switch on line 10 occurs.
3. T2 can now start executing UsbSamp_EvtRequestCancel, and another context switch happens on line 6 of T2.
4. T1 completes Request on line 11 and context switches again on line 12.
5. On line 8, T2 tries to access Request that has been completed in the previous step, which is an error.

It is important to note that although the scenario leading to this bug might seem simple, the bug has not been found before by extensively applying other software checkers on usbsamp. For instance, SLAM [1] failed to discover this bug since SLAM can check only sequential code. KISS [19], on the other hand, can check concurrent code, but only up to 2 context switches, and would therefore also miss this bug since the bug occurs only after at least 3 context switches.

5   Related Work

We roughly divide the related work into two areas — bounded approaches to concurrency and other techniques for analysis of concurrent C programs.

Bounded approaches to concurrency. The idea of context-bounded analysis of concurrent programs was proposed by Qadeer and Wu [19], and later context-bounded reachability analysis for concurrent boolean programs was shown to be decidable [18]. Many subsequent approaches have relied on bounding the number of contexts to tackle the complexity and scalability issues of concurrent program analysis [14,16,18,19,20].

KISS [19] transforms a concurrent program with up to two context switches into a sequential one by mimicking context switches using procedure calls. However, restricting the number of context switches can be limiting, as evidenced by the bug in Section 4.3 that STORM discovered.

Rabinovitz and Grumberg [20] propose a context bounded verification technique for concurrent C programs based on bounded model checking and SAT solving. The algorithm applies traditional BMC on each thread separately and generates sets of constraints for each. The constraints are instrumented to account for concurrency, by introducing copies of global variables and additional constraints for context switches. The resulting formula is solved by a SAT solver. Our work offers several important advantages: we support memory maps to deal with a possibly unbounded heap; our source-to-source program transformation allows us to leverage any sequential verification technique, including annotation-based modular reasoning; our experiments are performed on real-world benchmarks, whereas the authors apply the technique to handcrafted microbencmarks. Finally, it is unclear how to exploit techniques such as field slicing using their method.

Bounded model checking of concurrent programs was also explored by Ganai and Gupta [10], where concurrency constraints are added lazily and incrementally during bounded unrolling of programs. The number of context switches is not bounded a priori, but heap and stack are, and the number of program steps the bounded model checker explores is limited by the available resources.

Suwimonteerabuth et al. [22] present a context-bounded analysis of multithreaded Java programs. Their approach is different from ours because it translates a multithreaded Java program to a concurrent pushdown system by bounding the size of the program heap and using finite bitvector encoding for integers.

CHESS [16] is a tool for testing multithreaded programs that dynamically explores thread interleavings by iteratively bounding the number of contexts. On the other hand, STORM is a static analysis tool and therefore does not have to execute the code using tests and offers more coverage since it explores all possible paths in a program up to a given context bound.

Analysis of concurrent C programs. Kahlon et al. [12] focus their efforts on iteratively reducing the number of thread interleavings using invariants generated by abstract interpretation. The described techniques are complementary to our approach, since we could also use them to reduce the number of interleavings in our instrumented program. The authors then apply model checking, but only on program slices in order to resolve data-race warnings, and therefore fair comparison with our experiments would be hard.

Witkowski et al. [23] describe their experience with applying CEGAR-based predicate abstraction on concurrent Linux device drivers. Their results indicate that concurrency rapidly increases the number of predicates inferred by the refinement loop, which in turn causes a fast blow-up in the model checker. Before we derived our current technique based on SMT solvers, we attempted a similar approach where we used the Lal-Reps method to create a source-to-source transformation from a multithreaded to a sequential C program, which is then analyzed by the SLAM [1] verifier. Our experience was similar as we could not scale this approach beyond even simple microbenchmarks. Henzinger et al. [11] present a more scalable approach for CEGAR-based predicate abstraction of concurrent programs; their method checks each thread separately in an abstract stateful context that is iteratively constructed by a refinement loop.

Chugh et al. [4] introduce a framework for converting a sequential dataflow analysis into a concurrent one using a race detection engine. The race detection engine is used to ensure soundness of the sequential analysis by invalidating the dataflow facts influenced by concurrent writes. The analysis is scalable, but yields many false positives; our approach is much more precise, but not as scalable.

There also exists work that targets analysis of concurrent boolean program models [7,17]. However, these approaches do not clarify how to obtain these models from real-world programs, while our approach can automatically analyze C programs.

References

1. Ball, T., Majumdar, R., Millstein, T., Rajamani, S.K.: Automatic predicate abstraction of C programs. In: Conf. on Programming Language Design and Implementation (PLDI), pp. 203–213 (2001)
2. Barnett, M., Chang, B.-Y.E., DeLine, R., Jacobs, B., Leino, K.R.M.: Boogie: A modular reusable verifier for object-oriented programs. In: Intl. Symp. on Formal Methods for Objects and Components (FMCO), pp. 364–387 (2005)
3. Chatterjee, S., Lahiri, S.K., Qadeer, S., Rakamarić, Z.: A reachability predicate for analyzing low-level software. In: Grumberg, O., Huth, M. (eds.) TACAS 2007. LNCS, vol. 4424, pp. 19–33. Springer, Heidelberg (2007)
4. Chugh, R., Voung, J.W., Jhala, R., Lerner, S.: Dataflow analysis for concurrent programs using datarace detection. In: Conf. on Programming Language Design and Implementation (PLDI), pp. 316–326 (2008)
5. Clarke, E.M., Grumberg, O., Jha, S., Lu, Y., Veith, H.: Counterexample-guided abstraction refinement. In: Emerson, E.A., Sistla, A.P. (eds.) CAV 2000. LNCS, vol. 1855, pp. 154–169. Springer, Heidelberg (2000)
6. Condit, J., Hackett, B., Lahiri, S.K., Qadeer, S.: Unifying type checking and property checking for low-level code. In: Symp. on Principles of Programming Languages (POPL), pp. 302–314 (2009)
7. Cook, B., Kroening, D., Sharygina, N.: Symbolic model checking for asynchronous boolean programs. In: Godefroid, P. (ed.) SPIN 2005. LNCS, vol. 3639, pp. 75–90. Springer, Heidelberg (2005)
8. de Moura, L., Bjørner, N.: Z3: An efficient SMT solver. In: Ramakrishnan, C.R., Rehof, J. (eds.) TACAS 2008. LNCS, vol. 4963, pp. 337–340. Springer, Heidelberg (2008)
9. DeLine, R., Leino, K.R.M.: BoogiePL: A typed procedural language for checking object-oriented programs. Technical Report MSR-TR-2005-70, Microsoft Research (2005)
10. Ganai, M.K., Gupta, A.: Efficient modeling of concurrent systems in BMC. In: Havelund, K., Majumdar, R., Palsberg, J. (eds.) SPIN 2008. LNCS, vol. 5156, pp. 114–133. Springer, Heidelberg (2008)
11. Henzinger, T.A., Jhala, R., Majumdar, R.: Race checking by context inference. In: Conf. on Programming Language Design and Implementation (PLDI), pp. 1–13 (2004)
12. Kahlon, V., Sankaranarayanan, S., Gupta, A.: Semantic reduction of thread interleavings in concurrent programs. In: Kowalewski, S., Philippou, A. (eds.) TACAS 2009. LNCS, vol. 5505, pp. 124–138. Springer, Heidelberg (2009)
13. Kurshan, R.P.: Computer-Aided Verification of Coordinating Processes: The Automata-Theoretic Approach. Princeton University Press, Princeton (1995)

14. Lal, A., Reps, T.W.: Reducing concurrent analysis under a context bound to sequential analysis. In: Gupta, A., Malik, S. (eds.) CAV 2008. LNCS, vol. 5123, pp. 37–51. Springer, Heidelberg (2008)
15. Lal, A., Touili, T., Kidd, N., Reps, T.W.: Interprocedural analysis of concurrent programs under a context bound. In: Ramakrishnan, C.R., Rehof, J. (eds.) TACAS 2008. LNCS, vol. 4963, pp. 282–298. Springer, Heidelberg (2008)
16. Musuvathi, M., Qadeer, S.: Iterative context bounding for systematic testing of multithreaded programs. In: Conf. on Programming Language Design and Implementation (PLDI), pp. 446–455 (2007)
17. Patin, G., Sighireanu, M., Touili, T.: Spade: Verification of multithreaded dynamic and recursive programs. In: Damm, W., Hermanns, H. (eds.) CAV 2007. LNCS, vol. 4590, pp. 254–257. Springer, Heidelberg (2007)
18. Qadeer, S., Rehof, J.: Context-bounded model checking of concurrent software. In: Halbwachs, N., Zuck, L.D. (eds.) TACAS 2005. LNCS, vol. 3440, pp. 93–107. Springer, Heidelberg (2005)
19. Qadeer, S., Wu, D.: KISS: Keep it simple and sequential. In: Conf. on Programming Language Design and Implementation (PLDI), pp. 14–24 (2004)
20. Rabinovitz, I., Grumberg, O.: Bounded model checking of concurrent programs. In: Etessami, K., Rajamani, S.K. (eds.) CAV 2005. LNCS, vol. 3576, pp. 82–97. Springer, Heidelberg (2005)
21. Rakamarić, Z., Hu, A.J.: A scalable memory model for low-level code. In: Jones, N.D., Müller-Olm, M. (eds.) VMCAI 2009. LNCS, vol. 5403, pp. 290–304. Springer, Heidelberg (2009)
22. Suwimonteerabuth, D., Esparza, J., Schwoon, S.: Symbolic context-bounded analysis of multithreaded Java programs. In: Havelund, K., Majumdar, R., Palsberg, J. (eds.) SPIN 2008. LNCS, vol. 5156, pp. 270–287. Springer, Heidelberg (2008)
23. Witkowski, T., Blanc, N., Weissenbacher, G., Kroening, D.: Model checking concurrent Linux device drivers. In: Intl. Conf. on Automated Software Engineering (ASE), pp. 501–504 (2007)

Predecessor Sets of Dynamic Pushdown Networks with Tree-Regular Constraints

Peter Lammich, Markus Müller-Olm, and Alexander Wenner

Institut für Informatik, Fachbereich Mathematik und Informatik
Westfälische Wilhelms-Universität Münster
{peter.lammich,markus.mueller-olm,alexander.wenner}@uni-muenster.de

Abstract. Dynamic Pushdown Networks (DPNs) are a model for parallel programs with (recursive) procedures and process creation. The goal of this paper is to develop generic techniques for more expressive reachability analysis of DPNs.

In the first part of the paper we introduce a new tree-based view on executions. Traditional interleaving semantics model executions by totally ordered sequences. Instead, we model an execution by a partially ordered set of rule applications, that only specifies the per-process ordering and the causality due to process creation, but no ordering between rule applications on processes that run in parallel. Tree-based executions allow us to compute predecessor sets of regular sets of DPN configurations relative to (tree-) regular constraints on executions. The corresponding problem for interleaved executions is not effective.

In the second part of the paper, we extend DPNs with (well-nested) locks. We generalize Kahlon and Gupta's technique of acquisition histories to DPNs, and apply the results of the first part of this paper to compute lock-sensitive predecessor sets.

1 Introduction

Writing parallel programs is notoriously difficult, as concurrency-related bugs are hard to find and hard to reproduce due to the nondeterministic behavior of the scheduler. Hence there is a real need for automated methods for verifying parallel programs. The goal of this paper is to develop stronger techniques for reachability analysis of *Dynamic Pushdown Networks (DPNs)* [2], a formal model of parallel programs with (recursive) procedures and process creation.

DPNs generalize pushdown systems by rules that have the additional side effect of creating a new process that is then executed in parallel. The key concept for analyzing DPNs is computation of predecessor sets. Configurations of a DPN are represented as words over control and stack symbols, and for a regular set of configurations, the set of predecessor configurations is regular as well and can be computed efficiently [2]. Predecessor computations can be used for various interesting analyses, like kill/gen analysis on bitvectors, context-bounded model checking [1], and data race detection.

A. Bouajjani and O. Maler (Eds.): CAV 2009, LNCS 5643, pp. 525–539, 2009.

Usually, DPNs are analyzed w.r.t. an interleaving semantics, where an execution is a sequence of rule applications. Interleaving semantics models the execution on a single processor, that performs one step at a time and may switch the currently executing process after every step. However, the set of interleaved executions does not have nice properties, which makes them difficult to reason about. For example, it is undecidable whether there exists an execution with a given regular property. Moreover, a step of the interleaving semantics does not contain the information which process executed the step, making interleaving semantics inappropriate to track properties of specific processes, e.g. acquired locks.

In the first part of this paper, we introduce an alternative view on executions of DPNs. An execution is modeled as a partially ordered set of steps, rather than a (totally ordered) sequence. The new semantics only reflects the ordering between steps of the same process and the causality due to process creation, i.e. that steps of a created process must be executed after the step that created the process. However, it does not enforce any ordering between steps of processes running in parallel. The new semantics does not lead to any loss of information as the interleaved executions can be recovered as topological sorts of the partial ordering. The partial ordering of an execution has a tree shape, where thread creation steps have at most two successors and all other steps have at most one successor. Hence, we model an execution as a list of trees (called *execution hedge*), that contains one tree for each process in the start configuration of the execution.

Taking advantage of our new, tree-based view on executions, we increase the expressivity of predecessor computations. Specifically, we show that for a regular set of configurations C and a (tree-) regular set of execution hedges H, the set of configurations from which a configuration in C is reachable via an execution in H is, again, regular and can be computed efficiently. We call this set the H-constrained predecessor set of C. Note that the corresponding problem for the interleaving semantics, i.e. predecessor computation with a (word-)regular constraint on the interleaved execution, is not effective[1].

In the second part of this paper, we extend DPNs by adding mutual exclusion via well-nested locks. Locks are a commonly used synchronization primitive to manage shared resources between processes. A process may acquire and release a lock, and a lock may be owned by at most one process at the same time. If a process wants to acquire a lock that is already owned by another process, it has to wait until the lock is released. We assume that locks are used in a well-nested fashion, i.e. a process has to release locks in the opposite order of acquisition, an assumption that is often satisfied in practice. For instance, the

---

[1] We can use the regular constraint $(a\bar{a} + b\bar{b})^*$ to synchronize two pushdown systems, thus reducing the emptiness check of the intersection of two context free languages, which is well-known to be undecidable, to this problem. We should mention that, nevertheless, predecessor sets w.r.t. a special class of regular constraints, called *alphabetic path constraints*, can be computed. Alphabetic path constraints have the form $S_1^{m_1} \ldots S_n^{m_n}$ with $S_1, \ldots, S_n \subseteq L$ and $m_1, \ldots, m_i \in \{1, *\}$.

synchronized-blocks of Java guarantee well-nested lock usage syntactically. Note that for non-well-nested locks even simple reachability problems are undecidable [5]. We can describe lock-sensitive executions by a tree-regular constraint, thus obtaining an algorithm for precise computation of lock-sensitive predecessor sets of regular sets of computations (lock-sensitive pre*). For this purpose, we generalize acquisition histories [4,5] to DPNs.

Summarizing, the contributions of this paper are:

- We present a tree-based view on DPN executions, and an efficient predecessor computation procedure that takes tree-regular constraints on the executions into account.
- We generalize the concept of acquisition histories to programs with potentially recursive procedures and process creation.
- We characterize lock-sensitive executions by a tree-regular constraint. Applying the predecessor computation procedure, this leads to an algorithm for computing lock-sensitive pre*.

Related Work. The results presented in this paper have been formalized and verified with the interactive theorem prover Isabelle/HOL [11]. The proof document is available as a technical report [9]. The theorems in this paper are annotated with the section and name of the corresponding theorem in the technical report.

Acquisition histories have been introduced for the analysis of parallel pushdown systems without process creation [4,5], in a setting where it is sufficient to regard only two parallel processes. They have been applied for conflict analysis of DPNs [10], where it is also sufficient to regard just two parallel processes at a time. Our generalization of acquisition histories is non-trivial, as we have to consider unboundedly many parallel processes and process creation.

An efficient implementation of acquisition history based techniques for a model without process creation is currently studied in a joint work of one of the authors [7]. However, the focus of that work lies on exploiting symbolic techniques to get an efficient implementation, while the focus of this paper is the generalization to DPNs. The use of symbolic techniques for getting an efficient implementation is briefly discussed in the conclusion section.

Locks can be simulated by shared memory, and thus context bounded model-checking techniques for DPNs [1] can also handle locks. However, the number of lock operations is also limited by the context bound, while our technique handles unboundedly many lock operations. Moreover, the technique presented in [1] is based on predecessor computations, hence it is straightforward to extend it with our results, getting a model-checking algorithm that can handle boundedly many accesses to shared memory and unboundedly many lock operations.

2   Dynamic Pushdown Networks

Dynamic pushdown networks (DPNs) [2] are a model for parallel processes with potentially recursive procedures and process creation. They extend pushdown processes by the ability to create new processes. A DPN is a tuple $M = (P, \Gamma, L, \Delta)$, where P is a finite set of control states, Γ is a finite stack alphabet with $P \cap \Gamma = \emptyset$, L is a finite set of rule labels, and $\Delta = \Delta_N \cup \Delta_S$ is a finite set of *non-spawning* (Δ_N) and *spawning* rules (Δ_S). A non-spawning rule $p\gamma \xhookrightarrow{l} p'w \in \Delta_N \subseteq P\Gamma \times L \times P\Gamma^*$ enables a transition on a single pushdown process with state p and top of stack γ to new state p' and new top of stack $w \in \Gamma^*$. A spawning rule $p\gamma \xhookrightarrow{l} p'w \triangleright p_s w_s \in \Delta_S \subseteq P\Gamma \times L \times P\Gamma^* \times P\Gamma^*$ is a pushdown rule with the additional side-effect of creating a new process with initial state p_s and initial stack w_s. For the rest of this paper, we assume that we have a fixed DPN $M = (P, \Gamma, L, \Delta)$.

Interleaving Semantics. We briefly recall the interleaving semantics of a DPN as presented in [2]: Configurations $\mathsf{Conf}_M := (P\Gamma^*)^*$ are sequences of words from $P\Gamma^*$, each word containing the control state and stack of one of the processes running in parallel. The step relation $\to_M \subseteq \mathsf{Conf}_M \times L \times \mathsf{Conf}_M$ is the least solution of the following constraints:

$$[\mathsf{nospawn}] \ c_1(p\gamma r)c_2 \xrightarrow{l}_M c_1(p'wr)c_2 \qquad \text{if } p\gamma \xhookrightarrow{l} p'w \in \Delta_N$$

$$[\mathsf{spawn}] \quad c_1(p\gamma r)c_2 \xrightarrow{l}_M c_1(p_s w_s)(p'wr)c_2 \ \text{if } p\gamma \xhookrightarrow{l} p'w \triangleright p_s w_s \in \Delta_S$$

A [nospawn]-step corresponds precisely to a pushdown operation (manipulating the control state and the top of the stack), a [spawn]-step additionally creates a new process that is inserted to the left of the creating process. We define $\to_M^* \subseteq \mathsf{Conf}_M \times L^* \times \mathsf{Conf}_M$ to be the reflexive, transitive closure of $\to_M$. This semantics is an *interleaving semantics*, because steps of processes running in parallel are interleaved. It models the possible executions on a single processor, where preemption may occur after any step.

Example 1 (DPN-Execution). Consider a DPN with non-spawning rules $\Delta_N = \{p_1\gamma \xhookrightarrow{l_1} p_1\gamma_1\gamma_2, p_1\gamma_3 \xhookrightarrow{l_3} p_1, p_2\gamma \xhookrightarrow{l_4} p_2\gamma_2\gamma_3\}$ and spawning rules $\Delta_S = \{p_1\gamma_1 \xhookrightarrow{l_2} p_1\gamma_3 \triangleright p_2\gamma\}$. It has the execution: $p_1\gamma \xrightarrow{l_1} p_1\gamma_1\gamma_2 \xrightarrow{l_2} p_2\gamma p_1\gamma_3\gamma_2 \xrightarrow{l_4} p_2\gamma_2\gamma_3 p_1\gamma_3\gamma_2 \xrightarrow{l_3} p_2\gamma_2\gamma_3 p_1\gamma_2$.

Tree Semantics. The interleaving semantics involves two types of nondeterministic choice: First, there may be more than one rule with a left-hand side matching the state of a process. Second, there may be more than one process that can make a step. In each step, the interleaving semantics nondeterministically chooses a process and a matching rule. We now separate these two types of nondeterministic choice: In a first step, we just fix the choice of the applied rules. The interleaving is then chosen in a second step.

The interleaving semantics models an execution as a sequence of steps, i.e. a total ordering of steps. We now model an execution as a partial ordering of steps, that totally orders steps of the same process, and additionally orders steps of a created process to come after the step that created the process. However, it does not order steps running in parallel. This ordering has a tree shape (cf. Fig. 1, showing the partial ordering of steps corresponding to the execution in

Example 1). Formally, we model an execution starting at a single process as an *execution tree* of type $T_M ::= \mathsf{N}\ L\ T_M\ |$ $\mathsf{S}\ L\ T_M\ T_M\ |\ \mathsf{L}\ P\Gamma^*$. A tree of the form $\mathsf{N}\ l\ t$ models an execution that performs the non-spawning step l first, followed by the execution described by t. A tree of the form $\mathsf{S}\ l\ t_s\ t$ models an execution that performs the spawning step l first, followed by the execution of the spawned process described by t_s and the remaining execution of the spawning process described by t. A node of the form $\mathsf{L}\ pw$ indicates that the process makes no more steps and that its final configuration is pw. The an-

Fig. 1. Partial Ordering of Steps

notation of the reached configuration at the leafs of the execution tree increases expressiveness of regular sets of execution trees, e.g. one can characterize execution trees that reach certain control states. The distinction between spawned and spawning tree at S-nodes allows for keeping track of which steps belong to which process, e.g. when tracking the acquired locks of a process.

The relation $\Longrightarrow_M\ \subseteq\ P\Gamma^*\times T_M\times\mathsf{Conf}_M$ characterizes the execution trees starting at a single process. It is defined as the least solution of the following constraints:

$$[\text{leaf}] \qquad qw \xRightarrow{\mathsf{L}\ qw}_M qw$$

$$[\text{nospawn}]\ q\gamma r \xRightarrow{\mathsf{N}\ l\ t}_M c' \qquad \text{if } q\gamma \xhookrightarrow{l} q'w \in \Delta_N\ \wedge\ q'wr \xRightarrow{t}_M c'$$

$$[\text{spawn}] \qquad q\gamma r \xRightarrow{\mathsf{S}\ l\ t_s\ t}_M c_s c' \ \text{if } q\gamma \xhookrightarrow{l} q'w \rhd q_s w_s \in \Delta_S$$
$$\wedge\ q_s w_s \xRightarrow{t_s}_M c_s\ \wedge\ q'wr \xRightarrow{t}_M c'$$

An execution that starts at a configuration with multiple processes is modeled as a list of execution trees (called an *execution hedge*), with one tree per process. These executions are defined by overloading $\Longrightarrow_M$ with:

$$c \xRightarrow{t_1\dots t_n}_M c' \quad :\Leftrightarrow \quad \exists c'_1\dots c'_n \in \mathsf{Conf}_M,\ p_1\dots p_n \in P,\ w_1\dots w_n \in \Gamma^*.$$
$$c = p_1 w_1\dots p_n w_n\ \wedge\ c' = c'_1\dots c'_n$$
$$\wedge\ p_1 w_1 \xRightarrow{t_1}_M c'_1\ \wedge\dots\wedge\ p_n w_n \xRightarrow{t_n}_M c'_n$$

Intuitively, $c \xRightarrow{h}_M c'$ means that there is an execution from configuration c to configuration c' with execution hedge h. Figure 2 shows an execution tree t satisfying $p_1\gamma \xRightarrow{t}_M p_2\gamma_2\gamma_3 p_1\gamma_2$ for the DPN from Example 1. The execution tree of the spawned process is always drawn as the left successor of the S-node, and the corresponding edge is labeled with „spawn". Hence, the rightmost steps in an execution tree corresponds to the execution of the process at the root of the tree.

In order to relate the tree semantics to the interleaving semantics, we define a scheduler that maps execution hedges to compatible sequences of rules. From the ordering point of view, the scheduler maps the steps ordered by the execution hedge

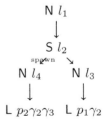

Fig. 2. Execution Tree

to the set of its topological sorts. As hedges are acyclic, there always exists a topological sort. The scheduler is modeled as a labeled transition system over execution hedges. A step replaces a root node in the hedge by its successors. Formally, the scheduler $\rightsquigarrow\ \subseteq T_M^* \times L \times T_M^*$ is the least relation satisfying the following constraints:

$$[\mathsf{nospawn}]\ h_1(\mathsf{N}\ l\ t)h_2 \overset{l}{\rightsquigarrow} h_1th_2$$
$$[\mathsf{spawn}]\quad h_1(\mathsf{S}\ l\ t_s\ t)h_2 \overset{l}{\rightsquigarrow} h_1t_sth_2$$

We call $\mathsf{sched}(h) := \{\bar{l} \in L^* \mid \exists h' \in (\mathsf{L}\ P\Gamma^*)^*.\ h \overset{\bar{l}}{\rightsquigarrow}^* h'\}$ the set of *schedules* of a hedge $h \in T_M^*$, where $(\mathsf{L}\ P\Gamma^*)^*$ is the set of all hedges that solely consist of L-nodes (i.e. have no more rules to execute), and $\rightsquigarrow^*$ is the reflexive, transitive closure of the scheduler $\rightsquigarrow$. It can be shown by straightforward induction that every execution of the interleaving semantics is a schedule of an execution of the tree semantics and vice versa:

Theorem 2 (Thm. sched-correct in Sec. 4 of [9]). *Let* $c, c' \in \mathsf{Conf}_M$ *and* $\bar{l} \in L^*$, *then* $c \overset{\bar{l}}{\rightarrow}_M^* c'$ *if and only if there is an execution hedge* $h \in T_M^*$ *with* $c \overset{h}{\Longrightarrow}_M c'$ *and* $\bar{l} \in \mathsf{sched}(h)$.

Predecessor Sets. Given a set $C' \subseteq \mathsf{Conf}_M$ of configurations, the set $\mathsf{pre}_M(C') := \{c \mid \exists c' \in C',\ l \in L.\ c \overset{l}{\rightarrow}_M c'\}$ is the set of *immediate predecessors* of C', i.e. the set of configurations that can make a transition to a $c' \in C'$ in exactly one step. Similarly, $\mathsf{pre}_M^*(C') := \{c \mid \exists c' \in C',\ \bar{l} \in L^*.\ c \overset{\bar{l}}{\rightarrow}_M^* c'\}$ is the set of *predecessors* of C', i.e. the set of configurations that can make a transition to a $c' \in C'$ by executing an arbitrary number of steps.

An important result on DPNs is that pre_M and pre_M^* preserve regularity, i.e. if C' is a regular set then $\mathsf{pre}_M(C')$ and $\mathsf{pre}_M^*(C')$ are regular as well, and given an automaton accepting C', automata accepting $\mathsf{pre}_M(C')$ and $\mathsf{pre}_M^*(C')$, respectively, can be computed in polynomial time [2]. This result is the key to analysis of DPNs, because it allows to cascade pre_M and pre_M^* computations and pose regular constraints on the intermediate configurations. For example, liveness of a global variable x at a control location u can be decided [2]: Let M be the DPN that models the program, $M|_{\mathsf{read}}$ be the DPN M restricted to those rules that correspond to program statements that read x, and $M|_{\mathsf{nowrite}}$ be the DPN M restricted to those rules that do not write x. Moreover, let $\mathsf{at}(u) \subseteq \mathsf{Conf}_M$ be the (regular) set of configurations where some process is at control location[2] u. Finally, let $c_0 \in \mathsf{Conf}_M$ be the initial configuration of the system. The variable x is live at control node u if and only if: $c_0 \in \mathsf{pre}_M^*(\mathsf{at}(u) \cap \mathsf{pre}_{M|_{\mathsf{nowrite}}}^*(\mathsf{pre}_{M|_{\mathsf{read}}}(\mathsf{Conf}_M)))$. In this fashion, all forward and backward kill/gen-bitvector problems can be decided in polynomial time. Other important analyses that can be done by predecessor computations are

---

[2] Usually, a control location is identified with the symbol at the top of the stack, such that $\mathsf{at}(u) = (P\Gamma^*)^* Pu\Gamma^* (P\Gamma^*)^*$.

context-bounded model-checking of DPNs with shared memory [1], and checking of reachability properties (e.g. data races).

Hedge-Constrained Predecessor Sets. In the introduction we indicated that reachability w.r.t. regular constraints on the interleaved executions is undecidable. Now, we constrain the execution hedges: For a set of configurations $C' \subseteq$ Conf_M and a set of execution hedges $H \subseteq T_M^*$, we define the *H-constrained predecessor set* of C' as: $\mathsf{pre}_M[H](C') := \{c \in \mathsf{Conf}_M \mid \exists c' \in C', h \in H. \ c \overset{h}{\Longrightarrow}_M c'\}$, i.e. those configurations that can make a transition with an execution hedge $h \in H$ to a configuration $c' \in C'$. We show that if H is (tree-)regular and C' is regular, then $\mathsf{pre}_M[H](C')$ is regular as well, and given a hedge automaton for H and an automaton for C', an automaton for $\mathsf{pre}_M[H](C')$ can be computed in polynomial time.

Hedge Automata. In order to characterize regular sets of execution hedges, we define a type of hedge automata [3] adjusted to acceptance of execution hedges: A hedge automaton $\mathcal{H} = (S, \mathcal{A}_0, D)$ consists of a finite set of states S, an initial automaton $\mathcal{A}_0$ with $L(\mathcal{A}_0) \subseteq S^*$, and a set $D = D_L \cup D_N \cup D_S$ of transition rules. Rules $s \hookrightarrow \mathcal{A} \in D_L$ consist of a state $s \in S$ and an automaton $\mathcal{A}$ that accepts process configurations, i.e. $L(\mathcal{A}) \subseteq P\Gamma^*$. These rules are used to label L-nodes with a state. Rules $s \overset{l}{\hookrightarrow} s' \in D_N$ with $s, s' \in S$ and $l \in L$ are used to label N-nodes and rules $s \overset{l}{\hookrightarrow} s' \triangleright s_s \in D_S$ with $s, s_s, s' \in S$ and $l \in L$ are used to label S-nodes[3].

A hedge $h = t_1 \ldots t_n \in T_M^*$ is accepted iff the trees $t_1, \ldots, t_n$ can be labeled bottom-up according to the rules in D such that the sequence of states $s_1, \ldots, s_n$ that label the roots of $t_1, \ldots, t_n$ is accepted by the initial automaton $\mathcal{A}_0$. Formally, we define the relation $\mathsf{lab}_{\mathcal{H}} \subseteq S \times T_M$ as the least relation satisfying the following rules:

[leaf] $\mathsf{lab}_{\mathcal{H}}(s, \mathsf{L} \ pw)$ if $s \hookrightarrow \mathcal{A} \in D_L \ \wedge \ pw \in L(\mathcal{A})$

[nospawn] $\mathsf{lab}_{\mathcal{H}}(s, \mathsf{N} \ l \ t)$ if $s \overset{l}{\hookrightarrow} s' \in D_N \ \wedge \ \mathsf{lab}_{\mathcal{H}}(s', t)$

[spawn] $\mathsf{lab}_{\mathcal{H}}(s, \mathsf{S} \ l \ t_s \ t)$ if $s \overset{l}{\hookrightarrow} s' \triangleright s_s \in D_S \ \wedge \ \mathsf{lab}_{\mathcal{H}}(s_s, t_s) \ \wedge \ \mathsf{lab}_{\mathcal{H}}(s', t)$

$\mathsf{lab}_{\mathcal{H}}(s, t)$ means that the root of the tree t can be labeled by the state s. We overload $\mathsf{lab}_{\mathcal{H}} \subseteq \bigcup_{n \in \mathbb{N}} S^n \times T_M^n$ for hedges by: $\mathsf{lab}_{\mathcal{H}}(s_1 \ldots s_n, t_1 \ldots t_n)$:$\Leftrightarrow$ $\mathsf{lab}_{\mathcal{H}}(s_1, t_1) \wedge \ldots \wedge \mathsf{lab}_{\mathcal{H}}(s_n, t_n)$ and define the language of the hedge automaton $\mathcal{H}$ by $L(\mathcal{H}) := \{h \mid \exists \bar{s} \in L(\mathcal{A}_0). \ \mathsf{lab}_{\mathcal{H}}(\bar{s}, h)\}$.

Assume we have a DPN $M = (P, \Gamma, L, \Delta)$, a regular set of configurations $C' \subseteq$ Conf_M, and a hedge automaton $\mathcal{H}$ that accepts a set of hedges $L(\mathcal{H}) \subseteq T_M^*$. In order to compute $\mathsf{pre}_M[L(\mathcal{H})](C')$, we define a new DPN $M \times \mathcal{H} = (P \times S, \Gamma, L, \Delta')$, a new regular set of configurations $C' \times \mathcal{H} \subseteq \mathsf{Conf}_{M \times \mathcal{H}}$, and an operator $\mathsf{proj}_{\mathcal{H}}$: $2^{\mathsf{Conf}_{M \times \mathcal{H}}} \to 2^{\mathsf{Conf}_M}$, such that $\mathsf{pre}_M[L(\mathcal{H})](C') = \mathsf{proj}_{\mathcal{H}}(\mathsf{pre}^*_{M \times \mathcal{H}}(C' \times \mathcal{H}))$. The

---

[3] A more standard notation of the rules would be $\mathcal{A}() \hookrightarrow s, l(s') \hookrightarrow s$, and $l(s_s, s') \hookrightarrow s$. However, our notation emphasizes the relation to DPN-rules.

constructions of $M \times \mathcal{H}$ and $C' \times \mathcal{H}$, as well as the operator $\mathsf{proj}_{\mathcal{H}}$, are effective, such that we can compute $\mathsf{pre}_M[L(\mathcal{H})](C')$ (for a given automaton for C') using the saturation algorithm for pre^* presented in [2]. The idea of this construction is to encode the states of the hedge automaton into the states of the DPN, and simulate the transitions of the hedge automaton within the transitions of the DPN. The new set of configurations $C' \times \mathcal{H}$ reflects the application of the D_L-rules of the hedge automaton, and the $\mathsf{proj}_{\mathcal{H}}$-operation removes configurations not compatible with the initial automaton $\mathcal{A}_0$, and projects the control states of $M \times \mathcal{H}$ back to states of M. The rules $\Delta' = \Delta'_N \cup \Delta'_S$ of the DPN $M \times \mathcal{H}$ are defined as follows:

[nospawn] $(p,s)\gamma \xrightarrow{l} (p',s')w \in \Delta'_N$ iff $p\gamma \xrightarrow{l} p'w \in \Delta_N$
$$\land \ s \xrightarrow{l} s' \in D_N$$

[spawn] $(p,s)\gamma \xrightarrow{l} (p',s')w \rhd (p_s,s_s)w_s \in \Delta'_S$ iff $p\gamma \xrightarrow{l} p'w \rhd p_s w_s \in \Delta_S$
$$\land \ s \xrightarrow{l} s' \rhd s_s \in D_S$$

Notice that this definition generates $O(|\Delta|D)$ rules and can be implemented in time $O(|\Delta|D)$. The new set of configurations $C' \times \mathcal{H}$ is defined as:

$$C' \times \mathcal{H} := \{(p_1,s_1)w_1 \ldots (p_n,s_n)w_n \mid p_1 w_1 \ldots p_n w_n \in C'$$
$$\land \ \forall 1 \leq i \leq n. \ \exists \mathcal{A}. \ s_i \hookrightarrow \mathcal{A} \in D_L \ \land \ p_i w_i \in L(\mathcal{A})\}$$

Finally, we define the projection operator as:

$$\mathsf{proj}_{\mathcal{H}}(C_\times) := \{p_1 w_1 \ldots p_n w_n \mid \exists s_1, \ldots, s_n \in S. \ s_1 \ldots s_n \in L(\mathcal{A}_0)$$
$$\land \ (p_1,s_1)w_1 \ldots (p_n,s_n)w_n \in C_\times\}$$

We can show that $\mathsf{pre}_M[L(\mathcal{H})](C') = \mathsf{proj}_{\mathcal{H}}(\mathsf{pre}^*_{M \times \mathcal{H}}(C' \times \mathcal{H}))$ (Theorem *xdpn-correct* in Section 8 of [9]). Moreover, we can write $C' \times \mathcal{H}$ and $\mathsf{proj}_{\mathcal{H}}(C_\times)$ using only operations that preserve regularity and are computable in polynomial time for given automata (Theorem *projH-effective* in Section 8 of [9]). With the polynomial time algorithm for computing pre^*_M [2] we get the following theorem:

Theorem 3 (Thm. prehc-effective[4] in Sec. 8 of [9]). *Given a DPN M, a hedge automaton $\mathcal{H}$ and a regular set of configurations C', the set $\mathsf{pre}_M[L(\mathcal{H})](C')$ is regular and given an automaton for C', an automaton for $\mathsf{pre}_M[L(\mathcal{H})](C')$ can be computed in polynomial time.*

3   Lock-Sensitive DPNs*

Locks are an important synchronization mechanism to guarantee mutual exclusion, e.g. to protect accesses to shared resources. Processes may *acquire* and

---

[4] This Theorem follows from Theorem *prehc-effective* in [9], some well-known results about tree-automata and the results from [2]. However, the tree-automata results and the results from [2] are not formally proven in [9].

release locks, but, at any time, each lock may be owned by at most one process. If a process wants to acquire a lock currently owned by another process, it blocks until the lock is released. We now extend DPNs by a finite number of locks and assume that they are acquired and released in a well-nested fashion, i.e. a process must release locks in the opposite order of acquisition. We assume locks to be non-reentrant, that is a process must not re-acquire a lock that it already owns. Note that we can simulate re-entrant locks with non-reentrant ones if the acquisition and release of locks is aligned with procedure calls [6] (like monitors and Java synchronized blocks).

Model Definition. Let $\mathbb{L}$ be a finite set of locks. We label the rules by their actions w.r.t. the locks in $\mathbb{L}$, i.e. the labels[5] are $L ::= \text{none} \mid \text{acq } \mathbb{L} \mid \text{rel } \mathbb{L}$. As mentioned, we assume that locks are accessed in a well-nested and non-reentrant fashion. In general there may exist executions from (unreachable) configurations that violate the well-nestedness or non-reentrance assumptions. Hence, we fix a start configuration $p_0\gamma_0 \in P\Gamma$, and make these assumptions only for executions from the start configuration. Moreover, we assume that, initially, a process does not own any locks, i.e. no execution from the start configuration or of a spawned process releases a lock that it has not acquired before. Note that it is straightforward to decide whether a given DPN satisfies our assumptions.

In order to simplify the presentation, we assume that the set of currently acquired locks is visible in the control state of a process, i.e. we assume that there is a function $\text{locks} : P \to 2^{\mathbb{L}}$ that maps control states to the set of allocated locks. This function must satisfy the constraints $\text{locks}(p_0) = \emptyset$ and

$$p\gamma \overset{l}{\hookrightarrow} p'w[\triangleright\, p_s w_s] \in \Delta \;\Rightarrow\; \text{locks}(p) \overset{l}{-\!\!\!\triangleright} \text{locks}(p') \; [\wedge\, \text{locks}(p_s) = \emptyset]$$

where $-\!\!\!\triangleright\, \subseteq 2^{\mathbb{L}} \times L \times 2^{\mathbb{L}}$ describes valid transitions on the set of acquired locks:

$$\begin{array}{lll} [\text{none}] & X \xrightarrow{\text{none}}\!\!\triangleright X' & :\Leftrightarrow X = X' \\[4pt] [\text{acquire}] & X \xrightarrow{\text{acq } x}\!\!\triangleright X' & :\Leftrightarrow x \notin X \wedge X' = \{x\} \cup X \\[4pt] [\text{release}] & X \xrightarrow{\text{rel } x}\!\!\triangleright X' & :\Leftrightarrow x \notin X' \wedge X = \{x\} \cup X' \end{array}$$

Note that DPNs where locks are not visible in the control state can be transformed to DPNs with a locks-function, involving a blowup that is, in the worst case, exponential in the maximum nesting depth of locks, which is typically small. We overload the locks-function to configurations by: $\text{locks}(p_1 w_1 \ldots p_n w_n) := \text{locks}(p_1) \cup \ldots \cup \text{locks}(p_n)$. Also note that for an execution hedge h, all configurations c where h can start (i.e. $\exists c'.\ c \overset{h}{\Longrightarrow}_M c'$) hold the same set of locks. This set can be derived from the annotation of the final configurations at the leafs and the lock operations at the inner nodes. For an execution hedge h, we overload $\text{locks}(h)$ to be the set of locks held by any configuration where h starts, i.e. we have $c \overset{h}{\Longrightarrow}_M c' \;\Rightarrow\; \text{locks}(c) = \text{locks}(h)$.

---

[5] Usually, one wants to make visible additional information in the labels. This could be done by using pairs of lock-actions and additional information as labels. However, we omit such a definition here for clarity.

The lock-sensitive step relation is defined as $c \xrightarrow{l}_{\mathsf{ls},M} c' :\Leftrightarrow c \xrightarrow{l}_M c' \wedge$ $\mathsf{locks}(c) \xrightarrow{l}\triangleright \mathsf{locks}(c')$. As usual, we write $\rightarrow^*_{\mathsf{ls},M}$ for its reflexive, transitive closure.

The extension of the tree-based semantics to locks can be described as a restriction of the scheduler. The $\Longrightarrow_M$-relation, that relates configurations to execution hedges, does not change. The original scheduler maps an execution hedge to all its topological sorts. However, we cannot model the set of lock-sensitive schedules as topological sorts. For example, Consider two processes that execute the steps 1:acq x, 2:rel x and 3: acq x, 4 : rel x for some lock x. When they are executed in parallel, the possible schedules are $1, 2, 3, 4$ and $3, 4, 1, 2$. However, if these would be topological sorts of some ordering, so would be the schedule $1, 3, 2, 4$, which is invalid.

The lock-sensitive scheduler $\leadsto_{\mathsf{ls}} \subseteq T^*_M \times L \times T^*_M$ is a restriction of the original scheduler to those schedules that respect the semantics of locks:

$$h \xrightarrow{l}_{\mathsf{ls}} h' :\Leftrightarrow h \xrightarrow{l} h' \wedge \mathsf{locks}(h) \xrightarrow{l}\triangleright \mathsf{locks}(h')$$

The set of *lock-sensitive schedules* of a hedge $h \in T^*_M$ is defined as: $\mathsf{sched}_{\mathsf{ls}}(h) :=$ $\{\bar{l} \mid \exists h' \in (L\ P\Gamma^*)^*.\ h \xrightarrow{\bar{l}}^*_{\mathsf{ls}} h'\}$, where $\leadsto^*_{\mathsf{ls}}$ is the reflexive, transitive closure of the lock-sensitive scheduler $\leadsto_{\mathsf{ls}}$. It is again straightforward to show that the lock-sensitive scheduler matches the interleaving semantics:

Theorem 4 (Thm. lsched-correct in Sec. 9 of [9]). *Let $c, c' \in \mathsf{Conf}_M$ and $\bar{l} \in L^*$, then $c \xrightarrow{\bar{l}}^*_{\mathsf{ls},M} c'$ if and only if there exists an execution hedge $h \in T^*_M$ with $c \xRightarrow{h}_M c'$ and $\bar{l} \in \mathsf{sched}_{\mathsf{ls}}(h)$.*

Acquisition Structures. As shown above, the lock-sensitive schedules cannot be characterized as the set of topological sorts of some order. However, in order to compute lock-sensitive predecessor sets, we do not need to consider every single schedule of an execution hedge, but just the existence of a schedule. We now introduce a finite state abstraction of execution hedges from which we can decide whether a lock sensitive schedule exists or not. Our approach generalizes *acquisition histories* [4,5].

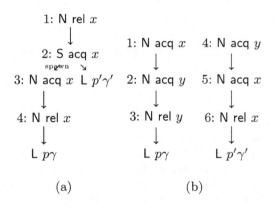

(a)   (b)

Fig. 3. Executions With Locks

In order to sketch the basic idea, we have to introduce some wording: An execution hedge that starts at a reachable configuration is called *reachable*. Note that, due to the well-nestedness and non-reentrance assumptions, reachable execution hedges also use locks in a well-nested and non-reentrant fashion. Given a (reachable) execution hedge, an acquisition of a lock x without a matching release is called a *final acquisition* of x. A matching release means, that the same process releases the lock, i.e. that there is a release of x on the rightmost path starting at the acquisition node. Symmetrically, a release of x without a matching acquisition is called an *initial release*. Acquisitions and releases that are not final acquisitions or initial releases are called *usages*. For example consider the execution tree from Figure 3a: Node 1 is an initial release of the lock x, Node 2 is a final acquisition of x, and Nodes 3 and 4 are usages of x.

Given a reachable execution hedge h, we define its *release graph* $g_r(h) \subseteq \mathbb{L} \times \mathbb{L}$ and its *acquisition graph* $g_a(h) \subseteq \mathbb{L} \times \mathbb{L}$: $g_r(h)$ contains an edge $x \rightarrow x'$, iff h contains an initial release of x' and the ordering induced by h enforces a usage of x to be scheduled before the initial release of x'. Symmetrically, $g_a(h)$ contains an edge $x \rightarrow x'$ iff h contains a final acquisition of x that has to be scheduled before a usage of x'. We now identify some necessary criteria for a reachable execution hedge h to have a lock-sensitive schedule:

1. All locks that are used or finally acquired in h are either also initially released in h or are not contained in the initial set of locks $\mathsf{locks}(h)$.
2. h does not contain multiple final acquisitions of the same lock.
3. The acquisition graph and the release graph of h are acyclic.

To justify Criterion 1, we observe that all locks in $\mathsf{locks}(h)$ that are not initially released remain allocated throughout the entire execution. Hence, no acquisition (neither a usage nor a final acquisition) of such a lock can be scheduled. The intuition behind Criterion 2 is, that a finally acquired lock will not be freed for the rest of the execution. Hence, if there are multiple final acquisitions of the same lock, only one of them can be scheduled. Note that we do not check the symmetric condition for initial releases, as reachable execution hedges cannot contain multiple initial releases of the same lock. To illustrate Criterion 3, assume that the acquisition graph $g_a(h)$ has a cycle $x_1 \rightarrow x_2 \rightarrow \ldots \rightarrow x_n = x_1$ with $n > 1$. Then, h has no lock sensitive schedule: From the definition of the acquisition graph, we see that, first, each lock $x_i, i < n$ has a final acquisition in h (because it has an outgoing edge in $g_a(h)$) and, second, that this final acquisition of x_i precedes a usage of x_{i+1} in each schedule of h. In a lock sensitive schedule, this usage of x_{i+1} must preceed the final acquisition of x_{i+1}. Because of the cycle $x_1 \rightarrow \ldots \rightarrow x_n = x_1$ this would imply that the final acquisition of x_1 precedes itself, which is a contradiction. The argumentation for a cycle in the release graph is similar. For example, the execution tree depicted in Figure 3a has no schedule, as the usage of x (Nodes 3 and 4) cannot be scheduled before the final acquisition of x (Node 2). Its acquisition graph $\{x \rightarrow x\}$ is trivially cyclic. The execution hedge from Figure 3b also has no schedule: We have to schedule the final acquisition of x (Node 1) or y (Node 4) as first step. However, if we schedule Node 1 first, we will not be able to schedule the usage of x (Nodes 5 and 6) and, symmetrically, if we schedule Node 4 first, we will not be able to schedule the usage of y (Nodes 2 and 3). The acquisition graph is $\{x \rightarrow y, y \rightarrow x\}$, which has the cycle $x \rightarrow y \rightarrow x$.

An *acquisition structure* is a finite domain abstraction of an execution hedge that can be computed inductively over the execution hedge and contains enough information to decide the criteria 1-3 depicted above. An acquisition structure is either the special symbol $\perp$ or a five-tuple (r, u, a, g_r, g_a), where $r \subseteq \mathbb{L}$ is the set of initially released locks, $u \subseteq \mathbb{L}$ is the set of used locks, and $a \subseteq \mathbb{L}$ is the set of finally acquired locks. $g_r, g_a \subseteq \mathbb{L} \times \mathbb{L}$ are the acquisition and release graphs. We define AS to be the set of all acquisition structures.

$$as(L\ pw) := (\emptyset, \emptyset, \emptyset, \emptyset, \emptyset)$$
$$as(N\ l\ t) := upd(l, as(t))$$
$$as(S\ l\ t_s\ t) := upd(l, as(t_s) \parallel as(t))$$
$$as(t_1 \ldots t_n) := as(t_1) \parallel \ldots \parallel as(t_n)$$

$$upd(none, s) := s$$
$$upd(n, \perp) := \perp$$
$$upd(acq\ x, (r, u, a, g_r, g_a)) := \text{if } x \in r \text{ then}$$
$$\quad (r \setminus \{x\}, u \cup \{x\}, a,$$
$$\quad\quad (g_r \setminus (\mathbb{L} \times \{x\})) \cup (\{x\} \times r \setminus \{x\}), g_a)$$
$$\quad \text{else if } x \notin a \text{ then}$$
$$\quad (r, u, a \cup \{x\}, g_r, g_a \cup (\{x\} \times u))$$
$$\quad \text{else } \perp$$
$$upd(rel\ x, (r, u, a, g_r, g_a)) := (r \cup \{x\}, u, a, g_r, g_a)$$

$$\_ \parallel \perp := \perp$$
$$\perp \parallel \_ := \perp$$
$$(r, u, a, g_r, g_a) \parallel (r', u', a', g_r', g_a') :=$$
$$\quad \text{if } r \cap r' = \emptyset \wedge a \cap a' = \emptyset \text{ then}$$
$$\quad (r \cup r', u \cup u', a \cup a', g_r \cup g_r', g_a \cup g_a')$$
$$\quad \text{else } \perp$$

Fig. 4. Definition of acquisition structures

Acquisition structures can be computed bottom-up along the structure of an execution hedge. Figure 4 shows the computation in a pseudo-functional language. The $upd(l, \_)$-function describes the effect of prepending a node labeled with l to the acquisition structure. The $\parallel$-operator composes the acquisition structures of two processes that are executed in parallel. An acquisition structure $(r, u, a, g_r, g_a) \in$ AS is called *consistent* w.r.t. a set of initial locks $X \subseteq \mathbb{L}$, if and only if $(X \setminus r) \cap (u \cup a) = \emptyset$ and both, g_r and g_a, are acyclic. This models Criteria 1 and 3. The acquisition structure $\perp$ is not consistent w.r.t. any set of locks. This models Criterion 2, as the acquisition structure becomes $\perp$ if it is violated. We define $cons(X)$ to be the set of all acquisition histories that are consistent w.r.t. X. We can show the following theorem:

Theorem 5 (Thm. acqh-correct in Sec. 11 of [9]). *For any reachable execution hedge h, we have $sched_{ls}(h) \neq \emptyset$ if and only if $as(h) \in cons(locks(h))$.*

The proof of the $\Rightarrow$-direction follows the intuition described above. For the proof of the $\Leftarrow$-direction, a valid schedule of an execution hedge with a consistent acquisition history is constructed inductively. For the details we refer to [9]. Note that Theorem 5 implies that the criteria 1-3 are not only necessary, but also sufficient for existence of a lock-sensitive schedule of an execution hedge.

Encoding Acquisition Structures into Hedge Automata. In this section, we show that the set of all execution hedges that have a lock-sensitive schedule is regular. For this purpose, we design a hedge automaton $\mathcal{H}_{ls}$ that computes $locks(h)$ and $as(h)$ within its states, and checks consistency by its initial automaton. The Definition of $\mathcal{H}_{ls}$ is shown in Figure 5. The rules label each tree t with $locks(t)$ and $as(t)$. The initial automaton $\mathcal{A}_0$ computes the locks and the acquisition structure of the hedge. A hedge h is accepted iff $\mathsf{as}(h)$ is consistent w.r.t. $\mathsf{locks}(h)$. The rules of the hedge-automaton use the function $\mathsf{eff}^{-1} : L \times 2^{\mathbb{L}} \to 2^{\mathbb{L}}$ for bottom-up computation of $\mathsf{locks}(h)$. It describes the reverse effect of a lock operation. With the definitions above and Theorem 5 we get the following theorem:

Theorem 6 (Thm. reachable-hls-char in Sec. 14 of [9]). *For any reachable configuration c and execution hedge h that starts at c (i.e. $\exists c'. \ c \xLongrightarrow{h}_M c'$), we have $\mathsf{sched}_{\mathsf{ls}}(h) \neq \emptyset$ if and only if $h \in L(\mathcal{H}_{\mathsf{ls}})$.*

$$\mathcal{H}_{\mathsf{ls}} := (2^{\mathbb{L}} \times \mathsf{AS}, \mathcal{A}_0, D_L \cup D_N \cup D_S)$$
$$\mathcal{A}_0 := (2^{\mathbb{L}} \times \mathsf{AS}, q_0, F_0, \delta_0)$$
$$q_0 := (\emptyset, (\emptyset, \emptyset, \emptyset, \emptyset, \emptyset, \emptyset))$$
$$F_0 := \{(X, s) \mid s \in \mathsf{cons}(X)\}$$
$$\delta_0 := \{(X, s) \xrightarrow{(X', s')} (X \cup X', s \parallel s') \mid$$
$$X, X' \subseteq \mathbb{L} \wedge s, s' \in \mathsf{AS}\}$$
$$D_L := \{(\mathsf{locks}(p), (\emptyset, \emptyset, \emptyset, \emptyset, \emptyset, \emptyset)) \hookrightarrow \{p\}\Gamma^* \mid p \in P\}$$
$$D_N := \{(X, \mathsf{upd}(l, s)) \xhookrightarrow{l} (\mathsf{eff}^{-1}(l, X), s) \mid$$
$$X \subseteq \mathbb{L}, \ s \in \mathsf{AS}, \ l \in L\}$$
$$D_S := \{(X, \mathsf{upd}(l, s_s \parallel s)) \xhookrightarrow{l} (\mathsf{eff}^{-1}(l, X), s) \rhd (\emptyset, s_s) \mid$$
$$X \subseteq \mathbb{L}, \ s, s_s \in \mathsf{AS}, \ l \in L\}$$

$$\mathsf{eff}^{-1}(\mathsf{none}, X) := X$$
$$\mathsf{eff}^{-1}(\mathsf{acq}\ x, X) := X \cup \{x\}$$
$$\mathsf{eff}^{-1}(\mathsf{rel}\ x, X) := X \setminus \{x\}$$

Fig. 5. Definition of $\mathcal{H}_{\mathsf{ls}}$

Cascaded, lock-sensitive predecessor sets can now be computed using the lock-insensitive, hedge-constrained predecessor computation presented in the first part of this paper: A lock-sensitive predecessor set is computed by $\mathsf{pre}_M[\mathcal{H}_{\mathsf{ls}} \cap \mathcal{H}_{\mathsf{addc}}]$, where $\mathcal{H}_{\mathsf{addc}}$ may contain additional constraints on the execution hedge, like restrictions of the rule labels or the number of applied rules (e.g. to compute immediate predecessor sets). Note that Theorem 6 is only applicable for reachable configurations. Hence, we have to ensure that we only derive information from reachable configurations during cascaded predecessor set computations. However, we observe that most applications of cascaded predecessor computations are used to query whether the start configuration $p_0\gamma_0$ is contained in the outermost predecessor set, i.e. they have the shape $p_0\gamma_0 \in \mathsf{pre}_M[\mathcal{H}_{\mathsf{ls}} \cap \_](\ldots \mathsf{pre}_M[\mathcal{H}_{\mathsf{ls}} \cap \_](\_) \ldots)$. By definition, only reachable configurations can be reached from the start configuration. Thus, the result of such a query depends only on reachable configurations in the intermediate predecessor sets, and, using Theorem 6, we can show that the result is sound and precise w.r.t. the lock-sensitive semantics.

Complexity. The problem of deciding whether the initial configuration is contained in the lock-sensitive predecessor set of some regular set of configurations is NP-hard, even if we store the set of allocated locks in the control states of the processes and have no procedures at all. This can be shown by a reduction from the boolean satisfiability problem (SAT). The reduction uses the same idea as [10], but uses multiple processes instead of recursive procedures. Hence, we cannot expect a polynomial time algorithm. And indeed, the number of states of the automaton $\mathcal{H}_{\mathsf{ls}}$ is exponential in the number of locks.

4 Conclusion

We have presented a tree-based semantics for DPNs, where executions are modeled as hedges, which reflect the ordering of steps of a single process and the causality due to process creation, but enforce no ordering between steps of processes running in parallel. We have shown how to efficiently compute predecessor sets of regular sets of configurations with tree-regular constraints on the execution hedges. Our algorithm encodes a hedge-automaton into the DPN, thus reducing the problem to unconstrained predecessor set computation, for which a polynomial time algorithm exists. In the second part of this paper, we have presented a generalization of acquisition histories to DPNs, and used it to construct tree-regular constraints for lock-sensitive executions. With the techniques from the first part of this paper, we obtained an algorithm to precisely compute cascaded, lock-sensitive predecessor sets.

As many analyses of DPNs are based on the computation of predecessor sets, it is now straightforward to make them lock-sensitive by substituting the original, lock-insensitive predecessor computation by our new, lock-sensitive one. For example, we can construct lock-sensitive bitvector analyses, and extend context-bounded analysis of DPNs with shared memory [1], as discussed in the introduction.

Future Research. A main direction of future research is implementation and experimental evaluation of the techniques presented in this paper. Possible starting points may be [8] and [7]. In [8], Java programs are abstracted to an intermediate model based on pushdown systems without process creation, and then analyzed using a semi-decision procedure. The techniques in this paper provide a decision procedure for an intermediate model that is more suited to the abstraction of Java programs, as thread creation can be abstracted more precisely. In a joint work of one of the authors [7], an acquisition history based decision procedure for the original intermediate model of [8], that does not support process creation, has been constructed. It uses many optimizations to increase the efficiency of the implementation. The most notable optimization is that the consistency check is not performed after each intermediate computation of a cascaded computation (which is likely to exponentially blow up the size of the automaton), but is delayed until all intermediate computations are completed. For this purpose, the analysis works with vectors of so called *extended acquisition histories*. Moreover, instead of encoding information into the control states, weighted pushdown systems [12] are used. Similar optimizations may apply to our technique, using vectors of acquisition structures and weighted DPNs [13], such that there is hope that an implementation might be practical despite of the NP-hardness of the problem.

Acknowledgment. We thank Ahmed Bouajjani, Nicholas Kidd, Thomas Reps, and Tayssir Touili for helpful and inspiring discussions on analysis of concurrent pushdown systems with and without process creation.

References

1. Bouajjani, A., Esparza, J., Schwoon, S., Strejcek, J.: Reachability analysis of multithreaded software with asynchronous communication. In: Ramanujam, R., Sen, S. (eds.) FSTTCS 2005. LNCS, vol. 3821, pp. 348–359. Springer, Heidelberg (2005)
2. Bouajjani, A., Müller-Olm, M., Touili, T.: Regular symbolic analysis of dynamic networks of pushdown systems. In: Abadi, M., de Alfaro, L. (eds.) CONCUR 2005. LNCS, vol. 3653, pp. 473–487. Springer, Heidelberg (2005)
3. Bruggemann-Klein, A., Murata, M., Wood, D.: Regular tree and regular hedge languages over unranked alphabets. Research report (2001)
4. Kahlon, V., Gupta, A.: An automata-theoretic approach for model checking threads for LTL properties. In: Proc. of LICS 2006, pp. 101–110. IEEE Computer Society, Los Alamitos (2006)
5. Kahlon, V., Ivancic, F., Gupta, A.: Reasoning about threads communicating via locks. In: Etessami, K., Rajamani, S.K. (eds.) CAV 2005. LNCS, vol. 3576, pp. 505–518. Springer, Heidelberg (2005)
6. Kidd, N., Lal, A., Reps, T.: Language strength reduction. In: Alpuente, M., Vidal, G. (eds.) SAS 2008. LNCS, vol. 5079, pp. 283–298. Springer, Heidelberg (2008)
7. Kidd, N., Lammich, P., Touili, T., Reps, T.: A decision procedure for detecting atomicity violations for communicating processes with locks (submitted for publication)
8. Kidd, N., Reps, T., Dolby, J., Vaziri, M.: Finding concurrency-related bugs using random isolation. In: Jones, N.D., Müller-Olm, M. (eds.) VMCAI 2009. LNCS, vol. 5403, pp. 198–213. Springer, Heidelberg (2009)
9. Lammich, P.: Isabelle formalization of hedge-constrained pre* and DPNs with locks. Technical Report, http://cs.uni-muenster.de/sev/publications/
10. Lammich, P., Müller-Olm, M.: Conflict analysis of programs with procedures, dynamic thread creation, and monitors. In: Alpuente, M., Vidal, G. (eds.) SAS 2008. LNCS, vol. 5079, pp. 205–220. Springer, Heidelberg (2008)
11. Nipkow, T., Paulson, L.C., Wenzel, M.: Isabelle/HOL. LNCS, vol. 2283. Springer, Heidelberg (2002)
12. Reps, T., Schwoon, S., Jha, S., Melski, D.: Weighted pushdown systems and their application to interprocedural dataflow analysis. Sci. Comput. Program. 58(1-2), 206–263 (2005)
13. Wenner, A.: Optimale Analyse gewichteter dynamischer Push-Down Netzwerke. Master's thesis, University of Münster (August 2008)

Reachability Analysis of Hybrid Systems Using Support Functions[*]

Colas Le Guernic[1] and Antoine Girard[2]

[1] Verimag, Université de Grenoble
[2] Laboratoire Jean Kuntzmann, Université de Grenoble
{Colas.Le-Guernic,Antoine.Girard}@imag.fr

Abstract. This paper deals with conservative reachability analysis of a class of hybrid systems with continuous dynamics described by linear differential inclusions, convex invariants and guards, and linear reset maps. We present an approach for computing over-approximations of the set of reachable states. It is based on the notion of support function and thus it allows us to consider invariants, guards and constraints on continuous inputs and initial states defined by arbitrary compact convex sets. We show how the properties of support functions make it possible to derive an effective algorithm for approximate reachability analysis of hybrid systems. We use our approach on some examples including the navigation benchmark for hybrid systems verification.

1 Introduction

Reachability analysis has been a major research issue in the field of hybrid systems over the past decade. An important part of the effort has been devoted to hybrid systems where the continuous dynamics is described by linear differential equations or inclusions. This work resulted in several computational techniques for approximating the reachable set of a hybrid system using several classes of convex sets including polyhedrons [1,2], ellipsoids [3,4], hyperrectangles [5] or zonotopes [6,7]. In these approaches, the set of continuous inputs is assumed to belong to the considered class; invariants and guards are usually given by polyhedrons or also sometimes by ellipsoids (e.g. in [3]).

In this paper, we propose an approach that can handle hybrid systems where invariants, guards and constraints on the continuous inputs and initial states are defined by arbitrary compact convex sets. It is based on the representation of compact convex sets using their support function. Algorithms based on support functions have already been proposed for reachability analysis of purely continuous systems in [8] and more recently in [9], using the efficient computational scheme presented in [7]. We extend this latter approach to handle hybrid dynamics. The paper is organized as follows. In section 2, we briefly present some results from [9] on reachability analysis of continuous linear systems. In section 3, we adapt these results for hybrid systems by taking care of the constraints

---

[*] This work was supported by the ANR SETIN project VAL-AMS.

A. Bouajjani and O. Maler (Eds.): CAV 2009, LNCS 5643, pp. 540–554, 2009.

imposed by invariants and guards. In section 4, we present the notion of support functions for convex sets. In section 5, we show how the properties of support functions make it possible to derive an effective implementation of the algorithm presented in section 3 for reachability analysis of hybrid systems. Finally, we use our approach on some examples including the navigation benchmark for hybrid systems verification [10].

Notations : Given a set $\mathcal{S} \subseteq \mathbb{R}^n$, CH($\mathcal{S}$) denotes its convex hull. For a matrix M, $M\mathcal{S}$ denotes the image of $\mathcal{S}$ by M, and for a real number λ, $\lambda\mathcal{S} = (\lambda I)\mathcal{S}$ where I is the identity matrix. For $\mathcal{S}, \mathcal{S}' \subseteq \mathbb{R}^n$, $\mathcal{S} \oplus \mathcal{S}'$ denotes the Minkowski sum of $\mathcal{S}$ and $\mathcal{S}'$: $\mathcal{S} \oplus \mathcal{S}' = \{x + x' : x \in \mathcal{S}, x' \in \mathcal{S}'\}$. For a matrix M, $M^\top$ denotes its transpose.

2   Reachability Analysis of Linear Systems

In this paper, we shall consider a class of hybrid systems where the continuous dynamics is described by linear differential inclusions of the form:

$$\dot{x}(t) \in Ax(t) \oplus \mathcal{U},$$

where the continuous state $x(t) \in \mathbb{R}^n$, A is a $n \times n$ matrix and $\mathcal{U} \subseteq \mathbb{R}^n$ is a compact convex set; note that $\mathcal{U}$ need not be full dimensional. Let $\mathcal{X} \subseteq \mathbb{R}^n$, we denote by $\mathcal{R}_C(s, \mathcal{X}) \subseteq \mathbb{R}^n$ the set of states reachable at time $s \geq 0$ from states in $\mathcal{X}$: $\mathcal{R}_C(s, \mathcal{X}) = \{x(s) : \forall t \in [0, s], \dot{x}(t) \in Ax(t) \oplus \mathcal{U}, \text{ and } x(0) \in \mathcal{X}\}$. Then, the reachable set on the time interval $[s, s']$ is defined as

$$\mathcal{R}_C([s, s'], \mathcal{X}) = \bigcup_{t \in [s, s']} \mathcal{R}_C(t, \mathcal{X}).$$

Let $\mathcal{X} \subseteq \mathbb{R}^n$ be a compact convex set of initial states and $T > 0$ a time bound. In the recent paper [9], we presented an improved computational scheme, adapted from [6], for the over-approximation of the reachable set $\mathcal{R}_C([0, T], \mathcal{X})$. Let $\|.\|$ be a norm and $\mathcal{B} \subseteq \mathbb{R}^n$ the associated unit ball. We denote $\delta_\mathcal{X} = \max_{x \in \mathcal{X}} \|x\|$, and $\delta_\mathcal{U} = \max_{u \in \mathcal{U}} \|u\|$. We use a discretization of the time with step $\tau = T/N$ ($N \in \mathbb{N}$). We have

$$\mathcal{R}_C([0, T], \mathcal{X}) = \bigcup_{i=0}^{N-1} \mathcal{R}_C([i\tau, (i+1)\tau], \mathcal{X}).$$

An over-approximation of $\mathcal{R}_C([0, T], \mathcal{X})$ can be obtained by computing over-approximations of the sets $\mathcal{R}_C([i\tau, (i+1)\tau], \mathcal{X})$. We consider the first element of the sequence.

Lemma 1. *[9] Let $\mathcal{Y}_0 \subseteq \mathbb{R}^n$ be defined by :*

$$\mathcal{Y}_0 = \text{CH}\left(\mathcal{X} \cup (e^{\tau A}\mathcal{X} \oplus \tau\mathcal{U} \oplus \alpha_\tau \mathcal{B})\right) \tag{1}$$

where $\alpha_\tau = (e^{\tau\|A\|} - 1 - \tau\|A\|)(\delta_\mathcal{X} + \frac{\delta_\mathcal{U}}{\|A\|})$. Then, $\mathcal{R}_C([0, \tau], \mathcal{X}) \subseteq \mathcal{Y}_0$.

This lemma can be roughly understood as follows, $e^{\tau A}\mathcal{X} \oplus \tau\mathcal{U}$ is an approximation of the reachable set at time τ; a bloating operation followed by a convex hull operation gives an approximation of $\mathcal{R}_C([0, \tau], \mathcal{X})$. The bloating factor α_τ is chosen to ensure over-approximation. We consider the other elements of the sequence. Let us remark that

$$\mathcal{R}_C([(i+1)\tau, (i+2)\tau], \mathcal{X}) = \mathcal{R}_C(\tau, \mathcal{R}_C(, [i\tau, (i+1)\tau], \mathcal{X})), \ i = 0, \dots, N-2.$$

For $\mathcal{Y} \subseteq \mathbb{R}^n$, the following lemma gives an over-approximation of $\mathcal{R}_C(\tau, \mathcal{Y})$:

Lemma 2. *[9] Let $\mathcal{Y} \subseteq \mathbb{R}^n$, $\mathcal{Y}' \subseteq \mathbb{R}^n$ defined by $\mathcal{Y}' = e^{\tau A}\mathcal{Y} \oplus \tau\mathcal{U} \oplus \beta_\tau \mathcal{B}$ where $\beta_\tau = (e^{\tau\|A\|} - 1 - \tau\|A\|)\frac{\delta_\mathcal{U}}{\|A\|}$. Then, $\mathcal{R}_C(\tau, \mathcal{Y}) \subseteq \mathcal{Y}'$.*

The set $e^{\tau A}\mathcal{Y} \oplus \tau\mathcal{U}$ is an approximation the reachable set at time τ; bloating this set using the ball of radius β_τ ensures over-approximation. We can define the compact convex sets $\mathcal{Y}_i$ over-approximating the reachable sets $\mathcal{R}_C([i\tau, (i+1)\tau], \mathcal{X})$ as follows. $\mathcal{Y}_0$ is given by equation (1) and

$$\mathcal{Y}_{i+1} = e^{\tau A}\mathcal{Y}_i \oplus \tau\mathcal{U} \oplus \beta_\tau \mathcal{B}, \ i = 0, \dots, N-2. \tag{2}$$

Then, it follows from Lemmas 1 and 2:

Proposition 1. *[9] Let us consider the sets $\mathcal{Y}_0, \dots, \mathcal{Y}_{N-1}$ defined by equations (1) and (2); then, $\mathcal{R}_C([0, T], \mathcal{X}) \subseteq (\mathcal{Y}_0 \cup \dots \cup \mathcal{Y}_{N-1})$.*

We refer the reader to our work in [9] for technical proofs and explicit bounds on the approximation error.

3   Reachability Analysis of Hybrid Systems

In this paper, we consider a class of hybrid systems with continuous dynamics described by linear differential inclusions, convex invariants and guards, and linear reset maps. Formally, a hybrid system is a tuple $H = (\mathbb{R}^n, Q, E, F, \mathcal{I}, \mathcal{G}, R)$ where $\mathbb{R}^n$ is the continuous state-space, Q is a finite set of locations and $E \subseteq Q \times Q$ is the set of discrete transitions. $F = \{F_q : q \in Q\}$ is a collection of continuous dynamics; for each $q \in Q$, $F_q = (A_q, \mathcal{U}_q)$ where A_q is a $n \times n$ matrix and $\mathcal{U}_q \subseteq \mathbb{R}^n$ is a compact convex set. $\mathcal{I} = \{\mathcal{I}_q : q \in Q\}$ is a collection of invariants; for each $q \in Q$, $\mathcal{I}_q \subseteq \mathbb{R}^n$ is a compact convex set. $\mathcal{G} = \{\mathcal{G}_e : e \in E\}$ is a collection of guards; for each $e \in E$, $\mathcal{G}_e \subseteq \mathbb{R}^n$ is either a compact convex set or a hyperplane. $R = \{R_e : e \in E\}$ is a collection of reset maps; for each $e \in E$, $R_e = (B_e, \mathcal{V}_e)$ where B_e is a $n \times n$ matrix and $\mathcal{V}_e \subseteq \mathbb{R}^n$ is a compact convex set. Let us remark that the sets $\mathcal{U}_q, \mathcal{I}_q, \mathcal{G}_e$ and $\mathcal{V}_e$ are only assumed to be compact and convex, these can be polyhedrons, ellipsoids or more complex convex sets. We distinguish the case where $\mathcal{G}_e$ is a hyperplane; in this case, we shall see that reachability analysis can be processed more accurately.

The state of the hybrid system at time t is a pair $(q(t), x(t))$ consisting of a discrete state $q(t) \in Q$ and a continuous state $x(t) \in \mathbb{R}^n$. The state of the hybrid system can evolve in a continuous or discrete manner. During the continuous evolution, the discrete state remains constant $q(t) = q$ and the continuous state evolves according to the linear differential inclusion:

$$\dot{x}(t) \in A_q x(t) \oplus \mathcal{U}_q \text{ and } x(t) \in \mathcal{I}_q.$$

The discrete evolution is enabled at time t if the state $(q(t), x(t)) = (q, x)$ satisfies $x \in \mathcal{G}_e$ for some $e = (q, q') \in E$. Then, the transition e can occur instantaneously: the state of the hybrid system jumps to $(q(t), x(t)) = (q', x')$ where

$$x' \in B_e x \oplus \mathcal{V}_e.$$

In the following, for simplicity of the presentation, we consider reachability analysis of hybrid systems on an unbounded time interval with the understanding that the termination of the described algorithms is not ensured.

Let $\Sigma_0 = \bigcup_{q \in Q} \{q\} \times \mathcal{X}_{0,q} \subseteq Q \times \mathbb{R}^n$ be a set of initial states where, for $q \in Q$, $\mathcal{X}_{0,q} \subseteq \mathbb{R}^n$ is a compact convex set. The set of states reachable under the evolution of the hybrid system from this set of initial states is denoted $\mathcal{R}_H(\Sigma_0)$. In a given location q, the set of continuous states reachable under the continuous evolution from a set of continuous states $\mathcal{X}$ is

$$\mathcal{R}_{\text{loc}}(q, \mathcal{X}) = \{x(s) : s \geq 0, \forall t \in [0, s], \dot{x}(t) \in A_q x(t) \oplus \mathcal{U}_q, x(t) \in \mathcal{I}_q, x(0) \in \mathcal{X}\}$$

A transition $e \in E$ of the form $e = (q, q')$ can occur if $\mathcal{R}_{\text{loc}}(q, \mathcal{X}) \cap \mathcal{G}_e \neq \emptyset$, the set of continuous states reachable just after the transition is

$$\mathcal{R}_{\text{jump}}(e, \mathcal{X}) = B_e \left(\mathcal{R}_{\text{loc}}(q, \mathcal{X}) \cap \mathcal{G}_e \right) \oplus \mathcal{V}_e.$$

Then, the set of reachable states $\mathcal{R}_H(\Sigma_0)$ can be computed by Algorithm 1.

Algorithm 1. Reachability analysis of a hybrid system

Input: Set of initial states $\Sigma_0 = \bigcup_{q \in Q} \{q\} \times \mathcal{X}_{0,q}$
Output: $\mathcal{R} = \mathcal{R}_H(\Sigma_0)$
1: $L \leftarrow \{(q, \mathcal{X}_{0,q}) : q \in Q\}$
2: $\Sigma \leftarrow \emptyset$
3: $\mathcal{R} \leftarrow \emptyset$
4: **while** $L \neq \emptyset$ **do**
5:     Pick $(q, \mathcal{X}) \in L$
6:     $\Sigma \leftarrow \Sigma \cup (\{q\} \times \mathcal{X})$
7:     $\mathcal{R} \leftarrow \mathcal{R} \cup (\{q\} \times \mathcal{R}_{\text{loc}}(q, \mathcal{X}))$ ▷ Reachable set by continuous evolution
8:     **for** $e \in E$ of the form $e = (q, q')$ **do**   ▷ Reachable set by discrete evolution
9:         **if** $\{q'\} \times \mathcal{R}_{\text{jump}}(e, \mathcal{X}) \nsubseteq \Sigma$ **then**
10:             Insert $(q', \mathcal{R}_{\text{jump}}(e, \mathcal{X}))$ in L ▷ Insert in L if not explored yet
11:         **end if**
12:     **end for**
13: **end while**
14: **return** $\mathcal{R}$

In the variable L, we store a list of sets from which reachability analysis has to be processed. $\Sigma \subseteq Q \times \mathbb{R}^n$ represents the set of explored states from which reachability analysis has already been made.

It is clear that an algorithm for computing over-approximations of $\mathcal{R}_{\mathrm{loc}}(q, \mathcal{X})$ and $\mathcal{R}_{\mathrm{jump}}(e, \mathcal{X})$ is sufficient for conservative reachability analysis of the hybrid system. This can be done using Algorithm 2 adapted from the method presented in the previous section for reachability analysis of linear systems. For lighter notations, the index q has been dropped. We use a discretization of time with a step $\tau > 0$. The real numbers α_τ and β_τ are those defined in Lemmas 1 and 2. Note that Algorithm 2 takes a convex set $\mathcal{X}$ as input; therefore, in order to use it in a straightforward implementation of Algorithm 1, it needs to compute a convex over-approximation of $\mathcal{R}_{\mathrm{jump}}(e, \mathcal{X})$.

Algorithm 2. Reachability analysis in a given location q

Input: Convex set of states $\mathcal{X}$, time step τ.
Output: $\mathcal{R} \supseteq \mathcal{R}_{\mathrm{loc}}(q, \mathcal{X})$; convex $\mathcal{X}_e \supseteq \mathcal{R}_{\mathrm{jump}}(e, \mathcal{X})$, for $e \in E$ such that $e = (q, q')$
1: $\mathcal{Z}_0 \leftarrow \mathrm{CH}\left(\mathcal{X} \cup (e^{\tau A}\mathcal{X} \oplus \tau\mathcal{U} \oplus \alpha_\tau \mathcal{B})\right) \cap \mathcal{I}$ ▷ Initialize the reachable set
2: $\mathcal{R} \leftarrow \mathcal{Z}_0$
3: $i \leftarrow 0$
4: **while** $\mathcal{Z}_i \neq \emptyset$ **do**
5:    $\mathcal{Z}_{i+1} \leftarrow \left(e^{\tau A}\mathcal{Z}_i \oplus \tau\mathcal{U} \oplus \beta_\tau \mathcal{B}\right) \cap \mathcal{I}$ ▷ Propagate the reachable set
6:    $\mathcal{R} \leftarrow \mathcal{R} \cup \mathcal{Z}_{i+1}$
7:    $i \leftarrow i + 1$
8: **end while**
9: **for** $e \in E$ such that $e = (q, q')$ **do**
10:    $\mathcal{H}_e \leftarrow \mathrm{CH}(\mathcal{R} \cap \mathcal{G}_e)$ ▷ Intersect with guards
11:    $\mathcal{X}_e \leftarrow B_e\mathcal{H}_e \oplus \mathcal{V}_e$ ▷ Reachable set after the transition
12: **end for**
13: **return** $\mathcal{R}$; $\mathcal{X}_e$, for $e \in E$ such that $e = (q, q')$

Proposition 2. *Let $\mathcal{R}$; $\mathcal{X}_e$, for $e \in E$ such that $e = (q, q')$ be computed by Algorithm 2. Then, $\mathcal{R}_{\mathrm{loc}}(q, \mathcal{X}) \subseteq \mathcal{R}$ and $\mathcal{R}_{\mathrm{jump}}(e, \mathcal{X}) \subseteq \mathcal{X}_e$.*

Proof. Let $z \in R_{\mathrm{loc}}(q, \mathcal{X})$, then there exists $s \geq 0$ and a function $x(.)$ such that $x(s) = z$, $x(0) \in \mathcal{X}$ and for all $t \in [0, s]$, $\dot{x}(t) \in Ax(t) \oplus \mathcal{U}$ and $x(t) \in \mathcal{I}$. Let $i^* \in \mathbb{N}$ such that $s \in [i^*\tau, (i^* + 1)\tau]$. Let us remark that $s - i^*\tau \in [0, \tau]$, then from Lemma 1 and since $x(s - i^*\tau) \in \mathcal{I}$, it follows that $x(s - i^*\tau) \in \mathcal{Z}_0$. Let us show, by induction, that for all $i = 0, \ldots, i^*$, $x(s + (i - i^*)\tau) \in \mathcal{Z}_i$. This is true for $i = 0$; let us assume that it is true for some $i \leq i^* - 1$. Then, from Lemma 2 and since $x(s + (i + 1 - i^*)\tau) \in \mathcal{I}$, it follows that $x(s + (i + 1 - i^*)\tau) \in \mathcal{Z}_{i+1}$. Therefore, for all $i = 0, \ldots, i^*$, $x(s + (i - i^*)\tau) \in \mathcal{Z}_i$, which implies for $i = i^*$ that $z = x(s) \in \mathcal{Z}_{i^*} \subseteq \mathcal{R}$. The first part of the proposition is proved. It follows that $\mathcal{R}_{\mathrm{jump}}(e, \mathcal{X}) \subseteq (B_e(\mathcal{R} \cap G_e) \oplus \mathcal{V}_e) \subseteq \mathcal{X}_e$.   ∎

In the following, we discuss the implementation of the Algorithm 2 based on the notion of support functions.

4   Support Functions of Convex Sets

The support function of a convex set is a classical tool of convex analysis. Support functions can be used as a representation of arbitrary complex compact convex sets. In this section, we present some properties of support functions and show how they can be used for the computation of polyhedral over-approximations of convex sets. The results are stated without the proofs that can be found in several textbooks on convex analysis (see e.g. [11,12,13]).

Definition 1. *Let $S \subseteq \mathbb{R}^n$ be a compact convex set; the support function of S is $\rho_S : \mathbb{R}^n \to \mathbb{R}$ defined by $\rho_S(\ell) = \max_{x \in S} \ell \cdot x$.*

The notion of support function is illustrated in Figure 1.

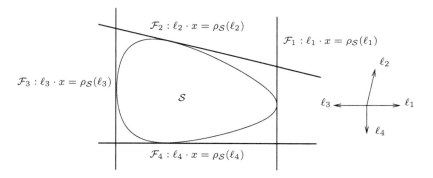

Fig. 1. Illustration of the notion of support function of a convex set S

4.1   Properties of Support Functions

It can be shown that the support function of a compact convex set is a convex function. For two compact convex sets, S and S', it is easy to see that $S \subseteq S'$ if and only if $\rho_S(\ell) \leq \rho_{S'}(\ell)$ for all $\ell \in \mathbb{R}^n$. It is to be noted that a compact convex set S is uniquely determined by its support function as the following equality holds:

$$S = \bigcap_{\ell \in \mathbb{R}^n} \{x \in \mathbb{R}^n : \ell \cdot x \leq \rho_S(\ell)\}.$$

From the previous equation, it is clear that a polyhedral over-approximation of a compact convex set can be obtained by "sampling" its support function:

Proposition 3. *Let S be a compact convex set and $\ell_1, \ldots, \ell_r \in \mathbb{R}^n$ be arbitrarily chosen vectors; let us define the following polyhedron:*

$$\overline{S} = \{x \in \mathbb{R}^n : \ell_k \cdot x \leq \rho_S(\ell_k), \ k = 1, \ldots, r\}.$$

Then, $S \subseteq \overline{S}$. Moreover, we say that this over-approximation is tight as S touches the faces $\mathcal{F}_1, \ldots, \mathcal{F}_r$ of $\overline{S}$.

An example of such polyhedral over-approximation of a convex set can be seen in Figure 1. The support function can be computed efficiently for a large class of compact convex sets. Let $\mathcal{B}_1$, $\mathcal{B}_2$, $\mathcal{B}_\infty$ denote the unit balls for the 1, 2 and ∞ norms. Then, $\rho_{\mathcal{B}_1}(\ell) = \|\ell\|_\infty$, $\rho_{\mathcal{B}_2}(\ell) = \|\ell\|_2$ and $\rho_{\mathcal{B}_\infty}(\ell) = \|\ell\|_1$. Let Q be a $n \times n$ positive definite symmetric matrix, then for the ellipsoid:

$$\mathcal{E} = \left\{ x \in \mathbb{R}^n : x^\top Q^{-1} x \leq 1 \right\}, \ \rho_{\mathcal{E}}(\ell) = \sqrt{\ell^\top Q \ell}.$$

Let $g_1, \ldots, g_r \in \mathbb{R}^n$, then for the zonotope:

$$\mathcal{Z} = \left\{ \alpha_1 g_1 + \cdots + \alpha_r g_r : \alpha_j \in [-1,1], \ j = 1, \ldots, r \right\}, \ \rho_{\mathcal{Z}}(\ell) = \sum_{j=1}^{r} |g_j \cdot \ell|.$$

Let $c_1, \ldots, c_r \in \mathbb{R}^n$ and $d_1, \ldots, d_r \in \mathbb{R}$, then for the polyhedron

$$\mathcal{P} = \left\{ x \in R^n : \ c_j \cdot x \leq d_j, \ j = 1, \ldots, r \right\},$$

$\rho_{\mathcal{P}}(\ell)$ can be determined by solving the linear program

$$\begin{cases} \text{maximize } \ell \cdot x \\ \text{subject to } c_j \cdot x \leq d_j, \ j = 1, \ldots, r \end{cases}$$

More complex sets can be considered using the following operations on elementary compact convex sets:

Proposition 4. *For all compact convex sets $\mathcal{S}$, $\mathcal{S}' \subseteq \mathbb{R}^n$, for all matrices M, all positive scalars λ, and all vectors ℓ of suitable dimension, the following assertions hold:*

$$\rho_{M\mathcal{S}}(\ell) = \rho_{\mathcal{S}}(M^\top \ell)$$
$$\rho_{\lambda\mathcal{S}}(\ell) = \rho_{\mathcal{S}}(\lambda \ell) = \lambda \rho_{\mathcal{S}}(\ell)$$
$$\rho_{\mathrm{CH}(\mathcal{S} \cup \mathcal{S}')}(\ell) = \max(\rho_{\mathcal{S}}(\ell), \rho_{\mathcal{S}'}(\ell))$$
$$\rho_{\mathcal{S} \oplus \mathcal{S}'}(\ell) = \rho_{\mathcal{S}}(\ell) + \rho_{\mathcal{S}'}(\ell)$$
$$\rho_{\mathcal{S} \cap \mathcal{S}'}(\ell) \leq \min \left(\rho_{\mathcal{S}}(\ell), \rho_{\mathcal{S}'}(\ell) \right)$$

Except for the last property, these relations are all exact. For the intersection, we only have an over-approximation relation. The inequality comes from the fact that the function $\min \left(\rho_{\mathcal{S}}(\ell), \rho_{\mathcal{S}'}(\ell) \right)$ may not be a convex function. An exact relation between $\rho_{\mathcal{S} \cap \mathcal{S}'}$, $\rho_{\mathcal{S}}$ and $\rho_{\mathcal{S}'}$ exists[1]; unfortunately, this relation is not effective from the computational point of view. Let us remark, though, that for a convex set $\mathcal{K}$, such that $\rho_{\mathcal{K}}(\ell) \leq \min \left(\rho_{\mathcal{S}}(\ell), \rho_{\mathcal{S}'}(\ell) \right)$, for all $\ell \in \mathbb{R}^n$, it follows that $\mathcal{K} \subseteq \mathcal{S}$ and $\mathcal{K} \subseteq \mathcal{S}'$, thus $\mathcal{K} \subseteq \mathcal{S} \cap \mathcal{S}'$.

We shall see, further in the paper, how the properties presented in this section allow us to compute an over-approximation of the set $\mathcal{R}_{\mathrm{loc}}(q, \mathcal{X})$, given as the union of convex polyhedrons.

---

[1] Indeed, it can be shown [13] that $\rho_{\mathcal{S} \cap \mathcal{S}'}(\ell) = \inf_{w \in \mathbb{R}^n} \left(\rho_{\mathcal{S}}(\ell - w) + \rho_{\mathcal{S}'}(w) \right)$.

4.2   Intersection of a Compact Convex Set and a Hyperplane

We now consider the problem of computing the support function of the inter-section of a compact convex set $\mathcal{S}$, given by its support function $\rho_{\mathcal{S}}$, and a hyperplane $\mathcal{G} = \{x \in \mathbb{R}^n : c \cdot x = d\}$ where $c \in \mathbb{R}^n$ and $d \in \mathbb{R}$. This will be use-ful to compute a polyhedral over-approximation of the intersection of $\mathcal{R}_{\text{loc}}(q, \mathcal{X})$ with a guard of the hybrid system given by a hyperplane. First of all, let us remark that checking whether $\mathcal{S} \cap \mathcal{G}$ is empty is an easy problem. Indeed, it is straightforward (see Figure 2) that $\mathcal{S} \cap \mathcal{G} \neq \emptyset$ if and only if $-\rho_{\mathcal{S}}(-c) \leq d \leq \rho_{\mathcal{S}}(c)$.

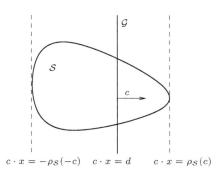

Fig. 2. Checking emptiness of $\mathcal{S} \cap \mathcal{G}$

In the following, we shall assume that $\mathcal{S} \cap \mathcal{G} \neq \emptyset$. Let $\ell \in \mathbb{R}^n$, we consider the problem of computing an accurate over-approximation of $\rho_{\mathcal{S} \cap \mathcal{G}}(\ell)$. The following result, adapted from [14], shows that the problem can be reduced to a two-dimensional problem by projecting on the subspace spanned by c and ℓ.

Proposition 5. *[14] Let $\Pi : \mathbb{R}^n \to \mathbb{R}^2$ be the projection operator defined by $\Pi x = (c \cdot x, \ell \cdot x)$. Then, $\rho_{\mathcal{S} \cap \mathcal{G}}(\ell) = \max\{y_2 \in \mathbb{R} : (d, y_2) \in \Pi\mathcal{S}\}$.*

Thus, the computation of $\rho_{\mathcal{S} \cap \mathcal{G}}(\ell)$ is reduced to a two dimensional optimization problem which essentially consists in computing the intersection of the two di-mensional compact convex set $\Pi\mathcal{S}$ with the line $\mathcal{D} = \{(y_1, y_2) \in \mathbb{R}^2 : y_1 = d\}$. We shall further reduce the problem. Let $\theta \in {]}0, \pi{[}$ and $v_\theta = (\cos\theta, \sin\theta)$, the equation of the line supporting $\Pi\mathcal{S}$ in the direction v_θ is $y_1 \cos\theta + y_2 \sin\theta = \rho_{\Pi\mathcal{S}}(v_\theta) = \rho_{\mathcal{S}}(\Pi^\top v_\theta)$. This line intersects the line $\mathcal{D}$ at the point of coordinates (y_1, y_2) with $y_1 = d$, $y_2 = (\rho_{\mathcal{S}}(\Pi^\top v_\theta) - d\cos\theta)/\sin\theta$, as shown on Figure 3. Then, let us define the function $f : {]}0, \pi{[} \to \mathbb{R}$ given by

$$f(\theta) = \frac{\rho_{\mathcal{S}}(\Pi^\top v_\theta) - d\cos\theta}{\sin\theta}.$$

It is easy to see that f is unimodal and that $\inf_{\theta \in {]}0,\pi{[}} f(\theta) = \sup\{y_2 \in \mathbb{R} : (d, y_2) \in \Pi\mathcal{S}\}$. Therefore, using a minimization algorithm for unimodal functions such as the golden section search algorithm [15], one can compute an accurate over-approximation of the minimal value of f and therefore of $\rho_{\mathcal{S} \cap \mathcal{G}}(\ell)$.

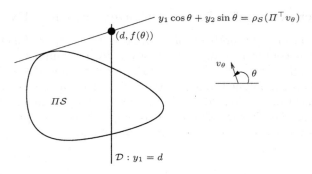

Fig. 3. Definition of the function $f(\theta)$

5 Support Functions Based Reachability Analysis

We now discuss effective reachability analysis in a location $q \in Q$ using support functions. For lighter notations, the index q has been dropped again. Let $\rho_{\mathcal{X}}$, $\rho_{\mathcal{U}}$, $\rho_{\mathcal{I}}$ denote the support functions of the sets $\mathcal{X}$, $\mathcal{U}$, $\mathcal{I}$; $\rho_{\mathcal{B}}$ denote the support function of the unit ball for the considered norm.

5.1 Over-Approximation of $\mathcal{R}_{\mathrm{loc}}(q, \mathcal{X})$

We first determine a union of convex polyhedrons over-approximating $\mathcal{R}_{\mathrm{loc}}(q, \mathcal{X})$.

Proposition 6. *Let $\mathcal{Z}_i$ be the sets defined in Algorithm 2, then*

$$\forall \ell \in \mathbb{R}^n, \ \rho_{\mathcal{Z}_i}(\ell) \le \min\left(\rho_{\mathcal{Y}_i}(\ell), \min_{k=0}^{i} \rho_{\mathcal{I}_k}(\ell) \right), \ \text{where}$$

$$\rho_{\mathcal{Y}_0}(\ell) = \max\left(\rho_{\mathcal{X}}(\ell), \rho_{\mathcal{X}}(e^{\tau A^\top}\ell) + \tau\rho_{\mathcal{U}}(\ell) + \alpha_\tau \rho_{\mathcal{B}}(\ell) \right),$$

$$\rho_{\mathcal{Y}_i}(\ell) = \rho_{\mathcal{Y}_0}(e^{i\tau A^\top}\ell) + \sum_{k=0}^{i-1}\left(\tau\rho_{\mathcal{U}}(e^{k\tau A^\top}\ell) + \beta_\tau \rho_{\mathcal{B}}(e^{k\tau A^\top}\ell) \right), \tag{3}$$

$$\rho_{\mathcal{I}_i}(\ell) = \rho_{\mathcal{I}}(e^{i\tau A^\top}\ell) + \sum_{k=0}^{i-1}\left(\tau\rho_{\mathcal{U}}(e^{k\tau A^\top}\ell) + \beta_\tau \rho_{\mathcal{B}}(e^{k\tau A^\top}\ell) \right). \tag{4}$$

Proof. For $i = 0$, by applying the rules of Proposition 4, it is straightforward to check that $\rho_{\mathcal{Z}_0}(\ell) \le \min(\rho_{\mathcal{Y}_0}(\ell), \rho_{\mathcal{I}_0}(\ell))$. Hence, the property holds for $i = 0$. Let us assume that it holds for some i, then by definition of $\mathcal{Z}_{i+1}$ and from Proposition 4, we have $\rho_{\mathcal{Z}_{i+1}}(\ell) \le \min(\rho_{\mathcal{Z}_i}(e^{\tau A^\top}\ell) + \tau\rho_{\mathcal{U}}(\ell) + \beta_\tau \rho_{\mathcal{B}}(\ell), \rho_{\mathcal{I}}(\ell))$. Then, by assumption

$$\rho_{\mathcal{Z}_i}(e^{\tau A^\top}\ell) + \tau\rho_{\mathcal{U}}(\ell) + \beta_\tau \rho_{\mathcal{B}}(\ell) \le$$
$$\min\left(\rho_{\mathcal{Y}_i}(e^{\tau A^\top}\ell) + \tau\rho_{\mathcal{U}}(\ell) + \beta_\tau \rho_{\mathcal{B}}(\ell), \ \min_{k=0}^{i} \rho_{\mathcal{I}_k}(e^{\tau A^\top}\ell) + \tau\rho_{\mathcal{U}}(\ell) + \beta_\tau \rho_{\mathcal{B}}(\ell) \right)$$

Further, by equation (3)

$$\rho_{\mathcal{Y}_i}(e^{\tau A^\top}\ell) = \rho_{\mathcal{Y}_0}(e^{(i+1)\tau A^\top}\ell) + \sum_{k=0}^{i-1}\left(\tau\rho_{\mathcal{U}}(e^{(k+1)\tau A^\top}\ell) + \beta_\tau\rho_{\mathcal{B}}(e^{(k+1)\tau A^\top}\ell)\right)$$

$$= \rho_{\mathcal{Y}_0}(e^{(i+1)\tau A^\top}\ell) + \sum_{k=1}^{i}\left(\tau\rho_{\mathcal{U}}(e^{k\tau A^\top}\ell) + \beta_\tau\rho_{\mathcal{B}}(e^{k\tau A^\top}\ell)\right).$$

Therefore, it follows that $\rho_{\mathcal{Y}_i}(e^{\tau A^\top}\ell) + \tau\rho_{\mathcal{U}}(\ell) + \beta_\tau\rho_{\mathcal{B}}(\ell) = \rho_{\mathcal{Y}_{i+1}}(\ell)$. Similarly, we can show from equation (4) that $\rho_{\mathcal{I}_k}(e^{\tau A^\top}\ell) + \tau\rho_{\mathcal{U}}(\ell) + \beta_\tau\rho_{\mathcal{B}}(\ell) = \rho_{\mathcal{I}_{k+1}}(\ell)$. This leads to

$$\rho_{\mathcal{Z}_i}(e^{\tau A^\top}\ell) + \tau\rho_{\mathcal{U}}(\ell) + \beta_\tau\rho_{\mathcal{B}}(\ell) \leq \min\left(\rho_{\mathcal{Y}_{i+1}}(\ell), \min_{k=0}^{i}\rho_{\mathcal{I}_{k+1}}(\ell)\right)$$

which implies that

$$\rho_{\mathcal{Z}_{i+1}}(\ell) \leq \min\left(\rho_{\mathcal{Y}_{i+1}}(\ell), \min_{k=0}^{i}\rho_{\mathcal{I}_{k+1}}(\ell), \rho_{\mathcal{I}}(\ell)\right) = \min\left(\rho_{\mathcal{Y}_{i+1}}(\ell), \min_{k=0}^{i+1}\rho_{\mathcal{I}_k}(\ell)\right)$$

Hence, by induction, the proposition is proved. ∎

It follows from the previous proposition that $\mathcal{Z}_i \subseteq \mathcal{Y}_i \cap \mathcal{I}_i \cap \cdots \cap \mathcal{I}_0$ where $\mathcal{Y}_i, \mathcal{I}_i, \ldots, \mathcal{I}_0$ are the convex sets determined by their support functions $\rho_{\mathcal{Y}_i}, \rho_{\mathcal{I}_i}, \ldots, \rho_{\mathcal{I}_0}$. Let us remark that the sets $\mathcal{Y}_i$ are actually the same than those in section 2 and thus give an over-approximation of the states reachable from $\mathcal{X}$ under the dynamics of the linear differential inclusion. The sets $\mathcal{I}_i, \ldots, \mathcal{I}_0$ allow us to take into account the constraint that the trajectories must remain in the invariant $\mathcal{I}$ during the evolution. We shall not discuss the efficient implementation of the evaluation of the support functions, this can be found for $\rho_{\mathcal{Y}_i}$, in [9]. A similar approach based on ideas from [7] can be used for the functions $\rho_{\mathcal{I}_i}, \ldots, \rho_{\mathcal{I}_0}$.

We can now compute polyhedral over-approximations $\overline{\mathcal{Z}}_i$ of the sets $\mathcal{Z}_i$ defined in Algorithm 2. Let $\ell_1, \ldots, \ell_r \in \mathbb{R}^n$ be a set of directions used for approximation. Let

$$\gamma_{i,j} = \min\left(\rho_{\mathcal{Y}_i}(\ell_j), \min_{k=0}^{i}\rho_{\mathcal{I}_k}(\ell_j)\right), \quad j = 1, \ldots r.$$

Then, it follows from Propositions 3 and 6 that

$$\mathcal{Z}_i \subseteq \overline{\mathcal{Z}}_i = \{x \in R^n : \ell_j \cdot x \leq \gamma_{i,j}, \ j = 1, \ldots, r\}.$$

Then, Proposition 2 leads to the following result:

Theorem 1. *Let $\overline{\mathcal{Z}}_i$ be the polyhedrons defined above, let $i^* \in \mathbb{N}$ be the smallest index such that $\overline{\mathcal{Z}}_{i^*} = \emptyset$. Then, $\mathcal{R}_{\mathrm{loc}}(q, \mathcal{X}) \subseteq \overline{\mathcal{Z}}_0 \cup \cdots \cup \overline{\mathcal{Z}}_{i^*-1}$.*

The choice of the vectors $\ell_1, \ldots, \ell_r \in \mathbb{R}^n$ is important for the quality of approximation. If the invariant is a polyhedron $\mathcal{I} = \{x \in \mathbb{R}^d : c_j \cdot x \leq d_j, \ j = 1, \ldots, m\}$

where $c_1, \ldots, c_m \in \mathbb{R}^n$ and $d_1, \ldots, d_m \in \mathbb{R}$, it is useful to include the vectors $c_1, \ldots, c_m$. This way, it is ensured that $\overline{Z}_0 \cup \cdots \cup \overline{Z}_{i^*-1} \subseteq \mathcal{I}$. Also, by considering vectors of the form $e^{-k\tau A^\top} c_1, \ldots, e^{-k\tau A^\top} c_m$, for some values of $k \in \{1, \ldots, i^* - 1\}$, the constraints imposed by the invariant on the reachable set at a given time step are also taken into account k time steps further.

5.2   Over-Approximation of $\mathcal{R}_{\mathrm{jump}}(e, \mathcal{X})$

Let $\mathcal{H}_e = \mathrm{CH}(\mathcal{R} \cap \mathcal{G}_e)$ be the set defined in Algorithm 2. Let us remark that $\mathcal{H}_e = \mathrm{CH}(\mathcal{H}_{e,0} \cup \cdots \cup \mathcal{H}_{e,i^*})$ where $\mathcal{H}_{e,i} = \mathcal{Z}_i \cap \mathcal{G}_e$.

Over-approximation of $\mathcal{H}_{e,i}$. If $\mathcal{G}_e$ is a compact convex set defined by its support function $\rho_{\mathcal{G}_e}$, let

$$\delta_{e,i,j} = \min\left(\rho_{\mathcal{G}_e}(\ell_j), \rho_{\mathcal{Y}_i}(\ell_j), \min_{k=0}^{i} \rho_{\mathcal{I}_k}(\ell_j) \right), \ j = 1, \ldots r.$$

Then, it follows from Propositions 3 and 6 that

$$\mathcal{H}_{e,i} \subseteq \overline{\mathcal{H}}_{e,i} = \{x \in R^n : \ell_j \cdot x \leq \delta_{e,i,j}, \ j = 1, \ldots, r\}.$$

If $\mathcal{G}_e$ is a hyperplane we can use the method presented in section 4.2 to compute a more accurate over-approximation of $\mathcal{H}_{e,i}$. First of all, let us remark that the over-approximation of the support function $\rho_{\mathcal{Z}_i}$ given by Proposition 6 is possibly non-convex. Then, it cannot be used to compute an over-approximation of $\rho_{\mathcal{Z}_i \cap \mathcal{G}_e}$ by the method explained in section 4.2 as the function to minimize might not be unimodal. However, from Proposition 6, it follows that

$$\mathcal{H}_{e,i} \subseteq (\mathcal{Y}_i \cap \mathcal{I}_0 \cap \cdots \cap \mathcal{I}_i) \cap \mathcal{G}_e = (\mathcal{Y}_i \cap \mathcal{G}_e) \cap (\mathcal{I}_0 \cap \mathcal{G}_e) \cap \cdots \cap (\mathcal{I}_i \cap \mathcal{G}_e). \quad (5)$$

We can check the emptiness of $\mathcal{Y}_i \cap \mathcal{G}_e$, $\mathcal{I}_0 \cap \mathcal{G}_e,\ldots, \mathcal{I}_i \cap \mathcal{G}_e$ using the simple test described in section 4.2. If one of these sets is empty, then $\mathcal{H}_{e,i} \subseteq \overline{\mathcal{H}}_{e,i} = \emptyset$. Otherwise, let

$$\delta_{e,i,j} = \min\left(\rho_{\mathcal{Y}_i \cap \mathcal{G}_e}(\ell_j), \min_{k=0}^{i} \rho_{\mathcal{I}_k \cap \mathcal{G}_e}(\ell_j) \right), \ j = 1, \ldots r$$

where the support functions $\rho_{\mathcal{Y}_i \cap \mathcal{G}_e}, \rho_{\mathcal{I}_0 \cap \mathcal{G}_e}, \ldots, \rho_{\mathcal{I}_i \cap \mathcal{G}_e}$ can be computed by the method explained in section 4.2. Then, from Proposition 3 and equation (5), it follows that

$$\mathcal{H}_{e,i} \subseteq \overline{\mathcal{H}}_{e,i} = \{x \in R^n : \ell_j \cdot x \leq \delta_{e,i,j}, \ j = 1, \ldots, r\}.$$

Over-approximation of $\mathcal{H}_e$. Let $\overline{\mathcal{H}}_{e,0} \ldots \overline{\mathcal{H}}_{e,i^*}$ be computed by one of the two methods described in the previous paragraph, let $I = \{i : \overline{\mathcal{H}}_{e,i} \neq \emptyset\}$. Let $\delta_{e,j} = \max_{i \in I} \delta_{e,i,j}$, then we have

$$\mathcal{H}_e \subseteq \mathrm{CH}(\overline{\mathcal{H}}_{e,0} \cup \cdots \cup \overline{\mathcal{H}}_{e,i^*}) \subseteq \overline{\mathcal{H}}_e = \{x \in R^n : \ell_j \cdot x \leq \delta_{e,j}, \ j = 1, \ldots, r\}.$$

Proposition 2 leads to the following result:

Theorem 2. *Let $\overline{\mathcal{H}}_e$ be the polyhedron defined above, let $\overline{\mathcal{X}}_e = C_e \overline{\mathcal{H}}_e \oplus \mathcal{V}_e$. Then, $\mathcal{R}_{\text{jump}}(e, \mathcal{X}) \subseteq \overline{\mathcal{X}}_e$.*

Let us remark that $\overline{\mathcal{X}}_e$ need not be effectively computed as it can be represented by its support function $\rho_{\overline{\mathcal{X}}_e}(\ell) = \rho_{\overline{\mathcal{H}}_e}(C_e^\top \ell) + \rho_{\mathcal{V}_e}(\ell)$.

6 Examples

In this section, we show the effectiveness of our approach on some examples. All computations were performed on a Pentium IV, 3.2 GHz with 1 GB RAM.

5-dimensional benchmark. We propose to evaluate the over-approximation due to our way of handling hybrid dynamics. For that purpose, we consider the 5-dimensional linear differential inclusion from [6]. This artificial system was generated from a block diagonal matrix and a random change of variables. The initial set $\mathcal{X}_0$ is a cube of side 0.05 centered at $(1, 0, 0, 0, 0)^\top$ and the set of inputs $\mathcal{U}$ is a ball of radius 0.01 centered at the origin.

By introducing a switching hyperplane, we artificially build a hybrid system that has the same set of reachable continuous states. The hybrid system has two locations 1 and 2 and one discrete transition $(1, 2)$. The continuous dynamics is the same in each location, given by the 5-dimensional linear differential inclusion. The invariants are $\mathcal{I}_1 = \{x \in \mathbb{R}^5 : c \cdot x \leq d\}$ where $c \in \mathbb{R}^5$ and $d \in \mathbb{R}$, and $\mathcal{I}_2 = \mathbb{R}^5$. The guard $\mathcal{G}_{(1,2)} = \{x \in \mathbb{R}^5 : c \cdot x = d\}$ and the reset map $R_{(1,2)}$ is the identity map. We assume that the initial location is 1. We computed the reachable sets of the linear differential inclusion and of the hybrid system over 800 time steps $\tau = 0.005$. Their projection on the first two continuous variables are shown in Figure 4, for two different choices of c and d.

We can see that hybrid dynamics introduces an additional over-approximation, especially for the second system where the reachable set intersects the guard almost tangentially. The accuracy can be improved in two ways, we can reduce the time step and we can consider more vectors for computing the polyhedral

Fig. 4. Reachable set of the hybrid system in the first (dark grey), and second (light grey) locations, and reachable set of the equivalent linear differential inclusion (in black)

over-approximations. However, as we use a convex hull over-approximation of the intersection of the reachable set in the first location with the guard (see Algorithm 2), we will not reach the accuracy of the reachable set of the linear differential inclusion.

Navigation benchmark. We now consider the navigation benchmark for hybrid systems verification proposed in [10]. It models an object moving in a plane, whose position and velocities are denoted $x(t)$ and $v(t)$. The plane is partitioned into cubes, each cube corresponds to one location of the hybrid system. At time t, a location q is active if $x(t)$ is in the associated cube; there, the object follows dynamically a desired velocity $v_q \in \mathbb{R}^2$. We use the instances NAV01 and NAV04 from [16]. We render the problem slightly more challenging by including an additional continuous input $u(t)$ modelling disturbances. In the location q, the four-dimensional continuous dynamics is given by

$$\dot{x}(t) = v(t), \ \dot{v}(t) = A(v(t) - v_q - u(t)), \ \|u(t)\|_2 \leq 0.1 \text{ where } A = \left(\begin{smallmatrix} -1.2 & 0.1 \\ 0.1 & -1.2 \end{smallmatrix}\right).$$

In Figure 5, we represented the projection of the reachable sets on the position variables as well as the partition of the plane and, in each cube of the partition the set of velocities $v_q \oplus 0.1\mathcal{B}$ in the associated location.

One can check in Figure 5(b) that the intersection of the over-approximation $\overline{\mathcal{Z}}_i$ of the reachable sets in one location with the guards does not coincide with the over-approximation $\overline{\mathcal{H}}_e$ of the intersection of the reachable set in one location with the guards. The latter is more accurate because of the use of the method presented in section 4.2 for computing the support function of the intersection of a convex set with a hyperplane.

In Figures 5(c) and 5(d), the support function of the intersection is sampled in 6 directions which results in $\overline{\mathcal{H}}_e$ defined as an interval hull. We need to add 12 sampling directions to get an octagon, used in Figures 5(a) and 5(b). The benefit of using more sampling directions for approximation is clearly seen for NAV04 where the reachable set appears to be actually much smaller in Figure 5(b) than in Figure 5(d). However, the support function of an interval hull can be computed very efficiently whereas the support function of an octagon requires solving a linear program. This explains the huge differences in execution times reported in Table 1.

Table 1 also contains time and memory used by the optimized tool PHAVer on a similar computer as reported in [16]. One should be careful when comparing these results. On one hand the navigation problem we consider here is more challenging than the original one since we add disturbances on the input. These disturbances add, in several locations, chattering effects that cannot occur without them, and produces larger reachable sets. On the other hand PHAVer uses exact arithmetic.

We believe that the performances of our algorithm can be significantly improved. First of all, our algorithm is slowed down due to an inefficient interface between our reachability algorithm and the LP solver used to evaluate support functions. Also, there is a lot of room for improvements in the implementation. A first improvement would be to initialize the LP solver with the last computed

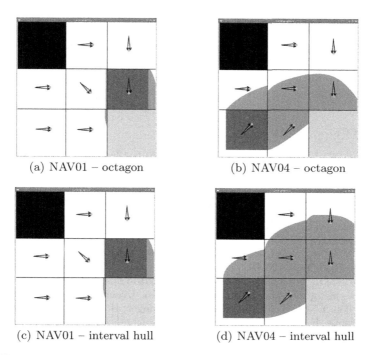

(a) NAV01 – octagon   (b) NAV04 – octagon

(c) NAV01 – interval hull   (d) NAV04 – interval hull

Fig. 5. Two navigation benchmarks with perturbations. In (a) and (b) the intersections with the guards are over-approximated by octagons, whereas in (c) and (d) they are over-approximated by their interval hulls. Dark grey: initial set. Grey: reachable sets. Light grey: Target State. Black: Forbidden State.

Table 1. Time and memory needed for reachability analysis of NAV01 and NAV04

	NAV01		NAV04	
	time (s)	memory (MB)	time (s)	memory (MB)
octagon	10.28	0.24	54.77	0.47
interval hull	0.11	0.24	0.88	0.47
PHAVer	8.7	29.0	13.6	47.6

optimizer, because ℓ and $e^{\tau A^{\top}}\ell$ are almost the same. Another improvement would be to over-approximate the intersections with the guards by several sets whose support function have growing complexity in order to avoid calling the LP solver as much as possible.

7   Conclusion

In this paper we presented a new method for conservative reachability analysis of a class of hybrid systems. The use of support functions allows us to consider a wide class of input sets, invariants, and guards. For the special case of guards defined by hyperplanes we showed how to transform the problem of intersecting the reachable set with a guard to the minimization of a unimodal function. Our algorithms have been implemented in a prototype tool that shows promising results on non-trivial examples. There is still a lot of room for improvements, future work should focus on the choice of the directions of approximation and LP optimizations.

References

1. Chutinan, A., Krogh, B.: Verification of polyhedral-invariant hybrid automata using polygonal flow pipe approximations. In: Vaandrager, F.W., van Schuppen, J.H. (eds.) HSCC 1999. LNCS, vol. 1569, pp. 76–90. Springer, Heidelberg (1999)
2. Asarin, E., Dang, T., Maler, O., Bournez, O.: Approximate reachability analysis of piecewise-linear dynamical systems. In: Lynch, N.A., Krogh, B.H. (eds.) HSCC 2000. LNCS, vol. 1790, pp. 20–31. Springer, Heidelberg (2000)
3. Kurzhanski, A., Varaiya, P.: Ellipsoidal techniques for reachability analysis. In: Lynch, N.A., Krogh, B.H. (eds.) HSCC 2000. LNCS, vol. 1790, pp. 202–214. Springer, Heidelberg (2000)
4. Botchkarev, O., Tripakis, S.: Verification of hybrid systems with linear differential inclusions using ellipsoidal approximations. In: Lynch, N.A., Krogh, B.H. (eds.) HSCC 2000. LNCS, vol. 1790, pp. 73–88. Springer, Heidelberg (2000)
5. Stursberg, O., Krogh, B.: Efficient representation and computation of reachable sets for hybrid systems. In: Maler, O., Pnueli, A. (eds.) HSCC 2003. LNCS, vol. 2623, pp. 482–497. Springer, Heidelberg (2003)
6. Girard, A.: Reachability of uncertain linear systems using zonotopes. In: Morari, M., Thiele, L. (eds.) HSCC 2005. LNCS, vol. 3414, pp. 291–305. Springer, Heidelberg (2005)
7. Girard, A., Le Guernic, C., Maler, O.: Efficient computation of reachable sets of linear time-invariant systems with inputs. In: Hespanha, J.P., Tiwari, A. (eds.) HSCC 2006. LNCS, vol. 3927, pp. 257–271. Springer, Heidelberg (2006)
8. Varaiya, P.: Reach set computation using optimal control. In: Proc. KIT Workshop on Verification of Hybrid Systems, Grenoble (1998)
9. Le Guernic, C., Girard, A.: Reachability analysis of linear systems using support functions. Nonlinear Analysis: Hybrid Systems (2009) (to appear)
10. Fehnker, A., Ivancic, F.: Benchmarks for hybrid systems verification. In: Alur, R., Pappas, G.J. (eds.) HSCC 2004. LNCS, vol. 2993, pp. 326–341. Springer, Heidelberg (2004)
11. Bertsekas, D., Nedic, A., Ozdaglar, A.: Convex analysis and optimization. Athena Scientific (2003)
12. Boyd, S., Vandenberghe, L.: Convex optimization. Cambridge University Press, Cambridge (2004)
13. Rockafellar, R., Wets, R.: Variational analysis. Springer, Heidelberg (1998)
14. Girard, A., Le Guernic, C.: Zonotope/hyperplane intersection for hybrid systems reachability analysis. In: Egerstedt, M., Mishra, B. (eds.) HSCC 2008. LNCS, vol. 4981, pp. 215–228. Springer, Heidelberg (2008)
15. Kiefer, J.: Sequential minimax search for a maximum. Proceedings of the American Mathematical Society 4, 502–506 (1953)
16. Frehse, G.: PHAVer: algorithmic verification of hybrid systems past HyTech. Int. J. on Software Tools for Technology Transfer 10(3), 263–279 (2008)

Reducing Test Inputs
Using Information Partitions*

Rupak Majumdar and Ru-Gang Xu

Department of Computer Science, University of California, Los Angeles
{rupak,rxu}@cs.ucla.edu

Abstract. Automatic symbolic techniques to generate test inputs, for example, through concolic execution, suffer from *path explosion*: the number of paths to be symbolically solved for grows exponentially with the number of inputs. In many applications though, the inputs can be partitioned into "non-interfering" blocks such that symbolically solving for each input block while keeping all other blocks fixed to concrete values can find the same set of assertion violations as symbolically solving for the entire input. This can greatly reduce the number of paths to be solved (in the best case, from exponentially many to linearly many in the number of inputs). We present an algorithm that combines test input generation by concolic execution with dynamic computation and maintenance of information flow between inputs. Our algorithm iteratively constructs a partition of the inputs, starting with the finest (all inputs separate) and merging blocks if a dependency is detected between variables in distinct input blocks during test generation. Instead of exploring all paths of the program, our algorithm separately explores paths for each block (while fixing variables in other blocks to random values). In the end, the algorithm outputs an input partition and a set of test inputs such that (a) inputs in different blocks do not have any dependencies between them, and (b) the set of tests provides equivalent coverage with respect to finding assertion violations as full concolic execution. We have implemented our algorithm in the Splat test generation tool. We demonstrate that our reduction is effective by generating tests for four examples in packet processing and operating system code.

1 Introduction

Automatic test case generation using symbolic execution and constraint solving has recently regained prominence as a comprehensive technique for generating all paths in a program with a bounded input [4,8,15]. In practice though, these techniques suffer from *path explosion*: the number of paths to be explored can increase exponentially with the number of inputs. This is particularly cumbersome for programs which manipulate data structures such as arrays. While compositional techniques [7,1] alleviate path explosion, full path coverage remains problematic

---

* This research was sponsored in part by the NSF grants CCF-0546170, CCF-0702743, and CNS-0720881, and a gift from Intel.

A. Bouajjani and O. Maler (Eds.): CAV 2009, LNCS 5643, pp. 555–569, 2009.

```
void test(int a₁, int a₂,        00 void free(int A[], int count[]) {
         ...,                     01   for (int i = 0; i < N; i++) {
         int aₙ) {               02     old_count[i] = count[i];
1:      if (a₁ = 0) a₁ := 1;     03   }
2:      if (a₂ = 0) a₂ := 1;     04   for (int i = 0; i < N; i++) {
        ...                       05     if (A[i] != 0)
n:      if (aₙ = 0) aₙ := 1;     06       count[i]++;
                                  07   }
n+1: if (a₁ = 0) error();        08   for (int i = 0; i < N; i++) {
n+2: if (a₂ = 0) error();        09     if (A[i] != 0)
        ...                       10       assert(count[i]==old_count[i]+1);
2n:     if (aₙ = 0) error();     11   }
}                                 12 }
```

Fig. 1. Examples with many independent inputs: (a) Example `test` (b) Example `free`

even for medium-sized applications within a reasonable testing budget, say, one night.

In this paper, we develop a technique that exploits the *independence* between different parts of the program input to reduce the number of paths needed to be explored during test generation. As a simple example, consider the function `test` shown in Figure 1(a). While there are 2^n syntactic paths through the code, we quickly recognize that it is sufficient to check only $2 \cdot n$ paths: two each for each of the inputs $a_1, a_2, \ldots, a_n$ being zero or non-zero. In particular, we conclude that `error()` is not reachable based only on these paths. The additional paths through the program do not add any more "interesting" behaviors, as the inputs are *non-interfering*: there is no data or control dependency between any two distinct inputs a_i, a_j for $i \neq j$. This indicates that by generating tests one independent input at a time (while holding the other inputs to fixed values), we can eliminate the combinational explosion of testing every arrangement of inputs, in this case, from an exponential number of paths (2^n for n inputs) to a linear number ($2 \cdot n$), while retaining all interesting program behaviors (e.g., behaviors that can cause assertion violations or behaviors that lead to an error). While the above example is artificial, there are many interesting examples where the input space can be partitioned into independent and non-interfering components, either through the application semantics (e.g., blocks in a file system, packet headers in network processors, permission-table entries in memory protection schemes) or due to security and privacy reasons (e.g., independent requests to a server).

We present an automatic test generation algorithm FlowTest that formalizes and exploits the independence among inputs. FlowTest is based on *concolic execution* [7,15] which explores executable paths of an input program using simultaneous concrete random simulation and symbolic execution. In contrast to the basic concolic execution algorithm, the main idea of FlowTest is to compute control and data dependencies among variables dynamically while performing concolic execution, and to use these dependencies to keep independent variables separated during test generation. FlowTest maintains a partitioning of the program inputs (where two variables in different blocks are assumed not to interfere), and generates tests by symbolically treating variables in each block in isolation while holding variables in other blocks to fixed values.

In case the partition does denote non-interfering sets of variables, and all program executions terminate, the test generation is relatively sound: any assertion violation detected by basic concolic execution is detected. To check for data or control dependencies between variables in separate blocks, FlowTest maintains a *flow map* during test generation which associates each variable with the set of input blocks in the current partition which can potentially influence the value of the variable. If there is some entry in the flow map which contains more than one input block, this indicates "information flow" between these input blocks. In this case, these input blocks are merged and test generation is repeated by tracking this larger block of inputs together.

The algorithm terminates when the input partitions do not change (and tests have been generated relative to this input partition). For example test, starting with the initial optimistic partition in which each variable is in a separate partition, FlowTest will deduce that this partition is non-interfering, and generate test cases that explore the $2n$ interesting paths. In contrast, concolic execution explores 2^n paths.

We have implemented FlowTest on top of the Splat directed testing implementation [18] to test and check information flow in C programs. The benefit of FlowTest is demonstrated on a memory allocator, a memory protection scheme, an intrusion detector module and a packet printer. FlowTest dramatically reduces the number of paths explored for all case studies without increasing much overhead per path due to flow-set generation and dependency checking. In all cases, FlowTest reduced the overall time for input generation and the number of paths generated. In two cases, FlowTest cut input generation in half. In one case, FlowTest terminated in less than ten minutes when the basic concolic execution algorithm failed to terminate even after a day.

Related Work. Test generation using concolic execution has been successfully applied to several large programs [8,15,4,18,3]. However, path explosion has been a fundamental barrier. Several optimizations have been proposed to prune redundant paths, such as function summarization [7,1] and the pruning of paths that have the same side-effects of some previously explored path through read-write sets (RWSets) [2]. FlowTest is an optimization orthogonal to both function summarization and RWSets.

Program slicing has been used to improve the effectiveness of testing and static analysis by removing irrelevant parts of the program [17,16,10,11]. One way to view FlowTest is as simultaneous path exploration by concolic execution and dynamic slicing across test runs: for each input block, the algorithm creates dynamic slices over every run, and merges input blocks that have common data or control dependencies. In contrast to running test generation on statically computed slices, our technique, by computing slices dynamically and on executable traces, can be more precise.

Our optimization based on control and data dependencies is similar to checking information flow [5,6,12]. For example, dynamic information flow checkers [5,12] are based on similar dependency analyzes.

2   Preliminary Definitions

We illustrate our algorithm on a simple imperative language with integer-valued variables while our implementation handles more general features such as pointers and function calls. We represent programs as *control flow graphs (CFG)* $P = (X, X_0, \mathcal{L}, \ell_0, op, E)$ consisting of (1) a set of variables X, with a subset $X_0 \subseteq X$ of *input* variables, (2) a set of control locations (or program counters) $\mathcal{L}$ which include a special start location $\ell_0 \in \mathcal{L}$, (3) a function op labeling each location $\ell \in \mathcal{L}$ with one of the following basic operations:

1. a termination statement halt,
2. an assignment $x := e$, where $x \in X$ and e is an arithmetic expression over X,
3. a conditional **if**(x)**then** ℓ' **else** ℓ'', where $x \in X$ and ℓ', ℓ'' are locations in $\mathcal{L}$,

and (4) a set of directed edges $E \subseteq \mathcal{L} \times \mathcal{L}$ defined as follows. The set of edges E is the smallest set such that (1) every node ℓ where $op(\ell)$ is an assignment statement has exactly one node ℓ' with $(\ell, \ell') \in E$, and (2) every node ℓ such that $op(\ell)$ is **if**(x)**then** ℓ' **else** ℓ'' has two edges (ℓ, ℓ') and (ℓ, ℓ'') in E. For a location $\ell \in \mathcal{L}$ where $op(\ell)$ is an assignment operation, we write $N(\ell)$ for its unique neighbor.

Thus, the locations of a CFG correspond to program locations with associated commands, and edges correspond to control flow from one operation to the next. We assume that there is exactly one node ℓ_{halt} in the CFG with $op(\ell_{\mathsf{halt}}) = \mathsf{halt}$. A *path* is a sequence of locations $\ell^1, \ell^2 \dots \ell^n$ in the CFG. A location $\ell \in \mathcal{L}$ is reachable from $\ell' \in \mathcal{L}$ if there is a path $\ell' \dots \ell$ in the CFG. We assume that every node in $\mathcal{L}$ is reachable from ℓ_0 and ℓ_{halt} is reachable from every node.

Semantics. The concrete semantics of the program is given using a *memory* that maps variables in X to values. For a memory M, we write $M[x \mapsto v]$ for the memory mapping x to v and every other variable $y \in X \setminus \{x\}$ to $M(y)$. For an expression e, we denote by $M(e)$ the value obtained by evaluating e where each variable x occurring in e is replaced by the value $M(x)$.

Execution starts from a memory M_0 containing initial values for input variables in X_0 and constant default values for variables in $X \setminus X_0$, at the entry location ℓ_0. Each operation updates the memory and the control location. Suppose the current location is ℓ and the current memory is M. If $op(\ell)$ is $x := e$, then the new location is $N(\ell)$ and the new memory is $M[x \mapsto M(e)]$. If $op(\ell)$ is **if**(x)**then** ℓ' **else** ℓ'' and $M(x) = 0$, then the new location is ℓ'' and the new memory is again M. On the other hand, if $M(x) \neq 0$ then the new location is ℓ' and the new memory remains M. If $op(\ell)$ is halt, the program terminates.

Execution of the program starting from a memory M_0 defines a path in the CFG in a natural way. A path is executable if it is the path corresponding to program execution from some initial memory M_0.

Symbolic and Concolic Execution. We shall also evaluate programs *symbolically*. Symbolic execution is performed using a *symbolic memory* μ, which maps variables in X to symbolic expressions over a set of symbolic constants, and a *path constraint* ξ, which collects predicates over symbolic constants along the execution path. Execution proceeds as in the concrete case, starting at ℓ_0 with an initial symbolic memory μ which maps each variable x in X_0 to a fresh symbolic constant α_x and each variable $y \in X \setminus X_0$ to some default constant value, and the path constraint *true*. For an assignment $x := e$, the symbolic memory μ is updated to $\mu[x \mapsto \mu(e)]$, where $\mu(e)$ denotes the symbolic expression obtained by evaluating e using μ and $\mu[x \mapsto v]$ denotes the symbolic memory that updates μ by setting x to v. The control location is updated to $N(\ell)$. For a conditional **if**(x)**then** ℓ' **else** ℓ'', there is a choice in updating the control location. If the new control location is chosen to be ℓ', the path constraint is updated to $\xi \wedge \mu(x) \neq 0$, and if the new control location is chosen to be ℓ'', the path constraint is updated to $\xi \wedge \mu(x) = 0$. In each case, the new symbolic memory is still μ. Symbolic execution terminates at halt.

For each execution path, every satisfying assignment to the path constraint ξ gives values to the input variables in X_0 that guarantee the concrete execution proceeds along this path. *Concolic execution* [8,15] is a variant on symbolic execution in which the program is run simultaneously with concrete and symbolic values.

Partitions. A *partition* $\Pi(X)$ of a set X is a set of pairwise disjoint subsets of X such that $X = \bigcup_{Y \in \Pi(X)} Y$. We call each subset in a partition a *block* of the partition. For a variable $x \in X$, we denote by $\Pi(X)[x]$ the block of $\Pi(X)$ that contains x.

Given a partition $\Pi(X)$ and a subset $Y \subseteq \Pi(X)$ of blocks in $\Pi(X)$, the partition $\mathsf{Merge}(\Pi(X), Y)$ obtained by merging blocks in Y is defined as $(\Pi(X) \setminus Y) \cup \{\cup_{b \in Y} b\}$.

A partition $\Pi(X)$ *refines* a partition $\Pi'(X)$ if every block in $\Pi'(X)$ is a union of blocks in $\Pi(X)$. In this case we say $\Pi'(X)$ is *as coarse as* $\Pi(X)$. If $\Pi'(X)$ is as coarse as $\Pi(X)$ but $\Pi'(X) \neq \Pi(X)$, we say $\Pi'(X)$ is coarser than $\Pi(X)$. When the set X is clear from the context, we simply write Π.

Control and Data Dependence. For two locations $\ell, \ell' \in \mathcal{L}$ we say ℓ' *post-dominates* ℓ if every path from ℓ to ℓ_{halt} contains ℓ'. We say ℓ' is the *immediate post-dominator* of ℓ, written $\ell' = idom(\ell)$, if (1) $\ell' \neq \ell$, (2) ℓ' post-dominates ℓ, and (3) every ℓ'' that post-dominates ℓ is also a post-dominator of ℓ'. It is known that every location has a unique immediate post-dominator [13], and hence the function $idom(\ell)$ is well-defined for every $\ell \neq \ell_{\mathsf{halt}}$.

A node ℓ is *control dependent* on ℓ' if there exists some executable path $\ell_0 \ldots \ell' \ldots \ell$ such that $idom(\ell')$ does not appear between ℓ' and ℓ in the path.

Algorithm 1. FlowTest

Input: Program P, initial partition $\Pi_0(X)$

1 **local** partitions Π and Π_{old} of X ;
2 **local** flow map $flow$;
3 $\Pi := \Pi_0(X)$;
4 $\Pi_{old} := \emptyset$;
5 $flow(x) := \{\Pi[x]\}$ for $x \in X$;
6 **while** $\Pi_{old} \neq \Pi$ **do**
7         $\Pi_{old} := \Pi$;
8   **for** $I \in \Pi_{old}$ **do**
9                $input := \lambda x \in X_0.random()$;
10               $flow := \mathsf{Generate}(P, \Pi, I, flow, input, -1)$;
11   **end**
12   **for** *each* $x \in X$ **do**
13               $\Pi := \mathsf{Merge}(\Pi, flow(x))$;
14   **end**
15 **end**

For an expression e, we write $\mathsf{Use}(e)$ for the set of variables in X occurring in e. For variables $x, y \in X$, we say x is *data dependent* on y if there is some executable path to a location ℓ such that $op(\ell)$ is $x := e$ and $y \in \mathsf{Use}(e)$.

3   The FlowTest Algorithm

Overall Algorithm. Algorithm 1 shows the overall FlowTest algorithm. It takes as input a program P and an initial partition $\Pi_0(X)$ of the set X of variables, and applies test generation with iterative merging of partitions. It maintains a "current" partition Π of the inputs, which is updated based on control and data dependence information accrued by test generation. The "old" partition Π_{old} is used to check when a round of test generation does not change the partition. Initially, Π is the input partition $\Pi_0(X)$, and Π_{old} is the empty-set (lines 3, 4).

The main data structure to store dependency information is called a *flow map*, $flow : X \to 2^\Pi$, a function mapping each variable $x \in X$ to a set of blocks of the current partition Π. Intuitively, $flow(x)$ denotes the set of input blocks that are known to influence (through data or control dependence) the value of x. Initially, we set $flow(x) = \{\Pi[x]\}$ for each $x \in X$ (line 5).

The main loop (lines 6–14) implements test generation and iterative merging of partitions. The procedure Generate (described next) implements a standard path exploration algorithm using concolic execution, but additionally updates the flow map. Generate is called to generate tests for each block I of the current partition Π (lines 8–11). In each call, the variables in the block I are treated symbolically, and every other variable is given a fixed, random initial value. Generate returns an updated flow map which is used to merge blocks in Π to get an updated partition (lines 12–14). For every $x \in X$ such that $|flow(x)| > 1$, the blocks in $flow(x)$ are merged into one block to get a new coarser partition. The main loop is repeated with this coarser partition until there is no change.

Algorithm 2. Generate

Input: Program P, partition Π, block $I \in \Pi$, flow map *flow*
Input: input *input*, last explored branch *last*
1 $(\xi, \mathit{flow}) := \mathsf{Execute}(P, \Pi, I, \mathit{flow}, \mathit{input})$;
2 *index* := $\mathsf{Length}(\xi) - 1$;
3 **while not empty**$(\xi) \wedge \mathit{index} \neq \mathit{last}$ **do**
4        $p := \mathbf{pop}(\xi)$;
5   **if** $\xi \wedge \neg p$ *is satisfiable* **then**
6   *input* := $\mathsf{Solve}(\xi, \neg p)$;
7   *flow* := $\mathsf{Generate}(P, \Pi, I, \mathit{flow}, \mathit{input}, \mathit{index})$;
8   *index* := *index* − 1;
9 **end**
10 **return** *flow*;

Algorithm Generate. Algorithm 2 describes the path enumeration algorithm, and is similar to the path enumeration schemes in [8,15,4]. It takes as input the program P, a partition Π of the inputs of P, a block I of the partition, an input *input* mapping input variables to initial values, and an index *last* tracking the last visited branch. It performs test case generation using a depth first traversal of the program paths using concolic execution. In the concolic execution, only inputs from I are treated symbolically and the rest of the inputs are set to fixed concrete values (chosen randomly). The procedure returns an updated flow map.

The main loop of Algorithm Generate implements a recursive traversal of program paths. In each call to Generate, the function Execute (described next) is used to perform concolic execution along a single path and update the flow map. The returned path constraint ξ is used to generate a sequence of new inputs in the loop (lines 3–9). This is done by popping and negating the last constraint in the path constraint and generating a new input using procedure Solve. The new input causes the program to explore a new path: one that differs from the last one in the direction of the last conditional branch. The function Generate is recursively invoked to explore paths using this new input (line 7).

Notice that the pure concolic execution algorithm, from e.g., [8], is captured by the call $\mathsf{Generate}(P, \{X\}, X, \lambda x.\{X\}, \lambda x.0, -1)$.

Algorithm Execute. Algorithm 3 describes the procedure for performing concolic execution and computing data and control dependencies along a single program path. It takes as input the program P, a concrete input i, and a partition Π. It returns a path constraint ξ and an updated flow map *flow*. Notice that the path constraint is maintained as a stack of predicates (instead of as a conjunction of predicates). This helps in simplifying the backtracking search in Generate.

Algorithm Execute, ignoring lines 10, 11, 16, 17, 20 and 21, is identical to the concolic execution algorithm [8,15]. It executes the program using both the concrete memory M and the symbolic memory μ. The extra lines update the flow map.

Algorithm 3. Execute

Input: Program P, partition Π, block $I \in \Pi$, flow map $flow$, input i
Result: Path constraint ξ and updated flow map $flow$

1 **for** $x \in X$ **do**
2 | $M(x) := i(x)$; **if** $x \in I$ **then** $\mu(x) := \alpha_x$;
3 **end**
4 $\xi :=$ **emptyStack**; $\ell := \ell_0$;
5 $\mathsf{Ctrl}(\ell_0) := \emptyset$;
6 **while** $op(\ell) \neq$ halt **do**
7 | **switch** $op(\ell)$ **do**
8 | | **case** $l := e$
9 | | | $M := M[l \mapsto M(e)]$; $\mu := \mu[l \mapsto \mu(e)]$; $\ell := N(\ell)$;
10 | | | $\mathsf{Ctrl}(N(\ell)) := \mathsf{Ctrl}(\ell) \setminus \mathsf{RmCtrl}(\mathsf{Ctrl}(\ell), N(\ell))$;
11 | | | $flow(l) := flow(l) \cup \bigcup_{x \in \mathsf{Use}(e)} flow(x) \cup \bigcup_{\langle \ell', x' \rangle \in \mathsf{Ctrl}(N(\ell))} flow(x')$;
12 | | **end**
13 | | **case** **if**(x)**then** ℓ' **else** ℓ''
14 | | | **if** $M(x) = 0$ **then**
15 | | | | $\xi :=$ **push**$(\mu(x) = 0, \xi)$; $\ell := \ell''$;
16 | | | | $\mathsf{Ctrl}(\ell'') := (\mathsf{Ctrl}(\ell) \cup \{\langle \ell, x \rangle\}) \setminus \mathsf{RmCtrl}(\mathsf{Ctrl}(\ell) \cup \{\langle \ell, x \rangle\}, \ell'')$;
17 | | | | $flow(x) := flow(x) \cup \bigcup_{\langle \hat{\ell}, y \rangle \in \mathsf{Ctrl}(\ell'')} flow(y)$;
18 | | | **else**
19 | | | | $\xi :=$ **push**$(\mu(x) \neq 0, \xi)$; $\ell := \ell'$;
20 | | | | $\mathsf{Ctrl}(\ell') := (\mathsf{Ctrl}(\ell) \cup \{\langle \ell, x \rangle\}) \setminus \mathsf{RmCtrl}(\mathsf{Ctrl}(\ell) \cup \{\langle \ell, x \rangle\}, \ell')$;
21 | | | | $flow(x) := flow(x) \cup \bigcup_{\langle \hat{\ell}, y \rangle \in \mathsf{Ctrl}(\ell')} flow(y)$;
22 | | |
23 | | **end**
24 | **end**
25 **end**
26 **return**$(\xi, flow)$;

We now describe the working of Algorithm Execute. The concrete memory is initialized with the concrete input i, and the symbolic memory is initialized with a fresh symbolic constant α_x for each $x \in I$ (lines 1–3). The path constraint is initialized to the empty stack and the initial control location is ℓ_0 (line 4).

The main loop of Execute (lines 6–25) performs concrete and symbolic evaluation of the program while updating the flow map. The loop executes while the program has not terminated (or, in practice, until some resource bound such as the number of steps has been exhausted).

We first ignore the update of the flow map and describe how the concrete and symbolic memories and the path constraint are updated in each iteration.

If the current location is ℓ and the current operation is an assignment $l := e$ (lines 8–12), the concrete memory updates the value of l to $M(e)$ and the symbolic memory updates it to $\mu(e)$ (line 9). Finally, the control location is updated to be $N(\ell)$.

If the current location is ℓ and the current operation is **if**(x) **then** ℓ' **else** ℓ'', the updates are performed as follows (lines 13–23). The concrete memory M

and symbolic memory μ remain unchanged. If $M(x) \neq 0$, then the constraint $\mu(x) \neq 0$ is pushed on to the path constraint stack ξ, and the new control location is ℓ' (line 19). If $M(x) = 0$, then the constraint $\mu(x) = 0$ is pushed on to the path constraint stack ξ, and the new control location is ℓ'' (line 15).

We now describe how the control dependencies and the flow maps are updated. We use a helper data structure Ctrl mapping each location to a set of pairs of locations and expressions. This data structure is used to maintain the set of conditionals on which a location is control dependent along the current execution. At the initial location ℓ_0, we set $\mathsf{Ctrl}(\ell_0) = \emptyset$ (line 5). Each statement updates the set Ctrl. We use the following definition. Let $L \subseteq \mathcal{L} \times X$ be a set of pairs of locations and variables. Let $\ell \in \mathcal{L}$. We define $\mathsf{RmCtrl}(L, \ell) = \{\langle \ell', x \rangle \in L \mid \ell \text{ is the immediate post-dominator of } \ell'\}$. Intuitively, these are the set of conditionals that on which ℓ is no longer control dependent.

Suppose the current location is ℓ and $op(\ell)$ is the assignment $l := e$. The set $\mathsf{Ctrl}(N(\ell))$ consists of the set $\mathsf{Ctrl}(\ell)$ minus the set of all locations which are immediate post-dominated by $N(\ell)$ (line 10). The flow map for the variable l is updated as follows (see line 11). There are three components in the update. The first component is $flow(l)$, the flow computed so far. The second component $\bigcup_{x \in \mathsf{Use}(e)} flow(x)$ captures data dependencies on l due to the assignment $l := e$: for each variable x appearing in e, it adds every input block known to influence x (the set $flow(x)$) to $flow(l)$. The third component captures dependencies from controlling conditionals. The controlling conditionals for $N(\ell)$ and their conditional variables are stored in $\mathsf{Ctrl}(N(\ell))$. For every $\langle \ell', x' \rangle \in \mathsf{Ctrl}(N(\ell))$, we add the set $flow(x')$ of inputs known to influence x' to $flow(l)$.

Now suppose the current location is ℓ and $op(\ell)$ is $\mathbf{if}(x)$ $\mathbf{then}$ ℓ' $\mathbf{else}$ ℓ''. In this case, depending on the evaluation of the conditional x, the execution goes to ℓ' or ℓ'' and the corresponding data structure $\mathsf{Ctrl}(\ell')$ or $\mathsf{Ctrl}(\ell'')$ is updated to reflect dependence on the conditional x (lines 16, 20). The pair $\langle \ell, x \rangle$ is added to the set of controllers to indicate that the conditional may control execution to ℓ' and ℓ'', and as before, the set of conditionals post-dominated by ℓ' (respectively, ℓ'') are removed. Finally, for each $\langle \hat{\ell}, y \rangle$ in $\mathsf{Ctrl}(\ell')$ (respectively, $\mathsf{Ctrl}(\ell'')$), the set of input blocks $flow(y)$ is added to the flow map for x.

The updated flow map is returned at the end of the loop.

Algorithm solve. Finally, procedure solve takes as input a stack of constraints ξ and a predicate p, and returns a satisfying assignment of the formula

$$\bigwedge_{\phi \in \xi} \phi \wedge p$$

using a decision procedure for the constraint language. In the following, we assume that the decision procedure is *complete*: it always finds a satisfying assignment if the formula is satisfiable.

Relative Soundness. As we have seen, FlowTest can end up exploring many fewer paths than pure concolic execution (i.e., the call Generate $(P, \{X\}, X, \lambda x.\{X\}, \lambda x.0, -1)$). However, under the assumption that all program executions terminate, we can show that FlowTest is relatively sound: for every location ℓ, if concolic execution finds a feasible path to ℓ, then so does FlowTest. In particular, if all program executions terminate, then FlowTest does not miss any assertion violation detected by concolic execution.

We say a location $\hat{\ell}$ is *reachable* in FlowTest(P, Π_0) or Generate $(P, \{X\}, X, \lambda x.\{X\}, \lambda x.0, -1)$ if the execution reaches line 7 of Execute with $\ell = \hat{\ell}$. Clearly, a location reachable in either algorithm is reachable in the CFG by an executable path.

Theorem 1. *Let* $P = (X, X_0, \mathcal{L}, \ell_0, op, E)$ *be a program and* Π_0 *an initial partition of the inputs of* P. *Assume* P *terminates on all inputs. If* FlowTest(P, Π_0) *terminates then every location* $\ell \in \mathcal{L}$ *reachable in* Generate $(P, \{X\}, X, \lambda x.\{X\}, \lambda x.0, -1)$ *is also reachable in* FlowTest(P, Π_0).

We sketch a proof of the theorem. We prove the theorem by contradiction. Suppose that there is a location ℓ that is reachable in concolic execution but not in FlowTest. Fix a path $\pi = \ell_0 \rightarrow \ell_1 \rightarrow \ldots \rightarrow \ell_k$ executed by concolic execution such that ℓ_k is not reachable in FlowTest but each location $\ell_0, \ldots, \ell_{k-1}$ is reachable by FlowTest. (If there are several such paths, choose one arbitrarily.) Notice that since π is executed by concolic execution, the path constraints resulting from executing π is satisfiable. Also, $op(\ell_{k-1})$ must be a conditional, since if it were an assignment and ℓ_{k-1} is reachable in FlowTest, ℓ_k would also be reachable in FlowTest.

Since every program execution terminates, we can construct a *path slice* [9] of π, i.e., a subsequence π' of operations of π, with the following properties: (1) every initial memory M_0 that can execute π can also execute π', and (2) every initial memory M_0 that can execute π' is such that there is a (possibly different) program path π'' from ℓ_0 to ℓ_k such that M_0 can execute π''. Such a slice can be computed using the algorithm from [9]. Since the path constraint for π is satisfiable, so is the path constraint for π'. Let $V(\pi')$ be the set of variables appearing in π', i.e., $V(\pi')$ is the smallest set such that for every operation $l := e$ in π' we have $\{l\} \cup \mathsf{Use}(e) \subseteq V(\pi')$ and for every operation $\mathbf{if}(x)$ $\mathbf{then}$ ℓ' $\mathbf{else}$ ℓ'' in π', we have $x \in V(\pi')$.

We show that each variable in $V(\pi')$ is eventually merged into the same input block. We note that every conditional operation in π' controls the next operation in π' and every assignment operation $l := e$ in π' either uses l in a subsequent assignment or in a conditional. Now, since every location along π' is reachable, we can show (by induction on the length of π') that all variables in $V(\pi')$ are merged into the same input block. Call this block I.

Consider the call to Generate made by FlowTest with the input block I. This call is made by FlowTest in the iteration after I is created. Since π' is a path slice of π, and π is executable, we know that the sequence of operations in π' can be executed by suitably setting values of variables in I, no matter how the rest of the variables are set. Moreover, since the path constraint for π is satisfiable, so is the path constraint for π'. Since every execution terminates, the backtracking search implemented in Generate is complete (modulo completentess of the decision procedure), so the call to Generate using input block I must eventually hit ℓ_k. This is a contradiction, since this shows ℓ_k is reachable in FlowTest.

While the theorem makes the strong assumption that all program paths terminate, in practice this is ensured by setting a limit on the length of paths simulated in concolic execution. In fact, if the program has an infinite execution, then the concolic execution algorithm does not terminate: it either finds inputs that show non-termination (and gets stuck in Execute), or finds an infinite sequence of longer and longer program execution paths.

4   Example

We illustrate the working of FlowTest on a simplified version of a virtual memory page-free routine in an OS kernel (the actual code was tested in our experiments). Figure 1(b) shows the `free` function which takes as input two arrays of integers A and count each of size N, a fixed constant. For this example, let us set $N = 2$. For readability, we use C-like syntax and an array notation as a shorthand for declaring and using several variables (our simple language does not have arrays, but our implementations deals with arrays).

Notice that the loop in lines 4–7 of the function `free` in has 2^N paths, because the conditional on line 5 could be true or false for $0 \le i < N$. So, even for small N, concolic execution becomes infeasible. For example, our implementation of concolic execution in the tool Splat [18] already takes one day on an Intel Core 2 Duo 2.33 Ghz machine when $N = 20$.

Now we show how FlowTest can reduce the cost of testing this function. Our intuition is that the behavior of one "page" in the system is independent of all other pages, so we should test the code one page at a time. Concretely, in the code, there is no control or data dependency between two separate indices of the arrays. For example, the value $A[0]$ is not control or data dependent on $A[1]$, and $count[0]$ is not control or data dependent on $count[1]$. However, there is dependence between $A[i]$ and $count[i]$ (through the conditional in lines 5–6).

Initially, we start with the optimistic partition

$$\{ \{A[0]\}, \{A[1]\}, \{count[0]\}, \{count[1]\}\}$$

in which each variable is in its own partition. Consider the run of Generate when $A[0]$ is treated symbolically, but all other variables are fixed to constant values. The concolic execution generates two executions: one in which $A[0]$ is 0 and a second in which $A[0]$ is not zero. For the run in which $A[0]$ is not zero, moreover, the flow map is updated with the entry:

$$flow(count[0]) = \{\{A[0]\}, \{count[0]\}\}$$

since the assignment to $count[0]$ is control dependent on the predicate $A[0] \ne 0$. Thus, the blocks $\{A[0]\}$ and $\{count[0]\}$ are merged. In a similar way, the blocks $\{A[1]\}$ and $\{count[1]\}$ are merged.

In the next iteration of the main loop of FlowTest, the function Generate generates tests individually for the blocks $\{A[0], count[0]\}$ and $\{A[1], count[1]\}$. This time, there is no additional merging of input blocks. Hence, the algorithm terminates. The assertion holds on all paths of the resulting test set. The relative soundness result implies that the assertions hold for every execution of `free`.

5   Evaluation

5.1   Implementation

We have implemented a subset of the FlowTest algorithm to generate inputs for C programs on top of the Splat concolic execution tool [18]. In our tool, we take as input a program and a manual partition of the inputs, and implement the test generation and dependence checking part of the algorithm (lines 8–11 in Algorithm 1). However, instead of merging input blocks and iterating, our tool stops if two different input blocks must be merged (and assumes that the merging is performed manually). Our experiments (described below) confirm the following hypotheses:

- The performance impact of the added checks for dependencies is small, and more than compensated by the reduction in the number of paths explored.
- A tester can find non-interfering input partitions by superficially examining the source code.

Our implementation is divided in four main components: control flow generation, tracking flow, symbolic execution, and test generation. We use CIL [14] to instrument C code and to statically build the post-dominators (assuming every loop terminates) using the standard backwards dataflow algorithm [13]. We use the concolic execution and test generation loop of Splat to additionally track information flow between input partitions. Our implementation handle function calls and dynamic memory allocation in the standard way [8,15]. In our experiments, we did not put a priori bounds on the lengths of executions, but ran each function to completion.

Functions. Statement labels are made to be unique across all functions, therefore, entering and exiting a function during an execution is similar to in-lining the function at each call site.

Pointers and Memory. Given a branch label ℓ, we track all writes from that branch label to the label that post-dominates ℓ. Because our algorithm executes the code, address resolution is done during runtime. This implies we do not require a static alias analysis or suffer from the imprecision associated with static alias analysis, especially in the presence of address arithmetic or complex data structures.

We merge all dynamically allocated memory by allocation site when computing data dependencies, but distinguish each memory location individually when performing concolic execution. This can merge different potentially independent locations into the same block, but does not introduce imprecision in concolic execution. For statically- and stack-allocated variables, each byte is distinguished individually. For multiple writes to the same address from the branch label ℓ to the immediate post-dominator of ℓ, we take the union of all blocks that flow into that address. This limits the memory tracked to be (stack size × static allocation points) per branch node and is conservative because writes to one allocation point flow into all dynamic memory allocated from that point. Experientially, we found that this trade off did not lead to false alarms and was sufficient to check that blocks did not interfere with each other – mostly because each field in a data structure is distinguished.

Performance. Experimentally, we found that the extra information stored and checked along each path results in doubling the time taken to generate and explore a path. However, this increase in the per path time was more than compensated by the reduction in the number of paths explored. The static analysis cost (to compute post-dominators) is negligible (< 1 second for each of our case studies). While we did not experiment with automatic merging of input blocks, we expect there would not be a significant performance hit because finer grain blocks would have few paths and merging would occur quickly.

5.2   Case Studies

We have compared our algorithm with Splat on the following case studies. pmap is the code managing creation and freeing of a new processes in a virtual memory system for an educational OS kernel (1.6 KLOC), mondrian is the insertion module in a memory protection scheme (2.6 KLOC), snort is a module in an intrusion detection system (1.7 KLOC), and tcpdump consists of eight printers in a packet sniffer (12 KLOC).

In all programs selected, it was possible to come up with a good partition of the input with only a cursory examination of the source code (even though we did not write the code ourselves). In pmap, each header representing a physical page is a separate block. In mondrian, the protection bits could be partitioned from all other inputs. In both of the packet processing programs snort and tcpdump, various parts of the packet header could be partitioned. For tcpdump, we looked at 10 different packet types that could be printed by tcpdump. The partition for all those packet types were destination address, source address and everything else.

The implementation automatically generated inputs to check if there was interference between the manually chosen partitions for each program. Table 1 shows the results. All experiments were performed on a 2.33 GHz Intel Core 2 Duo with 2 GB of RAM. The two columns compare partitioning with concolic execution. The **Input Size** is the size of the symbolic input buffer used for both implementations. **Blocks** is the number of input blocks found manually and used for FlowTest. **Paths** is the number of unique paths found. **Coverage** is the number of branches covered. For all experiments, we could not achieve 100% coverage because we were only testing a specific part of the program. While these partitions may not be the best partition, FlowTest finished in half the time

Table 1. Experimental Results: Comparing FlowTest and Splat. **Input** is the size of the symbolic input buffer in bytes. **Blocks** is the number of blocks into which the input was (manually) partitioned. **Coverage** is branch coverage for both FlowTest and Splat. **Paths** is the number of unique paths explored. **Time** is the time taken up to a maximum of one hour.

				FlowTest		Splat	
Program	**Input**	**Blocks**	**Coverage**	**Paths**	**Time**	**Paths**	**Time**
pmap	1024	512	50/120 = 42%	1536	8m29s	6238	>1hr
mondrian	12	2	57/192 = 30%	733	23m20s	2916	36m35s
snort	128	2	44/52 = 85%	45	4m44s	73	4m55s
tcpdump	128	3	404/2264 = 18%	1247	34m1s	4974	53m46s

of Splat in two cases. For `pmap`, FlowTest finished in less than 10 minutes. In contrast, Splat did not finish in one day (Table 1 shows the progress made by Splat after one hour (6238 paths).

We did not compare our algorithm with combinations of other optimizations such as function summaries [7,1] or RWSets [2], as these techniques are orthogonal and can be combined to give better performance.

Limitations. In several examples, we found artificial dependencies between inputs caused by error handling code. For example, the `snort` module first checks if a packet is an UDP packet, and returns if not:

```
if(!PacketIsUDP(p)) return;
```

This introduces control dependencies between every field checked in `PacketIsUDP` and the rest of the code. However, these fields can be separated into their own blocks if the `PacketIsUDP(p)` predicate holds. A second limitation is our requiring that inputs are *partitioned*. In many programs, there is a small set of inputs that have dependencies with all other inputs, but the rest of the inputs are independent. Thus, it makes sense to divide the inputs into subsets whose intersections may not be empty.

Acknowledgments. We thank the anonymous referees for their detailed suggestions.

References

1. Anand, S., Godefroid, P., Tillmann, N.: Demand-driven compositional symbolic execution. In: Ramakrishnan, C.R., Rehof, J. (eds.) TACAS 2008. LNCS, vol. 4963, pp. 367–381. Springer, Heidelberg (2008)
2. Boonstoppel, P., Cadar, C., Engler, D.: RWset: Attacking path explosion in constraint-based test generation. In: Ramakrishnan, C.R., Rehof, J. (eds.) TACAS 2008. LNCS, vol. 4963, pp. 351–366. Springer, Heidelberg (2008)
3. Cadar, C., Dunbar, D., Engler, D.R.: KLEE: Unassisted and automatic generation of high-coverage tests for complex systems programs. In: OSDI (2008)

4. Cadar, C., Ganesh, V., Pawlowski, P., Dill, D., Engler, D.: Exe: automatically generating inputs of death. In: CCS (2006)
5. Clause, J., Li, W., Orso, A.: Dytan: A generic dynamic taint analysis framework. In: ISSTA (2007)
6. Denning, D.E.: A lattice model of secure information flow. Commun. ACM 19(5), 236–243 (1976)
7. Godefroid, P.: Compositional dynamic test generation. In: POPL. ACM, New York (2007)
8. Godefroid, P., Klarlund, N., Sen, K.: Dart: directed automated random testing. In: PLDI (2005)
9. Jhala, R., Majumdar, R.: Path slicing. In: PLDI 2005, ACM, New York (2005)
10. Korel, B., Laski, J.: Dynamic program slicing. Information Processing Letters 29, 155–163 (1988)
11. Korel, B., Yalamanchili, S.: Forward computation of dynamic program slices. In: ISSTA (1994)
12. Masri, W., Podgurski, A., Leon, D.: Detecting and debugging insecure information flows. In: ISSRE (2004)
13. Muchnick, S.: Advanced Compiler Design and Implementation. Morgan Kaufmann, San Francisco (1997)
14. Necula, G.C., McPeak, S., Rahul, S.P., Weimer, W.: CIL: Intermediate language and tools for analysis and transformation of C programs. In: Horspool, R.N. (ed.) CC 2002. LNCS, vol. 2304, p. 213. Springer, Heidelberg (2002)
15. Sen, K., Marinov, D., Agha, G.: Cute: a concolic unit testing engine for c. In: FSE (2005)
16. Tip, F.: A survey of program slicing techniques. Journel of Programming Languages 3, 121–189 (1995)
17. Weiser, M.: Program slices: Formal, psychological, and practical investigations of an automatic program abstraction method. Ph.D Thesis (1979)
18. Xu, R., Godefroid, P., Majumdar, R.: Testing for buffer overflows with length abstraction. In: ISSTA (2008)

On Using Floating-Point Computations to Help an Exact Linear Arithmetic Decision Procedure[*]

David Monniaux

Verimag[**]

Abstract. We consider the decision problem for quantifier-free formulas whose atoms are linear inequalities interpreted over the reals or rationals. This problem may be decided using satisfiability modulo theory (SMT), using a mixture of a SAT solver and a simplex-based decision procedure for conjunctions. State-of-the-art SMT solvers use simplex implementations over rational numbers, which perform well for typical problems arising from model-checking and program analysis (sparse inequalities, small coefficients) but are slow for other applications (denser problems, larger coefficients).

We propose a simple preprocessing phase that can be adapted to existing SMT solvers and that may be optionally triggered. Despite using floating-point computations, our method is sound and complete — it merely affects efficiency. We implemented the method and provide benchmarks showing that this change brings a naive and slow decision procedure ("textbook simplex" with rational numbers) up to the efficiency of recent SMT solvers, over test cases arising from model-checking, and makes it definitely faster than state-of-the-art SMT solvers on dense examples.

1 Introduction

Decision procedures for arithmetic theories are widely used for computer-aided verification. A decision procedure for a theory T takes as input a formula of T and outputs a Boolean: whether the formula is satisfiable. For many decidable and potentially useful theories, however, decision procedures are sometimes too slow to process problems beyond small examples. This is for instance the case of the theory of real closed fields (polynomial arithmetic over the real numbers). Excessive computation times arise from two sources: the Boolean structure of the formulas to be decided (propositional satisfiability is currently solved in exponential time in the worst case), and the intrinsic hardness of the theory. In recent years, SAT modulo theory (SMT) techniques have addressed the former source of inefficiency, by leveraging the power of efficient SAT (Boolean satisfiability) solvers to deal with the Boolean structure. SMT solvers combine a SAT solver with a decision procedure for conjunctions of atoms in T. If T is linear

---

[*] This work was partially funded by the ANR ARPEGE project "ASOPT".

[**] VERIMAG is a joint laboratory of CNRS, Université Joseph Fourier and Grenoble-INP.

A. Bouajjani and O. Maler (Eds.): CAV 2009, LNCS 5643, pp. 570–583, 2009.

real arithmetic (LRA), then this decision procedure must decide whether a set of linear inequalities with rational or integer coefficients has rational solutions.

The problem of testing whether a set of linear inequalities has a solution and, if it has, to find a solution that maximizes some linear combination of the variables is known as linear programming and has been considerably studied in operational research. Very efficient implementations exist, whether commercial or not, and are able to solve very large problems. They are not directly applicable to our problems, however, if only because they operate over floating-point numbers and provide in general no assurance that their result is truthful, despite elaborate precautions taken against numerical instabilities. As a result, the decision procedures for LRA in SMT solvers are implemented with rational arithmetic, which is slower than floating-point, especially if coefficients become large, as often happens with dense linear problems: large coefficients force the use of costly extended precision arithmetic. It thus would seem desirable to leverage the speed and maturity of floating-point linear programming systems to enhance exact decision procedures.

This article describes a simple preprocessing phase that can be added, with minimal change, to existing rational simplex implementations used as decision procedures inside SMT solvers. The procedure was implemented on top of a naive and inefficient rational simplex implementation; the resulting procedure rivals recent SMT solvers.

A similar method has been proposed in the operational research field [4],[1] but there are reasons why it may perform less well for the typical optimization tasks of operational research than for decision tasks. The novelty of this article is the application of this technique as a simple modification of existing SMT algorithms.

2   Simplex

SMT solvers need a decision procedure capable of:

- being used incrementally: adding new constraints to the problem, and removing blocks of constraints, preferably without recomputing everything;
- telling whether the problem is satisfiable or not;
- if the problem is unsatisfiable, outputting a (preferably small or even minimal) unsatisfiable subset of the constraints;
- propagating theory lemmas, if possible at reasonable costs (from a conjunction $C_1 \wedge \ldots \wedge C_n$, obtain literals $L_1, \ldots, L_m$ that are consequences of that conjunction: $C_1 \wedge \ldots \wedge C_n \Rightarrow L_1 \wedge \ldots \wedge L_m$).

All current SMT solvers seem to decide general linear real arithmetic (as opposed to syntactic restrictions thereof such as difference logic) using the *simplex algorithm*. This algorithm is exponential in the worst case, but tends to perform

---

[1] We were not aware of this article when we started our work, and we thank Bernd Gärtner for pointing it to us.

well in practice; none of the current solvers seem to use a (polynomial-time) interior point method. Our method is a variant of the simplex algorithm; we shall thus first describe the "conventional" simplex.

2.1   Basic Simplex

We shall first give a brief summary on the dual simplex algorithm on which the LRA decision procedures in YICES[2] [5,6] and Z3[3] [3] are based. There otherwise exist many excellent textbooks on the simplex algorithm [2,15], though these seldom discuss the specifics of implementations in exact precision or incremental use.

Take a system of linear equations, e.g.

$$\begin{cases} x - 2y \leq 1 \\ -y + 3z \geq -1 \\ x - 6z \geq 4 \end{cases} \tag{1}$$

The system is first made canonical. Inequalities are scaled so that each left hand side only has integer coefficients with no common factors. Then, each inequality is optionally negated so that the first coefficient appearing (using some arbitrary ordering of the variables) is positive. This ensures that two inequalities constraining the same direction in space (e.g. $-y + 3z \geq -1$ and $2y - 6z \geq 3$) appear with the exact same left-hand side. For each left-hand side that is not a variable, a new variable is introduced; the system is then converted into a number of linear equalities and bound constraints on the variables. For instance, the above system gets converted into:

$$\begin{cases} \alpha = x - 2y \\ \beta = y - 3z \\ \gamma = x - 6z \end{cases} \quad \begin{cases} \alpha \leq 1 \\ \beta \leq 1 \\ \gamma \geq 4 \end{cases} \tag{2}$$

The problem is thus formulated as deciding whether a product of intervals intersects a linear subspace given by a basis.

The set of variables is partitioned into *basic* and *nonbasic* variables; the number of basic variables stays constant throughout the algorithm. Basic variables are expressed as linear combinations of the nonbasic variables. The main operation of the algorithm is *pivoting*: a basic variable is made nonbasic and a nonbasic variable is made basic, without changing the linear subspace defined by the system of equations. For instance, in the above example, $\alpha = x - 2y$ defines the basic variable in term of the nonbasic variables x and y. If one wants instead x to be made basic, one obtains $x = \alpha + 2y$. The variable x then has to be replaced by $\alpha + 2y$ in all the other equalities, so that the right-hand sides of these equalities only refer to nonbasic variables. This replacement procedure (essentially, replacing a vector $\mathbf{u}$ by $\mathbf{v} + k\mathbf{u}$) is the costly part of the algorithm. A more formal description is given in Alg. 1.

---

[2] http://yices.csl.sri.com/
[3] http://research.microsoft.com/en-us/um/redmond/projects/z3/

Let us insist that pivoting does not change anything to the validity of the problem: both the bounds and the linear subspace stay the same. The idea behind the simplex algorithm is to pivot until a position is found where it is obvious that the problem has a solution, or that it has not.

The algorithm also maintains a vector of "current" values for the variables. This vector is fully defined by its projection on the nonbasic variables, since the basic variables can be obtained from them. The current values of the nonbasic variables always stay within their respective bounds. If all current values of the basic variables also fit within the bounds, the current value is a solution to the problem and the algorithm terminates.

If there are basic variables that fall outside the prescribed bounds, one of them (say, α) is selected and the corresponding row (say, $x - 2y$) is examined. Suppose for the sake of the explanation that the current value for α, c_α, is strictly greater than the maximal prescribed value M_α. One can try making x smaller or y larger to compensate for the difference. If x is already at its lower bound and y at its upper bound, it is impossible to make α smaller and the system is unsatisfiable; the algorithm then terminates. In other words, by performing interval arithmetic over the equation defining α in terms of the nonbasic variables, one shows this equation to be unsatisfiable (replacing the nonbasic variables by their interval bounds, one obtains an interval that does not intersect the interval for α).

Let us now suppose that x is not at its lower bound; we can try making it smaller. α and x are pivoted: x becomes basic and α nonbasic. α is set to its lower bound and x is adjusted accordingly.

It can be shown that if there is a solution to the problem, then there is one configuration where any nonbasic variable is either at its lower or upper bound. Intuitively, if some nonbasic variables are "in the middle", then this means we have some "slack margin" available, so we should as well use it. The simplex algorithm appears to move between numerical points taken in an infinite continuous space, but in fact, its current configuration is fully defined by stating which variables are basic and nonbasic, and, for the nonbasic variables, whether they are at their lower or upper bound — thus the number of configurations is finite.

Remark that we left aside how we choose which basic variable and which basic variable to pivot. It can be shown that certain pivoting strategies (say, choose the suitable nonbasic and basic variables of least index) necessarily lead, maybe after a great number of pivots, to a configuration where either a solution is obtained, or the constraints of a nonbasic variable are clearly unsatisfiable.

The idea of our article is based on the following remark: the simplex algorithm, with a suitable pivoting strategy, always terminates with the right answer, but its execution time can vary considerably depending on the initial configuration. If it is started from a configuration where it is obvious that the system has a solution or does not have one, then it terminates immediately. Otherwise, it may do a great deal of pivoting. Our idea is to use the output of some untrusted floating-point simplex algorithm to direct the rational simplex to a hopefully good starting point.

2.2 Modifications and Extensions

The above algorithm is a quick description of "textbook simplex". It is not sufficient for obtaining a numerically stable implementation if implemented over floating-point; this is why, after initial trials with a naive floating-point implementation, we moved to a better off-the-shelf implementation, namely GLPK (GNU Linear Programming Kit) [9].

So far, we have only considered wide inequalities. A classical method to convert problems with strict inequalities into problems with only wide inequalities is to introduce *infinitesimals*: a coordinate is no longer one single rational number, but a pair of rational numbers a and b, denoted $a + b\varepsilon$, with lexicographic ordering. ε is thus a special number, greater than zero but less than all positive rationals. $x < y$ is rewritten into $x + \varepsilon \leq y$. The "current" values in the simplex algorithm are thus pairs (a, b) of rationals, noted $a + b\varepsilon$, the upper bounds are either $+\infty$ or $a + b\varepsilon$, the lower bounds either $-\infty$ either $a + b\varepsilon$. The "current" vector, a vector of pairs, can be equivalently represented as a pair of vectors of rationals $(\mathbf{u}, \mathbf{v})$, written $\mathbf{u} + \varepsilon\mathbf{v}$ — if $\mathbf{v} \neq \mathbf{0}$, it designates a point infinitely close to $\mathbf{u}$ in the direction of $\mathbf{v}$, if $\mathbf{v} = \mathbf{0}$ it only means the point $\mathbf{u}$.

In addition to a yes/no answer, decision procedures used in SMT need to provide:

- In case of a positive answer, a solution point. If only wide inequalities are used, this is given straightforwardly by the "current" values. For points of the form $\mathbf{u} + \varepsilon\mathbf{v}$, one considers the half-line $\mathbf{u} + t\mathbf{v}$, $t > 0$, inject it into the system of inequalities, and solve it for t — the solution set will be an interval of the form $(0, t_0)$. A suitable solution point is thus $\mathbf{u} + \frac{t_0}{2}\mathbf{v}$.
- In case of a negative answer, a contradiction witness: nonnegative coefficients such that by multiplying the original inequalities by those coefficients, one gets a trivially unsatisfiable inequality ($0 < c$ where $c \leq 0$, or $0 \leq c$ where $c < 0$). This contradiction witness is obtained by using an auxiliary tableau tracking how the equalities $b - \sum_n t_{b,n} n = 0$ defining the basic variables were obtained as linear combinations of the original equalities defined at the initialization of the simplex, as described in [6, Sec. 3.2.2].

3 Mixed Floating-Point/Rational Strategy

Our procedure takes as input a rational simplex problem in the format described at Sec. 2.1: a tableau of linear equalities and bounds on the variables. It initializes a floating-point simplex by converting the rational problem: the infinitesimals are discarded and the rationals rounded to nearest. It then calls, as a subroutine, a floating-point simplex algorithm which, on exit, indicates whether the problem is satisfiable (at least according to floating-point computation), and a corresponding configuration (a partition into basic and nonbasic variables, and, for each nonbasic variable, whether it is set to its upper or lower bound). There are several suitable packages available; in order to perform experiments, we implemented our method using the GNU Linear programming toolkit (GLPK) [9].

In order for the resulting mixed procedure to be used incrementally, the floating-point solver should support incremental use. Commercial linear programming solvers are designed for large problems specified as a whole; there may be a large overhead for loading the problem into the solver, even if the problem is small. Instead, we need solvers capable of incrementally adding and withdrawing constraint bounds at minimal cost. GLPK supports incremental use, since it keeps the factorization of the basis in memory between calls [9, p. 20]; this factorization is costly to compute but needs to be computed only if the basis matrix changes: in our case, this basis stays the same.

At this point, if successful, and unless there has been some fatal numeric degeneracy, the floating-point simplex outputs a floating-point approximation to a solution point. However, in general, this approximation, converted back into a rational point, is not necessarily a true solution point. The reason is that simplex produces solution points at a vertex of the solution polyhedron, and, numerically speaking, it is in general impossible to be exactly on that point; in general, the solution point obtained is found to be very slightly outside of the polyhedron when membership is tested in exact arithmetic. It is therefore not feasible to simply take this solution point as a witness.

The rational simplex tableau is then "forcefully pivoted", using Algorithm 2, until it has the same basic/nonbasic partition as the floating-point output. This amounts to a pass of Gaussian elimination for changing the basis of the linear subspace. This phase can partially fail if the final basic/nonbasic partition requested is infeasible in exact precision arithmetic — maybe because of bugs in the floating-point simplex algorithm, or simply because of floating-point inaccuracies.

The "current" values of the nonbasic variables are then initialized according to the output of the floating-point simplex: if the floating-point simplex selected the upper bound for nonbasic variable n then its current value in the rational simplex is set to its upper bound, and similarly for lower bounds. If the final basic/nonbasic partition produced by the floating-point simplex is infeasible, then there are nonbasic variables of the rational simplex for which no information is known: these are left untouched or set to arbitrary values within their bounds (this does not affect correctness). The current values of the basic variables are computed using the rational tableau.

The rational simplex is then started. If things have gone well, it terminates immediately by noticing that it has found either a solution, or a configuration showing that the system is unsatisfiable. If things have gone moderately well, the rational simplex does a few additional rounds of pivoting. If things have gone badly, the rational simplex performs a full search.

The rational simplex algorithms are well known, and we have already presented them in Sect. 2.1. The correctness of our mixed algorithm relies on the correctness of the rational simplex and the "forced pivoting" phase maintaining the invariant that the linear equalities define the same solutions as those in the initial system.

We shall now describe in more detail the "forced pivoting" algorithm (Alg. 2). This algorithm takes as input a simplex tableau, with associated partition of the

Algorithm 1. PIVOT(*tableau*, b, n): pivot the basic variable b and the nonbasic variable n. t_v is the line defining basic variable v, $t_{v,w}$ is the coefficient of t_v corresponding to the nonbasic variable w. The a_i are the optional auxiliary tableau described in Sec. 2.2.

Require: b basic, n nonbasic, $t_{b,n} \neq 0$

$p := -1/t_{b,n}; t_n := p.t_b; t_{n,n} := 0; t_{n,b} := -p; a_n = p.a_b$
$B := B \cup \{n\} \setminus \{b\}$
for all $b' \in B$ **do**
    $p := t_{b',n}; t_{b',n} := 0; t_{b'} := t_{b'} + p.t_b; a_{b'} := a_{b'} + p.a_b$
end for
$t_b := 0$

The "for all" loop is the most expensive part of the whole simplex algorithm. Note that, depending on the way the sparse arrays and auxiliary structures are implemented, this loop may be parallelized, each iteration being independent of the others. This gives a performance boost on dense matrices.

Algorithm 2. FORCEDPIVOT(*tableau*, B_f): force pivoting until the set of basic variables is B_f

$B := B_i$
repeat
    $hasPivotedSomething :=$ **false**
    for all $b \in B \setminus B_f$ **do**
        if $\exists n \in B_f \setminus B \; t_{b,n} \neq 0$ **then**
            Choose n in $B_f \setminus B$ such that $t_{b,n} \neq 0$
            PIVOT(*tableau*, b, n) {This involves $B := B \cup \{n\} \setminus \{b\}$}
            $hasPivotedSomething :=$ **true**
        end if
    end for
until $\neg hasPivotedSomething$
return $B = B_f$

set V of variables into basic (B_i) and nonbasic variables $(\bar{B}_i)$, and a final partition of basic (B_f) and nonbasic variables $(\bar{B}_f)$. For each basic variable b, the tableau contains a line $b = \sum_{n \in \bar{B}} t_{b,n} n$. Additional constraints are that the tableau is well-formed (basic variables are combination of only the nonbasic variables) and that $|B_i| = |B_f|$ (since $|B|$ is a constant).

Assuming that all arithmetic operations take unit time (which is not true when one considers dense problems, since coefficient sizes quickly grow, but is almost true for sparse problems with small coefficients), the running time of the forced pivoting algorithm is at most cubic in the size of the problem. This motivates our suggestion: instead of performing an expensive and potentially exponential-time search directly with rational arithmetic, we perform it in floating-point, with all the possibilities of optimization of floating-point linear arithmetic offered by modern libraries and compilers, and then perform a cubic-time pass with rational arithmetic.

Not all final configurations are feasible: it is possible to ask FORCEDPIVOT to perform an impossible transformation, in which case it returns "false". For instance, if the input system of equations is $x = a + b \wedge y = a + b$, thus with $B_i = \{x, y\}$, then it is impossible to move to $B_f = \{a, b\}$, for there is no way to express a and b as linear functions of x and y. More precisely, we say that a configuration is feasible if it is possible to write the basic variables of the configuration as linear function of the nonbasic variables and obtain the same solutions as the initial system.

Lemma 1. FORCEDPIVOT *succeeds (and returns "true") if and only if the final partition defined by B_f is feasible, otherwise it returns "false".*

Proof. Let S denote the space of solutions of the input system of equations. At all iterations, S is exactly defined by the system of equations, and $\dim S = |\bar{B}|$. The only way the procedure fails is when $B \neq B_f$ and yet, for all basic variable $b \in B \setminus B_f$ and nonbasic variable $n \in B_f \setminus B$, it is impossible to pivot b and n because $t_{b,n} = 0$. In other words, all such b are linear combinations of the nonbasic variables in $\bar{B} \cap \bar{B}_f$. All variables in $\bar{B}_f$ are thus linear combinations of variables in $\bar{B} \cap \bar{B}_f$, and since we have supposed that $B \neq B_f$, $\bar{B} \cap \bar{B}_f \subsetneq \bar{B}$ thus $|\bar{B} \cap \bar{B}_f| < |\bar{B}| = \dim S$. But then, $|\bar{B}_f| < \dim S$ and B_f cannot be a feasible configuration.

One can still add a few easy improvements:

- Before embarking into any simplex, we first test that the original problem does not contain a trivially unsatisfiable tableau row: one where the bounds obtained by interval arithmetic on the right-hand side of $b = \sum_n t_{b,n} n$ the equality have an empty intersection with those for b.
- During the forced pivoting procedure, we detect whether the new equality obtained is trivially unsatisfiable, in which case we terminate immediately.
- Forced pivots can be done in any order. At the beginning of the procedure, we sort the variables in $B_i \setminus B_f$ according to the number of nonzero coefficients in the corresponding equation. When choosing the basic variable to be pivoted, we take the least one in that ordering. The idea is that the pivoting steps are faster when the equation defining the basic variable to be pivoted has few nonzero coefficients.
- Similarly, one can pre-sort the variables in $B_f \setminus B_i$ according to their number of occurrences in equations.

The SMT procedure may have at its disposal, in addition to the "exact" theory test a partial and "fast" theory test, which may err on the side of satisfiability: first test satisfiability in floating-point, and test in exact arithmetic only if negative. The "fast" theory test may be used to test whether it seems a good idea to investigate a branch of the search tree or to backtrack, while the "exact" results should be used for theory propagation or when it seems a good idea to check whether the current branch truly is satisfiable. Various systems are possible, depending on how the SAT and theory parts interact in the solver [8].

Note that after an "exact" theory check, we have an exact rational simplex tableau corresponding to the constraints, from which it is possible to extract theory propagation information. For instance, if interval analysis on a row $x = 3y+5z$, using intervals from y and z, shows that $x < 3$, then one can immediately conclude that in the current SAT search branch, the literal $x \geq 4$ is false.

4   Implementation and Benchmarks

We implemented the above algorithm into a toy SMT solver.[4] The SAT part is handled by MINISAT [7]. Implementing a full SMT solver for LRA was useful for testing the software, against the SMT-LIB examples.[5] We however did not use SMT-LIB for benchmarking: the performance of a complete SMT solver is influenced by many factors, including the performance of the SAT solver, the ease of adding new clauses on the fly, etc., outside of the pure speed of the decision procedure.

The floating-point simplex used is the dual simplex implemented by option GLP_DUALP in GLPK [9], with default parameters. The rational simplex tableau is implemented using sparse vectors.[6] Rational numbers are implemented as quotients of two 32-bit numbers; in case of overflow, extended precision rationals from the GMP library [10] are used.[7] The reason behind a two-tier system is that GMP rationals inherently involve some inefficiencies, including dynamic memory allocation, even for small numerator and denominator. In many examples arising from verification problems, one never needs to call GMP. The simplex algorithm, including the pivot strategy, is implemented straight from [6,5]. It is therefore likely that our system be implemented as a preprocessor into any of the current SMT platforms for linear real arithmetic, or even those for linear integer arithmetic, since these are based on relaxations to rationals with additional constraints (branch-and-bound or Gomory cuts).

We benchmarked four tools:

- Our "naive" implementation of rational simplex.
- The same, but with the floating-point preprocessing and forced pivoting phase described in this article ("mixed simplex").
- Bruno Dutertre and Leonardo de Moura's (SRI International) Yices 1.0.9
- Nikolaj Bjørner and Leonardo de Moura's (Microsoft Research) Z3, as presented at SMT-COMP '08.

---

[4] Benchmarks and implementation are available from
http://www-verimag.imag.fr/~monniaux/simplexe/.
[5] http://goedel.cs.uiowa.edu/smtlib/benchmarks/QF_LRA.tar.gz
[6] More precisely, using boost::numeric::ublas::compressed_vector from the BOOST library, available at http://www.boost.org/.
[7] http://gmplib.org/

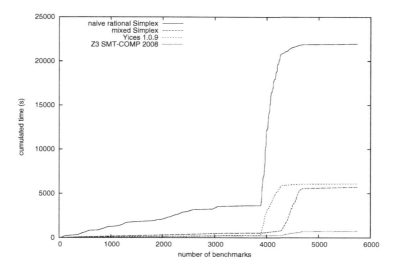

Fig. 1. Benchmarks on unsatisfiable conjunctions extracted from vSMT verification problems. Even though our implementation of sparse arithmetic and the rational simplex are not up to those in state-of-the-art solvers (as shown by the lack of performance on the "easy" examples on the left), and our procedure is not geared towards the sparse problems typical of verification applications, it still performs faster than Yices 1. In 4416 cases out of 5736 (77%), no additional simplex pivots are needed after FORCEPIVOT.

We used two groups of benchmarks:

- Benchmarks kindly provided to us by Leonardo de Moura, extracted from SMT-LIB problems. Each benchmark is an unsatisfiable conjunction, used by Z3 as a theory lemma. These examples are fairly sparse, with small coefficients, and rational simplex seldom needs to use extended precision rational arithmetic. Despite this, the performance of the "mixed" implementation is better than that of Yices 1 (Fig. 1). Since the source code of neither Yices nor Z3 are available, the reasons why Z3 performs better than Yices 1 and both perform much better than our own rational simplex implementation are somewhat a matter of conjecture. The differences probably arise from both a better sparse matrix implementation, and a better pivoting strategy.
- Random, dense benchmarks. On these, our mixed implementation performs faster than all others, including the state-of-the-art SMT solvers (Fig. 2).

On a few examples, GLPK crashed due to an internal error (failed assertion). We are unsure whether this is due to a bug inside this library or our misusing it — in either case, this is rather unsurprising given the complexity of current numerical packages. It is also possible that the numerical phase outputs incorrect results in some cases, because of bugs or loss of precision in floating-point computations. Yet, this has no importance — the output of the numerical phase does not affect

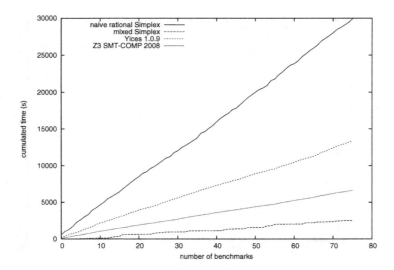

Fig. 2. Benchmarks on systems of 100 inequalities with 50 variables, where all coefficients are taken uniformly and independently distributed integers in $[-100, 100]$. 31 are unsatisfiable, 46 are satisfiable. For each solver, benchmarks sorted by increasing time spent. In 58 cases out of 82 (71%), no additional simplex pivots are needed after FORCEPIVOT.

the correction of the final result, but only the time that it takes to reach this result.

5   Related Work

The high cost of exact-arithmetic in linear programming has long been recognized, and linear programming packages geared towards operational research applications seldom feature the option to perform computations in exact arithmetic. In contrast, most SMT solvers (e.g. YICES, Z3) or computational geometry packages implement exact arithmetic.

Faure et al. have experimented with using commercial, floating-point SMT solvers such as CPLEX[8] inside an SMT solver [8]. Their approach is different from ours in that they simply sought to reuse the yes/no return value produced by the inexact solver, while we also reuse the basis structure that it produces. Many of the difficulties they report — for instance, not being able to reuse the output of the inexact solver for theory propagation — disappear with our system. Some of their remarks still apply: for instance, the floating-point solver should allow incremental use, which means that, for instance, it should not per-

---

[8] CPLEX is a professional optimization package geared towards large operational research problem, published by ILOG. http://www.ilog.com/products/cplex/

form LU matrix factorization every time a bound is changed but only at basis initialization.

The idea of combining exact and floating-point arithmetic for the simplex algorithm is not new. Gärtner proposed an algorithm where most of the computations inside the simplex algorithm are performed using ordinary floating-point, but some are performed using extended precision arithmetic (floating-point with an arbitrary number of digits in the mantissa), and reports improvements in precision compared to the industrial solver CPLEX at moderate costs [11]. It is however difficult to compare his algorithm to ours, because they are geared towards different kinds of problems. Our algorithm is geared towards the decision problem, and is meant to be potentially incremental, and to output both satisfiability and unsatisfiability witnesses in exact rational arithmetic. Gärtner's is geared towards optimization problems in computational geometry, and does not provide optimality or unsatisfiability witnesses.

The work that seems closest to ours seems to be LPex [4], a linear programming solver that first obtains a floating-point solution, then recreates the solution basis inside an exact precision solver and then verifies the solution and possibly does additional iterations in exact precision in order to repair a "wrong" basis. The original intent of the authors was to apply this technique to optimization, not decision problems, and there are in fact arguments against using this technique for optimization that do not apply to using it for decision. A simplex-based optimization solver actually runs two optimization phases:

1. A search for a feasible solution (e.g. the algorithm from Sec. 2.1), which can be equivalently presented as an optimization problem. A new variable δ is added, and all inequalities $\sum a_{i,j} x_j \leq b$ are replaced by $\sum a_{i,j} x_j - \delta \leq b$. By taking δ sufficiently large, one can find a solution point of the modified problem. Optimization iterations then reduce δ until it is nonnegative. Intuitively, δ measures how much afar we are from a solution to the original problem.

2. Once a solution point to the original problem is found, the original objective function f is optimized.

There are therefore two objective functions at work: one for finding a solution point, and the "true" objective function. The floating-point simplex process, optimizes δ, then f. Then, the rational simplex, seeking to "repair" the resulting basis, starts optimizing δ again; then it has to move back to optimizing f. In general, changing objective functions in the middle of an optimization process is bad for efficiency. However, since we are interested in decision, we optimize a single function and the objection does not hold.

This approach was later improved to computing exact solutions for all problems in NETLIB-LP, a popular benchmark library for linear programming problems [14]. One improvement was to re-run the floating-point simplex in higher precision rather than attempt to repair the "wrong" output basis using exact arithmetic — thus the suggestion to use extended-precision floating-point arithmetic[9] with increasing precisions until the solution found can be checked in exact precision. This last algorithm was implemented inside the QSopt_ex solver [1].[10]

These proposals are however different from ours in that they involve more modifications to the underlying exact arithmetic solver. For once, they compute exact precision factorizations of the input matrices, which probably saves time for the large operational research problems that they consider but may have a too high overhead for the smaller problems that arise in SMT applications. In contrast, our algorithm can be adapted as a preprossessing step to the simplex procedure used in existing SMT solvers with hardly any modification to that procedure.

6   Conclusion and Future Work

Our work leverages the maturity and efficiency of floating-point simplex solver (inherent efficiency of hardware floating-point versus rationals, advanced pricing and pivoting strategies...) in order to speed up exact decision procedures in cases where these perform poorly.

The main application of SMT solvers so far has been program or specification verification. Such problems are typically sparse, with small coefficients. On such problems, recent SMT solvers such as Yices and Z3 typically perform well using the simplex algorithm over rational numbers. Performance, however, decreases considerably if they are used over dense problems, since the size of numerators and denominators involved can become prohibitively large. In this case, running our preprocessing phase before embarking on costly extended precision simplex can save significant time. We suggest that our procedure be added to such implementations and activated, as a heuristic, when the rational coefficients become too large.

Allowing SMT solvers to scale beyond program analysis examples may prove useful if they are used for some other applications than program proofs, for instance, formal mathematical proofs. As an example of the use of formal arithmetic proofs outside of program verification, Hales proved Kepler's conjecture using many lemmas obtained by optimization techniques [13], but mathematicians objected that it was unclear whether these lemmas truly held. As a result, Hales launched a project to formally prove his theorem, including all lemmas obtained using numerical optimization. He proposed transformations of his original linear programming problems into problems for which it is possible to turn the bounds obtained by numerical techniques into numerical bounds [12]. This suggests that there are potential mathematical applications of efficient decision procedures for linear arithmetic.

The applications of our improvements are not limited to the linear theory of the reals or rationals. They also apply to the linear theory of integers, or the mixed linear theory of rationals/reals and integers. In most SMT solvers, decision for integer and mixed linear problems is implemented by relaxing the

---

[9] Available through GNU MP's `mpf` type or the MPFR library, for instance.

[10] `http://www2.isye.gatech.edu/~wcook/qsopt/index.html`

problem to the real case. If there is no real solution, then there is no integer solution; if there is a solution where the variables that are supposed to be integers are integers, then the integer or mixed problem has a solution. Otherwise, the search is restarted in parts of the state space, delimited by "branch and bound" or Gomory cuts. Any efficiency improvement in the rational simplex can thus translate into an improvement to the integer or mixed linear decision procedure.

The reason why we still have to perform expensive rational pivots even after computing a floating-point solution is that the floating-point solutions produced by the simplex algorithm almost always lie outside of the solution polyhedron when tested over exact arithmetic, as explained in Sec. 3. We therefore think of investigating interior point methods, searching both for a satisfiability witness and for an unsatisfiability witness.

References

1. Applegate, D., Cook, W., Dash, S., Espinoza, D.: Exact solutions to linear programming problems. Oper. Res. Lett. 35(6), 693–699 (2007)
2. Dantzig, G.: Linear Programming and Extensions. Princeton University Press, Princeton (1998)
3. de Moura, L., Bjørner, N.: Z3: An efficient SMT solver. In: Ramakrishnan, C.R., Rehof, J. (eds.) TACAS 2008. LNCS, vol. 4963, pp. 337–340. Springer, Heidelberg (2008)
4. Dhiflaoui, M., Funke, S., Kwappik, C., Mehlhorn, K., Seel, M., Schömer, E., Schulte, R., Weber, D.: Certifying and repairing solutions to large LPs: how good are LP-solvers? In: SODA 2003: Proceedings of the fourteenth annual ACM-SIAM symposium on Discrete algorithms, pp. 255–256. SIAM, Philadelphia (2003)
5. Dutertre, B., de Moura, L.: A fast linear-arithmetic solver for DPLL(T). In: Ball, T., Jones, R.B. (eds.) CAV 2006. LNCS, vol. 4144, pp. 81–94. Springer, Heidelberg (2006)
6. Dutertre, B., de Moura, L.: Integrating simplex with DPLL(T). Technical Report SRI-CSL-06-01, SRI International (May 2006)
7. Eén, N., Sörensson, N.: An extensible SAT-solver. In: Giunchiglia, E., Tacchella, A. (eds.) SAT 2003. LNCS, vol. 2919, pp. 502–518. Springer, Heidelberg (2004)
8. Faure, G., Nieuwenhuis, R., Oliveras, A., Rodríguez-Carbonell, E.: SAT modulo the theory of linear arithmetic: Exact, inexact and commercial solvers. In: Kleine Büning, H., Zhao, X. (eds.) SAT 2008. LNCS, vol. 4996, pp. 77–90. Springer, Heidelberg (2008)
9. Free Software Foundation. GNU Linear Programming Kit Reference Manual, version 4.34 (December 2008)
10. Free Software Foundation. GNU MP The GNU Multiple Precision Arithmetic Library, 4.2.4 edition (September 2008)
11. Gärtner, B.: Exact arithmetic at low cost — a case study in linear programming. In: SODA 1998: Proceedings of the ninth annual ACM-SIAM symposium on Discrete algorithms, pp. 157–166. SIAM, Philadelphia (1998)
12. Hales, T.C.: Some algorithms arising in the proof of the Kepler conjecture, arXiv:math/0205209v1
13. Hales, T.C.: A proof of the Kepler conjecture. Ann. Math. 162, 1065–1185 (2005)
14. Koch, T.: The final NETLIB-LP results. Op. Res. Letters 32(2), 138–142 (2004)
15. Schrijver, A.: Theory of Linear and Integer Programming. Wiley, Chichester (1998)

Cardinality Abstraction for Declarative Networking Applications

Juan Antonio Navarro Pérez, Andrey Rybalchenko, and Atul Singh

Max Planck Institute for Software Systems (MPI-SWS)

Abstract. Declarative Networking is a recent, viable approach to make distributed programming easier, which is becoming increasingly popular in systems and networking community. It offers the programmer a declarative, rule-based language, called P2, for writing distributed applications in an abstract, yet expressive way. This approach, however, imposes new challenges on analysis and verification methods when they are applied to P2 programs. Reasoning about P2 computations is beyond the scope of existing tools since it requires handling of program states defined in terms of collections of relations, which store the application data, together with multisets of tuples, which represent communication events in-flight. In this paper, we propose a cardinality abstraction technique that can be used to analyze and verify P2 programs. It keeps track of the size of relations (together with projections thereof) and multisets defining P2 states, and provides an appropriate treatment of declarative operations, e.g., indexing, unification, variable binding, and negation. Our cardinality abstraction-based verifier successfully proves critical safety properties of a P2 implementation of the Byzantine fault tolerance protocol Zyzzyva, which is a representative and complex declarative networking application.

1 Introduction

Declarative networking is a recent approach to the programming of distributed applications [29]. This approach allows the programmer to focus on a high-level description of the distributed system from the point of view of the global system, while the underlying runtime environment is responsible for the automatic distribution of computation and communication among nodes participating in the system. Declarative networking is increasingly employed by the distributed systems and networking community. It has been successfully applied to implement several network protocols, including sensor networks, Byzantine fault tolerance, and distributed hash tables, see [11,25,30,39], and is a subject of study from the compilation, debugging, and protocol design perspectives, see [14,40,39]. Complementing these lines of research, this work proposes a reasoning technique for declarative networking.

An implementation of the declarative networking approach is given by P2, a rule-based programming language [15]. The language is derived from distributed Datalog. Formally, P2 programs describe parameterized systems whose nodes

A. Bouajjani and O. Maler (Eds.): CAV 2009, LNCS 5643, pp. 584–598, 2009.

execute the same set of rules [20]. Application data of P2 programs is stored at network nodes in form of relations (i.e., sets of named tuples organized in tables) that satisfy programmer-defined projection constraints. These constraints require that the projection of each table on a specified subset of its columns does not contain duplicate elements. The P2 runtime environment enforces these constraints by pruning existing table rows whenever addition of new tuples leads to a violation. Nodes communicate by exchanging events that are represented by named tuples. P2 treats events in-flight as a collection of multisets. An event received by a node triggers evaluation of the program rules at the node. For each rule, this corresponds to computing all solutions of the relational query represented by the rule body with respect to the stored relations. Each one of these solutions determines an action to be executed that, according to the rule head, can either modify the relations stored at the node or send a new event.

Declarative networking imposes new challenges on existing analysis and verification methods that cannot be directly applied to P2 programs. First, reasoning about P2 computations requires dealing with relations and multisets. In contrast, existing verification methods represent the program state as a single tuple—a valuation of program variables in scope. Second, declarative statements used in P2 carry out complex operations on relations, e.g., joins and projections on tables, as well as addition and deletion of tuples. Such artifacts are beyond the scope of the existing verification tools.

In this paper, we present a *cardinality abstraction* technique for the analysis and verification of declarative networking applications. Cardinality abstraction aims at discovering quantitative information about data-storing relations and multisets of events such as those manipulated during the execution of P2 programs. This information is expressed in terms of *cardinality measures* that count the number of stored facts as well as the size of projections of the corresponding tables on their columns. Cardinality abstraction yields an over-approximation of the one-step transition relation represented by a P2 program, thus providing a basis for its further analysis and verification.

Cardinality abstraction keeps track of cardinality measures under the application of declarative operations during program execution. We represent the effect of these operations using a set of equations over cardinality measures. Given a P2 program, the corresponding set of equations is derived automatically. The equations are precise, i.e., for every satisfying valuation of cardinality measures there is a corresponding pair of states in the program's transition relation. Cardinality abstraction naturally handles data values, stored in tables and delivered by events, to the following extent. First, it takes into account the binding of variables during event matching, which triggers rule evaluation for the respective values, and the propagation of values through the rule. Second, the cardinality abstraction is sensitive to a priori fixed data values, possibly symbolic, by a syntactic program transformation that partitions tables according to the appearance of such data values.

The analysis and verification of declarative networking applications is then performed by applying abstract interpretation [17] to the cardinality abstraction of a P2 program. Since the abstracting equations provide a relational abstraction of the one-step transition relation given by a P2 program, cardinality abstraction can be used to verify temporal safety and liveness properties. The computation of the abstract semantics can be carried out using existing tools and techniques, e.g., ASTRÉE, BLAST, INTERPROC, SLAM, and TERMINATOR [4, 5, 6, 16, 27].

We implemented the cardinality analysis-based tool CARDAN for the verification of safety properties of P2 programs[1]. CARDAN uses the ARMC model checker for the computation of the abstract semantics.[2] We applied CARDAN to automatically prove crucial safety properties of a P2 implementation of the Zyzzywa protocol for Byzantine fault tolerance [39], which is a representative, complex declarative networking application.

In summary, our contribution is a cardinality abstraction technique that enables analysis and verification of declarative networking applications. It relies on a quantitative abstraction of complex program states consisting of relations and multisets and manipulated using declarative statements. Our experimental evaluation using the CARDAN tool indicates that cardinality abstraction can be successfully applied for the automatic verification of declarative networking applications.

2   Example

In this section, we briefly describe P2 and illustrate cardinality abstraction on a simple program, TOKEN in Figure 1, that implements a token passing protocol.

States. The first four lines in the figure define the structure of TOKEN states. Each node maintains two tables `token` and `neighbor` that keep track of the token ownership and the network connectivity between nodes, respectively. Communication events in the multisets `release` and `pass` initiate the token transfer and convey the act of passing between the nodes. Distribution in P2 is achieved by keeping the address of a tuple, where it should be stored or sent to, as the value in its first argument. The `keys` declarations in Figure 1 require that the projection of `neighbor` on its first column does not have duplicate elements, i.e., each node has at most one neighbor. In Figure 2 we show an example state s_0 of TOKEN, in a network with three nodes A, B and C, under an assumption that there are no events in-flight. We use the symbol "−" to denote an empty table.

```
data(token/1,    keys(1)).
data(neighbor/2, keys(1)).
event(release/1).
event(pass/1).


r1  del  token(X)   :-  release(X), token(X).
r2  snd  pass(Y)    :-  release(X), token(X), neighbor(X, Y).
r3  add  token(Y)   :-  pass(Y).
```

Fig. 1. Program TOKEN implementing a token passing protocol in P2

---

[1] Tool and examples available at: `http://www.mpi-sws.org/~jnavarro/tools`
[2] The choice is due to implementation convenience.

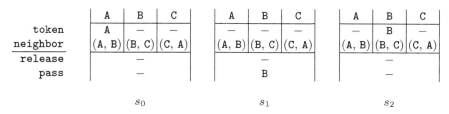

	A	B	C		A	B	C		A	B	C
token	A	−	−		−	−	−		−	B	−
neighbor	(A, B)	(B, C)	(C, A)		(A, B)	(B, C)	(C, A)		(A, B)	(B, C)	(C, A)
release		−				−				−	
pass		−				B				−	

$$s_0 \qquad\qquad\qquad\qquad s_1 \qquad\qquad\qquad\qquad s_2$$

Fig. 2. Sequence of TOKEN states s_0, s_1, and s_2 obtained by applying rules r1, r2, and r3 on the state s_0. Tables token and neighbor define the stored data, release and pass refer to the events in-flight. "−" denotes an empty table.

Rules. Program statements in P2 are represented by rules consisting of a head and a body separated by the symbol ":-". The rule head specifies the name of the rule, its action and the tuple on which the action is applied. TOKEN uses rules r1 and r3 to delete and add tuples from the table token, as specified by the keywords del and add. The rule r2 sends events in the form of pass tuples.

The body of each rule provides values for the variables appearing in the rule head. The evaluation is triggered by events arriving at a node. Assume that an event release is periodically broadcasted to all nodes from some external source whose nature is not important for this example, i.e., the nodes A, B, and C receive the tuples release(A), release(B), and release(C), respectively. Then, the runtime environment of each node triggers evaluation of rules whose first conjunct in the body matches with the event. Triggering consumes the corresponding event, i.e., the multiset of events in-flight becomes empty. At node A the rules r1 and r2 are triggered by release(A), but the rule r3 is not. The same rules are triggered at nodes B and C. For each triggered rule the set of all solutions to the rule body is computed. This step is similar to the bottom-up evaluation procedure of Datalog. Given the state s_0, the evaluation of r1 at A produces an action del token(A) by setting X = A, and for r2 we obtain snd pass(B) due to the presence of neighbor(A, B) which sets Y = B. Only a single snd action can be produced by TOKEN at A because of the projection constraint on neighbor. In fact, if TOKEN had the declaration data(neighbor/2, keys(1,2)) then each node could have multiple neighbors, and executing r2 would result in the event pass to be delivered at each of them. At nodes B and C no actions are produced since the rule evaluation fails due to the lack of token tuples.

The execution of rules produces actions to manipulate data and send events. After executing del token(A) we obtain a state s_1 shown in Figure 2. The runtime environment sends the event pass(B) to the node B. Upon arrival, this event triggers the execution of r3 at the node B, which consumes the event and adds the tuple token(B) to its tables. The resulting state s_2 is shown in Figure 2.

Property. If correct, the TOKEN program should satisfy the property of mutual exclusion when executed on a network with an arbitrary number of nodes. The property states that, at any given moment in time, at most one node can hold the token; under the assumption that the initial state of TOKEN already satisfies this condition and does not have any events in-flight.

This property relies on the invariant that the number of `token` and `pass` tuples together does not exceed one. This invariant is maintained in TOKEN through an interplay between the rules and the projection constraint on `neighbor`. Whenever the token leaves a node then only one of its neighbors will receive a `pass` tuple and will obtain the token.

Cardinality abstraction. Checking the validity of the mutual exclusion property for TOKEN requires reasoning about its set of reachable states. Instead of dealing with program states in full detail, we only consider their quantitative properties by applying cardinality abstraction.

We use cardinality measures to keep track of the size of tables and their projections on subsets of columns. For example, the measure $\#\text{neighbor}_{1,2}$, where the subscript "1,2" refers to its first and second column, represents the number of tuples in the table; whereas $\#\text{neighbor}_1$ represents the size of the table projected on its first column. The measures $\#\text{pass}$ refers to the number of `pass` events in-flight. This measure does not refer to any projection, since P2 treats events in-flight as multisets and multiset projection does not affect cardinality.

Cardinality abstraction over-approximates the semantics of rule execution in form of a binary relation over cardinality measures. For example, the execution of rules `r1` and `r2` triggered by an event `release` produces the following modification of the measures $\#\text{token}_1$ and $\#\text{pass}$, expressed in terms of a cardinality operator $|\cdot|$ and primed notation to denote measures after rule execution:

$$\#\text{token}_1' = \#\text{token}_1 - |\{X \mid \text{release}(X) \wedge \text{token}(X)\}| \,,$$
$$\#\text{pass}' = \#\text{pass} + |\{Y \mid \text{release}(X) \wedge \text{token}(X) \wedge \text{neighbor}(X,Y)\}| \,.$$

The cardinality expressions in the above equations are further constrained by applying algebraic properties of relational queries, the semantics of projection constraints, and the definition of measures, which are marked by (a), (b), and (c) respectively.

$$|\{X \mid \text{release}(X) \wedge \text{token}(X)\}| \leq |\{X \mid \text{release}(X)\}| \qquad (a)$$
$$|\{Y \mid \text{release}(X) \wedge \text{token}(X) \wedge \text{neighbor}(X,Y)\}| \leq |\{Y \mid \text{token}(X) \wedge \text{neighbor}(X,Y)\}| \qquad (a)$$
$$|\{Y \mid \text{token}(X) \wedge \text{neighbor}(X,Y)\}| \leq |\{X \mid \text{token}(X) \wedge \text{neighbor}(X,Y)\}| \qquad (b)$$
$$|\{X \mid \text{token}(X) \wedge \text{neighbor}(X,Y)\}| \leq |\{X \mid \text{token}(X)\}| \qquad (a)$$
$$|\{X \mid \text{token}(X)\}| = \#\text{token}_1 \qquad (c)$$

Additionally, we use the fact that only one event is consumed at a time, i.e.,

$$|\{X \mid \text{release}(X)\}| \leq 1 \,,$$

and that measures are always non-negative.

Cardinality abstraction-based verification. To verify TOKEN, we compute the set of reachable valuations of cardinality measures and show that it implies the assertion $\#\text{token}_1 \leq 1$, stating that at most one node holds the token. We apply a standard algorithm for assertion checking and obtain the following invariant that implies the property

$$\#\text{token}_1 \leq 1 \wedge \#\text{pass} + \#\text{token}_1 \leq 1 \,.$$

3   Preliminaries

In this section we briefly describe P2 programs [29] following the presentation in [34], which provides a better basis from the program analysis perspective.

Programs. A P2 program $P_2 = \langle \mathcal{L}, \mathcal{D}, \mathcal{K}, \mathcal{R}, S_0 \rangle$ is defined by a set of predicate symbols $\mathcal{L}$, a data domain $\mathcal{D}$, a function $\mathcal{K}$ defining projection constraints, a set of rules $\mathcal{R}$, and an initial state S_0. For the rest of the exposition we assume that variables are elements from a set of variables $\mathcal{V}$. We write $vars(W)$ to denote the set of variables occurring in an arbitrary expression W.

Given a predicate symbol $p \in \mathcal{L}$, with a positive arity n, a *predicate* is a term $p(u_1, \ldots, u_n)$, where each argument u_i is either a variable from $\mathcal{V}$, or a data element from $\mathcal{D}$. Variable-free predicates are called *tuples*. The first position in a predicate has a special role in P2 and is called *address*. The set of predicate symbols is partitioned into data and event symbols, which induces a partitioning of corresponding predicates and tuples.

The function $\mathcal{K}$ assigns to each data predicate symbol p of arity n a subset of its positions that includes the first one, i.e., $1 \in \mathcal{K}(p)$ and $\mathcal{K}(p) \subseteq \{1, \ldots, n\}$. Given a data tuple $P = p(v_1, \ldots, v_n)$, the projection operator $P\!\downarrow_{\mathcal{K}}$ computes a sub-tuple obtained from P by removing all of its arguments whose positions do not appear in the set $\mathcal{K}(p)$. For example, given $P = p(a, b, c, d)$ and $\mathcal{K}(p) = \{1, 3\}$, we obtain $P\!\downarrow_{\mathcal{K}} = p(a, c)$.

P2 uses *rules* of the form

$$r \; a \; H \; \text{:-} \; T, \; B$$

that consist of a head and a body separated by the symbol ":-". The head specifies the rule name r, determines the action kind $a \in \{\text{add}, \text{del}, \text{snd}\}$, and the action predicate H. For rules with the action kind snd, P2 requires H to be an event predicate, otherwise it must be a data predicate. The body consists of an event predicate T, called *trigger*, and a sequence of data predicates $B = B_1, \ldots, B_n$, called *query*. Each variable in the head must also appear in the body. We assume that all predicates in the body have the same address, i.e., they share the variable in the first position, and for each event name there is one rule in $\mathcal{R}$ with the equally named trigger predicate.[3]

Computations. The *state* of a P2 program $\langle \mathcal{M}, \mathcal{E} \rangle$ consists of a *data store* $\mathcal{M}$ and an *event queue* $\mathcal{E}$. The store $\mathcal{M}$ is a set of data tuples that satisfies the projection constraints given by $\mathcal{K}$. The queue $\mathcal{E}$ is a multiset of event tuples.

Figure 3 shows the procedure EVALUATE that defines the operational semantics of P2 programs. One iteration of the main loop, lines 2–12, defines the binary *transition relation* on program states, as represented by the P2 program. The state is given by the valuation of variables $\langle \mathcal{M}, \mathcal{E} \rangle$ in EVALUATE. Each transition starts selecting and removing an event tuple E from the event queue $\mathcal{E}$. Then, we select the rule with the matching trigger and compute all solutions to its query.

---

[3] These assumptions are not proper restrictions and can be removed at the expense of a more elaborate exposition of the proposed technique.

procedure EVALUATE
input
    $P_2 = \langle \mathcal{L}, \mathcal{D}, \mathcal{K}, \mathcal{R}, S_0 \rangle$: P2 program
vars
    $\langle \mathcal{M}, \mathcal{E} \rangle$: program state
    E: selected event tuple
    Δ: derived tuples
begin
1:     $\langle \mathcal{M}, \mathcal{E} \rangle := S_0$
2:     **while** $\mathcal{E} \neq \emptyset$ **do**
3:         $E :=$ take from $\mathcal{E}$
4:         **find** $r \ a \ H \ :- \ T, B \in \mathcal{R}$ **such that** T unifies with E
5:         $\Delta := \{ H\sigma \mid \sigma : \mathcal{V} \to \mathcal{D} \text{ and } E = T\sigma \text{ and } \mathcal{M} \models B\sigma \}$
6:         **case** a **of**
7:             snd: $\mathcal{E} := \mathcal{E} \setminus \{E\} \cup \Delta$
8:             add:
9:                 $\Delta^{\mathcal{K}} := \{ D{\downarrow}_{\mathcal{K}} \mid D \in \Delta \}$
10:                $\mathcal{M} := \{ D \mid D \in \mathcal{M} \text{ and } D{\downarrow}_{\mathcal{K}} \notin \Delta^{\mathcal{K}} \} \cup \Delta$
11:            del: $\mathcal{M} := \mathcal{M} \setminus \Delta$
12:        **end case**
13:    **done**
end.

Fig. 3. Operational semantics for P2

The resulting (multi)set Δ of tuples is further processed according to the action kind a. If the rule is of kind add, and to guarantee the satisfaction of projection constraints, conflicting tuples are deleted from $\mathcal{M}$ before adding the new ones.

4   Cardinality Abstraction

This section presents the cardinality abstraction technique.

Cardinality measures. *Cardinality measures* are expressions of the form $\#F_X$ and $\#E$, where F is a conjunction of predicates, X is a set of variables, and E is an event predicate. Sometimes we use an arbitrary expression W instead of X. In this case, we assume $X = vars(W)$. Given a substitution function $\sigma : \mathcal{V} \to \mathcal{V} \cup \mathcal{D}$ and a set of variables X, we write $\sigma{\downarrow}_X$ to denote the restriction of σ wrt. X, i.e., the function such that $x\sigma{\downarrow}_X = x\sigma$ if $x \in X$, and $x\sigma{\downarrow}_X = x$ if $x \notin X$. Note that $\sigma{\downarrow}_\emptyset$ is the identity function.

Given a program state $\mathcal{S} = \langle \mathcal{M}, \mathcal{E} \rangle$, the cardinality measures $\#F_X$ wrt. $\mathcal{S}$ counts the number of valuations for X that are determined by the solutions of F wrt. $\mathcal{M}$. Similarly, $\#E$ counts the number of events in $\mathcal{E}$ that unify with the event predicate E. Formally, we have

$$[\![\#F_X]\!]_{\mathcal{S}} = |\{ \sigma{\downarrow}_X \mid \sigma : \mathcal{V} \to \mathcal{D}, \mathcal{M} \models F\sigma \}| \,,$$

$$[\![\#E]\!]_{\mathcal{S}} = \sum \{ \mathcal{E}(E\sigma) \mid \sigma : vars(E) \to \mathcal{D} \} \,.$$

For an expression Φ over cardinality measures, we write $[\![\Phi]\!]_S$ to denote the expression where cardinality measures are replaced by their evaluation wrt. S.

The measure $\#F_\emptyset$ evaluates to one if the query F has at least one solution since all solutions are equal to the identity. If F does not have any solutions then $\#F_\emptyset$ evaluates to zero. We assume that variables in X that do not appear in F can be assigned arbitrary values from $\mathcal{D}$. Formally, in case X contains a set of variables X^- that do not occur in F, say $X = X^+ \uplus X^-$, we obtain

$$[\![\#F_X]\!]_S = [\![\#F_{X^+}]\!]_S \times |\mathcal{D}|^{|X^-|} .$$

Example 1 (Measure evaluation). We consider a case where $\mathcal{L} = \{p/2, q/2\}$, $\mathcal{D} = \{a, b, c, d, e, f\}$, $\mathcal{K}(p) = \{1, 2\}$, and $\mathcal{K}(q) = \{1\}$. Let $S = \langle \mathcal{M}, \mathcal{E} \rangle$ be a state such that $\mathcal{M}$ is given by the tables p and q below and $\mathcal{E} = \emptyset$. We present examples of cardinality measures and their evaluation wrt. S below.   □

p	q	F	X	$[\![\#F_X]\!]_S$	F	X	$[\![\#F_X]\!]_S$
a, b	a, b	$p(x, y)$	$\{x, y\}$	5	$p(x, y) \wedge q(y, z)$	$\{x, y, z\}$	4
a, c	b, c	$p(x, y)$	$\{x\}$	4	$p(x, y) \wedge q(y, z)$	$\{y, z\}$	2
b, b	d, a	$p(x, y)$	$\{y\}$	3	$p(x, y) \wedge q(y, z)$	$\emptyset$	1
c, a	e, a	$p(x, y)$	$\{y, z\}$	18	$p(x, y) \wedge q(y, x)$	$\emptyset$	0
d, b	f, a	$p(a, x)$	$\{x\}$	2	$p(x, y) \wedge p(y, x)$	$\{x, y\}$	3

4.1   Computing the Cardinality Abstraction

Figure 4 shows the CARDAN algorithm that together with a function STRUCT-CLOSURE computes the cardinality abstraction of P2 programs. The algorithm generates for each event, and corresponding triggered rule, a constraint that describes the state transition in terms of cardinality measures. Each constraint represents a relation between measures evaluated before and after the rule is executed. The primed cardinality measures $\#F'_X$ and $\#E'$ represent the next state of the program, and the evaluation $[\![\Phi]\!]_{S,S'}$ of an expression Φ is obtained by evaluating current and next state measures on the states S and S', respectively.

These constraints take into account how the measures on all tables (and their projections), as well as on all events, are updated according to the kind of rule executed (add, del, or snd) and the consumption of the selected event. A *structural closure*, computed by STRUCTCLOSURE, provides a set of constraints satisfied by the measures produced by the main algorithm. It constrains the values of measures for complex queries in terms of measures for their components. The execution of STRUCTCLOSURE terminates since at each iteration only cardinality measures with fewer predicates or fewer variables are introduced. Constraints computed by CARDAN are in the worst case exponentially larger than the input program. Section 4.2 presents optimizations that address this explosion in order to achieve a practical analysis.

Example 2 (Measure update). We show the constraints that CARDAN creates for an event $s(w_1)$ that triggers a rule

$$r \text{ add } p(x, y) :- s(x), \ B(x, y, z)$$

procedure CARDAN
input
    $P_2 = \langle \mathcal{L}, \mathcal{D}, \mathcal{K}, \mathcal{R}, S_0 \rangle$: a P2 program
vars
    Ψ, Φ : constraints over cardinality measures
begin
1:   $\Psi := \bot$
2:   **for each** event $S = s(w_1, \dots, w_m)$ **do**
3:     $\Phi := \top$
4:     **let** $r\ a\ H :\!- T, B \in \mathcal{R}$ **such that** T and S unify
5:     **for each** data predicate $P = p(v_1, \dots, v_n)$ and set $V \subseteq vars(P)$ **do**
6:       **if** there is a substitution σ **such that** $H = P\sigma$ **then**
7:         **if** $a = \mathbf{add}$ **then**
8:           $\Phi := \Phi \wedge (\#P'_V = \#P_V + \#B_{V\sigma} - \#(B \wedge (P\sigma{\downarrow}_V))_{V\sigma})$
9:         **else if** $a = \mathbf{del}$ **then**
10:           **if** $V = \{v_1, \dots, v_n\}$ **then**
11:             $\Phi := \Phi \wedge (\#P'_V = \#P_V - \#(B \wedge H)_{V\sigma})$
12:           **else**
13:             $\Phi := \Phi \wedge (\#P_V - \#(B \wedge H)_{V\sigma} \leq \#P'_V \leq \#P_V)$
14:         **else**
15:           $\Phi := \Phi \wedge (\#P'_V = \#P_V)$
16:     **for each** event predicate $E = e(v_1, \dots, v_n)$ **do**
17:       $\Delta := 0$
18:       **if** E and H unify **then**
19:         $\Delta := \#B_H$
20:       **if** E and T unify **then**
21:         $\Delta := \Delta - 1$
22:       $\Phi := \Phi \wedge (\#S' = \#S + \Delta)$
23:     $\Psi := \Psi \vee \textsc{StructClosure}(\Phi)$
24:   **end**
25:   **return** Ψ
end.

function STRUCTCLOSURE
input
    Φ : constraints over cardinality measures
begin
1:   **do**
2:     $\Phi := \Phi \wedge \bigwedge \{0 \leq \#F_\emptyset \leq 1 \mid \#F_X \text{ occurs in } \Phi\}$
3:     $\Phi := \Phi \wedge \bigwedge \{\#F_X \leq \#F_{X \cup Y} \leq \#F_X \times \#F_Y \mid \#F_{X \cup Y} \text{ occurs in } \Phi\}$
4:     $\Phi := \Phi \wedge \bigwedge \{\#(F \wedge G)_X \leq \#F_X \mid \#(F \wedge G)_X \text{ occurs in } \Phi\}$
5:     $\Phi := \Phi \wedge \bigwedge \{\#P_X = \#P_{P{\downarrow}_{\mathcal{K}}} \mid \#P_X \text{ occurs in } \Phi \text{ and } vars(P{\downarrow}_{\mathcal{K}}) \subseteq X \subseteq vars(P)\}$
6:     **for each** data predicate $P = p(v_1, \dots, v_n)$ and set $V \subseteq vars(P)$ **do**
7:       $\Phi := \Phi \wedge \bigwedge \{\#P\sigma_X \leq \#P_V \mid \#P\sigma_X \text{ occurs in } \Phi, |V| = |X|, \text{ and } X = V\sigma\}$
8:   **while** Φ is updated
9:   **return** Φ
end.

Fig. 4. CARDAN algorithm for computing cardinality abstraction

where $B(x, y, z)$ is some query over variables x, y, and z. For $P = p(v_1, v_2)$ and $V = \{v_1\}$, line 8 of CARDAN creates the constraint

$$\#p(v_1, v_2)'_{\{v_1\}} = \#p(v_1, v_2)_{\{v_1\}} + \#B(x, y, z)_{\{x\}} - \#(B(x, y, z) \wedge p(x, v_2))_{\{x\}} \,.$$

In this case, the substitution σ that unifies $p(v_1, v_2)$ with the head of the rule is given by $\sigma = \{v_1 \to x, v_2 \to y\}$ and its restriction is $\sigma\downarrow_{\{v_1\}} = \{v_1 \to x\}$.

This expression describes the change in the number of values in the p table—after executing the rule and projecting wrt. its first column—by adding first the number of solutions of the query projected on the variable x, and then subtracting the number of values that were already in the table. This is the role of the last term, which asks for those values of x that appear both as a solution to the query and as the first component in some tuple currently in the table. The second component of such tuple is free to contain any arbitrary value.

For other predicates, line 15 creates constraints encoding the frame conditions, e.g., for predicate $q(v_1, v_2)$ we obtain $\#q(v_1, v_2)'_V = \#q(v_1, v_2)_V$.   □

Example 3 (Structural closure). We illustrate the STRUCTCLOSURE function on expressions from Example 1. The set of computed constraints includes

$$0 \le \#(p(x, y) \wedge q(y, x))_\emptyset \le 1 \,, \tag{1}$$

$$\#p(x, y)_{\{x\}} \le \#p(x, y)_{\{x,y\}} \le \#p(x, y)_{\{x\}} \times \#p(x, y)_{\{y\}} \,, \tag{2}$$

$$\#(p(x, y) \wedge (y, z))_{\{y,z\}} \le \#p(x, y)_{\{y,z\}} \,, \tag{3}$$

$$\#q(x, y)_{\{x,y\}} = \#q(x, y)_{\{x\}} \,, \tag{4}$$

$$\#p(a, x)_{\{x\}} \le \#p(v_1, v_2)_{\{v_2\}} \,. \tag{5}$$

These constraints correspond to algebraic properties satisfied by cardinality measures (1-3), relations imposed by projection constraints (4), and relations between arbitrary single-predicate queries and table projections (5). One can check that all (1-5) are valid for the state $\mathcal{S}$ presented earlier in Example 1.   □

Correctness of Cardan. The constraints generated by STRUCTCLOSURE are valid for all possible states, as formalized in the following theorem.

Theorem 1. *Given an arithmetic constraint Φ over cardinality measures and a state $\mathcal{S}$, the constraint $[\![\Phi]\!]_\mathcal{S}$ holds if and only if $[\![\text{STRUCTCLOSURE}(\Phi)]\!]_\mathcal{S}$ does.*

Although we omit a proof for brevity, it is not hard to verify that all the constraints generated by CARDAN are valid. Moreover, as a direct consequence from the previous result, soundness of the approach follows.

Theorem 2. *Given a P2 program P_2, and a pair of states $\mathcal{S}$, $\mathcal{S}'$ related by the transition relation given by EVALUATE, the constraint $[\![\text{CARDAN}(P_2)]\!]_{\mathcal{S},\mathcal{S}'}$ holds.*

By Theorem 1, the STRUCTCLOSURE function gives a sound and relatively complete abstraction (modulo data values) of relations in terms of cardinality measures. Moreover, Skolem symbols can be used to refine the abstraction by taking into account particular data values and, in that sense, obtain completeness for the overall approach, see Section 5.

4.2   Extensions and Optimizations

The presentation in the previous sections was simplified with the assumption that, for each selected event, only one rule is executed. Programs in P2, including our TOKEN example from Section 2, often require the simultaneous execution of several rules in a single step. We automatically find sets of rules that have to be evaluated together (also propagating bindings of variables across rules), and prune combinations of rules that will never be evaluated concurrently. The algorithm presented earlier in Figure 4 can then to be modified to generate individual transitions not for each rule, but for each one of those groups of rules that perform atomic updates.

The implementation of many applications in P2, in particular the Zyzzyva protocol discussed in the next section, rely on rules that can also, as part of their evaluation, count the number of solutions of arbitrary queries on the store. To accommodate for this feature, the syntax of rules has to be extended to allow the use of *counting* operators on their bodies. However, since these counting operators can be expressed in terms of our cardinality measures, they don't impose any new challenges in the theory or implementation of the approach.

Finally, as an optimization to reduce the number of variables in queries, and therefore the number of constraints generated by the STRUCTCLOSURE function, we implement a *symbolic constant propagation* technique. This procedure simplifies rules by computing a set of variables that will be bound to at most one value, and replacing those variables with symbolic constants. This set of variables is initialized with those appearing in the trigger (since they have to exactly match the selected event), and then expanded to include more variables by propagating these symbolic constants through the projection constraints.

5   Experience

In this section we describe our experiences applying cardinality abstraction for the verification of the P2 implementation of the Zyzzyva protocol [39]. Zyzzyva is a state-of-the-art Byzantine fault tolerance (BFT) protocol designed to improve the reliability of client-server applications such as web services. In Zyzzyva, the service state and request processing logic is replicated on $3F+1$ computer hosts, where F is a non-negative integer. Zyzzyva guarantees correct and consistent execution of the service even when at most F replica hosts can fail *arbitrarily*, e.g., due to software bugs or malicious behavior caused by a computer virus.

To be correct, Zyzzyva must assign a distinct sequence number to each client request. This safety property is amenable to cardinality analysis since, by counting the number of messages that are sent between replicas and clients, it is possible to identify how many requests have been assigned to a given sequence number. Specifically, the safety property is violated if the table done, which collects the responses accepted by clients, contains two tuples with a different client or request values but the same sequence number. Our approach can show that the safety property is valid under the assumption that at most F hosts are faulty among the totaol of $3F + 1$ hosts. The BFT guarantees are not assumed, but rather derived from the basic assumption.

Since cardinality abstraction does not handle the data values stored in tuples (i.e., values of particular requests or sequence numbers), we represent this information by partitioning the original program tables with respect to a finite set of values of interest. For example, a table reply(Replica, Request, SeqNo) is partitioned to contain a table reply_a_s(Replica) whose elements correspond to tuples of the form reply(Replica, a, s).

We distinguish the behavior of *correct* and *faulty* replicas. To model Byzantine failures, we simulated the *worst possible* faulty behavior for replicas that, for this property, corresponds to sending (without the corresponding checks) confirmation messages agreeing to two conflicting request assignments for the same sequence number. Correct replicas behave according to the protocol implementation. We apply CARDAN on the resulting P2 program, which computes cardinality abstraction of the program. The model checking backend ARMC analyzes the resulting transition relation over cardinality measures and proves the property in five seconds.

In the on-going work, we consider further examples of BFT protocols [10,28,42], as well as other distributed applications.

6   Related work

Verification of distributed applications is a classical research topic. Recent efforts have been focused on the synthesis of quantified invariants [1, 3, 35] and counting abstraction [36] for parameterized, bounded-data systems. These techniques, however, are not directly applicable to P2 programs due to the complex program state and declarative representation of transition relations. Our approach, although closely related to counting abstraction, differs in that we count the number of solutions of complex relational queries, rather than the number of processes in one of finitely many possible states [36]. On the other hand, the network topology in P2 programs is abstracted away by a table of reachable neighbors. This eliminates the need to perform a network reachability analysis— one of the common difficulties of distributed protocol verification.

Program analysis has been extensively studied for Datalog and other forms of logic programming. Comprehensive abstract interpretation frameworks for Prolog exist, including [9, 18]. These frameworks are supported by state-of-the-art implementations, e.g., PLAI/CIAOPP [24] and ANALYSER [21]. These tools perform size analysis, cost analysis, determinacy analysis, non-failure analysis, termination analysis, and resource analysis. The cardinality analysis for Prolog, see e.g. [8], approximates number of solutions to a goal, but it does not handle indexing and bottom-up evaluation semantics, which we found crucial for declarative networking applications written in P2.

Existing approaches to the analysis of networking applications, see e.g. MACEMC [26] and CMC [32,33], focus on finding defects using symbolic executions techniques. While in theory they can be applied exhaustively to prove absence of defects, it is extremely difficult to achieve this in practice. In the context of declarative networking, early steps have been given by clarifying the semantics of P2 programs [34], and designing translations of program properties into formulas suitable for use in interactive theorem provers [41]. Our analysis complements these techniques by supporting automated proof discovery.

Abstraction of sets and relations for imperative programs focuses on dynamically allocated heap used to store graph structures of a particular shape, e.g., shape analysis [7, 38] and separation logic [37, 43]. [23] refines these approaches with information about the size of the allocated heap fragments. In contrast, declarative networking uses relations as a general purpose-data store without particular shape invariants and, unlike heap models, has to deal with database operations that manipulate tables. The result of cardinality abstraction can be analysed by existing tools and techniques for computing abstract semantics, including numerical abstract domains, e.g. [2, 19, 31], automatic abstraction refinement, invariant generation, and predicate abstraction [12, 13, 22].

References

1. Arons, T., Pnueli, A., Ruah, S., Xu, J., Zuck, L.D.: Parameterized verification with automatically computed inductive assertions. In: Berry, G., Comon, H., Finkel, A. (eds.) CAV 2001. LNCS, vol. 2102, p. 221. Springer, Heidelberg (2001)
2. Bagnara, R., Hill, P.M., Zaffanella, E.: The Parma Polyhedra Library: Toward a complete set of numerical abstractions for the analysis and verification of hardware and software systems. Science of Computer Programming (2008)
3. Balaban, I., Pnueli, A., Zuck, L.D.: Invisible safety of distributed protocols. In: Bugliesi, M., Preneel, B., Sassone, V., Wegener, I. (eds.) ICALP 2006. LNCS, vol. 4052, pp. 528–539. Springer, Heidelberg (2006)
4. Ball, T., Rajamani, S.K.: The SLAM project: Debugging system software via static analysis. In: POPL (2002)
5. Beyer, D., Henzinger, T.A., Jhala, R., Majumdar, R.: The software model checker blast. STTT (2007)
6. Blanchet, B., Cousot, P., Cousot, R., Feret, J., Mauborgne, L., Miné, A., Monniaux, D., Rival, X.: A static analyzer for large safety-critical software. In: PLDI (2003)
7. Bogudlov, I., Lev-Ami, T., Reps, T.W., Sagiv, M.: Revamping TVLA: Making parametric shape analysis competitive. In: Damm, W., Hermanns, H. (eds.) CAV 2007. LNCS, vol. 4590, pp. 221–225. Springer, Heidelberg (2007)
8. Braem, C., Charlier, B.L., Modart, S., van Hentenryck, P.: Cardinality analysis of Prolog. In: ILPS (1994)
9. Bruynooghe, M.: A practical framework for the abstract interpretation of logic programs. J. Log. Program. (1991)
10. Castro, M., Liskov, B.: Practical Byzantine Fault Tolerance (1999)
11. Chu, D., Popa, L., Tavakoli, A., Hellerstein, J.M., Levis, P., Shenker, S., Stoica, I.: The design and implementation of a declarative sensor network system. In: SenSys (2007)
12. Clarke, E.M., Grumberg, O., Jha, S., Lu, Y., Veith, H.: Counterexample-guided abstraction refinement. In: Emerson, E.A., Sistla, A.P. (eds.) CAV 2000. LNCS, vol. 1855. Springer, Heidelberg (2000)

13. Colón, M., Sankaranarayanan, S., Sipma, H.: Linear invariant generation using non-linear constraint solving. In: Hunt Jr., W.A., Somenzi, F. (eds.) CAV 2003. LNCS, vol. 2725, pp. 420–432. Springer, Heidelberg (2003)
14. Condie, T., Chu, D., Hellerstein, J.M., Maniatis, P.: Evita raced: metacompilation for declarative networks. In: PVLDB (2008)
15. Condie, T., Gay, D.E., Loo, B.T., et al.: P2: Declarative networking website (2008), http://p2.cs.berkeley.edu/
16. Cook, B., Podelski, A., Rybalchenko, A.: Terminator: Beyond safety. In: Ball, T., Jones, R.B. (eds.) CAV 2006. LNCS, vol. 4144, pp. 415–418. Springer, Heidelberg (2006)
17. Cousot, P., Cousot, R.: Abstract interpretation: a unified lattice model for static analysis of programs by construction or approximation of fixpoints. In: POPL, ACM, New York (1977)
18. Cousot, P., Cousot, R.: Abstract interpretation and application to logic programs. J. Log. Program. (1992)
19. Cousot, P., Halbwachs, N.: Automatic discovery of linear restraints among variables of a program. In: POPL (1978)
20. German, S.M., Sistla, A.P.: Reasoning about systems with many processes. J. ACM (1992)
21. Gobert, F.: Towards Putting Abstract Interpretation of Prolog Into Practice. Ph.D thesis, Université catholique de Louvain (2007)
22. Graf, S., Saïdi, H.: Construction of abstract state graphs with pvs. In: Grumberg, O. (ed.) CAV 1997. LNCS, vol. 1254. Springer, Heidelberg (1997)
23. Gulwani, S., Lev-Ami, T., Sagiv, M.: A combination framework for tracking partition sizes. In: POPL (2009)
24. Hermenegildo, M.V., Puebla, G., Bueno, F., López-García, P.: Program development using abstract interpretation (and the Ciao system preprocessor). In: Cousot, R. (ed.) SAS 2003. LNCS, vol. 2694, pp. 127–152. Springer, Heidelberg (2003)
25. Killian, C., Anderson, J.W., Braud, R., Jhala, R., Vahadat, A.: Mace: Language support for building distributed systems. In: PLDI (2007)
26. Killian, C.E., Anderson, J.W., Jhala, R., Vahdat, A.: Life, death, and the critical transition: Finding liveness bugs in systems code. In: NSDI (2007)
27. Lalire, G., Argoud, M., Jeannet, B.: The interproc analyzer, http://pop-art.inrialpes.fr/people/bjeannet/bjeannet-forge/interproc/index.html
28. Lamport, L.: The Part-Time Parliament. ACM Transactions on Computer Systems (1998)
29. Loo, B.T., Condie, T., Garofalakis, M., Gay, D.E., Hellerstein, J.M., Maniatis, P., Ramakrishnan, R., Roscoe, T., Stoica, I.: Declarative networking: Language, execution and optimization. In: SIGMOD (2006)
30. Loo, B.T., Condie, T., Hellerstein, J.M., Maniatis, P., Roscoe, T., Stoica, I.: Implementing declarative overlays. In: SIGOPS (2005)
31. Miné, A.: The octagon abstract domain. Higher-Order and Symb. Comp. (2006)
32. Musuvathi, M., Engler, D.R.: Model checking large network protocol implementations. In: NSDI (2004)
33. Musuvathi, M., Park, D.Y.W., Chou, A., Engler, D.R., Dill, D.L.: CMC: A pragmatic approach to model checking real code. In: OSDI (2002)
34. Navarro, J.A., Rybalchenko, A.: Operational semantics for declarative networking. In: PADL (2009)

35. Pnueli, A., Ruah, S., Zuck, L.D.: Automatic deductive verification with invisible invariants. In: Margaria, T., Yi, W. (eds.) TACAS 2001. LNCS, vol. 2031, p. 82. Springer, Heidelberg (2001)
36. Pnueli, A., Xu, J., Zuck, L.D.: Liveness with (0, 1, infty)-counter abstraction. In: Brinksma, E., Larsen, K.G. (eds.) CAV 2002. LNCS, vol. 2404, p. 107. Springer, Heidelberg (2002)
37. Reynolds, J.C.: Separation logic: A logic for shared mutable data structures. In: LICS (2002)
38. Sagiv, S., Reps, T.W., Wilhelm, R.: Parametric shape analysis via 3-valued logic. ACM Trans. Program. Lang. Syst. (2002)
39. Singh, A., Das, T., Maniatis, P., Druschel, P., Roscoe, T.: BFT protocols under fire. In: NSDI (2008)
40. Singh, A., Maniatis, P., Roscoe, T., Druschel, P.: Using queries for distributed monitoring and forensics. In: EuroSys, Leuven, Belgium (2006)
41. Wang, A., Basu, P., Loo, B.T., Sokolsky, O.: Declarative networking verification. In: PADL (2009)
42. Wood, T., Singh, R., Venkataramani, A., Shenoy, P.: ZZ: Cheap Practical BFT Using Virtualization. Technical Report TR14-08, University of Massachusetts (2008)
43. Yang, H., Lee, O., Berdine, J., Calcagno, C., Cook, B., Distefano, D., O'Hearn, P.W.: Scalable shape analysis for systems code. In: Gupta, A., Malik, S. (eds.) CAV 2008. LNCS, vol. 5123, pp. 385–398. Springer, Heidelberg (2008)

Equivalence Checking of Static Affine Programs Using Widening to Handle Recurrences

Sven Verdoolaege, Gerda Janssens, and Maurice Bruynooghe

Katholieke Universiteit Leuven, Department of Computer Science,
Celestijnenlaan 200A, B-3001 Leuven, Belgium

Abstract. Designers often apply manual or semi-automatic loop and data transformations on array and loop intensive programs to improve performance. The transformations should preserve the functionality, however, and this paper presents an automatic method for constructing equivalence proofs for the class of static affine programs. The equivalence checking is performed on a dependence graph abstraction and uses a new approach based on widening to handle recurrences. Unlike transitive closure based approaches, this widening approach can also handle non-uniform recurrences. The implementation is publicly available and is the first of its kind to fully support commutative operations.

1 Introduction

Embedded processors for multimedia and telecom systems are severely resource constrained. Developers apply aggressive loop and data transformations based on a combination of automated analysis and manual interventions to reduce memory requirements and power consumption. A crucial question is whether the transformed program is equivalent to the original. We address this problem for the case of static affine programs, i.e., programs with static control flow and piecewise affine expressions for all loop bounds, conditions and array accesses.

Figure 1 shows a toy example of a pair of programs for which we would like to prove equivalence. Both programs have the same input array In and output array Out (a scalar in this case) and the objective is to show that for any value of the input array(s), both programs produce the same value for the output array(s). We neither assume an a priori correspondence between the other arrays (the temporary arrays) of both programs nor between their loops.

The equivalence checking of static affine programs has been previously investigated by Barthou et al. [1, 6] and Shashidhar et al. [20, 21]. A major challenge in this line of research is posed by recurrences, i.e., a statement in a loop that (indirectly) depends on previous iterations of the same statement. Such recurrences render the representation of the values of the output arrays as a symbolic expression in terms of only the input arrays, as advocated by some symbolic simulation based techniques (e.g., [17]) impractical, as the whole loop needs to be effectively unrolled, or even impossible, if the number of iterations is unknown at analysis time, as is the case in our running example (Figure 1). All the previous work

A. Bouajjani and O. Maler (Eds.): CAV 2009, LNCS 5643, pp. 599–613, 2009.

```
1 A[0]=In[0];
2 for (i=1; i<N; ++i)
3    A[i]=f(In[i])+g(A[i-1]);
4 Out=A[N-1];
```
(a) Program 1

```
1  A[0]=In[0];
2  for (i=1; i<N; ++i) {
3     if (i%2 == 0) {
4        B[i]=f(In[i]);
5        C[i]=g(A[i-1]);
6     } else {
7        B[i]=g(A[i-1]);
8        C[i]=f(In[i]);}
9     A[i]=B[i]+C[i];}
10 Out=A[N-1];
```
(b) Program 2

Fig. 1. Two programs with a recurrence; assuming that + is commutative they are equivalent

mentioned above relies on the transitive closure operation [14] provided by the Omega library [13] to handle recurrences, effectively restricting the applicability of those techniques to programs containing only uniform recurrences.

Another challenge is posed by algebraic transformations, i.e., a transformation that depends on algebraic properties of operations, e.g., associativity or commutativity. Of the above, only Shashidhar has a proposal for handling algebraic transformations. However, as stated in Section 9.3.1 of [20], this proposal has not been implemented. Moreover, it is unable to handle the commutativity of + in Figure 1 as the order of the arguments has been reversed for only half of the iterations of the loop.

Furthermore, all the above approaches require both programs to be in dynamic single assignment (DSA) form [9], i.e., such that each array element is written at most once, and none of the implementations are publicly available.

Like the previous approaches, we handle recurrences in both programs *fully automatically* and we handle any per statement or per array piecewise quasi-affine loop or data transformation, including combinations of loop interchange, loop reversal, loop skewing, loop distribution, loop tiling, loop unrolling, loop splitting, loop peeling and data-reuse transformations. However, unlike those approaches, ours

- handles programs that perform destructive updates without a preprocessing step that converts them to dynamic single assignment form,
- handles both uniform and non-uniform recurrences by not relying on a transitive closure operation, and
- has a publicly available implementation,
- with full support for associative and commutative operations with a fixed number of arguments.

We define the concept of a dependence graph in Section 2, which we then use as input for the equivalence checking method of Section 3. Section 4 has implementation details and Section 5 the final discussion.

2   Program Model

Two programs will be considered to be equivalent if they produce the same output values given the same input values. As we treat all operations performed inside the programs as black boxes, this means that in both programs the same operations should be applied in the same order on the input data to arrive at the output. For our equivalence checking, we therefore need to know which operations are performed and how data flows from one operation to another. In this section, we introduce a program model that captures exactly this information. Unlike [20, 21] where an array based representation is used and some dependence analysis is implicitly performed during the equivalence checking, we separate the dependence analysis from the equivalence checking, the latter working on the output of the former. This separation allows us to use standard exact dataflow analysis [10] or, in future work, fuzzy dataflow analysis [5]. The resulting *dependence graph* is essentially a DSA representation of the program, but without rewriting the source program in that form as in [20, 21].

For simplicity we assume that input and output arrays are given, that input arrays are only read and output arrays only written, that each read value is either input or has been written before, and that there is only one output array. These assumptions can easily be relaxed. The use of exact dataflow analysis implies the usual restrictions of static affine programs, i.e., static control flow, quasi-affine loop bounds and quasi-affine index expressions. Recall that quasi-affine expressions consist of additions, constant multiplication and integer division by a constant. We also assume that all functions called in the program are pure.

We will now first present the definition of a dependence graph and then explain how such a dependence graph can be constructed from dataflow analysis. In what follows, "⊂" means "strict subset" and "⊆" means "subset". All sets and relations may involve parameters.

Definition 1 (Dependence Graph). *A dependence graph is a connected directed graph $G = <V, E>$ with a designated output vertex $v_0 \in V$ with in-degree 0 and a set $I \subset V$ of input vertices, each with out-degree 0. The graph may have loops and parallel edges. Each vertex $v \in V$ is adorned by a tuple $< d_v, D_v, f_v, r_v, l_v >$, with*

- *d_v a non-negative integer, called the* dimension *of the node*
- *D_v a set of d_v-tuples of integers, called the* iteration domain *of the node*
- *f_v a literal, called the* operation *of the node*
- *r_v a non-negative integer, called the* arity *of the node*
- *l_v a literal, called the* location *of the node*

and each edge $e = (u, v) \in E$ is adorned by a pair $< p_e, M_e >$, with

- *p_e a non-negative integer with $1 \le p_e \le r_u$, called the* argument position
- *M_e a set of $(d_u + d_v)$-tuples of integers, called the* dependence relation.

Moreover, the following constraints are satisfied. Firstly, $\forall u \in V, \forall \boldsymbol{x} \in D_u, \forall p \in [1, r_u] : \exists! e = (u, v) \in E : p_e = p$ and $\boldsymbol{x} \in dom(M_e)$, i.e., the domains of the *dependence relations of the edges emanating from a node for a given argument position partition the domain of the node. The unique edge corresponding to a point $\boldsymbol{x}$ and an argument position p is denoted $e_G(\boldsymbol{x}, p)$. Secondly, for any cycle in the graph, the composition of the dependence relations M_e along the cycle does not intersect the identity relation, i.e., no element of a domain (indirectly) depends on itself.*

To represent a program by a dependency graph, we use the vertices to represent *computations*. We distinguish three kinds of vertices/computations: An output computation for the output array, an input computation for each input array and a computation for each function call, each operation and each copy statement. The dependence graph of Program 1 (Figure 1(a)) is shown in Figure 2. The graph has one input and one output computation and five other computations, one for the copy statement in Line 4, one for the addition, one for the computation of f, and one for the computation of g (all from Line 3) and finally one for the copy statement in Line 1. As for the annotations of a node v, the pair (d_v, D_v) denotes the set of elements for which the computation is performed. For input and output computations, d_v is the dimension of the respective arrays and the domain is the set of its elements. As the output of Program 1 is a scalar, the dimension is 0 and the single element is denoted as (). The input array is one dimensional and the domain consists of the set of elements from 0 to $N - 1$. For other computations, the dimension is determined by the loop nest controlling the computation, while the domain describes the iterations for which the computation is performed (dimension 1 and elements 1 to $N - 1$ for the computations of Line 3). The pair (f_v, r_v) reflects the operation being performed and its arity. For input computations, f_v is the name of the input array while r_v is set to 0; for the output computation, f_v is the name of the output array and r_v is set to 1. Copy operations are represented by id (for identity) with arity 1 and the other operations by the name of the operation and its arity. The l_v annotation refers to the program line where the computation is performed; it is not defined for input and output computations.

Edges arise in three different ways. If, within a given statement, the result of some function f is used as the jth argument of some function g, then an edge e is added from the computation u corresponding to g to the computation v corresponding to f, with $p_e = j$ and $M_e = \{(\boldsymbol{i}; \boldsymbol{i}) \mid \boldsymbol{i} \in D_u\}$. Note that $D_u = D_v$ here since both operations appear in the same statement. Also note that for any relation $M \subseteq \mathbb{Z}^{d_u} \times \mathbb{Z}^{d_v}$, we separate the d_u input dimensions from the d_v output dimensions by a ";". In general, either or both of d_u and d_v may be zero. Examples of intra-statement dependences in Figure 2 are the edges from the addition (computation e) to respectively the computations c and d. If the function of computation u takes an array element as its jth argument and this array element has been "computed" by the function of computation v (this includes copy and input computations), then an edge $e = (u, v)$ is added, with $p_e = j$ and M_e relating the iterations of u with the corresponding iterations of v. Dataflow analysis is used to find v and to compute M_e by identifying the last statement iteration that wrote to the array. Since there is exactly one such last iteration for each of the array

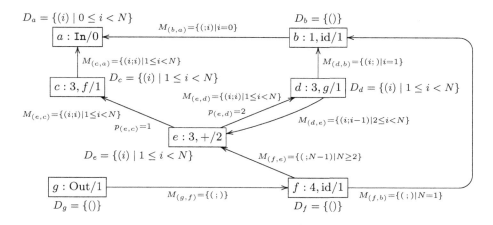

Fig. 2. Dependence graph of Program 1 in Figure 1. Computations are named from a to g with a the input and g the output computation. Each computation v is represented as "$v : l_v, f_v/r_v$" (l_v is absent for input and output computations). To avoid clutter, the dimension is omitted, while the domain is shown next to the box with the node; also the argument position p_e is only indicated on edges emanating from node e (it is 1 on all other edges).

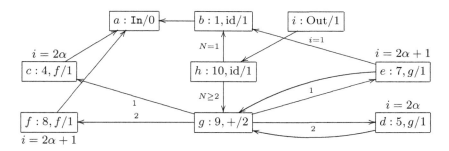

Fig. 3. Dependence graph of Program 2 in Figure 1 (some details omitted)

elements, the first constraint of Definition 1 is satisfied. The second constraint is satisfied because a statement iteration can only depend on a *previous* iteration in the execution order. For example, dataflow analysis identifies an edge from vertex f to vertex b with mapping $\{(;)\}$ (the single iteration in the zero-dimensional iteration domain of f is mapped to the single iteration of b) for $N = 1$ and an edge from vertex f to vertex e with mapping $\{(; N - 1)\}$ for $N \geq 2$ (the single iteration of f is mapped to iteration $N - 1$ of the one-dimensional iteration domain of computation e). Finally, for each computation v that last wrote an element of the output array (dataflow analysis determines which v), an edge is added from the output computation to v, with as M_e the reversed access relation of the write. In our running example, $M_{(g,f)} = \{(;)\}$ as a scalar of dimension 0 is written. Note that input computations do not have outgoing edges and the output computation does not have incoming edges.

The concept of the equivalence of two dependence graphs is defined inductively and follows the intuitive definition of the equivalence of two programs at the start of this section.

Definition 2 (Equivalence of Computation Iterations). *An iteration $x_1 \in D_{v_1}$ of a computation $v_1 \in V_1$ in a dataflow graph G_1 is equivalent to an iteration $x_2 \in D_{v_2}$ of a computation $v_2 \in V_2$ in a dataflow graph G_2 if one of the following conditions holds*

- *V_1 and V_2 are input computations with $f_{v_1} = f_{v_2}$ and $x_1 = x_2$,*
- *$f_{v_1} = \mathrm{id}$ and iteration $M_{e_{G_1}(x_1,1)}(x_1)$ of v_1' with $e_{G_1(x_1,1)} = (v_1, v_1')$ is equivalent to iteration x_2 of v_2 (and similarly for $f_{v_2} = \mathrm{id}$), or*
- *$(f_{v_1}, r_{v_1}) = (f_{v_2}, r_{v_2})$ and for each $p \in [1, r_{v_1}]$, iteration $M_{e_{G_1}(x_1,p)}(x_1)$ of v_1' with $e_{G_1(x_1,p)} = (v_1, v_1')$ is equivalent to iteration $M_{e_{G_2}(x_2,p)}(x_2)$ of v_2' with $e_{G_2(x_2,p)} = (v_2, v_2')$.*

Definition 3 (Equivalence of Dependence Graphs). *Two dependence graphs are equivalent if the iteration domains of their output computations are identical and if all iterations of these output computations are equivalent.*

3 Equivalence Checking

In order to prove equivalence of two dependence graphs we basically follow Definition 2 and propagate from the output to the input what correspondences between computation iterations we should prove. Once we hit computations with zero out-degree (either input computations or symbolic constants), we propagate back to the output what we have actually been able to prove. This two-way propagation is different from the approaches in [1, 6, 20, 21], the authors of which essentially only propagate information from output to input. There are several reasons for this difference in approach. Firstly, the discrepancy between what has to be proven and what is actually proven helps in debugging when the equivalence proof fails; secondly, as will become clear, propagating both ways will facilitate a better treatment of commutativity and recurrences.

The propagation from output to input constructs an equivalence tree. The nodes in this equivalence tree are annotated with *correspondences*, that reflect the correspondences that we intend to proof. During the reverse traversal of the equivalence tree, the correspondences are updated to reflect what we have actually been able to prove.

Definition 4 (Correspondence). *Let G_i ($i \in \{1, 2\}$) be the dependency graph of program P_i. A correspondence consists of a tuple $(v_1, v_2, R^{\mathrm{want}}, R^{\mathrm{got}})$ with v_i a computation in G_i with domain D_i, $R^{\mathrm{want}} \subseteq D_1 \times D_2$, and $R^{\mathrm{got}} \subseteq D_1 \times D_2$.*

R^{want} contains pairs of computation iterations for which we want to prove equivalence R^{got} is initially undefined and is later updated to the set of pairs of computation iterations that we have actually proven to be equivalent.

The initial equivalence tree consists of a single root node that models the equivalence to be proven between the output arrays of both programs. For this root, we have $R^{\text{want}} = \{(i, i) \mid i \in D\}$ with D the domain of the output computation (i.e., the domain of the output array). It expresses the intention to show that both arrays are identical. R^{got} is initially undefined; it is computed by up propagation when the R^{got} information of its children is available. The proof is successful when $R^{\text{want}} = R^{\text{got}}$. $R^{\text{want}} \setminus R^{\text{got}}$ shows for which elements of the output array equivalence could not be proven.

In our running example, the output is scalar, hence $R^{\text{want}} = \{(\,;)\}$. It is convenient to see more details in concrete examples, so instead of using $(v_1, v_2, R^{\text{want}}, R^{\text{got}})$, we use $\langle (l_{v_1}, f_{v_1}) \leftrightarrow (l_{v_2}, f_{v_2}) \rangle$ and keep R^{want} and R^{got} as separate annotations. Hence, we represent the root as $\langle \text{Out} \leftrightarrow \text{Out} \rangle$ (Figure 4).

The basic step in proving equivalence consists of *propagation*. We distinguish between *down* (from root to leaves) and *up* (from leaves to root) propagation.

Down Propagation. Down propagation reduces the correspondence $(v_1, v_2, R^{\text{want}}, \_)$ of a node n to a set of correspondences $(u_1, u_2, R_c^{\text{want}}, \_)$ in which u_i is the target of an outgoing edge of v_i in the dependency graph G_i. Each of these new correspondences annotates a child of node n. The dataflow encoded in the dependency graphs is used to derive the R_c^{want} relation of the children. More precisely, for each pair of computations u_1 and u_2 with (v_1, u_1) and (v_2, u_2) edges in the respective dependency graphs that refer to the same argument position (same p value), we have a child annotated with the correspondence $(u_1, u_2, R_c^{\text{want}}, \_, \_)$ where

$$R_c^{\text{want}} = \left(M_{(v_1, u_1)} \oplus M_{(v_2, u_2)} \right) R^{\text{want}}. \tag{1}$$

The $\oplus$ operator combines mappings of type $D_{v_1} \to D_{u_1}$ and $D_{v_2} \to D_{u_2}$ into one of type $D_{v_1} \times D_{v_2} \to D_{u_1} \times D_{u_2}$:

$$\{ (i_1, i_2; i_1', i_2') \in \mathbb{Z}^{(d_{v_1} + d_{v_2}) + (d_{u_1} + d_{u_2})} \mid (i_1, i_1') \in M_{(v_1, u_1)} \wedge (i_2, i_2') \in M_{(v_2, u_2)} \}.$$

Recall, the domains of the dependence relations M of all edges for a given argument position partition the domain of a node. Hence, for each argument position, R^{want} is partitioned by the domains of the combined dependence relations, i.e., each element of R^{want} is mapped to an element of the R_c^{want} of exactly one child corresponding to this argument position.

In our running example, the output computations have one outgoing edge, hence one child is created. We obtain the child $\langle (4, \text{id}/1) \leftrightarrow (10, \text{id}/1) \rangle$ with $R^{\text{want}} = \{(\,;)\}$; i.e., the copy operations in Line 4 of Program 1 and Line 10 of Program 2 should compute the same value. Each of these computations has two outgoing edges, but the constraints $N = 1$ and $N \geq 2$ are pairwise incompatible, so two of the four children have $R^{\text{want}} = \emptyset$. Of the two other children, one is constrained with $N = 1$ and the other with $N \geq 2$. The correspondence of the latter, $\langle (3, +/2) \leftrightarrow (9, +/2) \rangle$, has $R^{\text{want}} = \{(N - 1; N - 1) \mid N \geq 2\}$ expressing that the addition on Line 3 of Program 1 and the addition on Line 9 of Program 2 should compute the same value in iteration $N - 1$ (when $N \geq 2$).

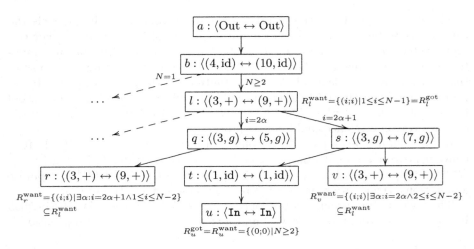

Fig. 4. Final state of part of the equivalence tree of the programs in Figure 1

In principle, this down propagation proceeds until correspondences are reached that cannot be further propagated. This holds when (i) $R^{\text{want}} = \emptyset$, in which case we can set $R^{\text{got}} = \emptyset$. (ii) R^{want} is a relation between input computations referring to the same input array: we can set $R^{\text{got}} = R^{\text{want}} \cap Id$ with Id the identity relation, i.e., the tuples in R^{want} between identical elements of the input arrays are proven, the others cannot be proven. (iii) The functions (f_{v_i} with arity r_{v_i}) of both computations are different; this includes the case of input computations referring to distinct input arrays. As we consider functions as black boxes, we cannot prove equivalences between different functions and we set $R^{\text{got}} = \emptyset$.

Up propagation. Once the R^{got} relations are obtained for all children of an equivalence node, up propagation can compute the R^{got} relation for that node. First, consider a single argument position. As we mentioned above, down propagation distributed the R^{want} relation of n over the R^{want} relation of the children of n that refer to the same argument position. Hence up propagation should take the union of the different parts. However, to prove an equivalence, it has to be proven for each of the r argument positions, so the results obtained for the different argument positions must be intersected. More formally, let $(v_1, v_2, R^{\text{want}}, R^{\text{got}})$ annotate node n and let $S_j = \{((v_1, u_1), (v_2, u_2)) \mid p_{(v_1, u_1)} = j \wedge p_{(v_2, u_2)} = j\}$. Finally, let $(u_1, u_2, R^{\text{want}}_{(u_1, u_2)}, R^{\text{got}}_{(u_1, u_2)})$ annotate the child of n with $((v_1, u_1), (v_2, u_2)) \in S_j$. Then, R^{got} is updated to

$$\bigcap_{j \in [1..r]} \bigcup_{((v_1, u_1), (v_2, u_2)) \in S_j} (M^{-1}_{(v_1, u_1)} \oplus M^{-1}_{(v_2, u_2)}) R^{\text{got}}_{(u_1, u_2)} \tag{2}$$

Algebraic operations. Associative operators can be nested differently in the two programs. A direct application of our technique would result in invalid pairings of argument positions and a failure of the proof. To solve this problem, we basically follow [21] and apply a preprocessing step to "flatten" associative operators in the dependency graph and reorganize the graph so that the functionality of the program is preserved. For example, a nesting of two binary associative operators introduces a ternary operator (possibly for only part of the domain of the outer node). Intuitively, an expression $+(a, +(b, c))$ with a nesting of two binary operators is replaced by the ternary expression $+(a, b, c)$.

Commutative operators pose more severe problems. For example, when propagating $\langle(3, +/2) \leftrightarrow (9, +/2)\rangle$ (correspondence l in Figure 4) as described above, the first argument of the first computation is paired with the first argument of the second computation, and also the second arguments are paired. When the operator is commutative as it is the case here, this does not suffice. The solution proposed in [21] (without implementation) is to consider all permutations of the arguments of the second computation separately and to use a look ahead mechanism to figure out which permutation is correct. However, this too is insufficient. Assume the above correspondence has $R^{\text{want}} = \{(i; i) \mid 1 \leq i \leq N - 1\}$. (This is not the initial value, but the recurrence handling described below updates it to this value.) Neither of the two possible permutations is correct on its own. One only holds for the even values of i ($i = 2\alpha$) and the other only for odd values of i ($i = 2\alpha + 1$); the proof attempt of [21] gets stuck.

Our approach is to try all permutations when the operator is commutative, and to extend the up propagation step so that it collects the results from the different permutations. Formally, let Π the set of permutations over $[1, \ldots, r]$. With π a permutation in Π, the set S_j used in Equation 2 is redefined as $S_j = \{((v_1, u_1), (v_2, u_2)) \mid p_{(v_1, u_1)} = j \wedge p_{(v_2, u_2)} = \pi(j)\}$. Then, with other symbols retaining the same meaning as in Equation 2, R^{got} is now computed as

$$\bigcup_{\pi \in \Pi} \bigcap_{j \in [1..r]} \bigcup_{((v_1, u_1), (v_2, u_2)) \in S_j} (M^{-1}_{(v_1, u_1)} \oplus M^{-1}_{(v_2, u_2)}) R^{\text{got}}_{(u_1, u_2)} \qquad (3)$$

(Definition 2 requires a similar change.)

In our running example, the $+/2$ computation of Program 1 (node e of Figure 2) has one outgoing edge for each argument, while node g in the model of Program 2 has 2 outgoing edges for each, yielding 8 possible combinations. However combinations leading to nodes where one computation has operator f and the other computation has operator g result in 4 children with $R^{\text{want}} = R^{\text{got}} = \emptyset$. The other cases result in 4 children that contribute to the proof, namely $\langle(3, f/1) \leftrightarrow (4, f/1)\rangle$ and $\langle(3, g/1) \leftrightarrow (5, g/1)\rangle$ with constraint $i = 2\alpha$, and $\langle(3, f/1) \leftrightarrow (8, f/1)\rangle$ and $\langle(3, g/1) \leftrightarrow (7, g/1)\rangle$ with $i = 2\alpha + 1$. Two of them are shown as children of node l in Figure 4. Once R^{got} is available in each of these children, up propagation can update R^{got} in this node l.

Recurrences: Induction, Widening and Narrowing. A given pair of computations may depend on itself, requiring special care. Termination is ensured when branches of the equivalence tree are finite and calculations in nodes are finite. The former will be ensured by allowing at most two occurrences of the same computation pair in a branch (the number of different pairs is finite); the latter by recomputing the R^{want} and R^{got} values in nodes only a finite number of times.

A pair (v_1, v_2) can only reappear in a branch when both dependency graphs have a cycle that passes through respectively v_1 and v_2, i.e., both programs have a recurrence. When a pair actually reappears, it means that both programs have performed the same computation since the first appearance of the pair. In the equivalence tree of our running example (Figure 4), nodes l and r (as well as l and v) form such a pair. Initially (node l) one wants to show that both computations are equivalent for the iteration pair $(N-1; N-1)$; down propagation creates nodes q, r, s, and v. In nodes r and v, the same equivalence has to be proven for the iteration pair $(N-2; N-2)$ (for respectively odd and even N). While in our running example, both programs have computed one iteration, the relationship can be more complex. For example, when one program is derived from the other by loop unrolling, the original one needs several iterations to perform the same computation as the transformed program does in one iteration.

More formally, let node a, annotated with $(v_1, v_2, R_a^{\text{want}}, R_a^{\text{got}})$ (with R_a^{got} undefined), be the first occurrence (the "ancestor") of the pair of computations (v_1, v_2) on a branch of an equivalence tree. Let node d annotated with $(v_1, v_2, R_d^{\text{want}}, R_d^{\text{got}})$ be the second occurrence (the "descendant"). If $R_d^{\text{want}} \subseteq R_a^{\text{want}}$, we can simply perform induction, setting $R_d^{\text{got}} = R_d^{\text{want}}$. When up-propagation reaches node a, we will of course need to validate our induction hypothesis. This will be discussed below. If $R_d^{\text{want}} \not\subseteq R_a^{\text{want}}$, then we want to extend the induction hypothesis R_a^{want} to include R_d^{want} so that we can perform induction also in this case. However, we cannot simply set the new R_a^{want} to the union of the old R_a^{want} and R_d^{want}, as this effectively corresponds to loop unrolling. This process would not terminate when the number of iterations is bounded by a symbolic constant (as in our running example) and would not scale when the bound is known.

Instead, we draw inspiration from the widening/narrowing technique of abstract interpretation [8] and apply a *widening* operator ∇. Such a widening operator turns a possibly infinite ascending chain, e.g., taking the union with R_d^{want} in each step as described above, into an eventually stationary chain. As our widening operator, we will essentially use the integer affine hull. However, as the induction hypothesis R_a^{want} needs to be a subset of $D_1 \times D_2$, with D_i the domain of v_i, we will intersect the affine hull with the aforementioned set. In the first iteration, R_a^{want} is then set to the intersection of $D_1 \times D_2$ with some affine subspace. Any additional widening step is only performed when R_d^{want} includes an element not in R_a^{want} (but still in $D_1 \times D_2$) and the widening operator will then increase the dimension of the affine subspace. So, after a finite number of widening steps, $R_a^{\text{want}} = D_1 \times D_2$, ensuring termination. At termination, we will have $R_d^{\text{want}} \subseteq R_a^{\text{want}}$. The affine hull not only ensures termination of the widening sequence, it is also a reasonable heuristic as an affine program will only remain affine if it is transformed using a (piecewise) affine transformation.

In our running example, the ancestor (node l) is created with $R_l^{\text{want}} = \{(N-1; N-1)\}$. Down propagation creates node r (or v, depending on the parity of N)

and computes $R_r^{\text{want}} = \{(N-2; N-2)\}$. This is not part of the initial induction hypothesis and so we need to revise the induction hypothesis. The affine hull of $\{(N-1; N-1)\}$ and $\{(N-2; N-2)\}$ is $\{(i; i)\}$ and intersection with $D_1 \times D_2$ yields the induction hypothesis shown in Figure 4.

As mentioned before, when up-propagation returns to a, we need to check whether the induction steps that have been made are valid. This is the case if $R_d^{\text{want}} \subseteq R_a^{\text{got}}$ for each descendant d, i.e., when $\cup_{d \in D} R_d^{\text{want}} \subseteq R_a^{\text{got}}$ with D the set of descendants for the computation pair (v_1, v_2). Note that there is no risk of circular reasoning ("unfounded sets") due to the second constraint of Definition 1: No individual iteration can (indirectly) depend on itself, hence no pair of individual iterations can depend on itself.

If R_d^{got} does not include R_d^{want}, then the performed induction is not founded by what we actually can prove. This means that R_a^{want}, the current hypothesis is an over-approximation of the correct induction hypothesis, or at least of the induction hypothesis that we are able to prove. In a second phase, we can then try to take successive subsets of R_a^{want}. However, as in the first phase, we need to be careful not to end up in a possibly infinite sequence. As in abstract interpretation, we therefore perform a (finite) number of *narrowing* steps. Our narrowing operator is fairly simply. The first time it is applied, we set $R_a^{\text{want}} = \cup_{d \in D} R_d^{\text{want}}$ with D the set of descendants that have used the induction hypothesis. Then, in the descendants, we perform induction, setting $R_d^{\text{got}} = R_d^{\text{want}} \cap R_a^{\text{want}}$. In particular, we do not allow any more widening steps on a once we have entered the narrowing phase. If the resulting R_a^{got} still does not include some R_d^{want}, then the second time we apply the narrowing operator, we simply set $R_a^{\text{want}} = \emptyset$.

The handling of recurrences can be summarized by the following algorithm. It uses a flag f to remember the status of the ancestor node. The flag is initialized to *undef* when a node is created by down propagation.

- If down propagation creates a node d, with $(v_1, v_2, R_d^{\text{want}}, R_d^{\text{got}}, undef)$, and there exists an ancestor node a with $(v_1, v_2, R_a^{\text{want}}, R_a^{\text{got}}, f_a)$ then
  - if $f_a = undef$, then set $f_a = widening$ (to indicate that a is the root of a recurrence);
  - if $f_a = widening$ and $\neg(R_d^{\text{want}} \subseteq R_a^{\text{want}})$ then $R_a^{\text{want}} \leftarrow R_a^{\text{want}} \nabla R_d^{\text{want}}$ (widening step) and remove all descendants of node a.
  - else $R_d^{\text{got}} = R_d^{\text{want}} \cap R_a^{\text{want}}$ (induction step, it will be checked later whether it was valid).
- If up propagation computes R_a^{got} for a node a, with $(v_1, v_2, R_a^{\text{want}}, R_a^{\text{got}}, f_a)$, and the node has a set D of descendant nodes with each node $d \in D$ annotated with $(v_1, v_2, R_d^{\text{want}}, R_d^{\text{got}}, f_d)$ then
  - if $\cup_{d \in D} R_d^{\text{want}} \subset R_a^{\text{got}}$ then done (the induction steps turn out to be valid and R_a^{got} can be used to perform up propagation on the parent of a)
  - else if $f_a = widening$ and $\neg(\cup_{d \in D} R_d^{\text{want}} \subseteq R_a^{\text{got}})$ then $f_a = narrowing$, $R_a^{\text{want}} = \cup_{d \in D} R_d^{\text{want}}$, and $R_a^{\text{got}} = undef$ (narrowing step) and remove all descendants of node a
  - else ($f_a = narrowing$) $R_a^{\text{got}} = \emptyset$ (no correct hypotheses found)

Proposition 1. *The equivalence checking algorithm terminates and for each node in the equivalence tree (including the root node) with correspondence* $(v_1, v_2, R^{\mathrm{want}}, R^{\mathrm{got}})$, *if* $(\boldsymbol{x}_1, \boldsymbol{x}_2) \in R^{\mathrm{got}}$ *then iteration* $\boldsymbol{x}_1$ *of* v_1 *is equivalent to iteration* $\boldsymbol{x}_2$ *of* v_2.

Our recurrence handling differs substantially from [21]. The program model used in that work makes it non trivial to find the ancestor/descendant pair over which both programs have performed the same computation. They need an unfolding operation to identify the pair, then they compute the across dependency mapping that corresponds to the computation performed between ancestor and descendant and use that mapping in a complex operation that involves the calculation of the transitive closure (implemented in the Omega library [13]) that yields the equivalences to be proven for the edges leaving the recurrence. This computation requires the recurrences to be uniform while our method can also handle non uniform recurrences. Furthermore, their representation of proof obligations only allows an element of an output array to depend on a single element of another array along any path in the program. In particular, if a program contains a loop with body `A[i] = A[i-1] + B[i]`, then they are unable to express that `A[N]` depends on `B[i]` for *all* iterations `i` of the loop. After stepping over the recurrence, they will therefore ignore all but one of these elements `B[i]`.

Tabling. A dependency graph is not necessarily a tree. This means that two computations may have some common subcomputation. Tabling can therefore be used to reuse already proven equivalences. A very simple table could store proven tuples $(v_1, v_2, R_t^{\mathrm{got}})$. When an equivalence has to be proven for the pair of computations (v_1, v_2), one needs only to prove it for $R^{\mathrm{want}} \setminus R_t^{\mathrm{got}}$. The same table can also be used to detect recurrences.

4   Implementation

The proof procedure of Section 3 has been implemented as part of our C++ isa (http://www.kotnet.org/~skimo/loop/isa-0.08.tar.bz2) prototype tool set. This set contains a polyhedral extractor from C based on SUIF [3] and an exact dependence analysis tool. We use our own C isl library, based on piplib [11], to manipulate sets of integers defined by linear inequalities and integer divisions. We avoid the Omega library [13] as it suffers from some unimplemented corner cases. Each set/relation is represented by a union of "basic sets", each of which is defined by a conjunction of linear inequalities. If a requested relation R^{want} is a union of basic sets, a node is created for each of its basic sets. All nodes with the same pair of computations are kept in a list accessible through a hash table keyed on the given pair, which is used both for tabling and detecting recurrences. The implemented algorithm differs slightly from the exposition above. In particular, we never remove any node from the equivalence tree or restart a proof, but instead extend the tree while keeping track of all the induction hypotheses that have been made. It also contains various other

```
A[0]  =  in;                    A[0]  =  g(in);
for (i = 1; i <= N; ++i)        for (i = 1; i <= N; ++i)
    A[i] = f(g(A[i/2]));            A[i] = g(f(A[i/2]));
out = g(A[N]);                  out = A[N];
```

Fig. 5. A pair of equivalent programs with a non-uniform recurrence

optimizations to avoid redundant computations and it supports multiple output arrays.

It is difficult to compare running times with the most closely related tool of [20] since the latter is not available to us and since the reported running times do not mention the CPU type. Furthermore, our isl library is relatively new and uses exact integer arithmetic, while the tool of [20] uses the more mature and presumably heavily optimized Omega library, which has only machine integer precision. As an indication, however, for the example in Figure 1, our tool takes about 0.04s on an Intel Core2@3GHz, 0.04s for the example of Figure 5 with a non-uniform recurrence and 0.02s for the example from [21], while for the USVD example pair from [20], with several hundred lines of code, the tool takes about 0.5s, most of which is spent reading in intermediate data structures. This kernel is often used in embedded systems and is the most complicated case study of [20].

For a more extensive experiment, we turned to the code generation tool CLooG [7], which previously used PolyLib to perform its iteration domain manipulations, but was recently extended to optionally use our own isl instead. Due to various differences in the internals of these tools, the outputs for CLooG's regression tests may not be textually identical, and we therefore want to verify that they are equivalent. Since the original statements are not available for these tests, we instead verify that the iterations of all statements are performed in the same order in both versions by passing around a token. Since each statement now writes to the same scalar, these tests constitute true stress tests for both the dependence analysis and the equivalence checking. In particular, using the original statements would result in a much easier equivalence checking problem. Of 105 tests, 97 were proven to be equivalent. Five contained a construct in the output that we currently cannot parse, while three produced memory overflows (1 during dependence analysis and 2 during equivalence checking). These overflows are probably due to the presence of a large number of integer divisions. The size of the 97 pairs of checked programs ranges from 2 to 800 lines (9478 lines in total), with running times up to 22 seconds (most are well below 1 second) and 62 seconds in total. The number of widening steps performed ranges from 0 to 228, with a grand total of 1018 widening steps.

5 Discussion and Conclusion

Unlike transitive closure based approaches [6, 21], our widening approach does not require uniform recurrences. Note that standard uniformization techniques [15] would only introduce an extra (easy) transitive closure, without resolving the original difficult transitive closure. However, our method will not be able to detect all kinds of equivalences, as the widening assumes that a piecewise affine transformation has been applied to the recurrences. The widening step may in rare cases also perform an inappropriate generalization, from which it will then be difficult to recover. In particular, this may occur in the presence of integer divisions more intricate than those in Figure 5. We are investigating if delaying the widening by one step or the use of more advanced widening or narrowing operators can solve these problems. The flattening of nested associative operators during preprocessing cannot handle reductions with a variable number of arguments such as in $\sum_{0 \leq i < N} a[i]$. Proving the equivalence of different ways of computing such reductions requires a further extension of our system.

Some forms of data-dependent or non-affine constructs can be handled by applying an if-conversion preprocessing [2] and/or using fuzzy [5] instead of exact dataflow analysis. Many other approaches exist to equivalence checking, including translation validation, e.g., [19], or fractal symbolic analysis [16]. Some of these approaches handle more general transformations than ours, but they typically rely on compiler hints or heuristics. SMT solvers such as CVC3 [4], used by many approaches, do not perform inductions. General theorem provers such as ACL2 [12] can perform induction, but even for the simple case of Figure 1 an encoding of the equivalence problem by an expert required a manual specification of the induction hypothesis, while we perform induction fully automatically. See [20] for a more detailed comparison to related work.

Another way of looking at our work is that we discover invariants between array indices of two programs. Tuples satisfying the invariant identify equal array elements. While the discovery is guided by the assumed invariant between program outputs, non trivial new invariants are induced when handling recurrences. Induction of variants —between scalars— is an active research area, e.g., [18].

We conclude that our method is the first static affine program equivalence checker that handles non-uniform recurrences with full support for commutativity and a publicly available implementation.

Acknowledgements. Research supported by FWO-Vlaanderen (G.0232.06N).

References

[1] Alias, C., Barthou, D.: On the recognition of algorithm templates. In: Int. Workshop on Compilers Optimization Meets Compiler Verification, Warsaw, April 2003. ENTCS, vol. 82, pp. 395–409. Elsevier Science, Amsterdam (2003)

[2] Allen, J.R., Kennedy, K., Porterfield, C., Warren, J.D.: Conversion of control dependence to data dependence. In: POPL 1983, pp. 177–189. ACM, New York (1983)

[3] Amarasinghe, S., Anderson, J., Lam, M.S., Tseng, C.-W.: An overview of the SUIF compiler for scalable parallel machines. In: Proceedings of the Seventh SIAM Conference on Parallel Processing for Scientific Computing (1995)

[4] Barrett, C., Tinelli, C.: CVC3. In: Damm, W., Hermanns, H. (eds.) CAV 2007. LNCS, vol. 4590, pp. 298–302. Springer, Heidelberg (2007)

[5] Barthou, D., Collard, J.-F., Feautrier, P.: Fuzzy array dataflow analysis. J. Parallel Distrib. Comput. 40(2), 210–226 (1997)

[6] Barthou, D., Feautrier, P., Redon, X.: On the equivalence of two systems of affine recurrence equations. In: Monien, B., Feldmann, R.L. (eds.) Euro-Par 2002. LNCS, vol. 2400, pp. 309–313. Springer, Heidelberg (2002)

[7] Bastoul, C.: Code generation in the polyhedral model is easier than you think. In: PACT 2004: Proceedings of the 13th International Conference on Parallel Architectures and Compilation Techniques, Washington, DC, USA, 2004, pp. 7–16. IEEE Computer Society, Los Alamitos (2004)

[8] Cousot, P., Cousot, R.: Comparing the Galois connection and widening/narrowing approaches to abstract interpretation. In: Bruynooghe, M., Wirsing, M. (eds.) PLILP 1992. LNCS, vol. 631, pp. 269–295. Springer, Heidelberg (1992)

[9] Feautrier, P.: Array expansion. In: ICS 1988: Proceedings of the 2nd international conference on Supercomputing, pp. 429–441. ACM Press, New York (1988)

[10] Feautrier, P.: Dataflow analysis of array and scalar references. International Journal of Parallel Programming 20(1), 23–53 (1991)

[11] Feautrier, P., Collard, J., Bastoul, C.: Solving systems of affine (in)equalities. Technical report, PRiSM, Versailles University (2002)

[12] Kaufmann, M., Moore, J.S., Manolios, P.: Computer-Aided Reasoning: An Approach. Kluwer Academic Publishers, Norwell (2000)

[13] Kelly, W., Maslov, V., Pugh, W., Rosser, E., Shpeisman, T., Wonnacott, D.: The Omega library. Technical report, University of Maryland (November 1996)

[14] Kelly, W., Pugh, W., Rosser, E., Shpeisman, T.: Transitive closure of infinite graphs and its applications. Int. J. Parallel Program. 24(6), 579–598 (1996)

[15] Manjunathaiah, M., Megson, G.M., Rajopadhye, S.V., Risset, T.: Uniformization of affine dependance programs for parallel embedded system design. In: Ni, L.M., Valero, M. (eds.) ICPP 2002, Proceedings, pp. 205–213. IEEE Computer Society, Los Alamitos (2001)

[16] Mateev, N., Menon, V., Pingali, K.: Fractal symbolic analysis. In: ICS 2001: Proceedings of the 15th international conference on Supercomputing, pp. 38–49. ACM, New York (2001)

[17] Matsumoto, T., Seto, K., Fujita, M.: Formal equivalence checking for loop optimization in C programs without unrolling. In: IASTED Proc. ACST 2007: Advances in Computer Science and Technology, Anaheim, CA, USA, pp. 43–48. ACTA Press (2007)

[18] Müller-Olm, M., Seidl, H.: Precise interprocedural analysis through linear algebra. In: Proceedings of the 31st ACM SIGPLAN-SIGACT Symposium on Principles of Programming Languages, POPL 2004, pp. 330–341 (2004)

[19] Necula, G.C.: Translation validation for an optimizing compiler. SIGPLAN Not. 35(5), 83–94 (2000)

[20] Shashidhar, K.C.: Efficient automatic verification of loop and data-flow transformations by functional equivalence checking. Ph.D thesis, Katholieke Universiteit Leuven, Belgium (May 2008)

[21] Shashidhar, K.C., Bruynooghe, M., Catthoor, F., Janssens, G.: Verification of source code transformations by program equivalence checking. In: Bodik, R. (ed.) CC 2005. LNCS, vol. 3443, pp. 221–236. Springer, Heidelberg (2005)

D-Finder: A Tool for Compositional Deadlock Detection and Verification

Saddek Bensalem, Marius Bozga, Thanh-Hung Nguyen, and Joseph Sifakis

Verimag Laboratory, Université Joseph Fourier Grenoble, CNRS

Abstract. D-Finder tool implements a compositional method for the verification of component-based systems described in BIP language encompassing multi-party interaction. For deadlock detection, D-Finder applies proof strategies to eliminate potential deadlocks by computing increasingly stronger invariants.

1 Methodology

Compositional verification techniques are used to cope with state explosion in concurrent systems. The idea is to aply divide-and-conquer approaches to infer global properties of complex systems from properties of their components. Separate verification of components limits state explosion. Nonetheless, components mutually interact in a system and their behavior and properties are inter-related. This is a major difficulty in designing compositional techniques [1,2,3,4,5,6,7,8]). As explained in [9], compositional rules are in general of the form

$$\frac{B_1 < \Phi_1 >,\ B_2 < \Phi_2 >,\ C(\Phi_1, \Phi_2, \Phi)}{B_1 \| B_2 < \Phi >} \tag{1}$$

That is, if two components with behaviors B_1, B_2 meet individually properties Φ_1, Φ_2 respectively, and $C(\Phi_1, \Phi_2, \Phi)$ is some condition taking into account the semantics of parallel composition operation and relating the individual properties with the global property, then the system $B_1 \| B_2$ resulting from the composition of B_1 and B_2 will satisfy a global property Φ.

In D-Finder, we implemented a novel approach for compositional verification of invariants based on the following rule:

$$\frac{\{B_i < \Phi_i >\}_i,\ \Psi \in II(\|_\gamma \{B_i\}_i, \{\Phi_i\}_i),\ (\bigwedge_i \Phi_i) \wedge \Psi \Rightarrow \Phi}{\|_\gamma \{B_i\}_i < \Phi >} \tag{2}$$

The rule allows to prove invariance of Φ for systems obtained by using a n-ary composition operation parameterized by a set of interactions γ. It uses global invariants which are the conjunction of individual invariants of components Φ_i and an interaction invariant Ψ. The latter expresses constraints on the global state space induced by interactions between components. It can be computed automatically from abstractions of the system to be verified. These are the composition of finite state abstractions B_i^α of the components B_i with respect to their

A. Bouajjani and O. Maler (Eds.): CAV 2009, LNCS 5643, pp. 614–619, 2009.

invariants Φ_i. They can be represented as a Petri net whose transitions correspond to interactions between components. Interaction invariants correspond to traps [10] of the Petri net and are computed symbolically as solutions of a set of boolean equations.

Our method differs from assume-guarantee methods in that it avoids combinatorial explosion of the decomposition and is directly applicable to systems with multiparty (not only binary) interactions. Furthermore, it needs only guarantees for components. It replaces the search for adequate assumptions for each component by the use of interaction invariants. These can be computed automatically from given component invariants (guarantees). Interaction invariants correspond to a *"cooperation test"* in the terminology of [11] as they allow to eliminate product states which are not feasible by the semantics.

1.1   Checking Deadlock-Freedom and Invariance Properties

D-Finder provides a method for automated verification of component-based systems described in BIP (Behavior-Interaction-Priority) language [12]. In BIP, a system is the composition of a set of atomic components which are automata extended with data and functions written in C. To prove a global invariant Φ for a system $\gamma(B_1, \ldots, B_n)$, obtained by composing a set of atomic components $B_1, ..., B_n$ by using a set of interactions γ, we use the rule (2) above, where $B_i < \Phi_i >$ means that Φ_i is an invariant of component B_i and Ψ is an interaction invariant of $\gamma(B_1, \ldots, B_n)$ computed automatically from Φ_i and $\gamma(B_1, \ldots, B_n)$. A key issue in the application of this rule is finding component invariants Φ_i. If the components B_i are finite state, then we can take $\Phi = Reach(B_i)$, the set of reachable state of B_i, or any upper approximation of $Reach(B_i)$. If the components are infinite state, $Reach(B_i)$ is approximated using techniques presented in [13,14].

- **Checking Invariance Properties.** We give a sketch of a semi-algorithm allowing to prove invariance of Φ by iterative application of the rule (2). The semi-algorithm takes a system $\langle \gamma(B_1, \ldots, B_n), Init \rangle$ and a predicate Φ. It iteratively computes invariants of the form $\mathcal{X} = \Psi \wedge (\bigwedge_{i=1}^{n} \Phi_i)$ where Ψ is an interaction invariant and Φ_i an invariant of component B_i. If $\mathcal{X}$ is not strong enough for proving that Φ is an invariant ($\mathcal{X} \wedge \neg\Phi = false$) then either a new iteration with stronger Φ_i is started or we stop. In this case, we cannot conclude about invariance of Φ.
- **Checking Deadlock-Freedom.** Checking global deadlock-freedom of a system $\gamma(B_1, \ldots, B_n)$ is a particular case of proving invariants - proving invariance of the predicate $\neg DIS$, where DIS is the set of the states of $\gamma(B_1, \ldots, B_n)$ from which all interactions are disabled.

1.2   Generating Component Invariants and Interaction Invariants

D-Finder provides methods for computing component invariants, particulary useful for checking deadlock-freedom. It also provides a general method for computing interaction invariants for $\gamma(B_1, \ldots, B_n)$ from a given set of component invariants Φ_i.

– **Computing Component Invariants.** Invariants for atomic components are generated by simple forward analysis of their behavior. A key issue is efficient computation of such invariants as the precise symbolic computation of reachable states requires quantifier elimination. An alternative to quantifier elimination is to compute over-approximations based on syntactic analysis of the predicates occuring in guards and actions. In this case, the obtained invariants may not be inductive. D-Finder uses different strategies which allow to derive local assertions, that is, predicates attached to control locations and which are satisfied whenever the computation reaches the corresponding control location. A more detailed presentation, as well as the techniques implemented in D-Finder for generating component invariants are given in [15,16].

– **Computing Interaction Invariants.** Interaction invariants express global synchronization constraints between atomic components. Their computation consists of the following steps. 1) For given component invariants Φ_i of the atomic components B_i, we compute a finite-state abstraction $B_i^{\alpha_i}$ of B_i where α_i is the abstraction induced by the elementary predicates occuring in Φ_i. This step is necessary only for components B_i which are infinite state. 2) The system $\gamma(B_1^{\alpha_1}, \cdots, B_n^{\alpha_n})$ which is an abstraction of $\gamma(B_1, \cdots, B_n)$, can be considered as a 1-safe Petri net. The set of the traps of the Petri net defines a global invariant which we compute symbolically. 3) The concretization of this invariant gives an interaction invariant of the initial system.

2   Tool Structure

D-Finder consists of a set of modules interconnected as shown in Figure 1.

It takes as input a BIP program and progressively finds and eliminates potential deadlocks. It basically works as follows. First, it constructs the predicate

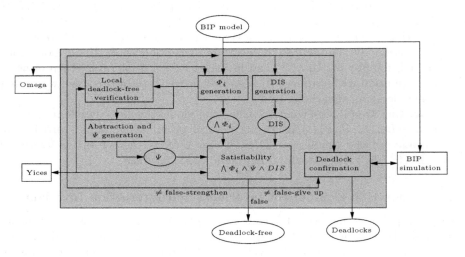

Fig. 1. D-Finder tool

characterizing the set of deadlock states (DIS generation module). Second, iteratively, it constructs increasingly stronger local invariants of components (Φ_i generation module). These invariants are used to compute finer finite state abstractions and increasingly stronger global interaction invariants (Abstraction and Ψ generation module). Third, it verifies deadlock-freedom by checking satisfiabilty of $\wedge\Phi_i \wedge \Psi \wedge DIS$ (satisfiability module). If it succeeds, the system is proven deadlock-free; otherwise it may continue or gives up, according to the user's choice.

For doing all this, D-Finder is connected with several external tools. It uses Omega [17] for quantifier elimination and Yices [18] for checking satisfiability of predicates. It is also connected to the state space exploration tool of the BIP platform, for finer analysis when the heuristic fails to prove deadlock-freedom. We provide non trivial examples showing the capabilities of D-Finder as well as the efficiency of the method.

3   Experimentation and Concluding Remarks

We provide experimental results for four examples. The first example is Utopar, an industrial case study of the European Integrated project SPEEDS[1] about an automated transportation system. A succinct description of Utopar can be found at http://www.combest.eu/home/?link=Application2. The system is the composition of three types of components: autonomous vehicles, called U-cars, a centralized Automatic Control System and Calling Units. The latter two types have (almost exclusively) discrete behavior. U-cars are equipped with a local controller, responsible for handling the U-cars sensors and performing various routing and driving computations depending on users' requests. We analyzed a simplified version of Utopar by abstracting from data exchanged between components as well as from continuous dynamics of the cars. In this version, each U-Car is modeled by a component having 7 control locations and 6 integer variables. The Automatic Control System has 3 control locations and 2 integer variables. The Calling Units have 2 control locations and no variables. In the second example, we consider Readers-Writer systems in order to evaluate how the method scales up for components without data. The third example is Gas Station in order to compare with other compositional method *assume-guarantee* [19]. Finally, as a last example, we consider Dinning Philosophers which is a well-known classical example.

The table below provides an overview of the experimental results obtained for these examples. In this table, n is the number of BIP components in the example, q is the total number of control locations, x_b (resp. x_i) is the total number of boolean (resp. integer) variables, $D_{\Phi\Psi}$ is the number of deadlock configurations remaining in $\wedge\Phi_i \wedge \Psi \wedge DIS$ and t is the total time for computing invariants and checking for satisfiability of $\wedge\Phi_i \wedge \Psi \wedge DIS$. Detailed results are available at http://www-verimag.imag.fr/~thnguyen/tool.

The results presented by Cobleigh and his colleagues in [19] raise doubts about the usefulness of assume-guarantee reasoning techniques. They undertook

---

[1] (http://www.speeds.eu.com/)

example	n	q	x_b	x_i	$D_{\Phi\Psi}$	t
Utopar System (40 U-Cars, 256 Calling Units)	297	795	40	242	0	3m46s
Utopar System (60 U-Cars, 625 Calling Units)	686	1673	60	362	0	25m29s
Readers-Writer (7000 readers)	7002	14006	0	1	0	17m27s
Readers-Writer (10000 readers)	10002	20006	0	1	0	36m10s
Gas station (100 pumps - 2000 customers)	1101	4302	0	0	0	14m06s
Gas station (300 pumps - 3000 customers)	3301	12902	0	0	0	33m02s
Philosophers (2000 Philos)	4000	10000	0	0	3	32m14s
Philosophers (3001 Philos)	6001	15005	0	0	1	54m34s

a study to determine if assume-guarantee reasoning provides an advantage over monolithic verification. In this work, they considered all two-way decomposition for a set of systems and properties, using two different verifiers, FLAVERS and LSTA. By increasing the number of repeated tasks in the systems, they evaluated the decompositions as they were scaled. They found that in only a few cases assume-guarantee reasoning can verify properties on larger systems than monolithic verification can, and in these cases the systems that can be analyzed are only a few sizes larger.

In our case, we also did some comparison with some well-known monolithic verification tools such as NewSMV (NuSMV). All the experimentations are done on a Linux machine Intel Pentium 4 3.0 GHz and 1G Ram.

The first comparison between NuSmv and D-Finder is on Dinning Philosopher example. We increase the number of Philosophers and compare the verification time between these two tools (figure 2). In the figure 2, NuSmv runs out of memory at the size 150 while D-Finder can go much further until the size 3000.

The second comparison between NuSmv and D-Finder is on Gas Station example. We consider a system with 3 pumps and increase the number of customers. The comparison of verification time is in figure 3. In this figure, NuSmv runs

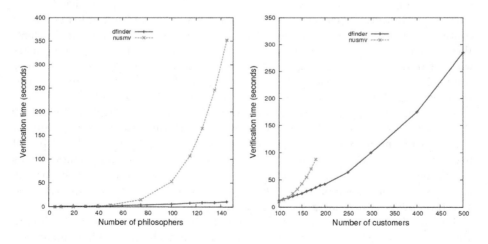

Fig. 2. Dinning Philosopher   **Fig. 3.** Gas Station

out of memory at the size 180 (Customers) while D-Finder can go much further until the size 3000.

References

1. Alur, R., Henzinger, T.: Reactive modules. In: Proceedings of the 11th Annual Symposium on LICS, pp. 207–208. IEEE Computer Society Press, Los Alamitos (1996)
2. Abadi, M., Lamport, L.: Conjoining specifications. Toplas 17(3), 507–534 (1995)
3. Clarke, E., Long, D., McMillan, K.: Compositional model checking. In: Proceedings of the 4th Annual Symposium on LICS, pp. 353–362 (1989)
4. Chandy, K., Misra, J.: Parallel program design: a foundation. Addison-Wesley Publishing Company, Reading (1988)
5. Grumberg, O., Long, D.E.: Model checking and modular verification. ACM Transactions on Programming Languages and Systems 16(3), 843–871 (1994)
6. McMillan, K.L.: A compositional rule for hardware design refinement. In: Grumberg, O. (ed.) CAV 1997. LNCS, vol. 1254, pp. 24–35. Springer, Heidelberg (1997)
7. Pnueli, A.: In transition from global to modular temporal reasoning about programs, pp. 123–144 (1985)
8. Stark, E.W.: A proof technique for rely/guarantee properties. In: Maheshwari, S.N. (ed.) FSTTCS 1985. LNCS, vol. 206, pp. 369–391. Springer, Heidelberg (1985)
9. Kupferman, O., Vardi, M.Y.: Modular model checking. In: de Roever, W.-P., Langmaack, H., Pnueli, A. (eds.) COMPOS 1997. LNCS, vol. 1536, pp. 381–401. Springer, Heidelberg (1998)
10. Peterson, J.: Petri Net theory and the modelling of systems. Prentice Hall, Englewood Cliffs (1981)
11. Apt, K.R., Francez, N., de Roever, W.P.: A proof system for communicating sequential processes. ACM Trans. Program. Lang. Syst. 2(3), 359–385 (1980)
12. Basu, A., Bozga, M., Sifakis, J.: Modeling heterogeneous real-time components in bip. In: SEFM, pp. 3–12 (2006)
13. Lakhnech, Y., Bensalem, S., Berezin, S., Owre, S.: Incremental verification by abstraction. In: Margaria, T., Yi, W. (eds.) TACAS 2001. LNCS, vol. 2031, pp. 98–112. Springer, Heidelberg (2001)
14. Bradley, A.R., Manna, Z.: Checking safety by inductive generalization of counterexamples to induction. In: FMCAD, pp. 173–180 (2007)
15. Bensalem, S., Lakhnech, Y.: Automatic generation of invariants. FMSD 15(1), 75–92 (1999)
16. Bensalem, S., Bozga, M., Sifakis, J., Nguyen, T.H.: Compositional verification for component-based systems and application. In: Cha, S., Choi, J.-Y., Kim, M., Lee, I., Viswanathan, M. (eds.) ATVA 2008. LNCS, vol. 5311, pp. 64–79. Springer, Heidelberg (2008)
17. Team, O.: The omega library. Version 1.1.0 (1996)
18. Dutertre, B., de Moura, L.: A fast linear-arithmetic solver for DPLL(T). In: Ball, T., Jones, R.B. (eds.) CAV 2006. LNCS, vol. 4144, pp. 81–94. Springer, Heidelberg (2006)
19. Cobleigh, J.M., Avrunin, G.S., Clarke, L.A.: Breaking up is hard to do: An evaluation of automated assume-guarantee reasoning. ACM TSEM 17(2) (2008)

HybridFluctuat: A Static Analyzer of Numerical Programs within a Continuous Environment

Olivier Bouissou[1], Eric Goubault[1], Sylvie Putot[1], Karim Tekkal[2],
and Franck Vedrine[1]

[1] CEA, LIST, Modelisation and Analysis of Systems in Interaction,
Boîte 65, Gif-sur-Yvette, F-91191 France
[2] FCS Digiteo, Route de l'Orme des Merisiers, Saint-Aubin, F-91190 France

Firstname.Lastname@cea.fr

Abstract. A new static analyzer is described, based on the analyzer
Fluctuat. Its goal is to synthetize invariants for hybrid systems, encompassing a continuous environment described by a system of possibly
switched ODEs, and an ANSI C program, in interaction with it. The evolution of the continuous environment is over-approximated using a guaranteed integrator that we developped, and special assertions are added
to the program that simulate the action of sensors and actuators, making
the continuous environment and the program communicate. We demonstrate our approach on an industrial case study[1], a part of the flight
control software of ASTRIUM's Automated Transfer Vehicle (ATV).

1   Introduction

An emerging trend in the software verification community is to extend the analysis of programs to take into account their interaction with the external world.
In the case of embedded programs, one of the most important interaction to
consider is the one between the program and a physical environment on which
it acts [4,5,9]. Generally, static analyzers abstract these interactions in a simple
way: inputs and outputs are abstracted by intervals. If this is obviously sound, it
leads to an important overestimation as it assumes that a continuously evolving
variable can instantaneously jump from its minimum to its maximum value.

In this paper we present a new static analyzer, named HybridFluctuat, that
makes it possible to analyze the interactions of an embedded program with its environment. Thanks to a language of assertions, it takes into account sensors (from
which the program reads the value of a physical variable) and actuators (with
which the program acts on the system behavior). The continuous environment is
modeled as a set of switched ODEs and its evolution is abstracted using the guaranteed integration solver GRKLib, while the analysis of the program itself relies
on the analyzer Fluctuat.

Running example. To illustrate this, let us look at a typical example of an
embedded, control command program. Listing 1 shows a simplified version of

---

[1] This work was partially funded by the ESA project ITI 19783 "Space Software
Validation using Abstract Interpretation". Thaks are also due to ASTRIUM SAS.

A. Bouajjani and O. Maler (Eds.): CAV 2009, LNCS 5643, pp. 620–626, 2009.

```
1   Initialize ();
2     for  ( i =1;; i++)  {
3       // Get new value for qnav and wnav
4       // Make two steps of RK4
5       a = ac[i −1];    (q1,w1) = RK4(a,qnav,wnav,h1);
6       a = ac[i];       (q,w) = RK4(a,q1,w1,h2);
7       (qest,west) = Fk(q,w,qnav,wnav);    // Kalman filter
8       ac[i+1] = Fa(qest,west,q,w);        // Next command
9       // Send ac to the actuator
10  }
```

Listing 1. Simplified algorithmic view of the ATV program

the MSU main control loop, part of the Automated Transfer Vehicle (ATV) control software. Its behavior is typical of embedded programs: at each cycle, its configuration (the position, speed, etc.) is read from sensors, then the program computes the command sent to actuators to achieve the desired thrust with the engines. In this application, the command is computed using a Kalman filter, where the prediction step is done using two Runge-Kutta integrations of order 4. The external environment (relating the position of the ATV to accelerations due to thrusters) is modeled by an ODE of dimension 7 that links the position of the ATV (recorded as qnav in the program) with its angular velocity (wnav). It also has three parameters that are linked with the vector ac of the program.

At line 3 of the program, the value of qnav and wnav is modified by the sensors: it takes its value from the solution of the system of ODEs. Then, the program computes the value of the command ac. This value is sent to the actuators that modify the thrust of the engines on line 9, and thus changes the parameters of the ODE and the evolution of the continuous system.

Contributions. The main contribution of HybridFluctuat is that it extends the static analysis of embedded programs by considering the physical environment in which they are executed. The analyzer considers programs written in C-ANSI and ordinary differential equations presented as a C++ function (see Listing 1.2 later). The tool then automatically derives invariants on the whole system.

Related work. Static analyzers for hybrid systems [2,7] mainly focus on high level models like hybrid automata and are generally used to prove the reachability of some state. Our approach differs from these as we consider the program itself and not a derived model of it, which allows us to analyze the impact of the implementation choices (e.g. the use of floating point numbers) on the behavior of the whole system (this feature is not yet implemented, but is a straightforward consequence of our approach).

2   HybridFluctuat: Description and User Point of View

In this section, we briefly describe the principles and use of HybridFluctuat. HybridFluctuat builds on two previously existing tools, Fluctuat and GRKLib,

```
void  on(double* res ,double* y ,double* param)
   { res [0] = param[0] − y [0] / 3 ; }
void  off(double* res ,double* y ,double* param)
   { res [0] = −y [0] / 3 ; }
```

Listing 1.2. Environment of the heater problem written as C++ functions

more details on which can be found in [3,8,11]. In practice, Fluctuat will be used to analyze a C program with special assertions specifying its interaction with the environment, and will call GRKlib whenever it encounters such assertions.

Fluctuat [8,11] is a static analyzer by abstract interpretation [6] that interprets a program written in ANSI-C with idealized semantics (real and integer numbers) and finite precision semantics (floating-point and machine integers). It gives bounds for variables with these two semantics, and bounds the error due to the use of finite precision numbers instead of real numbers. It decomposes this error on its provenance in the analyzed program, thus indicating which part of the program is responsible for the main imprecision.

GRKLib [3] is a C++ library that, given a system of ordinary differential equations (ODE) and an interval initial value, computes an interval overapproximation of its solution, either at a specific time stamp or over a whole time interval. To do so, the algorithm turns a numerical, non guaranteed Runge-Kutta method into a guaranteed integration method.

The input of HybridFluctuat is a system of ODEs given by the user as C++ functions, and a C program, in which the user added special assertions specifying the interaction between the program and the environment, i.e. between variables of the programs and the solutions or parameters of the ODEs.

There may be several systems of ODEs that model different parts of the environment, and interact with different parts of the program. We associate a different name system_i to each system. The program may modify a system system_i in two ways. Either the program makes a discrete change of mode, thus changing completely the evolution of the environment, or the program modifies a parameter in the ODE. To model these two kinds of interactions, we associate to each system_i several ODEs (named mode_j in the following), each representing one mode. Each mode mode_j also contains formal parameters that will be modified by the program. This models the action of actuators. For example, the ODEs of Listing 1.2 model the evolution of the temperature of a room with a heater that may be on (ODE on) or off (ODE off). The parameter param[0] represents the power of the heater (that may be changed by the controller).

In return, the environment influences the program: the program questions the values of physical variables (solutions of the ODEs), and uses them in the program. We suppose that the continuous time is computed by the program: when the program interacts with its environment, it must specify the time at which this interaction takes place. We now specify the assertions that represent these interactions in the C program.

Initializing the environment. First, the initial mode of each system `system_i` must be specified using the assertion `HYBRID_INIT_MODE(system_i, mode_j)`. Then, the initial value `param` of the jth parameter of the system `system_i` must be given using the assertion `HYBRID_PARAM_DINIT(system_i, j, param)`.

Finally, for each system `system_i`, the value of each component of the initial state must be set by `HYBRID_DINIT(system_i, j, value)`, where `j` means that we set the value of the jth component. When the analyzer encounters these assertions, it sends the information to the guaranteed integrator via XML files.

Getting values from the environment. As we said, the program can read values from the environment by calling `HYBRID_DVALUE(system_i, component_j, t)`. It reads the jth component of the state of `system_i` at global time `t`. When the analyzer encounters this assertion, it performs the guaranteed integration of the system `system_i` up to time `t`: the result of the assertion is the solution of this integration, transmitted again through an XML file.

Modifying the environment. Finally, the program can change the mode of a given system `system_i` at time `t` to the new mode `mod_j`. It uses the assertion: `HYBRID_MODE(system_i, mode_j, t)`. The assertion for changing the value of the jth parameters of the system `system_i` to the new value `value` at time `t` is: `HYBRID_PARAM(system_i, j, value, t)`. In practice, this changes the system of ODEs that will be used in order to compute the next values that will be read. Before that, the existing system is integrated until time t.

3   Experiments

The two tanks system [10]. This system is composed of two water tanks linked by a tube, and a controller that must keep the water levels in both tanks between safe bounds. We encoded the system as a C program [2] plus a set of ODEs and analyzed it with HybridFluctuat. We set the initial values of the levels to the range $[3, 8] \times [4, 7]$. As a result, HybridFluctuat proved that the water levels in both tanks remain in the range $[2.4, 8.5] \times [3.5, 7.8]$. We are thus able to automatically prove the correctness of the control command program on the whole state space with non-linear dynamics, which, to the best of our knowledge, cannot be done by existing verification tools. As the initial ranges of values are large, we used in the analysis regular subdivisions of width 0.1 on these initial ranges (this was done automatically by our tool). The analysis took one hour.

*The heating system [1].*This system is composed of n adjacent rooms, each with a heater, so that only m of them can be switched on at the same time. A controller must maintain a certain temperature in all the rooms. We used our tool to compute a range on the rooms temperature: this time, we set the initial condition to be a point (a temperature of 20 in all rooms) and introduced an uncertainty of 10% on all the parameters of the system (power of the heater, outside temperature...).

---

[2] The programs and ODEs mentioned in this article can be found at http://www.lix.polytechnique.fr/~bouissou/progs/hybridfluctuat/

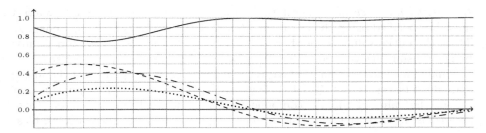

Fig. 1. Trajectory of the ATV over time in the quaternion coordinates. The black line is the first dimension of the quaternion, the dashed ones are the 3 others.

HybridFluctuat proved, in 28 seconds, that the temperature in all rooms remains above 11.5, which is similar to results obtained using PHAVer [7].

Industrial case study. We used HybridFluctuat to analyze the behavior of a simplified version of the MSU part of the safety ATV control program described in Section 1. The C program is about 400 lines of code including many array manipulations and non linear floating point computations. The ODE is of dimension 7 with 3 parameters. The open-loop system is particularly unstable, the continuous environment only converges under the action of the control program. This made this whole system hard to analyze. We first computed an overapproximation of the continuous trajectories on the 50 first seconds, with the initial condition being a point. We obtained Figure 1 that shows that the measured values converge towards $(1, 0, 0, 0)$, which is the safe state that the ATV is supposed to reach in this escape mode. This analysis, although performed on a finite time range, gives a good indication on the correctness of the control command program. Ideally, a fixpoint computation proving the convergence for unbounded time would be needed to prove the correctness. This is not implemented in HybridFluctuat yet.

We also measured the estimation error, i.e. the difference between the predicted position of the ATV and the position given by the sensors at the next cycle. The predictions were proved to be accurate: their error is around 5%.

4   Conclusion and Future Work

In this article, we presented the new static analyzer HybridFluctuat that extends the static analysis of numerical properties of embedded programs performed by Fluctuat, by accurately modeling their interaction with their physical environment. The evolution of the environment is overapproximated by GRKLib, a guaranteed integrator of ODEs. Although it is a preliminary work, we obtained very promising results and the case study we performed shows that it can be used for industrial applications. For the time being, we used HybridFluctuat to compute invariants on values of the variables of the program, and overapproximations of the continuous trajectories. We are thus able to prove the numerical stability of the implementation of a control-command algorithm. We next intend to extend this analysis in two natural directions described hereafter.

One specificity of Fluctuat is to model the propagation of initial uncertainties and rounding errors through numerical computations, pointing out the sources of the main errors on the outputs. In HybridFluctuat, we consider for now that the values sent to the actuators are error free, which is obviously not the case. We thus want to investigate the influence of the difference between the commands actually sent to the environment, and the ones that would be sent if the program used real numbers: this difference induces two distinct evolutions of the environment. We want to consider the difference between both evolutions to be the propagation of the computation errors. Secondly, we want to remove the current limitation of HybridFluctuat that imposes to analyze the system on a finite time range. To do so, we need to compute fixpoints of the continuous variables, i.e. fixpoints of the solutions of the ODEs: extrapolation algorithms may be of great help in this perspective. Finally, a current use of Fluctuat aims at bounding, when possible, not only the imprecision due to the implementation, but also the imprecision due to the method. In some applications (like the ATV case study), approximate ODE solvers are part of the program implemented. HybridFluctuat, with its guaranteed ODE solver, can give an estimation of the idealized result, and the difference with the result of the implementation, which can be seen and propagated as a method error.

References

1. Fehnker, A., Ivancic, F.: Benchmarks for hybrid systems verification. In: Alur, R., Pappas, G.J. (eds.) HSCC 2004. LNCS, vol. 2993, pp. 326–341. Springer, Heidelberg (2004)
2. Alur, R., Courcoubetis, C., Halbwachs, N., Henzinger, T.A., Ho, P.H., Nicollin, X., Olivero, A., Sifakis, J., Yovine, S.: The algorithmic analysis of hybrid systems. Theoretical Computer Science 138(1), 3–34 (1995)
3. Bouissou, O., Martel, M.: GRKLib: a guaranteed runge-kutta library. In: Follow-up of International Symposium on Scientific Computing, Computer Arithmetic and Validated Numerics. IEEE Press, Los Alamitos (2007)
4. Bouissou, O., Martel, M.: Abstract interpretation of the physical inputs of embedded programs. In: Logozzo, F., Peled, D.A., Zuck, L.D. (eds.) VMCAI 2008. LNCS, vol. 4905, pp. 1–3. Springer, Heidelberg (2008)
5. Cousot, P.: Integrating physical systems in the static analysis of embedded control software. In: Yi, K. (ed.) APLAS 2005. LNCS, vol. 3780, pp. 135–138. Springer, Heidelberg (2005)
6. Cousot, P., Cousot, R.: Abstract interpretation: A unified lattice model for static analysis of programs by construction of approximations of fixed points. Principles of Programming Languages 4, 238–252 (1977)
7. Frehse, G.: Phaver: Algorithmic verification of hybrid systems past hytech. In: Morari, M., Thiele, L. (eds.) HSCC 2005. LNCS, vol. 3414, pp. 258–273. Springer, Heidelberg (2005)
8. Goubault, E., Martel, M., Putot, S.: Asserting the precision of floating-point computations: A simple abstract interpreter. In: Le Métayer, D. (ed.) ESOP 2002. LNCS, vol. 2305, pp. 209–212. Springer, Heidelberg (2002)
9. Goubault, E., Martel, M., Putot, S.: Some future challenges in the validation of control systems. In: ERTS, SEE (2006)

10. Kowalewski, S., Stursberg, O., Fritz, M., Graf, H., Preuß, I.H.J., et al.: A case study in tool-aided analysis of discretely controlled continuous systems: the two tanks problem. In: Antsaklis, P.J., Kohn, W., Lemmon, M.D., Nerode, A., Sastry, S.S. (eds.) HS 1997. LNCS, vol. 1567, p. 163. Springer, Heidelberg (1999)
11. Putot, S., Goubault, E., Martel, M.: Static analysis-based validation of floating-point computations. In: Alt, R., Frommer, A., Kearfott, R.B., Luther, W. (eds.) Dagstuhl Seminar 2003. LNCS, vol. 2991, pp. 306–313. Springer, Heidelberg (2004)

The Zonotope Abstract Domain Taylor1+[*]

Khalil Ghorbal, Eric Goubault, and Sylvie Putot

CEA, LIST, Modelisation and Analysis of Systems in Interaction,
F-91191 Gif-sur-Yvette Cedex, France
firstname.surname@cea.fr

1 Introduction

Static analysis by abstract interpretation [1] aims at automatically inferring properties on the behaviour of programs. We focus here on a specific kind of numerical invariants: the set of values taken by numerical variables, with a real numbers semantics, at each control point of a program.

We present an implementation called Taylor1+, interfaced with the APRON library [2], of an abstract domain using affine forms [3], defined by E. Goubault and S. Putot in [4, 5].

Contributions and organisation of the paper. We recap, in Section 2 the semantics of the main operations implemented, both arithmetic and order-theoretic. We then explain in Section 3 how this real number semantics is implemented using finite precision arithmetic. We finally present, in Section 4, experimental results, which we compare to the results obtained with other domains of APRON, such as intervals [1], octagons [6] and polyhedra [7] abstract domains.

Related work. Geometrically, the representation of the abstract values (the joint range of all variables) in our domain is a center-symmetric polytope called zonotope. Zonotopes were successfully applied elsewhere, such as for reachability analysis in the model-checking of hybrid systems [8] or collision detection [9].

2 Abstract Domain Based on Affine Forms

Affine arithmetic [3] is an extension of Interval Arithmetic that keeps track of affine relations between values of variables. An affine form expresses a set of values as a central value plus a sequence of deviation terms over symbolic symbols, called noise symbols. Formally, the affine form, $\hat{x}$, describing the values that program variable x can take, is :

$$\hat{x} = \alpha_0^x + \sum_{i=1}^{n} \alpha_i^x \epsilon_i$$

where the real coefficients $(\alpha_i^x)_{1 \leq i \leq n}$ are the partial deviations and the noise symbols $(\epsilon_i)_{1 \leq i \leq n}$ have their unknown values within $[-1, 1]$. Its interval concretisation is

---

[*] This work was partially funded by the ANR project ASOPT.

A. Bouajjani and O. Maler (Eds.): CAV 2009, LNCS 5643, pp. 627–633, 2009.

$$\gamma(\hat{x}) = \left[\alpha_0^x - \sum_{i=1}^{n} |\alpha_i^x|, \alpha_0^x + \sum_{i=1}^{n} |\alpha_i^x| \right]$$

These noise symbols are introduced dynamically: $\imath$) for each new input whose value is given in an interval, or $\imath\imath$) when non linear operations are achieved (see section 2.1). For instance, the affine form abstraction of a new program variable x known to lie in $[a, b]$, is $\hat{x} = \frac{1}{2}(a + b) + \frac{1}{2}(b - a)\epsilon_{n+1}$, where ϵ_{n+1} is a fresh noise symbol, i.e. is not used by any existing affine form.

Abstract operations must be *sound*, that is, in our case, $\imath$) give guaranteed range over-approximations of the variables at the current control point of the program, and $\imath\imath$) give guaranteed range over-approximations for all other expressions on these variables that we might want to evaluate later (see [5]).

2.1   Arithmetic Operations

If performed with real number coefficients, affine arithmetic is exact on linear operations : addition and subtraction operations are defined componentwise. For non-linear unary operations, such as square root and inverse, our implementation relies on Taylor forms of first order with rigorous error bounds for the error term. For non-linear binary operations, an approximated affine form is computed, and the remaining non-linear term is bounded, then assigned to a fresh noise symbol. For instance, the multiplication of two affine forms $\hat{x} = \alpha_0^x + \sum_{i=1}^{n} \alpha_i^x \epsilon_i$ and $\hat{y} = \alpha_0^y + \sum_{i=1}^{n} \alpha_i^y \epsilon_i$ is :

$$\hat{x} \times \hat{y} = \alpha_0^x \alpha_0^y + \sum_{i=1}^{n} (\alpha_i^x \alpha_0^y + \alpha_i^y \alpha_0^x)\epsilon_i + \sum_{i=1}^{n} \sum_{j=1}^{n} \alpha_i^x \alpha_j^y \epsilon_i \epsilon_j \ . \tag{1}$$

We have implemented the method of [4]: $\epsilon_i \epsilon_j$ is taken within $[0, 1]$ whenever $i = j$, and $[-1, 1]$ otherwise. The method is cost-effective but not always the most precise one. A more accurate but more costly technique is to use SemiDefinite Programming (SDP) :

$$\max_{|\epsilon_i| \leq 1} \sum_{i=1}^{n} \sum_{j=1}^{n} \alpha_i^x \alpha_j^y \epsilon_i \epsilon_j = \max_{|\epsilon_i| \leq 1} \varepsilon^t . \Phi . \varepsilon \leq \inf_{\mu \in \mathbb{R}_+^n} \{ \text{trace}(\mu I_n) | \Phi - \mu I_n \preceq 0 \} \tag{2}$$

where $(\phi_{i,j})_{1 \leq i,j \leq n} = \frac{1}{2}(\alpha_i^x \alpha_j^y + \alpha_j^x \alpha_i^y)$ and $M \preceq 0$ means that matrix M is negative semidefinite. The equality holds when matrix Φ is negative semidefinite. The right hand side of (2) is a typical SDP problem. We give first experimental results in section 4.

2.2   Order-Theoretic Operations

Perturbed Affine Forms defined in [5] extend standard affine forms by adding special noise symbols ϵ_U, called join symbol, that allow simple and precise order-theoretic operations We define then exemplify the (pseudo) join operation.

Definition 1. *The join operation $\hat{z} = \hat{x} \cup \hat{y}$ defines an upper bound of $\hat{x}$ and $\hat{y}$, which is minimal in "generic" situations, and whose interval concretisation is the union of interval concretisations of $\hat{x}$ and $\hat{y}$:*

$$\alpha_0^z = mid(\gamma(\hat{x}) \cup \gamma(\hat{y})) \qquad\qquad\qquad \textit{(central value of } \hat{z})$$

$$\alpha_i^z = \underset{min(\alpha_i^x,\alpha_i^y)\leq\alpha\leq max(\alpha_i^x,\alpha_i^y)}{\operatorname{argmin}} (|\alpha|), \forall i \geq 1 \qquad \textit{(coeff. of } \epsilon_i)$$

$$\beta^z = \sup(\gamma(\hat{x}) \cup \gamma(\hat{y})) - \alpha_0^z - \sum_{i\geq1} |\alpha_i^z| \qquad \textit{(coeff. of } \epsilon_U)$$

where the γ function returns the interval concretisation of an affine form and $mid([a,b]) := \frac{1}{2}(a+b)$ and $\underset{a\leq x\leq b}{\operatorname{argmin}}(|x|) := \{x \in [a,b], |x| \text{ is minimal }\}.$

Example 1. By the formula of definition 1:
$$\begin{pmatrix} \hat{x} = 3 +\epsilon_1 +2\epsilon_2 \\ \hat{u} = 0 +\epsilon_1 +\epsilon_2 \end{pmatrix} \quad \cup \quad \begin{pmatrix} \hat{y} = 1 -2\epsilon_1 +\epsilon_2 \\ \hat{u} = 0 +\epsilon_1 +\epsilon_2 \end{pmatrix} \quad = \quad \begin{pmatrix} \hat{x} \cup \hat{y} = 2 \quad +\epsilon_2 +3\epsilon_U \\ \hat{u} \cup \hat{u} = 0 +\epsilon_1 +\epsilon_2 \end{pmatrix}$$

We also define the cyclic unfold, denoted by $(i, c, \mathcal{N})$, as the one obtained by initially unrolling i times the loop, and from then computing the fixpoint of the loop functional iterated c times until convergence, this with at most $\mathcal{N}$ iterations, after which a classical interval semantics is used [1]. As proved in [5], and shown in Section 4, the cyclic unfold schemes together with the join operator ensures termination with accurate fixpoint bounds for linear iterative schemes.

3   Implementation Aspects

The APRON Project [2] provides a uniform high level interface for numerical domains. For the time being, intervals, convex polyhedra, octagons, and congruences abstract domains are interfaced. We enrich here the library with a domain based on affine forms, called Taylor1+.

As we represent coefficients of affine forms by double precision floating-point numbers instead of real numbers, we have to adapt our transfer functions. For instance, instruction z = x + y; is abstracted by

$$\hat{z} = \hat{x} \oplus \hat{y} = float(\alpha_0^x + \alpha_0^y) + \sum_{i=1}^{n} float(\alpha_i^x + \alpha_i^y)\epsilon_i + \left(\sum_{i=0}^{n} dev(\alpha_i^x + \alpha_i^y)\right)\epsilon_{n+1}$$

where $float(x)$ is the nearest double-precision floating-point number to the real number x and $dev(x) := \rhd(|x - float(x)|)$, ($\rhd$ being rounding towards $+\infty$).

We are working on some techniques, namely those used in [8] and [10], to control the potential increase of the number of noise symbols during analysis.

However, in practise, the number of symbols reaches high levels very scarcely, since our join operator has the effect of reducing the number of noise symbols by collapsing some of them into a join symbol.

4   Experiments and Benchmarks

We analyse hereafter two simple iterative schemes. We used a laptop equipped with Intel(R) Core(TM)2 CPU (1.06GHz) and 2GB of RAM. All numerical values are rounded to two significant decimal digits for readability's sake.

4.1   Linear Iterative Schemes

Consider the following 2nd order filter :

$$S_n = 0.7E_n - 1.3E_{n-1} + 1.1E_{n-2} + 1.4S_{n-1} - 0.7S_{n-2}$$

where E_n are independent inputs with unknown values in range $[0, 1]$, and S_n is the output of the filter at iteration n. Pôles are inside the unit circle (norm close to 0.84), so the output in real numbers is provably bounded, and can be tightly estimated by manual methods to $[-1.09, 2.75]$. We also study a 8th order linear recursive digital filter used in an industrial test case (whose code is omitted for obvious reasons), whose output is provably bounded in $[-0.20, 1.20]$.

Unrolled schemes. We first fully unroll the 2nd order filter scheme to compute the abstract value at each iteration. Figure 1 compares accuracy and performance of Taylor1+ with three domains, provided in APRON: Boxes (Interval Analysis), Octagons, Polyhedra (both PK [11] and PPL [12] implementations were tested). The current version of the Octagonal domain does not integrate any of the symbolic enhancement methods of [13], which leads to inaccurate results. The Polyhedra domain with exact arithmetic (using GMP) gives the exact bounds for the filter output. One can see that Taylor1+ wraps very closely the exact range given by polyhedra (left figure) with great performance (right figure).

Fixpoint computation using Kleene-like iteration. For both filters, we detail results for two different $(i, c, \mathcal{N})$-iteration schemes (see end of Section 2.2) for Taylor1+, with $i = 0$ and $\mathcal{N} = 10^3$. Table 1 summarizes the results, for the 2nd order filter (left tables) and the 8th order filter (right tables). For boxes, octagons, and polyhedra domains, their respectively classical widening operator were used if a fixpoint is not reached after 100 iterations. For T1+ domain, beyond this threshold, i.e. 100, and before $\mathcal{N}$, we accelerated convergence of the fixpoint computation by only keeping noise terms with equal coefficients and collapsing all the others.

Since the output diverges for Boxes and Octagons domains, the fixpoint computation diverges as well. Polyhedra gives the least fixpoint in a short time for the second order filter, however it takes an enormous amount of time for the filter of order 8, so we aborted computation. For the 2nd (resp. 8th) order filter, the

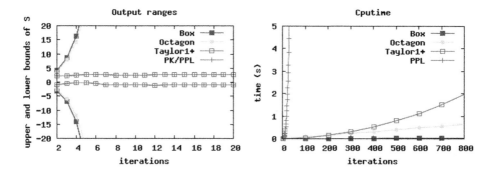

Fig. 1. Unrolled scheme for the 2nd order filter

Table 1. Fixpoint computation (2nd&8^{th}o filters) using Kleene-like iteration technique

filter o2	fixpoint	t(s)	filter o8	fixpoint	t(s)
Boxes	⊤	6×10^{-3}	Boxes	⊤	0.01
Octagons	⊤	0.19	Octagons	⊤	21
Polyhedra	$[-1.30 , 2.82]$	0.49	Polyhedra	abort	$> 24h$
T.1+(5)	$[-8.90 , 10.57]$	0.1	T.1+(5)	$[-19.77 , 20.77]$	0.74
T.1+(20)	$[-5.40 , 7.07]$	0.2	T.1+(20)	$[-3.81 , 4.81]$	0.5

fixpoint reached in Taylor1+ for the scheme $c = 20$ (i.e. for the loop functional iterated c times) is $[-1.18, 2.84]$ (resp. $[-0.27, 1.27]$). From there, the computation of the fixpoint of the loop is slightly wider: $[-5.40, 7.07]$ (resp. $[-3.81, 4.81]$); we are working on improvements.

4.2   Non-linear Iterative Scheme

The non-linear scheme we are considering is based on a Householder method of order 3 that converges towards the inverse of the square root of an input A. It originates from an industrial code, used as a test case in [14]; The current estimate of the inverse of the square root is updated as follows:

$$x_{n+1} = x_n + x_n \left(\frac{1}{2} h_n + \frac{3}{8} h_n^2 \right)$$

where $h_n = 1 - A x_n^2$, $A \in [16, 20]$ and $x_0 = 2^{-4}$.

We study the fully unrolled scheme for 5 iterations, then the fixpoint computation by the $(5, 1, 10^3)$-iteration scheme for Taylor1+, and compare different implementations of the multiplication; results are shown in Table 4.2. We compute here all possible values, whatever the stopping criterion (on $| x_{n+1} - x_n |$) of the loop may be. The fixpoint of $\sqrt{A}$ (right table), deduced from this estimate, thus encloses the first 5 iterations and is hence naturally wider than the result

Table 2. Comparison of domains on Householder (o3) example

Unrolling (5 It.)	$\sqrt{A} = Ax_n$	t(s)	Kleene Iteration	$\sqrt{A} = Ax_n$	t(s)
Boxes	[0.51 , 8.44]	1×10^{-4}	Boxes	$\top$	1×10^{-4}
Octagons	[0.51 , 7.91]	0.01	Octagons	$\top$	0.04
Polyhedra	[2.22 , 6.56]	310	Polyhedra	abort	$> 24h$
T.1+ :	[3.97 , 4.51]	1×10^{-3}	T.1+ :	[1.80 , 4.51]	0.01
• 10 subdivisions	[4.00 , 4.47]	0.02	• 10 subdivisions	[1.80 , 4.48]	0.2
• SDP	[3.97 , 4.51]	0.16	• SDP	[1.80 , 4.51]	0.86

of the unrolled scheme. We can see that results are tight even for non linear computations. The SDP solver is costly in time and does not seem to buy much more precision. However, for a larger range for input A, SDP gives tighter results than the standard multiplication. Moreover, the real advantage of SDP over subdividing is that the process of subdividing inputs might become intractable when several inputs would need subdividing. We tested here a non-guaranteed SDP solver [15], but we plan in the future to use guaranteed SDP solver such as the one described in [16].

References

[1] Cousot, P., Cousot, R.: Abstract interpretation: a unified lattice model for static analysis of programs by construction or approximation of fixpoints. In: ACM POPL 1977, pp. 238–252 (1977)
[2] APRON Project. Numerical abstract domain library (2007), http://apron.cri.ensmp.fr
[3] Comba, J.L.D., Stolfi, J.: Affine arithmetic and its applications to computer graphics. In: SIBGRAPI 1993 (1993)
[4] Goubault, E., Putot, S.: Static analysis of numerical algorithms. In: Yi, K. (ed.) SAS 2006. LNCS, vol. 4134, pp. 18–34. Springer, Heidelberg (2006)
[5] Goubault, E., Putot, S.: Perturbed affine arithmetic for invariant computation in numerical program analysis (2008), http://arxiv.org/abs/0807.2961
[6] Miné, A.: The Octagon abstract domain. Higher-Order and Symbolic Computation, 31–100 (2006)
[7] Cousot, P., Halbwachs, N.: Automatic discovery of linear restraints among variables of a program. In: ACM POPL 1978, pp. 84–97 (1978)
[8] Girard, A.: Reachability of uncertain linear systems using zonotopes. In: Morari, M., Thiele, L. (eds.) HSCC 2005. LNCS, vol. 3414, pp. 291–305. Springer, Heidelberg (2005)
[9] Guibas, L.J., Nguyen, A., Zhang, L.: Zonotopes as bounding volumes. In: Symposium on Discrete Algorithms, pp. 803–812 (2003)
[10] Kühn, W.: Zonotope dynamics in numerical quality control. In: Mathematical Visualization, pp. 125–134. Springer, Heidelberg (1998)
[11] Jeannet., B., et al.: Newpolka library, http://www.inrialpes.fr/pop-art/people/bjeannet/newpolka
[12] PPL Project. The Parma Polyhedra Library, http://www.cs.unipr.it/ppl/
[13] Miné, A.: Symbolic methods to enhance the precision of numerical abstract domains. In: Emerson, E.A., Namjoshi, K.S. (eds.) VMCAI 2006. LNCS, vol. 3855, pp. 348–363. Springer, Heidelberg (2005)

[14] Goubault, E., Putot, S., Baufreton, P., Gassino, J.: Static analysis of the accuracy in control systems: Principles and experiments. In: FMICS (2007)

[15] Borchers, B.: A C library for Semidefinite Programming (1999), `https://projects.coin-or.org/Csdp`

[16] Jansson, C., Chaykin, D., Keil, C.: Rigorous error bounds for the optimal value in semidefinite programming. SIAM J. Numer. Anal. 46(1), 180–200 (2007)

InvGen: An Efficient Invariant Generator

Ashutosh Gupta and Andrey Rybalchenko

Max Planck Institute for Software Systems (MPI-SWS)

Abstract. In this paper we present INVGEN, an automatic linear arithmetic invariant generator for imperative programs. INVGEN's unique feature is in its use of dynamic analysis to make invariant generation order of magnitude more efficient.

1 Introduction

Program verification relies on invariants for reasoning about sets of reachable states [3]. Synthesizing invariants that satisfy a given assertion is a difficult task. The scalability of existing approaches to invariant generation is severely limited due to the high computation cost of the underlying symbolic reasoning techniques.

We present INVGEN, an automatic tool for the generation of linear arithmetic invariants for imperative programs. INVGEN uses a constraint-based approach to generate invariants [2]. INVGEN combines it with static and dynamic analysis techniques to solve constraints efficiently [4]. INVGEN provides an order of magnitude efficiency improvement wrt. the existing tools, see [5]. This improvement enables INVGEN's application for automatic software verification, e.g., for refinement of predicate abstraction by generating invariants for program fragments determined by spurious counterexamples [1].

In this paper, we describe the design and implementation of INVGEN and present a collection of optimizations that were necessary to achieve the desired scalability. We also describe our experience with applying INVGEN on challenge benchmarks [8] and micro-benchmarks, which containing code fragments that are difficult to analyze automatically. The experimental results indicate that INVGEN is a practical tool for software verification.

2 Usage

INVGEN takes as input a program over linear arithmetic expressions that is given in C syntax or as a transition relation.[1] INVGEN uses a template based technique to compute invariants, which requires that a set of templates is given as input to the tool. A template is a Boolean combination of linear inequalities over program variables with coefficients that are kept as parameters. As a result, INVGEN either returns an invariant that proves the non-reachability of the error location or fails.

---

[1] See [5] for the syntax of transition relations.

A. Bouajjani and O. Maler (Eds.): CAV 2009, LNCS 5643, pp. 634–640, 2009.

INVGEN offers a collection of heuristics to improve scalability of invariant generation, and allows one to explore various combination of these heuristics. Support of dynamic/static analysis can be disabled/enabled with some parameters. Dynamic analysis can be performed using concrete or symbolic execution. Other tools can be used to generate test executions for INVGEN. INVGEN can run in the server mode, in which it communicates its input/output via standard input and output streams. The full set of options is described online [5].

3   Tool

In this section we briefly present the algorithm used by INVGEN and focus on the tool design and implementation.

3.1   Algorithm

INVGEN computes linear arithmetic invariants that prove the non-reachability of the error location. We will call such invariants *safe*. INVGEN applies the template based approach [2] for the invariant generation, which assumes an *invariant template* at each cut-point location in the program, i.e., at loop entry locations. Each invariant template consists of parameterized linear inequalities over the program variables. The specific goal of invariant generation is to find an instantiation of the template parameters that yields a safe invariant. The invariant templates at the start and error locations of the program are `true` and `false`, respectively. A template instantiation yields an invariant if each program path `stmt1;...;stmtN;` between each pair ℓ and ℓ' of adjacent cut-points satisfies the *inductiveness condition*: the instantiated invariant templates $\eta(\ell)$ and $\eta(\ell')$ at the respective cut-points together with the program path form a valid Hoare triple $\{\eta(\ell)\}\texttt{stmt1};...;\texttt{stmtN};\{\eta(\ell')\}$.[2] We translate the inductiveness condition into an arithmetic constraint over the template parameters. Each solution of this constraint yields a safe invariant.

```
1: x=0;
2: assume(n>0);
3: while(x<n){
4:   x++;
5: }
6: assert(x==n);
```

```
1: x=0;
2: while(x<n){
3:   x++;
4: }
5: if(n>0)
6:   assert(x==n);
```
(a)

```
1: assume(p);
2: while(p){
3:   ...
4:   assume(q);
5: }
6: assert(q);
```
(b)

Fig. 1. Example `simple.c`   **Fig. 2.** Examples requiring disjunctive invariants

---

[2] $\{P\}\texttt{stmts}\{Q\}$ is a valid Hoare triple if each computation that starts in a state satisfying the assertion Q either terminates in a state satisfying Q or diverges [7]. In our case, program paths are loop free and hence terminating.

See Figure 1. The example program `simple.c` contains a statement $\mathtt{assert}(p)$, which is a short form for `if (!p) ERROR;`. The entry location of the `while` loop is a cut-point location ℓ_3. At this location we assume an invariant template $\alpha_{\mathtt{x}}\mathtt{x} + \alpha_{\mathtt{n}}\mathtt{n} \leq \alpha$, where $\alpha_{\mathtt{x}}, \alpha_{\mathtt{n}}, \alpha$ are unknown parameters. The inductiveness condition for the path from the start location to the loop entry requires the validity of the triple $\{\mathtt{true}\}\mathtt{x} = 0; \mathtt{assume}(\mathtt{n} > 0); \{\eta(\ell_3)\}$, the condition for the loop iteration is $\{\eta(\ell_3)\}\mathtt{assume}(\mathtt{x} < \mathtt{n}); \mathtt{x} = \mathtt{x} + 1; \{\eta(\ell_3)\}$, and the path from the loop entry to the error location produces $\{\eta(\ell_3)\}\mathtt{assume}(\mathtt{x} \geq \mathtt{n}); \mathtt{assume}(\mathtt{x} \neq \mathtt{n}); \{\mathtt{false}\}$. The resulting arithmetic constraint has a following solution for template parameters: $\alpha_{\mathtt{x}} = 1$, $\alpha_{\mathtt{n}} = -1$, and $\alpha = 0$. Hence, $\mathtt{x} - \mathtt{n} \leq 0$ is a safe invariant.

Arithmetic constraints that encode the inductiveness condition contain non-linear arithmetic expressions and are difficult to solve. INVGEN improves performance of the constraint solving by adding information collected using dynamic and static analysis techniques.

In the dynamic analysis phase, we execute the program according to a coverage criterion and collect the reached states. By definition, each reached state must satisfy program invariants. For each reached state, we substitute the program variables occurring in the invariant template at the corresponding control location by their values in the state. Thus, we obtain linear constraints over template parameters. For `simple.c`, assume a reached state at the loop entry such that $(\mathtt{x} = 0, \mathtt{n} = 1)$. After substituting program variable by their values in the above template for the location ℓ_3 we obtain the constraint over template parameters $\alpha_{\mathtt{x}}0 + \alpha_{\mathtt{n}}1 \leq \alpha$. Such linear constraints improve the efficiency of constraint solving [4].

In the static analysis phase, we first apply abstract interpretation in a eager fashion to compute a collection of invariants – which are not necessarily strong enough to prove the non-reachability of the error location – that holds for the program, and then annotate the program with these invariants. The invariants obtain using abstract interpretation allow INVGEN to focus on the synthesis missing, complex invariants in a goal directed way. Such invariants may be missed by the abstract interpreter due to the necessary precision loss of join and widening operators and the limited precision of efficient abstract domains.

3.2   Design

We present the design of INVGEN in Figure 3. The input program is passed to the dynamic and static analyzers. The results of each analysis together with the program and the templates are passed to the constraint generator. The generated constraints are solved by a constraint solver. If the solver succeeds then INVGEN returns a safe invariants.

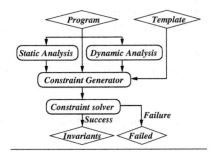

Fig. 3. INVGEN design

3.3 Implementation

Figure 4 outlines the implementation of IN-VGEN. It is divided into two executables, *frontend* and INVGEN.

The frontend executable contains a CIL [10] based interface to C and an abstract interpreter INTERPROC [9]. The frontend takes a program procedure written in C language as an input, and applies INTERPROC on the program three times using the interval, octagon, and polyhedral abstract domains. Then, the frontend outputs the transition relation of the program that is a annotated with the results computed by INTERPROC. Se [5] for the output format.

Next, we describe the components of IN-VGEN, following Figure 4.

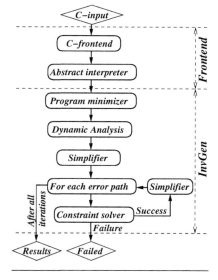

Fig. 4. INVGEN implementation

Program minimizer. INVGEN minimizes the transition relation of the program to reduce the complexity of constraint solving. INVGEN computes a minimal set of cut-point locations, and replaces each cut-point free path by a single, compound program transition. The unsatisfiable and redundant transitions are eliminated. At this phase, the invariants obtained from INTERPROC can lead to the elimination of additional transitions.

Dynamic analysis. INVGEN collects dynamic information for the minimized program using either concrete and symbolic execution. In case of concrete execution, INVGEN collects a finite set of reachable states by using a guided testing technique. Otherwise, INVGEN performs a bounded, exhaustive symbolic execution of the program. By default, the bound is set to the number of cut-points in the program. The user can limit the maximum number of visits for each cut-point during the symbolic execution.

Simplifier. INVGEN simplifies all arithmetic constraints locally at each step of the algorithm.

Consider the phase when the dynamic analysis using symbolic execution produces additional linear constraints over template parameters. These constraints contain existentially quantified variables, and the scope of the quantifier is rather limited. For simple.c, assume that a symbolic state $x = 0 \land n \geq 0$ is reached at the loop entry location. For any template evaluation, the symbolic state is subsumed by the invariant, hence $(x = 0 \land n \geq 0) \rightarrow (\alpha_x x + \alpha_n n \leq \alpha)$. After the elimination of program variables INVGEN obtains the constraints $\lambda \geq 0 \land -\lambda = \alpha_n \land \alpha \geq 0$, where λ is an existentially quantified variable.

λ does not appear anywhere in the constraint and can be eliminated locally. As a result, we obtain $\alpha_n \le 0 \wedge \alpha \ge 0$.

INVGEN also simplifies constraints obtained by the concrete execution and abstract interpretation.

Constraint solver. The inductiveness conditions result in non-linear arithmetic constraints. For `simple.c`, the inductiveness condition for the error path $\{\eta\}$`assume(x > n)`; $\{$`false`$\}$ translates to the implication $\alpha_x x + \alpha_n n \le \alpha \wedge x > n \to 1 \le 0$ with universal quantification over the program variables. After the elimination of the program variables, INVGEN obtains the non-linear constraint $\lambda \ge 0 \wedge \delta \ge 0 \wedge \lambda \alpha_x = \delta \wedge \lambda \alpha_n + \delta = 0 \wedge \lambda \alpha + 1 \le \delta$, where λ and δ are existentially quantified, non-negative variables that encode the implication validity. In practice, such existentially quantified variables range over a small domain, typically they are either 0 or 1.

INVGEN leverages this observation in order to solve the constraints by performing a case analysis on the variables with small domain. Each instance of case analysis results in a linear constraint over template parameters, which can be solved using a linear constraint solver. This approach is incomplete, since INVGEN does not take all possible values during the case analysis, however it is effective in practice.

Multiple paths to error location. A program may have multiple cut-point free paths that lead to the error location, which we refer to as error paths. INVGEN deals with multiple error paths in an incremental fashion for efficiency reasons. Instead taking inductiveness conditions for all error paths into account, INVGEN computes a safe invariant for one error path at a time. Already computed invariants are used as strengthening when dealing with the remaining error paths.

4   Discussion

We highlight several important aspects of INVGEN in detail.

Abstract interpretation. The template instantiation computed by INVGEN may rely on the invariants discovered during the abstract interpretation phase. INVGEN keeps track of such invariants and reports them to the user.

Template generation. The applicability of INVGEN depends on the choice of invariant templates. If the template is too expressive, e.g., if it admits a number of conjuncts that is larger than required, then the efficiency of INVGEN is decreasing due to the increased difficulty of constraint solving. A template that is not expressive enough cannot yield a desired invariant.

In our experience, the majority of invariants require a template that is a conjunction of two linear inequalities. This surprisingly small number of conjuncts is due to the strengthening using invariants obtained during the abstraction interpretation phase—INVGEN focuses on the missing invariants. By default, for each cut-point location INVGEN assumes a conjunction of two parametric linear inequalities as a template.

Table 1. Performance of INVGEN on benchmark inspired by [8]. INVGEN* does not apply dynamic analysis. INVGEN** applies neither static nor dynamic analysis. "T/O" means time out after 10 minutes.

Table 2. Application of INVGEN for the predicate discovery in BLAST using path invariants. We show the number of refinement steps required to prove the property.

File	INVGEN**	INVGEN*	INVGEN
Seq	23.0s	**0.5s**	**0.5s**
Seq-z3	23.0s	**0.5s**	**0.5s**
Seq-len	T/O	T/O	**2.8s**
nested	T/O	17.0s	**2.3s**
svd(light)	T/O	**10.6s**	14.2s
heapsort	T/O	19.2s	**13.3s**
mergesort	T/O	**142s**	170s
Spam-loop	T/O	**0.28s**	0.4s
apache-tag	**0.4s**	0.6s	0.7s
sendmail-qp	0.3s	0.3s	**0.3s**

File	BLAST	BLAST + INVGEN
Seq	diverge	8
Seq-len	diverge	9
fregtest	diverge	3
sendmail-qp	diverge	10
svd(light)	144	43
Spam-loop	51	24
apache-escape	26	20
apache-tag	23	15
sendmail-angle	19	15
sendmail-7to8	16	13

Disjunction. The user can provide disjunctive templates to INVGEN, which yields disjunctive invariants. Currently, INVGEN is not practical for disjunctive invariants.

Nevertheless, programs that require disjunctive invariants appear often in practice, as illustrated in Figure 2. Example 2(a) relies on a disjunctive loop invariant $n \geq x \vee n < 0$ to prove the assertion. Similarly, Example 2(b) requires a disjunctive loop invariant $p \vee q$.

Avoiding such program patterns improves the effectiveness of INVGEN. For example, adding a commonly used assumption $n \geq 0$ at the start location of the program in Figure 2(a) eliminates the need for disjunctive invariants.

Concrete vs. symbolic dynamic analysis. In our evaluation, dynamic analysis using symbolic execution performs better than with the concrete execution. Symbolic execution produces a smaller set of constraints and leads to the improvement of the constraint solving efficiency that is never worse the one achieved by the concrete execution.

5   Experiences

Verification benchmarks. We applied INVGEN on a collection of programs that are difficult for state-of-the-art software verification tools [8]. The collection consists of 12 programs. Due to short running times, we present the aggregated data and do not provide information for each program individually. Using the polyhedral abstract domain, INTERPROC computes invariants that are strong enough to prove the assertion for six programs in the collection. INVGEN handles 11 examples in 6.3 seconds, and times out on one program.

Effect of static and dynamic analysis. The collection [8] does not allow us to perform a thorough experimental evaluation of INVGEN, since the running times on these examples are too short. We constructed a set of more interesting programs that is inspired by [8] by extending the programs from this collection with additional loops and branching statements. Table 1 shows the effect of static and dynamic analysis when dealing with the constructed examples.

Random input. We developed a tool for the generation of random program. We try these random programs with INVGEN without testing then with testing feature. We generated 17 programs with three cut-point and one error location in each of them, see [5]. We observed that for these programs, dynamic analysis either improves or at least does not decrease the efficiency of invariant generation. In four cases, the efficiency of INVGEN increased by two orders of magnitude.

Integration with Blast. We have modified the abstraction refinement procedure of the BLAST software model checker [6] by adding predicate discovery using path invariants [1]. Table 2 indicates that constraint based invariant generation can be an effective tool for refining predicate abstraction. For several examples, BLAST diverged due to the disability to find the right set of predicates. In these cases, INVGEN enabled the successful termination of the verification attempt, while for other cases it reduced the number of the number of refinement iterations by 25–400%.

References

1. Beyer, D., Henzinger, T.A., Majumdar, R., Rybalchenko, A.: Path invariants. In: Proc. PLDI, pp. 300–309. ACM Press, New York (2007)
2. Colón, M., Sankaranarayanan, S., Sipma, H.: Linear invariant generation using non-linear constraint solving. In: Hunt Jr., W.A., Somenzi, F. (eds.) CAV 2003. LNCS, vol. 2725, pp. 420–432. Springer, Heidelberg (2003)
3. Floyd, R.W.: Assigning meanings to programs. In: Mathematical Aspects of Computer Science. AMS (1967)
4. Gupta, A., Majumdar, R., Rybalchenko, A.: From tests to proofs. In: Kowalewski, S., Philippou, A. (eds.) TACAS 2009. LNCS, vol. 5505, pp. 262–276. Springer, Heidelberg (2009)
5. Gupta, A., Rybalchenko, A.: InvGen: an efficient invariant generator, http://www.mpi-sws.org/~agupta/invgen/
6. Henzinger, T., Jhala, R., Majumdar, R., McMillan, K.: Abstractions from proofs. In: POPL 2004: Principles of Programming Languages, pp. 232–244. ACM, New York (2004)
7. Hoare, C.A.R.: An axiomatic basis for computer programming. Communications of ACM (1969)
8. Ku, K., Hart, T., Chechik, M., Lie, D.: A buffer overflow benchmark for software model checkers. In: Proc. ASE (2007)
9. Lalire, G., Argoud, M., Jeannet, B.: The interproc analyze, http://pop-art.inrialpes.fr/people/bjeannet/bjeannet-forge/interproc/index.html
10. Necula, G.C., McPeak, S., Rahul, S.P., Weimer, W.: CIL: Intermediate language and tools for analysis and transformation of C programs. In: Horspool, R.N. (ed.) CC 2002. LNCS, vol. 2304, pp. 213–228. Springer, Heidelberg (2002)

INFAMY: An Infinite-State Markov Model Checker*

Ernst Moritz Hahn, Holger Hermanns, Björn Wachter, and Lijun Zhang

Universität des Saarlandes, Saarbrücken, Germany
{emh,hermanns,bwachter,zhang}@cs.uni-sb.de

Abstract. The design of complex concurrent systems often involves intricate performance and dependability considerations. Continuous-time Markov chains (CTMCs) are a widely used modeling formalism, where performance and dependability properties are analyzable by model checking. We present INFAMY, a model checker for arbitrarily structured infinite-state CTMCs. It checks probabilistic timing properties expressible in continuous stochastic logic (CSL). Conventional model checkers explore the given model exhaustively, which is often costly, due to state explosion, and impossible if the model is infinite. INFAMY only explores the model up to a finite depth, with the depth bound being computed *on-the-fly*. The computation of depth bounds is configurable to adapt to the characteristics of different classes of models.

1 Introducing INFAMY

Continuous-time Markov chains (CTMCs) are widely used in performance and dependability analysis and biological modeling. Properties are typically specified in continuous stochastic logic (CSL) [1], a logic inspired by CTL. In CSL, the until operator is equipped with a time interval to express properties such as: *"The probability to reach a goal within 2 hours while maintaining a probability of at least 0.5 of communicating periodically (every five minutes) with a base station, is at least 0.9"* via $\mathcal{P}_{\geq 0.9}\left(\left(\mathcal{P}_{\geq 0.5}\diamondsuit^{\leq 5}\text{communicate}\right)\mathcal{U}^{\leq 120}\text{ goal}\right)$. CSL model checking amounts to analysis of the transient (time-dependent) probability vectors [1], typically carried out by *uniformization*, where the transient probability is expressed by a weighted infinite sum (weights are given by a Poisson process). The standard methodology in CSL model checking is to truncate the infinite sum up to some pre-specified accuracy [2]. Outside the model checking arena, ideas have been developed [3,4,5] which not only truncate the infinite sum, but also the matrix representing the system, which admits transient analysis of CTMCs with large or even infinite state spaces, provided they are given implicitly in a

---

* This work is supported by the NWO-DFG bilateral project VOSS, by the DFG as part of the Transregional Collaborative Research Center SFB/TR 14 AVACS and the Graduiertenkolleg "Leistungsgarantien für Rechnersysteme", and has received funding from the European Community's Seventh Framework Programme under grant agreement n° 214755.

A. Bouajjani and O. Maler (Eds.): CAV 2009, LNCS 5643, pp. 641–647, 2009.

modeling language. Harvesting and improving on these ideas, INFAMY is the first CSL model checker based on *truncation*. The underlying truncation technique was developed in [6]. Besides truncation, INFAMY features SPIN-like [7] state space exploration, and supports models given in a high-level description language.

Several other CSL model checkers exist, see [8] for an overview. Among them, PRISM [9] is a probabilistic model checker which uses advanced techniques for model representation and model checking for several stochastic model types. The model description language of INFAMY is based on the one of PRISM, but allows for infinite variable domains, while PRISM is restricted to finite models. Thus the tools are incomparable for infinite models. For several very large finite models, INFAMY is competitive with PRISM, as evident from Section 3. Model checkers based on discrete-event simulation [10,11,12,9] could, in principle, also analyze models with implicitly infinite state space, however they have not yet been applied to such models, and thus we cannot compare with them.

INFAMY is available at http://depend.cs.uni-sb.de/~emh/infamy.

2   Truncation-Based Model Checking

INFAMY reads models in a guarded-command language extending the one of PRISM. The semantics of a model is a CTMC in which each state is a valuation of model variables. Initial states are specified by an expressions over model variables. The rest of the description consists of commands. Each command comprises a guard and a set of rates. Each rate is associated with an update formula. If a state fulfills the guard of a command, this state has a rate to each state obtained by the respective update formula. Contrary to PRISM, we allow variables with infinite range. Properties are specified in the time-dependent fragment of CSL which involves the Boolean operators, timed until and next operators.

Using truncation, we compute a finite submodel which is sufficient for checking the validity of a property given in time-dependent CSL. This is done by descending into the CSL formula and at the same time exploring the model subject to the different time bounds given in the subformulas as well as the rates occurring in the model (details can be found in [13]). Beginning with a set of start states – either the initial states or, when descending into nested formulas, states determined by a subformula, the model is explored breadth-first up to

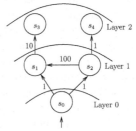

Fig. 1. Layers.

a certain depth. The lower the depth the higher the error in the probabilities computed during model checking. This error needs to be kept below a user-defined absolute error ε for all methods described in the following. As illustrated in Figure 1, our technique proceeds layer by layer exploring states with increasing *depth*, i.e. minimal distance from the start states, and estimates the error on the fly to determine if the depth is already sufficient. In the next paragraph, we discuss three error-estimation methods implemented in INFAMY, ranging from very precise and expensive to faster techniques with larger overestimation. An interesting trade-off arises between finding the smallest depth possible and the cost of error estimation.

Finite state projection (FSP). Munsky and Khammash [5] consider transient properties in the context of infinite-state biological models, including the one resulting from *Chemical Master Equation* problems. They build the CTMC incrementally in layers. Whenever adding a layer, they estimate the error by computing the probability of reaching the outermost layer from the initial states. FSP can find a minimal truncation point. However, as the exploration of new layers involves a stochastic analysis, relative computational cost of error estimation can be high.

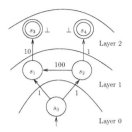

Fig. 2. FSP.

Uniform. While FSP performs error estimation on the full model, we recently developed the *Uniform* method [13], which abstracts the model to a chain, as illustrated in Figure 3. The probability of reaching the last state of the chain is an upper bound for the error. Compared to FSP, this admits a much faster error estimation, where the chain needs not even be constructed explicitly. We can just consider the maximal sum of rates λ_{max} leaving a state into the next layer. Using the Fox-Glynn algorithm [2], a right truncation point is computed by starting the algorithm with a value of $\lambda_{max} \cdot t$ where t is the time-bound of the current subformula. Whenever a state with a higher sum is seen, we adjust the right truncation point.

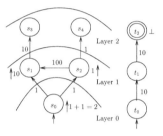

Fig. 3. Uniform method.

Layered. We consider more fine-grained chains than in the Uniform method that take into account maximal rates for individual layers, leading to a chain in which each edge is labeled with the maximal rate of the corresponding layer. This is depicted in Figure 4. Using the vector, we can construct a birth process in which the probability of reaching the last state within time bound t is larger than leaving the finite truncation. By building the birth process until we see a probability which is low enough, we obtain a method

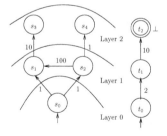

Fig. 4. Layered Method.

which may explore less layers than the Uniform one if the rates of the layers vary. However, we have to compute the probabilities within the birth process each time we explore a new layer. Thus model exploration may be more time-consuming. We call this the Layered method.

In all cases, after the exploration, usual CSL model checking is applied on the resulting submodel.

3 Results

We compare different configurations of INFAMY, i.e., FSP, Uniform and Layered method. Further, for finite models, we assess the effectiveness of truncation by comparing with PRISM. We denote the number of states on which model checking is performed by n. For INFAMY, this refers to the finite truncation, and, for PRISM, this refers to the full model. Where appropriate, we denote multiples of 1000 by "K". For all configurations, the probabilities listed in the experiments are exact up to $\varepsilon = 10^{-6}$ (or 10^{-12}, if the probability is close to 10^{-6}). The time column is of the form xx/yy, where xx is construction and yy is model check time. A full description of the models is given in [13].

Quasi-Birth-Death Processes [14]. We consider a system consisting of processors and an infinite queue for storing jobs. We compute the probability that, given all processors are busy and there are no jobs in the queue, within $t = 10$ time units a state is reached in which all processors are idle and the queue is empty. Results for different rates of incoming jobs λ are given below. The depth needed grows linearly with λ. Thus, the performance of the FSP method suffers from the high cost of repeated transient analysis.

λ	Uniform			Layered			FSP			prob.
	depth	time (s)	n	depth	time (s)	n	depth	time (s)	n	
40	609	1.1/0.2	2,434	533	1.1/0.2	2,130	473	28.1/0.2	1,890	4.21E-04
60	846	1.1/0.3	3,382	754	1.1/0.2	3,014	694	66.0/0.2	2,774	1.25E-04
80	1,077	1.1/0.3	4,306	971	1.1/0.3	3,882	911	125.5/0.3	3,642	5.26E-05
100	1,305	1.1/0.4	5,218	1,187	1.1/0.4	4,746	1,127	209.4/0.4	4,506	2.69E-05

Protein Synthesis [15]. We analyze a model of protein synthesis considering the property that, within time t but later than 10 time units, a state is reached, in which 20 or more proteins exist and the synthesizing gene is inactive. Overall, the FSP method is the most efficient here, because a rather low number of layers is relevant. In terms of model construction time, the Uniform method is best here.

t	Uniform			Layered			FSP			prob.
	depth	time (s)	n	depth	time (s)	n	depth	time (s)	n	
100	973	1.1/0.1	1,945	756	1.1/0.1	1,511	30	1.1/0.0	59	1.03E-03
500	3,636	1.1/6.0	7,271	3,308	1.2/5.0	6,615	35	1.2/0.0	69	4.39E-02
1000	6,830	1.1/39.3	13,659	6,420	1.4/34.7	12,839	36	1.4/0.0	71	9.99E-02
2000	13,103	1.1/276.9	26,205	12,577	2.3/255.3	25,153	37	1.7/0.0	73	2.02E-01

Grid-World Robot [11]. We consider a grid world in which a robot moves from the lower left to the upper right corner sending signals to a station. A janitor moves around and may block the robot for some time. In contrast to [11], the janitor can leave the $N \times N$ field of the robot, which leads to an infinite state space. We check a nested formula of the form mentioned in the introduction, namely whether the robot moves with probability 0.9 to the upper right corner within 100 time units while periodically communicating with the base. We give results for different N. Using the FSP method is advantageous, as each layer of the model contains quite a large number of states, and FSP only needs to explore a fraction of the layers compared to the other methods. As seen from the "prob." column, for $N = 2, 3$ the property holds, while, for $N = 4$, it does not. The reason for the decreasing probability is that the distance the robot has to travel increases with n. Thus the probability decreases that the robot will complete its travel in time.

An implicit representation of the edges of the model used to handle the large number of transitions. However, this increases the runtime in this example.

N	Uniform			Layered			FSP			prob.
	depth	time (s)	n	depth	time (s)	n	depth	time (s)	n	
2	905	15/4,479	9,807K	570	6/1,667	3,885K	107	1,417/37	135K	1.000
3	905	24/8,135	16,308K	571	11/2,979	6,475K	96	1,681/56	177K	0.902
4	905	33/13,323	22,781K	571	14/5,099	9,034K	98	2,754/99	253K	0.898

Workstation cluster [16]. We consider the *dependability of a fault-tolerant workstation cluster*, a model with finite state space. For the model with 512 workstations, we compute the probability that the QoS drops below minimum quality within one time unit, and compare with PRISM. Results are given for the fastest configuration of PRISM (sparse engine), and INFAMY (FSP) respectively.

The state space explored by PRISM has depth 1029 and includes 9.4 million states. Up to $t = 20$, INFAMY with FSP is faster than PRISM. However, for larger time bounds, the model construction time dominates, since for each layer the error estimate is recomputed. As observed by Munsky [5], this can be alleviated by adding more than one layer at each step. We consider a variant in which we double the number of layers we add per step, thus computing an error estimate every $1, 2, 4, 8, \ldots$ layers. We call this configuration *FSP exponential*. It is consistently the fastest method for $t \leq 50$, as shown in the last column of the table.

t	PRISM	FSP			FSP exponential			prob.
	time (s)	depth	time (s)	n	depth	time (s)	n	
5.0	4.8/147.3	37	7.1/0.4	23K	64	3.1/1.5	701K	1.21E-06
10.0	5.8/190.5	52	25.0/1.4	46K	64	4.4/2.4	701K	3.79E-06
20.0	6.0/315.3	80	209.1/7.8	111K	128	26.9/20.2	289K	1.01E-05
30.0	5.6/365.6	104	547.5/15.1	190K	128	38.7/28.3	289K	1.68E-05
50.0	5.4/502.5	147	2,610.5/46.2	382K	256	255.8/182.0	1,167K	3.04E-05

Tandem Queueing Network [17]. This model consists of two interconnected queues with capacity c. We consider the probability that the first queue becomes full before time 0.23. Larger time bounds are left out, since then this probability is one. The performance results for INFAMY using configuration Layered are better, while for large time bound ($t \geq 1$) the whole model will be explored thus PRISM will perform better.

c	PRISM			Layered			prob.
	depth	time	n	depth	time	n	
511	1,535	3.7/49.7	523,776	632	6.8/7.5	235,339	3.13E-02
1023	3,071	13.7/380.3	2,096,128	1,167	3.6/49.6	714,306	4.24E-03
2047	6,143	69.3/3,068.3	8,386,560	2,198	10.0/297.8	2,449,798	9.87E-05
4095	12,287	560.9/31,386.5	33,550,336	4,209	27.4/2,889.8	8,899,113	7.06E-08

4   Conclusion and Future Work

INFAMY enables model checking of infinite models and, for certain finite models, is competitive with the leading model checker PRISM in time and memory usage. As observed in our experiments, the appropriate truncation method strongly depends on the model and property under consideration. Therefore, INFAMY allows the user to select the method that fits best. We plan to implement heuristics that choose the estimation method automatically. Further, the approach implemented in INFAMY is applicable to richer languages than PRISM, e.g., languages that support dynamic process creation, as in the stochastic π-calculus.

References

1. Aziz, A., Sanwal, K., Singhal, V., Brayton, R.K.: Model-Checking Continuous-Time Markov Chains. ACM Trans. Comput. Log 1, 162–170 (2000)
2. Fox, B.L., Glynn, P.W.: Computing Poisson Probabilities. Commun. ACM 31, 440–445 (1988)
3. Grassmann, W.K.: Finding Transient Solutions in Markovian Event Systems Through Randomization. In: NSMC 1991, pp. 357–371 (1991)
4. van Moorsel, A.P.A., Sanders, W.H.: Adaptive Uniformization. Communications in Statistics - Stochastic Models 10, 619–647 (1994)
5. Munsky, B., Khammash, M.: The Finite State Projection Algorithm for the Solution of the Chemical Master Equation. Journal of Chemical Physics 124 (2006)
6. Zhang, L., Hermanns, H., Hahn, E.M., Wachter, B.: Time-Bounded Model Checking of Infinite-State Continuous-Time Markov Chains. In: ACSD, pp. 98–107 (2008)
7. Holzmann, G.J.: The Model Checker SPIN. IEEE Trans. Software Eng. 23, 279–295 (1997)
8. Baier, C., Haverkort, B.R., Hermanns, H., Katoen, J.P.: Model checking meets performance evaluation. SIGMETRICS Performance Evaluation Review 32, 10–15 (2005)
9. Hinton, A., Kwiatkowska, M.Z., Norman, G., Parker, D.: PRISM: A Tool for Automatic Verification of Probabilistic Systems. In: Hermanns, H., Palsberg, J. (eds.) TACAS 2006. LNCS, vol. 3920, pp. 441–444. Springer, Heidelberg (2006)
10. Hérault, T., Lassaigne, R., Magniette, F., Peyronnet, S.: Approximate Probabilistic Model Checking. In: Steffen, B., Levi, G. (eds.) VMCAI 2004. LNCS, vol. 2937, pp. 73–84. Springer, Heidelberg (2004)
11. Younes, H.L.S.: Ymer: A statistical model checker. In: Etessami, K., Rajamani, S.K. (eds.) CAV 2005. LNCS, vol. 3576, pp. 429–433. Springer, Heidelberg (2005)
12. Zapreev, I.S.: Model Checking Markov Chains: Techniques and Tools. Ph.D thesis, University of Twente, Enschede, The Netherlands (2008)

13. Hahn, E.M., Hermanns, H., Wachter, B., Zhang, L.: Time-Bounded Model Checking of Infinite-State Continuous-Time Markov Chains. Technical Report No. 47, SFB/TR 14 AVACS (2009); To appear in Fundamenta Informaticae
14. Katoen, J.P., Klink, D., Leucker, M., Wolf, V.: Three-Valued Abstraction for Continuous-Time Markov Chains. In: Damm, W., Hermanns, H. (eds.) CAV 2007. LNCS, vol. 4590, pp. 311–324. Springer, Heidelberg (2007)
15. Gross, P.J.E., Peccoud, J.: Quantitative modeling of stochastic systems in molecular biology by using stochastic Petri nets. Proc. Natl. Acad. Sci. USA 95, 6750–6755 (1998)
16. Haverkort, B.R., Hermanns, H., Katoen, J.P.: On the Use of Model Checking Techniques for Dependability Evaluation. In: SRDS, pp. 228–237 (2000)
17. Hermanns, H., Meyer-Kayser, J., Siegle, M.: Multi terminal binary decision diagrams to represent and analyse continuous time Markov chains. In: Plateau, B., Stewart, W., Silva, M. (eds.) NSMC, pp. 188–207 (1999)

Browser-Based Enforcement of Interface Contracts in Web Applications with BeepBeep

Sylvain Hallé[1] and Roger Villemaire[2]

[1] University of California, Santa Barbara
[2] Université du Québec à Montréal
shalle@acm.org, villemaire.roger@uqam.ca

Abstract. BeepBeep is a lightweight runtime monitor for Ajax web applications. Interface specifications are expressed internally in an extension of LTL with first-order quantification; they can be transparently enforced on the client side using a small and invisible Java applet. Violations of the specification are reported on-the-fly and prevent erroneous or out-of-sequence XML messages from reaching the server.

1   Introduction and Motivation

Asynchronous JavaScript and XML (Ajax) refers to a collection of technologies used to develop rich and interactive web applications. A typical Ajax client runs locally in the user's web browser and refreshes its interface using JavaScript according to user input. Popular Ajax applications, such as Google Maps and Facebook, communicate in the background with a remote server; in many cases, the server's functionality is made publicly available as an instance of a *web service*, which can be freely accessed by any third-party Ajax application. These services cannot be invoked arbitrarily: their public documentation specifies constraints on the content of each message and the proper sequence in which they can be exchanged. Yet, nothing prevents an Ajax application from sending messages violating this *interface specification*. In that event, the server can interrupt the communication, reply with an error message, or more insidiously, continue the conversation without warning and eventually send nonsensical or corrupt data. Preventing erroneous or out-of-sequence messages from being sent to the server is desirable, saving bandwidth and allowing client non-conformance to be detected early. To this end, we developed BeepBeep, a lightweight runtime monitor for Ajax applications. BeepBeep's input language is a rich extension of LTL, called LTL-FO$^+$, which includes first-order quantification over message elements and values of a global system clock. By transparently observing the trace of all incoming and outgoing messages inside an Ajax application, BeepBeep can monitor and enforce on-the-fly a wide range of interface contracts, including complex dependencies between message contents, sequences, and time.

A. Bouajjani and O. Maler (Eds.): CAV 2009, LNCS 5643, pp. 648–653, 2009.
© Springer-Verlag Berlin Heidelberg 2009

2   An Example

To illustrate our approach, we consider a library which makes its catalogue available online through a web service interface, allowing users to browse the library catalogue, borrow and return books. Each of these operations can be invoked by sending the proper XML message; for example, the following fragment represents a typical XML message for borrowing a list of books, identified by their book IDs:

$$
\begin{aligned}
&\texttt{<message xmlns=``http://example.com/library''>}\\
&\quad\texttt{<action>borrow</action>}\\
&\quad\texttt{<books>}\\
&\quad\quad\texttt{<id>837</id>}\\
&\quad\quad\texttt{<id>4472</id>}\\
&\quad\texttt{</books>}\\
&\texttt{</message>}
\end{aligned}
\tag{1}
$$

The documentation for the library web service imposes constraints on the messages that can be sent by a client, such as these ones:

1. Every "return" message must precede any "borrow" message
2. Any book can be involved in at most one borrow and/or return operation
3. Any two messages must be at most 60 seconds apart

3   The BeepBeep Runtime Monitor

A standard Ajax application communicates with a web service by sending and receiving messages through the standard `XMLHttpRequest` object provided by the local browser, as shown in the left part of Figure 1. BeepBeep is a lightweight tool that wraps around this object to monitor and enforce interface contracts at runtime (Figure 1, right).[1] The first part of BeepBeep is a small Java applet called the `BeepBeepMonitor`. This applet is responsible for actually keeping track and analyzing the incoming and outgoing messages with respect to an interface contract. The second part is a JavaScript file providing a class called `XMLHttpRequestBB`, which behaves exactly like the standard `XMLHttpRequest`, with the exception that incoming and outgoing messages, before being actually sent (or returned), are deviated to the applet and possibly blocked if violations are found.

Including BeepBeep into an existing Ajax application is simple. It suffices to host two files (the `.jar` applet and the `.js` include) in the same directory as the Ajax application, and to load BeepBeep by adding a single line at the beginning of the original client's code. Any invocations of the original `XMLHttpRequest` object can then be replaced by calls to `XMLHttpRequestBB`. No other changes to the code are required: from this point, BeepBeep intercepts the messages and transparently monitors the conversation.

---

[1] BeepBeep and its source code are available for download under a free software license at `http://beepbeep.sourceforge.net/`

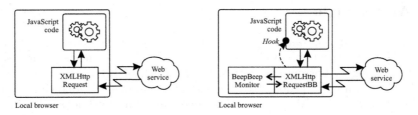

Fig. 1. Standard (left) and BeepBeep-enabled (right) Ajax applications

When BeepBeep detects that a message violates a contract property, its default behaviour is to block the message and to pop a window alerting the user, showing the plain-text description associated with that property. Alternatively, BeepBeep can be asked to call a function, called a *hook*, provided by the application developer.

4   The BeepBeep Contract Specification Language

BeepBeep's language for contract specification is an extension of Linear Temporal Logic called LTL-FO$^+$ [6], whose models are sequences of messages. *Filter expressions* are used to fetch values inside a message; they return a set of values, depending on the *current* message. They are expressed in a subset of the XML Path Language XPath [3]. For example, on the previous XML message (1), the filter /message/books/id returns the set $\{837, 4472\}$. *First-order quantifiers* are used to express universal or existential properties over sets returned by filter expressions. Hence the formula $\forall\, x \in$ /message/books/id : $x \neq 123$ states that, in the *current* message, no id element has value 123. These quantifiers can then be freely mixed with the traditional *LTL temporal modalities and Boolean connectives* to express complex properties correlating message contents and sequentiality. For example, consider the following formula:

$$\mathbf{G}\, \forall\, a_1 \in \texttt{/message/action} : (a_1 = \texttt{borrow} \rightarrow$$
$$\mathbf{X}\, \mathbf{G}\, (\forall\, a_2 \in \texttt{/message/action} : a_2 \neq \texttt{return}))$$

The formula states that in every message, if the action element has value **borrow**, then from now on, no message can have an action element with value **return**. This is the formal translation of constraint 1 mentioned in Section 2. Quantification can be used to compare values fetched in messages at different points in the trace. For example, the formal translation in LTL-FO$^+$ of constraint 2 stipulates that for any book ID i_1 appearing in a message, then no future message can have some book ID i_2 such that $i_2 = i_1$:

$$\mathbf{G}\, (\forall\, i_1 \in \texttt{/message/books/id} : \mathbf{X}\, \mathbf{G}\, (\forall\, i_2 \in \texttt{/message/books/id} : i_1 \neq i_2))$$

Finally, *metric constraints* can be expressed by providing a special filter expression, called "TIME", which always returns a single value: the time of a global system clock at the moment it is evaluated. Timed properties hence become a special case of quantification, as the translation of constraint 3 shows:

$$\mathbf{G} \, (\forall \, t_1 \in \text{TIME} \; : \; \mathbf{X} \, (\forall \, t_2 \in \text{TIME} \; : \; t_2 - t_1 < 60))$$

5   Tool Highlights and Related Work

Besides its ease of use, the main advantage of BeepBeep is that the specification of the contract is completely decoupled from the code required for its actual monitoring. The contract is located on the server side in a file separate from the monitor itself, which is generic. This is in contrast with [7, 9, 11], which require the compilation of a contract into executable Java code –an operation which must be repeated whenever the contract is changed. This requirement is ill-suited to the highly volatile nature of web service interactions. In BeepBeep, changing the contract can be done dynamically without changing anything to the clients: the monitoring plan is generated automatically from any LTL-FO$^+$ formula passed to the monitor.

This dynamicity is possible thanks to BeepBeep's monitoring algorithm. It is based on an algorithm presented in [5], which creates the Büchi automaton for a given LTL formula. This algorithm performs on-the-fly and generates the automaton as the sequence of states unwinds. Although LTL monitoring requires exponential space [12], in practice the on-the-fly algorithm generates a subset of the automaton with negligible space. BeepBeep's monitoring procedure, detailed in [6], is an extension of this algorithm, adapted for LTL-FO$^+$'s first-order quantification on message elements. It includes a number of optimizations, such as the simplification of unsatisfiable subformulæ and the use of three-valued logic [2] to allow for "inconclusive" trace prefixes.

BeepBeep distinguishes itself from related work in a number of aspects:

- Message monitoring. BeepBeep monitors conversations specified at the XML message level; it is independent from any client implementation and does not refer to any internal variable of the client's source code.
- Rich input language. BeepBeep's LTL-FO$^+$ allows first-order quantification over XPath expressions to fetch values inside messages, store them and compare them at a later time. Contrarily to similar message-based logics, such as LTL-FO [4], there is no restriction on the use of temporal operators inside quantifiers, and vice versa. BeepBeep can handle arbitrary nested structures; no upper bound on the arity of the messages needs to be fixed in advance.
- Client-side monitoring. Erroneous messages are trapped at the source, saving bandwidth and CPU time on the server. This contrasts with [10, 1] where monitoring of the conversation is done on the server side.
- Non-invasive. Runtime monitoring of arbitrary interface contracts can be enforced transparently with minor changes to the code, apart from including BeepBeep. Other approaches, such as [9], require heavier code instrumentation in order to correctly intercept non-compliant behaviour.

- Low footprint. The total volume that needs to be downloaded by an Ajax application using BeepBeep (JavaScript + applet) is less than 50 kb, and this must be done only once when the application starts.
- Universal. BeepBeep works off-the-shelf on any browser supporting Java applets, including proprietary software with closed source code. It does not require a modified version of the browser (hooks) to work, as is the case for Browser-enforced Embedded Policies (BEEP) described in [8].

6   Experimental Evaluation

BeepBeep has been tested on Ajax applications in various scenarios.[2] We compared a plain Ajax client using a real-world web service, the Amazon E-Commerce web service, against the same client communicating through BeepBeep and monitoring 11 different contract properties. Since we did not have access to Amazon's file server, the contract file was located on the same server as BeepBeep for the needs of the experiment. Each version of the client sent to Amazon the same set of randomly generated message sequences; the difference in the elapsed time was measured and plotted in Figure 2. Since the experiment involved actual communications with the service, it was repeated on 20 different traces to average out punctual differences caused by the variable latency of the network (explaining the negative values). Our findings indicate that on low-end computer (Asus EeePC with a 600 MHz processor), monitoring LTL-FO$^+$ contract properties produces an average overhead of around 3%, a negligible 10 ms per message in absolute numbers. As a rule, the state of the network accounts for wider variations than the additional processing required by the monitor.

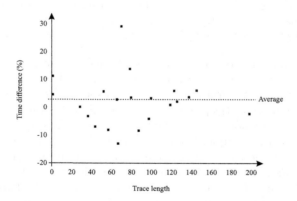

Fig. 2. Overhead for a BeepBeep-enabled Ajax client

Therefore, we conclude that BeepBeep can efficiently monitor LTL-FO$^+$ runtime properties at a very low cost. By providing a transparent and very simple

---

[2] See http://beepbeep.sourceforge.net/examples for more details.

way of enforcing rich interface contracts into virtually any existing Ajax application, BeepBeep contributes to increase the reach of logic and formal verification approaches in the development of everyday web applications.

References

1. Barbon, F., Traverso, P., Pistore, M., Trainotti, M.: Run-time monitoring of instances and classes of web service compositions. In: ICWS, pp. 63–71. IEEE Computer Society, Los Alamitos (2006)
2. Bauer, A., Leucker, M., Schallhart, C.: Monitoring of real-time properties. In: Arun-Kumar, S., Garg, N. (eds.) FSTTCS 2006. LNCS, vol. 4337, pp. 260–272. Springer, Heidelberg (2006)
3. Clark, J., DeRose, S.: XML path language (XPath) version 1.0, W3C recommendation (1999)
4. Deutsch, A., Sui, L., Vianu, V.: Specification and verification of data-driven web services. In: Deutsch, A. (ed.) PODS, pp. 71–82. ACM, New York (2004)
5. Gerth, R., Peled, D., Vardi, M.Y., Wolper, P.: Simple on-the-fly automatic verification of linear temporal logic. In: Dembinski, P., Sredniawa, M. (eds.) PSTV. IFIP Conference Proceedings, vol. 38, pp. 3–18. Chapman & Hall, Boca Raton (1995)
6. Hallé, S., Villemaire, R.: Runtime monitoring of message-based workflows with data. In: EDOC, pp. 63–72. IEEE Computer Society Press, Los Alamitos (2008)
7. Hughes, G., Bultan, T., Alkhalaf, M.: Client and server verification for web services using interface grammars. In: Bultan, T., Xie, T. (eds.) TAV-WEB, pp. 40–46. ACM, New York (2008)
8. Jim, T., Swamy, N., Hicks, M.: Defeating script injection attacks with browser-enforced embedded policies. In: Williamson, C.L., Zurko, M.E., Patel-Schneider, P.F., Shenoy, P.J. (eds.) WWW, pp. 601–610. ACM, New York (2007)
9. Krüger, I.H., Meisinger, M., Menarini, M.: Runtime verification of interactions: From MSCs to aspects. In: Sokolsky, O., Taşıran, S. (eds.) RV 2007. LNCS, vol. 4839, pp. 63–74. Springer, Heidelberg (2007)
10. Mahbub, K., Spanoudakis, G.: Run-time monitoring of requirements for systems composed of web-services: Initial implementation and evaluation experience. In: ICWS, pp. 257–265. IEEE Computer Society, Los Alamitos (2005)
11. Rosu, G., Chen, F., Ball, T.: Synthesizing monitors for safety properties: This time with calls and returns. In: Leucker, M. (ed.) RV 2008. LNCS, vol. 5289, pp. 51–68. Springer, Heidelberg (2008)
12. Rosu, G., Havelund, K.: Rewriting-based techniques for runtime verification. Autom. Softw. Eng. 12(2), 151–197 (2005)

HOMER: A Higher-Order Observational Equivalence Model checkER⋆

David Hopkins and C.-H. Luke Ong

Oxford University Computing Laboratory

Abstract. We present HOMER, an observational-equivalence model checker for the 3rd-order fragment of Idealized Algol (IA) augmented with iteration. It works by first translating terms of the fragment into a precise representation of their game semantics as visibly pushdown automata (VPA). The VPA-translates are then passed to a VPA toolkit (which we have implemented) to test for equivalence. Thanks to the fully abstract game semantics, observational equivalence of these IA-terms reduces to the VPA Equivalence Problem. Our checker is thus sound and complete; because it model checks *open* terms, our approach is also compositional. Further, if the terms are inequivalent, HOMER will produce both a game-semantic and an operational-semantic counter-example, in the form of a play and a separating context respectively. We showcase these features on a number of examples and (where appropriate) compare its performance with similar tools. To the best of our knowledge, HOMER is the first implementation of a model checker of 3rd-order programs.

1 Theory and Implementation

Motivation. Higher-order functions are commonly used in functional programming. The functions map and foldr are standard examples of 2nd-order programs. 3rd and higher-order functions arise naturally in language processors [10]. Higher-order programs also crop up in imperative / object-oriented languages. E.g. any algorithm or data structure parameterised by, say, a comparison function is 2nd-order. A program that relies on such a 2nd-order function (being defined in an external library, say) is 3rd-order. Perhaps the most significant higher-order program is Google's MapReduce system [11]. Here we present the first model checker for 3rd-order programs.

Reynold's **Idealized Algol** (IA) [9] is a higher-order procedural language that combines imperative constructs (such as block-allocated assignable variables, sequencing and iteration) with higher-order functional features. It is essentially a call-by-name variant of (core) ML. E.g. the imperative term while $!X > 0$ do $\{Y := !Y * !X$; $X := !X - 1;\}$ and the lambda-term $\lambda f^{A \to B \to C}.\lambda g^{A \to B}.\lambda x^A.f\, x\,(g\,x)$ are both valid in IA.

Here we consider the fragment of IA containing up to 3rd-order terms over finite base types. I.e. we allow functions of types $((b_1 \to b_2) \to b_3) \to b_4$, say, where each b_i is one of the base types: *com* (commands), *exp* and *var* (expressions and variables respectively, with values taken from a finite prefix of the natural numbers). In addition, we allow while-loops but not full recursion. We denote this fragment IA_3^*.

⋆ We thank A. Murawski for useful discussions and Microsoft Research PhD Scholarship Programme for funding this work. HOMER builds on and extends Hopkins' dissertation [7].

A. Bouajjani and O. Maler (Eds.): CAV 2009, LNCS 5643, pp. 654–660, 2009.

Two terms $\Gamma \vdash M_1, M_2 : A$ are **observationally** (or *contextually*) **equivalent**, written $\Gamma \vdash M_1 \cong M_2$, just if for every program context $C[-]$ such that both $C[M_1]$ and $C[M_2]$ are closed terms of type com, $C[M_1]$ converges if and only if $C[M_2]$ converges. I.e. two terms are observationally equivalent whenever no program context can possibly distinguish them. An intuitively compelling notion of program equivalence, observational equivalence has a rich theory. For example, $\lambda x^{exp}.\mathsf{new}\, X \,\mathsf{in}\, \{X := x; !X\} \cong \lambda x^{exp}.x$, because the internal workings of the function are not detectable from the outside. However, these terms are not equivalent to $\lambda x^{exp}.\mathsf{if}\, x \,\mathsf{then}\, x \,\mathsf{else}\, x$ — because expressions can have side-effects, the outcome of evaluating x twice may be different from evaluating x only once. A much less obvious equivalence is

$$p : com \rightarrow com \;\vdash\; \mathsf{new}\, x := 0 \,\mathsf{in}\, \{p\,(x := 1); \mathsf{if}\, !x = 1 \,\mathsf{then}\, \Omega \,\mathsf{else}\, \mathsf{skip}\} \;\cong\; p\,\Omega$$

where Ω is the term that immediately diverges. This example shows that "snapback" (i.e. a term that first evaluates its com-type arguments and then immediately undoes their side-effects) is not definable in IA. The above equivalence holds because in either case, if p ever evaluates its argument, the computation will diverge.

Game Semantics. The *fully abstract*[1] game semantics [1] of IA has proved extremely powerful. In this model, a type A is interpreted as a game $[\![A]\!]$ between P and O, and a term $\Gamma \vdash M : A$ as a *strategy* $[\![\Gamma \vdash M]\!]$ for P to play in the game $[\![\Gamma \vdash A]\!]$. A strategy is just a set of plays (forming a playbook for how P should respond at each step he is to play), and a *play* is a sequence of moves, each is a question or an answer equipped with a *pointer*[2] to an earlier move. A play is *complete* if every question in it has been answered, so the game has run to completion.

The highly accurate game semantics characterises observational equivalence in terms of complete plays i.e. $\Gamma \vdash M_1 \cong M_2$ if and only if $comp[\![\Gamma \vdash M_1]\!] = comp[\![\Gamma \vdash M_2]\!]$, where $comp\,\sigma$ is the set of complete plays in strategy σ. Murawski and Walukiewicz [8] have shown that the complete plays in the strategy denotation of an IA_3^*-term are recognisable by a visibly pushdown automaton.

Visibly Pushdown Automata. The *visibly pushdown automata* (VPA) [3] are a subclass of pushdown automata in which the stack actions (push, pop or no-op) are completely determined by the input symbol. They are more expressive than finite automata, yet enjoy many nice closure properties of the regular languages. Because they are closed under complementation and intersection, and have a decidable emptiness problem, the *VPA Equivalence Problem* ("Given two VPA, do they accept the same language?") is decidable. So by representing the set of complete plays in a strategy denotation of an IA_3^*-term as a VPA, it is decidable (in EXPTIME [8]) if a given pair of β-normal IA_3^*-terms are observationally equivalent.

Implementation. Following the algorithm of Murawski and Walukiewicz [8], we have created a tool, called HOMER, for checking observational equivalence of IA_3^* terms-in-context. Given two such terms, it first translates them to their VPA representations.

---

[1] Full abstraction is a strong goodness-of-fit measure. A denotational semantics is *fully abstract* if the theory of equality induced by the semantics coincides with observational equivalence.

[2] Which models the operand-to-operator, and variable-to-binder relation within a term.

These are then fed into a VPA toolkit, which we have created, to check for equivalence by complementing, intersecting and emptiness-checking to test for inclusion in both directions. The complementation and intersection operations are straightforward implementations from [3]. Since the VPA-translates are deterministic by construction, they are complemented just by complementing the final states. Intersection is by a product construction (which works for VPA – but not general PDA – because the two automata always perform the same stack action). More complex is the emptiness test. We experimented on a few algorithms before settling on Schwoon's pre* algorithm for general PDA, [12]. When the two terms are inequivalent, this will produce as a counter-example a play recognisable by exactly one of the two VPA-translates. The tool will use this play to generate a *separating context* - a context that converges when its hole is filled by one term, but diverges when filled by the other. HOMER is written in about 8 KLOC of *F#*, including about 600 LOC for the VPA toolkit.

2   Evaluation and Tests

All tests in the following have been run on a laptop with a 2.53GHz Intel Core 2 Duo processor and 4GB RAM under Windows Vista. The base type $exp\%N$ is $\{0, 1, \cdots N - 1\}$. Unless specified otherwise, exp coincides with $exp\%N$, which defaults to $N = 3$.

Sorting. Verifying sorting programs is a challenging test for model checkers because of the complex interplay between data flow and control flow [2]. An implementation of bubble sort is given below. Input to the program takes the form of an array of elements of the set $\{0, 1, 2\}$; we evaluate the model for different values of n, the length of the array. The program communicates with its environment only through the non-local variable x. In a call-by-name setting, because x can represent any *var*-typed procedure, it is legitimate to use it as an input/output stream. The program initially populates the array by reading from x, and after sorting writes the values back to x in order. These reads and writes are the only actions visible from the outside.

```
1   x : var%3 |-
2   new a[N]%3 in
3   {new i%N+1 in while !i < N do {a[!i] := !x; i := (!i + 1)}};
4   {
5     new flag%2 in
6     flag := 1;
7     while !flag do{
8       new i%N in
9       flag := 0;
10      while !i < N-1 do{
11        if !a[!i] > !a[!i + 1] then{
12          new temp%3 in
13          flag := 1;
14          temp := !a[!i] ;
15          a[!i] := !a[!i + 1];
16          a[!i + 1] := !temp
17        }
18        else skip;
19        i := !i + 1
20      }
21    }
22  };
23  {new i%N+1 in while !i < N do {x:= !a[!i];i := !i + 1}}
```

The automaton produced when $n = 2$ is shown in the following using Graphviz[3]. Since this is a 1st-order program, the VPA-translate degenerates to a deterministic finite automaton. It can be seen that there is a trace through the automaton for each of the 9 possible input combinations. [4]

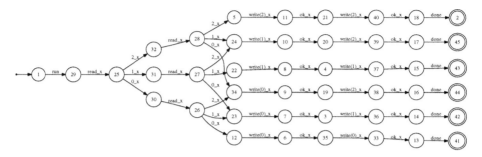

Since the internals of the sorting program are hidden, bubble sort is observationally equivalent to any other sorting algorithm. Replacing the body of the bubble sort algorithm above (but keeping the same input and output format) with the code for insertion sort, we can feed them both into HOMER and check that (for a given value of n) they are in fact equivalent. (Timing data are provided under *Related Work* in the sequel.)

Kierstead Terms. An interesting 3rd-order example are the family of *Kierstead terms*, $K_{n,i} := \lambda f^{(o \to o) \to o}.f(\lambda x_1.f(\lambda x_2. \cdots f(\lambda x_{n-1}.f(\lambda x_n . x_i))))$, where $1 \le i \le n$, and o is a base type. $K_{2,1}$ and $K_{2,2}$ are the simplest pair of terms for which the location of pointers is critical. In the VPA-translate, each 3rd-order question has a tag that indicates the target of its pointer. Over base-type *com*, the table below gives the times to compile $K_{n,i}$, and to determine $K_{n,i} \not\equiv K_{n,j}$ whenever $i \ne j$, as n varies.

n	Time (Compile)	Time (Compare)	State Space (Final)	State Space (Max)
10	1.5s	2.6s	64	1172
20	3.8s	6.5s	97	3340
80	35s	70s	250	8848
160	220s	7.5 mins	730	26128

Counter-Example: Separating Context. It is not at all obvious how to construct by hand a context that witnesses inequivalent Kierstead terms. Below is a context that separates $K_{2,1}$ and $K_{2,2}$, as generated by HOMER (suitably adjusted for readability). By following the (somewhat complex) execution process, we can see how the assignments and tests on the local variable X force the program to follow the single path from which the context was derived: it terminates on $K_{2,2}$, but diverges on $K_{2,1}$ when it tries to run its arguments' argument from the first time it is called (thus deviating from the path).

---

[3] http://www.graphviz.org/
[4] HOMER uses a somewhat naïve forward reachability checker to remove unreachable states at each intermediate stage. This is very fast, and reduces the state space considerably, but it does not make any attempt to merge bisimilar states or delete states that can never reach a final state.

```
1   (    fun G:(((com -> com) -> com) -> com).new X in
2     X:=1;
3     G ( fun z:(com -> com).
4       if !X = 1 then
5       (
6         X:=2;
7         z omega;
8         if !X = 5 then X:=6 else omega
9       )
10      else if !X = 2 then
11      (
12        X:=3;
13        z (if !X = 3 then X:=4 else omega);
14        if !X = 4 then X:=5 else omega
15      )
16      else
17        omega
18    );
19    if !X = 6 then X:=7 else omega
20  )([-])
```

Shortest Prefix. Let us represent a sequence of numbers by a function of type $exp \rightarrow exp$ that maps i to the ith value in the sequence. We assume that if i exceeds the length of the sequence then evaluation diverges. A predicate over such sequences has type $(exp \rightarrow exp) \rightarrow exp \rightarrow bool$ where the second argument is the length of the sequence being tested. Given such a predicate and a sequence, we can find the length of the shortest prefix of the sequence that satisfies the predicate using the following 3rd-order program.

```
1   |- fun p : (exp%N -> exp%M) -> exp%N -> exp%2 . fun xs : exp%N -> exp%M .
2     new i%N in
3     new done%2 in
4     new found%2 in
5     while not !done do{
6       if (p (fun index:exp%N . if index > !i then omega else (xs index)) !i) then {
7         found := 1;
8         done := 1
9       }
10      else if !i = N-1 then done := 1 else i := !i + 1
11    };
12    if !found then !i else omega
```

We construct sequences that agree with xs up to index i and then diverge and check whether p holds for such a sequence. The boolean flags are required because of a restriction on comparing values of different types (e.g. exp%N and exp%M with unequal N and M). Fixing the type of the data to exp%3 and varying the size of the input sequence, the timing and state space data are below.

n	Time (Compile)	State Space (Final)	State Space (Max)
5	2s	197	4706
10	4s	592	18486
15	9s	1187	47966
20	18s	1982	99146

Related Work. To our knowledge, HOMER is the first implementation of a model checker of 3rd-order programs. The tools most similar to ours are MAGE [4], and

GAMECHECKER [5]. Though these are model checkers based on game semantics, they only check up to 2nd-order programs, which are much simpler as they can be represented by finite automata. Further they check for reachability rather than equivalence, so a fair comparison is thus hard to make even for 2nd-order programs. However, if we augment bubble sort so that as it outputs each of the values, it also asserts that each element is less than the next one, we can use MAGE to check that none of the assertions fail.

In the table below, compile time is the time to just compile the model, paramaterised by n, the size of the array. Compare time is the total time to compile both bubble and insert sort and check that they are observationally equivalent. The times for MAGE are how long it took to assert that bubble sort always results in a sorted array.

n	Compile	Compare	State Space (Final)	State Space (Max)	Time (MAGE)
5	1.3s	2.3s	495	1983	0.6s
10	55s	7.5 mins	60501	353613	154s

For $n = 15$, both MAGE[5] and HOMER gave up complaining of insufficient memory.

Conclusions. Since HOMER is (we believe) the first third-order model checker, there are no benchmarks against which we can properly measure its performance. When compared to MAGE, HOMER's performance is of the order of magnitude. Given the complexity of model-checking observational equivalence of third-order problems (EXPTIME-complete), this is encouraging. Further, as this is a prototype implementation, we used a simple explicit representation of the state-space. We expect a significant performance gain when techniques that have proved successful in other model-checkers (including MAGE), such as symbolic representation, lazy model checking or CEGAR, are exploited. Another encouraging point is that the final models produced are compact. Though the intermediate VPA have larger state-spaces, they are still much smaller than that examined by a naive state space exploration.

References

1. Abramsky, S., McCusker, G.: Linearity, sharing and state. In: Algol-Like Langs. (1997)
2. Abramsky, S., et al.: Applying Game Semantics to Compositional Software Modelling and Verification. In: Jensen, K., Podelski, A. (eds.) TACAS 2004. LNCS, vol. 2988, pp. 421–435. Springer, Heidelberg (2004)
3. Alur, R., Madhusudan, P.: Visibly pushdown languages. In: Proc. STOC (2004)
4. Bakewell, A., Ghica, D.R.: On-the-fly techniques for game-based software model checking. In: Proc. TACAS (2009)
5. Dimovski, A.S., Ghica, D.R., Lazic, R.: Data-abstraction refinement. In: Hankin, C., Siveroni, I. (eds.) SAS 2005. LNCS, vol. 3672, pp. 102–117. Springer, Heidelberg (2005)
6. Ghica, D.R., McCusker, G.: Reasoning about Idealized Algol Using Regular Languages. In: Welzl, E., Montanari, U., Rolim, J.D.P. (eds.) ICALP 2000. LNCS, vol. 1853, p. 103. Springer, Heidelberg (2000)

---

[5] It may have been possible to increase the memory available to MAGE's Haskell compiler.

7. Hopkins, D.: A model checker for a higher-order procedural language. MCompSc dissertation, University of Oxford (2009), http://users.comlab.ox.ac.uk/luke.ong/publications/HopkinsReport.pdf
8. Murawski, A., Walukiewicz, I.: Third-order idealized algol with iteration is decidable. In: Sassone, V. (ed.) FOSSACS 2005. LNCS, vol. 3441, pp. 202–218. Springer, Heidelberg (2005)
9. Reynolds, J.C.: The essence of Algol. In: Algorithmic Languages. North-Holland, Amsterdam (1981)
10. Okasaki, C.: Even higher-order functions for parsing. J. Funct. Program. (1998)
11. Cataldo, A.: The Power of Higher-Order Composition Languages in System Design. Ph.D thesis, UC Bekerley (2006)
12. Schwoon, S.: Model-Checking Pushdown Systems. Ph.D thesis, Tech. Univ. of Munich (2002)

Apron: A Library of Numerical Abstract Domains for Static Analysis[*]

Bertrand Jeannet[1] and Antoine Miné[2]

[1] INRIA Rhône-Alpes, Grenoble, France
`Bertrand.Jeannet@inrialpes.fr`
[2] CNRS, École Normale Supérieure, Paris, France
`mine@di.ens.fr`

Abstract. This article describes APRON, a freely available library dedicated to the static analysis of the numerical variables of programs by abstract interpretation. Its goal is threefold: provide analysis implementers with ready-to-use numerical abstractions under a unified API, encourage the research in numerical abstract domains by providing a platform for integration and comparison, and provide teaching and demonstration tools to disseminate knowledge on abstract interpretation.

1 Introduction

Static analysis aims at discovering, at compile-time, properties on all the possible executions of a program, which is useful to, *e.g.*, automatically prove the absence of errors or optimize code. *Numerical* static analysis focuses on properties of numerical program variables. *Abstract Interpretation* [9] is a general theory of semantic approximation which allows constructing static analyses that are *sound* by construction (*i.e.*, always over-approximate the set of program behaviors). In the past 30 years, many *numerical abstract domains* [6,7,10,12,13,17,20,21] have been proposed, each defining a representation for a set of properties of interest and algorithms to manipulate them. They vary in expressiveness and in the cost/precision trade-off.

However, many abstract domains have no publicly available implementation while others (*e.g.*, early implementations of [10,20]) have diverging API which makes reuse and experimental comparison difficult. Most are tied to application domains, lacking operators to be useful in more general settings (*e.g.*, [5] does not support non-linear or floating-point expressions).

The APRON library aims at solving these problems and provides a uniform, rich, and user-friendly API, which is given a precise concrete semantics that underlying abstract domains are free to implement with safe approximations. It also provides reference implementations for a growing number of numerical abstract domains — including intervals, octagons [20], and polyhedra [10]. Static analyzers for all kinds of semantics (including non-linear and floating-point arithmetic)

---

[*] This work is supported by the INRIA project-team Abstraction common to the CNRS and the École Normale Supérieure, and the ANR project ASOPT.

A. Bouajjani and O. Maler (Eds.): CAV 2009, LNCS 5643, pp. 661–667, 2009.

can easily use APRON to perform their numerical abstractions. APRON also encourages the development of new domains by providing an abstraction toolbox library. New domains can then be plugged into APRON-powered static analyzers by changing a single line of code, as the API is essentially domain-independent.

The most closely related project is the Parma Polyhedra Library [5], which shares several features with APRON in its very last version (0.10). Its concrete semantics does not support however non-linear and floating-point expressions, and it supports only one global environment for mapping variable names to dimensions in vector spaces. However, the domains implemented in the PPL can be interfaced to APRON and can hence benefit from its additional functionalities.

2   Architecture

The architecture of the library is sketched in Fig. 1. A client analysis would first create a context manager object that specifies which abstract domain to use, and then interface to the bottom right part of Fig. 1 by constructing domain-independent operator argument objects and issuing calls to the library. Internally, the library will dispatch the call to the proper domain implementation (left part), which can in turn use built-in generic abstraction and utility libraries (top right part). Due to lack of space, it is not possible to present code samples in this paper, but short examples can be found on the web-site [1].

Data-types. To communicate with domains, APRON provides various domain-independent concrete data-types to represent scalars, intervals, linear expressions, expression trees, tests, and generators, as well as associated utility functions — constructors, destructors, conversions, etc. Intervals can appear in linear and non-linear expressions, where they model a non-deterministic choice. By soundness, all possible outcomes of non-deterministic assignments are taken into account, and

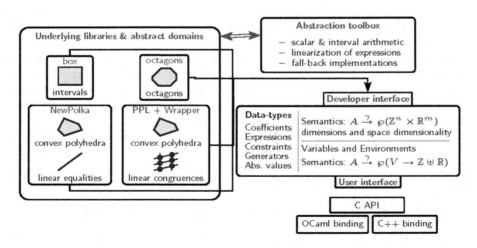

Fig. 1. Architecture of the APRON library

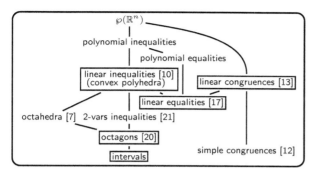

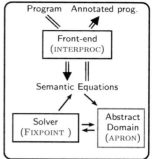

Fig. 2. Some abstract domains for numerical variables, partially ordered by their expressiveness

Fig. 3. Architecture of the INTERPROC analyzer

a program state passes a non-deterministic test if it does for at least one of its possible values. Non-determinism is useful to model program input but also to abstract complex operators into simpler ones. Operators in expressions include the four standard operations $(+, -, \times, /)$, modulo, and square root. Each can be tagged with a rounding target type (*e.g.*, integer, or some IEEE floating-point format [8]) and direction (towards 0, $+\infty$, $-\infty$, to nearest, or non-deterministic). Constants can be provided as integers, rationals, or floats, using either machine types or arbitrary precision types — using the GMP [2] and MPFR [3] libraries.

Abstract elements and operators. Abstract elements are completely opaque data-types that ultimately represent sets of points in $\mathbb{Z}^n \times \mathbb{R}^m$. In particular, floating-point variables can be modeled using real-valued dimensions and expression trees with explicit rounding tags. Standard operators include (linear and non-linear) assignments, substitutions, and constraint additions, joins, meets, widenings, projections, and various comparisons. Less common operators include n-ary joins, parallel assignments (useful to analyze automata), folds and expands (useful to analyze summarized arrays [11]).

An important rule is that the implementation is free to perform *any* sound approximation. Not imposing precision guarantees allows us to require that *all domains support all operators for all data-types*. Imprecision comes from the well-known limited expressiveness of each domain (*e.g.*, polyhedra cannot encode non-linear constraints nor disjunctions) but also from less obvious implementation details — *e.g.*, internal use of inexact arithmetic, such as floats. Thus, together with a sound result, domains may also return a flag telling whether the result is exact, optimal (w.r.t. the domain expressiveness), or neither. Also, operators have a generic cost-precision parameter that has a domain-specific but documented effect — *e.g.*, polyhedra may gain precision by using integer tightening on integer variables, or lose precision by soundly rounding large constraint coefficients to more memory-efficient ones.

Abstract domains. Fig. 2 presents a few abstract domain examples, organized as a lattice showing their respective expressiveness. The boxed domains are those currently available: intervals, octagons [20] (with either integer, rational or float bounds, using machine representation, or GMP and MPFR arbitrary precision numbers), polyhedra [10] (using GMP integers and the double description method), and linear equalities [17] (implemented as an abstraction of polyhedra). APRON can also act as a middle-ware and make foreign libraries available under its unified API. Linear congruences [13] and an alternate implementation of polyhedra are optionally available through the PPL [5]. Finally, APRON supports a generic reduced product which is instantiated to combine polyhedra and linear congruences. Fig. 2 also shows some of the domains we wish to add in the future to provide either improved expressiveness (*e.g.*, polynomial domains) or additional cost/precision trade-offs (*e.g.*, weakly relational domains).

Abstraction toolbox. APRON exposes a rich, high-level API to domain users that can chose among a large set of abstract operators and various data-type arguments. However, domain designers wish to implement a minimal set of low-level entry-points. To ease the burden of developing new domains, APRON provides several support libraries:

1. APRON provides an *environment* management package, so that the developer has only to manipulate dimensions in vector-spaces while the user can ¡manipulate named variables and environments — hence the two interfaces on the bottom right part of Fig. 1.

2. APRON provides a complete arithmetic package for scalar and outward-rounded intervals in a variety of types (integers, rationals, floats; machine types, GMP, and MPFR numbers). Sound conversion functions are provided so that the developer can choose the most convenient arithmetic type to use internally and still handle all the API data-types available to the user (*e.g.*, polyhedra are implemented using integers but can handle floating-point constants in expressions).

3. APRON provides *linearization* functions that domains can use to abstract arbitrary expression trees into linear ones (with or without interval coefficients). In particular, they can handle integer and floating-point expressions by abstracting away the non-linearity introduced by rounding, and output linear expressions with $\mathbb{R}$ semantics [19]. Linearization is not compulsory and developers may also access the raw expression trees provided by the user.

4. APRON provides a default implementation for many operators. For instance, compound operators provided for the user convenience (such as *n*-ary joins or parallel assignments) are implemented in terms of simpler ones (regular joins and assignments). Domain designers are always free to implement those operators if a specialized implementation would provide some efficiency gain.

Bindings. The core API is in C (27 KLOC) to ensure maximum interoperability, but it is designed in an object-oriented way. Additionally, a C++ binding (leveraging the object-orientation aspect and adding intelligent constructors, destructors, and operator overloading for improved user-friendliness) and an OCAML binding (providing stricter type-checking and fully automated memory management) are provided. Other API bindings may be easily designed. As for the C

API, these bindings are fully domain-independent and immediately benefit from the addition of new abstract domains.

Finally, the library is fully thread-safe and several instances (with possibly different domains) can be used concurrently through the use of context managers.

3   Applications

Distribution. The APRON library is freely available [1] and is released under the LGPL license.[1] Currently, we are aware of ten other research teams using APRON. Two of them plan to contribute to its development.

The INTERPROC *static analyzer.* INTERPROC [15] fulfills three goals: provide a library showcase, disseminate abstract interpretation techniques and help prototype new domains [6] and analyses [18,4] — *e.g.*, by encoding problems in the input language. Its architecture is depicted in Fig. 3. INTERPROC acts both as a front-end generating semantic equations from the input program, and as a driver interpreting the equations in the chosen abstract domain and solving them with the FIXPOINT [14] equation solver.

INTERPROC takes as input programs written in a small imperative language featuring numerical variables, loops, and recursive procedures. It performs either forward analysis that infers invariants at each program point, or backward analysis that infers necessary conditions to reach a given set of control points specified by `fail` instructions, or a combination of both analyses. Procedures are handled in a relational way using the formalisation of [16]. The output of INTERPROC is a program annotated with invariants that can also be interpreted as procedure summaries at the exit point of procedures. Any of the abstract domains provided by APRON can be selected, as well as several options regarding iteration strategies in fixpoint solving, thus allowing for easy experimentation and comparison. INTERPROC is written in OCAML (2 KLOC, excluding the FIXPOINT solver [14]) and released under the LGPL license. It has already been used in two research papers [18,4].

4   Conclusion

The APRON library provides several numerical abstract domains under a unified interface. It defines a precise concrete semantics for a quite complete set of operations — including non-linear and floating-point arithmetic — that domains are free to approximate in a sound way, and that are suitable to build many kinds of static analyses. APRON encourages the development and experimental comparison of new abstract domains by providing a toolbox enabling developers to focus on the core algorithms of their domain while benefiting for free from powerful features such as floating-point semantics. Thus, it conciliates two kinds of users with conflicting requirements: analysis designers wishing for a rich, high-level,

---

[1] However, *optional* dependencies [5] may be released under a more strict license.

and domain-independent API, and domain designers, wishing to implement a minimal set of low-level entry-points. Its effectiveness is illustrated by the number of research teams using it and developing new domains. A sample analyzer, INTERPROC, demonstrates its use.

In the future, we plan to integrate not only more numerical abstract domains, but also to develop abstract domains combining numerical and finite-type (such as boolean) variables, and extend INTERPROC accordingly.

References

1. The APRON abstract domain library, http://apron.cri.ensmp.fr/library/
2. GMP: The GNU multiple precision arithmetic library, http://gmplib.org/
3. The MPFR library, http://www.mpfr.org/
4. Amjad, H., Bornat, R.: Towards automatic stability analysis for rely-guarantee proofs. In: Jones, N.D., Müller-Olm, M. (eds.) VMCAI 2009. LNCS, vol. 5403, pp. 14–28. Springer, Heidelberg (2009)
5. Bagnara, R., Hill, P.M., Zaffanella, E.: The Parma Polyhedra Library: Toward a complete set of numerical abstractions for the analysis and verification of hardware and software systems. SCP 72(1-2), 3–21 (2008)
6. Chen, L., Miné, A., Cousot, P.: A sound floating-point polyhedra abstract domain. In: Ramalingam, G. (ed.) APLAS 2008. LNCS, vol. 5356, pp. 3–18. Springer, Heidelberg (2008)
7. Clarisó, R., Cortadella, J.: The octahedron abstract domain. In: Giacobazzi, R. (ed.) SAS 2004. LNCS, vol. 3148, pp. 312–327. Springer, Heidelberg (2004)
8. IEEE Computer Society. IEEE standard for binary floating-point arithmetic. Technical report, ANSI/IEEE Std. 745-1985 (1985)
9. Cousot, P., Cousot, R.: Abstract interpretation: a unified lattice model for static analysis of programs by construction or approximation of fixpoints. In: POPL 1977, pp. 238–252. ACM Press, New York (1977)
10. Cousot, P., Halbwachs, N.: Automatic discovery of linear restraints among variables of a program. In: POPL 1978, pp. 84–97. ACM Press, New York (1978)
11. Gopan, D., DiMaio, F., Dor, N., Reps, T., Sagiv, S.: Numeric domains with summarized dimensions. In: Jensen, K., Podelski, A. (eds.) TACAS 2004. LNCS, vol. 2988, pp. 512–529. Springer, Heidelberg (2004)
12. Granger, P.: Static analysis of arithmetical congruences. Int. Journal of Computer Mathematics 30, 165–190 (1989)
13. Granger, P.: Static analysis of linear congruence equalities among variables of a program. In: Abramsky, S. (ed.) CAAP 1991 and TAPSOFT 1991. LNCS, vol. 493, pp. 169–192. Springer, Heidelberg (1991)
14. Jeannet, B.: The Fixpoint solver, http://pop-art.inrialpes.fr/people/bjeannet/bjeannet-forge/fixpoint/
15. Jeannet, B., et al.: The Interproc analyzer, http://pop-art.inrialpes.fr/interproc/interprocweb.cgi
16. Jeannet, B., Serwe, W.: Abstracting call-stacks for interprocedural verification of imperative programs. In: Rattray, C., Maharaj, S., Shankland, C. (eds.) AMAST 2004. LNCS, vol. 3116, pp. 258–273. Springer, Heidelberg (2004)
17. Karr, M.: Affine relationships among variables of a program. Acta Informatica, 133–151 (1976)

18. Majumdar, R., Gupta, A., Rybalchenko, A.: An efficient invariant generator. In: Federrath, H. (ed.) Designing Privacy Enhancing Technologies. LNCS, vol. 2009. Springer, Heidelberg (2001)
19. Miné, A.: Relational abstract domains for the detection of floating-point run-time errors. In: Schmidt, D. (ed.) ESOP 2004. LNCS, vol. 2986, pp. 3–17. Springer, Heidelberg (2004)
20. Miné, A.: The octagon abstract domain. HOSC 19(1), 31–100 (2006)
21. Simon, A., King, A., Howe, J.: Two variables per linear inequality as an abstract domain. In: Leuschel, M.A. (ed.) LOPSTR 2002. LNCS, vol. 2664, pp. 71–89. Springer, Heidelberg (2003)

Beaver: Engineering an Efficient SMT Solver
for Bit-Vector Arithmetic

Susmit Jha, Rhishikesh Limaye, and Sanjit A. Seshia

EECS Department, UC Berkeley
{jha,rhishi,sseshia}@eecs.berkeley.edu

Abstract. We present the key ideas in the design and implementation of Beaver, an SMT solver for quantifier-free finite-precision bit-vector logic (QF_BV). Beaver uses an eager approach, encoding the original SMT problem into a Boolean satisfiability (SAT) problem using a series of word-level and bit-level transformations. In this paper, we describe the most effective transformations, such as propagating constants and equalities at the word-level, and using and-inverter graph rewriting techniques at the bit-level. We highlight implementation details of these transformations that distinguishes Beaver from other solvers. We present an experimental analysis of the effectiveness of Beaver's techniques on both hardware and software benchmarks with a selection of back-end SAT solvers.

Beaver is an open-source tool implemented in Ocaml, usable with any back-end SAT engine, and has a well-documented extensible code base that can be used to experiment with new algorithms and techniques.

1 Introduction

Decision procedures for quantifier-free fragments of first-order theories, also known as satisfiability modulo theories (SMT) solvers, find widespread use in hardware and software verification. Of the many first-order theories for which SMT solvers are available, one of the most useful is the theory of finite-precision bit-vector arithmetic, abbreviated as QF_BV [14]. This theory is useful for reasoning about low-level system descriptions in languages such as C and Verilog which use finite-precision integer arithmetic and bit-wise operations on bit-vectors. Recently, there has been a resurgence of work on new QF_BV SMT solvers such as BAT [10], Boolector [3], MathSAT [4], Spear [9], STP [8], UCLID [5] and Z3 [6].

In this article, we describe the design and implementation of BEAVER, a new open-source SMT solver for QF_BV that placed third in SMTCOMP'08. The novelty in Beaver is in its application-driven engineering of a *small* set of simplification methods that yield high performance. This set is: online forward/backward constant and equality propagation using event queues, offline optimization of Boolean circuit templates for operators, and the use of and-inverter graph (AIG) as back-end to perform problem specific bit-level simplifications. Additionally, we have done a systematic study of different Boolean encoding techniques for non-linear operations.

The goal in creating BEAVER was to engineer an efficient and extensible SMT solver around a small core of word-level and bit-level simplification techniques. One aim in writing this article is to succinctly describe the techniques we employed and evaluate

A. Bouajjani and O. Maler (Eds.): CAV 2009, LNCS 5643, pp. 668–674, 2009.
© Springer-Verlag Berlin Heidelberg 2009

them on the SMT-LIB benchmarks. We believe this paper could be useful to both users and designers of solvers. For example, our experiments suggest that online equality propagation is critical to software benchmarks while Boolean rewrites are needed for hardware benchmarks. For developers of SMT and SAT solvers, we present a comparison of Beaver with different SAT solvers as back-end. Our main observation is that the only available non-clausal SAT solver NFLSAT [11] performs significantly better than other SAT solvers.

We do not attempt to make a comprehensive survey and comparison of solvers here; the interested reader can find a survey of current and past bit-vector solvers in recent articles (e.g. [5]), our technical report [17], and the SMTCOMP'08 results [13]. Our focus is on improving the understanding of what makes a good SMT solver for QF_BV, and on identifying features of solvers and benchmarks that could be of interest to the SAT, SMT, and user community.

2 Approach

BEAVER is a satisfiability solver for formulas in the quantifier-free fragment of the theory of *bit-vector arithmetic* (QF_BV). For lack of space, we omit a detailed presentation of the logic and instead direct the reader to the SMT-LIB website [14] for the detailed syntax and semantics.

BEAVER operates by performing a series of rewrites and simplifications that transform the starting bit-vector arithmetic formula into a Boolean circuit and then into a Boolean satisfiability (SAT) problem. This approach is termed the *eager* approach to SMT solving [1]. A major design decision was to be able to use any off-the-shelf SAT solver so as to benefit from the continuing improvements in SAT solving. BEAVER can generate models for satisfiable formulas.

The transformations employed by BEAVER are guided by the following observations about characteristics of formulas generated in verification and testing.

- *Software verification and testing:* Formulas generated during program analysis are typically queries about the feasibility of individual program paths. They tend to be conjunctions of atomic constraints generated from an intermediate representation such as static single assignment (SSA). There are often multiple variables in the formula representing values of the same program variable. Linear constraints abound, and they tend to be mostly equalities.

  Thus, a major characteristic of software benchmarks tends to be the presence of many redundant variables, a simple Boolean structure comprising mostly of conjunctions, and an abundance of equalities amongst the atomic constraints.

- *Hardware verification:* SMT formulas generated in hardware verification arise in bounded model checking (BMC), equivalence checking, and simulation checking. These formulas tend to have a complicated Boolean structure, with several alternations of conjunctions and disjunctions. Many of the variables are Boolean. However, there are often several syntactically different sub-formulas which are nevertheless logically equivalent. These arise from structural repetitions in the formula, such as across multiple time-frames in BMC, or in the intrinsic similarities between two slightly different copies of a circuit being checked for equivalence. Word-level and bit-level rewrite rules are crucial to simplifying the formula and identifying equivalences. Thus, efficient solving of formulas from hardware verification requires word-level and bit-level simplification techniques.

- *Non-linear operations:* Non-linear operations such as multiplication and division are known to be difficult for SAT solvers. While many formulas arising in verification and testing do not contain these operators (or in a manner that makes the problem hard), every SMT solver needs efficient techniques to deal with hard non-linear constraints when they do arise.

How BEAVER **works.** BEAVER performs a sequence of simplifications starting from the original bit-vector formula F_{bv} and ending in a Boolean formula F_{bool} which is handed off to an external SAT engine. Currently BEAVER supports both clausal and non-clausal SAT solvers.

We briefly sketch the transformations performed by BEAVER below. (The first three bit-vector transformations are not necessarily performed in the sequence listed below). They transform F_{bv} to an intermediate Boolean formula F'_{bool}. Bit-level simplifications are then performed on F'_{bool} to yield the final formula F_{bool}.

- *Event-driven constraint propagation:* BEAVER uses an online event-driven approach to propagate constants and equality constraints through the formula in order to simplify it. In particular, a simple form of constraint that appears in many software benchmarks is an equality that uses a fresh variable to name an expression, often of constant value. Both backward (from root of the formula to its leaves) and forward constraint propagation are performed. The event-driven approach, similar to event-driven simulation, allows the simplifications to be performed as a succession of rewrite events. Potential applications of a constant/constraint propagation rewrite are put in a queue and execution of each rewrite rule can potentially generate more avenues of rewriting which are also queued. The rewriting continues till the queue is empty and no further constant/constraint propagation is possible. This propagation is in addition to preliminary simplifications using structural hashing.

- *Bit-vector rewrite rules:* BEAVER also uses a small set of bit-vector rewrite rules to simplify the formula. These interact with the above step by creating new opportunities for constraint propagation. For the current SMTCOMP benchmark suite, an example of a very useful rewrite is the removal of redundant extractions from bit-vectors that enables methods such as constraint propagation to further simplify the formula.

- *Non-linear operations:* In BEAVER, we have experimented with a range of techniques to translate non-linear arithmetic operations such as multiplication, division, and remainder into SAT. These include: (1) Using *magic numbers* when one of the arguments is a constant [19]; (2) decomposing a large bit-width operation into a set of smaller bit-width operations by computing residues modulo a set of primes and using the Chinese remainder theorem; and (3) bit-blasting using standard arithmetic circuits for multiplication by expressing $a \div b$ as q where $a = q*b + r \wedge r < b$ and $*$ and $+$ must not overflow.

  Of the three approaches, our experience has been that the third approach performs the best on most of the current SMT-LIB benchmarks. Thus, while all three options are available, we set the third approach to be the default option.

- *Boolean simplifications — offline and online:* After performing the above bit-vector simplifications, the resulting formula F'_{bv} is encoded into a Boolean formula F'_{bool} that is represented as an And-Inverter Graph (AIG). The translation is straightforward except for one novelty: we pre-synthesize optimized netlists from Verilog for different arithmetic operators for various bit-widths. These pre-synthesized *template circuits* are stored as AIGs and can be optimized offline using logic synthesis tools such as the ABC logic synthesis engine [16]. We explore the impact of logic optimization on template circuits in Section 3. When the solver runs on a specific benchmark, it can further perform bit-level rewrites on the AIG obtained after all operators have been instantiated with template circuits. The resulting formula is F_{bool}.

  F_{bool} can be solved using clausal (CNF-based) or non-clausal SAT engines. We have experimented with different CNF generation options from the ABC engine and also with a non-clausal SAT solver. Our results are presented in Section 3.

A more detailed description of the above transformations with examples is available from the BEAVER website listed below. BEAVER is implemented in OCaml (linked with the ABC library) and uses an external SAT engine. A source-code release of BEAVER has been publicly available since July 2008; the latest version can be downloaded from the URL `http://uclid.eecs.berkeley.edu/beaver/`.

3 Experimental Evaluation

Setup. Experiments were conducted with a selection of benchmarks from all families in the QF_BV section of the publicly available SMT-LIB benchmark suite [15]. A cluster of machines was used for experiments, with each workstation having an Intel(R) Xeon(TM) 3.00 GHz CPU, 3 GB RAM, and running 64-bit Linux 2.6.18. We enforced a memory limit of 1 GB on all runs and the timeout was set to 1 hour. A complete set of experimental data is available at the BEAVER website.

Impact of SAT solvers. First, we evaluate the impact of the choice of SAT solver on performance. We used the default setting of bit-vector transformations and Tseitin's encoding to CNF. Five SAT solvers were compared: Picosat v. 846 compiled in optimized mode [2], Minisat 2.0 [7], Rsat [12], ABC's version of Minisat 1.14 [16], and NFLSAT [11]. Of the five, NFLSAT is the only non-clausal SAT solver.

Figure 1 summarizes the comparison of the five SAT solvers. From Fig. 1(a), we can see that NFLSAT exhibits the smallest aggregate run-time over all benchmarks. Fig. 1(b) compares solvers in terms of the degree of speed-up obtained. We see that NFLSAT is the best performing SAT engine, achieving speed-ups by large factors, indicating that the use of a non-clausal SAT solver might be beneficial for bit-vector formulas.

Detailed pair-wise comparisons of SAT engines have also been performed; however, for lack of space, we omit these here and refer the reader to our technical report [17]. We have observed that the relative performance of SAT solvers can depend heavily on the benchmark family. For example, in comparing NFLSAT and Minisat 2.0, we found a set of benchmarks where the NFLSAT run-time is fairly stable between 1 and 20 sec. while the Minisat run-time goes from 10 to above 1000 sec. These benchmarks are almost all

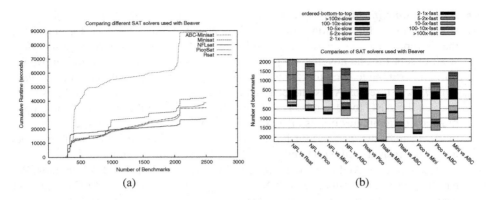

Fig. 1. Comparing five SAT solvers. (a) Plots of cumulative run-time over all benchmarks; (b) Comparing speed-ups. Each stacked bar compares two SAT solvers by counting the number of benchmarks with various ranges of speed-ups. Different colors represent different range of speed-ups (100x,20x,5x,2x,1x). The portion of a bar above 0 represents the number of benchmarks where the first solver is faster than the second solver and the part below represents benchmarks on which the first is slower than the second.

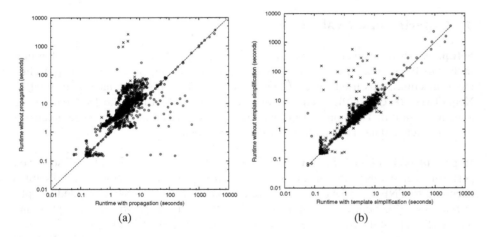

Fig. 2. (a) Impact of constant/equality constraint propagation; (b) Impact of template optimization. All scatterplots use log-scale axes. NFLSAT was the back-end SAT solver. For (a), the path feasibility queries are marked with ×; for (b), satisfiable benchmarks are marked with × and unsatisfiable benchmarks with ∘.

from the `spear` family, where formulas are verification conditions with rich Boolean structure and several kinds of arithmetic operations. On the other hand, there is also a set of benchmarks on which Minisat's run-time stays under 0.1 sec while NFLSAT's run-time ranges from 1 to 100 seconds. These benchmarks were from mostly from the `catchconv` family, with a few `crafted` benchmarks. Since the `catchconv` family comprises path feasibility queries that are conjunctions of relatively simple constraints (mostly equalities), it appears that the Boolean structure and form of atomic constraints could determine whether non-clausal solving is beneficial.

Impact of word-level simplifications. Figure 2(a) shows the impact of constraint propagation. Overall, constraint propagation helps, as can be seen by the big cluster of benchmarks above the diagonal. On a closer examination of the data, we noticed that *all* path feasibility queries (`catchconv`) benchmarks (indicated in plot using ×) benefited greatly from the use of constraint propagation, with a typical speed-up for the solver of 5-100X on these formulas.

Impact of circuit synthesis techniques. We evaluated two CNF generation techniques available in ABC – 1) standard Tseitin encoding, with some minimal optimizations like detection of multi-input ANDs, ORs and muxes, and 2) technology mapping based CNF generation [18], which uses optimization techniques commonly found in the technology mapping phase of logic synthesis to produce more compact CNF. A plot comparing these two techniques is given in our technical report [17]. The TM-based CNF generation significantly reduced the SAT run-time for the `spear` benchmarks, but actually increased the run-time for the `brummayerbiere` family of benchmarks. For other SAT solvers, there wasn't an appreciable difference. Also, neither CNF generation technique improved much on NFLSAT.

The use of logic optimization techniques on the template circuits for arithmetic operators was beneficial in general, as can be seen from Fig. 2(b). The speed-up obtained from optimizing the templates was especially large for the `spear` benchmarks. We hypothesize that this is because that family of benchmarks has a wide variety of arithmetic operations, including several non-linear operations, which are the ones for which template optimization helps the most.

Discussion. From our analysis of the different options in BEAVER, it seems that different settings of options will benefit different families, which indicates that some form of family-specific auto-tuning might be worth performing. It would also be worth further investigating the better performance of the non-clausal solver NFLSAT over the CNF-based solvers used in this study.

Acknowledgments. This work was supported in part by SRC contract 1355.001, NSF grants CNS-0644436, CNS-0627734, and CCF-0613997, and an Alfred P. Sloan Research Fellowship.

References

1. Barrett, C., Sebastiani, R., Seshia, S.A., Tinelli, C.: Satisfiability modulo theories. In: Biere, A., van Maaren, H., Walsh, T. (eds.) Handbook of Satisfiability, ch. 8, vol. 4. IOS Press, Amsterdam (2009)
2. Biere, A.: PicoSAT essentials. JSAT 4, 75–97 (2008)
3. Brummayer, R.D., Biere, A.: Boolector: An efficient SMT solver for bit-vectors and arrays. In: Proc. of TACAS (March 2009)

4. Bruttomesso, R., Cimatti, A., Franzen, A., Griggio, A., Hanna, Z., Nadel, A., Palti, A., Sebastiani, R.: A lazy and layered SMT(BV) solver for hard industrial verification problems. In: Damm, W., Hermanns, H. (eds.) CAV 2007. LNCS, vol. 4590, pp. 547–560. Springer, Heidelberg (2007)
5. Bryant, R.E., Kroening, D., Ouaknine, J., Seshia, S.A., Strichman, O., Brady, B.: Deciding bit-vector arithmetic with abstraction. In: Grumberg, O., Huth, M. (eds.) TACAS 2007. LNCS, vol. 4424, pp. 358–372. Springer, Heidelberg (2007)
6. de Moura, L., Bjorner, N.: Z3: An efficient SMT solver. In: Ramakrishnan, C.R., Rehof, J. (eds.) TACAS 2008. LNCS, vol. 4963, pp. 337–340. Springer, Heidelberg (2008)
7. Een, N., Sorensson, N.: An extensible SAT-solver. In: Giunchiglia, E., Tacchella, A. (eds.) SAT 2003. LNCS, vol. 2919, pp. 502–518. Springer, Heidelberg (2004)
8. Ganesh, V., Dill, D.: A decision procedure for bit-vectors and arrays. In: Damm, W., Hermanns, H. (eds.) CAV 2007. LNCS, vol. 4590, pp. 519–531. Springer, Heidelberg (2007)
9. Hutter, F., Babic, D., Hoos, H.H., Hu, A.J.: Boosting verification by automatic tuning of decision procedures. In: FMCAD 2007, pp. 27–34. IEEE Press, Los Alamitos (2007)
10. Manolis, P., Srinivasan, S.K., Vroon, D.: BAT Bit-level Analysis tool. In: Damm, W., Hermanns, H. (eds.) CAV 2007. LNCS, vol. 4590, pp. 303–306. Springer, Heidelberg (2007)
11. Jain, H., Clarke, E.M.: Efficient SAT solving for Non-Clausal Formulas using DPLL, Graphs and Watched Cuts. In: 46th Design Automation Conference (2009)
12. Pipatsrisawat, K., Darwiche, A.: Rsat 2.0: Sat solver description. Technical Report D–153, Automated Reasoning Group, Computer Science Department, UCLA (2007)
13. SMT-COMP 2008 results, http://www.smtexec.org/exec/?jobs=311
14. SMT-LIB QF_BV logic,
    http://goedel.cs.uiowa.edu/smtlib/logics/QF_BV.smt
15. SMT-LIB QF_BV benchmarks,
    http://combination.cs.uiowa.edu/smtlib/benchmarks.html
16. Berkeley Logic Synthesis and Verification Group. ABC: A system for sequential synthesis and verification, release 70930,
    http://www.eecs.berkeley.edu/~alanmi/abc/
17. Jha, S., Limaye, R., Seshia, S.A.: Beaver: Engineering an Efficient SMT Solver for Bit-Vector Arithmetic. Technical Report, EECS Department, UC Berkeley (April 2009)
18. Een, N., Mishchenko, A., Sorensson, N.: Applying logic synthesis to speedup SAT. In: Marques-Silva, J., Sakallah, K.A. (eds.) SAT 2007. LNCS, vol. 4501, pp. 272–286. Springer, Heidelberg (2007)
19. Warren Jr., H.S.: Hacker's Delight. Addison Wesley, Reading (2003)

CalFuzzer: An Extensible Active Testing Framework for Concurrent Programs

Pallavi Joshi[1], Mayur Naik[2], Chang-Seo Park[1], and Koushik Sen[1]

[1] University of California, Berkeley, USA
{pallavi,parkcs,ksen}@eecs.berkeley.edu
[2] Intel Research
mayur.naik@intel.com

Abstract. Active testing has recently been introduced to effectively test concurrent programs. Active testing works in two phases. It first uses predictive off-the-shelf static or dynamic program analyses to identify potential concurrency bugs, such as data races, deadlocks, and atomicity violations. In the second phase, active testing uses the reports from these predictive analyses to explicitly control the underlying scheduler of the concurrent program to accurately and quickly discover real concurrency bugs, if any, with very high probability and little overhead. In this paper, we present an extensible framework for active testing of Java programs. The framework currently implements three active testers based on data races, atomic blocks, and deadlocks.

1 Introduction

Multi-threaded programs often exhibit incorrect behavior due to unintended interference between threads. These concurrency bugs—such as data races and deadlocks—are often difficult to find using conventional testing techniques because they typically happen under very specific thread interleavings. Testing done in a particular environment often fails to come up with interleavings that could happen in other environments, such as under different system loads. Moreover, testing depends on the underlying operating system or the virtual machine for thread scheduling—it does not try to explicitly control the thread schedules; thus, it often ends up executing the same interleaving repeatedly.

Numerous program analysis techniques [1,2,4] have been developed to *predict* concurrency bugs in multi-threaded programs by detecting violations of commonly used synchronization idioms. For instance, accesses to a memory location without holding a common lock are used to predict data races on the location, and cycles in the program's lock order graph are used to predict deadlocks. However, these techniques often report many false warnings because violations of commonly used synchronization idioms do not necessarily indicate concurrency bugs. Manually inspecting these warnings is often tedious and error-prone.

Recently, we have proposed a new technique for finding *real* bugs in concurrent programs, called *active testing* [3,5,7]. Active testing uses a randomized thread scheduler to verify if warnings reported by a predictive program analysis are

A. Bouajjani and O. Maler (Eds.): CAV 2009, LNCS 5643, pp. 675–681, 2009.

real bugs. The technique works as follows. Active testing first uses an existing predictive off-the-shelf static or dynamic analysis, such as Lockset [4,6], Atomizer [1], or Goodlock [2], to compute potential concurrency bugs. Each such potential bug is identified by a set of program statements. For example, in the case of a data race, the set contains two program statements that could potentially race with each other in some execution. For each potential concurrency bug, active testing runs the given concurrent program under random schedules. Further, active testing biases the random scheduling by pausing the execution of any thread when the thread reaches a statement involved in the potential concurrency bug. After pausing a thread, active testing also checks if a set of paused threads could exhibit a real concurrency bug. For example, in the case of a data race, active testing checks if two paused threads are about to access the same memory location and at least one of them is a write. Thus, active testing attempts to force the program to take a schedule in which the concurrency bug actually occurs. In previous work, we have developed active testing algorithms for detecting real data races, atomicity violations, and deadlocks.

In this paper, we describe an extensible tool for active testing of concurrent Java programs, called CALFUZZER. CALFUZZER provides a framework for implementing both predictive dynamic analyses and custom schedulers for active testing. We elaborate upon each of these next.

CALFUZZER provides a framework for implementing various predictive dynamic analyses to obtain a set of program statements involved in a potential concurrency bug. We have implemented three such techniques in CALFUZZER: a hybrid race detector [4], the Atomizer algorithm [1] for finding potential atomicity violations, and iGoodlock [3] which is a more informative variant of the Goodlock algorithm [2] for detecting potential deadlocks. More generally, CALFUZZER provides an interface and utility classes to enable users to implement additional such techniques.

CALFUZZER also provides a framework for implementing custom schedulers for active testing. We call these custom schedulers *active checkers*. We have implemented three active checkers in CALFUZZER for detecting real data races, atomicity violations, and deadlocks. More generally, CALFUZZER allows users to specify an arbitrary set of program statements in the concurrent program under test where an active checker should pause. Such statements may be thought of as "concurrent breakpoints".

We have applied CALFUZZER to several real-world concurrent Java programs comprising a total of 600K lines of code and have detected both previously known and unknown data races, atomicity violations, and deadlocks. CALFUZZER could easily be extended to detect other kinds of concurrency bugs, such as missed notifications and atomic set violations.

2   The Active Testing Framework

In this section, we give a high-level description of our active testing framework. We consider a concurrent system composed of a finite set of threads. Given a

---

Algorithm 1. CalFuzzer with user defined `analyze` and `check` methods

1: **Inputs:** the initial state s_0 and a set of transitions *breakpoints*
2: *paused* := $\emptyset$
3: $s := s_0$
4: **while** `Enabled`$(s) \neq \emptyset$ **do**
5:     $t :=$ a random transition in `Enabled`$(s) \setminus$ *paused*
6:     `analyze`(t)
7:     **if** $t \in$ *breakpoints* **then**
8:         *paused* := `check`$(t,$ *paused*$)$
9:     **end if**
10:    **if** $t \notin$ *paused* **then**
11:        $s :=$ `Execute`(s, t)
12:    **end if**
13:    **if** *paused* $=$ `Enabled`(s) **then**
14:        remove a random element from *paused*
15:    **end if**
16: **end while**
17: **if** `Alive`$(s) \neq \emptyset$ **then**
18:     **print** "ERROR: system stall"
19: **end if**

---

concurrent state s, let `Enabled`(s) denote the set of transitions that are enabled in the state s. Each thread executes a sequence of transitions and communicates with other threads through shared objects. We assume that each thread terminates after the execution of a finite number of transitions. A concurrent system evolves by transitioning from one state to another state. If s is a concurrent state and t is a transition, then `Execute`(s, t) executes the transition t in state s and returns the updated state.

The pseudo-code in Algorithm 1 describes the CalFuzzer algorithm. The algorithm takes an initial state s_0 and a set of transitions (denoting a potential concurrency bug), called *breakpoints*, as input. The set of transitions *paused* is initialized to the empty set. Starting from the initial state s_0, at every state, CalFuzzer randomly picks a transition enabled at the state and not present in the set *paused*. It then calls the user defined method `analyze` to perform a user defined dynamic analysis, such as Lockset, Atomizer, or Goodlock. The `analyze` method can maintain its own local state; for example, the local state could maintain locksets and vector clocks in the case of hybrid race detection. If transition t is in the set *breakpoints*, CalFuzzer invokes the user defined method `check`, which takes t and the *paused* set as input and returns an updated *paused* set. The `check` method could be used to implement various active checkers. A typical implementation of the `check` method could add t to the *paused* set and remove some transitions from the *paused* set. After the invocation of `check`, CalFuzzer executes the transition t if it has not been added to the *paused* set by the `check` method. At the end of each iteration, CalFuzzer removes a random transition from the *paused* set if all the enabled transitions have been

---

Algorithm 2. The `check` method for active testing of data races

1: **Inputs:** transition t and a set of transitions *paused*
2: **if** $\exists t' \in$ *paused* s.t. t and t' access same location and one is a write **then**
3:     **print** "Real data race between t and t'" (* next resolve race randomly to check if something could go wrong due to the race *)
4:     **if** `random()` **then**
5:         add t to *paused* and remove t' from *paused*
6:     **end if**
7: **else**
8:     add t to *paused*
9: **end if**
10: **return** *paused*

---

paused. The algorithm terminates when the system reaches a state that has no enabled transitions. At termination, if there is at least one thread that is alive, the algorithm reports a system stall.

3   An Example Instantiation of the Framework

CALFUZZER takes two user defined methods: `analyze` and `check`. In order to implement an active testing technique, one needs to define these two methods. For example, an active testing technique for data races [7] would require us to implement the hybrid race detection algorithm [4] in the `analyze` method and a `check` method as shown in Algorithm 2. Recall that the `check` method takes an enabled transition t in *breakpoints* and the set of paused transitions, *paused*, as input. If there exists a transition t' in *paused* such that both t and t' access the same memory location, and one of them is a write to that location, then we have exhibited a thread schedule which has a real race, namely the race between transitions t and t'. In principle, we could stop at this point, but we go further and determine if this race is benign or harmful (e.g. causes an exception). For this purpose, we randomly decide whether we want t' to execute before t, or vice versa. If `random()` returns true, then we let t' to execute before t, by adding t to *paused* and removing t' from it. Otherwise, we let t to execute before t'. Since t' is already paused, we keep it paused, and let t execute.

4   Implementation Details

We have implemented the CALFUZZER active testing framework for Java. CAL-FUZZER (available at `http://srl.cs.berkeley.edu/~ksen/calfuzzer/`) instruments Java bytecode using the SOOT compiler framework [8] to insert callback functions before or after various synchronization operations and shared memory accesses.[1] These callback functions are used to implement various predictive dynamic analyses and active checkers. Each predictive dynamic analysis

---

[1] We decided to instrument bytecode instead of changing the Java virtual machine or instrumenting Java source code because Java bytecode changes less frequently than JVM and Java source may not be available for libraries.

implements an interface called `Analysis`. The methods of these interface implements the `analyze` function in Algorithm 1. Likewise, each active checker is implemented by extending a class called `ActiveChecker` which implements the `check` functions in Algorithm 1. The methods of these two classes are called by the callback functions.

The framework provides various utility classes, such as `VectorClockTracker` and `LocksetTracker` to compute vector clocks and locksets at runtime. Methods of these classes are invoked in the various callback functions described above. These utility classes are used in the hybrid race detection [4] and iGoodlock [3] algorithms; other user defined dynamic analyses could also use these classes.

The instrumentor of CALFUZZER modifies all bytecode associated with a Java program including the libraries it uses, except for the classes that are used to implement CALFUZZER. This is because CALFUZZER runs in the same memory space as the program under analysis. CALFUZZER cannot track lock acquires and releases by native code and can therefore go into a deadlock if there are synchronization operations inside uninstrumented classes or native code. To avoid such scenarios, CALFUZZER runs a low-priority monitor thread that periodically polls to check if there is any deadlock. If the monitor discovers a deadlock, then it removes one random transition from the *paused* set.

CALFUZZER can also go into livelocks. Livelocks happen when all threads of the program end up in the *paused* set, except for one thread that does something in a loop without synchronizing with other threads. We observed such livelocks in a couple of our benchmarks including `moldyn`. In the presence of livelocks, these benchmarks work correctly because the correctness of these benchmarks assumes that the underlying Java thread scheduler is fair. In order to avoid livelocks, CALFUZZER creates a monitor thread that periodically removes those transitions from the *paused* set that are waiting for a long time.

5 Results

Table 1 summarizes some of the results of running active testing on several real-world concurrency Java programs comprising a total of 600K lines of code. Further details are available in [7,5,3]. Note that the bugs reported by the active checkers (RaceFuzzer, AtomFuzzer, and DeadlockFuzzer) are real, whereas those reported by the dynamic analyses (hybrid race detector, Atomizer, and iGoodlock) could be false warnings. Although active testing may not be able reproduce some real bugs, all previously known real bugs were reproduced, with the exception of AtomFuzzer (see [5] for a discussion on its limitations).

The runtime overhead of CALFUZZER is from 1.1x to 20x. Normally, the slowdown is low since only the synchronization points and memory accesses of interest are instrumented. However, in some cases the slowdown is significant—this is caused when CALFUZZER pauses redundantly at an event. We use precise abstractions [3] to distinguish relevant events, which lessens redundant pauses.

Table 1. Average execution time and number of bugs reported for each checker implemented with the CALFUZZER framework (LoC: Lines of Code, Norm: Uninstrumented code, RF: RaceFuzzer, DF: DeadlockFuzzer, AF: AtomFuzzer, HRD: Hybrid Race Detection, KR: Previously known real bugs, iG: iGoodlock, Az: Atomizer)

Benchmark	LoC	Avg. runtime(s)				Number of reported bugs								
		Norm	RF	DF	AF	HRD	RF	KR	iG	DF	KR	Az	AF	KR
moldyn	1,352	2.07	42.4	-	-	5	2	0	0	-	-	-	-	-
jspider	10,252	4.62	4.81	-	51	29	0	-	0	0	-	28	4	0
sor	17,718	0.163	0.23	-	1.0	8	0	0	0	0	-	0	0	0
hedc	25,024	0.99	1.11	-	1.8	9	1	1	0	0	-	3	0	1
DBCP	27,194	0.60	-	1.4	-	-	-	-	2	2	2	-	-	-
jigsaw	160,388	-	-	-	-	547	36	-	283	29	-	60	2	1
Java Swing	337,291	4.69	-	28.1	-	-	-	-	1	1	1	-	-	-

6   Conclusion

CALFUZZER provides a framework for implementing predictive dynamic analyses to find potential concurrency bugs and custom randomized schedulers, called active checkers, to automatically verify if they are real bugs. We have implemented three active checkers in this framework for detecting data races, atomicity violations, and deadlocks. We have shown the effectiveness of these checkers on several real-world concurrent Java programs comprising a total of 600K lines of code. We believe CALFUZZER provides a simple extensible framework to implement other predictive dynamic analyses and active checkers.

Acknowledgements. This research was supported in part by a generous gift from Intel, Microsoft and Intel funding (award #20080469), matching funding by U.C. Discovery (award #DIG07-10227), and NSF Grant CNS-0720906.

References

1. Flanagan, C., Freund, S.N.: Atomizer: a dynamic atomicity checker for multi-threaded programs. In: 31st ACM SIGPLAN-SIGACT Symposium on Principles of Programming Languages (POPL), pp. 256–267 (2004)
2. Havelund, K.: Using runtime analysis to guide model checking of java programs. In: Havelund, K., Penix, J., Visser, W. (eds.) SPIN 2000. LNCS, vol. 1885, pp. 245–264. Springer, Heidelberg (2000)
3. Joshi, P., Park, C.-S., Sen, K., Naik, M.: A randomized dynamic program analysis technique for detecting real deadlocks. In: ACM SIGPLAN Conference on Programming Language Design and Implementation (PLDI 2009) (2009) (to appear)
4. O'Callahan, R., Choi, J.-D.: Hybrid dynamic data race detection. In: ACM SIGPLAN symposium on Principles and practice of parallel programming, pp. 167–178. ACM, New York (2003)
5. Park, C.-S., Sen, K.: Randomized active atomicity violation detection in concurrent programs. In: 16th ACM SIGSOFT International Symposium on Foundations of software engineering, pp. 135–145. ACM, New York (2008)

6. Savage, S., Burrows, M., Nelson, G., Sobalvarro, P., Anderson, T.E.: Eraser: A dynamic data race detector for multithreaded programs. ACM Trans. Comput. Syst. 15(4), 391–411 (1997)
7. Sen, K.: Race directed random testing of concurrent programs. In: PLDI 2008: Proceedings of the 2008 ACM SIGPLAN conference on Programming language design and implementation, pp. 11–21. ACM, New York (2008)
8. Vallee-Rai, R., Hendren, L., Sundaresan, V., Lam, P., Gagnon, E., Co, P.: Soot - a Java optimization framework. In: CASCON 1999, pp. 125–135 (1999)

MCMAS: A Model Checker for the Verification of Multi-Agent Systems*

Alessio Lomuscio[1], Hongyang Qu[1], and Franco Raimondi[2]

[1] Imperial College London, UK
[2] University College London, UK

1 Overview

While temporal logic in its various forms has proven essential to reason about reactive systems, agent-based scenarios are typically specified by considering high-level agents attitudes. In particular, specification languages based on epistemic logic [7], or logics for knowledge, have proven useful in a variety of areas including robotics, security protocols, web-services, etc. For example, security specifications involving anonymity [4] are known to be naturally expressible in epistemic formalisms as they explicitly state the lack of different kinds of knowledge of the principals.

More generally, various extensions of temporal logic have been studied in agents and AI contexts to represent properties of autonomous systems. In addition to epistemic operators, at the very core of these approaches is the importance of deontic modalities expressing norms and compliance/violation with respect to previously agreed commitments, and ATL-like modalities expressing cooperation among agents.

While these languages have been long explored and appropriate semantics developed, until recently there has been a remarkable gap in the availability of efficient symbolic model checking toolkits supporting these. In this paper we describe MCMAS, a symbolic model checker specifically tailored to agent-based specifications and scenarios. MCMAS [12] supports specifications based on CTL, epistemic logic (including operators of common and distributed knowledge) [7], Alternating Time Logic [2], and deontic modalities for correctness [16]. The release described in this abstract is a complete rebuild of a preliminary experimental checker [14]. The model input language includes variables and basic types and it implements the semantics of interpreted systems, thereby naturally supporting the modularity present in agent-based systems. MCMAS implements OBDD-based algorithms optimised for interpreted systems and supports fairness, counter-example generation, and interactive execution (both in explicit and symbolic mode). MCMAS has been used in a variety of scenarios including web-services, diagnosis, and security. MCMAS is released under GNU-GPL.

2 Multi-Agent Systems Formalisms

Multi-Agent Systems (MAS) formalisms are typically built on extensions of computational tree logic (CTL). For the purposes of this abstract we consider specifications

---

* The research described in this paper is partly supported by the European Commission Framework 6 funded project CONTRACT (IST Project Number 034418).

A. Bouajjani and O. Maler (Eds.): CAV 2009, LNCS 5643, pp. 682–688, 2009.

given in the following language $\mathcal{L}$ built from a set of propositional atoms $p \in P$, and a set of agents $i \in A$ ($G \subseteq A$ denotes a set of agents):

$$\phi ::= \neg\phi \mid \phi \wedge \phi \mid \langle\langle G \rangle\rangle X\phi \mid \langle\langle G \rangle\rangle F\phi \mid \langle\langle G \rangle\rangle [\phi U \psi] \mid K_i\phi \mid D_G\phi \mid C_G\phi \mid O_i\phi.$$

$\mathcal{L}$ extends ATL (hence CTL) by considering epistemic modalities representing "agent i knows ϕ" ($K_i\phi$), "group G has distributed knowledge of ϕ" ($D_G\phi$), "group G has common knowledge of ϕ" ($C_G\phi$), and deontic modalities encoding "whenever agent i is working correctly ϕ holds" ($O_i\phi$). The ATL modalities above are read as customary: $\langle\langle G \rangle\rangle X\phi$ stands for "group G can enforce ϕ at the next step" and $\langle\langle G \rangle\rangle F\phi$ stands for "group G can enforce ϕ at some point in the future". As standard, CTL modalities for AG, AU, AX and their existential counterparts may be derived from the ATL modalities, and, similarly, epistemic modalities for E_G ("everyone in G knows") may be rewritten as a conjunction of appropriate $K_i, i \in G$, formulas. The specification language above is very rich as it includes AI-based modalities representing various notions of knowledge [7], deontic conditions [16], ATL-style modalities for cooperation [2], as well as standard CTL.

A computationally grounded semantics for the family of MAS formalisms above (in the sense of [19], i.e., one in which the interpretation to all modalities is defined in terms of the computational states of the system) can be given by suitably extending *interpreted systems*. Interpreted systems [7], originally proposed for linear time only, are an agent-based semantics where the components, or agents, are defined by a set of possible local states, a set of actions that they may perform according to their local protocol, and transition functions returning the target local state given the current local state and the set of actions performed by all agents. An environment (described similarly to an agent) is also modelled as part of the system. ATL and CTL modalities are interpreted on the induced temporal relation given by the protocols and transition functions [15], the epistemic modalities are defined on the equivalence relations built on the equality of local states [7], and the deontic modalities are interpreted on "green states", i.e., subsets of local states representing states of locally correct behaviour for the agent in question. Specifically, satisfaction for the epistemic modalities is defined by $(IS, s) \models K_i\phi$ iff for all $s' \in S$ we have that $s \sim_i s'$ implies $(IS, s') \models \phi$, where IS is an interpreted system, s, s' reachable global states, and $\sim_i$ is defined on the local equality of global states, i.e., $s \sim_i s'$ iff $l_i(s) = l_i(s')$ where l_i is the function returning the local state of agent i in a given global state. Satisfaction for common knowledge is defined by $(IS, s) \models C_G\phi$ iff for all $s' \in S$ we have that $s \sim^* s'$ implies $(IS, s') \models \phi$, where $\sim^*$ is the reflexive and transitive closure of the union of the relations $\sim_i, i \in G$. We refer to the user manual available from [12] for satisfaction of distributed knowledge D_G and correctness modalities O_i, as well as more details and examples.

The language $\mathcal{L}$ has been used to specify a wide range of scenarios in application areas such as web-services, security, and communication protocols. For example, in a communication protocol we can use $EF(K_{sender}(K_{receiver}(bit = 0)))$ to specify that at some point in the future the sender will know that the receiver knows that the bit being sent is equal to 0; in a game-based setting, we can write $AGO_{p_1}\langle\langle p_1, p_2 \rangle\rangle X(p_1\_p_2 win)$ to represent that it is always the case that, as long as player 1 is functioning correctly, player1 and player2 can together force a win at any step.

The complexity of the model checking problem of $\mathcal{L}$ against compact representations (e.g., via reactive modules, or ISPL modules as below) is given by its more expensive fragment (ATL) and so it is EXPTIME-complete [9]. Note, however, that the problem of checking its temporal-epistemic-deontic fragment is only PSPACE-complete [13], i.e., the same as CTL [11].

3   The MCMAS Toolkit

MCMAS is implemented in C++ and compiled for all major platforms. It exploits the CUDD [18] library for BDD operations. MCMAS implements standard algorithms for CTL and ATL [3,2], and dedicated BDD-based algorithms for the epistemic and deontic operators [17], in particular, the algorithms for satisfaction for K_i and C_G are sketched in Algorithm 1 (S represents the set of reachable states).

Algorithm 1. Algorithms for $SAT_K(\phi, i)$(left) and $SAT_C(\phi, G)$ (right)

	1: $X \Leftarrow \Sigma; Y \Leftarrow SAT(\neg\phi)$;
	2: **while** $X \neq Y$ **do**
1: $X \Leftarrow SAT(\neg\phi)$;	3: $X \Leftarrow Y$;
2: $Y \Leftarrow \{s \in S \mid \exists s' \in X \text{ s.t. } s \sim_i s'\}$;	4: $Y \Leftarrow \{s \in S \mid \exists s' \in X \text{ and } i \in G \text{ s.t. } s \sim_i s'\}$;
3: **return** $\neg Y \cap S$;	5: **end while**
	6: **return** $\neg Y \cap S$;

A number of optimisations are implemented in MCMAS in an attempt to minimise the memory consumption and verification time. For example, the checker does not build a single OBDD for the global transition relation, but performs any required operation against the local evolutions. Also, MCMAS does not compute the union of equivalence relations $\sim_i$ in Algorithm 1 when checking common knowledge, but instead repeatedly operates on all $\sim_i$. MCMAS provides counterexamples and witnesses for a wide range of formulas including epistemic modalities thereby giving guidance to the user. The algorithm used to return witnesses and counterexamples is novel and inspired by the tree-like construction of [5].

MCMAS takes ISPL (Interpreted Systems Programming Language) descriptions as input. An ISPL file fully describes a multi-agent system (both the agents and the environment), and it closely follows the framework of interpreted systems described above. We refer to the user manual for examples and usage. Essentially, an ISPL agent is described by giving the agents' possible local states, their actions, protocols, and local evolution functions. Local states are defined by using variables of type `Boolean`, `integer`, and `enumeration`. An optional section `RedStates` permits the definition of non-green states by means of any Boolean formula on the variables of the local states to interpret the correctness modalities O_i. The local transition function is given as a set of *evolution items* of the form `A if C`, where C is a Boolean condition over local variables, global variables (see below), and actions by the agents and the environment, and A is a set of assignments on the agent's local variables. All variables not present in A remain constant in the local transition. Any enabling condition and synchronisation among the agents is specified in C; note also that any non-deterministic

Table 1. ISPL snippet for the Train/Gate/Controller (Agent T2, similar to Agent T1, is omitted)

```
Agent Environment                          Agent T1
Vars: s: {g, r}; end Vars                  Vars: s: {w, t, a}; end Vars
Actions={E1, L1, E2, L2};                  Actions={E1, L1, B1};
Protocol:                                  Protocol:
 s=g: {E1, E2};                             s=w: {E1}; s=t: {L1}; s=a: {B1};
 s=r: {L1, L2};                            end Protocol
end Protocol                               Evolution:
Evolution:                                  s=w if s=a and Action=B1;
 s=g if s=r and ((Action=L1 and T1.Action=L1)   s=t if s=w and Action=E1 and
         or (Action=L2 and T2.Action=L2));          Environment.Action=E1;
 s=r if s=g and ((Action=L1 and T1.Action=E1)   s=a if s=t and Action=L1 and
         or (Action=L2 and T2.Action=E2));          Environment.Action=L1;
end Evolution                              end Evolution
end Agent                                  end Agent
```

behaviour may be specified by using several evolution items. Compared to that of an agent, an environment definition may have additional features, including the definition of global variables observable to some or all agents. Table 1 shows an example of a self-explanatory ISPL file for the Train/Gate/Controller scenario with two trains.

An ISPL file also contains sections for the definition of the initial states (given by Boolean conditions on the agents' local variables), any fairness constraints, groups of agents (to be used in epistemic and ATL formulas) and the actual formulae in the language $\mathcal{L}$ to be checked. The interpretation for the propositional atoms used in the specifications is also given; among these the predefined atoms GreenStates, and RedStates have their interpretation fixed to the locally green local states and their set complement respectively. We refer to the user manual for more details and examples.

The graphical user interface (GUI) is an essential part of the MCMAS release. It is built as an Eclipse plug-in and provides a rich number of functionalities, some of which reported below.

ISPL program editing. The GUI guides the user to create and edit ISPL programs by performing dynamic syntax checking (an additional ISPL parser was implemented in ANTLR for this). The GUI also provides outline view, text formatting, syntax highlighting, and content assist automatically.

Interactive execution mode. The user can use MCMAS interactively to explore the model. This can be done both in symbolic and explicit way. The explicit exploration does not require installation of the checker itself and is provided entirely by the GUI. Obviously large models are best explored symbolically. Users can choose which state to visit among the possibilities presented, backtrack, etc.

Counterexample display. The user can launch the verification process via the GUI which, in turns, calls the checker. The GUI shows which specifications are satisfied and which are not. For a wide range of specifications (see the user manual) the user can visualise counterexamples or witnesses (the Graphviz package is used to display the submodel representing the counterexample/witness). The user has a variety of options once a submodel is displayed including inspecting the agents' states in the system, projecting the whole system onto agents, etc.

4   Experimental Results and Conclusions

MCMAS has been used in our group and in a limited number of other institutions to verify a range of scenarios, including agent-based web services, networking protocols, and security protocols. Some of these examples are available from the MCMAS website. To evaluate the tool we discuss the experimental results obtained while verifying the protocol of the *dining cryptographers* [4]. This is a scalable anonymity protocol in which lack of knowledge needs to be preserved following a round of announcements. We refer to [8,10] for more details.

On a Linux x86_64 machine with Intel Core 2 Duo 2.2GHz and 4GB memory, we tested the protocol (code on the website) against two temporal epistemic specifications:

$$AG((\text{odd} \wedge \neg \text{payer}_1) \rightarrow ((K_{\text{cryptographer}_1} \bigvee_{i=2}^{n} \text{payer}_i) \wedge (\bigwedge_{i=2}^{n} \neg K_{\text{cryptographer}_1} \text{payer}_i))),$$

$AG(\text{even} \rightarrow C_{\{\text{cryptographer}_1,....,\text{cryptographer}_n\}} \neg (\bigvee_{i=1}^{n} \text{payer}_i))$. We checked the second formula specifically to evaluate the performance of the tool against common knowledge.

Table 2. Verification results for the dinning cryptographers protocol

n crypts	possible states	reachable states	knowledge		common knowledge	
			bdd memory (MB)	time (s)	bdd memory (MB)	time (s)
10	1.86×10^{11}	33792	12.5	1	12.5	1
11	2.23×10^{12}	73728	12.4	3	12.6	2
12	2.67×10^{13}	159744	12.8	4	12.9	4
13	3.21×10^{14}	344064	28.2	23	28.4	23
14	3.85×10^{15}	737280	15.8	14	16.1	13
15	4.62×10^{16}	1.57×106	17.1	24	18.0	24
16	5.55×10^{17}	3.34×106	42.3	149	42.3	150
17	6.66×10^{18}	7.07×106	60.0	612	60.0	612
18	7.99×10^{19}	1.49×107	222.8	2959	222.8	2959

The table reports the results for different numbers of cryptographers, indicated in the first column. The size of the state space (equal to 3×12^n) is reported in the second column, and the third reports the number of actual reachable states in the corresponding model. Memory usage and time required for the verification of the two formulas follow in the last four columns respectively.

A direct efficiency comparison with other toolkits is problematic. Apart from the different input languages, other tools with overlapping functionalities support different variable types making any comparison difficult. In terms of pure size of the model, we found that MCMAS can explore the full state space of models whose size is approximately two orders of magnitude larger than most examples available for temporal-epistemic model checkers [8,6,20], and comparable to the size of the models analysed with BDD-based temporal-only model checkers such as NuSMV.

As mentioned in the introduction, MCMAS is a complete reimplementation of the original proof-of-concept described in [14]. Compared to the original prototype, the current version is several orders of magnitude faster. This is due to improved algorithms for the verification of epistemic and ATL modalities, and the computation of the reachable state space. Additionally, the revised input language now enables the user to write code that naturally generates smaller models, e.g., by using globally observable variables in the environment. Several functionalities, e.g., counterexample generation, witnesses, fairness, a fully-fledged GUI, etc., are also now included.

From the point of view of supported functionalities, MCMAS is the only checker we are aware of that supports the specification language $\mathcal{L}$ described above. Epistemic modalities are also treated in [8] although not via an observation-based semantics as here and not with the CUDD package. BMC based approaches for epistemic modalities have also been presented [6]: a comparison with [6] reveals the known advantages and disadvantages of BDD vs SAT-based approaches. Finally, ATL is of course supported by MOCHA [1]. However, MOCHA is an on-the-fly checker tailored to assume/guarantee analysis, whose efficiency crucially depends on the learning of successful decompositions and assumptions for the scenario under analysis.

References

1. Alur, R., Henzinger, T., Mang, F., Qadeer, S., Rajamani, S., Tasiran, S.: MOCHA: Modularity in model checking. In: Y. Vardi, M. (ed.) CAV 1998. LNCS, vol. 1427, pp. 521–525. Springer, Heidelberg (1998)
2. Alur, R., Henzinger, T.A., Kupferman, O.: Alternating-time temporal logic. Journal of the ACM 49(5), 672–713 (2002)
3. Burch, J.R., Clarke, E.M., McMillan, K.L., Dill, D.L., Hwang, L.J.: Symbolic model checking: 10^{20} states and beyond. Information and Computation 98(2), 142–170 (1990)
4. Chaum, D.: The dining cryptographers problem: Unconditional sender and recipient untraceability. Journal of Cryptology 1(1), 65–75 (1988)
5. Clarke, E., Lu, Y., Jha, S., Veith, H.: Tree-like counterexamples in model checking. In: the 17th IEEE Symposium on Logic in Computer Science. IEEE Computer Society Press, Los Alamitos (2002)
6. Dembiński, P., Janowska, A., Janowski, P., Penczek, W., Pólrola, A., Szreter, M., Woźna, B., Zbrzezny, A.: VerICS: A tool for verifying Timed Automata and Estelle specifications. In: Garavel, H., Hatcliff, J. (eds.) TACAS 2003. LNCS, vol. 2619, pp. 278–283. Springer, Heidelberg (2003)
7. Fagin, R., Halpern, J.Y., Moses, Y., Vardi, M.Y.: Reasoning about Knowledge. MIT Press, Cambridge (1995)
8. Gammie, P., van der Meyden, R.: MCK: Model checking the logic of knowledge. In: Alur, R., Peled, D.A. (eds.) CAV 2004. LNCS, vol. 3114, pp. 479–483. Springer, Heidelberg (2004)
9. van der Hoek, W., Lomuscio, A., Wooldridge, M.: On the complexity of practical atl model checking knowledge, strategies, and games in multi-agent systems. In: Proceedings of AAMAS 2006, pp. 946–947. ACM Press, New York (2006)
10. Kacprzak, M., Lomuscio, A., Niewiadomski, A., Penczek, W., Raimondi, F., Szreter, M.: Comparing BDD and SAT based techniques for model checking Chaum's dining cryptographers protocol. Fundamenta Informaticae 63(2,3), 221–240 (2006)
11. Kupferman, O., Vardi, M.Y., Wolper, P.: An automata-theoretic approach to branching-time model checking. Journal of the ACM 47(2), 312–360 (2000)
12. Lomuscio, A., Qu, H., Raimondi, F.: MCMAS, http://www-lai.doc.ic.ac.uk/mcmas/

13. Lomuscio, A., Raimondi, F.: The complexity of model checking concurrent programs against CTLK specifications. In: Proceedings of the 5th international joint conference on Autonomous agents and multiagent systems (AAMAS 2006), pp. 548–550. ACM Press, New York (2006)
14. Lomuscio, A., Raimondi, F.: MCMAS: A model checker for multi-agent systems. In: Hermanns, H., Palsberg, J. (eds.) TACAS 2006. LNCS, vol. 3920, pp. 450–454. Springer, Heidelberg (2006)
15. Lomuscio, A., Raimondi, F.: Model checking knowledge, strategies, and games in multi-agent systems. In: Proceedings of AAMAS 2006, pp. 161–168. ACM Press, New York (2006)
16. Lomuscio, A., Sergot, M.: Deontic interpreted systems. Studia Logica 75(1), 63–92 (2003)
17. Raimondi, F., Lomuscio, A.: Automatic verification of multi-agent systems by model checking via OBDDs. Journal of Applied Logic 5(2), 235–251 (2005)
18. Somenzi, F.: CUDD: CU decision diagram package - release 2.4.1 (2005), http://vlsi.colorado.edu/~fabio/CUDD/cuddIntro.html
19. Wooldridge, M.: Computationally grounded theories of agency. In: Proceedings of ICMAS, International Conference of Multi-Agent Systems, pp. 13–22. IEEE Press, Los Alamitos (2000)
20. Wooldridge, M., Fisher, M., Huget, M., Parsons, S.: Model checking multiagent systems with MABLE. In: Proceedings of AAMAS 2002, pp. 952–959 (2002)

TASS: Timing Analyzer of Scenario-Based Specifications

Minxue Pan, Lei Bu, and Xuandong Li

State Key Laboratory for Novel Software Technology, Nanjing University
Department of Computer Science and Technology, Nanjing University
Nanjing, Jiangsu, P.R. China 210093
panmx@seg.nju.edu.cn, bl@seg.nju.edu.cn, lxd@nju.edu.cn

Abstract. In this paper, we present TASS which is a timing analyzer of scenario-based specifications. TASS accepts UML2.0 interaction models with general and expressive timing constraints and can be used for three kinds of timing analysis problems: the reachability analysis, the constraint conformance analysis, and the bounded delay analysis. The underlying technique of TASS is to reduce the timing analysis problems into linear programming problems.

1   Introduction and Motivations

Scenario-based specifications (SBSs) such as message sequence charts (MSCs) [1] and UML interaction models [2] offer an intuitive and visual way of describing design requirements. Such specifications can describe concrete interactions among communicating entities and therefore are playing an increasingly important role in the design of software systems. For real-time systems, timing constraints are introduced into SBSs to describe timed behaviors. However compared with numerous theoretical studies on timing analysis of SBSs, tools are rather scarce. This paper introduces our tool TASS which supports timing analysis of SBSs expressed by UML interaction models.

The models analyzed by TASS consist of UML sequence diagrams (SDs) and UML2.0 interaction overview diagrams (IODs) [2] which are illustrated in Figure 1. We use the UML sequence diagram to describe exactly one scenario without alternatives and loops, and the UML2.0 interaction overview diagram which combines references to SDs to describe sequential, iterating and non-deterministic executions of SDs. This manner of breaking down SBSs into different hierarchies can make complicated SBSs more comprehensible.

The existing mechanisms of describing timing constraints in MSCs and UML sequence diagrams include timers [1], interval delays [3,4], and timing marks [2,5,6]. However all these mechanisms are just suitable to describe simple timing constraints which are only related to the separation in time between two events. In practical problems, we often need to describe more complex timing constraints which are about the relation among multiple separations in time between events. Another issue is that although the topic of timing analysis

A. Bouajjani and O. Maler (Eds.): CAV 2009, LNCS 5643, pp. 689–695, 2009.
© Springer-Verlag Berlin Heidelberg 2009

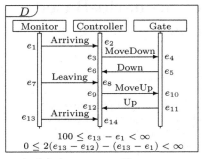

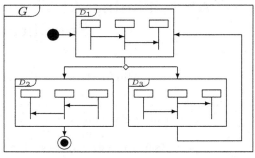

(a) A sequence diagram   (b) An interaction overview diagram

Fig. 1. UML interaction models

of SBSs has been thoroughly studied [3,4,5,6,7,8], to our knowledge, all previous work is about checking SBSs for timing consistency, which is a basic property. In practical situations, there are a lot of properties about the accumulated delays on the traces of systems. For example, we often need to check if all the traces of a system satisfy that the separation in time between two given events is in a given time interval, which is called *bounded delay analysis*. This problem has been considered for timed automata in [9] but to our knowledge no tool has been implemented for this timing analysis problem of SBSs so far.

These issues motivate us to develop TASS. TASS accepts more general and expressive timing constraints which depict relations among multiple separations in time between events. Additionally TASS can be used to solve three timing analysis problems:

- Reachability analysis (RA): to check if a given scenario of an SBS is reachable along a behavior of the SBS with regard to all the timing constraints.
- Constraint conformance analysis (CCA): to check if the given several scenarios, which occur consecutively in the behavior of an SBS, satisfy a given timing constraint.
- Bounded delay analysis (BDA): to check if the separation in time between two given events, which may occur in different sequence diagrams, is not smaller or greater than a given real number in any behavior of an SBS. This is called the *minimal bounded delay analysis* or the *maximal bounded delay analysis* respectively.

The above timing analysis problems of SBSs are undecidable in general [10]. Therefore we developed a decision procedure for a decidable subset of SBSs and a bounded timing analyzer for general SBSs respectively. The bounded timing analyzer gets its name for utilizing the *bounded model checking* [11] techniques.

2   Architecture and Underlying Techniques

Fig. 2 illustrates the architecture of TASS. TASS accepts two types of timing constraints. One are the timing constraints enforced on SDs which describe the relations among multiple separations in time between events. By events we mean the message sending and the message receiving in the diagram. We use event names to represent the occurrence time of events, and linear inequalities on event names to represent the timing constraints. A timing constraint is of the form $a \leq c_0(e_0 - e_0') + c_1(e_1 - e_1') + \ldots + c_n(e_n - e_n') \leq b$, where e_i and e_i' $(0 \leq i \leq n)$ are event names which represent the occurrence time of e_i and e_i', a, b and $c_0, c_1, \ldots, c_n$ are real numbers (b may be ∞). For example, for the scenario of the railroad crossing system depicted in Figure 1(a), the timing constraint $0 \leq 2(e_{13} - e_{12}) - (e_{13} - e_1) < \infty$ specifies the requirement that from the time one train is arriving to the time the next train is arriving, the gate stays open for at least half of this period.

The other type of timing constraints is enforced on IODs of the form $a \leq e - e' \leq b$ where e and e' occur in different sequence diagrams and $0 \leq a \leq b$ (b may be ∞), which can describe the timed relations between two events from different sequence diagrams.

TASS is composed of three timing analyzers. The *path-oriented timing analyzer* is a basic analyzer that takes a finite path as its input. If the path is infinite then a length threshold is required. The underlying technique of the analyzer is to reduce the timing analysis problems into linear programming problems, which is described in details in [12]. In a nutshell, for a finite path in an SBS, since all the timing constraints along the path can form a group of linear inequalities, the timing analysis problems are encoded into linear programs which can be solved efficiently by the *linear program solver*. The solver is a free collection of Java classes from OR-Objects of DRA Systems [13]. The *bounded timing analyzer* requires a threshold as input, traverses all the paths within the threshold in a depth-first manner, and checks the related paths one by one by calling the path-oriented timing analyzer. This is one of the key functions of TASS. Although the timing analysis problem of general SBSs is undecidable, based on

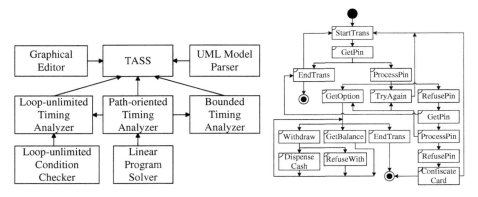

Fig. 2. TASS Architecture   **Fig. 3.** ATM SBS

the "bounded" approach we can verify all the SBSs as long as a threshold is provided, and thereby increase the faith in the correctness of the system.

Moreover, we developed the *loop-unlimited timing analyzer* which is a decision procedure for a set of SBSs named *loop-unlimited SBSs*. They are SBSs with the following three characteristics: (i) The concatenation of two consecutive SDs in an SBS is interpreted as the "synchronous mode": when moving one node to the other, all events in the previous SD finish before any event in the following SD occurs; (ii) No timing constraint is enforced on the repetition of any loop: for any timing constraint in an IOD of the form $a \leq e - e' \leq b$ (note that e and e' belong to different SDs) there is no loop between the nodes in which e and e' occur; and (iii) One unfolding of a loop is time independent of the other unfolding: there is no "reverse constraint" in an IOD of the form $a \leq e - e' \leq b$ such that e and e' occurs in the same loop and e occurs before e'. Otherwise the reverse constraint would be enforced on two consecutive unfolds of the same loop which means one unfolding of the loop is time dependent of the other.

The loop-unlimited timing analyzer first calls the *loop-unlimited condition checker* to check whether an SBS is loop-unlimited. If so, it can reduce the possible infinite number of infinite paths in the SBS to a finite set of finite paths, which is the other key function of TASS. The reduction process, roughly speaking, is to unfold the loops related to the timing constraints finite times and remove the unrelated ones. Afterwards it calls the path-oriented timing analyzer to analyze each finite path. It is a decision procedure for loop-unlimited SBSs, and a semi-decision procedure for general SBSs.

There are ways other than our linear programming based approach to solve the timing analysis problems of SBSs. In [6] a simple sequence diagram is transformed to a set of timed automata and in [14] MSC specifications are interpreted as global state automata. Compared with the way of transforming SBSs to other representations of models, the advantage of our approach includes two aspects. On the one hand, our approach avoids the generation of the state space of transformed models altogether and also the involved complexity. On the other hand, the timing constraints considered in our approach can be used to describe relations among multiple separations in time between events which means we need to compare multiple clocks if the timed automata based approach is adopted, which is undecidable [15].

3   Performance Evaluation

TASS is implemented in Java and is now available on the website [16]. We briefly describe the performance of TASS with two well-known examples: the automatic teller machine (ATM) system and the global system for mobile communication (GSM). The experiment platform is a Pentium 4/2.2GHz/2.0GB PC.

Fig. 3 is the IOD of the ATM SBS. It has 16 nodes and each node refers to an SD that consists of 3 communicating components. The GSM SBS has 32 nodes and each refers to an SD with 8 components. The GSM SBS and the SDs of the ATM SBS are too large to display here but can be found in TASS website [16].

Table 1. Performance data of case studies

Problem / Case	RA Result	RA Time	CCA Result	CCA Time	BDA Result	BDA Time
ATM	yes	62ms	yes	1.420s	no	63ms
GSM	yes	62ms	yes	780ms	yes	125ms

(a) Sample results of loop-unlimited timing analysis

Problem / k	Path: $StartTrans\hat{\ }\cdots\hat{\ }(Withdraw\hat{\ }RefuseWith)^k\hat{\ }\cdots\hat{\ }EndTrans$				
	constraints	events	RA	CCA	BDA
100	3496	1645	93.224s	90.662s	90.559s
200	6896	3245	695.683s	695.659s	696.276s
300	10296	4845	2299.692s	2299.753s	2302.140s
400	13696	6445	4999.113s	5009.316s	5067.740s

(b) Sample results of path-oriented timing analysis of ATM SBS

Problem / k	RA of GSM path	RA of GSM time	CCA of GSM path	CCA of GSM time	BDA of GSM path	BDA of GSM time	BDA of ATM path	BDA of ATM time
15	1	78ms	28	374ms	27	250ms	1	78ms
20	1	125ms	922	23.276s	816	13.244s	1	156ms
25	1	156ms	22574	947.778s	19374	546.515s	1	343ms
30	1	192ms	495570	32741.155s	419365	19463.581s	1	671ms

(c) Sample results of bounded timing analysis

Both the ATM SBS and GSM SBS are loop-unlimited, so we first evaluated the loop-unlimited timing analyzer. It reported a violation for the bounded delay analysis of the ATM SBS, and satisfactions for the rest five analyses as expected (Table 1(a)). The results are fascinating since we only assigned 50M memory to the Java Virtual Machine (JVM) and all the analysis tasks are finished in split second including the time to check whether the SBS is loop-unlimited. This indicates that TASS is capable of dealing with substantially larger SBSs.

We also assessed the performance of the path-oriented timing analyzer on the path "StartTrans^GetPin^ProcessPin^GetOption^(Withdraw^RefuseWith)^k^ Withdraw^DispenseCash^EndTrans" of the ATM SBS. Table 1(b) illustrates its processing ability. It is shown that when the repetition times k of the loop "Withdraw^RefuseWith" was set to 400, the length of the single path analyzed could be as long as 800 (400*2) steps and the number of constraints reached to 13696 with 6445 timed events. However, the analyzing time was no more than one and a half hours because we directly encoded the timing analysis problem into a linear program which can be solved efficiently.

Finally we evaluated the bounded timing analyzer. We performed all three timing analyses of the GSM SBS and the bounded delay analysis of the ATM SBS. From results shown in Table 1(c) we can see that:

1. TASS took little time to prove the satisfaction of reachability analysis and the dissatisfaction of constraint conformance analysis and bounded delay analysis (cf. columns of "RA of GSM" and "BDA of ATM"), because the bounded timing analyzer would stop immediately once it witnesses a feasible path for RA or a violating path for CCA and BDA.
2. With only 50M memory assigned to the JVM, TASS verified more than four hundred thousand paths when the threshold k was set to 30 (cf. columns

of "CCA of GSM" and "BDA of GSM"). This is because the underlying technique of TASS is to recursively traverse directly on the structure of the SBS and check paths within the threshold in a depth-first manner, one by one. No matter how big the whole model state is, TASS only cares for the currently visiting path and therefore consumes little memory.

4   Conclusion

In this paper, we present our tool TASS, a timing analyzer of scenario-based specifications. TASS accepts general and expressive timing constraints and can be used for three kinds of timing analysis problems: the reachability analysis, the constraint conformance analysis, and the bounded delay analysis. It provides a path-oriented timing analyzer to check one single path, a bounded timing analyzer to check the whole SBSs in a given threshold, and a powerful loop-unlimited timing analyzer to check loop-unlimited SBSs. The experiments show that TASS has good performance and scalability, and indicate its clear potential.

Acknowledgement

This work is supported by the National Natural Science Foundation of China (No.90818022, No.60721002, No.60673125), the National 863 High-Tech Programme of China (No.2009AA01Z148, No.2007AA010302), and by the Jiangsu Province Research Foundation (BK2007714).

References

1. ITU-TS. ITU-T. Recommendation Z.120. ITU - Telecommunication Standardization Sector, Geneva, Switzerland (May 1996)
2. Object Management Group, Framingham, Massachusetts. UML 2.0 Superstructure Specification (October 2004)
3. Alur, R., Holzmann, G., Peled, D.: An analyzer for message sequence charts. Tools and Algorithms for the Construction and Analysis of Systems, 35–48 (1996)
4. Ben-Abdallah, H., Leue, S.: Timing Constraints in Message Sequence Chart Specifications. In: Proc. of FORTE X/PSTV XVII, pp. 91–106. Chapman & Hall, Boca Raton (1998)
5. Seemann, J., von Gudenberg, J.W.: Extension of UML Sequence Diagrams for Real-Time Systems. In: Bézivin, J., Muller, P.-A. (eds.) UML 1998. LNCS, vol. 1618, pp. 240–252. Springer, Heidelberg (1999)
6. Firley, T., Huhn, M., Diethers, K., Gehrke, T., Goltz, U.: Timed sequence diagrams and tool-based analysis - A case study. In: France, R.B., Rumpe, B. (eds.) UML 1999. LNCS, vol. 1723, pp. 645–660. Springer, Heidelberg (1999)
7. Li, X., Lilius, J.: Timing analysis of UML sequence diagrams. In: France, R.B., Rumpe, B. (eds.) UML 1999. LNCS, vol. 1723, pp. 661–674. Springer, Heidelberg (1999)
8. Li, X., Lilius, J.: Checking compositions of UML sequence diagrams for timing inconsistency. In: Proc. of APSEC 2000, pp. 154–161. IEEE Computer Society, Los Alamitos (2000)

9. Courcoubetis, C., Yannakakis, M.: Minimum and maximum delay problems in real-time systems. Form. Methods Syst. Des. 1, 385–415 (1992)
10. Alur, R., Yannakakis, M.: Model Checking of Message Sequence Charts. In: Baeten, J.C.M., Mauw, S. (eds.) CONCUR 1999. LNCS, vol. 1664, p. 114. Springer, Heidelberg (1999)
11. Biere, A., Cimatti, A., Clarke, E., Strichman, O., Zhu, Y.: Bounded model checking. Advances in Computers 58, 118–149 (2003)
12. Li, X., Pan, M., Bu, L., Wang, L., Zhao, J.: Timing Analysis of Scenario-Based Specifications (manuscript), `http://cs.nju.edu.cn/lxd/TASS/`
13. OR-Objects, `http://OpsResearch.com/OR-Objects/index.html`
14. Ladkin, P., Leue, S.: Interpreting Message Sequence Charts. Technical Report TR 101, Dept. of Computing Science, University of Stirling, United Kingdom (1993)
15. Alur, R., Dill, D.L.: A theory of timed automata. Theor. Comput. Sci. 126 (1994)
16. TASS Website, `http://cs.nju.edu.cn/lxd/TASS/`

Translation Validation: From Simulink to C

Michael Ryabtsev[1] and Ofer Strichman[2]

[1] Computer Science, Technion, Haifa, Israel
`michaelr@cs.technion.ac.il`
[2] Information Systems, IE, Technion, Haifa, Israel
`ofers@ie.technion.ac.il`

Abstract. Translation validation is a technique for formally establishing the semantic equivalence of the source and the target of a code generator. In this work we present a translation validation tool for the REAL-TIME WORKSHOP code generator that receives as input Simulink models and generates optimized C code.

1 Introduction

Translation Validation [8,7,5] is a formal method for validating the semantic equivalence between the source and the target of a compiler or a code generator. A translation validation tool receives as input the source and target programs as well as a mapping between their input, output and state variables (frequently this mapping can be derived automatically). Based on the semantics of the source and target languages, it then builds a verification condition that is valid if and only if the generated code faithfully preserves the semantics of the source code. Hence, translation validation is applied separately to each translation, in contrast to the alternative of verifying the code generator itself. It has the advantage of being less sensitive to changes in the code generator – such changes invalidate correctness proofs of the code generator – and simpler, since verifying the code generator amounts to functional verification of a complex program. Further, when the code generator is not open-source this is the only option.

In this work we present TVS (Translation Validation tool for Simulink). TVS applies translation validation to the (commercial) REAL-TIME WORKSHOP (RTW) code generator [3], which translates Matlab/Simulink models to optimized C code.[1] We will briefly describe Simulink in the next section. In Sect. 3 we will describe the verification condition generated by TVS, and in Sect. 4 we will highlight various technical issues such as automatic generation of invariants that are needed for the proof and abstraction based on uninterpreted functions. We must assume here, owing to lack of space, that the reader is familiar with such proof techniques.

---

[1] TVS only handles 'classic' Simulink models. Simulink also allows integration of state diagrams in the model, called STATEFLOW, which TVS does not support.

A. Bouajjani and O. Maler (Eds.): CAV 2009, LNCS 5643, pp. 696–701, 2009.

2   Simulink

Simulink [4,3], developed by *The MathWorks*, is a software package for model-based design of dynamic systems such as signal processing, control and communications applications. Models in Simulink can be thought of as executable specifications, because they can be simulated and, as mentioned earlier, they can be translated into a C program via the RTW code generator.

Simulink's graphical editor is used for modeling dynamic systems with a block diagram, consisting of blocks and arrows that represent signals between these blocks. A wide range of signal attributes can be specified, including signal name, data type (e.g., 16-bit or 32-bit integer), numeric type (real or complex), and dimensionality (e.g., one-dimensional or multidimensional array). Each block represents a set of equations, called *block methods*, which define a relationship between the block's *input* signals, *output* signals and the *state* variables. Blocks are frequently parameterized with constants or arithmetical expressions over constants.

Simulink diagrams represent synchronous systems, and can therefore be translated naturally into an *initialization* function and a *step* function. The block diagram in the left of Figure 1, for example, represents a counter; the corresponding initialization and step functions that were generated by RTW appear to the right of the same figure. These two functions appear within a template program that includes all the necessary declarations.

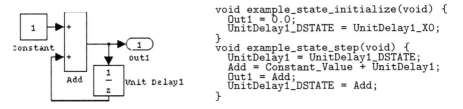

```
void example_state_initialize(void) {
    Out1 = 0.0;
    UnitDelay1_DSTATE = UnitDelay1_X0;
}
void example_state_step(void) {
    UnitDelay1 = UnitDelay1_DSTATE;
    Add = Constant_Value + UnitDelay1;
    Out1 = Add;
    UnitDelay1_DSTATE = Add;
}
```

Fig. 1. A Simulink diagram representing a counter (the Unit Delay1 block represents a state element), and the corresponding generated code. The variable UnitDelay1_DSTATE is a state variable, which is initialized to a constant stored in UnitDelay1_X0 (by default this value is 0).

Model simulation and code generation. Model simulation is done in several phases. In the first phase the code generator converts the model to an executable form following these steps: 1) it evaluates the block's parameter expressions; 2) it determines signal attributes, e.g., name, data type, numeric type, and dimensionality (these are not explicitly specified in the model file) and performs type-checking, i.e., it checks that each block can accept the signals connected to its inputs; 3) it flattens the model hierarchy by replacing subsystems with the blocks that they contain; and 4) it sorts the blocks according to the execution order. After this phase, the blocks are executed in a single loop corresponding to a single step of the model.

Many optimizations are performed during the code generation phase, such as loop unwinding, introduction of auxiliary variables, elimination of variables by expression propagation, simplifications of expressions, etc. Some of these optimizations cause a simple proof of equivalence by induction to fail, as we will demonstrate in Sect. 4.

3   The Verification Condition

When considering reactive control systems, code equivalence can be stated in terms of system outputs equivalence, given the same input stream. The output in such systems in each step depends on the current inputs and the values of the state variables. The proof of equivalence is based on induction, assuming we have a correct mapping between the state variables and inputs in both programs.[2]

The inductive verification condition with which TVS attempts to establish the equivalence between the two transition systems can be formulated as follows. For a transition system M, let $init(M)$ be its initial-state predicate over M's state-variables, and let $TR(M)$ be its transition relation over M's inputs, outputs, current and next-step state variables. Denote by $inp(M)$, $out(M)$ and $state(M)$, the sets of M's input, output and state variables respectively (these sets are assumed to be disjoint). We use v' to denote the next-state version of a state variable v. Let S and T be two transition systems corresponding to the source and target of the code generator, and let map be a mapping function between their variables. The verification condition corresponding to the base case is:

$$\bigwedge_{s \in state(S)} s = map(s) \wedge init(T) \Rightarrow init(S) \wedge Inv \,, \tag{1}$$

where Inv is an invariant over T's variables that is possibly needed in order to strengthen the induction claim.[3] This condition ensures that the initial states of the target are legitimate initial states in the source, as well as the validity of the invariant in the initial step.

The verification condition corresponding to the step is:

$$Inv \wedge \bigwedge_{i \in inp(S)} i = map(i) \wedge \bigwedge_{s \in state(S)} s = map(s) \wedge TR(S) \wedge TR(T) \quad \Rightarrow$$
$$Inv' \wedge \bigwedge_{s \in state(S)} s' = map(s') \wedge \bigwedge_{o \in out(S)} o' = map(o') \,.$$
$$\tag{2}$$

This condition ensures that if values of corresponding inputs are the same and the state variables in the current state are the same, then the transition relation implies that the outputs and states in the next step are equal. It also guarantees the propagation of the invariant.

---

[2] Incorrect mapping of the variables leads to incompleteness. Yet the process is incomplete due to other reasons as well. Automatic variable mapping is possible when the code generator preserves variable names in the translation.

[3] The need for such an invariant was already recognized in the original translation validation article [6].

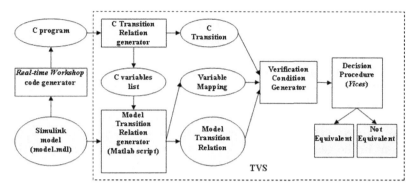

Fig. 2. The architecture of TVS

After the construction of the two verification conditions, it is left to check them with a decision procedure. For this purpose any one of the existing off-the-shelf SMT solvers can be used. Our tool invokes Yices [2].

The architecture of the translation validation tool appears in Figure 2.

4 Various Technical Issues

Generating the target transition relation. is rather straightforward because RTW uses a rather simple subset of the C language (e.g., no unbounded loops or dynamic memory allocation). However since C represents asynchronous computations whereas the transition relation is a formula, TVS uses Static Single Assignment (SSA) [1] – based on the observation that there are no unbounded loops in the target code – in order to cope with variables that have different values in the course of the computation of the step function. For example, the code a = b; b = b + 1 is translated into $a_0 = b_0 \wedge b_1 = b_0 + 1$. Multiple assignments to the same variable in a single step (such as b in this example) are common in code generated by RTW owing to its various optimizations.

Generating the source transition relation. is more difficult for two reasons. First, the transitions entailed by each type of block should be defined according to the block's semantics. The large number of such blocks and the fact that the semantics are not formally defined (at least not in the public domain), makes this task difficult. Second, the *model.mdl* file, which represents the Simulink model, is not sufficient when taken out of Matlab's workspace. TVS uses the 'Matlab script language' for retrieving information missing from this file such as the signals' type and constants from the Matlab workspace, for evaluating various expressions, and for working with an internal data structure that represents the model.

Invariants. While variables in a synchronous model are *volatile* (i.e., they have an undefined value in a step in which they are not updated), the corresponding global variables in the generated C code preserve their values between steps.

If not all state variables are updated explicitly at each step the inductive proof can fail. Indeed, RTW generates code that updates the variables only as needed, while relying on their previous value otherwise.

Consider, for example, the following code fragments. The code on the left is a representation of the model according to Simulink's semantics, whereas the code on the right was generated by RTW for the same model. In the generated code MODE is declared as global and is being updated only in the step function. It can therefore avoid an update when the value has not changed. As a result, while in the Simulink model this variable is assigned a value in every step, it performs an assignment in the generated C code only when the value of `condition` changes. This clearly invalidates the inductive argument.

```
if (condition)              if (condition)
  MODE = ENABLED;             {if (MODE == DISABLED) MODE = ENABLED;}
else                        else
  MODE = DISABLED;            {if (MODE == ENABLED) MODE = DISABLED;}
```

In order to solve this problem TVS adds an invariant Inv (see Eq. (1) and (2)) of the form MODE = DISABLED $\vee$ MODE = ENABLED. Such cases are associated with conditional executions of blocks, and can be identified automatically.

Abstraction. Whereas the functions in the verification condition range over finite domains (integer, float...), deciding it without abstraction has little chance to scale. A standard solution in the translation validation literature is to make some or all the functions uninterpreted. For example, instead of proving:

$$a_1 = (x_1 * x_2) \wedge a_2 = (y_1 * y_2) \wedge z = a_1 + a_2 \Rightarrow (z = (x_1 * x_2) + (y_1 * y_2)) ,$$

we can attempt to prove the more abstract formula:

$$a_1 = f(x_1, x_2) \wedge a_2 = f(y_1, y_2) \wedge z = g(a_1, a_2) \Rightarrow (z = g(f(x_1, x_2), f(y_1, y_2))) ,$$

where f and g are uninterpreted. In general this type of abstraction may introduce incompleteness, unless we know in advance the type of transformations done by the code generator, and change the verification conditions accordingly. Two examples of such modifications that we found necessary and TVS accordingly supports are *commutativity* and *constant propagation*. As for the former, consider a case in which the code generator swapped the arguments of a multiplication expression, e.g., from $a * b$ to $b * a$. We need to declare the uninterpreted function that replaces the multiplication function as commutative. In Yices this is possible by adding a quantifier of the following form, for an uninterpreted function f:[4]

$$(forall \ (a :: int \ b :: int) \ (= \ (f \ a \ b) \ (f \ b \ a))) .$$

As for the latter, constant propagation is required in a case such as the following: whereas the blocks in the model correspond to two consecutive statements

---

[4] Using this construct leads to incompleteness in Yices. We rarely encountered this in practice.

`c = 1; y = c * x;`, in the target C code there is only the statement `y = x;` owing to constant propagation. This trivial propagation invalidates the proof if the multiplication is replaced with an uninterpreted function. TVS, therefore, performs constant propagation before the abstraction phase.

4.1   Summary and Experiments

We introduced TVS, a translation validation tool for the code generator REAL-TIME WORKSHOP, which generates optimized C code from Simulink models. TVS works according to the classic induction-based proof strategy introduced already a decade ago in [6,7]. Each language, however, poses a new challenge since the verification condition depends on the semantics of the operators used in this language. Further, each code generator poses a challenge owing to its particular optimizations that may hinder the inductive argument. We presented several such problems and the way TVS solves them.

The largest model that we verified automatically (with some minor manual modifications listed in a technical report [9]) with TVS is called "rtwdemo_fuelsys", which is a model of a fuel injection controller that is distributed together with Matlab. This model has about 100 blocks, and the generated C code for the step has about 250 lines. The generated verification condition in the format of Yices has 790 lines. Yices solves it in about a second. Small perturbations of the verification condition that invalidates it cause Yices to find counterexamples typically within 10 seconds.

References

1. Cytron, R., Ferrante, J., Rosen, B.K., Wegman, M.N., Zadeck, F.K.: Efficiently computing static single assignment form and the control dependence graph. ACM Transactions on Programming Languages and Systems 13(4), 451–490 (1991)
2. Dutertre, B., Moura, L.D.: The Yices SMT solver. Technical report, SRI international (2006)
3. Mathworks, T.: Simulink 7 user-guide,
   `http://www.mathworks.com/access/helpdesk/help/pdf_doc/simulink/sl_using.pdf`
4. Mathworks, T.: Simulink getting started guide,
   `http://www.mathworks.com/access/helpdesk/help/pdf_doc/simulink/sl_gs.pdf`
5. Necula, G.C.: Translation validation for an optimizing compiler. In: PLDI 2000 (June 2000)
6. Pnueli, A., Siegel, M., Shtrichman, O.: Translation validation for synchronous languages. In: Larsen, K.G., Skyum, S., Winskel, G. (eds.) ICALP 1998. LNCS, vol. 1443, pp. 235–246. Springer, Heidelberg (1998)
7. Pnueli, A., Siegel, M., Shtrichman, O.: The code validation tool (CVT)- automatic verification of a compilation process. Int. Journal of Software Tools for Technology Transfer (STTT) 2(2), 192–201 (1999)
8. Pnueli, A., Siegel, M., Singerman, E.: Translation validation. Technical report, SACRES and Dept. of Comp. Sci., Weizmann Institute (April 1997)
9. Ryabtsev, M., Strichman, O.: Translation validation: From Simulink to C (full version). Technical Report IE/IS-2009-01, Industrial Engineering, Technion (2009)

VS³: SMT Solvers for Program Verification

Saurabh Srivastava[1,*], Sumit Gulwani[2], and Jeffrey S. Foster[1]

[1] University of Maryland, College Park
{saurabhs,jfoster}@cs.umd.edu
[2] Microsoft Research, Redmond
sumitg@microsoft.com

Abstract. We present VS³, a tool that automatically verifies complex properties of programs and infers maximally weak preconditions and maximally strong postconditions by leveraging the power of SMT solvers. VS³ discovers program invariants with arbitrary, but prespecified, quantification and logical structure. The user supplies VS³ with a set of predicates and invariant templates. VS³ automatically finds instantiations of the unknowns in the templates as subsets of the predicate set. We have used VS³ to automatically verify ∀∃ properties of programs and to infer worst case upper bounds and preconditions for functional correctness.

1 Introduction

There are two major hurdles in the widespread adoption of current verification tools for program analysis. The first is their inability to express invariants with the detailed logical structure (specifically, quantifiers and disjunctions) that is required for almost all non-trivial programs. The second is the annotation burden and effort required on the part of the programmer in reasoning formally about inductive invariants. The sophisticated invariants required for most non-trivial programs are hard for the programmer to come up with and impose a significant annotation burden.

In this tools paper, we describe VS³ (Verification and Synthesis using SMT Solvers), a tool that partly addresses the above mentioned limitations by leveraging the engineering advances made in constraint solving in the past decade. VS³ takes as input a set of invariant templates and a set of candidate predicates to populate the templates' unknowns. VS³ then infers required program invariants and, optionally, required maximally weak preconditions. By allowing the invariants to have an arbitrary, but prespecified, logical structure, VS³ can verify sophisticated (e.g., ∀ and ∀∃) properties of programs. Additionally, by automatically inferring maximally weak preconditions, VS³ reduces the burden on the programmer, both in coming up with difficult preconditions and in specifying them alongside the code. In the future, we plan to augment VS³ with template inference and abstraction refinement to build a powerful system for software verification with minimal user input.

* The work reported here was supported in part by NSF CCF-0430118 and was in part done during an internship at Microsoft Research.

A. Bouajjani and O. Maler (Eds.): CAV 2009, LNCS 5643, pp. 702–708, 2009.
© Springer-Verlag Berlin Heidelberg 2009

(a)
```
    BinarySearch(Array A, int e, int n)
1     low := 0; high := n − 1;
2     while (low ≤ high)
3         mid := ⌈(low + high)/2⌉;
4         if (A[mid] < e)
5             low := mid + 1;
6         else if (A[mid] > e)
7             high := mid − 1;
8         else return true;
9     Assert (∀j : (0 ≤ j < n) ⇒ A[j] ≠ e)
10    return false;
```

(b)
```
    SetInclusion(Array A, int n,
                 Array B, int m)
1     for (i = 0; i < n; i++)
2         exists := false;
3         for (j = 0; j < m; j++)
4             if (A[i] = B[j])
5                 exists := true; break;
6         if (¬exists) return false;
7     Assert (∀y∃x : (0 ≤ y < n)
8         ⇒ (A[y] = B[x] ∧ 0 ≤ x < m))
9     return true;
```

User Input:

Template: $v_1 \land (\forall j : v_2 \Rightarrow v_3)$
        $\land (\forall j : v_4 \Rightarrow v_5) \land (\forall j : v_6 \Rightarrow v_7)$

Predicate Set:
`AllPreds`($\{j, n, low, high\}, \{0\}, \{\leq, <\}$) $\cup$
`AllPreds`($\{A[t] \,|\, t \in \{j, j \pm 1\}\} \cup \{e\}, \{0\},$
                                $\{\leq, \neq\}$)

User Input:

Template: $v_1 \land (\forall y\exists x : v_2 \Rightarrow v_3)$
        $\land (\forall y\exists x : v_4 \Rightarrow v_5)$

Predicate Set:
`AllPreds`($\{x, y, i, j, m\}, \{0\}, \{\leq, <\}$) $\cup$
`AllPreds`($\{exists\}, \{\text{true}, \text{false}\}, \{=\}$) $\cup$
`AllPreds`($\{A[t], B[t] \,|\, t \in \{x, y\}\}, \{0\}, \{=\}$)

Tool Output: "Precondition required":

Precondition:
$\forall j : (0 \leq j < n) \Rightarrow A[j] \leq A[j + 1]$
Loop Invariant:
$0 \leq low \land high < n$
$\forall j : (low \leq j \leq high) \Rightarrow A[j] \leq A[j + 1]$
$\forall j : (0 \leq j < low) \Rightarrow A[j] \neq e$
$\forall j : (high < j < n) \Rightarrow A[j] \neq e$

Tool Output: "Assertion valid":

Outer loop invariant:
$\forall y\exists x : 0 \leq y < i \Rightarrow (A[y] = B[x] \land 0 \leq x < m)$
Inner loop invariant:
$j \geq 0$
$\forall y\exists x : 0 \leq y < i \Rightarrow (A[y] = B[x] \land 0 \leq x < m)$
$\forall y\exists x : (y = i \land exists = \text{true})$
        $\Rightarrow (A[y] = B[x] \land 0 \leq x < m)$

Fig. 1. (a) VS³ computes the maximally weak precondition for correctness of binary search (b) VS³ computes the ∀∃ invariants required to prove the correctness of a program that checks set inclusion. (`AllPreds`(Z, C, R) denotes the set of predicates $\{z \text{ op } z' \mid z, z' \in Z \cup C, \text{op} \in R\}$.)

We have used VS³ with great success to verify a wide array of difficult program properties, such as the full functional correctness of standard implementations of all major sorting algorithms [1], and have additionally used it to infer difficult preconditions for functional correctness. VS³ interfaces with off-the-shelf SMT solvers for its core reasoning and provides a rich source for SMT benchmark instances from the domain of verification and property inference of programs.

1.1 Motivating Examples and Tool Usage

We now illustrate the power of VS³ by considering two motivating examples.

Precondition Inference. Consider the program shown in Fig. 1(a), which implements a binary search for the element e in an array A. The functional specification of the program is given as the assertion[1] on Line 9, which essentially states that if the procedure returns false, then A indeed does not contain e.

For this function, VS^3 automatically infers the maximally weak precondition for functional correctness, shown in Fig. 1(a), which is that the input array is sorted. VS^3 also infers the loop invariant, also shown in Fig. 1(a), encoding the semantics of binary search (that the array elements between low and $high$ are sorted and those outside do not equal e).

In automatic CUTPOINT mode, VS^3 searches for inductive program invariants at loop headers. Alternatively, in some cases the invariants are simpler if inferred at specific locations, which should form a valid cutset such that each cycle in the CFG contains at least one location [2]. VS^3 also supports a MANUAL mode for user-specified cutsets.

The user also specifies a *global* invariant template and a *global* predicate set, as shown. The template is used for invariants at each cutpoint and the predicate set specifies the candidate predicates for the unknowns in the template. In practice, the user starts by guessing simple templates and predicates. If the analysis fails then the user iteratively increases the sophistication of the templates and predicates until VS^3 finds a solution.

In practice, the logical structure (quantification and boolean connectives) of the templates is easily derived from given program assertions and discovered by iterative guessing. For instance, for BinarySearch we first tried a template with one unquantified and one quantified conjunct, but VS^3 failed to infer an instantiation. We then iteratively increased the number of quantified conjuncts until a solution was found. Also, typically we used a predicate set consisting of inequality relations between relevant program and bound variables. In our experience (over a large set of programs [1]), coming up with the templates and predicate set is typically easy for the programmer.

Verification using invariants with arbitrary logical structure. Consider the program shown in Fig. 1(b), which checks whether all elements of A are contained in B. The loop invariant required contains $\forall\exists$ quantification, which VS^3 infers. We do not know of any other tool that can automatically discover such invariants. Note how the conjuncts in the invariant template in this case follow the schematic of the given assertion and therefore are $\forall\exists$-quantified. As before, we discovered the appropriate number of conjuncts by iterative guessing.

2   Tool Architecture

VS^3 uses Microsoft's Phoenix compiler framework [3] as a front end parser for ANSI-C programs and Z3 [4] to solve the SMT queries. Our implementation is approximately 15K non-blank, non-comment lines of C# code.

---

[1] VS^3 allows the user to specify assertions and assumptions with arbitrary logical structure up to those expressible in the underlying SMT solver. Assumptions may be required to model expressions not handled by the solver. For instance, in the current system, the assignment on Line 3 is modeled as Assume($low \leq mid \leq high$).

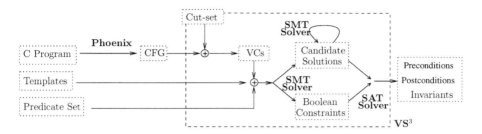

Fig. 2. The VS³ tool. In addition to the ANSI-C program, the user provides the templates, the predicate sets, and optionally, a cutset. The tool provides the option of choosing between an iterative and a constraint-based fixed-point computation.

The tool architecture is shown in Fig. 2. VS³ uses Phoenix to generate the control flow graph (CFG) of the program. The CFG is then split into simple paths using a cutset (either generated automatically with a cutpoint at each loop header or specified by the user). The tool then generate a verification condition (VC) corresponding to each simple path. For fixed-point computation the tool provides two alternatives:

Iterative Fixed-Point [1]. The iterative scheme performs a variant of a standard dataflow analysis. It maintains a set of candidate solutions, and by using the SMT solver to compute the best transformer it iteratively improves the candidates until a solution is found. See [1] for details.

Constraint-based Fixed-Point [5,1]. In the constraint-based scheme, a predicate p at location l is identified by boolean indicator variables $b_{p,l}$. For verification condition vc, VS³ generates the minimal set of constraints over the indicator variables that ensures that vc is satisfiable. These constraints are accumulated and solved using a SAT solver that yields a fixed-point solution. See [1] for details.

2.1   Solver Interface

Compensating for current limitations of SMT solvers. The generic primitives provided by SMT solvers are expressive but lacking in some aspects that are needed for our application.[2] We augment the solver by providing a wrapper interface that preprocesses the SMT queries and adds hints for the solver.

Patterns for quantifier instantiation. The current state-of-art for reasoning over quantified facts uses the now commonly known technique of E-matching [6] for quantifier instantiation. E-matching uses *patterns* to match against ground terms. Because individual SMT queries in our system are over simple quantified terms, a simple heuristic to automatically generate patterns suffices: Given a quantified fact with bound variables $\bar{k}$ and bound boolean term F, VS³ recursively parses F and returns valid patterns from F's subterms. A subterm f is a

---

[2] Our current implementation uses the Z3 solver, but the limitations we discuss here apply to all state-of-the-art solvers, as far as we know.

valid pattern if it contains all the bound variables and at least one subterm of f does not contain all the variables. For example, for the fact $\forall k : k > 10 \Rightarrow A[k] < A[k+1]$, VS^3 computes the set of patterns $\{\{k > 10\}, \{A[k]\}, \{A[k+1]\}\}$, and for $\forall k : k \geq 0 \wedge k < v \Rightarrow A[k] < min$, VS^3 computes the set $\{\{k \geq 0\}, \{k < v\}, \{A[k] < min\}\}$. This simple heuristic is potentially expensive, but allows for automatic and, in practice, fast proofs or disproofs of the implication checks.

Saturating inductive facts. SMT solvers have difficulty instantiating relevant facts from inductive assumptions. For instance, in our experiments, we encountered assumptions of the form $k_n \geq k_0 \wedge \forall k : k \geq k_0 \Rightarrow A[k] \leq A[k+1]$ from which $A[k_0] \leq A[k_n + 1]$ was needed for the proof. Z3 times out without finding a proof or disproof of whether $A[k_0] \leq A[k_n+1]$ follows from the assumption. Notice that the pattern $k \geq k_0$ will only allow the prover to instantiate $A[k_n] \leq A[k_n + 1]$ from the ground fact, which does not suffice to prove $A[k_0] \leq A[k_n + 1]$.

VS^3 therefore syntactically isolates inductive facts and saturates them. To do this, it pattern matches quantified assumptions such as the above (consisting of a base case in the antecedent and the induction step in the consequent of the implication) and asserts the quantified inductive result. For example, for the case above, the saturated fact consists of $\forall k_2, k_1 : k_2 \geq k_1 \geq k_0 \Rightarrow A[k_1] \leq A[k_2 + 1]$. Using the ground term $k_n \geq k_0$, the tool can now instantiate $A[k_0] \leq A[k_n + 1]$. This heuristic allows the tool to deal with inductive reasoning for particular cases that arise in program analysis.

Explicit Skolemization for $\forall \exists$. Z3 v1.0 does not correctly instantiate global skolemization functions for existentials under a quantifier and so VS^3 infers these functions from the program[3]. An approach that suffices for all our benchmark examples is to rename the skolemization functions at the endpoints of a verification condition and to insert axioms relating the two functions. VS^3 syntactically infers the appropriate axioms over the skolem functions for the two specific cases that we describe below.

VS^3 can infer appropriate skolemization functions for the two cases of the verification condition containing array updates and assumptions equating array values. Suppose in the quantified formulae at the beginning and end of a simple path, the skolemization functions are $\mathtt{skl}$ and $\mathtt{skl'}$, respectively. For the case of array updates, suppose that locations $\{l_1, l_2, \ldots, l_n\}$ are overwritten with values from locations $\{r_1, r_2, \ldots, r_n\}$. Then the tool introduces two axioms. The first axiom states that the skolemization remains unchanged for locations that are not modified (Eq. 1), and the second axiom defines the (local) changes to the skolemization function for the array locations that are modified (Eq. 2):

$$\forall y : (\wedge_i (\mathtt{skl}(y) \neq r_i \wedge \mathtt{skl}(y) \neq l_i)) \Rightarrow \mathtt{skl'}(y) = \mathtt{skl}(y) \qquad (1)$$

$$\bigwedge_i \forall y : \mathtt{skl}(y) = r_i \Rightarrow \mathtt{skl'}(y) = l_i \qquad (2)$$

---

[3] We are aware of work being pursued in the solving community that will eliminate this restriction. Therefore in the future we will not need to infer skolemization functions.

For the case of assumptions equating array values, VS³ asserts the corresponding facts on skl', e.g., if Assume($A[i] = B[j]$) occurs and skl' indexes the array B then the tool adds the axiom $skl'(i) = j$.

Axiomatic support for additional theories. Some program verification tasks require support for non-standard expressions, e.g., reachability in linked-list or tree data structures. SMT solvers, and in particular Z3, support the addition of axioms to support these kind of predicates.

There are two steps towards the verification of such programs. First, VS³ defines the semantics of field accesses and updates on record datatypes using sel and upd. A field access $s \rightarrow f$, is encoded as $sel(f, s)$ and an update $s \rightarrow f := e$ is encoded as $upd(f, s, e)$. Second, VS³ asserts a set of axioms to define the semantics of higher level predicates, such as reachability, in terms of the constructs that appear in the program. Let $x \rightsquigarrow y$ denote that y can be reached by following pointers starting at x. Then for the case of reasoning about singly linked lists connected through next fields, the tool augments the SMT solver with the following reachability axioms:

$$\begin{array}{ll}
\forall x \,.\, x \rightsquigarrow x & \text{Reflexivity} \\
\forall x, y, z \,.\, x \rightsquigarrow y \wedge y \rightsquigarrow z \;\Rightarrow\; x \rightsquigarrow z & \text{Transitivity} \\
\forall x \,.\, x \neq \bot \;\Rightarrow\; x \rightsquigarrow (x \rightarrow \text{next}) & \text{Step: Head} \\
\forall x, y \,.\, x \rightsquigarrow y \;\Rightarrow\; x = y \vee (x \rightarrow \text{next}) \rightsquigarrow y & \text{Step: Tail} \\
\forall x \,.\, \bot \rightsquigarrow x \;\Rightarrow\; x = \bot & \text{End}
\end{array}$$

Using these axioms the solver can, for instance, prove that $head \rightsquigarrow tail \wedge tail \rightsquigarrow n \wedge n \neq \bot \Rightarrow head \rightsquigarrow (n \rightarrow \text{next})$.

3   Summary of Experiments and Conclusions

We have used VS³ to verify a wide variety of properties of programs manipulating arrays. We have verified the full correctness of standard implementations of five major sorting algorithms. Showing sortedness for these examples required ∀ invariants, and showing permutation required ∀∃ invariants (which have received little previous attention [7,8]).

Additionally, we have successfully used VS³ for inferring maximally weak preconditions. We have derived maximally weak preconditions for functional correctness and for proving worst case upper bounds for programs, e.g., inferring the input that yields the worst case run of a sorting program. See [1] for details.

Our experiments with VS³ have demonstrated its promise for the verification and inference of difficult program properties.

References

1. Srivastava, S., Gulwani, S.: Program verification using templates over predicate abstraction. In: PLDI (2009)
2. Gulwani, S., Srivastava, S., Venkatesan, R.: Program analysis as constraint solving. In: PLDI, pp. 281–292 (2008)

3. Microsoft Research: Phoenix (2008), http://research.microsoft.com/Phoenix/
4. de Moura, L., Bjørner, N.: Z3: Efficient SMT solver. In: Ramakrishnan, C.R., Rehof, J. (eds.) TACAS 2008. LNCS, vol. 4963, pp. 337–340. Springer, Heidelberg (2008)
5. Gulwani, S., Srivastava, S., Venkatesan, R.: Constraint based invariant inference over predicate abstraction. In: Jones, N.D., Müller-Olm, M. (eds.) VMCAI 2009. LNCS, vol. 5403, pp. 120–135. Springer, Heidelberg (2009)
6. Moura, L.: Bjørner, N.: Efficient E-matching for SMT solvers. In: CADE-21 (2007)
7. Balaban, I., Fang, Y., Pnueli, A., Zuck, L.D.: IIV: An invisible invariant verifier. In: Etessami, K., Rajamani, S.K. (eds.) CAV 2005. LNCS, vol. 3576, pp. 408–412. Springer, Heidelberg (2005)
8. Kovács, L., Voronkov, A.: Finding loop invariants for programs over arrays using a theorem prover. In: FASE (2009)

PAT: Towards Flexible Verification under Fairness

Jun Sun[1], Yang Liu[1], Jin Song Dong[1], and Jun Pang[2]

[1] School of Computing, National University of Singapore
[2] Computer Science and Communications, University of Luxembourg

Abstract. Recent development on distributed systems has shown that a variety of fairness constraints (some of which are only recently defined) play vital roles in designing self-stabilizing population protocols. Current practice of system analysis is, however, deficient under fairness. In this work, we present PAT, a toolkit for flexible and efficient system analysis under fairness. A unified algorithm is proposed to model check systems with a variety of fairness effectively in two different settings. Empirical evaluation shows that PAT complements existing model checkers in terms of fairness. We report that previously unknown bugs have been revealed using PAT against systems functioning under strong global fairness.

1 Introduction

In the area of system/software verification, liveness means something good must eventually happen. A counterexample to a liveness property is typically a loop (or a deadlock state) during which the good thing never occurs. Fairness, which is concerned with a fair resolution of non-determinism, is often necessary and important to prove liveness properties. Fairness is an abstraction of the fair scheduler in a multi-threaded programming environment or the relative speed of the processors in distributed systems. Without fairness, verification of liveness properties often produces unrealistic loops during which one process or event is unfairly favored. It is important to systematically rule out those unfair counterexamples and utilize the computational resource to identify the real bugs.

The population protocol model has recently emerged as an elegant computation paradigm for describing mobile ad hoc networks [1]. A number of population protocols have been proposed and studied [6]. Fairness plays an important role in these protocols. For instance, it was shown that the self-stabilizing population protocols for the complete network graphs only works under *weak fairness*, whereas the algorithm for network rings only works under *strong global fairness* [2]. It has further been proved that with only *strong local fairness* or weaker, uniform self-stabilizing leader election in rings is impossible [2]. In order to verify (implementations of) those algorithms, model checking techniques must take the respective fairness into account. However, current practice of model checking is deficient with respect to fairness.

One way to apply existing model checkers for verification under fairness is to reformulate the property so that fairness become premises of the property. A liveness property ϕ is thus verified by showing the truth value of the following formula: *fairness assumptions* $\Rightarrow \phi$. This practice is deficient for two reasons. Firstly, a typical system may have multiple fairness constraints, whereas model checking is PSPACE-complete in the size of the formula. Secondly, partial order reduction which is one of

A. Bouajjani and O. Maler (Eds.): CAV 2009, LNCS 5643, pp. 709–714, 2009.
© Springer-Verlag Berlin Heidelberg 2009

the successful reduction techniques for model checking becomes ineffective. Partial order reduction ignores/postpones invisible actions, whereas all actions/propositions in *fairness constraints* are visible and therefore cannot be ignored or postponed. An alternative method is to design specialized verification algorithms which take fairness into account while performing model checking. In this work, we present a toolkit named PAT (http://www.comp.nus.edu.sg/~pat) which checks linear temporal logic (LTL) properties against systems functioning under a variety of fairness (e.g., weak fairness, strong local/global fairness, process-level weak/strong fairness, etc.). A unified on-the-fly model checking algorithm is developed. PAT supports two different ways of applying fairness, one for ordinary users and the other for advanced users. Using PAT, we identified *previously unknown bugs* in the implementation of population protocols [2,6]. For experiments, we compare PAT and SPIN over a wide range of systems.

This work is related to research on categorizing and verifying fairness [2,8,9]. We investigate different forms of fairness and propose a verification algorithm (and a tool) which handles many of the fairness notions. In automata theory, fairness/liveness is often captured using accepting states. Our model checking algorithm is related to previous works on emptiness checking for Büchi automata and Streett automata [4]. In a way, our algorithm integrates the two algorithms presented in [3,7] and improves them in a number of aspects.

2   Background

Models in PAT are interpreted as labeled transition systems (LTS) implicitly. Let a be an action, which could be either an abstract event (e.g., a synchronization barrier if shared by multiple processes) or a data operation (e.g., a named sequential program). Let Σ be the set of all actions. An LTS is a 3-tuple $(S, init, \rightarrow)$ where S is a set of states, $init \in S$ is an initial state and $\rightarrow \subseteq S \times \Sigma \times S$ is a labeled transition relation.

For simplicity, we write $s \xrightarrow{a} s'$ to denote that (s, a, s') is a transition in $\rightarrow$. $enabled(s)$ is the set of enabled actions at s, i.e., a is in $enabled(s)$ if and only if there exist s' such that $s \xrightarrow{a} s'$. An execution is an infinite sequence of alternating states and actions $E = \langle s_0, a_0, s_1, a_1, \cdots \rangle$ where $s_0 = init$ and for all i such that $s_i \xrightarrow{a_i} s_{i+1}$. Without fairness constraints, a system may behave freely as long as it starts with an initial state and conforms to the transition relation. A fairness constraint restricts the set of system behaviors to only those fair ones. In the following, we focus on event-level fairness. Process-level fairness can be viewed as a special case of event-level fairness.

Definition 1 (Weak Fairness). *Let $E = \langle s_0, a_0, s_1, a_1, \cdots \rangle$ be an execution. E satisfies weak fairness, or is weak fair, iff for every action a, if a eventually becomes enabled forever in E, $a_i = a$ for infinitely many i, i.e., $\Diamond \Box$ a is enabled $\Rightarrow \Box \Diamond$ a is engaged.*

Weak fairness [8] states that if an action becomes enabled forever after some steps, then it must be engaged infinitely often. An equivalent formulation is that every computation should contain infinitely many positions at which a is disabled or has just been taken, known as justice condition [9]. Weak fairness has been well studied and verification under weak fairness has been supported to some extent [5].

Definition 2 (Strong Local Fairness). *Let* $E = \langle s_0, a_0, s_1, a_1, \cdots \rangle$ *be an execution. E satisfies strong local fairness iff for every action* a, *if* a *is infinitely often enabled, then* $a = a_i$ *for infinitely many* i, *i.e.,* $\Box\Diamond$ a *is enabled* $\Rightarrow$ $\Box\Diamond$ a *is engaged.*

Strong local fairness [8,9,2] states that if an action is infinitely often enabled, it must be infinitely often engaged. This type of fairness is useful in the analysis of systems that use semaphores, synchronous communication, and other special coordination primitives. Strong local fairness is stronger than weak fairness (since $\Diamond\Box$ a *is enabled* implies $\Box\Diamond$ a *is enabled*). Verification under strong local fairness or compassion conditions has been discussed previously [3,4,7]. Nonetheless, there are few established tool support for formal verification under strong local fairness.

Definition 3 (Strong Global Fairness). *Let* $E = \langle s_0, a_0, s_1, a_1, \cdots \rangle$ *be an execution. E satisfies strong global fairness iff for every* s, a, s' *such that* $s \xrightarrow{a} s'$, *if* $s = s_i$ *for infinite many* i, *then* $s_i = s$ *and* $a_i = a$ *and* $s_{i+1} = s'$ *for infinitely many* i.

Strong global fairness [2] states that if a *step* (from s to s' by engaging in action a) can be taken infinitely often, then it must actually be taken infinitely often. Strong global fairness concerns about both actions and states. It can be shown by a simple argument that strong global fairness is stronger than strong local fairness. Strong global fairness requires that an infinitely enabled action must be taken infinitely often in *all* contexts, whereas strong local fairness only requires the enabled action to be taken in *one* context. A number of population protocols reply on strong global fairness, e.g., self-stabilizing leader election in ring networks [2] and token circulation in rings [1]. As far as the authors know, there are no previous work on verification under strong global fairness.

A number of other fairness notions have been discussed by various researchers. We remark that our approach can be extended to handle other kinds of fairness.

3   Verification under Fairness

Verification under fairness is to examine only fair executions of a given system and to decide whether certain property is true. Given a property ϕ, model checking is to search for an infinite fair execution which fails ϕ. In the following, we present PAT's unified algorithm to verify whether a system is feasible under different fairness constraints. A system is feasible if and only if there exists at least one infinite execution which satisfies the fairness constraints. Applied to the product of the system and (the negation of) the property, the algorithm can be easily extended to do model checking under fairness. The soundness of the algorithm and a discussion on its complexity is discusssed in [10].

Without loss of generality, we assume that a system contains only finite states. A system is feasible under fairness if and only if there exists a loop which satisfies the fairness. Feasibility checking is hence reduced to loop searching. In this work, we develop a unified algorithm, shown below, extending existing SCC-based algorithms to cope with fairness. Notice that nested DFS is not ideal as whether an execution is fair or not depends on the path instead of one state [5]. The algorithm is based on Tarjan's algorithm for identifying SCCs. It searches for fair strongly connected subgraph on-the-fly. The basic idea is to identify one SCC at a time and then check whether it is fair or not. If it is, the search is over. Otherwise, the SCC is partitioned into multiple smaller strongly connected subgraphs, which are then checked recursively one by one.

procedure *feasible*(S, T)
1. **while** there are states which have not been visited
2.   **let** $scc := findSCC(S, T)$;
3. $pruned := \boldsymbol{prune(scc,T)}$;
4.   **if** $pruned = scc$ **then**;
5.   generate a feasible path; **return** true;
6.   **endif**
7.   **if** $feasible(pruned, T)$ **then return** $true$; **endif**
8. **endwhile**
9. **return** $false$;

Let S and T be a set of states and transitions. The main loop is from line 1 to 8. Line 2 invokes Tarjan's algorithm (implemented as *findSCC*) to identify one SCC within S and T. In order to perform on-the-fly verification, *findSCC* is designed in such a way that if no S and T are given, it explores states and transitions on-the-fly until one SCC is identified. Function *prune* (at line 5) is used to prune *bad states* from the SCC. Bad states are the reasons why the SCC is not fair. The intuition is that there may be a fair strongly connected subgraph in the remaining states. If the SCC satisfies the fairness assumption, no state is pruned and a fair loop (which traverses all states/transitions in the SCC) is generated and we conclude true at line 5. If some states have been pruned, a recursive call is made to check whether a fair strongly connected subgraph exists within the remaining states. The recursive call terminates in two ways, either a fair subgraph is found (at line 5) or all states are pruned (at line 9). If the recursive call returns false, there is no fair subgraph and we continue with another SCC until there is no state left.

By simply modifying function *prune*, the algorithm can be used to handle a variety of fairness. For instance, the following defines the function for weak fairness.

$$prune_{wf}(scc, T) = \begin{cases} S \text{ if } always(scc) \subseteq engaged(scc); \\ \varnothing \text{ otherwise.} \end{cases}$$

where $always(scc)$ is the set of events which are enabled at every state in scc and *engaged* is the set of events labeling a transition between two states in scc. If there exists an event e which is always enabled but never engaged, by definition scc does not satisfy weak fairness. *If scc does not satisfy weak fairness, none of its subgraphs does.* As a result, either all states are pruned or none of them are. The following defines the function for strong local fairness.

$$prune_{slf}(scc, T) = \{s : scc \mid once(scc) \subseteq engaged(scc)\}$$

where $once(scc)$ contains events which are enabled at one or more states in scc. A state is pruned if and only if there is an event enabled at this state but never engaged in scc. By pruning the state, the event may become never enabled and therefore not required to be engaged. The following defines the function for strong global fairness.

$$prune_{sgf}(S, T) = \begin{cases} \varnothing & \text{if there exists } s : scc \text{ such that } s \xrightarrow{a} s' \text{ and } s' \notin scc; \\ scc & \text{otherwise.} \end{cases}$$

All states are pruned if there is a transition from a state in the SCC to a state not in the SCC. *If an SCC is not strong global fair, none of its subgraphs is (since the subgraph must contain a step to a pruned state and thus can not be strong global fair).*

Action Annotated Fairness. In PAT, we offer an alternative approach, which allows users to associate fairness to only part of the systems or associate different parts with different fairness constraints. The motivation is twofold. Firstly, previous approaches treat every action or state equally, i.e., fairness is applied to every action/state. In verification practice, it may be that only certain actions are meant to be fair. Our remedy is to allow users to associate fairness constraints with individual actions. The other motivation of action annotated fairness is that *for systems with action annotated fairness, it remains possible to apply partial order reduction to actions which are irrelevant to the fairness annotations.*

A number of different fairness may be used to annotate actions. Unconditional action fairness is written as $f(a)$. An execution of the system is fair if and only if a occurs infinitely often. It may be used to annotate actions which are known to occur periodically. For instance, a discrete clock may be modeled as: $Clock() = f(tick)\{x = x + 1\} \rightarrow Clock()$ where x is a discrete clock variable. By annotating $tick$ with unconditional fairness, we require that the clock must progress infinitely and the system disallows unrealistic *timelock*, i.e., execution of infinite actions which takes finite time. Weak (strong) action fairness is written as $wf(a)$ $(sf(a))$. An execution of the system is fair if and only if a occurs infinitely often given it is always (once) enabled. Unconditional action fairness does not depend on whether the action is enabled or not, and therefore, is stronger than weak/strong action fairness. The algorithm can then be applied to check systems with action annotated fairness with small modifications.

Model	Property	Size	Weak Fair		Strong Local Fair		Strong Global Fair	
			Result	PAT	SPIN	Result	PAT	Result	PAT
LE_C	$\Diamond\Box oneleader$	5	Yes	4.7	35.7	Yes	4.7	Yes	4.1
LE_C	$\Diamond\Box oneleader$	6	Yes	26.7	229	Yes	26.7	Yes	23.5
LE_C	$\Diamond\Box oneleader$	7	Yes	152.2	1190	Yes	152.4	Yes	137.9
LE_C	$\Diamond\Box oneleader$	8	Yes	726.6	5720	Yes	739.0	Yes	673.1
LE_OR	$\Diamond\Box oneleader$	3	No	0.2	0.3	No	0.2	Yes	11.8
LE_OR	$\Diamond\Box oneleader$	5	No	1.3	8.7	No	1.8	−	−
LE_R	$\Diamond\Box oneleader$	4	No	0.3	< 0.1	No	0.7	Yes	19.5
LE_R	$\Diamond\Box oneleader$	5	No	0.8	< 0.1	No	2.7	Yes	299.0
LE_R	$\Diamond\Box oneleader$	6	No	1.8	0.2	No	4.6	−	−
TC_R	$\Diamond\Box onetoken$	5	No	< 0.1	< 0.1	No	< 0.1	Yes	0.6
TC_R	$\Diamond\Box onetoken$	7	No	0.2	0.1	No	0.2	Yes	13.7
TC_R	$\Diamond\Box onetoken$	9	No	0.4	0.2	No	0.4	Yes	640.2
$peterson$	bounded bypass	3	Yes	0.1	1.25	Yes	0.1	Yes	0.1
$peterson$	bounded bypass	4	Yes	1.7	> 671	Yes	1.8	Yes	2.4
$peterson$	bounded bypass	5	Yes	58.9	−	Yes	63.7	Yes	75.4

Experiments. In the following, we show PAT's capability and efficiency over a range of systems where fairness is necessary. The following data are obtained by executing SPIN 4.3 and PAT 2.2 with Core 2 CPU 6600 at 2.40GHz and 2GB RAM.

The models include recently proposed self-stabilizing leader election protocols [6], e.g., for complete networks (LE_C), odd sized rings (LE_OR), and network rings (LE_R), token circulation for network rings (TC_R), and Peterson's algorithm for mutual exclusion. All models, with configurable parameters, are embedded in the PAT package. Because of the difference between process-level weak fairness and weak fairness, the models are manually twisted in order to compare PAT with SPIN fairly (refer to [10] for details). SPIN has no support for strong local or global fairness. The only way to perform verification under strong local/global fairness in SPIN is to encode the fairness constraints as part of the property. However, even for a network of 3 nodes, SPIN needs significant amount of time to construct the (very large) Büchi automata, which makes it infeasible for such purpose.

In summary, PAT complements existing model checkers with the improvement in terms of the performance and ability to handle different forms of fairness. We remark that fairness does play an important role in these models. All of the algorithms fail to satisfy the property without fairness. Model LE_C and *peterson* require at least weak fairness, whereas the rest of the algorithms require strong global fairness. It is thus important to be able to verify systems under strong local/global fairness. Notice that TC_R satisfies the property for a network of size 3 under weak fairness. There is, however, a counterexample for a network with more nodes. The reason is that a particular sequence of message exchange which satisfies weak fairness but fails the property needs the participation of at least 4 network nodes. This suggests that our approach has its practical values. *We highlight that previously unknown bugs in implementation of LE_OR [6] have been revealed using PAT.* We translated the algorithms *without* knowing how it works and generated a counterexample within seconds. SPIN is infeasible for this task because the algorithm requires strong global fairness [6].

References

1. Angluin, D., Aspnes, J., Fischer, M.J., Jiang, H.: Self-stabilizing Population Protocols. In: Anderson, J.H., Prencipe, G., Wattenhofer, R. (eds.) OPODIS 2005. LNCS, vol. 3974, pp. 103–117. Springer, Heidelberg (2006)
2. Fischer, M.J., Jiang, H.: Self-stabilizing Leader Election in Networks of Finite-state Anonymous Agents. In: Shvartsman, M.M.A.A. (ed.) OPODIS 2006. LNCS, vol. 4305, pp. 395–409. Springer, Heidelberg (2006)
3. Geldenhuys, J., Valmari, A.: More efficient on-the-fly LTL verification with Tarjan's algorithm. Theoritical Computer Science 345(1), 60–82 (2005)
4. Henzinger, M.R., Telle, J.A.: Faster Algorithms for the Nonemptiness of Streett Automata and for Communication Protocol Pruning. In: Karlsson, R., Lingas, A. (eds.) SWAT 1996. LNCS, vol. 1097, pp. 16–27. Springer, Heidelberg (1996)
5. Holzmann, G.J.: The SPIN Model Checker: Primer and Reference Manual. Addison Wesley, Reading (2003)
6. Jiang, H.: Distributed Systems of Simple Interacting Agents. Ph.D thesis, Yale Univ. (2007)
7. Kesten, Y., Pnueli, A., Raviv, L., Shahar, E.: Model Checking with Strong Fairness. Formal Methods and System Design 28(1), 57–84 (2006)
8. Lamport, L.: Proving the Correctness of Multiprocess Programs. IEEE Transactions on Software Engineering 3(2), 125–143 (1977)
9. Lehmann, D.J., Pnueli, A., Stavi, J.: Impartiality, Justice and Fairness: The Ethics of Concurrent Termination. In: Even, S., Kariv, O. (eds.) ICALP 1981. LNCS, vol. 115, pp. 264–277. Springer, Heidelberg (1981)
10. Sun, J., Liu, Y., Dong, J.S., Pang, J.: Towards a Toolkit for Flexible and Efficient Verification under Fairness. Technical Report TRB2/09, National Univ. of Singapore (December 2008)

A Concurrent Portfolio Approach to SMT Solving

Christoph M. Wintersteiger[1], Youssef Hamadi[2], and Leonardo de Moura[3]

[1] Computer Systems Institute, ETH Zurich, Switzerland
christoph.wintersteiger@inf.ethz.ch
[2] Microsoft Research Cambridge, 7 JJ Thomson Avenue, Cambridge CB3 0FB, UK
youssefh@microsoft.com
[3] Microsoft Research, One Microsoft Way, Redmond, WA, 98074, USA
leonardo@microsoft.com

Abstract. With the availability of multi-core processors and large-scale computing clusters, the study of parallel algorithms has been revived throughout the industry. We present a portfolio approach to deciding the satisfiability of SMT formulas, based on the recent success of related algorithms for the SAT problem. Our parallel version of Z3 outperforms the sequential solver, with speedups of well over an order of magnitude on many benchmarks.

1 Introduction

Z3 is a Satisfiability Modulo Theories (SMT) solver from Microsoft Research [4]. It is targeted at solving problems that arise in software verification and analysis applications. Consequently, it integrates support for a variety of theories. Z3 participated in SMT-COMP'08, where it won 9 first places (out of 15), and 6 second places. Z3 uses novel algorithms for quantifier instantiation [2] and theory combination [3]. The first external release of Z3 was in September 2007, and the latest version was released in the beginning of 2009. Z3 integrates a modern DPLL-based SAT solver, a core theory solver that handles equalities and uninterpreted functions, satellite solvers (for arithmetic, arrays, etc.), and an E-matching abstract machine (for quantifiers). Z3 is implemented in C++; Figure 1 (left box) gives an overview of the architecture of the solver.

The ManySAT parallel SAT solver [6] won the parallel track of the 2008 SAT-Race.[1] It includes all the classical features of modern DPLL-based solvers like two-watched literals, unit propagation, activity-based decision heuristics, lemma deletion strategies, and clause learning. In addition to the classical first-UIP scheme, it incorporates a new technique which extends the classical implication graph used during conflict-analysis to exploit the satisfied clauses of a formula [1]. Unlike other parallel SAT solvers, ManySAT does not implement a divide-and-conquer strategy based on some dynamic partitioning of the search space. On the contrary, it uses a portfolio philosophy which lets several sequential DPLLs compete and cooperate to be the first to solve the common instance.

---

[1] http://www-sr.informatik.uni-tuebingen.de/sat-race-2008/

A. Bouajjani and O. Maler (Eds.): CAV 2009, LNCS 5643, pp. 715–720, 2009.

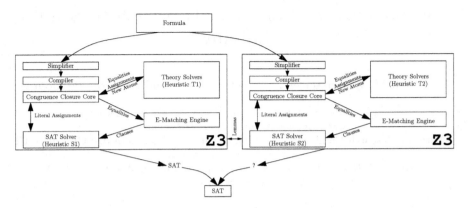

Fig. 1. Schematic overview of the Z3 parallelization.

These DPLLs are differentiated in many ways. They use complementary restart strategies, VSIDS and polarity heuristics, and learning schemes. Additionally, all the DPLLs exchange learnt clauses up to some static size limits, which allows for super-linear speedups that would be difficult to reach in a portfolio without sharing.

The portfolio approach is very attractive for SMT because it allows the use of different encodings of a problem, as well as different theory solvers at the same time. Moreover, SMT solvers frequently have to handle problems that are in undecidable fragments (e.g., first-order logic and arithmetic, or non-linear arithmetic). In these fragments, the solvers are much more fragile, and different heuristics may dramatically affect performance.

On the following pages we present an integration of those two award-winning techniques. To the best of our knowledge, this constitutes the first implementation of a parallel SMT solver available to the public.

2   Portfolios

Modern SMT solvers are based on a decomposition of the input problem into a propositional problem, and theory-specific problems over the formula atoms. This allows the use of modern SAT solving techniques alongside theory-specific solvers. Each of them employs a great number of heuristics to solve industrial size problems efficiently.

In our parallel version of Z3, we parallelize the sequential solver by running multiple solvers, each configured to use different heuristics, i.e., by running a *portfolio* of solvers. If two heuristics are known to work well on disjoint benchmark sets, then we can expect speedups from this technique.

To further improve the performance of our solver, we *share* derived lemmas between solvers. New lemmas are derived as part of conflict analysis in the SAT and theory solvers. When running multiple solvers in parallel, they are likely to investigate different parts of the search space at a given point in time. Sharing lemmas may prevent a solver from entering a search space that was previously investigated by another solver, thus improving the performance of the first solver.

Z3 has a portfolio of theory solvers. For example, Z3 supports multiple arithmetic solvers: a trivial solver that treats all arithmetic functions as uninterpreted, two difference-logic solvers (based on the Bellman-Ford and Floyd-Warshall algorithms), as well as a simplex based solver. Since Z3 cannot tell which of the arithmetic solvers would be the quickest to decide the formula beforehand, we can run them in parallel and abort the computation as soon as one of them is able to deliver a definite result. Note that using the first three solvers is equivalent to constructing conservative over-approximations of the formula. If either of them decides the formula to be unsatisfiable, then so must the simplex-based solver. Sharing information in a portfolio of over-approximating solvers is sound, as solvers decide the formula only for unsatisfiable input formulas. It is also a way of implicit approximation refinement, as approximations become more precise by importing lemmas derived from the precise formula. When sharing information in a portfolio of under-approximations, or mixed under- and over-approximations, sharing is only sound in one direction, i.e., from precise to less precise formulas.

3 Implementation

In this section we discuss the main components of our implementation. The parallel version of Z3 is based on the newest version of the sequential Z3 SMT solver. The implementation of the multi-core (shared-memory) functionality was implemented with the help of the OpenMP library, while multi-node functionality was added using an MPI library. Here, we focus on multi-core operation.

We made the observation that most benchmarks in the SMT library require a relatively small amount of memory to solve, when compared to SAT benchmarks, e.g., it is rare to see benchmarks that require more than 100 MB of memory. We thus made the design decision to copy all input data to all cores, once it is read from a file or handed to the solver using the Z3 API. This eliminates the need for locks on the formula, and enables us to use unlocked reference counters. Furthermore, it allows us to modify the input formula before (or after) handing it to a core, which is important if different (precise or approximating) encodings are to be solved, or if we would like to split the search space (e.g., by adding constraints on variables). Our experiments indicate that the additional memory overhead is of consequence only on very large instances.

Lemma exchange between cores is achieved by the help of lockless queues that hold references to all lemmas that a core wants to export. Upon reaching decision level 0 in the SAT solver, every core checks his queues for new lemmas to import.

3.1 Challenges

While working on our parallelization of Z3, we met two important challenges that we propose to discuss. First, we noticed that there is a considerable overhead when simply running multiple identical solvers in parallel. This overhead is induced by cache and memory bus congestion, and has a considerable impact on the performance of each solver in our portfolio. Figure 2a shows the average number of propositional propagations that each core is able to perform in a setup of identical solvers. This number drops dramatically from almost 2.5 million propagations per second to only 2.3 million when eight cores are employed. This corresponds to a 7 % decrease in solver performance.[2]

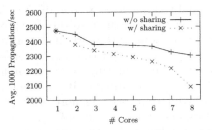 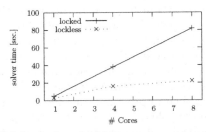

(a) Avg. Core performance with and without sharing of lemmas up to size 2

(b) Locked vs. lockless memory manager

Fig. 2. Parallelization and Sharing Overhead

Another challenge that we faced was memory allocation. While the sequential version of Z3 uses a global memory manager, we found that locking the global manager in the parallel version imposes far too much overhead. We solved this problem by reserving memory in separate heaps for each thread. Figure 2b depicts the difference in runtime that we witnessed on a small, but memory intense benchmark when running identical solvers on all cores. Clearly, the reduction in runtime by using a lockless memory manager is significant.

3.2   Portfolio

The default configuration of our implementation uses the same portfolio as ManySAT on the first four cores, i.e., it only diversifies based on heuristics specific to the built-in SAT-solver. Additional cores are configured by using different combinations of settings. Other configurations may be set from the command line, a feature available to the user in order to define their own portfolios.

3.3   Lemma Sharing

We experimented with different lemma sharing strategies, and found that sharing of lemmas up to a size of 8 literals performed best on our benchmarks. This is not surprising, as it is also the best performing sharing strategy in ManySAT (cf. [5]).

---

[2] These numbers were obtained from a single, statistically non-relevant file. The number of propagations per second varies greatly across different benchmarks; the relative change in performance is typical, however.

4   Experimental Evaluation

We present results on experiments on benchmarks from the SMT library[3], more specifically, the `QF_IDL` category, which consists of 1673 benchmark files. The results we present here were obtained on AMD Opteron 2.0 GHz machines with 8 cores and 16 GB of RAM. For our experiments we used four cores on each of the machines, and we compare against the sequential version of Z3 (using the configuration that was used in SMT-COMP'08); the timeout was set to 300 seconds. Our results indicate, that running four different arithmetic solvers achieves speedups only on very few benchmarks, and due to the parallelization overhead many benchmarks take more time to solve than in the sequential version (Fig. 3a). This changes considerably when sharing is enabled, as demonstrated in Fig. 3a. Many benchmarks are now solved faster, with speedups between 1 and 25. Due to the large number of small benchmarks in the set, the average speedup is only 1.06. Excluding files that can be solved in less than 60 seconds by the sequential version, the average speedup is 3.2.[4]

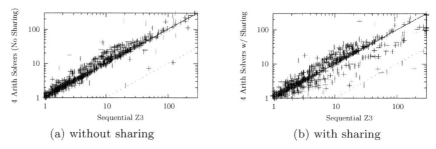

(a) without sharing   (b) with sharing

Fig. 3. Four arithmetic solvers

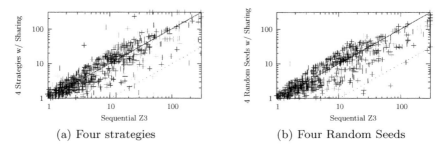

(a) Four strategies   (b) Four Random Seeds

Fig. 4. Four SAT solvers with sharing

---

[3] `http://www.smt-lib.org`

[4] Below this point the parallelization overhead dominates. For further investigation the full benchmark data set may be obtained from
`http://research.microsoft.com/~leonardo/z3-cav2009-results.zip`

We achieve similar results by diversifying the SAT strategies in our solver (Fig. 4). Using the four strategies used in ManySAT, we see an average speedup of 1.14, resp. 2.6 on the 60+ seconds benchmarks. As Fig. 4a shows, the speedup on many of the benchmarks is super-linear, with a maximum speedup of 40.

The best results we have seen during our experiments, were produced by a portfolio of identical solvers with sharing, each initialized by a different random seed. Those results are presented in Fig. 4b; the average speedup is 1.28 and the speedup on the 60+ seconds benchmarks is 3.5, i.e., close to linear on average. The maximum speedup we see in this configuration is 50.

5   Status and Availability

We currently investigate different portfolios and their performance on SMT-lib benchmarks. The parallel version of Z3 is also used on internal projects to improve the performance of multiple software-verification projects, and we expect more and better portfolios to arise from the use of our solver in practice.

The parallel version of Z3 is released alongside the sequential version. It is available from the Z3 project website.[5]

References

1. Audemard, G., Bordeaux, L., Hamadi, Y., Jabbour, S., Sais, L.: A Generalized Framework for Conflict Analysis. In: Kleine Büning, H., Zhao, X. (eds.) SAT 2008. LNCS, vol. 4996, pp. 21–27. Springer, Heidelberg (2008)
2. de Moura, L., Bjørner, N.: Efficient E-matching for SMT Solvers. In: Pfenning, F. (ed.) CADE 2007. LNCS, vol. 4603, pp. 183–198. Springer, Heidelberg (2007)
3. de Moura, L., Bjørner, N.: Model-based Theory Combination. In: SMT 2007 (2007)
4. de Moura, L., Bjørner, N.: Z3: An Efficient SMT Solver. In: Ramakrishnan, C.R., Rehof, J. (eds.) TACAS 2008. LNCS, vol. 4963, pp. 337–340. Springer, Heidelberg (2008)
5. Hamadi, Y., Jabbour, S., Sais, L.: ManySAT: A Parallel SAT Solver. Journal of Satisfiability (2008) (to appear)
6. Hamadi, Y., Jabbour, S., Sais, L.: ManySAT: Solver Description. Technical Report MSR-TR-2008-83, Microsoft Research (May 2008)

---

[5] http://research.microsoft.com/projects/z3/

Author Index